MASTER VISUALLY™

Photoshop® 6

MASTER VISUALLY™

Photoshop® 6

by Ken Milburn

From

maranGraphics®

&

HUNGRY MINDS, INC.
New York, NY • Cleveland, OH • Indianapolis, IN

Master VISUALLY™ Photoshop® 6

Published by
Hungry Minds, Inc.
909 Third Avenue
New York, NY 10022

maranGraphics, Inc.
5755 Coopers Avenue
Mississauga, Ontario, Canada
L4Z 1R9

Library of Congress Control Number: 00-109415
ISBN: 0-7645-3541-2
Printed in the United States of America
10 9 8 7 6 5 4 3 2 1

1O/RZ/QT/QR/IN

Distributed in the United States by Hungry Minds, Inc.
Distributed by CDG Books Canada Inc. for Canada; by Transworld Publishers Limited in the United Kingdom; by IDG Norge Books for Norway; by IDG Sweden Books for Sweden; by IDG Books Australia Publishing Corporation Pty. Ltd. for Australia and New Zealand; by TransQuest Publishers Pte Ltd. for Singapore, Malaysia, Thailand, Indonesia, and Hong Kong; by Gotop Information Inc. for Taiwan; by ICG Muse, Inc. for Japan; by Intersoft for South Africa; by Eyrolles for France; by International Thomson Publishing for Germany, Austria and Switzerland; by Distribuidora Cuspide for Argentina; by LR International for Brazil; by Galileo Libros for Chile; by Ediciones ZETA S.C.R. Ltda. for Peru; by WS Computer Publishing Corporation, Inc., for the Philippines; by Contemporanea de Ediciones for Venezuela; by Express Computer Distributors for the Caribbean and West Indies; by Micronesia Media Distributor, Inc. for Micronesia; by Chips Computadoras S.A. de C.V. for Mexico; by Editorial Norma de Panama S.A. for Panama; by American Bookshops for Finland.

For corporate orders, please call maranGraphics at 800-469-6616 or fax 905-890-9434.

For general information on Hungry Minds' products and services please contact our Customer Care Department within the U.S. at 800-762-2974, outside the U.S. at 317-572-3993 or fax 317-572-4002.

For sales inquiries and reseller information, including discounts, premium and bulk quantity sales, and foreign-language translations, please contact our Customer Care Department at 800-434-3422, fax 317-572-4002, or write to Hungry Minds, Inc., Attn: Customer Care Department, 10475 Crosspoint Boulevard, Indianapolis, IN 46256.

For information on licensing foreign or domestic rights, please contact our Sub-Rights Customer Care Department at 650-653-7098.

For information on using Hungry Minds' products and services in the classroom or for ordering examination copies, please contact our Educational Sales Department at 800-434-2086 or fax 317-572-4005.

Please contact our Public Relations Department at 212-884-5163 for press review copies or 212-884-5000 for author interviews and other publicity information or fax 212-884-5400.

For authorization to photocopy items for corporate, personal, or educational use, please contact Copyright Clearance Center, 222 Rosewood Drive, Danvers, MA 01923, or fax 978-750-4470.

Screen shots displayed in this book are based on pre-released software and are subject to change.

Trademark Acknowledgments

Permissions

maranGraphics

U.S. Corporate Sales

Contact maranGraphics
at (800) 469-6616 or
fax (905) 890-9434.

U.S. Trade Sales

Contact Hungry Minds
at (800) 434-3422
or (317) 572-4002.

Praise for Visual books...

"If you have to see it to believe it, this is the book for you!"

–PC World

"I would like to take this time to compliment maranGraphics on creating such great books. I work for a leading manufacturer of office products, and sometimes they tend to NOT give you the meat and potatoes of certain subjects, which causes great confusion. Thank you for making it clear. Keep up the good work."

–Kirk Santoro (Burbank, CA)

"I write to extend my thanks and appreciation for your books. They are clear, easy to follow, and straight to the point. Keep up the good work! I bought several of your books and they are just right! No regrets! I will always buy your books because they are the best."

–Seward Kollie (Dakar, Senegal)

"What fantastic teaching books you have produced! Congratulations to you and your staff."

–Bruno Tonon (Melbourne, Australia)

"Compliments To The Chef!! Your books are extraordinary! Or, simply put, Extra-Ordinary, meaning way above the rest! THANKYOUTHANKYOU THANKYOU! for creating these. They have saved me from serious mistakes, and showed me a right and simple way to do things. I buy them for friends, family, and colleagues."

–Christine J. Manfrin (Castle Rock, CO)

"A master tutorial/reference — from the leaders in visual learning!"

–Infoworld

"Your books are superior! An avid reader since childhood, I've consumed literally tens of thousands of books, a significant quantity in the learning/teaching category. Your series is the most precise, visually appealing and compelling to peruse. Kudos!"

–Margaret Rose Chmilar (Edmonton, Alberta, Canada)

"You're marvelous! I am greatly in your debt."

–Patrick Baird (Lacey, WA)

"Just wanted to say THANK YOU to your company for providing books which make learning fast, easy, and exciting! I learn visually so your books have helped me greatly – from Windows instruction to Web page development. I'm looking forward to using more of your Master Books series in the future as I am now a computer support specialist. Best wishes for continued success."

–Angela J. Barker (Springfield, MO)

"A publishing concept whose time has come!"

–The Globe and Mail

"I have over the last 10-15 years purchased $1000's worth of computer books but find your books the most easily read, best set out and most helpful and easily understood books on software and computers I have ever read. You produce the best computer books money can buy. Please keep up the good work."

–John Gatt (Adamstown Heights, Australia)

"The Greatest. This whole series is the best computer learning tool of any kind I've ever seen."

–Joe Orr (Brooklyn, NY)

maranGraphics is a family-run business
located near Toronto, Canada.

At maranGraphics, we believe in producing great computer books – one book at a time.

maranGraphics has been producing high-technology products for over 25 years, which enables us to offer the computer book community a unique communication process.

Our computer books use an integrated communication process, which is very different from the approach used in other computer books. Each spread is, in essence, a flow chart – the text and screen shots are totally incorporated into the layout of the spread. Introductory text and helpful tips complete the learning experience.

maranGraphics' approach encourages the left and right sides of the brain to work together – resulting in faster orientation and greater memory retention.

Above all, we are very proud of the handcrafted nature of our books. Our carefully-chosen writers are experts in their fields, and spend countless hours researching and organizing the content for each topic. Our artists rebuild every screen shot to provide the best clarity possible, making our screen shots the most precise and easiest to read in the industry. We strive for perfection, and believe that the time spent handcrafting each element results in the best computer books money can buy.

Thank you for purchasing this book. We hope you enjoy it!

Sincerely,

Robert Maran
President
maranGraphics
Rob@maran.com
www.maran.com
www.hungryminds.com/visual

CREDITS

Acquisitions, Editorial, and Media Development

Project Editors
Rev Mengle
Dana Lesh
Maureen Spears

Acquisitions Editor
Martine Edwards

Product Development Supervisor
Lindsay Sandman

Copy Editor
Paula Lowell

Technical Editor
Dennis R. Cohen

Permissions Editor
Carmen Krikorian

Media Development Specialist
Brock Bigard

Media Development Coordinator
Marisa Pearman

Editorial Manager
Rev Mengle

Media Development Manager
Laura Carpenter

Editorial Assistant
Amanda Foxworth

Production

Book Design
maranGraphics®

Project Coordinator
Maridee Ennis

Layout
Joe Bucki
Adam Mancilla
Kristin Pickett

Screen Artists
Craig Dearing
Mark Harris
Jill A. Proll

Illustrator
David E. Gregory

Proofreaders
David Faust
Dwight Ramsey
Marianne Santy
Charles Spencer

Indexer
York Production Services, Inc.

Special Help
Timothy J. Borek, copy editor
Jill Mazurczyk, copy editor
Amy Pettinella, copy editor

GENERAL AND ADMINISTRATIVE

Hungry Minds, Inc.: John Kilcullen, CEO; Bill Barry, President and COO; John Ball, Executive VP, Operations & Administration; John Harris, CFO

Hungry Minds Technology Publishing Group: Richard Swadley, Senior Vice President and Publisher; Mary Bednarek, Vice President and Publisher; Walter R. Bruce III, Vice President and Publisher; Joseph Wikert, Vice President and Publisher; Mary C. Corder, Editorial Director; Andy Cummings, Publishing Director, General User Group; Barry Pruett, Publishing Director, Visual Group

Hungry Minds Manufacturing: Ivor Parker, Vice President, Manufacturing

Hungry Minds Marketing: John Helmus, Assistant Vice President, Director of Marketing

Hungry Minds Online Management: Brenda McLaughlin, Executive Vice President, Chief Internet Officer

Hungry Minds Production for Branded Press: Debbie Stailey, Production Director

Hungry Minds Sales: Roland Elgey, Senior Vice President, Sales and Marketing; Michael Violano, Vice President, International Sales and Sub Rights

The publisher would like to give special thanks to Patrick J. McGovern, without whom this book would not have been possible.

ABOUT THE AUTHOR

Ken Milburn is a photo-digital illustrator and author. More than 250 of his articles and reviews on computer graphics and multimedia have appeared in *InfoWorld, PC World, MacWeek, Mac User, Popular Computing, PC Computing, Computer Graphics World, Publish,* and *Windows* magazines, and Ken is a contributing editor to Pictureit.msn.com. Ken has also worked as a user-interface design consultant for Mannequin, an application developed by the HumanCAD division of Biomechanics Corp. of America and the predecessor to Fractal Design's Poser. Milburn began his career as a fashion and travel photographer in Beverly Hills and now specializes in photo-digital illustration.

AUTHOR'S ACKNOWLEDGMENTS

First, I'd like to thank everyone else who's written a Photoshop book. I can't scientifically claim to have read them all, but certainly most of them have contributed to the background that went into the writing of this book. So have the galleries and clients who buy my work.

Next, if it weren't for family (my ex-wife Nancy Miller is definitely still family) and close friends, I'd never be able to take the pressure of writing books. These people nurture and sustain you even when you don't give them nearly as much love or pay as much attention to them as they deserve. I especially have to thank those who have been extraordinarily supportive these past few months: Nancy Miller, Lane Milburn (my son, who is turning out to have a real talent for both art and computers), Janine Warner, Bob Cowart, Markus Baue, Sonita Malan, and Elke Savala are among those whose names I have to mention.

The publishing crew on this book is one of my all time favorites. Not only have they been as professional as they come, but they are just downright pleasant and fun to work with. Martine Edwards was the original acquisitions editor, Rev Mengle was the editorial manager, Paula Lowell was the copy editor, and Project Editors Dana Lesh and Maureen Spears also helped out. I don't know the technical editor, Dennis R. Cohen, personally but the man certainly had his eye on the ball.

I especially want to thank my assistant, Bob Matutat, for doing an enormous amount of preparatory work — including re-shooting every screen shot in the book in order to match them up with the latest requirements of the Master Visually series.

PHOTOSHOP® 6

I GETTING STARTED

1) Photoshop Basics

2) Photoshop File Management

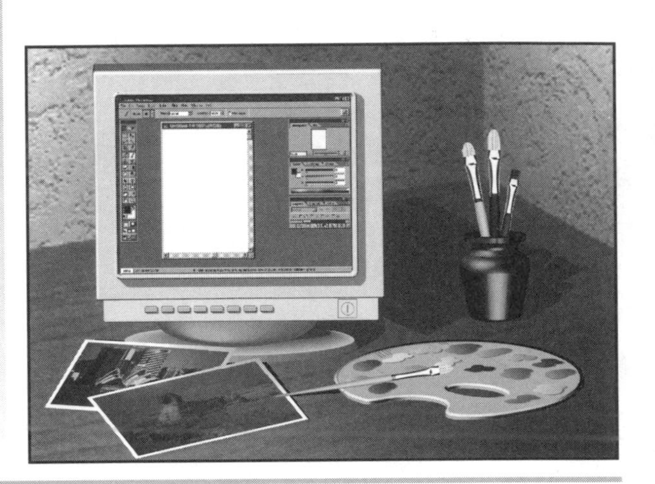

II MAKING IMAGE ADJUSTMENTS

3) Changing the Size of an Image

4) Adjusting Image Quality

5) Retouching Images

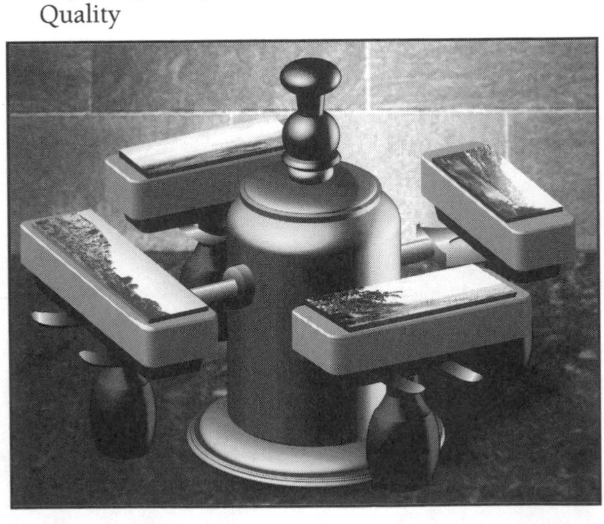

WHAT'S INSIDE

III ISOLATING PARTS OF THE IMAGE

IV PHOTOSHOP FOR ART'S SAKE

V ADVANCED TECHNIQUES

VI PREPARING IMAGES FOR THE WEB

VII APPENDIXES

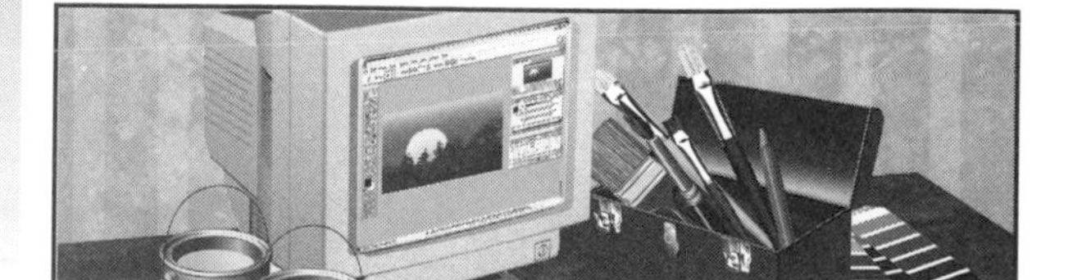

1 GETTING STARTED

1) PHOTOSHOP BASICS

2) PHOTOSHOP FILE MANAGEMENT

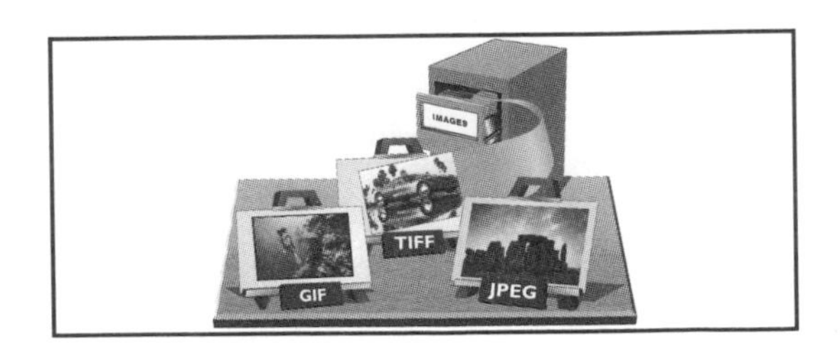

TABLE OF CONTENTS

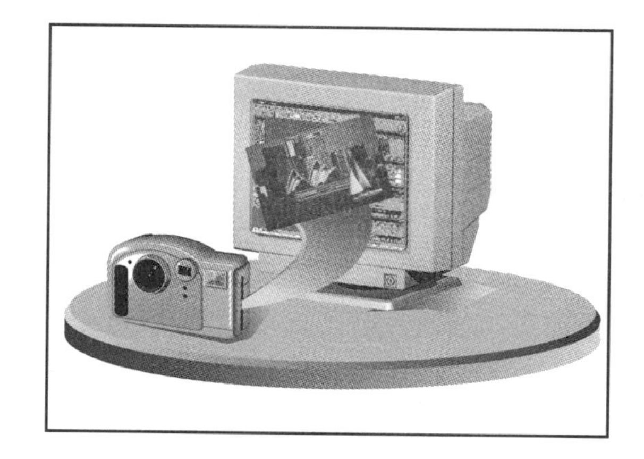

4) ADJUSTING IMAGE QUALITY

5) RETOUCHING IMAGES

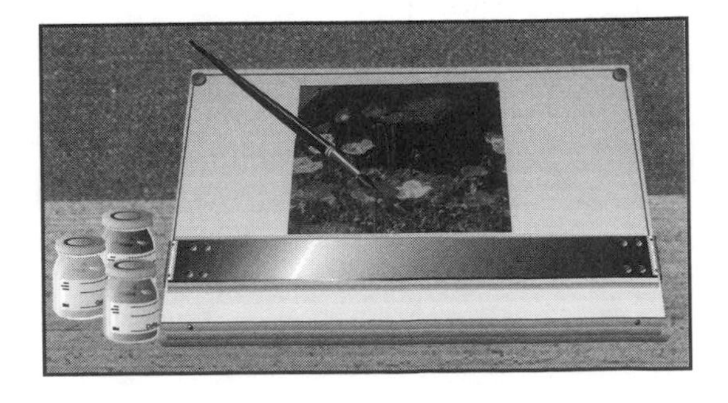

TABLE OF CONTENTS

3 ISOLATING PARTS OF THE IMAGE

6) MAKING SELECTIONS

7) WORKING WITH VECTOR PATHS

8) WORKING WITH MASKS

9) WORKING WITH LAYERS

TABLE OF CONTENTS

10) CHANNEL OPERATIONS

11) TEXT AND TEXT EFFECTS

4 PHOTOSHOP FOR ART'S SAKE

12) USING PHOTOSHOP'S BRUSHES

13) APPLYING DARKROOM EFFECTS

14) WORKING WITH TEXTURES

TABLE OF CONTENTS

15) USING THE ARTISTIC FILTERS

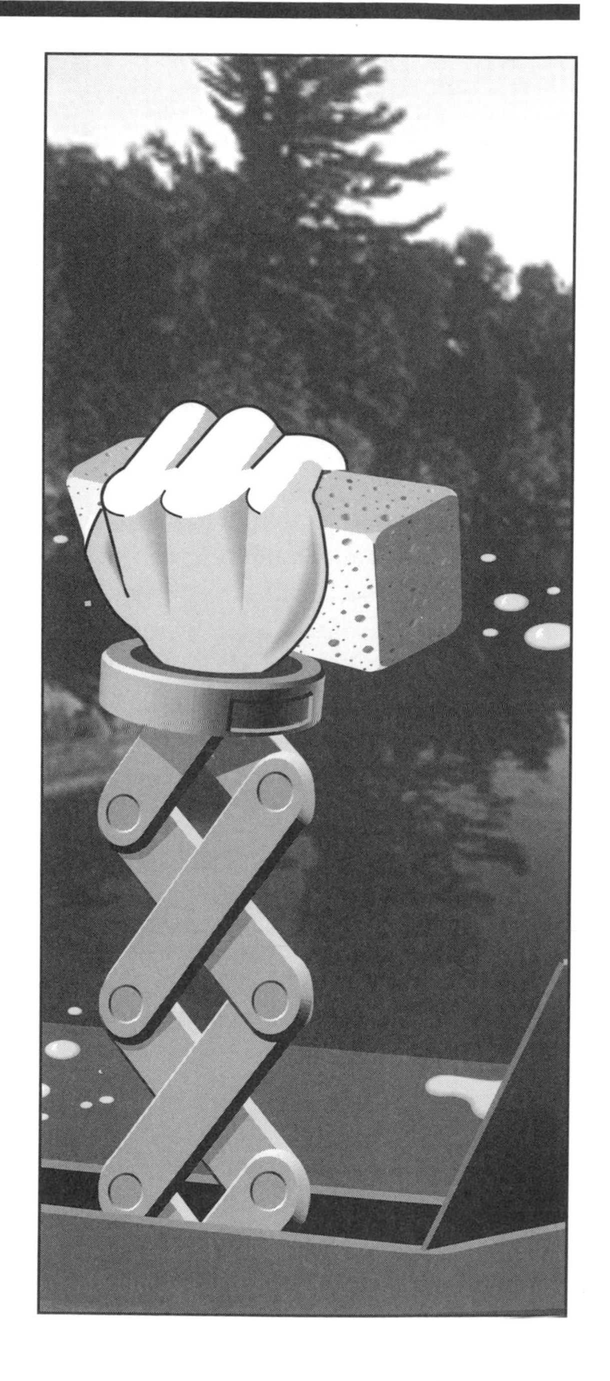

16) USING THE DISTORT FILTERS

17) USING THE NOISE, PIXELATE, AND STYLIZE FILTERS

5 ADVANCED TECHNIQUES

18) USING LAYERS TO COMBINE EFFECTS

19) AUTOMATING PHOTOSHOP WITH ACTIONS

20) PREPARING IMAGES FOR A COMPOSITE

6 PREPARING IMAGES FOR THE WEB

21) PREPARING AND PREVIEWING WEB PAGES

22) DESIGNING INTERACTIVE GRAPHICS

23) MAKING ANIMATIONS FROM PHOTOGRAPHS

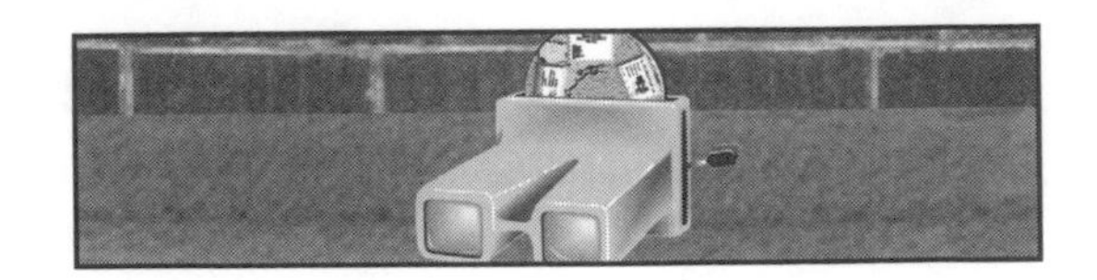

7 APPENDIXES

APPENDIX A

APPENDIX B

APPENDIX C

APPENDIX D

PHOTOSHOP® 6

Master Visually Photoshop 6 is a visual reference for professionals and serious hobbyists to quickly discover how to complete the most frequently needed creative tasks in Photoshop.

About seventy-five percent of the book is devoted to these visual task quides. In addition, extensive reference appendixes explain the uses and options for each tool and command that Photoshop has to offer.

Who This Book Is For

This book is for you if you're a creative professionals or serious hobbyists whose work is producing photo-graphics and continuous-tone artwork for documentation, illustration, advertising, fine art, and (of course) for making Web sites more dynamic and compelling.

Although this book doesn't require an extensive pre-knowledge of Photoshop, it does expect that you have some experience with the program. This is not because the tasks are difficult to understand (after all, you just do what you see), but because the book isn't organized as a tutorial. *Teach Yourself VISUALLY Photoshop 6* by Mike Wooldridge (Hungry Minds, Inc.) is a better place for beginners to start.

What You Need To Use This Book

To perform the tasks in this book, you need a computer with Microsoft Windows 95, 98, ME or 2000 or a Macintosh computer with OS 8.5 or better. Your computer should have at least 64MB of RAM, and you'll need 128 MB of hard disk space to install the program code. However, be forewarned that professional bit-mapped graphics will benefit from just about as much RAM and storage space as you can muster. You also need a color monitor capable of displaying at least 256 colors, although if you intend to be serious about photography (and given the price of Photoshop, you'd better be) a monitor capable of displaying the full-range of 16.8 million color is a must. Also, monitors capable of displaying at least 1024x768 pixels will give you room to dock palettes on the Options bar, which will speed your work flow. Flatter monitors are more desirable because they are less prone to picking up reflections from windows and room lights. If you are working on Web graphics (and, these days, who isn't?), having a Web browser, such as Microsoft Internet Explorer, installed will make it possible to preview your Web graphics as they will actually appear on the Web.

The Conventions In This Book

The terminology used in this book for what you should do with your mouse/pen is very specific to the type of operation you will be performing. The terms you want to watch for are: Select, Choose, Click, Drag, and Scrub.

* **Select** means to indicate which part of the image will be affected by the use of the next tool or command. Specifically, either highlight the name bar in a palette to select such things as a layer or channel, use one of the selection tools — such as the marquee or lasso — to restrict the operation to a limited portion of the image that resides on the active layer.

* **Choose** means to specify the use of a command or tool by picking it from the Toolbox or one of Photoshop's menus.

* **Click** means to place the cursor in the designated place and to press the *left* (or, in the case of most Mac mice, *only*) mouse button. If you are asked to use another mouse button, it will be specified before the word "click," e.g. "Right-click to bring up the in-context menu."

* **Drag** means to click and then immediately move the mouse (usually in a specific direction). Since the click is implied, you will never see the words "click and drag."

* **Scrub** is similar to *drag*, except that the movement of the mouse is erratic back-and-forth or side-to-side, as though scrubbing a stubborn food speck from an old skillet. Scrubbing is a mouse action that is nearly unique to image editing applications because it is often needed for retouching small portions of an image by hand.

number of typographic and layout styles have been used hroughout *Master Visually Photoshop 6.*

old

ndicates information that must be typed by you.

talics

ndicates a new term being introduced.

Many tasks in the book are supplemented with a section called Master It. These are tips, hints, and tricks that extend your use of the task beyond what you learned by performing the task itself.

he Organization Of This Book

he main part of this book is organized into Photoshop's unctional areas by seven parts, each of which consists of visual asks in which you are literally shown where and what to point at nd click on in order to get something done. Each of these tasks as a short introduction that explains why on Earth you would ver want to do this task

art I: Getting Started has two chapters. The first chapter explains he new features in Photoshop 6, shows you how to setup your omputer to best compliment Photoshop, how to recover from nistakes using the History palette, how to use Quick Edit Mode, nd how to set each of Photoshop's preferences. The second chapter has to do with various techniques that can be used for visually managing files in Photoshop.

Part II: Making Image Adjustments consists of three chapters. Chapter 3 shows you how to change the size of an image, both by re-scaling and by cropping (trimming). Chapter 4 shows you a host of techniques for changing the overall characteristics of an image. The part concludes with Chapter 5, which demonstrates essential retouching techniques.

Part III: Isolating Parts of the Image uses six chapters to cover making selections, working with vector paths, and working with masks, channels and text.

Part IV: Photoshop for Art's Sake covers the use of Photoshop's brushes, darkroom effects, and filters (separated into four chapters for texture, artistic, distortion, and image breakup).

Part V. Advanced Techniques covers using layers to combine effects, using actions to automate repetitive tasks, and techniques for preparing to combine multiple images into one.

Part VI: Preparing Images for the Web is three chapters long. The first deals with the art of image optimization — that is, tweaking an image for peak Web performance. The next addresses designing images for interactive graphics and discusses image maps, image slicing, rollover events, and animation.

The balance of the book is devoted to referencing Photoshop's nuances in a series of appendixes.

Appendix A is a reference that discusses all the Photoshop 6 commands and palettes.

Appendix B covers the Photoshop 6 and Image Ready 3.0 toolbox and options bars.

Appendix C focuses on all of the *current* keyboard shortcuts and modifiers that can be used to help you do things faster.

Appendix D explains what's on this book's CD-ROM, including trial versions of complimentary programs; images that can be used for practicing the tasks in this book; and a searchable e-version of the book.

SECTION I

1) PHOTOSHOP BASICS

2) PHOTOSHOP FILE MANAGEMENT

THE PHOTOSHOP 6 INTERFACE FOR WINDOWS

You can start Photoshop 6 in Windows by clicking Start, choosing Programs and then choosing Adobe, and then clicking Adobe Photoshop 6. You can also start Photoshop from the desktop, if you have a shortcut present, or double-clicking a Photoshop document icon in the Windows desktop or in Windows Explorer. Finally, you can start Photoshop by dragging a Photoshop file from Windows Explorer to the desktop shortcut. This opens Photoshop as well as the file you dragged onto the shortcut icon.

The typical Windows interface for Photoshop looks like the following:

THE PHOTOSHOP 6 INTERFACE FOR WINDOWS

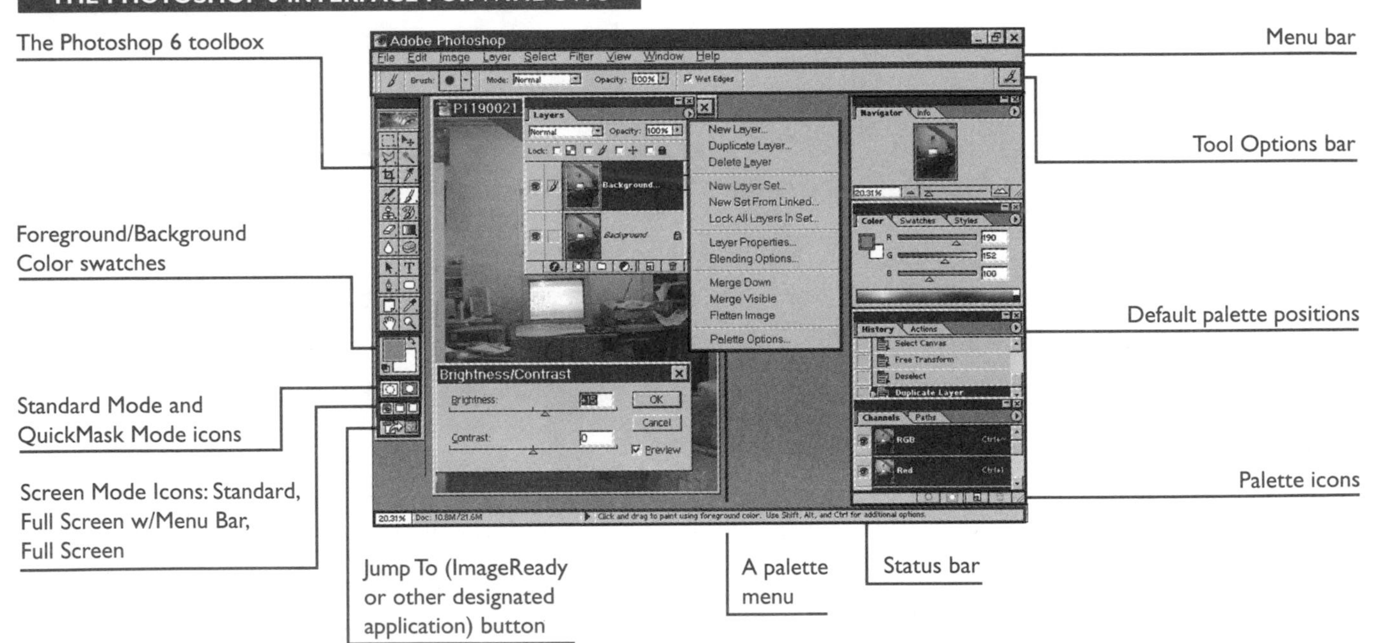

THE PHOTOSHOP 6 INTERFACE FOR MACS

You can start Photoshop 6 on a Mac by double-clicking the Photoshop 6 icon in a folder or an alias of that icon (usually placed on the desktop).

You can also double-click a Photoshop document, have an alias in the Apple menu, or drag a compatible document icon onto either the Photoshop application icon or an alias to it.

The typical Mac interface looks like the following:

THE PHOTOSHOP 6 INTERFACE FOR MACS

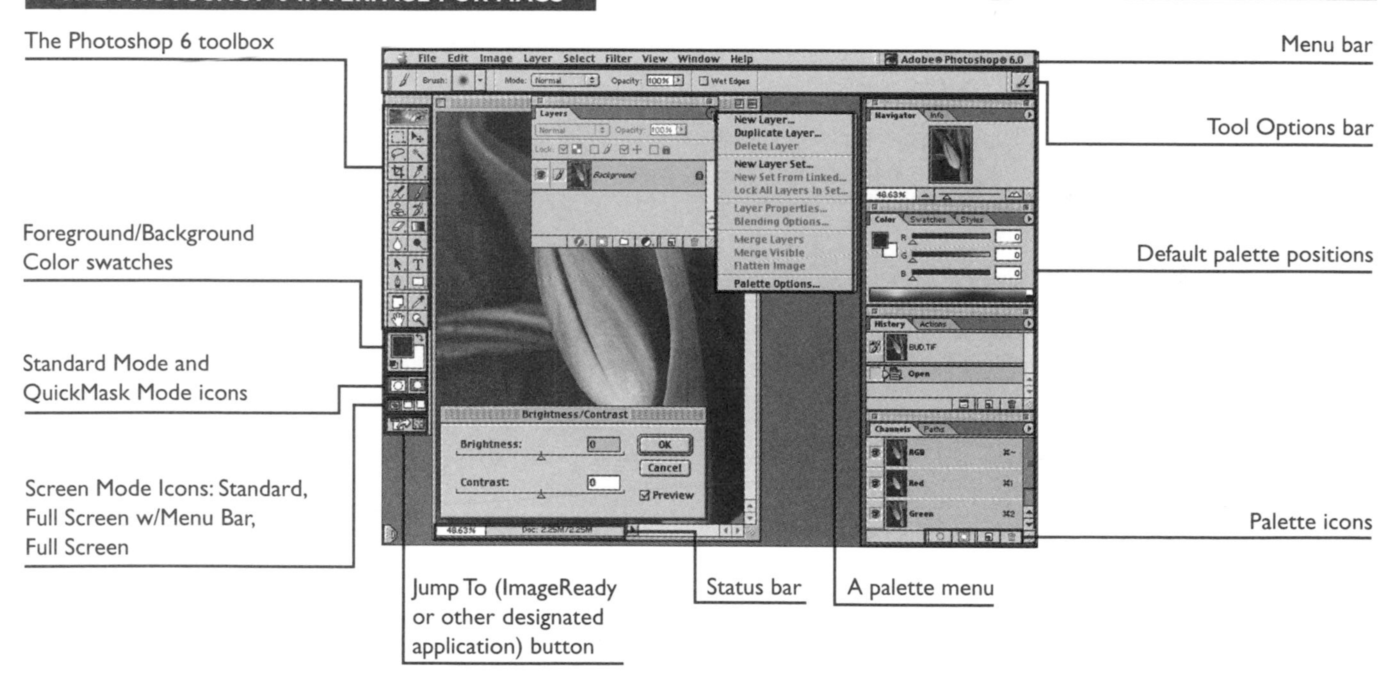

WHAT IS NEW IN PHOTOSHOP 6

Photoshop 6 features a significant redesign of the user interface, much tighter coordination of interface and features with ImageReady (now up to version 3.0), and the addition of enough new tools and features to make the upgrade irresistible to both image makers and Web designers.

Additional Interface Improvements

The basic Windows and Mac interfaces (see the previous pages) include many improvements, including the following:

- Restyled tool fly-out menus: The new fly-outs appear as a vertical menu with the name of each individual tool alongside the tool's icon.
- Instant changing of units: If you have the Show Rulers command in effect, you can right-click (Windows)/Ctrl-click (Mac) the ruler to access a menu that gives you the choice of Pixels, Inches, Centimeters, Points, Picas, and Percent.
- Palette docking: You can keep your favorite palettes accessible, but out of your workspace, by docking them on the right side of the Options bar. Palette docking works best with a screen resolution of 1024 x 768 or greater and a screen greater than 17 inches. You just choose Window, then click Show palette to open the palette, then drag it to the palette well on your current Options bar.
- A streamlined interface for accessing brush sizes and styles quickly: The new Brushes Styles Library replaces the old Brushes palette, and it can be accessed directly from the new Options bar. You can click a button to view the drop-down library. The button automatically appears on the Options bar for any tool that uses brush shapes. (See Chapter 12.)

- Faster and more intuitive file-loading capabilities in Windows: You can now load several files by clicking File and then shift-clicking several files before clicking Open, whether you are using a Mac or a PC. Also, Photoshop 6 lets you designate certain folders as "favorites," which you can access from a Favorites button in the upper-right corner of the File Open dialog box. Click the button, and the designated folders appear in a short list.

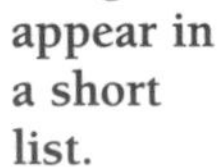

Expanded Format Support

Photoshop 6 supports several new formats including layered TIFF files, TIF files that use JPEG and ZIP compression, PBM files, Wavefront RLA, and Alias PIX. In addition, the redesigned Import dialog box makes importing PhotoCD images easier.

You can now view 16-bit Lab images in Photoshop and convert them to other modes. Also, you can apply a number of the most essential filters to 16-bit images, including Gaussian Blur, Add Noise, Median, Unsharp Mask, High Pass, Dust & Scratches, and Gradient Map. (See Chapters 15 and 16.)

More Powerful Vector Paths

Photoshop 6 adds the ability to draw predefined vector shapes to any size and proportion in a single click-and-drag operation. New buttons in the Options bar enable you to create new shapes by adding, subtracting, restricting, and inverting standard shapes. (See Chapter 7.)

The geometric shape tools enable you to create raster shapes through vectors without having to convert the shape into a selection and then fill it. You can also use any of the shape tools, including the Pen tool, to draw either a workpath or a clipping path on a new shape layer prefilled with the current foreground color.

Although the existing Pen tool, which draws industry-standard Bezier-curve vector shapes, stays intact, it offers flexible selection tools in a separate Toolbox location. (See Chapter 7.)

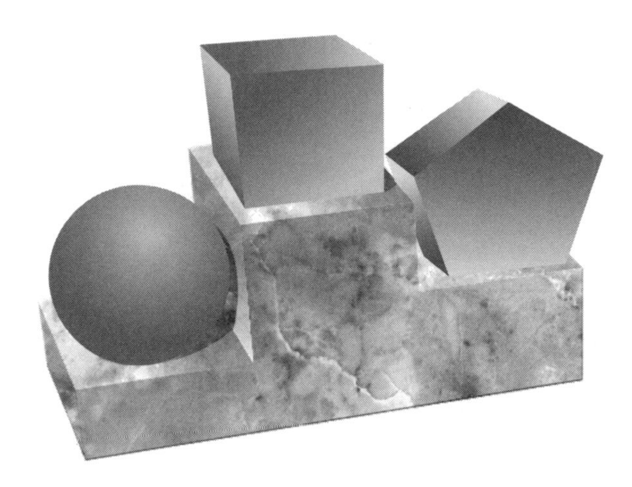

Quicker and Smoother Image Extraction

With Photoshop 6, you can create complex image knockouts using three new features in the Extract dialog box:

- A Smart Highlighting option, which automatically marks the edge, highlights the optimum width, and gives the edge the optimum overlap between foreground and background.
- The Cleanup tool, which acts just like the Background Eraser and almost automatically cleans up smudgy "leftovers."
- The Edge Touchup tool, which acts like the History brush to "paint in" overclipped areas. (See Chapter 12.)

WHAT IS NEW IN PHOTOSHOP 6

CONTINUED

Layers and New Layers

Photoshop 6 offers a number of improvements for working with layers:

- You can manage as many layers as you like by grouping them in sets (much like placing files in folders). You can click the triangle in the Layer Set name bar to expand or hide the layers in that set.
- Layer Effects are no longer under that name on the Layer menu. Instead, you look for Layer Styles. However, Effects Layers are still a layer type.
- Photoshop 6 offers a new layer type called a *Fill Layer*, so called because it is entirely occupied by any one of the Photoshop fill types: solid color, gradient, or pattern.
- You can now change Adjustment Layer types without deleting the Adjustment Layer. You can also readjust Adjustment and Fill layers. (See Chapter 9.)
- The new Layer Styles dialog box and shape tools enable you to (almost) automatically create 3D text, textured text, and button shapes. (See Chapter 9.)
- Photoshop 6 lets you save a group of settings, created in the Layer Styles dialog box, to a specialized palette called a library. (See "Manage Presets with the Preset Library," in this chapter.) You can apply Photoshop's Styles presets, or you can create and save your own styles by clicking an icon of that style in the Layer Effects library, shown below.

PDF Support Extended

You can now output files to PDF and, in the process, save layers, transparencies, and vector objects. You can send these files to any organization equipped with Acrobat prepress plug-ins and publish quality printed materials.

Enhanced Text Capabilities

With Photoshop 6, you can directly type text onto an image. You can also apply a variety of impressive transformations, warping, and styles to the text without affecting its editability. Enhanced character and paragraph palettes mimic those in Illustrator and InDesign. (See Chapter 11.)

You can also twist and warp text with a great deal of control, although there is still no text-on-a-path command. (Read more about warping in Chapters 11 and 13.)

Interactive Warping

You can now interactively warp sections of the image in an endless variety of ways. With the new Liquify command on the Image menu, you can refine already created strokes and distortions.

By turning on the mesh, you can preview the effect of each stroke and distortion tool. Also, you can easily protect those parts of the image that you want to make sure do not warp. You can either select part of the image before you employ the Liquify command or you can use the Freeze tool to paint a rubylith (transparent red). (See Chapter 13.)

WHAT IS NEW IN PHOTOSHOP 6 CONTINUED

More Versatile Actions

Photoshop 6 offers you more options for opening and renaming files by an Action. This feature makes Actions far better at batch operations, where you apply a number of commands on a whole group of files. Now, when you save an Action's results to a whole group of files, you can include the following information in the original filename: original name, date, serial number, and file extensions.

If you have an Action selected in the Actions palette, you can turn it into a droplet automatically. In case you are new to droplets, a *droplet* is a mini-application that applies an action to any file that you drop on it. Droplets can be placed in directories or on desktops, so you do not even have to open the files in Photoshop in order to have them processed by the Action in the droplet.

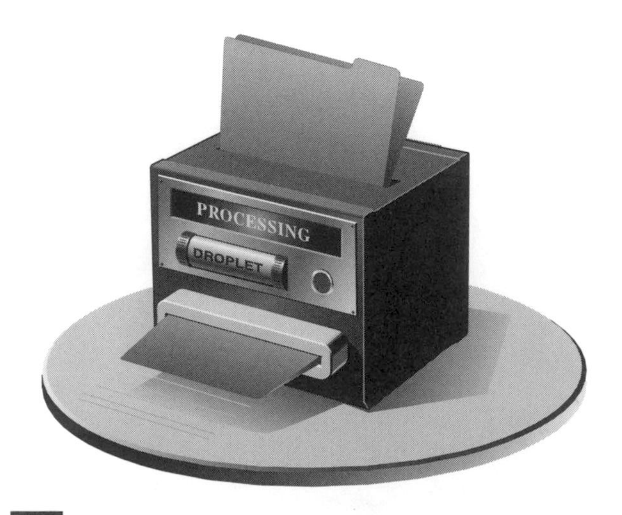

Better Print Previews

You can now preview the image as it appears in print, thanks to a new Print Options dialog box. You can even specify halftone screens and transfer functions, as well as crop marks, registration marks, captions, and labels.

You can view and change the assigned ICC profile to see the effect of your color management settings. You can also control whether vector data outputs with your image at print time.

More Powerful Web Graphics

Photoshop 6 makes the production of Web graphics a more flexible, controllable and professional process. It does so in several ways:

- More Web graphics capabilities built into Photoshop: You can now slice images in Photoshop without jumping into ImageReady (unless you want to attach JavaScript rollovers to the slices). ImageReady now incorporates more new Photoshop features—such as layer management, text control enhancements, text warping, and the Liquify command. (For more information regarding ImageReady, see Section VI, Preparing Images for the Web.)
- Greater control over the optimization of Web graphics in both Photoshop and ImageReady 3.0: You can now use channels (masks) to selectively optimize specific parts of an image without resorting to slicing, which restricts you to rectangular areas. You can also size a graphic as you save it for the Web—a great time-saver.
- Integrated Vector shape tools: The new Photoshop shape tools and Layer Styles effect now appear in ImageReady 3.0 as well as Photoshop 6.
- Dynamic layer-based slices: You can add layer effects to buttons and text. You can also add JavaScript rollovers in ImageReady 3.0. (See Chapter 22.)
- Easier jumping between Photoshop 6 and ImageReady 3.0: You can now literally jump between Photoshop 6 and ImageReady 3.0 by clicking the Jump To button. The program no longer prompts you to save your file when you make a jump.

- New animation capabilities, such as the ability to animate warped text: You can animate "liquified" text so that it morphs between one liquified effect and another. (See Chapter 13.)
- Flexible handling of JavaScript rollover automation, including a styles library for rollovers: You can either use standard events as triggers for a rollover action (for example, Mouse Over, Mouse Down) or insert any custom JavaScript code that you are clever enough to write. (See Chapter 22.)
- New image map shapes and capabilities: You can now use circles and freeform polygons to define hotspots in image maps. You can easily associate URLs with these hotspots and jump to other Web pages by clicking a button.
- More accessible controls: You can preview images in a browser, and preview rollover effects and image map effects instantaneously with four new buttons near the bottom of the Toolbox in both Photoshop 6 and ImageReady 3.0.

SET UP WINDOWS TO COMPLEMENT PHOTOSHOP

You do not really have to do anything special to make Windows and Photoshop work well together. Still, you can do certain things to enhance their coexistence. The default Windows color scheme leans toward garish and can seriously hamper your judgment of color relationships and dynamics in a photograph.

First, set your monitor to display as much of the subtle tonalities in a photo as possible. Set your monitor to either High Color (thousands of colors) or True Color (millions of colors).

Second, get rid of as many of the extraneous colors surrounding a photo as possible. Do not use colored wallpapers and screen savers or any of the appearance schemes provided by Windows or invented by others. Colors outside the picture you are working on can influence your ability to accurately adjust and choose colors within the image.

If you just occasionally use Photoshop to edit and size a Web graphic or to enhance photos for a family album, you can leave your desktop color scheme alone. But if you are a serious artist, graphic designer, or prepress specialist, your ability to judge colors accurately becomes much more critical.

SET UP WINDOWS TO COMPLEMENT PHOTOSHOP

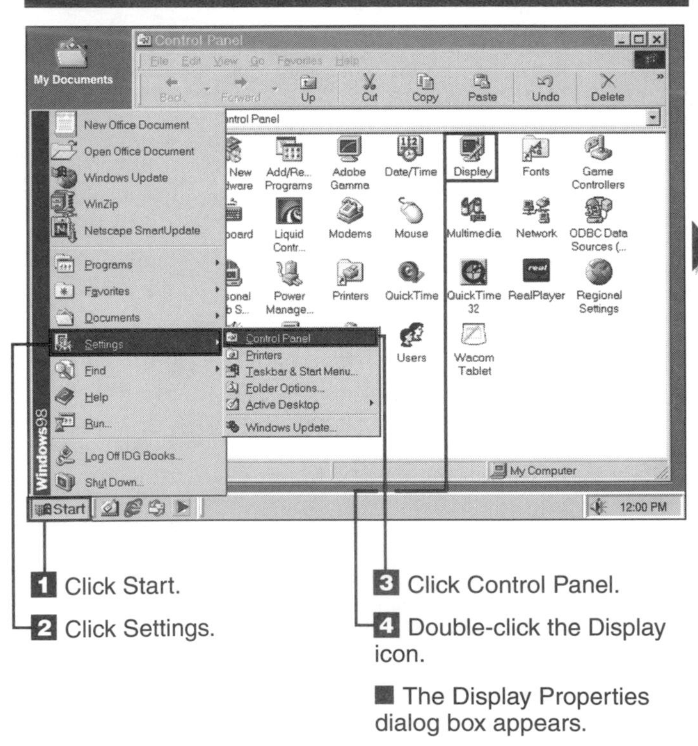

1 Click Start.

2 Click Settings.

3 Click Control Panel.

4 Double-click the Display icon.

■ The Display Properties dialog box appears.

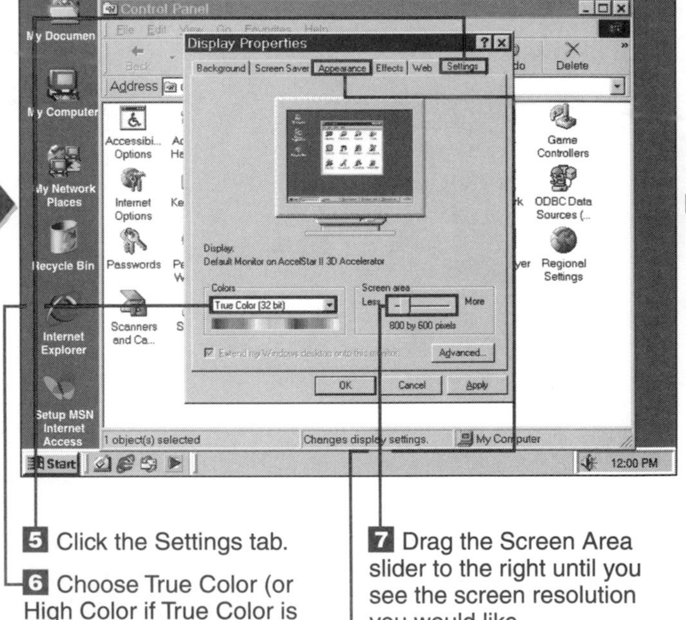

5 Click the Settings tab.

6 Choose True Color (or High Color if True Color is not available) from the Color palette menu.

Note: Not all Photoshop commands work in color modes other than RGB (though most will work in CMYK or LAB).

7 Drag the Screen Area slider to the right until you see the screen resolution you would like.

8 Click the Appearance tab.

Is there a way to switch settings more quickly?

✔ Yes. Place the cursor on the desktop and right-click, then choose Properties from the In-Context menu. The Display Properties dialog box appears. You avoid having to go through the My Computer route.

Is there a way to save my new settings and wallpaper so I do not have to repeat these steps every time I want the same look?

✔ Yes. First, make sure all your appearance settings are okay. Then, in the Display Properties window, click the Appearance tab. Click Save As. Name the scheme and click OK. Then you can always retrieve the entire scheme by clicking its name.

Can I use a black or gray background (wallpaper) for the Windows desktop?

✔ Yes. Open a new file in Photoshop and make it approximately 16 pixels square (see Chapter 3 to find out how to do this). Select Edit, then Fill or the Paint Bucket tool to fill the image with solid black. Save the image as a Windows bitmap (BMP) file. Place it in the C:\Windows directory (folder). In the Display Settings window, click the Background tab. In the Wallpaper box, choose the Tile radio button and click Browse. Locate the file you saved and click OK.

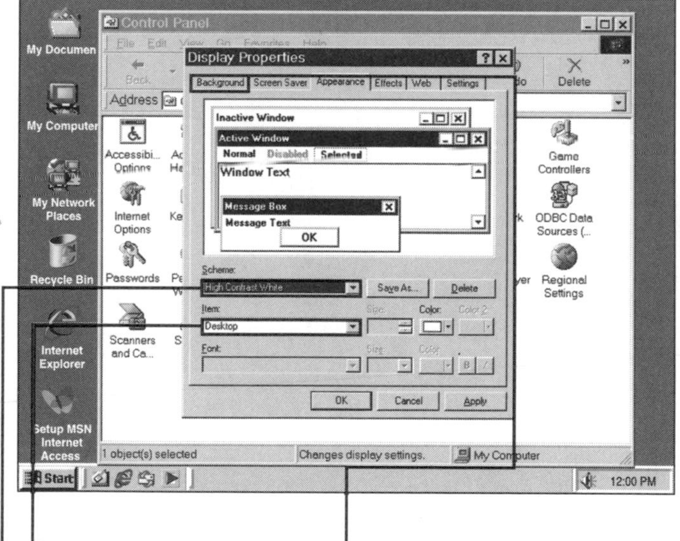

9 Choose Desktop from the Item menu.

10 Choose High Contrast White in the Scheme menu.

Note: You can choose to use smaller or larger letters. Smaller letters let you see more of the image you are editing, but larger letters in window titles and menu names are easier to read.

11 Click the Background tab.

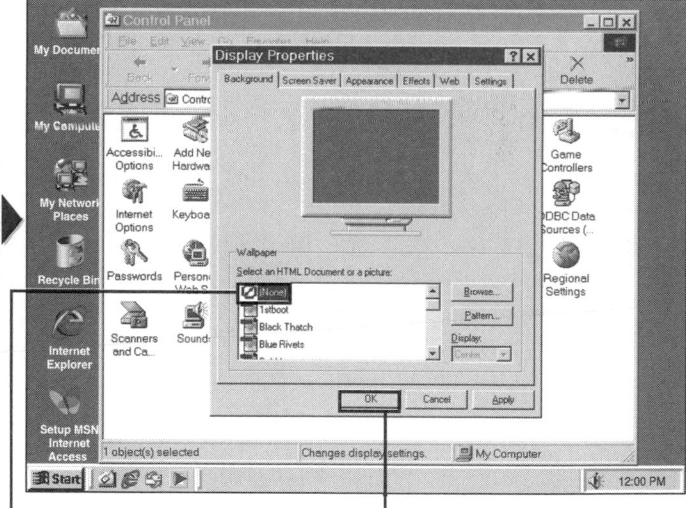

12 Choose None from the Wallpaper list.

13 Click OK.

SET UP YOUR MAC TO COMPLEMENT PHOTOSHOP

Setting up the Macintosh desktop to give the most accurate preview of color images is even easier than in Windows.

First, unless your work will strictly be in black and white, set your monitor to display as much of the subtle tonalities in a photo as possible. Set your monitor to either High Color (thousands of colors) or True Color (millions of colors).

Second, get rid of as many of the extraneous colors surrounding a photo as possible. Do not use colored backgrounds, background patterns, or pictures for the desktop. The colors outside the picture you are working on can influence your ability to accurately adjust and choose colors within the image.

Choosing the appropriate resolution setting based on the size of your monitor is important for image quality. Here is a hint: If your CRT monitor is 12 to 15 inches, set the resolution to 640 x 480; set 17-inch monitors to 800 x 600; and set 19- to 21-inch monitors to 1024 x 768. Flat panel LCD monitors play by each manufacturer's own rules.

The steps shown in the task on this page are appropriate to all revisions of Mac OS 9. If you use a different version, these steps are slightly different, but not so much that you will not know what to do.

SET UP YOUR MAC TO COMPLEMENT PHOTOSHOP

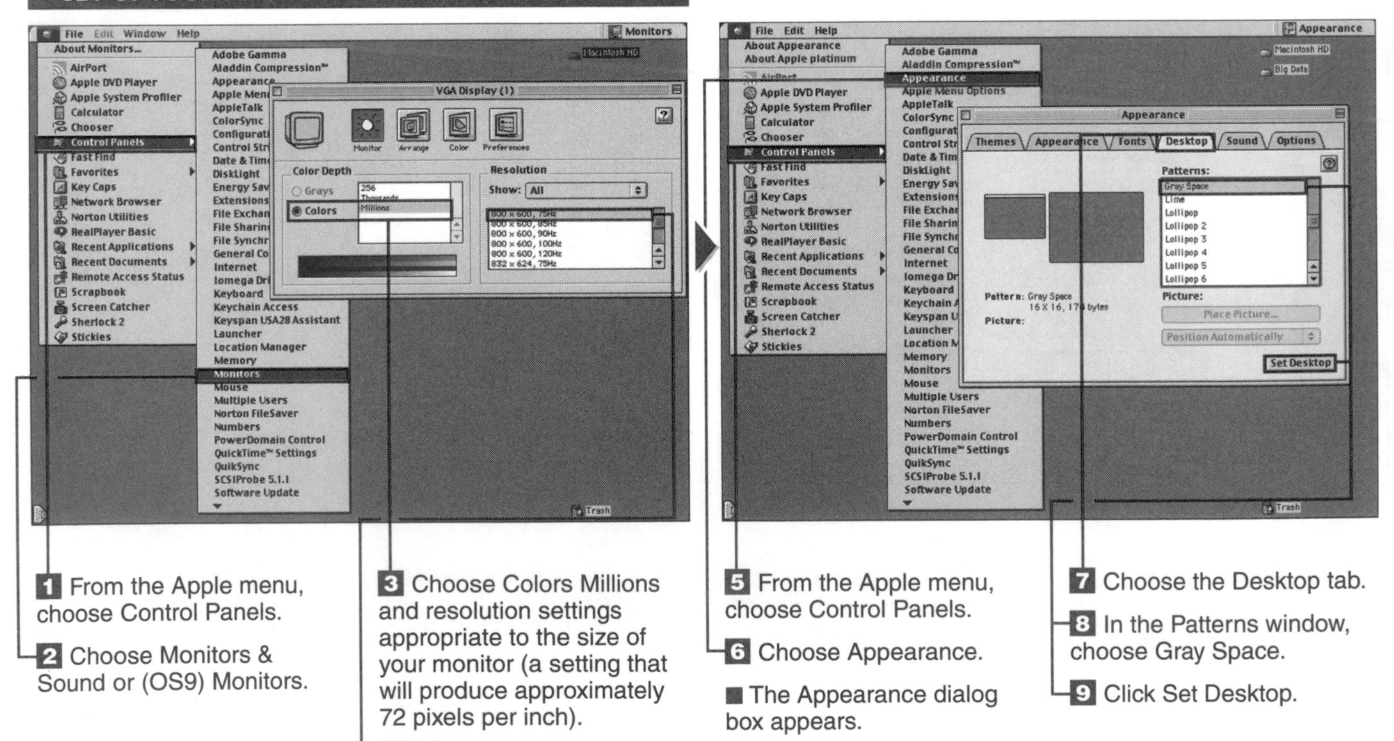

1 From the Apple menu, choose Control Panels.

2 Choose Monitors & Sound or (OS9) Monitors.

3 Choose Colors Millions and resolution settings appropriate to the size of your monitor (a setting that will produce approximately 72 pixels per inch).

4 Choose the correct profile for your monitor (consult your monitor manual or the manufacturer).

5 From the Apple menu, choose Control Panels.

6 Choose Appearance.

■ The Appearance dialog box appears.

7 Choose the Desktop tab.

8 In the Patterns window, choose Gray Space.

9 Click Set Desktop.

SET GENERAL PREFERENCES

Before you start working in Photoshop, you can organize Photoshop so that the program works the way you want it to.

The first thing you need to do is open the Preferences dialog box, which you access with the Preferences command. (Note that in Photoshop 6, the location of the Preferences command has been moved to the Edit menu from the File menu.)

You can choose your preferred type of Color Picker, either Photoshop's, your Windows native picker, or one of the pickers offered on a Mac. All the exercises in this book that use the Color Picker use Photoshop's, so you should set yours that way at least until you have the confidence to use another scheme. However, the Photoshop Color Picker is by far the most widely used (even in many other programs) Color Picker on both Macs and PCs.

You can also choose the type of Interpolation that Photoshop will use when you enlarge an image. Unless you are using a really slow computer that is short on memory, choose Bicubic.

Note: From the Preferences dialog box, you also can change the settings for all the Preferences categories: General, Saving Files, Display & Cursors, Transparency & Gamut, Units & Rulers, Guides & Grid, Plug-ins & Scratch Disk, and Memory & Image Cache. This chapter discusses many of those settings later.

SET GENERAL PREFERENCES

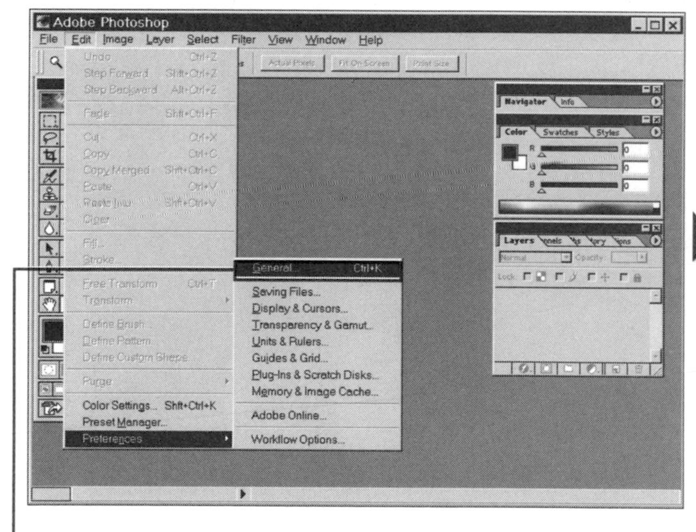

1 Choose Edit, Preferences, and then click General.

■ The General Preferences dialog box appears.

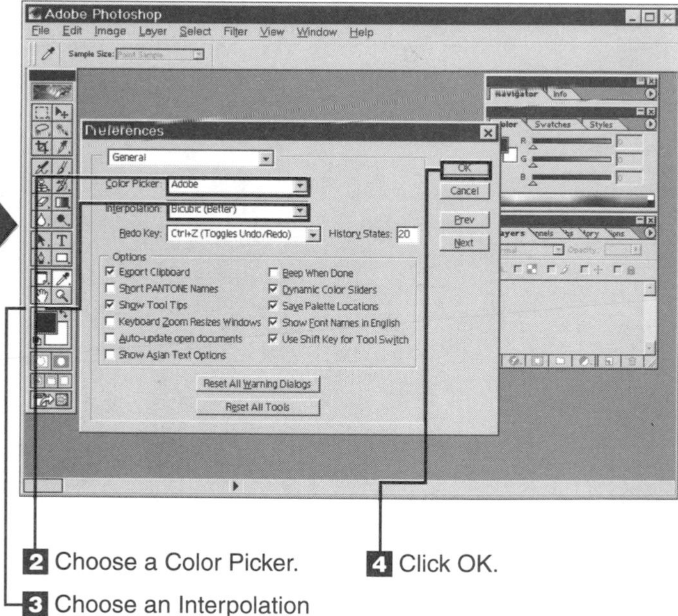

2 Choose a Color Picker.

3 Choose an Interpolation setting.

4 Click OK.

SET PREFERENCES FOR SAVING FILES

Photoshop enables you to define exactly how you want your files to be saved. Setting preferences for saving files is the simplest job in the series of setting preferences—and one of the most important.

Using the Preferences dialog box, you can define

- Whether you want an image preview or whether you want Photoshop to ask. If you are saving JPEG, GIF, or PNG files for Web use, you should select Never Save, because previews are of little use with the Web and add to download time. You are better off using Photoshop's Save for Web command. (See Section VI.)
- Whether you want the file extension to be Upper Case or Lower Case. Stick with Lower Case, the default.
- What file compatibility options you want. Photoshop 6 offers two: maximizing backward compatibility to previous versions of Photoshop (highly recommended), and enabling advanced TIFF save options.

Macintosh users get a few more options for saving files than PC users do. For example, the Mac can save picture icons to the desktop and full-size 72 dpi thumbnails for use as accurate size placeholders in publishing programs.

SET PREFERENCES FOR SAVING FILES

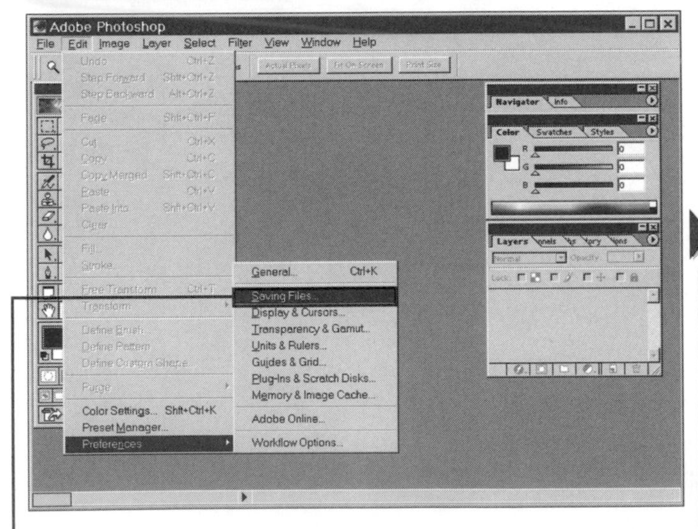

1 Choose Edit, Preferences, and then click Saving Files.

■ The Preferences dialog box appears with Saving Files in the pop-up menu (Mac) or drop-down list (Windows).

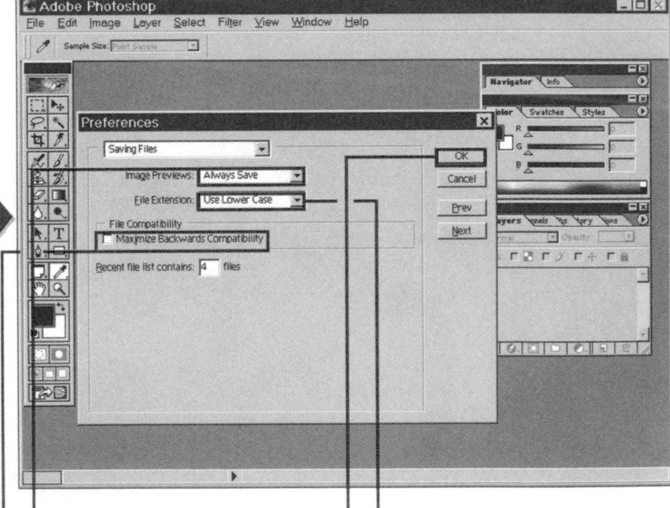

2 Choose Always Save (unless photo is destined for Web — see intro).

3 Check if you want to maximize compatibility with files for earlier versions of Photoshop.

4 Choose Use Lower Case (for most consistent compatibility with other operating systems).

5 Mac only: Choose Always (from the Append Extensions menu), and check Thumbnail.

6 Click OK.

SET PREFERENCES FOR DISPLAY AND CURSORS

The Photoshop Display & Cursors Preferences dialog box lets you choose the methods for displaying the shapes in which the cursors will appear.

The Display options include showing Color Channels in Color, rather than the default grayscale. Most users find grayscale a more readable and easier-to-use choice. Use Diffusion Dither should be used only when you are forced to work on a display that cannot show all 16 million colors, while Use Pixel Doubling enables previews to display more quickly.

Photoshop differentiates between the cursors used by brushes (called *painting cursors*) and all other cursors. The Painting Cursors options are

- Standard, which displays the icon for the tool, so you know which brush you are using. However, you will have a hard time knowing how much area your brush stroke is going to affect. Pros rarely use this setting.
- Precise, which displays a target for the exact tip of the brush, so you know exactly on which pixel your brush is centered.
- Brush size, which displays a circle that describes the limits of the brush's coverage. Brush size is a very helpful option.

SET PREFERENCES FOR DISPLAY AND CURSORS

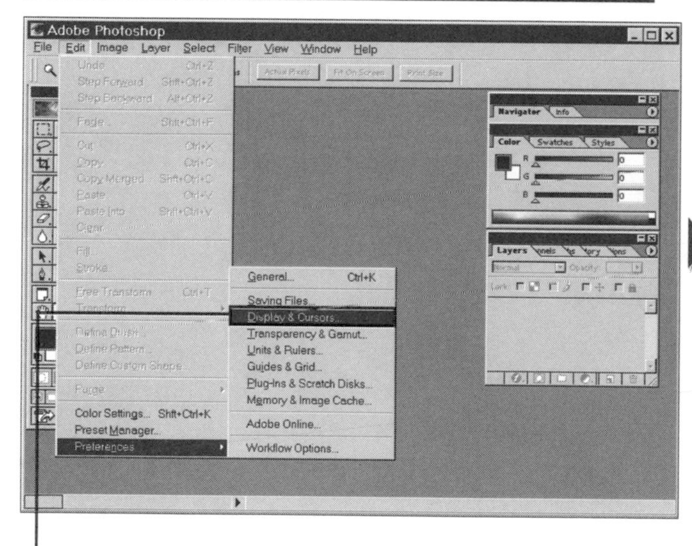

1 Choose Edit, Preferences, and then click Display & Cursors.

■ The Display & Cursors Preferences dialog box appears.

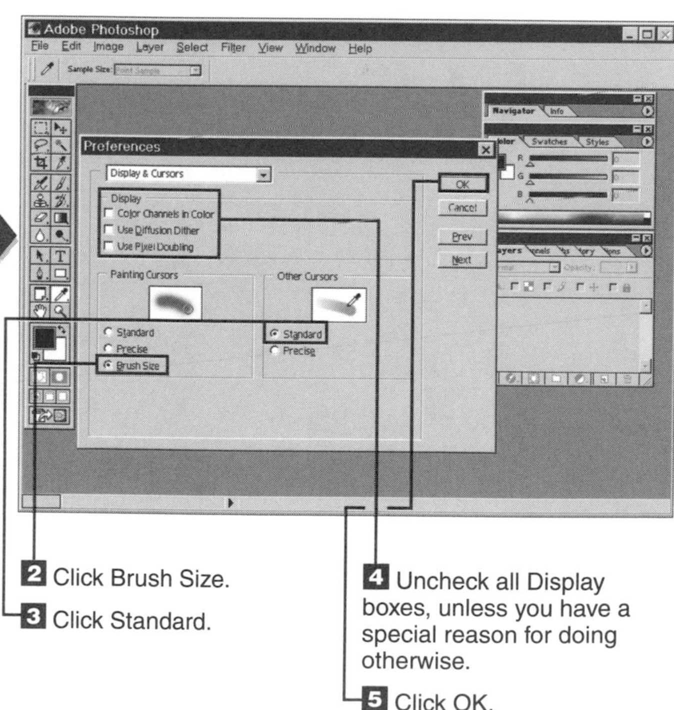

2 Click Brush Size.

3 Click Standard.

4 Uncheck all Display boxes, unless you have a special reason for doing otherwise.

5 Click OK.

SET PREFERENCES FOR TRANSPARENCY AND GAMUT

You can use the Transparency & Gamut Preferences dialog box to determine how Photoshop displays a transparent background and how it alerts you when you have chosen colors for your image that are outside the range of the intended CMYK color printer.

Most color printers use the CMYK (cyan-magenta-yellow-black) color scheme, while the default color scheme used by your monitor is RGB (red-green-blue). RGB colors that cannot be accurately interpreted by a CMYK color printer are called *out-of-gamut colors*. Photoshop can show these as a garish, flat color to let you know that you had better make image adjustments to get the proper printed output.

To alert you when part (or all) of your image contains absolutely nothing—in other words, is transparent—Photoshop displays a checkerboard pattern. The Transparency Settings portion of the Transparency & Gamut Preferences dialog box lets you choose the color of the darker squares in the checkerboard so it will appear in obvious contrast to the rest of your image. You can also choose the size of the squares—small, medium, large, or none—in the checkerboard.

Note: Chapter 4 covers how to make color adjustments.

SET PREFERENCES FOR TRANSPARENCY AND GAMUT

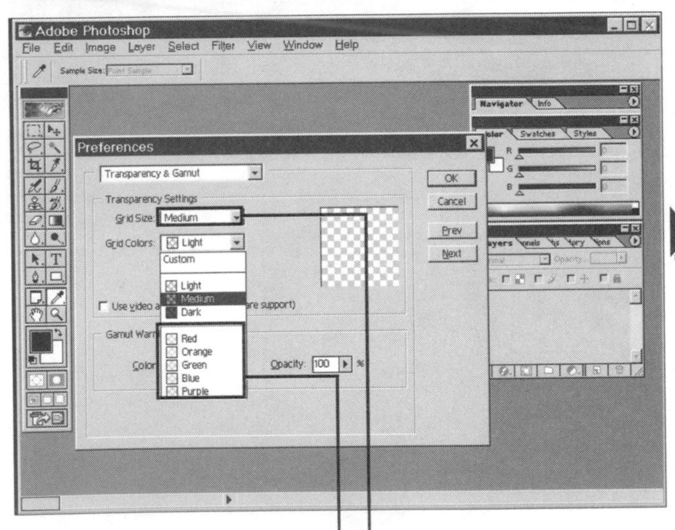

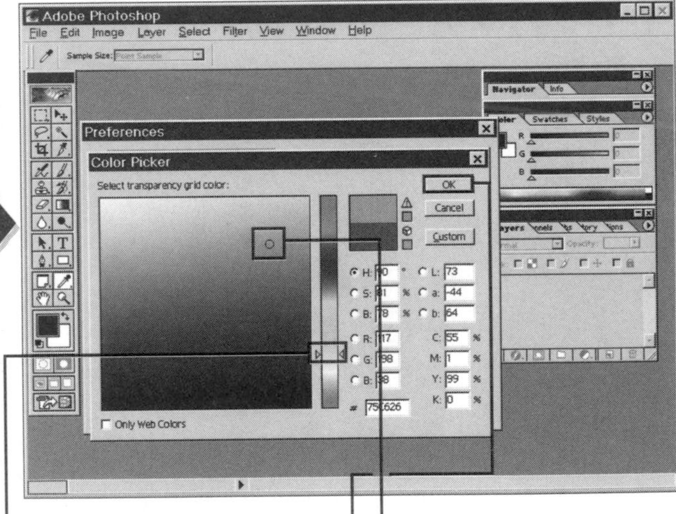

1 Choose Edit, Preferences, and then click Transparency & Gamut.

■ The Transparency & Gamut Preferences dialog box appears.

2 Choose Grid Size: Small, Medium, Large, or None.

3 If you want to change the color for any of the items, click the appropriate color square.

■ The Color Picker dialog box appears.

4 Click the sliding Hue bar to choose color.

5 Click the Select transparency grid color area to choose color intensity.

6 Click OK.

SET PREFERENCES FOR UNITS AND RULERS

The Units & Rulers Preferences dialog box lets you choose the system of measurement that will be used throughout your Photoshop session to measure the size of images, selections, layers, and canvas (the work area, including the image and its borders). You can also set column size and point/pica size.

Photoshop gives you the option of measuring in

- pixels
- picas (the standard unit of measurement for typesetting)
- or more conventional inches and centimeters

In general, you should use pixels as your ruler's unit of measurement, as pixels are constant and resolution is variable. In other words, an image 1 inch wide could be any number of pixels wide. On the other hand, if most of your images will be printed in a specific publication at a particular resolution, you may want to use inches or picas.

If type is a major element of your image, the decision as to which measurement unit to use is tougher. Choose pixels if you are going to use the image on the Web and picas if you will be targeting the image for print.

SET PREFERENCES FOR UNITS AND RULERS

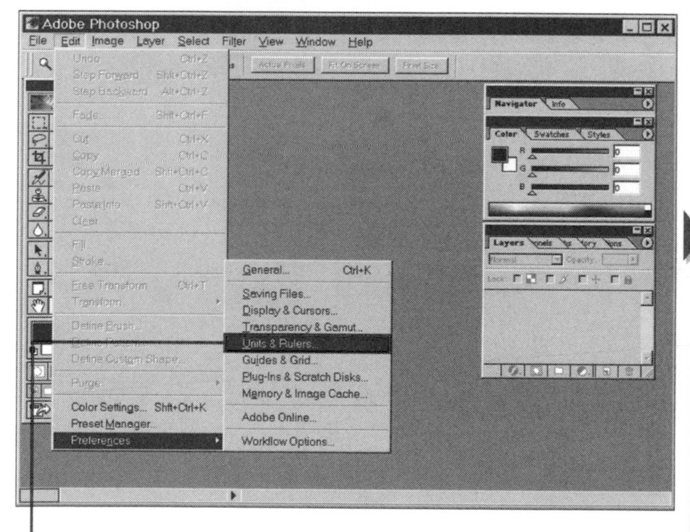

1 Choose Edit, Preferences, and then Units & Rulers.

■ The Units & Rulers Preferences dialog box appears.

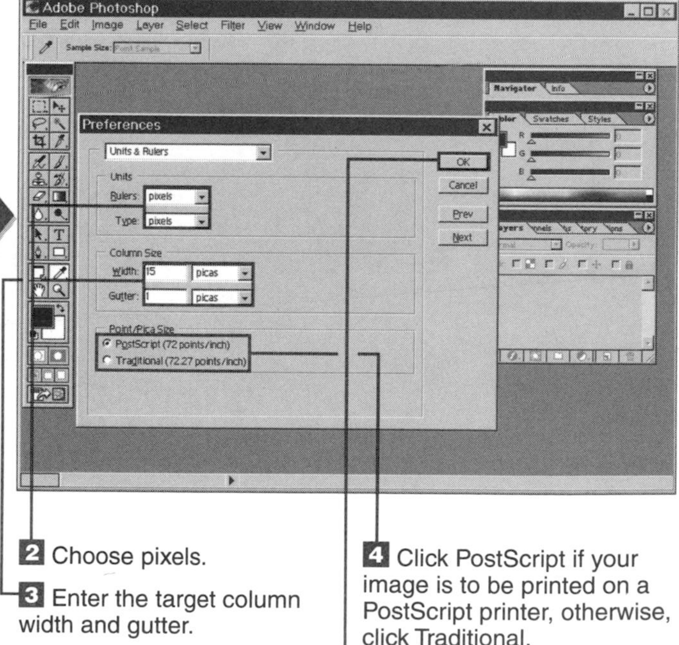

2 Choose pixels.

3 Enter the target column width and gutter.

4 Click PostScript if your image is to be printed on a PostScript printer, otherwise, click Traditional.

5 Click OK to finish.

SET PREFERENCES FOR GUIDES AND GRID

You can use guides and grids to help you space and place objects, type, and brush strokes on the screen.

Guides and grids are nonprinting visual aids in the form of single-pixel lines in a color (bright blue by default) that contrasts with the image. If you are a beginning artist, you may also find painting from scratch easier if you draw on grid paper or make ruler guides for the compositional "rule of thirds." Here, the computer beats the traditional methods because you can hide your "amateur" guidelines when you have finished your image.

The Guides & Grid Preferences dialog box enables you to choose a color for your grids and guides. Picking separate colors for these is a good idea, just in case you find a reason to use the two together. Also, there may be times when the default blue is not visible due to a predominant amount of blue in your image.

Finally, you can choose to use either solid lines or dashed lines for both grids and guides. Grids can also be dotted lines. If you have an image that uses a lot of straight lines (such as venetian blinds or mattress-ticking type fabric patterns), broken lines can be easier to see.

SET PREFERENCES FOR GUIDES AND GRID

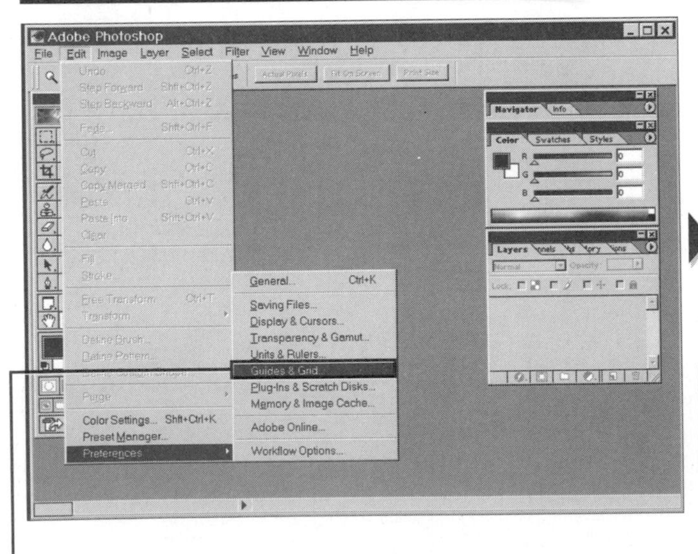

■1 Choose Edit, Preferences, and then Guides & Grid.

■ The Guides & Grid Preferences dialog box appears.

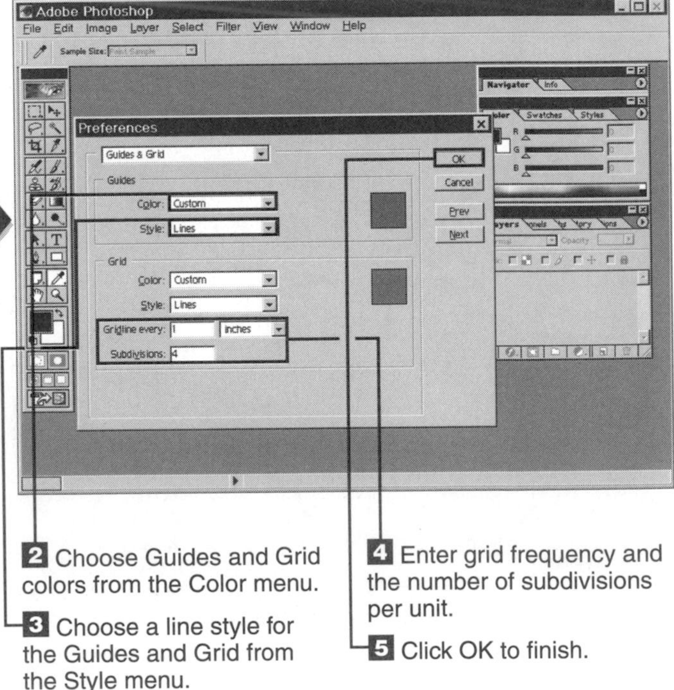

■2 Choose Guides and Grid colors from the Color menu.

■3 Choose a line style for the Guides and Grid from the Style menu.

■4 Enter grid frequency and the number of subdivisions per unit.

■5 Click OK to finish.

SET PREFERENCES FOR PLUG-INS AND SCRATCH DISKS

Using the Plug-ins & Scratch Disks Preferences dialog box, you can choose where Photoshop should look for installed plug-in programs and where it stores the data it is temporarily swapping out from active RAM.

Plug-ins are programs written so that they will work inside Photoshop to add greater functionality to Photoshop. You can put plug-ins in any folder you like. Use defaults whenever possible, because you will remember where a plug-in resides long after you have forgotten how you set up the program.

Some folks like to put plug-ins in a top-level folder outside of Photoshop so that there will be a shorter path to them from other applications that are compatible with Photoshop plug-ins.

Scratch disks refers to where Photoshop stores its temporary virtual memory files. If you have more than one hard disk, you can tell Photoshop to store its temporary files elsewhere.

Note: Unlike most other preference settings, Plug-ins & Scratch Disk settings you make now will not take effect until you restart Photoshop.

SET PREFERENCES FOR PLUG-INS AND SCRATCH DISKS

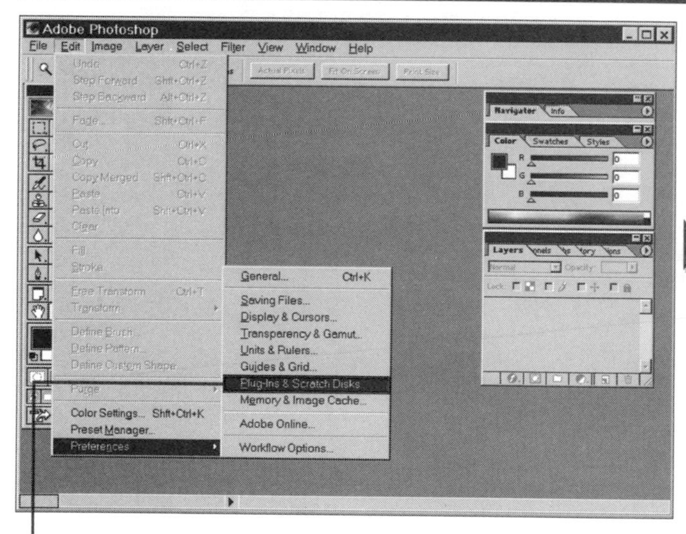

1 Choose Edit, Preferences, and then Plug-Ins & Scratch Disks.

■ The Plug-Ins & Scratch Disk Preferences dialog box appears.

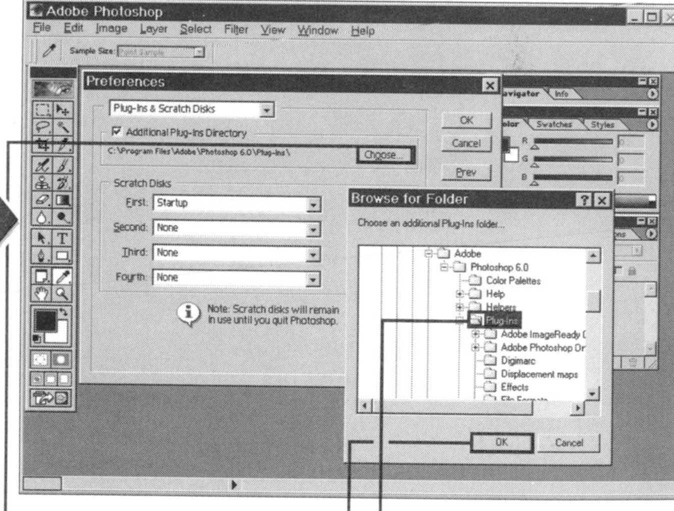

2 Click the Choose button.

■ The Browse for Folder dialog box appears in Windows. On a Mac, a standard Choose Folder (Open) dialog box appears; click the Choose button.

3 In Windows, navigate to the folder where you want to save your additional plug-ins in and select it.

4 Click OK.

SET PREFERENCES FOR MEMORY AND IMAGE CACHE

Photoshop, in versions since 4.0, uses a memory-caching scheme to speed its operations. Photoshop stores multiple resolutions of the currently active file in a cache, for example, so the program can access the resolution closest to the zoom level you are working in.

You can set two preferences for the image cache:

- the number of cache levels
- whether to use the cache for drawing histograms

Histograms are the graphs Photoshop draws in the Levels and Histogram dialog boxes (both found on the Image menu). If you check the box, histograms will be drawn faster but will not be as accurate, so leave the box unchecked unless you really need the speed or until you can afford more memory.

If you set more levels of cache, Photoshop operations will run faster, but you will have less memory to run them in.

Note: Memory & Image Cache (just Image Cache on the Mac) Preferences dialog box settings will not take effect until you restart Photoshop.

SET PREFERENCES FOR MEMORY AND IMAGE CACHE

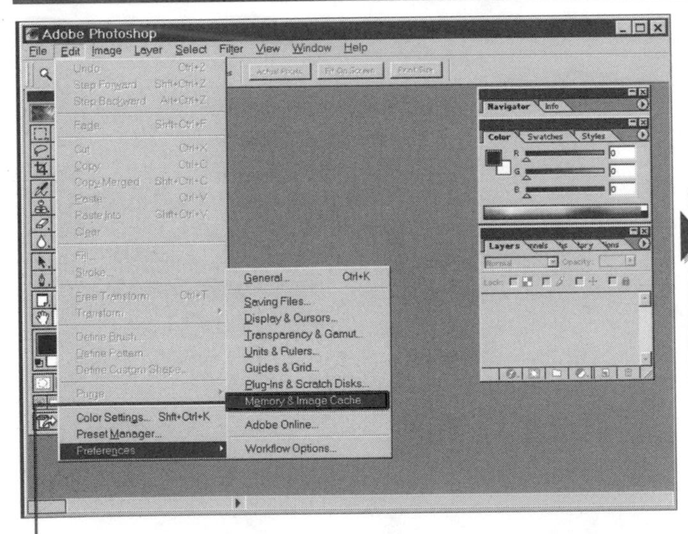

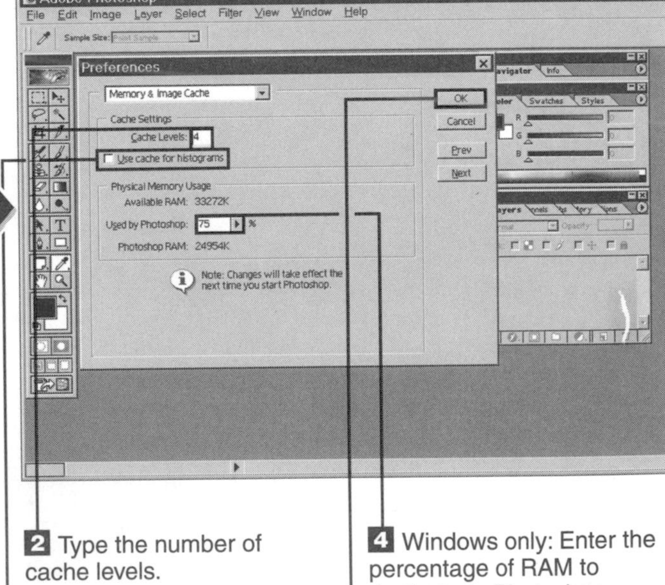

1 Choose Edit, Preferences, and then Memory & Image Cache.

■ The Memory & Image Cache Preferences dialog box (just Image Cache on the Mac) appears.

2 Type the number of cache levels.

3 Uncheck the Use Cache for Histograms box.

4 Windows only: Enter the percentage of RAM to dedicate to Photoshop.

5 Click OK.

Note: The settings do not take effect until you restart Photoshop.

RECOVER FROM MISTAKES: UNDO

If you make an error or a change that you decide you do not want to keep, Photoshop 6 gives you several ways to recover from your mistake.

One of the most fundamental things to understand about Photoshop is that it mostly works with *raster* (sometimes called *bitmap*) images. You cannot edit items in a raster image, such as an orange or a face, for example. Instead, you must edit the pixels that make up those items—and those pixels are part of a matrix that encompasses the whole layer. So, if you goof on part of the picture, you mess up the entire layer.

Photoshop 6 gives you six ways to recover from such mistakes without having to recreate the entire image: use Undo or Revert, duplicate a layer, use the History list, take a snapshot, or take a merged snapshot. If you understand the fundamental methods of recovery, and which to use when, you can save enormous amounts of time in the long run.

Undo is the fastest way to recover from a single-step mistake, such as a misplaced brush stroke. Undo is useless after performing more than one action, however.

The following pages describe the other five recovery methods.

RECOVER FROM MISTAKES: UNDO

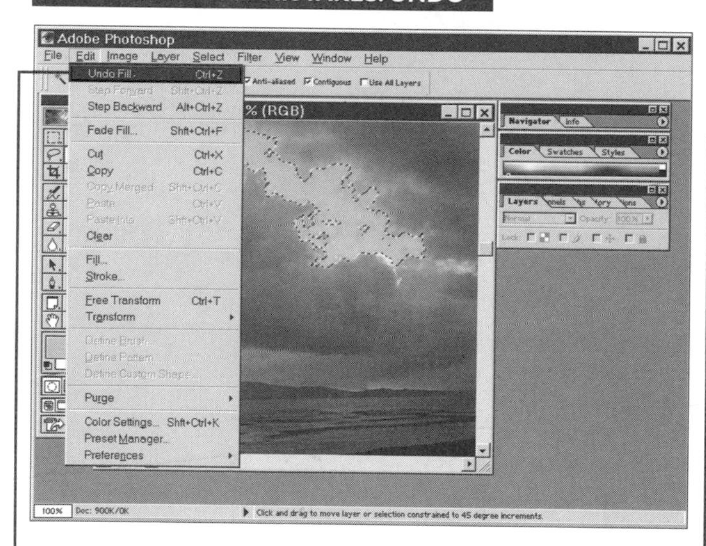

UNDO COMPLETELY

1 Choose Edit, then Undo (or press ⌘/Ctrl+Z).

Note: The name of the previous operation follows the Undo command. Undo also removes the last operation from the History list.

Note: If you change your mind, you can repeat this operation or press ⌘/Ctrl+Z again. The second time you repeat the operation, the command is called Redo (last operation).

FADE THE UNDO

1 Choose Edit, then Fade Fill.

■ The Fade dialog box appears.

2 Drag the slider to set opacity, then choose a Mode, then click OK.

Note: The quickest and most important way to undo is ⌘/Ctrl+7. Getting in thc habit of keeping your fingers near those keys is a good idea.

RECOVER FROM MISTAKES: REVERT

Although immediately undoing anything you do not like is smart, sometimes you do not realize that you have taken the wrong path until you are several steps down the path. In that case, you can choose Edit, then Revert to retrieve the last saved version of your image.

To take maximum advantage of the Revert method, always keep your project saved to Photoshop (.PSD) format until the project is complete. This way you will have access to all layers, channels, and most other Photoshop features when you revert to the last-saved version.

There is one exception: You cannot retrieve the History list with the Revert command. (See "Recover from Mistakes: Use the History List," later in this chapter, for more about the History list.) Photoshop does not save the History list when the file is saved in order to conserve disk space.

One tip: Get in the habit of saving the file each time you get to a stage where you know you are pleased with the overall effect. Then you can always revert without wasting RAM with unneeded snapshots.

RECOVER FROM MISTAKES: REVERT

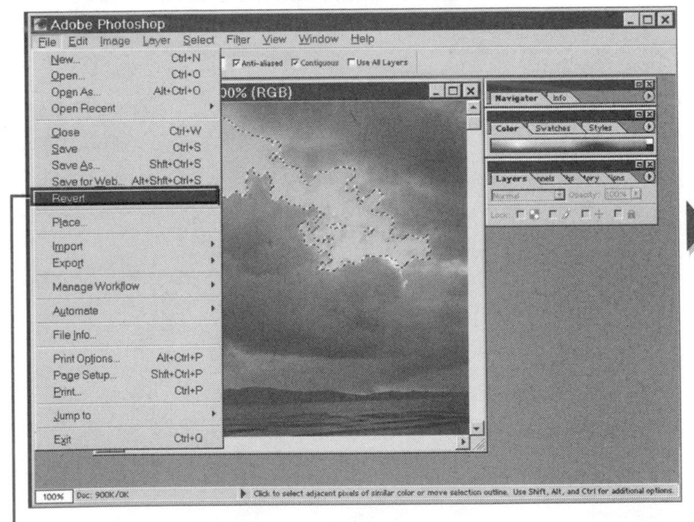

1 Choose Edit, then Revert.

■ The file is immediately restored to the last saved version.

■ Any steps taken since the last save are gone. You cannot recover those steps.

RECOVER FROM MISTAKES: DUPLICATE A LAYER

Most Photoshop commands work only on the currently selected layer. If you want to experiment with the content of a layer and then be able to recover quickly if you (or your client) hate the result, you can make a duplicate of the target layer.

By duplicating the target layer, if you do not like the result, you can just trash the layer. You can also turn it off and on until you decide which layer looks best to you.

You can have multiple duplicate layers for any number of layers, each showing variations in treatment when compared to the original layer. In addition to the advantage mentioned previously, you may discover that the best effect is a combination of the effects on several different layers that depict the same subject.

One problem with creating several duplicate layers is that having lots of layers requires lots of file space (and RAM, if you are a Mac user). Be sure to delete or merge layers (see Chapter 9) after the need to keep them independent has passed.

RECOVER FROM MISTAKES: DUPLICATE A LAYER

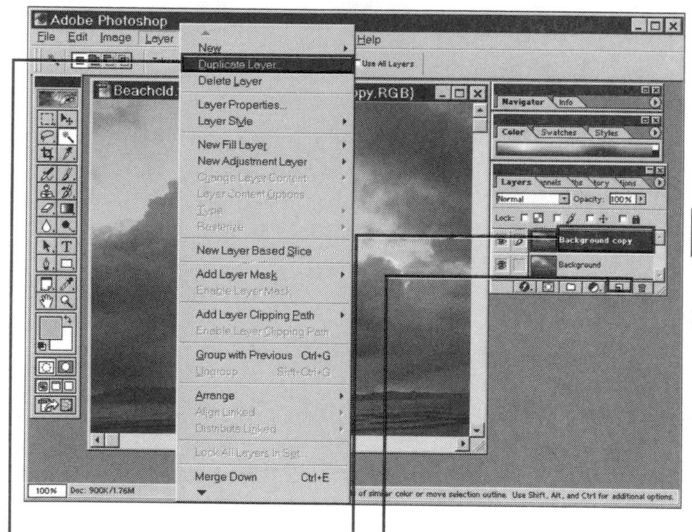

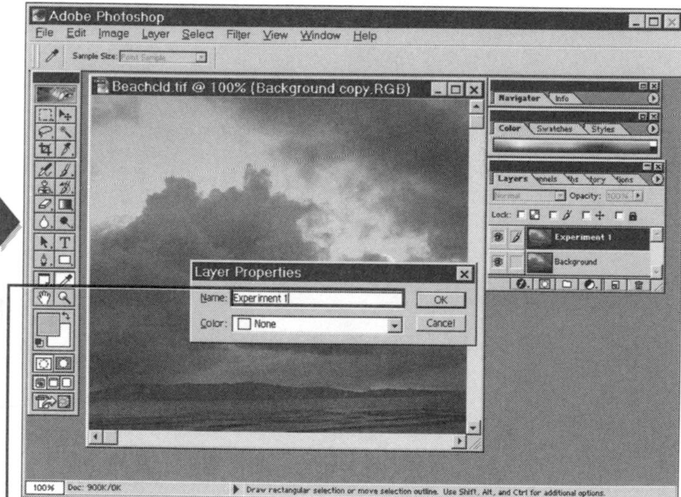

1 Choose Layer and then Duplicate Layer.

2 Drag the existing Layer bar to the New icon.

3 Control/right-click the new layer to bring up the Layer Properties dialog box so you can enter a new name.

4 Type a descriptive name for your new layer.

Note: Be sure to delete layers you are sure you will no longer need. Unneeded layers make unnecessarily large files.

RECOVER FROM MISTAKES: USE THE HISTORY LIST

The Photoshop 6 History list provides a means for recording each brush stroke, command, or any other operation. Everything you do is entered onto a list in the History palette by the name of the command or tool used. You can return to any stage of the creation of your project by selecting (highlighting) an operation's name bar.

You can no longer set the number of operations that the History list will record in the History Options dialog box. The limit is now 20. If you want to record a state before the 20-step limit is reached, be sure to make a new snapshot.

You can also choose to automatically create the first snapshot (for more about snapshots, see "Recover from Mistakes: Snapshots," next in this chapter) and whether to allow a nonlinear history.

If you check Allow Non-Linear History in the History Options dialog box, you can go back and insert steps anywhere in the sequence without deleting the steps that follow. Otherwise, if you make a change at any step, those that follow are automatically deleted.

RECOVER FROM MISTAKES: USE THE HISTORY LIST

SET HISTORY OPTIONS

1 Choose Window, then Show History.

■ The History palette appears or comes to the front.

2 Choose History Options from the palette menu.

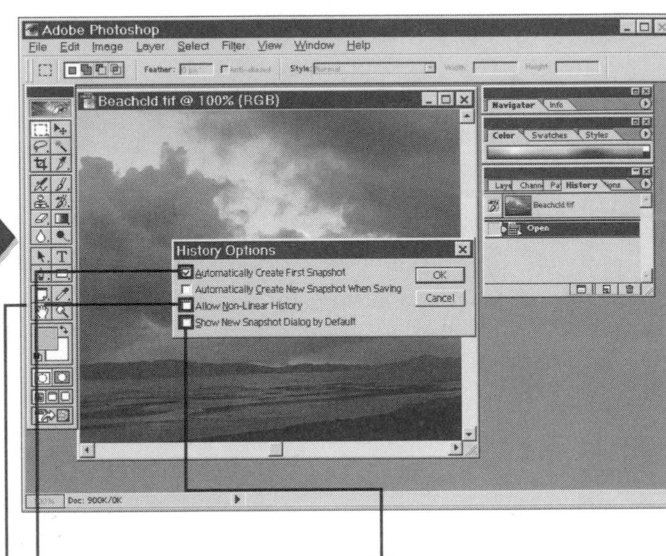

3 Check Automatically Create First Snapshot.

4 Check Allow Non-Linear History if you want to be able to insert steps out of order.

5 Check Show New Snapshot Dialog by Default to remind you to name the snapshot.

RECOVER FROM MISTAKES: SNAPSHOTS

Whenever you want to record an image that is the result of all the steps you have performed up to that point, use the History palette menu to take a snapshot of the image. You can then recreate the image as it looked at that stage simply by selecting the snapshot in the History list. You can also "erase to the snapshot" by selecting the snapshot and using the History Brush.

When you want to record all the visible layers as a single image to the History list, use the New Snapshot command. When the New Snapshot dialog box appears, choose Merged Layers from the pull-down menu. You can choose which layers are visible by clicking the Eye icon box so that the Eye icon is visible. Layers that have no Eye icon showing in the Layers palette list will not be merged.

Note: Shoot a new snapshot any time you change the size of the image. Photoshop does not let you restore parts of a snapshot that are a different size than the file you are currently working on.

RECOVER FROM MISTAKES: SNAPSHOTS

TAKE A SNAPSHOT

1 Choose Window, then Show History.

2 Click the History palette arrow to show the palette menu.

3 Choose New Snapshot to summon the New Snapshot dialog box.

4 Type a name and then click OK.

■ The Snapshot icon appears at the top of the History palette list.

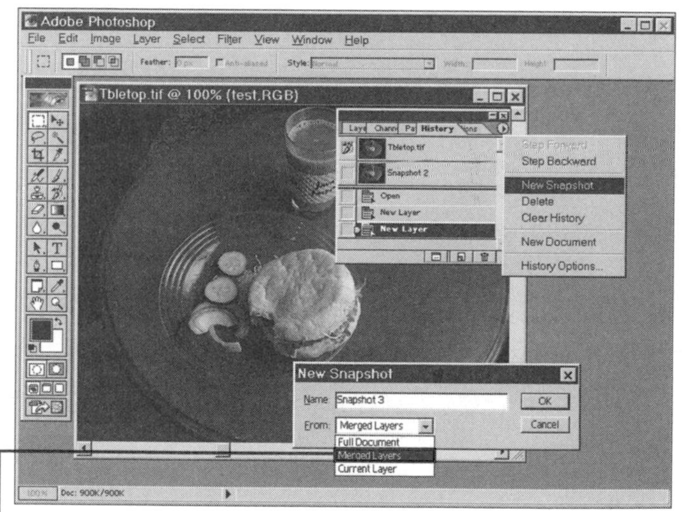

TAKE A MERGED SNAPSHOT

1 Choose Merged Layers from the From menu in the New Snapshot dialog box.

Note: You can also make a snapshot of all layers, visible or not, by choosing Full Document. If you just want a snapshot of a single layer, choose Current Layer. Make sure the layer you want to shoot is the one that is currently chosen.

MANAGE PRESETS WITH THE PRESET LIBRARY

You can use the Preset Library to manage preset attributes for all the pop-up libraries that you access from the Options bar: brushes, custom shapes, contours, gradients, patterns, swatches, and styles. The advantage to using the Preset Library is that you can access these libraries without having to select the tool that calls up the appropriate Options bar. Besides, some folks like to work with the Options bar hidden.

Suppose that you want to access one of the menus attached to a Library pane, but the Options bar that houses that pane is hidden. You can just choose Edit, then Preset Manager. A menu lets you choose each library. After you choose a library, its Library pane and associated pop-up menu appear in the dialog box.

You can then create, save, load, or delete libraries by using the pop-up menu.

MANAGE PRESETS WITH THE PRESET LIBRARY

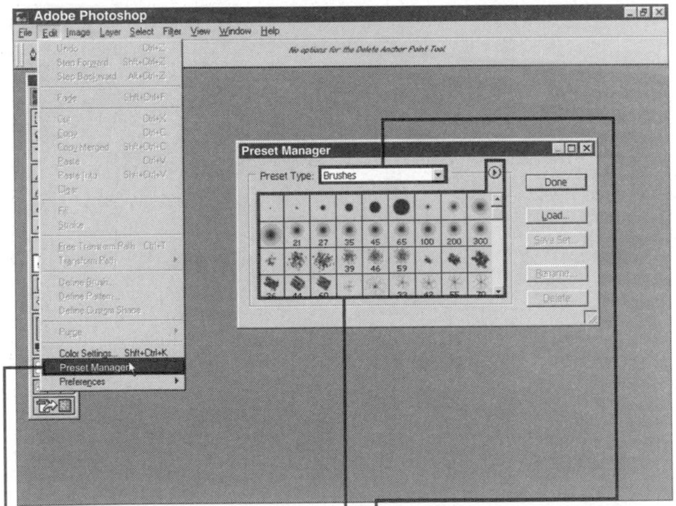

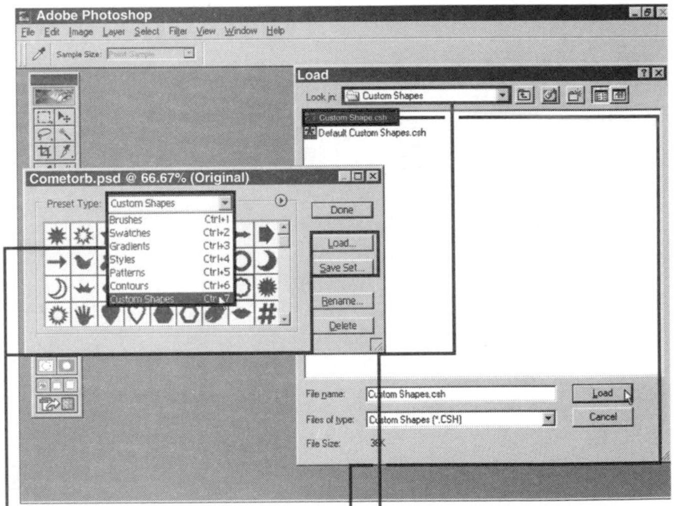

OPEN THE PRESET MANAGER

1 Choose Edit, then Preset Manager.

■ The Preset Manager dialog box appears.

2 Choose the library you want to manage.

■ The Library pane and its associated menu appear in the dialog box.

LOAD OR SAVE A LIBRARY

1 Choose the library you want to manage.

■ The Library pane appears.

2 Click either Load or Save Set.

3 Navigate to the folder where you want to load or save.

4 If saving, type a name and click Save. If loading, click the name of the file you want to load and click Load.

Can I load a library that completely replaces the current library?

✔ Ordinarily, when you load a library, that library's assets are added to those of the current library. If you click Replace Library from the Library's pop-up menu, the library you designate in the resulting Load dialog box completely replaces the current assets.

Can I save part of a library to another name?

✔ Sure. Press the Shift key as you select all the assets (such as different styles and shapes of brushes) that you want to keep. Then, click the Save Set button in the Preset Manager menu.

What if I want to save the whole library under another name?

✔ Press ⌘/Ctrl+A to select all the assets and then click the Save Set button. When the Save dialog box appears, enter a new name for the library.

Can I create an individual preset while working with the Preset Manager?

✔ No. You have to show the Options bar and go about creating the preset in the usual manner.

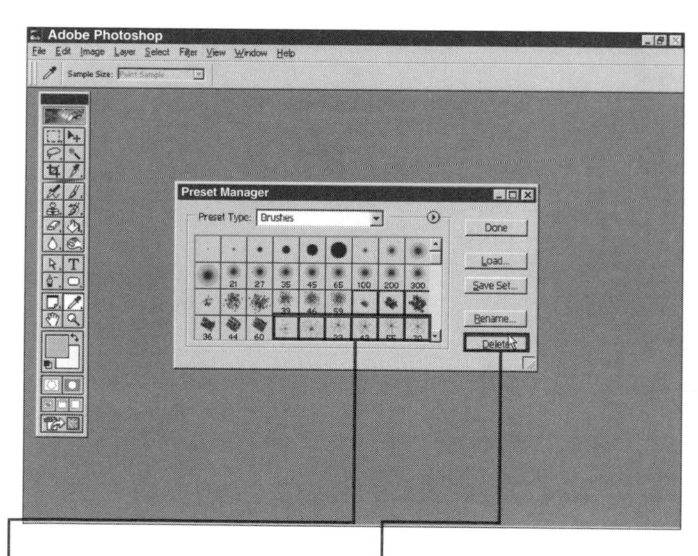

DELETE ITEMS FROM A LIBRARY

1 Shift-click to highlight each preset you want to delete from the currently chosen library.

2 Click Delete.

■ The chosen presets disappear.

Note: If you delete presets from a default library, you can always restore them.

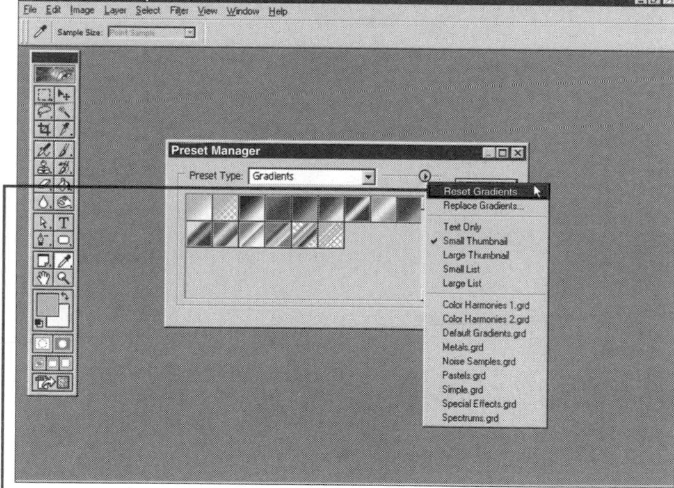

RESET A LIBRARY TO ITS DEFAULTS

1 From the Preset Manager menu, choose Reset [Library], where [Library] is the name of the current library (such as Gradients, shown here).

■ The default assets are immediately and obviously restored.

MAKE CONTACT SHEETS

Finding your image resources can be much easier if you use Photoshop's Automate plug-in to make contact sheet files for each of your image directories.

A *contact sheet* is a collection of thumbnail images organized by directory, enabling you to quickly view each image. You can print out these contact sheets (in full-color, if you have a color printer) or keep them in a contact sheet directory where you can refer to them online.

If you have a CD-ROM recorder to enable you to store files on CDs or if you have had Kodak PhotoCDs made of your images, you can also keep contact sheets of the images contained on a CD in the CD's jewel case or envelope.

Contact sheets make distinguishing between multiple versions of the same image or completely different shots with similar filenames easy.

See "Create Contact Proof Sheets Automatically" later in this chapter to learn about automating the contact sheet creation process.

MAKE CONTACT SHEETS

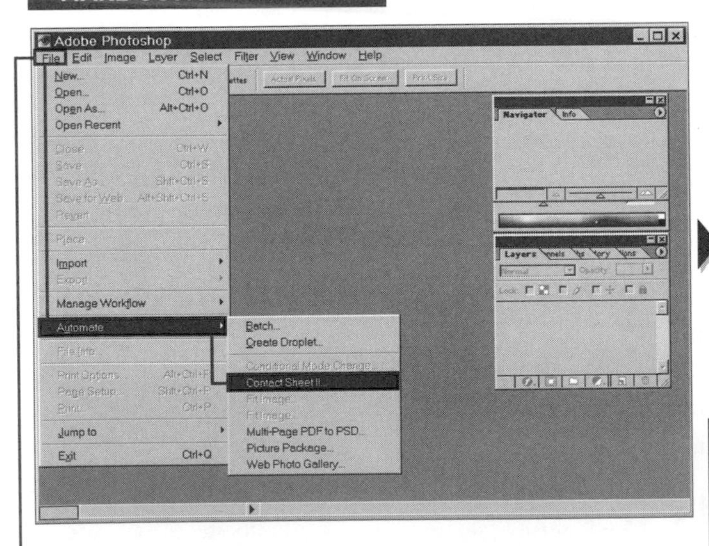

1 Click File, then Automate, then Contact Sheet II.

■ The Contact Sheet II dialog box appears.

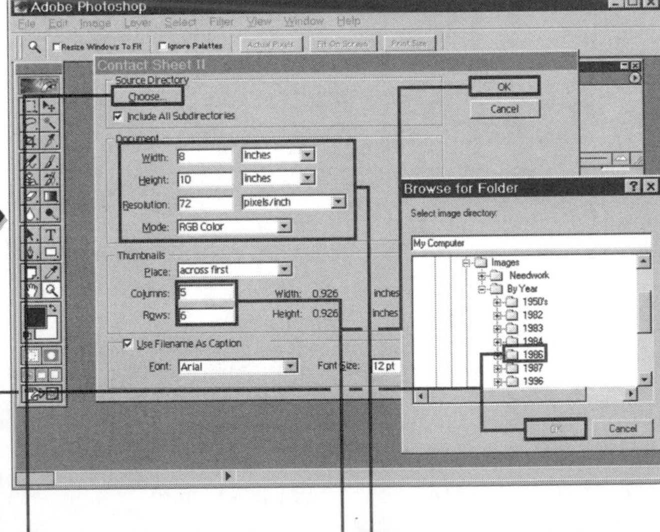

2 Click Choose to display the Browse for Folder (Windows) or Select Image Directory (Mac) dialog box.

3 Navigate to the target directory and either click OK (Windows) or Choose (Mac).

4 Match the settings shown here in the Document area.

5 Specify the number of columns and rows you want and click OK.

■ Photoshop creates the contact sheet.

OPEN A NEW FILE

You can click File, then New to start with a blank canvas. To start a new image, Photoshop needs to know several things that are not required by other types of programs: the output resolution of the file you want to create, the units of measurement you want to use while you create your image, and the size of the canvas you want to create the image on.

Photoshop also wants to know what color you want the canvas (the background the image will be seen against if there are transparent areas) to be, or whether you want a transparent background. Choose Transparent if you want to paint or paste an irregular shape that can later be combined with new layers without the need for further masking.

Photoshop automatically enters the dimensions and Color mode of any image currently on the Clipboard. If you want the canvas to be smaller because you intend to crop the image after you paste it, do not worry. Using the cropping tool automatically resizes the canvas to match.

If you paste a Clipboard image onto a smaller canvas, the image will be automatically cropped to fit the canvas, keeping the pixels from the upper-left corner down.

OPEN A NEW FILE

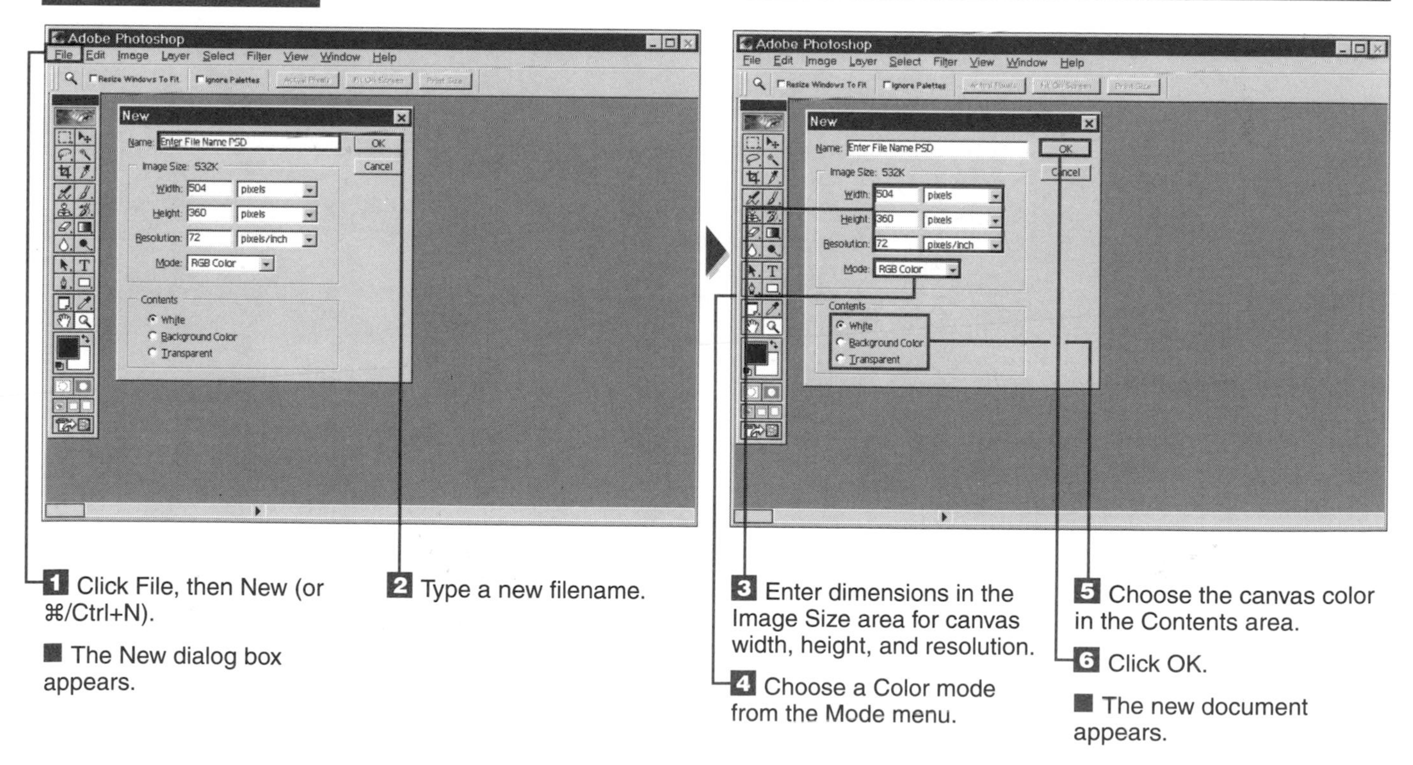

1 Click File, then New (or ⌘/Ctrl+N).

■ The New dialog box appears.

2 Type a new filename.

3 Enter dimensions in the Image Size area for canvas width, height, and resolution.

4 Choose a Color mode from the Mode menu.

5 Choose the canvas color in the Contents area.

6 Click OK.

■ The new document appears.

OPEN EXISTING FILES

You can open an existing file in Photoshop in basically the same way as that for any other application running under the Mac OS or Windows. There are a few things to know and a few caveats, however.

Although Photoshop is compatible with most bitmap and some vector (Encapsulated PostScript, Adobe Illustrator, Quark Generic EPS files) image formats, you may encounter incompatible formats. If you need to open a format that is not on the Open dialog box's Files of Type menu (Windows)/Show menu (Mac), you have several options for opening the non-Photoshop-compatible file:

- Check the Adobe Web site (www.adobe.com) for a plug-in.
- Open the file in the program native to that format and then save it to a Photoshop-compatible one.
- Use a file conversion program such as DeBabelizer from Equilibrium Software or, on the Mac, GraphicConverter from Lemke Software (www.lemkesoft.de).

If you want to open a file using a plug-in (a small special-purpose program that installs into Photoshop), click File, then Import, then the format name. If you want to open a file under a new name, click File, then Open As (Windows only).

OPEN EXISTING FILES

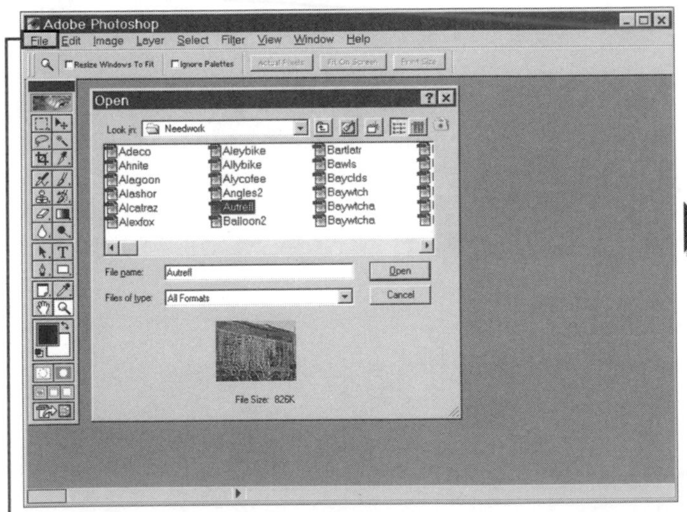

OPEN A PHOTOSHOP OR COMPATIBLE FILE

1 Click File, then Open.

■ The Open dialog box appears.

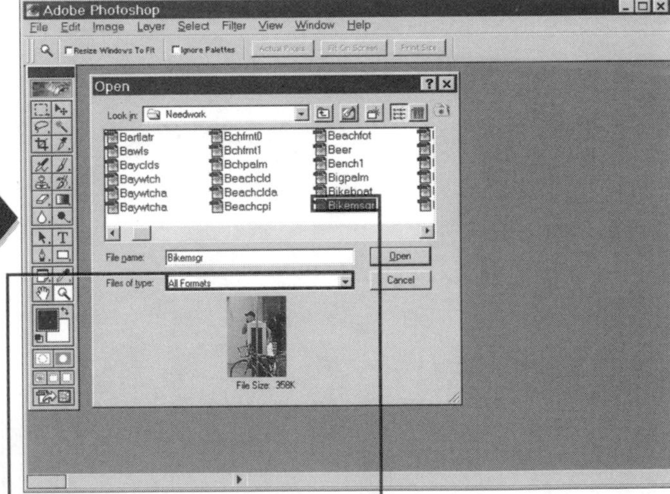

2 Choose All Formats from the Files of Type menu (Windows) or All Readable Documents from the Show menu (Mac).

■ All types of Photoshop-compatible files in the target directory appear in the list.

3 Double-click the file that you want to load.

Note: Any Photoshop-compatible file will open in Photoshop.

What should I do if Photoshop will not open the file, even though it appears to be in a compatible format?

✔ Open the file in the application that created it (or use DeBabelizer/ GraphicConverter) and save it to another Photoshop-compatible format. Reopen the file in Photoshop and save it again in the format you want to use.

I tried the preceding, and it did not solve the problem. Any other suggestions?

✔ You may have a damaged file, or you may have given the file the wrong extension (Windows) when you saved it. Try using the Open As command and test some different formats until one of them works.

What if I cannot find the file I want to open?

✔ Use the OS's Find command (Sherlock or Sherlock 2 on the Mac) to search all the local drives. Then use it on all your CDs and removable media.

How do I figure out which image goes with which filename in a long list of files?

✔ Just click a filename in the Open dialog box. A thumbnail appears in the dialog box (provided one was saved with the image). If you are on the Mac, make sure that the preview area is not hidden.

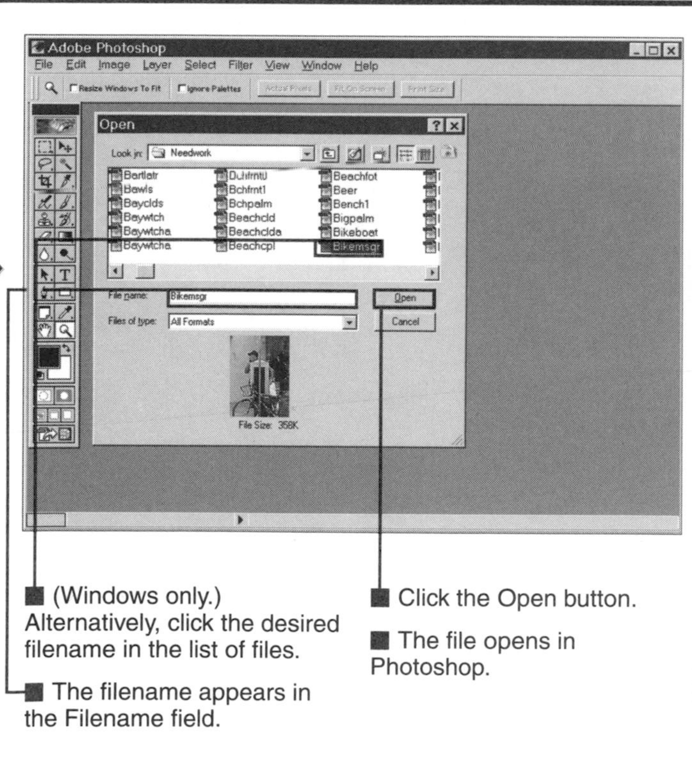

■ (Windows only.) Alternatively, click the desired filename in the list of files.

■ The filename appears in the Filename field.

■ Click the Open button.

■ The file opens in Photoshop.

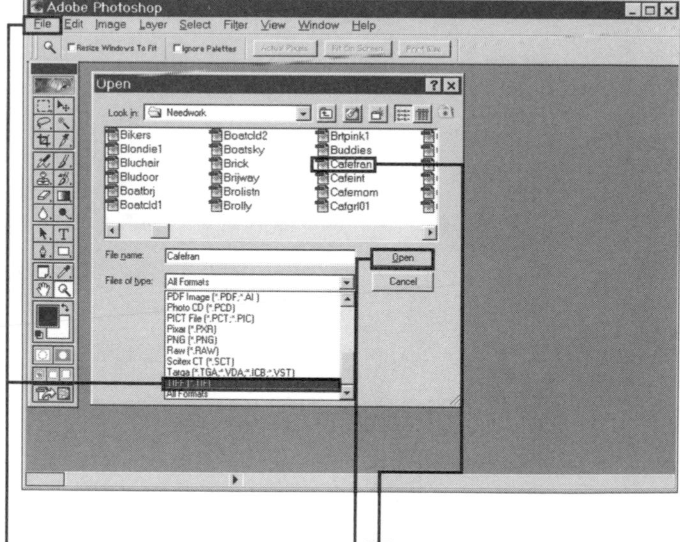

OPEN A FILE IN A GIVEN FORMAT

1 Click File, then Open.

2 Choose the format you think the file was stored in from the Files of Type menu (Windows) or the Show menu (Mac).

3 Click the name of the file you want to open.

4 Click Open (or press Return/Enter).

■ The file opens in the given format.

SAVE THE CURRENT FILE

You should get in the habit of using the Save command any time you make changes that you do not want to lose. Remembering to save at regular intervals ensures that you can retrieve all the successful work you have done to that point by choosing File, then Revert. You are also ensuring you can recover your work after an unexpected computer crash.

You can save the current, or open, file several ways. You can perform a simple save by pressing ⌘/Ctrl+S or choosing File, then Save.

A slightly more complicated alternative to the Save command is to click File, then Save As. Save As lets you convert the file to a different file format, save it under a new name, or save it to a different disk location. This command is the one to use when you want to try a risky experiment, because you can always go back to the original.

Using the Save As command is also the route to take when you want to save your file to a different format. For example, you may want to save a PSD file as a GIF file for the Web.

SAVE THE CURRENT FILE

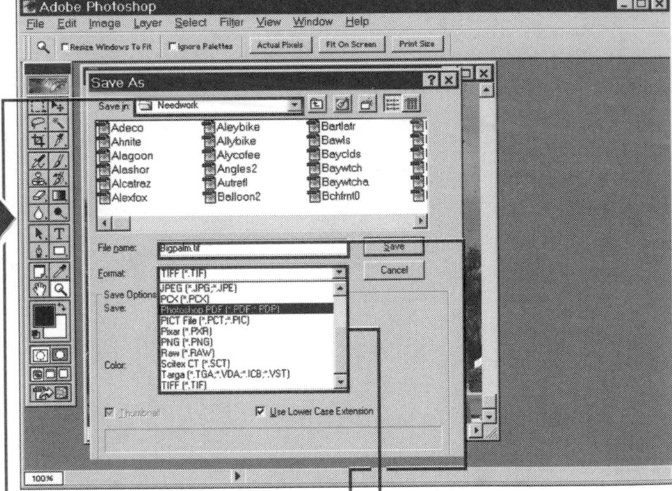

1 Click File, then Save As.

■ The Save As dialog box appears.

2 Navigate to the folder where you want to save this file.

Note: Mac users can navigate to other drives or folders using the menu buttons above the file list.

3 Choose the format that you want to save to from the Format menu.

4 Type the filename you want to use in the Filename field (Windows) or Name field (Mac).

Is there a faster way to save files in several different formats?

✔ Use an external file conversion application, such as DeBabelizer (Windows or Mac) or GraphicConverter (Mac). They can automatically convert a whole disk or directory (folder) of PSD files to several different formats in one operation.

Should I always save image previews?

✔ Not when saving files for use on the Web. Preview thumbnails add to the file space size. It is also a waste of space if the file is not going to be reopened by an application that can preview the thumbnail.

Does more than one version of the Photoshop file format exist?

✔ Almost every new version of Photoshop introduces features to the PSD file format that were not supported in an earlier version. Photoshop 6 includes the following features that were not supported in earlier versions: layer sets, layer color coding, layer clipping paths, fill layers, layer styles, paragraph type, and advanced type formatting.

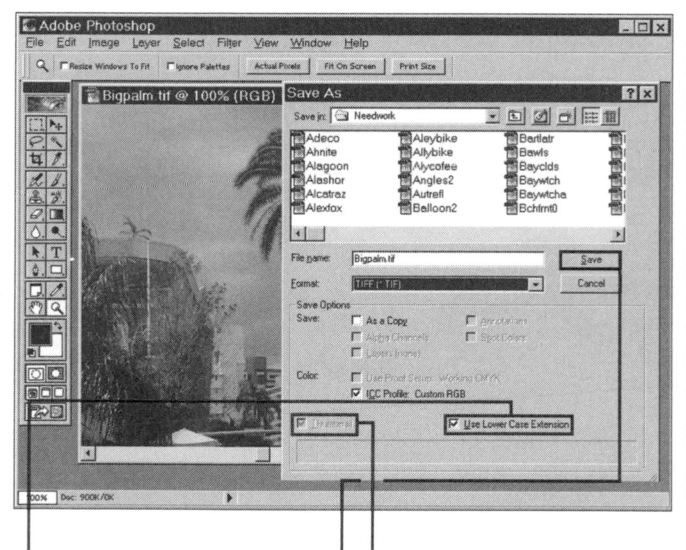

5 Click the Use Lower Case Extension check box (Windows only) to make files cross-platform compatible with UNIX.

Note: Compatibility with UNIX may be especially important if UNIX is the OS used by your Web server or service provider.

6 Click the Thumbnail check box if you are saving a file to be opened later (Windows only).

7 Click Save.

PERFORM A QUICK SAVE

1 Click File, then Save or press ⌘/Ctrl+S.

■ The file is saved to the same drive and folder to which it was last saved (or from which it was originally opened).

SAVE A COPY OF THE CURRENT FILE

The As A Copy check box in the Save As dialog box does far more than its name suggests. You can use it to flatten all the layers, save to another file format, save the file under an entirely different name, exclude any data that does not belong to the image, and exclude all alpha channels. All these options can help you minimize file size.

Using As A Copy is the most direct way to save a version of the current file for use in another program without affecting your original. This way, you can keep the layers and masks intact in the original in case you want to make changes later. At the same time, you create a file that is more portable or that works in another application (such as a desktop publishing program that requires a flattened file).

The keyboard shortcut for saving a copy is ⌘/Ctrl+Opt/Alt+S. You can also force the use of a lowercase extension — an especially good idea when sending files to a Web server or placing them on a cross-platform or hybrid CD-ROM.

SAVE A COPY OF THE CURRENT FILE

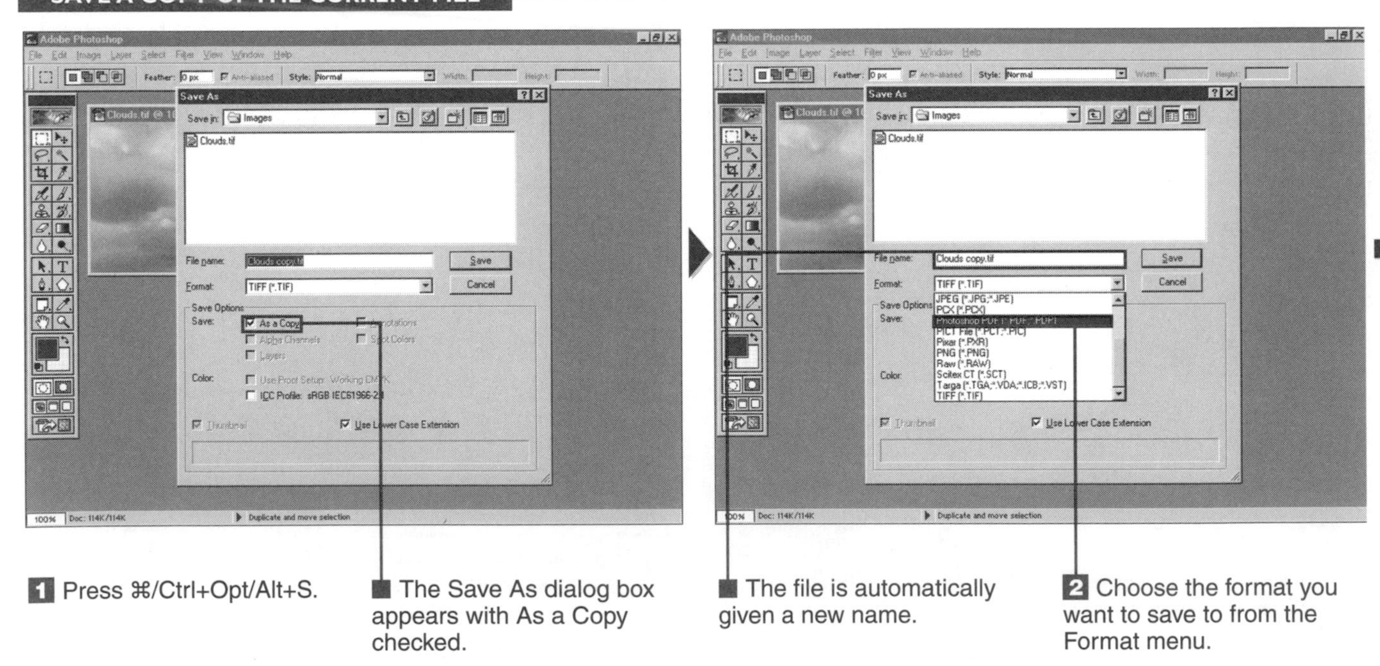

1 Press ⌘/Ctrl+Opt/Alt+S.

■ The Save As dialog box appears with As a Copy checked.

■ The file is automatically given a new name.

2 Choose the format you want to save to from the Format menu.

Why should I press ⌘/Ctrl+Opt/Alt+S instead of just clicking File, then Save As?

✔ Pressing ⌘/Ctrl+Opt/Alt+S automatically checks the As A Copy check box in the Save As dialog box for you. Saving a copy duplicates the current file and saves it as well. So whatever you have done in the original that is valuable is backed up and protected. Saving a copy also lets you convert the file to another format, customize the minimization of file size, and rename the file — all within a single operation. However, remember that the copy file is now not open in Photoshop — it is only saved to your drive.

The Layers check box is almost always grayed out. Why?

✔ If there are no layers in your file or if the destination format does not support layers, the box will be grayed. If you are saving a layered Photoshop file to TIFF format, you now have the option to save layers — an option available only in Photoshop 6.

Why would I decide not to include alpha channels?

✔ Alpha channels are masks. Masks can increase file size by 25 to 35 percent. So if you do not need the masks, unload them by unchecking the Alpha Channels check box.

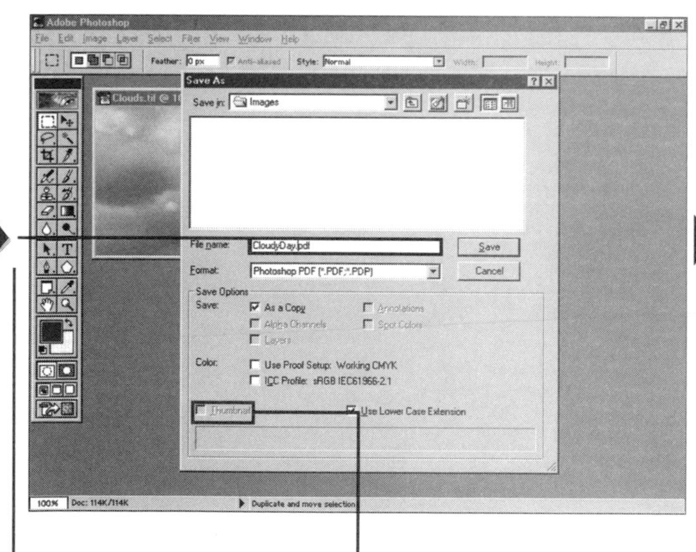

3 Alternatively, type a new, more descriptive filename in the File Name field.

4 Check Thumbnail (Windows only).

Note: In Windows, Thumbnail will be grayed out if you have chosen Always Save Thumbnail in Photoshop Preferences. (See Chapter 1 for more about preferences.)

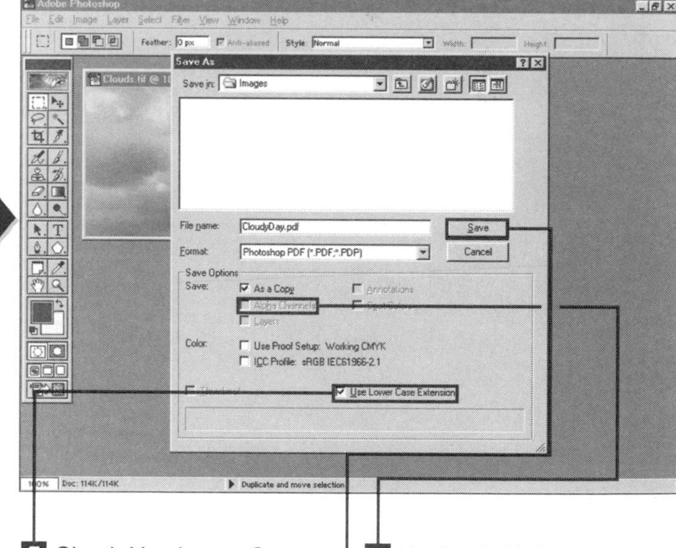

5 Check Use Lower Case Extension (Windows only).

Note: Checking Use Lower Case Extension ensures universal portability between different platforms. You can set this on the Mac under Edit, then Preferences, then Saving Files.

6 Uncheck Alpha Channels.

7 Click Save.

ADD AND RETRIEVE INFORMATION ABOUT A FILE

Finding the right image in a collection of hundreds (or thousands) could take an ungainly amount of time unless you can attach verbal descriptions to those files. With Photoshop 6, you can store and retrieve six categories of information about the current file:

- Captions
- Keywords
- Categories
- Credits
- Origins
- Copyright and URLs

As you gain experience with Photoshop, you will discover more and more uses for this information.

Each category of information has its own fill-in form dialog box. These dialog boxes let you enter information according to standards set up by the Newspaper Association of America (NAA) and the International Press Telecommunications Council (IPTC) to help identify remotely transmitted news images.

You can save file information when you save any file in Photoshop, TIFF, and JPEG formats. If you are on the Macintosh, you can save file information in any supported format.

ADD AND RETRIEVE INFORMATION ABOUT A FILE

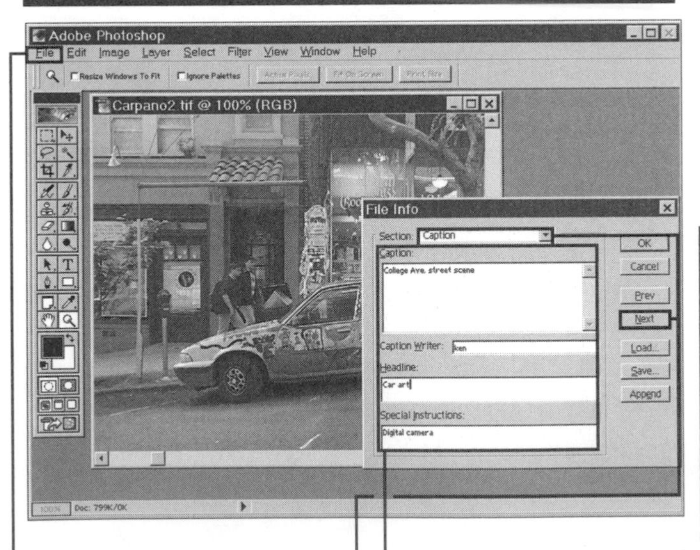

ADD CAPTION INFORMATION

1 Click File, then File Info.

■ The File Info dialog box appears with Caption chosen in the Section box.

2 Enter the caption information you want.

3 Click the Next button to move to the next section or choose a specific dialog box from the Section menu.

ADD KEYWORDS INFORMATION

1 Choose Keywords from the Section menu if it is not already selected.

2 Type a keyword to add to the list for this picture.

3 Click the Add button to add the word to the keyword list.

4 Click OK or choose the next dialog box in the Section menu.

How can I make this data easier to search?

✔ Use the Urgency menu in the Categories section of the File Info dialog box to order a group of files by their importance, sequence, or viewing priority.

Can I use the information in the current file for another file?

✔ Yes. Just click the Load and Save buttons that reside on the right side of all the File Info dialog boxes. To modify the record that stays with your image, just edit the contents of the newly loaded file in the normal way.

Can you tell me when I might need this data?

✔ You may be asked to supply information as to how the file was created or to prove the date and circumstances of creation in a copyright case.

What are the buttons on the right side of the various dialog boxes?

✔ The Prev and Next buttons move you up or down the list of dialog boxes. Load and Save let you save the information for this file to an external file. Append lets you store the file info at the end of an existing list.

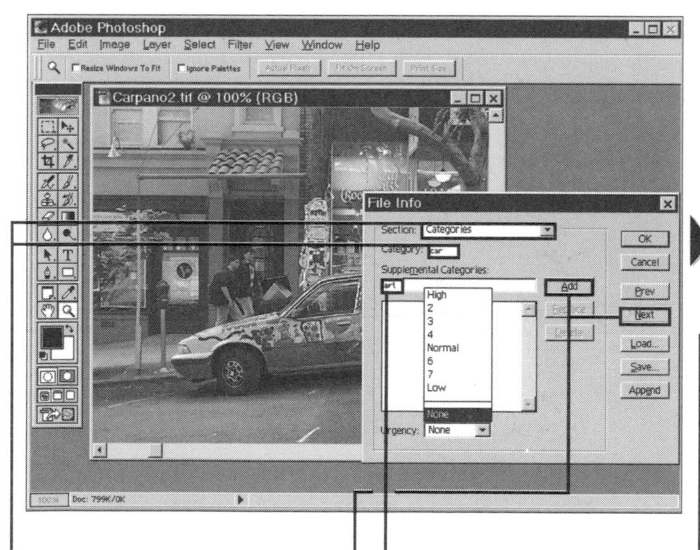

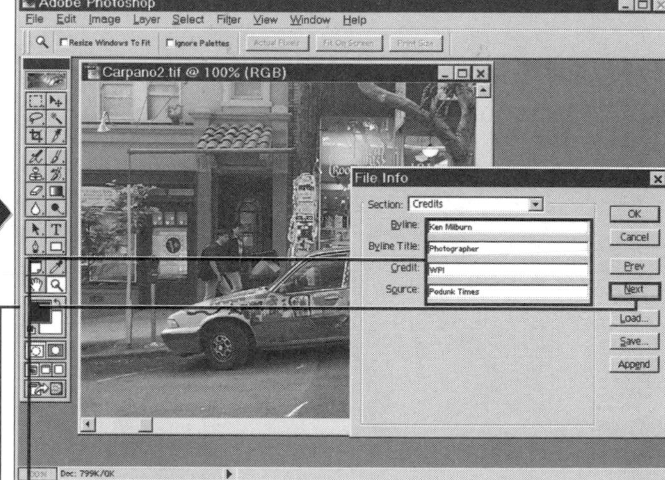

ADD CATEGORIES INFORMATION

1 Choose Categories from the Section menu.

2 Enter a three-character category name.

3 Enter a name for the supplemental category.

4 Click Add and then click Next to display the Credits section of the File Info dialog box.

5 Type the information that you want to include.

6 Click Next.

■ The File Info Origin dialog box appears.

Note: You are free to enter any information that will fit in most fields. However, if you want to subscribe to the NAA/NTPC standards for transmitting news photos, follow the guidelines of those organizations at www.iptc.org/iptc/catguide.html.

CREATE CONTACT PROOF SHEETS AUTOMATICALLY

You can automatically create proof sheets in Photoshop 6. *Proof sheets* let you see images for a whole folder of files at once, making it much easier to find exactly the file you are looking for — especially if there are multiple images of the same subject with only slight differences between them.

Most Photoshop users tend to create a lot of images. Then they complicate matters by creating numerous variations of those images. Before long, you may find yourself opening several versions of the same file just to figure out which file is the file you want. Contact proofs are the solution to this problem.

You may wonder why you would use contact proofs, because Mac users get thumbnail previews of images and Windows offers a preview mode. However, neither of these is an ideal solution. The Mac thumbnails are too small, and the Windows previews take a long time to generate. The best solution is to create printed proof sheets of all your images. Finding images in a paper catalog is much faster.

CREATE CONTACT PROOF SHEETS AUTOMATICALLY

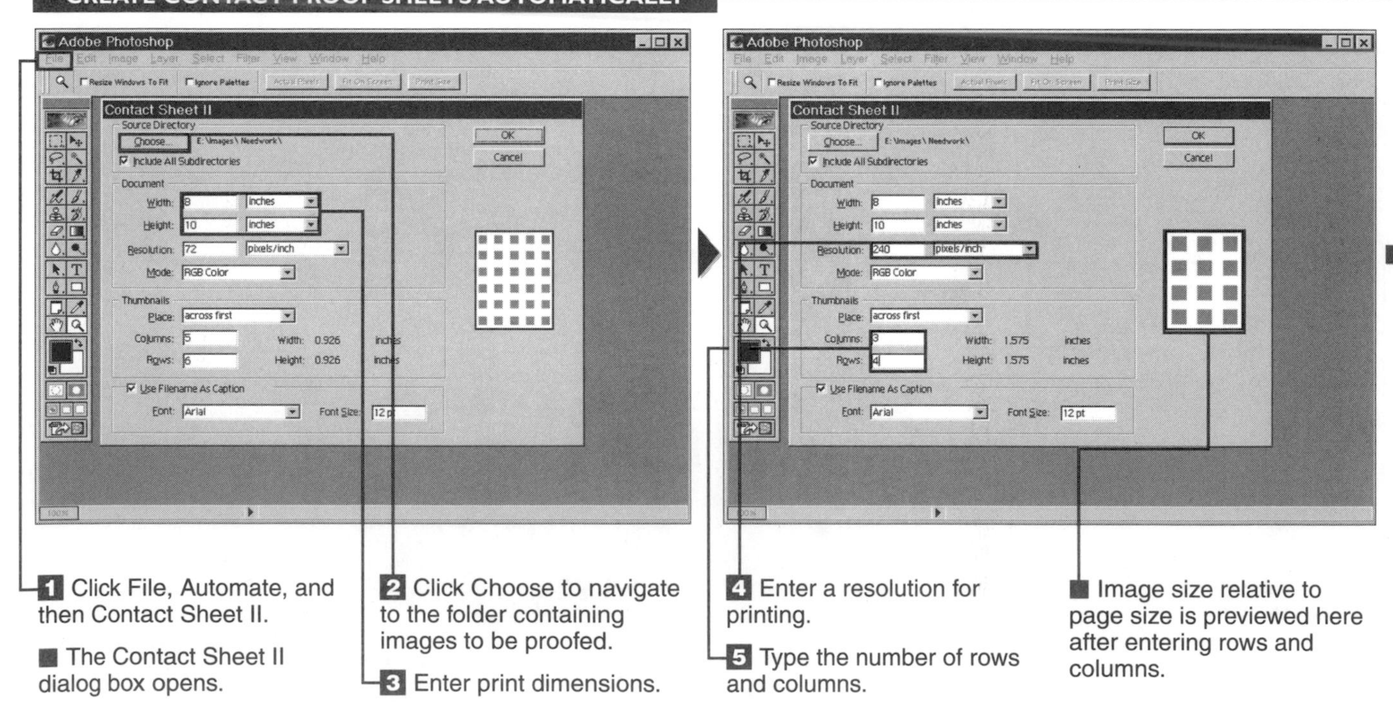

1 Click File, Automate, and then Contact Sheet II.

■ The Contact Sheet II dialog box opens.

2 Click Choose to navigate to the folder containing images to be proofed.

3 Enter print dimensions.

4 Enter a resolution for printing.

5 Type the number of rows and columns.

■ Image size relative to page size is previewed here after entering rows and columns.

What resolution should I use for printing the contact sheet?

✔ Typically, about one-third of the resolution of your color printer, because the resolution of your printer is the number of dots made by all three color printheads. (Black does not count because it is added to the image wherever needed to add contrast.)

What color mode should I use?

✔ Read your printer manual. Most modern inkjet printers print in CMYK colors but print from an RGB image. Therefore, most of the time you should use RGB.

How many rows and columns should I use?

✔ You can preview to see what works best for you. Three columns and three rows works best for easy viewing in most cases.

What if I want to use a label other than the filename?

✔ Not a good idea. The thumbnail will not tell you what file it relates to. You can use long, descriptive filenames if you do not have to save these images to the Web or to a CD-ROM.

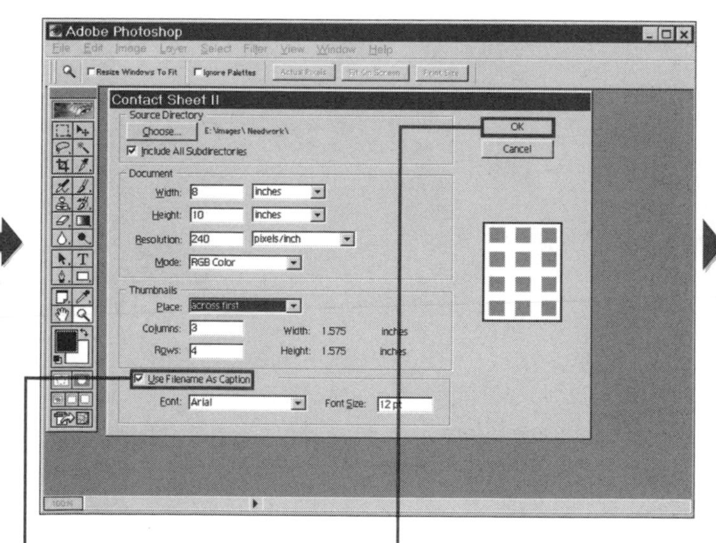

6 Check Use Filename As Caption if you want to label thumbnails with the existing filename.

7 Click OK when you are ready to execute.

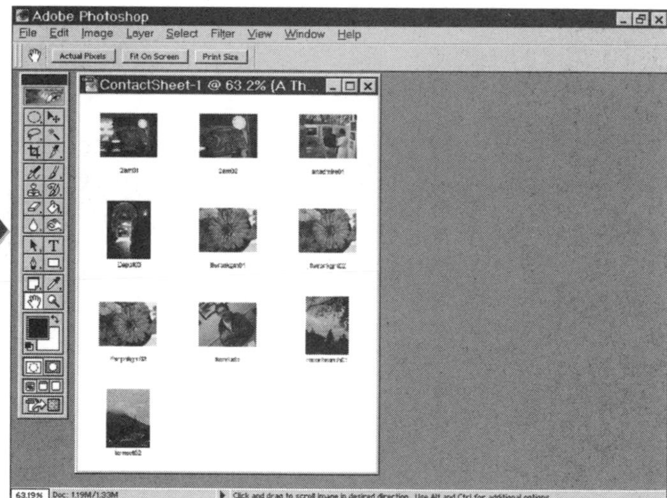

■ The finished contact sheet appears.

Note: If there had been more than the number of images in the folder than would fit on the page, Photoshop would have made as many contact sheets as necessary.

MAKE A PICTURE PACKAGE OR JOB PRINT

If you need to make numerous small prints of an image, you may find it tedious and wasteful to cut paper into small sizes and then print one image at a time. You can use the Picture Package command to eliminate that tedium. *Picture packages* and *job prints* are interchangeable trade terms for making multiple prints (often in different sizes) of the same subject on the same sheet of paper.

Making a picture package is a straightforward task. You choose the Picture Package command from the Automate menu, and the Picture Package dialog box appears. You choose the file that you want to print, choose a layout, resolution, and color mode (RGB, CMYK, and so on), and then click OK. All that is left is to make sure that your printer is turned on and the paper is loaded.

The Photoshop 6 Picture Package command gives you a much wider choice of picture size mixes than that in Photoshop 5.5. You can also print on 11-x-17-inch paper (provided that your printer can use this paper size).

MAKE A PICTURE PACKAGE OR JOB PRINT

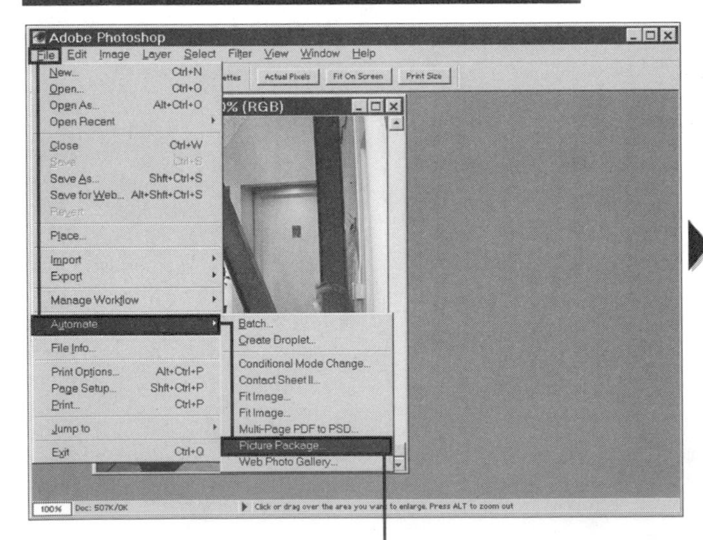

1 Open the image that you want to print as a Picture Package.

2 Click File, Automate, and then Picture Package.

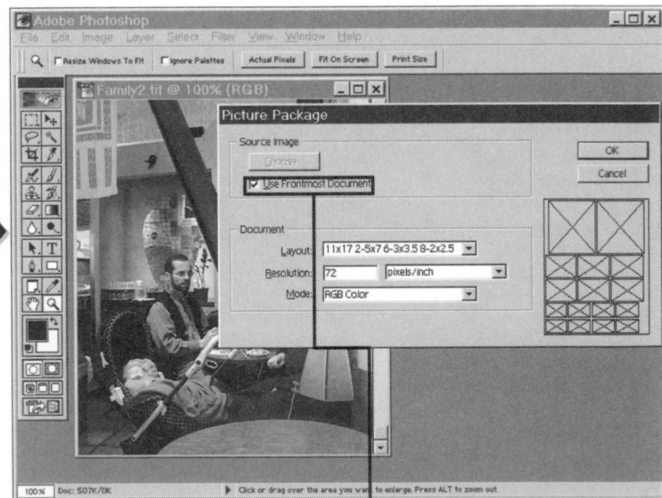

■ The Picture Package dialog box appears.

3 Check Use Frontmost Document.

Note: If you have not opened the file that you want to print, you can click Choose to browse for it. You will not be able to make image adjustments before printing, however.

What image resolution is best for my printer?

✔ Most printers have several options for the printing resolution. For photographs, you generally want to set the printer for the highest resolution possible. The image resolution should be one-third of the resolution that you choose for your printer because there are three primary color dots for each pixel in an image. If you use a higher resolution, you do not gain appreciable image quality, and your files use significantly more disk space.

When making a job print automatically, can I use any mixture of sizes that is not on the menu?

✔ No. You can, however, manually place different images on separate layers and then use the Transform command under the Image menu to scale them to any size you like.

Why did you choose the RGB color mode for your CMYK printer?

✔ Using RGB mode is the procedure recommended by most inkjet printer manufacturers. However, you should check with your manufacturer. If you want to make CMYK proofs from your inkjet printer, you should look into the availability of software for converting the image to PostScript called a PostScript Raster Image Processor (RIP).

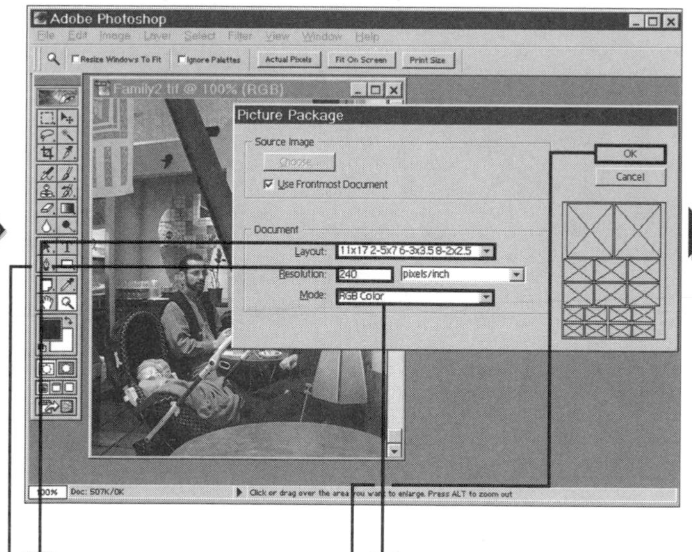

4 Choose the layout that you want to use.

5 Enter the desired printing resolution.

6 Choose the color mode for your printer.

7 Click OK.

■ Photoshop creates the picture package, showing the same image laid out on a sheet of paper in multiple sizes.

MAKE A SCRAPBOOK PAGE

A scrapbook page procedure differs from the Picture Package command in that it lets you print multiple *different* images on the same sheet of paper. This is a procedure, not a built-in command, but this means that it is more versatile because you can print as many different images on a single sheet of paper as you choose to. The borders between images can be whatever you want them to be. Furthermore, you can print on any size paper you like. You can also make the background color anything you like.

This procedure is handy for making up scrapbook pages, doing a very rough layout for a catalog or magazine page, or simply for printing a series of mixed-subject small images. I use it to print my business cards in color — each with a different illustration from my portfolio as the centerpiece.

The procedure involves creating a new file, then opening all the files you want to put on the page at once, rotating and sizing them, and then dragging each image onto the new page.

MAKE A SCRAPBOOK PAGE

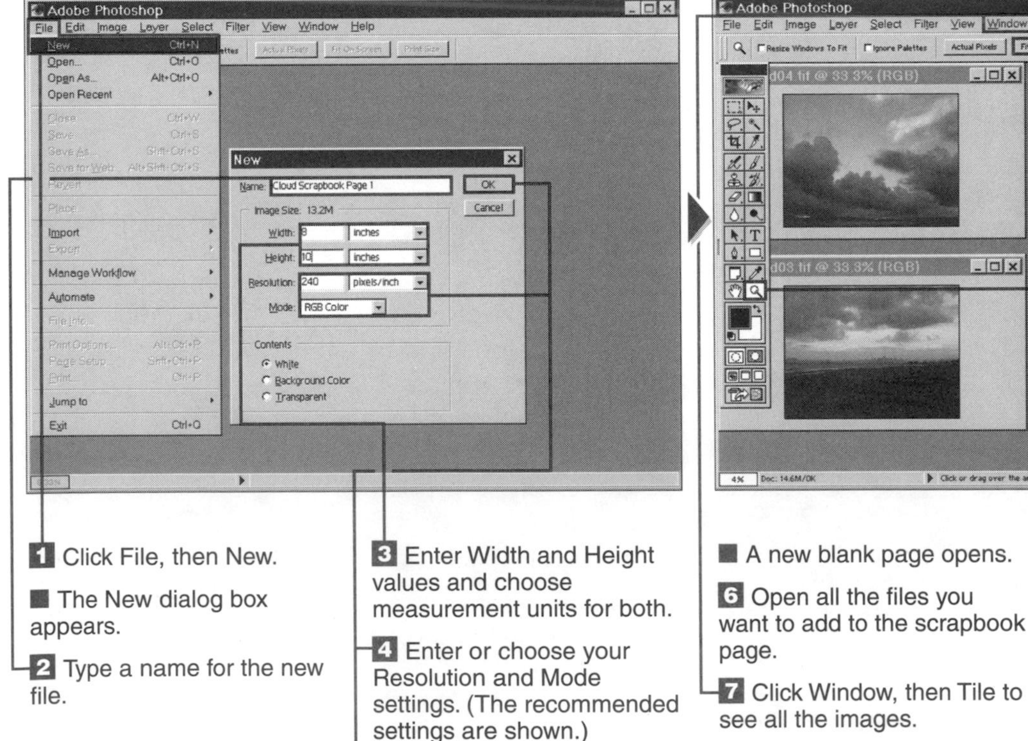

1 Click File, then New.

■ The New dialog box appears.

2 Type a name for the new file.

3 Enter Width and Height values and choose measurement units for both.

4 Enter or choose your Resolution and Mode settings. (The recommended settings are shown.)

5 Click OK.

■ A new blank page opens.

6 Open all the files you want to add to the scrapbook page.

7 Click Window, then Tile to see all the images.

Note: On a Mac, you need to resize and drag the windows manually.

8 Click the Zoom tool.

9 Click each image and then click Fit on Screen.

■ You can now see the full image in each window.

Do you really print on 8-x-10-inch paper, rather than letter size?

✔ No. Letter-size would be the most economical choice. You need to leave at least a half-inch margin. Also, if you put the contents into an 8-x-10-inch area, they will fit inside a standard-size picture frame. Of course, if your printer prints on larger sheets of paper, you can make the whole scrapbook page larger.

Can you use this technique with large format printers?

✔ There is no problem with composing scrapbook pages of any size, provided they are supported by your printer. The larger the paper, the more different images and sizes you can print at once.

Is there an easy way to mix printing several of the same image with other images?

✔ Click the window of the image you want to duplicate, then Click Image, then Duplicate as many times as you want multiples of the image. Or, you can duplicate the layer of the image, then move it.

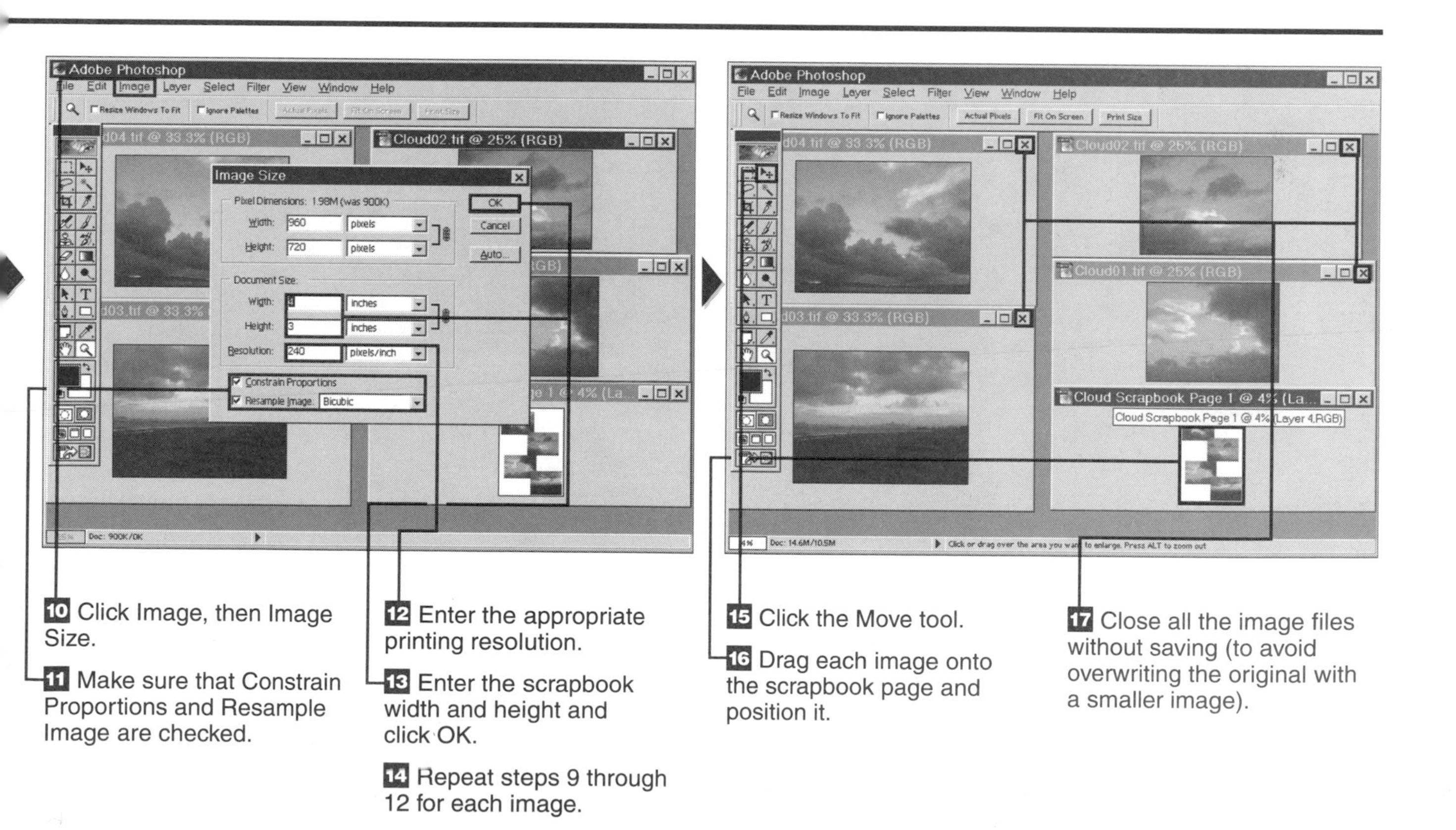

10 Click Image, then Image Size.

11 Make sure that Constrain Proportions and Resample Image are checked.

12 Enter the appropriate printing resolution.

13 Enter the scrapbook width and height and click OK.

14 Repeat steps 9 through 12 for each image.

15 Click the Move tool.

16 Drag each image onto the scrapbook page and position it.

17 Close all the image files without saving (to avoid overwriting the original with a smaller image).

IMPORT IMAGES FROM A TWAIN DEVICE

You can use Photoshop to import images from a TWAIN device. TWAIN (short for Technology Without An Interesting Name) is a protocol used on PCs and Macs to communicate with all types of image-acquisition devices, including digital cameras, video cameras, scanners, and slide scanners.

The advantage of TWAIN is that the manufacturer of the device does not need to write a driver for each specific type of software or application. If the software (such as Photoshop) understands TWAIN, the device will automatically work with that software.

To use a TWAIN device, follow the instructions in that device's manual for installing the TWAIN drivers in your operating system. Then, when you select a TWAIN device (shown in the steps that follow), all the devices that have been installed on your system will show up in your Windows or System: Extensions folder, depending on your platform. After you select the device, you then have to import your images from the TWAIN device. The software for whichever device you have preselected will appear on your desktop to prompt you through this process.

IMPORT IMAGES FROM A TWAIN DEVICE

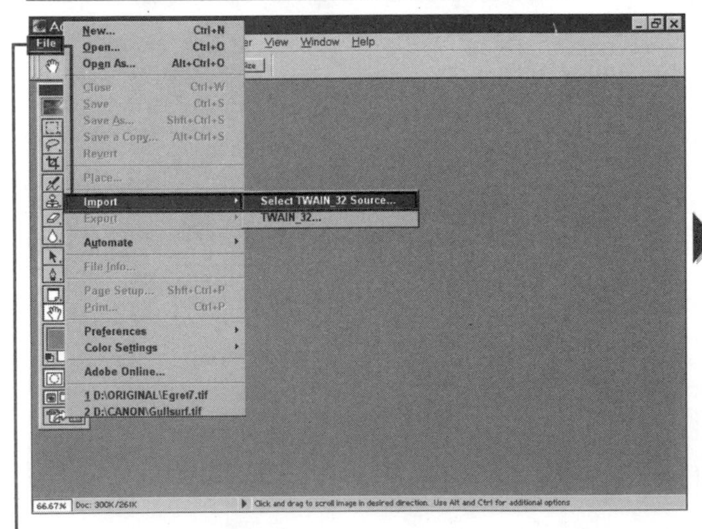

1 Click File, then Import, then Select TWAIN_32 Source (or Select TWAIN Source if you have an older 16-bit operating system or device [Windows only]).

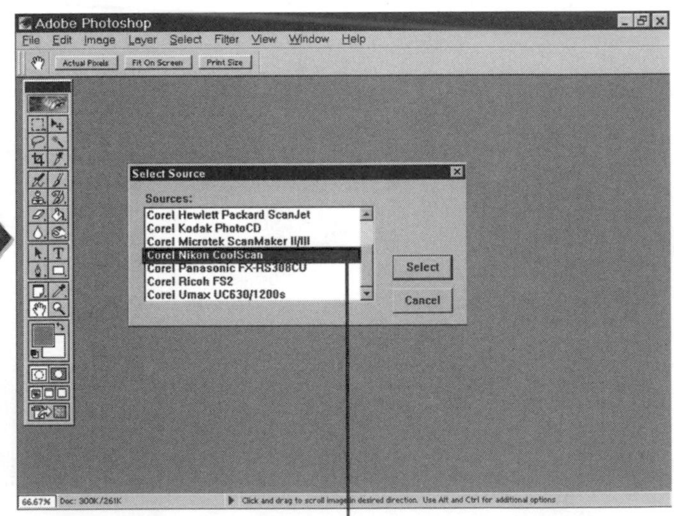

■ The Select Source dialog box opens.

2 Choose the source (device) from which you want to import images.

My TWAIN device has a much different-looking interface than that shown here. Where do I find out what to do next?

✔ All TWAIN software interfaces are unique. The only thing they have in common is the protocol used to make the device "talk" to your software. Most are fairly obvious and work much like those for the three types of devices shown on these pages. If you have more specific questions, refer to the user manual that came with your device.

What should I do if my device does not have a TWAIN driver or a Photoshop plug-in?

✔ You will have to run stand-alone software outside of Photoshop. If you have allocated most of your system's memory to Photoshop operation, you may have to first close Photoshop, and then open the device's software. If your device has a Photoshop plug-in, then it will work, regardless of whether or not it uses TWAIN protocol.

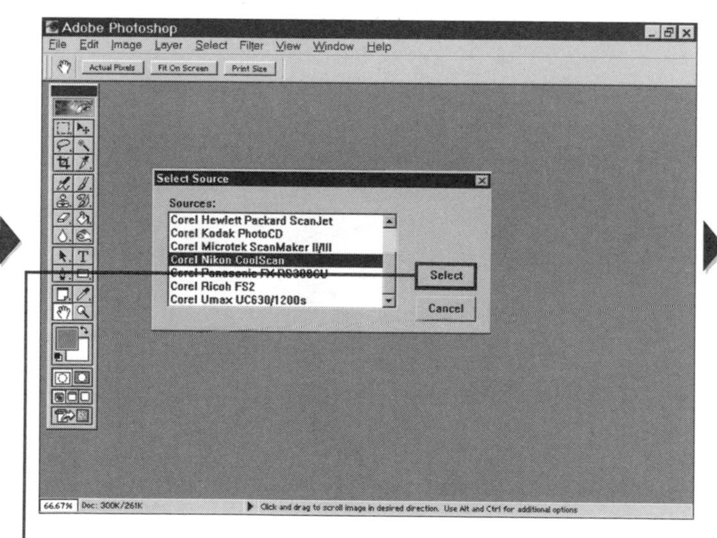

3 Click Select.

Note: What happens at this point depends on the software for the TWAIN device you have chosen.

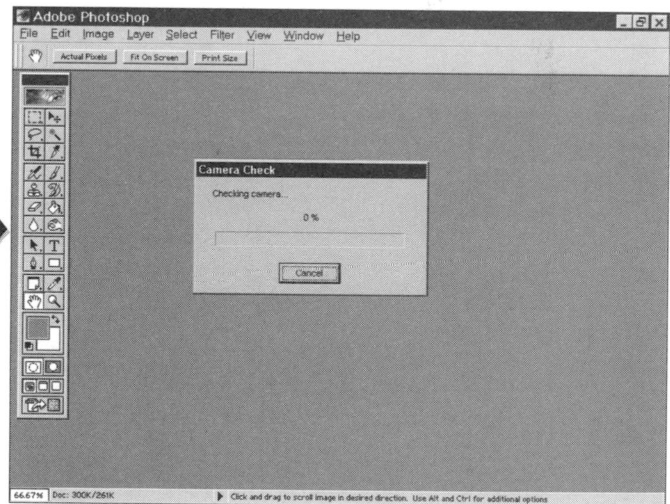

■ A dialog box may appear to advise you that information is being transferred.

■ Or, you may jump straight to the software interface for the TWAIN device you have chosen.

Note: Again, what happens at this point depends on the software for the TWAIN device you have chosen.

IMPORT IMAGES FROM A DIGITAL CAMERA

You can import digital camera images directly into Photoshop very easily. You can import the images three ways:

- Using the TWAIN device procedure, as shown here.
- Using a plug-in. Almost all the popularly priced digital cameras come with a Photoshop import plug-in for both Macs and PCs. If your camera has a plug-in, check your manual for instructions on how to use it with Photoshop.
- Importing the file straight into Photoshop. Many digital cameras store their images on smart cards or flash memory cards. You can place these into a Personal Computer Memory Card Interface Adapter (PCMCIA) that can be read as an external disk by most of today's laptop computers. You can also buy PCMCIAs for desktop computers. Files are usually stored in JPEG format, so you can open them by choosing File, then Open in Photoshop.

A huge variety of digital cameras are available, ranging in resolution from 300 x 220 pixels to better-than-film resolution. In price, they range between $90 and $50,000. You will get the best compromise from a sub-$1,000 point-and-shoot camera with "megapixel" resolution and a zoom lens.

IMPORT IMAGES FROM A DIGITAL CAMERA

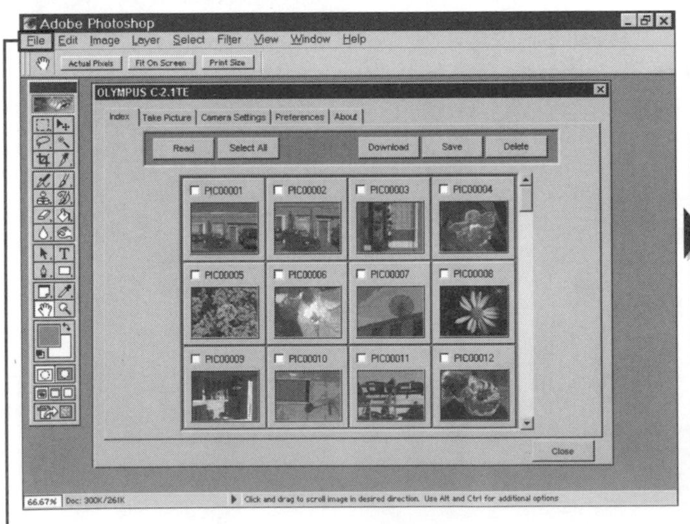

1 Click File, then Import, then TWAIN_32 Source.

■ The Select Source dialog box appears.

2 Choose the digital camera from which you want to import images.

3 Click Select.

■ The digital camera's software dialog box appears.

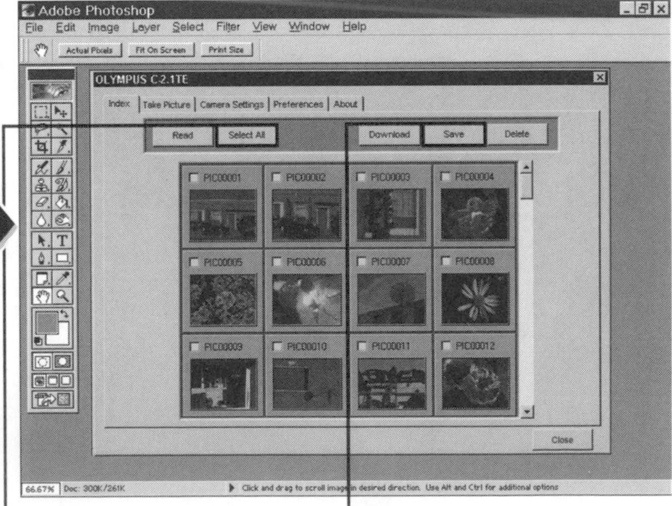

4 Click Select All.

■ The thumbnails turn gray to show that they have been selected.

5 Click Save.

■ The File Save dialog box appears.

If the resolution of popularly priced digital cameras is limited to making a 5 x 7 photographic-quality print, are these cameras worth the investment?

✔ Probably, but that really depends on your goals. For example, I often use digital camera images as "instant sketches" for illustrations that are heavily processed by special effects filters and overpainted by hand. The original resolution is thus of little consequence. They are also practical for collecting details to be included later in larger compositions for record-keeping purposes (such as insurance photos or employee databases). Finally, for Web publication purposes, the creative potential of these cameras is unlimited.

What effect does the number of images saved in a digital camera have on image definition?

✔ Some manufacturers actually give you a choice of resolution. Obviously, you can save more 640 x 480 images than 1280 x 1024 images. Also, most digital cameras give you a choice of quality (compression) levels. More compression results in blotches and smears called artifacts, which are tolerable for record-keeping and sketchpad purposes. Artifacts become more pronounced when you click Image, then Adjust.

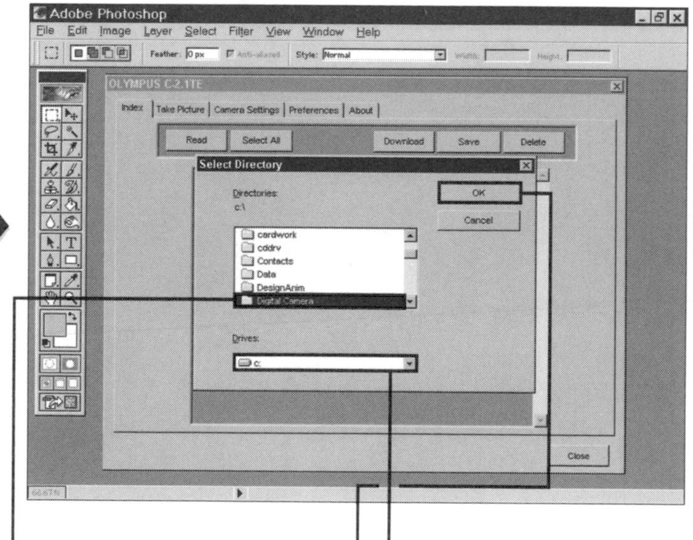

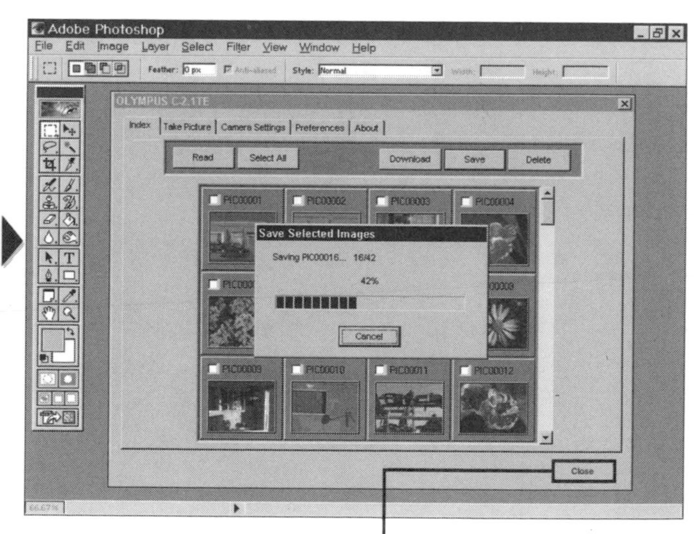

6 Navigate to the folder where you want to store these images.

Note: This folder should not contain other files that may have the same names as those in the camera. Creating a new folder for each download is best.

7 Use the Drives menu if you want to store the images on a different drive.

8 Click OK.

9 Wait until the Save Selected Images meter reaches 100% and the dialog box disappears.

10 Click Close.

IMPORT IMAGES FROM A FLATBED SCANNER

You can import images into Photoshop from the most versatile of all image acquisition devices: a flatbed scanner. Flatbed scanners tend to have higher optical resolution and greater color depth than the sheet-fed variety. Furthermore, you can scan small 3D objects and thick books on a flatbed scanner. Flatbed scanners are ideal for capturing patterns in fabrics and printed materials, as well as photographs.

Although painting an original image in Photoshop is certainly possible, most of us use the program to enhance images acquired from another source.

Most makes and models of scanners work with Photoshop. Make sure that the glass of your scanner is clean. Also check that the art you want to scan is clean. Photoshop is good at retouching, but why make work for yourself?

Finally, make sure that the scanner is turned on and that its plug-in software has been installed properly.

Be sure to keep your scanner manual handy, too. Some scanners require that you scan using independent software and then save the resulting file in a Photoshop-compatible format. If you have such a scanner, refer to its manual.

IMPORT IMAGES FROM A FLATBED SCANNER

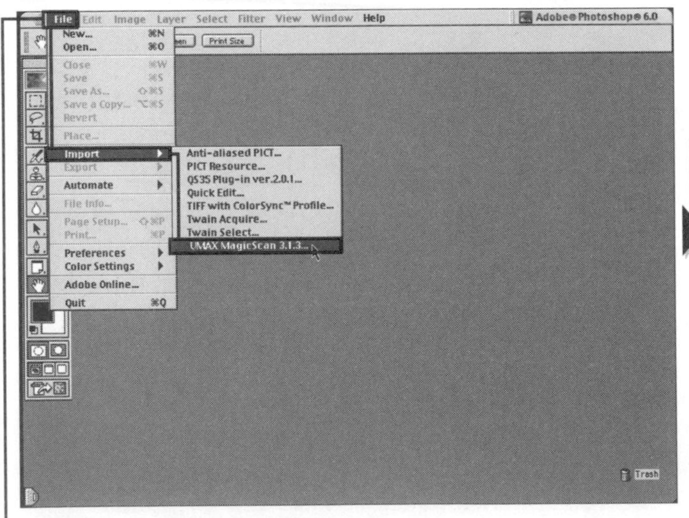

1 Click File, then Import, then *Your Scanner Software* (in this case, UMAX MagicScan).

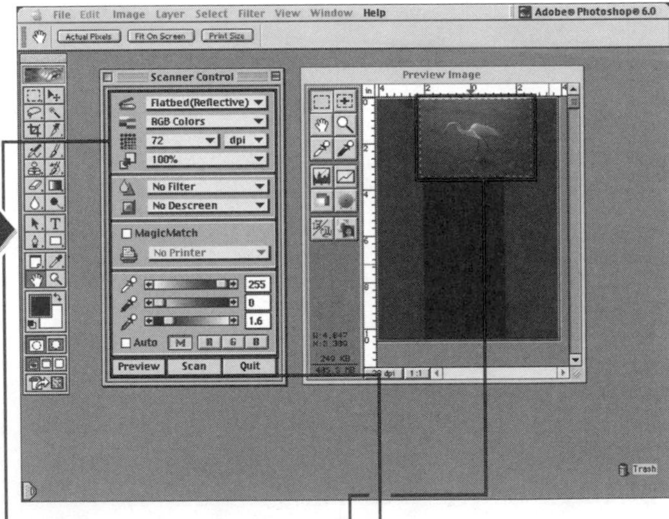

■ The scanner's software dialog box appears inside Photoshop.

2 Use settings similar to those shown here.

3 Click Preview to see the picture in position on the scanner bed.

4 Drag the selection marquee to restrict the scan to the intended picture.

What do the image size controls do in the scanner software?

✔ They have nothing to do with image size control in Photoshop, although the resolution in pixels helps you to preview how large the Photoshop image will be onscreen. Setting the units for those measurements in pixels is a good idea.

What criteria should I use in judging the scanner preview?

✔ Scan an image that has the truest color balance and the widest possible range of tones. Then you will have a library image that will give you the most flexibility when modifying the image later.

What should I look for in a scanner?

✔ At least 600 dpi optical resolution and 30-bit color. You can get both of these qualities today in scanners that cost less than $100.

Are transparency adapters worth the extra cost?

✔ Transparency adapters are very useful for making contact sheets from 35mm and roll film negatives. Because they eliminate the need to make prints, they return their extra costs pretty quickly. Most, however, do not scan at high enough optical resolutions to substitute for a film scanner.

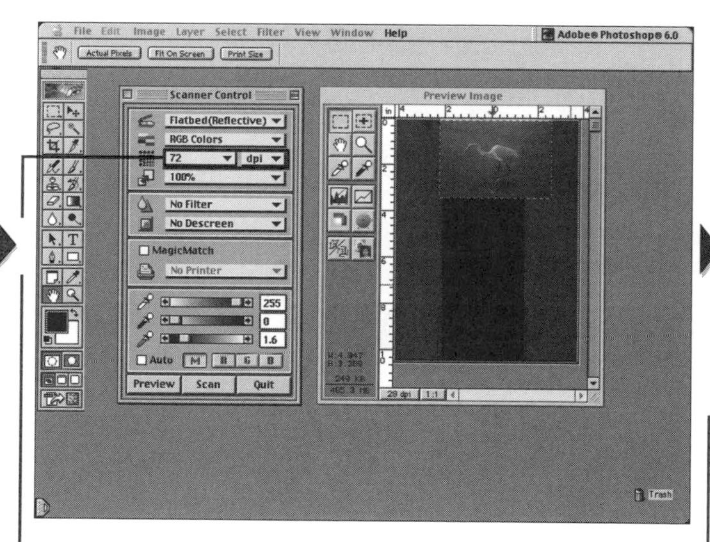

5 Specify the resolution of the file you want to bring into Photoshop.

Note: Stick to your scanner's range of optical resolutions, per the scanner's manual. This way, you will have an easier time enlarging the image in Photoshop.

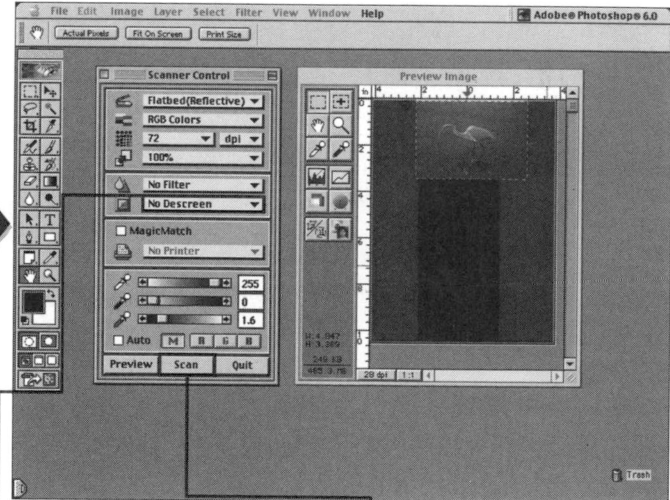

Note: Use the scanner software to make your scanner preview look like you want your end product to look.

6 If scanning publications, click Descreen or Despeckle.

7 Make any other adjustments that seem appropriate. (Options vary from scanner to scanner.)

8 Click Scan.

■ After a few moments, the image appears in Photoshop, ready to be edited.

IMPORT IMAGES FROM A SLIDE SCANNER

You can easily import images from a slide scanner into Photoshop, using either the scanner's TWAIN device interface or a plug-in provided by the scanner's manufacturer. If you want the highest quality images from your original photos at the most affordable price, a slide scanner is the way to go.

A scanner resolution of about 2,700 dpi is adequate to reproduce the detail in a 35mm image shot on ISO 100 film. Scanning at 30 or 36 bits per pixel greatly increases shadow range and depth. The resulting file is approximately 27MB, which is large enough to produce a professional-quality, full-page magazine ad.

Some of the newest desktop slide scanners go up to 4,000 dpi. You can get even more detail and much greater dynamic range from a drum scan, but the cost per scan goes up dramatically.

The drawback to slide scanners is their cost and lack of versatility. You can spend between $400 and $2,000, and you will still need another scanner for reflective materials. The least expensive scanners can work with APS (24mm Advance Photo System) as well as 35mm film, but generally resolve only 1,800 dpi. Transparency scanners are also available for larger format images, but count on paying close to $5,000.

IMPORT IMAGES FROM A SLIDE SCANNER

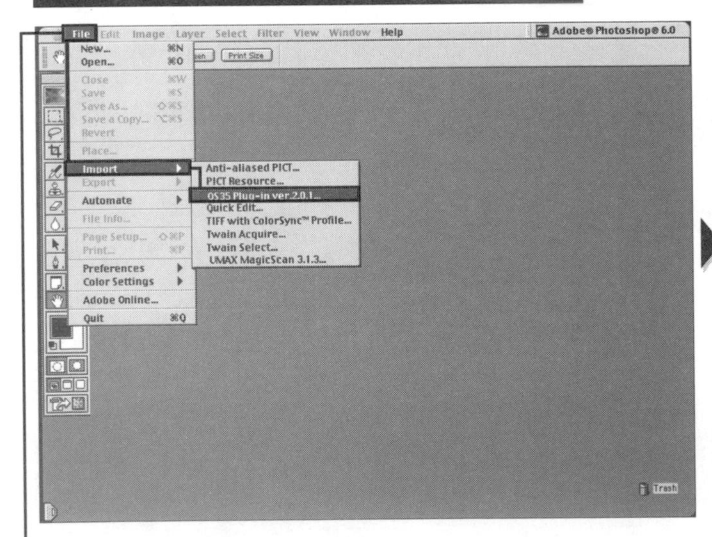

1 Click File, then Import, then *Your Slide Scanner* (in this case, Minolta QuickScan 35).

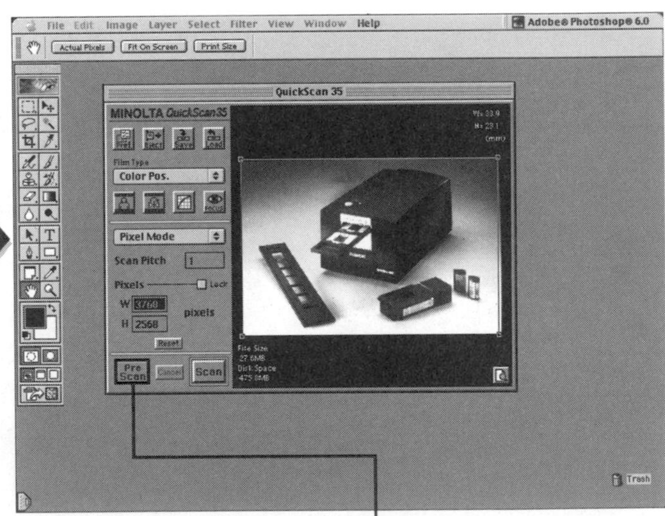

■ The slide scanner's software dialog box appears.

2 Insert the slide or the film holder into the slot in the scanner.

3 Click Preview or Prescan.

■ After about a minute, an image appears in the preview box.

If I have negatives, do I have to make prints and scan them on a flatbed scanner?

✔ No. Most popular slide scanners will scan negatives and convert them. There is no need to make a print at all.

Why not use a transparency attachment on my flatbed scanner to scan slides?

✔ Resolution is not good enough for full page publication-quality work. If the format is 6 x 9 or larger, you are more likely to get a large enough scan at high enough resolution from a scanner with 1200-dpi optical resolution.

Is a transparency adapter good for anything?

✔ A transparency adapter is a great way to make contact sheets of 35mm negatives. An adapter also works for scanning Web images, which typically have a maximum of 800 x 600 pixels.

What do I do about film strips that are too long to fit in the film holder?

✔ Film holders usually accommodate up to six frames. If you have already cut your film into longer strips, you will have to cut them again.

4 Click to rotate the image, if necessary.

5 Adjust color balance and contrast (slider area).

6 Drag the selection marquee to crop out any unneeded part of the image.

7 Click Scan.

■ The scanned image appears in a work window in Photoshop.

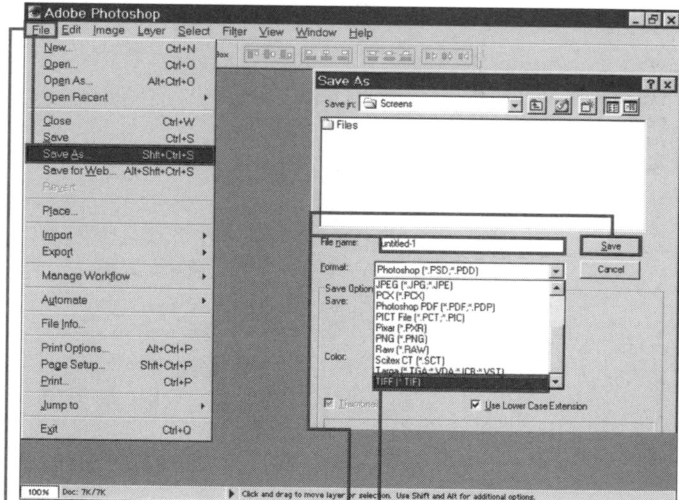

SAVE THE FILE TO A PORTABLE FORMAT

1 Click File, then Save As.

■ The Save As dialog box appears.

2 Choose TIFF (or another preferred format) from the Format menu.

3 Type the filename that you want to use.

4 Click Save.

SECTION II

3) CHANGING THE SIZE OF AN IMAGE

4) ADJUSTING IMAGE QUALITY

5) RETOUCHING IMAGES

CHANGE THE IMAGE SIZE

Photoshop includes two commands that you can use to change the size of an image: Image Size and Canvas Size.

If you want to change the size or proportions of an image — for instance, to make it fit into a Web page or print layout — choose Image, then Image Size. You can learn more about the Canvas Size command in the section "Change the Canvas Size."

Photoshop can add pixels and blend the transition between added and the new pixels so that the brightness and color of the image do not look unnaturally pixilated.

This process also softens or unfocuses the edges, so you may want to run the Unsharp Mask filter after doing any resampling (see Chapter 13, "Applying Darkroom Effects").

Remember that Photoshop cannot add detail when resampling; it has to guess, according to various mathematical formulae, which pixels to duplicate and whether to duplicate them exactly or to change their colors according to the colors of their surrounding pixels.

If you want a large image to show fine detail, the original, unscaled image has to contain enough pixels to record that detail.

CHANGE THE IMAGE SIZE

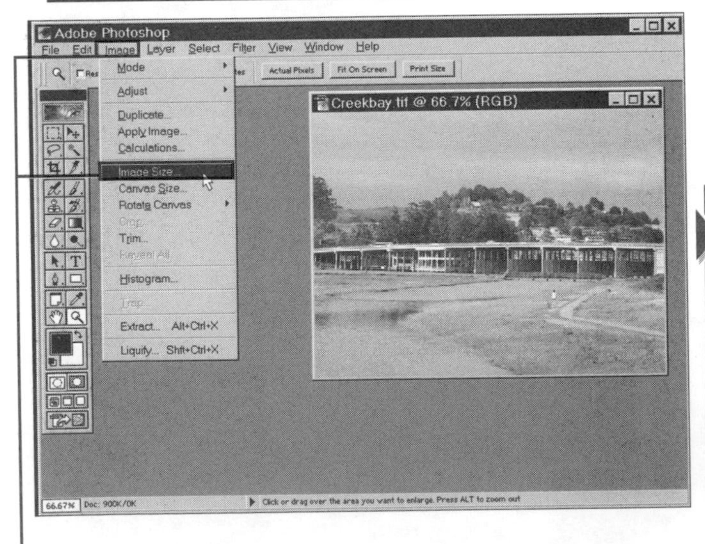

1 Choose Image, then Image Size.

■ The Image Size dialog appears.

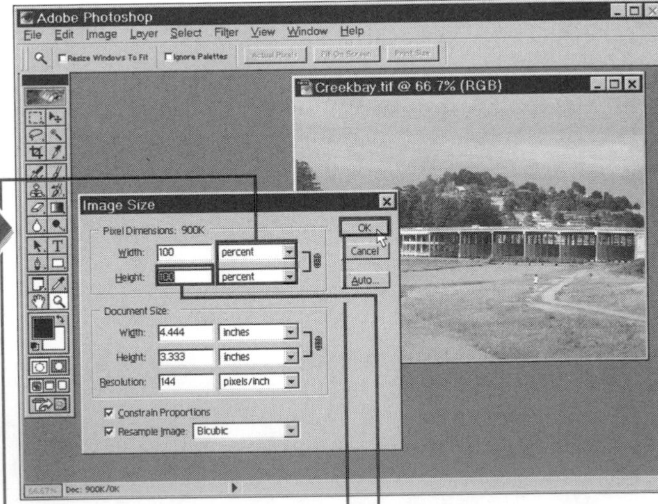

2 To change the size of the image by a percentage without changing the proportions, choose Percent from the Height and Width menus.

3 Enter the percentage.

Note: If Constrain Proportions is checked, you need to enter the percentage in only one field. The other is entered automatically.

4 Leave other settings at the defaults (shown) and click OK.

What does Resample accomplish?

✔ If you turn Resample off (☑ becomes ☐), Photoshop assigns more pixels to the representation of each original pixel by the amount specified.

How do I know what resolution is needed for a particular size output from a particular printer?

✔ Divide the printer's vertical output resolution by the number of colors used, excluding black. For example, an Epson Stylus color printer at 720 dpi prints one dot of each color. So the resolution of the image does not need to be more than 240 dpi.

How do I get rid of the out-of-focus effect that seems to occur when I change the size of an image significantly?

✔ You can use the Unsharp Mask filter (see Chapter 13). The most beneficial settings depend on the colors and contrast of the image, so you need to experiment. One technique is to use the default settings and then repeat the command by pressing ⌘/Ctrl+F. If the sharpness of the image deteriorates press ⌘/Ctrl+Z to undo the last filtration.

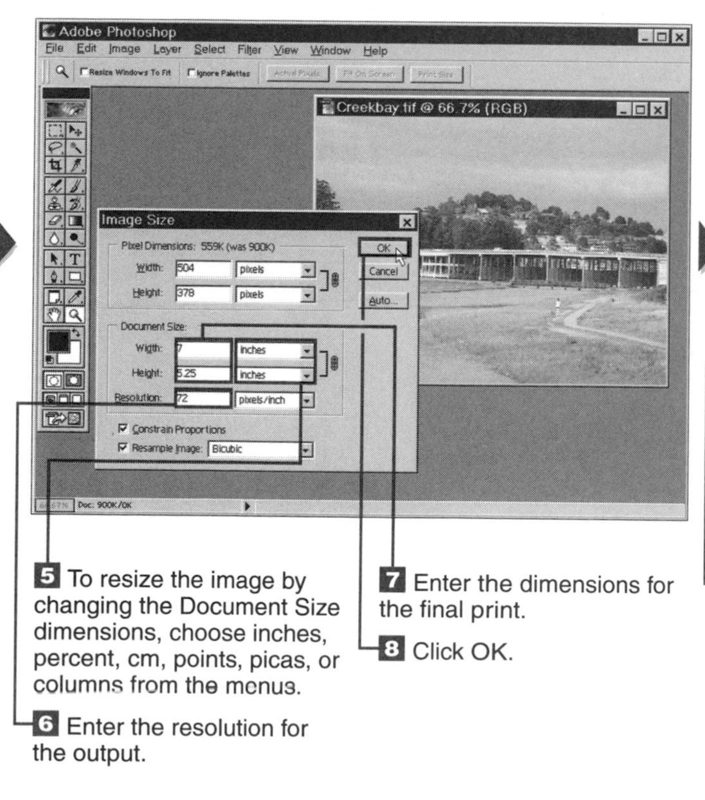

5 To resize the image by changing the Document Size dimensions, choose inches, percent, cm, points, picas, or columns from the menus.

6 Enter the resolution for the output.

7 Enter the dimensions for the final print.

8 Click OK.

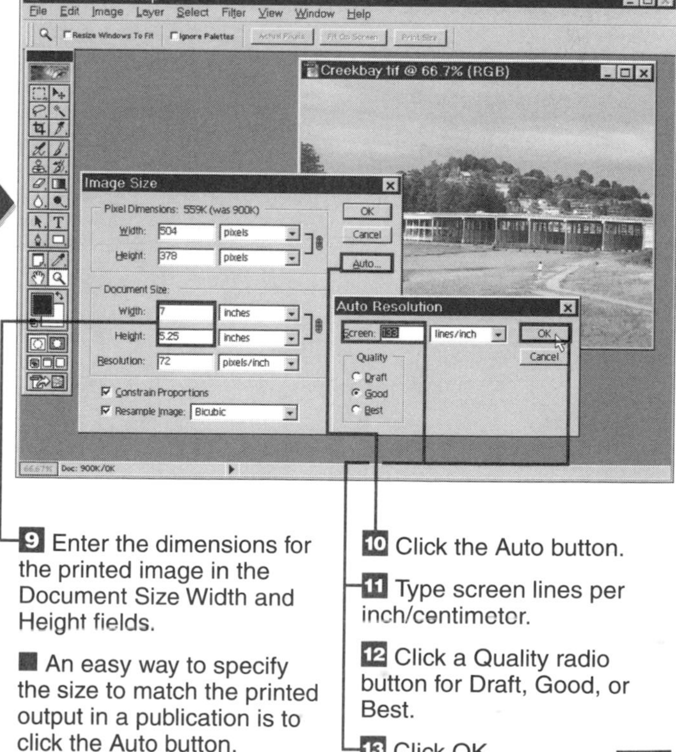

9 Enter the dimensions for the printed image in the Document Size Width and Height fields.

■ An easy way to specify the size to match the printed output in a publication is to click the Auto button.

10 Click the Auto button.

11 Type screen lines per inch/centimeter.

12 Click a Quality radio button for Draft, Good, or Best.

13 Click OK.

CHANGE THE CANVAS SIZE

You can use the Canvas Size command to change the size of the workspace (background) without changing the size of the picture. In this manner, you can change the proportions of the image and leave room outside the image for a border, border effect, or drop shadow.

When you make the canvas larger than the image, the border automatically fills with the current background color. Be sure to choose the background color you like before issuing the Canvas Size command.

If you dislike the background color, and it is too late to Undo your change, choose the foreground color you want for the border. Next, choose the Paint Bucket tool and use it to fill the border. Be sure to type **1** in the Paintbucket Options Tolerance field, or the fill may bleed into the image.

The location of the gray square in the Canvas Size dialog box's Anchor box dictates where the outside borders fall. If you add a symmetrical border (or border effect or drop shadow), be sure to leave the image centered (the default position).

CHANGE THE CANVAS SIZE

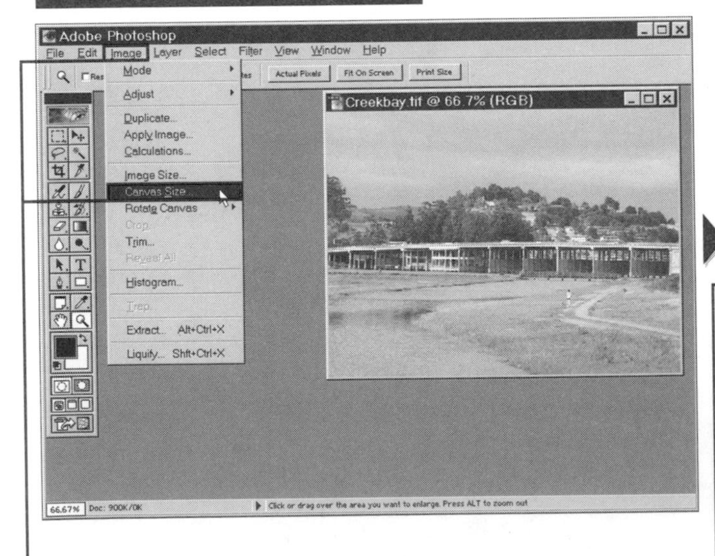

1 Choose Image, then Canvas Size.

■ The Canvas Size dialog box appears.

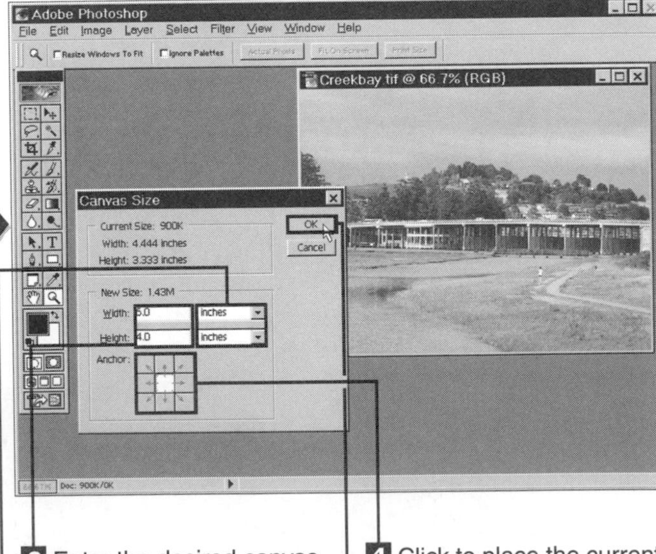

2 Enter the desired canvas dimensions in the Width and Height boxes.

3 Select the desired units of measurement.

4 Click to place the current image in the desired location on the canvas.

5 Click OK.

■ The canvas increases as specified and assumes the current background color.

Can I have a transparent canvas?

✔ Yes. You may want to have this canvas so you can place another background or a textured border around the image.

How can I make a drop shadow on the canvas border?

✔ Select the image and press ⌘/Ctrl+ J to lift the image to a new layer. From the menu bar, choose Layer, then Layer Style, then Drop Shadow. Adjust the dialog settings according to your preferences and click OK.

What if I want to place the image on the canvas so that the borders are not equidistant on all sides?

✔ Make the canvas large enough so that you can crop the image. Then use the Crop tool (see the section "Crop the Image.") to define the borders on the top and sides. Or, create a new transparent background layer and then select the original layer and use the Move tool to drag the image to any position you want.

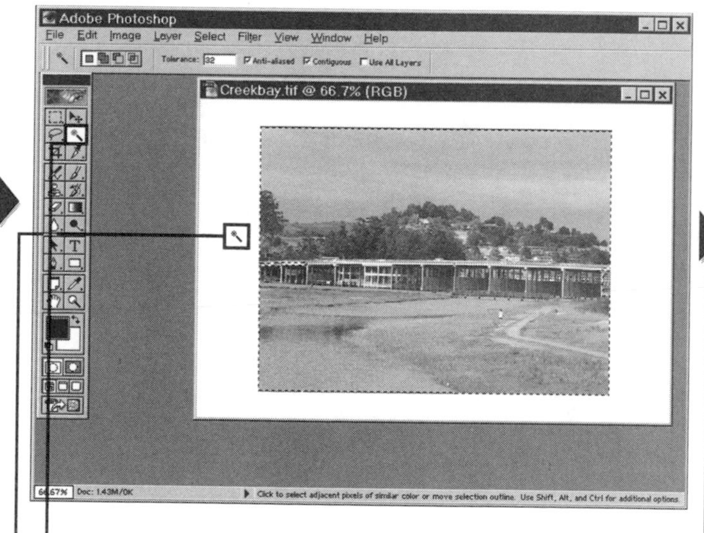

6 If the borders of the image contrast with the border color, click the Magic Wand.

7 Click in the border.

8 Press /Ctrl+Shift+I to invert the selection.

9 Press /Ctrl+J to lift the contents of the selection to a new layer.

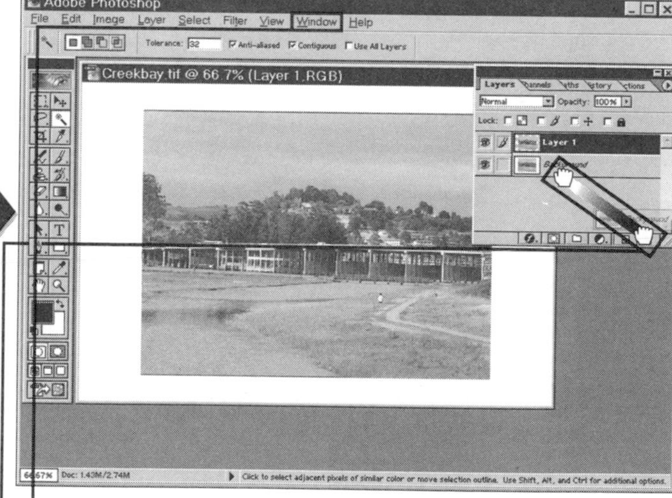

10 Choose Window, then Show Layers.

11 Drag the Background layer to the trash.

■ The border around the canvas is now transparent.

CROP THE IMAGE

Often, information close to the borders of the image detracts from the main subject. Sometimes the image's dimensions are out of proportion with your intended layout or print frame. You can fix these problems by trimming, or cropping, the edges of the image.

The first lesson you learn when you study the art of photographic composition is to crop out any subject matter that detracts from the intended center of attention. So, though cropping may be simple, it is also important.

Photoshop gives you two means of cropping an image:

- the Crop tool
- the Marquee tool

This example illustrates how to use the Crop tool and the Rectangular Marquee selection tool. Photoshop has four different Marquee tools: rectangular, elliptic, row, and column. You can access these tools from the fly-out menu that appears when you click and hold down the Marquee tool.

CROP THE IMAGE

CROP WITH THE CROP TOOL

1 Click the Crop tool.

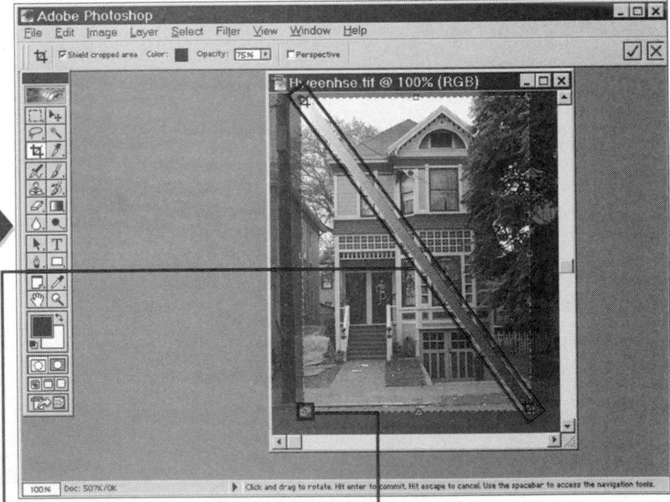

2 Drag diagonally across the image to create a marquee approximating the area of the image to be cropped.

■ Sizing handles appear around the marquee with a target to indicate the image center.

Note: You need not be precise in dragging the marquee. Use the sizing handles to get the exact trim.

Which is the more versatile of the two cropping methods?

✔ The Crop tool enables you to size and rotate after you have dragged the marquee. It is definitely the more versatile of the two tools.

Is there a way to crop the image without reducing the Canvas size?

✔ You have to cheat. Indicate the area you want to crop to with the Marquee tool. Press ⌘/Ctrl+Shift+I to invert the selection. Choose Edit, then Fill, then Background Color. Because the color of the canvas is the background color, you have accomplished your goal.

Is there a method for cropping the image without cropping the original?

✔ Yes. Choose Image, then Duplicate. Crop the duplicate image that results, then save it to a different name than the original.

How do I keep the cropping tool from snapping to the edges when I just want to trim a little?

✔ Use the Marquee tool and the Image menu's Crop command.

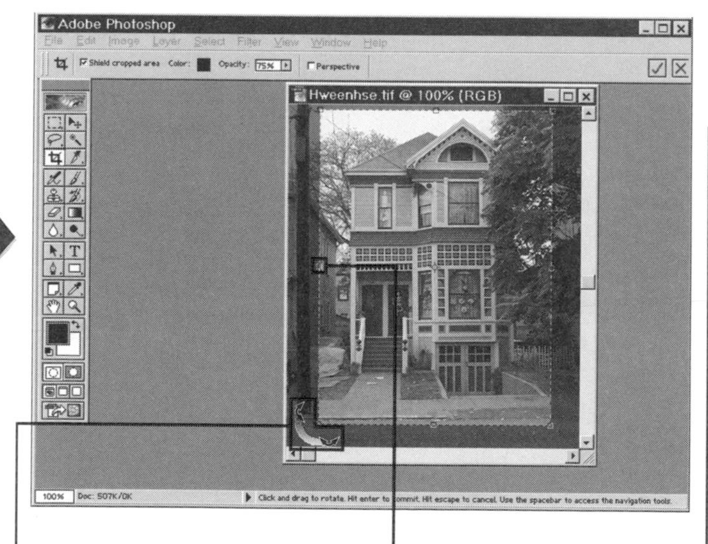

3 To rotate the area to be cropped, place the cursor just outside any corner handle, then, when the cursor changes to a curved double-headed arrow, drag to indicate rotation.

4 To resize the trim border, drag any sizing handle.

■ To resize proportionately, press Shift and drag your cursor.

5 To crop, double-click inside the marquee or press Return/Enter.

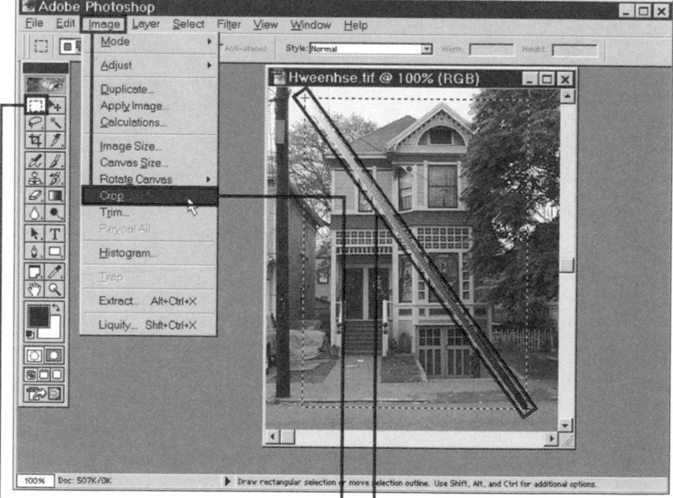

CROP WITH THE MARQUEE TOOL

1 Choose the Rectangular Marquee tool or press M until the Rectangular Marquee tool appears in the toolbox.

2 Drag to indicate the border you want to crop to.

3 When the marquee is the right size, choose Image, then Crop.

CROP AN IMAGE TO A SPECIFIC PROPORTION

Often you may be required to produce an image that is a specific proportion. For instance, you might want to produce Web thumbnails or components in an ad layout that all have the same proportionate shape. You can do this task easily with the Marquee tool and the Image menu's Crop command.

Cropping to a Specific Proportion is not the same as making proportionately correct images all the same size. To make all images a uniform size, choose Window, then Show Info, noting the size of the first image you cropped to a specific proportion. You then change the Marquee Options Style menu choice to Fixed Size and enter the size you noted on your first image. Until you change the settings, every subsequent image you crop with the Marquee tool has the exact same size and proportions of the first image.

To make images cropped to the same proportion the same size, you can click the Image, then Image Size command after cropping. Remember, however, that the greater the size change, the greater the chance of losing detail.

CROP AN IMAGE TO A SPECIFIC PROPORTION

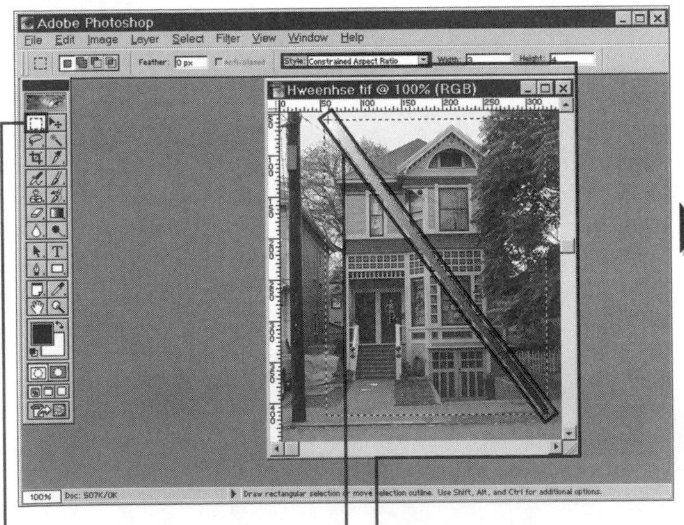

1 Click the Rectangular Marquee tool or choose it from the Marquee tools fly-out menu.

■ The Marquee Options bar appears.

2 Choose Constrained Aspect Ratio from the Style menu.

3 Drag to size the marquee.

■ Proportions are maintained at any size.

Note: Drag inside the marquee to position the marquee as desired.

4 Choose Image, then Crop.

■ Everything outside the marquee is cropped.

CROP AN IMAGE TO A SPECIFIC SIZE

You can use the Rectangular Marquee tool to crop out an area of specific height and width from an image.

This is another useful technique for making thumbnails, and is also extremely useful for cropping out sections of textures for use as seamless tiles for texture mapping (see Chapter 14).

You can crop to a fixed size by choosing the Fixed Size setting from the Style menu in the Marquee Options bar. You then type the desired height and width for your image.

In Photoshop 6, you can also choose the unit of measurement by typing px for pixels, in for inches, cm for centimeters, and so forth.

After you enter a fixed size in the Width and Height fields of the Marquee Options bar, any place you click with the Marquee tool is where the upper-left corner of a marquee of those dimensions appears. If the marquee is bigger than the image, the entire image is selected, even if you click inside the image.

CROP AN IMAGE TO A SPECIFIC SIZE

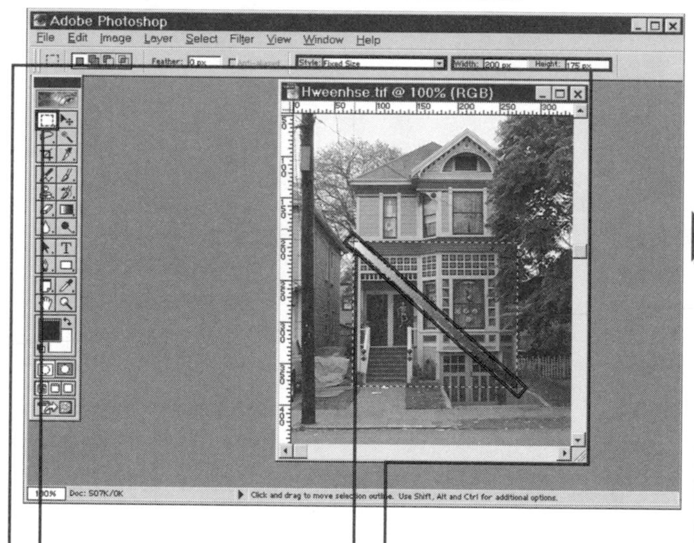

1 Click the Rectangular Marquee tool or choose it from the Marquee tools menu.

2 Choose Fixed Size from the Style menu.

3 Enter the desired measurements and units in the Height and Width fields.

4 Drag to place the marquee.

■ The marquee immediately assumes its designated size.

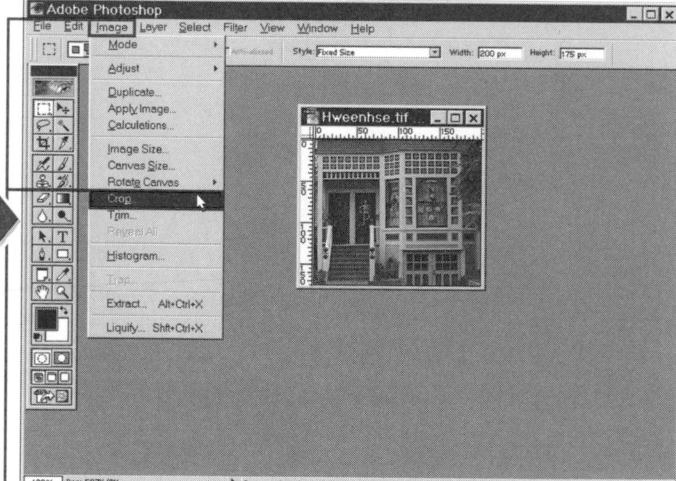

Note: Drag inside the marquee to position it as desired.

5 Choose Image, then Crop.

■ Everything outside the marquee is cropped.

CROP AN IMAGE TO A FIXED SIZE AND RESOLUTION

At times you may want to trim an image to a specific pixel width and height and, at the same time, render it at a specific resolution. For example, you may need a specific size to fit the image in a page layout, and a specific resolution for output to a printer. In Photoshop you do so by using the Crop tool and checking the Fixed Target Size option in the Crop Options palette.

The objective is to produce a cropped image with a specific proportion, as well as a specific resolution. In the Crop Options palette, if you change the height or width and do not reenter resolution, the resolution automatically changes in the end result. On the other hand, if you do not change the height and width entries, but do change the pixels per inch (or centimeter) of resolution, the Image Size specification changes the height and width to make the image the correct size at the specified resolution.

If you click the Front Image button, the current dimensions and resolution become your starting point. If you do not click the Front Image button, simply specify height and width and resolution. The image sizes itself accordingly.

CROP AN IMAGE TO A FIXED SIZE AND RESOLUTION

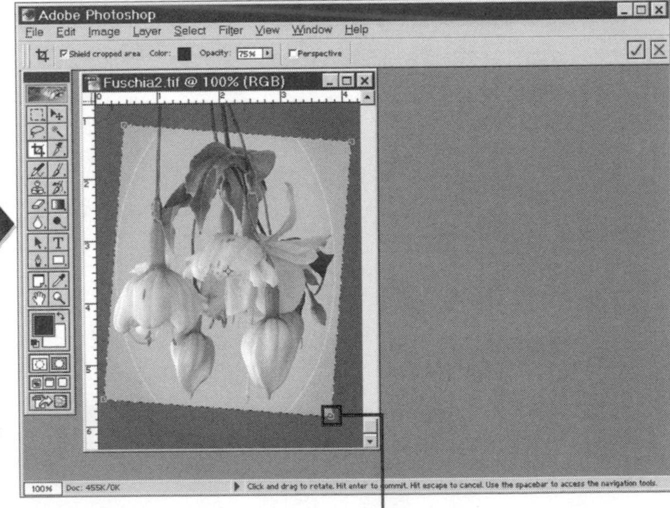

1 Click the Crop tool.

■ The Crop options appear in the Options bar.

2 Click Front Image.

■ The current image size information appears.

3 Enter the desired dimensions and resolution for the resized image.

4 Drag diagonally to create a marquee approximating the area of the image to be cropped.

■ Sizing handles appear around the marquee.

5 Drag corners to change size of the crop boundaries or drag outside to rotate boundaries.

CROP AN IMAGE TO A SPECIFIC PROPORTION OR DIMENSION

You can crop a series of images to a consistent size and resolution or to a set proportion of height and width by using the Rectangular Marquee tool.

These options can save you significant time and hassles when you want to crop images to fit in uniform spaces on a print page (think of the portraits in a year book) or on a Web page (think of image thumbnails). You can also find fixed-size crops handy for cutting out patterned portions of an image for use as tiled fill patterns.

You need to either write down the dimension you want to make consistent, so that you can re-enter it, or create an Action that automatically enters the desired dimensions. Otherwise, you have to be sure to open and crop all the images in the series before you make any changes in the Width and Height fields of the Crop tool Options bar.

CROP AN IMAGE TO A SPECIFIC PROPORTION OR DIMENSION

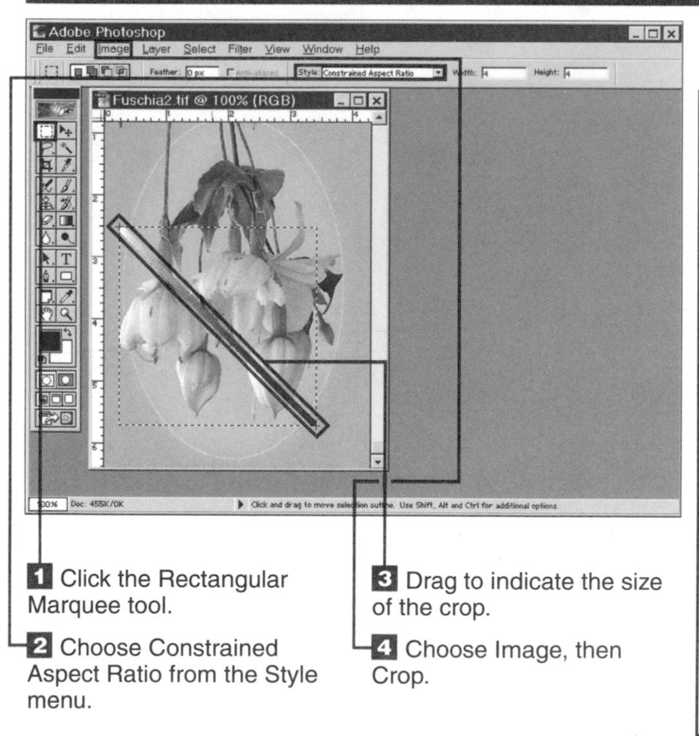

1 Click the Rectangular Marquee tool.

2 Choose Constrained Aspect Ratio from the Style menu.

3 Drag to indicate the size of the crop.

4 Choose Image, then Crop.

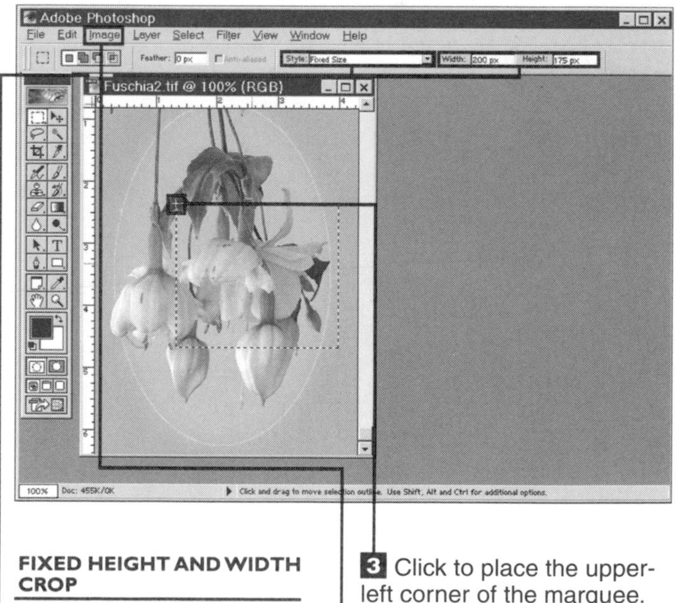

FIXED HEIGHT AND WIDTH CROP

1 Choose Fixed Size from the Style menu in the Marquee Options bar.

2 Enter the pixel dimensions you desire.

3 Click to place the upper-left corner of the marquee.

4 Choose Image, then Crop.

ADJUST A SPECIFIC AREA

You can limit image quality adjustments to a specific area of the layer you are working on or, if you are using an adjustment layer, to a specific area of all layers below the adjustment layer. (To find out how to use adjustment layers, see the section "Correct Overall Color Balance" later in this chapter.) All it takes is to make a selection that includes only the area that you want to affect (see Chapter 6).

Another way to limit any adjustments you make to a specific area of the image is to place that section of the image on a layer that contains nothing but the information you want to select. Select the portion you want to change and then press ⌘/Ctrl+J to lift the selection to a new layer.

Often you will want the selected area to blend smoothly with its surroundings. You can do that by feathering the selection. Choose Select, then Feather. When the dialog box appears, enter a number representing the distance (in pixels) to graduate the effect along the edge of the selection marquee.

ADJUST A SPECIFIC AREA

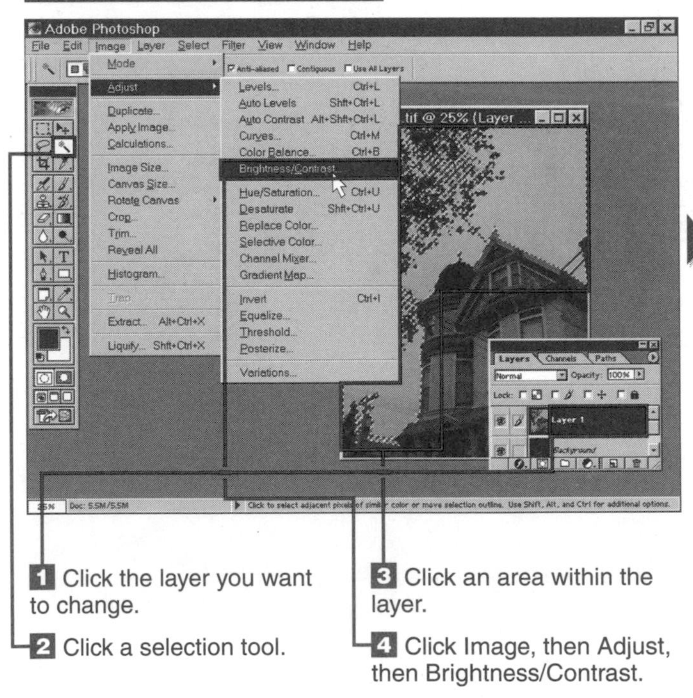

Adobe Photoshop
File Edit Image Layer Select Filter View Window Help
Sample Size: Point Sample
house.tif @ 25% (Layer ...
Brightness/Contrast
Brightness: -45
Contrast: +45
OK
Cancel
Preview
Layers Channels Paths
Layer 1
Background
Doc: 5.5M/5.5M

1 Click the layer you want to change.

2 Click a selection tool.

3 Click an area within the layer.

4 Click Image, then Adjust, then Brightness/Contrast.

■ The Brightness/Contrast dialog box appears.

5 Click Preview.

■ The image is now in Preview mode.

6 Drag the Brightness and Contrast sliders until you achieve the appearance you want.

7 Click OK.

■ Photoshop adjusts the area you specified.

8 Press /Ctrl+D to remove the selection.

ADJUST A SPECIFIC LAYER

You can restrict any image quality adjustment to a single layer. In fact, that is what happens by default if you choose to make your adjustment directly from the Image menu instead of first adding an adjustment layer.

When you adjust only one layer, you maintain the effect of any blending commands that have been applied to that layer. Also, the relationship of transparent areas on different layers remains the same. In other words, opaque areas do not hide one another in unexpected ways. You also use this procedure when you specifically do not want to affect any other layers.

The main difference between the steps in this section and the section "Adjust a Specific Area" is that you want to affect an entire layer (although sometimes it can be the only layer in the image anyway).

ADJUST A SPECIFIC LAYER

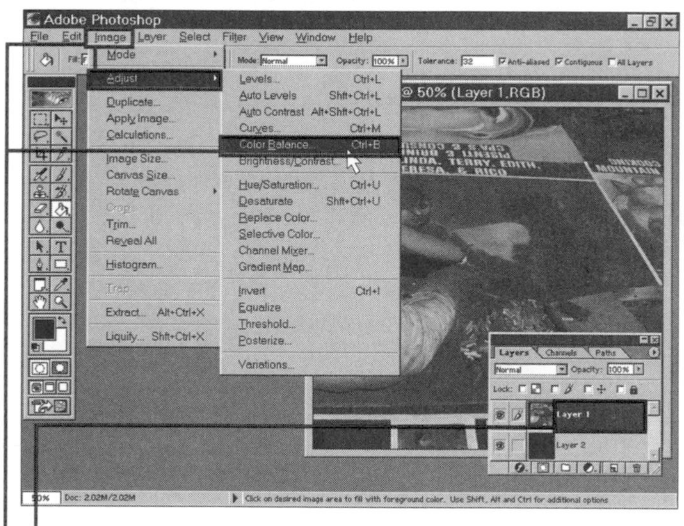

1 Click the layer you want to affect.

2 Click Image, then Adjust.

3 Click the desired command from the menu.

Note: This example illustrates Color Balance, but the steps also apply to the other Adjust commands. Some adjustment commands execute immediately, making the remaining steps in this section unnecessary.

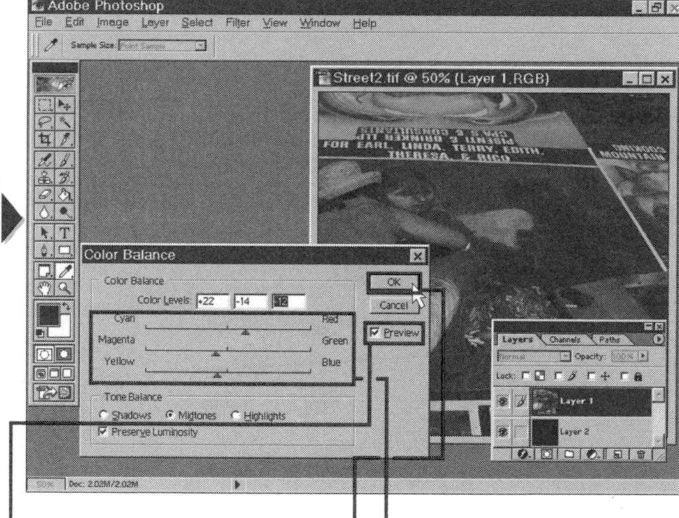

■ The dialog box for your selected command appears.

4 Click Preview to activate an instant preview of the image (☐ becomes ☑).

5 Drag the sliders until you achieve the desired appearance.

6 Click OK.

■ Photoshop adjusts your layer.

CORRECT OVERALL COLOR BALANCE

You can correct the overall color balance of an image to fix unattractive color casts that result from poor film quality or film intended for a different type of light source, correct a hastily made scan, change the mood of a photo, or create a special effect. In any of these cases, the Color Balance command on the Image menu is the best candidate.

You usually want to use the Color Balance command after adding an adjustment layer so that it affects all the layers in the image—as demonstrated in this section.

If you want to apply Color Balance to an individual layer, select the layer in question and click Image, Adjust, and then Color Balance. Then follow the steps that occur in this section after the Color Balance dialog box appears.

When making composite images that were shot in different circumstances and locations, apply the Color Balance command to each layer so that your images look like they belong in the same place and time when you place them together.

CORRECT OVERALL COLOR BALANCE

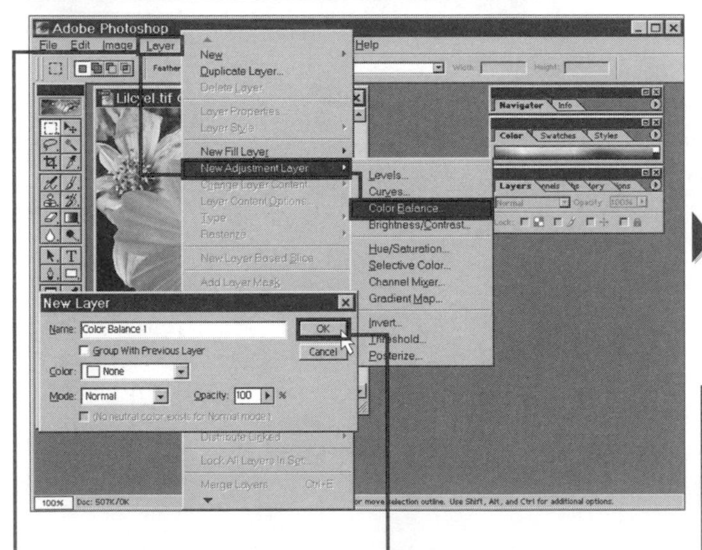

1 Click Layer, then New Adjustment Layer, then Color Balance.

■ The New Layer dialog box appears.

2 Click OK.

■ The Color Balance dialog box appears. This dialog box is the same one that appears if you choose Color Balance from the Adjust menu under Image.

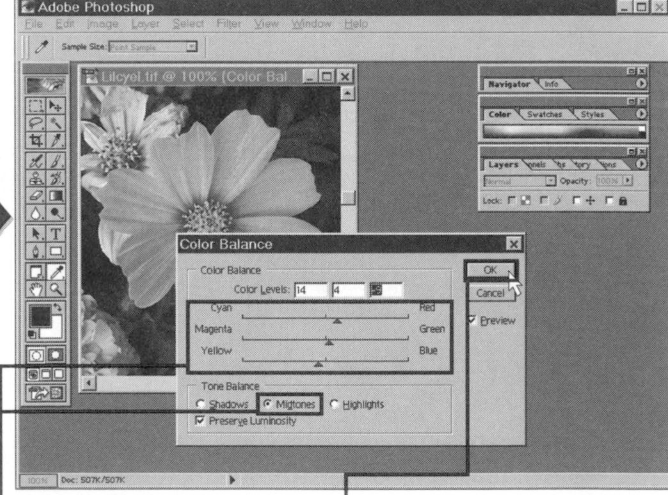

■ The Preview and Preserve Luminosity boxes are checked by default.

3 Click Midtones.

4 Drag the sliders to increase the intensity of color in the direction of the label.

Note: You can make Shadow, Midtone, and Highlight adjustments before you close the dialog box. You should do so if you want to adjust color over the full range of image brightness.

5 Click OK.

Is there a shortcut to the Color Balance command?

✔ Yes. You can press ⌘/Ctrl+B to activate the Color Balance command, but the result affects only the current layer.

Which is better—correcting a poor scan with the Color Balance command or rescanning the image?

✔ On rare occasions, you might be able to improve on the best your scanner can do, because not all scanners are created equal. Still, you owe it to yourself to get the best you can out of your scanner. Remember, the more detail you have to work with in the first place, the better.

How can I view my image when the Color Balance dialog box covers most of it?

✔ When balancing overall color, most users find seeing the whole image advantageous. Before you open the Color Balance dialog box, drag the image window to about one-quarter of your active screen size and then zoom out until the image is small enough to fit within that window. Drag the window to the upper-right corner of the screen and open the Color Balance dialog box. Another solution is to click the Color Balance dialog box's title bar and drag it out of the way.

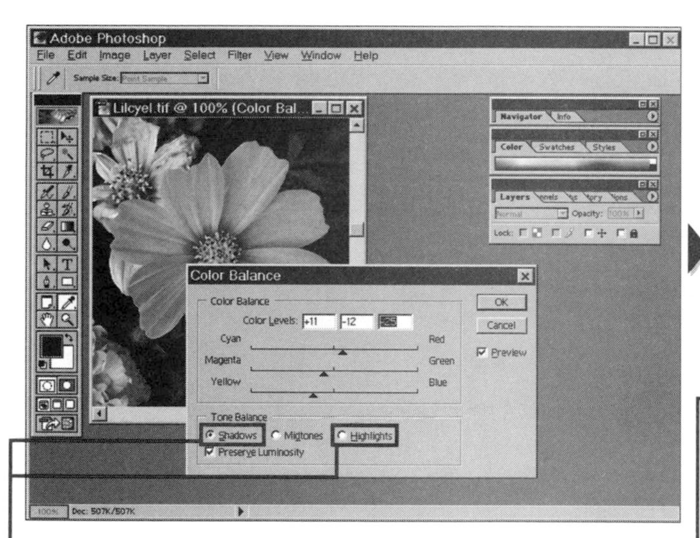

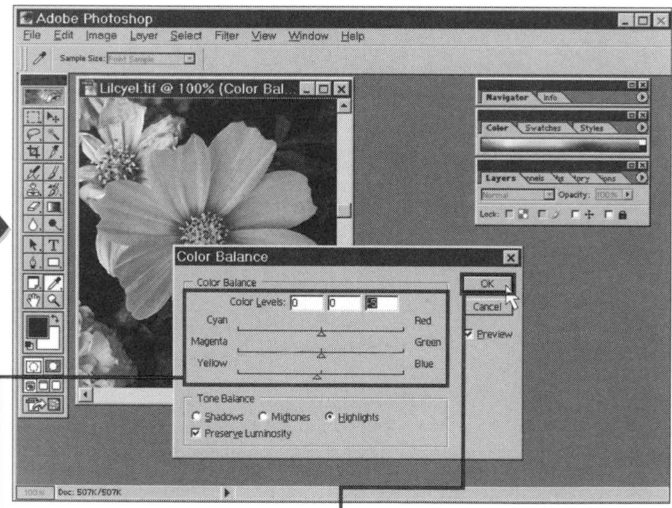

MODIFY THE BALANCE IN THE SHADOWS OR HIGHLIGHTS

1 Click Shadows to modify the shadows or click Highlights to modify Highlights.

2 On any or all slider bars, either drag sliders or type values to indicate the desired color shift.

■ Typing positive numbers moves the slider right and typing negative numbers moves the slider left of center.

■ You can press Tab to cycle through the three number boxes.

3 Click OK.

■ Photoshop makes the appropriate adjustments.

USING COLOR CORRECTION AIDS

You can use a pair of palettes (you can always find palettes under the Window menu) to help you in making color corrections: the Color palette and the Info palette. When used in tandem, these two palettes can give you precise feedback on your color changes.

To use this technique, you open the Info palette (click Window, then Show Info) and then use the Eyedropper tool to test up to four samples of color from the image itself. Place the pickup points in the areas that most need to be changed by your image adjustments.

Next, open the Color palette (click Window, then Show Color). Now, suppose you want to make a color correction, and you want to know the exact color in a particular part of the image. Place the cursor anywhere in the image, and it changes to the Eyedropper cursor. Click in the color areas that concern you most. Now, any change you make with the correction command is reflected in the setting of the Color palette sliders and in the color samples in the Info palette.

USING COLOR CORRECTION AIDS

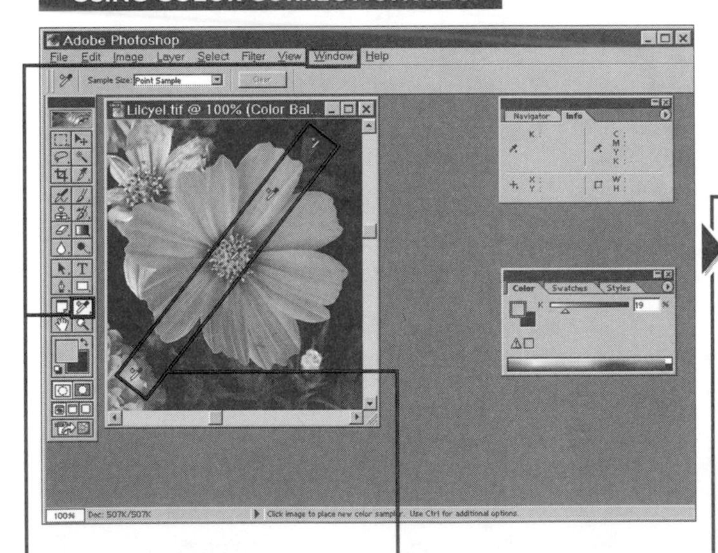

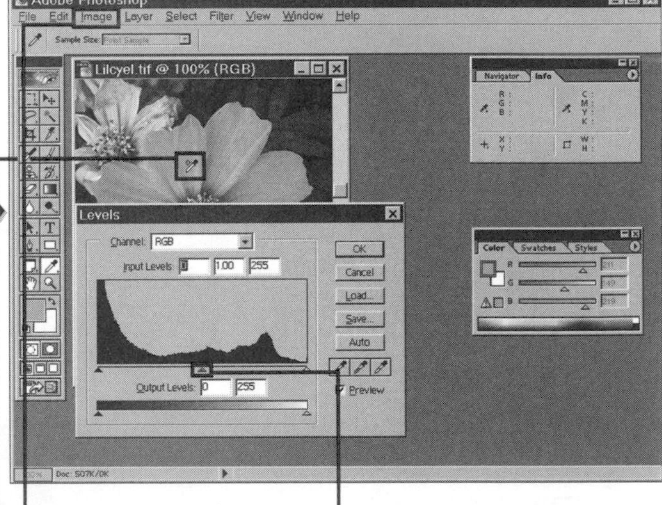

1 Click Window, then Show Info to display the Info palette.

2 Click Window, then Show Color to display the Color palette.

3 Click the Eyedropper tool.

4 Click up to four sample spots.

■ The exact colors of each sampled pixel are shown graphically in the Color palette and numerically in the Info palette.

5 Choose any of the color correction commands you want to use (such as Image, then Adjust, then Levels).

■ The command's dialog box appears.

6 Click a color in the workspace.

■ The color settings change in response.

7 Make the desired adjustment in the command's dialog box.

■ The change is instantly reflected in the image.

ADJUST BRIGHTNESS AND CONTRAST

You can use the Brightness/Contrast command to uniformly adjust those qualities across highlights, midtones, and shadows. The Brightness/Contrast dialog box is very simple and easy to understand. In it are two slider bars, one for brightness, the other for contrast. If you drag the slider above the midpoint, the image becomes brighter or gains contrast (depending on which slider you move). If you drag a slider below the midpoint, the image becomes darker or flatter.

The advantage of this tool is that you can easily make "quick-and-dirty" overall changes. The disadvantage is that you cannot separately modify the intensity of highlights, midtones, and shadows—as you can when using the Levels or Curves commands. If you sense that a quick and simple adjustment is best—or if you are only working inside a small selected area of the image—the Brightness/Contrast command is a timesaver.

Because no shortcut key exists for the Brightness/Contrast command, consider making it an action and assigning it to a function key (see Chapter 19 for more information on how to automate Photoshop with actions).

ADJUST BRIGHTNESS AND CONTRAST

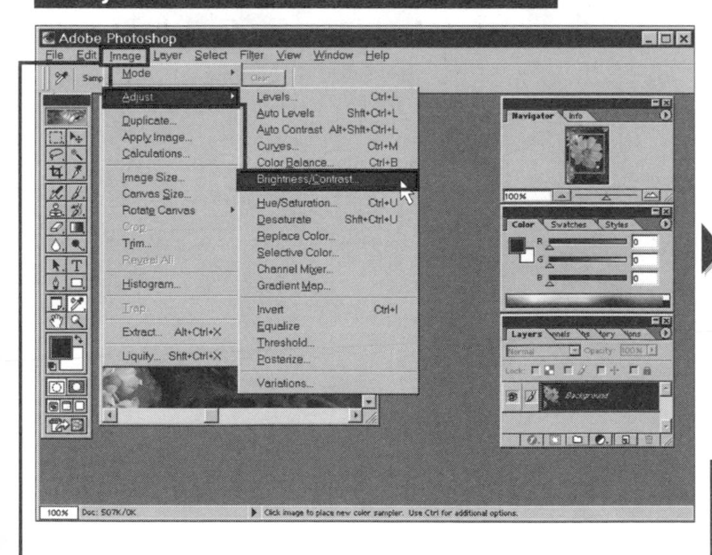

1 Click Image, then Adjust, then Brightness/Contrast.

■ The Brightness/Contrast dialog box appears.

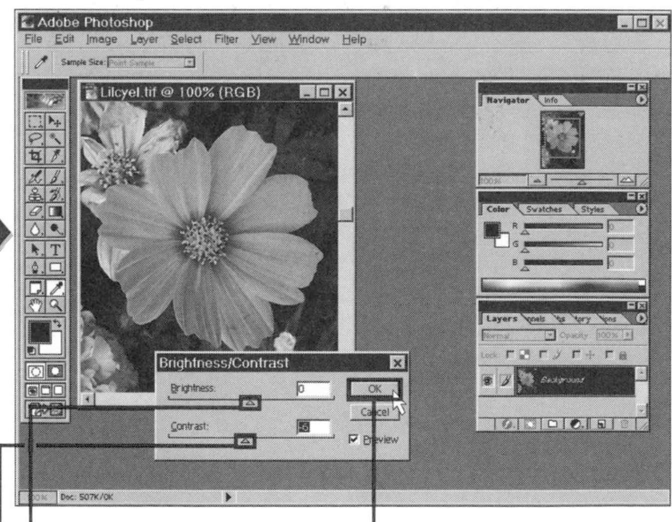

2 Drag the Brightness slider to the left of center to darken or to the right of center to brighten the image.

3 Drag the Contrast slider to the left of center to lower contrast or to the right of center to increase contrast.

4 When you are satisfied with the result, click OK.

Note: Be sure you check the Preview box; otherwise, you may not be able to judge the results of your adjustments.

ALTER COLOR WITH HUE/SATURATION

You can change any combination of color balance, color saturation, or image brightness for the overall image—all in one dialog box—by using the Hue/Saturation command. This command is most often used for increasing or decreasing the intensity of all colors in the image (saturation). You can also work on individual channels of color and their complements. Finally, by checking the Colorize box, you can change the overall color of the image.

You can use the Hue/Saturation command to either affect the current layer and selection or multiple layers in an adjustment layer. (For more on layers, see Chapter 9.)

The spectrum bar at the bottom of the Hue/Saturation dialog box serves two purposes. If you choose Master and move the Hue slider, the lower spectrum bar moves to show the relationship between it and the old colors. If you choose a color, the area affected is shown by a bar and a pair of movable brackets, which you can drag to increase the chosen color range on either side of the primary color.

ALTER COLOR WITH HUE/SATURATION

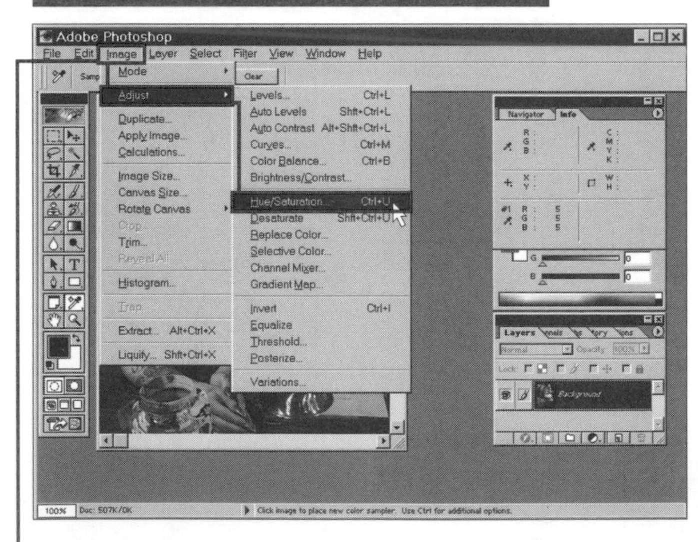

1 Click Image, then Adjust, then Hue/Saturation.

■ The Hue/Saturation dialog box appears.

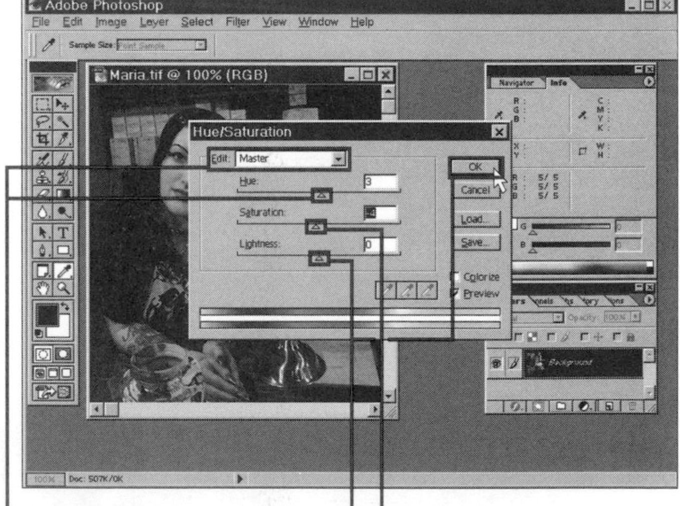

MAKE OVERALL ADJUSTMENTS TO THE LAYER

1 Choose Master from the Edit menu.

2 Drag the Hue slider if you want to change the overall color tint.

3 Drag the Saturation slider to increase or decrease color intensity.

4 Drag the Lightness slider to lighten or darken.

5 Click OK.

Can I make several adjustments in series?

✔ Adjustments made in the Hue/Saturation dialog box are cumulative. You can make an adjustment to all colors, then several individual colors, and then within a selection. All the changes will be registered when you click OK.

When I choose a color from the Hue/Saturation dialog box's Edit menu, am I limited to affecting areas in the image that are in that color family?

✔ Click any color in the image, and it, too, will be changed when you make adjustments for the color family chosen from the Edit menu.

When I choose a specific color from the Hue/Saturation dialog box's Edit menu, will I be modifying only that exact color?

✔ No. You are adjusting all tones that are in that color's family. You can also widen or narrow the range of colors to be modified by dragging the bracket on either side of the color bar that appears between the spectrum bars.

How can I select a range of colors that matches a specific area in the image?

✔ Shift+drag the cursor over the area in the image that you want to affect.

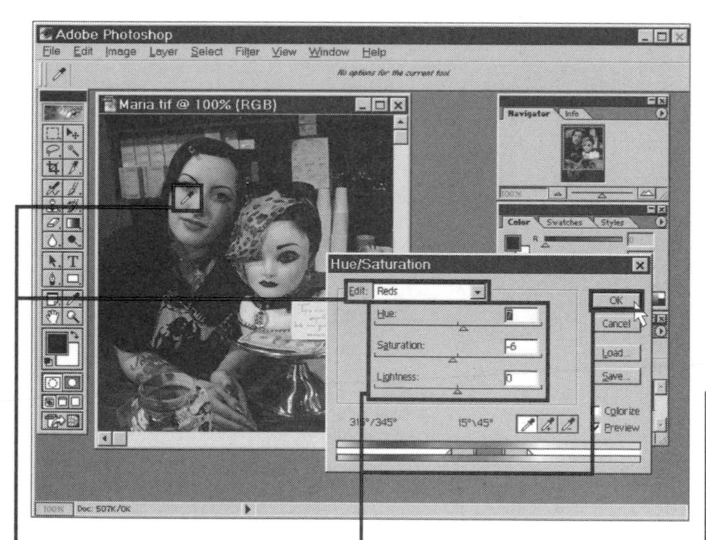

MAKE ADJUSTMENTS TO A RANGE OF COLORS

1 From the Edit menu, choose the range of colors to be modified.

2 Click the color you want to change.

Note: You can expand the range of colors surrounding the chosen color by moving the bracket sliders.

3 Drag the sliders to modify the color range.

4 Click OK.

CHANGE THE IMAGE TO AN OVERALL MONOTONE

1 Check the Colorize check box.

2 Drag the sliders to change the tint, intensity, and image brightness of the monotone.

3 Click OK.

Note: The settings shown in this example create a nice sepia tone, like that of an antique photograph.

LOSE ALL COLOR WITH DESATURATE

Using the Desaturate command (click Image, then Adjust, then Desaturate or Shift+⌘/Ctrl+U) is a one-step no-brainer. After choosing the command, your image suddenly becomes grayscale, without your having to specify options in an intervening dialog box. If the result is not what you wanted, press ⌘/Ctrl+Z to undo; click File, then Revert; or delete the command from the History list. (No Reset button exists because no dialog box exists.)

You may well ask, why not simply change the Color mode to Grayscale? If you do so, you do not accomplish the same thing. You must be in a Color mode (Indexed, RGB, CMYK, or Lab) when you issue the Desaturate command. Because you are still in that Color mode, you can now directly recolor the image.

To recolor a monochrome image, choose a brush and, on the Brush Options bar, choose Color from the Mode menu.

LOSE ALL COLOR WITH DESATURATE

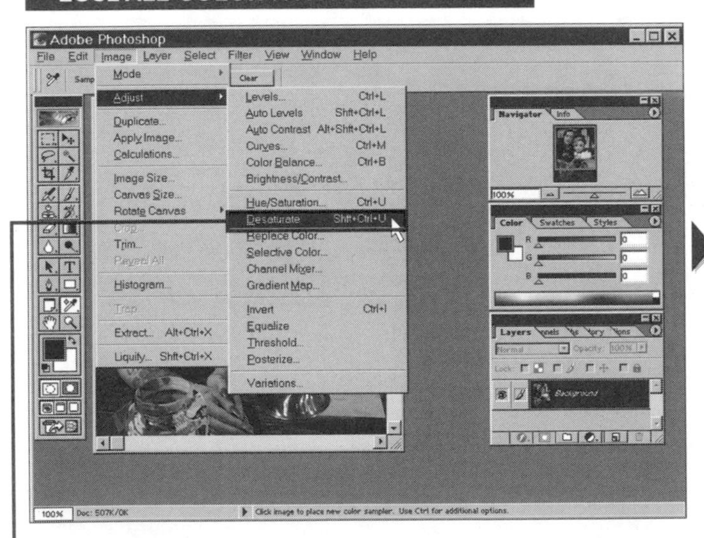

1 Click Image, then Adjust, then Desaturate.

■ The image loses all color but is still in full-color mode, which means that you can color the image or add additional colored layers.

Note: You can have the image fade from grayscale to full color by first making a mask that is filled with a white-to-black gradient. Load the mask as a selection, and then issue the Desaturate command.

CREATE A TONAL EFFECT WITH INVERT

Issuing the Invert command (click Image, Adjust, and then Invert or ⌘/Ctrl+I) causes a reversal of all the tones in an image. In other words, Invert makes a photographic negative of a positive image. Invert is also useful for converting scans of black-and-white negatives into positives. Unfortunately, this does not work on color negatives because those negatives use an orange mask, which Photoshop does not take into account.

To use Invert, you execute the command and immediately have a negative (or a positive, if you started with a negative).

You may also find Invert useful for making a channel mask, especially if the mask is subsequently hand-retouched so that the masking is limited to very specific areas. You can make a negative mask in the Channels palette by dragging any of the color channels to the New Channel icon. Click the resulting new alpha channel, and press ⌘/Ctrl+I.

CREATE A TONAL EFFECT WITH INVERT

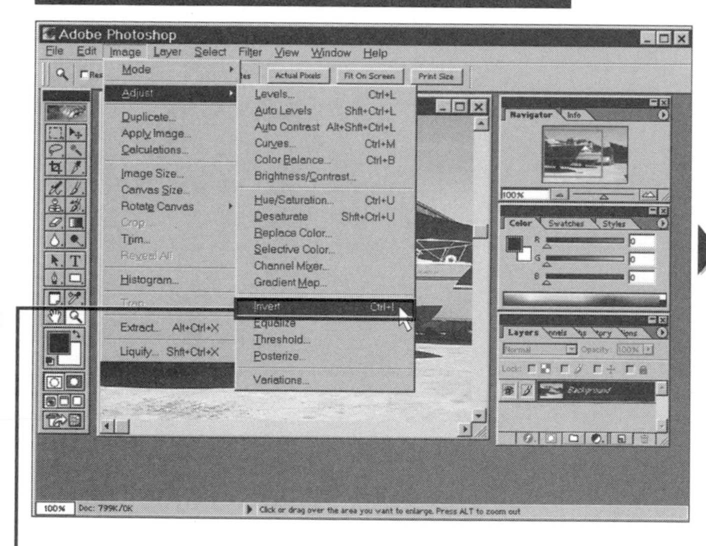

1 Click Image, then Adjust, then Invert.

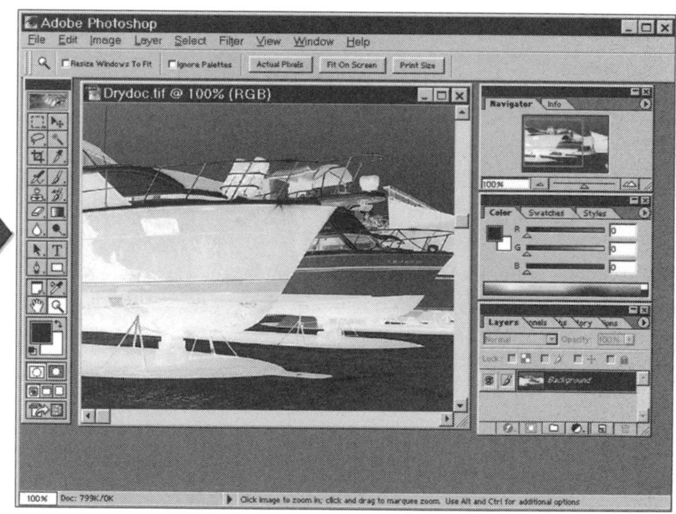

■ All tonal values are reversed in the current image.

■ Notice the resulting negative image.

SWAP ONE COLOR FOR ANOTHER

The Replace Color command (click Image, then Adjust, then Replace Color) enables you to recolor parts of an image. It does so by making a mask and then letting you adjust the hue, saturation, and color. In other words, it is the Replace Color and Brightness/Hue/Saturation commands in one dialog box. Often, you may want to restrict the area for recoloring. In such a case, select the area or areas to be affected before issuing the Replace Color command.

Making adjustments is a matter of dragging sliders to alter the degree of change. You choose the color you want to change by simply clicking in the image. You can add and subtract colors to and from the selection by choosing the plus (+) and minus (–) Eyedropper tools and continuing to click in the image. The Fuzziness slider broadens or narrows the range of color surrounding the chosen colors. It is not just the color itself that you can change—you can also control the saturation and lightness of the color you swap.

SWAP ONE COLOR FOR ANOTHER

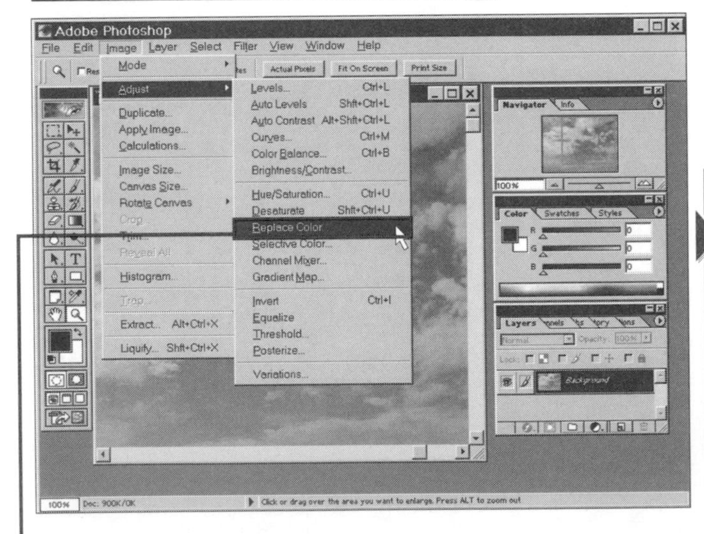

1 Click Image, then Adjust, then Replace Color.

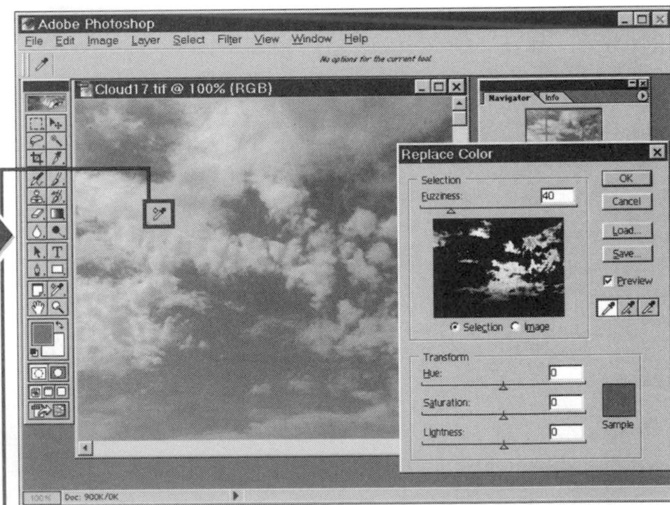

■ The Replace Color dialog box appears.

2 Click in the image to indicate the color you want to replace.

■ The area covered by your selection appears as white in the Preview box.

Note: The Sample box at lower right displays the color (including hue, saturation, and lightness) that replaces the color that you have chosen. To change this color, adjust the sliders.

The Replace Color dialog box seems very familiar. Does another Photoshop dialog box work in much the same way?

✔ The Color Range dialog box (which you access by clicking Select, then Color Range) has almost identical controls. You could use it to replace color by first choosing the replacement color as the foreground color and then using the Edit, then Fill command in conjunction with the Color Apply mode.

How can I see the whole image when I am zoomed in on the image?

✔ You can see the whole image in the Preview window if you click the Image radio button under the Preview window.

Do I have to click the plus and minus Eyedroppers to add and select colors?

✔ No. In the Replace Color dialog box (or any other that features plus and minus Eyedroppers), you can Shift-click in the current image to add colors or Option/Alt-click to subtract colors. This technique is much faster because the cursor never needs to leave the image.

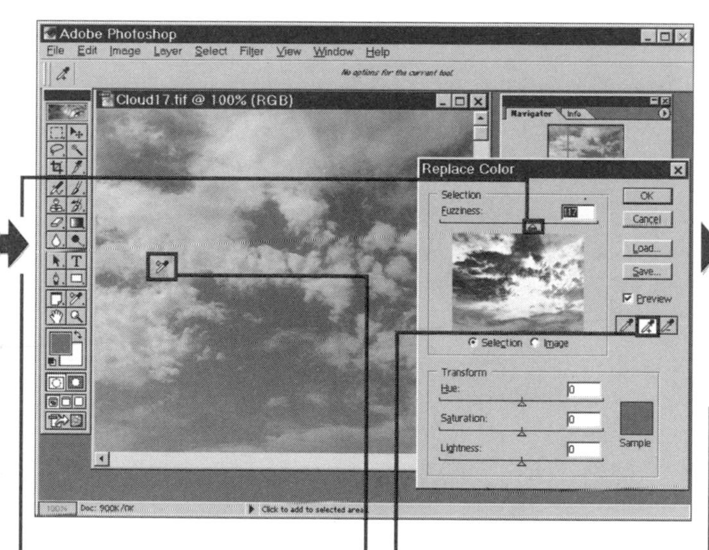

3 Drag the Fuzziness slider to increase the selected range of color.

■ The area of white in the Preview window expands and contracts as you move the slider.

4 Click the plus Eyedropper to add other colors to the selection or the minus Eyedropper to subtract colors.

5 Click in the image to add or subtract colors, as needed.

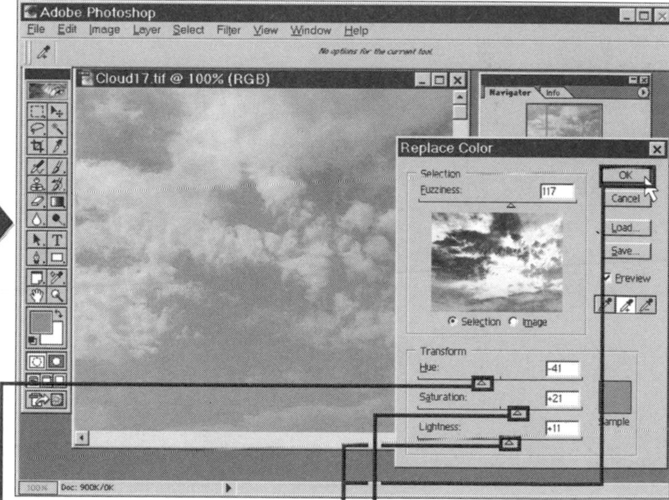

6 Drag the Hue slider to replace the chosen color.

Note: If the Preview box is checked, you see the color change previewed in the image. You can also click the Image radio button to see the change in the Preview box.

7 Drag the Saturation slider to change the intensity of the replacement color.

8 Drag the Lightness slider to change the brightness of the replacement color.

9 Click OK.

MIX COLOR CHANNELS

You can click Image, then Adjust, then Channel Mixer to change the mix of colors that contribute to a particular color channel. Although changing color balance (drastically) is possible by this method, its real purpose is to create special effects. The most readily understandable and useful applications include custom sepia tinting of grayscale images and using channel data to create a mask. Mathematically, the Channel Mixer creates output channels that reflect your adjustments to the existing channels plus a constant brightness value. The constant value is adjustable by dragging the Constant slider at the bottom of the Channel Mixer dialog box.

The Channel Mixer is meant to replace operations that would require channel calculations or layer blending in earlier versions of Photoshop. These effects generally fall into the areas of grayscale conversions, mixing and matching of channels for making custom masks, and bizarre special effects. Talented prepress types can also use the Channel Mixer command for making custom-mixed separation plates.

Note that you cannot use the Channel Mixer unless you are viewing the Composite channel (RGB, CMYK, Lab).

MIX COLOR CHANNELS

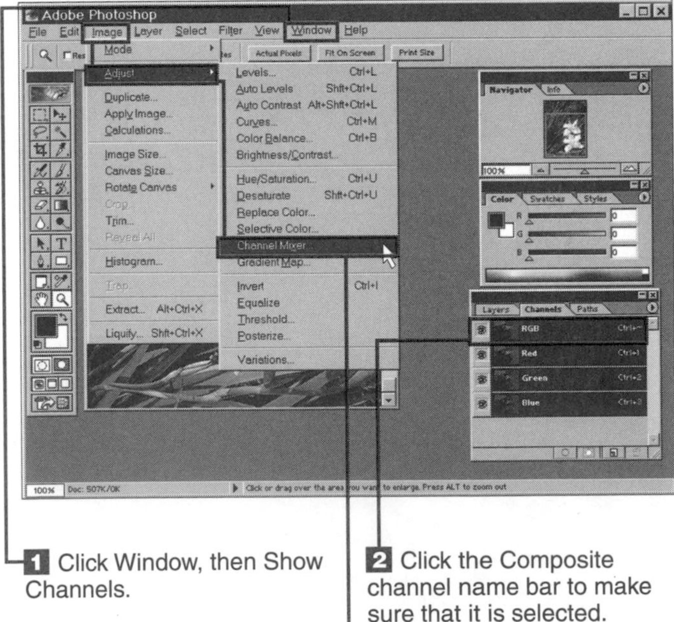

1 Click Window, then Show Channels.

2 Click the Composite channel name bar to make sure that it is selected.

3 Click Image, then Adjust, then Channel Mixer.

■ The Channel Mixer dialog box appears.

4 Choose the primary color channel you want to adjust from the Output Channel menu.

5 If not checked, click the Preview box.

How do I use the Channel Mixer to create a monochrome or duotone effect, such as a sepia tone?

✔ Try setting the source channels for the Red output channel at Red = +132, Green = 0, and Blue = 0. For the Green source channel, try Red = 0, Green = +42, and Blue = +22. For the Blue source channel, try Red = 0, Green = 0, and Blue = +32. Using the Channel Mixer produces a sepia effect that still has some hint of color.

How can I use the Channel Mixer to make a custom mask?

✔ Copy the layer you want to mask. Click the Monochrome box to check it and make adjustments to the channels until you see the contrasts you are looking for in the mask. When you see something close to the mask you want, click OK. Press ⌘/Ctrl+A to Select All and then ⌘/Ctrl+C to copy the contents of the layer to the Clipboard. Switch to the Channels palette, and click the New Channel icon. Select the new channel, and press ⌘/Ctrl+V to paste in the layer contents.

6 Drag the color sliders until you see the approximate effect you want.

■ The colors shift in the workspace window.

7 Drag the Constant slider to change the image contrast and to fine-tune the effect of the channel adjustments.

8 To make a monochrome image, layer, or mask, click the Monochrome check box (☐ becomes ☑).

■ The layer becomes monochromatic.

9 Drag any combination of sliders to achieve the desired tonal values in the monochromatic image.

10 Click OK.

Note: This monochromatic mode can be used to create mask channels.

MAKE AN ADJUSTMENT WITH VARIATIONS

The Variations command (click Image, then Adjust, then Variations) is the easiest way for the uninitiated and the most efficient way for the experienced to make adjustments in color balance, exposure, and contrast. It is easy because the image is shown as it will look if adjusted in several different ways. You can make any combination of adjustments.

The Variations command is best for making corrections that apply to the entire layer (or image, if it is used on an adjustment layer). It will, of course, work on masked areas, but you cannot see the effect very well. The Variations dialog box occupies almost your entire screen, so there is no workspace preview. Generally, the thumbnails prove too small to give you a good preview of even smaller masked areas.

The Variations dialog box is set up so that commands across from one another in the color area have opposite effects. For instance, if you click "More Yellow" and then "More Blue" (the opposite command), the image does not change—the commands cancel out each other.

MAKE AN ADJUSTMENT WITH VARIATIONS

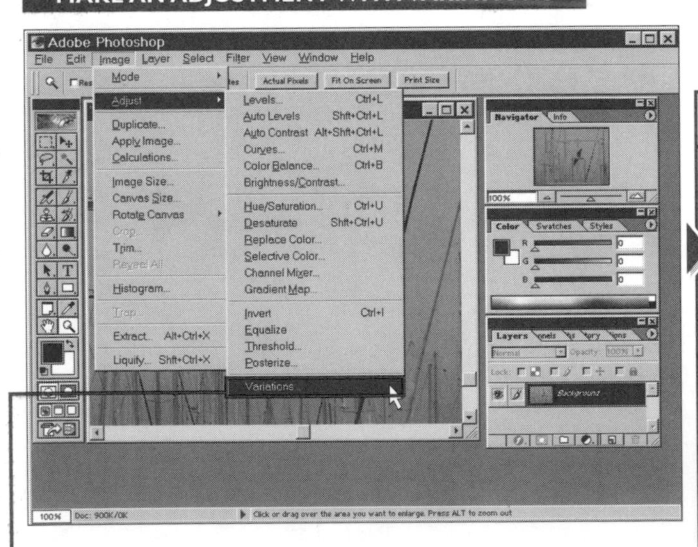

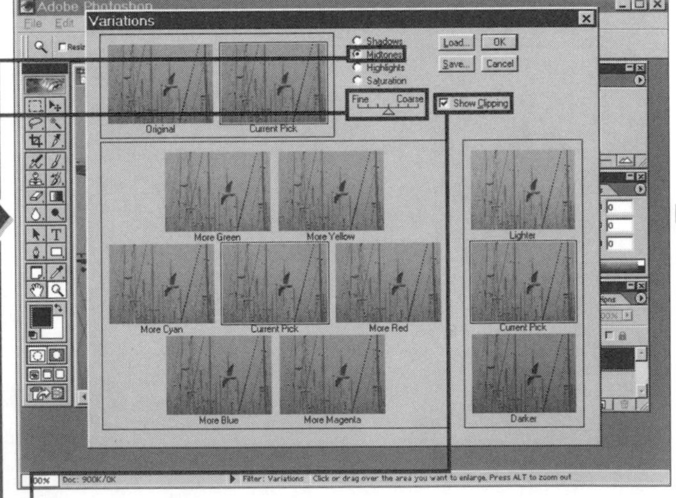

1 Click Image, then Adjust, then Variations.

■ The Variations dialog box appears, covering nearly the entire Photoshop workspace. It is purposely large to give you the largest possible thumbnails, as no workspace preview is provided.

2 Click Show Clipping.

3 Click Midtones (○ becomes ◉).

4 Drag the Slider to make the differences between thumbnails more or less pronounced.

Note: Each tickmark on the Slider scale indicates a doubling (or halving) of the intensity of the effect.

Is an experienced user likely to ever use the Variations command?

✔ The Variations command can be a good way to get an image closer to the desired final result. You could then use any of the Adjust commands for fine-tuning. The Variations command is also a quick check for loss of detail due to clipping. Clipping occurs when the colors go to pure black (in the shadows) or pure white (in the highlights). Make sure that the Show Clipping box is checked.

If I use Variations as a prelude to tweaking with other Adjust commands, am I likely to lose data?

✔ You could, if you make adjustments that cause clipping. You can give yourself additional headroom by working in 16-bit-per-channel mode.

What if I overadjust?

✔ You can recover in many ways. First, you can click the complementary color thumbnail opposite the one that caused the overadjustment. If you want to return to the state of the original image, press ⌘/Ctrl and Option/Alt-click the Cancel button when it changes to Reset or click the image box titled Original. Of course, you can also press ⌘/Ctrl-Z to undo the change.

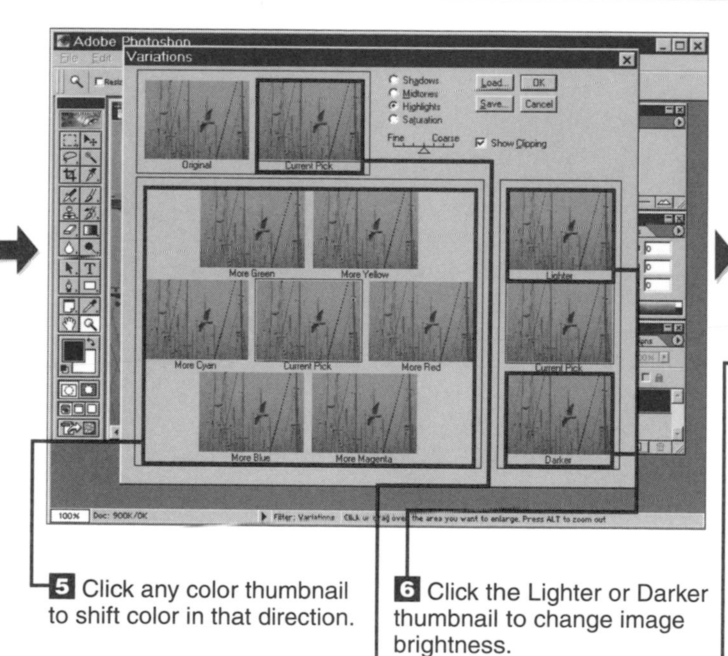

5 Click any color thumbnail to shift color in that direction.

6 Click the Lighter or Darker thumbnail to change image brightness.

■ The result appears in the Current Pick thumbnail.

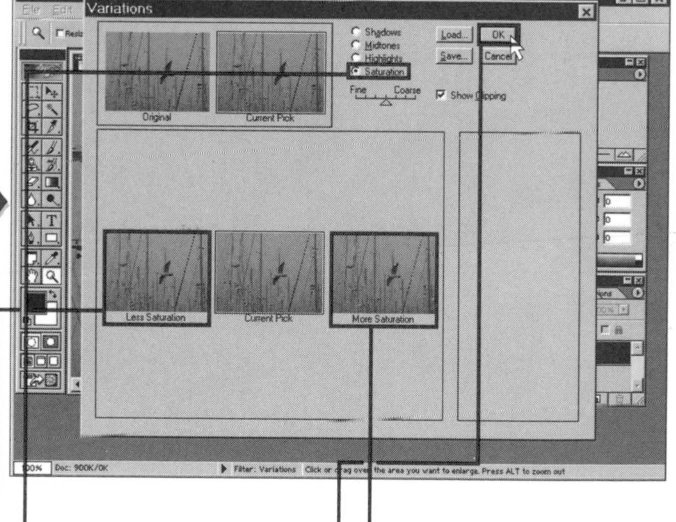

7 To change the hue intensity (color brightness) of an image, click Saturation (○ becomes ◉).

8 Click Less Saturation to dull colors.

9 Click More Saturation to brighten colors.

10 Click OK when you are satisfied with the appearance of the Current Pick thumbnail.

CREATE A TONAL EFFECT WITH EQUALIZE

Choosing Image, then Adjust, then Equalize causes all the tonal values in an image to be evenly distributed in a single step. You may wonder why on earth someone would want to use this command. Usually, it is because an image (from a camera or scanner) has been acquired that is messed up to the extent that all its values are compressed. In other words, the picture has too much contrast or is flat as a pancake. Fortunately for us, most digital capture devices produce files that have more color depth than is apparent on-screen.

Another way to use Equalize is to make a selection first. You can then choose whether to equalize only within the selected area or to equalize the entire image according to the tonal range contained within the selection.

After you have used the Equalize command, you may very well want to use the Levels, Curves, or other Adjust commands to further refine or interpret the values in the image.

CREATE A TONAL EFFECT WITH EQUALIZE

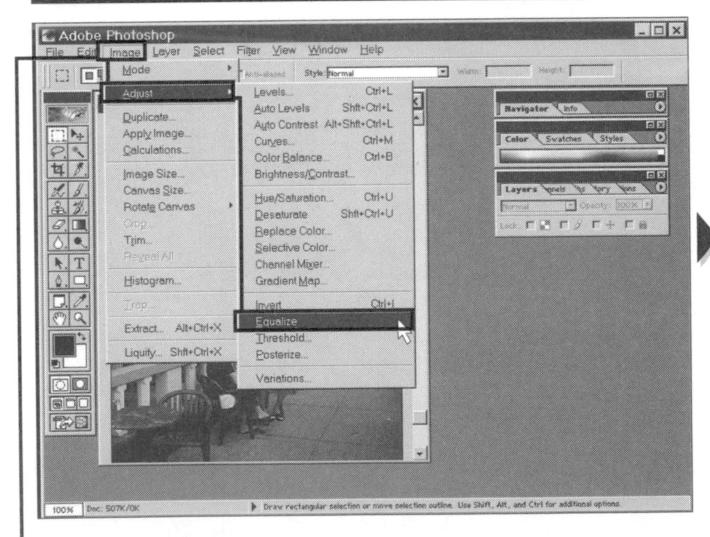

1 Click Image, then Adjust, then Equalize.

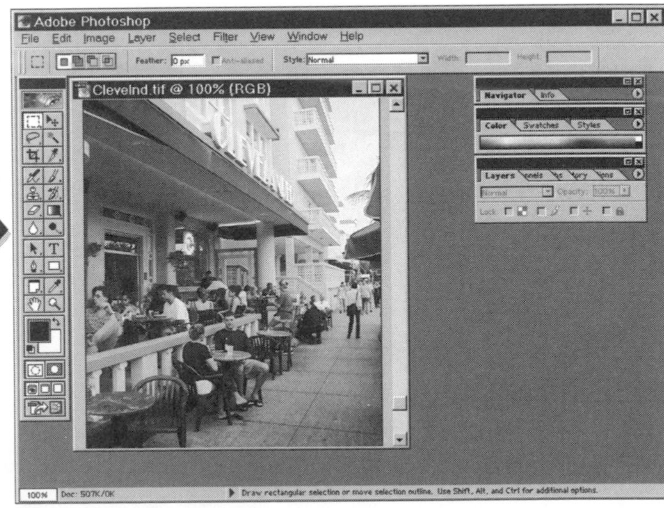

■ Photoshop finds the absolute highlight (white point) and absolute shadow (black point) in the image's data and evenly distributes all data in between according to brightness value.

Is the Equalize Entire Image Based On Selected Area option a good way to increase shadow detail in a specific area of the image?

✔ It can be a good starting point. Usually, however, you will get too much shadow detail for the image to seem realistic. Use the Levels or Curves commands after applying the Equalize command (but while the selection is still active) to darken the selection.

Can I use the Equalize Entire Image Based On Selected Area option to highlight and separate an object from its surroundings?

✔ That is one of the most useful things you can do with this command.

Are any other commands commonly used before or after the Equalize command to create special effects?

✔ Of course. Here is one I like: Copy the image to a new layer and equalize the whole image to a shadow area. Edges become more defined. Run a Stylize filter such as Find Edges. Now try combining the new layer with the old layer (see Chapter 10).

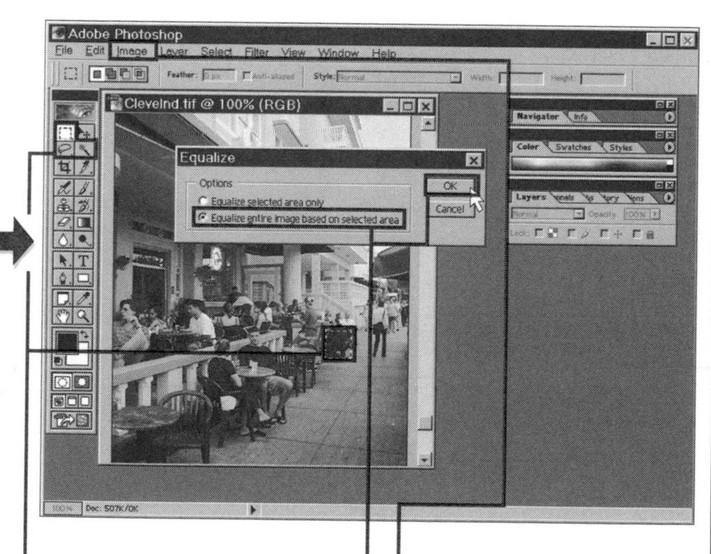

EQUALIZE A LAYER BASED ON A SELECTION

1 Click any of the selection tools.

2 Make a selection.

3 Click Image, then Adjust, then Equalize.

4 Click the Equalize Entire Image Based on Selected Area radio button.

5 Click OK.

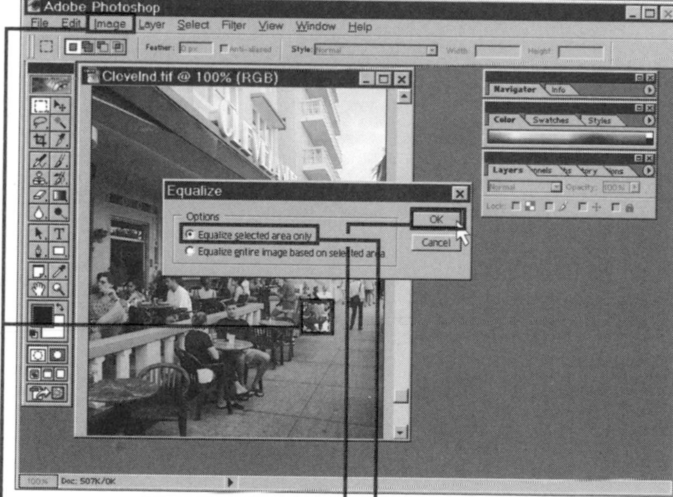

EQUALIZE A SELECTION AREA ONLY

1 Make a selection with one of the selection tools.

2 Click Image, then Adjust, then Equalize.

3 Click the Equalize Selected Area Only radio button.

4 Click OK.

Note: Experiment with using this method when the selection has been made with the Magic Wand or Lasso tool.

SWITCH COLOR PALETTES

The use of Color palettes applies only to indexed color images, which means that you cannot access these commands unless you first convert your image to indexed color. At that point, you have two ways to influence which palette is used:

- You can specify which palette and dithering method to use initially.
- You can subsequently switch to another palette by using the Image, then Mode, then Color Table command.

The two main uses for the Image, then Mode, then Color Table command are to view the colors assigned to each palette position (index), and to change the colors assigned to the current color table (often called a Color palette).

The Color Table dialog box enables you to load any saved palette file for use with the current image. This feature is useful for creating a new image from scratch that uses only colors assigned to a specific palette, such as the Web palette or the System palette of an operating system.

SWITCH COLOR PALETTES

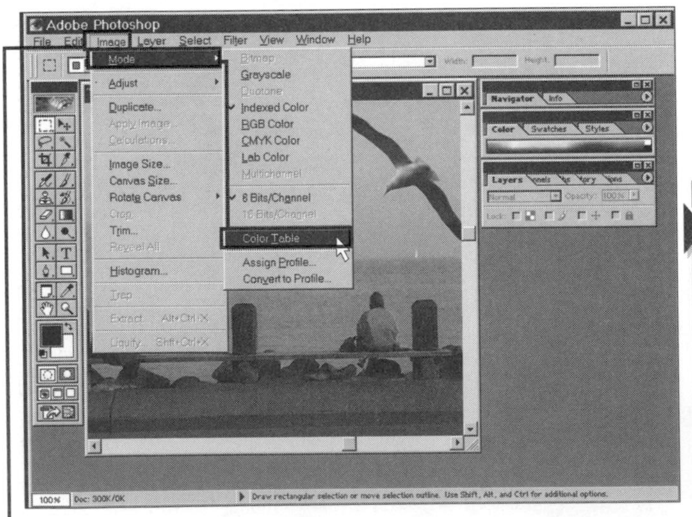

1 Click Image, then Mode, then Color Table.

■ The Color Table dialog box appears.

Note: The Color Table command is only available in Indexed Color mode. To place a image in Indexed Color mode, click Image, Mode, Indexed Color, and then click OK.

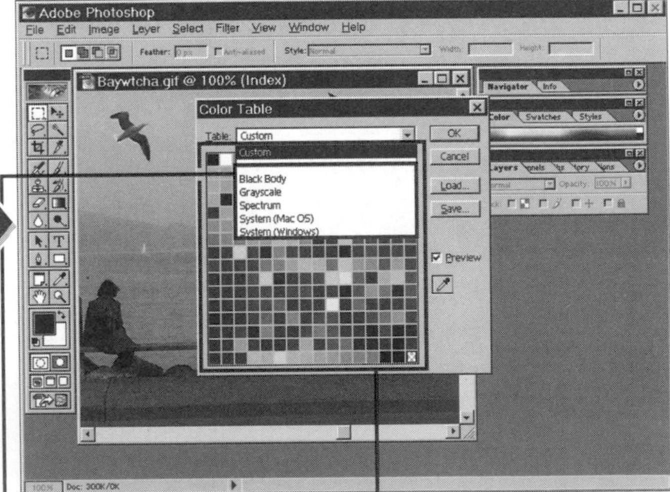

■ You can choose from one of Photoshop's preset palettes in the Table menu.

Note: You can experiment with the preset tables. Simply choose the default, Custom, when done experimenting. Click OK to commit to the palette change.

2 To change an individual color in the color table, click the color you want to change.

Can I access the color table at the same time I convert to indexed color?

✔ Yes. Click Image, then Mode, then Indexed Color. The Indexed Color dialog box appears. From the Palette menu, choose Custom. The Color Table dialog box appears. From here you can take any of the steps shown in this section.

Can I use the color table to create special effects?

✔ Yes. The easiest and most effective trick is to convert the image to grayscale and then back to indexed color. The color table will then consist entirely of shades of gray. Now, substitute the same color for a whole range of grays. You will end up with a bizarre pop-art effect.

How can I load the color table used by another image?

✔ Open the file containing the color table you want to borrow. Click Image, then Mode, then Color Table. When the image's color table appears, click the Save button and name the file. In Windows, the required .act extension is automatically added by Photoshop. On Mac, the letters *CLUT* (for Color Lookup Table) appear on the icon.

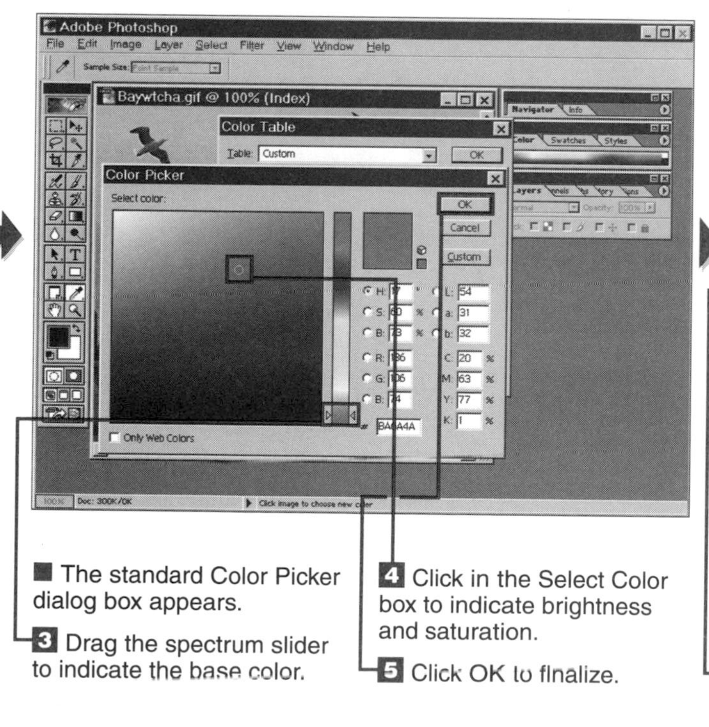

■ The standard Color Picker dialog box appears.

3 Drag the spectrum slider to indicate the base color.

4 Click in the Select Color box to indicate brightness and saturation.

5 Click OK to finalize.

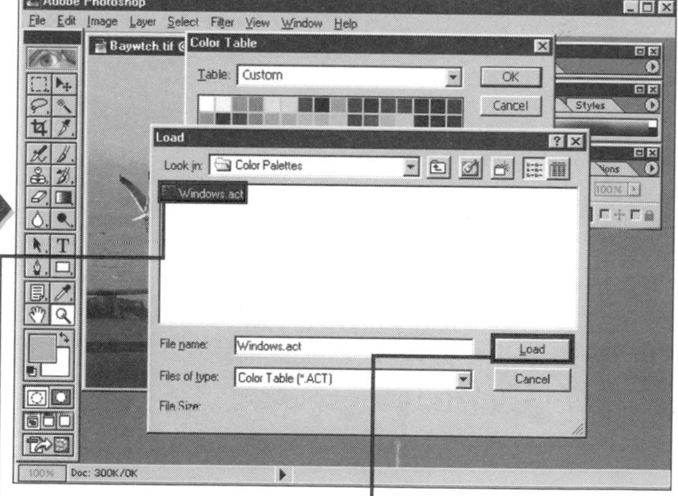

6 To load a specific, presaved palette, click the Load button.

7 Click the name of the file you want to load, which then appears in the File Name field.

8 Click the Load button.

Note: You can also save any changes you make to the color table. After making the changes, click the Save button and follow the normal procedures for saving a file.

CORRECT TONAL VALUES WITH THE LEVELS COMMAND

The Levels command enables you to make layerwide changes (or imagewide changes, if used on an adjustment layer) in the intensity of shadows, midtones, and highlights by dragging the corresponding slider. You can also make more precise changes by entering exact numbers in the corresponding Input Levels fields.

You can also use the Levels dialog box to control overall image contrast by dragging the Shadow and Highlight sliders to specify output and input levels. The Shadow slider controls the maximum density, and the Highlight slider controls maximum brightness.

Activating the Preview check box enables you to see the effect on the image of any changes you make in the output. Finally, Highlight, Midtone, and Shadow Eyedroppers let you set levels visually. Do so by selecting the Shadow Eyedropper and then clicking its tip on the darkest part of the image. Click the Highlight Eyedropper and then click its tip on the part of the image you want to be absolute white. Use the Midtone Eyedropper to indicate the pixel that should be 50% gray.

CORRECT TONAL VALUES WITH THE LEVELS COMMAND

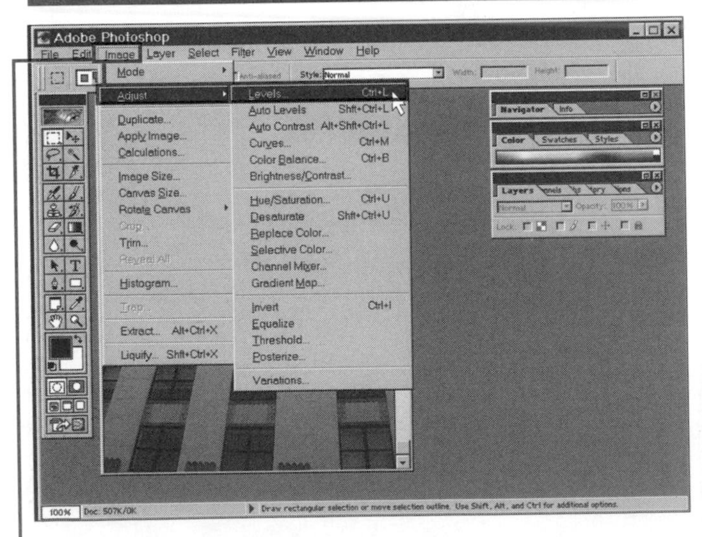

1 Click Image, then Adjust, then Levels (or press /Ctrl+L).

■ The Levels dialog box appears.

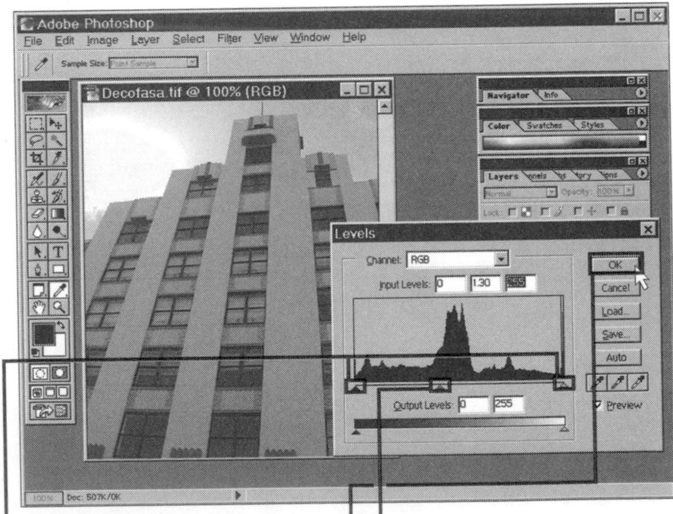

USING THE HISTOGRAM TO SET LEVELS

1 Drag the Highlight slider to the point where brightness should be maximum.

2 Drag the Shadow slider to the point below which everything should turn to black.

3 Drag the Midtone slider to adjust the brightness of midtones.

4 If you are satisfied with the results, click OK.

I have a hard time using the Eyedroppers accurately. What am I doing wrong?

✔ Zoom in on the image (about 200%) and use the Navigation palette to help you move to the exact pixels you want to pick for the darkest, median, and brightest points.

Can I do color balancing with the Levels dialog box?

✔ Yes, to some extent. The Highlight Eyedropper "white balances" any pixel you click. If that pixel really should have been white, you will get a fairly accurate overall color balance. Of course, if you pick a point that was not originally white, you may throw the color balance way off.

Can I apply the same settings to a whole series of images?

✔ Yes. Make the adjustments to a typical image until you are satisfied with the result. Next, click the Save button. When the Save dialog box appears, follow normal file-saving procedures. Open the next image in the series and load the saved Level settings. The settings thus retrieved will automatically apply to the image.

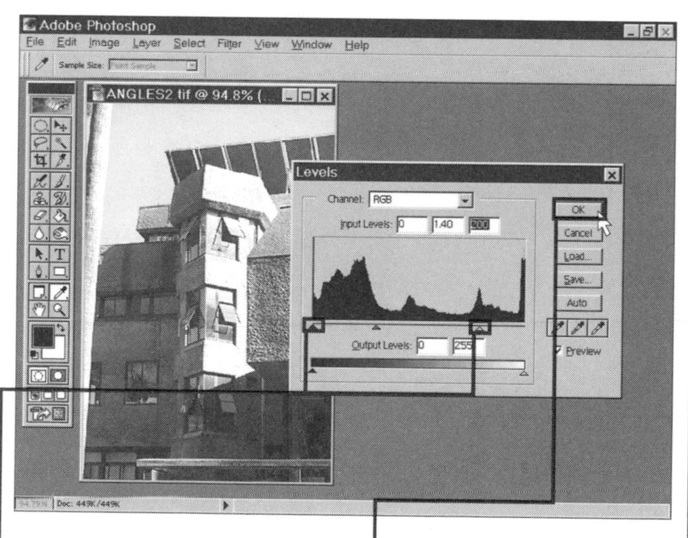

CHANGE THE CONTRAST OF THE IMAGE

1 Drag the Highlight slider to lower the white point.

2 Drag the Shadow slider to raise the black point.

3 Click OK when satisfied with the result.

Note: Saving the image before making tonal adjustments is a good idea. This way you can return to the original state by clicking File, then Revert.

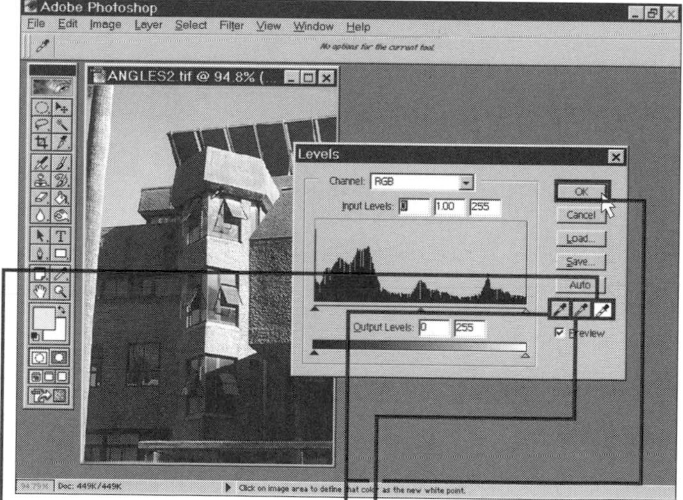

ADJUST HIGHLIGHTS

1 Click the Set White Point Eyedropper.

2 Click a white point in the image.

3 Repeat using the Set Gray Point Eyedropper to pick the midtone point.

4 Repeat with the Set Black Point Eyedropper to pick the black point.

5 When satisfied, click OK.

CORRECT TONAL VALUES WITH THE CURVES COMMAND

The Curves command presents many more options for controlling tonal values, in more precise fashion, than any of the other image adjustment controls. You can control tonal values for any point on the curve of any color in the current color model. In other words, you can use the Curves command for color correction of specific areas as well as brightness and contrast correction.

As with the Levels command, you can try automatically adjusting tonal values and color balance by simply clicking the Auto button. You can immediately preview the results of this or any other curves adjustment by checking the Preview box.

Because the Curves command is so appropriate for correcting specific tonal ranges, knowing exactly where the tonal ranges occur on the curve helps. If you place the pointer on an image and click, a circle appears on the portion of the curve that affects that tone in the image. Drag the circle to correct the tonal range.

CORRECT TONAL VALUES WITH THE CURVES COMMAND

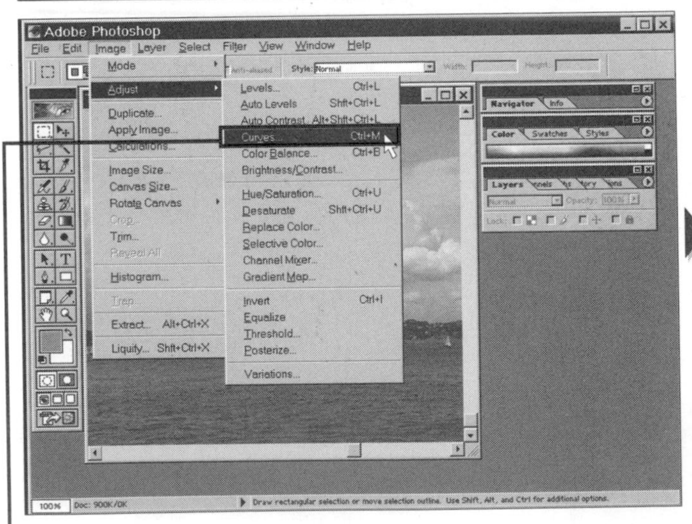

1 Click Image, then Adjust, then Curves.

■ The Curves dialog box appears.

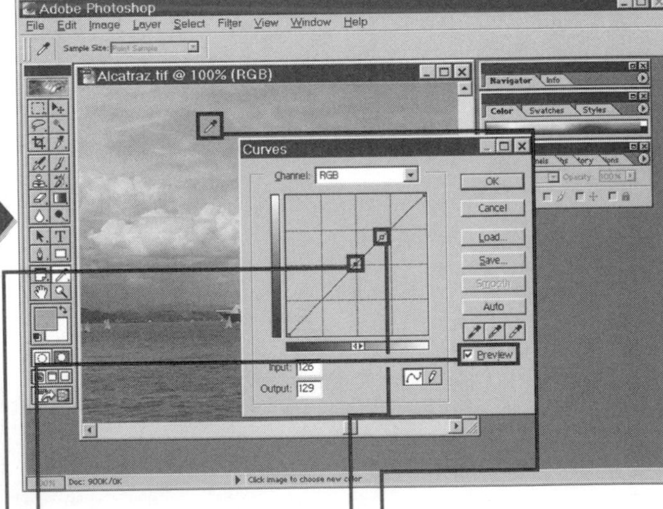

2 Click Preview (☐ becomes ☑).

3 If you want to maintain a current value, click to place an anchor at the point of the value you want to preserve.

■ A solid dot appears to indicate the anchor point.

4 Place the cursor over an area in the image where you want to change values and click and hold.

■ A hollow circle appears to indicate where that tonal value lies on the curve. Note the circle's position.

Can I apply the same curves to a series of images?

✔ Yes, by using the Save and Load buttons. Set the curves for a typical image and then save the setting by clicking the Save button and following normal procedures for saving a file. Open the other images to which you want to apply that curve and click the Load button. Follow normal file-loading procedures, and the chosen curve will automatically be applied to the current image.

What is the quickest and most direct route to adjusting for acceptable image quality?

✔ The Shadow and Highlight Eyedropper method is the most direct.

If I use the Eyedropper or Auto methods, can I still make adjustments to specific parts of the range?

✔ Yes. And, in practice, you will often want to lighten or darken the midtones by dragging the middle (or near middle) of the curve. This method is usually a better one than using the Midtone Eyedropper, because the Eyedropper will change the color balance to 50% gray at that point— which may shift the entire color balance of the image.

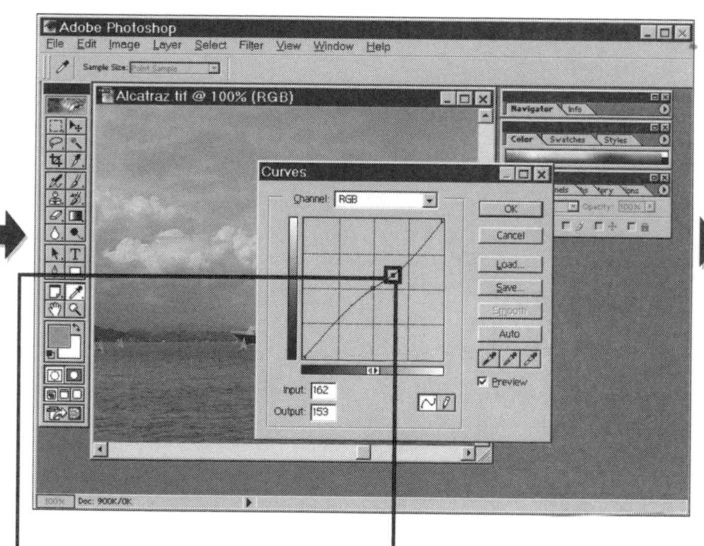

■ The circle disappears when you release the mouse button.

5 Click to place an anchor point at the approximate location of the circle.

6 Drag the point you placed in step 5 up to lighten, down to darken.

Note: To delete an anchor point you no longer need, select the point and press Delete or simply drag the point off the edge of the window.

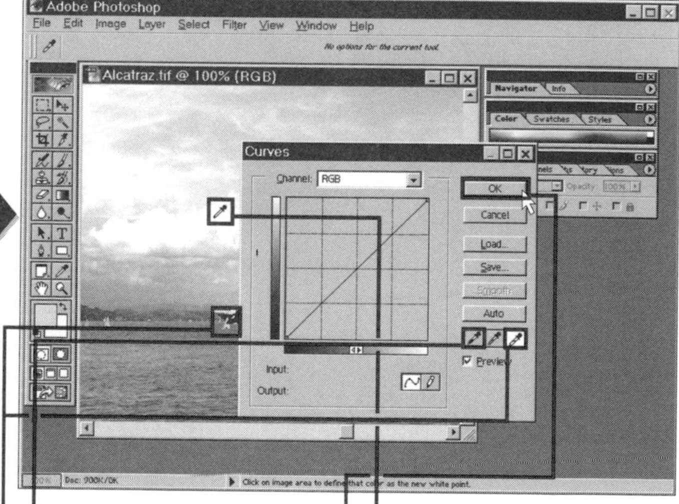

7 Click the Set Black Point Eyedropper.

8 Click in the area of the image you want to be 100% black.

9 Click the Set White Point Eyedropper.

10 Click in the area you want to represent absolute white.

11 Click OK.

■ The tonal range between highlight and shadow automatically adjusts.

CORRECT COLOR VALUES WITH THE CURVES COMMAND

In addition to providing a way to modify tonal value in a particular area for all colors simultaneously, the Curves command lets you modify the same characteristics for each color channel. This method is especially useful when you want to exaggerate color in a particular part of the spectrum for a mood effect. Also, many make this method their primary one for color correction (rather than relying on the Color Balance command). For that matter, experimenting with other possibilities for special effects is worth it.

If your goal is correction of the overall color balance of the image, using the Curves command is not the easiest method to do so. You may want to try Image, then Adjust, then Variations or Image, then Adjust, then Color Balance. You may also be able to achieve certain effects with the Image, then Adjust, then Hue/Saturation command.

You can make all the adjustments made here on an adjustment layer or on only the active layer within the current selection.

CORRECT SOME COLOR VALUES WITH THE CURVES COMMAND

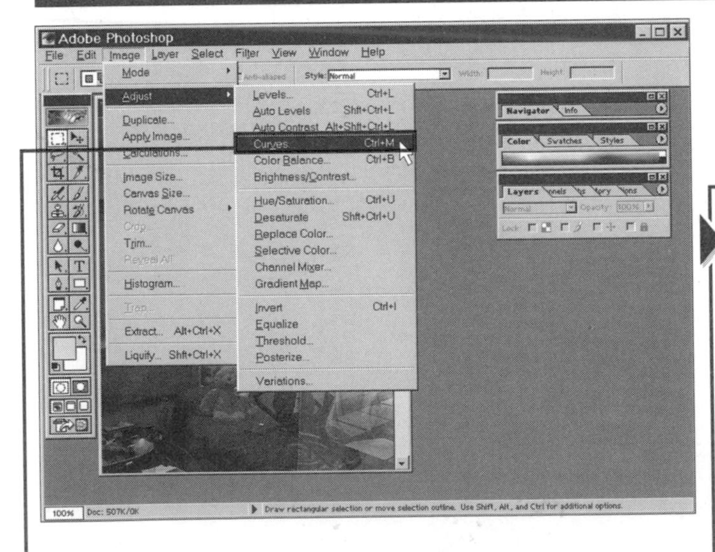

1 Click Image, then Adjust, then Curves.

■ The Curves dialog box appears.

2 Click the Preview box so that you can see your results the instant you make an adjustment.

3 Click the Color channel you want to modify.

4 Click and hold in the area of the image in which you want to modify color balance.

5 Click to place an anchor point where the circle was.

What if I want to make exactly the same degree and area of correction to multiple (but not all) color channels?

✔ Press Shift and choose the channels you want to simultaneously modify in the Channels palette. Keep an eye on RGB values so that you can see what you are doing when you go to the Curves dialog box to make the change to more than one channel.

What if I want to change the overall color balance of the image?

✔ You can do it with the Curves command, but unless you want to emphasize some part of the spectrum in a limited number of color channels, the other methods (Levels, Color Balance, Variations) will save you time and confusion.

Why do I not get a single color preview when I choose a single color channel?

✔ Every change you make in a single color channel affects the overall color balance, so you get a much more accurate idea of the effect of your changes.

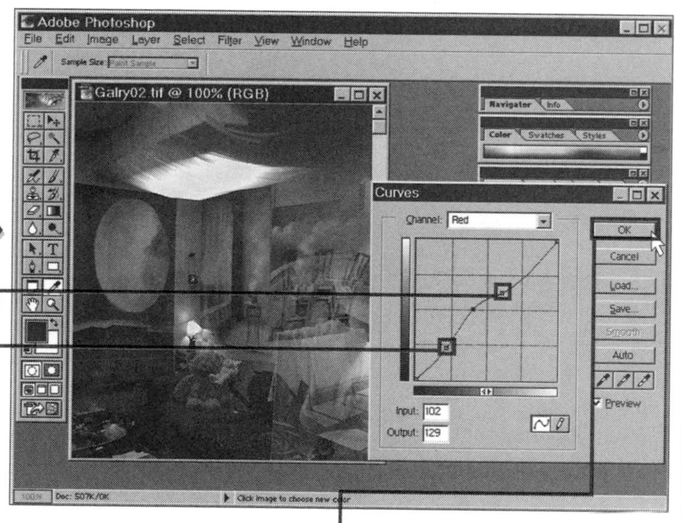

Note: To make a smooth adjustment where the curve peaks in the chosen area, drag the control point up to brighten, down to darken, and click OK.

6 Place two anchor points on either side of the last anchor point.

■ These anchors hold the rest of the curve more in line while you move the center point.

7 Use this method to make adjustments in other color channels until you are satisfied.

8 Click OK.

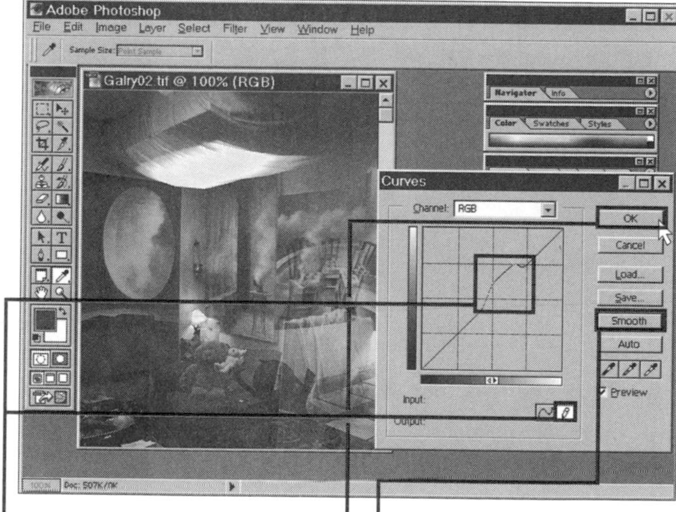

CORRECT COLOR WITH THE ARBITRARY METHOD

1 Click the Pencil tool.

2 Draw a line parallel to the diagonal line to indicate the brightness range you want modified.

3 Click the Smooth button.

4 Click OK.

Note: You can use variations of this method to create special effects. (See the next task in this chapter.)

CREATE SPECIAL EFFECTS COLOR CHANGES WITH CURVES

In a sense, using the Curves dialog box to alter part of the color spectrum is a special effect. For example, by adding a little pink to the sky, you could change the time of day to sunset. In this case, the special effects are far less subtle and much more freeform.

You can use the control-point method to create special effects, but these will always display smooth transitions. Most find that using the Freehand or Pencil tool to draw the curve is easier and faster. Adobe calls this the *arbitrary method.*

The result of certain attempts at special effects is highly experimental. Remember to press Option/Alt and click Reset in the Curves dialog box whenever you want to start over. If you come up with an effect that might work on several images, remember that you can save the curve and load it from any image.

CREATE SPECIAL EFFECTS COLOR CHANGES WITH CURVES

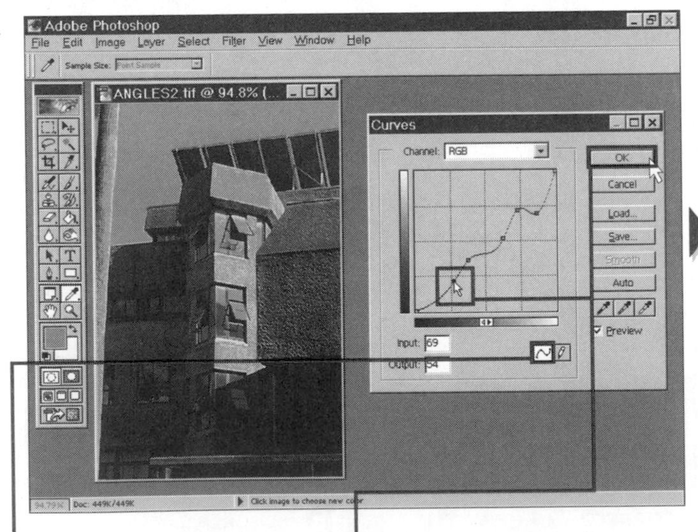

1 Choose Image, then Adjust, then Curves.

2 Click the Curves button and place a number of points along the diagonal line.

■ You can add more points. To subtract a point, you can select it and press Delete.

3 Drag the points in alternating directions. The wider the curves, the more pronounced the effect.

4 When you are satisfied with the result, click OK.

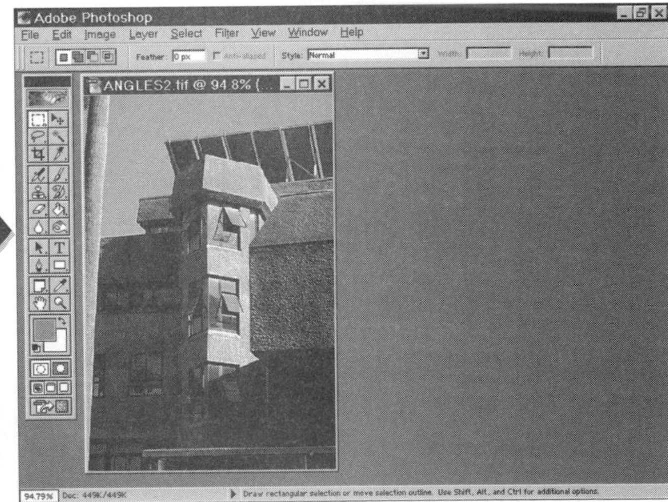

■ This example shows the result of the curve using the points method on an otherwise well-balanced landscape photo.

Does any way exist for *white balancing* (removing any tint caused by the color of ambient light) all the photos shot in a particular time and location?

✔ Get a Kodak 50% gray card from a photography store and set it near your subject in one of the photos. Shoot one photo, take the card away, and finish the shoot. Bring the test image into Photoshop and use Curves or Levels to correct exposure (if necessary). Next, choose the Neutral (Gray) Eyedropper and click the gray card. The image will now be white balanced. Click the Save button and save the settings. Bring the other photos into Photoshop by the same methods and settings. Open the Curves dialog box, click the Load button, retrieve the original settings file, and then click OK to preserve the result.

Does any way exist for making the grid smaller so that judging the exact distance between points is easier?

✔ Press Option/Alt and click on the grid. Each time you do this, the grid switches between the default 4 x 4 grid and a 10 x 10 grid.

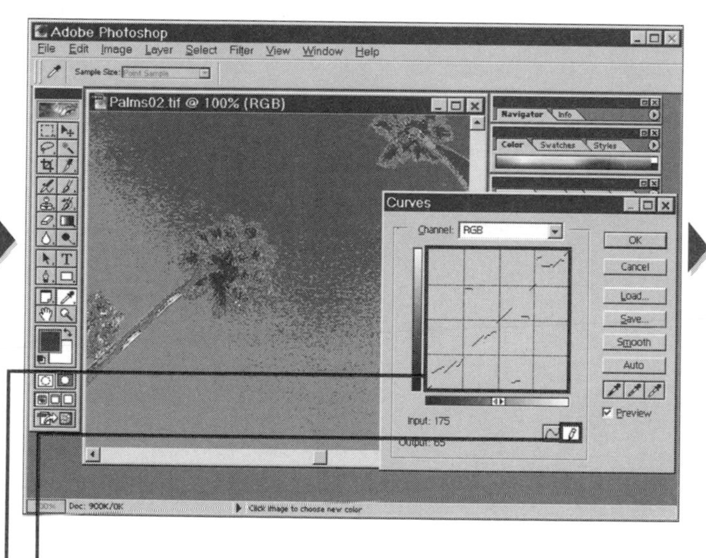

5 Click the Arbitrary (Pencil) Curves tool.

6 Experiment with drawing lines in random directions at various angles and lengths.

Note: Clicking randomly, making very short lines or dots with the pencil, creates dramatic special effects.

■ If the Preview box is checked, the results of your experiment appear in the image window.

■ This time, the result is more posterized, with hard edges.

Note: If you click the Smooth button, the hard edges disappear, and you will get a much different effect. The more times you click the Smooth button, the less pronounced the effect will be.

USING THE EYEDROPPER TO PICK UP COLOR

The Eyedropper tool allows you to transfer the exact same color from one image to another. You can use the Eyedropper tool to pick up the exact color of a single pixel in the image.

You can access the Eyedropper tool in one of three ways:

- Press I.
- Click the Eyedropper tool icon in the toolbox.
- When using the Airbrush, Paintbrush, Pencil, Paint Bucket, or Gradient tool, press the Option/Alt key. The Eyedropper cursor appears in place of the standard cursor.

The behavior of the Eyedropper, no matter how you ultimately access it, is determined in the Eyedropper Options bar. You can decide whether you want to use the default single-pixel sample or to average the foreground color via a 3-x-3 or 5-x-5 matrix of pixels.

To pick up background color, press X once to swap the background color for the foreground color and then press X again. Or press Option/Alt and click with the Eyedropper to select the background color directly.

USING THE EYEDROPPER TO PICK UP COLOR

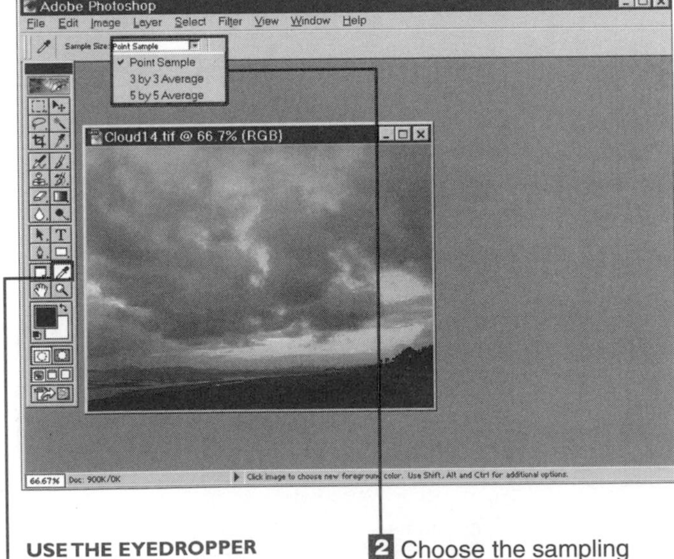

USE THE EYEDROPPER

1 Click the Eyedropper ( ).

2 Choose the sampling method from the Sample Size menu.

Note: If pickup colors do not match, check to see whether sampling is set at Point Sample.

■ Photoshop picks up the color.

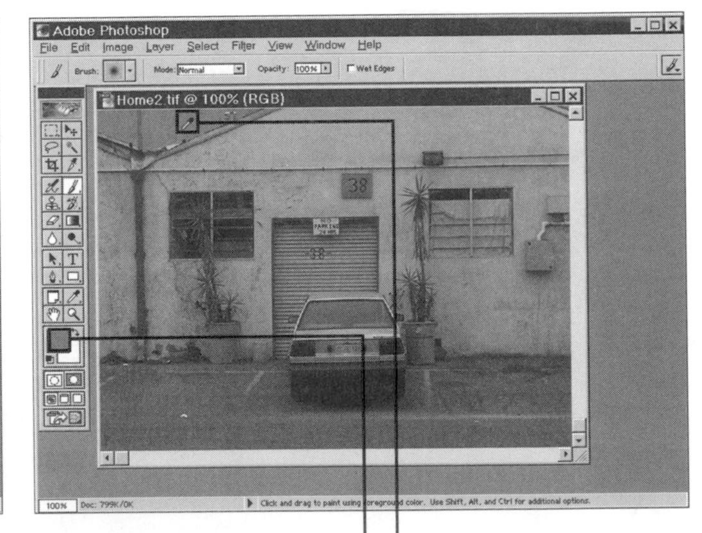

USE THE EYEDROPPER WITH OTHER TOOLS

1 Press Option/Alt.

■ The cursor changes to an Eyedropper.

2 Click inside the image window to pick up a color.

■ Photoshop picks up the color. The color appears in the Foreground Color box.

USING OFFSET CLONING

Offset cloning is the method most often used for retouching because it lets you transfer the color and shading from one area of a picture to another area of the picture. Most of the time, the Rubber Stamp tool (also known as the *Clone tool*) is used to duplicate the many shades in the grain of the film or fine textures, such as grass, leaves, and hair.

Using the Rubber Stamp requires two steps:

- First, defining the area of the image to be cloned.
- Second, clicking and dragging to clone the area onto another part of the image.

The example depicted on these pages uses the Rubber Stamp tool to create another flower from the original flower image, utilizing colors and textures from the rest of the image.

You may find that changing brush sizes frequently helps in this process (especially if you are using a mouse). The square bracket keys cycle up (]) and down ([) the brushes in the library.

USING OFFSET CLONING

1 Click the Rubber Stamp tool (🖾).

2 Choose Normal from the Mode menu.

■ You also have the option of cloning from overlaid objects as though the image were flat. To clone from all the layers, click Use All Layers.

3 Press Option/Alt and click the pixel from which you want to start your clone.

4 Paint in the area to which you want to clone.

■ Photoshop transfers the selected color.

Note: When you release and start cloning again, the pickup point moves relative to the source point if you have the option set on Aligned. Blending the retouched area by cloning repeatedly from different pickup points is a good idea.

USING ALIGNED CLONING

Sometimes you may want to replace a whole section of an image with another section of the image.

For example, you may want to place an extra car in an otherwise empty parking space or duplicate a window to fill a blank wall.

You can use cut and paste to place objects. Often, however, blending the objects with their old surroundings by painting them in is easier.

You can do this easily with *aligned cloning*. Click the Aligned check box in the Options bar to turn on (☑) or turn off (❑) aligned cloning.

When you check Aligned, you can reproduce an entire area of the image in another area of the image.

The Aligned option is useful when you want to use different brush sizes to clone elements in your image.

USING ALIGNED CLONING

1 Click the Rubber Stamp tool (🖃).

2 Click the Aligned check box if it is unchecked.

■ To clone from all the layers, you can click Use All Layers.

3 Press Option/Alt and click in the center of the area from which you want to clone.

■ The Rubber Stamp tool displays a white arrow until you release Option/Alt.

4 Paint in the area in which you want to clone part of the image.

■ Photoshop transfers your image.

Note: When you release and start cloning again, the pickup point moves. Blend the retouched area by cloning repeatedly from different pickup points.

AUTOMATIC SPOTTING WITH THE DUST & SCRATCHES FILTER

Some scanned images may be marred by tiny dust and scratches. If the areas in which these blemishes appear are smooth-shaded, rather than textured detail, Photoshop provides a nearly instant fix: Choose Filter, then Noise, then Dust & Scratches.

The Dust & Scratches dialog box contains a pair of sliders called Radius and Threshold. *Radius* refers to the width of the largest blemish. As a rule, do not try to remove lines and blobs more than a few pixels across, or you may see unacceptable blurring in the overall image. *Threshold* refers to the contrast between the blemish and its surrounding pixels. The higher you set Threshold number, the higher the contrast has to be before the filter takes effect.

The best use of the Dust & Scratches filter usually involves compromise: Get rid of all the blemishes, and you may start losing file detail. Get rid of most of them, and the time you spend retouching by hand is greatly reduced. Remember, you can always run the filter again within selected areas.

AUTOMATIC SPOTTING WITH THE DUST & SCRATCHES FILTER

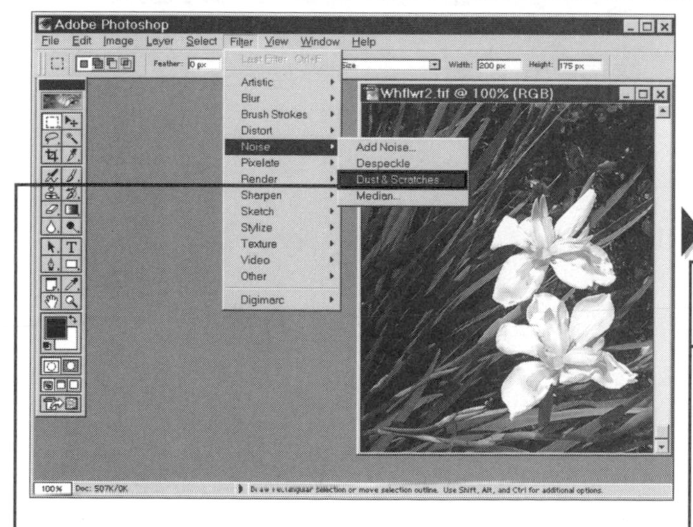

1 Choose Filter, then Noise, then Dust & Scratches.

■ The Dust & Scratches dialog box appears.

2 Click to check the Preview box.

3 Drag the Radius slider until most of the dust and/or scratches disappear.

Note: If you set Radius too high, the image starts to lose sharpness.

4 Drag the Threshold slider until the least contrasting scratches disappear.

■ The dust and scratches disappear from your image.

AUTOMATIC SPOTTING WITH THE GAUSSIAN BLUR FILTER

Under some circumstances, the Gaussian Blur filter can automatically eliminate small defects that the Dust & Scratches filter does not fix.

If the defects are in an even-toned, nontextured area, you may be able to simply blur that area enough to hide the problem. If so, the filter command that enables you to control the exact amount of blur is Filter, then Blur, then Gaussian Blur. This technique works best when you shoot photos against a highly out-of-focus background, seamless paper studio backdrops, or bare sky.

You need to employ this technique within a selection; otherwise you may blur the entire image. You can refer to Chapter 6 if you want to polish your ability to make those selections. Most of the time, however, simply drawing a freehand selection with the Lasso or Polygon Lasso tool works adequately.

Note: If you blur an area to eliminate small defects or artifacts, you may want to match the grain in the rest of the image by using one of the Noise filters.

AUTOMATIC SPOTTING WITH THE GAUSSIAN BLUR FILTER

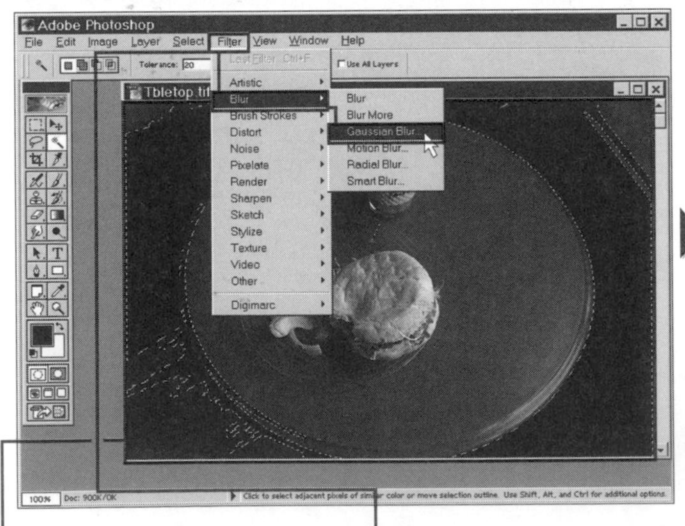

1 Click to select the area to be blurred.

2 Choose Filter, then Blur, then Gaussian Blur.

■ The Gaussian Blur dialog box appears.

3 Click to check the Preview box.

4 Drag the Radius slider until the pixels blend together.

Note: Do not feather the edges of the selection. If you see a border when you hide the selection, you blurred too much, or you need to use the Noise filter to match the grain.

CORRECT BLENDING DEFECTS

You can eliminate defects in small, isolated areas with the Smudge and Blur tools. These tools are especially appropriate for fixing the jagged edges that occur in some parts of an image when it is enlarged or collaged into an existing scene.

The Smudge and Blur tools work especially well when the defect is less than 2 pixels wide. These tools change the picture of the grain and texture painted by the original pixels, so make sure that your brush is no more than 3 pixels wide and follow the defect with care. Also be sure to zoom in very tightly (to at least 200%).

The Blur tool works by lowering the contrast between neighboring pixels. The Smudge tool actually pushes pixels around so that they exchange places. You can use it to push light pixels into a dark area or vice versa.

When you finish retouching with either tool, try matching the surrounding grain pattern by carefully selecting the area you retouched and then using the Add Noise filter (Filter, then Noise, and then Add Noise).

CORRECT BLENDING DEFECTS

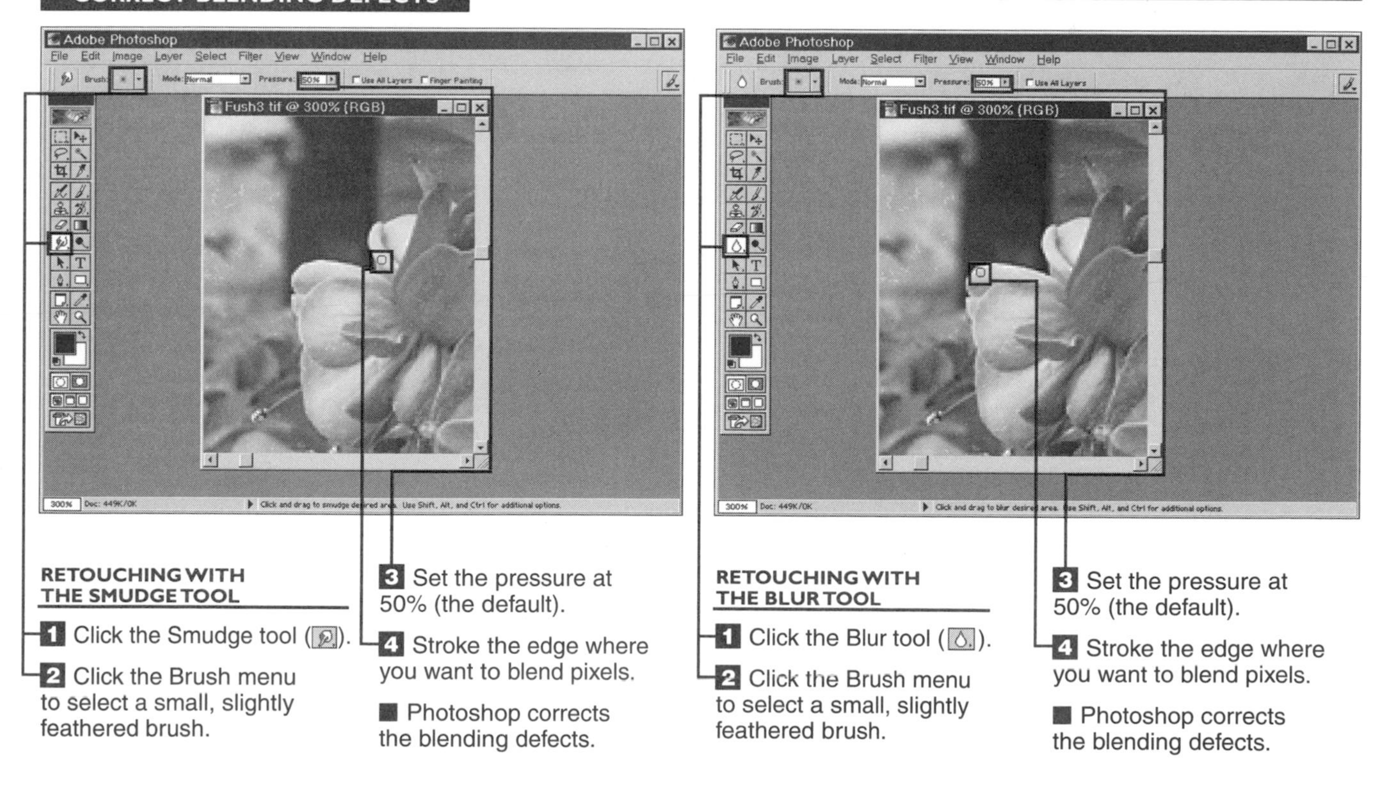

RETOUCHING WITH THE SMUDGE TOOL

1 Click the Smudge tool ( ).

2 Click the Brush menu to select a small, slightly feathered brush.

3 Set the pressure at 50% (the default).

4 Stroke the edge where you want to blend pixels.

■ Photoshop corrects the blending defects.

RETOUCHING WITH THE BLUR TOOL

1 Click the Blur tool ( ).

2 Click the Brush menu to select a small, slightly feathered brush.

3 Set the pressure at 50% (the default).

4 Stroke the edge where you want to blend pixels.

■ Photoshop corrects the blending defects.

HAND-SPOTTING WITH THE BRUSHES

If the picture detail in the area to be retouched is important and unique, you may have to paint it in by hand with the Paintbrush, Airbrush, or Pencil tool. If your time is precious, this technique should be a last resort.

Which tool you use depends mostly on what the problem is. For example, the Pencil tool is best for making exact pixel matches because the tool is hard edged.

The main thing to remember when retouching by hand is to keep it subtle. Pay particular attention to blending the retouching seamlessly with surrounding pixels. If a large area needs to be retouched, you may be better off using a clone of another image or another part of the picture. Zoom in far enough to exaggerate the pixel structure so you can follow the pattern—but not so closely that you cannot stay oriented.

You will do the best job of "hand retouching" with the brushes if you combine these strokes with some of the other techniques discussed in this chapter to blend your painting efforts.

HAND-SPOTTING WITH THE BRUSHES

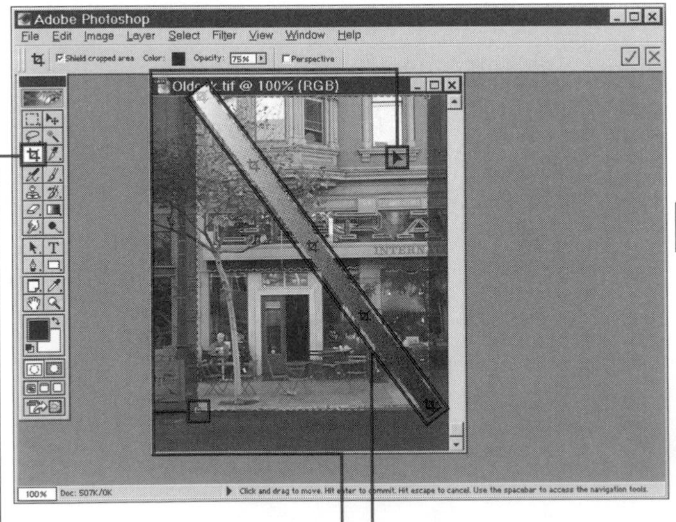

Note: Starting your retouching by cropping out any unneeded portions of the picture is always best. You get better composition and there will be less to retouch.

1 Click the Crop tool ( ).

2 Drag the cursor to include the area to be kept.

3 Drag the handles to adjust the selection.

4 Double-click inside the selection to crop.

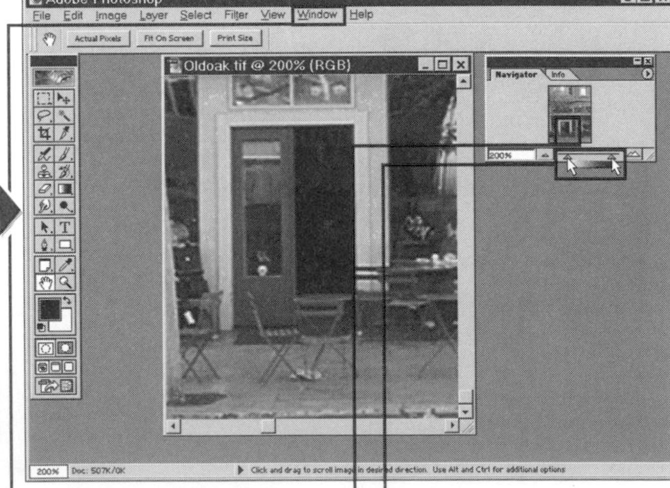

5 Choose Window, then Show Navigator.

■ The Navigator palette appears.

6 Drag the slider to Zoom in to 200% to see detail.

7 Drag the window to inspect retouched areas.

What is the best way to retouch textured areas of a picture, such as a tweed coat?

✔ Use the Clone tool with the Alignment box unchecked. Find an area of the image that contains the texture you want in the right shade and color and clone from there.

What should I do if I cannot find an area to clone that is as light or dark as the area I want to retouch?

✔ You can compensate to some degree by judiciously using the Burn and Dodge tools. Keep the exposure slider at a very low setting and do your burning and dodging carefully. If you overdo it, go back a few strokes in the History palette.

What is the best tool for retouching pimples, wrinkles, and other skin blemishes?

✔ Working with the Clone tool so that you duplicate skin texture in the retouched areas is usually easier and more effective. Be sure to clone from several different spots around the retouched area so that the retouching blends smoothly.

8 Click the Airbrush, Paintbrush, or Pencil tool.

9 Click the Brush menu to select a 3-pixel brush.

10 Press Option/Alt and click a pixel of the color you want to use.

11 Paint into the spot that you want to retouch.

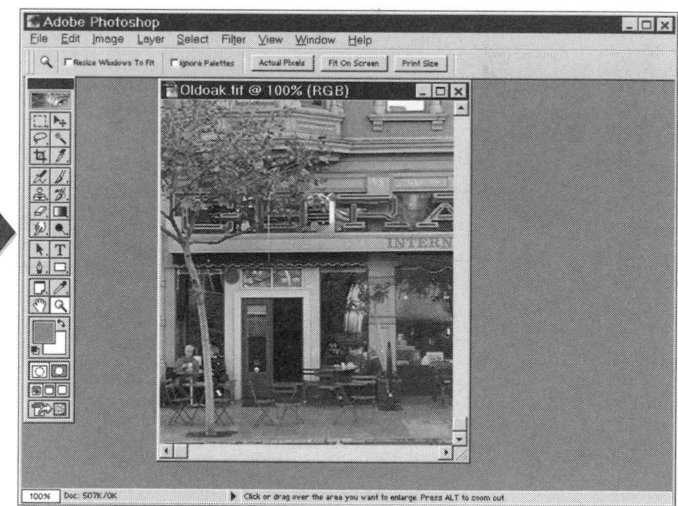

■ Here is the finished retouched image.

SECTION III

6) MAKING SELECTIONS

7) WORKING WITH VECTOR PATHS

ISOLATING PARTS OF THE IMAGE

8) WORKING WITH MASKS

9) WORKING WITH LAYERS

10) CHANNEL OPERATIONS

11) TEXT AND TEXT EFFECTS

MAKE POLYGON SELECTIONS

You can use the Polygon Lasso tool to make straight-line selection marquees between successive clicks. This tool can be a lifesaver when you have to select the straight edges of buildings, boxes, and computer monitors.

Using the Polygon Lasso is easy. Click the tool, click the pixel where the marquee will start, move the cursor to stretch the line, and click to end the line and start the next segment. Double-click to end the Polygon Lasso selection, and the selection will close between the first and last points clicked.

You do not need to select the Polygon Lasso tool to make a Polygon Lasso selection. Pressing Opt/Alt while drawing with the Lasso tool makes stretching a straight line possible. Likewise, pressing the Opt/Alt key while using the Polygon Lasso tool toggles to the Lasso tool. Thus, you can combine both techniques into a single selection.

Later in this chapter, the section "Make Compound Selections" demonstrates how handy the Polygon Lasso is for quickly making rough selections that you can refine later.

MAKE POLYGON SELECTIONS

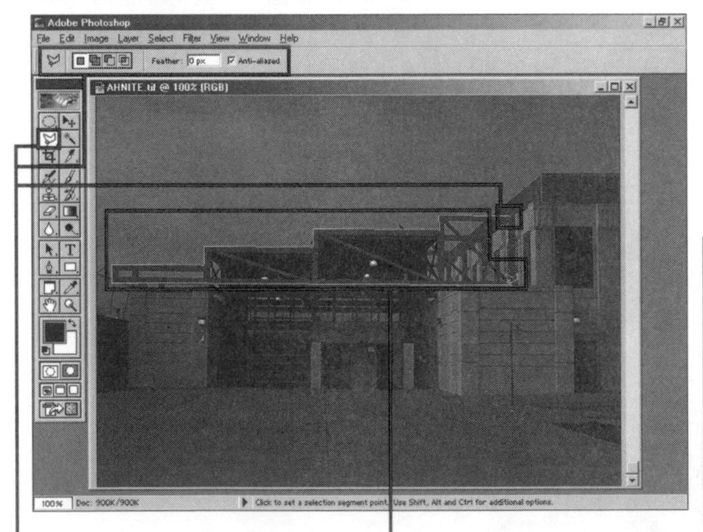

SELECT USING THE TOOL

1 Click the Polygon Lasso tool ( ).

2 Set the desired Options in the Options bar.

3 Click to place the start point of the first line segment.

4 Without dragging, click to define each subsequent connection point.

5 Double-click when you are ready to close the selection, or click the first point.

SELECT WHILE DRAWING

1 To start a polygon selection with the Lasso tool, press Opt/Alt at the pixel where the straight line is to start.

2 Move the cursor without dragging to stretch the straight line.

3 Click to set the end of the first straight line.

4 Continue making polygonal selections with the Opt/Alt key pressed.

Note: You can resume freehand by releasing the Opt/Alt key.

AUTOMATE SELECTION WITH THE MAGIC WAND

You can use the Magic Wand to automatically select all the pixels that fall within a specified contrast range surrounding the click point.

The Magic Wand can either save you many hours or waste a lot of your time. You can save time if you know when to use Magic Wand appropriately, what to specify for the contrast range (more a matter of practice than anything else), and how to edit a selection after you make it.

Using the Magic Wand is simply a matter of choosing the tool and clicking somewhere in the image. If the resulting marquee does not include enough of the area you want, increase the Tolerance setting in the Magic Wand Options palette.

Hint: Try using the Magic Wand in conjunction with the Magnetic Lasso (covered on the next page). Select a large area, such as the sky or a building, with the Magic Wand. Then choose the Magnetic Lasso and press Shift to add the exact edges you had in mind to the wand's selection.

AUTOMATE SELECTION WITH THE MAGIC WAND

1 Choose the Magic Wand tool (🪄).

2 Check the Anti-aliased check box in the Options bar.

3 Specify a tolerance (a number between 1 and 255).

4 Click on a pixel that represents the middle of the tonal range you want to select.

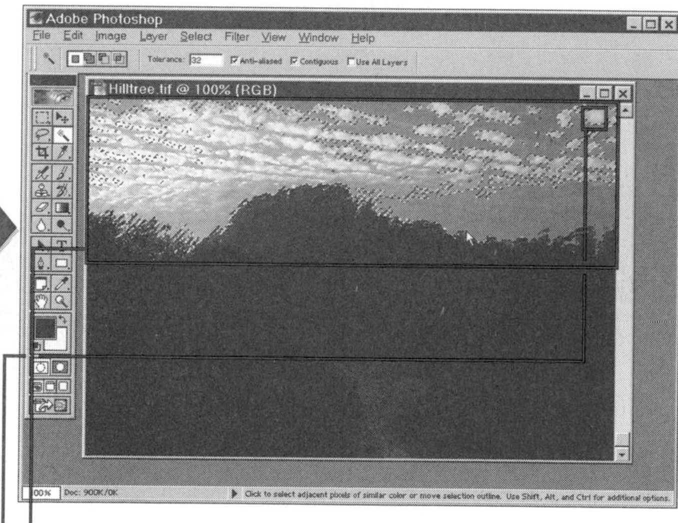

■ Photoshop selects most of the desired edges.

■ If needed, you can add to the selection by pressing Shift and clicking in an area outside the selection.

Note: Unless you photograph your subject on a plain and contrasting background, you may have some edges to edit.

AUTOMATE SELECTION WITH THE MAGNETIC LASSO

Although Photoshop lacks a shrink-to-fit tool or a command to eliminate the holes in a selection, the Magnetic Lasso and Magnetic Pen tools make it easier to automate making selections. Both work in exactly the same way, except one draws a selection marquee, whereas the other creates a path (see Chapter 7 for more about paths).

The Magnetic Lasso makes creating a selection that precisely follows the shape of an object easy. If enough contrast exists between the pixels in the object and the surrounding background, and if you keep the cursor within a specified number of pixels of the desired edge, the Magnetic Lasso works quite nicely.

The Magnetic Lasso does not work perfectly, however. Often there will not be enough contrast, which can result in imprecise selections. You can press the Backspace key to back up to a previous control point (yes, even the Magnetic Lasso uses control points) and try again.

Hint: In some cases, you can temporarily increase the contrast in your image by selecting a different channel in the Channels palette, which can then allow you to make your Magnetic Lasso selection.

AUTOMATE SELECTION WITH THE MAGNETIC LASSO

1 Choose the Magnetic Lasso tool ( ).

2 Specify feathering and anti-aliasing in the Options bar.

3 Type a percentage for edge contrast.

Note: Edge contrast refers to the difference in lightness between pixels that form one shape versus the pixels in the background.

4 Click the Stylus Pressure check box if you have a digitizing tablet and want stylus pressure to determine Lasso width.

Can I move or edit the control points?

✔ No. They merely serve to anchor the selection to a given pixel so that if you back up, you do not deselect the edge preceding the control point.

What do I do when the selection starts following an edge I do not want it to follow?

✔ This problem often occurs if you are working in an area of low contrast. When it does happen, just move the cursor backward (you do not need to drag). To eliminate unwanted control points, press Delete/Backspace.

How many ways can I close the selection?

✔ The most popular is to click on the start point. If you want to close from the current point to the start point and have the in-between edges automatically selected, double-click. If you want to close the shape with a straight line between the first and last points, press Opt/Alt and then double-click.

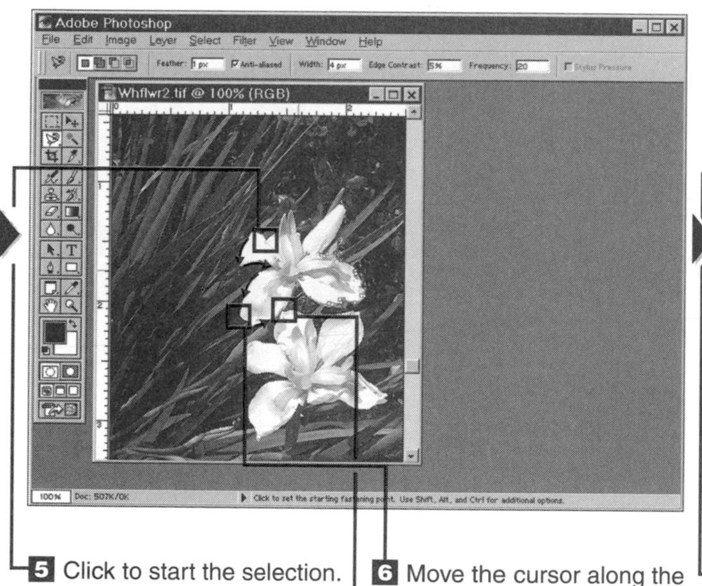

5 Click to start the selection.

6 Move the cursor along the desired edge of the selection within the distance set by the path.

7 Click to set the control point to change direction.

8 To close the selection between the first and last points with a straight line, press Opt/Alt and then double-click.

■ To continue the selection, press Shift and draw as before.

Note: This two-point selection technique is especially useful with the Magnetic Lasso tool. Otherwise, controlling the behavior of the tool when you need to pan, scroll, or zoom to complete the selection is difficult.

DEFINE A PATTERN

You can capture any part of any image and then save it to the Pattern Library. After that, you can always fill with that pattern — or even use the History brush to paint with it.

You may want to make your pattern seamless, so that you do not see a border between one of its edges and another when you fill or paint with it. How you go about that depends on the type of pattern you want to create. The easiest way is to paint your own pattern before you define it. Over a solid color background, make a square marquee selection by holding down the Shift key and dragging the Marquee tool. Then paint objects inside the selection and equidistant from and not touching the marquee border. The more symmetrical your design, the better. Then follow the instructions below for defining a pattern.

If you want to make a pattern from a natural texture in a photograph, make sure it is lighted evenly and photographed when the film is perfectly perpendicular with respect to the object.

DEFINE A PATTERN

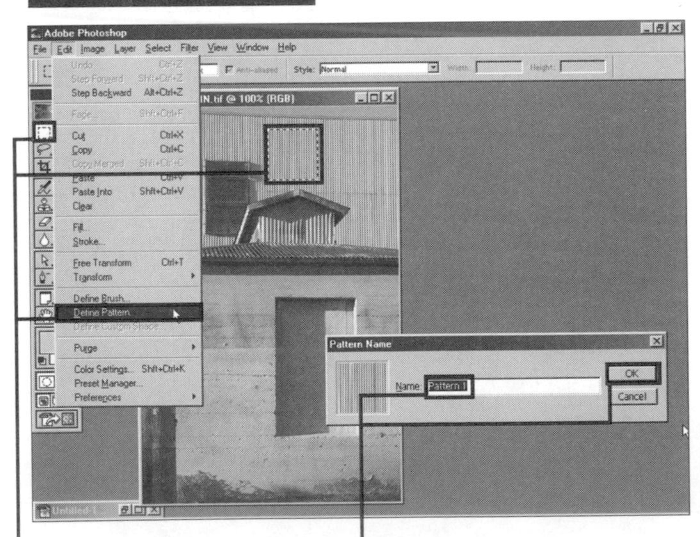

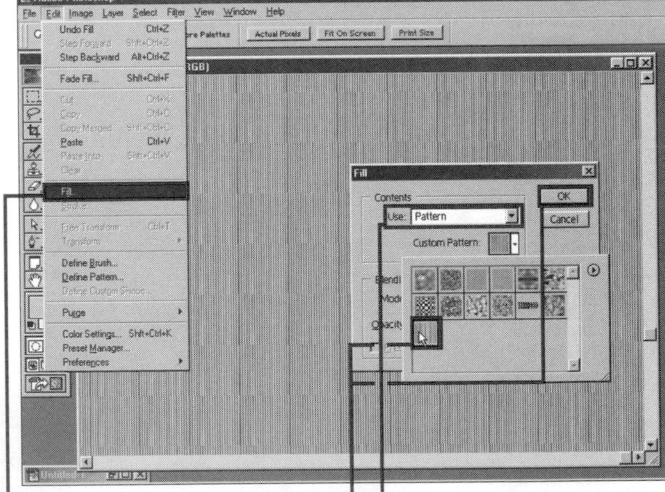

DEFINE THE PATTERN

1 Click the Marquee tool ( ).

2 Drag a rectangle to surround the pattern you want to define.

3 Choose Edit, then Define Pattern.

■ The Pattern Name dialog box appears.

4 Type a name for the pattern.

5 Click OK.

■ Photoshop defines your pattern.

FILL WITH A PATTERN

1 Open a new file, create a new layer, or select a layer that you want to fill.

2 Choose Edit, then Fill.

■ The Fill dialog box appears.

3 Choose Pattern from the Use menu.

4 Choose the pattern from the Custom Pattern menu.

5 Click OK.

■ The designated area fills with the pattern you created and chose.

USING THE COLOR RANGE COMMAND

You can select a whole range of colors and interactively specify a tolerance for that range of colors by dragging a slider. Then, if you want to refine that selection by adding or subtracting colors, you can choose the add or subtract Eyedropper and click in the image to indicate the specified color range.

With the Magic Wand command (see "Automate Selection with the Magic Wand"), you may have times when you want to select more of a given area than the command can cover in a single stroke. For example, you might want to select the spaces between the leaves of a tree to separate it from the sky. You can use the Magic Wand to make these selections and then click additional areas. However, Color Range may allow you to achieve the same result in one step.

The Color Range command is good for intricate images. For example, editing the sky from the section "Automate Selection with the Magic Wand" takes less time with the Color Range command than if you were to use the Magic Wand and Shift-click.

USING THE COLOR RANGE COMMAND

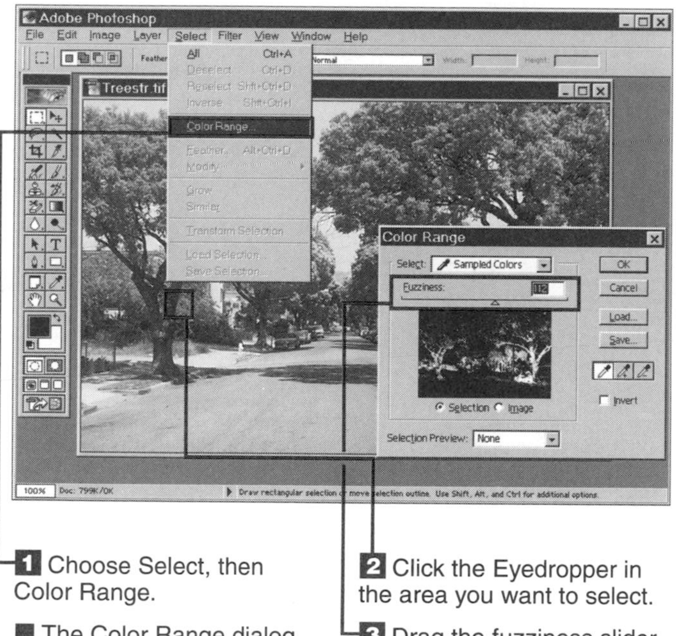

1 Choose Select, then Color Range.

■ The Color Range dialog box appears.

2 Click the Eyedropper in the area you want to select.

3 Drag the fuzziness slider to increase the size of the selection (tonal range).

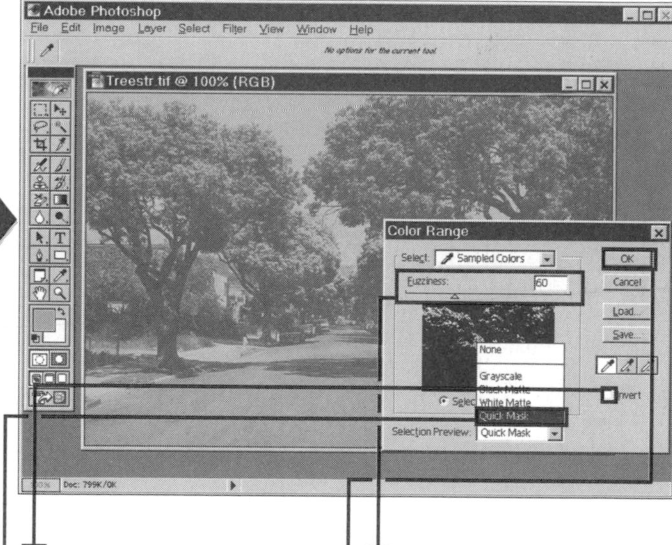

4 Click Invert (☐ changes to ☑) to test your selection.

5 Choose Quick Mask from the Selection Preview menu.

■ If the selection's colors vary, you can add colors to the range using the Eyedropper.

6 Drag the slider until most of the area you want selected is the mask color.

7 Click OK.

USING QUICK MASK MODE

Photoshop's Quick Mask mode allows you to create a selection using the painting tools (paintbrush, airbrush, and pencil). To use this mode, you click the Edit in Quick Mask Mode button in the toolbox and then use a painting tool to create a mask defining your selection. Upon completion, the familiar dashed selection outline appears.

You can change the mask color to one that contrasts more obviously with the colors in your image. Just double-click the Edit in Quick Mask Mode button and then click the Color Swatch in the dialog box that appears. Then make your choice from the standard Color Picker.

You can combine the Quick Mask feature with other selection tools. To quickly clean up a selection like the one in the section "Using the Color Range Command," click the Quick Mask button. Press D to select the default foreground and background colors, press X to switch the foreground color to white, press B to select the brush, and paint out any mask color that does not belong there. If you miss an edge, press X to switch the foreground color to black and paint the masking color back in.

USING QUICK MASK MODE

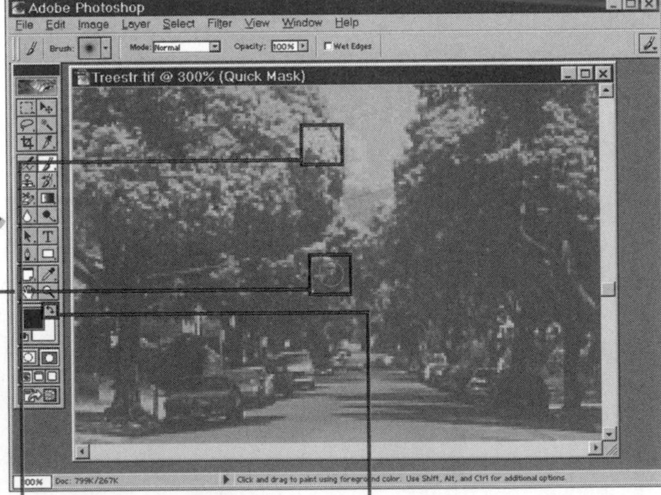

1 Starting with an active selection marquee, click the Edit in Quick Mask Mode button or press Q.

2 Click default foreground/background colors (or press D).

3 Click the curved double-arrow (or press X) to switch to white as foreground color.

■ Painting with white allows you to remove the mask and extend your selection.

4 Click the Paint Brush tool ( ) or press B.

5 Paint white where the mask infringes on areas that should not be masked.

6 Paint black in areas to extend the mask and shrink your selection.

7 Press the double-arrow to switch foreground and background colors.

Note: Paint in gray when you want the mask to be partly effective or to indicate atmospherics. Lighter grays make the mask more transparent.

When would I find painting the entire mask in Quick Mask mode to be easier?

✔ You might find that painting the entire mask is easier most of the time, especially if you are using a pressure-sensitive digitizing pad, which makes painting seem more natural and prevents you from having to switch brush sizes constantly.

How else can I make the mask color contrast more with the image?

✔ Choose Window then Show Channels and pick a single-color channel that contrasts the most sharply with the area to be selected (masked). Paint to correct your mask; then switch back to Normal mode (click the Normal mode icon and save the selection).

Is there another way to check to make sure I have not missed painting out any areas?

✔ Before you scroll to the next section of the image, press Q to toggle Quick Mask mode off. If you see a little marquee inside the target marquee, press Q again and paint white over that area.

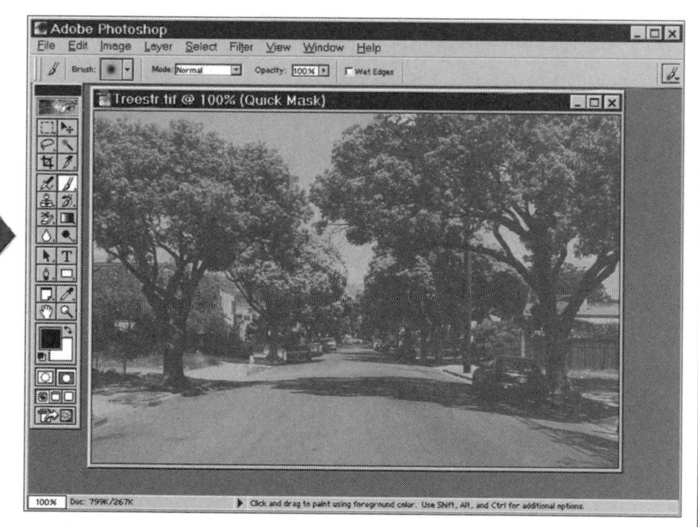

■ This selection is completely cleaned up as a result of painting in Quick Mask mode. Compare it to the previous screen.

Note: When cleaning up or editing images in zoomed-in windows, move one full window at a time from left to right, move down one window, move right to left, and then move down one window — repeating until you are sure you have covered the entire image.

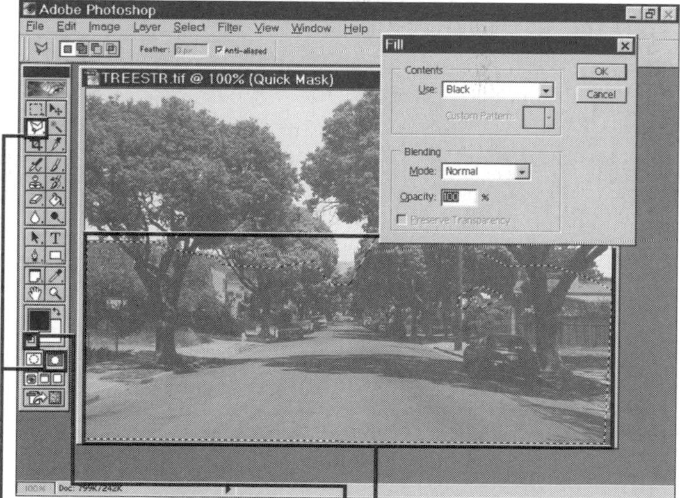

CLEAN UP LARGE QUICK MASK AREAS

1 Click the Edit in Quick Mask Mode button (or press Q).

2 Choose the Polygon Lasso tool (☐).

3 Click to start a selection. Each subsequent click makes a straight-line selection.

4 If necessary, click the default icon to select white as the background color (or press D).

5 Press Delete.

MAKE COMPOUND SELECTIONS

You can make selections using more than one tool, and you can combine multiple selections in Photoshop.

You can, for instance, use the Polygon Lasso tool to select a building in an image, press the plus (+) key and use the Magic Wand to select the sky, then press the plus key again. You can then use a rectangular marquee to select most of the foreground, and then press the plus key and use the Lasso tool to pick up the odd shapes.

Compound selections are often used to speed the selection of the desired area while improving accuracy. The most accurate way to make freehand selections is to select most of the inside of the subject, and then zoom in and work around the edges.

Making compound selections is also the first step in learning to change the shape of selections by editing them. Pressing Shift adds a selection to an existing selection, Opt/Alt subtracts a selection from an existing selection, and ⌘/Ctrl leaves whatever the previous and current selections both had in common.

MAKE COMPOUND SELECTIONS

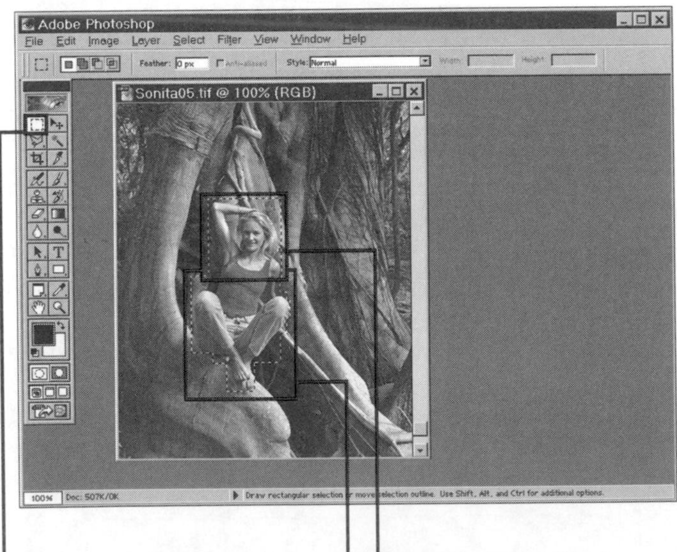

1 Click the Rectangular Marquee icon (⬚) or press M/Shift+M until it cycles into view.

2 Drag to select the first rectangle.

3 Press Shift and drag to add other overlapping rectangles as necessary.

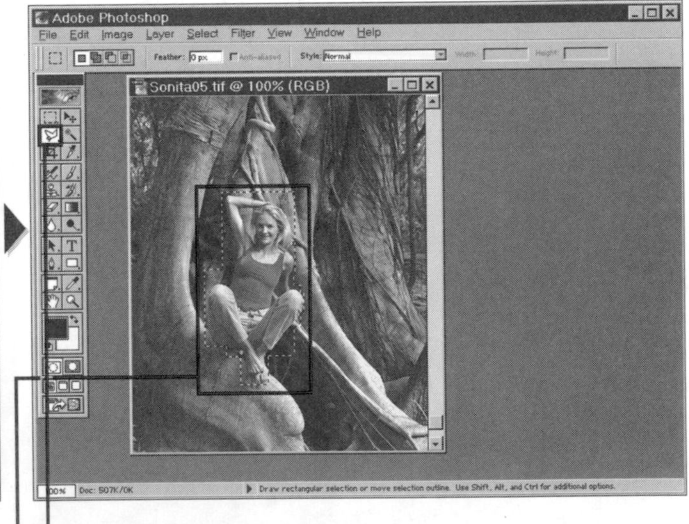

4 Choose the Polygon Lasso tool (⛉).

5 Press Opt/Alt and drag just inside the previous selection, then outside it to close the selection.

■ Each time you use this method, portions of the selection are trimmed away.

Can I draw a perfect circle or square and add it at the same time?

✔ Believe it or not, it is possible (but it takes some practice). Press Shift before you drag to add the elliptical or rectangular marquee selection. While dragging, release and then press Shift. The marquee will be constrained to a square or circle.

What if I want to subtract from my selection instead of add?

✔ When you have to subtract, press the Opt/Alt key instead of the Shift key. Otherwise, the process is the same.

Do other key modifiers exist that help in making selections?

✔ Yes. You can draw a geometric selection from the center by pressing Shift+Opt/Alt while dragging.

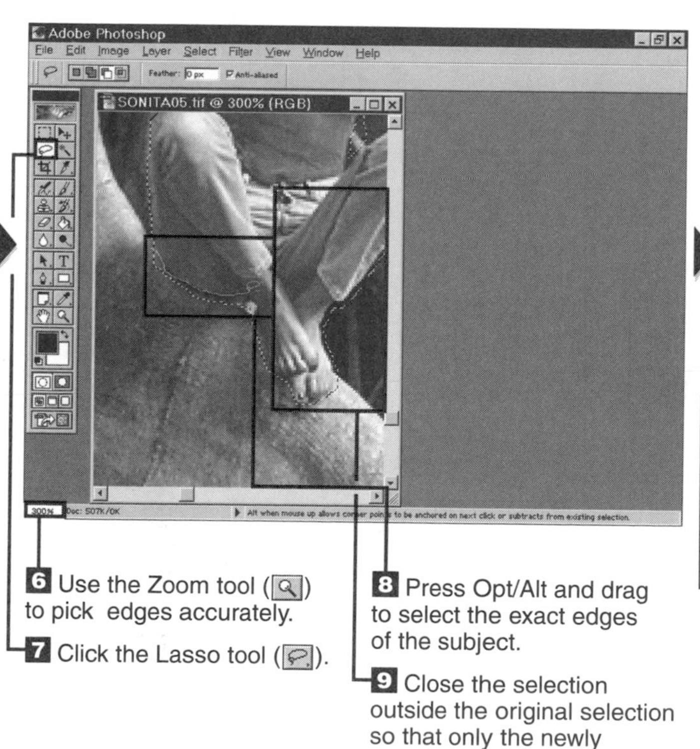

6 Use the Zoom tool ( ) to pick edges accurately.

7 Click the Lasso tool ( ).

8 Press Opt/Alt and drag to select the exact edges of the subject.

9 Close the selection outside the original selection so that only the newly selected edge remains.

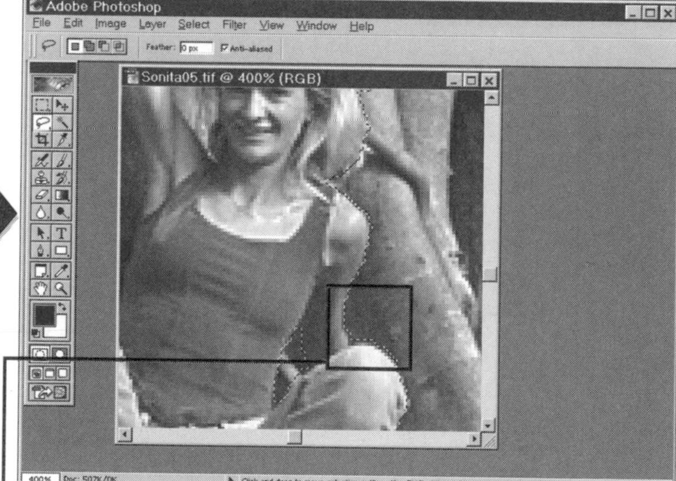

10 Zoom in very tight and continue to trim the exact edges more carefully.

Note: You can use Shift to add to or Opt/Alt to subtract from any selection, with any selection tool.

EDIT SELECTIONS

You can easily change the shape of a selection. By using selection tools a second time in combination with keyboard commands, you can

- Add a shape to the existing selection. Simply click a selection tool, press Shift, and then drag the mouse to draw the addition.
- Subtract a shape from the existing selection. Click a selection tool, press Opt/Alt, and then drag the mouse to draw the area to be deleted.
- Draw a shape that intersects the existing shape, then select only the area those shapes have in common. Click a selection tool, press Shift+Opt/Alt, and then drag.

You might have several reasons to change the shape of selections. The most common is the need to refine a rough selection so that it defines exactly the edges of the image within which you want to confine your modifications. Another is to accurately draw complex geometric shapes by combining ellipses and rectangles.

You can also use the same processes to add, subtract, and intersect saved selections, channel masks, and selection commands.

EDIT SELECTIONS

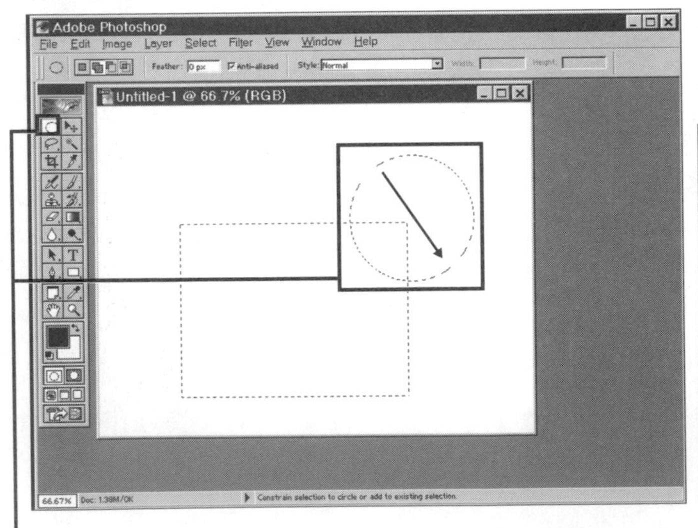

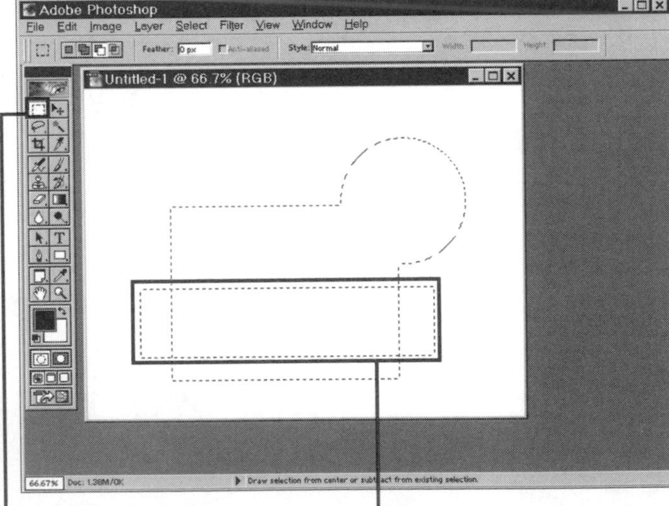

ADD A SHAPE TO A SELECTION

1 Click the selection tool that makes the shape you want to add.

2 Press Shift and drag to make and position the shape.

■ The shape is added to the existing shape. If the two shapes do not touch, you have two separate marquees.

SUBTRACT A SHAPE FROM A SELECTION

1 Click the selection tool that makes the shape you want to subtract.

■ Photoshop subtracts the shape from the existing shape, leaving a gap, indent, or hole.

When the marquee sits right over the seam, how can I tell how an edge affects the blending of the selection with the rest of the image?

✔ You can hide the marquee. Just press ⌘/Ctrl+H. Be sure you press ⌘/Ctrl+D to drop the selection the second you are through with it — or press ⌘/Ctrl+H again to make the selection visible.

These edits have been demonstrated with geometric tools. Will the Lasso and Magic Wand tools behave in the same way?

✔ Absolutely. The geometrics were used only because the result would be more obvious.

What if my compound edits turn out to be a mess?

✔ Use the History Palette (see Chapter 1). You can go back to exactly the point before your selection started going astray.

Can I draw or paint with a compound selection?

✔ Actually, drawing or painting with a compound selection is one of the most useful ways to use compound selections. Combine circles, ellipses, and rectangles to make a simple shape (such as an icon). Then use the Edit, then Stroke command.

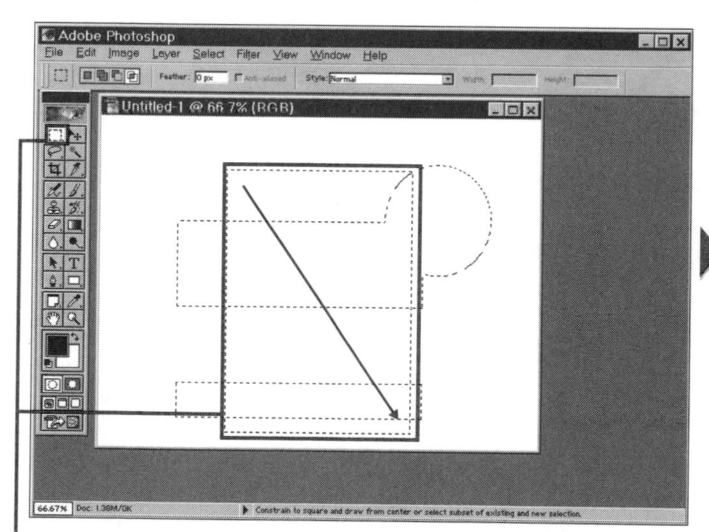

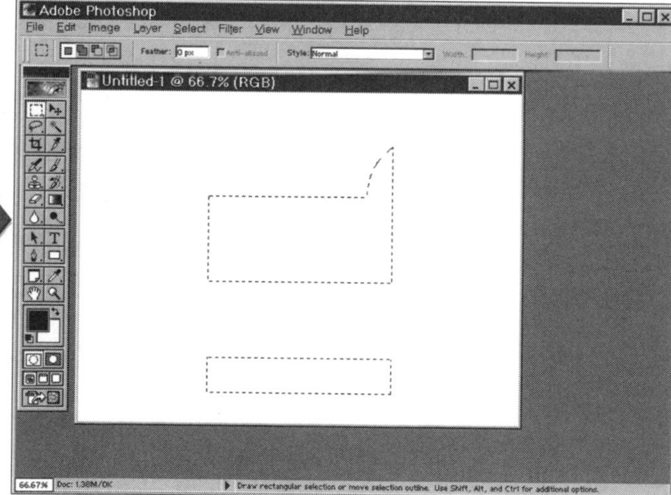

INTERSECT A SELECTION WITH A SELECTION

1 Click the selection tool you want.

2 Press Opt/Alt+Shift and drag to make and position the shape.

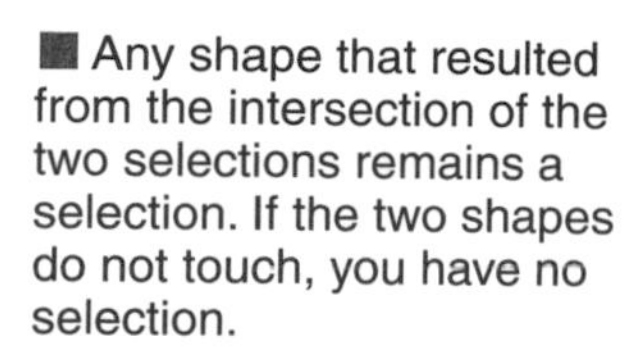

■ Any shape that resulted from the intersection of the two selections remains a selection. If the two shapes do not touch, you have no selection.

■ Here is the result of the intersection in the previous figure.

MODIFY SELECTIONS

Using commands found under the Select menu, you can modify existing selections. Specifically, you can make a selection that borders either side of the original selection by a specified number of pixels; round the corners of straight-edged selections; or make a selection larger or smaller by a specified number of pixels.

You access the commands by clicking Select, then Modify. The commands are

- Border: This command makes a selection around the edge of the current selection border that is as wide as the number of pixels you specify.
- Smooth: This command rounds the "corners" or sharp turns in a selection by a radius of a specified number of pixels (up to a maximum of 100).
- Expand: This command increases the size of the selection marquee by any number of pixels, up to 100. Sharp corners will be rounded in the process.
- Contract: This command decreases the size of the selection marquee by any number of pixels, up to 16. Rounded corners will be sharpened in the process. *Note that if you specify a number so large that the selection shrinks to nothing, then you have no selection.*

MODIFY SELECTIONS

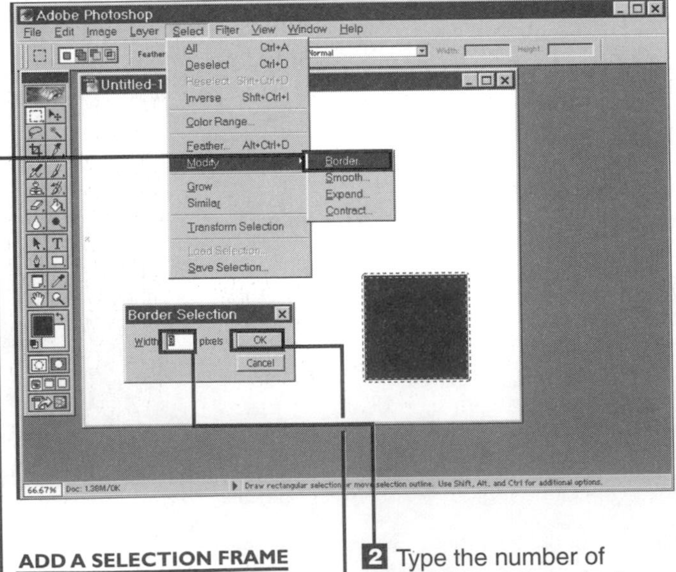

ADD A SELECTION FRAME

1 Choose Select, then Modify, then Border.

■ The Border Selection dialog box appears.

2 Type the number of pixels (up to 64) desired for the frame width.

3 Click OK.

■ Photoshop drops the original selection and the border selection appears on either side of it.

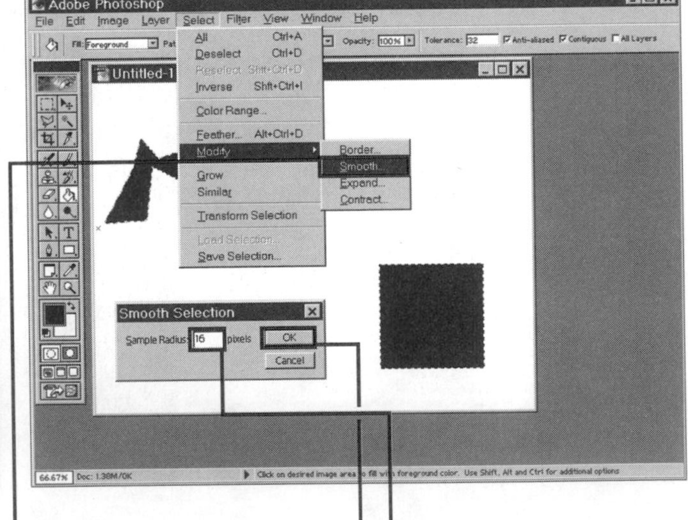

SMOOTH A SELECTION

1 Choose Select, then Modify, then Smooth.

■ The Smooth Selection dialog box appears.

2 Type the number of pixels (no longer limited to 16) desired for the rounding radius.

3 Click OK.

■ Photoshop drops the original selection and the smoothed selection appears.

Can I use Select, then Modify, then Smooth to smooth marquees created by an unsteady hand?

✔ Yes, but you may find that the smoothing causes the selection of pixels you did not want to have selected. Take a look at the smoothed path in the "Enlarge a Selection's Size" screen on this page.

How do I make a rounded-corner polygon selection?

✔ You can make a rounded-corner polygon selection by making a selection with straight edges, then choosing Select, then Modify, then Smooth and entering the desired corner radius.

The limit for the options Smooth, Expand, and Contract is 100 pixels. What if I want more?

✔ Divide the number you want by 2 until you get below 100, and enter that number in the dialog box. Then repeat the command as many times as it takes to get back to the number you want. If you want an odd number, repeat until you are within a few pixels, and then reissue the command and enter the exact number of pixels you want to add to the last border.

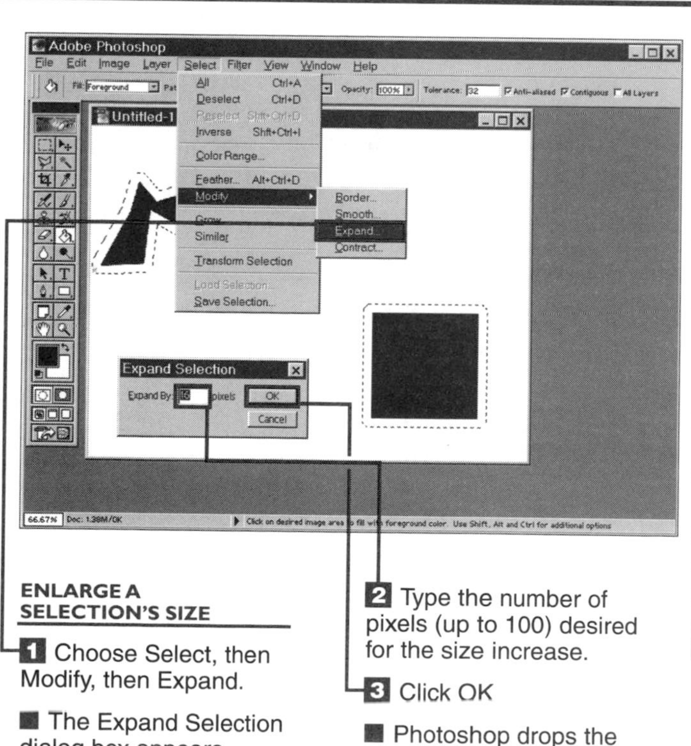

ENLARGE A SELECTION'S SIZE

1 Choose Select, then Modify, then Expand.

■ The Expand Selection dialog box appears.

2 Type the number of pixels (up to 100) desired for the size increase.

3 Click OK

■ Photoshop drops the original selection and a larger selection appears.

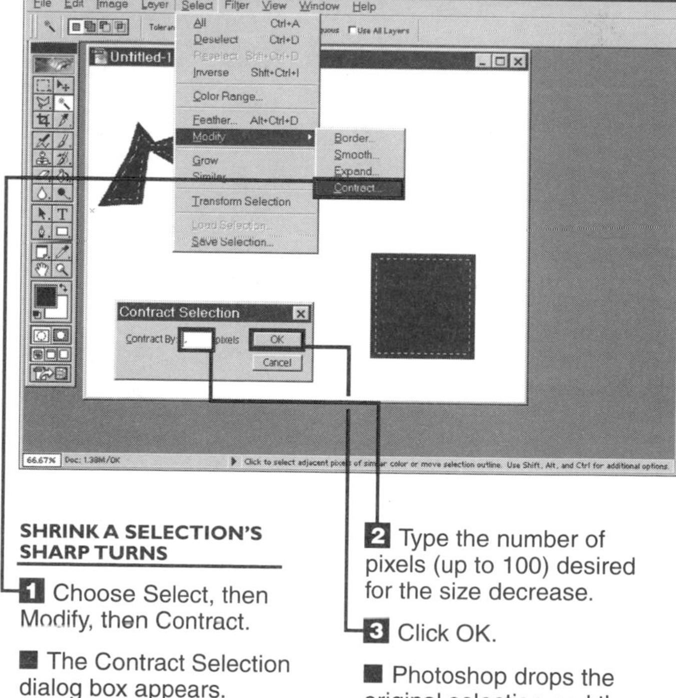

SHRINK A SELECTION'S SHARP TURNS

1 Choose Select, then Modify, then Contract.

■ The Contract Selection dialog box appears.

2 Type the number of pixels (up to 100) desired for the size decrease.

3 Click OK.

■ Photoshop drops the original selection and the reduced selection appears.

MODIFY SELECTIONS WITH GROW AND SIMILAR

In addition to the four commands discussed in "Modify Selections," earlier in this chapter, you can also modify selections with two additional commands on the Select menu: Grow and Similar. Both of these can enlarge a selection on the basis of the colors that are currently selected within them. Using these commands means the borders of the resulting selection will include more of the image.

Choosing Select then Grow immediately expands the current selection by the same grayscale range as exists in the current selection's Magic Wand Tolerance options — as long as the pixels within that range are contiguous. If the Magic Wand happens to be the chosen selection tool, whether you have checked Contiguous in the Options bar does not matter — the selection still only grows contiguously.

Choosing Select, then Similar immediately selects all shades that fall within the same range of tones as those in the original, regardless of any tolerance settings and whether the newly selected pixels are contiguous.

The results of this command are unaffected by the Magic Wand's Contiguous check box.

MODIFY SELECTIONS WITH GROW AND SIMILAR

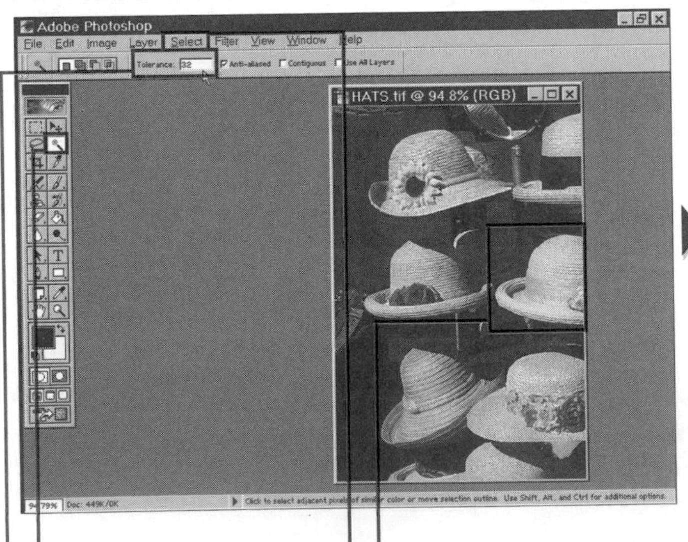

1 Click the Magic Wand tool (🪄) to bring up its Options palette.

2 Set a tolerance (between 1 and 255) in the selection tool's Options palette.

3 Make a selection.

4 Choose Select, then Grow.

■ The selection instantly grows to double the previously chosen tool tolerance, as shown in this example.

How do I keep the Grow command from making the selection grow too much?

✔ Open the Magic Wand Options palette and set the tolerance level to a fairly low number (try 8). Now issue the Grow command. If the selection does not grow enough, press ⌘/Ctrl+F to repeat the command at the same setting until the selection includes everything you want. If you go one step too far, press ⌘/Ctrl+Z to go back a step. If you are still not dead on, drop the selection and try again at a lower tolerance setting.

What is the best use for the Similar command?

✔ Selecting all the instances of a particular color — for example, the colors in lace or in particular interface elements. Suppose you wanted to place a frame around all the Web page buttons: Select a button, choose Select, then Similar, and then choose Select, then Modify, then Border.

Are selections made with the Grow and Similar commands anti-aliased?

✔ Only if the Anti-aliased box is checked in the Magic Wand Options palette.

SELECT SIMILAR SHADES

1 Make a selection.

2 Press Shift and make as many more selections as necessary to include the tones you want selected.

3 Choose Select, then Similar.

■ The selection instantly grows to include all the shades in the image that were included in your original selection, as shown in this example.

MAKE WHOLESALE SELECTION CHANGES

Many of the methods described in this chapter require you to make highly refined and accurate selections. However, if you want to make simpler, broader selections, you can use several options under the Select menu.

Choosing Select, then All (⌘/Ctrl+A) places a rectangular marquee around the entire layer. You can then float the image, make it into another layer, drag it into another file, or use any of the transformation commands on it.

Choosing Select, then Deselect might be the most valuable selection command of all. It lets you get rid of all the selections and adjustments you made so you can start all over again.

Choosing Select, then Inverse makes choosing everything in the image except what is already chosen easy. Best of all, you only need to make one selection. This method is usually the easiest way to separate an object from its surroundings — and then go to work on its surrounding.

MAKE WHOLESALE SELECTION CHANGES

SELECT THE ENTIRE LAYER

1 Choose Select, then All.

■ A selection marquee covers the entire image, indicating the currently chosen layer is selected. Any pre-existing selections disappear.

Note: If you are zoomed in, you may not see any of this marquee, because it is outside the borders of the workspace window.

CANCEL (DROP) ALL CURRENT SELECTIONS

1 Choose Select, then Deselect.

■ Any existing selections in the image window are canceled.

Note: Execute this command just before you do anything intended to affect the whole layer. You may have forgotten to unhide a selection marquee or may have made selections too subtle to allow the marquee to be visible.

Is Select All truly the fastest way to duplicate a layer?

✔ Yes. Press ⌘/Ctrl+A, press ⌘/Ctrl+J, and you will have copied the current layer without ever having to pull down a menu or drag a layer name bar.

What is all this about hiding selections?

✔ I thought you would never ask. Finding a spot to show something invisible is tough in a book such as this one, so let me elaborate here: If you want to hide the edges of a selection so you can see how smoothly the effect of a command blends, press ⌘/Ctrl+H.

Can you give me an example of why I would want to invert a selection?

✔ Inverting is a great way to throw the background out of focus (using the Gaussian Blur command — see "Control Focus" in Chapter 13) or to knock out the background entirely (just press the Delete/Backspace key). If you knock out the background, you can put a new background on a layer beneath the current one.

✔ **Can I reselect a selection?**
Yes. Click Select and then Reselect. Photoshop reselects the last selection that you deselected in your image.

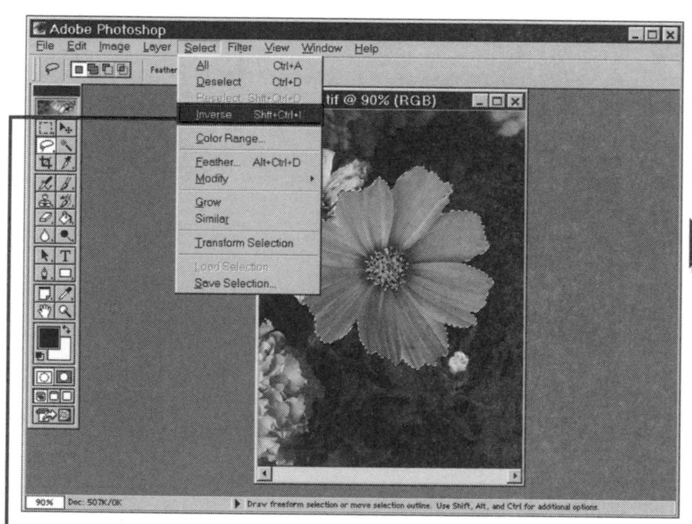

REVERSE (INVERT) THE SELECTION

1 Choose Select, then Inverse.

■ The marquee instantly surrounds all of the previously unselected image, as shown in this example.

■ This example uses Image, then Adjust, then Brightness/Contrast to darken the other flowers and foliage so that the foreground daisy stands out more.

SOFTEN EDGES WITH ANTI-ALIASING AND FEATHERING

The secret to making realistic composite photos lies in subtly and gradually making the edges of selections transparent (in imitation of persistence of vision). You can have a lot of control over how the edge of a selection fades into its surroundings, thanks to anti-aliasing and feathering.

Anti-aliasing is simply a matter of alternating the edge pixels with pixels of a lighter shade, which creates an optical illusion that makes the edges seem smoother. *Feathering* graduates the transparency of the edge over a user-specified number of pixels. Photoshop feathers a selection's edges by applying a bell-curve grayscale gradient for a specified number of pixels on either side of the selection marquee.

Anti-aliasing and feathering are controlled in the Options bar for most of the selection tools. You can also apply feathering to a selection by clicking Select and then Feather.

You can use feathering to "fade" almost any image adjustment, brush stroke, or filter effect. Feathering is also useful in collage compositions, creating cross-fades between some or all of the composition's images.

SOFTEN EDGES WITH ANTI-ALIASING AND FEATHERING

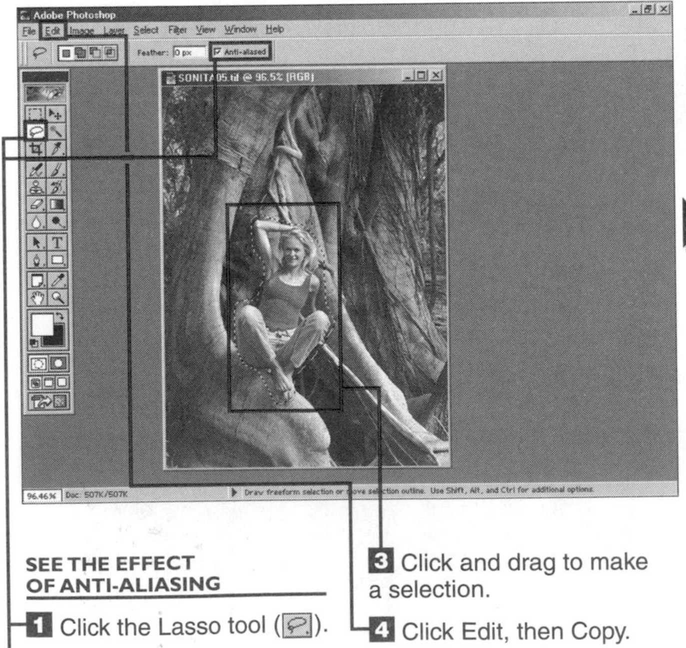

SEE THE EFFECT OF ANTI-ALIASING

1. Click the Lasso tool.
2. Check Anti-aliased in the Options bar.
3. Click and drag to make a selection.
4. Click Edit, then Copy.

■ To see the effect of anti-aliasing, paste the copied selection onto a solid-colored background.

5. Make a selection with the Lasso tool where you want to place the selection, then click Edit, then Paste.
6. Repeat steps 1 through 5 leaving the Anti-aliased box unchecked.

■ The example above shows magnified versions of selections that have anti-aliasing turned on (note the blurred edge) and turned off (note the jagged edge).

Does a way exist to feather the selection less than 1 pixel?

✔ If you are doing this for a composite, the answer is yes. Before making any selection, cut the image you want and paste it into another file of the same size. Double the size of the image, make the selection, and feather it 1 pixel. Invert the selection and press the Delete key to cut out the background. Reduce the image to its original size and drag it back to the original file. The feathering now takes place in half the space. This task is possible because a 1-pixel feather actually affects a 4-pixel radius.

Does a difference exist between setting feathering in a tool's Options palette and choosing the Select, then Feather command?

✔ Yes. Any setting you make in the Options palette affects all subsequent selections, but not any current selection. Any degree of feathering you specify in the Feather command's Feather Selection dialog box affects the current selection, regardless of which tool(s) you used to make that selection.

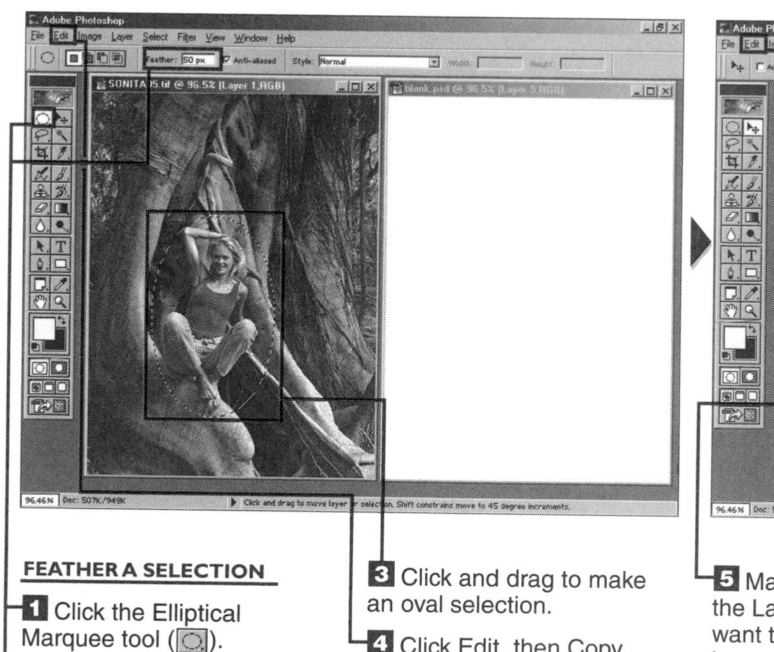

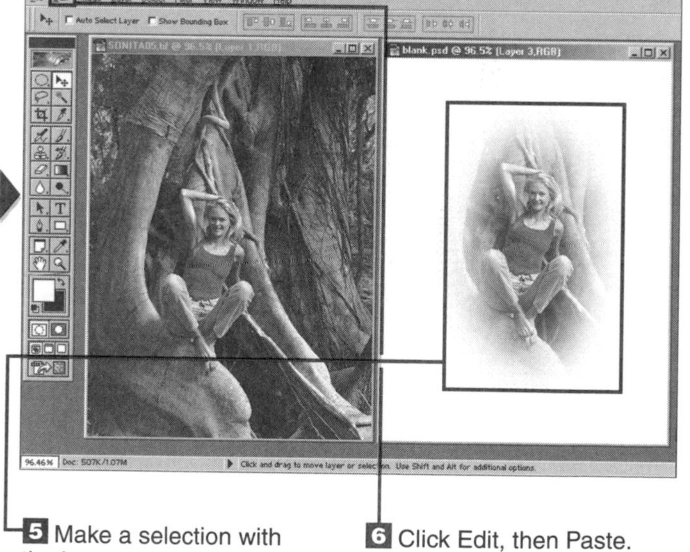

FEATHER A SELECTION

1 Click the Elliptical Marquee tool (◯).

2 Type a Feather value in the Options bar.

3 Click and drag to make an oval selection.

4 Click Edit, then Copy.

5 Make a selection with the Lasso tool where you want to place the selection in your image.

6 Click Edit, then Paste.

■ Photoshop feathers the edges of your selection.

ERASE WITH THE MAGIC ERASER

The Magic Eraser makes solid-color, fairly evenly lit areas of the image (such as a sky or a wall) disappear — like magic.

Like the Magic Wand or the Paint Bucket, you set a tolerance between 1 and 255. The tones you erase do not need to be identical; they just need to fall within the brightness range you specify in the Tolerance field. Also like the Magic Wand and Paint Bucket, the Magic Eraser's effects are not always perfect near low-contrast edges of your image. Be prepared to do some cleanup afterwards in some cases.

The three check box options in the Magic Eraser Options palette are

- Use All Layers: If you check Use All Layers, the erasure will take place on all visible tones that fall within the specified tonal range, regardless of layer.
- Anti-aliased: Checking Anti-aliased ensures that edges will be smooth (rather than pixilated).
- Contiguous: Check Contiguous if your foreground subject has lots of holes — that is, spaces where the background shows through.

ERASE WITH THE MAGIC ERASER

1 Click the Lasso tool ( ).

2 Make a selection that includes the area you want to erase. Be sure to include edges with holes.

3 Click the Magic Eraser ( ).

4 To erase pixels that are not necessarily connected, uncheck Contiguous.

5 Specify a tolerance value between 1 and 255.

6 Click inside the area you want to erase. Click a pixel of intermediate brightness in that area.

■ The area is deleted. If you erased wanted edges, Tolerance was set too high. Undo, decrease the tolerance, and try again.

Should I always check Anti-alias?

✔ No. Sometimes the anti-aliased pixels contain unexpected colors that create a halo around your foreground object. If you see this problem occur, try again with anti-aliasing turned off.

When should I use the Contiguous option?

✔ You use the Contiguous option when you want to make sure that Photoshop only erases the area you have not clicked. At times, making several clicks is better than having to subtract a large number of areas that you did not want selected in the first place.

How do I know how much Tolerance to specify?

✔ You have to practice. When you want to erase an evenly lit seamless background, consider starting at around 10. If it is a cloudless sky, something around 30 seems to work. You may have to an adjustment or two after you initial selection to achieve the effect you want.

What application seems tailor made for the Magic Eraser?

✔ Getting rid of the sky behind sparse or bare tree branches when I want to substitute a new or more interesting sky.

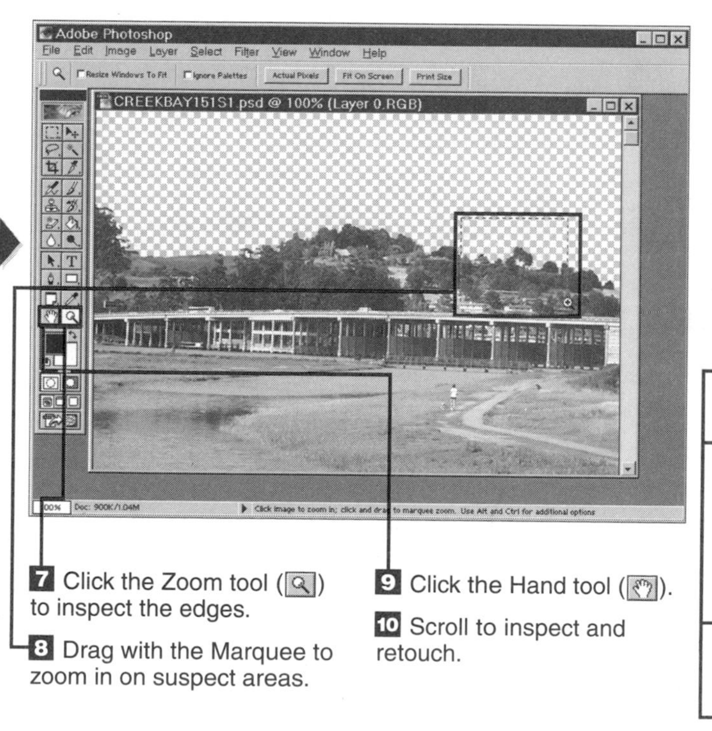

7 Click the Zoom tool (🔍) to inspect the edges.

8 Drag with the Marquee to zoom in on suspect areas.

9 Click the Hand tool (✋).

10 Scroll to inspect and retouch.

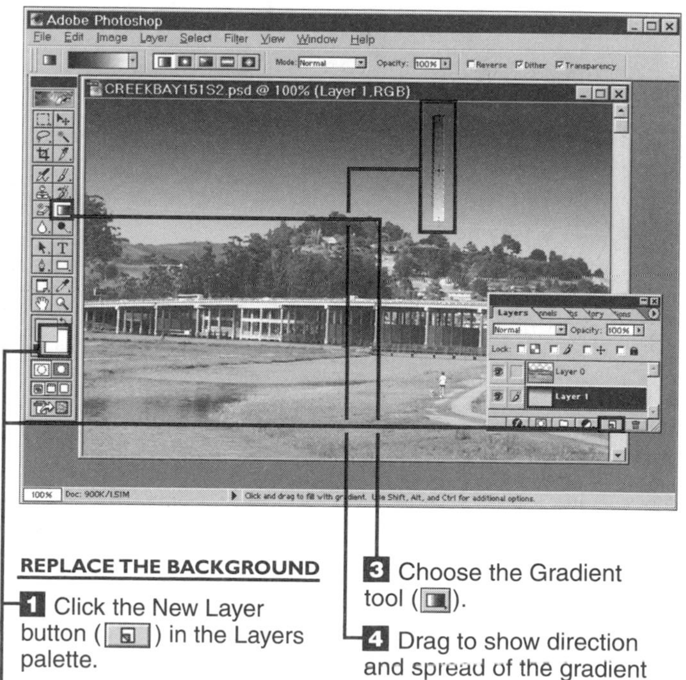

REPLACE THE BACKGROUND

1 Click the New Layer button (▣) in the Layers palette.

2 Choose a color for the background.

3 Choose the Gradient tool (▣).

4 Drag to show direction and spread of the gradient fill.

ERASE BACKGROUNDS

The Background Eraser dynamically deletes similarly colored pixels as you drag it, making it ideal for painting out evenly colored backgrounds in images.

The cursor for the Background Eraser is a circle with a cross in the center. The Background Eraser works by erasing all the colors within a specified range of the color that the center of that cross passes over. Similar to the Magic Eraser, you specify the color range by setting a tolerance value. Unlike the Magic Eraser, the Background Eraser works only on the currently active layer.

Note that when used on a background layer, the Background Eraser erases pixels to the current background color. So if you want the tool to erase a background layer to transparency, you must first convert the background layer to a regular layer (for more about layers, see Chapter 9).

The Background Eraser is also an excellent tool for retouching the results of the Extract Image command.

ERASE BACKGROUNDS

1 Click the background layer in the Layers palette.

2 Choose Layer, then Layer Properties.

■ The Layer Properties dialog appears.

3 Rename the Background layer.

4 Make a rough selection of the object whose background you want to erase, invert the selection (/Ctrl+Shift+I), and press Delete/Backspace.

■ A checkerboard pattern indicates the transparent area of the image.

5 Press /Ctrl+D to Deselect All.

6 Click the Eyedropper tool ( ).

■ The Eyedropper Options appear.

7 Choose a 5 x 5 sample size.

What do the choices in the Limits menu mean?

✔ The choices are Contiguous (erases all colors within range of the color sampled click); Discontiguous (erases all colors within range as cursor is dragged); and Find Edges (does not erase colors on the other side of an obvious edge).

What about the choices in the Sampling menu?

✔ The choices are Continuous (samples continuously as the mouse is dragged); Once (samples only once when the mouse is first clicked); and Background (erases only the Background color wherever it is found).

What other options do I have for erasing the background around elements in my image?

✔ For elements that have well-defined edges and relatively evenly colored backgrounds, using the Magic Wand (see "Automate Selection with the Magic Wand"), Color Range command (see "Using the Color Range Command"), or the Magic Eraser (see "Erase with the Magic Eraser") can be simpler, faster, and easier than the Background Eraser.

8 Click the Eyedropper and click the predominant color in the object you want to keep.

9 Click the Background Eraser (![]).

10 Set tolerance in the Background Eraser Options bar.

11 Choose Contiguous.

12 Check Protect Foreground Color.

13 Drag around subject.

■ The background erases to the edge of the subject.

■ If too much or too little is erased, press /Ctrl+Z to Undo, adjust the Tolerance, and try again.

14 Continue until the background is erased.

DRAW A PATH

You can use Photoshop to draw the smooth and scalable vector paths popular in illustration programs.

Although you can easily "draw" a path by converting a mask or selection into a path, or by importing an Adobe Illustrator path into Photoshop, you can create and edit your own path. You can draw and correct paths without using the Eraser tool.

If you work in Adobe Illustrator, Macromedia FreeHand, or CorelDRAW!, you are probably already familiar with the concepts in this section. If you are unfamiliar with drawing paths, you may find this section a bit different than other processes in Photoshop.

If you are new to drawing paths, remember that clicking, repositioning, and clicking again results in a straight line, while clicking and dragging creates a curve.

DRAW A PATH

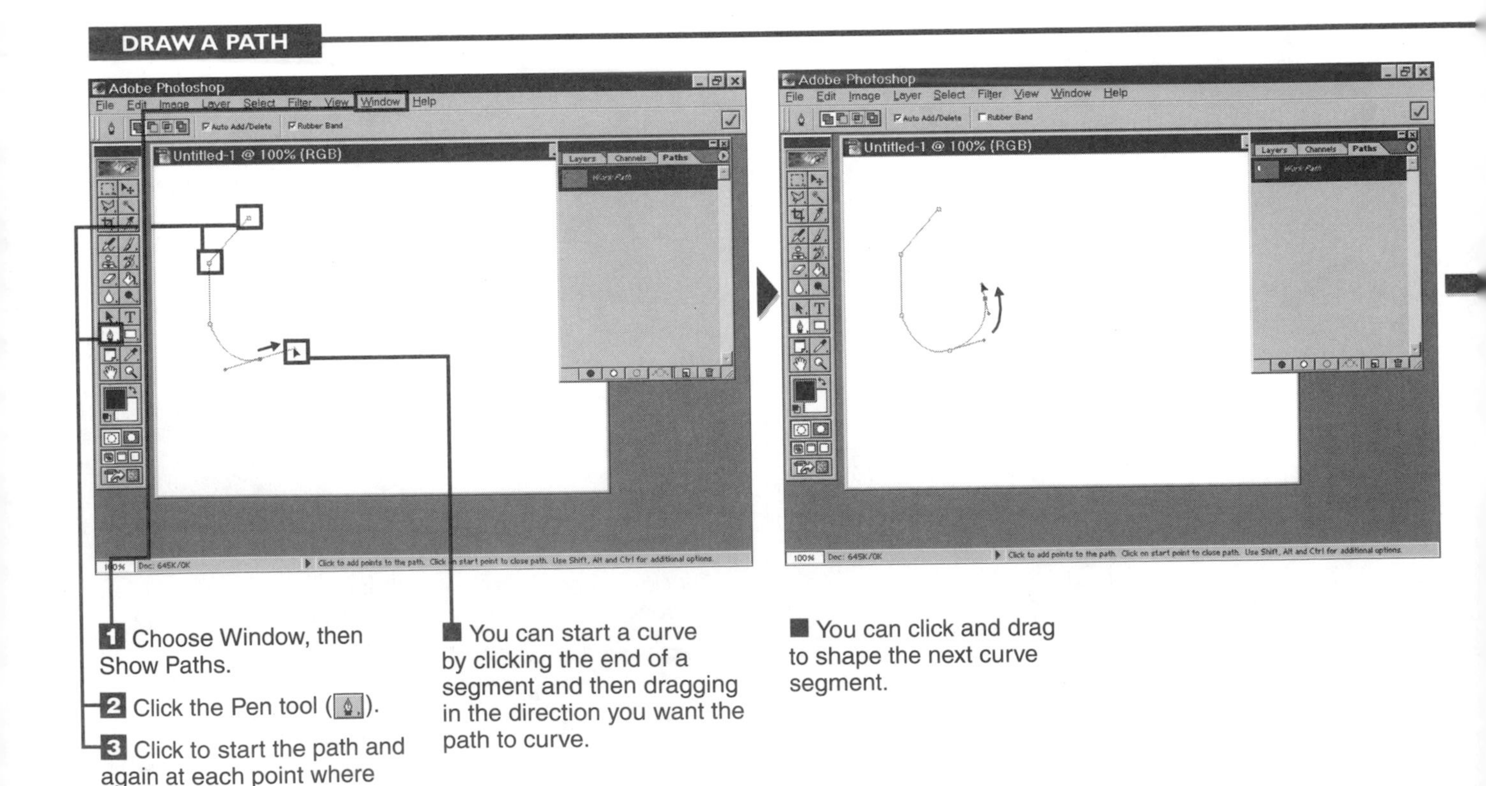

1 Choose Window, then Show Paths.

2 Click the Pen tool ( ).

3 Click to start the path and again at each point where you want a straight segment.

■ You can start a curve by clicking the end of a segment and then dragging in the direction you want the path to curve.

■ You can click and drag to shape the next curve segment.

Why would I use the Pen tools rather than the Freehand Pen?

✔ The Freehand Pen places a control point whenever you inadvertantly jiggle the cursor. If you want paths that are perfectly smooth and simple, draw with the Pen tools.

How can I use paths to make geometric shapes?

✔ Choose View, then Show Grid, and then choose View, then Snap to Grid. You can now place anchor points at exact distances from one another. This technique is great for creating round-cornered buttons, rectangular banners, and other functional graphics.

What is the most efficient way to trace the outline of highly irregular shapes?

✔ You can make a new layer immediately above the object you want to trace. Then draw a rough path around the object and drag the major points into exact alignment. Next, use the Add Point tool to insert any needed control points. You can then drag the additional control points into place and edit the curve until it fits.

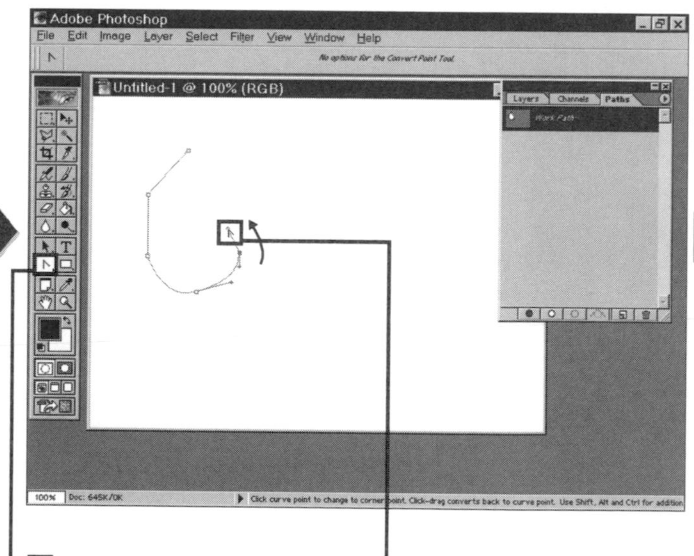

4 To draw a straight line from a curve point, click the Convert Anchor Point tool ( ).

5 Click and drag the upper direction point until it points in the direction of the next straight-line segment.

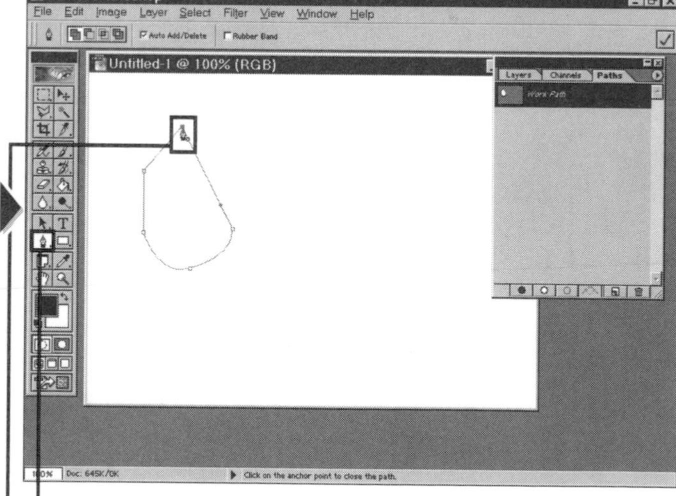

6 Click the Pen tool ( ).

7 Place the Pen tool cursor directly over the first point.

■ A circle appears next to the Pen tool cursor, indicating that you are about to close the path.

8 Click your beginning point.

■ The path closes, completing your path.

DRAW COMPLEX PATHS

You can draw much more complicated paths than the path illustrated in the section "Draw a Path." Rarely do you draw paths with simple requirements; rather, you draw paths that suddenly change direction and have severe curves.

Suppose you want to create a path with a combination of straight and curved lines, and smooth and asymmetrical curves. Photoshop allows you to create complex paths with the modifier keys in the Pen tools.

When drawing complex paths, first draw a simple polygon. Next, click each of the main points along the edge of the shape where the curves change direction. Finally, zoom in and add points so that you can drag them onto the more irregular edges of your shape.

Remember that you must complete or deselect a path before you can start another path.

DRAW COMPLEX PATHS

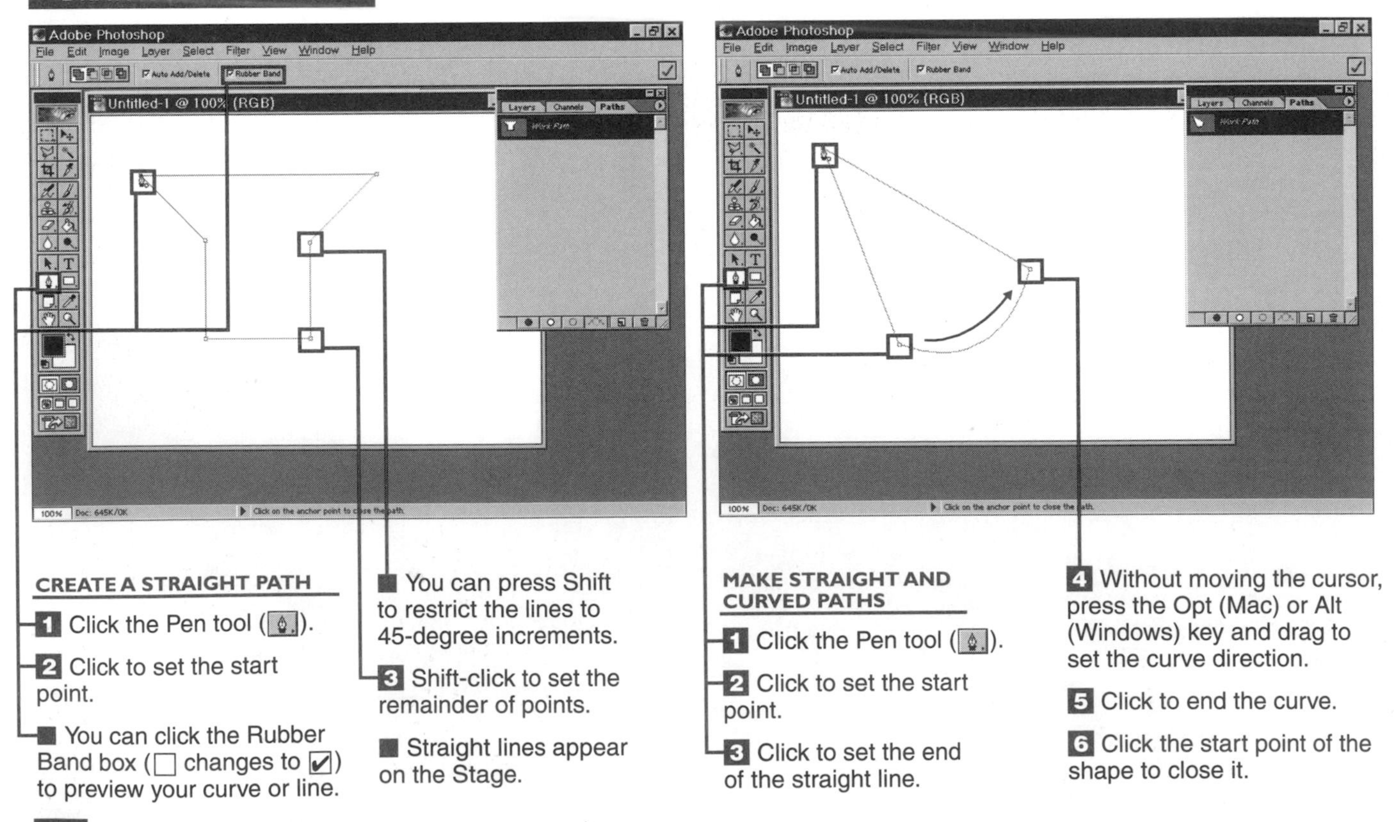

CREATE A STRAIGHT PATH

1 Click the Pen tool ( ).

2 Click to set the start point.

■ You can click the Rubber Band box (☐ changes to ☑) to preview your curve or line.

■ You can press Shift to restrict the lines to 45-degree increments.

3 Shift-click to set the remainder of points.

■ Straight lines appear on the Stage.

MAKE STRAIGHT AND CURVED PATHS

1 Click the Pen tool ( ).

2 Click to set the start point.

3 Click to set the end of the straight line.

4 Without moving the cursor, press the Opt (Mac) or Alt (Windows) key and drag to set the curve direction.

5 Click to end the curve.

6 Click the start point of the shape to close it.

Can I change tools from the Pen tools menu while I draw?

✔ Changing tools from the Toolbox while drawing can be very confusing because success depends on exactly when you press a modifier key or switch tools. Also, if you check the Rubber Band box and change tools, Photoshop draws erratic lines when you select another tool.

How do I get the "tracing paper" effect?

✔ You can create a new layer between your photo and the new layer on which you want to trace. Fill the in-between layer with white (choose Edit, then Fill) and set the layer transparency to 50%. The final image looks as if you are viewing it through tracing paper.

How do I force a sharp change in the direction of a path?

✔ You have to change the control point(s) through which the curve passes to a corner point. Make sure you select the curve and the Pen tool. Place the cursor over the point you want to change, press the Opt (Mac) or Alt (Windows) key and then click the point.

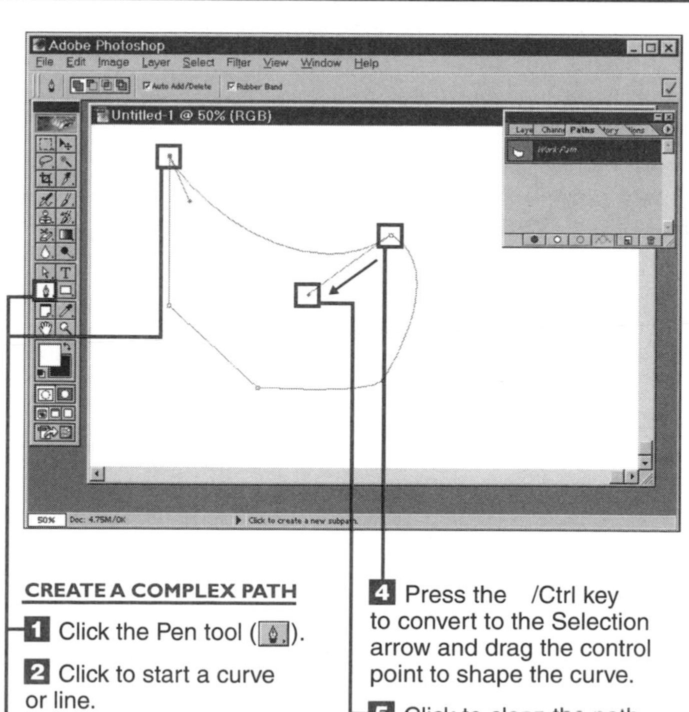

CREATE A COMPLEX PATH

1 Click the Pen tool ( ).

2 Click to start a curve or line.

3 Click to place a few points to start a shape.

4 Press the /Ctrl key to convert to the Selection arrow and drag the control point to shape the curve.

5 Click to close the path, dragging down to position the direction point.

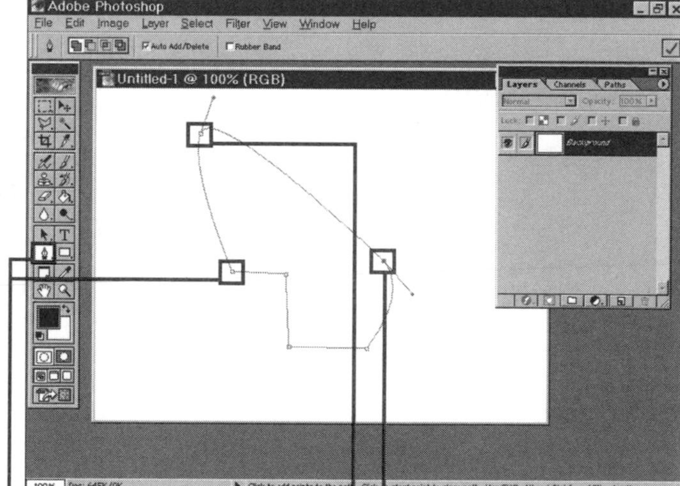

START A COMPLEX PATH WITH A CURVE

1 Click the Pen tool.

2 Click and drag to start the shape.

3 Click a few more times to make straight lines.

4 Click and drag to curve the next point. Press the Opt/Alt key. Click to convert to a corner point.

5 Click and drag to set the curve's direction. Press the Opt/Alt key and click the direction arrows to shape the curves.

DRAW FREEHAND PATHS

You can draw paths freehand by using the Freeform Pen tool. Drawing paths using this method requires a certain level of skill. You must draw the paths accurately, or you run the risk of spending a lot of time editing them. If you do not draw precisely, you might produce a large file with an unmanageable (and virtually uneditable) number of control points.

Several techniques make drawing paths freehand easier. You can purchase a pressure-sensitive tablet to reduce the number of unintentional control points. You can also experiment with the Curve Fit setting in the Freeform Pen Options palette to control the number of points you add as you draw.

You can also draw more accurately if you do so at over 100% zoom, because the Curve Fit settings apply to screen pixels. If you must pan to complete the path, you risk accidentally dropping the path. To avoid this situation, pause drawing, press the spacebar, and click the Hand button. With the Hand tool, you can then drag the screen view, release the spacebar, and continue drawing.

DRAW FREEHAND PATHS

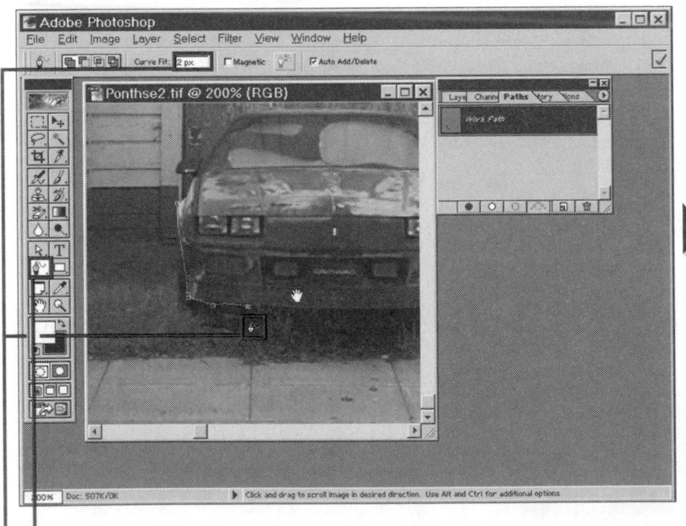

1 Click the Freeform Pen tool (✎).

2 Type the number of pixels you want to smooth the curve.

3 Outline your image until you return to the origin point.

Note: See the section "Draw Complex Paths" to outline your image.

4 Release the mouse button.

■ The path closes.

■ This example shows a composite. You do not see two cursors on screen at one time.

■ To switch to the Direct Selection tool, you can press the ⌘ (Mac) or Ctrl (Windows) key and then drag the point.

■ To change the nature of a control point, you can press the Opt (Mac) or Alt (Windows) key to switch to the Convert Point tool.

CONVERT SELECTIONS TO A PATH

You can create a new path by converting any selection into a path. You can use this technique to convert hard-edged flat symbols, such as photos, into paths. Converting a selection is a very fast process, especially if you use the Magic Wand selections. You can make the selection with the Magic Wand and then click the Make Path button at the bottom of the Paths palette.

You can use the feathering options in the converting process, although the effects of the options vary. With the feathering option, you can produce smooth curves. However, if you want your path to accurately follow the selection marquee, you might consider turning off this option because the path centers itself in between the edges of the feathered area.

Converting selections into paths might not be the answer to all your path problems. Feathered selections and selections made from channels may not follow the edge you desire. Small details, such as hair or leaves, overly complicate the edge of the mask. For more about making complex selections, see Chapter 6.

CONVERT SELECTIONS TO A PATH

1 Click a selection tool.

2 Type **0** pixels in the Options palette to turn off feathering.

3 Make your selection.

Note: For more on making a selection, see Chapter 6.

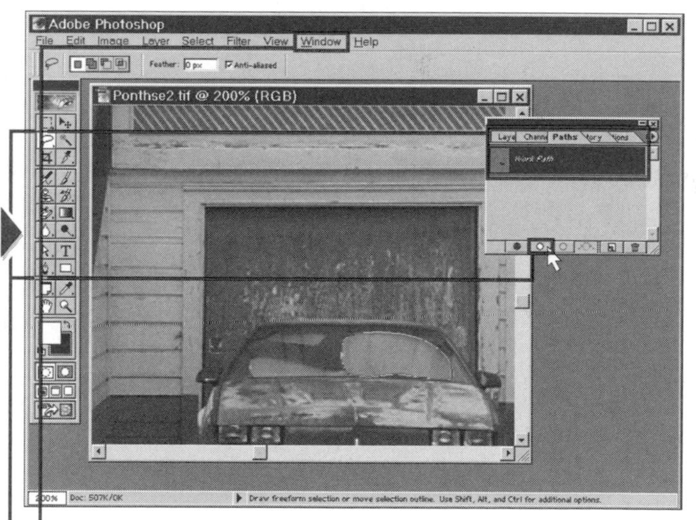

4 Choose Window, then Show Paths.

■ The Paths palette appears.

5 Click the Make Path from Selection icon.

■ Photoshop converts your selection according to the setting in the Make Work Path dialog box (accessible from the Paths palette menu).

AUTOMATE PATH TRACING WITH THE MAGNETIC PEN

You can automatically trace edges with the Magnetic Pen tool, which is a property you can select on the Pen tool's Option bar.

The Magnetic Pen draws a path precisely on the edge of an image that you trace. The Magnetic Pen works best with sharp edges, when there are minor directional changes, and when the contrast along the edge is fairly consistent. If your image does not meet these requirements, the tool draws randomly.

The Magnetic Pen also works best when you click to place a start point and move the cursor along the edge without depressing the mouse button. When you reach a point where the contrast or direction of the edge changes, click to set a point, and then continue tracing your path. If the Magnetic Pen tool begins to draw randomly, press the Delete or Backspace key to move backward until you reach a control point where you can resume.

AUTOMATE PATH TRACING WITH THE MAGNETIC PEN

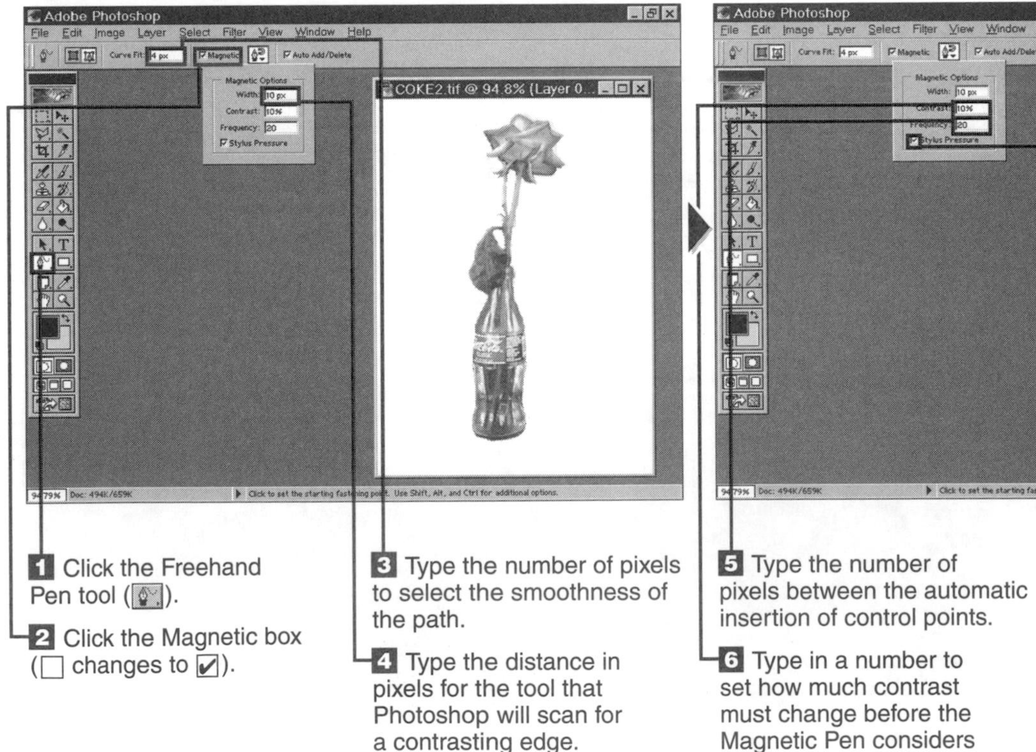

1 Click the Freehand Pen tool.

2 Click the Magnetic box (☐ changes to ☑).

3 Type the number of pixels to select the smoothness of the path.

4 Type the distance in pixels for the tool that Photoshop will scan for a contrasting edge.

5 Type the number of pixels between the automatic insertion of control points.

6 Type in a number to set how much contrast must change before the Magnetic Pen considers something an edge.

■ If you use a pressure pen, you can click the Stylus Pressure on (☐ changes to ☑). Only use this option after you practice.

What are the best conditions for using the Magnetic Pen tool?

✔ The Magnetic Pen can save time when the image has pronounced, obvious edges.

If I cannot use the Magnetic Pen tool for complicated shapes with low contrast, fuzzy, or thin thread edges, what can I use?

✔ The Magnetic Pen is not as accurate as the human eye. Remember that paths are straight, smooth lines. If a shape has fuzzy edges, transparent areas, and shadows, you might need to work with grayscale masks. (See Chapter 8 for information on masks.)

Can you close the path without clicking the last point?

✔ Yes. You have two ways to do so. If you double-click, the path automatically closes while attempting to follow any edges it finds along the way. If you press the Opt (Mac) or Alt (Windows) key and click the first point, the path closes and places a straight line between the first and last points.

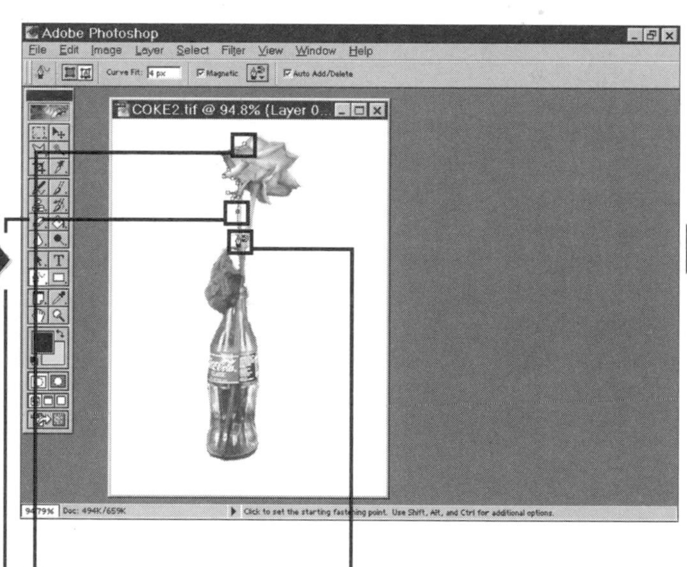

7 Click to set the start point.

8 Release the mouse button and move the cursor along the edge.

■ The path automatically begins to attach itself to the edge.

■ You can click the mouse to change direction of the path.

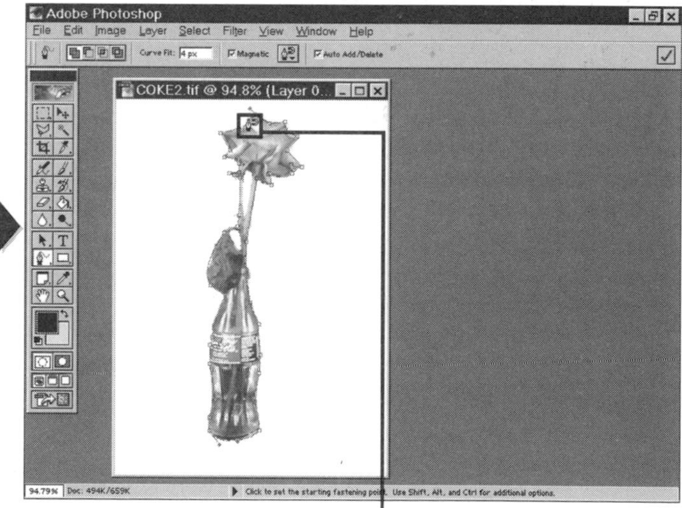

■ To erase the most recent anchor points along your path, you can press the Delete or Backspace key. This can be helpful if your path begins to wander from your intended path.

9 To close the path, click the start point.

■ To edit the path, see the section "Edit and Reshape a Path."

EDIT AND RESHAPE A PATH

You can edit and reshape paths by moving and dragging the control points and their handles. Direction handles are attached to control points. A control point can have zero (corner point), one (combination curve-line point), or two handles.

Knowing the structure of curve types makes understanding how to edit them easier. A control point with two handles can be one of three types:

- A smooth curve with its two direction points equidistant but opposed 180 degrees.
- An asymmetrical curve with its direction points of unequal distance but opposed 180 degrees.
- A cusp (corner) point with the two direction points not directly opposed.

If you do not have enough curves, you can add points and adjust the point handles. If you have too many curves, you can subtract points. To change a corner point to a curve, you can add and position the needed control points.

EDIT AND RESHAPE A PATH

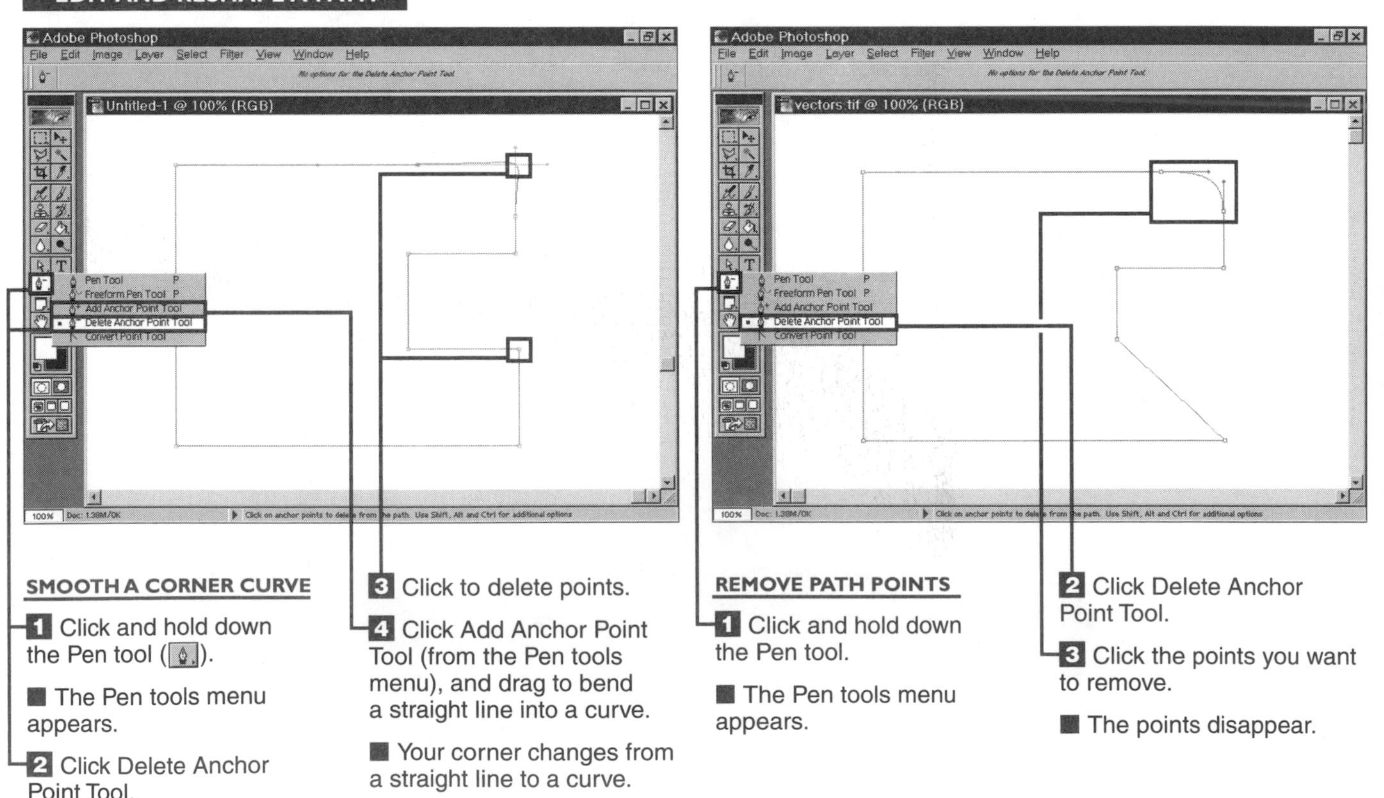

SMOOTH A CORNER CURVE

1 Click and hold down the Pen tool ( ).

■ The Pen tools menu appears.

2 Click Delete Anchor Point Tool.

3 Click to delete points.

4 Click Add Anchor Point Tool (from the Pen tools menu), and drag to bend a straight line into a curve.

■ Your corner changes from a straight line to a curve.

REMOVE PATH POINTS

1 Click and hold down the Pen tool.

■ The Pen tools menu appears.

2 Click Delete Anchor Point Tool.

3 Click the points you want to remove.

■ The points disappear.

How do I transform a path?

✔ Transformations are overall edits, such as scaling, rotating, and stretching. If the path is selected, Photoshop allows you to transform a path by choosing Edit, then Free Transform Path or Edit, Transform Path.

Does Photoshop permit open paths?

✔ Yes. You are no longer forced to close a path. Of course, if you convert a selection to a path, it becomes a closed path. If you want to open it, select a single segment and press the Delete or Backspace key.

Can I join two open paths?

✔ Yes. Click the Pen tool. Click the end point of one of the open paths and, if you want their intersection to be a curve, drag to indicate the direction. Then click an end point of the other open path. Drag if necessary to complete the curve.

Can I edit the shape of a line by dragging the line itself?

✔ Yes. You need to use the Direct Selection tool. Click and drag the Selection tool to make its menu appear. The Direct Selection tool is white.

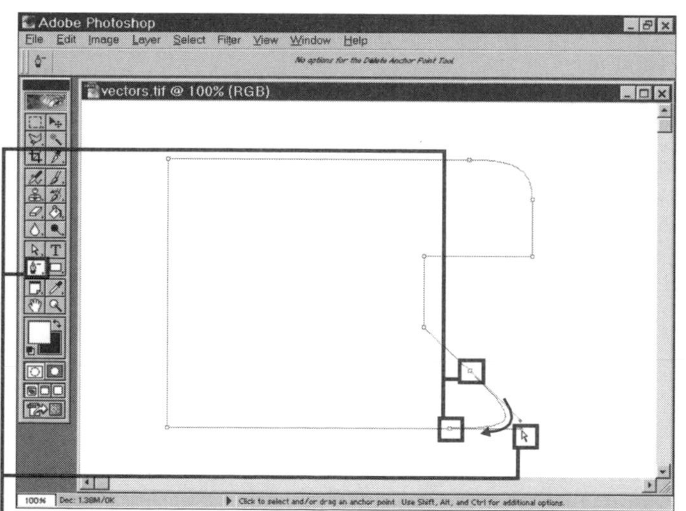

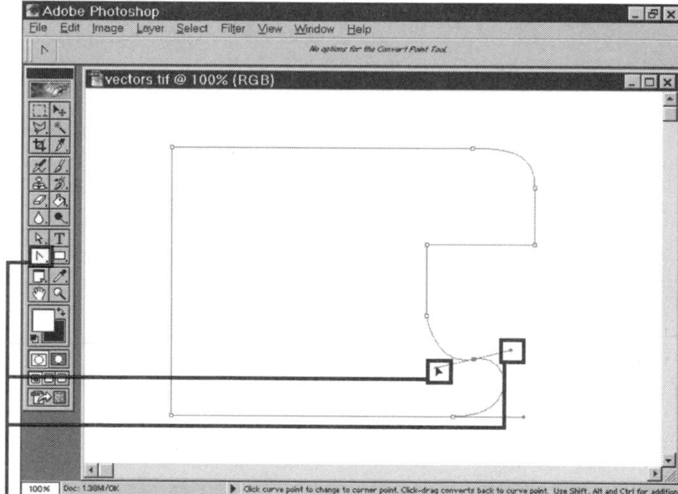

ROUND A CORNER

1 Click the Add Anchor Point Tool ( ) in the Pen tools menu and click to add points to prevent the path from curving.

2 Click the Delete Point tool.

3 Click to delete the corner point.

■ The cursor changes to the selection arrow.

4 Drag the direction points to round the corner as desired.

■ The curve rounds to your specifications.

IRREGULAR CURVES

1 Click the Convert Point Tool in the Pen tools menu.

2 Drag from the control point you want to change.

3 Drag a direction point to reshape the curve.

■ You can drag the opposite direction point to reshape the curve in that direction.

■ The curve changes into an asymmetric curve.

MAKE AND USE A CLIPPING PATH

You can designate a path as a clipping path. Clipping paths trim the image outside the path to give it a nonrectangular shape in a publication. Clipping paths are nothing more than ordinary Photoshop paths that you designate as clipping paths.

A clipping path has no effect in Photoshop. To use the path, you must export the image to a PostScript-based illustration or page-makeup program, such as QuarkXPress, Adobe Illustrator or PageMaker, Macromedia FreeHand, Adobe InDesign or CorelDRAW!.

You can designate any path in the Paths palette as a clipping path. Highlight the path you want to use and choose Clipping Path. The Clipping Path dialog box lets you choose any of the named paths (not working paths).

When you export the file to EPS format, the clipping path goes with it. You can designate it as a clipping path as you are saving in EPS format. PageMaker and some other programs also recognize clipping paths saved to TIFF format.

MAKE AND USE A CLIPPING PATH

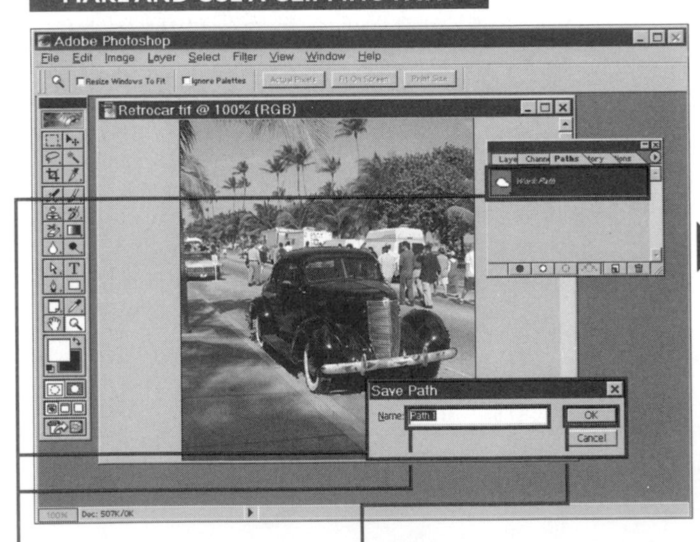

CREATE A PATH

1 Double-click the path's name bar.

■ The Save Path dialog box appears.

2 Type a new name for the path or accept the default.

■ By default, Photoshop automatically numbers paths.

3 Click OK.

■ Photoshop saves the path with the new name.

CONVERT TO A CLIPPING PATH

4 Click Clipping Path in the Paths palette menu to display its dialog box.

■ Type a flatness value to convert the path into a series of polygons.

■ You can leave this option blank and let the output device decide what flatness to apply.

5 Click OK.

■ Photoshop designates your path as a clipping path.

EXPORT AND SAVE PATHS

You can export the paths you draw in Photoshop to virtually all vector illustration programs, including Web animation programs, such as Macromedia Flash and Adobe LiveMotion. Their space efficiency makes them a good way to keep your saved selections while eliminating alpha channels in favor of file size. However, exporting paths may cause you to lose virtually all softness or transparency you might have in your masks.

Saving a path takes so little disk space that you can save a number of them without seeing a difference in overall file size. If you make a lot of selections for later use, convert them to paths and save them. Converting them back to selections is much easier than making the selection all over again.

To export paths to Illustrator, choose File, then Export to Illustrator. The Export Paths dialog box is typical of all file-saving dialog boxes except that you can choose to export a specific path, all paths, or the document boundaries.

EXPORT AND SAVE PATHS

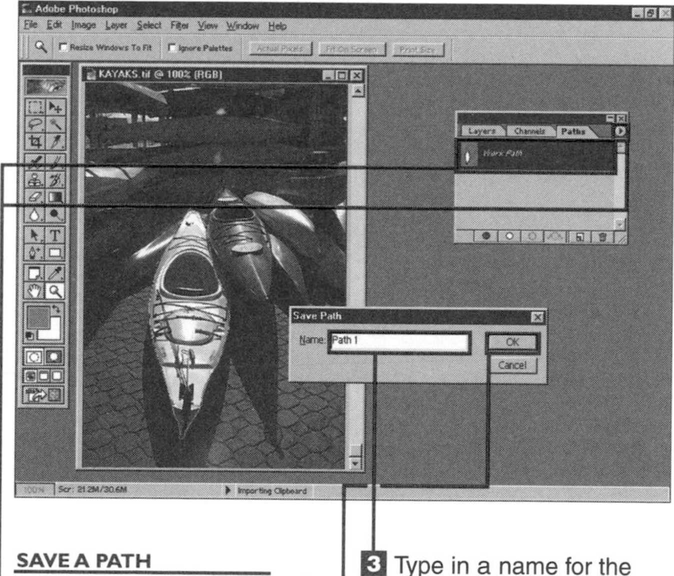

SAVE A PATH

1 Click the workpath.

2 Click (▶) and click Save Path.

■ The Save Path dialog box appears.

3 Type in a name for the path or accept the default.

4 Click OK.

■ Photoshop saves your path in a file.

EXPORT A PATH TO ILLUSTRATOR

1 Choose File, then Export, then Paths to Illustrator.

■ The Export Paths (Mac) or Save (Windows) dialog box appears.

2 Click the path you want to export in the Path box.

3 Navigate to the directory in which you want to save the file.

4 Click OK (Mac) or Save (Windows).

■ Photoshop saves your path to Illustrator.

PAINT A PATH

You can paint along an existing path using any of Photoshop's paintbrushes. You can also fill the space inside the path. This technique is very much like filling or stroking a selection, but with important differences.

When you stroke a path, the stroke uses the foreground color, and you can specify the width. You can also choose which brush and brush style to use — including the Pattern Clone, History Brush, and Darkroom tools. All the settings currently in effect for that brush are applied.

When you fill a path, your only options are to anti-alias the outline and to feather the edges of the fill. Nonetheless, this command is very useful. You can use it to shade and feather channel masks that you save as paths.

You can also use paths and selections in combination with one another. If you fill a path and a selection overlaps it, Photoshop only fills that part of the path inside the selection. You can use this technique to paint a variety of shapes, using only a single mask.

PAINT A PATH

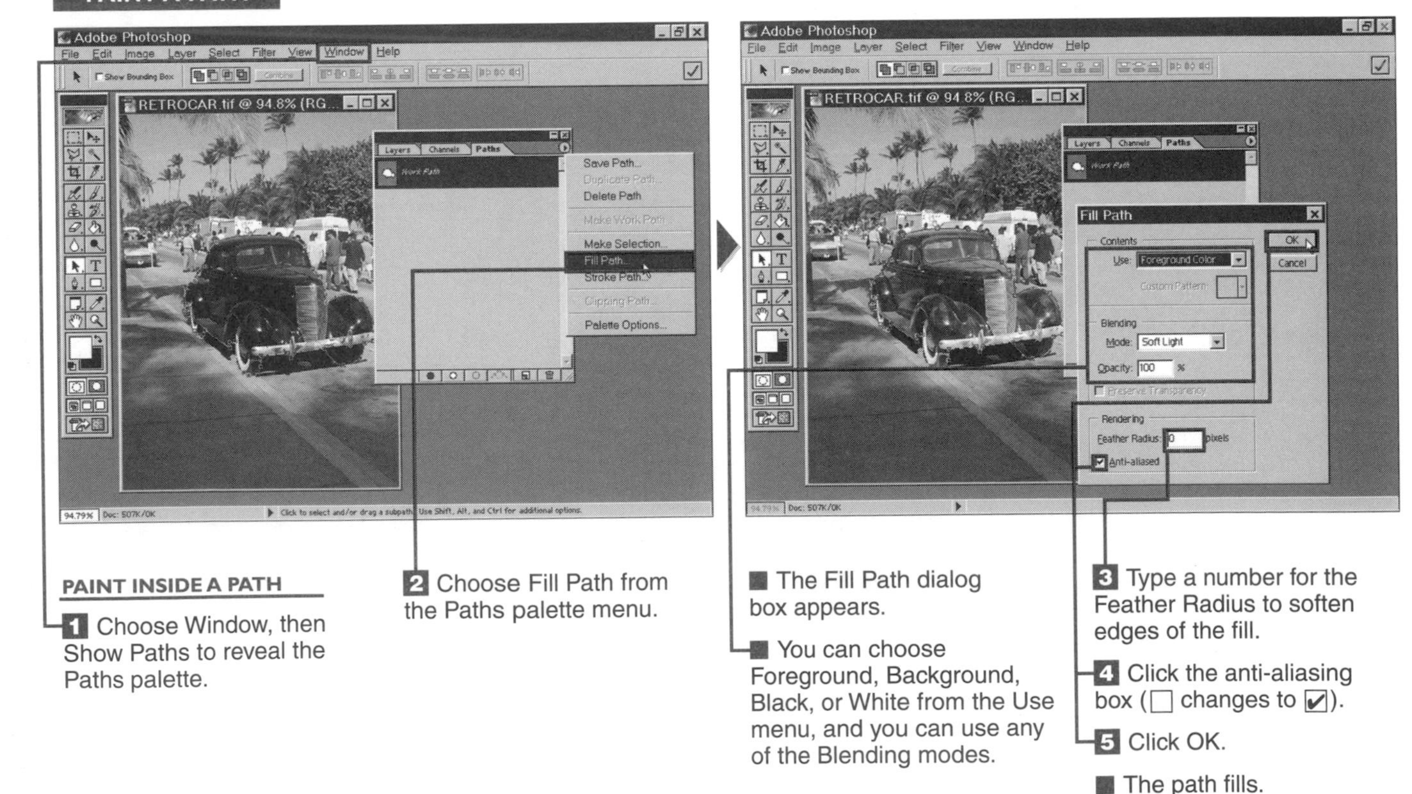

PAINT INSIDE A PATH

1 Choose Window, then Show Paths to reveal the Paths palette.

2 Choose Fill Path from the Paths palette menu.

■ The Fill Path dialog box appears.

■ You can choose Foreground, Background, Black, or White from the Use menu, and you can use any of the Blending modes.

3 Type a number for the Feather Radius to soften edges of the fill.

4 Click the anti-aliasing box (☐ changes to ☑).

5 Click OK.

■ The path fills.

Should I just save every selection I make as a path, even if I cannot imagine ever using it again?

✔ Doing so is probably a good idea. You can always turn a path back into a selection and modify the selection in less time than it takes to make the whole selection again. Even if you only need a hand-painted grayscale mask, starting with a pre-made selection saves you time.

What if I want to transform part of a path?

✔ Click any sequence of points in the path. Choose Edit, then Transform Points. You can use any of the Photoshop transformations, including entering a transformation numerically.

Why I would want to use Fill Path when making alpha channel masks?

✔ You can store dozens of selection shapes as paths and then recall and fill or stroke them in any sequence or arrangement you like. Also, paths use significantly less storage space.

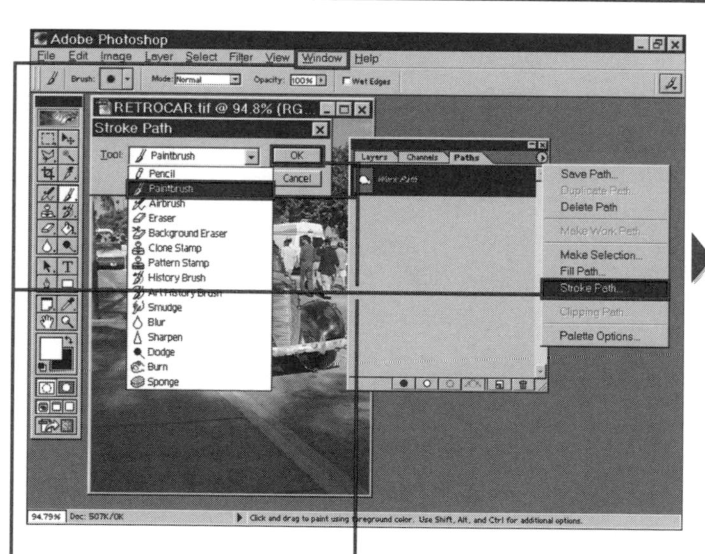

STROKE A PATH

1 Display the Paths palette by choosing Window, then Show Paths.

2 Choose Stroke Path from the Paths palette menu.

■ The Stroke Path dialog box appears.

3 Click a brush type.

4 Click OK.

■ Photoshop strokes the path according to your brush settings. For more about using the brush tools, see Chapter 12.

DRAW AUTOMATIC GEOMETRIC SHAPES

You can draw specific vector shapes by using the new Custom Shapes tools: Rectangle, Rounded Rectangle, Ellipse, Polygon, Line, and Custom Shape. All it takes to draw any of these shapes is to choose the desired tool, click the upper-left corner of the shape, drag a diagonal line, and release the mouse button. To jazz up the shapes, you can treat them with any one of a number of layer styles.

Photoshop has also made these tools amazingly versatile in other ways. This task shows you each of the shapes you can draw as basic vector graphic shapes. This information is good to know for a number of reasons. First, a vector shape is a geometric entity, rather than a mosaic of pixels. So, no matter how many shapes you draw overlapping one another, you can always select and manipulate them as an entity. Also, they will be as high in resolution as the currently available output device. Finally, you can always add and subtract other shapes and control points to create new shapes.

DRAW AUTOMATIC GEOMETRIC SHAPES

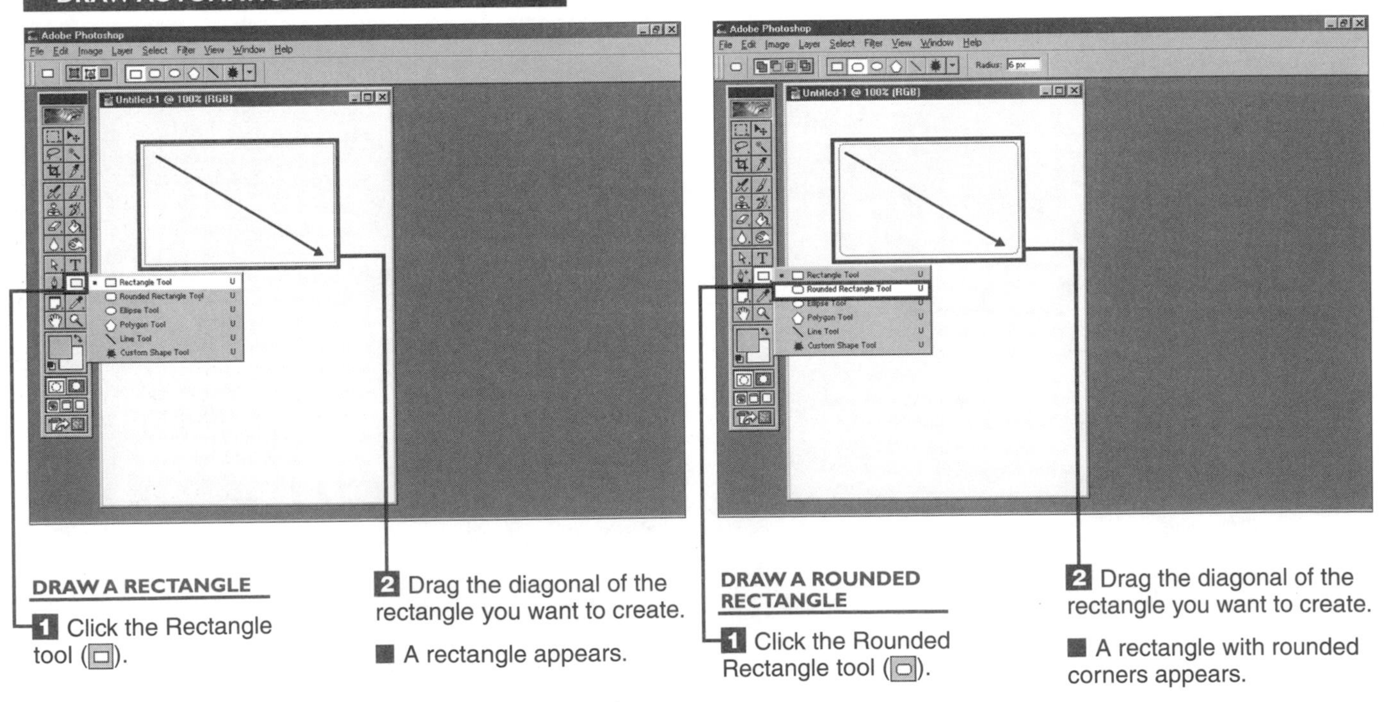

DRAW A RECTANGLE

1 Click the Rectangle tool (▭).

2 Drag the diagonal of the rectangle you want to create.

■ A rectangle appears.

DRAW A ROUNDED RECTANGLE

1 Click the Rounded Rectangle tool (▢).

2 Drag the diagonal of the rectangle you want to create.

■ A rectangle with rounded corners appears.

What if I want to turn one of these shapes into a button?

✔ You can do that by placing the shape on its own layer and then using the Layer Styles command. However, starting by using the Create New Shape Layer mode is much easier.

Why do the shape outlines disappear when I click the Dismiss Target path check box?

✔ You may not always want the vector paths to be visible. If you want to see them again, click their layer in the Paths palette.

Can I edit these shapes?

✔ Yes. They are normal vector paths. You can use the selection arrow tools to make the control points visible and you can use the Pen tools to add points, subtract points, and to move the control point handles.

Are these paths always stored in the Paths palette, even if I cannot see them in the workspace?

✔ Yes, as long as you keep the file in Photoshop file format.

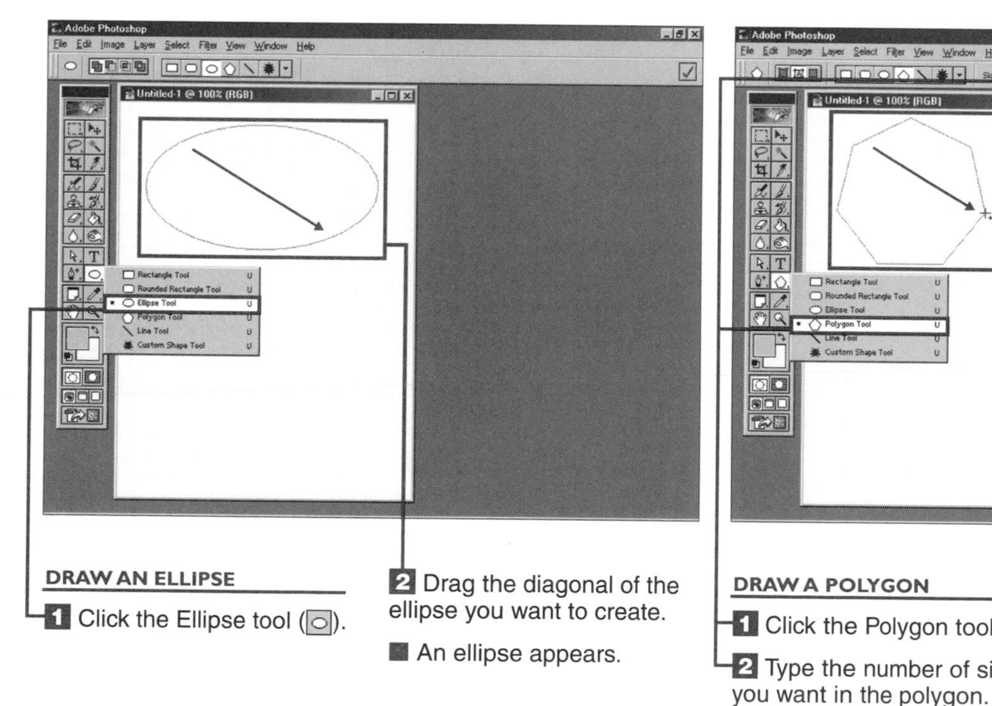

DRAW AN ELLIPSE

1 Click the Ellipse tool (◯).

2 Drag the diagonal of the ellipse you want to create.

■ An ellipse appears.

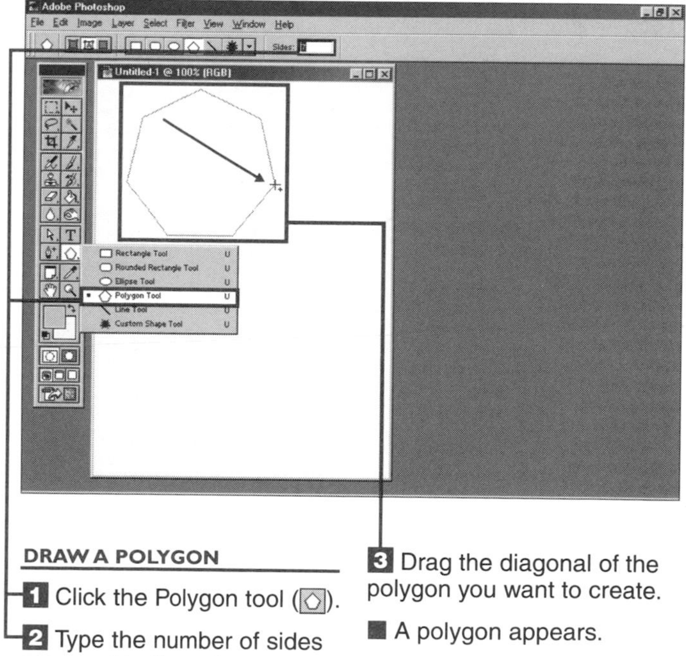

DRAW A POLYGON

1 Click the Polygon tool (⬡).

2 Type the number of sides you want in the polygon.

3 Drag the diagonal of the polygon you want to create.

■ A polygon appears.

EDIT AND RESHAPE A SHAPE

You can easily edit and reshape paths, whether drawn with the Pen tools or the shape tools. The tools you use to select the path for editing are the Direct Selection tool (white arrow) and the Path Component Selection tool (black arrow). The tools you use to reshape the path itself are the Pen tools, including the Pen, Add Anchor Point, Delete Anchor Point, and Convert Point tools.

If you have been drawing paths with the Pen tools and editing them, you are already familiar with the procedure. If you are just starting to draw paths or are beginning to experiment with the shape tools, this task will get you up to speed.

Even if you have little drawing experience, making simple drawings is easy when you can simply modify a path. It is also a quick and easy way to make custom shapes.

You can use the techniques illustrated in this section to modify any of the basic geometric shapes: rectangle, rounded rectangle, ellipse, and polygon.

EDIT AND RESHAPE A SHAPE

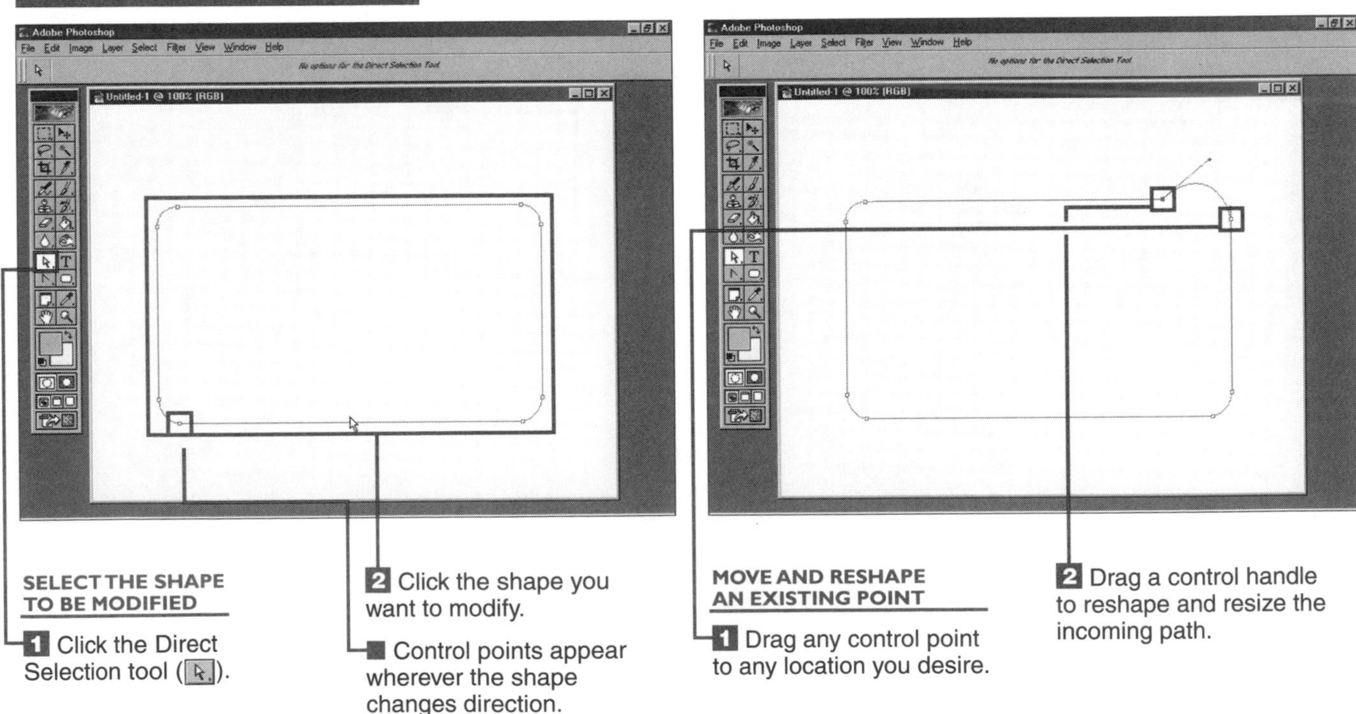

SELECT THE SHAPE TO BE MODIFIED

1 Click the Direct Selection tool ( ).

2 Click the shape you want to modify.

■ Control points appear wherever the shape changes direction.

MOVE AND RESHAPE AN EXISTING POINT

1 Drag any control point to any location you desire.

2 Drag a control handle to reshape and resize the incoming path.

Can I drag a line to change the shape of a path?

✔ Yes, you can. If you drag a straight line, you can move it perpendicular to its original position and the rest of the shape stretches to accommodate the move.

What if I drag a curved line?

✔ The control handles at either end of the line move as the line bends into a new shape. It is more intuitive to drag the curve, but more precise to reshape the line by dragging the control handles.

What does the Delete Anchor Point tool do?

✔ The Delete Anchor Point tool completely removes the anchor point. When you remove an anchor point, the object reshapes to stretch between the two points that had been adjacent to the deleted point.

Does Photoshop provide a way to cut a line into two segments?

✔ Not yet.

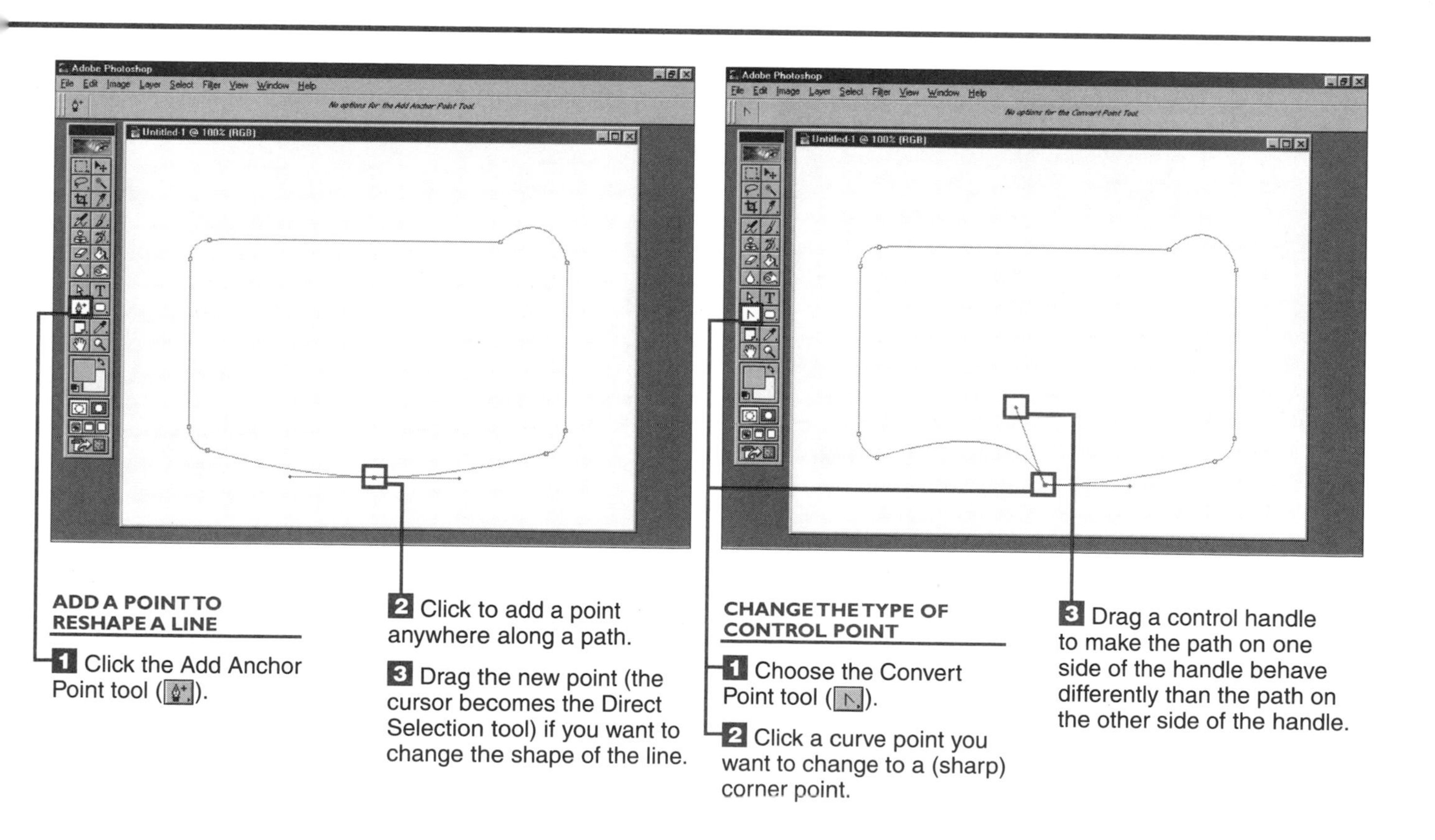

ADD A POINT TO RESHAPE A LINE

1 Click the Add Anchor Point tool ( ).

2 Click to add a point anywhere along a path.

3 Drag the new point (the cursor becomes the Direct Selection tool) if you want to change the shape of the line.

CHANGE THE TYPE OF CONTROL POINT

1 Choose the Convert Point tool ( ).

2 Click a curve point you want to change to a (sharp) corner point.

3 Drag a control handle to make the path on one side of the handle behave differently than the path on the other side of the handle.

MAKE RASTER SHAPES WITH PATH TOOLS

With Photoshop 6, you can use all the shape drawing tools to draw bitmapped shapes directly. No longer must you first convert a workpath to a selection and then fill or trace it. This capability is restricted to the shape tools and does not yet apply to shapes drawn with the Pen tools. However, you can use a Pen tool to create a custom shape—and then save it as a custom shape.

Raster shapes are handy for making custom brushes or for making small atmospheric elements. They are also useful for making symbols, such as company logos or tattoos, when you want to attach them to objects in a photograph.

Creating raster shapes on their own layer is a good idea. You always have the option to apply a layer style to the object or to use a layer Blend mode and layer transparency for compositing a shape to another object.

You can use Blend modes and transparency settings right on the Options bar when you draw the object. The difference is that by putting the object on its own layer, you can exercise or change those options at any time.

MAKE RASTER SHAPES WITH PATH TOOLS

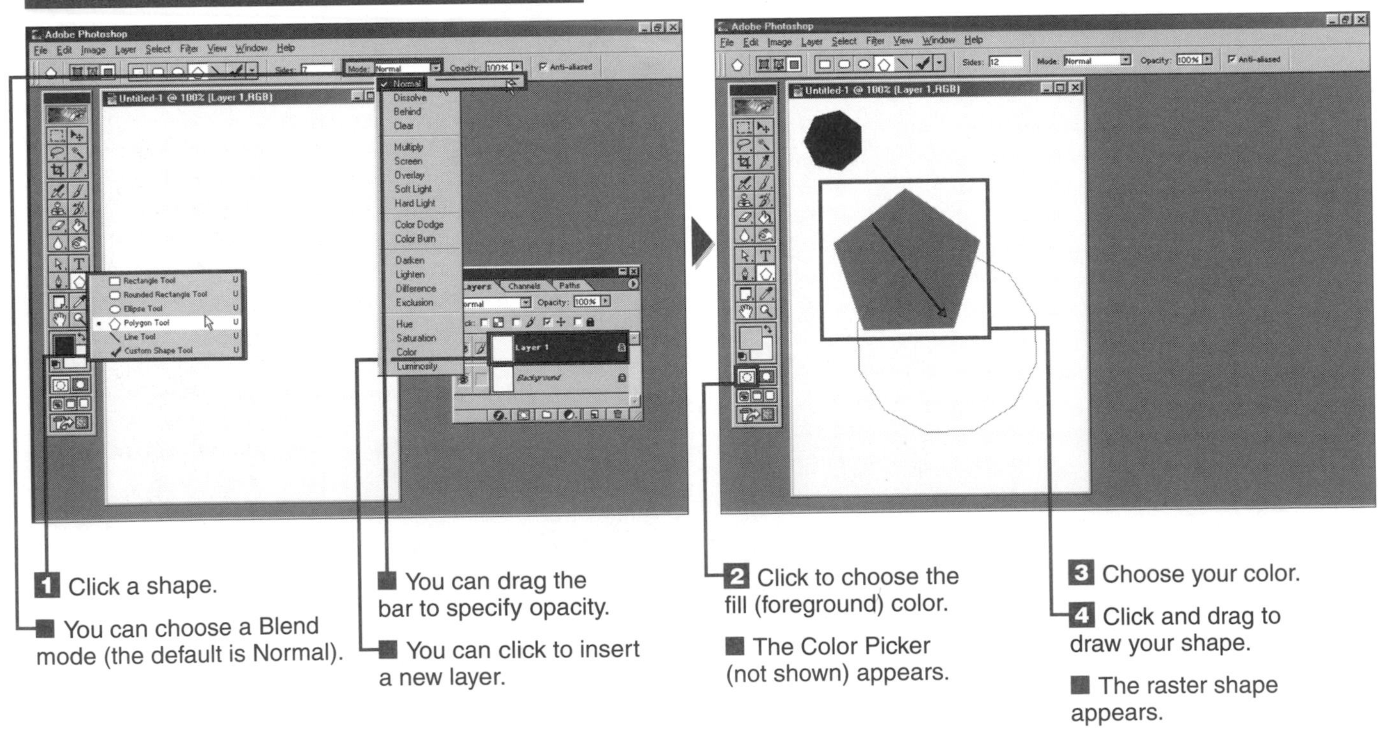

1 Click a shape.

■ You can choose a Blend mode (the default is Normal).

■ You can drag the bar to specify opacity.

■ You can click to insert a new layer.

2 Click to choose the fill (foreground) color.

■ The Color Picker (not shown) appears.

3 Choose your color.

4 Click and drag to draw your shape.

■ The raster shape appears.

DRAW WITH CUSTOM SHAPES

You can turn any work path you have created in Photoshop into a custom shape. Then you can draw that shape just as easily as if it were a simple rectangle. You just use the custom shape tool and then choose the custom shape from a menu.

You can copy, paste, and rescale any vector shape into any number of other locations. However, you can save custom shapes, such as arrows, buttons, and symbols into separate libraries. Then you can load, unload, and exchange libraries. To save a workpath as a custom shape, you simply select its path in the Path palette and then choose Edit, then Define Custom Shape. A dialog box immediately pops up allowing you to name the shape. At the same time, the shape automatically appears on the custom shapes menu.

You create new libraries of custom shapes by deleting the old shapes, creating new ones, and then choosing Save Shapes from the Custom Shapes pop-up palette menu.

DRAW WITH CUSTOM SHAPES

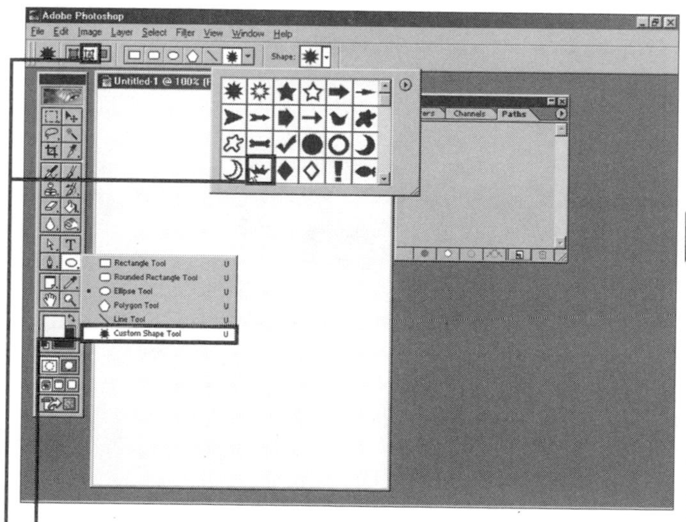

1 Click and drag to choose the Custom Shape Tool (✹).

2 Click the New Workpath button.

3 Click the shape you want from the Custom Shapes palette.

■ In this example, we've first loaded additional custom shapes by selecting Load Shapes from the Shapes drop-down menu.

Note: Keeping the Paths palette open when working with paths is always a good idea so that you can access its commands more readily.

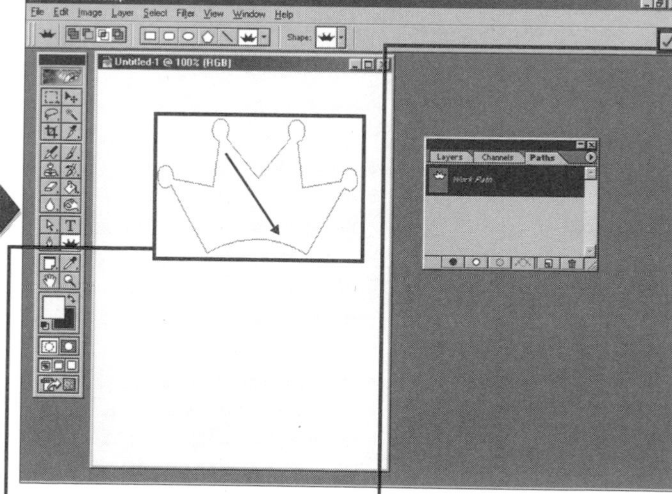

4 Click and drag.

■ Changing the angle and distance of the drag changes the size and proportion of the shape.

5 Click the Dismiss button to hide the shape and permanently store it in the Paths palette.

■ The path reappears when selected in the Paths palette (the workpath is highlighted).

INTRODUCING MASKS

Masks are grayscale images that allow you to restrict any of Photoshop's commands, tools, or filters to the portion of the current layer that is not completely blocked by that portion of the mask image that is not solid black.

Selections and masks are essentially the same, with two distinctions:

- A selection does not become a permanent mask until it is saved to an *alpha channel*, or a noncomposite channel not needed for recording a file's color information. (See Chapter 10 for more about channels.) As soon as you save a selection, you have made a grayscale, alpha-channel mask.
- Masks are more editable than selections (although both are highly editable), because masks are actually bitmapped images that you can modify with any of Photoshop's tools and commands.

To help you visualize how masks work, this figure shows a mask made by saving a selection.

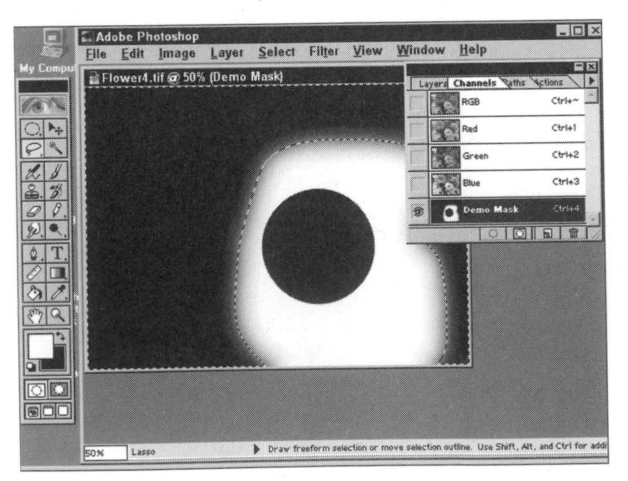

This selection was made with the Lasso tool and then edited with the Elliptical Marquee tool. The selection made with the Lasso tool was feathered by 20 pixels, so the mask, which is white on the inside, fades to black on the outside. The selection made with the Elliptical Marquee tool is unfeathered and was subtracted from the first selection, so it cuts a sharp-edged hole into the center of the mask.

Prior to saving, the selection from which the mask was made would behave just as the mask would: The black areas would totally block the effect of any Photoshop command or tool. The white areas would be affected 100 percent by those same commands. The gray areas would be partially affected, in direct proportion to their brightness. This process is demonstrated in the following figure:

White areas are unmasked (100 percent transparent), while black areas are fully masked (100 percent opaque). Gray areas are transparent in inverse proportion to their percentage of gray: If an area is 10 percent gray, the area is 90 percent transparent. Almost anything you do to the image when that mask is active (such as making a brush stroke, adjusting the image, or running a filter) will have only 90 percent of its unmasked effect.

SAVE AND LOAD MASKS

Because a mask is a saved selection, making a mask is very easy. And by saving a selection and making a mask, you can reference a selection repeatedly simply by loading the mask.

As a general rule, save every selection you make, unless you are 100 percent sure you will never need the selection again. Loading a mask — or making changes to an existing mask — is far quicker than making a brand-new selection. More importantly, the selection will remain consistent each time you use it, and you may want to reuse a selection for purposes other than those originally intended.

When you save a mask, you can designate whether you want the mask to be a new channel or be added to, intersected with, or subtracted from another channel.

If you need to mask a group of items, you can either save all the selections as a group or save all the selections individually. The latter gives you more editing flexibility, because you can adjust and filter each mask separately.

SAVE AND LOAD MASKS

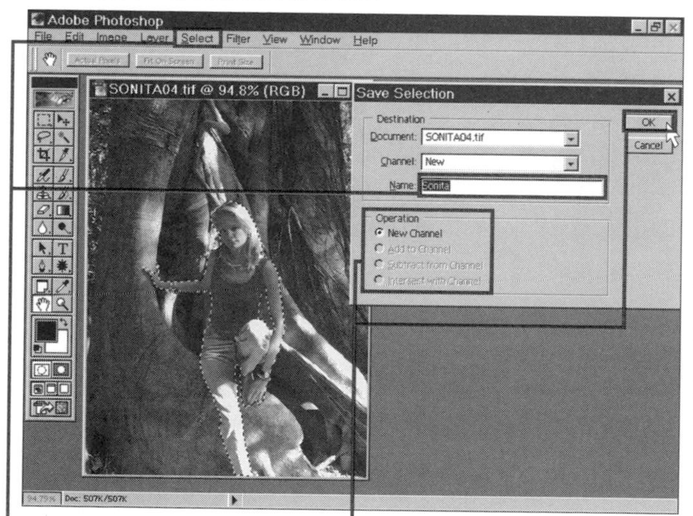

SAVE A SELECTION

1 Choose Select, then Save Selection.

■ The Save Selection dialog box appears.

2 In the Save Selection dialog box, type a name for your mask.

■ If the selection is to interact with another channel, choose the target channel in the Channel box; otherwise, leave it New.

3 Click the appropriate Operation button.

4 Click OK.

RETRIEVE (LOAD) A SELECTION

1 Choose Select, then Load Selection.

■ The Load Selection dialog box appears.

2 Choose the selection in the Channel list.

3 To add to, subtract from, or intersect the current selection with an existing channel, click the appropriate radio button.

4 Click OK.

EDIT MASKS: EDIT EDGES

You can edit a mask with any of Photoshop's commands and tools. Think of a mask as a grayscale painting: the blacker the mask, the more opaque.

The three most commonly used mask editing techniques are

- Blurring edges to control feathering, demonstrated on this page.
- Painting the mask with a brush (see "Edit Masks: Painting with Brushes," next in this chapter).
- Filling the mask, perhaps with a gradient fill (see "Edit Masks: Using Fills," later in this chapter).

This example demonstrates the use of a combination of a blur filter and a selection to make a sharp edge that graduates into the image. This effect is useful for making rounded-edge buttons or for creating the illusion that part of the image is raised from the rest of the image. The example assumes that you have already made a mask.

EDIT MASKS: EDIT EDGES

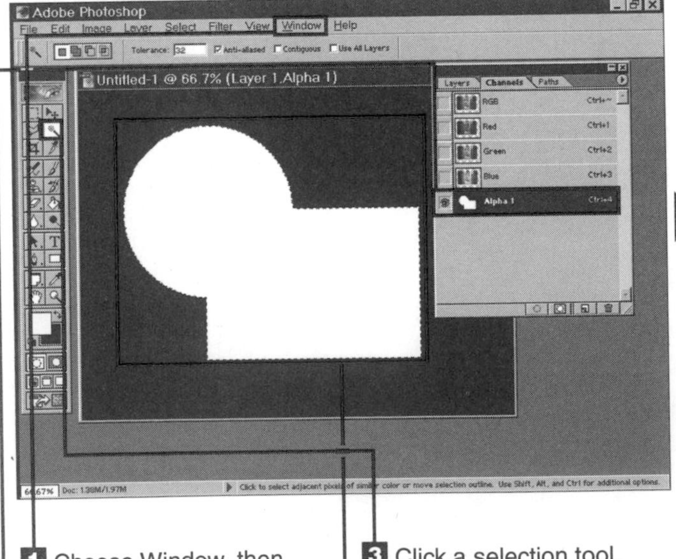

1 Choose Window, then Show Channels.

■ The Channels palette appears.

2 Click to choose the mask you want to edit.

3 Click a selection tool.

4 Click (or drag) to create a selection around the mask segment to be edited.

■ In this example, the Magic Wand tool selects the white portion of the mask.

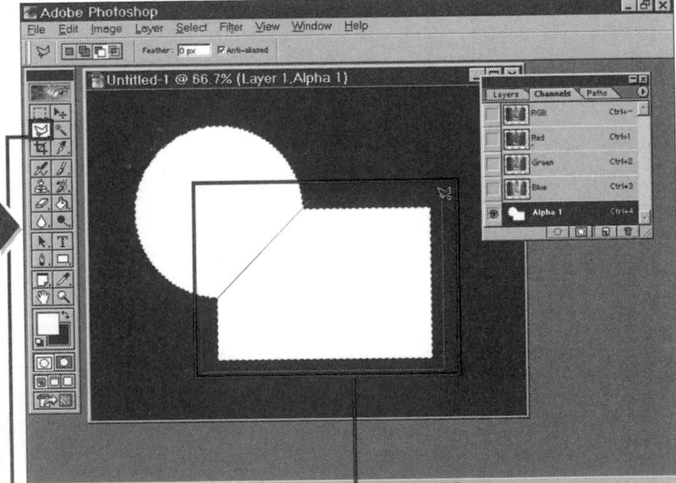

Note: To feather only part of this shape, subtract the part of the selection you want to leave unaffected.

5 Click the appropriate Lasso tool ( ) and select what you want to subtract from the image.

6 Press Opt/Alt to subtract from the selection while clicking or dragging to designate the part of the selection you wish to have subtracted.

Why would I want to use a partially transparent mask?

✔ On occasion you may need to partially blend an effect into its surroundings while limiting the blending to a restricted area. As mentioned, this technique is also excellent for creating the illusion of a rounded edge when making 3D buttons or picture frames.

Can I save a selection made from a mask?

✔ You can save a selection made from a mask in exactly the same way as saving any other selection.

Are there useful variations of the technique shown in this example?

✔ Endless variations exist. The two most useful are limiting the blur to a specific area and blending an effect smoothly with the surrounding area by creating the blur without using a selection.

Can I use a filter effect on a mask?

✔ Absolutely. A filter effect is a good way to "texturize" the mask. You could then paint or fill through the mask to create all manner of effects.

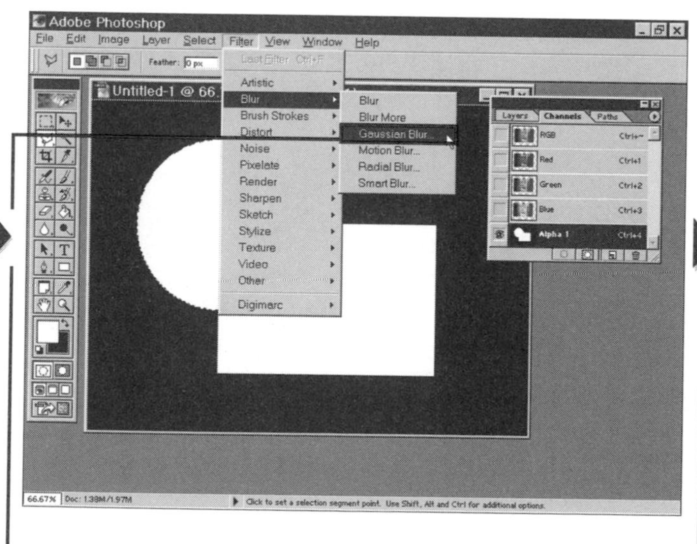

7 Choose Filter, then Blur, then Gaussian Blur.

■ The Gaussian Blur dialog box appears.

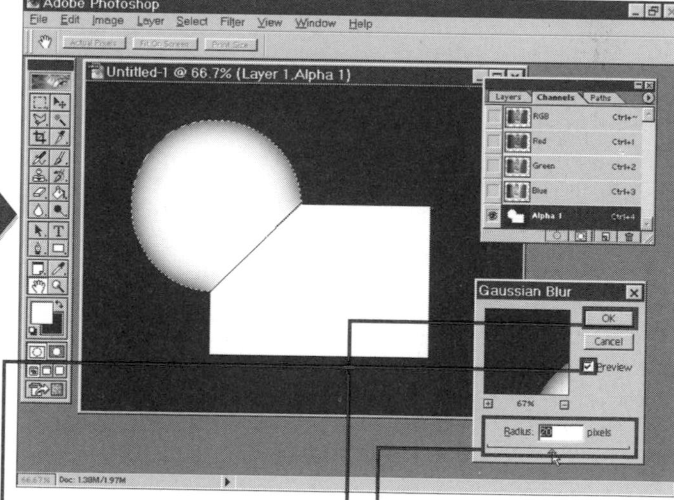

8 Check the Preview check box.

■ You should be able to see the effect of your blurring in the workspace.

9 Drag to the desired level of blur or type a specific pixel radius to the blur.

10 When satisfied, click OK.

EDIT MASKS: PAINT WITH BRUSHES

You may occasionally find simply painting on a mask easier or more intuitive than creating it from a selection. For example, you may want to select a large portion of the image (such as a wall or sky) with the Magic Wand to isolate a contrasting main subject. However, this technique almost always leaves holes in the selection. Fortunately, you can save the selection as a mask and then simply paint out the holes with any of Photoshop's brushes.

You can also use brushes to fine-tune the edges of selections. For example, if an edge is a bit jagged, you can try smoothing it with the Blur brush.

Also, you can simply paint into blank space to create texture or atmospheric effects, such as smoke or raindrops. When you load a selection from such a mask, any subsequent fill or filter will be effective only in the transparent or semitransparent areas of the mask.

You could also texturize areas of the mask by painting with a pattern brush or by using the History or Art History brushes.

EDIT MASKS: PAINT WITH BRUSHES

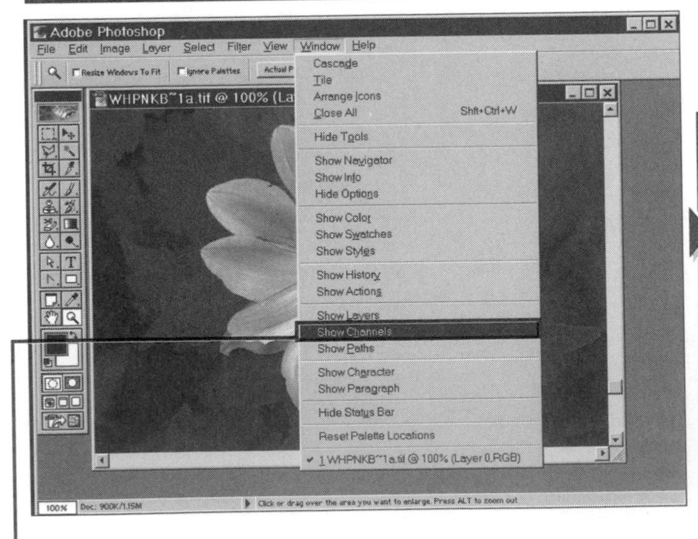

1 Choose Window, then Show Channels.

■ The Channels palette appears.

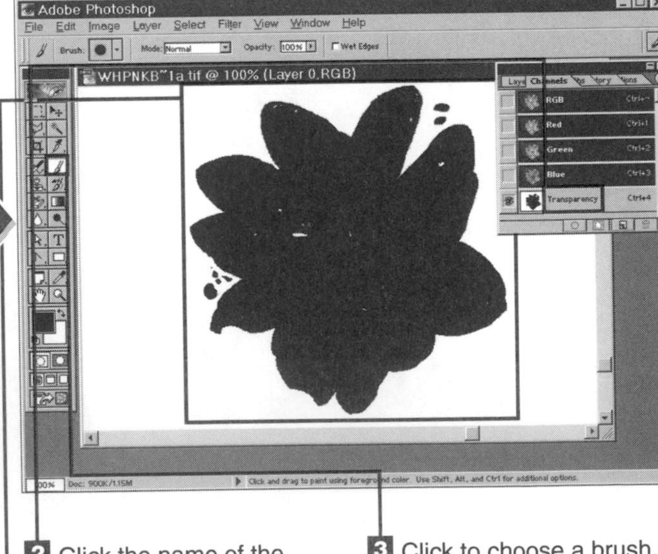

2 Click the name of the mask you want to edit.

■ The mask appears in the workspace.

3 Click to choose a brush.

Note: The Paintbrush and Airbrush are the most commonly used, but you can use any of the tools in this space.

Would eliminating holes by selecting and filling the area surrounding them be simpler than painting on a mask?

✔ That method is often a better solution, but not always. As a rule, painting out holes in small, tight areas is better. You have to decide which works best for you in any given situation.

How do I paint a texture mask and how is it used?

✔ Rough textures, such as graffiti or raindrops, are fairly easy. Choose New Channel from the Channels palette menu and select the newly created channel so that it appears in the workspace. Then paint in your texture, using the Paintbrush, Cloner, Airbrush, or other appropriate tools.

How do I know how transparent a given portion of the mask is?

✔ Select the color with the Eyedropper. Click the foreground color to bring up the Color Picker. Check the brightness percentage in the HSB fields. The percentage of transparency is the additive inverse of the percentage of brightness.

What is the fastest way to blur part of the edge of a mask?

✔ Make a selection around that part that you want to blur. Feather the selection so that the effect of the next step will graduate into the hard edge of the rest of the mask. Finally, use the Gaussian Blur filter to blur that part of the edge that is within the selection.

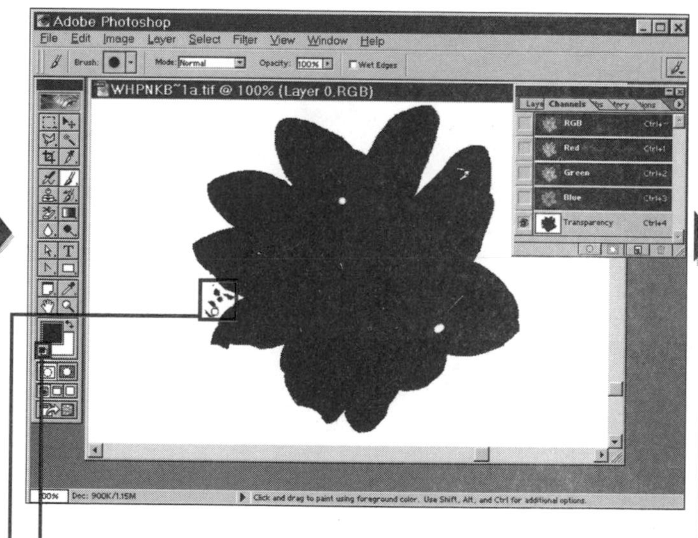

4 Click to switch to default foreground and background colors (white and black) or press D.

5 Drag to paint out any black holes.

■ If you want to paint out white holes in a black portion of the mask, make white the foreground color.

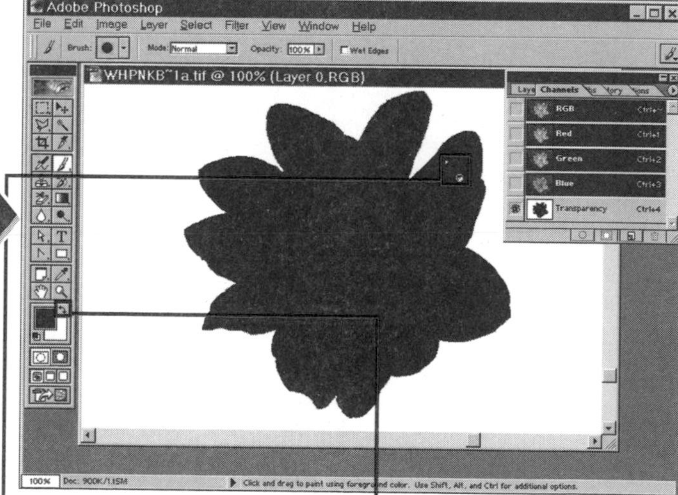

■ If you accidentally paint into an area that should remain unmasked, you have two options. You can Undo (or back up in the History Palette if you went several strokes too far).

■ Or, you can click to switch the foreground color to black.

EDIT MASKS: USING FILLS

You can quickly clean up holes and other "dirt" in masks by using a combination of selections and fills.

For example, to get rid of a large area full of holes or partially masked areas that should be solid, simply surround the area with a quick Lasso selection and fill it with black.

Another type of fill that is useful in masking is the gradient fill. Gradient fills are especially good for blending transitions between images in a collage. Gradient fills are also useful for shading areas that will be adjusted for brightness or color or for areas that will be filtered with a special effect.

Remember that you can combine masks, which means that you can make a mask from a gradient and combine it with other masks specific to individual shapes within the image. The effect of the gradient will be consistent with the position of the object in the overall image.

Finally, you can fill a selected area of a mask with a seamless texture. See Chapter 14, "Working with Textures."

EDIT MASKS: USING FILLS

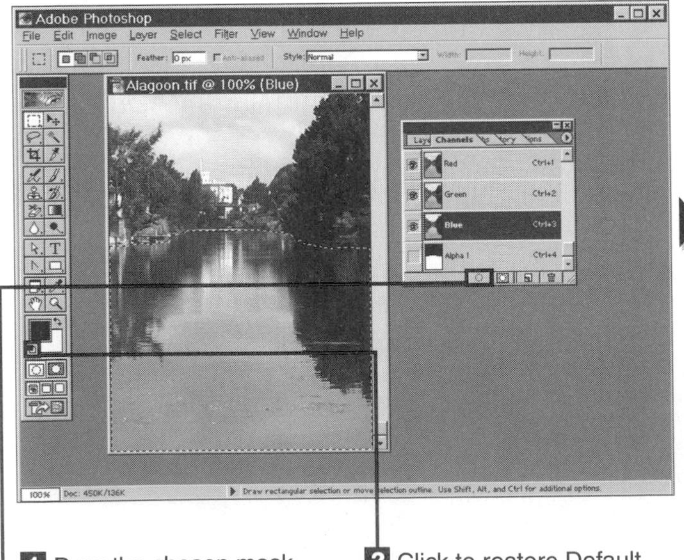

1 Drag the chosen mask to the Make Selection icon.

■ A selection appears in the workspace. Your gradient is restricted to the area within the selection.

2 Click to restore Default colors.

3 Click the Quick Mask icon ( ) to make an orange mask visible over the image.

4 Click the channel name to make the mask the active workspace.

Note: You can still see the full color image under the orange mask.

5 Click to change the Background color.

Can I also paint with the orange mask showing (Quick Mask mode)?

✔ Yes. Actually, painting the orange (or whatever color you use for Quick Mask mode) mask is the best way to correct edges by hand. (Unfortunately, space considerations prevent this technique from being demonstrated here.) Just click the Quick Mask icon in the Toolbox.

Can you give me an example of how I might use a gradient fill?

✔ Suppose you wanted to create a reflection of your subject on one of the surrounding surfaces. If you masked the reflecting surface with a gradient, the "reflection" could be more intense as it receded into the distance — thus making it look more natural.

What other types of fills might prove useful?

✔ You can use a solid fill to restrict the effect of an adjustment, filter, or subsequent brush strokes to the transparency of the filter. You could also achieve the same effect by choosing Filter, then Fade (Last adjustment or filter), but the mask works better when you have to do several operations at the same level of intensity.

Are there any other useful fills?

✔ You can fill with a pattern to create a texture mask. See "Make Texture Masks," later in this chapter, for more information.

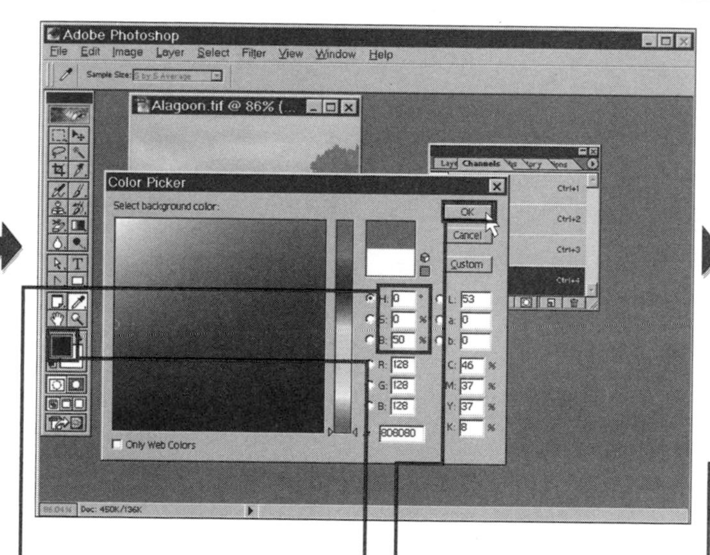

■ The Color Picker dialog box appears.

6 Type in the hue, saturation, and brightness values for your desired background color.

■ Press Tab to jump from one field to the next.

7 Click OK.

8 Click the Foreground chip to again summon the Color Picker, and repeat the selection process for the foreground color.

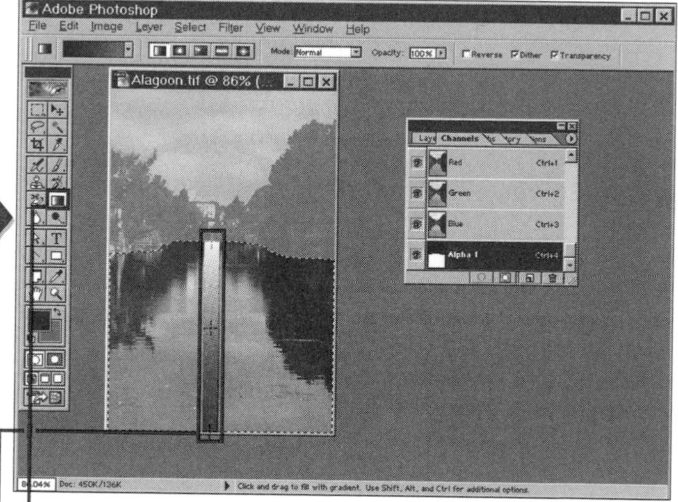

9 Click the Gradient tool (▣).

10 Drag from top to bottom.

■ The mask area fills with a gradient between the foreground and background colors. In Quick Mask mode, you see this effect in translucent orange. To see the full effect in the mask, click the Eye icon and make sure the mask is chosen.

EDIT MASKS WITH QUICK MASK MODE

You can edit a mask in place over your image so that you can see exactly how the edges of your mask register with the edges in your image. You just load the mask as a selection and then click the Quick Mask button to edit it in Quick Mask mode, which shows the mask as a colored (transparent red by default) overlay.

Quick Mask mode has two main benefits over the other mask-editing methods:

- You can edit the mask before you even save the selection (if, indeed, you ever save it).
- You can always see the edits in precise registration with the image, because the mask is represented as a 50 percent transparent solid color overlay.

You edit the mask just as if it were grayscale: black masks, white unmasks, and grays create varying degrees of transparency. Furthermore, all the Photoshop tools and commands are applicable in the same ways.

Also, you can create selections while in Quick Mask mode to limit the extent of your edits. Note, however, that Quick Mask can be set to show selected areas or masked areas — each of which is the inverse of the other.

EDIT MASKS WITH QUICK MASK MODE

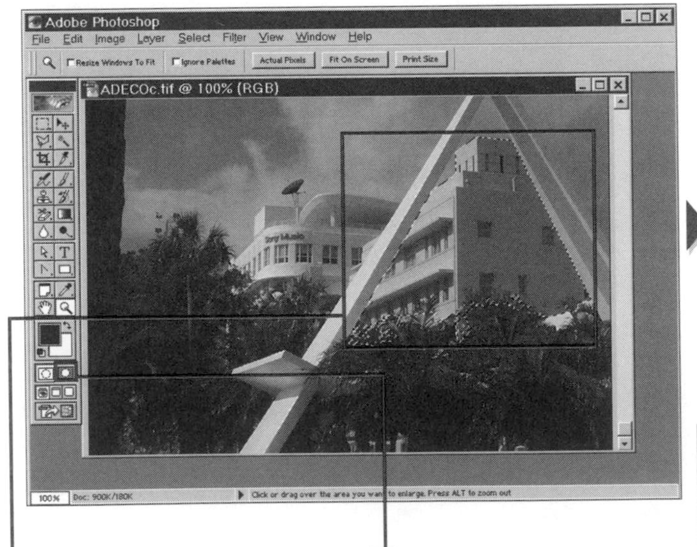

1 Load the selection for the mask you want to edit.

■ In this example, a selection appears in the workspace. Note that the selection leaves some holes in some areas of the mask.

2 Click the Quick Mask icon (◙) or press Q to switch to Quick Mask mode.

■ A transparent red mask appears over the masked portion of the image.

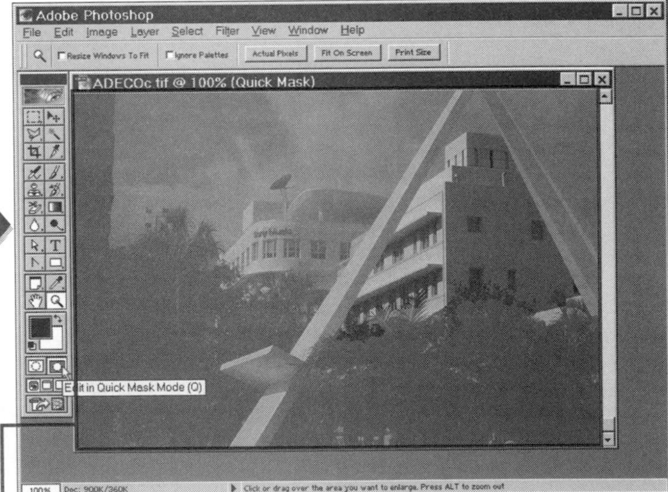

■ The image as it appears in Quick Mask mode. Even in this grayscale version, you can see light areas that the mask does not cover.

3 Zoom in to about 200%.

■ You will likely see small defects in the mask, which you can correct by painting over, erasing, or blurring.

What if I want the mask color to indicate the unmasked area?

✔ You can specify this option in the Quick Mask Options dialog box. Double-click the Quick Mask icon, click the Selected Areas radio button, and then click OK.

Can I change the color of the Quick Mask so that it shows up better against my red subjects?

✔ Easily. Double-click the Quick Mask icon, and the Quick Mask Options dialog box appears. Click in the color box, and the standard Color Picker dialog box appears. You can then choose from any of the 16.8 million colors.

Why do I sometimes see unwanted blotchiness in the image after filling a masked area?

✔ The mask was not really clean. This problem often happens after using automatic masking methods such as third-party masking plug-ins, "blue screen" compositing plug-ins, or the Select, then Color Range command. The blotchiness occurs because the masking algorithm finds certain protected colors inside the area to be masked. Moral: Examine each mask after saving the selection, and make any necessary edits by hand.

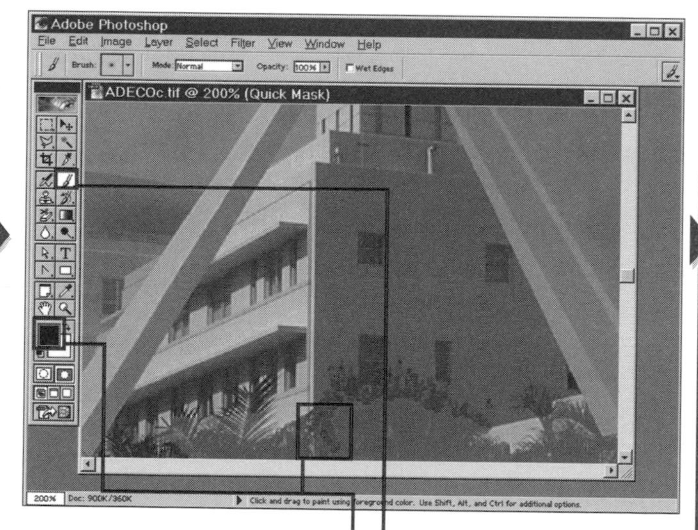

Note: Just as when editing the mask itself, you edit the Quick Mask by choosing black to create opacity (solid red, in this case), white to clear the mask, and gray for any level of transparency in between.

4 Choose the brush with which you want to retouch.

5 Click a shade of gray with which to paint.

6 Paint on or erase the mask.

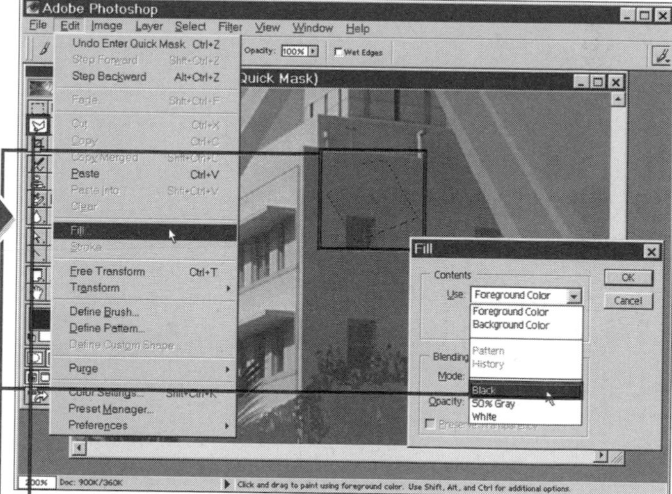

7 To mask large areas uniformly, choose a selection tool.

8 Make the selection.

9 Choose Edit, then Fill, and then Black from the Fill dialog box's Use menu.

■ Any holes in the mask are filled. To clear large areas of the mask, follow the preceding steps, but choose Edit, then Fill, then (from the dialog box) White.

MAKE TEXTURE MASKS

You can use a texture mask to superimpose a texture onto an image. You can create the mask from a photograph, a seamless texture tile, or a special effects filter. You turn the mask into a selection, then fill with colors, patterns, or images.

All you need to do to make the texture mask is to create a new channel and then paste a textured image into it, run a filter compatible with Photoshop on it, and fill it with a pattern tile or simply paint a freehand texture on it.

Because masks are channels, keeping the Channels palette visible (choose Window, then Show Channels) is a good idea. Then you can change the channel mask into a selection by clicking the channel that has the mask you want to use and clicking the Load Channel as Selection button at the bottom of the palette.

To make a texture mask using a brush stroke filter, you need a pattern to stroke. Use the noise filter to create a heavy grain pattern first, and then use any of the other filters, such as the brush stroke filters.

MAKE TEXTURE MASKS

1 Open the file to which you want to add the texture mask and the image that contains the texture.

■ Both must be the same size.

2 Choose Window, then Show Channels.

■ The Channels palette appears.

3 Choose New Channel.

■ The New Channel dialog box appears.

4 Click OK to accept the defaults.

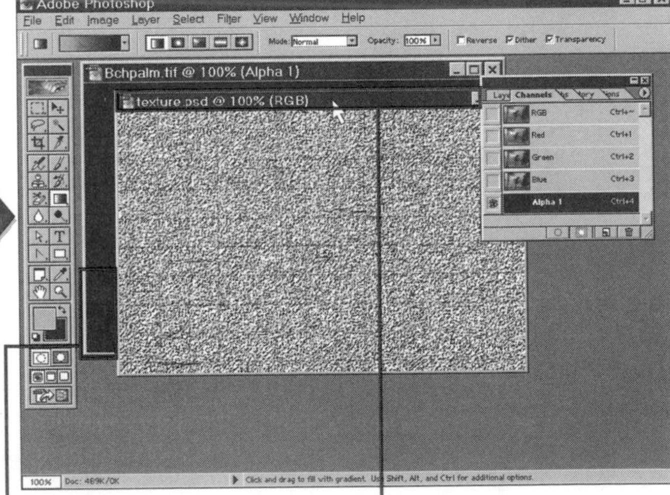

■ The workspace becomes black because the new channel that has been created is the active channel.

5 Activate the texture image window by clicking on its title bar.

What are some good sources for textures?

✔ Try fabrics and papers. You can scan those on a flatbed scanner or photograph them and scan the film. Photographs of textures such as concrete, sand, pebbles, and wood grain are also valuable.

How about some specific examples of how textures might be used?

✔ Using a texture mask, you can simulate the texture of cracked plaster, sand, or watercolor paper; make a photo appear to be lighted through a gauze curtain; or create the appearance of falling raindrops or snowflakes.

Can I use several of these masks in conjunction with one another?

✔ In fact, copying the mask's channel, making it active, and then inverting it (⌘/Ctrl+I) is a good idea. Now you have both positive and negative versions of the texture. Load one of the channels as a selection, press the right and down arrow keys a couple of times to offset the selection, and then save it to the original channel. Now you can fill these two masks with different colors to create highlights and shadows.

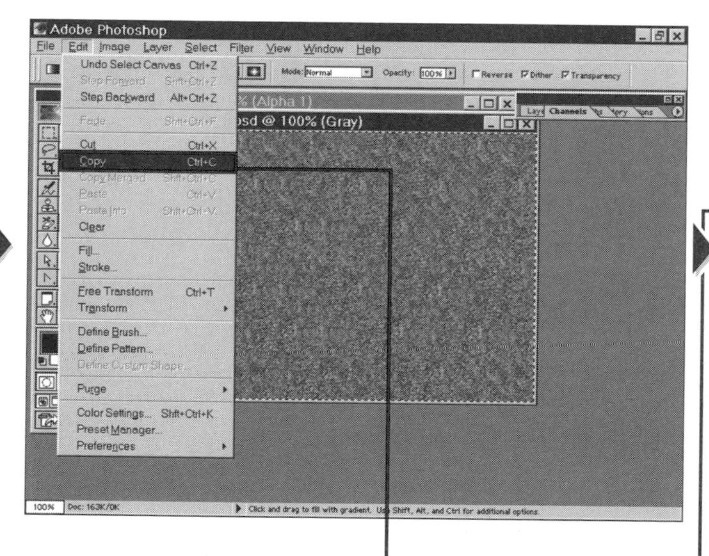

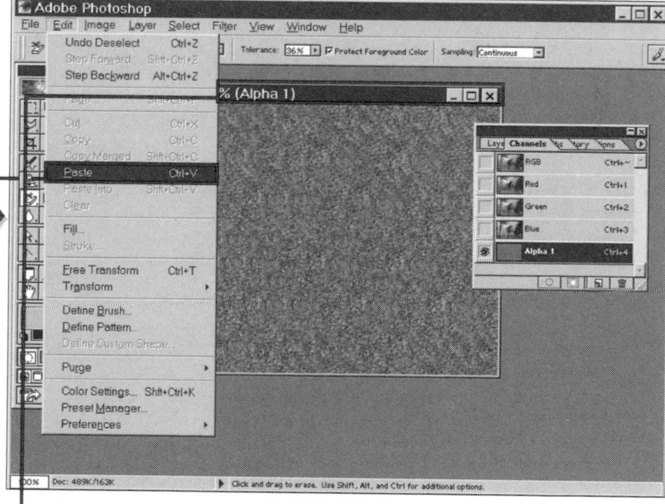

■ Now you need to copy the texture image and paste it into the new channel.

6 Choose Select, then All or press /Ctrl + A.

7 Choose Edit, then Copy or press /Ctrl + C.

■ Photoshop makes a copy of the texture image.

8 Click the target image's title bar to switch windows.

9 Choose Edit, then Paste, or press /Ctrl + V.

■ The texture appears in the new channel.

USING TEXTURE MASKS

You can use texture masks to achieve many different effects — so many, in fact, that the possibilities are limitless. However, understanding the basic principles for using them will give you a solid basis for further experimentation.

Any channel in your image can become an Alpha channel mask. All you have to do is duplicate the channel by selecting it and then clicking the New Channel button at the bottom of the Channels palette.

The same options that apply to the use of any type of mask can also add versatility to your texture masks. Think about layers. You could use the mask selection to cut out portions of layers so one texture is superimposed on another. Or, you could copy the same layer, apply the texture to each in different ways, and then use different transparencies, combine modes, and offsets for each layer.

If you want to move a selection made from a texture mask in small increments, press the arrow keys. Each press will move the mask one screen pixel.

You can apply virtually any Photoshop command to the texture mask. These steps demonstrate the most common: using it to filter a fill.

USING TEXTURE MASKS

1 Open a file that contains a texture mask.

2 If the Channels palette is not visible, choose Window, then Show Channels.

3 Drag the texture channel to the Make Selection icon ( ).

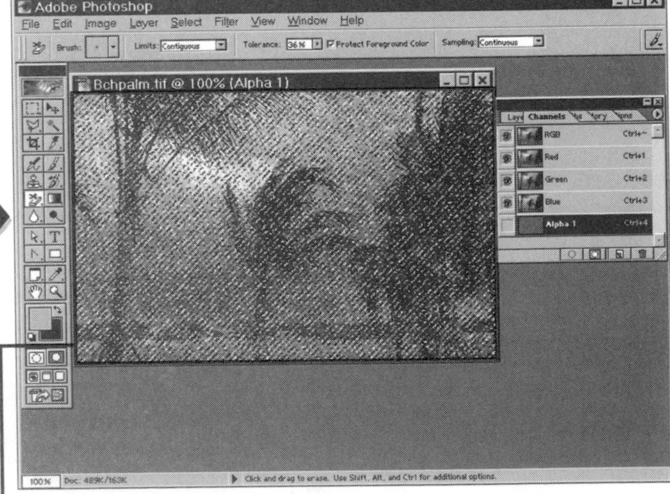

■ The selection appears in the workspace.

Note: If you want to add, subtract, or intersect channels to this selection, choose the next channel you want to combine and click the radio button for the desired operation.

What else can I do with the texture mask besides using it to filter a fill?

✔ The possibilities are endless. For example, you can paint with random colors, or apply an image adjustment. You can also make the texture mask into a layer mask.

What are Blend modes?

✔ They control how the colors in a layer or brush stroke interact with the colors in an underlying image layer or layers by applying mathematical formulae to the interaction of the colors. For instance, multiplying, adding, or subtracting the values of one layer or stroke and the values of the underlying layer(s).

Can I use texture masks to create a 3D texture?

✔ Yes. Use the texture mask on a transparent layer and apply it three times. Use the arrow keys to move it a pixel or two off center and apply a light version of the texture. Then move the mask a pixel or two below center and apply a dark version to create a shadow. Finally, move it back to the original position and apply the normal fill.

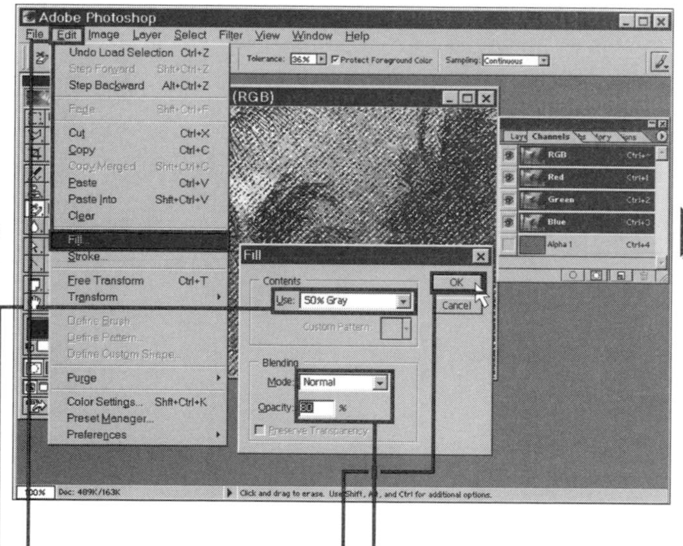

4 Click Edit, then Fill.

■ The Fill dialog box appears.

5 Choose a fill type from the Use menu.

6 Choose a blend mode and type a percentage for opacity.

7 Click OK.

■ The result appears. This example shows the result of applying a 50% gray fill at 80% opacity, using the Multiply Combine mode with the texture mask as a selection.

MAKE A MASK FROM A COLOR CHANNEL

You can make a channel mask from any image. You do so in one of two ways:

- Copy one of the channels in the existing image
- Copy (via the Clipboard) another image into an Alpha channel. You can then use any of Photoshop's tools and commands to modify the resulting Alpha channel mask.

Of course, before you can do any of this, you need to know how to copy a channel to an Alpha channel. The short answer is to drag the Color channel to the New Channel icon at the bottom of the Channels palette.

Suppose you want to knock out a wild-haired author from her background. First, you make a mask of the channel with the most contrast between hair and background. Then, boost the contrast. (Choosing the Image, then Adjust, then Threshold command can help here. See Chapter 8.) Finally, you paint and fill the interior details to mask/unmask areas that are not masked to your liking by the original image.

MAKE A MASK FROM A COLOR CHANNEL

1 Open the file you want to mask.

2 Choose Window, then Show channels.

■ The Channels dialog box appears.

3 Click each channel to see which has the greatest contrast between the desired mask edge and the background.

4 Drag the channel with the most contrast to the Create New Channel icon ( ).

5 Choose Image, then Adjust, then Brightness/Contrast.

■ The Brightness/Contrast dialog box appears. Watch the image to make sure you do not eliminate subtleties in the edge.

6 Click the Preview check box if it is unchecked.

7 Drag the sliders until you see a clean contrast between mask edge and background, then click OK.

What if I cannot adjust the contrast properly for all edges of the selection?

✔ This problem happens when the background changes color or when one side of the subject is in deep shadow and the other is in highlight. You can usually solve the problem by selecting each area separately and then making contrast adjustments for each of the areas.

Can I use adjustments other than Brightness/Contrast?

✔ Fine-tuning your adjustments with the Image, then Adjust Curves or Image, then Adjust Levels commands may be easier. This is especially true when the areas that contrast with the edge are more subtle than those shown here.

What if I get specks when I select a large area with the Magic Wand?

✔ That is pretty common. Choose the Lasso, press Shift (to add to the selection), and make a selection around the holes or specks so they are included in the overall selection. Now, when you fill, the specks will be covered.

What is the best tool to use when I just want to slightly soften the edges of a mask?

✔ While there is no best tool for all situations, the one that helps most frequently is the Blur tool.

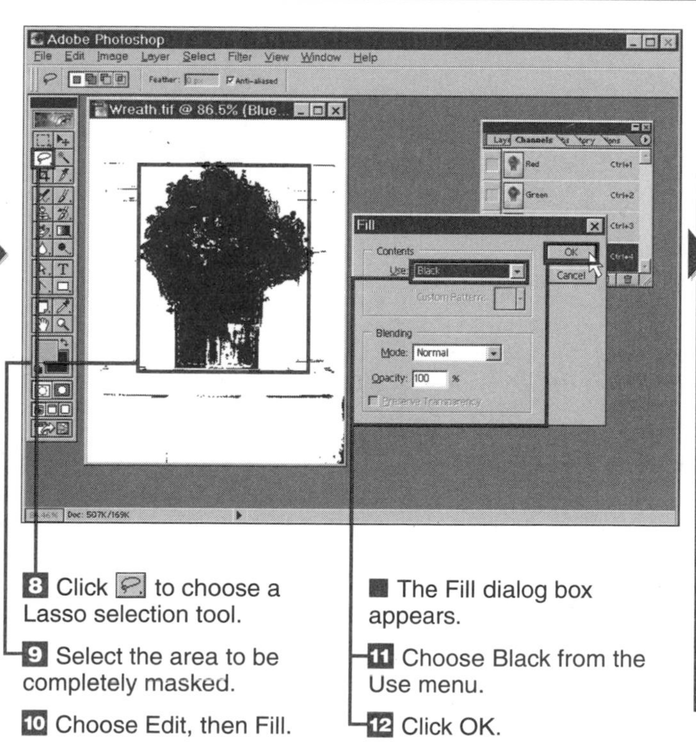

8 Click [lasso icon] to choose a Lasso selection tool.

9 Select the area to be completely masked.

10 Choose Edit, then Fill.

■ The Fill dialog box appears.

11 Choose Black from the Use menu.

12 Click OK.

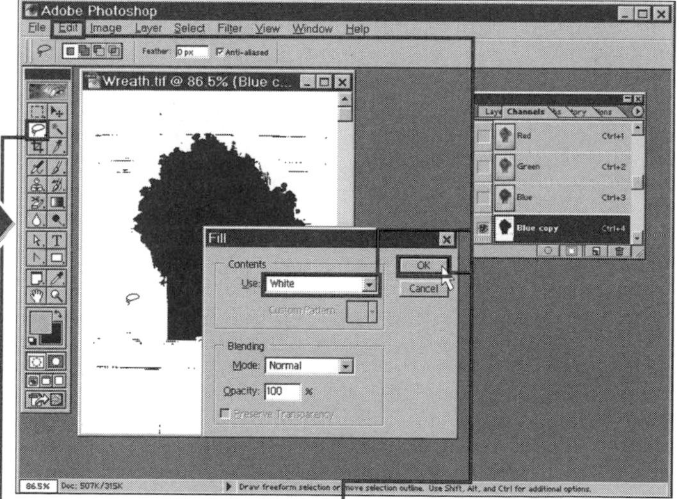

■ There may also be masked (gray) areas in the portion of the mask you wish to make unmasked.

13 Choose a selection tool that will surround the area to be unmasked.

14 Select the area to be unmasked.

15 Choose Edit, then Fill.

16 Choose White from the Use menu.

17 Click OK.

MAKE A THRESHOLD MASK

You can sometimes use an Alpha channel mask to separate a subject from its background.

This technique works best if the subject has been shot against a fairly solid background that is predominantly brighter or darker than the subject, and if that subject has a reasonably hard-edged silhouette.

Choose Image, then Adjust, then Threshold to turn all the shades above a certain threshold to white and all those below it to black. The idea is to make the background a solid white, then invert the channel so that the background is black (masked) and the subject is white (unmasked).

Threshold masks usually work best if the object you want to mask has a narrow range of brightness values that contrast strongly with the subject.

The channel you should duplicate as a mask is the one that is closest in color to that of either the subject or the background. For instance, the flower in these examples is bright fuchsia, so there is considerably more contrast in the red channel.

MAKE A THRESHOLD MASK

1 Open the image you want to mask.

2 Choose Window, then Show Channels.

■ The Channels dialog box appears.

3 Drag the channel with the most contrast between the object you want to mask and its background to the New Channel icon.

■ The channel is duplicated as an Alpha channel, and you should see the mask in the workspace.

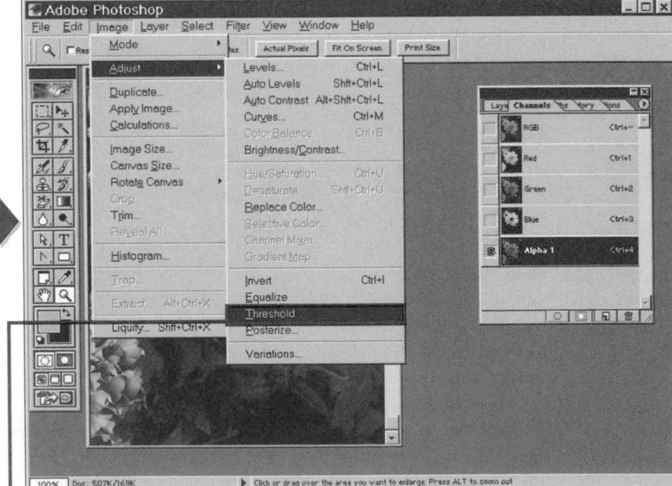

4 Choose Image, then Adjust, then Threshold.

■ The Threshold dialog box appears.

One of the problems with making threshold masks is that the edge quality will be very hard with no anti-aliasing. The masks are often a little bit off or have jagged edges. How can I check and correct for this problem?

✔ Edit in Quick Mask mode. Drag the mask channel to make a selection and click the Quick Mask icon. Press D to restore the default foreground and background colors. Next, use the Paintbrush or the Blur tool to retouch the edges.

Which type of brushes should I use for cleaning up masks?

✔ The block eraser is best for cleaning up larger areas. If you want a soft-edged mask for soft-edged objects, use the Blur tool.

What if the block eraser is too big for retouching?

✔ The block eraser is always the same size, no matter how far you zoom in. So if you want a smaller block eraser, zoom in tighter. Remember, the block eraser always uses the background color.

Is there a quicker way to soften the edges of a Threshold mask?

✔ Yes. If you want to soften the whole mask (or part of it within a selection), try the Blur or Blur More filters to anti-alias the edges.

5 Click the Preview check box if it is unchecked.

6 Drag the slider until your subject is (mostly) white and its surroundings mostly black.

7 Click OK.

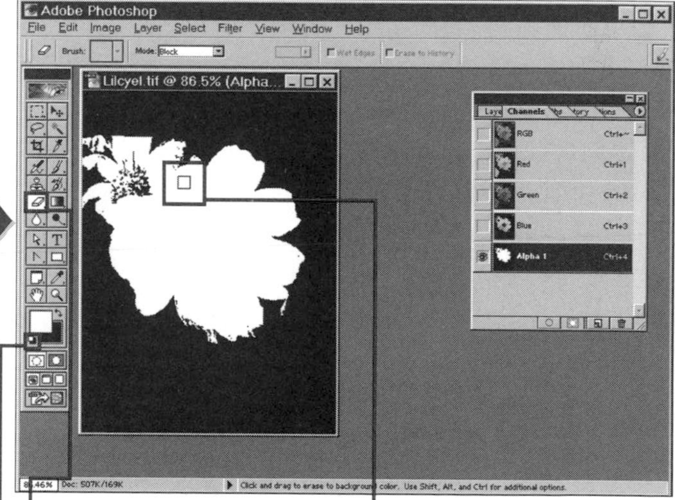

8 Choose the Eraser. Double-click it to show Eraser Options and choose Block from the Mode menu.

9 Click to restore colors (or Press D).

10 Erase unwanted blacks from the unmasked (subject) area.

11 Press X to switch foreground and background colors and erase unwanted whites from the background.

MAKE A LAYER MASK

You can attach one mask (Alpha channel) to a specific layer. Turning on the mask for a layer makes the masked area of the layer transparent, so the subject of the layer floats above the images on underlying layers.

The easiest way to mask a layer is to make a selection, press ⌘/Ctrl+C, and choose Edit, then Paste Into. A new layer is automatically made and the selection shape is the shape of the layer mask. Of course, you can edit that mask by all the methods described in this chapter.

You can also make a mask for any existing layer: In the Layers palette, click the name of the layer you want to activate. Make a selection on the image in the workspace (or in a color channel, if that makes the edges easier to distinguish). Next, while the target layer is still active, click the Make Mask icon at the bottom of the layers palette. Presto! The layer mask's thumbnail appears to the right of the image thumbnail in the Layers palette.

MAKE A LAYER MASK

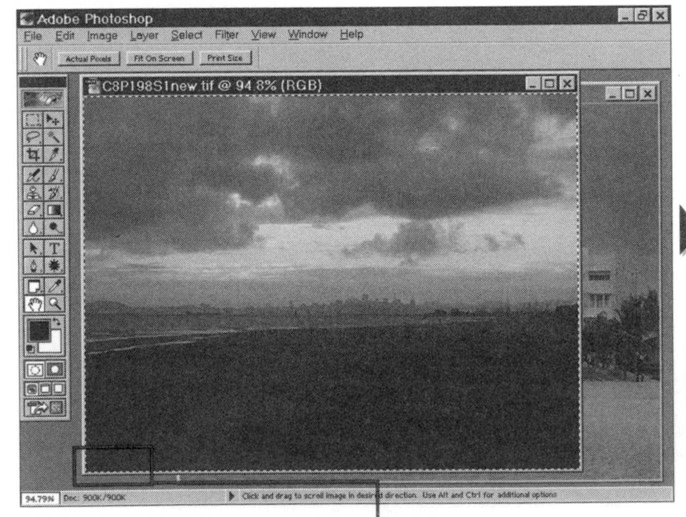

1 Open both the file to which you want to add the layer and the one you want to use as a masked layer.

2 With the layer file window active, press /Ctrl + A to select the entire image.

3 Press /Ctrl + C to copy the selection.

4 Click the target window.

5 Make the selection to paste into.

6 Choose Edit, then Paste Into.

■ The Clipboard image appears inside the selected area, and the selection marquee disappears.

■ A new layer appears in the Layers palette. A mask thumbnail automatically appears to the right of the new layer's image thumbnail.

What advantages does using a layer mask provide over other methods of making portions of a layer transparent?

✔ You can turn the layer mask on and off, making it easy to show two different backgrounds for the same subject.

What if I want to blur the object that is in a layer mask?

✔ Only that part of the blur that is inside the mask will show. Use the Gaussian Blur filter to blur the mask slightly. Then, when you blur the masked object, the edges will be softened as well.

What happens to a layer mask if I make a new selection on that layer and then click the Add Layer Mask icon?

✔ The cursor will turn into a "Cancel" sign and you will be unable to execute the command.

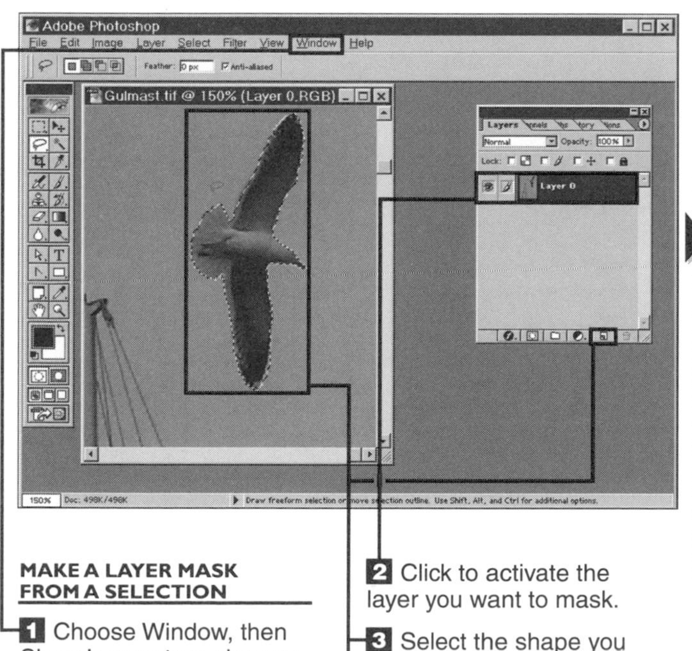

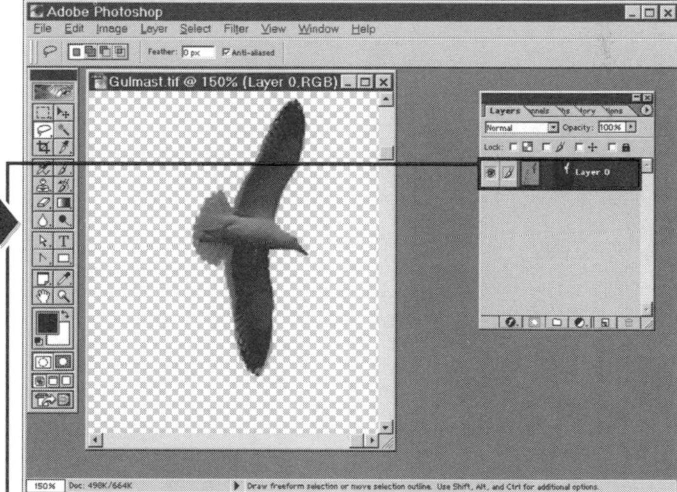

MAKE A LAYER MASK FROM A SELECTION

1 Choose Window, then Show Layers to make sure the Layers palette is visible.

2 Click to activate the layer you want to mask.

3 Select the shape you want to mask.

4 Click the Add Layer Mask button ( ).

■ The layer mask appears here.

■ The masked portions of the layer are invisible to the underlying layers.

CREATE A NEW LAYER

You can create a new layer any time you want to keep one part of an image separate from the rest of the image.

For example, you may want to paste something into an image that you cut out of another image. You might also want to make some annotations using freehand brush strokes that you could erase later.

Several methods exist for creating a new layer. Which method you use depends partly on whether you want an empty (transparent) layer or one that contains a new image.

If you want an empty layer, the easiest way to create a new one is to click the New Layer icon at the bottom of the Layers palette. If you want to duplicate one of the layers in your current image, just drag that layer onto the New Layer icon. If you want to create a new layer from an image in another file, open the other file and drag the image (or a layer from that image) into the current file. The layer from the other file automatically appears as an independent layer in the Layers palette.

CREATE A NEW LAYER

ADD A LAYER FROM ANOTHER FILE

1 Open the image to which you want to add the layer.

2 Open the image from which you want to get a layer.

3 Click the Move tool (▸+).

4 Click and drag the image to the window containing the target image.

■ A new layer appears in the target image's Layers palette.

How do I access the Layers palette?

✔ Choose Window, then click Show Layers.

Why would I want to create a layer that contains nothing?

✔ So that you can create original work on the layer without having that work alter the original. Of course, this work can be simple, such as painting color into an area so you can try using a Blend mode without having the experiment endanger the original.

What is so great about making annotations on a new, empty layer?

✔ You can make annotations about things you would like to do later or annotations for a client or assistant, then erase them from the image when you have finished working on it.

Can you paint on a layer to help with darkroom effects?

✔ Absolutely. You can paint in areas you want to affect, then change the brightness and contrast values of the layer by choosing Image, then Adjust, then Brightness/Contrast.

How do I delete a layer?

✔ You can delete a layer several ways. The easiest way is to drag the layer to the Trash Can icon at the bottom of the Layers palette. You can also click the layer to activate it, then click the Trash Can icon. Or, if you prefer using menus, choose Layer, then click on Delete Layer. You can retrieve a deleted layer as long as the layer is still in the History palette (see Chapter 12).

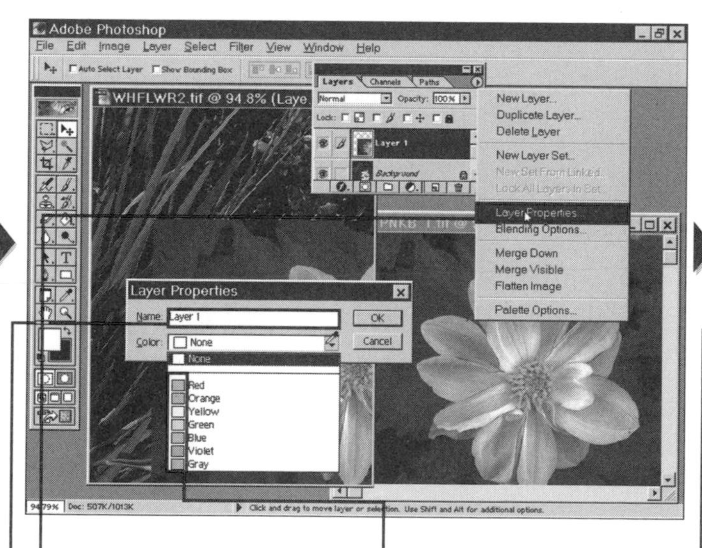

5 To set properties for the new layer, choose Layer Properties from the Layers palette menu.

6 Type a layer name (or accept the default).

■ You can choose a color for the Layer bar in the Layers palette for easy visual identification.

7 To make the layer thumbnail larger so you can more easily distinguish layers, choose Palette Options from the Layers palette menu.

8 Click the thumbnail size you prefer.

9 Click OK.

■ Photoshop creates the new layer.

STACK AND REORDER LAYERS

One of the benefits of layers is that you can change their stacking order easily, enabling you to decide which objects should appear to be in the foreground and which should appear farther back on overlapping layers. Because the visible portions of layers can be any size smaller than the overall image (or, of course, the same size), the ability to stack layers also makes seeing which layers you may want to remove, mask, or partially erase easier.

This exercise shows you how to reorder layers using the Layers palette and gives you some shortcuts to speed things along:

- Opt/Alt+] or [moves up (]) or down ([) one layer at a time.
- Shift+Opt/Alt+] or [takes you to the top (]) or the bottom ([) of the stack.
- ⌘/Ctrl+Opt/Alt+click takes you directly to the layer you clicked.

Pressing Ctrl+click (Mac) or right-clicking when using the Move tool over any layer brings up a context-sensitive menu of the layers under the cursor.

STACK AND REORDER LAYERS

MOVE A LAYER BETWEEN TWO TARGET LAYERS

1 Drag the layer name bar into the target position.

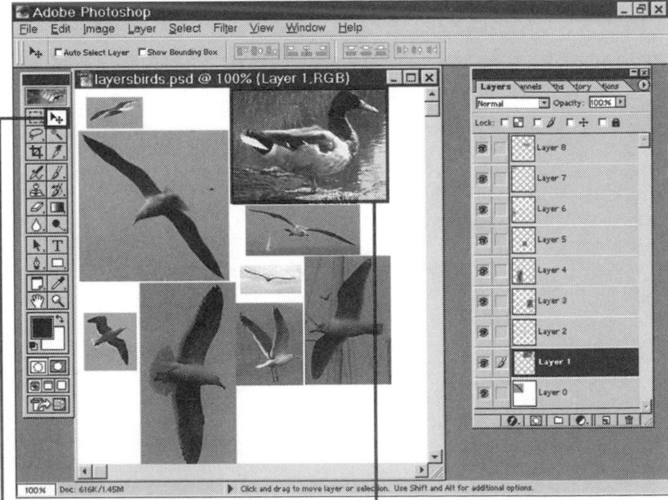

MOVE THE LAYER IN RESPECT TO THE OVERALL IMAGE

1 Click the Move tool (or press V).

2 Drag the desired image to reposition it.

SHOW AND HIDE LAYERS

You can show or hide layers simply by clicking the Eye icon in the Layers palette. If you can see the Eye icon, you can see the layer.

At times, you may want to show some layers and hide others for these reasons:

- To see and work on all of a layer without changing its stacking order.
- To change the apparent distance of objects from the viewer.
- To merge or link a select number of layers.

If operations are slowing down because you have too many layers, you can remove layers from the file without changing them. Create a new file (⌘/Ctrl+N) and enter dimensions large enough for the biggest layer. Drag the layers you want to set aside to the new file, and then (in the original file) drag them to the trash. Name and save the new file. When you are ready, you can open the original file and drag the layers back — unscathed.

Note: In Photoshop, hiding a layer also protects it from editing, even if it is the active layer.

SHOW AND HIDE LAYERS

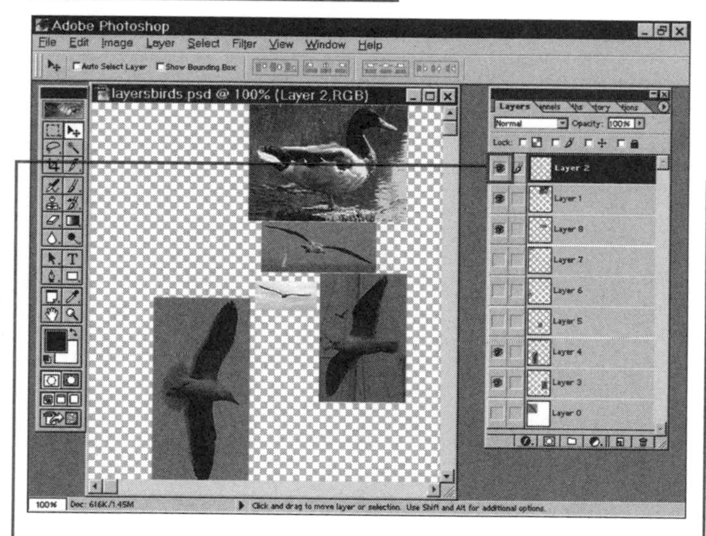

HIDE A LAYER

1 Click the layer's Eye icon.

■ The layer and its Eye icon disappear.

■ By turning off all but the layers you want to move, you can easily position and size the other layers in relation to one another.

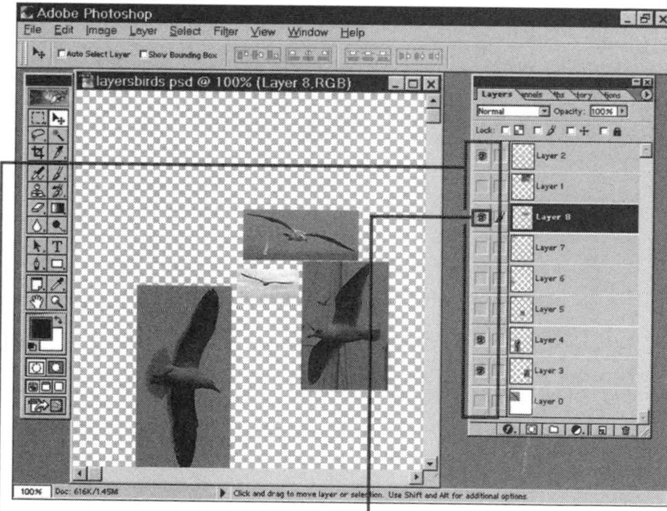

SHOW A LAYER

1 Click the blank box next to the layer's name in the Eye icon column.

■ The layer and its Eye icon appear.

MERGE LAYERS

You can combine specified layers into one — a process called *merging* layers. The more layers you have, the more memory you need to store them; so, merging layers whenever you are sure you no longer need to keep them separate is a good idea. The commands for merging layers can be most easily accessed from the Layers palette menu by clicking the arrowhead in the upper right corner of the Layers palette.

Sometimes you may want to merge layers so that you can use them as a single element. For example, you may want to create a whole field of grass by selecting a grassy area and then copying the selection to a new layer. You could then copy the new layer several times and move the individual copies until they cover the whole field. Then you can paint out the seams with the Clone tool.

You can merge all the visible layers, merge all the linked layers, merge with the layer immediately below, or just flatten the whole file.

MERGE LAYERS

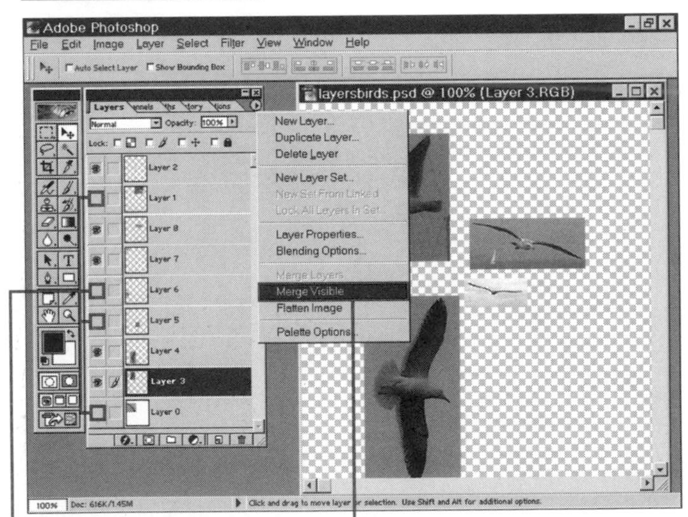

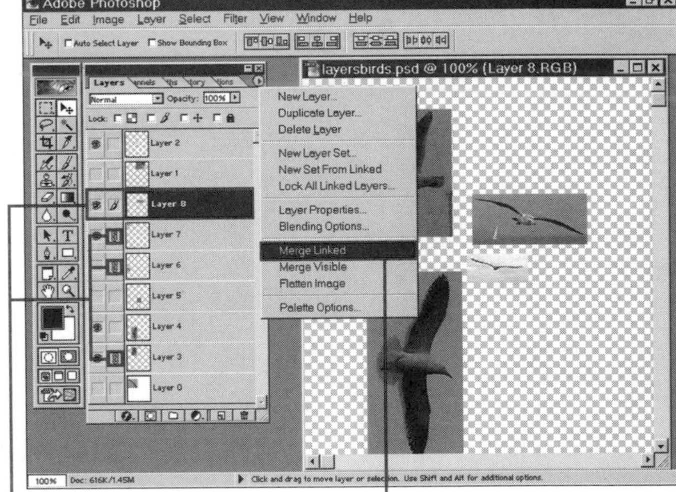

MERGE ALL THE VISIBLE LAYERS

Note: If the Layers palette is not on screen, choose Window, then Show Layers.

1 Click to hide layers you do not want to merge.

Note: See the section "Show and Hide Layers" to hide your layer.

2 Choose Merge Visible from the Layers palette menu.

■ The layers with the Eye icons visible become one layer, with the name of the layer that was active when you issued the command.

MERGE SOME OTHER LAYER(S), VISIBLE OR NOT

1 Click the layer(s) to link to.

2 Click to toggle linking.

3 Choose Merge Linked from the Layers palette menu.

■ The layers with the link icons become one and have the name of the active layer.

Why do so many different ways exist to merge layers?

✔ Photoshop is a thoroughly professional program; as such, it tries to be adaptable to any working style and set of requirements. Some images are composed of hundreds of layers, but keeping them all active at once is rarely practical.

How much memory does a layer use?

✔ It depends on the layer. If the layer consists of a full-color photograph that covers the entire image, it will be quite large. Adjustment layers, on the other hand, use virtually no extra memory.

What if I want to move a layer while I am painting? Is there a way to choose the Move tool without losing the current brush?

✔ Press ⌘/Ctrl. The Move tool stays in effect until you release the key. It is very much like pressing the spacebar to pan and scroll with the Hand tool.

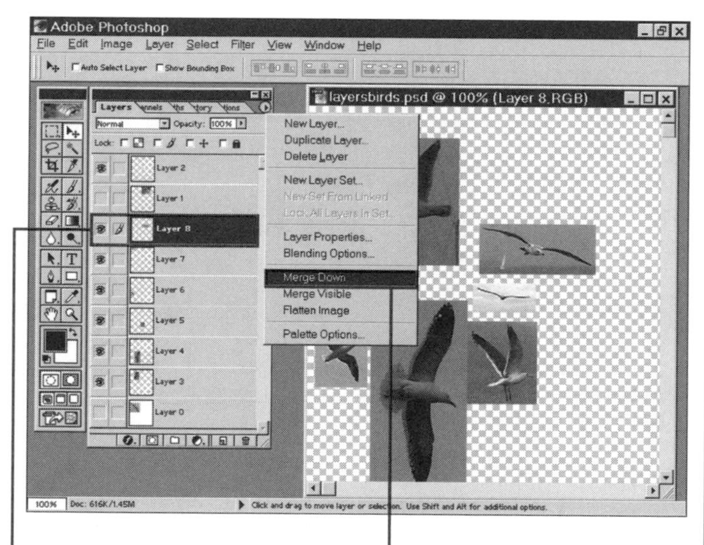

MERGE THE ACTIVE LAYER WITH THE LAYER BELOW IT

1 Click the layer you want to merge with the layer below it.

2 Choose Merge Down from the Layers palette menu.

■ The merged layer bears the name of the active layer.

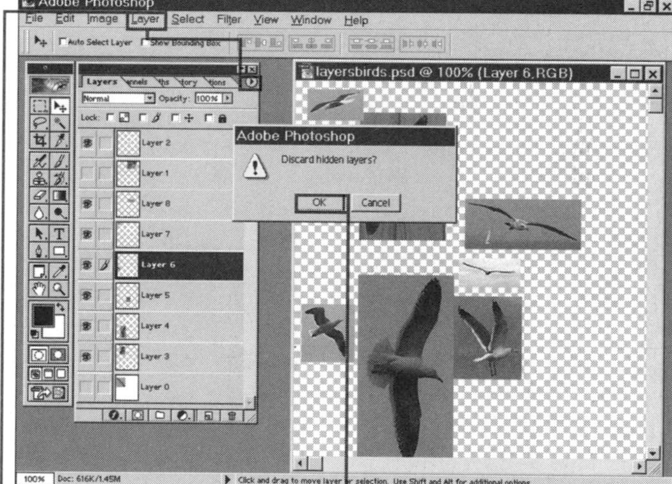

MERGE ALL VISIBLE LAYERS INTO ONE FLATTENED FILE

1 Choose Merge Visible from either the Layer menu or the Layers palette menu.

2 Click OK if a dialog box appears asking whether you want to discard hidden layers.

■ All visible layers automatically become one.

USE TRANSPARENCY WITH LAYERS

You can change the transparency of any layer at any time using one of the following methods:

- In the Layers palette, enter a number between 1(transparent) and 100 (opaque) in the Opacity field.
- Click the slider button (a right-facing arrow next to the Opacity box on the Layer Options palette). A slider appears. You can drag the Opacity slider to change opacity.
- Double-click the layer name bar to bring up the Layer Options palette. Enter a number between 1 and 100 in the Layer Options dialog box.

Opacity changes are never permanent unless you merge or flatten the layers (or save the image to a file format other than Photoshop's).

There are several reasons to make layers transparent, the most common being to temporarily see underlying layers. You can also reposition overlapping layers and blend their borders or erase a portion of a layer to reveal something on the layer below. Partially transparent layers are also useful in making collages and in creating double-exposure effects. Changing the transparency of a layer also changes the apparent effect of a special effects filter or Blending mode.

Note: You can transform several layers at the same time by linking them.

USE TRANSPARENCY WITH LAYERS

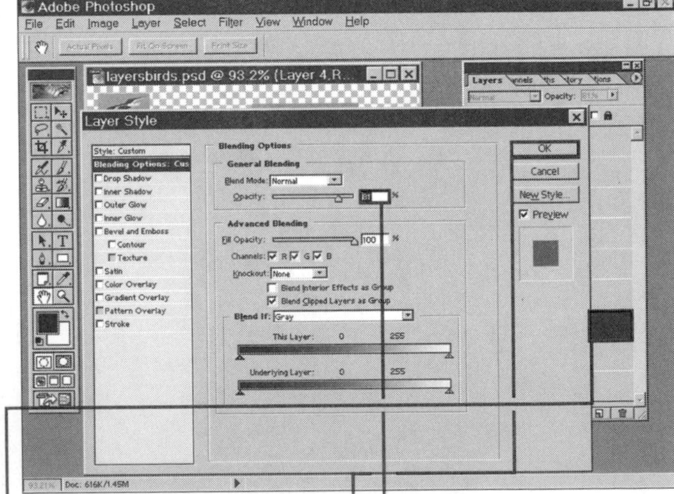

CHANGE THE TRANSPARENCY

1 Choose Window, then Show Layers.

2 Type a number between 1 (transparent) and 100 (opaque) in the Opacity field.

■ Alternatively, you can click the slider button next to the Opacity box on the Layers Option palette to bring up a slider, which you can drag to change the transparency.

■ Photoshop changes the layer's transparency.

CHANGE THE TRANSPARENCY IN THE LAYER STYLE DIALOG BOX

1 Double-click the layer name bar.

■ The Layer Style dialog box appears.

2 Type a number between 1 and 100 (100 percent is opaque) in the Opacity field.

3 Click OK.

■ Photoshop changes the layer's transparency.

STAMP LAYERS

You can condense several layers into a new layer without destroying the original layers. This new capability, called *stamping*, is very handy when you want to subject a group of layers to the same treatment without affecting any of the other layers in the composition.

One reason you may want to stamp layers is so that you can fill them with a color, then blur them to create a shadow or glow that you can then filter to create a special effect that is not possible with the Styles effects.

You can also break these shadows into individual objects and then apply perspective to them in order to approximate the effect of casting shadows on horizontal planes.

The three ways to stamp layers are

- Merging all linked layers into a new layer
- Merging all the layers in a set into a new layer
- Merging all the visible layers into a new layer

No menu command exists for stamping — only a keystroke combination: ⌘/Ctrl+Opt/Alt+E.

STAMPING LAYERS

STAMP A LAYER OR LINKED LAYERS

1 Click to choose the topmost layer to be stamped or

2 Click to indicate layers to be linked.

3 Press /Ctrl+Opt/Alt+E.

■ If no layers are linked, the layer below the selected layer is stamped into the selected layer. Otherwise, all linked layers are stamped into the selected layer.

STAMP A LAYER SET TO A NEW LAYER

1 Click to choose the layer set to be stamped.

2 Press /Ctrl+Opt/Alt+E.

■ The entire set is stamped to a single new layer.

CHANGE THE SIZE OF LAYERS

You can change the size of layers, as well as perform all the other types of transformations on them: Scale, Rotate, Distort, Skew, Perspective, Flop, and Flip. You can also do all of these things to the contents of any active selection.

By far the most common transformation is scaling. Scaling a layer differs from choosing the Image Size command on the Image menu in that the scaling is always done within the specified confines of a layer or selection, rather than for an entire image and all of its layers simultaneously.

As is the case with all other types of transitions, you can scale using several methods:

- In precise mathematical increments.
- By dragging control handles.
- In Free Form mode, where you can combine several types of transformations in the same operation. Free form transformations are handled in a separate spread so you can see how all the types of transformations work at once.

Using specific numbers for scaling and other transformations is no longer a special command, as of Photoshop 6. Now you enter numbers in the Options bar for any transformation command, including Free Transform.

CHANGE THE SIZE OF LAYERS

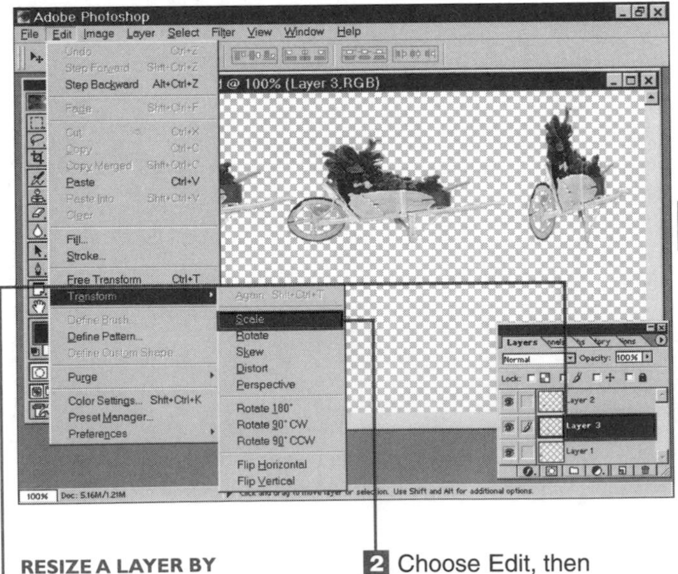

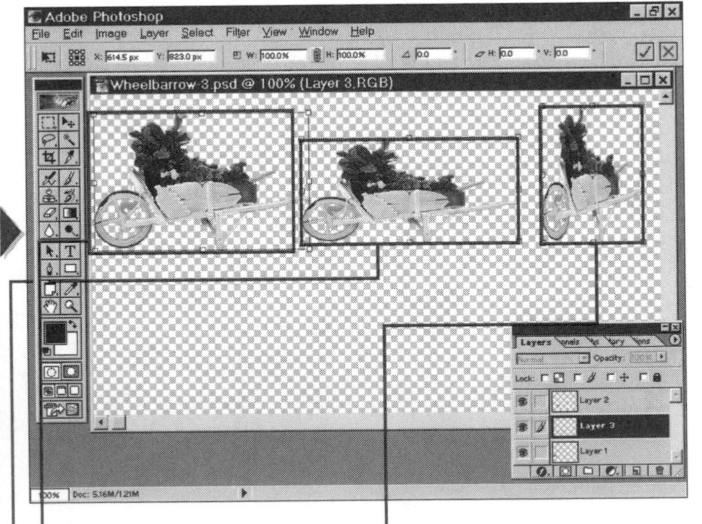

RESIZE A LAYER BY DRAGGING

1 Click to select the layer to be transformed.

2 Choose Edit, then Transform, then Scale.

■ A transformation box appears around a layer. In the next figure, a single transformation box is shown as it would appear after each of the three steps.

■ To maintain the original proportions press Shift and drag a corner.

■ To scale to fit an area without regard to height and width proportions drag a corner.

■ To scale the image in only one direction drag a side handle.

Note: Photoshop transforms layers and selections using the interpolation method specified in Preferences.

Besides saving time, is there any other advantage to combining several types of transformations into a single operation?

✔ You can use the Transform options bar to specify all the transformation settings before any of the transformations are made. Working this way gives you a big quality advantage, because pixels only have to be recalculated once. Of course, if you only need to make one type of transformation, the individual method produces the same result.

What if I start to make a transformation and need to get out of it?

✔ Press Escape or ⌘+Opt+. (Mac only). Until then, you will be unable to do anything else.

If I choose a conventional unit of measure, such as inches or centimeters, for transformation, will the image be that size on paper?

✔ Not unless you have already set the resolution of your file to match that of your printing device.

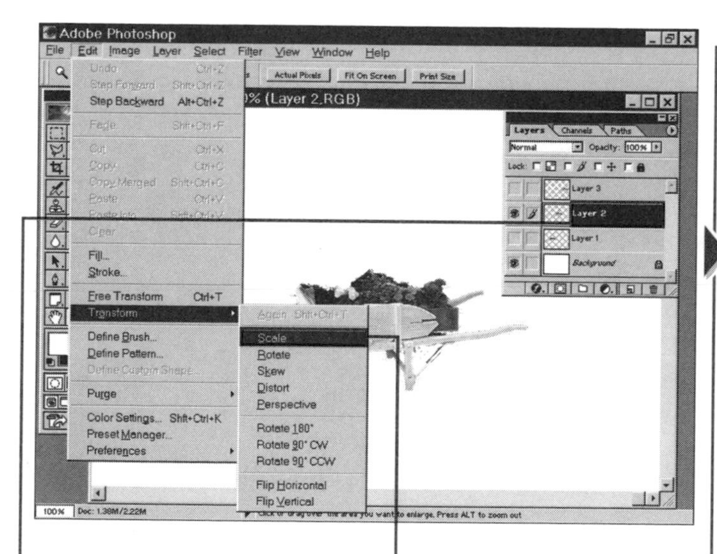

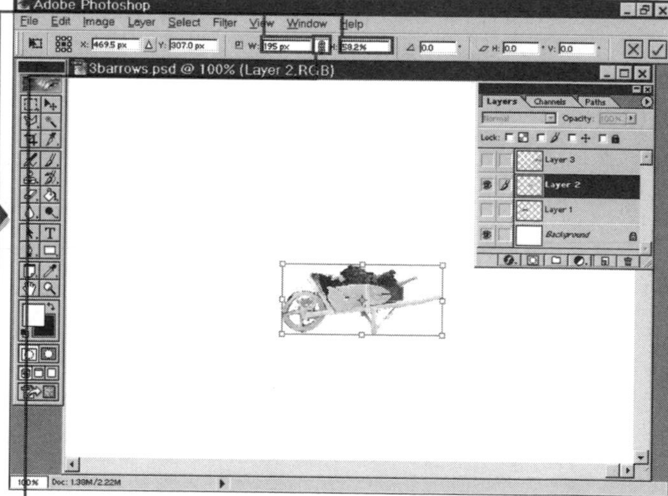

SCALE A LAYER (OR THE SELECTION CONTENTS) TO EXACT DIMENSIONS

1 Click to select the layer to be transformed.

2 Choose Edit, then Transform, then Scale.

■ A transformation box appears around the layer.

3 Click the Link icon to make scaling proportionate.

4 Enter the figure for either dimension.

■ The image instantly changes size.

Note: You can enter the dimension as a percentage or by abbreviating any Photoshop unit type: in = inches, px = pixels, cm = centimeters, and so on.

USING LAYER BLEND MODES

You can apply mathematical calculations between the current layer and the visible colors of any pixels underlying it. You can also change the opacity of any layer, thus making it more or less translucent.

For example, you can duplicate a layer, offset it from the original, and reduce the transparency to create a double-exposure effect.

A layer's Blend modes (also often called Apply modes) do the math. Photoshop features 17 Blend modes. Each mathematical formula creates a different visual effect.

The names of the 17 Blend modes are Normal, Dissolve, Multiply, Screen, Overlay, Soft Light, Hard Light, Color Dodge, Color Burn, Darken, Lighten, Difference, Exclusion, Hue, Saturation, Color, and Luminosity.

You can get a much better idea of how each of these Blend modes affect their underlying layers by checking out the Blend modes section in the color insert of this book.

To access a Blend mode, choose Window, then Show Layers, and use the Mode menu to choose the desired mode.

USING LAYER BLEND MODES

Note: For Layer Blend modes to work, you must have more than one layer. Here, a texture layer has been created to illustrate the interaction between blended layers.

1 Choose the desired mode from the Mode menu on the Layers palette.

■ The effect is immediately visible in the workspace window.

2 Enter a percentage of transparency to modify the intensity of the effect.

■ This figure shows the effect of using the Multiply Blend mode on these two layers. Notice how the texture almost seems to be projected onto the surface of the flowers.

CREATE SHAPE LAYERS FOR 3D BUTTONS

You can create instant 3D buttons by drawing shapes in the Shape Layers mode and choosing a layer style from the Layer Style Library window.

Buttons that are 3D are good because they look like they are meant to be pushed, because they appear to stick out from the background. They are very useful for all sorts of interactive applications, such as CD-ROM–based tutorials, computer-generated presentations, and (of course) Web pages.

All it takes to create one of these buttons is to choose the Shape Layers button after choosing any of the Geometric Shape tools and then choosing a style from the Layer Style Library window. Then, just draw your shape.

Speaking of making buttons for Web sites, you can make these buttons just as easily in ImageReady as in Photoshop. Because the shapes are automatically drawn on their own layer, you can assign URLs and events to their layers as well. However, ImageReady does not support custom shapes. You have to import those from Photoshop.

CREATE SHAPE LAYERS FOR 3D BUTTONS

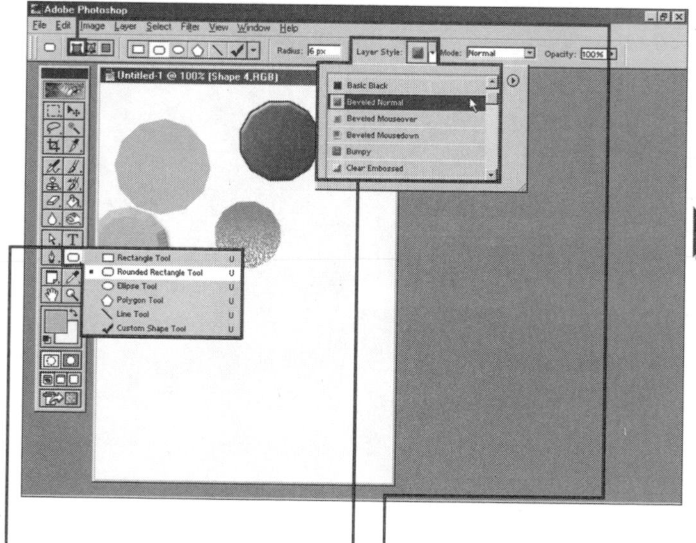

■ Here we see several layer effects that have already been executed on a polygon shape.

1 Click and drag to choose a shape tool.

2 Click to choose the Shape Layers mode.

3 Choose a layer effect from the Layer Style library window.

4 Click and drag to draw your button.

■ It automatically appears with all the style parameters added to it.

STRETCH LAYERS, SELECTIONS, AND PATHS

You can Stretch, Skew, Distort, Perspective Distort, and Rotate selections and paths, as well as layers. In Photoshop 6, you can use these techniques in several ways: You can press modifier keys to stretch, skew, or distort while using the Edit, then Free Transform command. You can choose Edit, then Transform to get directly to any of these operations. Finally, any time a transformation marquee is present, you will see a Transform Options bar that lets you enter exact numeric values for any of the types of transformation.

Stretch scales the target (layer, selection, or path) either vertically or horizontally.

Skew slants opposite sides of the bounding box at the same angle so that the image seems to lean.

Distort lets you change a layer by pulling one of the corner handles without moving the others; pressing Opt/Alt enables you to drag opposing handles simultaneously.

Perspective lets you distort by moving both of the corner handles on a given side to the same degree.

STRETCH LAYERS, SELECTIONS, AND PATHS

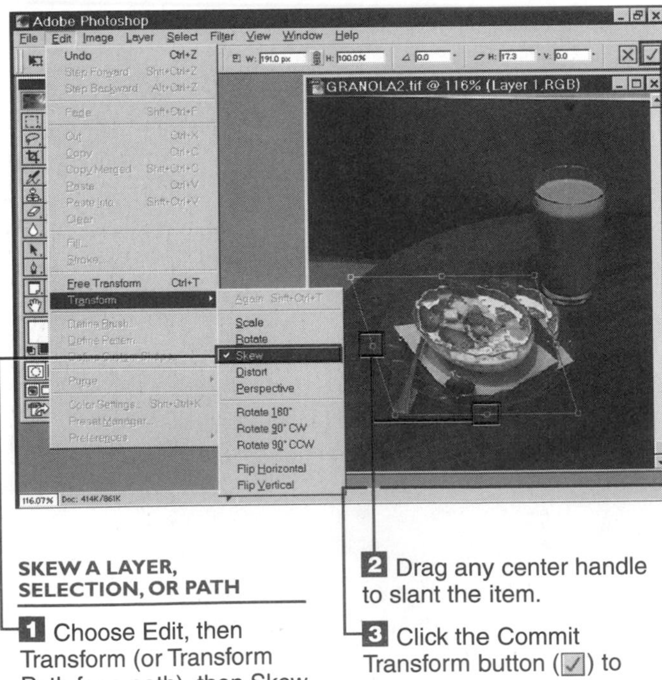

SKEW A LAYER, SELECTION, OR PATH

1 Choose Edit, then Transform (or Transform Path for a path), then Skew.

2 Drag any center handle to slant the item.

3 Click the Commit Transform button (✓) to render.

■ You can also distort simply by dragging a corner handle.

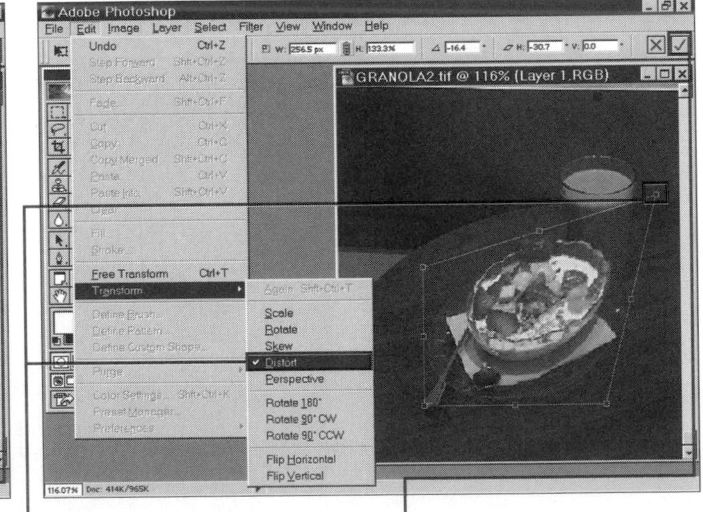

STRETCH A SINGLE CORNER

1 Choose Edit, then Transform, then Distort.

2 Drag any corner handle.

■ Drag other corners if needed.

3 Click the Commit Transform button (✓) to render.

Note: Distort allows you to make a convex selection concave by successively dragging opposite corners in the same direction. A Skew does not go concave.

I have been trying to transform the whole image and it does not work. Any idea why?

✔ Probably because you are trying to transform the background layer, which is illegal. Here are two workarounds: 1) Select the entire layer and then transform the selection. (You will see the background color wherever the transformation has moved the image away from the edges.) 2) Double-click the background layer and rename it in the Layers Options dialog box. It is now a standard image layer.

Can I slant in two different directions?

✔ You can repeat the reshaping, using different handles, as many times as you like until you are ready to render (calculate the pixel modifications and make them permanent) the item.

Is the Commit Transform button the same for the Mac as it is for Window?

✔ Although the Commit (checkmark) and Reject (X) Transform buttons look the same for both Mac and Windows, their order is reversed. In Windows, the Reject button is on left, while the Mac has the Commit button on the left.

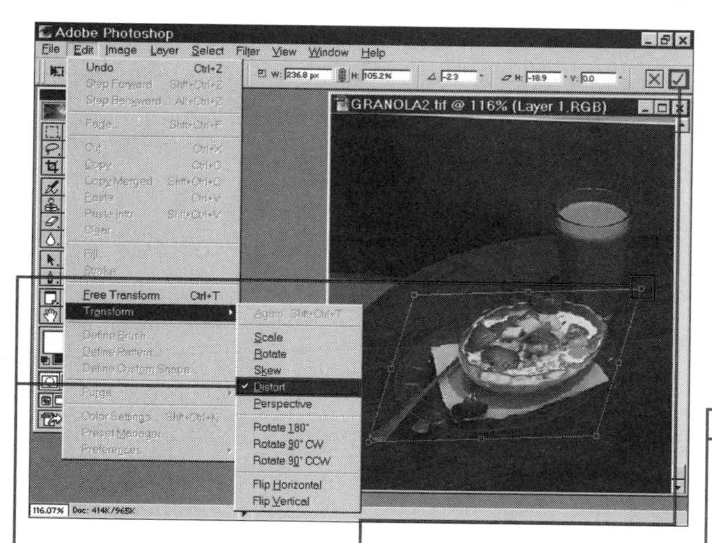

STRETCH BY MOVING TWO CORNERS EQUIDISTANTLY IN OPPOSITE DIRECTIONS

1 Choose Edit, then Transform, then Distort.

2 Press Opt/Alt and drag a corner.

■ The opposite corner moves the same distance in the opposite direction.

3 Click the Commit Transform button (☑) to render.

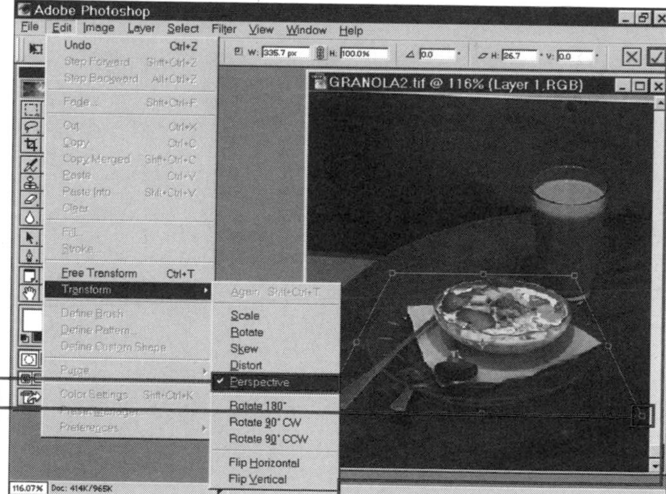

CHANGE THE APPARENT POINT OF VIEW OF A SELECTION LAYER OR PATH

1 Choose Edit, then Transform, then Perspective.

2 Drag a corner handle.

■ The opposite handle on the same side moves the same distance from the center.

3 Click the Commit Transform button (☑) to render.

MAKE MULTIPLE FREEHAND TRANSFORMATIONS

You can make several types of transformations interactively before finalizing the result. You do so by choosing Edit, then Free Transform. Because you can make several transformations before finalizing the result, the actual pixels are recalculated only once, which means that you get a higher fidelity result than if you performed several individual transformation operations.

Choosing to use the Free Transform command in Photoshop 6 can also be just as mathematically accurate as using the individual transformation commands because you can enter exact dimensions and coordinates into fields in the Transform Options bar.

Using Free Transform is also the fastest and easiest method for making transformations because you issue only one command and then use modifier keys and cursor location to control the type of transformation made when you drag one of the transformation box's handles.

Choosing Edit, then Free Transform allows all types of transformations: scaling, rotating, skewing, distorting, and changing perspective. You can even do flips and flops by entering negative numbers in the Transform Options bar's Height and Width fields.

MAKE MULTIPLE FREEHAND TRANSFORMATIONS

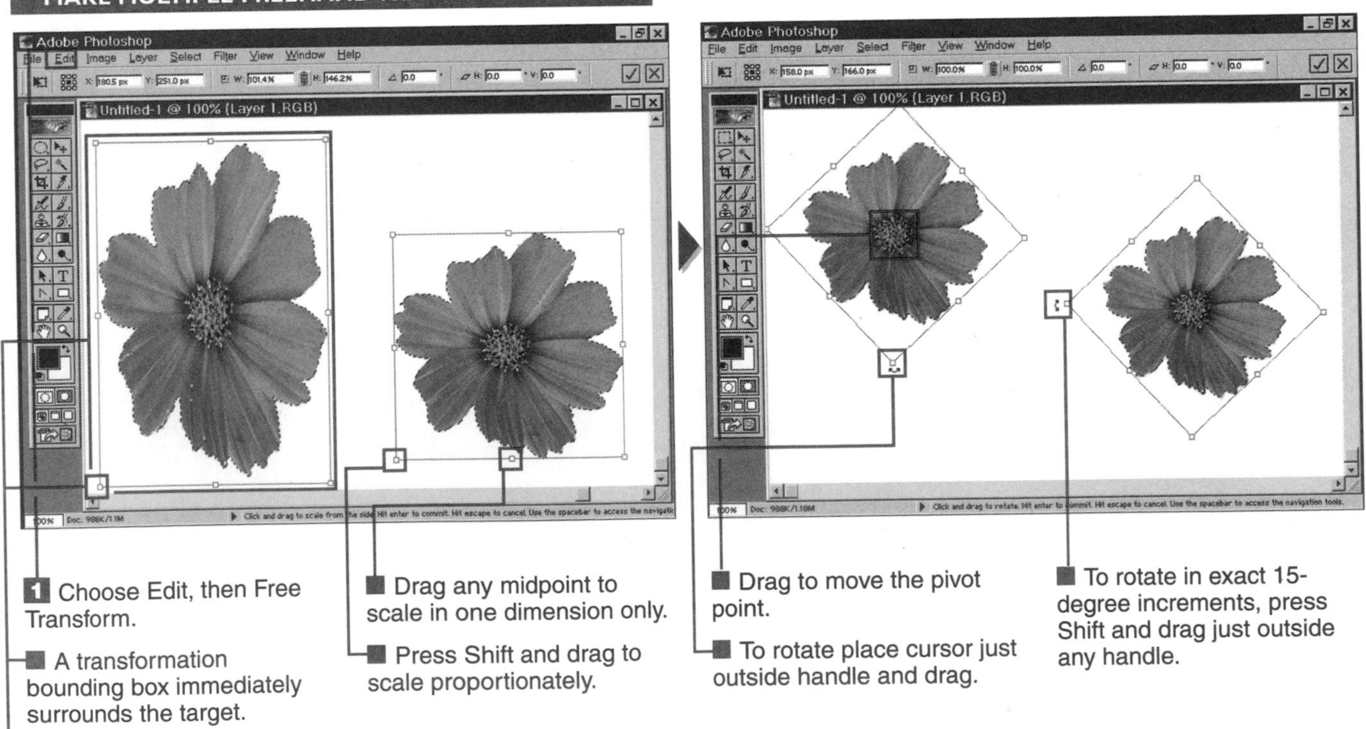

1 Choose Edit, then Free Transform.

■ A transformation bounding box immediately surrounds the target.

■ Drag any corner to scale disproportionately.

■ Drag any midpoint to scale in one dimension only.

■ Press Shift and drag to scale proportionately.

■ Drag to move the pivot point.

■ To rotate place cursor just outside handle and drag.

■ To rotate in exact 15-degree increments, press Shift and drag just outside any handle.

Do I have to choose Edit, then Free Transform to perform several types of transformations before I render the item?

✔ Not really. If you have trouble remembering the modifier keys to use with Free Transform, you can just choose Edit, then Transform as many times as you like before you render. You still get the benefit of rendering just once.

Can I make both freeform and numeric transformations before rendering?

✔ Yes. You will even see the numeric results of your freeform transformations appear in the Transform Options bar. Then you can make any perceived numeric changes.

Is there any advantage to using the Transform Options bar for numeric transformations?

✔ Yes. As soon as you enter a number, you see the result of the transformation. You can numerically enter numbers for several different types of transformations before finalizing (rendering) the transformation.

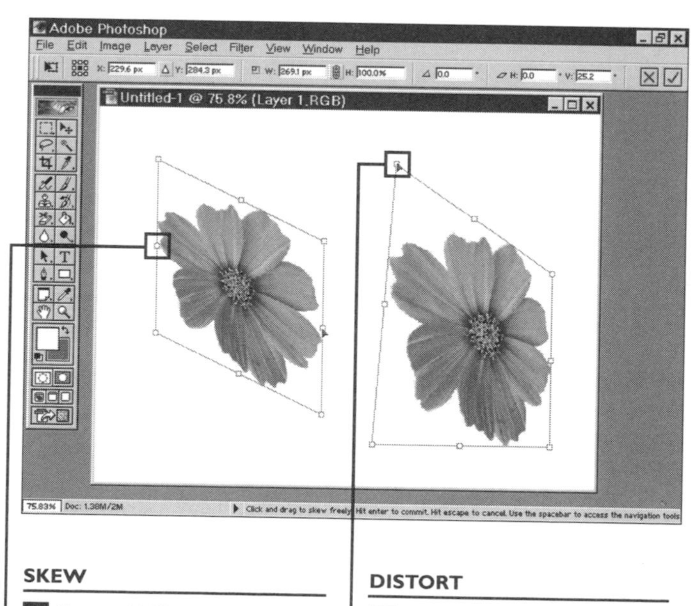

SKEW

1 Press ⌘/Ctrl and drag a center handle (add Shift key to constrain in single direction or Opt/Alt for a constrained tilt).

DISTORT

1 Press ⌘/Ctrl and drag a corner handle (add Shift key to constrain in 45- and 90-degree increments).

Note: In both cases, the cursor arrow turns gray.

CREATE PERSPECTIVE

1 Press Opt/Alt+⌘/Ctrl+Shift.

2 Drag horizontally or vertically.

3 Click the Commit Transform button (✓) to render.

MAKE NUMERICALLY PRECISE TRANSFORMATIONS

If you want a layer, selection, or path to have a perfectly precise location, size, orientation, or slant, choose Edit, then Free Transform. The Options bar will display fields that will enable you to perform each of the transformations described in this section. You can also perform any or all of these numerically precise transformations before clicking the Commit Transform button to render the transformation. Making transformations in this way leaves you with a much higher-fidelity result.

The Numeric Transform fields allow you to make the following transformations: Position, Scale, Skew, Rotate, Flip (mirror), and Flop (invert).

Unfortunately, you cannot perform a perspective or distortion transformation by choosing Edit, then Free Transform, but you can choose either Edit, then Transform, then Perspective, or Edit, then Transform, then Distort before you finalize your transformations. You can then drag a handle to make the distortion for that command and still have access to all the mathematical entry fields in the Transform Options bar.

If you want to return all the fields to their original state, just click the Cancel Transform button (the X).

MAKE NUMERICALLY PRECISE TRANSFORMATIONS

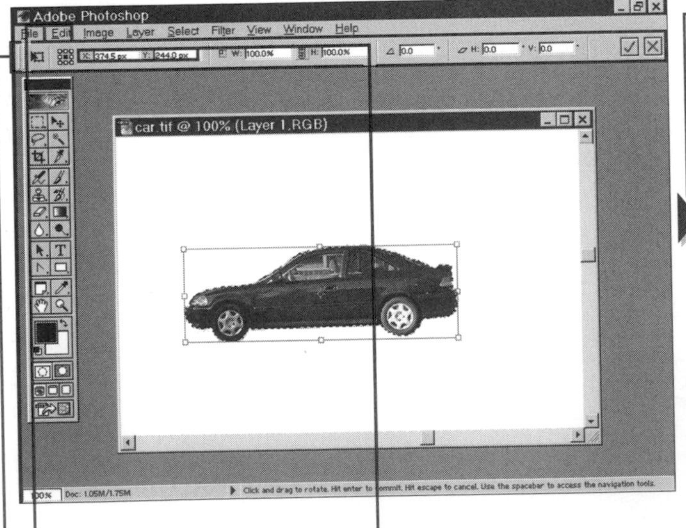

1 Choose Edit, then Free Transform (or Edit, then Transform, then Scale, Rotate, Perspective, Distort, and so on).

■ The Transform Options bar appears.

2 To change the position of the active layer, type X and Y values.

3 To resize the item, enter width and height.

■ To constrain proportions, you can click to activate a link. Then entering either dimension will automatically size the other.

What happened to the Transform Numeric command found in earlier editions of Photoshop?

✔ It is gone. You can now make any transformation either by dragging the transformation handles or by entering numeric data in the fields in the Transform Options bar. However, you can no longer transform several items so that they have the same characteristics by applying pre-existing numeric field entries. If your targets are all on individual layers, you can simply link the layers. Then all will transform simultaneously when you enter numeric specifications.

How many decimal points can I use?

✔ As many as you like, but Photoshop will round it off to two.

Can I enter negative numbers in any field?

✔ Yes, except for Scale. A negative number positions left of center or up from center. If you enter a negative number for the rotation angle, you will rotate the item counterclockwise.

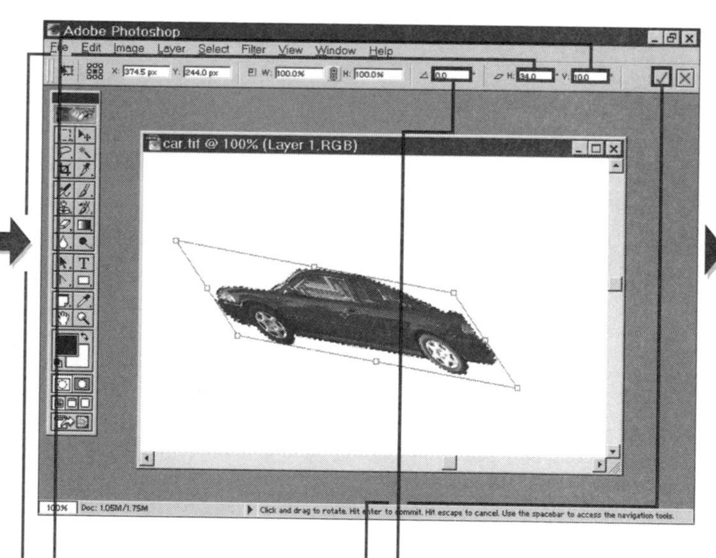

4 To slant the item vertically, type degrees of slant.

5 To slant the item horizontally, type degrees of slant.

6 To rotate the item, type a number with up to two decimal points (or drag to indicate the angle).

7 Click the Commit Transform button (☑) to render.

Note: Click the Cancel Transform button (☒) if you want to cancel the transformation.

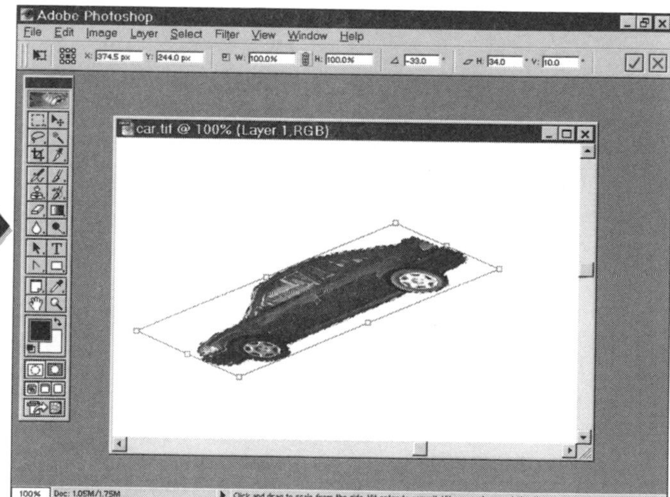

■ Here is the result produced by the numbers entered in the preceding example.

Note: You can make several types of transformations at once. Just make entries for each of the desired types of transformations. The transformation is previewed instantly but is not rendered until you click the Commit Transform button.

LINK LAYERS

You can link layers so that they all react to a command in the same way. This feature is another huge Photoshop timesaver. Imagine having an image with dozens of layers. If you need to rotate ten of them to the same degree, or if you want to merge six of those dozens of layers into one, all you need to do is link them.

Linking layers is easy. Just click the box in the second column of the Layers palette. If a Link icon appears, that layer is linked to the active layer. No menu commands exist for linking layers, so this instance is one of the rare ones where Photoshop provides you with only one way of doing things.

You can have multiple links in an image file. However, if you change the links to one of the linked layers, all the formerly associated links are dropped. You can affect layers in three ways: move them, merge them, or transform them. Other Photoshop commands simply do not work on multiple image layers.

LINK LAYERS

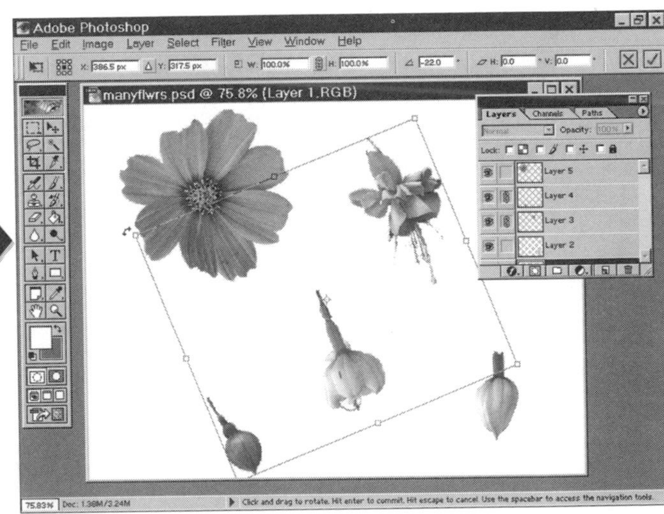

1 Click the name of the layer you wish to activate.

2 Click in the Link column of the layer(s) you want to link.

■ A Link icon appears next to all layers linked to the active layer.

Note: Linked layers need not be in any stacking order.

■ Merge, transform, or stamp the linked layers. (See the "Merging Layers" and "Stamping Layers" sections in this chapter.)

■ Here, the result of rotating linked layers is shown.

MAKE AND USE A CLIPPING GROUP

You can use the silhouette (transparency mask) of the active layer as a cutout for the visible layers in a group. The result is called a *clipping group*. For the clipping group to be effective, you need an item(s) that has been isolated on a layer(s) by lifting it (them) from a selection on another layer or by erasing portions of the layer it is on. In other words, you want the object's silhouette(s) to be surrounded by transparency.

You can get a similar effect by adding a mask to a layer; however, more steps are involved, especially if the mask shape you want is already present as a transparent background layer. Clipping groups are often confused with clipping paths, but they have no relationship. Clipping paths are used to place an irregularly shaped, bitmapped graphic into a DTP document in such a way that the program knows how to wrap text around the object.

You can ungroup layers by selecting one layer of the group and pressing Shift+⌘/Ctrl+G or by clicking the dotted line between grouped layers.

MAKE AND USE A CLIPPING GROUP

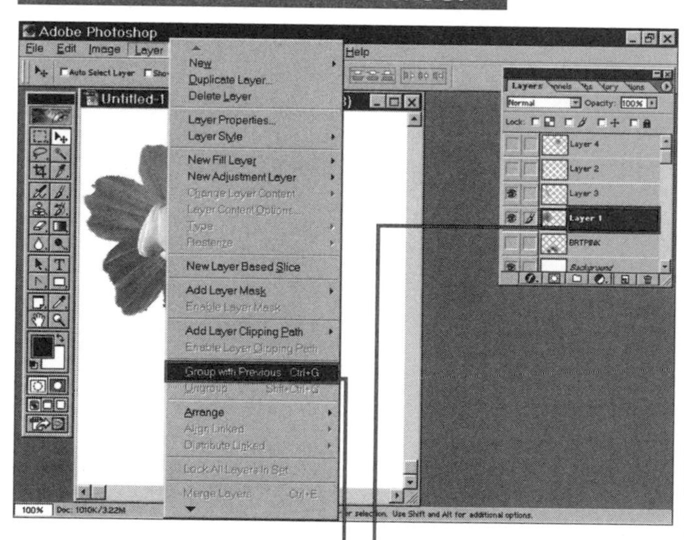

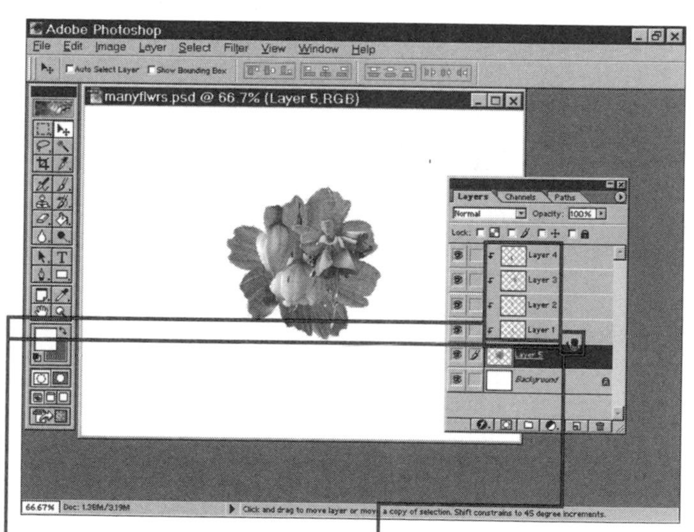

MAKE A CLIPPING GROUP WITH THE MENU COMMAND

1 Drag to arrange layers so that the image you want clipped is above the image that will become the mask shape.

2 Click to choose the bottommost layer of the layers you want masked.

3 Choose Layer, then Group With Previous (or press /Ctrl+G).

MAKE A CLIPPING GROUP WITH THE LAYERS PALETTE

1 Drag to arrange all the layers you want masked above the mask layer.

2 Press Opt/Alt and click the border between layers.

■ The cursor changes to overlapping circles and the border between grouped layers is dotted.

■ The lower layer's image shows through the mask, but grouped layers are trimmed to fit inside.

MAKE AND USE ADJUSTMENT LAYERS

You can apply Image, then Adjust commands simultaneously to all visible layers below the active layer when you use adjustment layers. Adjustment Layers make it possible to apply virtually all the Adjust commands on the Image menu to everything beneath them that is visible.

The three advantages of using the Adjust commands on the Image menu are that

- You do not have to apply the adjustment to each individual layer.
- The effect of the adjustment can be changed for as long as the file remains in Photoshop format and as long as the adjustment layer is not merged with other layers or deleted.
- You can vary the overall effect (intensity) of the adjustment in respect to other adjustment layers by changing their stacking order and opacity.

You must have a different adjustment layer for each type of layer adjustment. The adjustments available in adjustment layers include Levels, Curves, Color Balance, Brightness/Contrast, Hue/Saturation, Selective Color, Channel Mixer, Gradient Map, Invert, Threshold, and Posterize.

You can preview the effects of several different image adjustments, image adjustment types, or any combination of the above by using the Layers palette: Click the Eye icon in the Layer Name bar to toggle that layer's visibility.

MAKE AND USE ADJUSTMENT LAYERS

1 Choose Layer, then New Adjustment Layer.

■ You can also click the New Fill or Adjustment Layer button ( ) at the bottom of the Layers palette.

2 Choose the adjustment layer type from the submenu that appears.

3 If applicable, click the Preview box in the adjustment dialog box so you can see the effect of your adjustment settings.

4 When you are satisfied, click OK.

Does a way exist to have the adjustment layer affect only *some* of the underlying layers?

✔ No. The only option is to drag the layer you want to be unaffected to a Layers palette position above the adjustment layer's. Be aware that this method can affect how the visible portions of layers overlap.

Can I use adjustment layers in ImageReady?

✔ You cannot create them, but you can view them. If you need to create them, use the Jump To button to go back to Photoshop, create your adjustments, then jump back to ImageReady.

Can you have more than one adjustment layer of the same type?

✔ Yes. This method is a very good way to decide between several different sets of adjustments of the same type. You can also use a layer mask to make the adjustment in one adjustment layer affect only one part of the image and then use a layer mask on another adjustment layer of the same type to affect another part of the image.

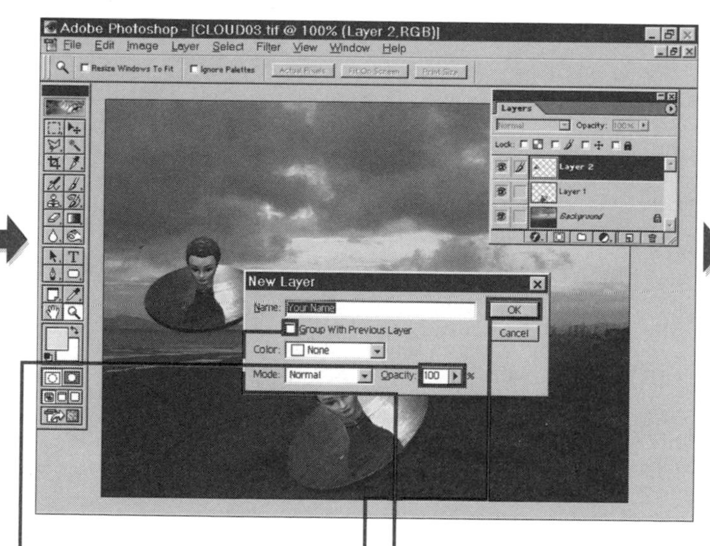

5 Enter the percentage of the effect you want for the adjustment.

6 Click the Group With Previous Layer check box.

7 Click OK.

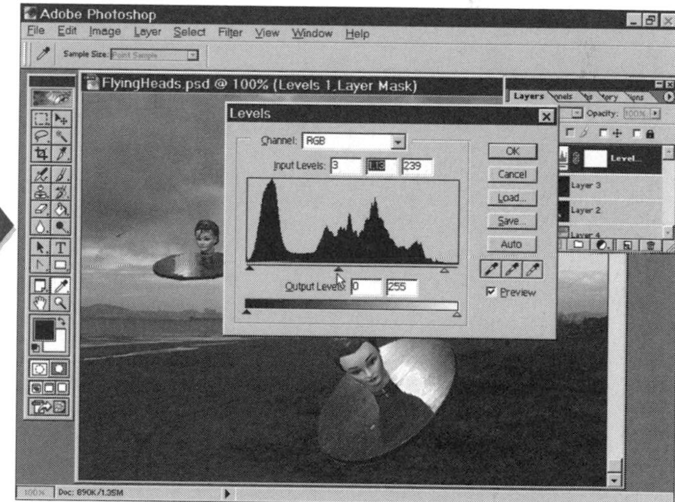

■ The dialog box for your chosen adjustment type appears.

■ The background image shows you the effects of these adjustments.

Note: If you double-click the mask (thumbnail) part of the adjustment layer in the Layers palette, you can rename it, change what you call the Blend mode, and adjust the Blend If sliders. Double-click the layer itself to bring up the appropriate adjustment window.

MAKE A LAYER MASK

You can have one mask associated with each layer so that the mask protects a given area of that layer no matter where you move or stack it. Like an ordinary channel mask, a layer mask can dictate specific areas of the layer as transparent, semitransparent, or graduating from transparent to opaque. The difference is that you can alter and turn on and off layer masks without affecting the pixels on that layer or anything else in the rest of the image. Of course, if you merge the layer with another or flatten the image, the layer mask becomes integrated with the final product and is no longer editable.

You can make layer masks in several ways. The simplest way is to click the Layer Mask icon at the bottom of the Layers palette. If a selection is active, the mask reveals the contents of the selection (the rest of the layer is transparent). If there is no selection, the mask reveals the entire layer. You can then protect areas of that layer by painting into the mask (see Chapter 8). You can also create Layer Masks by choosing Layer, then Add Layer Mask, then Reveal All/Selection or Hide All/Selection.

MAKE A LAYER MASK

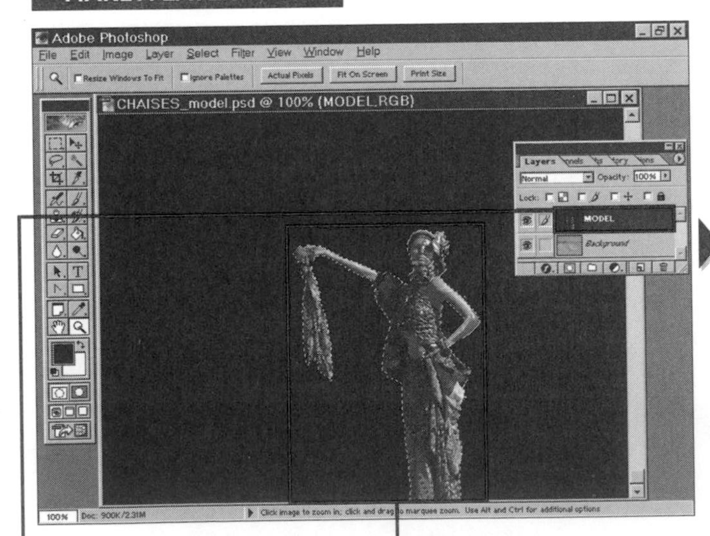

MAKE A LAYER MASK FROM A SELECTION

1 Click to activate the layer to which you want to add a mask.

2 Select the area of the layer you want to mask.

Note: Be sure to invert the selection if you have selected the portion of the image you want kept clear.

3 Click the Layer Mask icon ( ).

■ Alternatively, choose Layer, then Add Layer Mask, then Hide/Reveal selection.

■ The image appears with the masked portion transparent. In other words, you can see the underlying layer through the masked area.

How do I delete a layer mask?

✔ Drag the layer mask to the Trash Can icon at the bottom of the Layers palette or choose Layer, then Remove Layer. A dialog box appears asking whether you want to apply the mask before it is removed. To remove the mask and leave the layer intact, click Discard.

How do I link a layer mask so that it stays registered with the layer when I move it?

✔ Layer masks are linked by default, but checking that the link is still in effect before you move the layer is good practice. If the layer mask is linked, you should see a Link icon between the Layer icon and the Layer Mask icon. You can turn linking on and off by clicking the icon.

Does a way exist to defringe (matte) a layer mask?

✔ Edit the layer mask in the Channels palette. Use the Magic Wand to select the interior of the mask. Choose Select, then Modify, then Contract, and enter the number of pixels to defringe the mask. Click OK, and then invert the selection and fill it with black. If you want to soften the edge, feather the selection before filling it.

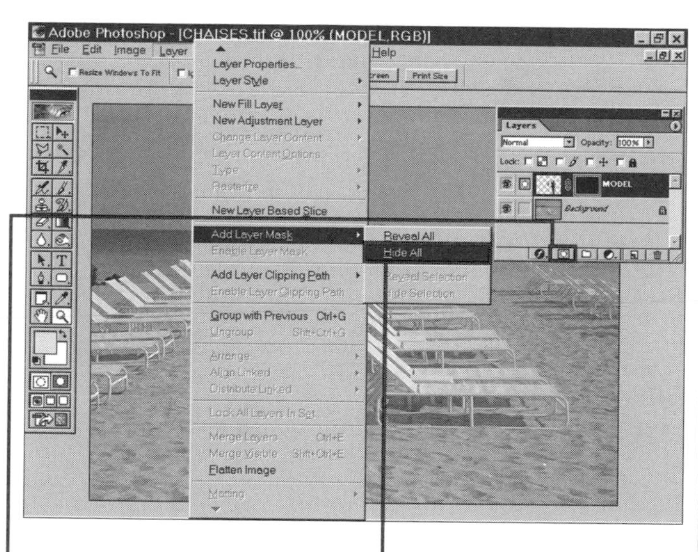

MAKE A NEW, SOLID MASK

1 Press Opt/Alt and click the Layer Mask icon ( ).

■ Alternatively, choose Layer, then Add Layer Mask, then Reveal All/Hide All.

■ The Layer Mask icon (either solid white or black) and the Layer Mask link appear.

EDIT THE LAYER MASK

1 Click to activate the layer mask.

2 Use any of Photoshop's image-editing tools to alter the mask.

■ This example is painted with a white brush. You could fill a selection, run a filter, or do many other things to alter this mask.

MAKE AND USE LAYER STYLES

You can now do much more than simply create text and button effects using the new Layer Styles command in Photoshop 6. Layer Styles replace the Layer Effects that were brand-new to Photoshop 5. Meant mostly to enhance the appearance of text and button layers (see Chapter 11 for information on making text layers), the Layer Styles dialog box gives you a wider range of settings for creating layer effects and also gives you added flexibility over layer blending controls.

The following effects are available: Drop Shadow, Inner Shadow, Outer Glow, Inner Glow, Bevel, and Emboss — and new in Photoshop 6— Satin, Color Overlay, Gradient Overlay, Pattern Overlay, and Stroke Effects. An *f* icon appears on the right side of the layer name bar when a Layer Style effect has been applied. You can apply multiple effects to a single layer. Normally, Layer Style effects are linked to the layer so that if you move the layer, you move the effect. You have the option to move the effect to its own layer. You can also clear, copy, and paste effects.

MAKE AND USE LAYER STYLES

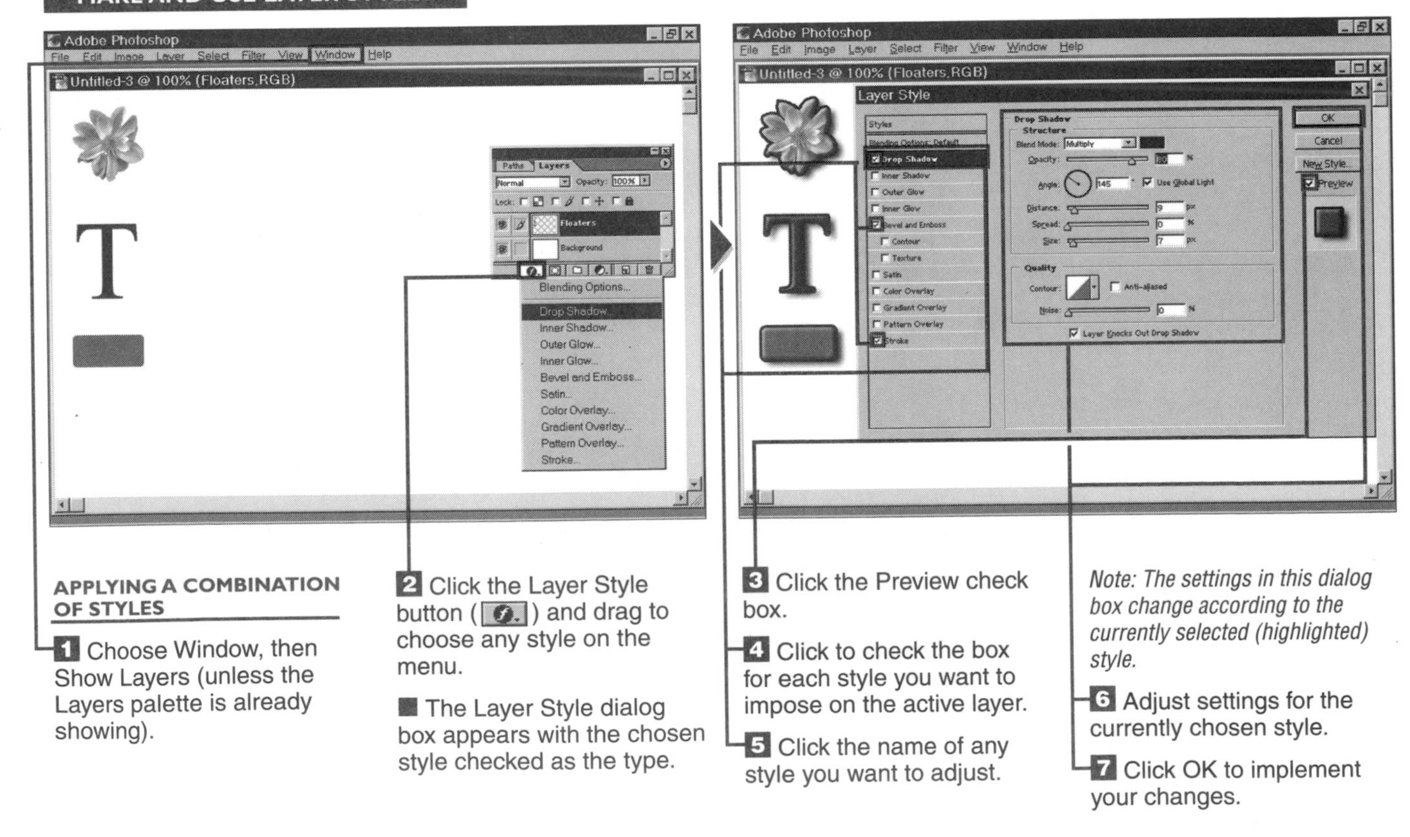

APPLYING A COMBINATION OF STYLES

1 Choose Window, then Show Layers (unless the Layers palette is already showing).

2 Click the Layer Style button ( ) and drag to choose any style on the menu.

■ The Layer Style dialog box appears with the chosen style checked as the type.

3 Click the Preview check box.

4 Click to check the box for each style you want to impose on the active layer.

5 Click the name of any style you want to adjust.

Note: The settings in this dialog box change according to the currently selected (highlighted) style.

6 Adjust settings for the currently chosen style.

7 Click OK to implement your changes.

Will the Blending modes within the Styles layer give me more effects?

✔ Yes, especially when you consider how you can combine them with all the other adjustments on screen.

Why do I need Blending modes in the Styles palettes when I have them on the Layers palette?

✔ The Layers palette Blend modes affect the way a layer's colors are mathematically combined with those on the layer below. The Styles Blend modes affect only the way one characteristic in that Blend affects another.

Will the effect render faster if I turn off Preview?

✔ Slightly. The difference will add up if you create this effect as part of an action that will be applied to numerous layers or if you have several effects checked.

Why does Photoshop not just impose a shadow blur automatically, based on distance?

✔ A hard edge will make the letter (or other layer edge) look more three-dimensional. The combination of blurring and distance, on the other hand, makes the layer seem to float at different distances above the background.

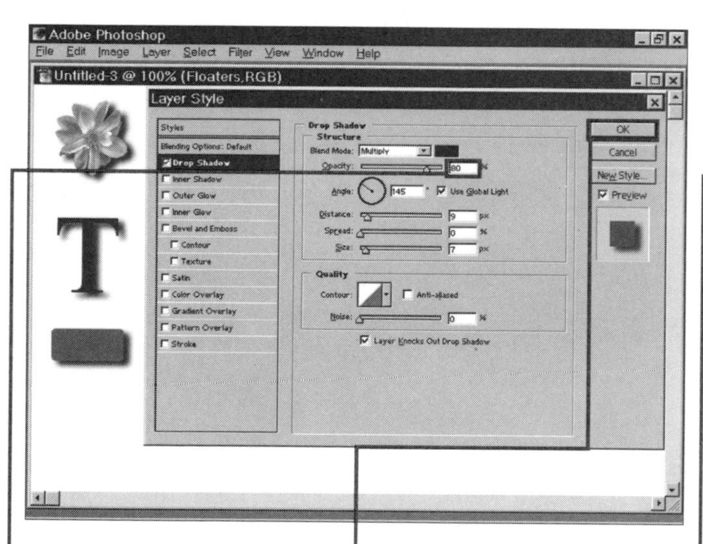

IMPOSE A DROP SHADOW

1 With the Layer Style dialog box open (see previous page), enter a number between 1 and 100 for percentage of opacity – or drag slider.

Note: You can drag a slider to indicate the figures for Opacity, Distance, Spread, Size, and Noise. See the next Master It section for what these settings do.

2 Click OK to finalize.

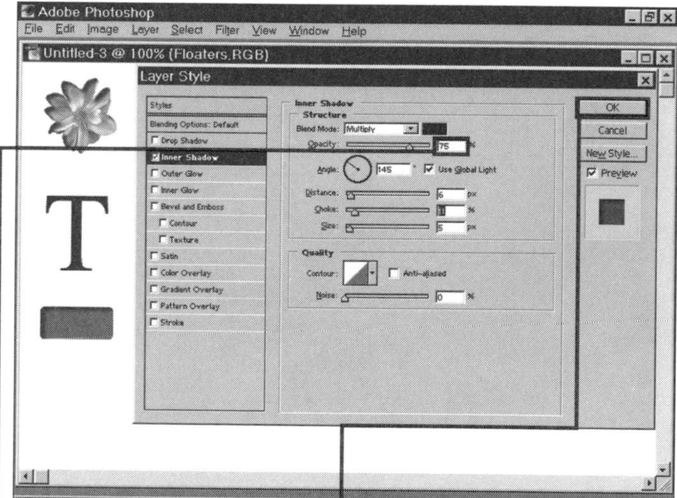

CREATE AN INNER SHADOW

1 With the Layer Style dialog box open (see previous page), enter a number between 1 and 100 for percentage of opacity – or drag slider.

Note: You can drag a slider to indicate the figures for Opacity, Distance, Spread, Size, and Noise. See the next Master It section for what these settings do.

2 Click OK to finalize.

CONTINUED

MAKE AND USE LAYER STYLES CONTINUED

One of the things that Layer Styles does that can save enormous amounts of time is saving the compound (several different effects) Styles you can create in the Styles dialog box to a styles library. The library applies the styles to a square button, so you immediately see the visual effect of the styles. Then you can apply the compound effect in a click or two.

All you have to do is create style effects that you want, using the techniques demonstrated in this chapter. Then, while you still have the new style's layer selected, choose Window, then Show Styles. The Styles Library appears. Just click to choose the style icon you want to apply to the layer and you are done.

MAKE AND USE LAYER STYLES (CONTINUED)

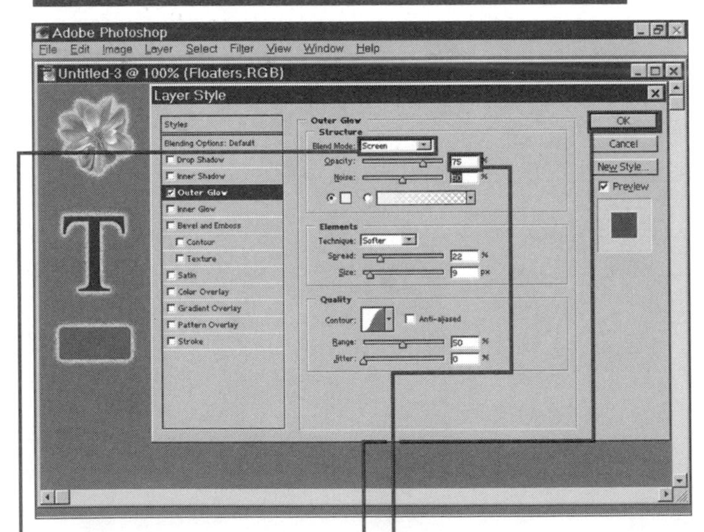

EXUDE AN OUTER GLOW

1 With the Layer Style dialog box open (see previous pages), choose a Mode (other than the default Multiply) from the menu.

■ The most effective is usually Screen but will depend on the background.

2 Enter a number between 1 and 100 for percentage of opacity – or drag the slider.

Note: You can drag a slider to indicate the figures for Opacity, Noise, Spread, Size, Range, and Jitter.

3 Click OK to finalize.

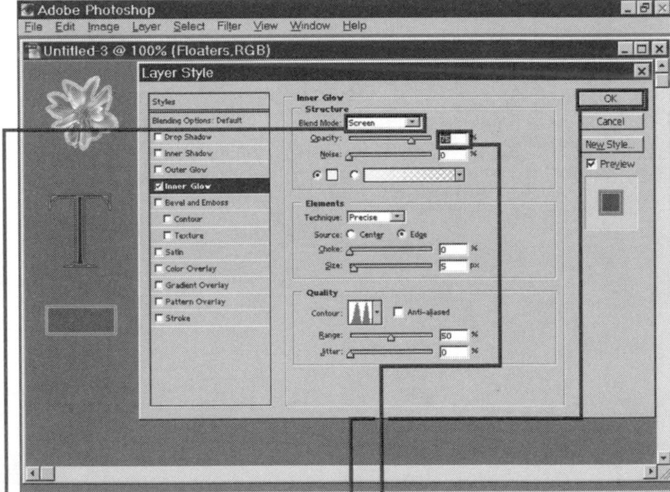

ACQUIRE AN INNER GLOW

1 With the Layer Style dialog box open (see previous pages), choose a Mode (other than the default Multiply) from the menu.

■ The most effective is usually Screen but will depend on the background.

2 Enter a number between 1 and 100 for percentage of opacity – or drag the slider.

Note: You can drag a slider to indicate the figures for Opacity, Noise, Choke, Size, Range, and Jitter.

3 Click OK to finalize.

Can you explain the meaning of the Drop Shadow and Inner Shadow drag bars?

✔ Opacity determines how much of the underlying layer shows through the shadow. Distance refers to the space between the layer's edge and the shadow. Spread determines how fuzzy the edges of the shadow will be. Size means the size of the shadow's shape. Noise makes the shadow break up into a grain pattern.

What if other styles are checked when the Layer Style dialog box appears?

You can click the check marks to toggle

✔ them on or off at any time before you merge or flatten the associated layer.

How do I edit a style after it has been applied?

✔ Just double-click its bar in the Layers palette, and the Styles palette that contains the settings appears. You can then change the settings any way you want.

How do I edit a contour?

✔ Click the Contour button (the larger icon, not the smaller button for the Library window). A dialog box appears that is very similar to the Curves dialog box (see Chapter 4).

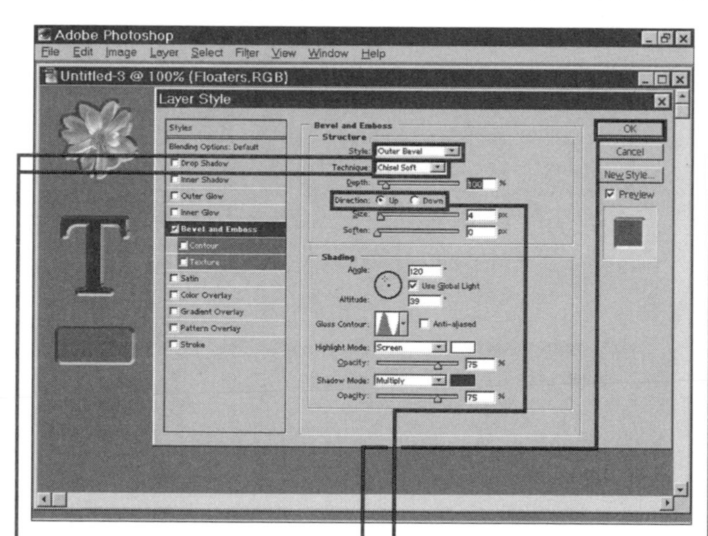

BEVEL AND EMBOSS: OUTER BEVEL

1 With the Layer Style dialog box open (see previous pages), choose Outer Bevel from the Style menu.

2 Choose an edge-carving Technique (Smooth, Chisel Hard, or Chisel Soft).

3 Click to push the layer in or out of the background.

Note: You can drag a slider to indicate the figures for Depth, Size, Soften, Highlight Mode Opacity, and Shadow Mode Opacity.

4 Click OK to finalize.

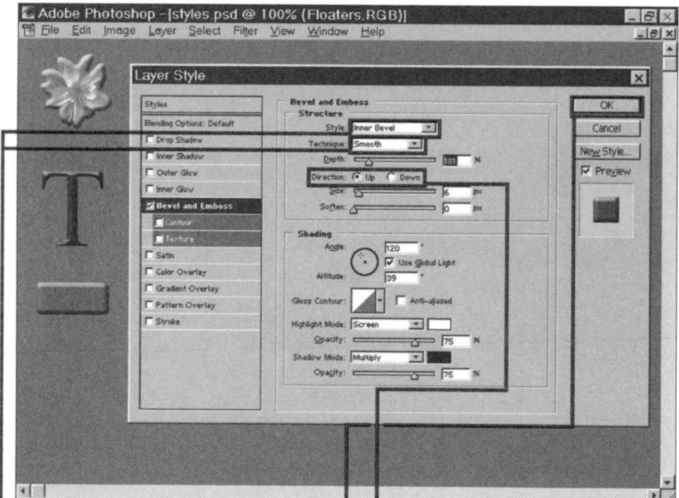

BEVEL AND EMBOSS: INNER BEVEL

1 With the Layer Style dialog box open (see previous pages), choose Inner Bevel from the Style menu.

2 Choose an edge-carving Technique (Smooth, Chisel Hard, or Chisel Soft).

3 Click to push the layer in or out of the background.

Note: You can drag a slider to indicate the figures for Depth, Size, Soften, Highlight Mode Opacity, and Shadow Mode Opacity.

4 Click OK to finalize.

CONTINUED

MAKE AND USE LAYER STYLES

CONTINUED

Best of all, you can create new layer styles just by applying an existing style, then choosing Layer, then Layer Style, then any of the effects. When the Layer Style dialog box appears, add any new effects you please, then click to choose the New Style button. You can (optionally) enter a name for the style and can check boxes to indicate that you want to include Layer Effects and/or Blending Options.

Most people use Layer Styles for one of two purposes: to create buttons or to create effects for text — especially for that which is used on the Web. However, there is no reason to limit yourself to those two purposes. Any subject that exists on any layer other than the background layer can be treated with a layer style. One possibility is to create unusual-looking art by selecting objects in a scene, then lifting each to its own new layer, then applying layer styles to each of the resulting layers. You can do the same with line-art drawn in vectors — whether abstract or representational. Don't be afraid to experiment. You could be the Museum of Modern Art's next new hero.

MAKE AND USE LAYER STYLES (CONTINUED)

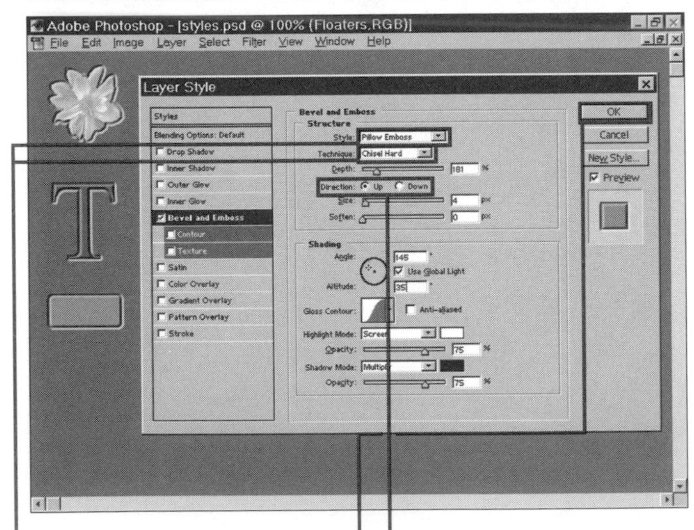

BEVEL AND EMBOSS: EMBOSS

1 In the Layer Style dialog box, choose Pillow Emboss (or any of the other Emboss styles) from the Style menu.

2 Choose an edge-carving Technique (Smooth, Hard or Soft Chisel).

3 Click to push the layer in or out of the background.

Note: You can drag a slider to indicate the figures for Depth, Size, Soften, Highlight Mode Opacity, and Shadow Mode Opacity.

4 Click OK to finalize.

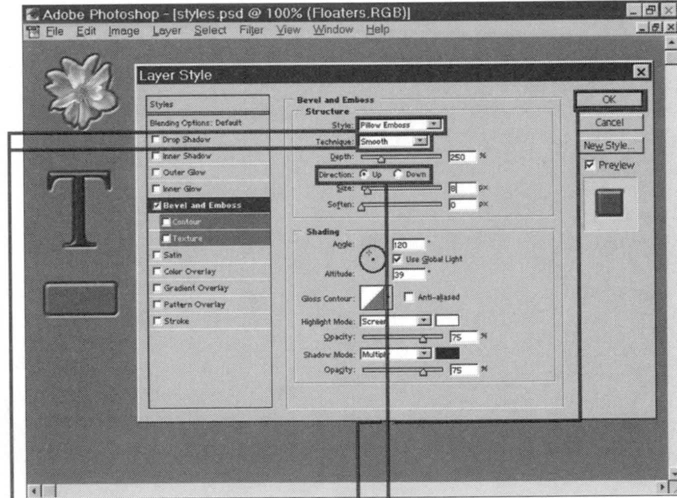

BEVEL AND EMBOSS: PILLOW EMBOSS

1 In the Layer Style dialog box, choose Pillow Emboss from the Style menu.

2 Choose an edge-carving Technique (Smooth, Hard or Soft Chisel).

3 Click to push the layer in or out of the background.

Note: You can drag a slider to indicate the figures for Depth, Size, Soften, Highlight Mode Opacity, and Shadow Mode Opacity (see tips for this task).

4 Click OK to finalize.

What does the Contour Library do when it appears in settings for a style?

✔ The Contour Library's apparent effect seems to vary from one style to another. Basically, it determines how the style gets broken up, reflected, or cast. For example, the triple-wave contour casts three concentric shadows.

What does the Use Global Light check box do? I see it in many different style's settings.

✔ The Global Light check box makes the direction of lighting consistent for all the individual styles that make up a combination of styles (that is, when several styles' name boxes are checked).

Can I create as many contours as I like?

✔ There is probably a practical limit to how many you would want to crowd into the Library window. You save an edited contour with the Save button in the Edit dialog box. If you want to create an entirely new Contour, click the New button before you start editing.

What does *jitter* mean?

✔ Jittering is an effect that randomizes the pixel pattern in a gradient by the percentage you indicate when you drag the slider or enter a number. It is a very subtle effect that takes some experimentation to understand.

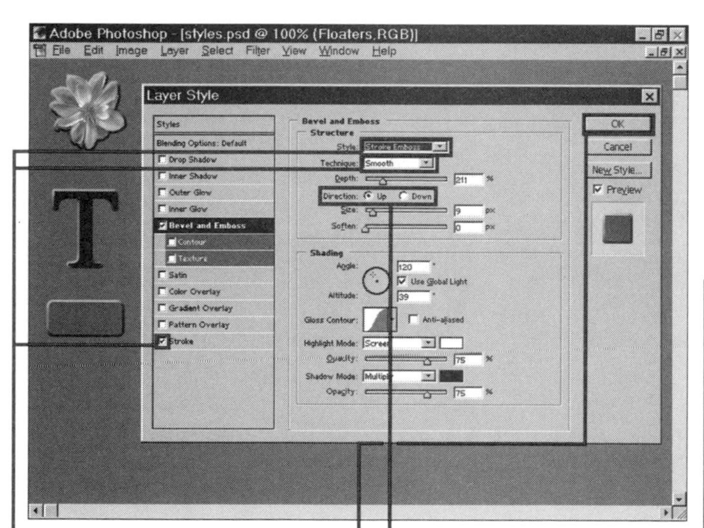

BEVEL AND EMBOSS: STROKE EMBOSS

1 In the Layer Style dialog box, click the Stroke box.

2 Choose Stroke Emboss from the Style menu.

3 Choose an edge-carving Technique (Smooth, Hard or Soft Chisel).

4 Click to push the layer in or out of the background.

Note: You can drag a slider to indicate the figures for Depth, Size, Soften, Highlight Mode Opacity, and Shadow Mode Opacity.

5 Click OK to finalize.

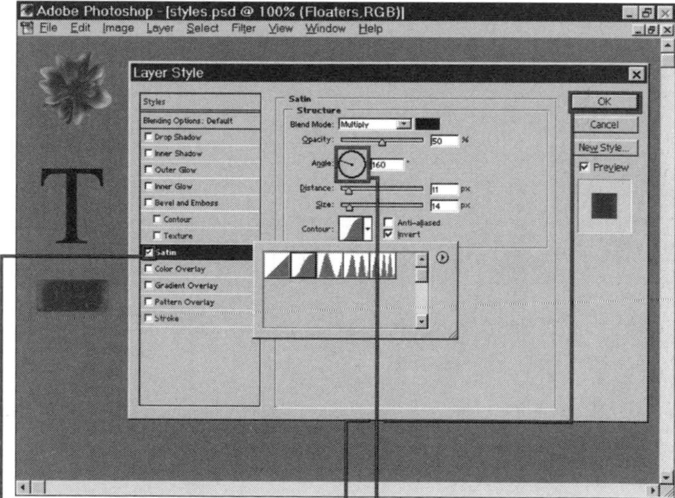

2D EFFECTS: SATIN

Note: 2D Style effects are usually (but not necessarily) used with 3D effects. They affect only the surface — not the edge — of the visible portion of the layer.

1 In the Layer Style dialog box, click the Satin box to activate the Satin options.

2 Drag to experiment with the Angle setting.

Note: You can drag a slider to indicate the figures for Opacity, Distance, and Size (see tips for this task).

3 Click OK to finalize.

CONTINUED

MAKE AND USE LAYER STYLES

CONTINUED

One layer effect that is especially useful on image layers is the pattern effect. You can apply any pattern you like to the entire layer. This gives a textured pattern to the effect. You could use this to create all sorts of natural materials that a viewer would think could be felt with the fingertips — everything from skin to hair to grass.

To do this, use the normal method for defining a pattern, then add that pattern to the Pattern Library. So you do not have to go look it up, here's the quick drill for doing that: Use the Rectangular Marquee tool to select part of an image, such as blades of grass, that shows a reasonably even pattern.

Next, choose Edit, then Define Pattern. When the Pattern Name dialog box appears, enter a name for the pattern and click OK.

That's all there is to it. The pattern you created can now be found in the Pattern Library when you want to apply the pattern as a layer effect.

MAKE AND USE LAYER STYLES (CONTINUED)

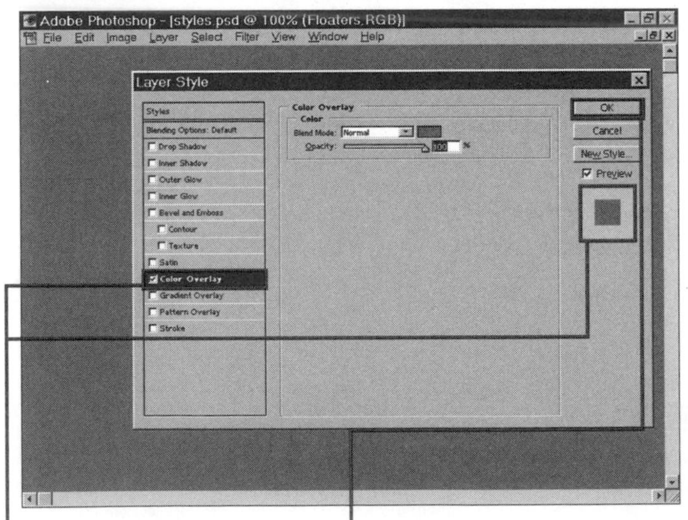

2D EFFECTS: COLOR OVERLAY

1 In the Layer Styles dialog box, click to check the Color Overlay box and to activate the Color Overlay options.

2 Choose a Color. The standard Color Picker dialog box appears.

■ Choose a color from the color picker in the standard manner.

3 Click OK.

■ The items on the layer change to the new color. The method of application can be changed by your choice of Blend Modes.

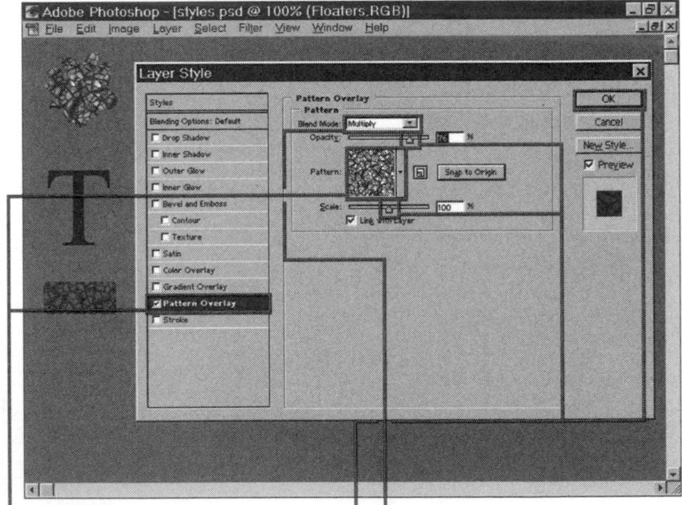

2D EFFECTS: PATTERN OVERLAY

1 In the Layer Styles dialog box, click to check the Pattern Overlay box and to activate the Pattern Overlay options.

2 Choose a Pattern.

3 Choose a Blend mode.

4 Drag to vary the pattern's transparency.

5 Drag to scale the pattern in relationship to the layer elements.

6 Click OK.

Can I create a surface style and then add other styles to it on a layer-by-layer basis?

✔ Easily. Apply the surface style, then edit the style. When the Styles dialog box appears, check additional styles. Then change the settings for each of the checked styles to suit your preferences.

What if I want to make the effect of a style permanent?

✔ Create a new layer and drag it below the Styles layer. Select the Styles layer and click the Link box in the new layer's Name bar, then choose Merge Linked from the Layers palette menu.

Can I have multiple Style libraries?

✔ Certainly. Just give each library a unique name. Then, when you want to use that library, bring up the Styles palette and click the Load button. Browse for the Library you want, double-click its name, and the library will load.

How do I apply a predefined style?

✔ The handiest way is to open the Styles palette by clicking the Styles button at the bottom of the Layers palette. Then click Styles in the Styles panel (on the left). The Styles Library will appear on the right side of the Styles palette. All you need to do to apply the style is click the desired icon in the Library.

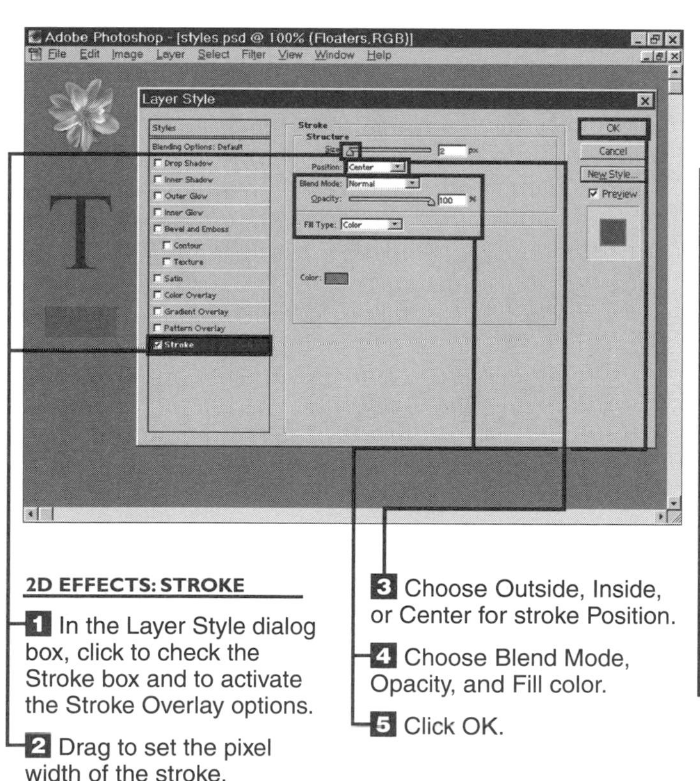

2D EFFECTS: STROKE

1 In the Layer Style dialog box, click to check the Stroke box and to activate the Stroke Overlay options.

2 Drag to set the pixel width of the stroke.

3 Choose Outside, Inside, or Center for stroke Position.

4 Choose Blend Mode, Opacity, and Fill color.

5 Click OK.

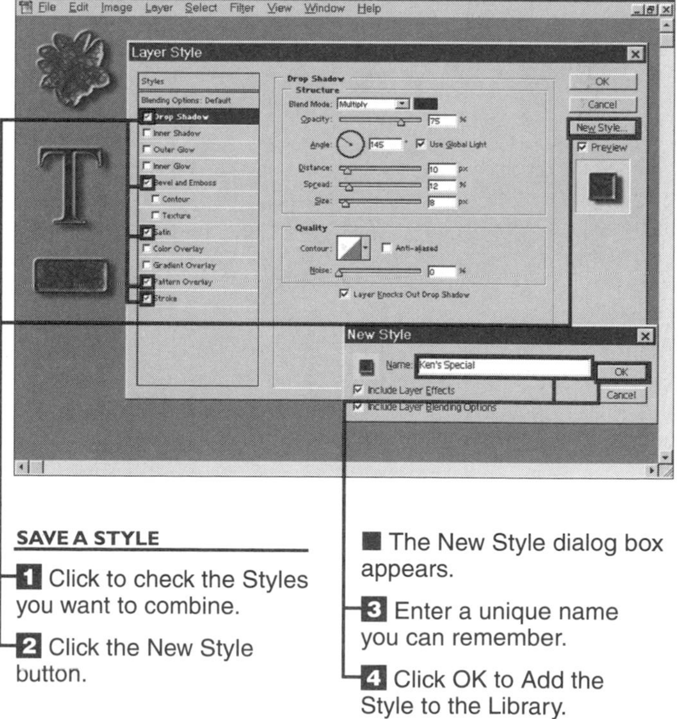

SAVE A STYLE

1 Click to check the Styles you want to combine.

2 Click the New Style button.

■ The New Style dialog box appears.

3 Enter a unique name you can remember.

4 Click OK to Add the Style to the Library.

ORGANIZE LAYERS

You can organize layers into folders called *sets*, with Photoshop 6. You can then perform operations on whole sets of layers at once, which can save you considerable time. Organizing layers into sets also makes both finding and isolating elements in complex compositions much easier. Finally, you can toggle the hiding and showing of entire sets, making it easy to show a client or colleague several variations of a technique before making a final decision as to which one survives.

The two primary ways of organizing existing layers into sets are creating a new set and then dragging layers into it, and linking the layers you want to place into the set and then choosing New Set From Linked from the Layers palette menu. All the linked layers automatically appear in the set.

The one thing to watch for when you put Layers into sets is stacking order. The layers will appear in the stacking order of the location of the set.

ORGANIZING LAYERS

CREATE A SET FROM LINKED LAYERS

1 Click to select the first layer in the target set.

2 Click to display the Link icon for each additional layer you want to place in the new set.

3 Choose New Set From Linked from the Layers palette menu.

■ The New Layer Set dialog box appears.

4 Enter a name for the new set and click OK.

■ All the formerly linked layers automatically appear in a new set.

5 Drag the new set to place it in the desired layer stacking order.

6 Click to reveal or hide all layers in the set.

How do you show/hide whole sets?

✔ The same way you show or hide a single layer: Click the layer visibility box until the Eye icon appears to show all the layers in the set; click again to turn off the Eye icon and hide all the layers in the set.

Can I collapse a whole set and stamp it to another layer?

✔ Yes. See the "Stamping Layers" section earlier in this chapter.

Can I lock all the layers in a set to protect them from changes?

✔ Just select the set by clicking its name in the Layers palette. Then, choose Lock All Layers In Set from the Layers palette menu. A Lock All Layers in Set dialog box appears, and you can lock Transparency, Image, Position, or All — just as you can by using the Layer palettes check boxes for locking those characteristics for an individual layer. You can also Lock All by clicking the set's name bar, then checking the Lock All box at the top of the palette.

CREATE A NEW LAYER SET

1 Choose New Layer Set from the Layers palette menu.

■ A New Layer Set dialog box appears.

2 Enter a new name for the set and click OK.

■ The folder name bar for the new set automatically appears in the Layers palette.

3 Drag the Layer name bar to the new set's folder icon to place a layer in the set.

■ Repeat step 3 until all the layers you want placed in the set have been moved.

MANAGE LAYERS

You can manage layers to conserve memory and disk space. Why bother? Well, a nontransparent layer consumes virtually as much file space as the original image. So does every such layer you add. If you do not get rid of or merge layers when you no longer need them, you will soon run out of resources. Even sooner, you will find your hot-rod graphics computer running at a snail's pace.

First, you need to know how to keep track of how large your files have become while you are working. Then you can judge how much RAM you need to complete the job and how much disk space you need to store the file.

Second, you want to know that you have enough scratch disk space left for Photoshop to be able to swap the image to disk when RAM becomes overcrowded. As the following exercises show, Photoshop makes both those jobs easy.

Finally, you need to know how to delete or merge layers when you no longer need them so that file sizes do not get unmanageable.

MANAGING LAYERS

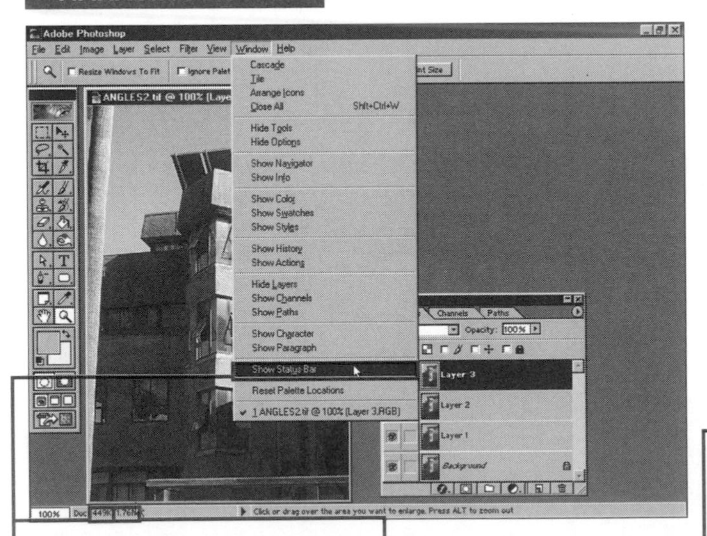

TRACK FILE SIZE

1 In Windows, if the status bar is not visible, choose Window, then Show Status Bar.

■ Size of file, if flattened, appears here.

■ Current size of file, with all layers, appears here.

Note: On a Mac, choose Show Sizes from the pop-up menu next to the status area in the bottom of the window. The status area is always visible on a Mac.

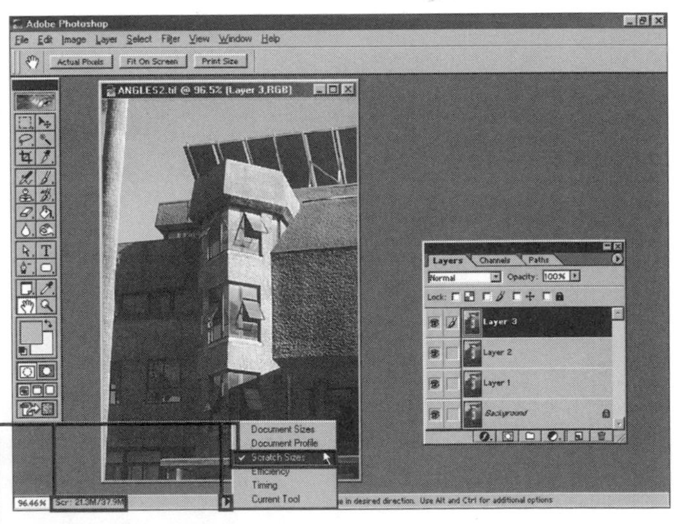

TRACK SCRATCH DISK SIZE REQUIREMENTS

1 Click the arrowhead to get the pop-up menu.

2 Choose Scratch Sizes.

■ Scratch disk file size requirements appear here.

Note: The actual amount of scratch disk space available is equal to the amount of free disk space on those hard drives designated as scratch disks.

What if I just want to flatten the entire file into one layer?

✔ It happens automatically as soon as you choose the Flatten Image command, which you can access from either the Layer menu or the Layers palette's pop-up menu.

Will carefully managed layers result in faster print times?

✔ Yes, especially if you are working with photographic-quality prints at larger sizes. This is even more important if your printer has no built-in memory of its own. You can keep a layered file while printing a flattened file. Just choose Image, then Duplicate and then Layer, then Flatten, and then print from the Duplicate file.

What are the layer management considerations for files that will appear on Web pages?

✔ You almost always want to flatten the image before placing it on a Web page because special plug-ins are required for reading layered images and most viewers have not installed such plug-ins. Also, the smaller the file size, the faster the image loads into the viewer's browser.

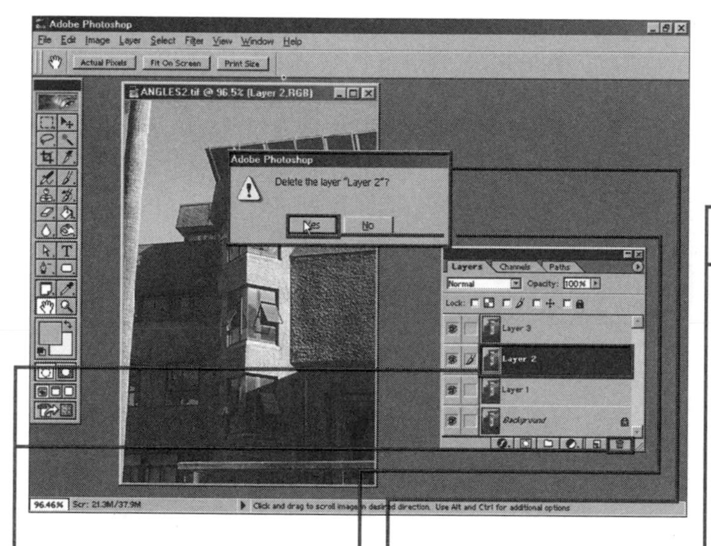

DELETE UNNEEDED LAYERS

1 Click the layer to be deleted.

2 Click the Trash icon.

■ A warning dialog box appears asking if you are sure you want to delete the file.

3 Click Yes.

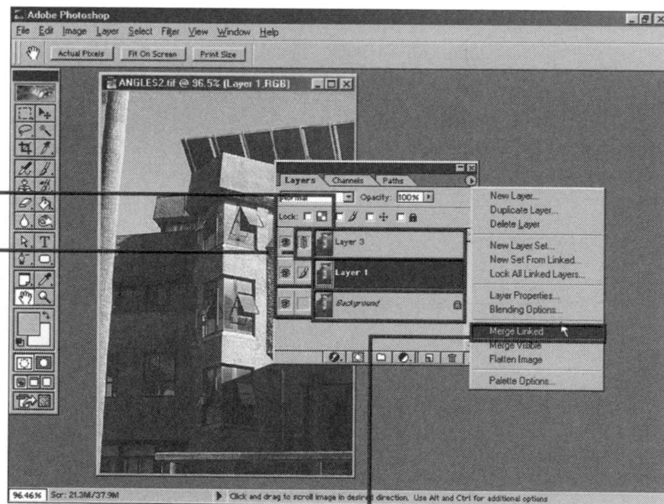

MERGE LAYERS

1 Click the layers you want to merge.

2 Click the Link icon to link.

■ You may link as many layers as you like in this way.

3 Choose Merge Linked from the menu that appears.

■ The chosen layer and all the layers with a link icon appearing in the second column will be merged together.

SPLIT OUT THE CHANNELS

You can place each channel in an image file—whether color, spot, or alpha—into a separate file.

Each of the channels is a grayscale channel, so if you need a black-and-white photo that looks more dramatic, one of these images might just do the job. The red channel even looks a little like a photograph shot on infrared film.

You can do many other things with split-out channels. Most importantly, you can edit any flaws in the individual channels and then recombine them all. Or, you can run different special effects in each channel and then recombine them.

You can also merge the separated alpha channels into a new file so that you end up with all the masks for your file in a separate file.

One common use for this feature is for transportation purposes. You can put a 3MB or larger RGB file on three floppy disks by splitting the file into three grayscale files—one per disk—and then reassembling them to recreate the color file.

SPLIT OUT THE CHANNELS

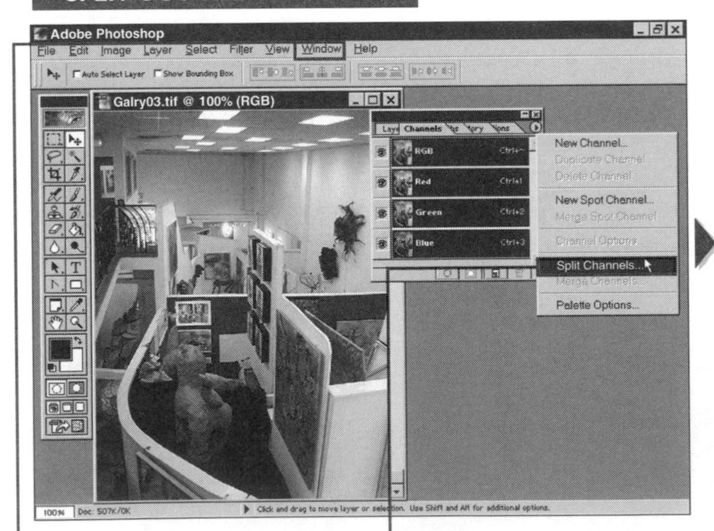

1 Choose Window, then Show Channels.

■ The Channels palette appears.

2 Choose Split Channels from the palette menu.

Note: Each channel is written out to a separate file (but not saved to disk — that is up to you).

■ The individual channels each appear in a separate window.

Note: You can merge these channels into a new file or merge them with other grayscale files (as long as all have exactly the same dimensions in pixels).

MAKE A SEPARATE CHANNEL FOR SPOT COLORS

You can create a specific channel for printing a specific spot color atop the continuous tone image. Spot color is usually used to introduce a brilliant blue, purple, orange, or fluorescent (which cannot be produced accurately with process color), or it can be used for a varnish or metallic ink.

When this file is printed, the traditional color separation is made for the C, M, Y, and K channels. Separate plates are then made for the spot color channels. These spot color plates are then used to overprint colors on the full-range print with a single ink of a specific color.

When you choose the color for a spot color, you will generally not want to use the standard process colors. Instead, choose your color from one of the color swatch books that are supported in the Color Picker. You can find out what these are by clicking one of the color swatches to open the Color Picker, then clicking the Custom button to open the Custom Colors dialog, then choosing the book from the Book menu.

MAKE A SEPARATE CHANNEL FOR SPOT COLORS

1 Unless you want a new blank channel, select the area you want the spot color to cover.

2 Choose Window, then Show Channels.

■ The Channels palette appears.

3 Choose New Spot Channel from the Channels palette menu.

■ The New Spot Channel dialog box appears.

4 Accept the default name or type a new one for the spot color channel.

5 Click the color swatch to bring up the Color Picker.

6 In the Color Picker, click the Custom button and choose your color.

7 Type a percentage of solidity for the spot color and click OK.

■ The new channel automatically appears and is activated in the Channels palette.

MERGE CHANNELS TO CREATE SPECIAL EFFECTS

You can create a new channel by merging two or more existing channels. You can merge channels from any files you like. If you specify more channels than are in the color model, the remaining channels become alpha (mask) channels. When you merge channels, Photoshop looks for all the open grayscale files that have the same number of vertical and horizontal pixels. If you are off by one pixel, the files cannot merge.

The most common reason for splitting and merging channels is so that you can edit each channel individually without having to worry about messing up the original image. However, this exercise adds a few extra steps so you can see the dramatic results that can be produced by merging channels.

This exercise turns a photograph into a uniquely rendered poster by treating each split channel with an artistic filter. You can experiment with any Photoshop process on the individual channels. You are bound to get some exciting results (and more than a few really ugly ones). This exercise assumes that you have used the Split Channels command (see "Split Out the Channels," earlier in this chapter) to create a separate grayscale file for each active channel.

MERGE CHANNELS TO CREATE SPECIAL EFFECTS

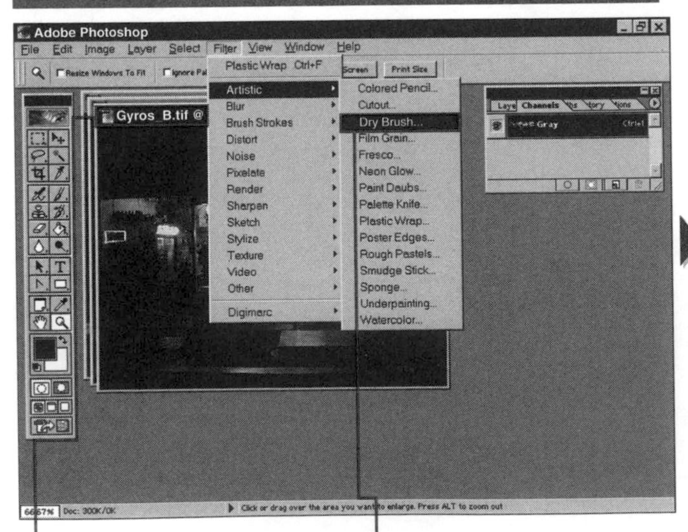

1 Click the title bar of the window you want to activate.

2 Use any Photoshop command to change the individual versions of each channel.

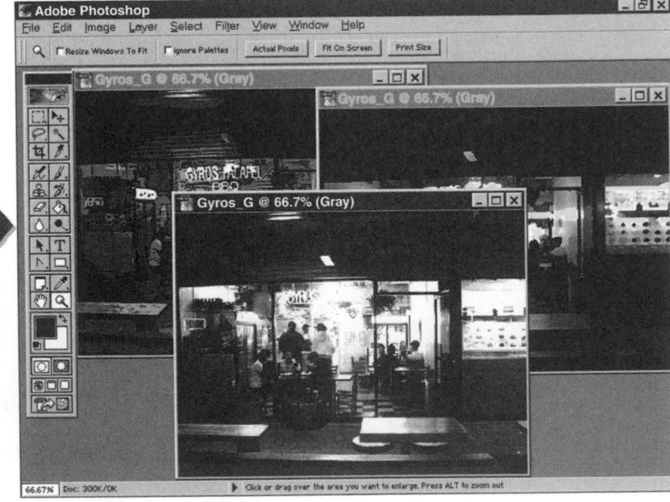

■ Here you see the result of running a different artistic filter on each of the grayscale files.

Which processes for each channel are most likely to be effective?

✔ On each channel, choose Image, then Adjust, then Auto Levels or Image, then Adjust, then click Equalize. Another effect that can prove interesting is to run a different distortion filter or a different texture filter on each channel document.

What happens when I create the three (or four) color channels from different pictures?

✔ If you do this with pictures of textures or patterns, you get textures you never saw or expected, which can be quite beautiful. This technique can also be very effective for photo-collage or a great way to make a big mess.

Is there an everyday use for merge channels?

✔ The most common use is improving the blue channel from low-end scanners and overcompressed JPEG files. This channel is the one in which mistakes and artifacts are most likely to appear. Often, you can improve the image by using a combination of the Gaussian Blur filter and the Unsharp mask filter on the blue channel.

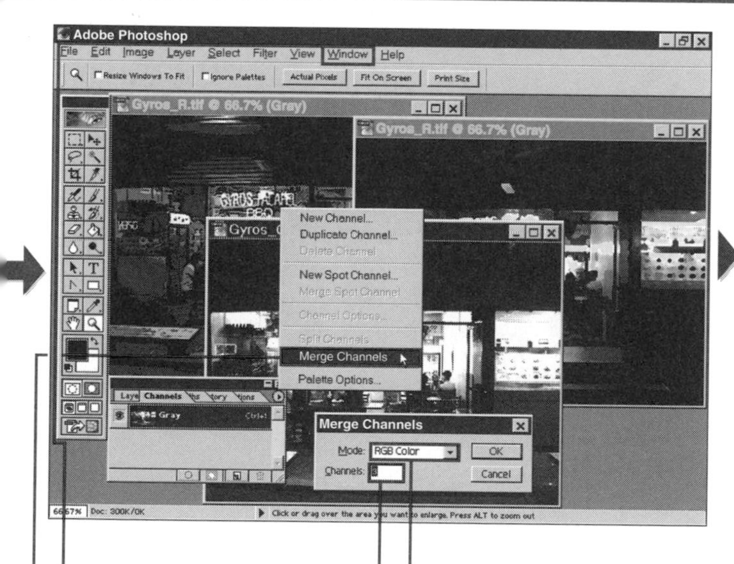

3 Choose Window, then Show Channels.

4 Choose Merge Channels from the Channels palette menu.

5 Choose the target color mode.

6 Type the number of channels and click OK.

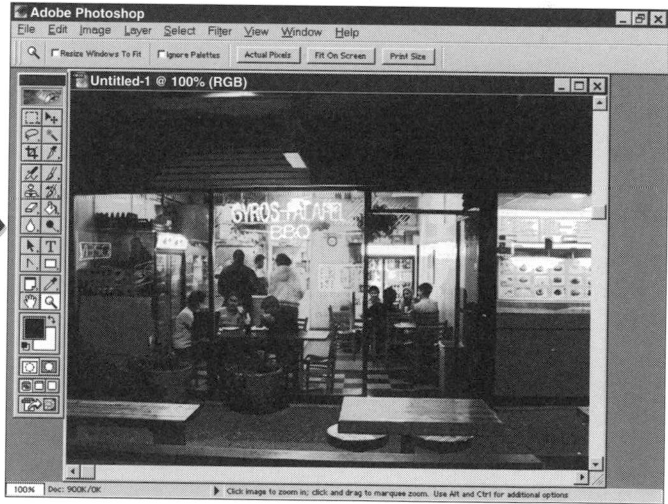

■ Here is the result of running three separate artistic filters, one in each of the channels, and then merging them.

MERGE CHANNELS FROM DIFFERENT FILES

You can merge any number of channels into a single file, as long as they are all grayscale and all the same size. This method is one way to import masks and spot color channels from other files. Merging can be handy for compositing, special effects, spot color compositions, and generic masks (such as those for vignettes and picture frames).

If you want to merge more files than a particular color model has channels (three for RGB and LAB, four for CMYK), you have to select Multichannel from the Mode menu in the Merge Channels dialog box. You will not have a color model in the merged file, so after merging, you need to choose Image, then Mode, then the appropriate color model.

When the image converts, Photoshop makes a composite channel of the first three or four (depending on mode) channels. If these channels are not the ones you want to use as the first three, simply use the Channels palette to select the channel you want to move and then drag and drop it into the new position in the stack.

MERGE CHANNELS FROM DIFFERENT FILES

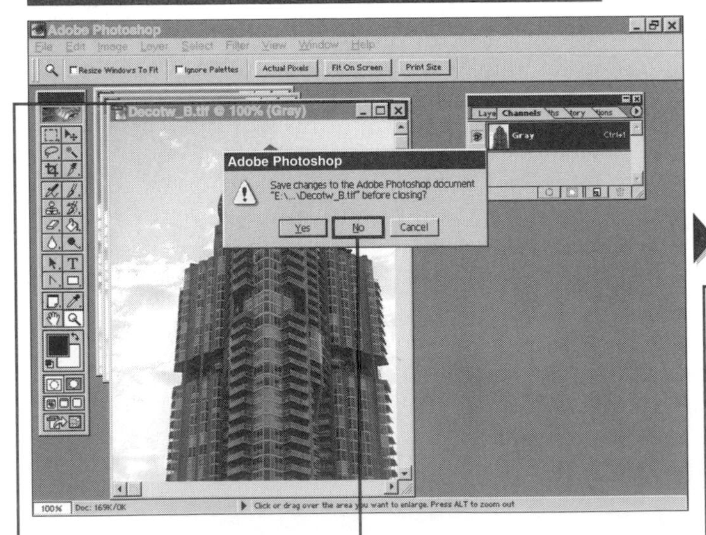

1 Split the channels from all the files you want to recombine.

Note: See "Split Out the Channels," earlier in this chapter.

2 Close the windows for channels you do not want to use in the new file.

Note: The preceding is not a requirement, but visually picking channels is often easier than (later) picking them by name only.

3 Click No to permanently dump unwanted channels.

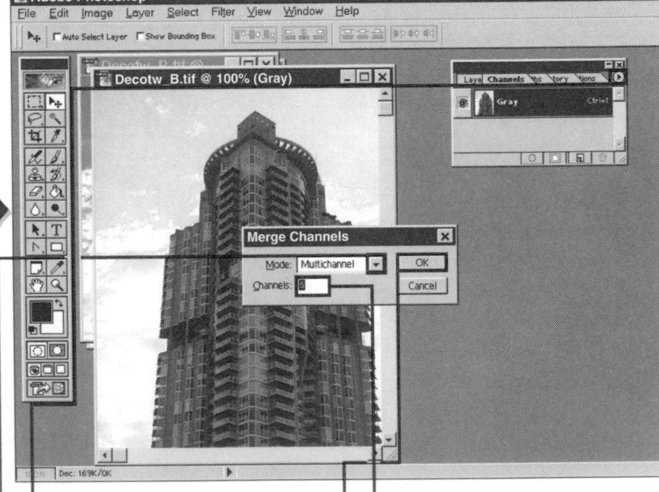

4 Choose Merge Channels from the Channels palette menu.

5 Choose Multichannel from the menu.

6 Type how many channels you want to recombine.

7 Click OK.

Can I use a collection of masks made from the silhouettes of shapes to create drawings?

✔ Yes. You can convert the mask to a selection, convert the selection to a path, save the path as an EPS file, and read that file into (almost) any illustration program. Remember, paths can also be converted to selections, so you can collect masks from any number of files, turn them all into paths, and save them in a single, tiny file.

How much can I vary the influence of each channel over the overall effect?

✔ You can apply any of the commands that you can access by choosing Image, then Adjust to any of the individual channels. First, select the channel in the Channels palette by clicking its name bar. Then use the Adjust command. When you select the composite channel, you will see the result of your adjustment(s).

Can I use Color Balance on an individual channel?

✔ No. The individual channels are grayscale images. You can use the Brightness/Contrast command, however.

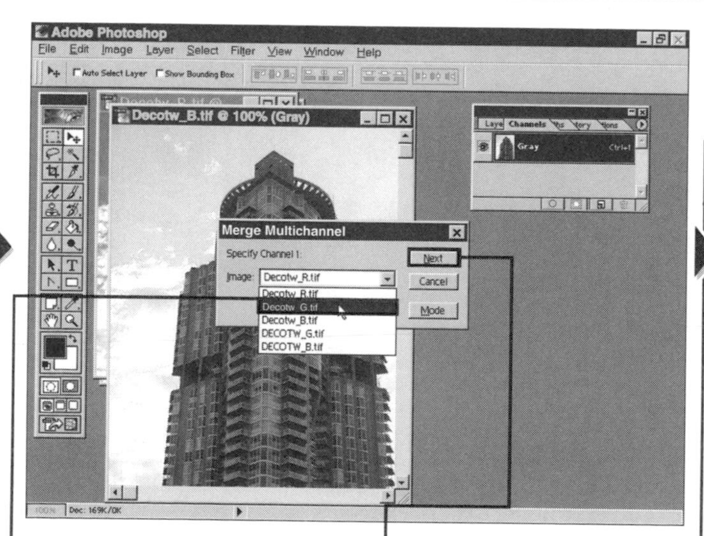

■ The Merge Multichannel dialog appears.

8 Choose the channels you want to merge into Channel 1.

9 Click Next.

10 Repeat steps 8 and 9 until you have chosen all the files you want to merge.

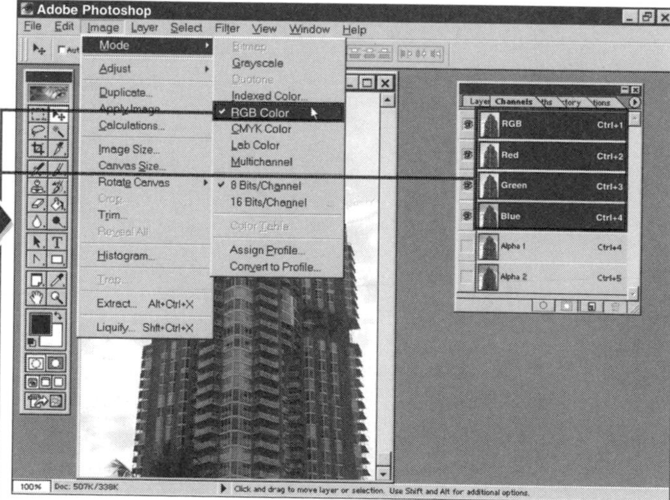

PLACE THE FILE BACK IN RGB MODE

11 Drag channels into proper order.

12 Choose Image, then Mode, then RGB (or any other color model you want to use).

■ A composite channel appears at the top of the Channels palette. If you merged channels into a model other than the model they were split from, the result is unpredictably weird.

USING THE APPLY IMAGE COMMAND

You can use the Apply Image command to create the channel mathematics known to Photoshop geeks as CHOPS. For years, real Photoshop geeks prided themselves on knowing their CHOPS—short for CHannel OPerationS. This term referred to the amazing effects you can apply if you fully understand the mathematics behind combining channels.

Today, you can perform almost all CHOPS by using the Blend modes in the Layers palette. You can still, however, selectively apply one specific channel to another and use Blend modes (Multiply, Add, and Screen, for example) in the process. These commands are Apply Image and Calculations on the Image menu —the simplest being the Apply Image command.

Through the Apply Image dialog box, you can combine channels, either in the current file or from another open file of the same dimensions, and store them in the current channel of the active file (document). You can achieve an infinite number of effects in this way: texturing, intensification of colors, framing—you name it.

Coming up with the exact effect you want requires some experimentation. Fortunately, by checking the Preview box, you can see any effect before committing to it.

USING THE APPLY IMAGE COMMAND

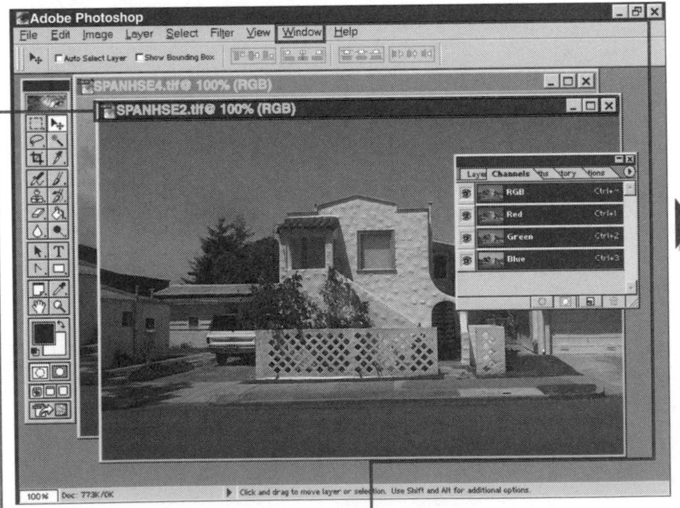

1 Open the target file and the file from which you want to apply either the whole image or a channel.

2 Make your target image active (click its title bar).

3 Choose Window, then Show Channels.

■ The Channels palette displays. Showing the Channels palette makes deciding which channels you want to combine, and from which images, easier.

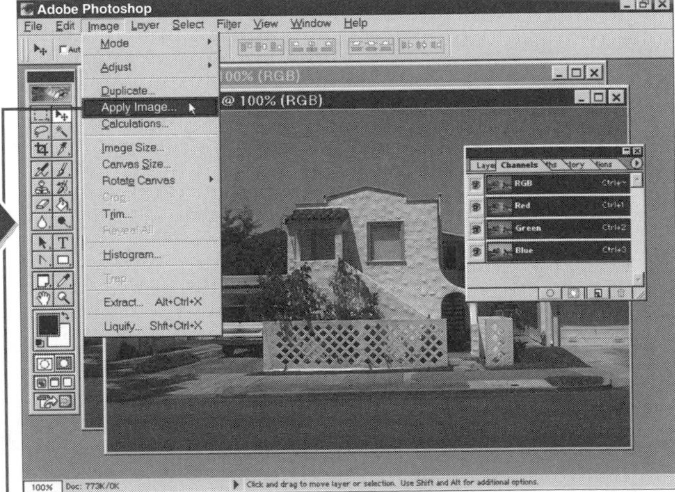

4 Choose Image, then Apply Image.

■ The Apply Image dialog appears.

Is using the Apply Image command an even faster way to collect alpha channels into a separate file?

✔ It is an easy way to do it, because you can simply get rid of all the color channels. You should make sure that you save the finished file under a name that clearly identifies it as an alpha channel file.

If I do not get the transparency right for the blend, or I want to lower it, can I use the Fade command on the Filter menu?

✔ Actually, this way is the best to deal with transparency, because it gives you a way to visualize the result interactively. Also, the huge Apply Image dialog box is no longer covering your image.

How can I use this command to texture an image?

✔ Use a scanned photograph of the texture you have in mind; use one of the many texture files available in CD-ROM libraries; or use one of the texture-generating plug-in filters, such as Real Texture or Terrazo from Xaos Tools. Make a file the same size as the target file and apply any of its channels in any of the Blend modes. Or, you can apply one of its channels and use another as a mask.

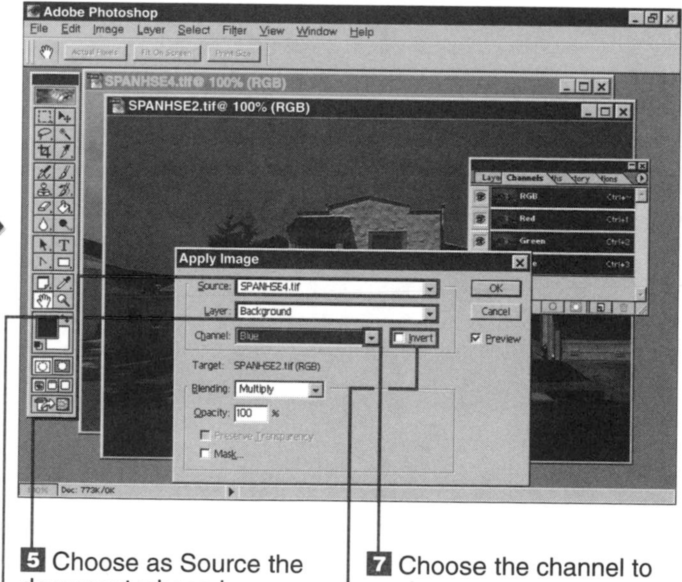

5 Choose as Source the document whose image you want to apply.

6 Choose the layer that holds the image.

7 Choose the channel to apply.

Note: To apply the entire layer, choose the composite (RGB/CMYK/LAB) channel.

■ Optional: Click to invert (make negative) the source channel.

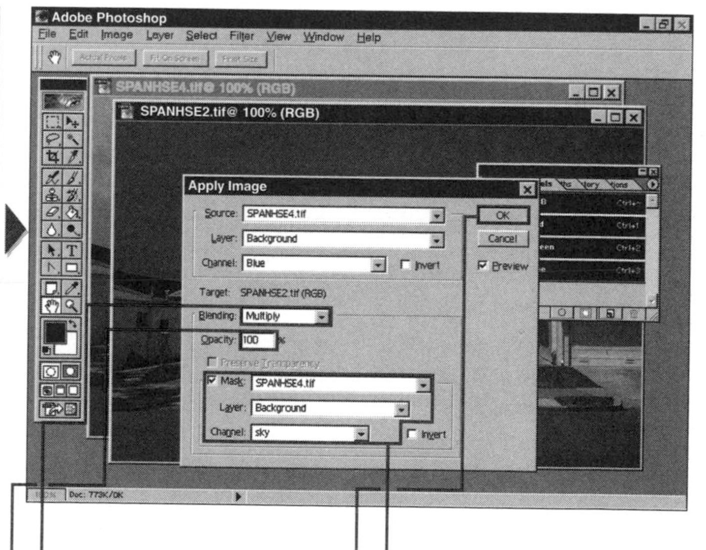

8 Choose the Blend mode you want to use.

■ Optional: Type an opacity for the Blend mode.

9 Click the Mask check box and choose the source, masking channel, and layer (applicable only if you want to use a layer mask).

10 Click OK.

USING THE CALCULATIONS COMMAND

You can also apply CHOPS (*Channel Operations*) with the Calculations command on the Image menu. The Calculations command is similar to the Apply Image command. Both commands require that you blend images between open files having the same pixel dimensions.

The big difference is that the result of the application of channels or images does not take place in the composite channel. You can choose whether the result appears as a layer mask (only if you are working with an active layer that has a layer mask), a new channel within the current file, or an alpha channel in an entirely new file. Furthermore, the target image may or may not be the active image and can even be a brand-new image. To put it another way, you mix two different channels from up to two different sources into one, which may or may not be a new file.

Blending options are the same as for the Apply Image command. You can see the visual effect of all Blend modes, regardless of which tool is used to apply them, pictured in the full-color section of this book.

USING THE CALCULATIONS COMMAND

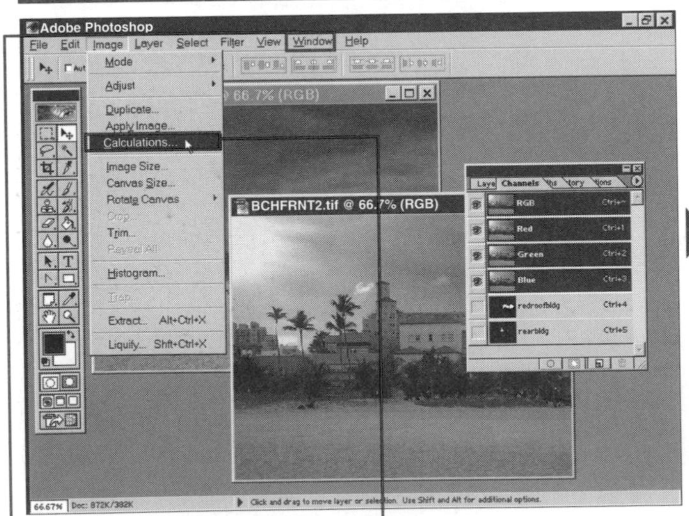

1 Open one or two files from which you want to combine channels.

2 Choose Window, then Show Channels to see which channels you want to blend.

3 Choose Image, then Calculations.

■ The Calculations dialog box appears.

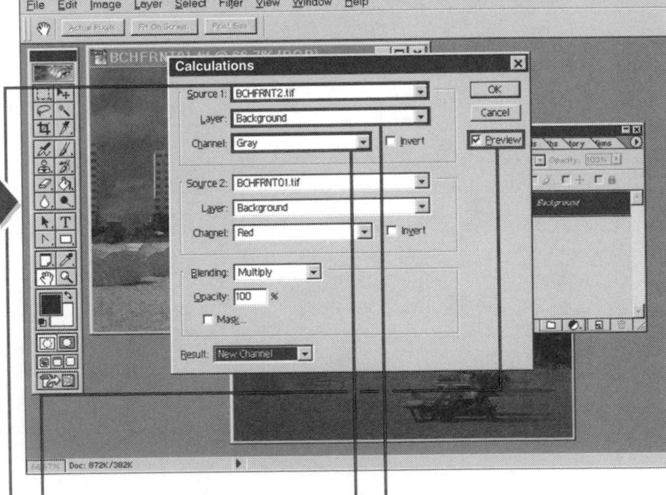

4 Click the Preview check box (default) until the checkmark toggles on.

5 Choose from the list of open files of the same size.

■ The front window appears as the default.

6 Choose the image layer you want calculated.

7 Choose the color channel you want calculated.

8 Repeat steps 5-7 for the fields in Source 2.

Can I get rid of the Calculations dialog box so that I can see what I am doing in the preview area?

✔ Just use its title bar to drag it out of the way.

What is the gray channel? I do not see it in the Channels palette.

✔ Because the gray channel is not there. If you choose gray, Photoshop makes the blend from a grayscale version of the composite channel.

Are any of the Blend modes in the Apply Image and Calculations dialog boxes unique to channel calculations?

✔ Yes, Add and Subtract. These modes add and subtract the brightness values of the two source channels. (Add lightens and Subtract darkens.) The offset value divides the sum or difference. The Scale value is then added to the result. Add the ability to set transparency, and you have total control over the intensity of the result.

Can I apply a mask with the Calculations command?

✔ Yes, but the mask always applies to the first source and protects the second source. The white portions of the mask show the result of the calculations, and the black portions show only the second source image.

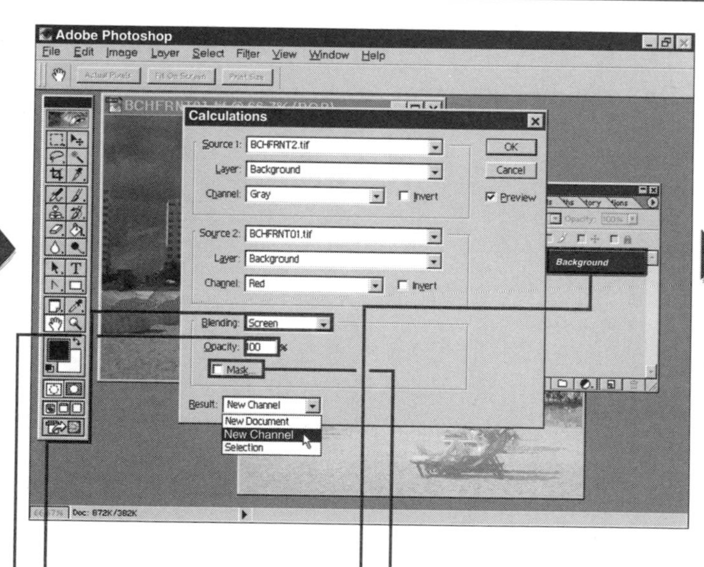

9 Choose a Blend mode.

10 Type a number for the opacity of the Blend.

11 Click to check whether you want to use any of the mask channels in either source to limit the effect of the blend.

12 Choose the channel to be used as a mask.

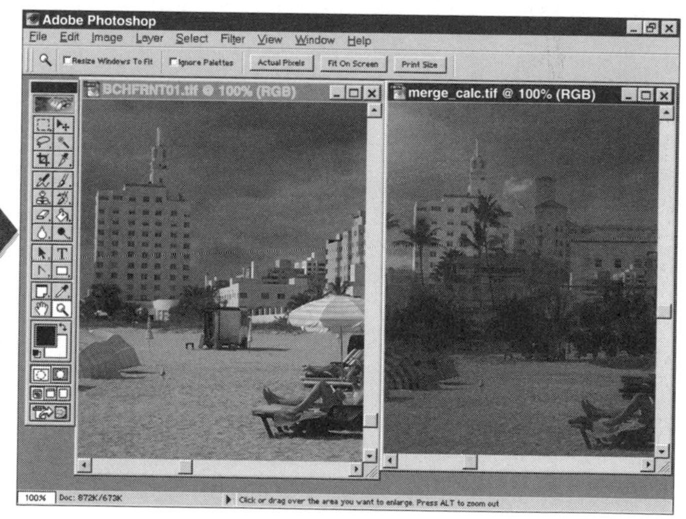

■ This image shows the effect of the channel operation on the target channel.

Note: An unlimited number of these effects are available, depending on the number and type of channels in the target and source and depending on which Blend modes you use.

USING THE TYPE TOOLS

You can enter text as either solid text or as a selection in the exact shape of the text you are entering. Each of these is divided into horizontal and vertical varieties. Type tools actually enter outline type that is converted to a bitmap once the type layers are merged or flattened.

Type tools automatically fill text with the current foreground color and place the text on its own layer. You can edit that text after it has been entered—as long as you do not merge or flatten its text layer.

You can enter either *point type* or *paragraph type*.

- To enter point type, you just click in the image at the point where you want the type to start.
- To enter paragraph type, use the Type tool to drag a marquee rectangle bounding box (see the next section, "Enter Paragraph Text"). Type will then wrap to fit within the box.

Type is not created on its own layer when you work in indexed color, bitmap, or multichannel modes, because those modes do not support layers.

USING THE TYPE TOOLS

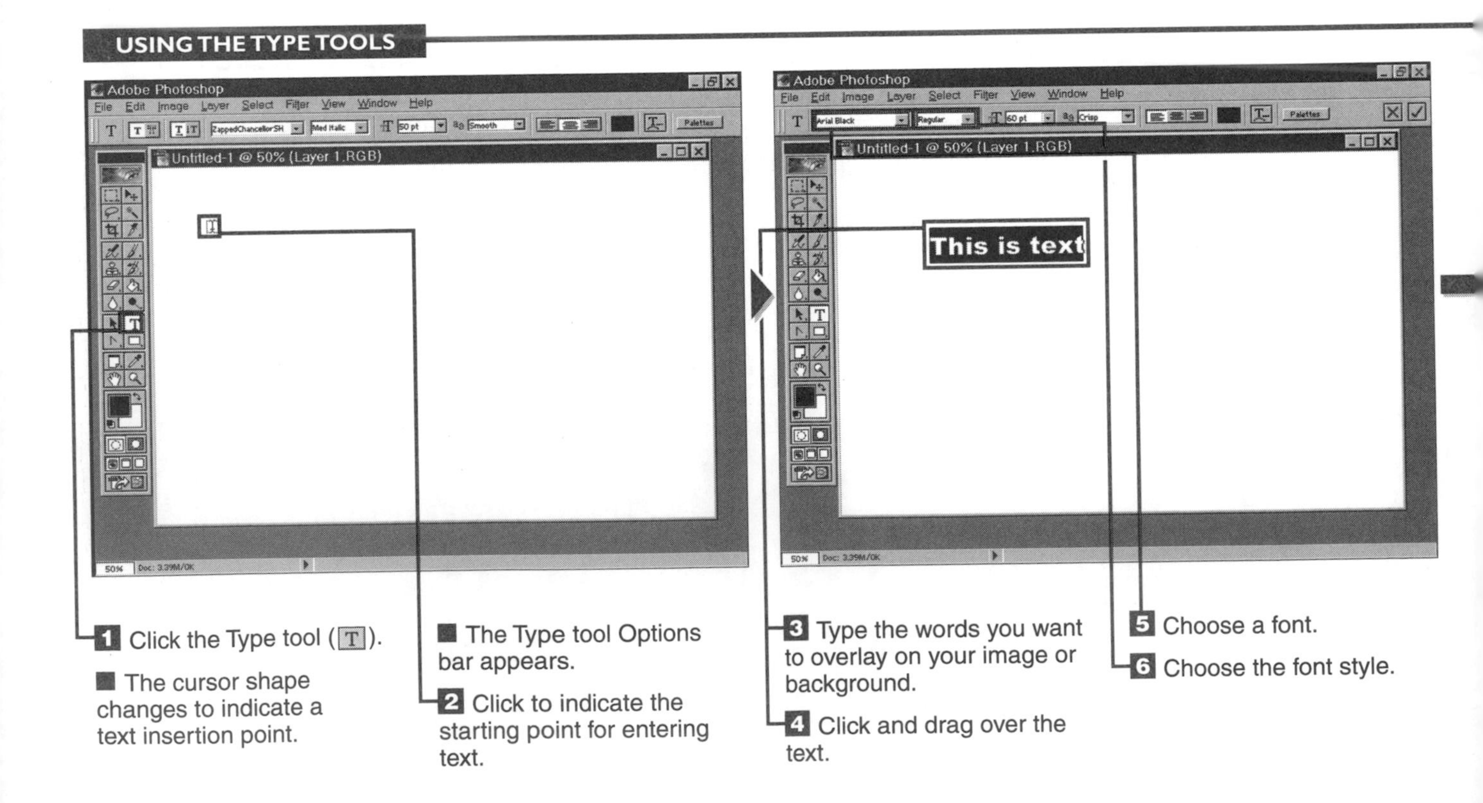

1 Click the Type tool (T).

■ The cursor shape changes to indicate a text insertion point.

■ The Type tool Options bar appears.

2 Click to indicate the starting point for entering text.

3 Type the words you want to overlay on your image or background.

4 Click and drag over the text.

5 Choose a font.

6 Choose the font style.

How do I get type to be a specific size on paper?

✔ Use a vector graphics-based illustration program, such as Adobe Illustrator or CorelDRAW!, or a page layout program, such as Adobe PageMaker, InDesign, or QuarkXPress. You can place your Photoshop document as an image in one of these programs and use the program's typesetting capabilities to specify type for print. If you are trying to size the type in Photoshop, make sure your inch dimensions and dpi are correct and then use point sizes.

How do I know what point size to choose?

✔ Choose the point size that makes the lettering the right size in relationship to the image on which you are overlaying it.

Then why bother to set type in Photoshop?

✔ Photoshop works well for setting type destined to be used on-screen and for setting type to be treated with artistic effects or integrated into an image as part of a collage.

What are some of the other character settings used for?

✔ *Kerning* adjusts the spacing between individual letters. *Tracking* adjusts the spacing between all the letters in a line or paragraph. *Leading* indicates the space between lines. *Baseline shift* moves a character up or down to produce superscript or subscript.

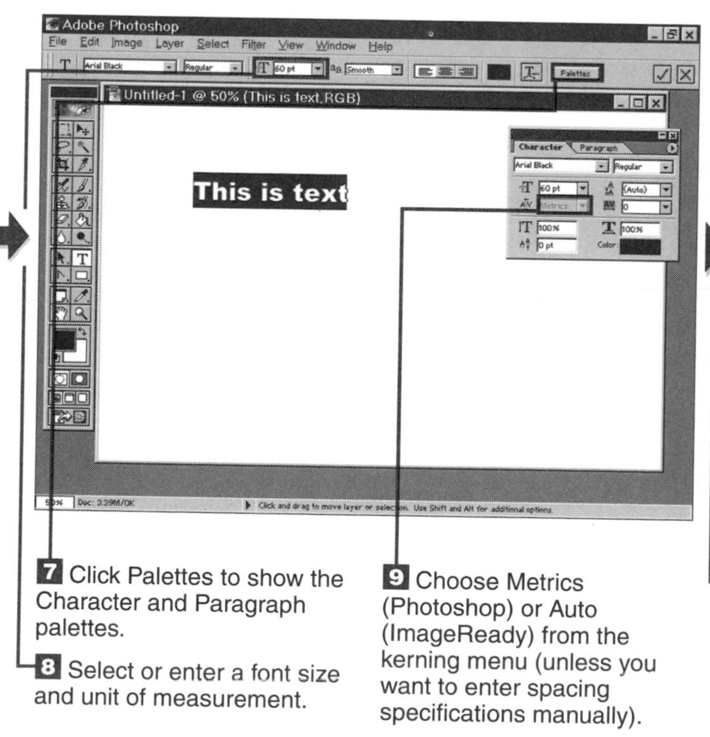

7 Click Palettes to show the Character and Paragraph palettes.

8 Select or enter a font size and unit of measurement.

9 Choose Metrics (Photoshop) or Auto (ImageReady) from the kerning menu (unless you want to enter spacing specifications manually).

Note: You must insert the blinking text insertion bar between letters you want to kern manually.

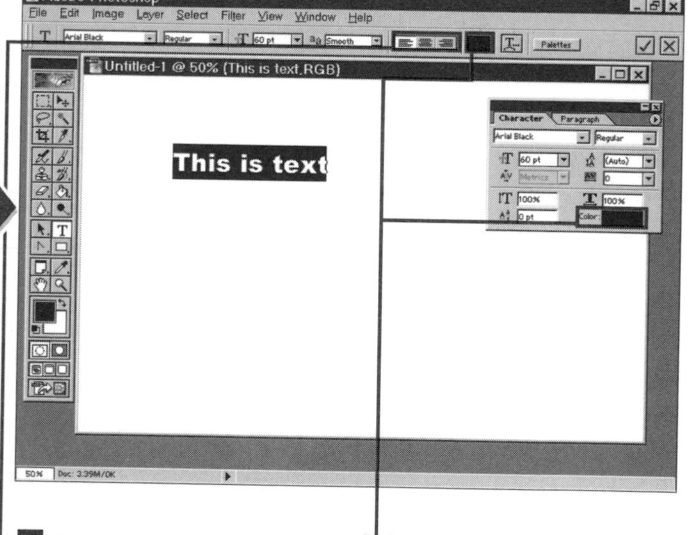

10 Click the desired justification button.

Note: If justification is set to Left, all text aligns at the left margin; if set to Center, text aligns equidistant on both sides; if set to Right, it aligns to the right margin.

11 Click the Color swatch to change the text color. (The Color Picker appears when you click the swatch.)

ENTER PARAGRAPH TEXT

You can enter text as paragraphs so that it automatically wraps when it reaches the end of the text line. Doing so is as easy as using the Type tool to drag a rectangular marquee that is the size of the area that is to contain the paragraph text. After you do that, you can use a palette to change the characteristics of the paragraph such as indentation and justification.

Another advantage of using paragraph text in Photoshop 6 is the ability to rescale or rotate the text box. You scale the text box by dragging the handles. This action does not scale the text. It just scales the box so that the text wraps differently. Rotation, on the other hand, works just like any other transform command. You can turn the text to any angle you like.

You can control a great many aspects of paragraph type by setting controls in both the Character and Paragraph palettes. You now access both of these controls from the Palettes button in the Type tool's Options bar. See the "Text Tool Options" section of Appendix B for more information.

ENTER PARAGRAPH TEXT

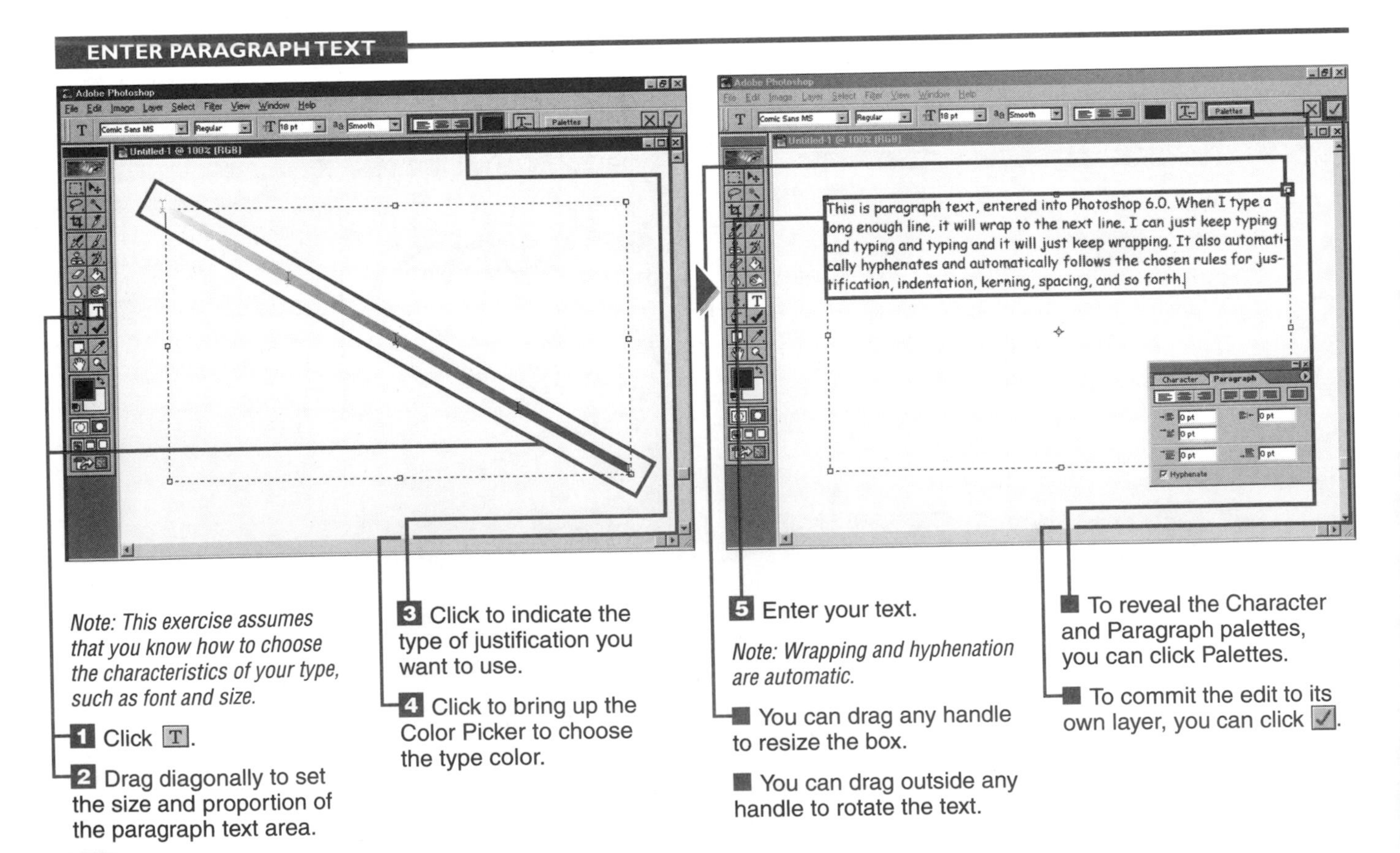

Note: This exercise assumes that you know how to choose the characteristics of your type, such as font and size.

1 Click T.

2 Drag diagonally to set the size and proportion of the paragraph text area.

3 Click to indicate the type of justification you want to use.

4 Click to bring up the Color Picker to choose the type color.

5 Enter your text.

Note: Wrapping and hyphenation are automatic.

■ You can drag any handle to resize the box.

■ You can drag outside any handle to rotate the text.

■ To reveal the Character and Paragraph palettes, you can click Palettes.

■ To commit the edit to its own layer, you can click ✓.

DISTORT TEXT

You can distort text in 15 prebuilt envelopes with control over bend, horizontal distortion, and vertical distortion. This feature is not the same as being able to have text follow a path but is very useful for creating emotional-impact text effects for illustration and presentation purposes.

The tools you use for distorting text are right on the text Options bar. You choose a style from a pull-down menu to bring up a dialog box with four controls: Bend, Horizontal/Vertical radio buttons, Horizontal Distortion, and Vertical Distortion.

Bend causes the text to follow a smooth curve path. The Horizontal/Vertical radio buttons let you choose whether the effect will be applied along the whole line of text (horizontally) or vertically on each letter. Of course, if the text is entered vertically, these effects are reversed.

Horizontal and Vertical Distortion refer to perspective distortion. Horizontal Distortion makes the text get smaller from one side to the other. Vertical Distortion makes the line of type shorter at the top or bottom.

DISTORT TEXT

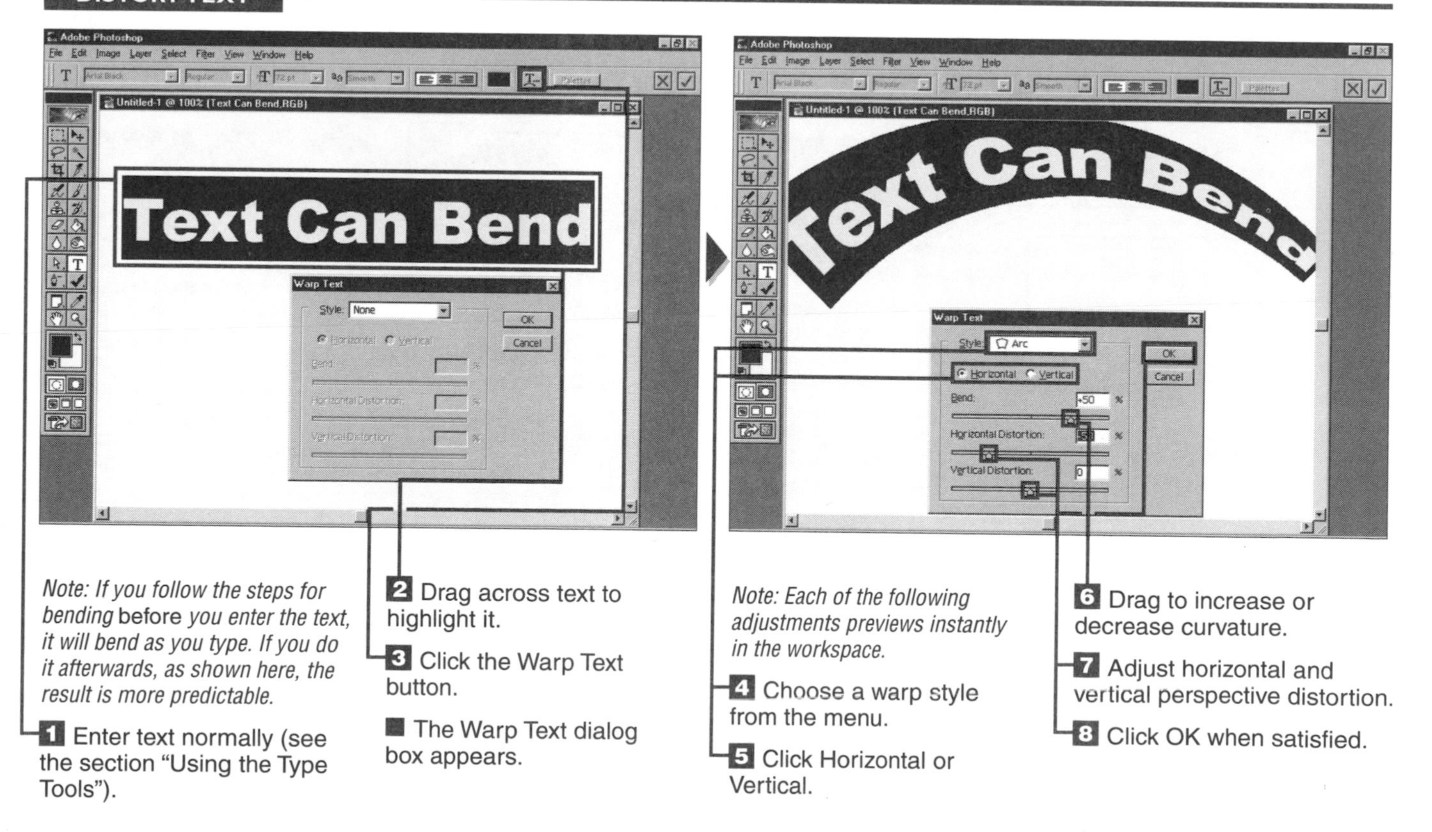

Note: If you follow the steps for bending before *you enter the text, it will bend as you type. If you do it afterwards, as shown here, the result is more predictable.*

1 Enter text normally (see the section "Using the Type Tools").

2 Drag across text to highlight it.

3 Click the Warp Text button.

■ The Warp Text dialog box appears.

Note: Each of the following adjustments previews instantly in the workspace.

4 Choose a warp style from the menu.

5 Click Horizontal or Vertical.

6 Drag to increase or decrease curvature.

7 Adjust horizontal and vertical perspective distortion.

8 Click OK when satisfied.

EDIT A TYPE LAYER

You can correct misspellings or even change the entire content of a paragraph, even after you have committed it to a layer (clicked the Check Mark button at the right side of the Options bar), without having to delete a text layer and start all over.

To edit text, you have to show the Layers palette (click Window, then Show Layers, or press Opt/Alt+F7 if you have not changed the default function key assignments). You can only edit text that has been entered with the Type tool. Text entered with the Type Selection tool is bitmapped and cannot be edited.

To edit text, you just choose the Type tool (unless it is already chosen) and click the type. The text entry cursor automatically appears where you clicked. Highlight any text you want to replace and then just start typing. When done, click the Commit Edits (check mark) button in the Options bar to commit the changes to the layer. You can also just highlight text to change type characteristics.

EDIT A TYPE LAYER

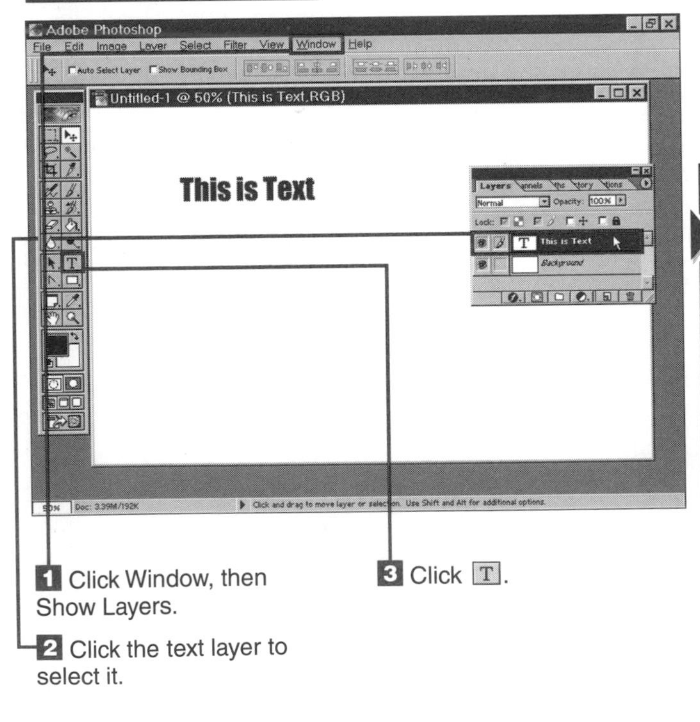

1 Click Window, then Show Layers.

2 Click the text layer to select it.

3 Click T.

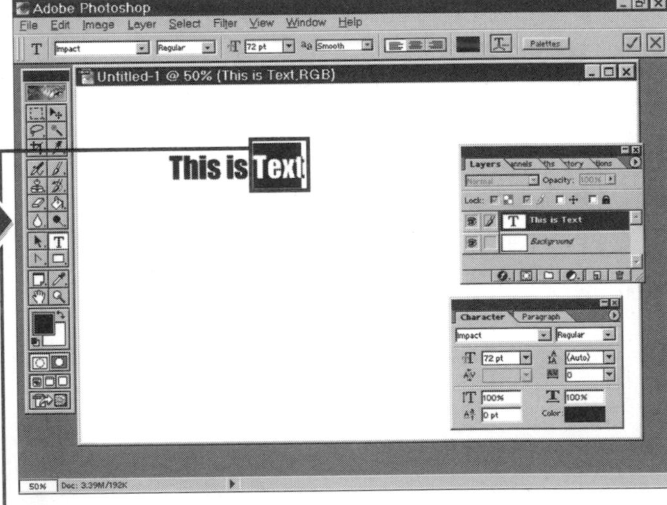

4 Click and drag to highlight any text that you want to edit.

■ You can start entering new text or change the selected text as you want.

Note: Changes in almost all settings affect only the highlighted letters.

Note: The changes are not permanent because you can always edit them, unless you merge type layers or rasterize the type.

Can I change the color of part of the text?

✔ Photoshop 6 makes this very easy. Click the Type tool, highlight the text whose color you want to change, and then click the Palettes button in the Options bar. The Character and Paragraph palettes appear. Click the Color Swatch in the Character palette and the Color Picker appears. Choose a new color and click OK. The color of the highlighted text changes automatically. If you are satisfied, click OK.

What advantage does setting type in Photoshop have that cannot be had in vector programs?

✔ The big advantages are transparency and the ability to apply layer styles. Although illustration programs are just beginning to introduce transparency, all you have to do to get transparency in Photoshop is drag the slider that controls the transparency of the layer.

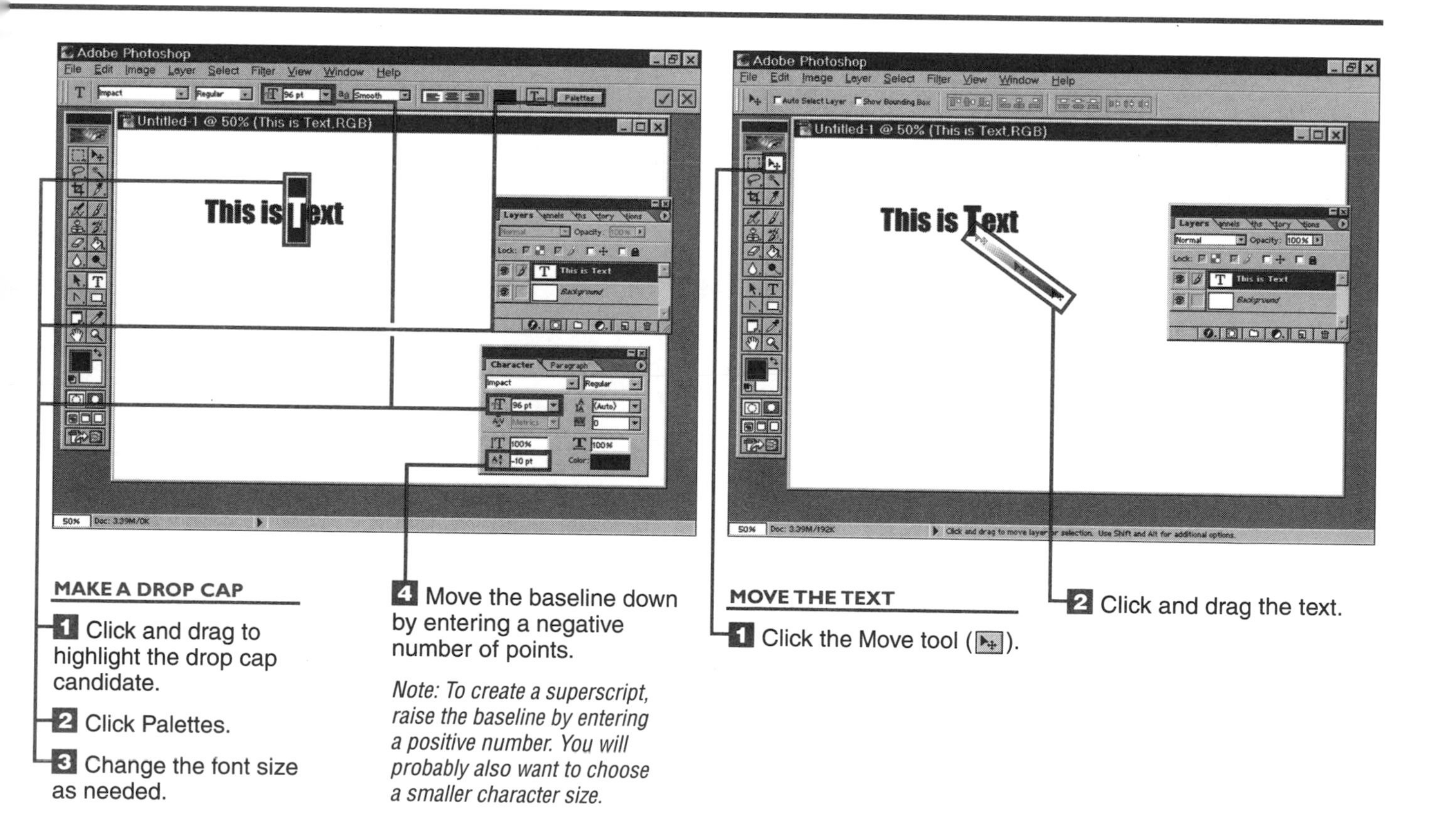

MAKE A DROP CAP

1 Click and drag to highlight the drop cap candidate.

2 Click Palettes.

3 Change the font size as needed.

4 Move the baseline down by entering a negative number of points.

Note: To create a superscript, raise the baseline by entering a positive number. You will probably also want to choose a smaller character size.

MOVE THE TEXT

1 Click the Move tool ( ).

2 Click and drag the text.

USING THE TYPE SELECTION TOOL

You can create selections in the shape of any type font. You can then use that selection in the same way as any other selection in Photoshop. This capability is useful if you want to fill type with the image in a layer, paint colors into type, or fill type with a pattern or texture.

Unlike the Type tool, using the Type Selection tool does not automatically place the type on its own layer; however you may create or fill text on its own layer. Just create a new, empty layer (click the New Layer icon at the bottom of the Layers palette) and enter the type you want to have appear as a selection. This gives you the advantage of being able to control the transparency of the text and of being able to throw out the layer if you make a mistake.

The big disadvantage of text entered with the Type Selection tool is that you cannot edit it (except, of course, by painting over it).

USING THE TYPE SELECTION TOOL

1 Click T.

■ The Type tool Options bar appears.

2 Click the Create a Mask or Selection button.

3 Click the point where you want the selection to start.

■ The Type Options bar loses the Create a Mask and Vertical/Horizontal buttons. Also, the screen automatically goes into Quick Mask mode.

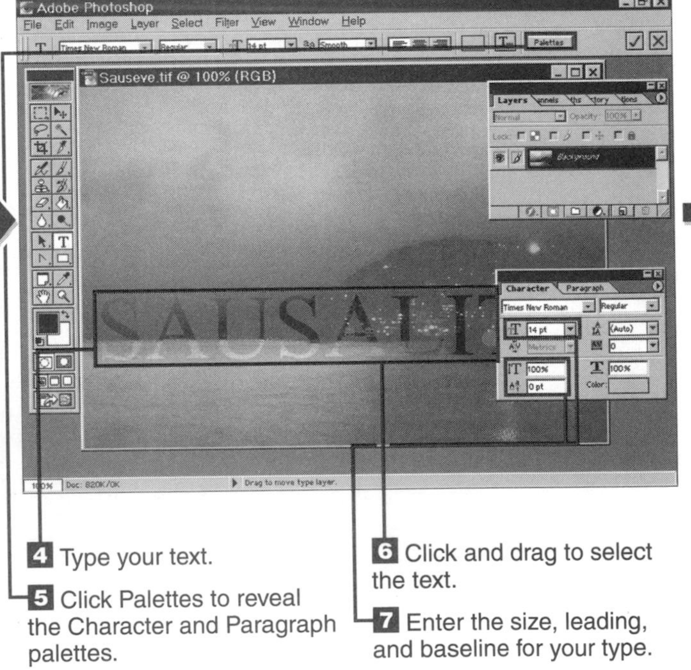

4 Type your text.

5 Click Palettes to reveal the Character and Paragraph palettes.

6 Click and drag to select the text.

7 Enter the size, leading, and baseline for your type.

What is the difference between type on a layer and any other irregular shape on a layer?

✔ If the type was made with the Type Selection tool, there is no difference. Anything you can do to any image on any layer you can do to type created in this way.

What if I created the type with the Type tool and then wanted to treat it like any other graphic on an independent layer?

✔ No problem. Create a new, empty layer, and then merge the type layer with the empty layer. To do that, link the type layer and the new layer, and then choose Merge Linked from the Layers palette menu.

Can I use the transparency slider and the Blend modes just as with any other layer?

✔ You can do anything with a type layer that you can do with any other layer. Transparency and Blend modes enable you to do some things with type that are especially attractive, for example, superimposing two different fonts and then blending them.

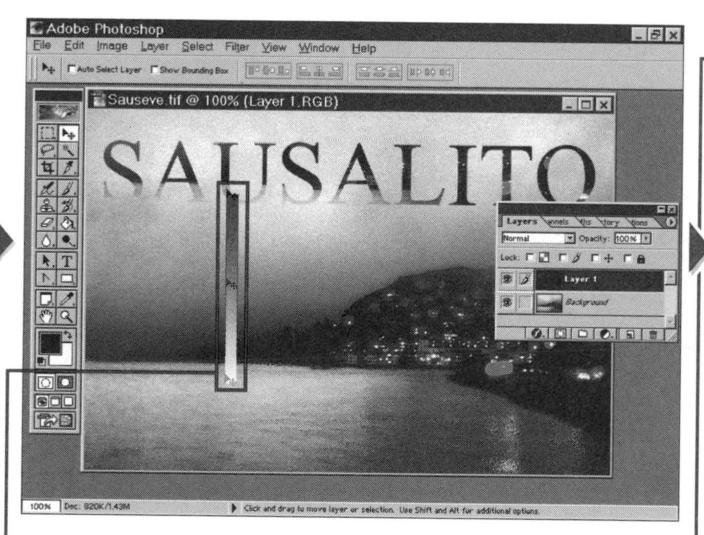

8 Place the cursor anywhere inside the orange quick mask and drag to move the text to the desired position.

Note: To cut out the contents of the selection and place them on their own layer, click ☑. When the marquee appears, press ⌘/Ctrl+J.

Note: If you move the contents of the text selection to a new layer, it seems to disappear. However, a look at the Layers palette reveals a new layer.

Note: Now that this text is on its own layer, you can enhance it with any of the layer effects. You can also paint on or fill the text and automatically confine the effect to the shape of the text.

9 Click Window, then Show Layers.

10 Click to check Lock Transparent Pixels.

■ Paint the text or click Edit, then Fill to change the color of the text or to fill it with a pattern.

USING TRANSPARENCY AND BLEND FOR TYPE EFFECTS

You can use the layer Blend modes and the Transparency control for unique type effects. Traditionally, Photoshop books devoted a chapter or two (or even the whole book) to special type effects. Nowadays, the new Layer Style feature (covered in Chapter 9) makes child's play of creating some of the most useful type effects. However, layer effects still cannot touch a few worthwhile tricks.

The most interesting of these tricks are that you can blend layers, make them semitransparent, and transform them. Blending and transparency work the same way for text layers as for normal layers; however, you cannot use Distort and Perspective (see Chapter 9) when transforming text layers.

If you do need to do a perspective or distort transformation on text, you must first rasterize the text. Then you can treat it just like any other image layer. To transform a text layer to a normal layer, click Layer, then Rasterize, then Type. You will no longer be able to edit the text.

USING TRANSPARENCY AND BLEND FOR TYPE EFFECTS

PLACE ONE FONT ATOP OR INSIDE ANOTHER

1 Select the type layer that you want to place type over.

2 Click Layer, then Rasterize.

3 Click [T].

4 Change the font to something different, but with similarly proportioned letters.

5 Click the insertion point at the exact beginning of the existing type.

BLEND NEW TEXT WITH THE UNDERLYING TEXT

6 Finish entering the text you started in the previous steps and click [✓].

7 Click Window, then Show Layers.

8 Click the layer of the text you want to blend.

9 Click [move tool] and drag to position the new type.

10 Choose a Blend mode.

11 Adjust the Transparency setting.

Can I use layer effects on the rendered text layers?

✔ Absolutely—any and all of them. You can also make things even more interesting (or messy—take your pick) by running layer effects on the individual layers before you do the blending and transparency. You can then run the layer effects again after the layers have been combined.

What do I do when I take it too far and things get really ugly?

✔ Open the History palette (see Chapter 1) and back up to the last step in which you liked the result. Then delete all that followed and either quit making changes or take a different path.

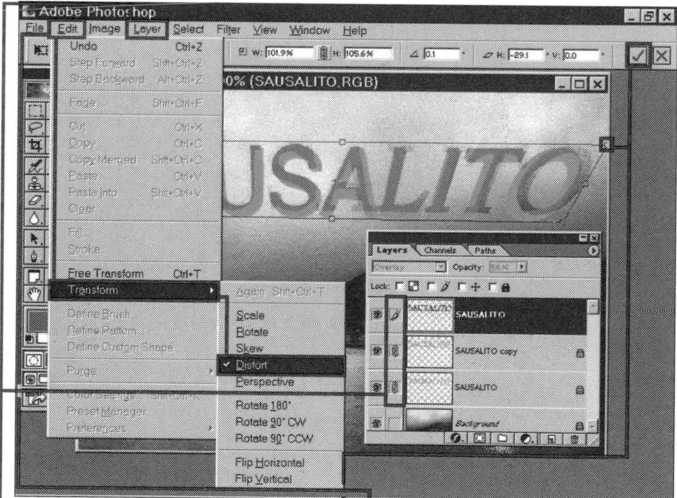

CREATE AN OFFSET DUPLICATE OF A LAYER

1 Drag the original layer to [icon].

2 Click the new layer's name bar.

3 Click to lock transparent pixels.

4 Click the Color swatch to bring up the Color Picker and choose a new color.

5 Click Edit, then Fill.

6 Choose Foreground Color and click OK.

TRANSFORM THE TEXT

1 Activate each text layer and click Layer, then Rasterize, then Type.

2 Click to link the layers that now contain rendered text.

3 Click Edit, then Transform, then Distort.

4 Drag the transformation handles to get the shape you want.

5 Click ✓ to render.

ENTER VERTICAL TYPE

You can enter type vertically instead of horizontally. Just click the Vertical Type button in the Type tool Options bar. Everything about entering type and type selections in the other sections of this chapter pertains to entering vertical type.

Entering type, whether horizontally or vertically, is a two-stage operation in Photoshop 6. The first stage occurs when you click the Type tool. The Options bar lets you choose the style of entry (solid or marquee text, horizontal or vertical orientation), the type style, point size, anti-aliasing method, justification, and color. You can also choose to enter text in one of many warping styles.

The second stage occurs when you click to start entering text. At this point, the icons for the entry method disappear from the Options bar and the Cancel Edits and Commit Edits buttons appear.

One thing to remember about entering vertical text: You can create a bounding box to wrap text, just as you can when entering text horizontally.

ENTER VERTICAL TYPE

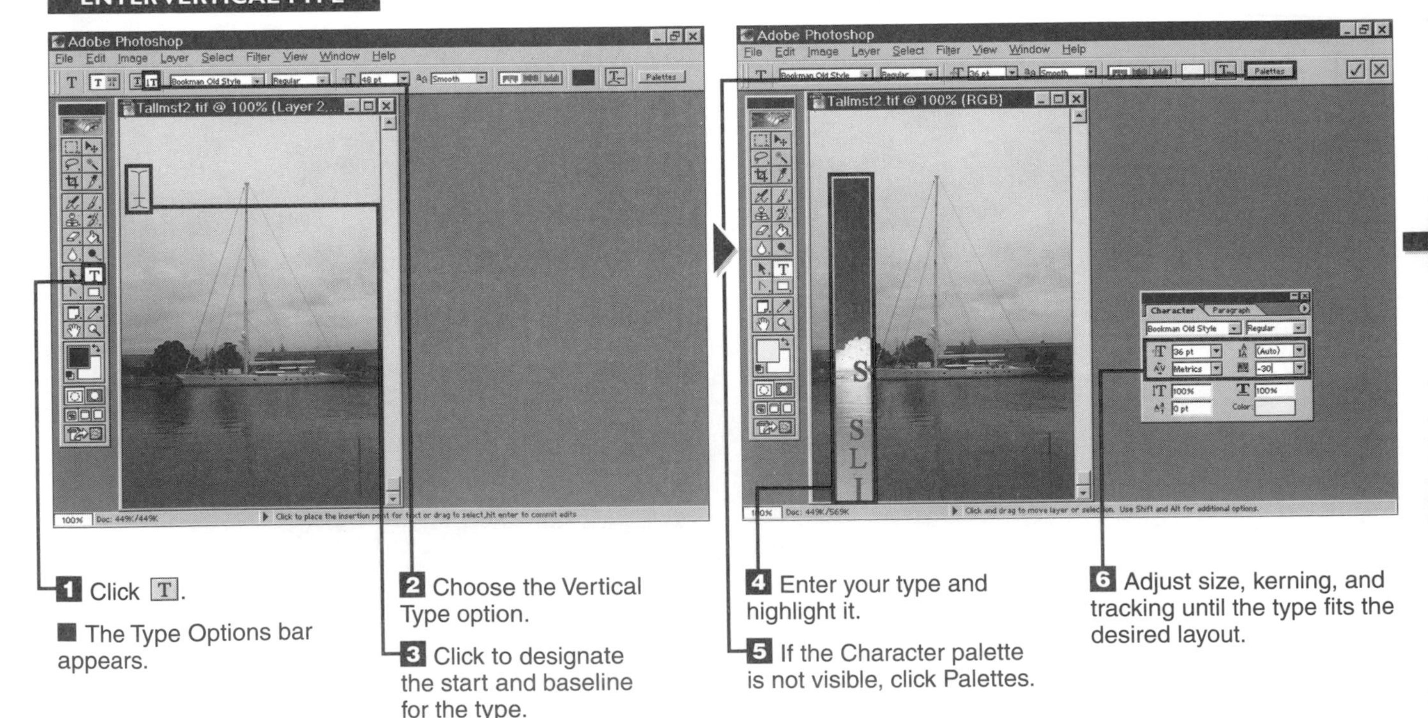

1 Click T.

■ The Type Options bar appears.

2 Choose the Vertical Type option.

3 Click to designate the start and baseline for the type.

4 Enter your type and highlight it.

5 If the Character palette is not visible, click Palettes.

6 Adjust size, kerning, and tracking until the type fits the desired layout.

Can I warp type that is entered vertically?

✔ No problem. Just follow the same procedures detailed in the section "Distort Text." However, you may have to experiment a bit more to get the result you are looking for.

Can I still use the alignment icons when entering vertical text?

✔ Yes. The type will appear equidistant from the insertion point if you specify the alignment as Center and will appear from the bottom up if you specify the alignment as Right. Although you can use the Move tool to place your type precisely where you want it, these choices help you position type more quickly.

What if I need to shorten the line of type without rotating it?

✔ Use the leading and tracking adjustments in the Character palette. If that does not do the job, you will have to choose a smaller size of type. Of course, if your type line is too long because of too many words, you need to use more than one line of type or change your copy.

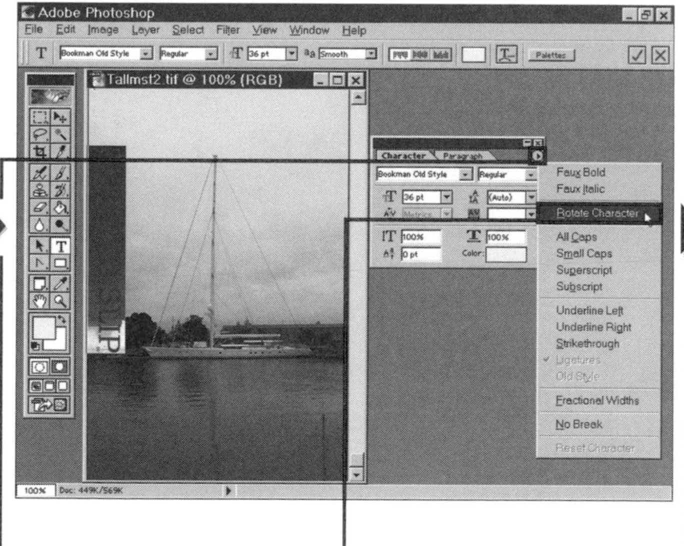

Note: Sometimes, as in this case, the line of type is still too long. You can shorten it by rotating the letters.

7 Click ▶.

■ The Character palette menu appears.

8 Click Rotate Character.

■ The letters turn on their right sides, taking far less space.

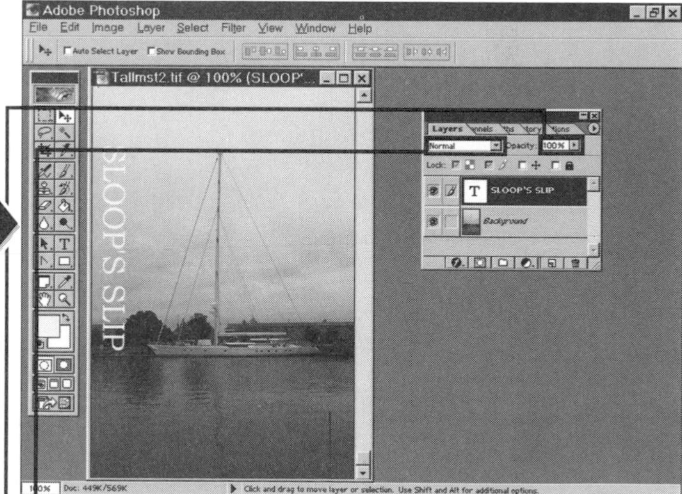

9 To change the blending of the type and underlying layers, choose a Blend mode.

10 Enter a number for the opacity.

■ The appearance of the type automatically changes to reflect your new Blend mode and Opacity settings.

SECTION IV

12) USING PHOTOSHOP'S BRUSHES

13) APPLYING DARKROOM EFFECTS

14) WORKING WITH TEXTURES

15) USING THE ARTISTIC FILTERS

16) USING THE DISTORT FILTERS

17) USING THE NOISE, PIXELATE, AND STYLIZE FILTERS

MANAGE PRESETS WITH THE PRESET LIBRARY

You can use the Preset Library to manage preset attributes for all the libraries that you access from the Options bar: brushes, custom shapes, contours, gradients, patterns, swatches, and styles.

The advantage to using the Preset Library is that you can access these libraries without having to select the tool that calls up the appropriate Options bar. Besides, some folks like to work with the Options bar hidden.

Suppose that you want to access one of the menus attached to a Library pane, but the Options bar that houses that pane is hidden. You can just choose Edit, then Presets Manager. A menu lets you choose each library. After you choose a library, its Library pane and associated menu appear in the dialog window.

You can then create, save, load, or delete libraries by using the menu.

Note: There is no way to create an individual preset while working with the Preset Manager.

MANAGE PRESETS WITH THE PRESET LIBRARY

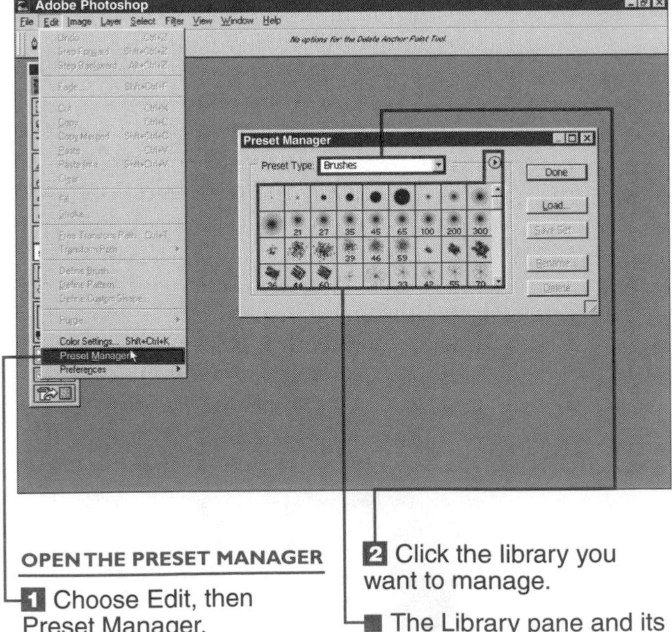

OPEN THE PRESET MANAGER

1 Choose Edit, then Preset Manager.

■ The Preset Manager dialog box appears.

2 Click the library you want to manage.

■ The Library pane and its associated menu appear in the dialog box.

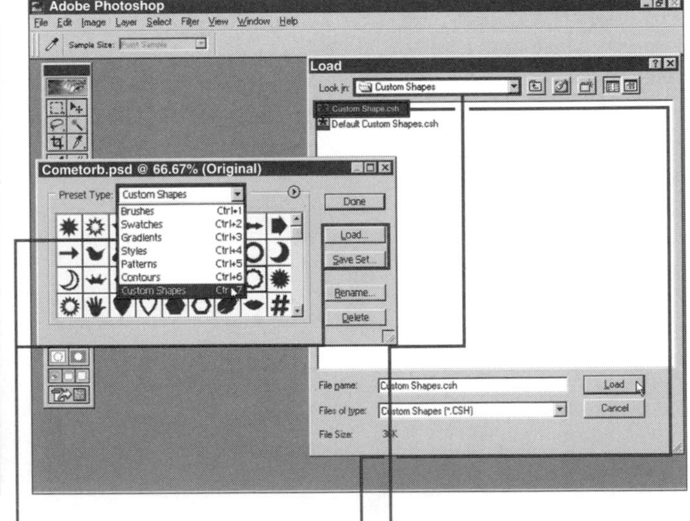

LOAD OR SAVE A LIBRARY

1 Click the library you want to manage.

■ The Library pane appears.

2 Click either Load or Save Set.

3 Navigate to the folder where you want to load or save.

4 If saving, enter a name and click Save; if loading, click the name of the file and click Load.

Note: Mac dialog boxes are slightly different.

Is there a way to load a library that completely replaces the current library?

✔ Ordinarily, when you load a library, that library's assets are added to those of the current library. If you click Replace Library from the Library's menu, the Library you designate in the resulting Load dialog box completely replaces the current assets.

Can I save part of a library to another name?

✔ Sure. Press the Shift key as you select all the assets (such as different styles and shapes of brushes) that you want to keep. Then, click the Save Set button in the Preset Manager menu.

What if I want to save the whole library under another name?

✔ Press ⌘/Ctrl+A to select all the assets and then click the Save Set button. When the Save dialog box appears, enter a new name for the library.

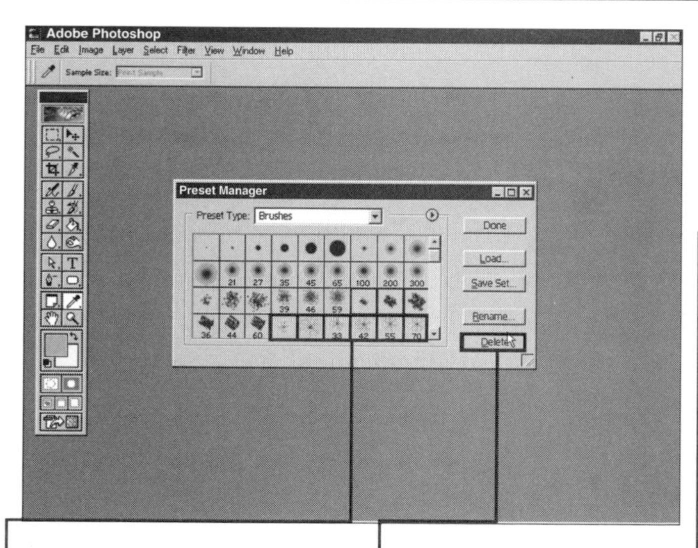

DELETE ITEMS FROM A LIBRARY

1 Shift-click to highlight each preset you want to delete from the currently chosen library.

2 Click Delete.

■ The chosen presets disappear.

Note: If you delete presets from a default library, you can always restore them.

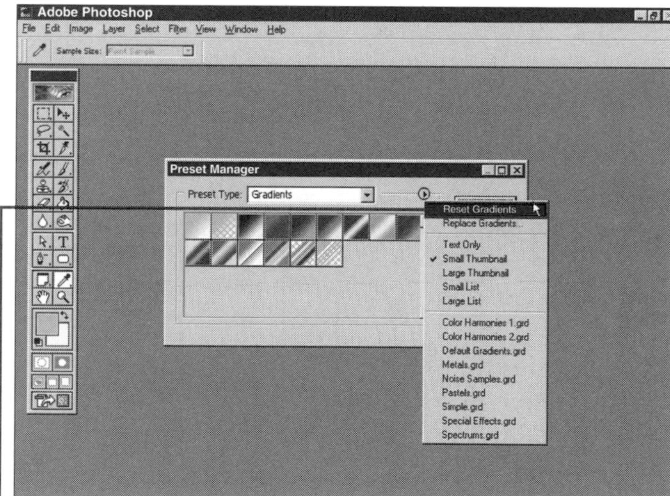

RESET A LIBRARY TO ITS DEFAULTS

1 From the Preset manager menu, choose Reset [Library], where [Library] is the name of the current library (such as Gradients, shown here).

■ The default assets are immediately and obviously restored.

CHOOSE THE RIGHT BRUSH

You can choose between the Airbrush, Paintbrush, and Pencil when you want to make freehand strokes of a single color. All of these tools apply the current foreground color, using the currently chosen brush shape. All also enable you to control the opacity of the colors and to choose a Blend mode. Finally, all three can use custom brush shapes that you create in the Brushes palette.

Of course, differences also exist among the three brushes. The Pencil is unique in that it always strokes with hard, aliased edges. Unlike with other program's pencils, you can use different sizes and shapes of strokes with Photoshop's pencil.

In most respects, the Airbrush and Paintbrush are hard to distinguish. However, the Paintbrush lets you use the Wet Edges option to make colors that mix with underlying colors. Only the Airbrush can simulate paint buildup (although you can never get it to drip) and paints in user-specified burst intervals and fall-off rates.

The fourth brush, the Eraser, paints in the background color or (if transparency is locked) erases to transparency.

CHOOSE THE RIGHT BRUSH

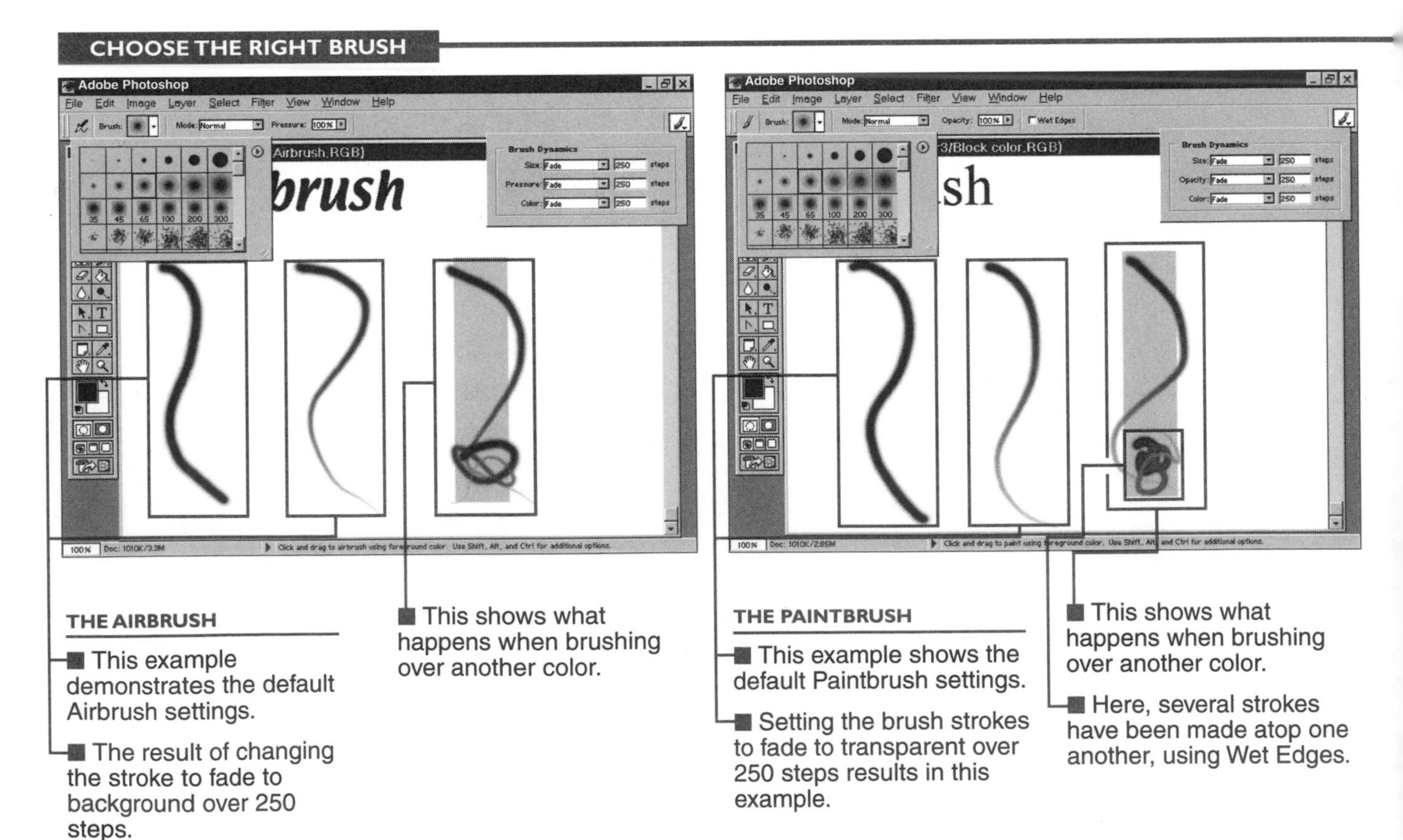

THE AIRBRUSH

■ This example demonstrates the default Airbrush settings.

■ The result of changing the stroke to fade to background over 250 steps.

■ This shows what happens when brushing over another color.

THE PAINTBRUSH

■ This example shows the default Paintbrush settings.

■ Setting the brush strokes to fade to transparent over 250 steps results in this example.

■ This shows what happens when brushing over another color.

■ Here, several strokes have been made atop one another, using Wet Edges.

How can I make exactly the same brush stroke for each brush?

✔ First, make a path with the Pen tools, and then choose Window, then Show Paths. From the Paths palette menu, choose Stroke Subpath. When the Stroke Subpath dialog box appears, choose the tool you want to use for the stroke. All the brushes, focus tools, and darkroom tools are available for autostroking.

What about calligraphy strokes?

✔ Make an elliptical selection on a white background, fill it with black, rotate it 45 degrees, and then save it as a brush.

Can I make strokes that expand and taper like a real brush stroke?

✔ Yes. The best way is to use pressure-sensitive digitizing pads, such as those made by Wacom or Cal Comp. They respond to pressure just as if you were painting with a real brush.

What does the Wet Edges option do?

✔ If you check the Wet Edges box in the Options bar, color builds at the edges of the stroke, much as if you were painting with loaded watercolors.

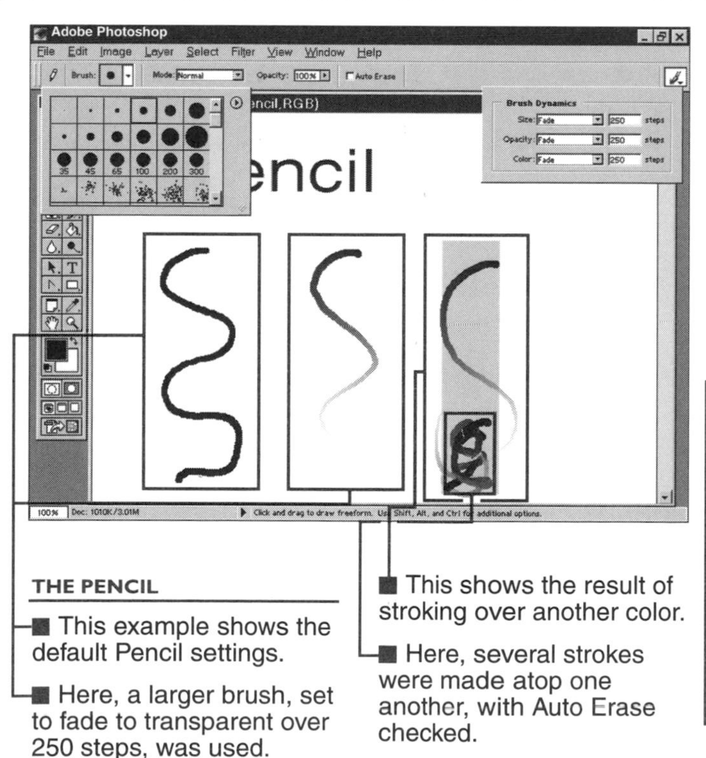

THE PENCIL

■ This example shows the default Pencil settings.

■ Here, a larger brush, set to fade to transparent over 250 steps, was used.

■ This shows the result of stroking over another color.

■ Here, several strokes were made atop one another, with Auto Erase checked.

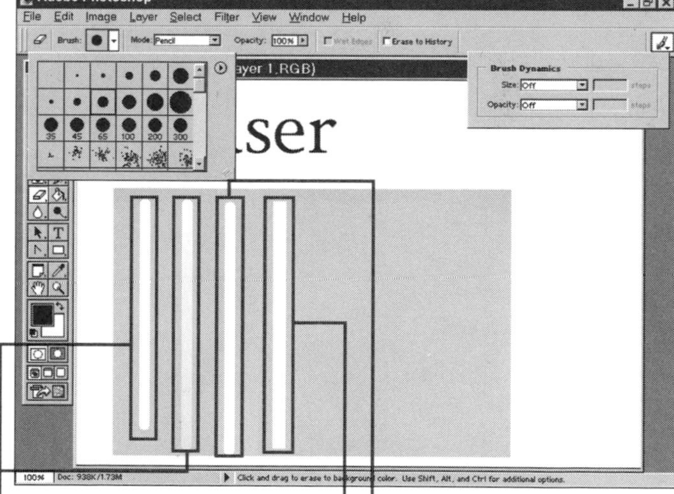

THE ERASER

■ This example demonstrates the default Eraser settings.

■ Setting the strokes to fade to transparency over 250 steps results in this example.

■ Here is how the stroke looks brushed over another color.

■ This results from using the Eraser in block mode.

SET AIRBRUSH OPTIONS

You can modify the look of Airbrush strokes by changing settings in the Airbrush Options bar. The options settings for the Airbrush include Blend mode, Pressure, and the settings in the Brush Dynamics palette: Size, Pressure, and Color.

The Airbrush's Pressure setting behaves exactly the same as the Opacity setting for the Paintbrush and has nothing to do with the effect of a pressure-sensitive tablet.

You can change the behavior of the brush by using the Brush Dynamics palette. The three settings for each of three brush characteristics are

- Pressure (opacity)
- Size
- Color

The three settings for each of these characteristics are Off, Fade, and Stylus.

At first, this is confusing because they sound like they all do the same thing. However, the effect of these three settings is different for each characteristic and may depend on whether you use a mouse or a pressure-sensitive tablet and pen.

SET AIRBRUSH OPTIONS

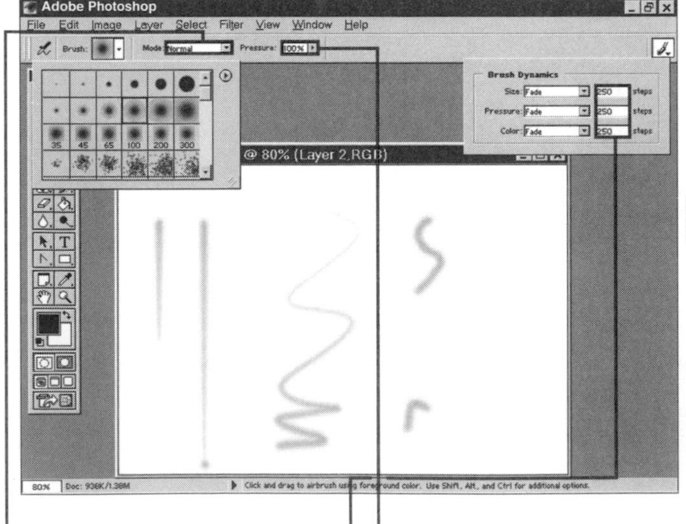

■ Click the Airbrush tool in the toolbox.

■ The Airbrush Options bar immediately appears.

2 Click a mode.

3 Enter a pressure setting or click the button and drag the slider.

4 Type a number in the Fade steps boxes.

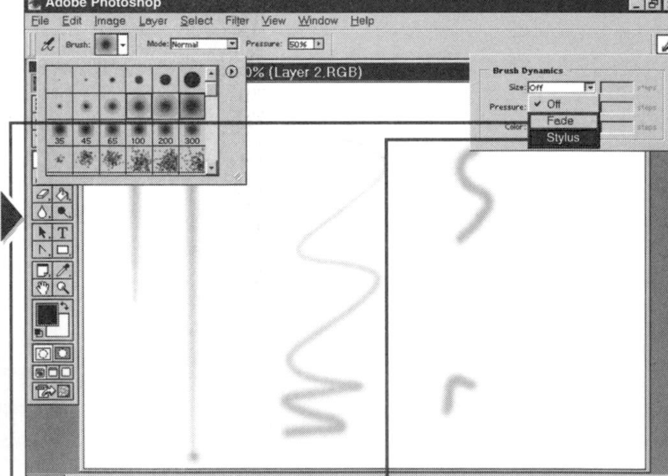

5 Select to make the pressure-sensitive pen increase the width of the brush stroke as pressure is increased.

6 Select to cause the pressure-sensitive pen to blend from the foreground color to the background color with pressure.

7 Experiment with different settings.

SET PAINTBRUSH OPTIONS

You can use settings for the Paintbrush that are almost identical to those for the Airbrush. However, an Opacity entry field (and a slider that appears when you click the button) take the place of the Airbrush's Pressure slider and entry field. Also, a Wet Edges check box makes the stroke darker on the edges and more transparent in the center, producing a water or turpentine effect.

The settings for Brush Dynamics are Size, Opacity, and Color. For Size, choosing Off means that there is no effect on size regardless of whether you use a pen or mouse. If you choose Fade, size changes from the maximum size of the chosen brush to 1 pixel over a specified number of pixels (steps). If you use a pen, choosing Stylus means size changes with pressure.

For Opacity, Fade increases transparency over the specified number of steps, and Stylus lets pressure control opacity.

For Color, Fade causes the stroke to change from the foreground to the background color over the specified number of steps. Stylus lets pressure control the amount of the mix between foreground and background color.

SET PAINTBRUSH OPTIONS

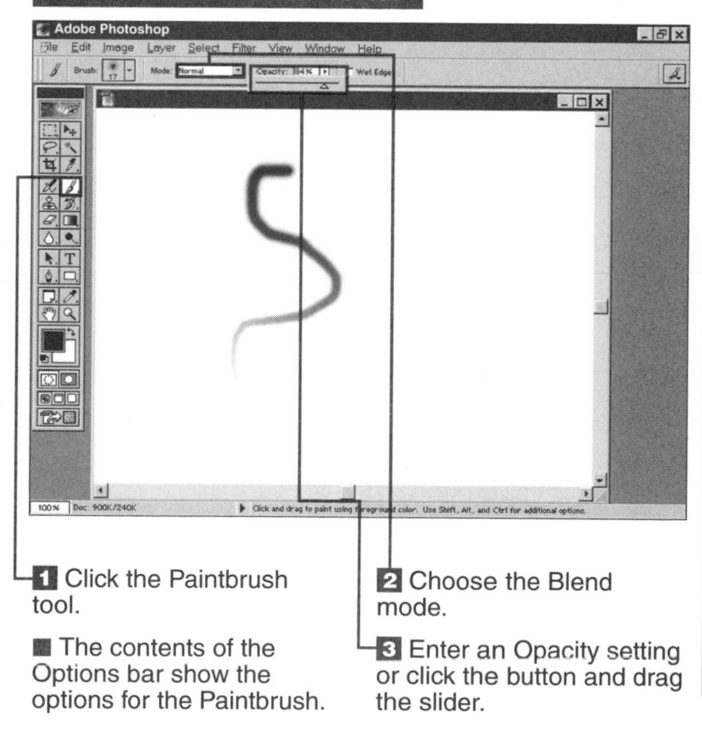

1 Click the Paintbrush tool.

■ The contents of the Options bar show the options for the Paintbrush.

2 Choose the Blend mode.

3 Enter an Opacity setting or click the button and drag the slider.

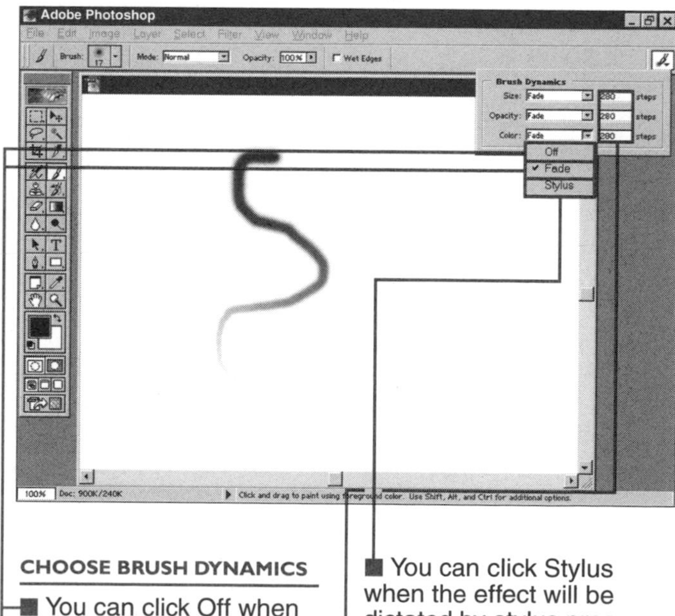

CHOOSE BRUSH DYNAMICS

■ You can click Off when you want no effect.

■ You can click Fade when you want the effect to diminish.

■ You can click Stylus when the effect will be dictated by stylus pressure.

■ If you are using a mouse and Fade is checked, type the number of brush diameters before the effect diminishes.

COMPARE PENCIL OPTIONS

You can use the Pencil tool when you want solid-color, hard-edged strokes.

The Pencil options are the same as the Paintbrush options in all but one respect: In place of the Wet Edges check box is an Auto Erase check box.

Auto Erase is useful for quickly refining a monochrome drawing without having to switch to the Eraser tool. Check this box, and the tool paints with the background color over any area where the foreground color already exists.

You must start painting with the cursor inside the foreground color for the effect to occur. If you click and drag in any other area, the Pencil paints with the foreground color.

If you combine this capability with the use of a pressure-sensitive pen and you select a setting other than Off in the Opacity or Color boxes, you get much more erratic results because Photoshop considers each shade of a color to be an entirely different color.

COMPARE PENCIL OPTIONS

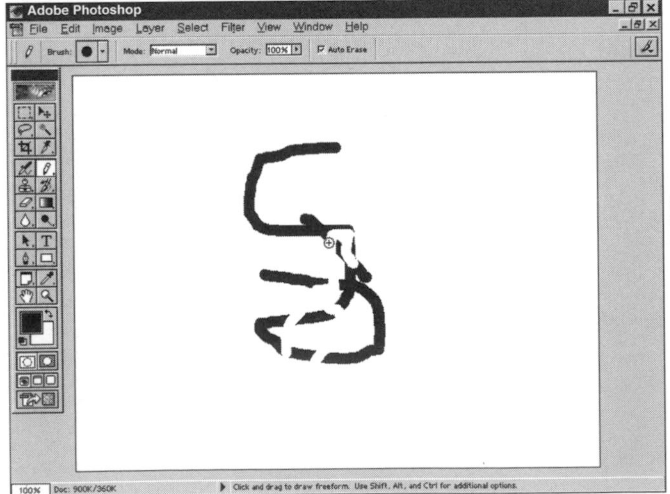

■ This example shows you Pencil strokes made with a mouse while Auto Erase is checked.

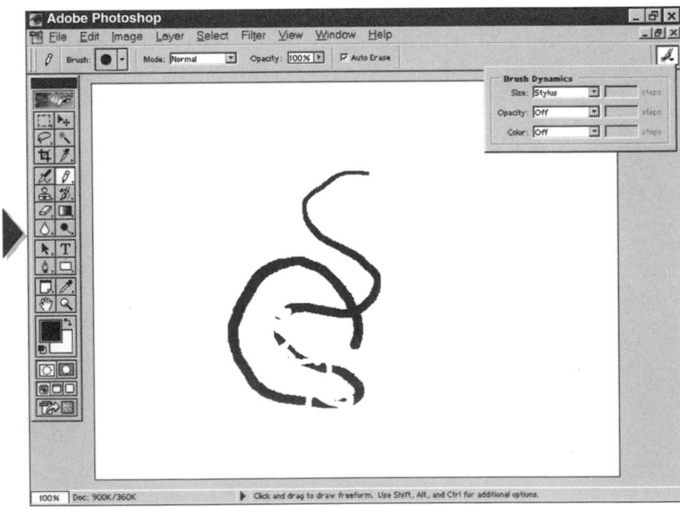

■ Here, Pencil strokes are made with a pressure-sensitive pen while Auto Erase is checked.

COMPARE ERASER OPTIONS

The Eraser options are unusual in that, except in Block mode, the effect of these options is dependent on the options settings for the Airbrush, Paintbrush, or Pencil. You can choose all four of these modes from the menu that occupies the position normally used by the Mode menu. In other words, if you choose Airbrush as the mode for the Eraser, the currently chosen options for the Airbrush are applied. Also, the interface for settings changes to reflect the chosen Eraser mode.

Although the settings may change to reflect the Eraser mode, this does not mean that they are identical to the options for the corresponding brush. For example, if you are in Airbrush mode, no Background option exists for the Fade To field.

The Eraser always erases to the current background color—unless, of course, you have checked the Erase to History box. In this case, the Eraser will paint in whatever state the file was in at the point in the History palette when you checked the History Brush Source box.

COMPARE ERASER OPTIONS

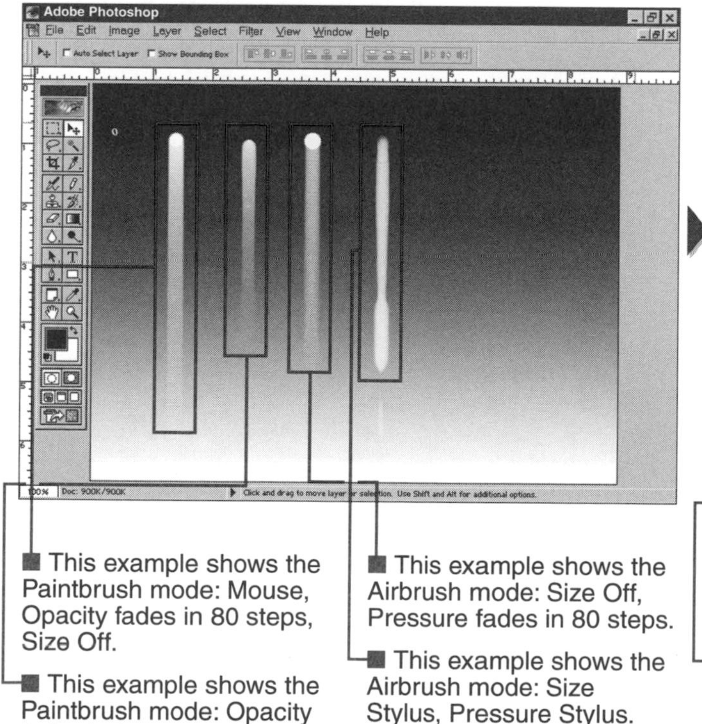

■ This example shows the Paintbrush mode: Mouse, Opacity fades in 80 steps, Size Off.

■ This example shows the Paintbrush mode: Opacity fades in 80 steps, Size Stylus.

■ This example shows the Airbrush mode: Size Off, Pressure fades in 80 steps.

■ This example shows the Airbrush mode: Size Stylus, Pressure Stylus.

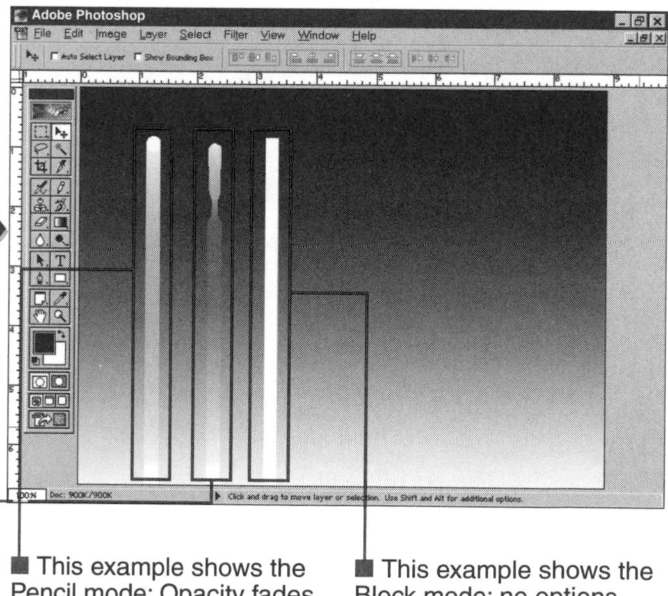

■ This example shows the Pencil mode: Opacity fades in 80 steps, Size Off.

■ This example shows the Pencil mode: Opacity fades in 80 steps, Size Stylus.

■ This example shows the Block mode: no options available.

SAVE AND LOAD BRUSH PALETTES

Photoshop comes with several brush palettes: Assorted, Drop Shadows, and Square. You can find an even more extensive set of brush shapes on the CD-ROM that accompanies this book. Also, you will quickly create dozens (or hundreds) of your own. All of these collections can be consolidated, intermingled, and saved as different collections of brushes.

When you save brushes, you save all the brushes in your palette to the new file. If you want to save just the new brushes you have made, you have to first delete all the existing brushes—one at a time.

You could also use the Preset Manager dialog to save collections of only a few chosen brushes. (See "Manage Presets with the Preset Library" earlier in the chapter.)

When you load brushes, you can either add the brushes to those in the current palette, or you can replace the current palette with a new palette by choosing Replace Brushes from the Brushes Palette menu.

SAVE AND LOAD BRUSH PALETTES

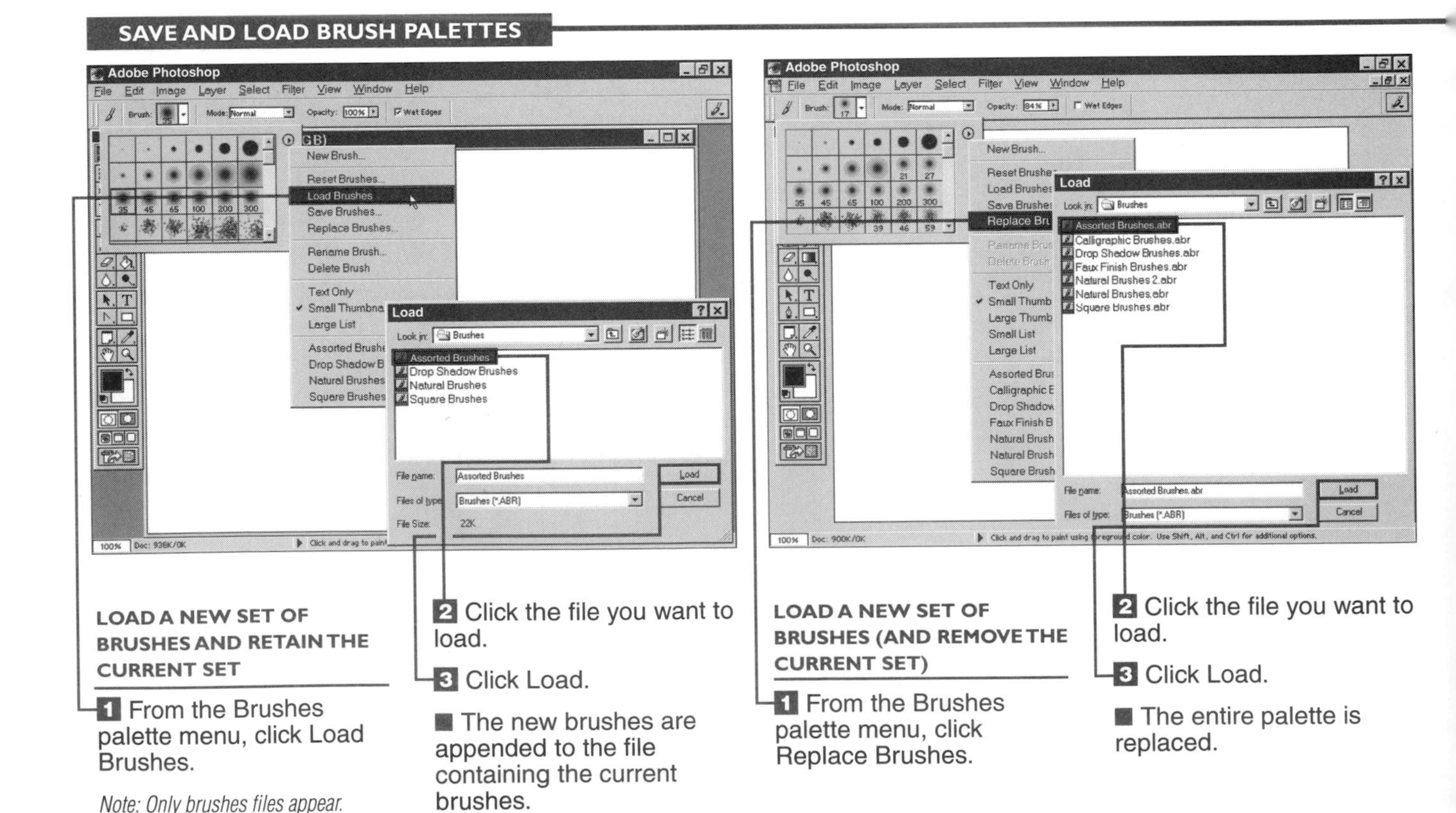

LOAD A NEW SET OF BRUSHES AND RETAIN THE CURRENT SET

1 From the Brushes palette menu, click Load Brushes.

Note: Only brushes files appear.

2 Click the file you want to load.

3 Click Load.

■ The new brushes are appended to the file containing the current brushes.

LOAD A NEW SET OF BRUSHES (AND REMOVE THE CURRENT SET)

1 From the Brushes palette menu, click Replace Brushes.

2 Click the file you want to load.

3 Click Load.

■ The entire palette is replaced.

If I want to save a newly created set of brushes into a file exclusive to them, can I avoid having to individually delete a horde of brushes?

✔ The new Presets Manager dialog makes this much easier. Choose Edit and then choose Presets Manager. When the dialog appears, choose Brushes from the Preset Type menu and then press Shift while clicking the brushes you want to keep. When you click Save Set, only the highlighted brushes are included.

Can I transfer a Brushes palette from a Mac to Windows and back?

✔ Yes. In earlier editions of Photoshop, for the Windows version of Photoshop to recognize the palette, you had to rename the file in Windows Explorer to include the extension .abr (The Mac automatically recognizes the file type regardless of extension.) Photoshop 6 automatically adds the .abr, making this transfer easier.

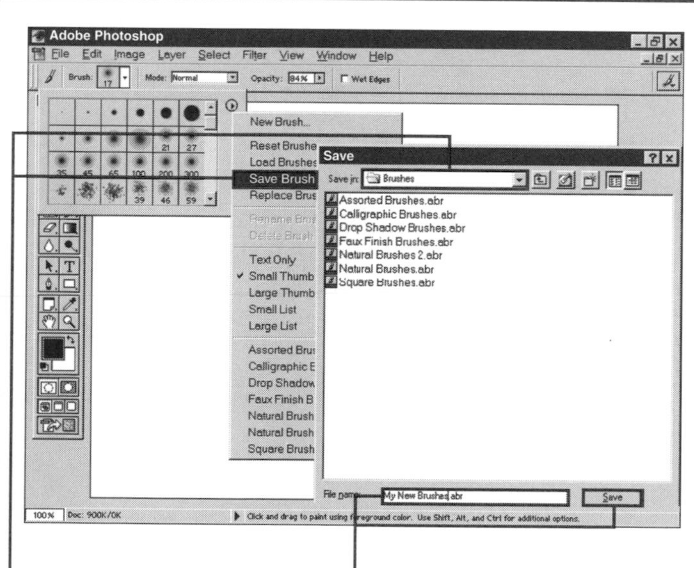

SAVE THE CURRENT SET OF BRUSHES

1 From the Brushes palette menu, click Save Brushes.

2 In the Save dialog box, navigate to the Photoshop 6/Extras/Brushes folder.

Note: The Mac version of Photoshop automatically navigates to this folder.

3 Enter the name you want to give this set.

4 Click Save.

Note: The .abr extension is added automatically.

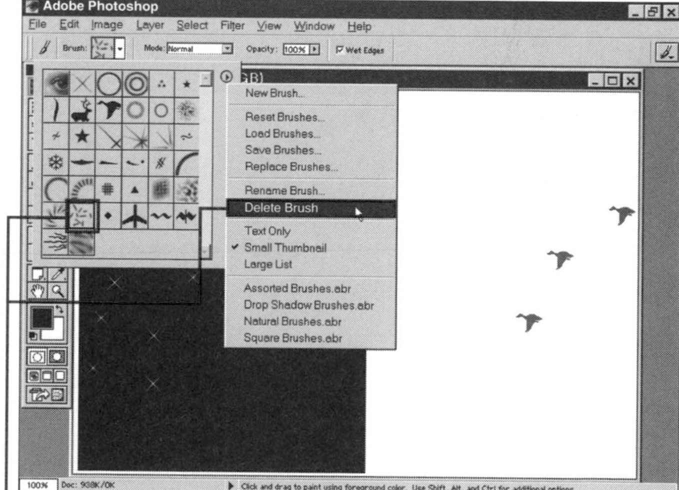

DELETE BRUSHES

1 Click the brush you want to delete.

2 From the Brushes palette menu, click Delete Brush.

Note: A nice shortcut is to hold down the /Ctrl key. The scissors icon replaces the cursor. Click a brush to delete it.

3 Repeat Steps 1 and 2 until you remove all the brushes you do not want.

CREATE CUSTOM BRUSH SHAPES

On its own, Photoshop does not have any natural media brushes. It does, however, enable you to create brushes from the content of any selection.

This feature does have some practical limits. Cutting out a solid portion of a photo and then using it as a brush does not make much sense, because the brush is grayscale—so all you get is a gray square.

Light colors make translucent brushes, imparting an effect like that of watercolors. You can make speckles and stripes to simulate hairy brushes. You can make starbursts, raindrops, and odd little shapes like confetti to add atmosphere to an image. Finally, you can make silhouette shapes that can act as components for patterns and textures. Basically, you can use any shape or texture as a new brush.

You cannot change the size of custom brushes if you are using a mouse. Pressure pen users are luckier—you can make the size of even the largest shape range from a few pixels to over a hundred by utilizing the Size box in the chosen tool's Options palette.

CREATE CUSTOM BRUSH SHAPES

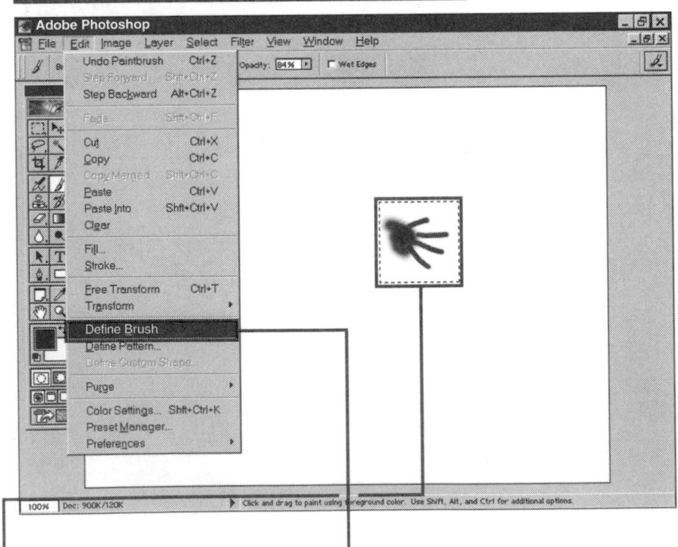

1 Open a file that contains the shape you want to use, or paint some strokes to make a texture brush.

2 Select the area you want to use as a shape.

3 Click Edit, then Define Brush.

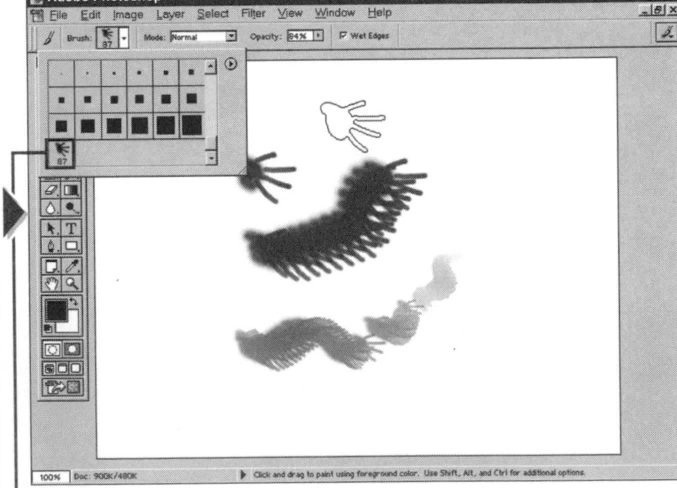

■ The brush immediately appears in the Brushes palette.

■ This example shows the result of painting when using the shape with a pressure-sensitive tablet.

Do you have any suggestions for cutting the time it takes to create a whole series of brushes?

✔ Here is an idea that has helped me quite a bit if I am importing and rasterizing a lot of line art. First, I import and rasterize as many files as my RAM can stand. Then I make an action that reduces the files to a common size (typically about 30 pixels high), fills them with black, and selects the images. Next, while the action is still recording, I ⌘/Ctrl-click the layer name bar to select the imported shapes and then choose Define Brush from the Brushes palette menu. Finally, I close the current files and stop recording.

What if the shapes are not on a transparent background?

✔ Crop each file to its minimum size before running the preceding action.

What are some good sources for brushes?

✔ Virtually all the inexpensive clip art collections—just make sure that the files are in EPS format. You can also use raster images, but the shapes do not tend to be as clean and well defined.

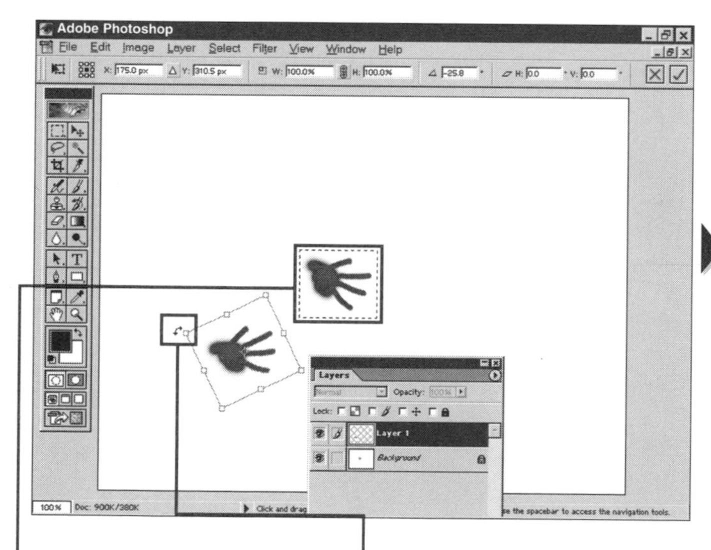

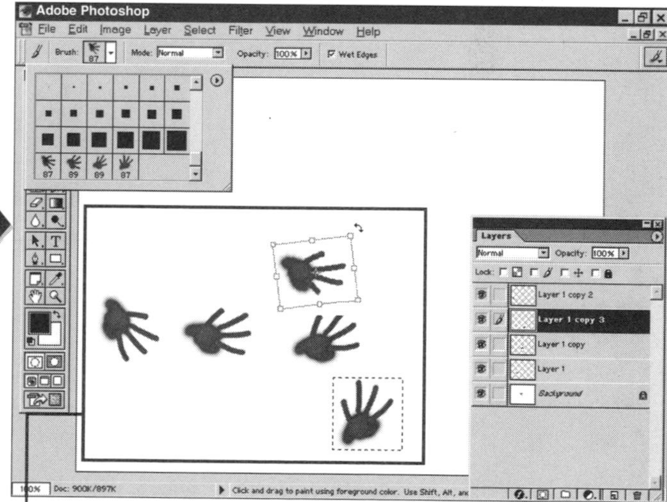

MAKE A BRUSH YOU CAN ROTATE

1 Select the original brush shape.

2 Press ⌘/Ctrl+J to copy the shape to a new layer.

3 Press ⌘/Ctrl+T.

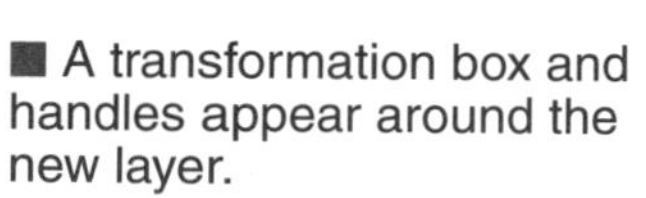

■ A transformation box and handles appear around the new layer.

4 Drag outside the transformation box to rotate the new layer as desired.

5 Repeat Steps 1–4 as many times as necessary to make additional rotated brushes.

6 Select each brush in turn and choose Define Brush from the Brushes palette menu, as shown earlier.

CREATE A BRUSH FROM TYPE

One of the easiest ways to capture useful shapes for brushes is to capture text—especially from the many dingbats and symbol libraries available. If you have a fairly sizable type library, you could also make a set of brushes consisting of nothing but asterisks or exclamation points—one from each typeface. Entering type in various sizes and then capturing each size as a different brush is very easy.

Why might you want to use type as a brush shape? Well, for one thing, letters can produce some interesting effects when you smear them. You can also use type brushes to hide messages in strange places or to create textures and patterns. They also have artistic applications, such as painting graffiti on walls or adding verbal backgrounds. You can even create tattooed bodies using rasterized text in conjunction with the new Liquify command in order to stretch the type to match the curves of a body.

This section shows you the procedure for making a brush from type by demonstrating the creation of a series of brushes from one character in a number of fonts.

CREATE A BRUSH FROM TYPE

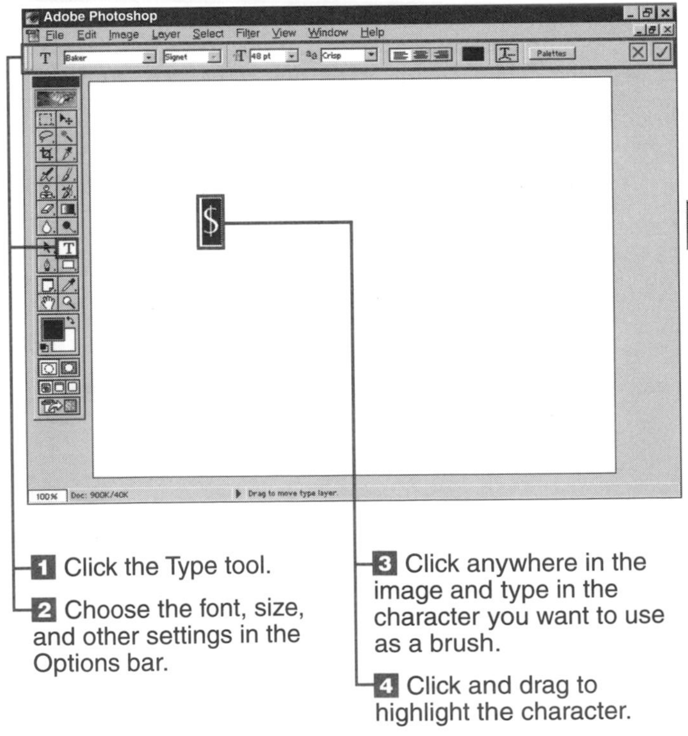

1 Click the Type tool.

2 Choose the font, size, and other settings in the Options bar.

3 Click anywhere in the image and type in the character you want to use as a brush.

4 Click and drag to highlight the character.

5 Choose Window, then Show Layers to display the Layers palette.

6 Click the layer name bar of the shape you want to use as a brush.

7 Choose Edit, then Define Brush.

■ The Brush Name dialog box appears.

8 Type a name.

9 Click OK.

■ The character appears as a new brush in the Brushes palette.

CREATE A BRUSH FROM A POSTSCRIPT IMAGE

You can import many useful brush shapes from the inexpensive and voluminous libraries of vector clip art made for use in illustration and page makeup programs.

You start by dragging any EPS file or icon from a folder (or the desktop) onto the Photoshop alias or into its workspace. Alternatively, you can select the EPS image in its own application and copy it to the Clipboard and then switch to Photoshop and paste, as shown in this section.

Tip: To make several sizes or rotations of this brush, size the brush to the largest you will want, choose Define Brush, and then use the Transform, then Numeric command to reduce the image to the next largest size and rotation. Capture the brush again and repeat the process for the next size as many times as desired.

CREATE A BRUSH FROM A POSTSCRIPT IMAGE

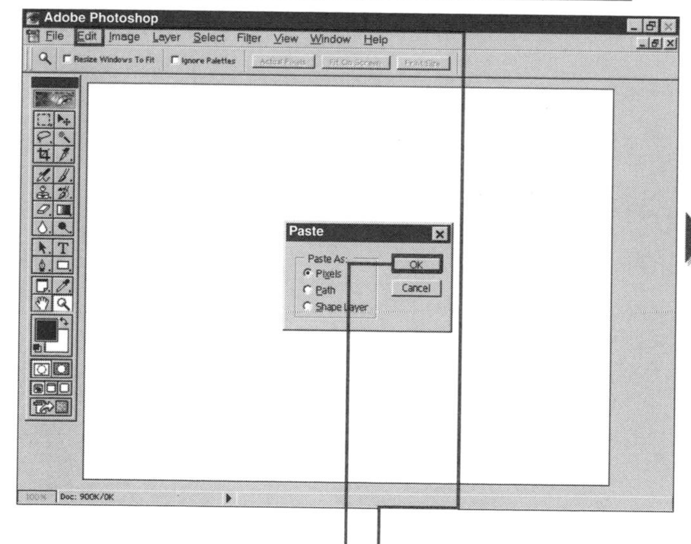

1 In the originating drawing program, select and copy the shape you want to turn into a brush and then switch to Photoshop.

2 Click Edit, then Paste.

3 Click OK.

■ The drawing appears inside a scaling box.

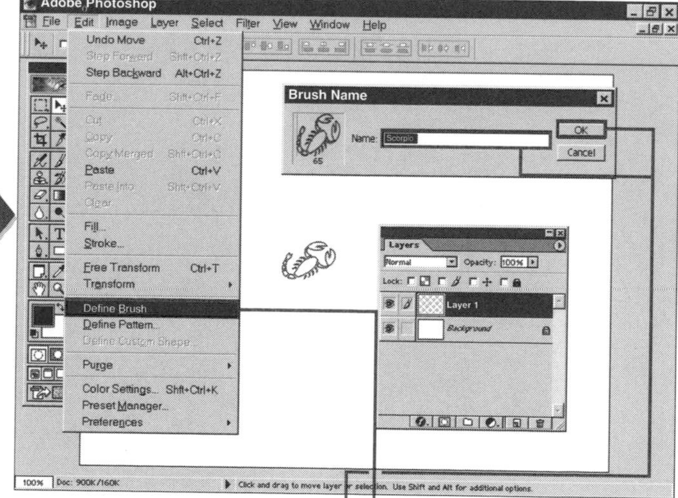

■ The image appears on a transparent layer, in its own window.

4 Drag the transform handles to scale and stretch the image.

5 Choose Window, then Show Layers.

6 Click the new layer to select it.

7 Choose Edit, then Define Brush.

■ The Brush Name dialog box appears.

8 Name the brush.

9 Click OK.

■ The new brush appears in the Brushes palette.

DEFINE A BRUSH FROM A RASTER IMAGE

You can create a new brush shape from an image, but knowing the threshold trick (described below) helps. When you define a brush from an image, it is always captured as a purely black-and-white shape. If you let the program do the black-and-white conversion automatically, you may find yourself in for some disappointments.

Do not worry: You simply convert the image to pure black and white before you define the brush by choosing Image, then Adjust, then Threshold. The Threshold dialog box then lets you choose the exact point along the image's tonal range at which tones drop to black or intensify to pure white.

The other advantage is that you can paint out any details you do not want included by simply covering them with pure white. You can either brush in the white or select around the areas you want to eliminate and then choose Edit, then Fill, then White. Then place a rectangular marquee around the area you want to turn into a brush and choose Edit, then Define Brush.

DEFINE A BRUSH FROM AN IMAGE

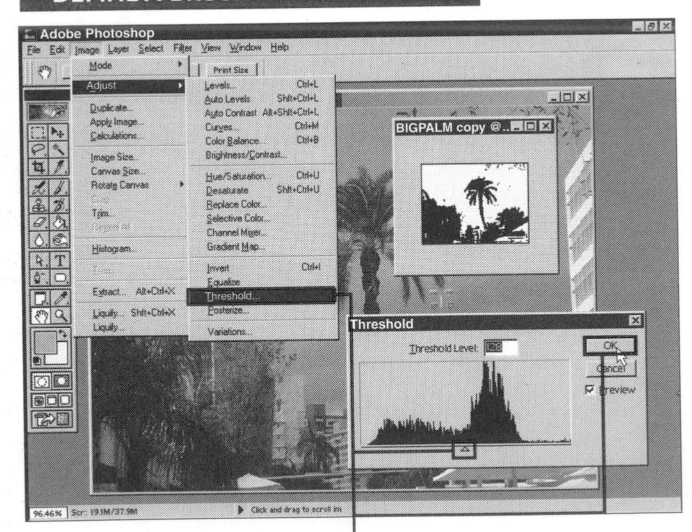

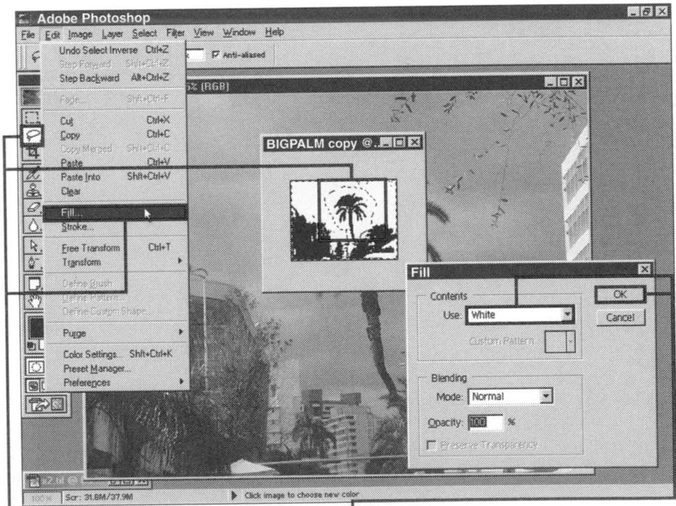

DUPLICATE AND SIZE THE IMAGE

1. Choose Image, then Duplicate.
2. Choose Image, then Image Size and enter the information for the brush size you want.

ESTABLISH A THRESHOLD POINT

1. Choose Image, then Adjust, then Threshold.
- The Threshold dialog box appears.
2. Drag to establish the threshold point.
3. Click OK.

ELIMINATE UNWANTED BLACK AREAS

1. Click the Lasso tool.
2. Drag a loose selection around the item that is to be the brush, and press ⌘/Ctrl+Shift+I to invert the selection.
3. Click Edit, then Fill.
- The Fill dialog box appears.
4. Choose White.
5. Click OK.

What subjects make the best brushes?

✔ Look for objects that are easily defined by their silhouette and that are positioned against a simple background such as the sky or a wall. Of course, you can always paint out superfluous "black blobs."

Can I turn a texture into a brush?

✔ You can turn anything into a brush. The question is will you be able to use it effectively? Try to pick textures with well-defined edges that will look good in black and white. You may want to erase around the edges of the captured texture so that the shape of the brush is not square.

How do I keep the image from smearing when I paint?

✔ You have two ways. You can use the brush like a rubber stamp. Just click, rather than clicking and dragging. The other is to double-click the Brush icon, check Spacing, and drag the slider to the right. Then, when you stroke, you get repetitions of the brush image at regular intervals.

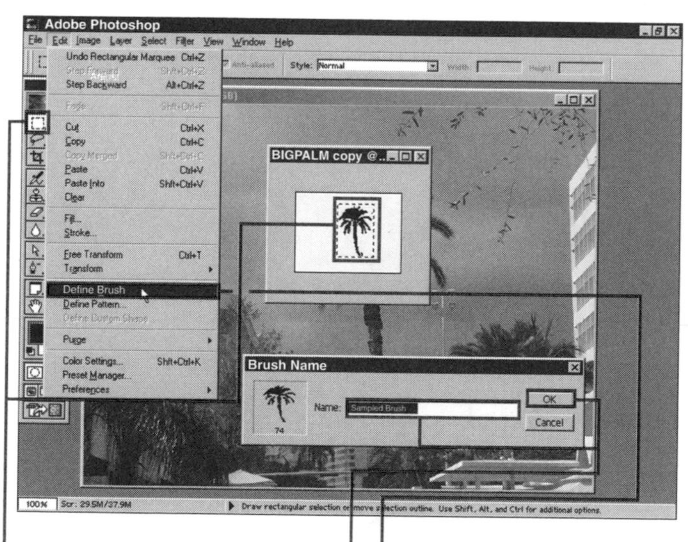

DEFINE THE BRUSH

1 Click the Rectangular Marquee tool.

2 Drag to enclose the subject of the brush.

Note: Leave as little white space as possible.

3 Choose Edit, then Define Brush.

■ The Brush Name dialog box appears.

4 Type the name for the brush.

5 Click OK.

PAINT WITH THE BRUSH

1 Click the brush tool.

2 Click the brush you just saved from the Brush Library.

3 Click the Brush icon in the Options bar and drag to set spacing.

4 Drag in the image to paint.

PAINT FROM A SNAPSHOT

Photoshop has a tool called the History Brush that was introduced in Version 5 and that few realize the value of. The History Brush lets you paint in any effect that Photoshop can do to an image, including all the filters, all the third-party filters, all the Image controls, any sort of compositing—anything you can imagine.

The two areas in which I find the History Brush invaluable are

- Extending the tonal range of the image
- Turning photos into paintings

To do either of these tasks, you want to create one or more new layers, run the process(es) that you want to paint into areas on those whole layers, take a snapshot, and then delete the layers (if you are tight on memory or want to speed things up).

Now all you need to do is select the snapshot of the original image, choose the History Brush, and click the box to the right of the layer that you want to paint in. Then, just paint in the effect from that layer.

PAINT FROM A SNAPSHOT

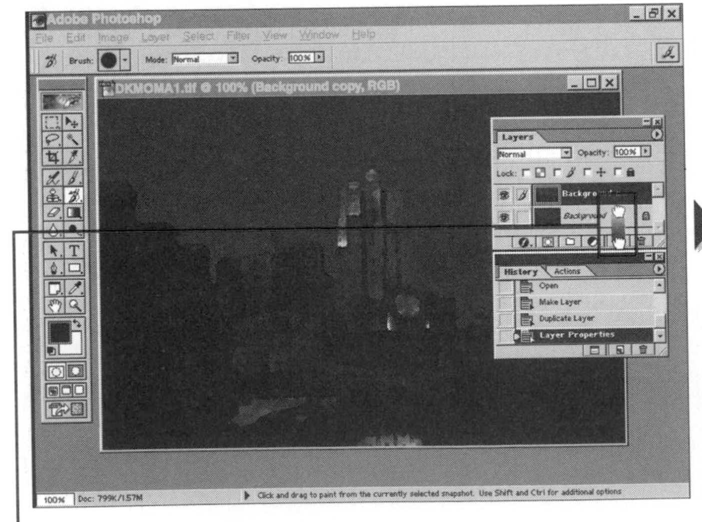

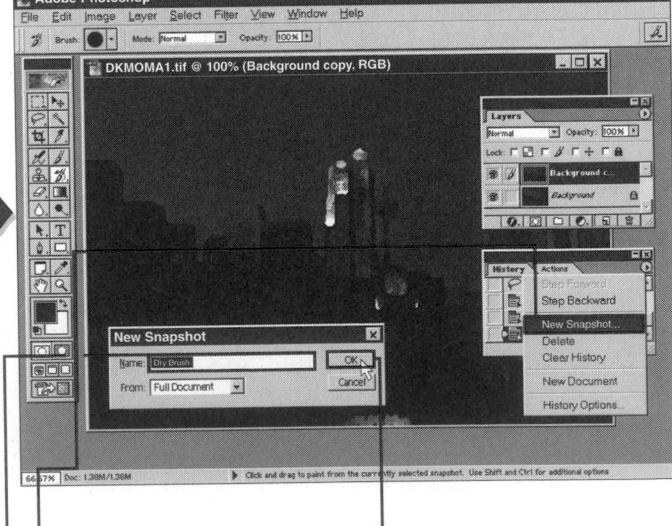

1 Open your image and make sure that the Layers and History palettes are showing.

2 Drag the layer the image is on to the New Layer button to duplicate it.

3 Run a filter on the image (anything you want).

4 Click New Snapshot from the History palette menu.

5 Type a descriptive name for the stage of the image.

6 Click OK.

■ The new snapshot appears in the History palette.

Why am I not seeing any results when I try to paint?

✔ Make sure the History Brush icon is showing in the box to the left of the Snapshot that you are supposed to be painting from. Also make sure you are painting into an active and visible layer.

What if I want to blend the effects of the History Brush?

✔ No problem. In the History Brush Options palette, drag the Opacity setting to a lower level to obtain a less intense effect. If you are using a pressure-sensitive stylus, you can also check the Stylus Opacity box; then less pressure will mean less effect.

How many snapshots can I paint from?

✔ As many as your computer's memory can handle. Very likely, you will want to impose several different effects. If you are short on memory, create a snapshot, paint in the needed changes, flatten, and save the file. Then open it again and create a new effect with a new snapshot.

7 Click the History brush.

8 Click the box to the left of the snapshot from which you want to paint.

9 Click to hide any layers covering the layer you want to paint to.

■ Make any needed changes in the Options bar settings.

10 Paint into the area you want to cover.

11 Eliminate any layers and snapshots you no longer need and then save.

GET EVEN MORE PAINTERLY WITH THE ART HISTORY BRUSH

The Art History brush, like the History brush, paints from a snapshot, but at the same time, it imposes its own style.

The brush works by sampling the color from a snapshot at the moment you press the mouse button and then smearing and changing the color of those pixels as you drag.

You have a choice of ten stroke styles: Tight Short, Tight Medium, Tight Long, Loose Medium, Loose Long, Dab, Tight Curl, Tight Curl Long, Loose Curl, Loose Curl Long.

The names are somewhat descriptive of how much farther and in what shape the pixels will be smeared as the strokes are moved. The size of these smears is dictated by the size of the brush chosen in the Brushes palette.

As you become familiar with the Art History brush, set Tolerance at a very low setting, the Blend Mode at Normal, and Fidelity at a fairly high level. These settings guarantee the lowest number of rude surprises.

GET EVEN MORE PAINTERLY WITH THE ART HISTORY BRUSH

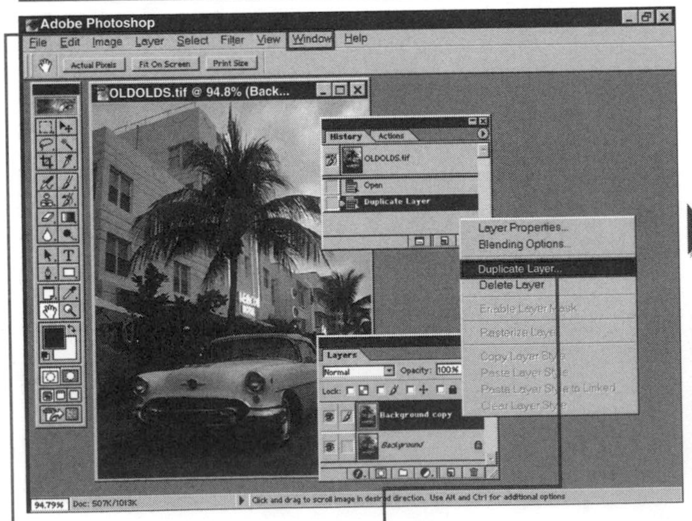

1 Choose Window, then Show History.

2 Choose Window, then Show Layers.

3 Control/right-click the Background Layer and click Duplicate Layer from the menu.

4 Click the duplicated layer and run a filter or make any overall change to the new layer.

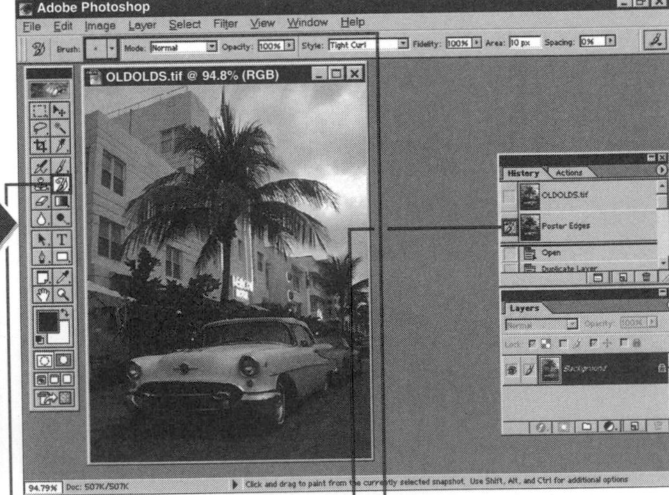

5 Click and hold the History brush and select the Art History brush from the box that appears.

■ The Art History brush Options bar appears.

6 Click a brush style from the Brush styles palette.

7 Click in the Snapshot box to select the snapshot as the source.

What do I do if I set the brush size too large and really mess up the image?

✔ This problem happens all the time. Sometimes it can even produce some nice effects. All you have to do is pick a smaller brush and paint over the area again. You can keep painting over areas with different brushes until you get the effect you are looking for.

But what if I want photographic detail in some areas?

✔ Use the History (not Art History) brush and paint it back in. However, you must make a Snapshot of the photographic image before you start using filters or other effects that may make it less photographic.

What is the secret to success in using the Art History brush?

✔ Choose Image, then Duplicate and experiment with a copy of your image. Also, be sure to shoot a snapshot of the image *before* you start using the Art History Brush and *after* you do any re-scaling. Then you can always use the History Brush to tune your images.

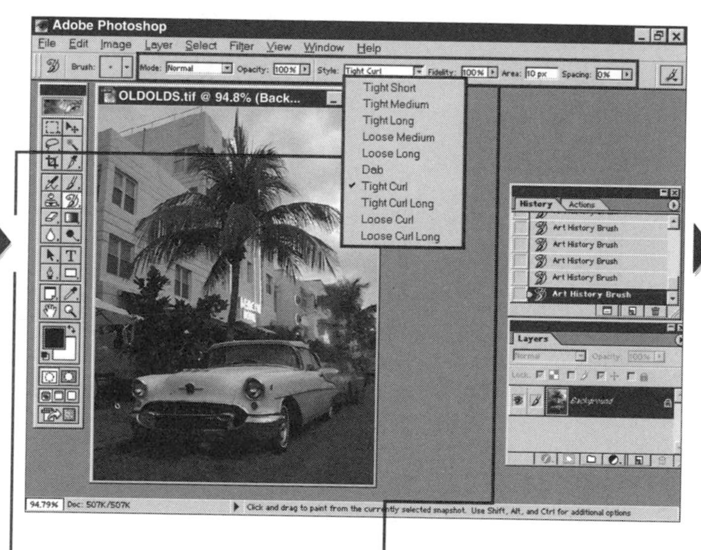

8 Click a brush size and style.

■ These options determine how much area a stroke will cover.

9 For starters, set the Art History Brush options as shown.

10 Start painting.

11 To enlarge or reduce the stroke, press the [or] keys.

12 Change the options and strokes as you paint.

■ You can blend strokes by varying the transparency of the strokes by changing the Opacity setting in the Options bar or by using a pressure-sensitive stylus and making the Brush Dynamics settings Stylus.

BURN AND DODGE SMALL AREAS

Two of the oldest darkroom tricks in the business are known as *burning* and *dodging*. Burning and dodging are techniques for correcting or emphasizing the luminosity values over a specific portion of the image. In traditional photographic printmaking, dodging is done by blocking some light from the enlarger over an area with a small piece of cardboard taped to coat-hanger wire. Burning is done by cutting a hole in cardboard (or using your hands as shown in the Burn Tool icon) so exposure can be increased over a small area.

Photoshop has always featured electronic equivalents of these tools. To darken an area, choose the Burn tool. To lighten an area, choose the Dodge tool. Then, wiggle the tool so the affected area blends with its surroundings.

You can also lighten or darken by selecting a specific area and using the image adjustment tools, as discussed next in this chapter.

BURN AND DODGE SMALL AREAS

USE THE DODGE TOOL

1 Click the Dodge tool (🔍).

■ Its options bar will appear.

2 Set exposure at about 10%.

3 Zoom in to see small details, and click the Dodge tool again.

4 Click to show brushes.

5 Choose a brush size slightly smaller than the area you want to dodge.

6 Drag the tool over the area several times until you achieve the desired degree of lightening/darkening.

How do I avoid streaking the image, which seems to happen easily?

✔ Here are some tips for avoiding streaks: First, make sure you set the exposure low enough to keep the effect of a single drag subtle. Second, choose a feathered brush so that the tool will not have a hard-edged path. Finally, avoid trying to work on too large an area.

Does any way exist for correcting streaking after it has been noticed?

✔ Just step back in the History palette until the streaking disappears and then delete the subsequent steps. Now you can resume the operation.

How do I decide whether to use Burn and Dodge or to adjust within a selection?

✔ If the area is more than a few times larger than the largest brush in the brush palette (100 pixels), a selection is probably more appropriate. Adjusting within a selection also promises more exact control over the effect and over shadows, midtones, and highlights.

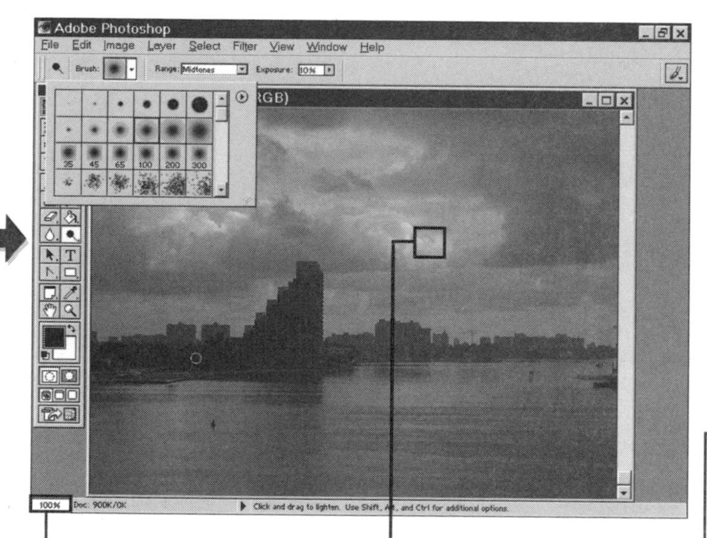

7 To work on larger areas, zoom out so that you can see the entire area.

8 Scrub the tool over the area to be affected.

9 Repeat until the desired degree of lightening is achieved.

USE THE BURN TOOL

■ Darkening (burning in) an area is done in the same way, but it darkens the area covered.

1 Click the Burn tool ( ).

2 Choose a brush size appropriate to the area you want to darken.

3 Drag repeatedly in the area to be affected until you achieve the desired effect.

BURN AND DODGE USING A SELECTION

The Burn and Dodge tools are wonderful for making freehand exposure adjustments to small areas of the image, but they can produce disturbingly uneven results over large areas. For larger areas of the image, simply select that area with the selection tools and choose Image, then Adjust to make the adjustment. After you make the selection, you probably want to feather it slightly so that the newly brightened or darkened area does not show an obvious border.

Choosing Image, then Adjust, then Brightness/Contrast is usually the quickest and easiest for this purpose. Depending on the subject, AutoLevels and Equalize might also be worth a try. Keep the Preview box checked while you make adjustments.

Of course, sometimes neither using the Burn or Dodge tools nor adjusting within a selection is the whole answer. Often, after you make the adjustments within the selection, you want to use the Burn or Dodge tool on smaller details.

BURN AND DODGE USING A SELECTION

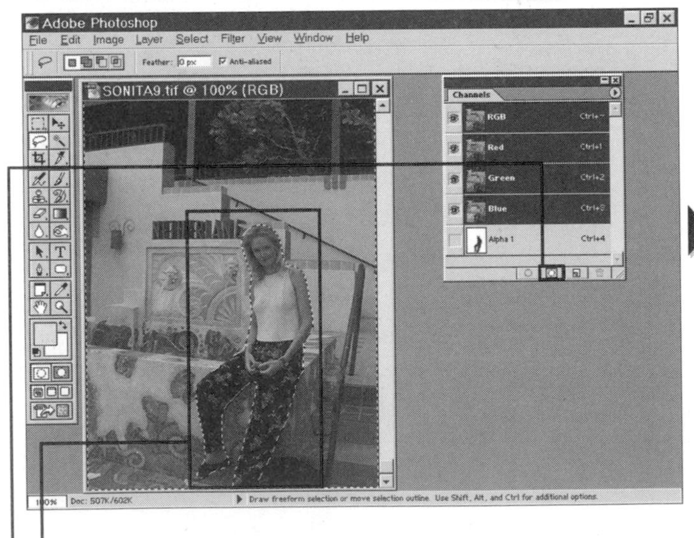

1 Make an accurate selection of the target area.

2 Click the Mask icon in the Channels palette.

■ The selection is saved as a mask.

Note: Saving the selection is not mandatory, but making accurate selections takes time.

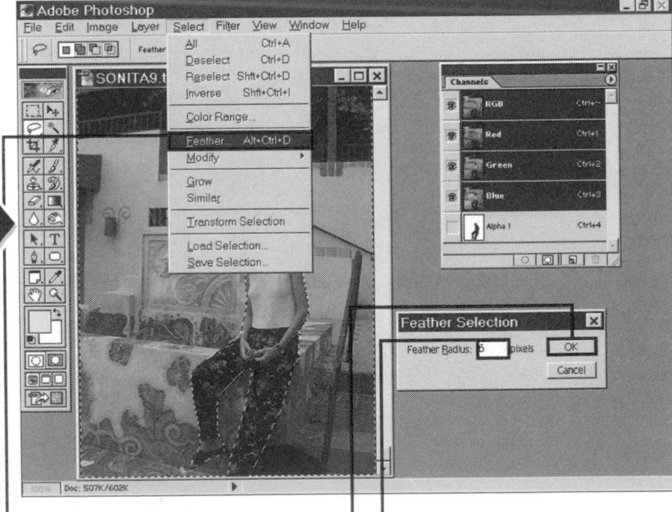

3 Choose Select, then Feather (/Ctrl+Opt/Alt+D).

■ The Feather Selection dialog box appears.

4 Enter a number of pixels over which the fade will occur.

5 Click OK.

How do I avoid making the edge of the selection obvious?

✔ Several techniques can help. The most common is to feather the selection (Opt/Alt+⌘/Ctrl+D). In the Feather Selection dialog box, be sure to enter a number of pixels high enough to ensure a smooth transition.

✔ At times, you may want to feather one part of the selection edge to a different degree than another. Feather the first selection. Now press Shift and add another selection that covers the edge you want to feather to a different degree. Press Opt/Alt+⌘/Ctrl+D again, and this time enter a different number of pixels in the Feather Selection dialog box.

✔ Finally, lighten or darken the area you want to burn or dodge by using the Curves command (⌘/Ctrl+M) to raise and lower only the midtones.

What if I want to darken or lighten a sky?

✔ Use the Magic Wand to select the colors in the sky. If you don't check the Contiguous box in the Magic Wand's options bar, you'll also select all the little gaps in the foreground that show the sky. Feather the selection slightly, then use the Image, Adjust, and then Brightness/Contrast to get the brightness value you want.

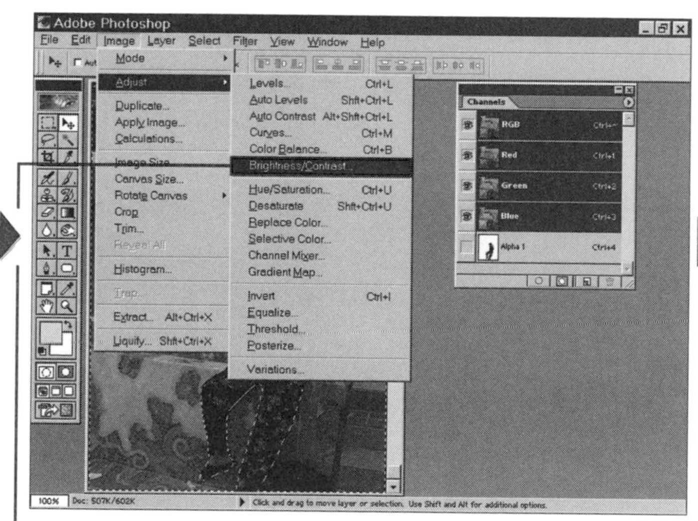

6 Choose Image, then Adjust, then Brightness/Contrast.

■ The Brightness/Contrast dialog box appears.

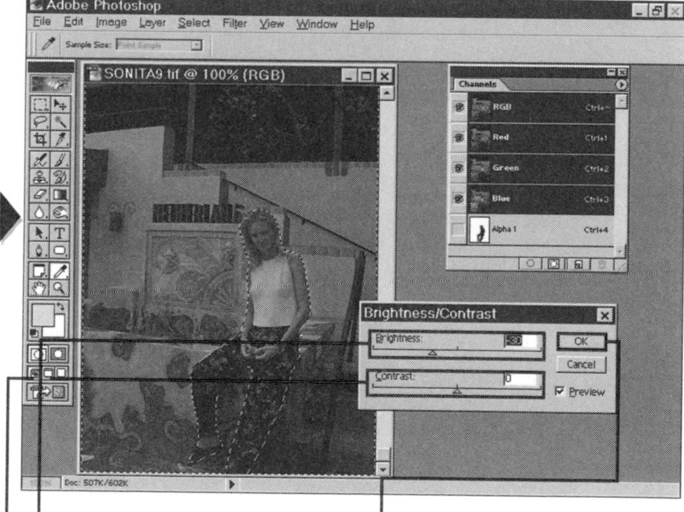

7 Drag the Brightness level until the luminosity seems correct.

8 Drag the Contrast slider until all the tonal values look natural for the subject.

9 Click OK to accept the changes.

SUCK UP COLOR WITH THE SPONGE TOOL

The Sponge is the third tool on the Burn and Dodge tool menu. The purpose of the Sponge tool is to help you tone down overintense colors or jazz up dull ones by changing the saturation. Tone down too much, and you end up with a gray tone.

You choose the Sponge tool by selecting it from the menu or by pressing the letter O (Shift+O) until you see the Sponge tool appear in place of the Dodge or Burn tools. Click the Sponge tool to bring up its Options bar. Choose Saturate or Desaturate from the menu, and set a pressure percentage. Next, choose the appropriate brush size, and drag repeatedly until the adjustment blends properly.

One of the most useful applications for the Sponge tool is toning down blotchiness in skin tones. Take out the redness (or blue in veins) with this tool. Complementary operations would include matching the surrounding skin tones by using the Paintbrush in Color Blend mode and then lightening or darkening with the Dodge or Burn tools (see "Match Color with the Paintbrush Tool" later in this chapter).

SUCK UP COLOR WITH THE SPONGE TOOL

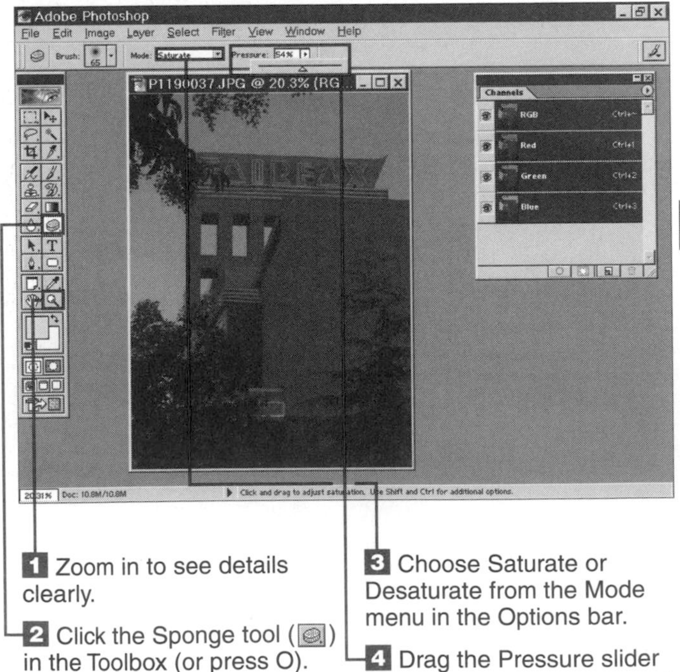

1 Zoom in to see details clearly.

2 Click the Sponge tool ( ) in the Toolbox (or press O).

3 Choose Saturate or Desaturate from the Mode menu in the Options bar.

4 Drag the Pressure slider to indicate the percentage of change.

5 Drag the cursor over the saturated area to change saturation.

MATCH COLOR WITH THE PAINTBRUSH TOOL

Usually, you use the Paintbrush tool for painting, but when you use it with Blend modes (available from the Paintbrush Options palette menu), the Paintbrush tool can serve a variety of other purposes as well. One of the most popular of these is retouching to change the color of small areas of the image.

You may want to change color to match the surrounding colors, to make the image more colorful (replacing ivory-colored flowers with red ones, for example), or simply to enhance composition in the image.

Tip: Remember when retouching that pressing the square bracket keys cycles you through the brushes, so changing sizes is easy. Also, if you are working on small areas, zoom in by using the Zoom tool to drag a marquee around the area you will be retouching.

MATCH COLOR WITH THE PAINTBRUSH TOOL

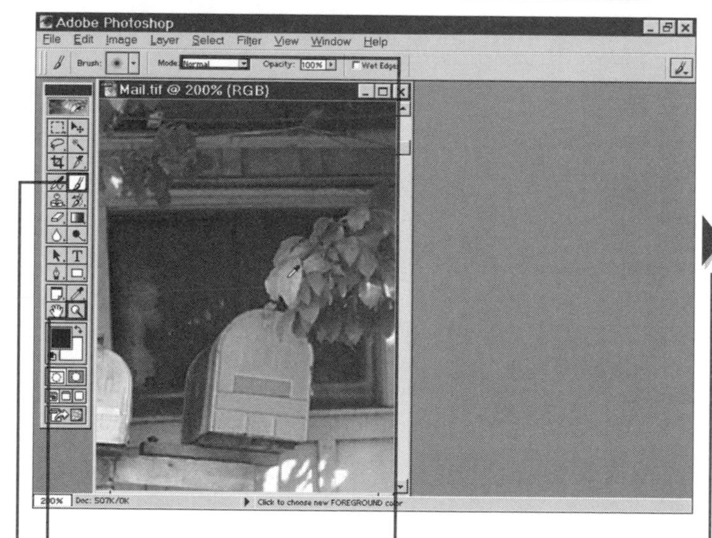

1 Zoom in to see details clearly.

2 Click the Paintbrush tool (🖌) to choose the tool and show its Options palette.

■ You can also access the tool by pressing B.

3 Choose Color from the Mode menu in the Options palette.

4 Press Opt/Alt to switch to the Eyedropper tool.

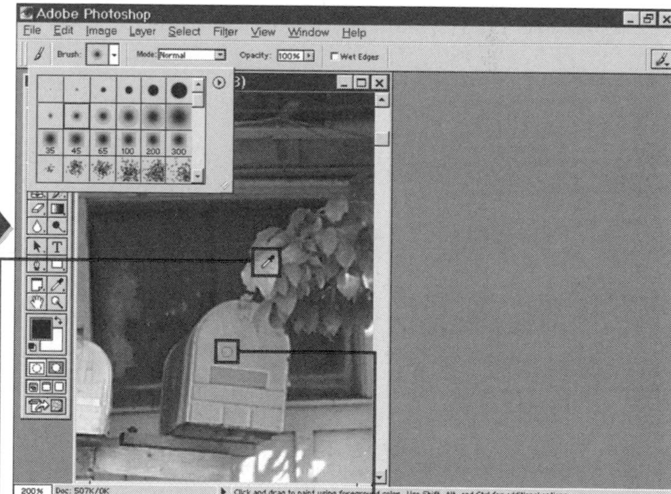

5 Pick up the color you want to match.

6 Paint in the area where you want to replace the original color to match the surrounding color.

CONVERT AN IMAGE TO MONOCHROME

Black-and-white photography is a treasured art form that we are in danger of losing, thanks to the overwhelming popularity of color. You have the power with Photoshop, however, to instantly turn color into monochrome.

You may want to do this for several reasons, and you can use more than one method to do it. First, the reasons: Black-and-white images can strengthen composition and impact. Black-and-white images cost far less to print and load much faster on the Web. Finally, they are the perfect starting point for hand-coloring (which you can do either in Photoshop or with transparent oils).

If you plan to do hand-coloring, the basic pigment color should be the one you want to dominate in the image. This is somewhat less important if you are going to do your coloring in Photoshop, because the coloring technique will recolor the pixels. Still, making your monochrome a particular color could save you from having to hand-color everything.

CONVERT AN IMAGE TO GRAYSCALE

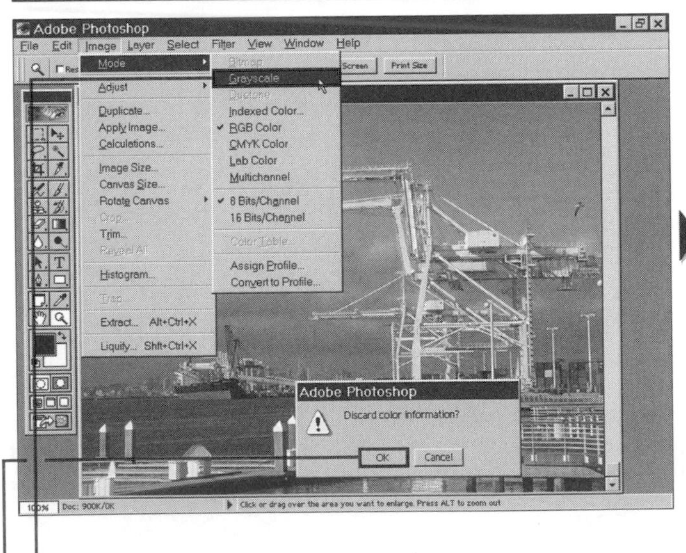

1 Choose Image, then Mode, then Grayscale.

2 Click OK in the Photoshop warning dialog box.

■ The Image becomes black and white. For toning, it has to be converted back to a color mode.

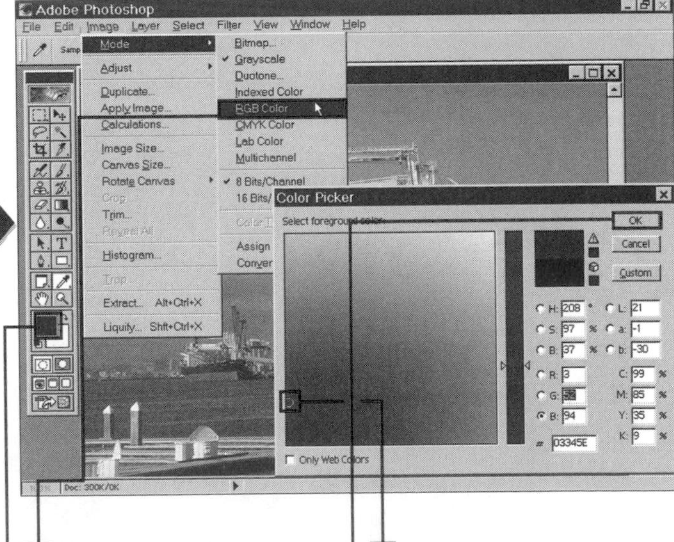

3 Choose Image, then Mode, then RGB Color.

4 Click the Foreground Color swatch.

■ The Color Picker dialog box appears.

5 Select as the foreground color the shade you want to use as the toning color.

6 Click OK.

What colors are best for toned prints?

✔ That really depends on the print. Sepia (reddish-brown) and blue are the two colors most commonly used, mostly because sepia produces fairly natural-looking skin tones, and blue is the color of sky and water. If you are after a special effect, anything goes.

Can I choose to tone an image with a spot color ink?

✔ Definitely. You can choose from such leading spot color systems as Pantone, DIC, Focoltone, Toyo, and TRUMATCH. You can reach these color books by clicking the Custom button in the Color Picker dialog box.

Can I tone images any other way?

✔ You can create toned images from grayscale in many ways. One is to use a Hue/Sat adjustment layer: Choose Colorize and click the foreground color box with a preselected color to change the foreground color, or just dial the color in with the sliders. Choosing Image, Mode, and then Duotone produces a smaller file size (closer to grayscale). Finally, you can use the Channel Mixer to create toned images.

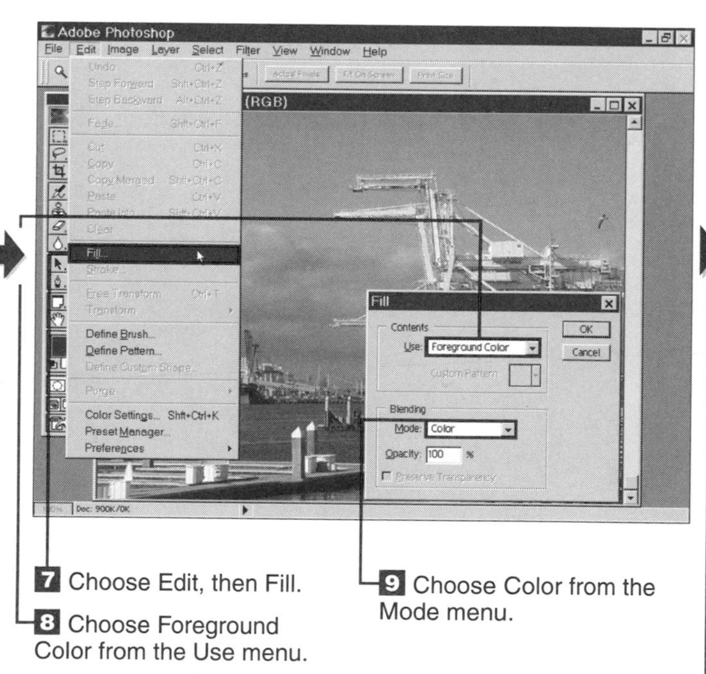

7 Choose Edit, then Fill.

8 Choose Foreground Color from the Use menu.

9 Choose Color from the Mode menu.

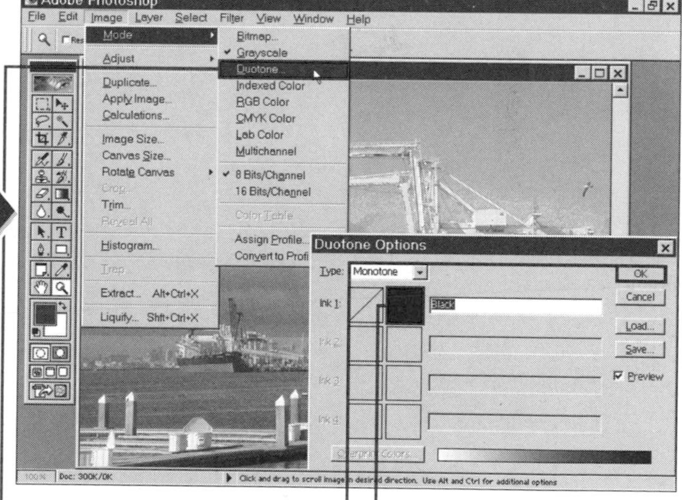

10 Starting from the color image, repeat steps 1 and 2.

■ The image is now Grayscale.

11 Choose Image, Mode, and then Duotone.

12 Click the color box and choose a color from the resulting Color Picker dialog (as in step 4).

13 Click OK.

MAKE DUOTONES

You can create duotones from any image, though you must first make sure that image is in Grayscale mode.

Duotones are images printed in two overlaid ink colors. The result is generally a richer tonal range than can be accomplished by printing a standard monotone image with only black ink. Usually you create duotones because the publication in which you are going to place the image is printed in spot (custom) colors, and you want to use the same inks to print the images. Another reason to create duotones is to jazz up the otherwise grayscale images in a particular print job. However, you can create a duotone just for the effect that mixing specific inks produces, and then change back to RGB and add your own colors.

The Duotone command gives you access to monotone, duotone, tritone, and quadtone, which means you can choose as many as four colors. You can also choose the percentage of ink that will be applied at any 10 percent increment of the tonal range from highlight to shadow.

MAKE DUOTONES

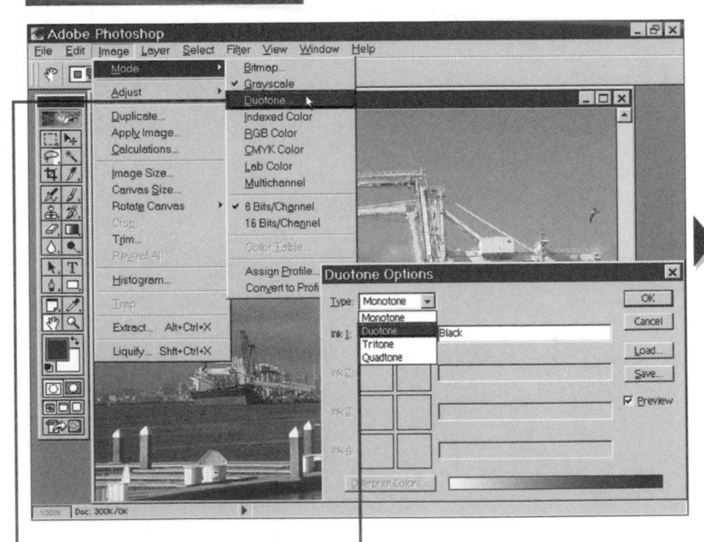

1 Start with or convert to a Grayscale image.

■ See "Convert an Image to Grayscale," earlier in this chapter.

2 Choose Image, Mode, and then Duotone.

■ The Duotone Options dialog box appears.

3 Choose Duotone from the Type menu.

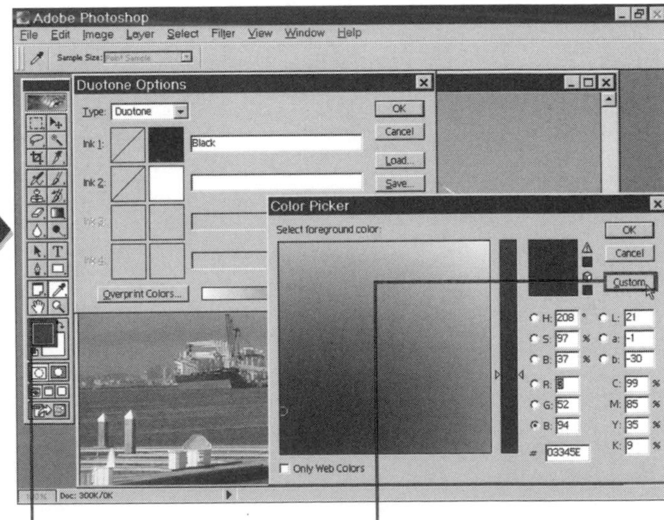

4 Click the Foreground Color swatch to bring up the Color Picker.

5 Click Custom in the Color Picker dialog box to bring up the Custom Colors dialog box.

Note: You usually want Custom Colors because most duotones are printed in spot colors already used elsewhere on the page.

Must I choose colors from color books?

✔ No. If the Custom Colors dialog box appears first, click the Color Picker button. If you choose colors from the Color Picker, remember that they cannot be printed from spot colors. However, if you are going to hand-color the image, feel free to choose colors from the Color Picker because you will need to print in CMYK (all colors) anyway.

What if I want to use three or four colors?

✔ The procedures are exactly the same as for a duotone, except you must choose Tritone (three colors) or Quadtone (four colors) from the Type menu in the Duotone Options dialog box.

What if I want to use more than four specific colors?

✔ You will have to use a different method. You can create as many custom color channels as you want by choosing Image, Mode, and then Multichannel. You can use Image, then Adjust commands on each of many different channels.

How can I be sure which colors and what intensity will work best?

✔ If you're already using spot colors in your print job, you have no choice. Otherwise, pick the colors that are most likely to set the mood that you're looking for. If you don't like what you see on screen, pick another set of colors.

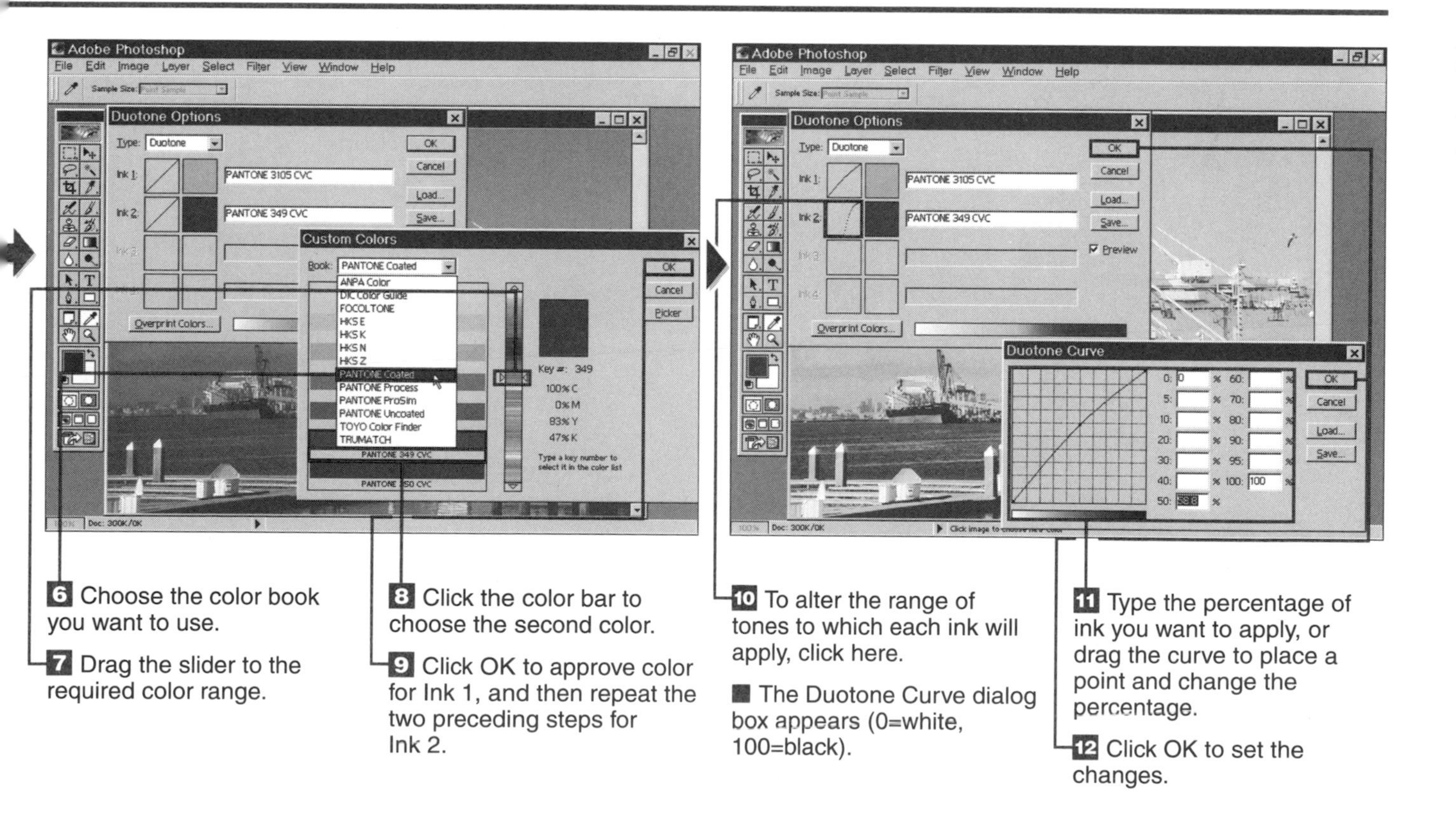

6 Choose the color book you want to use.

7 Drag the slider to the required color range.

8 Click the color bar to choose the second color.

9 Click OK to approve color for Ink 1, and then repeat the two preceding steps for Ink 2.

10 To alter the range of tones to which each ink will apply, click here.

■ The Duotone Curve dialog box appears (0=white, 100=black).

11 Type the percentage of ink you want to apply, or drag the curve to place a point and change the percentage.

12 Click OK to set the changes.

HAND-COLOR A MONOTONE IMAGE

You are not stuck with the colors with which your images were born. Photoshop provides you with several ways to recolor images. Converting an image to grayscale and making duotones are covered earlier in this chapter. You can also recolor any selection, layer, or channel using Edit, then Fill or using Image, then Adjust, then Replace Color to replace all of a particular range of colors within the image.

If you want absolute control over the color of every specific area of the image, however, use hand-coloring techniques. You can hand-color any part of a full-color image, using the techniques described in this exercise. If you want a completely hand-tinted photograph, however, start with a grayscale or duotone image. Convert that image back to full color, click the Paintbrush tool, and pick Color from the Blend Mode menu. When you color, the original luminance and saturation stay intact. Only the color changes.

You can employ this same technique with more control by creating a new layer, say, for each basic color, setting the layer to Color mode, and painting. You can later adjust the colors according to what you grouped per layer, and you can adjust opacity.

HAND-COLOR A MONOTONE IMAGE

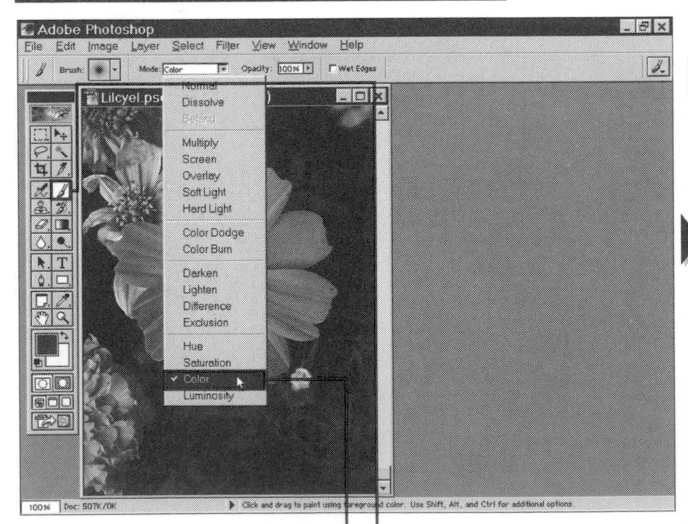

Note: The image used for this exercise was first converted to a duotone, which gives a different effect than working on a color image.

1 Click a brush (Paintbrush, Airbrush, or Pencil).

2 From the brush's Options bar, choose Color from the Mode menu.

3 Set zoom at about 200% so you can easily see the edges you want to stay within.

4 Click to bring up the Brushes library.

5 Click the brush you want to work with.

6 Reselect the Paintbrush tool and paint in the area where you want to change the color.

Sometimes boundaries are hard to see after converting to grayscale. How can I make seeing what I want to select easier?

✔ You make and save selections before converting to gray. You can retrieve the selections by dragging the channel mask to the Selection icon at the bottom right of the Channels palette.

Can the technique of hand-coloring be extended in any way?

✔ Hand-coloring can also mean that you use other Blend modes that will change the colorization in the original. Remember, too, that you can set opacity for your brush, which will affect the intensity of the color you are painting with.

Is there any way to save time over constantly having to choose colors from the Color Picker?

✔ Two suggestions: If you are recoloring an image that was formerly in color, save the image under another name as soon as you convert to monochrome. Then open the original in another window, and use the Eyedropper to pick from the original colors. If you want to stick to more basic colors, choose Window, then Show Swatches and pick your colors from that palette.

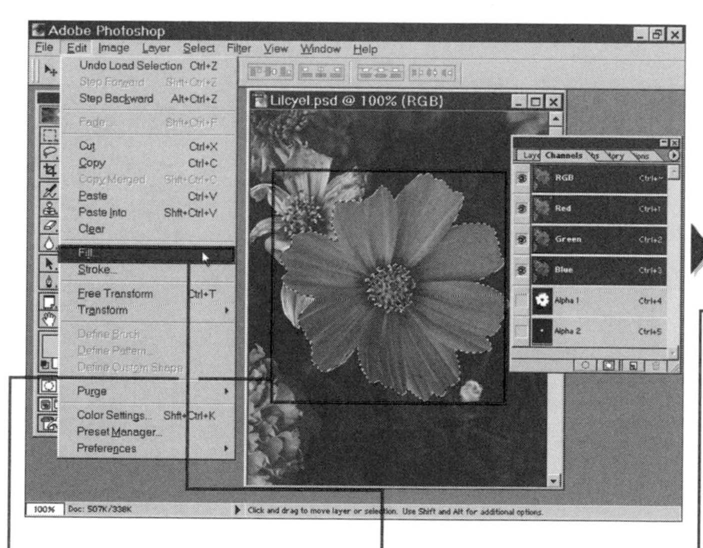

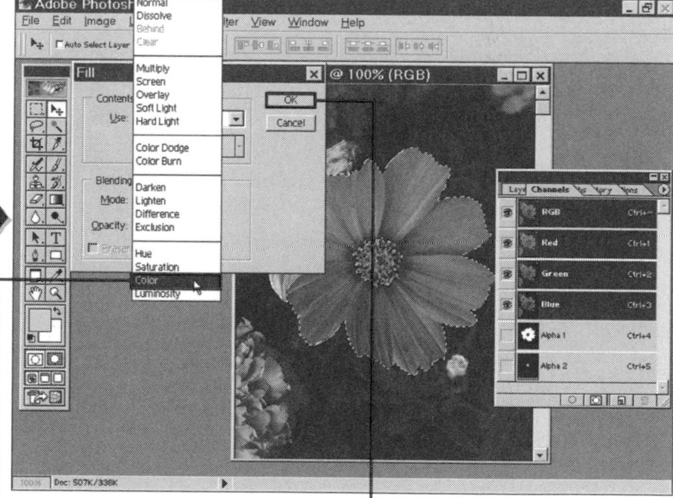

CHANGE COLOR BY FILLING A SELECTION

1 Select the area you want to fill.

Note: If you save your selections, you will be able to change colors more quickly when you want to make other interpretations of the image.

2 Choose Edit, then Fill.

■ The Fill dialog box appears.

3 Choose Color from the Mode menu.

■ Make sure other settings are at their defaults, as shown.

4 Click OK.

■ The selected area fills with the current foreground color.

CHANGE DEPTH OF FIELD

Often an image is more effective if the focus is, literally, on the subject. In conventional photography, this effect is achieved by keeping the subject in sharp focus while throwing foreground and background objects dramatically out of focus. This effect is known as *depth-of-field control.*

Depth of field is only controllable in-camera when the right equipment is used: a telephoto lens or a large-format camera, a wide aperture, and a camera that allows for exact focus control. Today's point-and-shoot and digital cameras generally sport wide-angle lenses, small imaging sensors (especially true of digital cameras), and automatic focusing.

Photoshop to the rescue! Thanks to the capability to precisely select any portion of the image (covered in the next chapter) and to Photoshop's Blur and Sharpen filters, you can reinvent depth of field after the fact. This layout shows you how to focus attention where you want it by blurring certain portions of the picture. (Sharpening is covered later in this chapter.)

CHANGE DEPTH OF FIELD

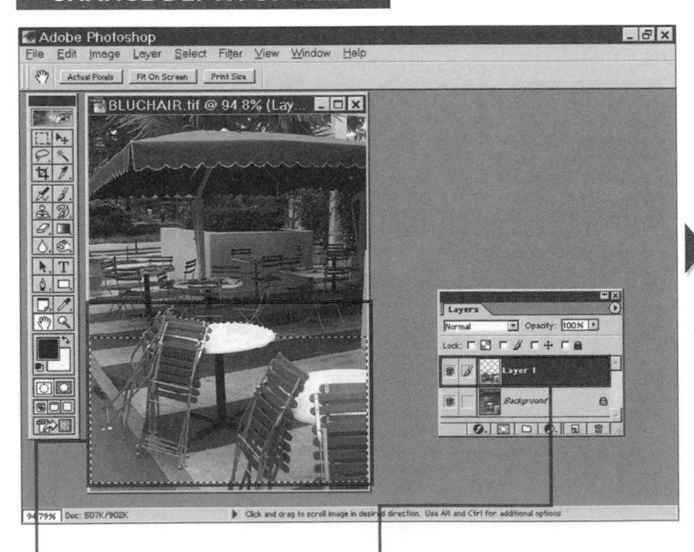

1 Select the area you want to keep in focus.

2 Press /Ctrl+J to lift the selection to a new layer (you may want to add and subtract from it later).

Note: See Chapter 6 for specific selection techniques, which varies according to image characteristics and the type of selection needed.

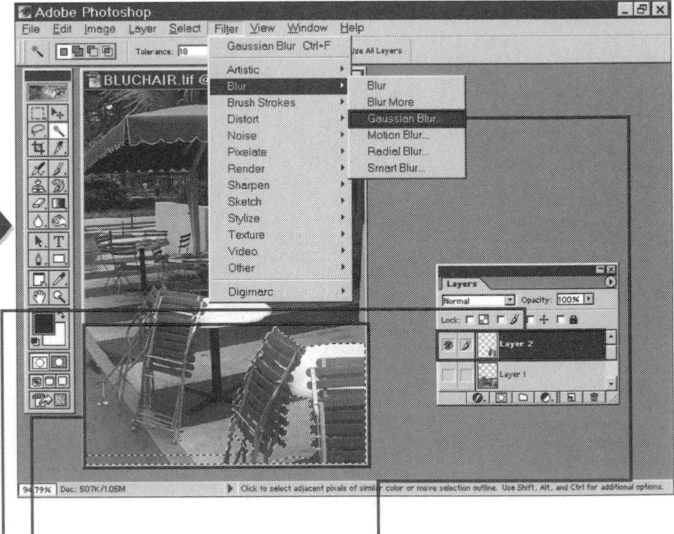

3 Select the area closest to the camera.

4 Press /Ctrl+J to lift the selection(s) to a new layer.

5 Choose Filter, Blur, and then Gaussian Blur.

Is there a better way if I want to create numerous interwoven planes of focus?

✔ If you have enough memory, which depends on the size of your image, you can copy the image to the same number of layers as the planes of focus you desire, and then blur each layer to the desired degree of focus. Erase those parts of a given layer not at the desired level of focus. Finally, change the stacking order of the layers so that the closest objects are at the top, the most distant at the bottom.

What if I want to just slightly blur an area to smooth blemishes or give a soft portrait effect?

✔ Although the Gaussian Blur filter seems a likely choice, you can easily overdo it with that filter. You are better off choosing Filter, then Blur, then Blur. The effect will be barely discernible, but you can press ⌘/Ctrl+F repeatedly until you see exactly the effect you want.

Is there a third-party Photoshop filter that makes depth-of-field blurring easier?

✔ Yes, Andromeda Software (www.andromeda.com) makes the Varifocus filter. It gives you a number of pre-set masks that cause the blurring to occur gradually over space. Of course, you can create the same effect, it just takes a bit longer.

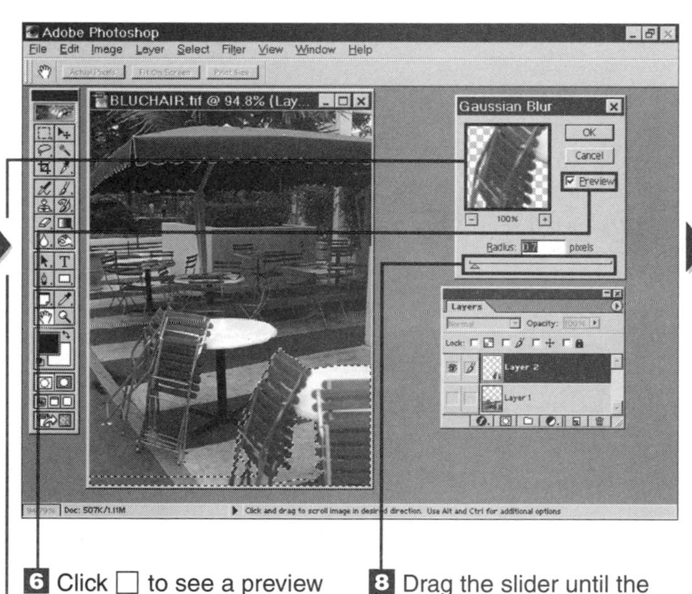

6 Click ☐ to see a preview (if unchecked).

7 Drag in the Preview box to center the area that will be defocused.

8 Drag the slider until the item is mildly blurred.

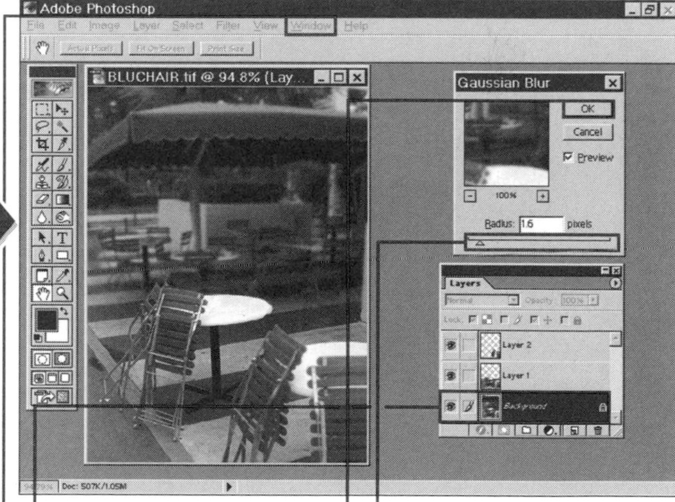

9 Click to select the Background layer.

10 Choose Filter, Blur, and then Gaussian Blur.

■ The Gaussian Blur dialog box appears.

11 Drag the slider until you see the degree of blurring you want in the background.

12 Click OK.

CREATE MOTION BLUR

Sometimes today's cameras—particularly the automated ones—are just too good: They freeze motion in bright light, whether you want them to or not. That is actually perfectly okay because Photoshop enables you to create as much motion blur as you like. You can even control the angle of that motion blur.

Motion blur is just a directional blur. To apply it to any selection, layer, or channel, all you need to do is choose Filter, then Blur, then Motion Blur. When the Motion Blur dialog box appears, drag a slider to indicate the degree of the blur, and drag an angle wheel to indicate the directional angle of the blur.

The example in this exercise shows you how to apply a comic-strip type blur that smears the trailing edge of an isolated object. You can modify these selections and settings to create different effects.

For instance, if you want to make an object on a transparent layer look as though it were flying upward, drag the angle wheel until the upward angle seems right for the upward flight path. Next, enter a number of pixels accross which you want the smear to spread. Click OK, and the motion blur is rendered.

CREATE MOTION BLUR

1 Carefully select the object you want to put in motion.

2 Press /Ctrl+C to copy the selection to the Clipboard.

3 Press /Ctrl+V to paste the object.

■ The object is now isolated on a new layer.

4 Choose Window, then Show Layers.

5 Make sure Preserve Transparency is unchecked.

6 Select the portion of the image within which you want the blur to occur.

7 Choose Select, then Feather.

8 Enter a fairly broad range of pixels to graduate the effect and click OK.

How do I blur the selection so that it is not just blurred inside the selection?

✔ Float the selection, or place it on its own, transparent layer. This technique also enables you to select only part of the layer, such as the trailing edge, so that the effect will look more natural. Be sure the option Preserve Transparency is unchecked; otherwise, the blur will not extend past the object itself.

How can I best combine the effects of Motion Blur and Wind?

✔ Duplicate the layer containing the Motion Blur effect and run the Wind filter on the topmost of the two layers. Then adjust the transparency of the two layers so that you get a blend of the two effects.

What if I want more of a streaked comic-strip type blur?

✔ Try choosing Filter, then Stylize, then Wind to bring up the Wind dialog box. This effect actually streaks the image from either the left or right edge. No slider exists for continuously varying the effect, but you could scale the layer up, run the filter, and then scale it back down if the effect is too dramatic. The wind effect always "blows" in the same direction.

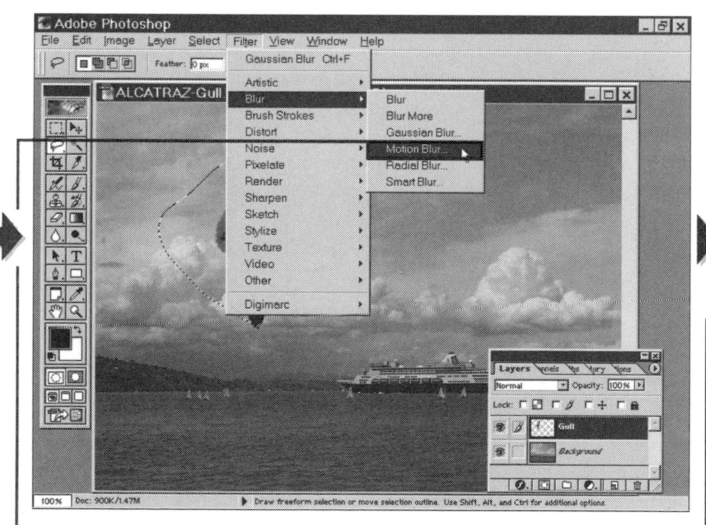

9 Choose Filter, Blur, and then Motion Blur.

■ The Motion Blur dialog box appears.

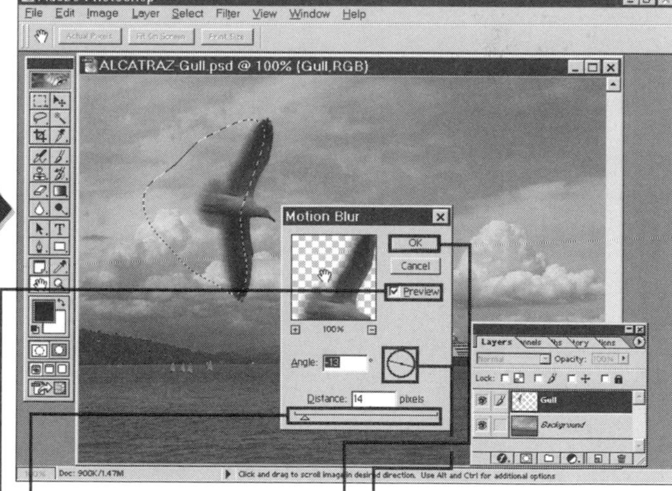

10 Drag the Distance slider until you see the degree of streaking you desire.

11 Check the Preview box if it is not already checked.

12 Drag to indicate the angle of blur.

13 Click OK when you are happy with the result.

CREATE A RADIAL BLUR

The Radial Blur filter can produce one effect that cannot be produced by any camera setting (although you could do it in the darkroom by spinning the paper during the exposure of an enlargement). The other effect you can create with this filter can be produced in-camera by rapidly zooming the lens during the course of a long exposure.

Once again, Photoshop gives you a great deal more control than you would have in real life. You can use a feathered selection to freeze the center of the blur and graduate the effect. The conventional process is going to blur the center as well as the edges, although the edges are blurred more because they move a greater distance during exposure.

The three quality settings in the Radial Blur dialog box are

- Draft
- Good
- Best

The Good and Best settings produce a fairly smooth diffusion of pixels, but processing takes significantly longer. The Draft mode is quicker, but produces pixelation.

CREATE A RADIAL BLUR

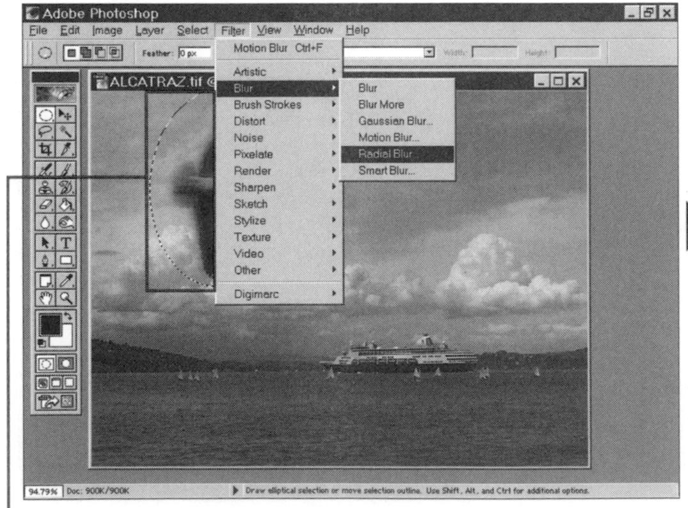

1 Use any of the Selection tools to select an area around or within the subject that you want to keep sharply focused.

2 Feather the selection for about one-fourth of the radius.

3 Choose Filter, then Blur, then Radial Blur.

■ The Radial Blur dialog box appears.

4 Click to set the Blur Method to Spin.

5 Drag the slider to set the distance the image will spin.

6 Drag the center of the Preview window to approximate the center of the spin.

7 Click to set the degree of quality.

8 Click OK.

Does a way exist to speed the processing of these filters?

✔ The quality you choose affects the speed of the filter: The better the interpolation method, the slower the processing time. Short of that, you just have to spend the money to buy the fastest possible state-of-the-art computer.

Can I use the Spin mode to make objects (wings or limbs, for instance) spin in opposite directions?

✔ Select and place a limb on a separate layer. Place an elliptical selection around the limb that places the limb on the outside radius of the selection. Now the Spin mode of the Radial Blur filter can blur the limb in one direction.

Does an easy way exist to control the blending of these effects with the information in the target image?

✔ At last! An opportunity to mention the fact that you can use the Fade command in conjunction with all the Image, then Adjust and Filter commands, as well as many other operations. Just press Shift+⌘/Ctrl+F, and the Fade dialog box appears. Drag the slider until you get the desired degree of blending.

Is there a way to keep the whole object from blurring?

✔ Yes. Select only that part of the object that you do want blurred.

USE THE ZOOM MODE OF THE RADIAL BLUR FILTER

1 Follow steps 1–4 from the preceding task.

2 Click to set the Blur method.

3 Drag to set the center of the zoom.

4 Drag to set the degree of zoom effect.

5 Click to set the image interpolation quality and click OK.

■ This is the way the image looks after processing at High Quality. Notice that there is no scattering of pixels when compared to the second screen in this spread. Notice how dramatically attention is focused on the bird.

ADD A SMART BLUR

Choosing Filter, then Blur, then Smart Blur enables you to blur lighter or neutral tones in the image while retaining the sharpness of darker edges. This feature is useful in portraits for keeping the hair, eyelashes, and pupils sharp while smoothing skin defects. A Smart Blur is also a nice way to keep some tonal gradations while "averaging" the neutral tones in preparation for running a special or artistic effects filter.

Four settings appear in the Smart Blur dialog box: Radius, Threshold, Quality, and Mode. Radius is the number of pixels included in the blur. If you set this number too high, the blur encroaches on the sharpness of edges. Threshold is the darkness value assigned to edges. You achieve the best results when the Radius is about half that of the Threshold.

You control edge smoothness by choosing High, Medium, or Low from the Quality menu. Of course, higher quality affects processing speed. The Mode options enable you to trace edges: white against black or vice versa.

ADD A SMART BLUR

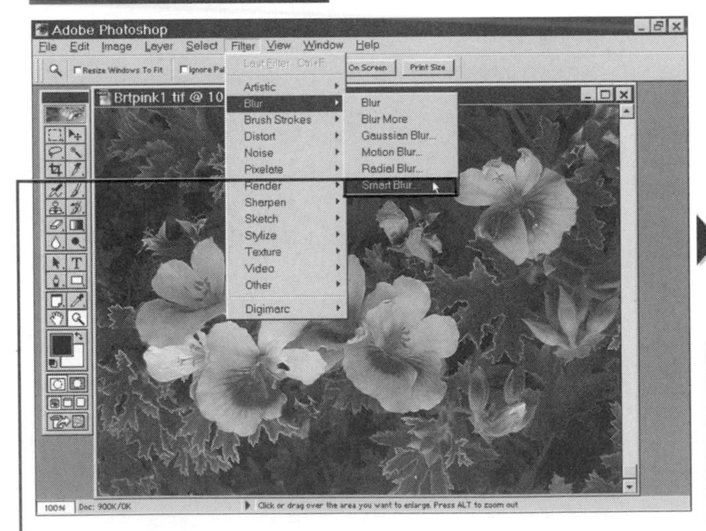

1 Choose Filter, then Blur, then Smart Blur.

■ The Smart Blur dialog box appears.

2 Click here to raise or lower magnification in the Preview window.

3 Drag to change the approximate radius, or type in a number.

4 Drag to change the approximate threshold value, or type in a number.

Why would I use the Edge Only or Overlay Edge settings?

✔ Good question. If the Overlay Edges were black, these settings could be a nice way to outline a painting. Use the Edge Only option after copying the image to another layer. Then invert the layer, choose Select, then Color Range, set Fuzziness to a fairly low number (3–6), click the Eyedropper in the white area, and click OK. Finally, press Shift+⌘/Ctrl+I and click the layer mask icon at the bottom of the Layers palette. The original image shows through the outline.

Can I use Smart Blur to make creating selections easier?

✔ Yes, especially when it comes to automated selection tools such as the Magic Wand and Magnetic Lasso and Pen, which can be easily thrown off-track by texture irregularities. Make an extra layer, select it, set Smart Blur Threshold and Radius at fairly high numbers, and click OK. Make your automated masks in that layer and save them. Then delete the layer and use the masks wherever they are needed.

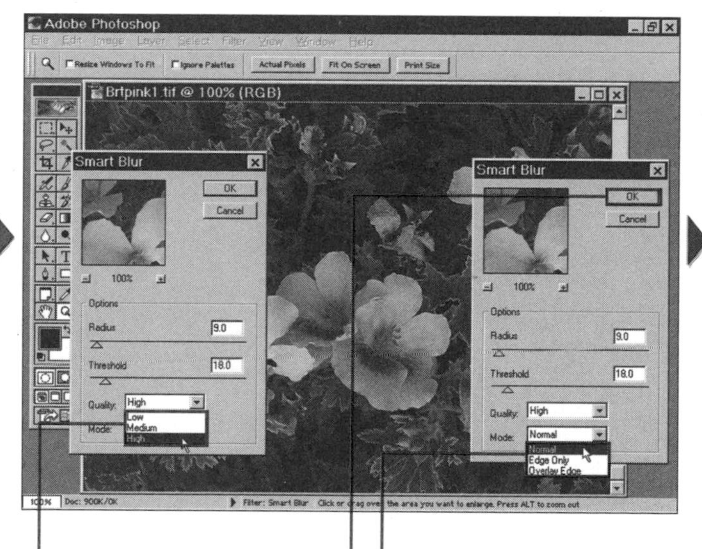

5 Choose desired edge smoothness from the Quality menu.

6 Choose edge-tracing mode from the Mode menu.

7 Click OK.

■ The left side of the image shows Edge Only tracing.

■ The right side of the image shows the result of the settings made in the preceding screens.

CONTROL FOCUS: BLURRING AND SHARPENING

Although Photoshop does a passable job of throwing portions of the image out of focus, Photoshop cannot do much to rescue hopelessly fuzzy images. On the other hand, if your camera optics are not up to Carl Zeiss standards or you were a little nervous when you pressed the shutter button, you are in several kinds of luck. Not only can you make the image crisper, but you can also be selective about it.

The preset Sharpen filters are Sharpen, Sharpen More, and Sharpen Edges. Using them involves nothing more than choosing them from the menu. You can, however, intensify their effect by pressing ⌘/Ctrl+F to repeat their application. Watch the image carefully while using this method. The second it becomes too harsh, press ⌘/Ctrl+Z to undo the last application.

Sharpen and Sharpen More work by simply increasing the contrast between adjacent pixels. Sharpen edges increases contrast only where pixels pass a certain contrast threshold.

CONTROL FOCUS: BLURRING AND SHARPENING

■ This is the original photo at 100% zoom. As you can see, it is a little soft.

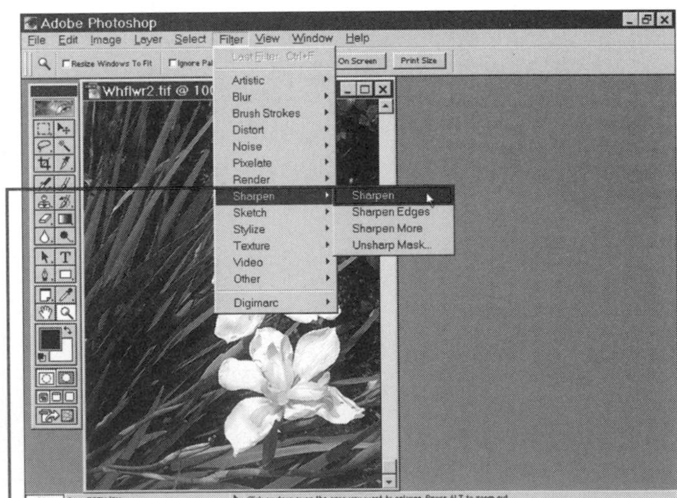

USE THE SHARPEN FILTER

1 Choose Filter, then Sharpen, then Sharpen.

■ The result appears almost immediately. No dialog box exists for setting options.

Can I sharpen only part of the image without having to make a selection?

✔ Photoshop makes this easy. Choose the Eraser to bring up the Options palette. Click the Erase to History box and drag the Opacity slider to about 50 percent. Now you can scrub areas of the image back to the original.

Can I control the focus of very small areas without resorting to making many selections?

✔ Yes—use the Focus brushes in the Toolbar. The Sharpen brush sharpens within the area covered by the chosen brush. The Blur tool has the opposite effect. You can intensify either effect by repeatedly stroking the same area.

What if I cannot get enough control by repeatedly applying the filter and then undoing?

✔ If the closest you can get is either a bit too hard or a bit too soft, use the Fade Last command. (Fade Last actually names the last "fadeable" command you executed.) Drag the slider in the resultant dialog box until you see the effect you want.

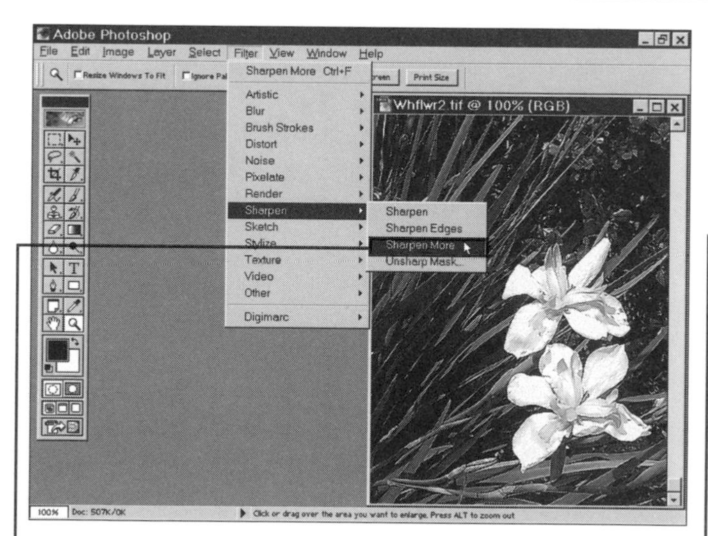

USE THE SHARPEN MORE FILTER

1 Choose Filter, then Sharpen, then Sharpen More.

■ The effect is immediate, with no intervening dialog box.

■ Here is the same portrait after one pass with the Sharpen More filter. The effect can be a bit much.

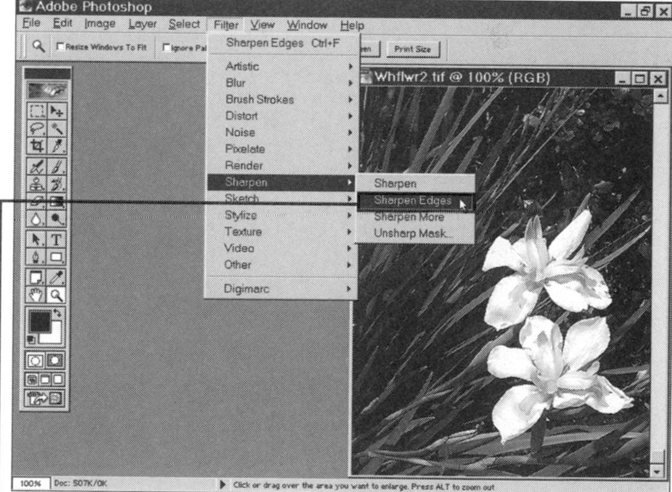

USE THE SHARPEN EDGES FILTER

1 Choose Filter, then Sharpen, then Sharpen Edges.

■ The effect is immediate, with no intervening dialog box.

■ Here is the same image after one pass with the Sharpen Edges filter. This is a pretty good quick fix.

CONTINUED

CONTROL FOCUS: BLURRING AND SHARPENING CONTINUED

The Unsharp Mask filter lets you balance the sharpening of edges (where dissimilarly colored pixels meet) and the sharpening or blurring of the rest of the image. Exactly how it works depends on how you set the Amount, Radius, and Threshold settings in the dialog box.

Understanding the Amount setting is easy: Set it for the desired degree of overall sharpening. The other two settings sound similar to settings found on some other filters, but they behave differently. Radius controls the thickness of edges. Higher values produce more overall image sharpness; lower values soften neutral tones and exaggerate the edges. Threshold determines the degree of contrast that must exist between neighboring pixels before they will be sharpened.

Unlike the other sharpening filters, Unsharp Mask has a Preview window of the entire image. You should preview at 100% magnification so you can see the effects of your changes on the final image.

CONTROL FOCUS: BLURRING AND SHARPENING (CONTINUED)

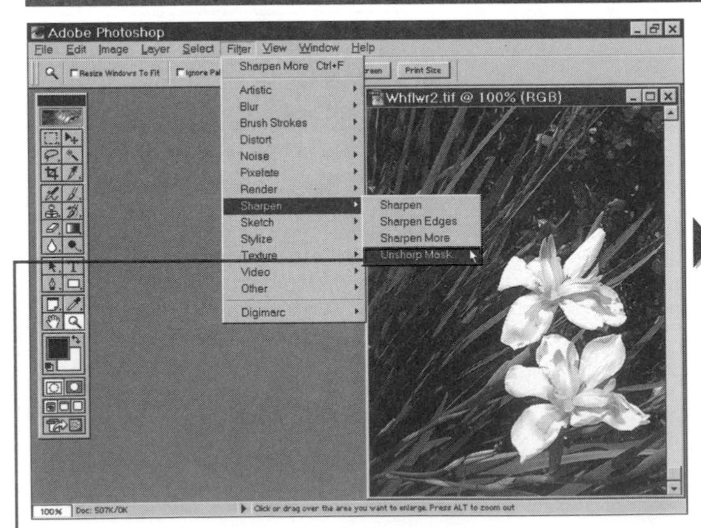

1 Choose Filter, Sharpen, and then Unsharp Mask.

■ The Unsharp Mask dialog box appears.

■ The default settings, shown here, will work best for most situations, in which case, you can just click OK.

What is the most frequent application for the Unsharp Mask filter?

✔ Transformations, image resizing, and filters can all cause the image to be resampled. Resampling can scramble some pixels, causing an overall softening of the image. You can usually fix this problem by running the Unsharp Mask filter.

What is the best way to experiment with this filter?

✔ Keep the settings low and repeat the execution of the filter until you get an effect that is just slightly overdone. Then Undo (⌘/Ctrl+Z) to move back a step.

What settings are usually the most successful?

✔ The answer depends on the contrast and colors in your image as well as the overall resolution of the image. The higher the image resolution, the higher the settings need to be. Having said that, you usually want to keep the numbers low: Keep Amount below 150%, and Threshold and Radius between 0 and 2. For prepress work (images that are to be screened and printed), it is generally recommended that you slightly oversharpen from what you think looks good on your screen.

2 Drag to determine the degree of overall sharpening.

■ Note the increase in sharpening along the contrasting edges.

3 Drag in the Preview window to center the area of interest.

4 Drag the Radius slider to adjust thickness of edges and overall contrast.

5 Drag the Threshold slider to specify brightness contrast between pixels before they are considered edges.

Note: You can also type exact numbers into the Radius and Threshold entry fields.

ELIMINATE ARTIFACTS FROM COMPRESSED IMAGES

The popularity of digital cameras and the Web have resulted in our having to deal with many compressed images. Compression can sacrifice accuracy of detail and color for efficiency of storage. The visible results are blotchiness in midtones and shadows and pixelated highlights near edges. These pixel aberrations are called *artifacts*.

This exercise deals with four techniques for minimizing artifacts, all of which involve blurring some aspect of the image:

- Adding a blurry layer and applying the Color Blend mode
- Converting to Lab color and blurring a chosen channel
- Blurring the blue channel
- Using the Blur brush to smooth any artifacts you may have missed with the other techniques

You will probably want to use all of these techniques on the same image to get the best effect, although at times one of these techniques will do the job.

ELIMINATE ARTIFACTS FROM COMPRESSED IMAGES

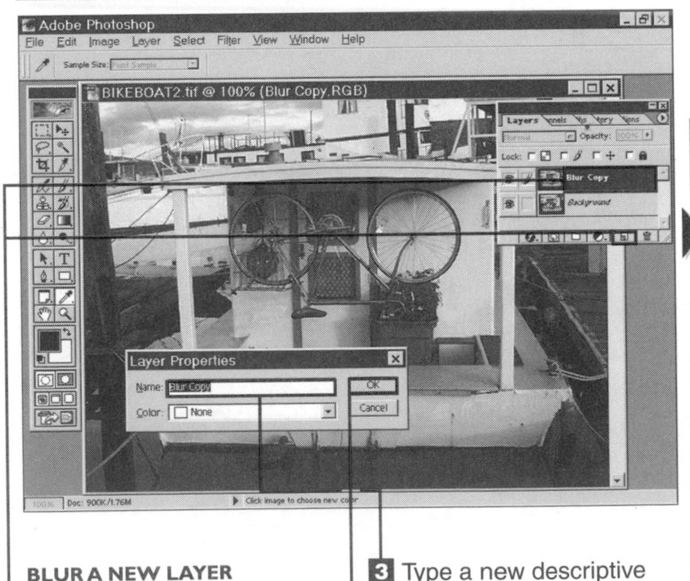

BLUR A NEW LAYER

1 Drag the background layer to the New Layer icon.

2 Double-click the background layer copy's name.

■ The Layer Properties dialog box appears.

3 Type a new descriptive name for the layer.

4 Click OK.

5 Choose Filter, then Blur, then Gaussian Blur.

6 Type a small pixel radius (or drag the slider).

7 Click OK.

How is Lab mode used to get rid of artifacts?

✔ Lab is actually Photoshop's native mode, used for converting images from color mode to color mode. If the artifacts are the same level of lightness, they can be blended in any channel without affecting sharpness, which is defined by the brightness (L) channel.

In RGB mode, why does blurring the blue channel help to eliminate artifacts?

✔ The blue channel tends to exhibit more artifacts than the other channels, so if you blur the blue channel slightly, you kill many artifacts without having much effect on overall sharpness.

Should I use the Unsharp Mask filter after performing all these steps?

✔ Sometimes it helps, and sometimes it takes you right back to where you started. Do not try it until you save your work. This way, you can choose File, then Revert if you are not happy with the results.

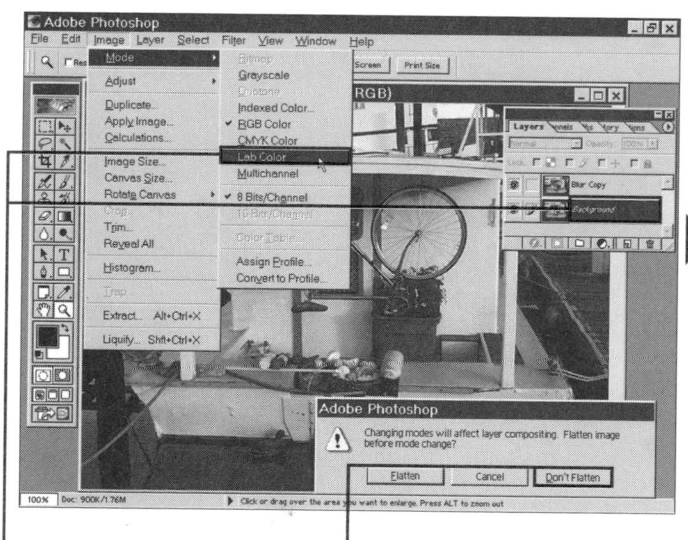

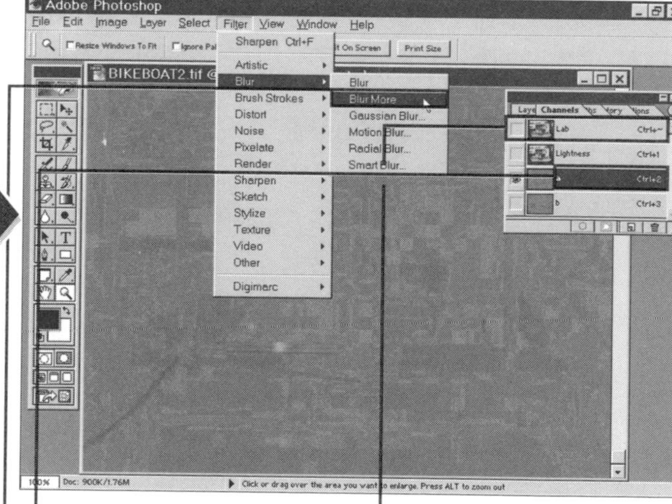

BLUR THE A CHANNEL

1 Click to target the background layer.

2 Choose Image, then Mode, then Lab Color.

■ Because multiple layers exist, a warning dialog box appears.

3 Click Don't Flatten.

■ You are now in Lab Color mode.

4 Click to target the A channel.

5 Choose Filter, then Blur, then Blur More.

6 Click to target the Lab channel.

■ The results of your efforts up to this point appear. Unless you want to perform other operations in Lab mode, choose Image, then Mode, then RGB color.

CONTINUED

ELIMINATE ARTIFACTS FROM COMPRESSED IMAGES CONTINUED

Blurring the blue channel in an RGB image is often an easy way to eliminate most scanning and digital camera artifacts because the blue channel tends to show artifacts more prominently.

At the same time, blurring the blue channel does little to distort our perception of the end result.

Although blurring the blue channel is seldom enough to remove all visible artifacts, it is the technique that most effectively minimizes them without over-softening the image.

Be very careful not to overdo the blurring in the Blue channel (or in either of the preceding two techniques). The idea is to minimize the effect of artifacts without making your picture too mushy and without creating strange color halos around contrasting pixels (edges).

ELIMINATE ARTIFACTS FROM COMPRESSED IMAGES (CONTINUED)

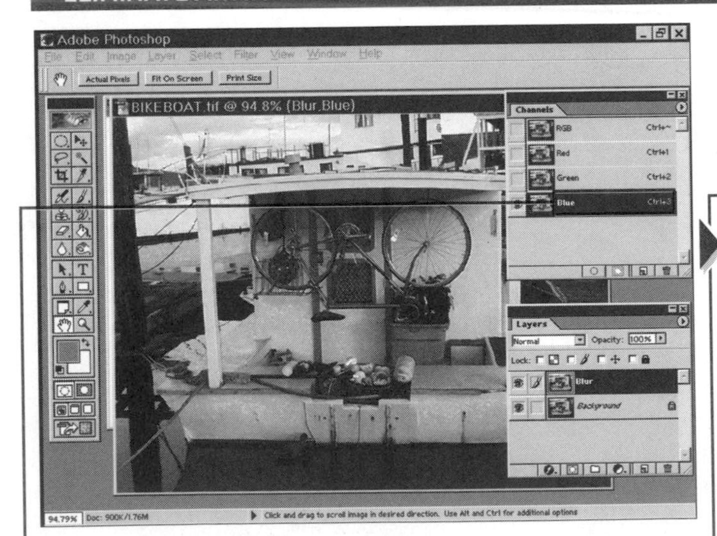

BLUR THE BLUE CHANNEL

1 Click to target the blue channel.

■ The blue channel image appears in the workspace. You can clearly see the edges of artifacts in this channel, so slight blurring will minimize the effect without blurring the overall image.

2 Choose Filter, then Blur, then Blur More (or if you have not used another filter in the meantime, press /Ctrl+F to repeat the Blur More filter).

3 Click to target the RGB channel.

■ You now see the result of what you have done. At this point, virtually all artifacts should have disappeared. You may still have some streaking near highly contrasting edges. If so, consider using the blur brush, as covered on the next page.

Why not just blur the whole image and then use the Sharpen Edges filter?

✔ Because you will probably end up with something that looks worse than the image you started with. Some of the most bizarre edges may be overemphasized. Try it if you like to go in search of "happy accidents," but be sure to do it on a duplicate copy of your image.

Would some of the retouching methods help in getting rid of artifacts?

✔ You bet. Often, the really objectionable artifacts are limited to small areas anyway. So you do not need to go through all the steps outlined in these two spreads. Just clone, blur, or use any other retouching technique to get rid of them.

If the artifacts are limited to a few shadow areas and the detail does not matter anyway, can I not just blur the whole area with a filter?

✔ Yes, this technique is another one that works well in certain situations. Two caveats: Be sure to feather the edges of your selections so that the blurring blends. And be sure to use the Add Noise filter on the same selection to match the grain in the rest of the image.

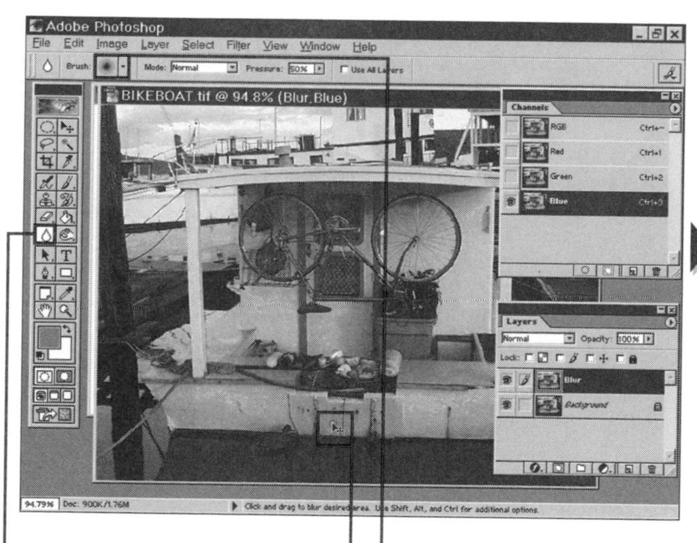

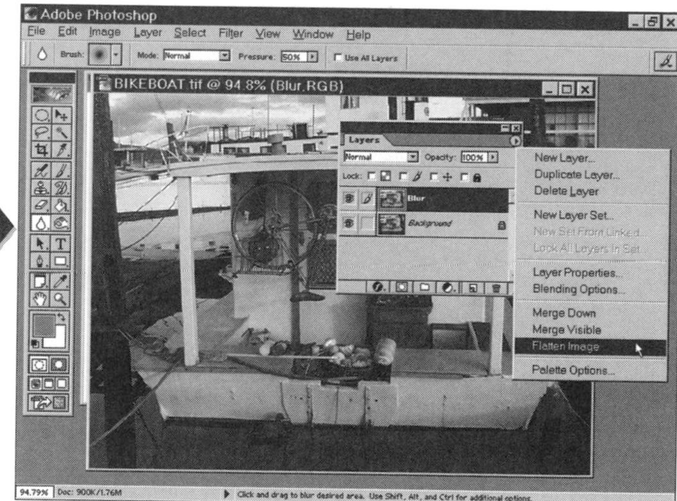

ELIMINATE SMALL ARTIFACTS WITH THE BLUR BRUSH

1 Click the Blur tool (💧).

2 Choose an appropriate brush size with some feathering.

■ Scrub to blend rough borders.

■ This image is now artifact free (at least for the ordinary viewer). Brush retouching required only a few strokes and took only about five minutes.

CONTROL FOCUS

You can use Photoshop to control focus in many ways that you cannot do with a camera. This news is especially good to those using consumer digital cameras. Digital cameras priced under $1,000 generally show everything in fairly sharp focus from about 2 feet from the lens to infinity. But blurring the background can greatly improve your composition. It also helps to focus interest on the subject of the photo.

You can find the three focus filters built-in to Photoshop—Blur, Blur More, and Gaussian Blur—by choosing Filter, then Blur. The other types of blur are generally meant for purposes other than focus because they create an effect, such as motion or zoom streaking. In fact, the Gaussian Blur filter is the one that you should almost always use because the other two filters do not give you any control over the amount of blurring.

These filters are best used if you just want a slight softening of the image for cosmetic reasons or to set a mood.

CONTROL FOCUS

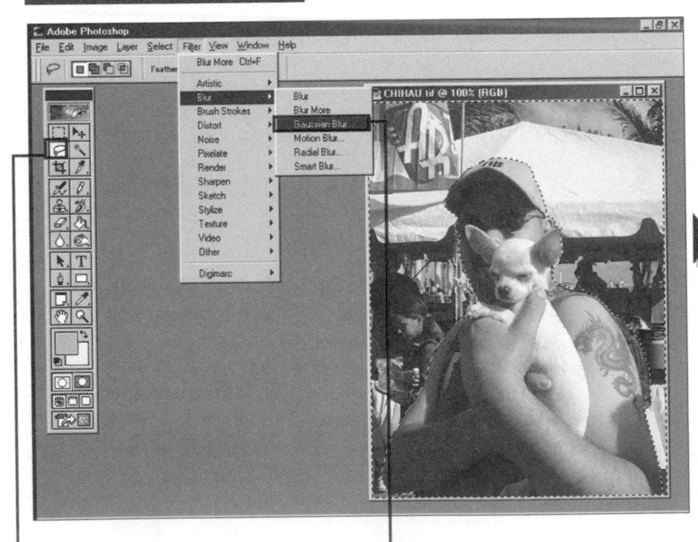

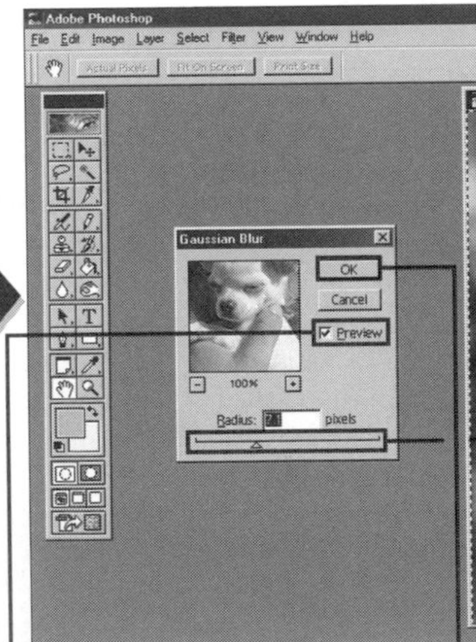

1 Click the Lasso tool ( ).

■ You can also use any other selection tool.

2 Select the area you want to throw out of focus.

3 Choose Filter, Blur, and then Gaussian Blur.

■ The Gaussian Blur dialog box appears.

4 Click Preview.

■ The result of your adjustment immediately appears in the Photoshop workspace window.

5 Drag to adjust the degree of blurring.

6 Click OK when you are happy with the degree of blurring.

ADD PSYCHEDELIC COLORING WITH A GRADIENT MAP

You can map the colors in any grayscale image to the colors in any linear gradient you can create in Photoshop. The blackest tone becomes the leftmost color in the gradient, and the whitest tone becomes the rightmost color in the gradient.

All the other grays become the colors in the gradient, according to their distance along the scale of brightness in the original. You can picture this by placing two identical-size rectangles one above the other and filling the top with a black-to-white gradient and the bottom one with a color gradient. Any given shade of gray becomes the color that is immediately below it in the color gradient.

You can use the Gradient Map to colorize an image as though it has been subjected to a toner such as Sepia by applying a gradient that ranges from the darkest to the lightest shade of one color. If you use multicolored gradients, you will create truly "wild and woolly" color effects.

ADD PSYCHEDELIC COLORING WITH A GRADIENT MAP

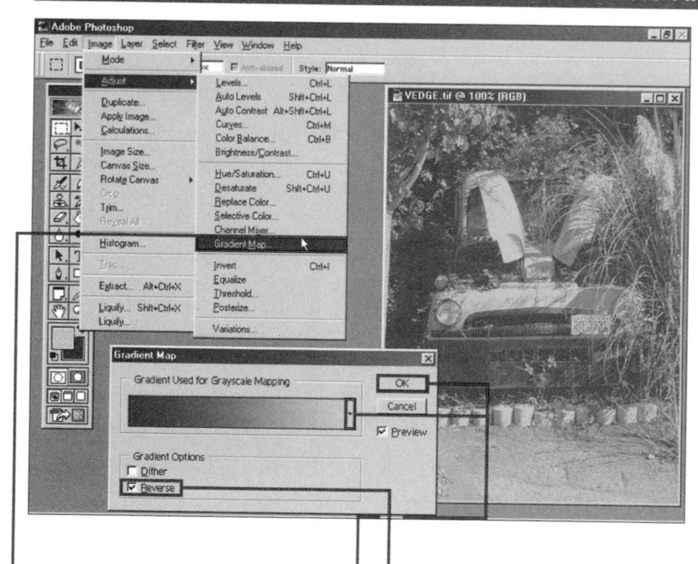

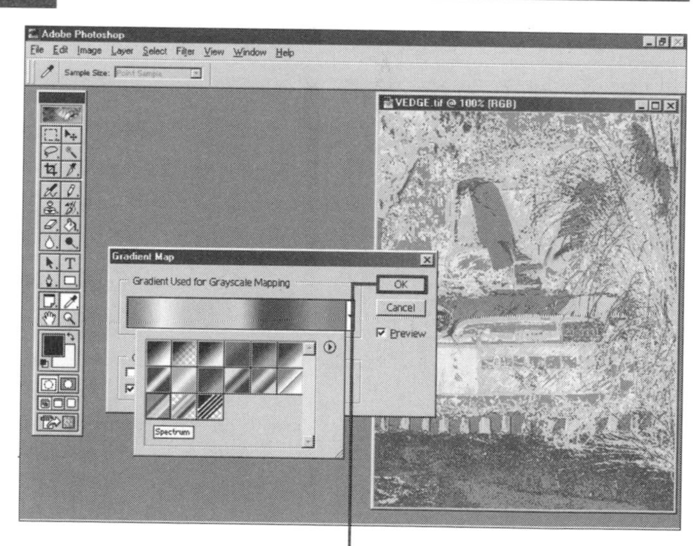

TONE WITH A DARK TO LIGHT GRADIENT

1 Choose Image, Adjust, and then Gradient Map.

■ The Gradient Map dialog box appears.

2 Optional: Click the Reverse box. Doing so changes the image from positive to negative.

3 Choose the gradient you want to use from this menu.

4 Click OK.

APPLY PSYCHEDELIC TONING

1 Follow steps 1–3 in the exercise at left, but choose a custom gradient, such as a spectrum or metallic one.

■ You can preview the result instantly in the workspace window.

2 Click OK when you are satisfied with the preview.

USING THE LIQUIFY COMMAND

You can use the Liquify command to distort portions of the image as if they were molten lava. You can stir the liquid to make all sorts of strange twists and whirls. You can stretch it as if a bubble were coming to the surface. You can even "swish" it to make zigzag distortions.

The tools within the Liquify preview mode include:

- Warp "goos" the image forward under the brush.
- Twirl Clockwise and Twirl Counterclockwise make the image look as if it were spiraling down a drain.
- Pucker squeezes the image toward the center of the brush.
- Bloat makes the image seem to bubble outward.
- Shift Pixels pulls pixels to the right or left. Dragging with Shift pulls pixels to the right; in conjunction with Opt/Alt, it pulls pixels to the left.
- Reflection vertically flips pixels just above the brush and paints them into the area you drag across.

The portion of the image that is affected by your strokes is determined by the size of the current brush.

USING THE LIQUIFY COMMAND

1 Click the Lasso tool ( ).

2 Click to select the area around the portion of the image that you want to Liquify.

3 Choose Image, then Liquify (or press Shift+ /Ctrl+X).

■ The portion of the image you have selected appears in the Liquify preview area.

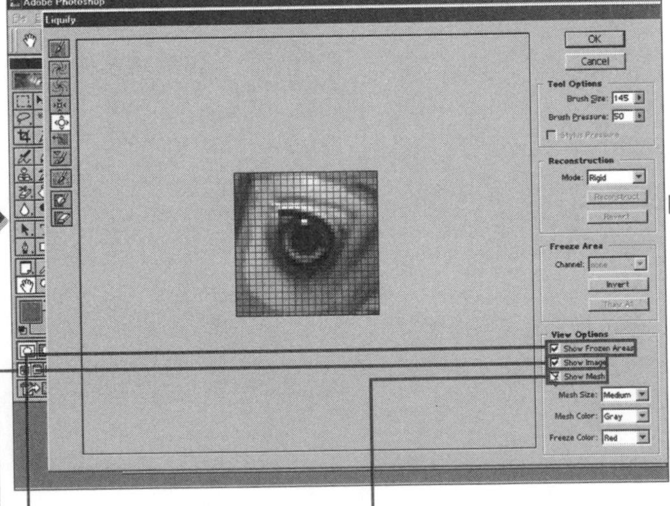

4 Click to show the mask over frozen areas (default).

5 Click to show the image that will be affected (default).

6 Click to show mesh.

■ You see the mesh swell and distort according to how you use the tools.

What if I want to see only an enlarged portion of the image in the Liquify preview?

✔ Before you enter the preview, select only the portion of the image you want to work on. The selected portion will be automatically zoomed in.

Can I warp in a straight line?

✔ You can use the Shift key to make straight line drag strokes just as you do with the Pencil and Brush tools. Click once to establish where you want the stroke to start, press Shift, and then click a second time to end the line. You will get a straight stroke between the two points.

Can I use this tool on type?

✔ Yes, but you have to rasterize it first. Then you can follow any of the procedures for liquification.

Can I "turn down" the effect I created in the Liquify preview?

✔ Choosing Edit, then Fade works just as well for this command as for the Filter and Extract commands. The percentage of fade chosen will lessen the amount of distortion by that percentage.

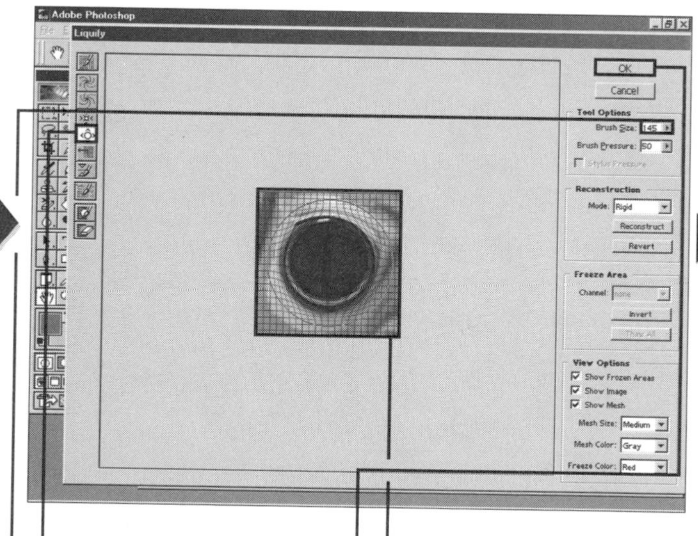

7 Click the Bloat tool ( ).

8 Enter the size of the brush you want to use. It should cover the area you want to bloat.

9 Center the brush over the area you want to bloat, click and hold the mouse button (left button if using Windows) until the swelling suits you.

10 When satisfied with the preview, click OK.

■ This is how the image appears after bloating the eye.

11 Press /Ctrl+D to drop the selection.

■ You can now select another area for the same or another type of selection. The next task spreads demonstrate the use of some of the other Liquify tools.

REFLECT AND SHIFT WITH THE LIQUIFY COMMAND

You can, of course, do all the other types of distortions that the Liquify command offers through the tools mentioned in the preceding section, "Using the Liquify Command." This section shows you how to use two of those tools, Reflect and Shift. You use the Shift tool to give a more violent atmosphere in the clouds. You then use the Shift tool to make ripples in the water.

One thing that you often want to do is to exercise control over the area in which you want the effect to be seen. You can do that in one of two ways:

- Make a selection of the area you want to liquify before issuing the command.
- Use the Freeze brush in the Liquify preview area to paint over the areas you do not want affected. It matters not one whit, outside of personal preference and working methods, as to which of these techniques you use.

When you work with the Liquify brushes, try pressing the ⌘/Ctrl and Opt/Alt keys at the same time. They will have different effects (or no effect) with different brushes.

REFLECT AND SHIFT WITH THE LIQUIFY COMMAND

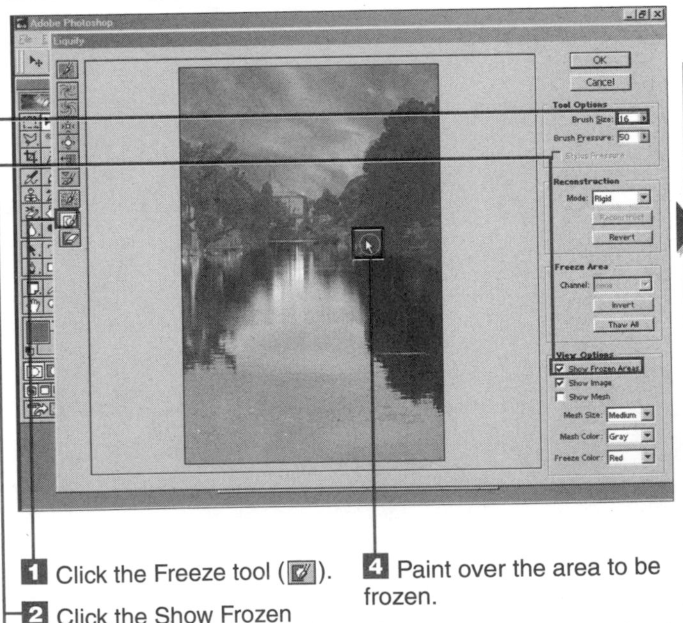

1 Click the Freeze tool.

2 Click the Show Frozen Areas checkbox.

3 Enter or drag a brush size.

4 Paint over the area to be frozen.

■ You can change the size of the brush and continue to paint.

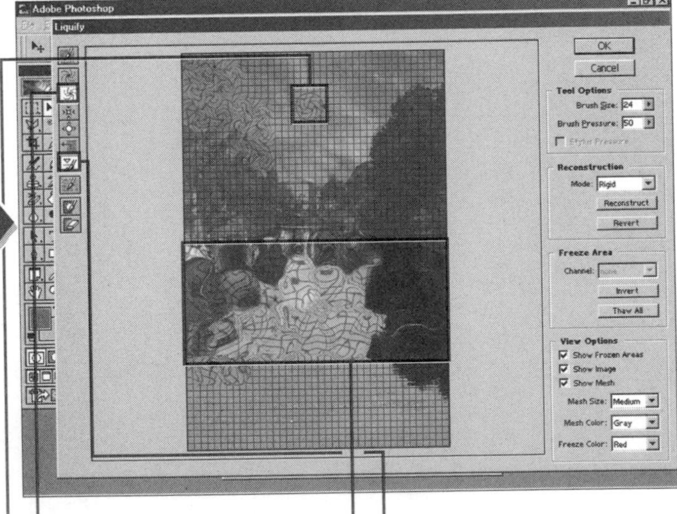

5 Click the Twirl tool.

6 Click and hold with the brush centered over the area you want to twist.

7 Click the Reflect tool.

8 Drag in the area where you want the reflection to appear.

Note: This image is a composite screen shot so that you can see the effect of using both tools at once.

USING LIQUIFIED WARPING AND TWISTING

You can use the Liquify command to give you an effect very similar to that of heating a Polaroid print and then physically pushing the emulsion around to get an almost Van Gogh effect. Some filters and paint programs can give you Van Gogh effects, but Liquify lets you do it your way. You can stroke to place the effects where you want and you can change the size of the brush to vary the size of the warping and twisting.

The Liquify tools that most readily lend themselves to these effects are the Warp and Shift tools. The Twist tools, discussed in the preceding task, are also good candidates.

Both the Warp and Shift tools seem to work best when you drag them.

The Warp tool pushes pixels in front of it. You can easily get zigzag effects by pushing one way, moving over a few pixels, and then pushing the other way. The Shift tool pushes pixels at a 90-degree angle to itself. It pulls them closer when you stroke to the right and pushes them further away when you stroke to the left.

USING LIQUIFIED WARPING AND TWISTING

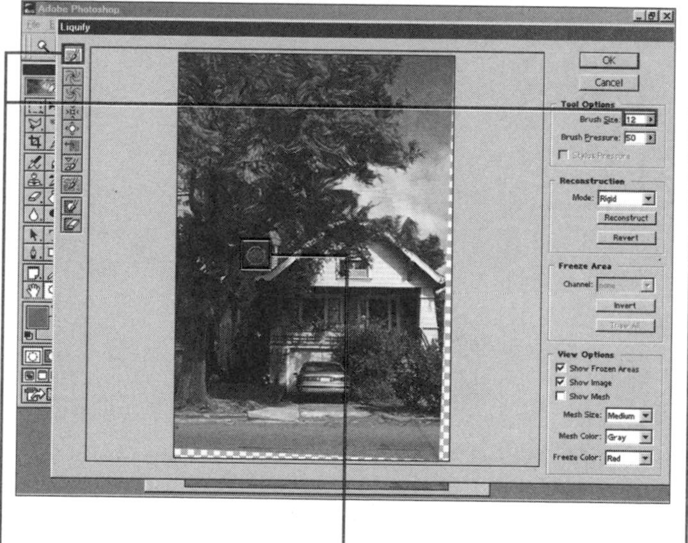

WARP

1 Click the Warp tool ( ).

2 Type your brush diameter in pixels.

■ You can also change the size of the brush by pressing the [key to make the brush smaller and the] key to make the brush larger.

3 Drag to push pixels in front of the brush.

SHIFT

1 Click the Shift tool ( ).

2 Type a number in pixels for your brush size.

3 Drag left to push pixels away from the sides of the stroke.

■ Dragging to the right "sucks" the pixels in along the sides of the stroke.

Note: You can use the Shift key while dragging to push pixels away along the edges of a straight line.

MAKE ADJUSTMENTS BY STROKING SMALL AREAS

You can hand-stroke to lighten, darken, or change the color saturation of small local areas. You may sometimes need to bring a bit more detail into a local highlight or to lighten the wrinkles under someone's chin. Using the Dodge, Burn, or Sponge tools is often the best way to darken a highlight or lighten a shadow, because you can watch the effect as it builds and keep changing the brush size until the effect blends exactly as you visualized the effect.

The Dodge, Burn, and Sponge tools take their names from tools used in photographic labs. Burning passes light from the enlarger through a hole in the hands or a piece of cardboard to continue exposing (darkening) a particular area of the picture. Dodging lightens an area by holding back light. Sponging lowers contrast or saturation by applying cold water to part of the image as it is being developed.

Note that for all three of the local area adjustment tools, you choose a brush style and size, just as you would for a painting tool.

MAKE ADJUSTMENTS BY STROKING SMALL AREAS

LIGHTEN (DODGE) A LOCAL AREA

1 Click and drag the Dodge tool ( ).

2 From the Options bar, choose the tonal range you want affected. (Midtones is the default.)

3 Set a low (around 15%) exposure range, so that your strokes build the effect slowly.

4 Scrub (drag back and forth or in circles) to darken the area until you see the desired result.

DARKEN (BURN IN) AN AREA

1 Click and drag to choose the Burn tool ( ).

2 From the Options bar, choose the tonal range you want to affect. (Midtones is the default.)

3 Set a low (around 15%) exposure range, so that your strokes build the effect slowly.

4 Scrub (drag back and forth or in circles) to lighten the area until you see the desired result.

How do I keep the border from being obvious when I protect an area with a selection?

✔ Choose Select, then Feather. Enter the number of pixels for the radius of the softened edge.

Why not just make a selection and then use one of the Image, Adjust commands?

✔ That is a very good technique, as long as you want the adjustment to be absolutely uniform. Often, it looks more natural and better blended if the adjustment is not quite so uniform.

What is the best way to ensure a smooth blend along the edges?

✔ Choose a fairly large brush relative to the area to be affected and set the Hardness to a very low number. Keep your exposure (pressure) low and keep moving the brush over the area until it slowly builds up.

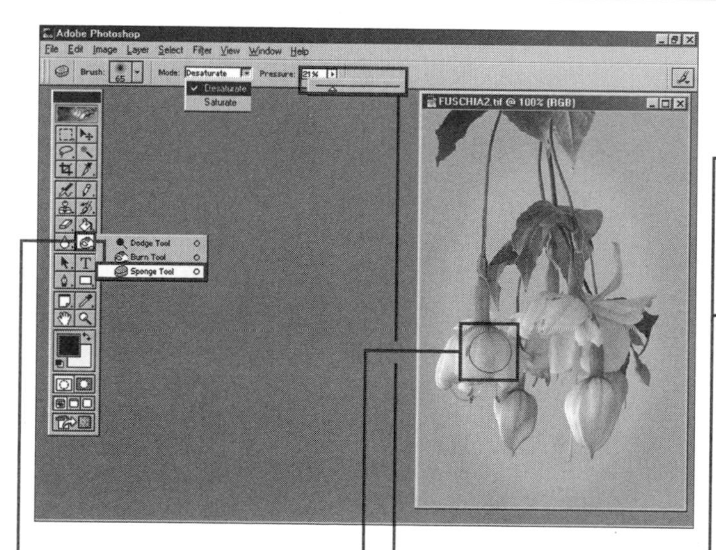

SATURATE OR DESATURATE AN AREA

1 Click and drag to choose the Sponge tool.

2 Choose Saturate to brighten colors or Desaturate to dull them from the Options bar Mode menu.

3 Set a low (around 15%) exposure range, so that your strokes build the effect slowly.

4 Scrub (drag back and forth or in circles) to affect the area until you see the desired result.

PROTECT AREAS YOU DO NOT WANT TO AFFECT

1 Click the Lasso tool ( ).

2 Carefully select the local areas you want to adjust.

■ Perform any of the three preceding exercises, as needed.

■ Press /Ctrl + D to drop the selection when you have finished. You can now make a new selection.

EXTRACT AN IMAGE FROM ITS BACKGROUND

You can quickly isolate objects from their backgrounds, even if their edges are not very well defined and even if the background is colored or patterned. The keyword here is "quickly." Isolating images from their backgrounds has long been possible in Photoshop, but the Image Extract command lets you paint a border around your object. The border can be any thickness, and Photoshop treats the border as a transitional area. If the colors inside the border match colors within the border, those colors are not erased. If colors within the transitional area match those outside the border, they are erased.

Of course, the Extract command can do its best if the background is an untextured, solid color. If that is the case, the program almost always guesses right, even in the case of partially transparent areas or when the edge is all hair and leaves.

The following exercise shows you the basic method for removing an object from its background. The next two exercises show you how to refine the selection before creating the final extraction.

EXTRACT AN IMAGE FROM ITS BACKGROUND

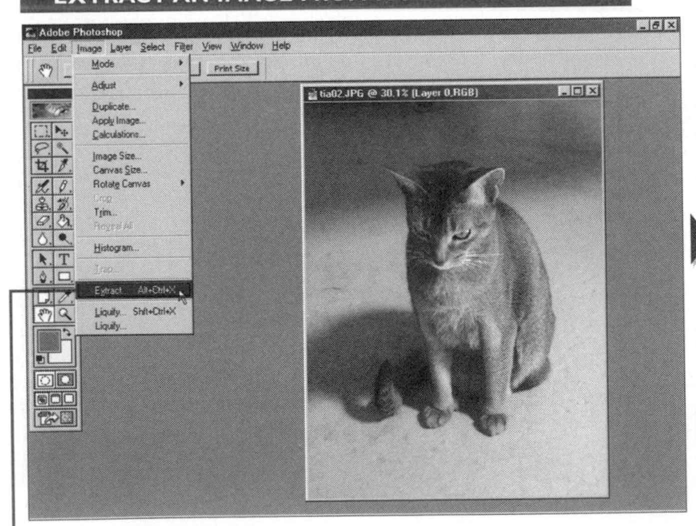

1 Choose Image, then Extract.

■ The screen fills with the Extract interface. Photoshop's usual commands become unavailable.

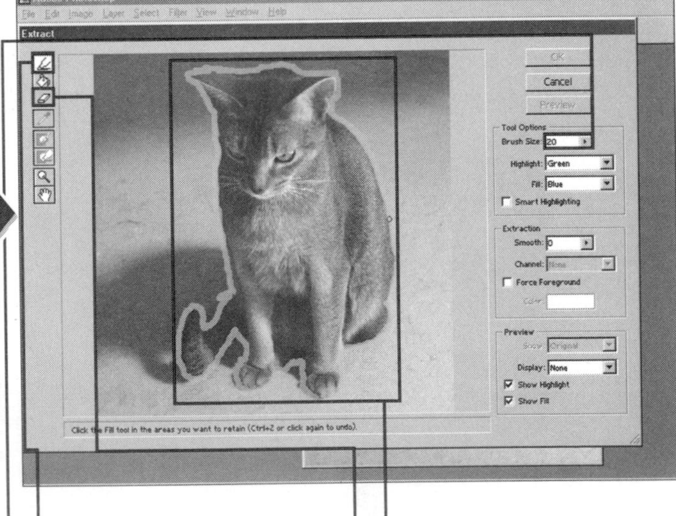

2 Click the Edge Highlighter tool ( ).

3 Enter the desired brush size in pixels (edge highlight thickness).

4 Highlight outside edge of subject so that all partially transparent areas are covered.

5 Click the Eraser ( ) to erase highlights that bleed too far into completely opaque areas.

What is the secret to using Extract successfully?

✔ When in doubt, make the marker thicker and make sure that as little of it as possible is inside the area you want to keep opaque.

Can the marker be too thick?

✔ Of course. You do not want to cover a lot of the colors that you definitely want to leave out. Also, make sure that some of the colors you definitely want to leave out are *not* covered by the marker color.

What is the best way to select fly-away hair or partially transparent edges such as found in a glass of tea?

✔ Cover all the hair or glass that shows the background through it. Be sure *not* to cover areas that do not reveal any background.

How do I get rid of smudgy areas around the edges of the extracted image?

✔ First, try re-highlighting the edges so that the highlight is narrower. If that does not help, use the Cleanup tool along the edges of the previewed image while the Extract dialog box is still open. Remember, you can zoom in if you need to check detail before you click OK.

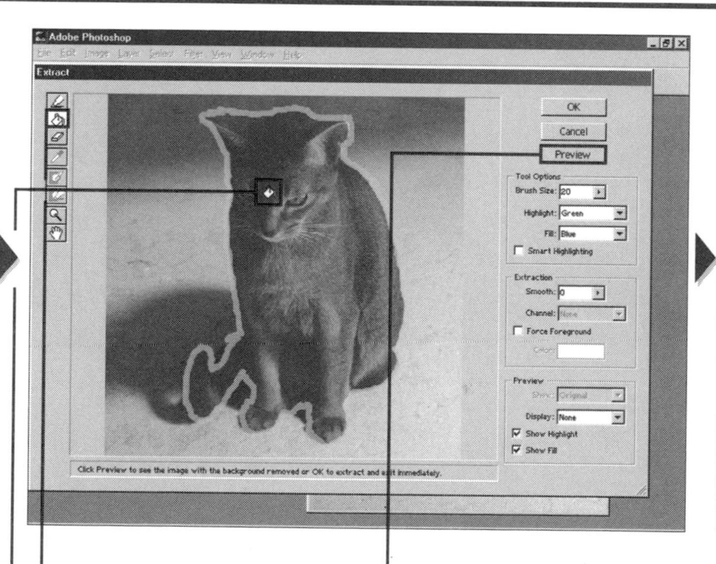

6 Click the Fill tool (◈).

7 Click inside the area surrounded by the Edge Highlight.

Note: If the fill color spills outside the Edge Highlight, use the Edge Highlighter to paint over the gap that allowed this to happen.

8 Click Preview.

■ The extracted (knocked out) image appears.

■ If no other layers exist, the image appears to float on a checkerboard background. You can now drag it into another Photoshop image, where it appears on its own layer. This feature makes compositing objects from one photograph with objects from another photograph easy.

CLEAN UP EDGES IN THE EXTRACT COMMAND

You can use two tools, Cleanup and Edge Touchup, that are brand new in Photoshop 6 to clean up edges while you are still working in the Extract command's window. After all, very seldom do you find yourself extracting a subject from a busy background and ending up with absolutely spotless edges.

The first thing you need to do is edit your Edge Highlight by checking the Show Highlight box and then using the Edge Highlighter and the Eraser to fine-tune the amount of the background that has been considered transitional. Generally, that means thinning the transition highlight wherever blotchiness comes through from the background.

Zoom in with the Magnifier tool so that you can see the edge more precisely. Click the Eraser tool and thin the outer edges of the highlight wherever they cover a color or colors that you would like to erase.

After you do that, click the Preview button again and then use the Cleanup tool and the Edge Touchup tool, as shown below.

CLEAN UP EDGES IN THE EXTRACT COMMAND

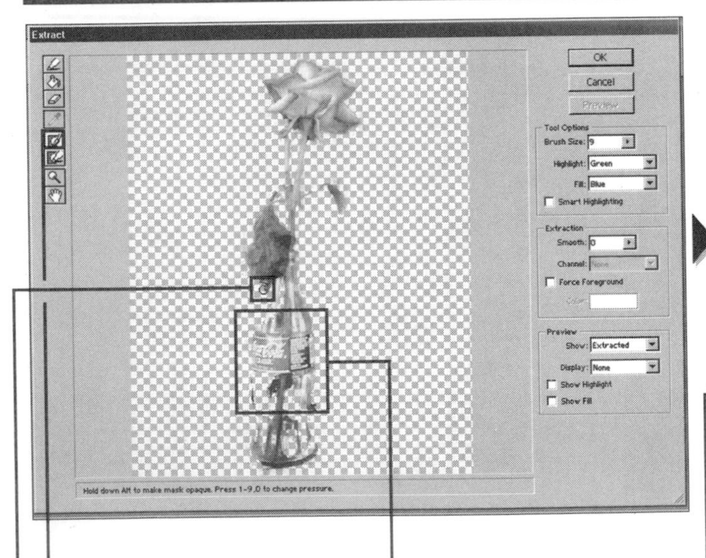

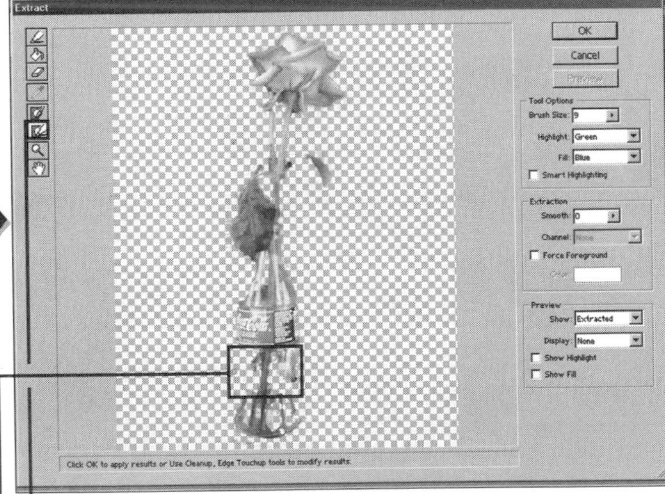

1 Click the Edge Touchup tool (), which works on the same principle as the Background Eraser (see Chapter 6).

2 Place the center of the brush circle on the color you want to eliminate.

3 Drag to erase.

■ You may want to reduce opacity on some edges and increase it on others.

4 Click the Cleanup tool ().

5 Pass the cursor over the edge to be made more transparent.

■ The more you scrub an edge, the more transparent it becomes.

■ To restore opacity, press Opt/Alt while using the Cleanup tool.

CLEAN EXTRACTED EDGES IN PHOTOSHOP

You can also clean edges after you have clicked the Extract window's OK button. You may sometimes find that cleaning Extract-ed edges in Photoshop works better than in the Extract dialog box. For one thing, you can place the new background behind the image before you complete the final edge processing. Then you can see exactly how well the edges blend with their new surroundings.

This exercise works with the other layers turned off. In order to work with only the transparent background visible, choose Window, then Show Layers, and then click the Eye icon in the Layer Visibility box to turn off all the other layers. A layer is off when the Eye icon disappears.

If you want a new solid color background, create a new layer and then fill it with the color you want. For a new image background, open it and use the Move tool to drag the image into the extracted image's window. It automatically forms a new layer. In the Layers palette, drag the new layer below the extracted image's layer.

CLEAN EXTRACTED EDGES IN PHOTOSHOP

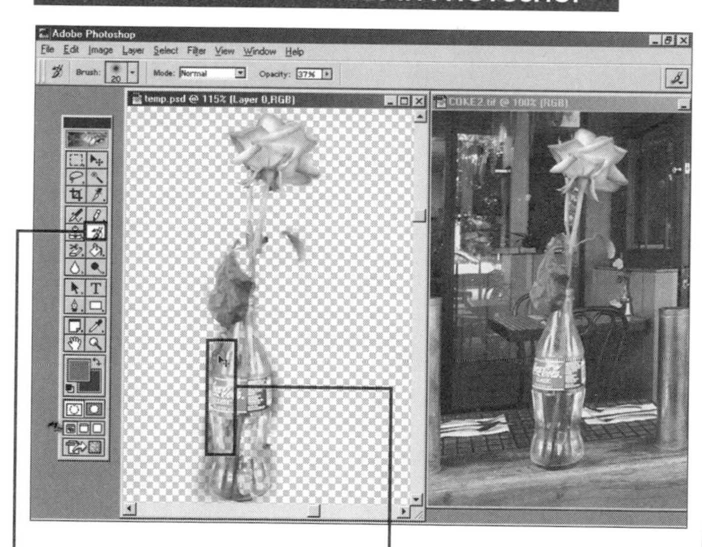

RESTORE EDGES WITH THE HISTORY BRUSH

1 Click the History brush ( ).

2 Enter a low Opacity setting on the Options bar so that you can add opacity from the snapshot.

3 Scrub the edges where you want to restore opacity.

■ The original of this photo is in the window at right.

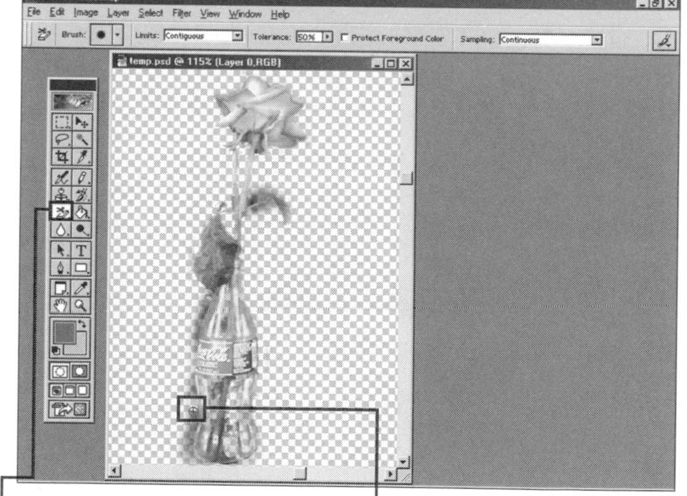

TRIM RESTORED EDGES WITH THE BACKGROUND ERASER

1 Click the Background eraser ( ).

Note: You may have to click and drag to choose this tool from the menu in this toolbox position.

2 Center the cursor on the color you want to erase and scrub.

■ Portions of the background have been cleaned.

APPLY TEXTURE FILTERS

You can create an endless variety of textures using Photoshop's built-in texture filters to impose a textured pattern on the active image layer.

You will find six texture filters available for use by selecting Filter, then Texture:

- Craquelure makes the image look as though it were projected onto a stucco wall.
- Grain simulates film grain and is useful for making a photograph look as though it were shot in adverse conditions.
- Mosaic Tiles divides the image into small squares and separates them to simulate grout.
- Patchwork divides the image into perfectly regular 3D rectangles.
- Stained Glass does a pretty fair job of simulating the real thing.
- Texturizer is the most useful and versatile of all these filters. Texturizer enables you to use any grayscale Photoshop (PSD) file as a texture. Lighter areas in the grayscale image make the subject appear to rise from the surface while darker areas seem to recess the image.

APPLY TEXTURE FILTERS

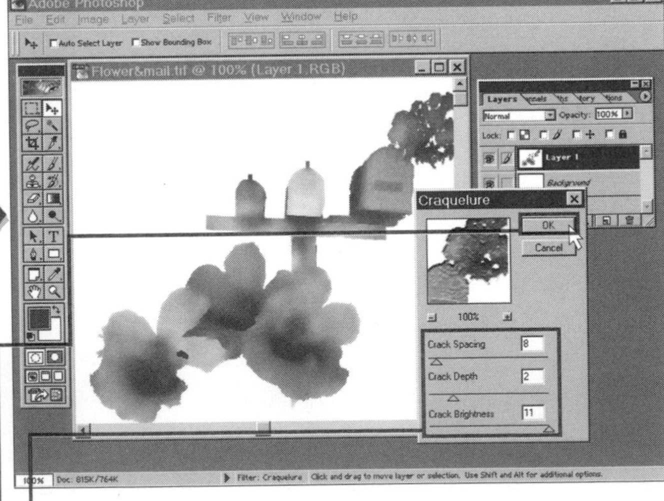

1 Choose Filter, then Texture, then Craquelure, Grain, Mosaic Tiles, Patchwork, Stained Glass or Texturizer.

■ The dialog box for the filter you chose appears.

2 Adjust the sliders in the dialog box.

3 Click OK when you are satisfied with what you see in the preview area.

■ The selected filter settings are applied to your image.

APPLY CRAQUELURE TEXTURE

You can create a stucco-like texture that is also useful for making artwork look like old, cracked paintings by using the Craquelure filter. This filter, like many other texture filters, tends to obscure fine details, such as single-pixel lines.

The Craquelure dialog box has three controls:

- The Crack Spacing slider adjusts the spacing between cracks from almost invisible to very widely spaced. For an ancient oil-on-canvas look, try a medium-low setting.
- Crack Depth has to do with the width of the shadow cast into the cracks.
- Crack Brightness controls the difference between the brightness of the main surface and that of the cracks in between.

Faded text on a sunny wall is one effect that you can create using Craquelure and other tools. Create your large, block text on a reddish-yellow background. "Age" the text with the Add Noise filter (which you can call up by choosing Filter, then Noise, then Add Noise), and by deleting/erasing portions of the text, leaving jagged edges. Finally, run the Craquelure filter.

APPLY CRAQUELURE TEXTURE

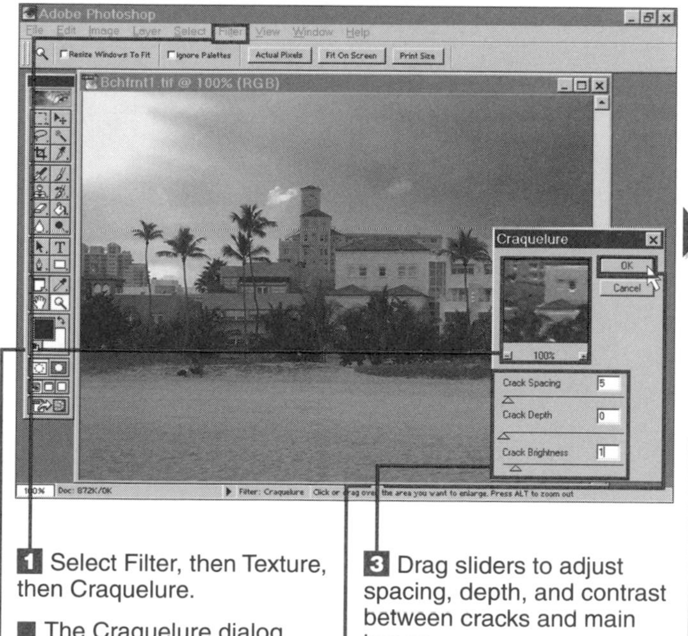

1 Select Filter, then Texture, then Craquelure.

■ The Craquelure dialog box appears.

2 Drag inside the preview area to frame the desired portion of the image.

3 Drag sliders to adjust spacing, depth, and contrast between cracks and main image.

Note: Click [+] to zoom in and [−] to zoom out.

4 Click OK.

■ The effect of the designated settings appears.

■ Here is the result of the settings shown in the previous figure.

■ The result of Spacing = 48, Depth = 6, Brightness = 7.

■ The result of Spacing = 11, Depth = 4, Brightness = 7.

APPLY GRAIN TEXTURE

The Grain texture actually lets you choose between film grain (an excellent way to match film grain in images composited from different photos with different grain patterns) and several other grainy effects: Soft, Sprinkles, Clumped, Contrasty, Enlarged, Stippled, Horizontal, Vertical, and Speckle. Sliders in the Grain dialog box let you control the intensity and contrast of the effect.

Most of the names for these grain types are self-descriptive. It is worth mentioning, however, that Sprinkles gives the look of a high-contrast overenlargement, meaning that photos have the look of being shot in adverse conditions.

Clumped produces a sort of plaster texture. Stippled makes a high-contrast, grainy monochrome in the foreground color. Speckle has virtually no effect on solid colors but can give the look of an impressionist painting to photos.

If for some reason you want your viewers to think a photograph was shot with grainier film (that is, ISO = 800 instead of the actual 100), the Regular effect is what you should use, but you are going to have to experiment to make it appear realistic.

APPLY GRAIN TEXTURE

1 Select Filter, then Texture, then Grain.

■ The Grain dialog box appears.

2 Choose the grain type.

3 Drag the Intensity slider to indicate grain fineness/coarseness.

4 Drag the Contrast slider to make grain more or less apparent.

5 Click OK.

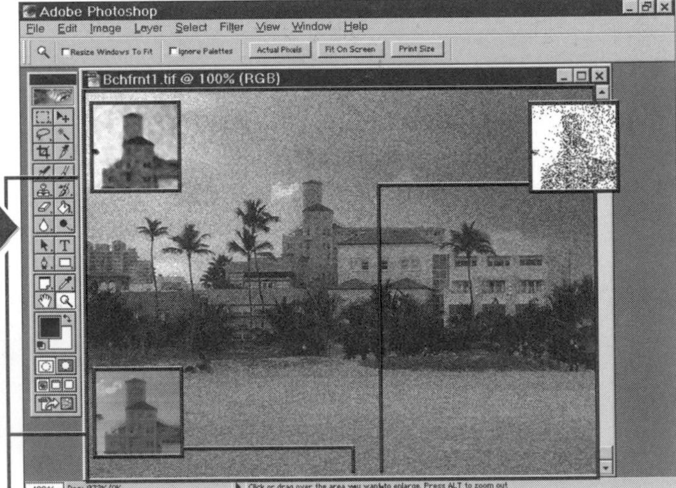

■ The settings take effect.

■ The settings in the previous figure yield this result.

■ The result of choosing Contrasty with Intensity = 26, Contrast = 69.

■ The result of choosing Horizontal with Intensity = 10, Contrast = 5.

■ The result of choosing Stippled with Intensity = 20, Contrast = 22.

CREATE MOSAIC TILES

You can use the Mosaic Tiles filter to divide the image into irregularly shaped tiles. These tiles have a three-dimensional appearance and are separated by a darker, recessed "grout." Actually, this texture looks more like an image that has been broken into irregular pieces and then glued back together than the traditional mosaic made of solid-color tiles.

The space between the tiles is not white or light gray, as real grout would likely be, either. The space is just a darker version of the same color that is in the image, which imparts a cool effect, reminiscent of cobblestone. You can lighten grout with one of the three Mosaic Tile filter controls, Lighten Grout. The other two controls set the size of the tile and the width of the grout.

You could use this effect on another texture to create quite a realistic-looking tiled or brick wall and then use the wall as the background for an extracted subject.

Try creating a new file, filling it with brick red and then using the Texturize filter to give it a sandstone texture. Run the Mosaic Tiles filter on it, then save it as a separate file.

CREATE MOSAIC TILES

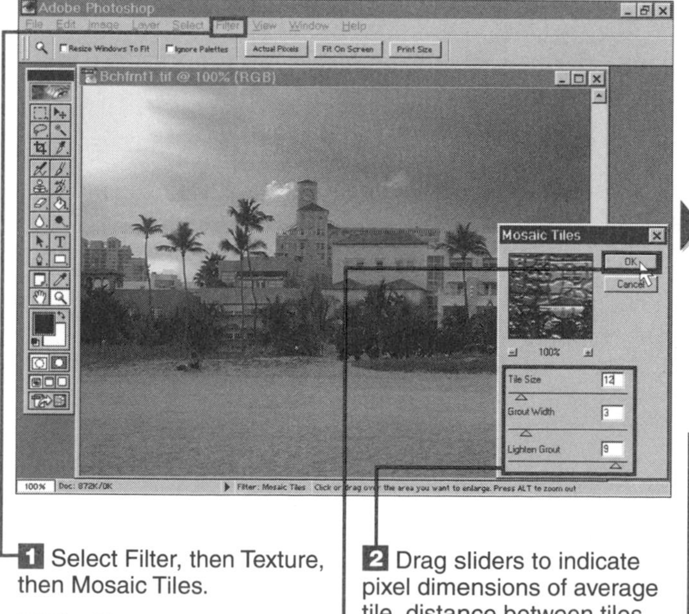

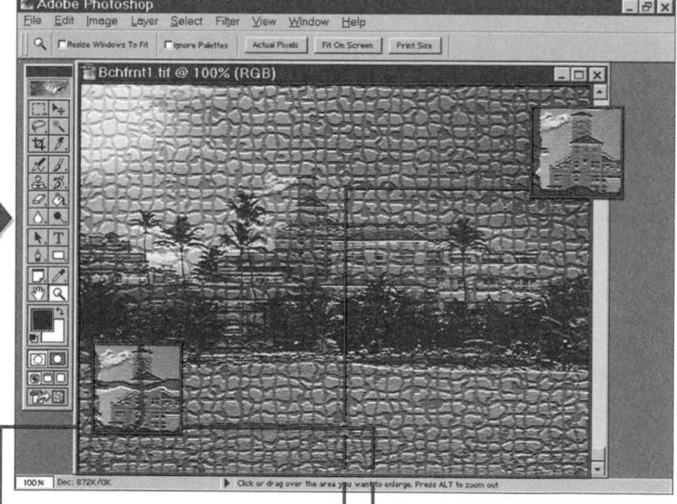

1 Select Filter, then Texture, then Mosaic Tiles.

■ The Mosaic Tiles dialog box appears.

2 Drag sliders to indicate pixel dimensions of average tile, distance between tiles, and to make grout more or less apparent.

3 Click OK.

■ The effect of the designated settings appears.

■ Here is the result of the settings shown in the previous figure.

■ The result of setting Tile Size = 50, Grout Width = 5, Lighten Grout = 5.

■ The result of setting Tile Size = 100, Grout Width = 10, Lighten Grout = 10.

CREATE A PATCHWORK

You can create some textures with the Patchwork filter that look as much like a patchwork quilt as the Mosaic Tiles texture (see previous page) looks like suede.

The weird thing is that the Patchwork texture makes the image look like a traditional mosaic — except that it is made of very small tiles, even at the largest tile size. Also, the horizontal grout is always darker than the vertical grout.

The controls in the Patchwork dialog box are:

- Square Size — Controls the size of the individual squares in the "patchwork." Sizes are scaled from 1 to 10, but there is no unit of measurement involved.
- Relief — Dragging the slider to the right exaggerates the 3D shading of the squares, making them appear to stand out more.

If you ever need to create a view through a screen or a net, the Patchwork filter might do the trick — provided the rendition does not have to be too literal.

CREATE A PATCHWORK

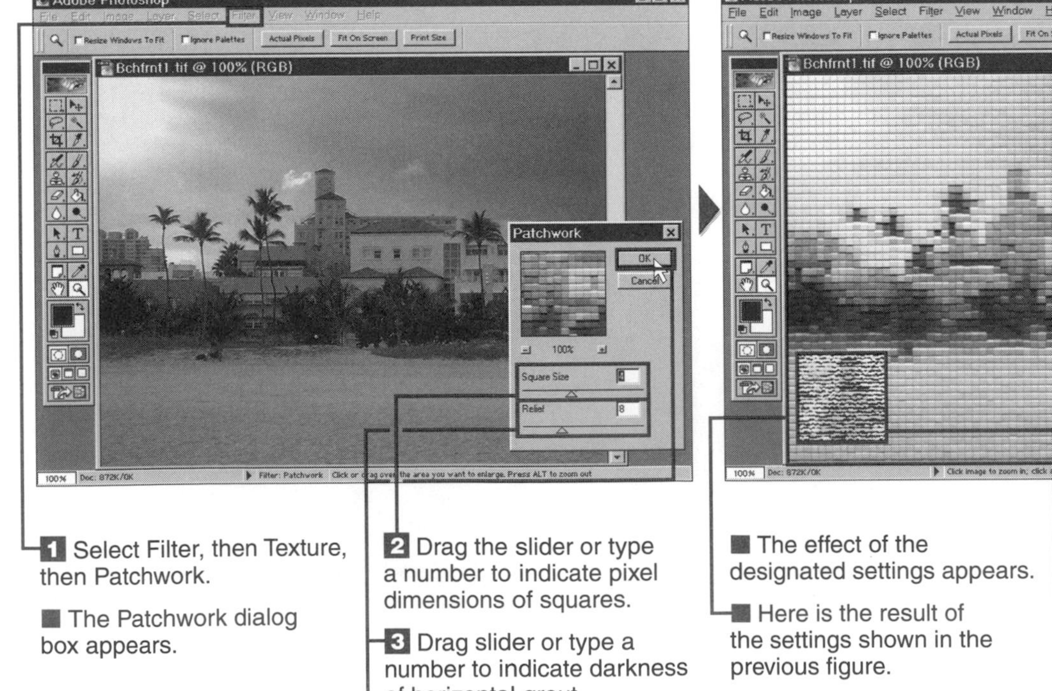

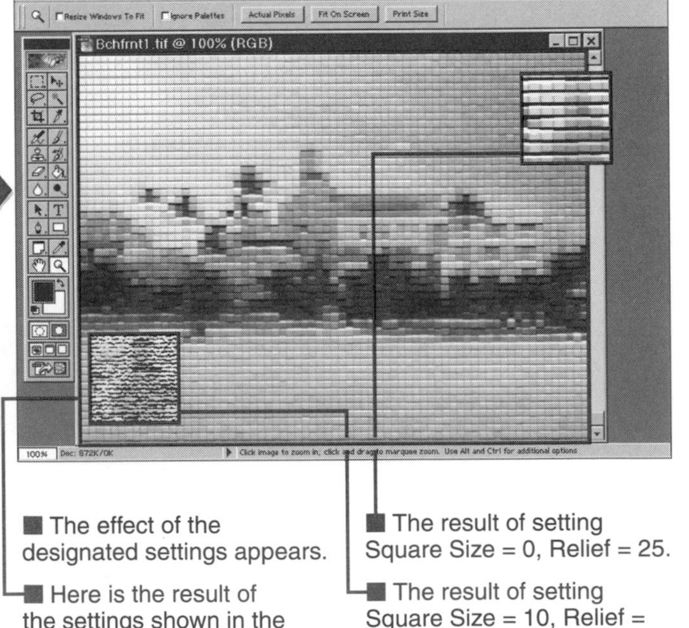

1 Select Filter, then Texture, then Patchwork.

■ The Patchwork dialog box appears.

2 Drag the slider or type a number to indicate pixel dimensions of squares.

3 Drag slider or type a number to indicate darkness of horizontal grout.

4 Click OK.

■ The effect of the designated settings appears.

■ Here is the result of the settings shown in the previous figure.

■ The result of setting Square Size = 0, Relief = 25.

■ The result of setting Square Size = 10, Relief = 25.

CREATE STAINED GLASS

You can really create something that looks like stained glass with the Stained Glass filter. Mosaic Tiles and Patchwork may not look much like their namesakes, but Stained Glass resembles the real thing. Each cell is a solid color, and the individual pieces of "glass" are of different sizes and shapes.

The Stained Glass filter provides three controls:

- Cell Size — This slider determines the size of the individual pieces of "stained glass."
- Border Thickness — Determines the width of the "leading" between panes.
- Light Intensity — Controls the overall brightness of the image.

Note that the "leading" is the same as the foreground color, so be sure to choose the color you want before you call up the filter. Also, the bigger you make the tiles the more detail you lose.

You may want to retouch some panes of your stained glass rendition to give the result a more authentic or aged look. Another solution: Run the filter on a duplicate of the target layer, then change its transparency to enable some of the original to show through.

CREATE STAINED GLASS

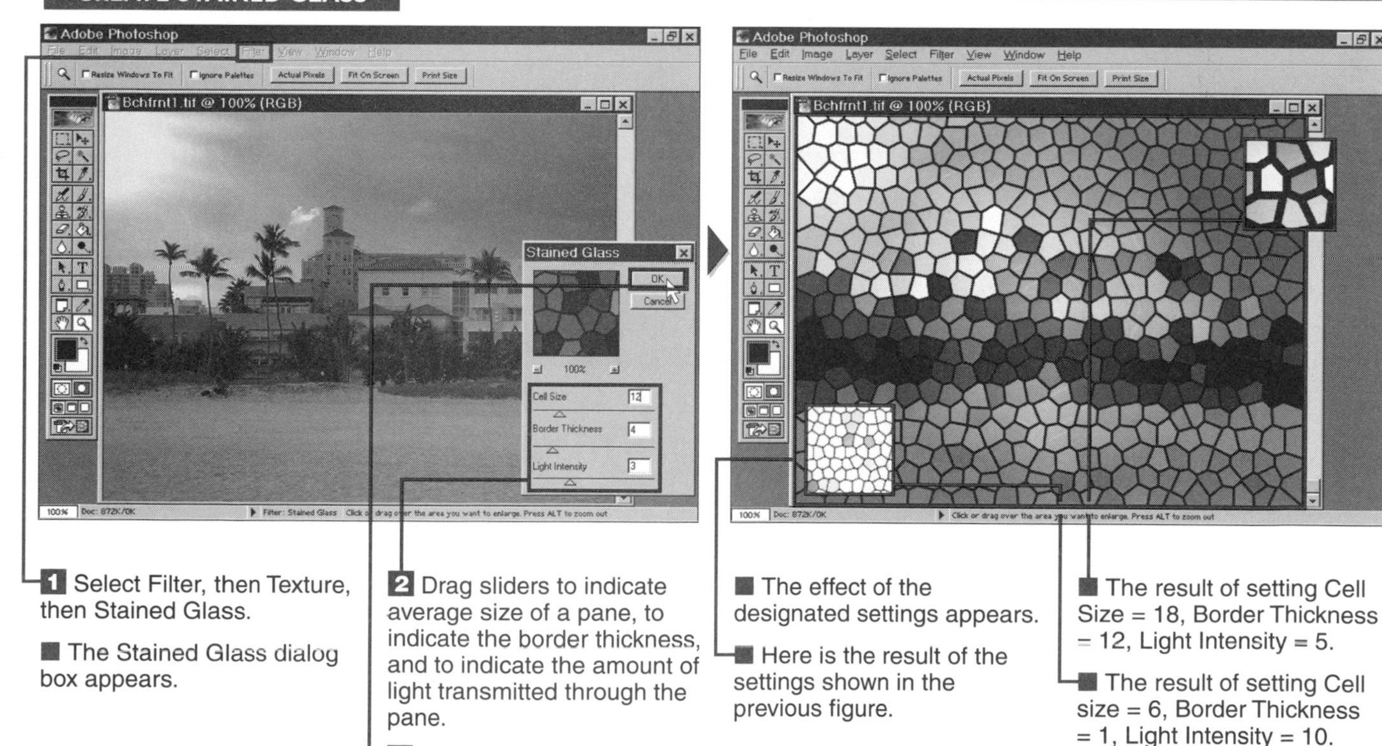

1 Select Filter, then Texture, then Stained Glass.

■ The Stained Glass dialog box appears.

2 Drag sliders to indicate average size of a pane, to indicate the border thickness, and to indicate the amount of light transmitted through the pane.

3 Click OK.

■ The effect of the designated settings appears.

■ Here is the result of the settings shown in the previous figure.

■ The result of setting Cell Size = 18, Border Thickness = 12, Light Intensity = 5.

■ The result of setting Cell size = 6, Border Thickness = 1, Light Intensity = 10.

APPLY TEXTURIZER TEXTURES

You can use the Texturizer filter to apply any texture you can photograph or scan. At the bottom of the menu that you get when you choose Filter then Texture is Texturizer, which comes with premade textures that mimic canvas, burlap, and sandstone. A Load Texture item on the same menu enables you to load any grayscale Photoshop image as a texture.

If an image was created to be a seamless tile, use a small image to texture the entire picture. The texture image repeats itself in rows and columns from upper left to lower right.

On the Photoshop CD are texture files for bumpy leather, hard linear grain, regular paper, and soft linear grain. You can also photograph or scan any texture, turn it into a seamless tile (see "Create Seamless Pattern and Texture Tiles" later in this chapter), save it as a grayscale file, and then load it into Texturizer.

Try scaling these textures to suit the overall size of the image you are producing. You can also adjust the apparent depth of the texture and change the angle of lighting in 45-degree increments.

APPLY TEXTURIZER TEXTURES

1 Choose Filter, then Texture, then Texturizer.

■ The Texturizer dialog box appears.

2 Choose one of the standard textures.

3 Select the settings shown here.

4 Check to invert the selection and click OK.

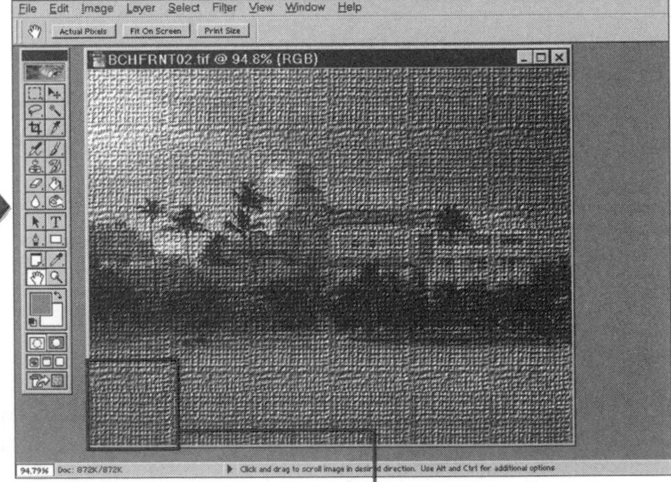

■ The effect of the designated settings appears.

■ Here is the Burlap texture, using the settings shown in the previous figure.

Can I create textures with other filters?

✔ You can create an almost endless variety of them. Most filters do not affect a solid color, but the following ones definitely work: Mezzotint, Add Noise, Pixelate, Grain, Craquelure, Mosaic Tiles, Patchwork, and Stained Glass. After you have made a pattern or texture with any of the aforementioned filters, you could use any of the other filters to modify them.

Why can I not create textures from scratch with all other filters?

✔ Most of the Photoshop filters modify the colored pixels by moving them, smearing them, highlighting them and so forth. If you do those things to solid colors, there is no visible difference.

What is the best way to create textures?

✔ You can create different kinds of textures in many ways. One of the easiest is to scan textures such as grained leather, various fabrics, and any kind of printed patterns. Then you can make a seamless tile texture (see "Create Seamless Pattern and Texture Tiles" later in this chapter). Then you can apply the textures as either fills or texturizers.

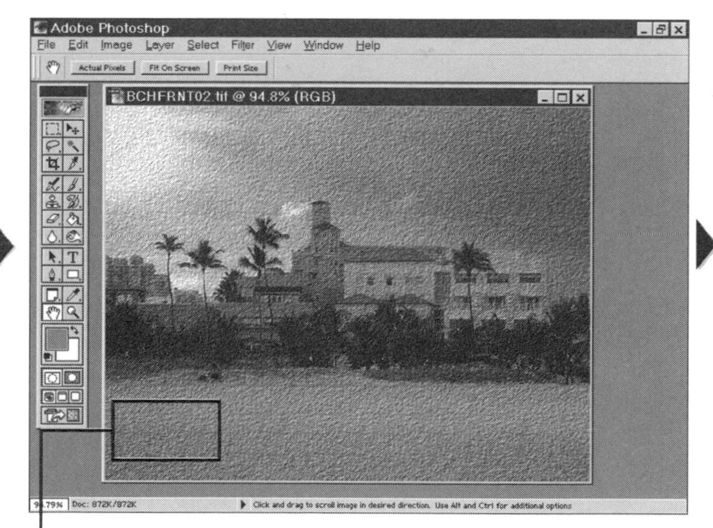

■ Here is the Sandstone texture.

■ Here is the Canvas texture.

Note: You can also choose Load Texture from the Texture menu to use any Photoshop-format grayscale file as a texture map.

CREATE NEW TEXTURES FROM PHOTOS

You can use Photoshop to turn any digitized image into a texture that can be loaded by any filter that utilitizes a Load Texture command.

You must use a grayscale Photoshop-format image. When such a photo is loaded into Texturizer, Photoshop repeats the texture image as often as necessary to fill the current image. For that reason, if your target images are bigger than your textures, you want to make a seamless tile (see "Create Seamless Pattern and Texture Tiles" later in this chapter).

You can readily make a texture image of just about anything under the sun. Having a macro lens or a close-up lens and a tripod helps. If you do not have a sophisticated studio and strobe lights available to you, shoot outdoors so that the amount of light falling on the surface is even, yet there is good contrast between highlights and shadows (you want to see the texture, remember). Use a tripod, and make sure the camera back is parallel to the subject surface. Finally, transfer the image to a data file.

CREATE NEW TEXTURES FROM PHOTOS

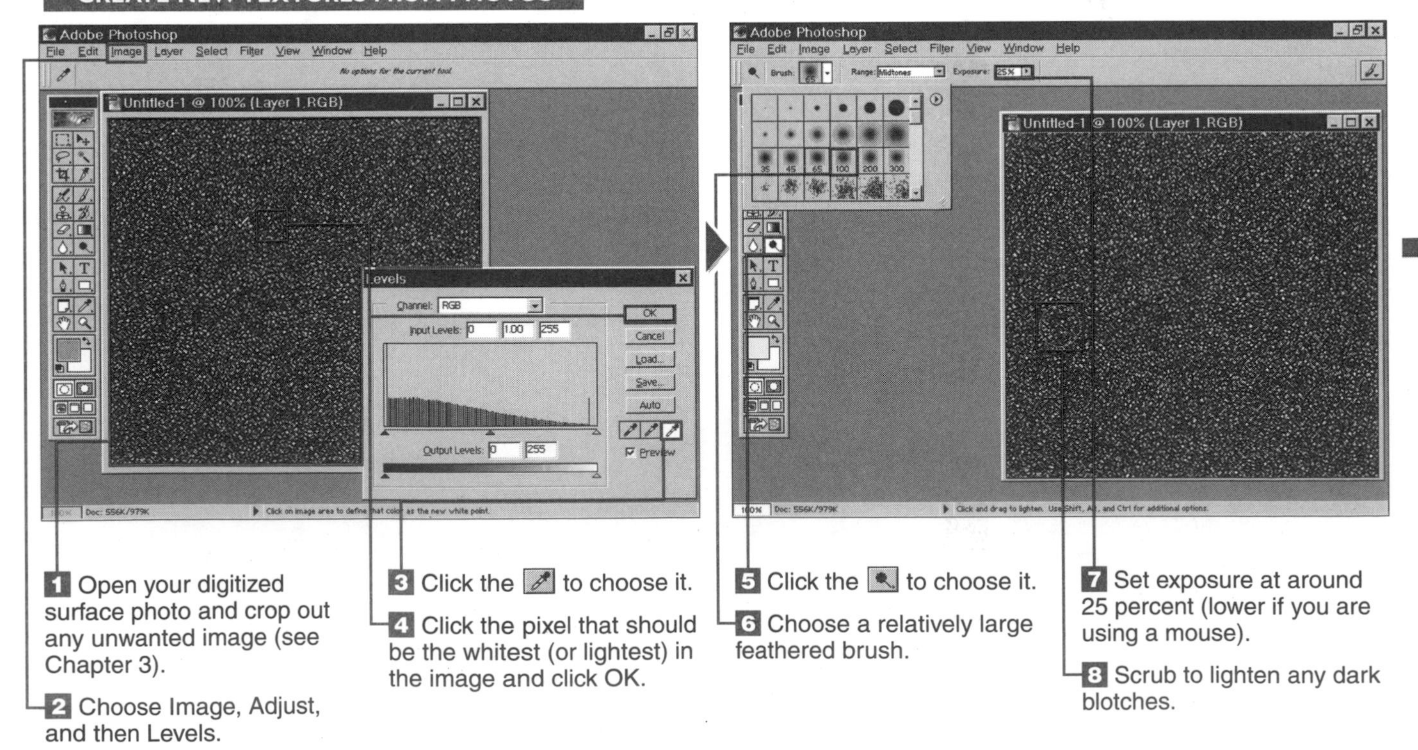

1 Open your digitized surface photo and crop out any unwanted image (see Chapter 3).

2 Choose Image, Adjust, and then Levels.

■ The Levels dialog box appears.

3 Click the [eyedropper icon] to choose it.

4 Click the pixel that should be the whitest (or lightest) in the image and click OK.

5 Click the [dodge tool icon] to choose it.

6 Choose a relatively large feathered brush.

7 Set exposure at around 25 percent (lower if you are using a mouse).

8 Scrub to lighten any dark blotches.

Color Plates

This section is a visual guide to the effects generated by Photoshop's Apply Modes, Blend Modes, and Filters. Apply and Blend Modes are illustrated as one, as the results they produce are the same. The effect is called a *Blend Mode* when it pertains to the way one of the tools applies color to the active layer. The same effect is called an *Apply Mode* when one layer is blended with one or more others.

The Filters chart shows you a single setting for each of Photoshop's built-in filters. Each of these filters' effects can be varied over a wide range of settings. It is less confusing, however, if you see each filter demonstrated at its most popular setting (usually the default) so that you get a clearer idea of the difference between the filters themselves. Of course, when you use that filter, you should experiment for the optimum settings.

Apply/Blend Modes

Blend Modes are available to all of the Photoshop tools that are used to paint, including selecting Edit, then Fill from the menu bar. To apply a Blend Mode, simply select the mode to be used by a tool from the tool's Options dialog box, or select the mode to be used by the Fill command from the Fill dialog box. To select the mode to be used by a layer you must go to the Layers window. Shown here are samples of the Apply/Blend Modes at their default setting.

Normal

Dissolve

Behind

Multiply

Screen

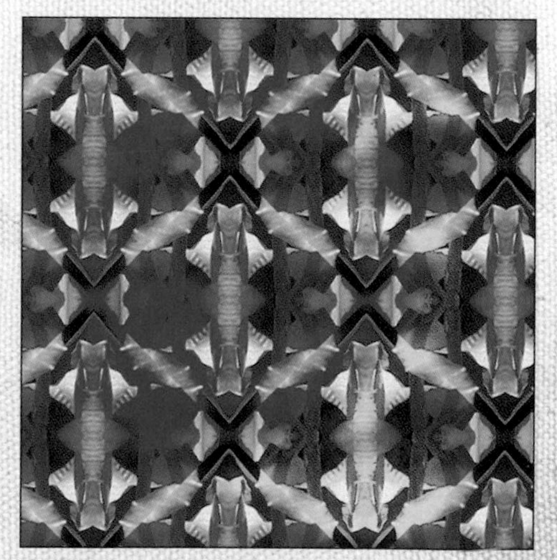
Overlay

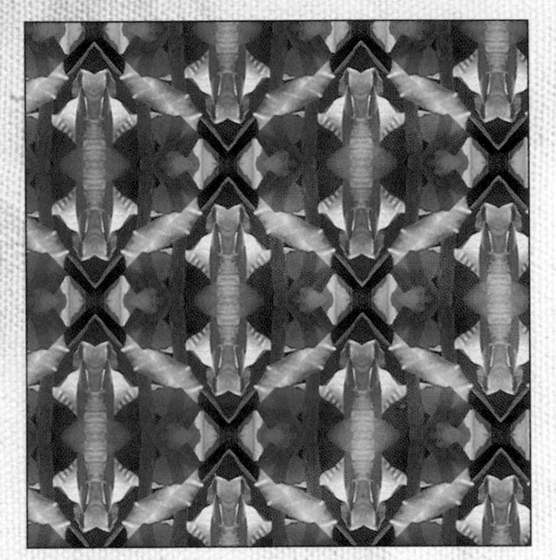
Soft Light

Hard Light

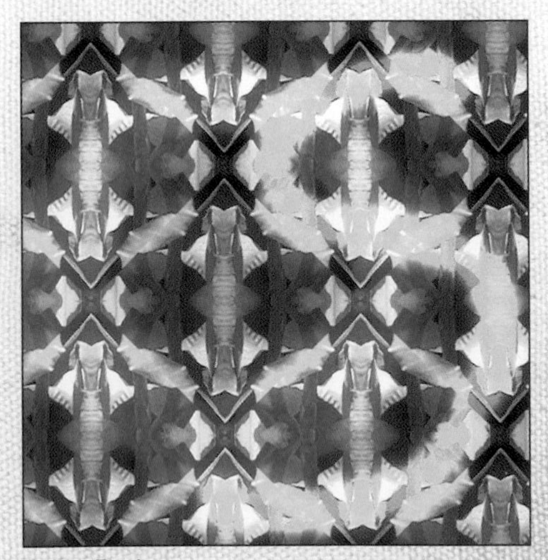
Color Dodge

Color Burn

Darken

Lighten

Difference

Exclusion

Hue

Saturation

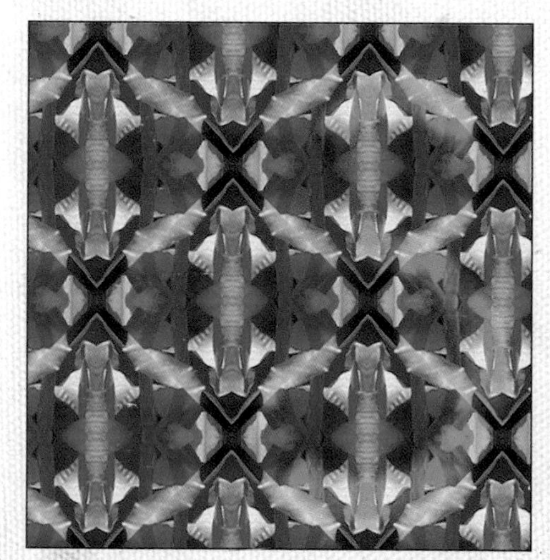

Color

Luminosity

PHOTOSHOP FILTERS

Following is a chart of all of the built-in Photoshop filters, organized by category. Order of appearance follows the order on the Filters menu. If you see a filter effect you think might be appropriate to the image you are working in, you will know exactly where to find it on the menu.

ARTISTIC

Colored Pencil

Cutout

Dry Brush

Film Grain

Fresco

Neon Glow

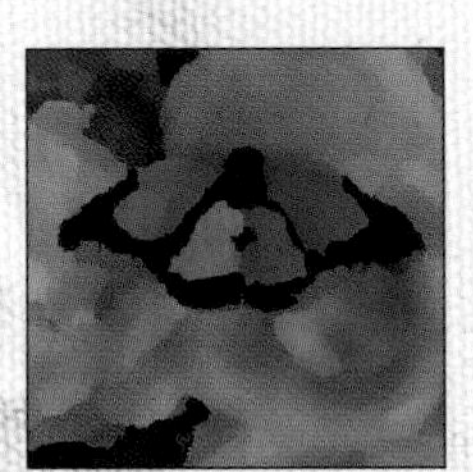

Palette Knife

Plastic Wrap

Artistic

Poster Edges

Rough Pastels

Smudge Stick

Sponge

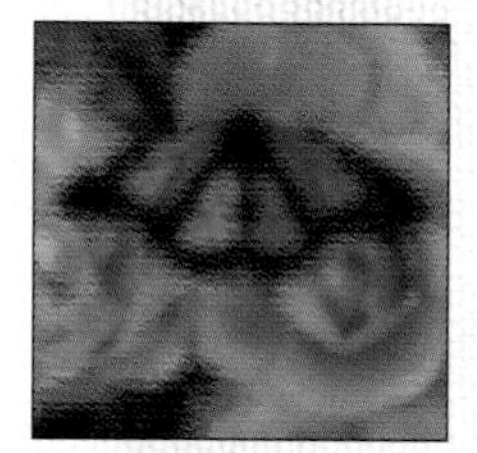
Underpainting

Watercolor

Blur

Blur

Blur More

Gaussian Blur

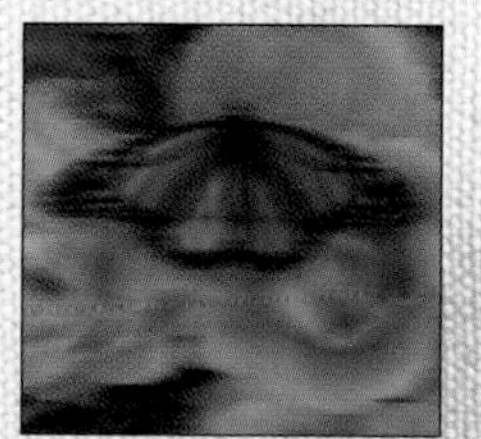
Motion Blur

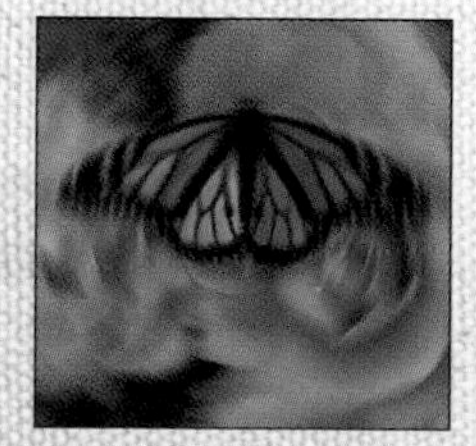
Radial Blur

Smart Blur

Brush Strokes

Accented Edges

Angled Strokes

Crosshatch

Dark Strokes

Ink Outlines

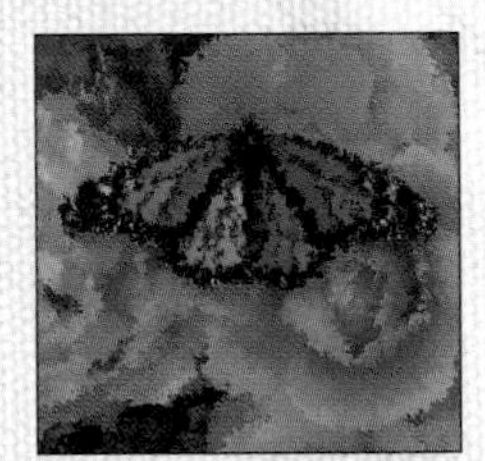

Spatter

Sprayed Strokes

Sumi-e

Diffuse Glow

Displace

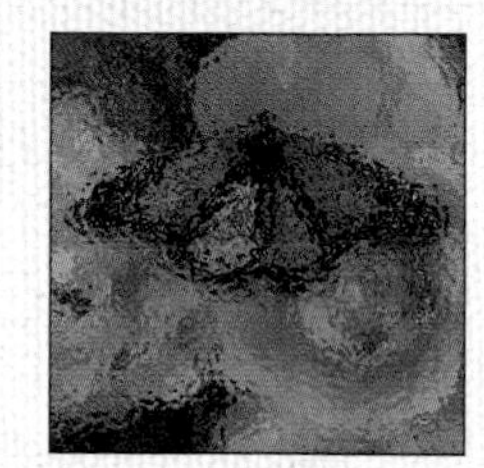
Glass

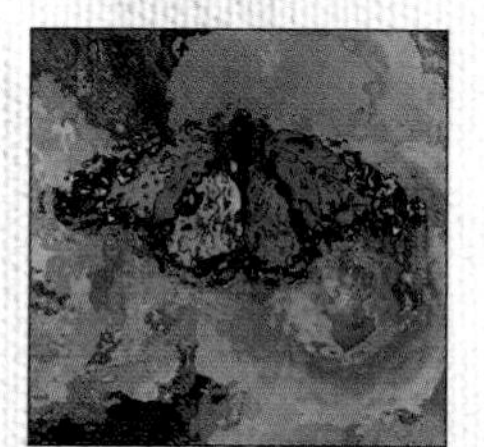
Ocean Ripple

Pinch

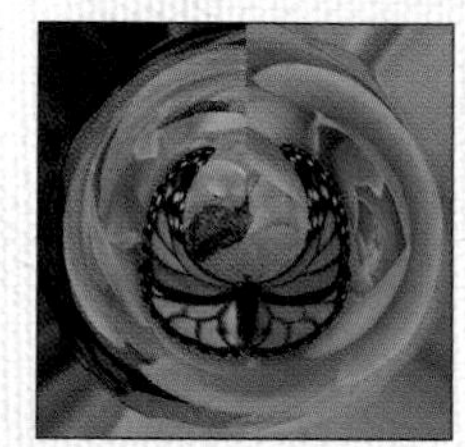
Polar Coordinates

Ripple

Shear

Spherize

Twirl

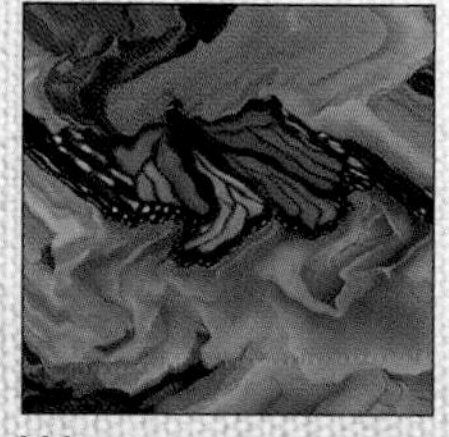
Wave

ZigZag

Noise

Add Noise

Despeckle

Dust & Scratches

Median

Pixelate

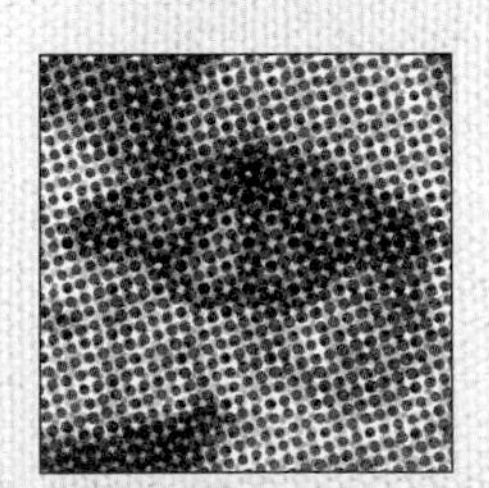
Color Halftone

Crystalize

Facet

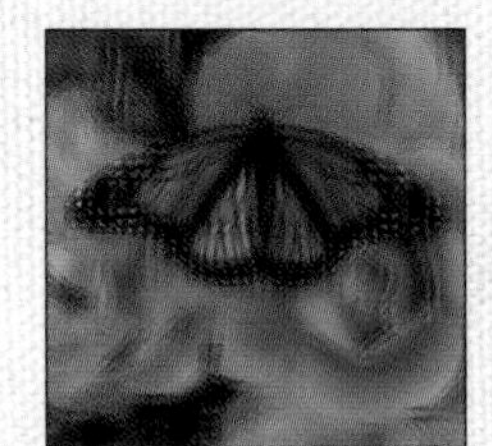
Fragment

Mezzotint

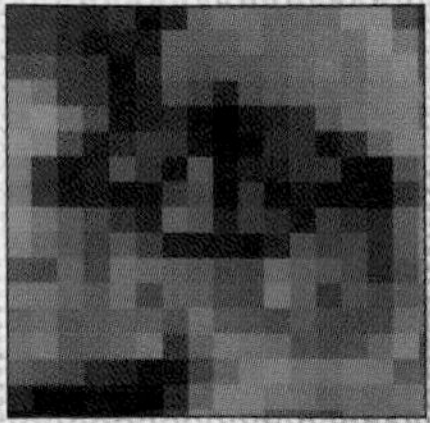
Mosaic

Pointillize

RENDER

3D Transform

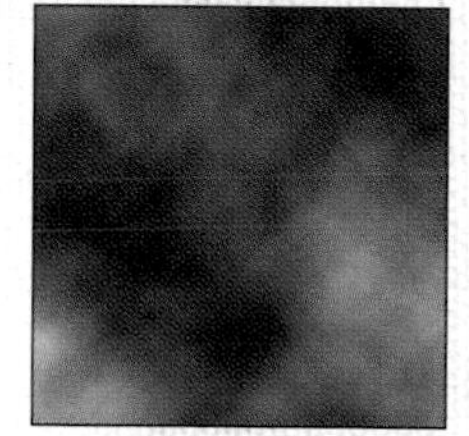
Clouds

Difference Clouds

Lens Flare

Lighting Effects

Texture Fill

SHARPEN

Sharpen

Sharpen Edges

Sharpen More

Unsharp Mask

Bas-Relief

Chalk & Charcoal

Charcoal

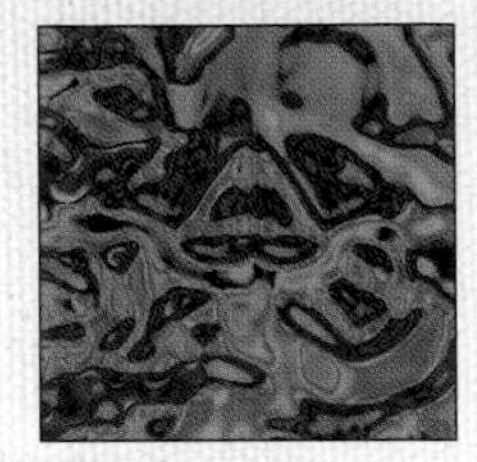
Chrome

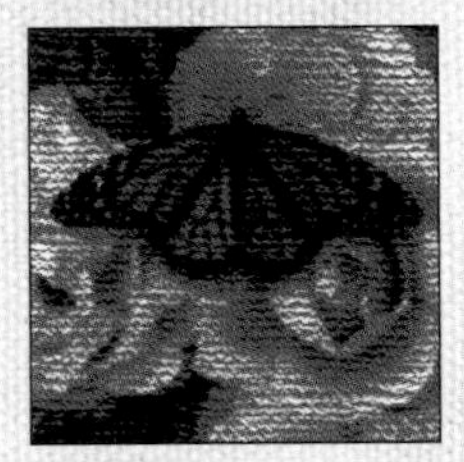
Conte Crayon

Graphic Pen

Halftone Pattern

Note Paper

Photocopy

Plaster

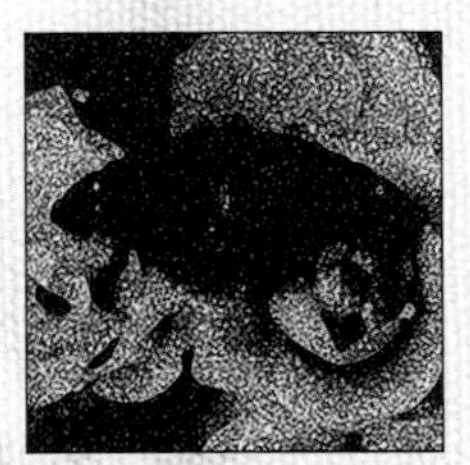
Reticulation

Stamp

Torn Edges

Water Paper

Diffuse

Emboss

Extrude

Find Edges

Glowing Edges

Solarize

Tiles

Trace Contour

Wind

Texture

Craquelure

Grain

Mosaic Tiles

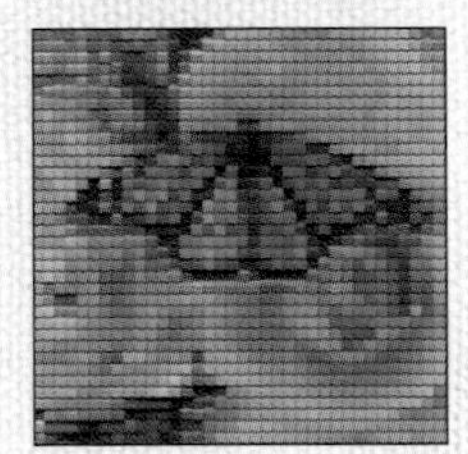
Patchwork

Stained Glass

Texturizer

Other

High Pass

Maximum

Minimum

Offset

Why am I setting only the Highlight dropper in the Levels dialog box?

✔ This adjustment is usually the one that works best with the least amount of fiddling. No hard and fast rule says you cannot make other adjustments; in fact, experimentation is encouraged. Remember that you are after a grayscale file that maps the texture, not color or other photographic details. Also, you do not want contrast to be significantly higher than is natural to the texture of the surface of the material you are recording (unless, of course, you are after a special effect).

Why does the image get more uneven when I try to burn and dodge?

✔ Doing this well takes practice. Keep your exposure setting low (5 percent might be good), so that each stroke makes only a mild adjustment. Use a highly feathered brush, so that the strokes tend to blend together. Use the History palette to go back several strokes if you suddenly notice you have made a mess.

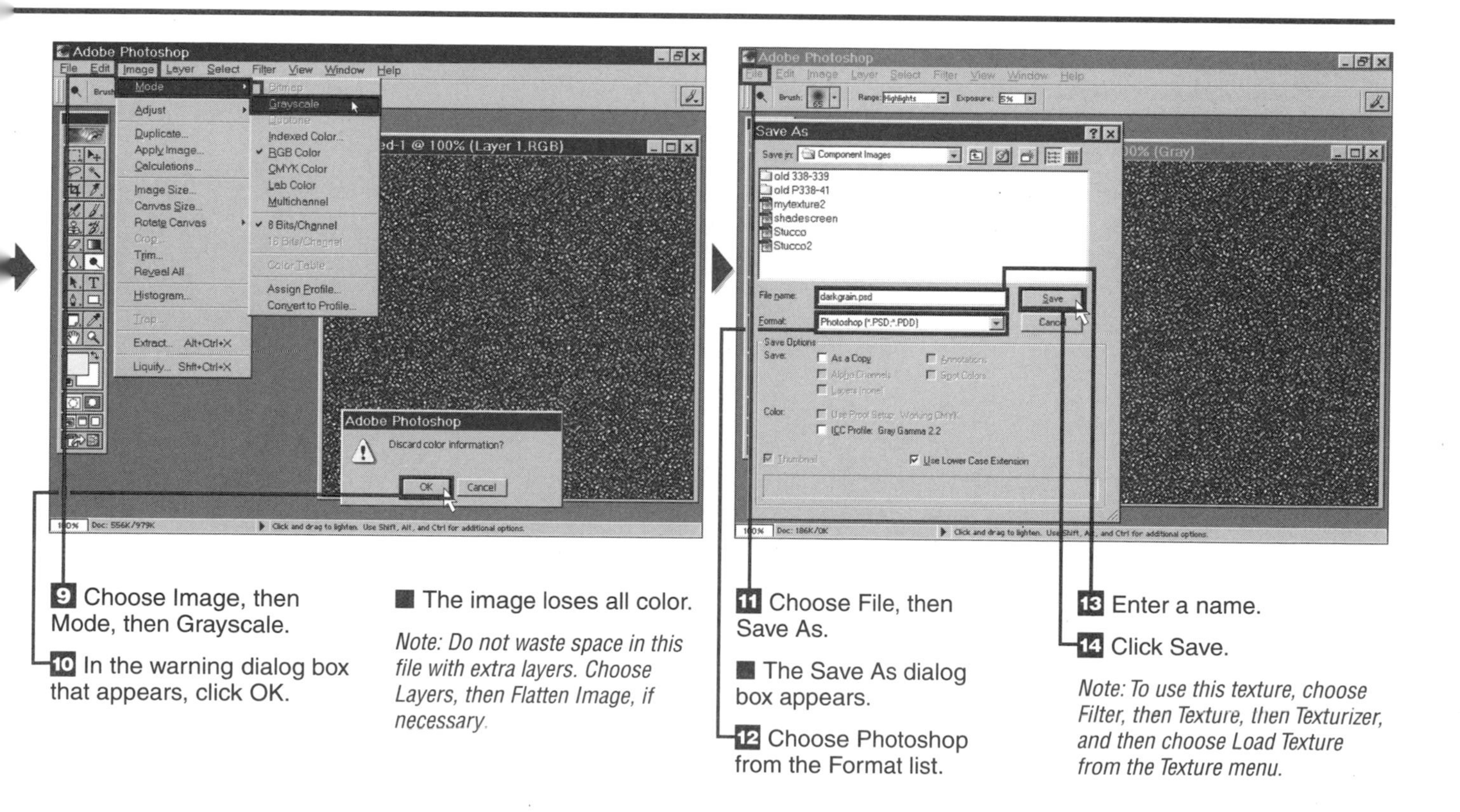

9 Choose Image, then Mode, then Grayscale.

10 In the warning dialog box that appears, click OK.

■ The image loses all color.

Note: Do not waste space in this file with extra layers. Choose Layers, then Flatten Image, if necessary.

11 Choose File, then Save As.

■ The Save As dialog box appears.

12 Choose Photoshop from the Format list.

13 Enter a name.

14 Click Save.

Note: To use this texture, choose Filter, then Texture, then Texturizer, and then choose Load Texture from the Texture menu.

CREATE SEAMLESS PATTERN AND TEXTURE TILES

You can create a seamless texture that can be repeated to cover an image of any size by making something called a "seamless texture tile."

Making a seamless texture tile is easy. Use the Marquee tool to select the area you want to turn into a tile. Choose Image, then Crop to make this area a new image and immediately save it to a unique name. Flatten the image (choose Layers, then Flatten Image) and, if the image is to be a texture for Texturizer, make sure it is grayscale (choose Image, then Mode, then Grayscale). Finally, choose File then Save As, choose Photoshop (PSD) file format, and give the file a name.

You will get an obvious edge between the tiles. To make seamless tiles, you need to select an exact size rectangle and choose Filter, then Other, then Offset. Wrap the contents halfway across, both side to side and top to bottom. You then use the Clone tool (see Chapter 12) to eliminate the seam. Finally, reverse the overlap and save the tile.

CREATE SEAMLESS PATTERN AND TEXTURE TILES

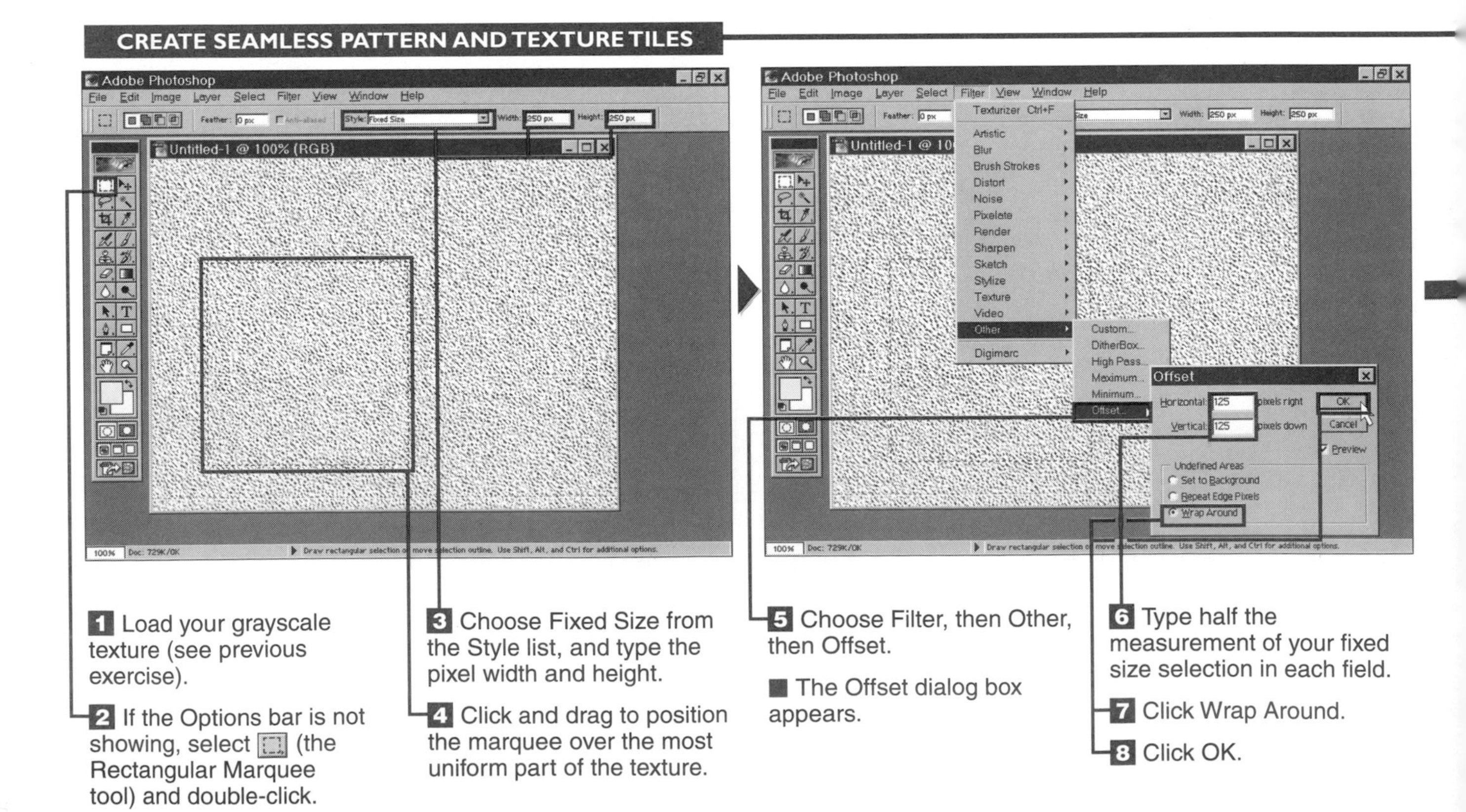

1 Load your grayscale texture (see previous exercise).

2 If the Options bar is not showing, select (the Rectangular Marquee tool) and double-click.

3 Choose Fixed Size from the Style list, and type the pixel width and height.

4 Click and drag to position the marquee over the most uniform part of the texture.

5 Choose Filter, then Other, then Offset.

■ The Offset dialog box appears.

6 Type half the measurement of your fixed size selection in each field.

7 Click Wrap Around.

8 Click OK.

What is the best way to test my seamless tile?

✔ Open a new file of sufficient dimensions to hold several repetitions of the tile. Open the texture file and press ⌘/Ctrl+A to Select All. Then choose Define Pattern from the Edit menu. Finally, activate the window of the new, empty file, and choose Edit, then Fill, then Pattern.

What do I do if the tile is not seamless?

✔ Try selecting a smaller portion of the texture so that you have a better chance at an even pattern. At least try selecting a different area of the texture that has a more even pattern.

What if I still cannot get an even pattern?

✔ First, work on a duplicate of the original file. Then use the Clone tool to copy areas of texture into other areas of texture until it is all evened out. You can even up lighting by burning and dodging and you can use the Color Apply mode with your brush to even up color.

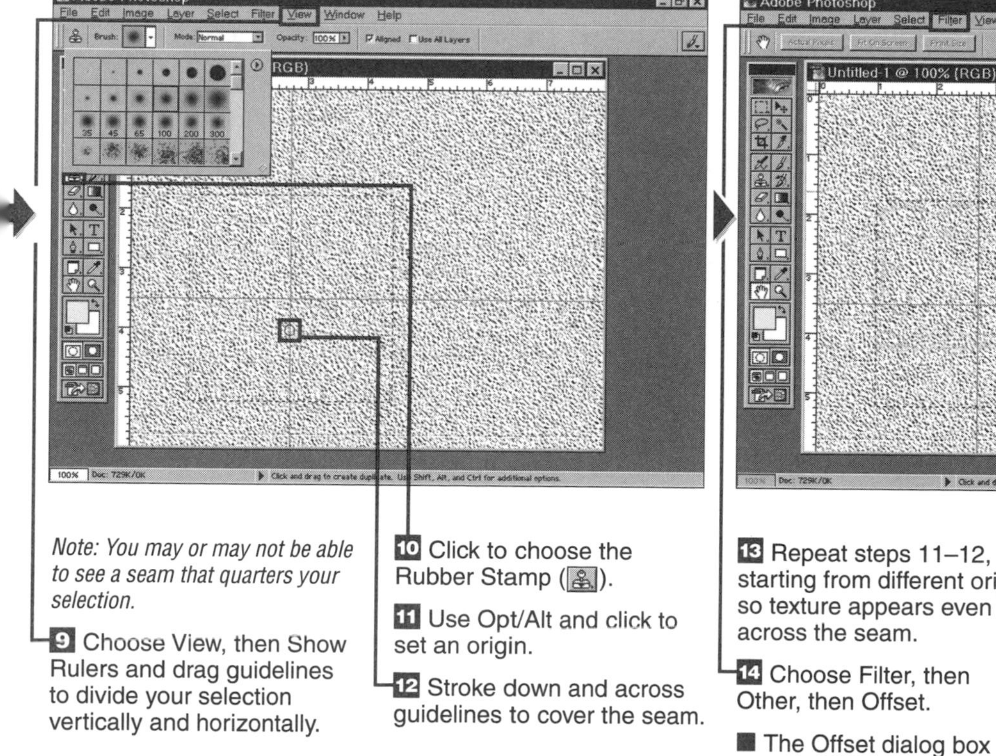

Note: You may or may not be able to see a seam that quarters your selection.

9 Choose View, then Show Rulers and drag guidelines to divide your selection vertically and horizontally.

10 Click to choose the Rubber Stamp (![]).

11 Use Opt/Alt and click to set an origin.

12 Stroke down and across guidelines to cover the seam.

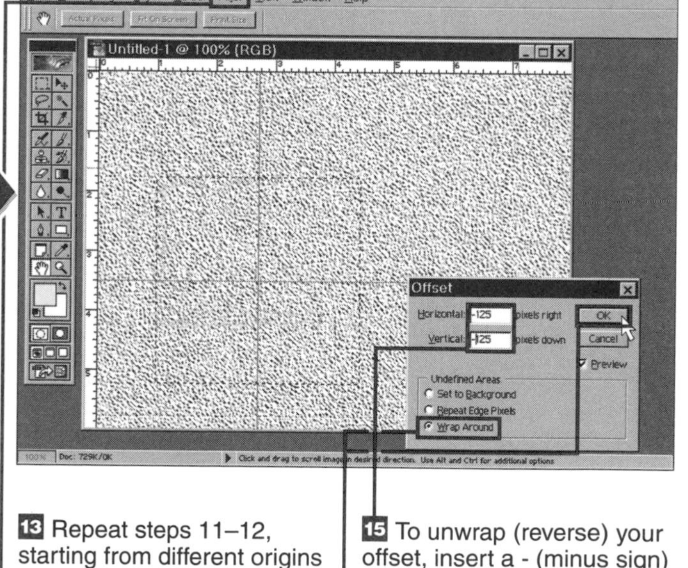

13 Repeat steps 11–12, starting from different origins so texture appears even across the seam.

14 Choose Filter, then Other, then Offset.

■ The Offset dialog box appears.

15 To unwrap (reverse) your offset, insert a - (minus sign) in front of the numbers you first entered.

16 Make sure Wrap Around is still chosen.

17 Click OK.

CREATE A PAINTING BY FILTERING SPECIFIC AREAS

You can combine several filter effects to overcome the mechanical look that usually results when you apply a single filter over the entire image. Most of the time, using a single filter to create a painting makes for flat, dull-looking images. Besides, a filter that flatters one area of the picture may really not be that flattering to another area.

A much better plan is to isolate specific areas of an image so that you can create a variety of textures and effects. You can then use a filter (or a different setting for the same filter) that works best for each area.

The process is pretty simple. Select each area of focus (or texture) separately, and save the selection. Name each selection for the area it represents. After you do that, choose Window then Show Channels and, one at a time, drag each channel to the Make Selection icon. Feather a particular selection (Opt/Alt+ ⌘/Ctrl+D) if it seems appropriate. Then run the filter you have chosen for that area.

Note that the following steps assume that you have selected each target area, saved each selection under a separate name, and then selected Windows, then Show Channels.

CREATE A PAINTING BY FILTERING SPECIFIC AREAS

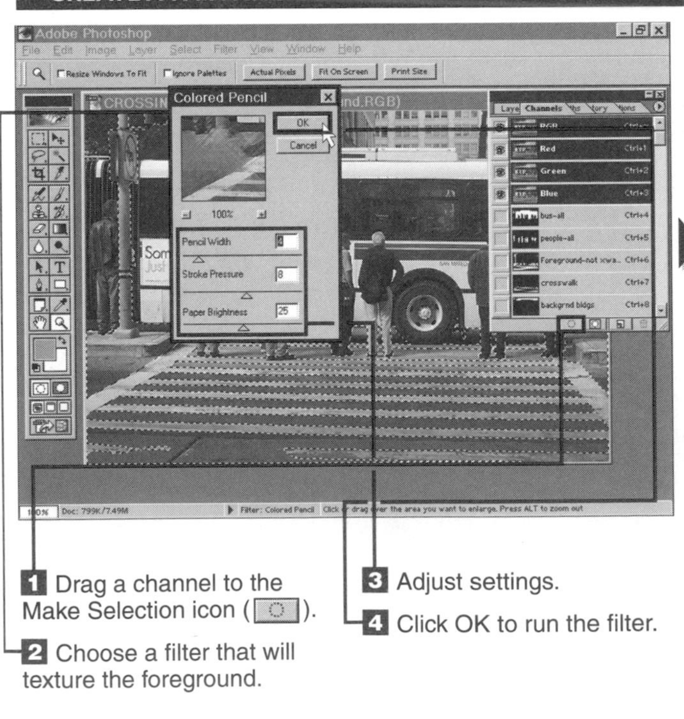

1 Drag a channel to the Make Selection icon ( ).

2 Choose a filter that will texture the foreground.

3 Adjust settings.

4 Click OK to run the filter.

5 Activate the selection for the background area (see steps 1–3).

6 Choose a filter that will soften (throw slightly out of focus) the background.

7 Make adjustments.

8 Click OK to run the filter.

How do I get rid of seams that show up between selected areas?

✔ Try feathering selections slightly before running the filters. Usually, this method ends up in a pleasant overlapping of the two effects. Sometimes you will need to use the Rubber Stamp tool to mend seams. You can also select objects with plenty of extra room inside the selection, mask them more precisely with a layer mask on their own layer, and then interactively fine-tune the seams later.

Are the Artistic filters the only ones I can treat this way?

✔ No. You apply any filter using a selection as a mask. The only limitation is whether you like the result.

What about using this technique to fade the same filter to different degrees?

✔ Fading is the best way to vary the look while keeping the character and direction of filter strokes consistent throughout the painting. Some purists would say that this technique is the only way to do it. Just choose Filter, then Fade (Last Command), and then enter a specific level of fade.

9 Select the area that is the secondary point of interest.

10 Choose a filter that mimics paint strokes, and texture this area in the way that looks most appropriate to you.

11 Make adjustments.

12 Click OK to run the filter.

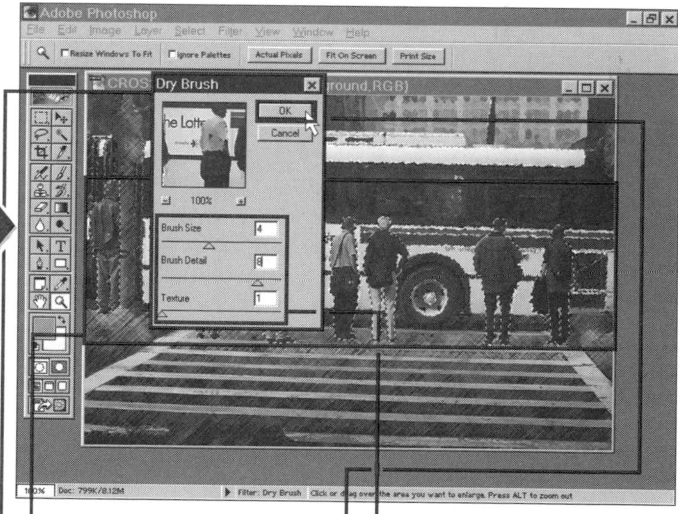

13 Select the area that surrounds the main point of interest.

14 Choose a filter that will paint and texture this area in the most appropriate way.

15 Make adjustments.

16 Click OK to run the filter.

Note: This example is a combined screen, created so you can see the result of the filter in the background painting.

TEXTURIZE AN IMAGE WITH A SKETCH FILTER

You can use both the Texturizer and Lighting Effects filters in combination with one of the two-color Sketch filters to create textures that look like techniques for applying heavy paints, such as oils and acrylics.

In traditional painting, this thick application of layers of paint is called *impasto*.

Regardless of how expertly you use the Artistic filters to paint an image, the result can still look flat, because most natural media has a texture to give it some of its appealing feel and character.

Oil paint, for example, can go on thicker or thinner, forming little ridges. Sometimes you can even see the underlying texture of the canvas. Watercolors, on the other hand, tend to soak into the paper, but the paper itself has a texture.

Here is a way to create an impasto texture: Open the image to which you want to apply impasto. Run one of the Sketch filters over it (each produces a different stroke style) and save the result to a unique name. Reopen the original file and apply the new file to it as a Texturize filter.

TEXTURIZE AN IMAGE WITH A SKETCH FILTER

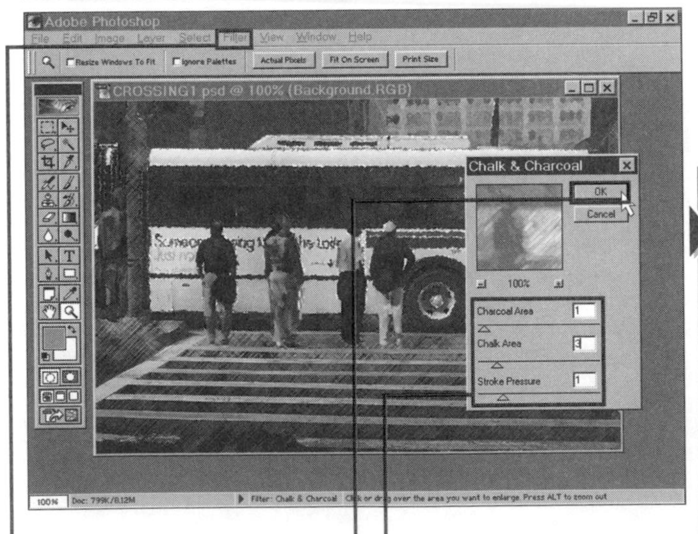

1 Choose Filter, then Sketch, then a specific filter name.

■ The filter's dialog box appears. Chalk & Charcoal was chosen for this example to create a subtle, palette knife-type patina.

2 Adjust the filter's controls.

■ Higher contrast and a more defined stroke produce more complex textures.

3 Click OK to render the filter.

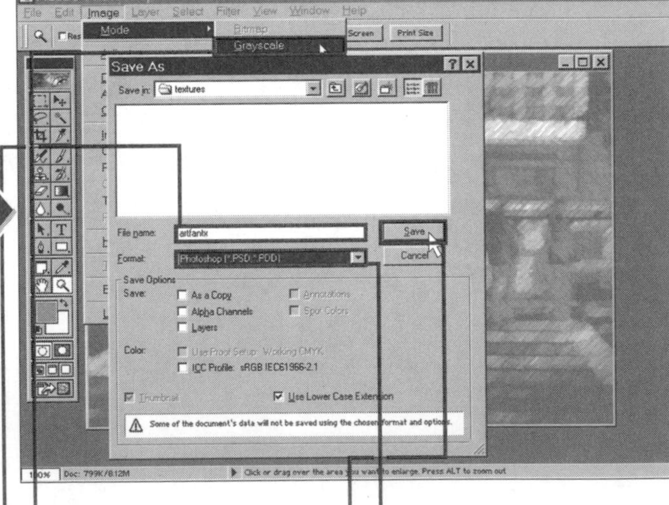

4 Choose File, then Save As.

■ The Save As dialog box appears.

5 Give the file a new name that indicates it is to be used as a texture.

6 Choose Photoshop (.PSD) from the Format menu.

7 Click Save.

8 Close the file you just renamed and reopen the original file.

Are any of the Sketch filters more likely to produce pleasing results?

✔ Yes. Bas Relief, Chrome, and Note Paper can produce excellent results. Some of the filters produce thin lines that do not look like impasto. You can use them to make it appear that you have hand-stroked edges by using the Darken mode on the duplicate filtered layer.

Can I use any of the filters other than Sketch for this purpose?

✔ You can try this technique with any filter—even those from third-party manufacturers. The Mezzotint filters from Andromeda can produce some especially interesting results.

Can I create a texture with more than one Sketch filter?

✔ You can simply keep using different Sketch filters on the same image and save the result as a grayscale or RGB PSD file. Then change the result using Texturizer, or any of the other filters that enable you to import a texture.

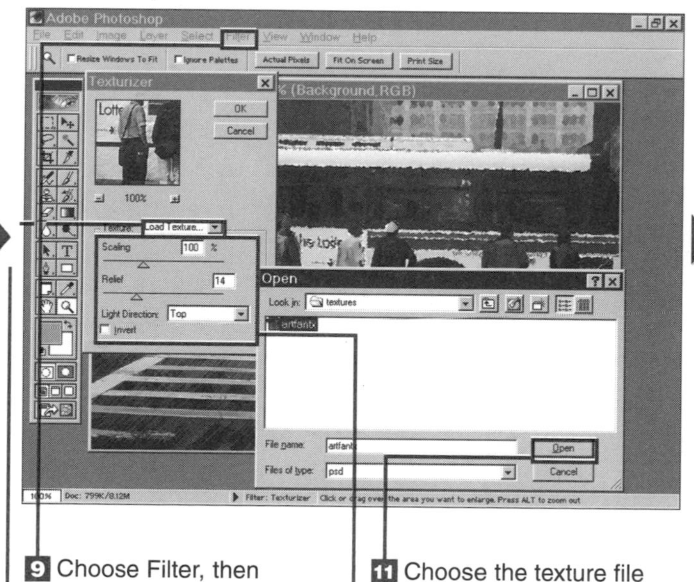

9 Choose Filter, then Texture, then Texturizer.

■ The Texturizer dialog box appears.

10 Choose Load Texture.

11 Choose the texture file you just created and click Open.

12 Make adjustments.

13 Click OK in the Texturizer dialog box.

■ Here is the result of the preceding steps for this exercise.

APPLY THE COLORED PENCIL FILTER

You can use the Colored Pencil filter to create "scrubbed" or cross-hatched drawings.

The exact effect depends on the mixture of settings you use in the Colored Pencil dialog box and on the background color that is current at the time. The background color determines the color of the background "paper."

Nevertheless, the Colored Pencil filter offers three variable effects — Pencil Width, Stroke Pressure, and Paper Brightness.

Paper Brightness determines the gray level of the background on which the rubbing is made. Stroke Pressure controls the intensity (brightness) of the strokes. Pencil Width determines whether the cross-hatched strokes appear to be made with a newly sharpened pencil or a fat, worn crayon.

One particularly effective trick to use with this filter is to run it twice on the same layer. Run it once using the current background color, click the Switch Foreground and Background colors icon, then run the filter again. If you want to keep the same settings, you can just press ⌘/Ctrl+F.

APPLY THE COLORED PENCIL FILTER

1 Choose Filter, then Artistic, then Colored Pencil.

■ The Colored Pencil dialog box appears.

2 Drag the Pencil Width slider to indicate thickness of stroke.

3 Drag the Stroke Pressure slider to indicate brightness of stroke.

4 Drag the Paper Brightness slider to change whiteness of the paper or background.

5 When you are happy with what you see in the preview area, click OK.

■ Wait a few moments and you will see an effect that looks approximately like the effect in this figure.

APPLY THE CUTOUT FILTER

You can create an illustration that uses flat colors and hard edges, similar to what you see in some posters, with the Cutout filter. The process is similar to the Posterize command in that the Cutout filter reduces the number of colors in an image to the number of colors you specify in the dialog box. However, it does a better job because it also smoothes the edges and lets you choose how closely you want to follow the original edge curves.

This filter is very useful for preparing images to be hand-painted in a natural-media paint program such as Corel Painter or Studio Artist.

The Cutout filter dialog box has three adjustments:

- No. of Levels determines the number of colors.
- Edge Simplicity determines how smooth or jagged the edges of shapes are.
- Edge Fidelity determines accuracy in tracing the original image's shapes.

In determining the number of colors to be used in the result, No. of Levels also determines the number of shapes (or the simplicity) you see in the result.

APPLY THE CUTOUT FILTER

1 Choose Filter, then Artistic, then Cutout.

2 Drag the No. of Levels slider to indicate degree of posterization.

3 Drag the Edge Simplicity slider to control border smoothness.

Note: A lower number equals a more normal edge; a higher number equals straighter edges

4 Drag the Edge Fidelity slider to make edge tracing more or less faithful to the original shapes.

5 When you are happy with what you see in the preview area, click OK.

■ Wait a few moments and you will see an effect that looks approximately like the effect in this figure.

APPLY THE DRY BRUSH FILTER

You can use the Dry Brush filter to produce an effect similar to that of the Cutout filter. However, with the Dry Brush filter, the edges are softer, you can have more levels (up to ten) of detail, and you can add a level of stroke texturing.

The Dry Brush dialog box has three adjustments:

- Brush Size determines the width of the stroke, which translates to the individual areas of color.
- Brush Detail determines the smoothness of the edges.
- Texture gives the strokes less or more of an impasto texture.

You will especially want to experiment with the brush size. The larger the brush, the more abstract the "painting" becomes.

My experiments have shown me that those images in which colors are predominantly one or two hues work better than most. However, as is the case with all these filters, experimentation is the real key to success.

For a really interesting effect, try running this filter twice in succession.

APPLY THE DRY BRUSH FILTER

1 Choose Filter, then Artistic, then Dry Brush.

■ The Dry Brush dialog box appears.

2 Drag the Brush Size slider to determine the width of the brush stroke.

3 Drag the Brush Detail slider to indicate levels of color.

4 Drag the Texture slider to intensify apparent thickness of paint.

5 When you are happy with what you see in the preview area, click OK.

■ Wait a few moments and you will see an effect that looks approximately like the effect in this figure.

APPLY THE FILM GRAIN FILTER

You can create the illusion that your image was shot on high-speed, grainy film with the Film Grain filter. For that reason, the Film Grain filter is really more of a photo-effect or darkroom filter than an artistic one, but the filter is contained within the Artistic filters menu.

The Film Grain filter (like the Grain filter in the Texture filter group) is very useful when you need to match sections of a composite image that were photographed on different film emulsions or enlarged to different degrees.

The Film Grain filter is also useful for making photos look as though they were shot on fast film at low light levels and then overdeveloped to bring up the underexposed image. In traditional photography, this method always produces excess grain.

In the Film Grain filter dialog box:

- Grain controls the size or coarseness of the grain.
- Highlight area adjusts the brightness of highlights.
- Intensity controls the contrast between the grain pattern and the image, which results in determining how widely the grain is distributed.

APPLY THE FILM GRAIN FILTER

1 Choose Filter, then Artistic, then Film Grain.

■ The Film Grain dialog box appears.

2 Drag the Grain slider to determine the size of grain.

3 Drag the Highlight Area slider to determine the brightness of highlights.

4 Drag the Intensity slider to spread or reduce the overall occurrence of a grain pattern.

5 When you are happy with what you see in the preview area, click OK.

■ Wait a few moments and you will see an effect that looks approximately like the effect in this figure.

APPLY THE FRESCO FILTER

You can imitate the effect of painting on wet plaster by using the Fresco filter. Highlights become wet and fuzzy, whereas darker colors become deeper and sharper. Saturation and contrast are both increased over the original image.

Frescos are painted on plaster, so the paints tend to be absorbed. The colors flatten and tend to bleed into one another. The darker colors become even darker. Take a look at the color section of this book to get a visual idea of the differences in these filters.

The Fresco filter's controls are identical to those for the Dry Brush filter. Brush Size determines the width of the stroke, which translates to the individual areas of color. Brush Detail determines the smoothness of the edges. Both Brush Size and Brush Detail have a possible range of 1–10.

The Texture control changes the roughness of the plaster that is the traditional substrate for a Fresco painting. As is the case with other filters that have a Texture control, there are three possible levels of texture.

APPLY THE FRESCO FILTER

1 Choose Filter, then Artistic, then Fresco.

■ The Fresco dialog box appears.

2 Drag the Brush Size slider to determine the width of the brush stroke.

3 Drag the Brush Detail slider to indicate levels of color.

4 Drag the Texture slider to intensify apparent thickness of paint.

5 When you are happy with what you see in the preview area, click OK.

■ Wait a few moments and you will see an effect that looks approximately like the effect in this figure.

APPLY THE NEON GLOW FILTER

You can create very interesting solarization effects using the Neon Glow filter. *Solarization* is a traditional darkroom procedure that causes a partial reversal of the image, and midtones tend to form a bit of a halo — thus the Neon Glow appellation for this filter.

When you run the Neon Glow filter, the colors in the image are reduced to shades of the foreground and background colors.

The Neon Glow filter controls let you adjust glow size, glow brightness, and glow color. Glow Size really determines how unfocused the image becomes. Glow Brightness determines the intensity and spread of the glow color. Glow Color is the only color (other than the already chosen foreground color) you can choose in this duotone effect. Clicking the Glow Color swatch brings up the standard Color Picker to let you choose any color.

Try combining this effect with another of the artistic effects by duplicating the filtered layer and then using the top layer's Blend modes and the transparency slider to combine the effect of the two filters. The possible combinations are endless.

APPLY THE NEON GLOW FILTER

1 Choose Filter, then Artistic, then Neon Glow.

■ The Neon Glow dialog box appears.

2 Drag the Glow Size slider to determine the degree to which the glow color will blur.

3 Drag the Glow Brightness slider to determine how intensely the glow color will appear.

4 Click the Glow Color Swatch to choose a color from the Color Picker.

5 When you are happy with what you see in the preview area, click OK.

■ Wait a few moments and you will see an effect that looks approximately like the effect in this figure.

APPLY THE PAINT DAUBS FILTER

You can create pointillist impressionist paintings (or something very much like them) by using the Paint Daubs filter.

The Paint Daubs filter has a menu of six different brushes, each of which creates a very different look. The basic idea is that the strokes imitate those made by a brush dipped into heavy paint and then applied by tapping the tip of the brush on the canvas.

The three controls are Brush Size, Sharpness, and Brush Type:

- Brush Size controls the spread of areas of different color (which most brush types tend to fade or blend into one another). You can choose a range of brush sizes from 1 to 50.
- Sharpness makes the borders between colors more or less distinct.
- The Brush Types are Simple, Light Rough, Dark Rough, Wide Sharp, Wide Blurry, and Sparkle. Each of these is shown, in order from left to right and top to bottom, in the second figure below.

If you want a really impressionistic, painterly look, choose a large brush size and move the sharpness slider up.

APPLY THE PAINT DAUBS FILTER

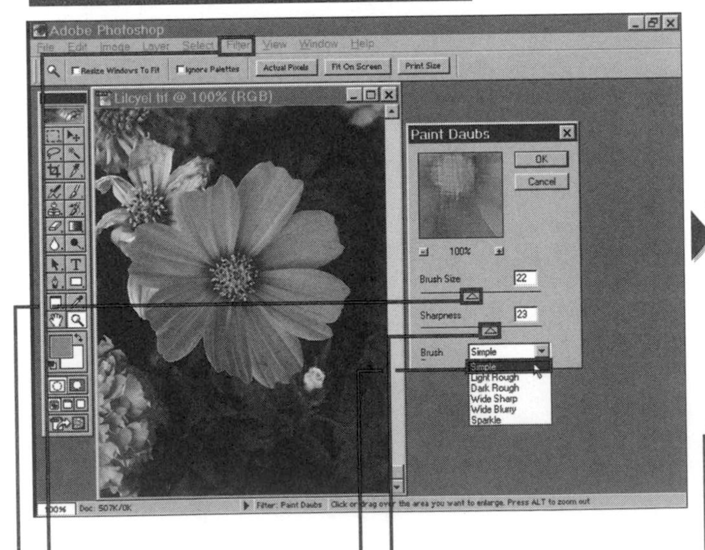

1 Choose Filter, then Artistic, then Paint Daubs.

■ The Paint Daubs dialog box appears.

2 Drag the Brush Size slider to determine the size of the brightest areas.

3 Drag the Sharpness slider to determine the sharpness of borders.

4 Choose a brush type for the effect.

5 When you are happy with what you see in the preview area, click OK.

■ After a few moments, the effects of your selections are displayed.

Note: The effects of the six brushes, from left to right, top to bottom: Simple, Light Rough, Dark Rough, Wide Sharp, Wide Blurry, and Sparkle.

APPLY THE PALETTE KNIFE FILTER

You can flatten colors into broad strokes with the Palette Knife filter. You can vary the softness of edges and the amount of apparent detail in the strokes. The effect is a pleasing variation that does not appear anything like the impasto effect of actually smearing on thick paint with a palette knife.

The Palette Knife dialog box has three controls:

- Stroke Size controls not only the size of the paint blobs but the amount of detail you see in the painting.
- Stroke Detail makes the strokes more or less bristled. The lower the detail, the more "pointillist" the strokes.
- Softness controls the softness of the edges of the strokes.

If you want the impasto effect, use the Duplicate command in the Image menu to copy your image, then choose Mode, and then Grayscale to turn the duplicate into a texture map for use in the Texturizer filter.

If you desire, however, you can use one of the other brushes in a texture channel and then use Lighting Effects to create an impasto effect.

APPLY THE PALETTE KNIFE FILTER

1 Choose Filter, then Artistic, then Palette Knife.

■ The Palette Knife dialog box appears.

2 Drag the Stroke Size slider to determine the size of the brightest areas.

3 Drag the Stroke Detail slider to determine the number of colors (areas of color).

4 Drag the Softness slider to determine the sharpness of borders.

5 When you are happy with what you see in the preview area, click OK.

■ Wait a few moments and you will see an effect that looks approximately like the effect in this figure.

■ An impasto effect was created by using the Glowing Edges filter on a copy of this file, putting the result into an alpha channel, and then using that as the texture channel for the Lighting Effects filter.

APPLY THE PLASTIC WRAP FILTER

You can use the Plastic Wrap feature to make the image look as though you have smothered everything in plastic food wrap.

The Plastic Wrap filter is one of my favorite Photoshop filters because it can actually lend a three-dimensional look to an image, which is useful for giving depth and roundness to such textured areas of a photo as the leaves of a tree.

Plastic Wrap's three controls are Highlight Strength, Detail, and Smoothness:

- Highlight Strength controls the apparent shininess of the plastic wrap.
- Detail controls the number of wrinkles and bumps (highlights) in the plastic wrap.
- Smoothness controls the abruptness of the transition between the highlights (plastic) and the underlying color.

You can get a very interesting effect by combining the Plastic Wrap and Stained Glass filters. Run the Plastic Wrap filter and then duplicate that layer. Run the Stained Glass filter from the Filter menu's Texture submenu on the duplicated layer. Make sure the foreground color is black so that the leading will be black. Change the Blend mode for the Stained Glass layer to Darken.

APPLY THE PLASTIC WRAP FILTER

1 Choose Filter, then Artistic, then Plastic Wrap.

■ The Plastic Wrap dialog box appears.

2 Drag the Highlight Strength slider to determine the shininess of the effect.

3 Drag the Detail slider to determine how tightly the wrap should adhere to the underlying shapes.

4 Drag the Smoothness slider to soften or harden the transition between plastic highlights and other image details.

5 When you are happy with what you see in the preview area, click OK.

■ Wait a few moments and you will see an effect that looks approximately like the effect in this figure.

APPLY THE POSTER EDGES FILTER

You can use the Poster Edges filter to create an effect reminiscent of the technique of artist Toulouse-Lautrec. Colors are flattened and then outlined with dark edges. This filter works extremely well when you use one of the texturizing methods described in Chapter 14.

The Poster Edges dialog box has three controls:

- Edge Thickness controls the thickness of the edge outlines.
- Edge Intensity controls how dark the edges become.
- Posterization reduces the number of colors in the image to between zero and six levels.

There may be times when you want the edges produced by Poster Edges without flattening the image. Duplicate the target layer, run the Poster Edges filter, then choose Blending Options from the Layers palette menu, then choose Darken from the Blend Modes menu. You can do an even cleaner job if you choose Image, then Adjust, then the Threshold command to turn all the details in the image except the edges to pure white.

APPLY THE POSTER EDGES FILTER

1 Choose Filter, then Artistic, then Poster Edges.

■ The Poster Edges dialog box appears.

2 Drag the Edge Thickness slider to determine the thickness of edge outlines.

3 Drag the Edge Intensity slider to determine the darkness of edge outlines.

4 Drag the Posterization slider to increase or reduce the number of colors in the image.

5 When you are happy with what you see in the preview area, click OK.

■ Wait a few moments and you will see an effect that looks approximately like the effect in this figure.

APPLY THE ROUGH PASTELS FILTER

You can imitate the look of rough pastels on textured paper. The Rough Pastels filter is dependent on the use of a texture file. Make your own watercolor paper texture, or use the one provided on the CD-ROM that accompanies this book (see Appendix D for more about all the goodies on the CD-ROM).

The look of this filter is a bit like oil pastels, but with all the strokes moving in a parallel direction. If the filter had an angle control, you could make the result more natural by filtering selected areas one at a time.

Rough Pastels has seven controls:

- Stroke Length—controls the distance over which strokes are smeared.
- Stroke Detail—controls the width of the stroke.
- Texture—Brick, Burlap, Canvas, or Sandstone, or load a texture.
- Texture Scaling—Drag to right for larger pattern, left for smaller pattern.
- Texture Relief—Drag to right for "deeper" texture, left for "smoother" texture.
- Light Direction (called Light Dir. in the Mac version)—Menu lets you choose from any 45-degree angle.
- Invert check box—Inverts the highlights and shadows in the texture.

APPLY THE ROUGH PASTELS FILTER

1 Select Filter, then Artistic, then Rough Pastels.

■ The Rough Pastels dialog box appears.

2 Set the Stroke Length and the Stroke Detail.

3 Choose a texture from the menu or load a custom texture file.

4 Set the Texture Scaling, the Texture Relief, and the Light Direction.

5 When you are happy with what you see in the preview area, click OK.

■ Here is the result of applying the settings in Steps 2–4.

APPLY THE SMUDGE STICK FILTER

You can use the Smudge Stick filter to create an effect that is a little like Rough Pastels without the texture. The image is highly posterized (you have no direct control over the number of levels of color) and is smeared in diagonal strokes.

You access the Smudge Stick dialog box by choosing Filter, then Artistic, then Smudge Stick. The Smudge Stick dialog box has three controls:

- Stroke Length controls the distance over which strokes are smeared. Stroke Length can be varied from 1–10.
- Highlight Area controls the brightness of highlights. Highlight Area has 20 levels.
- Intensity controls color saturation and contrast. Intensity has ten levels.

The Highlight Area control has a heavy on the overall lightness or darkness of the image. Keep this influence in mind, because the Smudge Stick filter tends to darken the image—especially if dark tones are dominant. You can also lower Intensity to lower contrast and brighten the shadow areas.

APPLY THE SMUDGE STICK FILTER

1 Choose Filter, then Artistic, then Smudge Stick.

■ The Smudge Stick dialog box appears.

2 Drag the Stroke Length slider to adjust the length of smear.

3 Drag the Highlight Area slider to control highlight brightness.

4 Drag the Intensity slider to change contrast and saturation.

5 When you are happy with what you see in the preview area, click OK.

■ Wait a few moments and you will see an effect that looks approximately like the effect in this figure.

APPLY THE SPONGE FILTER

You can use the Sponge filter to flatten and posterize colors with darker blotches imposed in a seemingly random pattern. The result is a sort of "faux finish" effect.

I use the Magic Wand to select spaces between the Poster Edges and then treat them with the Sponge filter, using different settings for each selection. Combining filter effects in this way is much easier and faster if you use Actions to assign several filters to a set of function keys.

The Sponge filter dialog box—which you can access by choosing Filter, then Artistic, then Sponge—contains the following three controls:

- Brush Size enlarges or reduces the sponge blobs.
- Definition lightens and darkens the blobs.
- Smoothness anti-aliases the edges of the blobs.

The Sponge filter is useful for creating faux finish backgrounds. You can use the Sponge filter in conjunction with the Poster Edges filter for an excellent effect. Create a new file using the background color that you want to predominate in the finish. Use the painting tools to make random strokes. When you get a pattern you like, run the Sponge filter.

APPLY THE SPONGE FILTER

1 Choose Filter, then Artistic, then Sponge.

■ The Sponge dialog box appears.

2 Drag the Brush Size slider to adjust blotch size.

3 Drag the Definition slider to intensify blotches.

4 Drag the Smoothness slider to smooth blotch edges.

5 When you are happy with what you see in the preview area, click OK.

■ Wait a few moments and you will see an effect that looks approximately like the effect in this figure.

APPLY THE UNDERPAINTING FILTER

You can use the Underpainting filter to do a credible job of making an image look as if it were washed onto a textured surface with highly thinned paints. This technique is a basic one for starting an oil painting and is a good first step when you are planning to combine increasingly detailed or textured Artistic filters.

Because Underpainting works with texture maps, its dialog box contains seven controls:

- Brush Size determines the size of flattened areas of color.
- Texture Coverage dictates how thin the paint must be before the texture shows through.
- The Texture menu lets you choose between Brick, Burlap, Canvas, and Sandstone. You can also load a texture file.
- Scaling enlarges or reduces the size of the texture.
- Relief determines the apparent depth of the texture.
- The Light Direction menu (called Light Dir. on a Mac) determines the direction of highlights and shadows on the texture.
- Finally, the Invert check box reverses the apparent highs and lows in the texture pattern by reversing the highlights and shadows in the texture file.

APPLY THE UNDERPAINTING FILTER

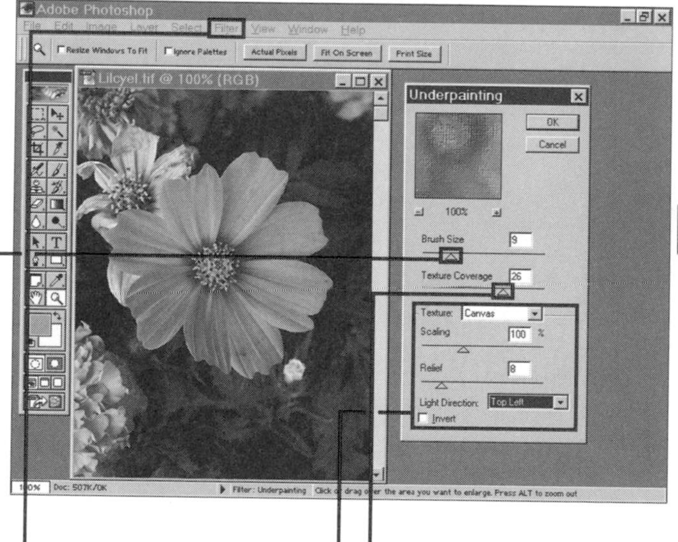

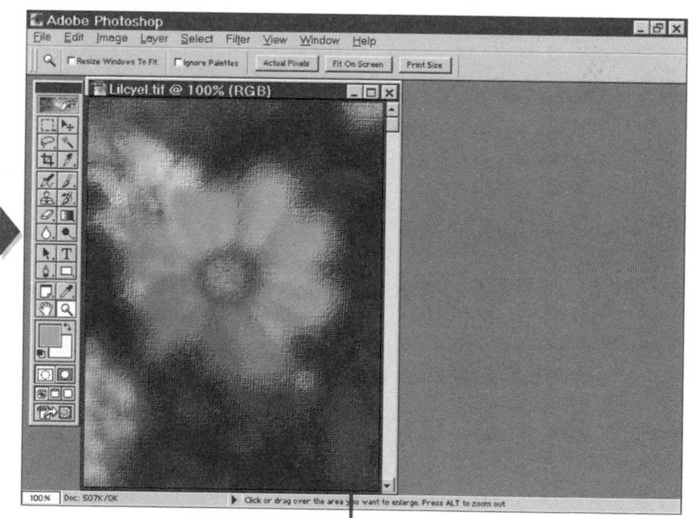

1 Choose Filter, then Artistic, then Underpainting.

■ The Underpainting dialog box appears.

2 Drag the Brush Size slider to adjust size of solid color areas.

3 Drag the Texture Coverage slider to determine the threshold for texture bleed-through.

4 Choose settings in this area to adjust the texture.

5 When you are happy with what you see in the preview area, click OK.

■ Wait a few moments and you will see an effect that looks approximately like the effect in this figure.

APPLY THE WATERCOLOR FILTER

You can make your image look as if it were painted with watercolors by using the Watercolor filter. Colors are posterized and then made to bleed into one another with soft edges. Darker colors below a certain threshold (which you cannot control) get much darker (you can control how much darker). The result looks a lot like the Fresco filter, but with softer borders and much less contrast between strokes.

The Watercolor filter dialog box—which you access by choosing Filter, then Artistic, then Watercolor—contains three controls:

- Brush Detail dictates the range of color reduction, as well as the size of the strokes. Photoshop 6 offers 14 levels of brush detail.
- Shadow Intensity lowers or raises contrast between highlights and shadows over a range of 10 levels.
- Texture does not use the standard art surfaces but controls the edge smoothness of the "paint strokes."

If you want to make the image look more like a water color, try hand-stroking with the Blur tool after running the Watercolor filter, then use a watercolor paper texture image in the Texturizer filter.

APPLY THE WATERCOLOR FILTER

1 Choose Filter, then Artistic, then Watercolor.

■ The Watercolor dialog box appears.

2 Drag the Brush Detail slider to adjust color reduction.

3 Drag the Shadow Intensity slider to determine shadow contrast.

4 Drag the Texture slider to control edge smoothness.

5 When you are happy with what you see in the preview area, click OK.

■ Wait a few moments and you will see an effect that looks approximately like the effect in this figure.

APPLY THE ACCENTED EDGES FILTER

You can create edge accents that range in brightness from pure white to pitch black using the Accented Edges filter, which works by reducing the number of colors and outlining the edges with a jagged dry-brush stroke. You can vary the width of this stroke to the extent that the edge can almost become the image. Altering brightness and smoothness also greatly changes the effect and texture of the image.

You summon the Accented Edges dialog box by choosing Filter, then Brush Strokes, then Accented Edges. The dialog box contains three controls:

- Edge Width controls the thickness of the brush-stroked border between colors.
- Edge Brightness adjusts the border color from white to black.
- Smoothness anti-aliases and blurs the edge stroke.

Using a selection to isolate the main subject from the background and then running the Accented Edges filter with the Edge Brightness slider at maximum is very effective. Then, invert the selection (⌘/Ctrl+Shift+I) and run the Accented Edges filter on the background.

APPLY THE ACCENTED EDGES FILTER

1 Choose Filter, then Brush Strokes, then Accented Edges.

■ The Accented Edges dialog box appears.

2 Drag the Edge Width slider to adjust the width of the outline brush stroke.

3 Drag the Edge Brightness slider to whiten/blacken the outline stroke.

4 Drag the Smoothness slider to anti-alias the border stroke.

5 When you are happy with what you see in the preview area, click OK.

■ Wait a few moments and you will see an effect that looks approximately like the effect in this figure.

Note: To make outlined edges in a variety of colors within the same image, choose Image, then Adjust, then Posterize and set the number of colors that suits your image. Select each area of color with the Magic Wand and choose Edit, then Stroke.

APPLY THE ANGLED STROKES FILTER

You can use the Angled Strokes filter to create an effect similar to the Rough Pastels filter (see "Apply the Rough Pastels Filter," earlier in this chapter). The difference is that you can control the main direction of the strokes with the Angled Strokes filter; however, strokes are automatically angled in different directions in contrasting areas of the image, giving the image The appearance of having been created with a very dry, very thick oil brush.

The Angled Strokes dialog box is accessed by choosing Filter, then Brush Strokes, then Angled Strokes. The three dialog box controls are

- Direction Balance, which changes the overall angle of the strokes
- Stroke Length, which shrinks and stretches the strokes
- Sharpness, which softens the edges of the strokes by anti-aliasing them

Of the three controls, Direction Balance is the most interesting. If the slider is at the left end, all strokes are at a 45-degree angle from upper left to lower right. If the slider is at the right end, all strokes are at a 45-degree angle from upper right to lower left. If the slider is in the middle, strokes are completely cross-hatched.

APPLY THE ANGLED STROKES FILTER

1 Choose Filter, then Brush Strokes, then Angled Strokes.

■ The Angled Strokes dialog box appears.

2 Drag the Direction Balance slider to change the principal direction of the brush stroke angle.

3 Drag the Stroke Length slider to lengthen or shorten the brush stroke.

4 Drag the Sharpness slider to anti-alias the strokes.

5 When you are happy with what you see in the preview area, click OK.

■ Wait a few moments and you will see an effect that looks approximately like the effect in this figure.

APPLY THE CROSSHATCH FILTER

You can create cross-stroked color etching using the Crosshatch filter. You could easily turn this image into a pen-and-ink etching by converting the image to grayscale and then choosing Image, then Adjust, then Threshold or High Pass.

The Crosshatch filter dialog box (which you get to by choosing Filter, then Brush Strokes, then Crosshatch) contains three controls:

- Stroke Length determines how far the stroke will smear before it fades out.
- Sharpness can increase the apparent effect but, if you are not careful, can also cause objectionable pixelization.
- Strength makes the effect more or less obvious, chiefly by broadening the strokes (actually, the "bristles"). Increase the Strength value to 3, and you get something that looks almost like a basket weave.

You can create a cross-hatch pattern without a highlight or with only a highlight. Duplicate the layer and run the Crosshatch filter on the new layer. Then use the new layer's Blend mode Darken or Lighten commands. The Darken command will leave only the black cross-hatching, the Lighten command only the white cross-hatching.

APPLY THE CROSSHATCH FILTER

1 Choose Filter, then Brush Strokes, then Crosshatch.

■ The Crosshatch dialog box appears.

2 Drag the Stroke Length slider to change the stroke distance.

3 Drag the Sharpness slider to harden or soften the strokes.

4 Drag the Strength slider to narrow or widen the strokes.

5 When you are happy with what you see in the preview area, click OK.

■ Wait a few moments and you will see an effect that looks approximately like the effect in this figure.

Note: Try selecting different areas of an image, feathering each selection, and then using different Strength settings in each area. You can use this trick to create an enhanced illusion of depth between foreground, midplane, and background.

APPLY THE DARK STROKES FILTER

You can make angular (not cross-hatched) smudged strokes using the Dark Strokes filter. This filter greatly heightens the difference between highlights and shadows, while midtones are left more or less alone. The darkest areas of the image are painted with variably dark strokes. The lighter areas of the image are painted with variably light strokes.

The Dark Strokes filter dialog box (which you can get to by choosing Filter, then Brush Strokes, then Dark Strokes) has three controls: Balance, Black Intensity, and White Intensity. Balance controls the ratio of black to white strokes (actually the overall contrast of the image). Black Intensity varies the blackness of the dark strokes while White Intensity varies the whiteness of the light strokes.

The Dark Strokes filter can produce very dramatic and classical-looking portraits if you double the size of the image, run the filter, and then reduce the image to its original size. This technique has the effect of increasing the apparent contrast between highlights and shadows. This technique works best if you reduce the contrast of the image before running the Dark Strokes filter so that highlights don't wash out.

APPLY THE DARK STROKES FILTER

1 Choose Filter, then Brush Strokes, then Dark Strokes.

■ The Dark Strokes dialog box appears.

2 Drag the Balance slider to change the midpoint of midtones.

3 Drag the Black Intensity slider to lighten or darken shadows.

4 Drag the White Intensity slider to lighten or darken highlights.

5 When you are happy with what you see in the preview area, click OK.

■ Wait a few moments and you will see an effect that looks approximately like the effect in this figure.

APPLY THE INK OUTLINES FILTER

You can create a mixture of cross-hatching and ink outline sketching using the Ink Outlines filter, which makes images look like they were painted with a mixture of color and inked sketch lines. The Ink Outlines filter also darkens the background and increases saturation and contrast in a manner very similar to the Dark Strokes filter (see previous page).

Access the Ink Outlines filter dialog box by choosing Filter, then Brush Stroke, then Ink Outlines. The dialog box controls are Stroke Length, Dark Intensity, and Light Intensity. Dark Intensity and Light Intensity work just like Black Intensity and White Intensity, respectively, in the Dark Strokes filter dialog box.

Stroke Length controls how much contrast must exist between edges before a stroke is made. For that reason, Stroke Length also controls the number of outline strokes. What any of that has to do with stroke length is anybody's guess.

Dark Intensity determines how black the black strokes and outlines will be. Light Intensity determines how white the light strokes will be.

APPLY THE INK OUTLINES FILTER

1 Choose Filter, then Brush Strokes, then Ink Outlines.

■ The Ink Outlines dialog box appears.

2 Drag the Stroke Length slider to change the number and length of outline strokes.

3 Drag the Dark Intensity slider to lighten or darken shadows.

4 Drag the Light Intensity slider to lighten or darken highlights.

5 When you are happy with what you see in the preview area, click OK.

■ Wait a few moments and you will see an effect that looks approximately like the effect in this figure.

APPLY THE SPATTER FILTER

You can use the Spatter filter to create an effect that is somewhere between a spray gun painting and pointillism. How far in between depends on where you set the sliders.

Applying the Spatter filter is fairly straightforward, and only two sliders are in the filter's dialog box:

- The Spray Radius slider controls the size of the spray dots. The larger the number, the larger the dots. The Spray Radius slider has a range of 1–25, but the actual size of the dots depends on the pattern in the underlying image. As usual, experimentation is the key to success.
- The Smoothness slider anti-aliases the edges of the spray dots so that the colors blend more smoothly.

You can make this filter much more effective if you vary the size of the dots by running it in different selected parts of the image. Try using larger dots for more distant areas and smaller dots for closer subjects.

The Spatter filter can be excellent for giving a softening effect to an image. Just apply the filter, and then choose the Edit, then Fade command to diminish the effect of the filter.

APPLY THE SPATTER FILTER

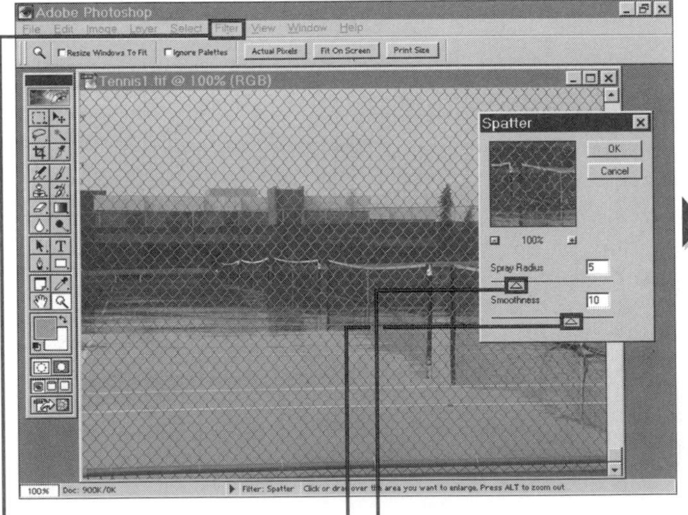

1 Choose Filter, then Brush Strokes, then Spatter.

■ The Spatter dialog box appears.

2 Drag the Spray Radius slider to increase/decrease the radius of a "splat" (pixel clump).

3 Drag the Smoothness slider to blend or sharpen the dots. Sharper dots heighten the spatter effect.

4 When you are happy with what you see in the preview area, click OK.

■ Wait a few moments and you will see an effect that looks approximately like the effect in this figure.

APPLY THE SUMI-E FILTER

You can use the Sumi-e filter to achieve an effect that is a cross between the Watercolor and Dark Strokes filters. The Sumi-e filter produces an effect with softer edges and colors than the Dark Strokes filter. The strokes are diagonal daubs whose size and intensity can be varied over a wide range. You cannot control the direction of strokes; they are all diagonal from top right to bottom left. Use this filter when you want your illustration to take on the look of an Oriental watercolor.

The Sumi-e filter dialog box is accessed by choosing Filter, then Brush Strokes, then Sumi-e. The dialog box has three controls:

- Stroke Width controls the distance over which details in the image are smeared.
- Stroke Pressure controls the density and intensity of the strokes.
- Contrast controls the width of the black strokes.

If you use the Sumi-e filter on an image that has been posterized or that has been subjected to the Underpainting filter, the result looks more like its namesake Japanese watercolor painting.

APPLY THE SUMI-E FILTER

1 Choose Filter, then Brush Strokes, then Sumi-e.

■ The Sumi-e dialog box appears.

2 Drag the Stroke Width slider to increase or decrease the area over which colors are blended.

3 Drag the Stroke Pressure slider to increase or decrease blackness of the stroke.

4 Drag the Contrast slider to increase or decrease width of black strokes.

5 When you are happy with what you see in the preview area, click OK.

■ Wait a few moments and you will see an effect that looks approximately like the effect in this figure.

APPLY THE BAS RELIEF FILTER

You can use the Bas Relief filter to create a grayscale embossed effect.

At least, the Bas Relief effect is grayscale if you leave colors at the default; otherwise, whatever colors are there for foreground and background will predominate. You can adjust the Bas Relief filter's effect to give the impression of more or less depth and detail.

Access the Bas Relief filter dialog box by choosing Filter, then Sketch, then Bas Relief. The dialog box has three controls:

- Detail controls the number of colors that are blended to make a relief plane.
- Smoothness controls the softness of edges.
- Light Direction lets you choose 45-degree angles of lighting from a menu.

This filter is also a wonderful way to give a color image the look of impasto oils: Run the filter, convert the image to grayscale, flatten it if necessary, and then save it under a new filename. Reload the original file and run the Texturizer filter using the Bas Relief-treated file as the texture.

APPLY THE BAS RELIEF FILTER

1 Choose Filter, then Sketch, then Bas Relief.

■ The Bas Relief dialog box appears.

2 Drag the Detail slider to increase or decrease the area of a shape or depth plane.

3 Drag the Smoothness slider to sharpen or blur the edges of planes.

4 Choose the lighting direction.

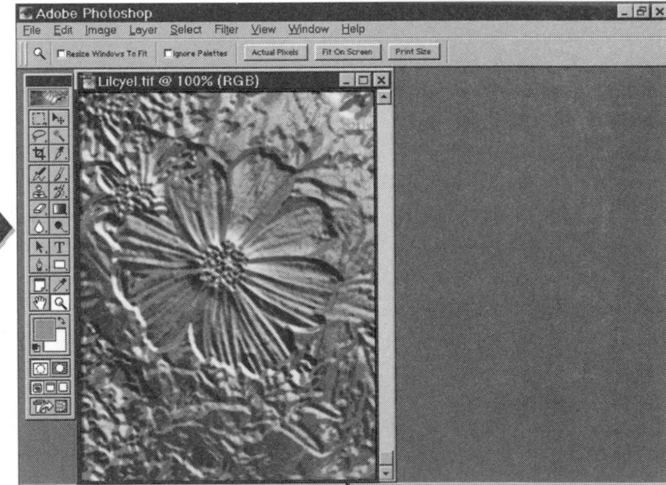

5 When you are happy with what you see in the preview area, click OK.

■ Wait a few moments and you will see an effect that looks approximately like the effect in this figure.

APPLY THE CHALK & CHARCOAL FILTER

You can use the Chalk & Charcoal filter to create a duotone version of the Rough Pastels filter. (See "Apply the Rough Pastels Filter," earlier in this chapter.) The filter applies angular, smudgy strokes that are a mixture of chalk (background color) and charcoal (foreground color).

You access the Chalk & Charcoal filter dialog box by choosing Filter, then Sketch, then Chalk & Charcoal. The dialog box has three controls:

- Charcoal Area controls the threshold below which the image is covered with strokes in the foreground color. The filter paints that area in the foreground color.
- Chalk Area controls the brightness level above which the image is covered with strokes in the background color. This happens because the default foreground color is black and the default background color is white. However, the filter will use any two colors that you assign to the foreground and background.
- Stroke Pressure controls the width of the strokes (and thus, how much area the strokes cover) and the degree to which the strokes bleed into one another.

APPLY THE CHALK & CHARCOAL FILTER

1 Choose Filter, then Sketch, then Chalk & Charcoal to bring up the Chalk & Charcoal dialog box.

2 Drag the Charcoal Area slider to increase or decrease the area stroked with the foreground color.

3 Drag the Chalk Area slider to increase or decrease the area stroked with the background color.

4 Drag the Stroke Pressure slider to narrow or widen the strokes (also has an effect on edge sharpness).

5 When you are happy with what you see in the preview area, click OK.

■ Wait a few moments and you will see an effect that looks approximately like the effect in this figure.

APPLY THE CHARCOAL FILTER

You can create a finer cross-hatched effect with the Charcoal Filter than with the Chalk & Charcoal filter (see previous page). The Charcoal filter uses the foreground and background colors of the image (as do all the Sketch submenu filters), but the borders between colors are more emphasized.

The Charcoal filter dialog box controls are Charcoal Thickness, Detail, and Light/Dark Balance.

- Charcoal Thickness controls the width of the stroke.
- Detail controls the number of colors within a given shape.
- Light/Dark Balance determines the point at which highlights become entirely white (untouched paper).

The Charcoal Filter is very high contrast, so you may occasionally find highlight and shadow areas of the image blocked up. Try duplicating the layer and changing the Charcoal Thickness and Light/Dark balance to gain detail in the lost areas. Place the blocked layer on top and erase the blocked areas so you can see the detail on the layer below.

You can get an even more interesting effect by first running the Ink Outlines filter (see "Apply the Ink Outlines Filter," earlier in this chapter), then the Charcoal filter over the same layer.

APPLY THE CHARCOAL FILTER

1 Choose Filter, then Sketch, then Charcoal to summon the Charcoal dialog box.

2 Drag the Charcoal Thickness slider to increase or decrease the thickness of the crosshatched strokes.

3 Drag the Detail slider to increase or decrease the number of shapes that can be distinguished.

4 Drag the Light/Dark Balance slider to control image contrast. This control also has a profound effect on how much detail is seen.

5 When you are happy with what you see in the preview area, click OK.

■ Wait a few moments and you will see an effect that looks approximately like the effect in this figure.

APPLY THE CHROME FILTER

You can use the Chrome filter to create a grayscale version of the Plastic Wrap filter (see "Apply the Plastic Wrap Filter," earlier in this chapter). Of course, you could convert the Chrome filter result to grayscale, but that would convert all of the layers in the file. You may have reason to want to use only one layer as grayscale, and that is where the Chrome filter comes in handy.

The Chrome filter dialog box controls are Detail and Smoothness.

- Detail determines the levels of color that are blended together.
- Smoothness softens the edges between shades of gray.

The Chrome filter can produce some lovely impasto effects when the file you create is saved as a grayscale .PSD file and then used with the Texturizer filter. In fact, all the Sketch filters are useful for creating texture effects with any of the filters that can use a grayscale texture.

Another way to use the Chrome filter effectively is to copy the filtered layer and then combine the original and the copy, using one of the Blend modes. The Color and Overlay modes are particularly appealing.

APPLY THE CHROME FILTER

1 Choose Filter, then Sketch, then Chrome.

■ The Chrome dialog box appears.

2 Drag the Detail slider to increase or decrease the number of recognizable shapes.

3 Drag the Smoothness slider to increase or decrease the smoothness of the transitions from highlights to shadows.

4 When you are happy with what you see in the preview area, click OK.

■ Wait a few moments and you will see an effect that looks approximately like the effect in this figure.

APPLY THE CONTÉ CRAYON FILTER

You can use the Conté Crayon filter to produce a soft-edge duotone sketch. You can use the Conté Crayon filter on its own (to make a fast-loading Web graphic, for instance) or for all sorts of interesting effects by choosing unexpected background colors.

The Conté Crayon filter dialog box controls are Foreground Level, Background Level, the Texture menu, Scaling, Relief, the Light Direction (Light Dir. on Mac) menu, and the Invert check box.

- Foreground and Background Levels control the intensity of the foreground and background colors, respectively.
- The Texture pull-down menu lets you choose from the standard four textures or load a grayscale Photoshop (PSD) texture file.
- Scaling adjusts the size of the texture file in relation to the target image.
- Relief determines the contrast between highlight and shadow.
- Light Direction determines the angle, in 45-degree increments, at which light appears to fall on the texture.
- The Invert checkbox inverts the texture when checked.

The midtones in Conté Crayon are always reduced to about 50 percent gray. The highlights are then reinterpreted as the background level and the shadows as the foreground level. Remember, the default foreground color is black.

APPLY THE CONTÉ CRAYON FILTER

1 Choose Filter, then Sketch, then Conté Crayon.

2 Drag the Foreground Level slider to increase or decrease the range of shades to be painted in the foreground color.

3 Drag the Background Level slider to increase or decrease the range of shades to be painted in the background color.

4 Choose and adjust the settings of a texture.

5 When you are happy with what you see in the preview area, click OK.

■ Wait a few moments and you will see an effect that looks approximately like the effect in this figure.

APPLY THE GRAPHIC PEN FILTER

You can use the Graphic Pen filter to produce something that looks like a pen-and-ink etching made with unidirectional strokes.

The best candidates for the Graphic Pen filter (as is the case for most of the Sketch filters) are those images with good contrast and have sharp, well-defined edges that are not too close together. Knowing this, you may want to use image and retouching commands on the image before applying any of the Sketch filters, including the Graphic Pen filter.

The Graphic Pen filter dialog box controls are Stroke Length, Light/Dark Balance, and the Stroke Direction (Stroke Dir. on Mac) pull-down/pop-up menu (which contains the options Right Diagonal, Horizontal, Left Diagonal, and Vertical). Light/Dark balance establishes the threshold for highlights and shadows.

This filter can produce some especially nice results using colors other than black and white as the foreground and background colors. Try a dark brown and a light tan or ochre for a sepia effect. Two shades of blue or blue and purple work well for sea- and skyscapes.

APPLY THE GRAPHIC PEN FILTER

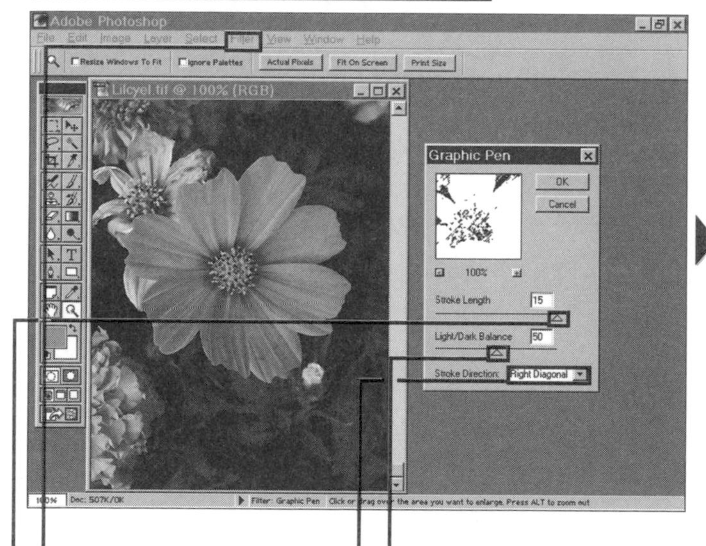

1 Choose Filter, then Sketch, then Graphic Pen.

2 Drag the Stroke Length slider to increase or decrease the length of the black ink stroke (foreground color).

3 Drag the Light/Dark Balance slider to increase or decrease the range of shades to be painted in the background color.

4 Choose a pen stroke direction.

5 When you are happy with what you see in the preview area, click OK.

■ Wait a few moments and you will see an effect that looks approximately like the effect in this figure.

APPLY THE HALFTONE PATTERN FILTER

You can "fake" a halftone pattern with the Halftone Pattern filter, which actually produces a halftone pattern atop the image. To put it another way, the filter masks the image with a halftone pattern.

The Halftone Pattern filter offers three types of halftone patterns: Dot (which imitates the standard printer halftone pattern), Circle (a concentric pattern that can create some very interesting texture effects), and Line (which looks a bit like TV scan lines).

The Halftone Pattern filter dialog box controls are Size, Contrast and Pattern Type:

- Size controls the size of the pattern element (circle, dot, or line).
- Contrast controls the overall contrast of the image and, therefore, how much of it is shown through the pattern mask.
- Pattern Type is a menu that lets you choose between Circle, Dot, and Line pattern types.

By duplicating layers and using different foreground and background colors with different Blend modes for the layers, you can create any number of postmodern-type stylizations. For instance, try this: After duplicating the layer, run a dot pattern in black and white on the lower layer. Select the upper layer and run a line pattern in red and blue. Now apply the Multiply blend mode.

APPLY THE HALFTONE PATTERN FILTER

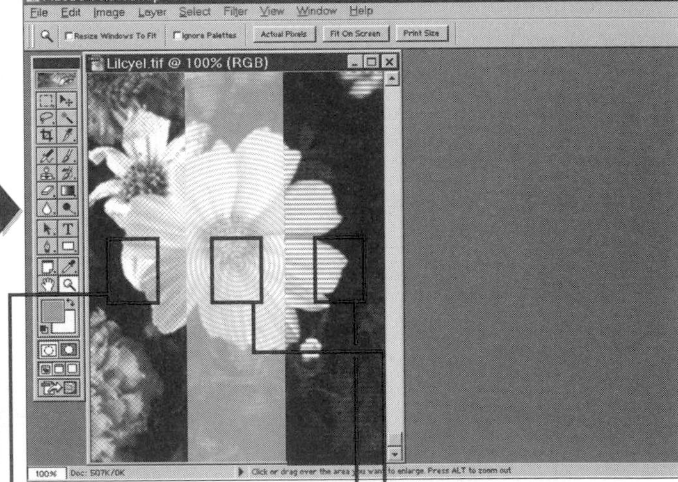

1 Choose Filter, then Sketch, then Halftone Pattern.

■ The Halftone Pattern dialog box appears.

2 Drag the Size slider to increase or decrease the size of the pattern element.

3 Drag the Contrast slider to increase or decrease the overall contrast of the underlying image.

4 Choose a pattern type.

5 When you are happy with what you see in the preview area, click OK.

■ This shows the results of the Dot pattern type.

■ This shows the results of the Circle pattern type.

■ This shows the results of the Line pattern type.

APPLY THE NOTE PAPER FILTER

The Note Paper filter creates an interesting effect that bears little obvious resemblance to its name. Application of this filter results in a two-color, high-contrast rendition of the image on textured paper. You can control the graininess of the paper texture, but not the texture pattern.

You access the Note Paper filter dialog box by choosing Filter, then Sketch, then Note Paper.

The Note Paper filter dialog box has three controls:

- Image Balance is a threshold control that determines which parts of the image become the foreground and which the background.
- Graininess determines how pronounced the paper texture will be.
- Relief controls the intensity of the highlights and shadows that separate the edges of shapes.

The Note Paper filter is a very good way to create a grayscale PSD texture file that can be used by other filters that are capable of loading a texture. Just open a new file in a solid color (white or black) and then open the filter and make adjustments until you see the degree of texture you like.

APPLY THE NOTE PAPER FILTER

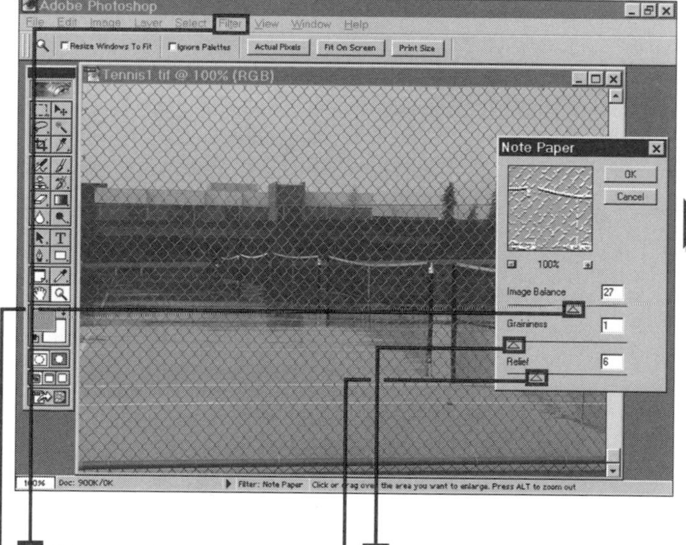

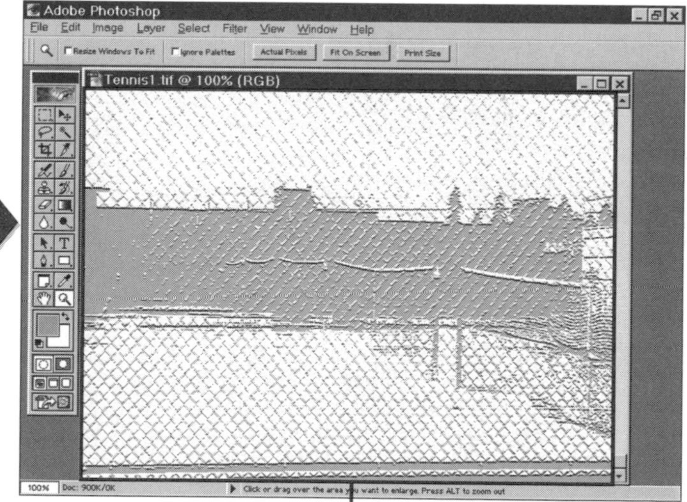

1 Choose Filter, then Sketch, then Note Paper.

■ The Note Paper dialog box appears.

2 Drag the Image Balance slider to change the foreground/background threshold.

3 Drag the Graininess slider to decrease or increase the definition of edge shadows and highlights.

4 Drag the Relief slider to adjust the brightness of highlights and shadows.

5 When you are happy with what you see in the preview area, click OK.

■ Wait a few moments and you will see an effect that looks approximately like the effect in this figure.

APPLY THE PHOTOCOPY FILTER

The Photocopy filter makes the image look as if it were copied on a copy machine incapable of producing grays.

The Photocopy filter is similar to the Threshold filter (see "Make a Threshold Mask" in Chapter 8) in that all color below a certain level goes to the background color and all color above that level goes to the foreground color. The Photocopy filter results in softer edges and a few more apparent shades of gray, however.

Access the Photocopy filter dialog box by choosing Filter, then Sketch, then Photocopy. The dialog box controls are Detail and Darkness. Applied to the test image, moving the Detail slider did not have much effect. The results it produces would be subtle on any image. The Darkness slider controls the intensity of the foreground color.

Because the Photocopy filter is such a pleasing version of a Threshold filter, this filter can be an excellent one to use in combination with some of the other Sketch filters. Run the Photocopy filter on a duplicate of your image and paste it into the original, then use the Layer Blend modes to blend both effects.

APPLY THE PHOTOCOPY FILTER

1 Choose Filter, then Sketch, then Photocopy.

■ The Photocopy dialog box appears.

2 Drag the Detail slider to change the shadow threshold.

3 Drag the Darkness slider to decrease or increase the intensity of the foreground color (shadow).

4 When you are happy with what you see in the preview area, click OK.

■ Wait a few moments and you will see an effect that looks approximately like the effect in this figure.

APPLY THE PLASTER FILTER

The Plaster filter reduces the image to a few tones below an adjustable threshold in shades of the background color and embosses the shapes over a solid foreground color. You can easily reverse the effect by switching the foreground and background colors before running the filter.

What this all has to do with plaster is hard to understand, but the effect is interesting nevertheless. Just how interesting depends on the image to a greater-than-usual degree. This filter becomes even more interesting when used on a duplicate layer together with a Blend mode.

You summon the Plaster filter dialog box by choosing Filter, then Sketch, then Plaster.

The dialog box has three controls:

- Image Balance changes the threshold for the background color and determines what is shown as a shape versus what is shown as flat foreground color.
- Smoothness softens the transition between the embossed shape and the background color.
- Light Direction (or Light Dir. on the Mac) lets you choose the direction of highlights and shadows on the embossed shapes.

APPLY THE PLASTER FILTER

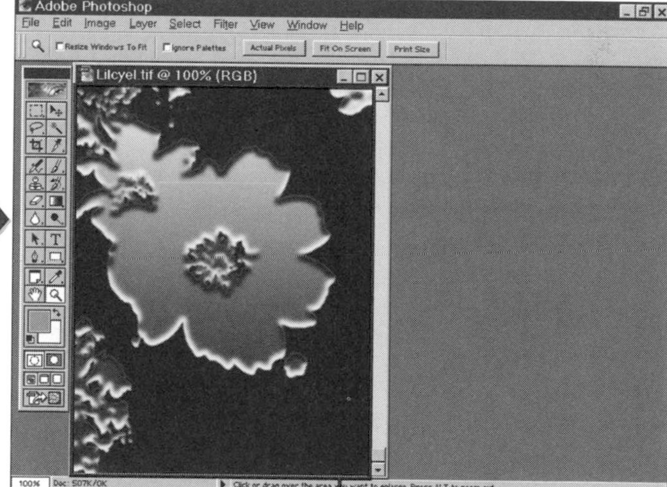

1 Choose Filter, then Sketch, then Plaster.

■ The Plaster dialog box appears.

2 Drag the Image Balance slider to change the shadow threshold.

3 Drag the Smoothness slider to sharpen or smooth the border between foreground color and embossed shapes.

4 Choose a lighting direction.

5 When you are happy with what you see in the preview area, click OK.

■ Wait a few moments and you will see an effect that looks approximately like the effect in this figure.

APPLY THE RETICULATION FILTER

The Reticulation filter imitates what happens when photographic film is overheated during processing and film grain clumps together in worm-like forms.

Access the Reticulation filter dialog box by choosing Filter, then Sketch, then Reticulation. The dialog box has three controls:

- Density actually dictates the number and size of grain dots. You can make a huge difference in the apparent pattern with this slider.
- Black Level controls at what gray point the image turns black.
- White Level controls at what gray point the image turns white.

Use the last two controls to create contrast in the pattern. This is a terrific filter for creating grain and stained glass patterns. Paste the pattern onto a new layer in your image and try using the Darken Only or Lighten Only blend modes.

Oddly, the effect can produce interesting results when used as a texture. Blurred slightly with the Gaussian Blur filter, the Reticulation filter makes great watercolor paper. Used on a duplicate layer applied with a Blend mode, you can get some nicely reticulated color photos, too.

APPLY THE RETICULATION FILTER

1 Choose Filter, then Sketch, then Reticulation.

■ The Reticulation dialog box appears.

2 Drag the Density slider to change the number of dots.

3 Drag the Black Level slider to delineate the black threshold.

4 Drag the White Level slider to delineate the white threshold.

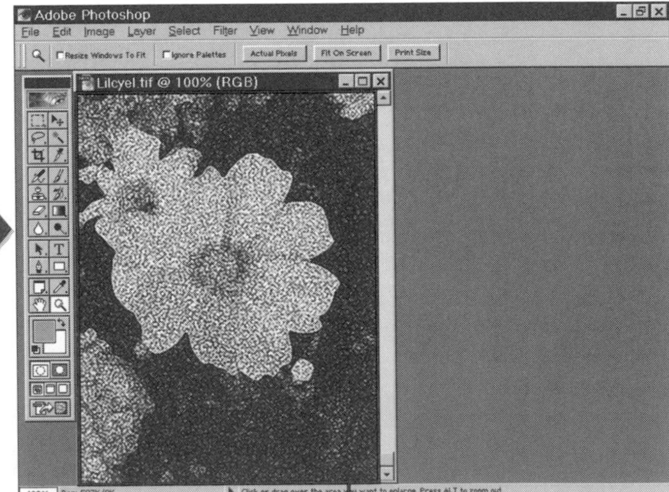

5 When you are happy with what you see in the preview area, click OK.

■ Wait a few moments and you will see an effect that looks approximately like the effect in this figure.

APPLY THE STAMP FILTER

The Stamp filter carves the image out in much the same way as rubber is carved to make a rubber stamp — thus the filter's name. You can control the smoothness of lines and the point at which black and white divide.

Access the Stamp filter dialog box by choosing Filter, then Sketch, then Stamp.

The box has two controls:

- Light/Dark Balance moves the threshold (brightness level dividing point) up and down the grayscale. By itself, this would have the same effect as the Threshold filter — but you cannot use it by itself.
- Smoothness hardens or softens the border between black and white. This is the control that really makes a difference in the look of the finished effect.

The Stamp filter is an excellent filter for making channel masks, by the way, especially because you can visually control the softness of the edges. Create a new layer and apply the filter to the layer. Copy the layer to the clipboard, then delete it. Create a new Alpha Channel and paste the clipboard image into it.

APPLY THE STAMP FILTER

1 Choose Filter, then Sketch, then Stamp.

■ The Stamp dialog box appears.

2 Drag the Light/Dark Balance slider to change the dividing point between black and white.

3 Drag the Smoothness slider to sharpen or blur edges.

4 When you are happy with what you see in the preview area, click OK.

■ Wait a few moments and you will see an effect that looks approximately like the effect in this figure.

APPLY THE TORN EDGES FILTER

The Torn Edges filter is a Threshold filter that converts everything in the image to the exact foreground or background color. A Threshold filter or command (that is, Image, then Adjust, then Threshold) is one that pushes all the tones in the image closer and closer to the current foreground/background colors. The "threshold" is the exact gray-level or brightness level of the dividing line between black and white. The difference between the Torn Edges filter and similar filters is that the borders between foreground color and background color give the impression that the shapes have been torn from newsprint. (Actually, the edges are just grainy.)

Summon the Torn Edges filter dialog box by choosing Filter, then Sketch, then Torn Edges. The Torn Edges filter dialog box has three controls:

- Image Balance selects the dividing line (threshold) between foreground and background (usually black and white).
- Smoothness dictates the graininess of the edges.
- Contrast would seem the same as Image Balance but really has to do with how much detail is shown in the grainy border areas.

APPLY THE TORN EDGES FILTER

1 Choose Filter, then Sketch, then Torn Edges.

2 Drag the Image Balance slider to select the dividing tone between what is translated to foreground or background color.

3 Drag the Smoothness slider to increase or decrease graininess of "torn edges."

4 Drag the Contrast slider to increase or decrease detail (or clumping) in grainy areas.

5 When you are happy with what you see in the preview area click OK.

■ Wait a few moments and you will see an effect that looks approximately like the effect in this figure.

APPLY THE WATER PAPER FILTER

The Water Paper filter is the only Sketch filter that works in full color. The Water Paper filter makes a kind of watercolor painting of your image, but the result looks more like an ink image painted on fibrous paper and soaked in water. Highlights flare into shadows, and lots of blurring occurs. The three sliders in the filter's dialog box give quite a bit of control over what stays recognizable and what blurs beyond recognition.

The Water Paper filter dialog box controls are Fiber Length, Brightness, and Contrast:

- Fiber Length controls blurriness, which actually becomes more or less pronounced as a result of the settings you use for Brightness and Contrast. The longer the Fiber Length, the less detailed the resulting image.
- Brightness and Contrast are used in the same way as the controls in the Adjust commands on the Image menu. Drag the Brightness slider to the right to make the image more "high key." Drag the Contrast slider to the right to increase the difference between light tones and dark tones.

APPLY THE WATER PAPER FILTER

1 Choose Filter, then Sketch, then Water Paper.

2 Drag the Fiber Length slider to change the blurriness and texture of the image.

3 Drag the Brightness slider to increase or decrease image brightness.

4 Drag the Contrast slider to increase or decrease image contrast.

5 When you are happy with what you see in the preview area, click OK.

■ Wait a few moments and you will see an effect that looks approximately like the effect in this figure.

DISTORT WITH THE DIFFUSE GLOW FILTER

You can use the Diffuse Glow filter to "bleed" the current background color into the lighter (highlight) areas of your image. Put another way, the Diffuse Glow filter can add noise of the same color as the background to the rest of the image.

Although the Diffuse Glow filter is the first filter found under the Distort submenu, the Diffuse Glow filter is unique in this group in that it actually does not distort at all, but rather adds noise, or pixels, to images.

Access the Diffuse Glow filter dialog box by choosing Filter, then Distort, then Diffuse Glow. The box has three controls:

- Graininess — Controls the amount of grain noise imposed on the image. Drag slider right to increase, left to decrease.
- Glow Amount — Increasing (dragging to the right) causes highlights to brighten and to bleed into shadow areas.
- Clear Amount — Dragging to the right increases detail in highlights.

Each of these has an effect on the amount of background color that spreads into the highlights.

DISTORT WITH THE DIFFUSE GLOW FILTER

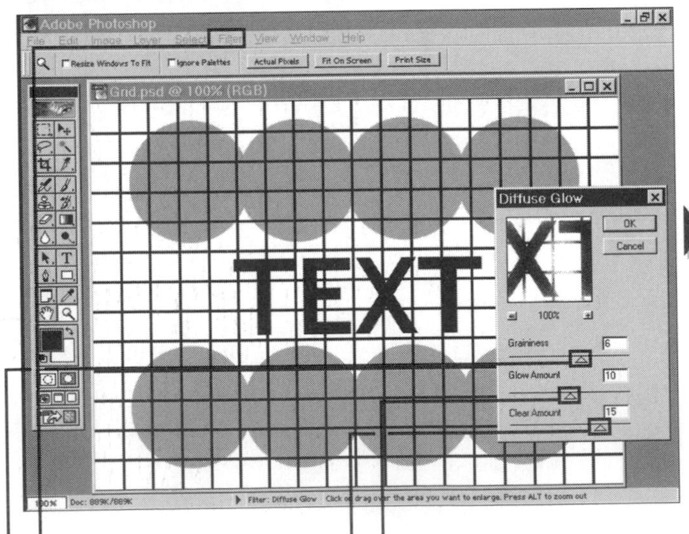

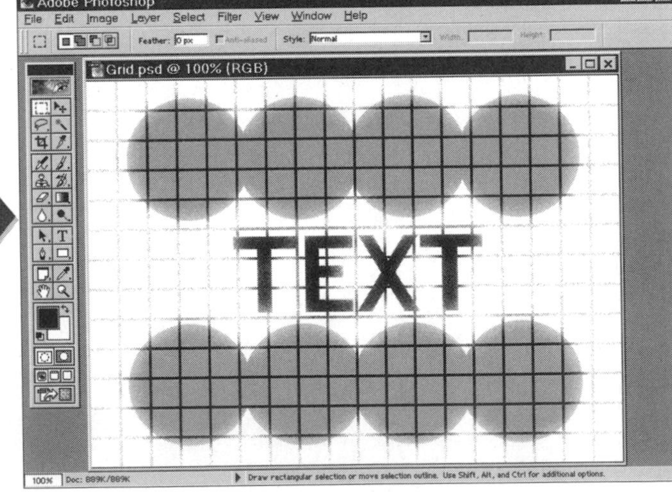

1 Choose Filter, then Distort, then Diffuse Glow.

■ The Diffuse Glow filter dialog box appears.

2 Drag the Graininess slider to enlarge or reduce speckling of scattered highlights.

3 Drag the Glow Amount slider to control spreading of highlights.

4 Drag the Clear Amount slider to control detail in highlights.

5 When you are happy with what you see in the preview area, click OK.

■ Photoshop implements the Diffuse Glow filter settings you selected.

■ This example shows the effect of running the Diffuse Glow filter on the test image. Notice that all the lines and shapes are unmoved.

DISTORT WITH THE DISPLACE FILTER

You can use the Displace filter, one of the most powerful filters on the Distort submenu, to make impressive changes in your image. The Displace filter must be used in conjunction with a grayscale texture map because the white tones in the image move the image to an extreme in one direction, while the black tones move it to the extreme in the other direction. (Gray tones cause movement proportionate to their lightness or darkness.)

Using the Displace filter can be confusing because the Displace dialog box asks you to make the settings before it asks you to pick a file to use as the displacement map. As soon as you click OK in the Displace dialog box, a conventional File Open dialog box appears, and you simply choose any grayscale Photoshop (PSD) file. Using a single-layer file is best, because multiple layers use more storage, have slow processing, and can cause unpredictable results.

DISTORT WITH THE DISPLACE FILTER

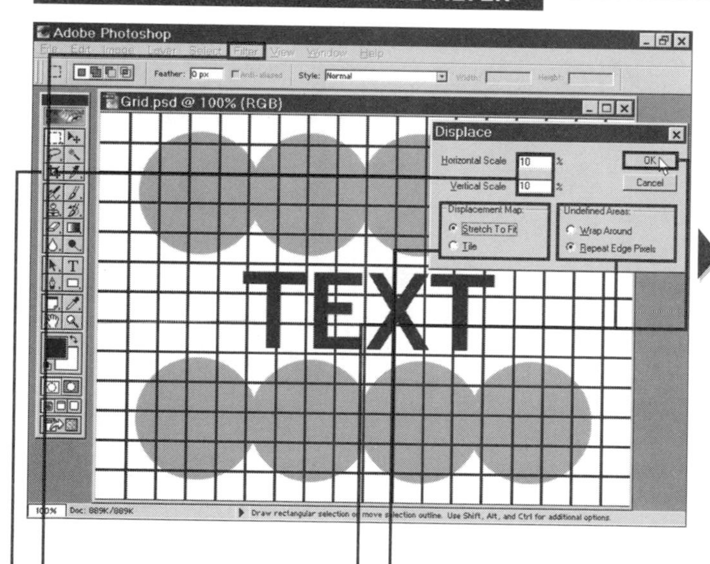

1 Choose Filter, then Distort, then Displace.

■ The Displace dialog box appears.

2 Type a percentage of the amount of horizontal and vertical displacement you want.

3 Click to select whether the displacement map scales to fit, or tiles to fill the target image.

4 Click to select how the image behaves in undefined areas.

5 Click OK.

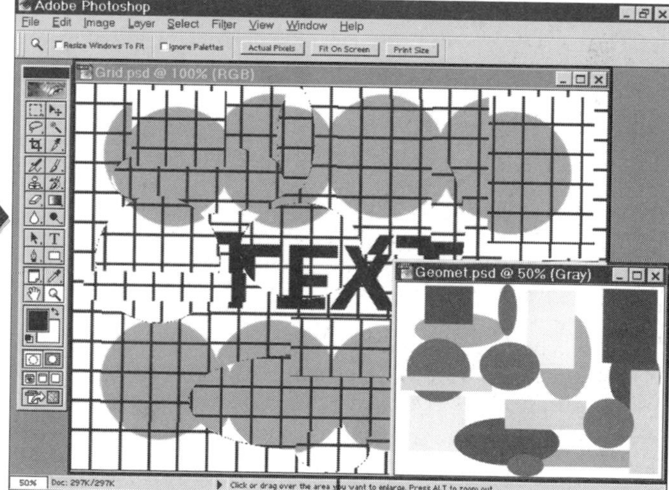

■ A File Open dialog box appears.

6 Navigate to choose the grayscale PSD file you want to use for the placement map.

7 Click OK.

■ This example shows the result of running the Distort filter on the test image. The displacement map is shown in the lower-right corner.

DISTORT WITH THE GLASS FILTER

You can use the Glass filter to make your image look as though you are viewing it through glass.

The effects of the Glass filter are easy to see. Some portions of the image are magnified, some reduced, and all are somewhat distorted.

The Glass filter is a versatile filter due to its five controls, Distortion, Smoothness, Texture, Scaling, and Invert:

- Distortion controls the amount of the distortion.
- Smoothness controls the size and blends the edges of the distorted areas at the same time.
- Texture contains further options for built-in textures: Blocks, Canvas, Frosted, Tiny Lens, and Load Texture. If you choose Load Texture, you can choose any grayscale Photoshop (PSD) file that is accessible to your system.
- Scaling controls the size of the texture pattern relative to your image.
- Checking the Invert check box reverses light and dark in the texture map, thus inverting the apparent high and low points in the texture.

DISTORT WITH THE GLASS FILTER

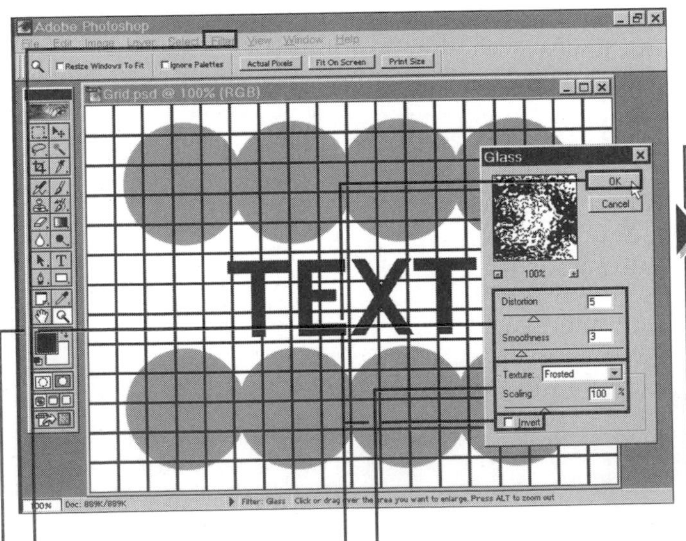

1 Choose Filter, then Distort, then Glass.

■ The Glass dialog box appears.

2 Drag the appropriate slider to adjust the light-bending of the image or to smooth the image's edges.

3 Choose a texture map, then drag the slider to enlarge or reduce the map.

4 Check Invert to make a negative of the texture map and then click OK.

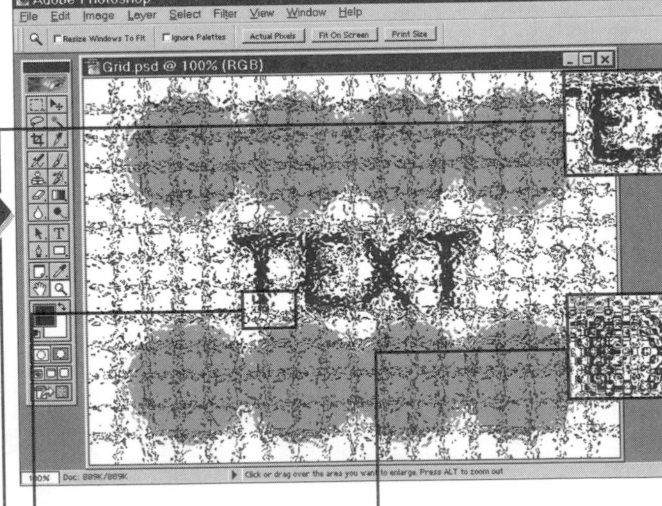

■ This example shows the result of running the Glass filter on a sample image. The texture map used is the built-in Frosted texture.

■ This example shows the same settings, using the Canvas texture map.

■ Again with the same settings, this example uses the Tiny Lens texture map.

DISTORT WITH THE OCEAN RIPPLE FILTER

You can use the Ocean Ripple filter to produce a distortion that is much like the distortion created by the Glass filter (see "Distort with the Glass Filter," previously in this chapter), but the Ocean Ripple filter creates ripple shapes that are more random in size. You can also alter the size of the various shapes with the Ocean Ripple filter dialog box.

I suppose it would have been a bit wordy to call this the "Light Breeze on a Calm Sea Ripple" filter — but that's much more descriptive of this filter's effect. You never get the waves that a stiffer breeze would create.

Note that the Ocean Ripple filter does not let you select a displacement map, making this filter easy to use. You can select one of two settings in the Ocean Ripple dialog box: Ripple Size and Ripple Magnitude. These may sound redundant, but you can think of Magnitude as height to make the distinction clearer.

Ocean Ripple is a good filter for making surfaces look like water or for making images look submerged.

DISTORT WITH THE OCEAN RIPPLE FILTER

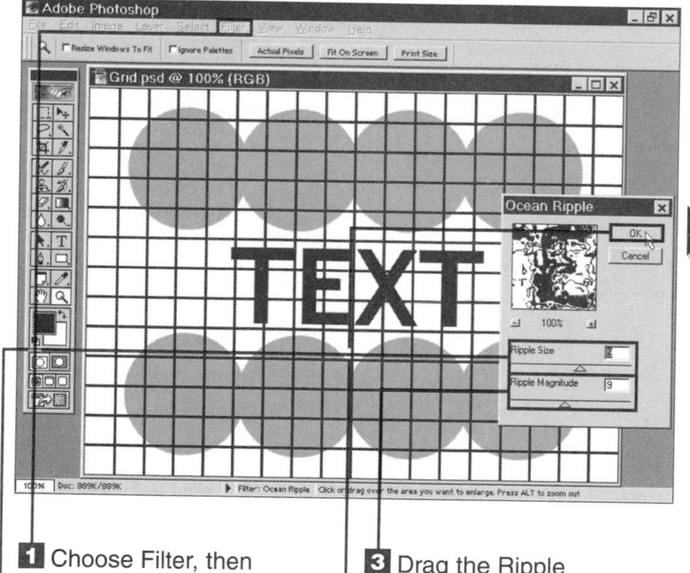

1 Choose Filter, then Distort, then Ocean Ripple.

■ The Ocean Ripple dialog box appears.

2 Drag the Ripple Size slider to indicate the size of shape distortions.

3 Drag the Ripple Magnitude slider to indicate apparent height or thickness of ripples.

4 Click OK.

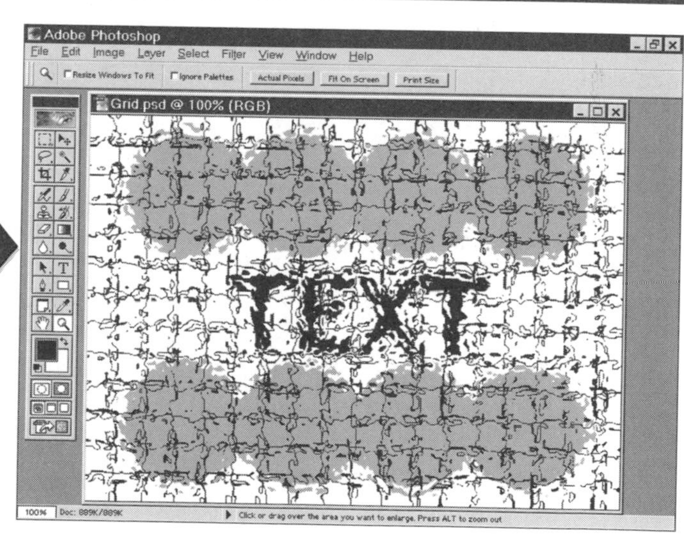

■ This example shows the result of running the Ocean Ripple filter on the test image.

DISTORT WITH THE PINCH FILTER

You can use the Pinch filter to make an image appear as if it is printed on a piece of rubber sheeting that has been made to sag in the center. You can also make it look as though a big ball is pushing the center of the rubber sheet toward you.

This filter is good for stretching an object so that you can blend it with a concave or convex surface in a photo composite.

The Pinch filter dialog box has only a single setting: Amount. If the slider is in the center, there is no distortion. You can drag the slider to the left to make the distortion expand (or blow out). Conversely, you can drag the slider to the right to make the distortion push in (suck in).

A preview grid at the bottom of the dialog box shows the exact degree of distortion. A zoomable preview box also shows you how your actual image looks at the distortion setting you are using.

DISTORT WITH THE PINCH FILTER

1 Choose Filter, then Distort, then Pinch.

■ The Pinch dialog box appears.

2 Drag the Amount slider to indicate the depth and spread of the pinch's depression or expansion.

3 Click OK.

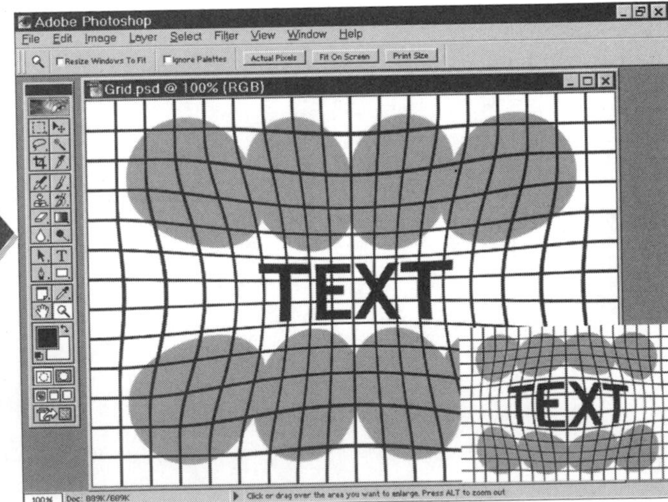

■ This shows the result of running the Pinch filter on the test image. At the lower right is the same image with the Amount pointer moved to the left.

DISTORT WITH THE POLAR COORDINATES FILTER

You can perform some impressive distortions with the Polar Coordinates filter; however, it is one of the most difficult to understand. You can apply either the Rectangular to Polar or the Polar to Rectangular options with this filter. If you apply the Rectangular to Polar option, the entire upper edge of the image reduces to a single pixel, taking all the other elements with it. If you select the Polar to Rectangular option, something entirely different happens. Look at the second figure in this exercise to get a better idea of how this filter works.

There are no other controls for the Polar Coordinates filter. What you click is what you get.

You might want to try using the Rectangular to Polar option when you want to create a photo that you can wrap (map) around a 3D globe in a 3D program. It is a little harder to imagine a use for the Polar to Rectangular option, but if you want to view the image through a mirrored cylinder, it will appear normal.

DISTORT WITH THE POLAR COORDINATES FILTER

1 Choose Filter, then Distort, then Polar Coordinates.

■ The Polar Coordinates dialog box appears.

2 Click to choose either the Rectangular to Polar or the Polar to Rectangular option.

3 Click OK.

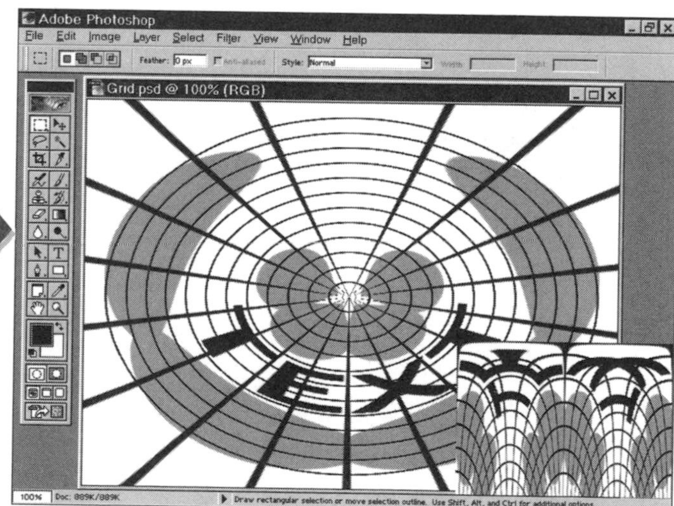

■ This example shows the result of running the Polar Coordinates filter on the test image.

■ The example in the lower-right corner is the same image distorted using the Polar to Rectangular.

DISTORT WITH THE RIPPLE FILTER

You can use the Ripple filter to produce effects similar to those of the Sprayed Strokes filter (see Chapter 15). However, the wavy edges it creates are much lower in frequency and more rounded. The ripples are regular in frequency (evenly spaced) and can be adjusted to a wide variety of wave heights.

Ripple Filter is simple to use. Only two controls appear in the dialog box: an Amount slider and a Size menu. The Amount slider pushes the wave in a positive or negative direction. The Size menu offers three choices — Small, Medium, and Large — which dictate the wave frequency.

If you choose Small from the Size Menu, you get a viable alternative to the Glass filter described earlier in this chapter. If you choose Large, you get a truly exaggerated zigzag effect that could be useful for creating fabric designs or abstract paintings.

Try these effects on hard-edged solid-color abstracts at various sizes and magnifications.

DISTORT WITH THE RIPPLE FILTER

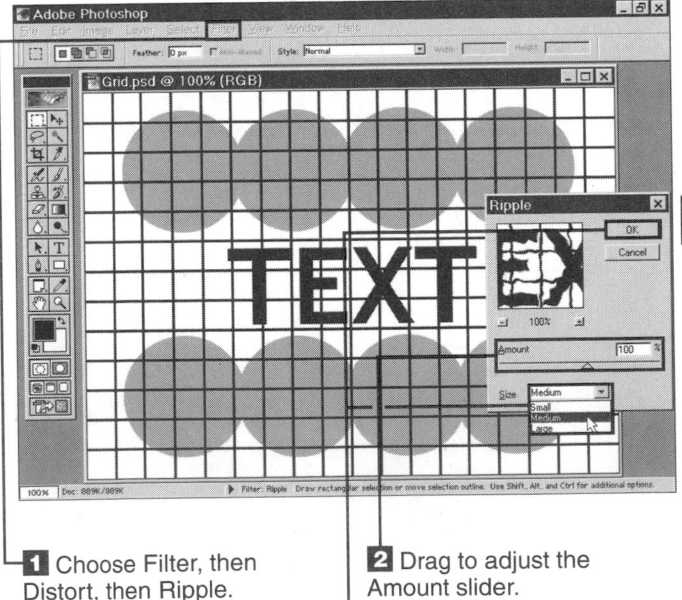

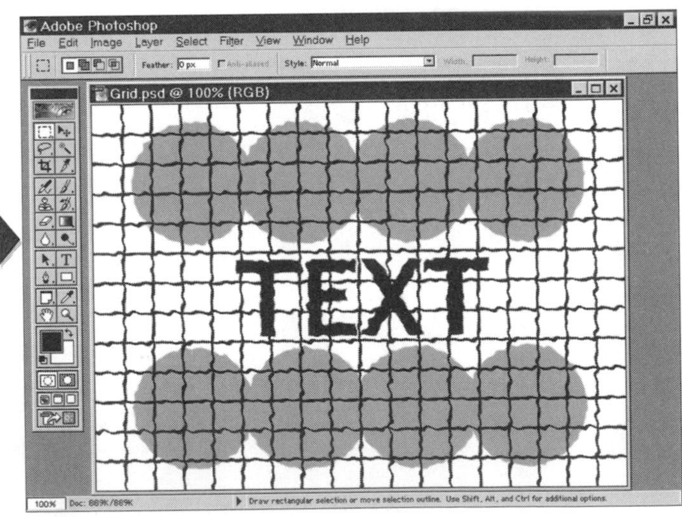

1 Choose Filter, then Distort, then Ripple.

■ The Ripple dialog box appears.

2 Drag to adjust the Amount slider.

3 Click to choose the size.

4 Click OK.

■ This example shows the result of running the Ripple filter on the test image

DISTORT WITH THE SHEAR FILTER

You can use the Shear filter, a powerful and highly useful warping tool, to "wrinkle" the surface of an image. An easy way to visualize the effect is to think of a photo in which a flat flag is made to appear to be furled in the breeze. You can also warp a texture so it can be blended atop a curved surface — think of a tattooed arm or a woodgrain pencil cup.

The application method for Shear is intuitive. You can create drag points by clicking on the grid and delete drag points by dragging them off the edge of the grid. You can then click the point and drag it so that it curves on the grid. The image warps to match. You can view your changes in the preview area.

If you choose Wrap Around, the parts of the image that get pushed off one side of the screen re-appear on the opposite side. If you choose Repeat Edge, the pixels that get pushed away from one side of the screen are repeated out to the edge of the image, so that it doesn't appear to be wavy or uneven.

DISTORT WITH THE SHEAR FILTER

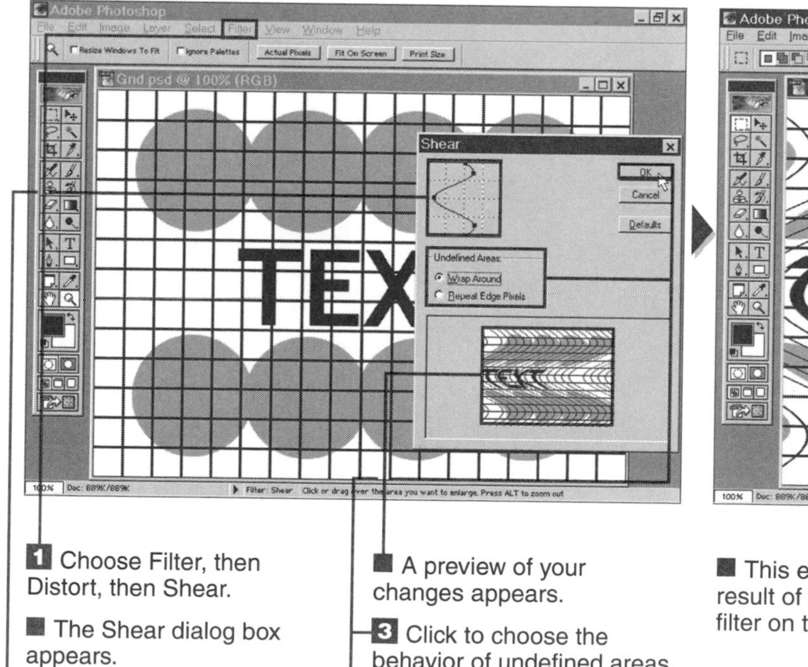

1 Choose Filter, then Distort, then Shear.

■ The Shear dialog box appears.

2 Click anywhere on the curved line to insert a point, and then drag the point to warp the image.

■ A preview of your changes appears.

3 Click to choose the behavior of undefined areas.

4 Click OK.

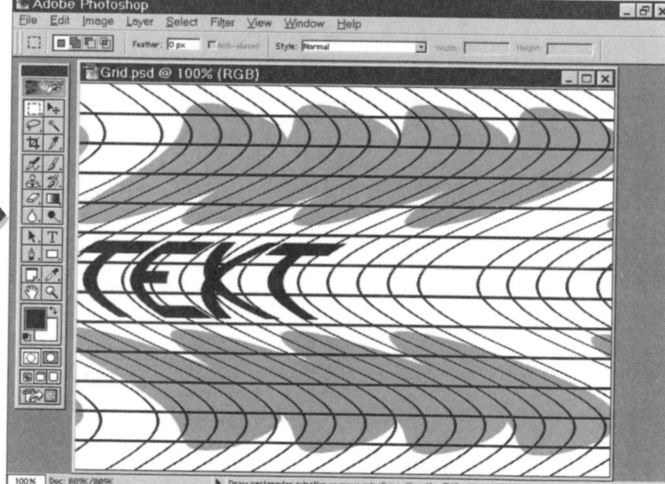

■ This example shows the result of running the Shear filter on the test image.

DISTORT WITH THE SPHERIZE FILTER

You can use the Spherize filter to warp your image halfway around a globe. You can then blend your subject onto a planet and place it in space, or blend it onto a ball and then make a racquet. . . . You get the idea.

The warp effect produced by the Spherize filter can be over any percentage of the surface of a sphere up to 50 percent. In other words, you cannot wrap around the sphere. There is some overlapping of visual effect with the Pinch filter (see "Distort with the Pinch Filter," earlier in this chapter), but Sphere's warp is perfectly spherical, whereas the Pinch filter effect is a bit more conical. As with the Pinch filter, you can drag to make your warps concave or convex. Also, the Spherize filter can make tubular warps in your choice of horizontal or vertical direction, which makes it an even better candidate than the Pinch filter for warping a tattoo to match the curve of an arm, for example.

The Spherize filter is easy to use because you only drag a single slider to indicate the percentage of the sphere over which you want to warp your image.

DISTORT WITH THE SPHERIZE FILTER

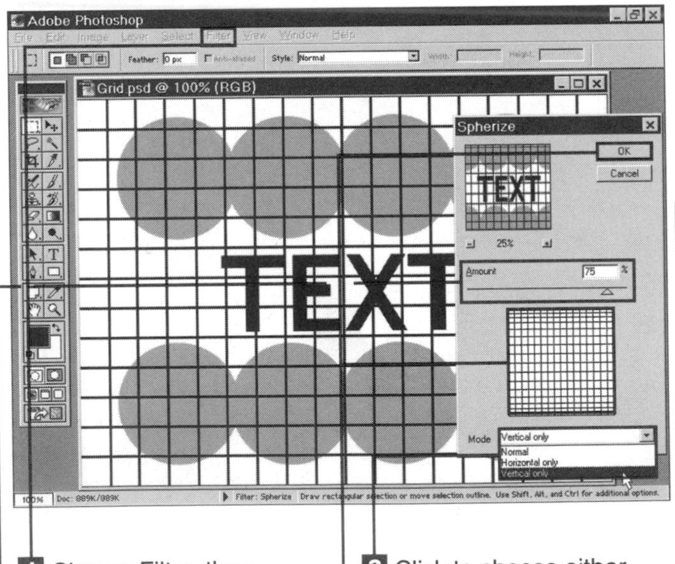

1 Choose Filter, then Distort, then Spherize.

■ The Spherize dialog box appears.

2 Drag the slider to adjust the amount of curve. Negative numbers create a concave surface.

3 Click to choose either spherical or tubular warps.

■ You can view a grid that represents the degree of warp.

4 Click OK.

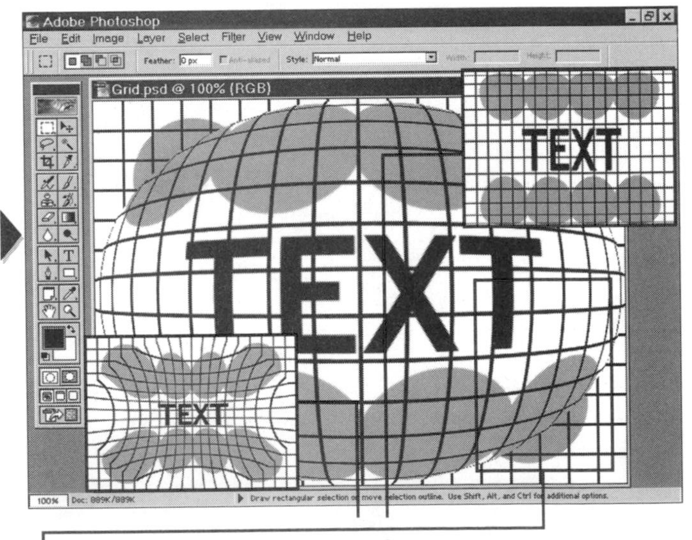

■ This example shows the result of running the Spherize filter on the test image.

■ This example shows a tubular warp.

■ This example shows a concave warp.

DISTORT WITH THE TWIRL FILTER

You can use the Twirl filter to twist the image into a spiral, as if it were being pulled down a giant drain. If you need to create a stock photo of money going down the drain, then this filter is the one for the job.

The Twirl filter dialog box contains a single slider that lets you spin the image counterclockwise if you drag to the left of center. There are two preview areas. One shows the effects of your changes on the image. The other diagrams the angle adjustments made with the slide bar. Both work in real time (as do all the other preview areas in Photoshop's built-in filters).

There is no Preview check box for the Distort submenu filters, so you will not see the actual effect until you click OK in the Twirl dialog box. Using the hand cursor to show a complex part of your image may be helpful, so that you can get a better idea of this filter's effect.

DISTORT WITH THE TWIRL FILTER

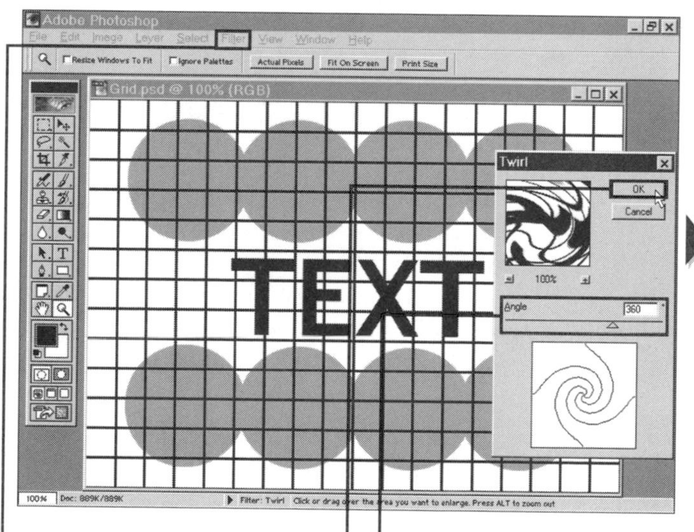

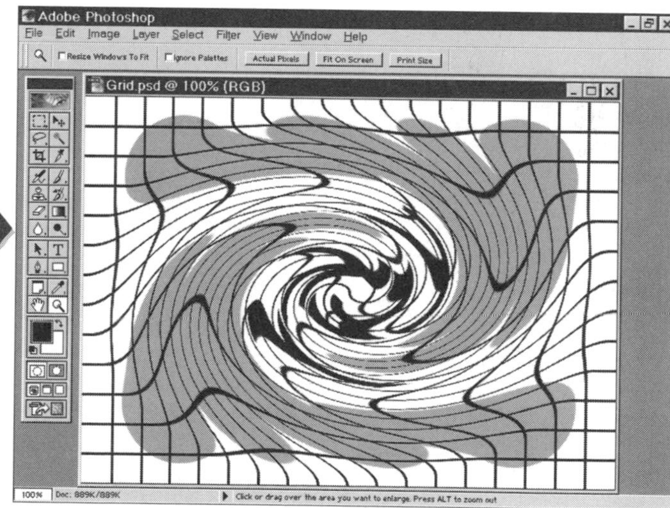

1 Choose Filter, then Distort, then Twirl.

■ The Twirl dialog box appears.

2 Drag the Angle slider to indicate the direction of the twist and the number of turns.

3 Click OK.

■ This example shows the result of running the Twirl filter on the test image.

DISTORT WITH THE WAVE FILTER

You can use the flexible Wave filter options to produce a wide variety of chaotic changes in your image. If you want to convert elements of the image into a watery, marble-like, or zigzag texture, this filter is the one to use. Think of it as a much more powerful and less predictable version of the Ocean Ripple and Ripple filters.

Seven controls are in the Options palette: Number of Generators, Minimum and Maximum Wavelength, Amplitude, Horizontal and Vertical Scale, Type, Randomize, and Undefined Areas.

Number of Generators determines the number of patterns Photoshop applies. Wavelength has two sliders for minimum and maximum amounts. Amplitude has the same two sliders. Scale determines the size of the texture in relationship to the size of the image. Undefined Areas determines what happens to edges left blank when the image distorts. Type, the most important control, determines the shape of the wave: smooth curves, right-angle peaks and straight edges, and straight peaks and valleys. When in doubt, click Randomize.

DISTORT WITH THE WAVE FILTER

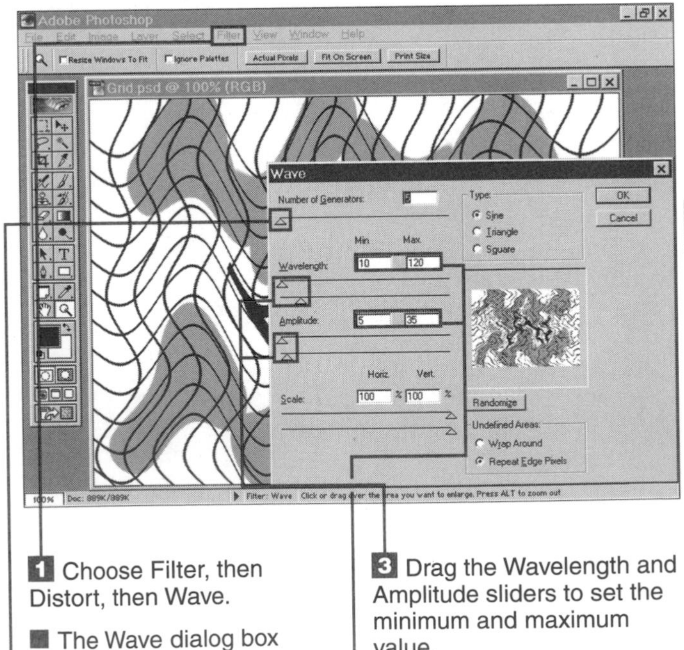

1 Choose Filter, then Distort, then Wave.

■ The Wave dialog box appears.

2 Drag the slider to make distortion more or less complex.

3 Drag the Wavelength and Amplitude sliders to set the minimum and maximum value.

■ You can type the same number for uniform wave frequency.

4 Drag the Scale sliders to change the percentage of the overall distortion effect.

5 Click to determine whether edges wrap or fill with pixels of the edge colors in undefined areas.

6 Click to choose wave shape.

■ Click Randomize to let Photoshop determine the settings.

7 When you click OK, your image appears as a wave.

DISTORT WITH THE ZIGZAG FILTER

You can use the ZigZag filter to produce an effect similar to what you see when you pitch a stone into a quiet pond. This filter can be very useful for creating the illusion that waves are emanating from something like a radio tower or a floating boat.

The controls in the ZigZag filter are Amount, Ridges, and Style. The Amount option controls wave size.

The Ridges option determines the number of wave peaks.

Style is a menu containing three additional style choices:

- Around Center, which creates a whirlpool effect.
- Out from Center, which creates the illusion that something is bubbling up from under the surface.
- Pond Ripples, which creates concentric waves like those that appear when you throw a pebble into a pond.

You can use the ZigZag filter on sections of the image as well as the entire image. For example, you can select a number of sections on a water-blue color, then apply the ZigZag filter to each section to create the appearance of rain falling on a pond.

DISTORT WITH THE ZIGZAG FILTER

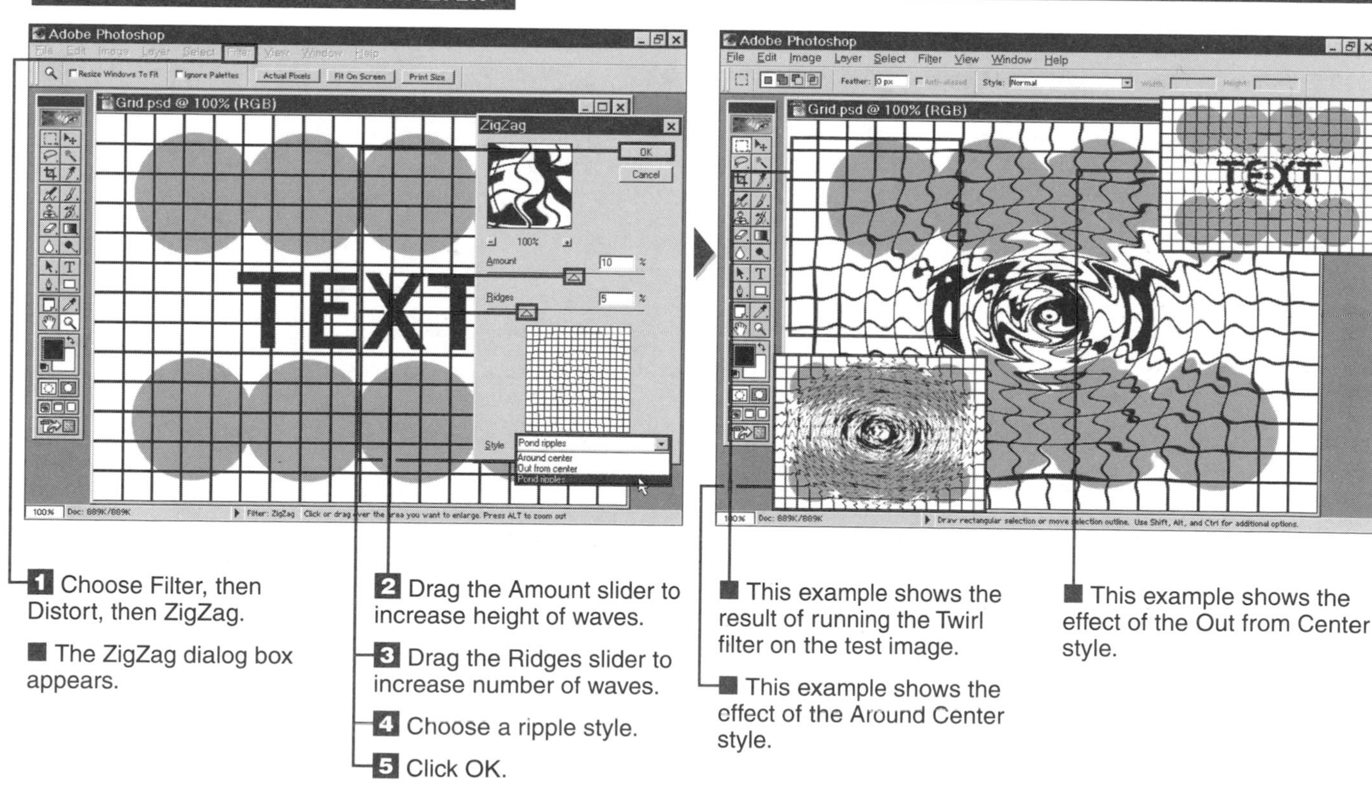

1 Choose Filter, then Distort, then ZigZag.

■ The ZigZag dialog box appears.

2 Drag the Amount slider to increase height of waves.

3 Drag the Ridges slider to increase number of waves.

4 Choose a ripple style.

5 Click OK.

■ This example shows the result of running the Twirl filter on the test image.

■ This example shows the effect of the Around Center style.

■ This example shows the effect of the Out from Center style.

APPLY THE ADD NOISE FILTER

You can use the Add Noise filter to granulate an image regardless of the image's content. In fact, you can create textures by adding grain to a solid-color image and then use other filters to smear, enlarge, or move it.

In the Distribution area of the Add Noise filter dialog box, you can add grain in a uniform pattern (by clicking Uniform) or have it clump according to highlights and shadows (Gaussian), simulating the grain of photographic emulsions. Leaving the Monochromatic check box blank tells the filter to work in color; checking it switches the appearance (but not the Color mode) of the image to monochrome.

The Add Noise filter is an excellent choice—along with the Film Grain filter and the Grain filter (see Chapters 14 and 15)—for helping you match the grain pattern in an image after another image is composited into it. For example, if you are creating a new background for a subject that is quite granular, experiment with the Add Noise filter on the background.

This method works especially well when applied to solid colors. You will also want to match grain patterns with this filter after using any of the blur filters.

APPLY THE ADD NOISE FILTER

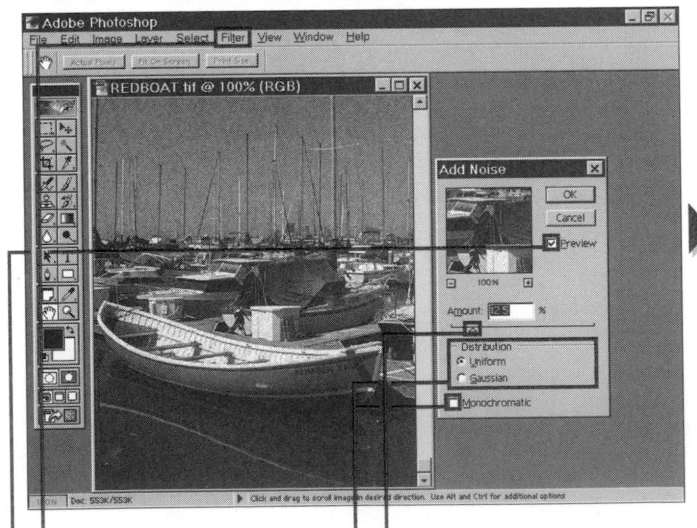

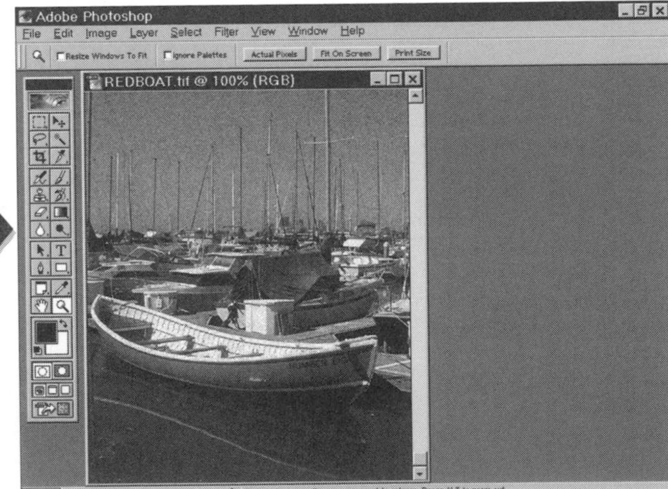

1 Choose Filter, then Noise, then Add Noise.

■ The Add Noise dialog box appears.

2 Check the Preview box to preview all changes in the work area.

3 Drag to increase or decrease graininess.

4 Click to choose between even and random grain distribution.

5 Check only to render image as grayscale.

6 When you like the effect created by the changes, click OK.

■ The result appears in the window. This example shows the result of using the default settings in the Add Noise filter dialog box.

APPLY THE DESPECKLE FILTER

You primarily use the Despeckle filter to get rid of those unsightly oil-slick patterns that often appear when you scan an already published image.

This pattern (called a *moiré pattern* in technospeak) occurs because the position and size of the dots in the halftone pattern of the printed image are out-of-register with the dots (pixels) that make up the digitized image.

Think of the Despeckle filter as more or less the opposite of the Add Noise filter (see previous page). Used judiciously, the Despeckle filter can soften or eliminate harsh details brought out in a scan or by applying an Unsharp Mask.

The Despeckle filter has no adjustments or controls, thus it does not have a dialog box. You simply choose Filter, then Noise, then Despeckle. If the filter does not remove all the noise the first time, run it again. Run it too many times, and the image will become fuzzier and fuzzier.

Careful: If you run the Unsharp Mask filters to cure the softness, you might get the moiré pattern back.

APPLY THE DESPECKLE FILTER

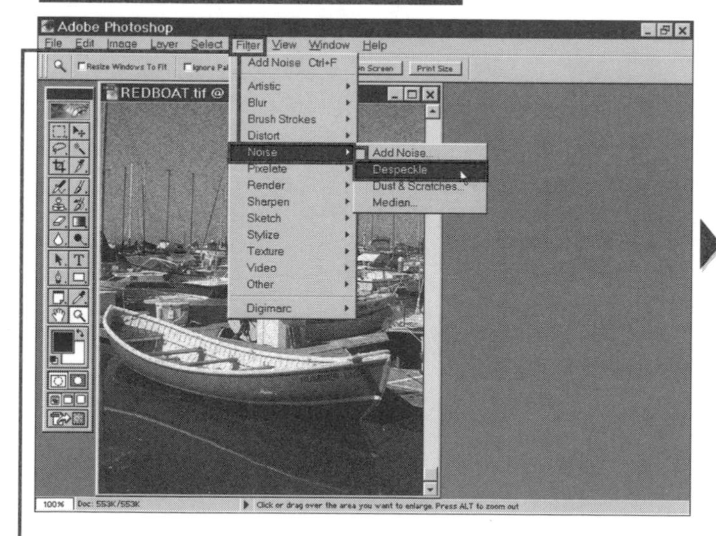

1 Choose Filter, then Noise, then Despeckle.

■ The pattern, or most of it, disappears.

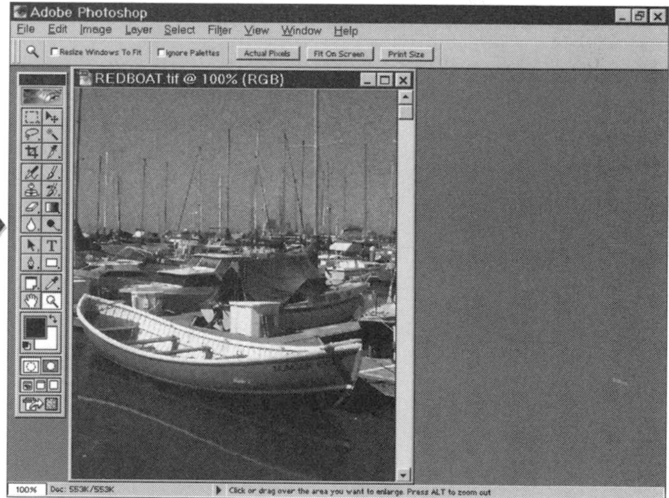

■ This example shows the result of running the Despeckle filter on the image from the previous exercise after it had been speckled by Add Noise.

APPLY THE DUST & SCRATCHES FILTER

You can perform automated retouching with the Dust & Scratches filter — sort of. The Dust & Scratches filter looks for abrupt breaks in the overall pattern of the image and blends those breaks together.

You can use the filter on the overall image, but it is likely to blur unpredictably in areas of the image. The filter can also be used on selections, just not an entire image. For example, you might want clean up a dirty background of an old photo without losing the clarity of the subject.

The Dust & Scratches filter dialog box contains a Preview check box and slider controls for Radius and Threshold. Radius determines the maximum width of a spot or scratch that Photoshop will consider repairing. Increase this setting too much, and the whole picture will appear fuzzy. Threshold determines degree of contrast between defects and surrounding pixels that must exist before Photoshop will attempt a repair. Check the Preview box if you want the results of your settings to simultaneously appear in the active workspace.

Note that you can use Dust & Scratches on an image that has no blemishes to produce a *chiaroscuro* (Rembrandt-like) effect, where highlights spread into shadows.

APPLY THE DUST & SCRATCHES FILTER

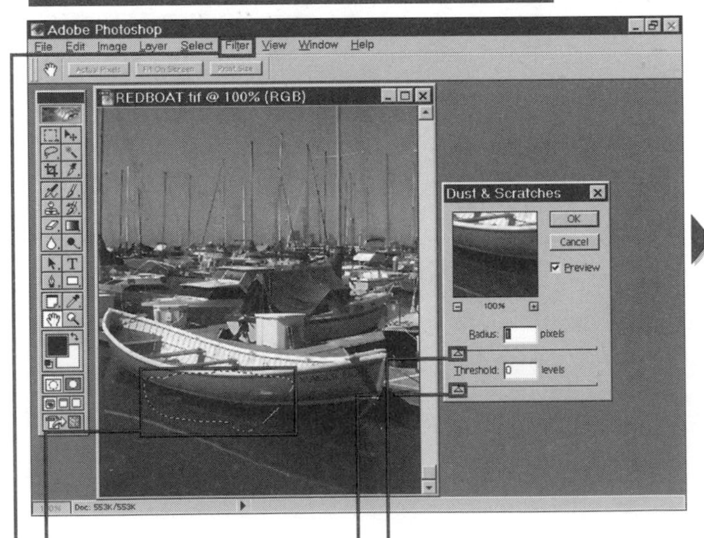

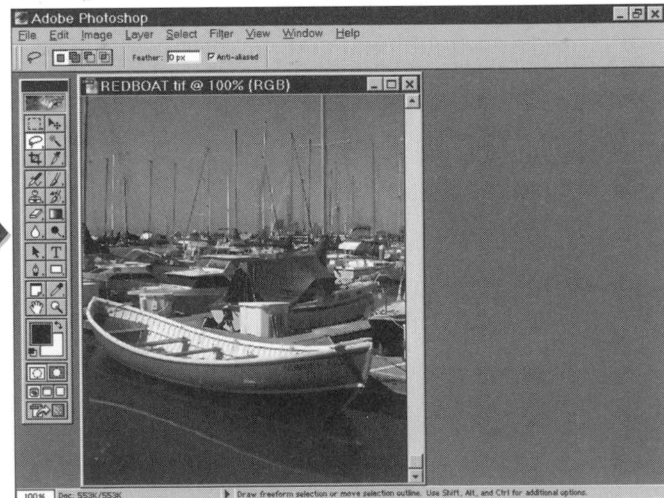

1 Select the area(s) that need repair.

2 Choose Filter, then Noise, then Dust & Scratches.

■ The Dust & Scratches dialog box appears.

3 Drag to increase radius of defects to be mended.

4 Drag to indicate contrast between pixels that must exist before Photoshop will consider a repair.

5 When you like the effect created by the changes, click OK.

■ The result appears in the window. This example shows the result of running the Dust & Scratches filter on an intentionally scratched, dust-laden image.

APPLY THE COLOR HALFTONE FILTER

You can use the Color Halftone filter as a pop-art effects filter, but the filter is not actually usable for making color-separation halftones for color printing. The Color Halftone filter simulates the effect of using an enlarged halftone screen on all image channels. Photoshop does have the capability to do true halftones, but first you need to make the separations and then make a grayscale halftone screen for each separation.

The Color Halftone filter divides the image into dots that you can exaggerate to your liking. There are five controls, one to specify dot size and one each for screen angles (the angle at which the rows of dots appear in the pattern) for Channels 1 through 4. The settings you use will depend on the overall size of your image and the size at which it will be reproduced. The filter does not have a Preview box.

Be careful about using this filter on images that are to be reproduced by halftone printing methods. If the dots are too small, two out-of-register dot patterns could end up creating a moiré pattern. The bigger the dots in the Color Halftone effect, the safer you will be.

APPLY THE COLOR HALFTONE FILTER

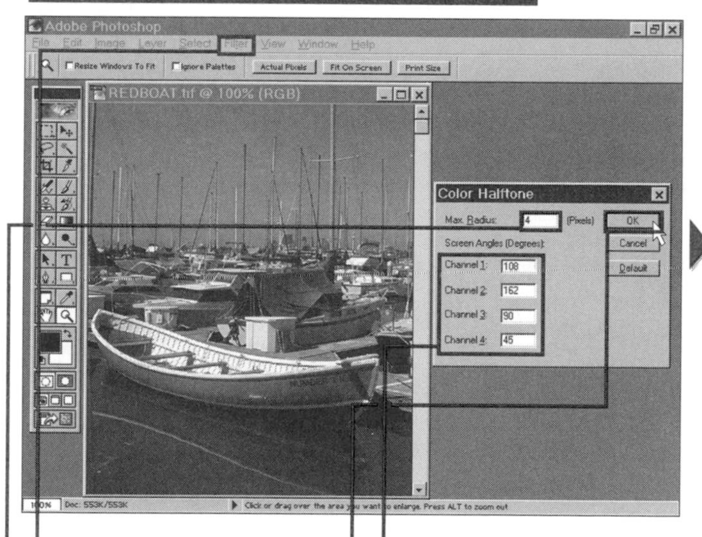

1 Choose Filter, then Pixelate, then Color Halftone.

■ The Color Halftone dialog box appears.

2 Type the radius of the largest dot in number of pixels.

3 Type a screen angle for all four channels, even if you are in RGB mode.

4 Click OK to render.

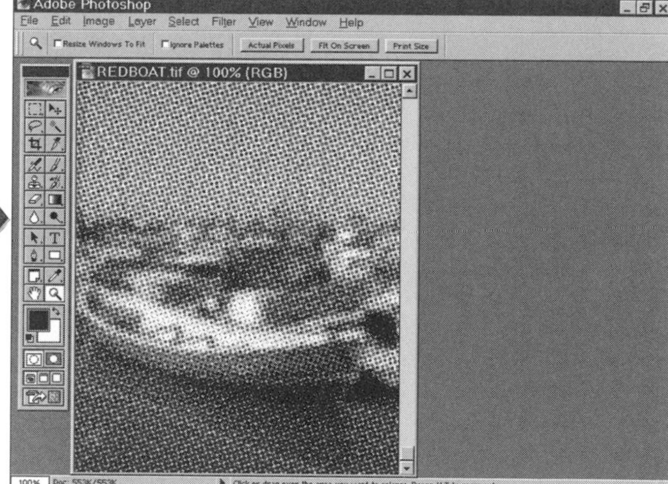

■ Here is the result of running the filter on the test image with a Maximum Radius of 4 pixels.

Note: The default screen angles usually give the best results, so start by changing the Maximum Radius (dot size) to suit the size of the image you are working on and the effect you want.

APPLY THE CRYSTALLIZE FILTER

You can simulate a variation on Pointillist expressionism with the Crystallize filter if you apply it to a whole image, as shown in the example on this page.

This filter (which you get to by choosing Filter, then Pixelate, then Crystallize) averages pixels into irregular solid-color polygons. The effect is due to a reduction of colors and is a form of blurring.

Only one control appears in the Crystallize filter dialog box—a slider that dictates the size of the polygonal crystals (cells). For images with lots of fine details, crystals that are too large can render them unrecognizable.

If you drag the slider far enough to the right, you get a stained glass effect, with no leading between the panes, and a more random-appearing scattering of colors.

By making careful masks for different sections of a scene, you can use the Crystallize filter to simulate moisture on a pane of glass. You will want to make the crystals vary in size and transparency and keep the crystal size relatively small overall.

APPLY THE CRYSTALLIZE FILTER

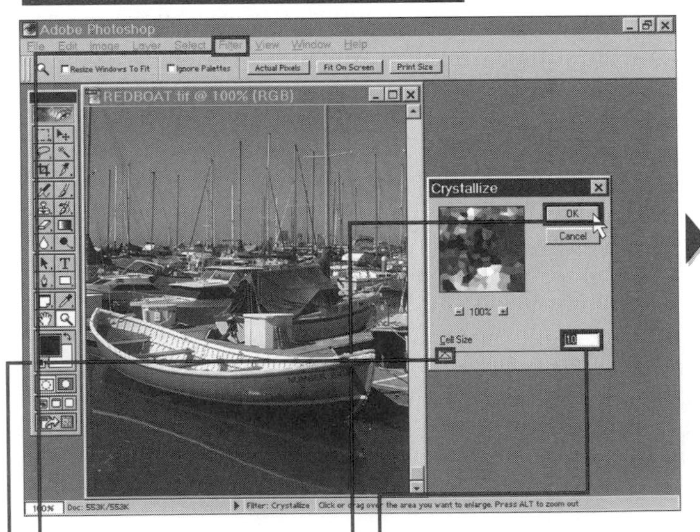

1 Choose Filter, then Pixelate, then Crystallize.

■ The Crystallize dialog box appears.

2 Drag to reduce or enlarge the size of the crystals.

■ Alternatively, type a number of pixels to indicate each crystal's size.

Note: A cell size of 3 is the smallest number that has any effect.

3 Click OK to render.

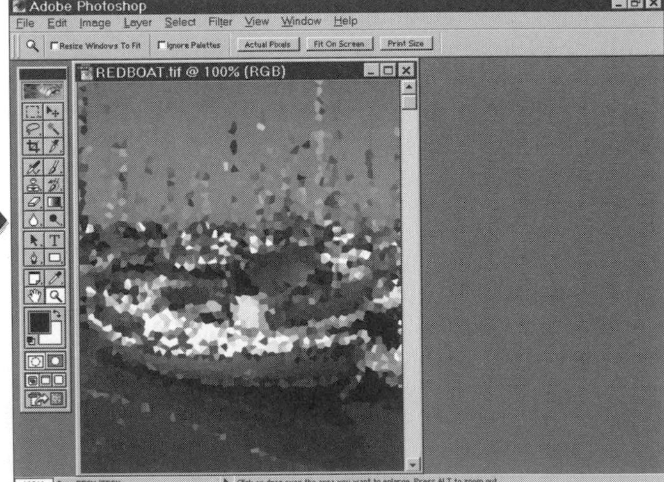

■ This example is the result of running the filter on the test image at the default settings.

Note: If you make the crystals large, you can produce a nice palette knife effect — especially if you then texturize the image by using Lighting Effects and one of the color channels as a texture map.

APPLY THE FACET FILTER

You can flatten colors with the Facet filter and remove anti-aliasing from edges, making them more jagged.

You can use this filter to make a scanned image look hand painted, or to make a realistic image resemble an abstract painting.

The Facet filter is a single-step filter with no adjustments, thus the filter has no dialog box. In addition, the effect of the Facet filter is so subtle that you may think that nothing has happened.

The Facet filter is a good filter to run on images you want to paint over in a natural-media program, such as Corel's Painter and Painter Classic. Put the result into one of these programs and then use a brush that moves the existing paint, such as the Palette knife or Turpentine brush.

You may actually want to reverse the anti-aliased look of text that has already rendered. Try the Facet filter on an image with large, smooth text that has been saved in the JPEG format. You will make that image less refined-looking.

APPLY THE FACET FILTER

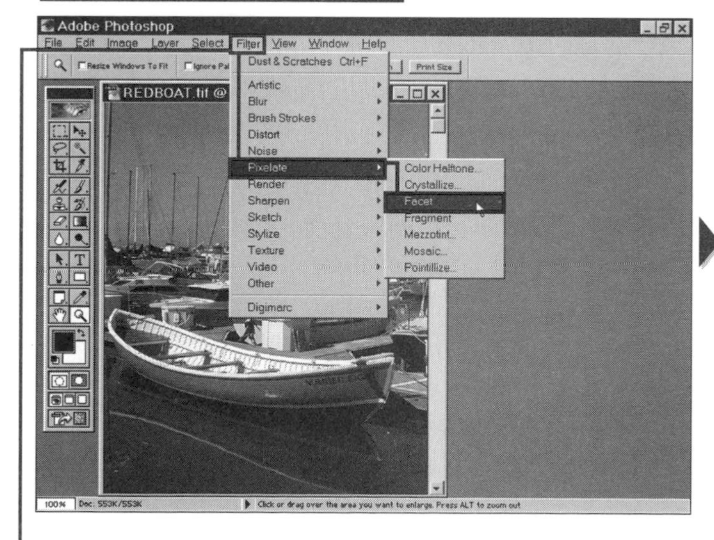

1 Choose Filter, then Pixelate, then Facet.

■ The progress meter runs for a moment (unless you are running a fast Pentium II/III or G3/G4 processor), and then the image changes very slightly.

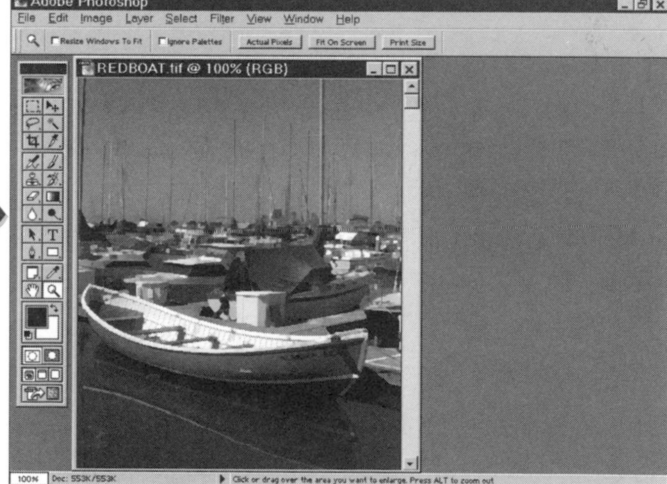

■ Here is the test image after running the Facet filter on it. You have to look carefully to notice much of a difference.

Note: You can magnify the effect of this filter by running it several times. Press /Ctrl+F until you get the result you want.

APPLY THE FRAGMENT FILTER

You can find something to do with the Fragment filter, another one-step Pixelate filter, but it requires a little imagination to find a use for it. The filter causes an image to blur and its elements to duplicate and offset just subtly enough that you will think that you need new glasses.

Indeed, you can bet that more than a few businesses, from optician's offices to high-pressure insurance agencies, have used this filter to generate advertisements. This one-trick pony probably works fine for newspaper ads or throwaway ad flyers.

The Fragment filter does not have any options to control, thus it has no dialog box. Just choose it from the menu, and your image is modified immediately.

One option that you might try is to see whether this filter works best with all or just a portion of your image. If the image below were an illustration of an earthquake, a clear sky as a background would work better than clouds, because the sky would not shake.

APPLY THE FRAGMENT FILTER

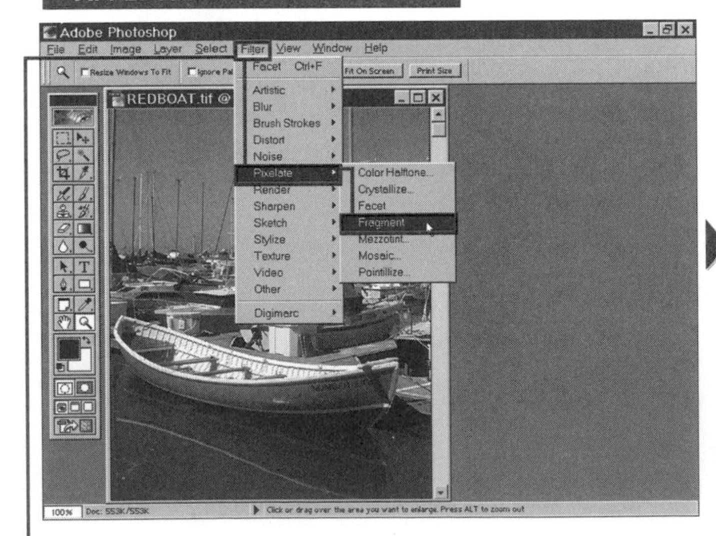

1 Choose Filter, then Pixelate, then Fragment.

■ The progress meter runs for a moment (unless you are running a fast Pentium II/III or G3/G4 processor) and then the image changes very slightly.

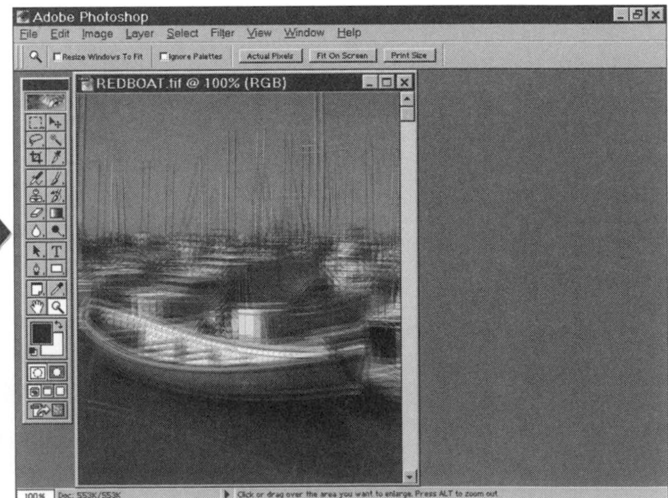

■ Here is the result of running the Fragment filter.

Note: You might use this as a background for earth-shaking news or as a prelude to the coming of Godzilla.

APPLY THE MEZZOTINT FILTER

A *mezzotint* is a halftone pattern created by replacing dots with enlarged versions or with short lines and strokes. Using the Mezzotint filter, you can embellish your image with up to ten dot, line, or stroke variations.

The variations are accessible through the Type menu on the Mezzotint filter dialog box. The options include

- Fine, medium, grainy, or coarse dots
- Short, medium, or long lines
- Short, medium, or long strokes

As you can see in the illustration below, the different types of options can yield dramatically different effects on an image. Are you looking to keep some clarity in your picture, or do you want to just fuzz-tone everything to the point of abstraction? Also, do not forget to try this filter on selections, not just the entire image.

One note about the Mezzotint filter dialog box: The preview area on the dialog box is unusually large and cannot be moved from its position in the middle of your image.

The Mezzotint filter can be of great use in creating texture patterns. See "Create a Texture with the Mezzotint Filter," next in this chapter, for more information.

APPLY THE MEZZOTINT FILTER

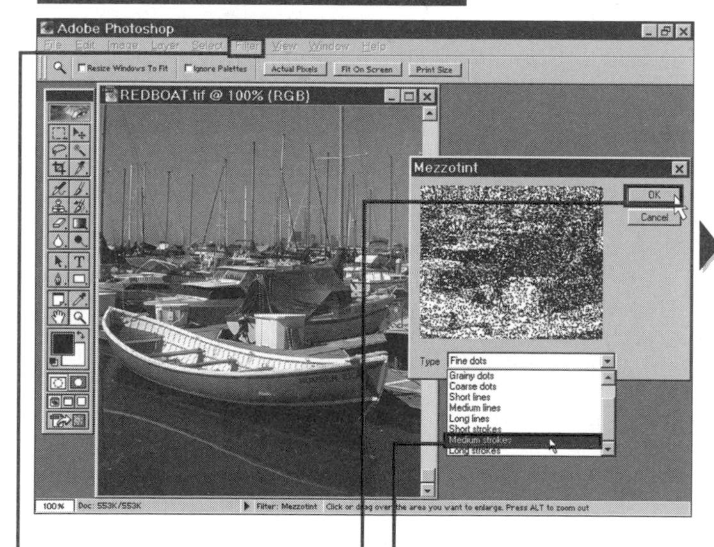

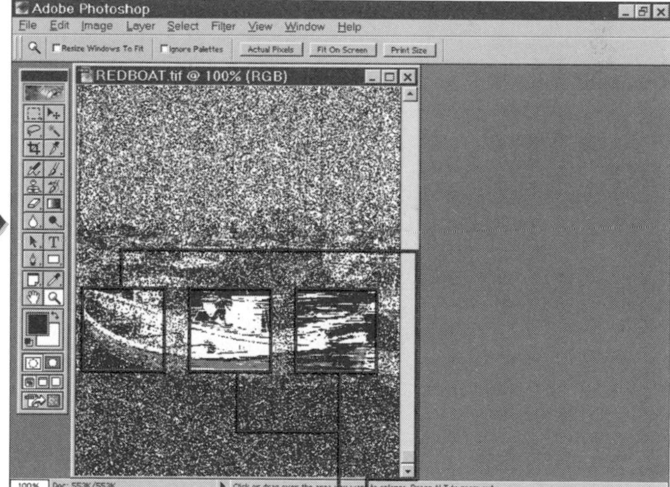

1 Choose Filter, then Pixelate, then Mezzotint.

■ The Mezzotint dialog box appears.

2 Choose a mezzotint pattern.

3 Click OK.

■ The image reflects the desired selection.

■ This example shows the result of running the Mezzotint filter at the Fine dots setting.

■ The result of specifying Medium dots.

■ The result of specifying Medium lines.

■ The result of specifying Medium strokes.

CREATE A TEXTURE WITH THE MEZZOTINT FILTER

You can make any image grainy with the Mezzotint filter—even one that is a solid color. This capability makes the Mezzotint filter ideal for use as a texture pattern maker.

You can further modify the grain patterns with Photoshop's built-in blur and distortion filters and then make multiple copies of layers and blend them to get a final texture. In other words, use the Mezzotint filter as just one step in the process of creating new textures. After all, this is the beauty of Photoshop—combining and mixing.

The steps to create a texture with the Mezzotint filter are shown in this section, but you can repeat any of these steps in any combination to make an infinite number of texture patterns. These patterns are especially useful as an easy way to create natural-looking textures that mimic things, such as hand-made papers, concrete, newsprint, and watercolor paper.

You can get many pre-made textures from Adobe or via download from other sources, but you may be just fussy enough to want to create some yourself.

CREATE A TEXTURE WITH THE MEZZOTINT FILTER

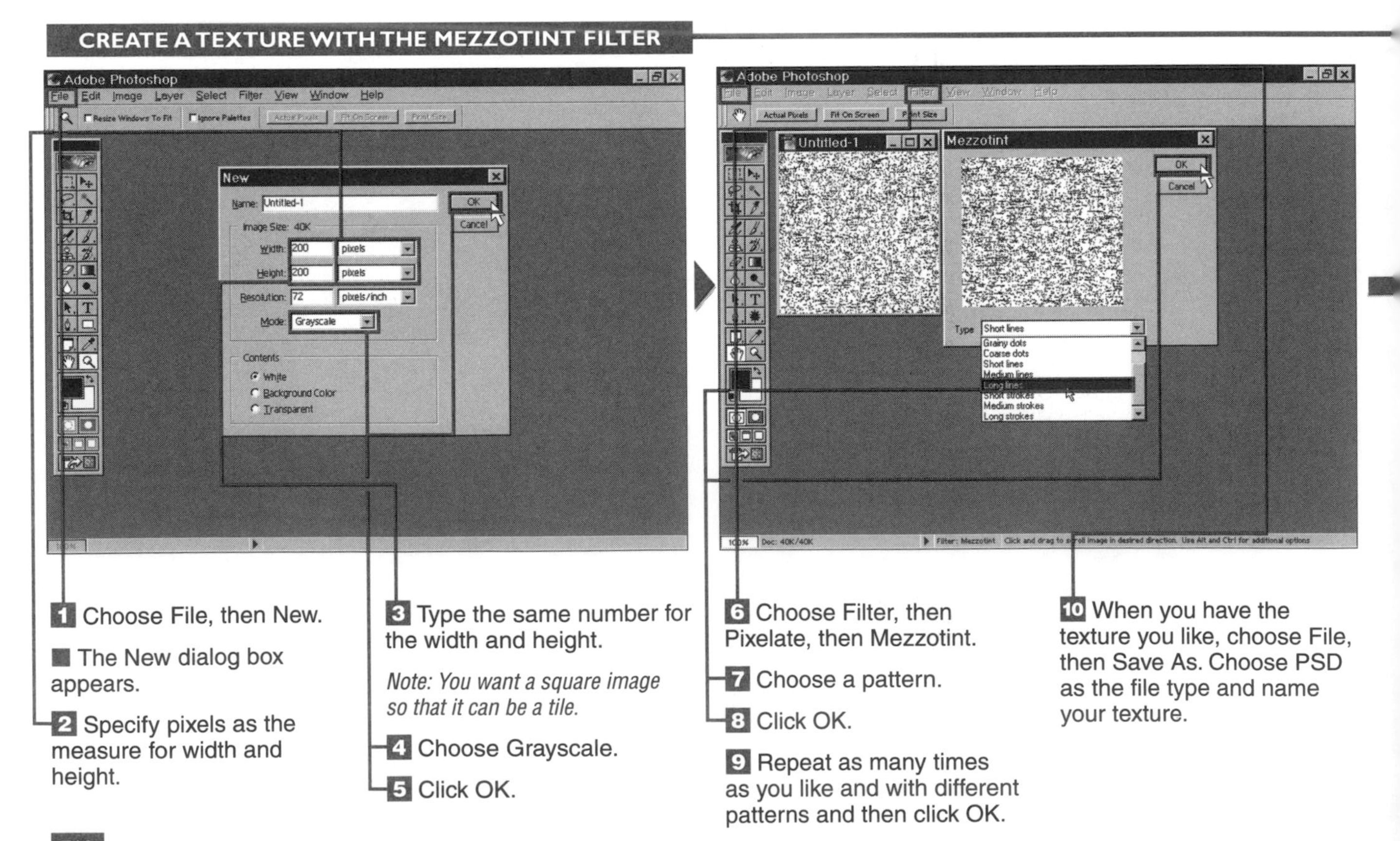

1 Choose File, then New.

■ The New dialog box appears.

2 Specify pixels as the measure for width and height.

3 Type the same number for the width and height.

Note: You want a square image so that it can be a tile.

4 Choose Grayscale.

5 Click OK.

6 Choose Filter, then Pixelate, then Mezzotint.

7 Choose a pattern.

8 Click OK.

9 Repeat as many times as you like and with different patterns and then click OK.

10 When you have the texture you like, choose File, then Save As. Choose PSD as the file type and name your texture.

Is there any way to make a texture that uses more than one of the Mezzotint effects?

✔ Duplicate the unfiltered background layer once for each effect you want to create. Apply a different effect to each layer. Use the transparency slider in the layer's palette to adjust the transparency for each layer. Apply distortion effects to each layer or wait until you have flattened the entire file. After flattening, you may want to use the Threshold filter to boost contrast. Finally, make a seamless tile of the texture (or make the texture big enough to cover an entire image or selection).

Are any particular distortion filters more useful for making textures?

✔ The Diffuse Glow filter is excellent for softening the edges of the Mezzotint patterns so you can get more natural-looking paper and marble textures. Also, the Glass filter is good for adding random streaks that look like paper fibers. From the right source, the Wave filter can give a texture that looks like chain-link fence. See Chapter 16 for more on the Diffuse Glow and Glass filters.

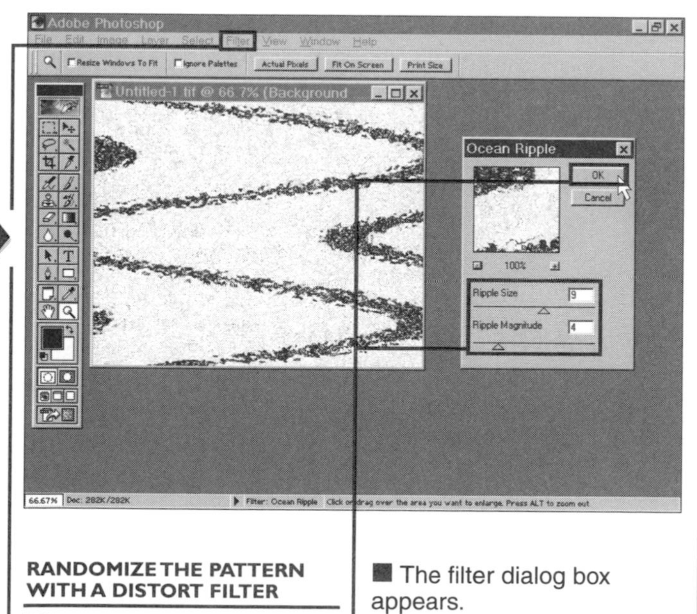

RANDOMIZE THE PATTERN WITH A DISTORT FILTER

1 Choose Filter, then Distort, then whichever Distort filter you want to use.

■ The filter dialog box appears.

2 Adjust controls.

3 Click OK.

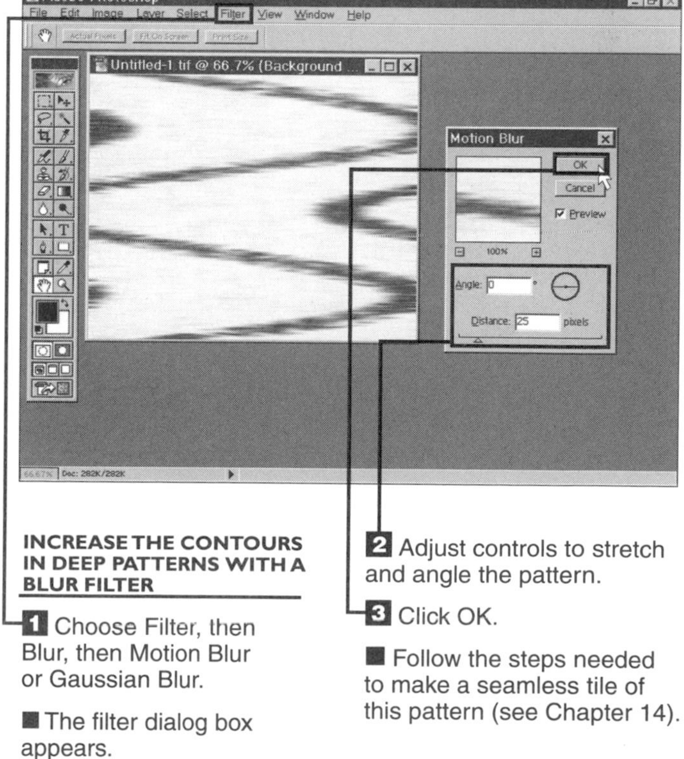

INCREASE THE CONTOURS IN DEEP PATTERNS WITH A BLUR FILTER

1 Choose Filter, then Blur, then Motion Blur or Gaussian Blur.

■ The filter dialog box appears.

2 Adjust controls to stretch and angle the pattern.

3 Click OK.

■ Follow the steps needed to make a seamless tile of this pattern (see Chapter 14).

APPLY THE POINTILLIZE FILTER

The Pointillize filter can help you do a fairly credible job of turning your image into a pointillist painting.

You can do this more effectively by running the filter so that the dots, or points of paint, vary in size from one area of the image to another. Also, the space between the dots will be in the current background color. You may want one space color for some areas of the image and another for other areas of the image.

The Pointillize filter dialog box has a single control for the size of the dot. The dialog box does not contain a Preview check box.

Try duplicating the layer on which you want to use the Pointillize filter. Run the same filter on the new layer, using white as the background color. Use the Underpainting filter on the underlying layer. Next, make the background color transparent by selecting white with the Color Range command on the Select menu and pressing Backspace/Delete. The Underpainted layer will now show through.

APPLY THE POINTILLIZE FILTER

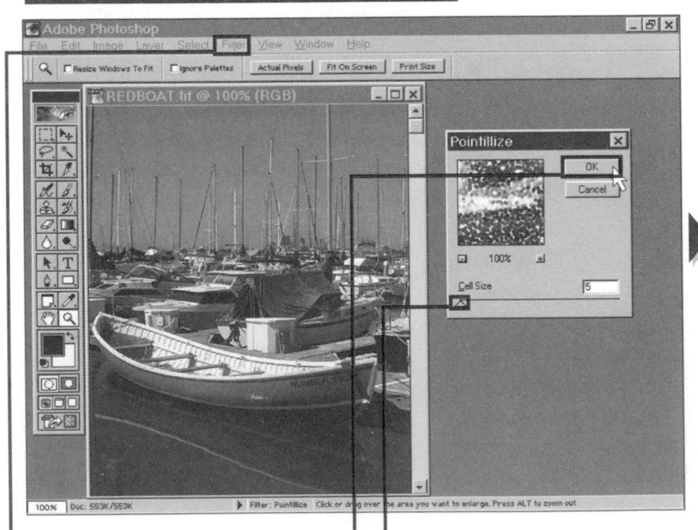

1 Choose Filter, then Pixelate, then Pointillize.

■ The Pointillize dialog box appears.

2 Drag to set the size of a color dot.

3 Click OK.

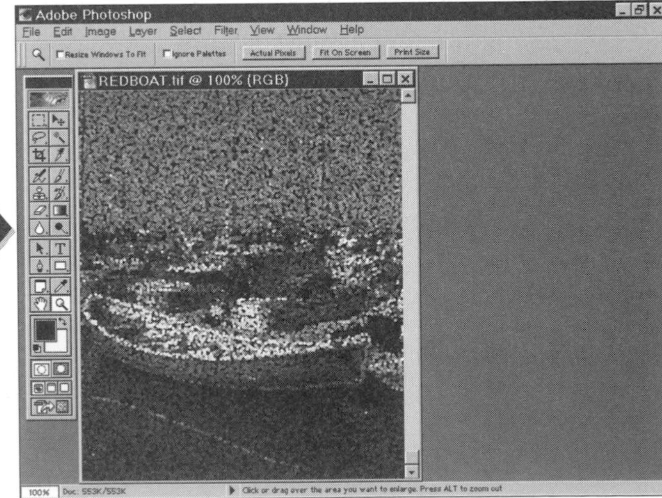

■ The effect appears. Here is the result of running the Pointillize filter at a Cell Size set to 5.

APPLY THE DIFFUSE FILTER

You can make an image look as if it were sprayed with paint from an aerosol can by using the Diffuse filter, which results in a diffused grainy effect.

This filter has little effect on solid colors or smooth gradients, so, for example, blue sky backgrounds will remain relatively unchanged, compared to the subject in the foreground.

If you are seeking a more photographic graininess, do not use this filter — the Film Grain filter is what you want. (See Chapters 14 and 15 for details.)

The Diffuse filter dialog box does not contain slider controls for modifying the size of the effect in relationship to the resolution of the image. Instead, three radio buttons enable you to choose between three variations of the effect: Normal, Darken only, and Lighten only. With the hand cursor, move your image around in the preview area.

You may not like the effect on your whole image of just one of these radio button options. Try the different settings on duplicate layers, then blend the layers to your liking.

APPLY THE DIFFUSE FILTER

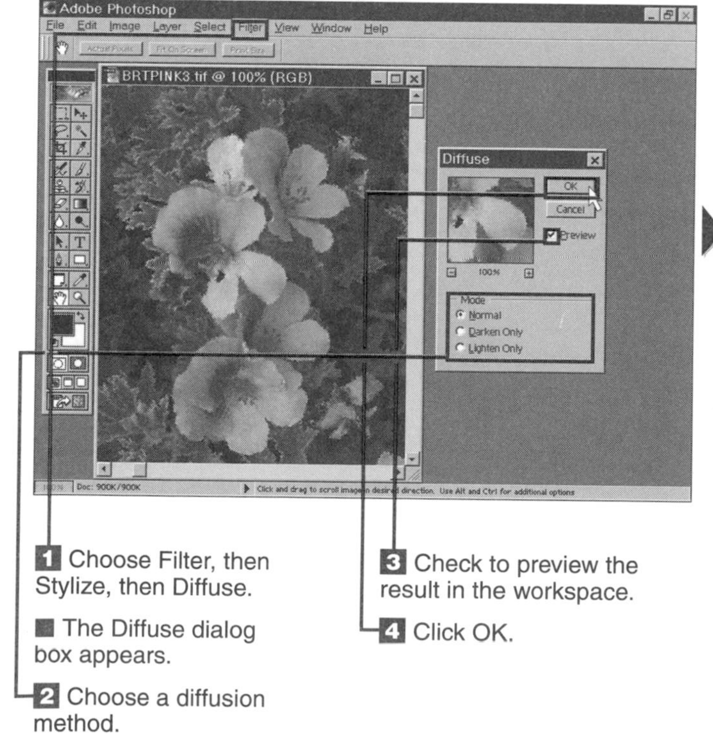

1 Choose Filter, then Stylize, then Diffuse.

■ The Diffuse dialog box appears.

2 Choose a diffusion method.

3 Check to preview the result in the workspace.

4 Click OK.

■ The effect appears. This example shows the result of running the Diffuse filter in Normal mode.

■ This result shows the Darken Only mode.

■ This result shows the Lighten Only mode.

APPLY THE EMBOSS FILTER

You can create a monochrome image with the Emboss filter that looks as if the elements in the image are stamped into paper—similar to embossed stationery.

The Emboss filter dialog box has a Preview check box and three settings:

- Angle refers to the apparent lighting angle.
- Height controls the depth of the most prominent edges in the image.
- Amount refers to the amount of detail that will be shown between the most contrasting edges.

You will see some color in the image if you move the settings to their upper limits and if you have a very colorful subject.

Emboss is an excellent filter to use as a texture map. The Emboss filter always produces grayscale tones, but you still have to choose Image, then Mode, then Grayscale, and then save the result in Photoshop (PSD) format. You can also duplicate the layer, use the Emboss filter on the underlying layer, and then use a Blend mode for a different kind of 3D effect.

APPLY THE EMBOSS FILTER

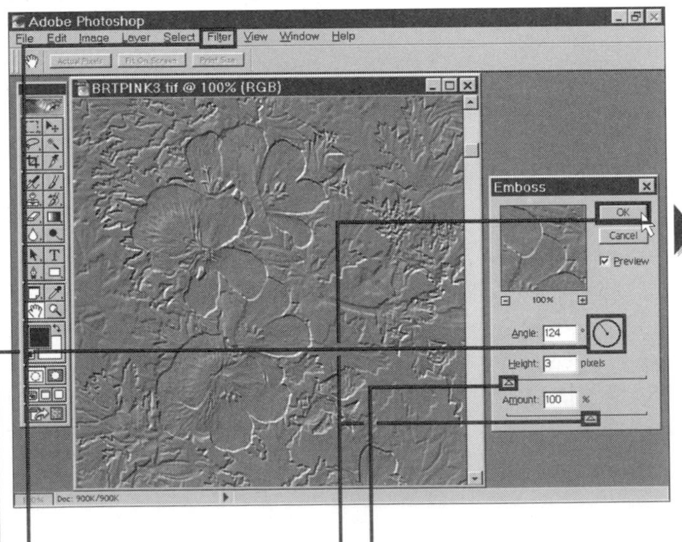

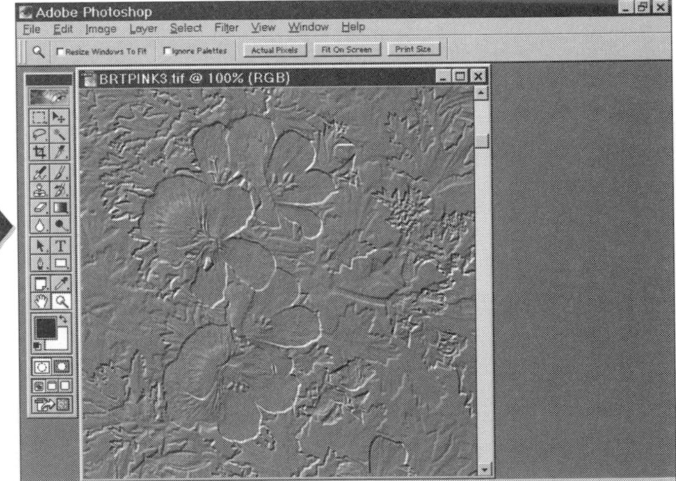

1 Choose Filter, then Stylize, then Emboss.

■ The Emboss dialog box appears. Any changes appear in the image as you make them.

2 Drag to set the angle of lighting.

3 Drag to make major edges cast deeper shadows.

4 Drag to increase amount of detail.

5 Click OK.

■ Here is the result of running the Emboss filter.

Note: The actual image updates while the dialog box is up.

APPLY THE EXTRUDE FILTER

You can make your image look like it has been glued to raised blocks with the Extrude filter. You can also use the Extrude filter to convert the image to solid-color 3D blocks or pyramids. Like most of the built-in Photoshop filters, Extrude makes the changes visible in the image while its dialog box is open.

The Extrude filter dialog box has no sliders, but it contains two entry fields, two pairs of radio buttons, and two check boxes. The Type control features a pair of radio buttons with which you can choose between square blocks or four-sided pyramids. You can enter the size of a block or pyramid as a number of pixels. You can also specify the depth, but then the depth of individual0 squares can be either based on color level or randomly assigned, depending on which radio button you choose.

Checking Solid Front Faces makes the face of each block a solid color (kind of like using the Mosaic filter at a large size). Checking Mask Incomplete Blocks drops any blocks that cannot be completed because of their proximity to the edge.

APPLY THE EXTRUDE FILTER

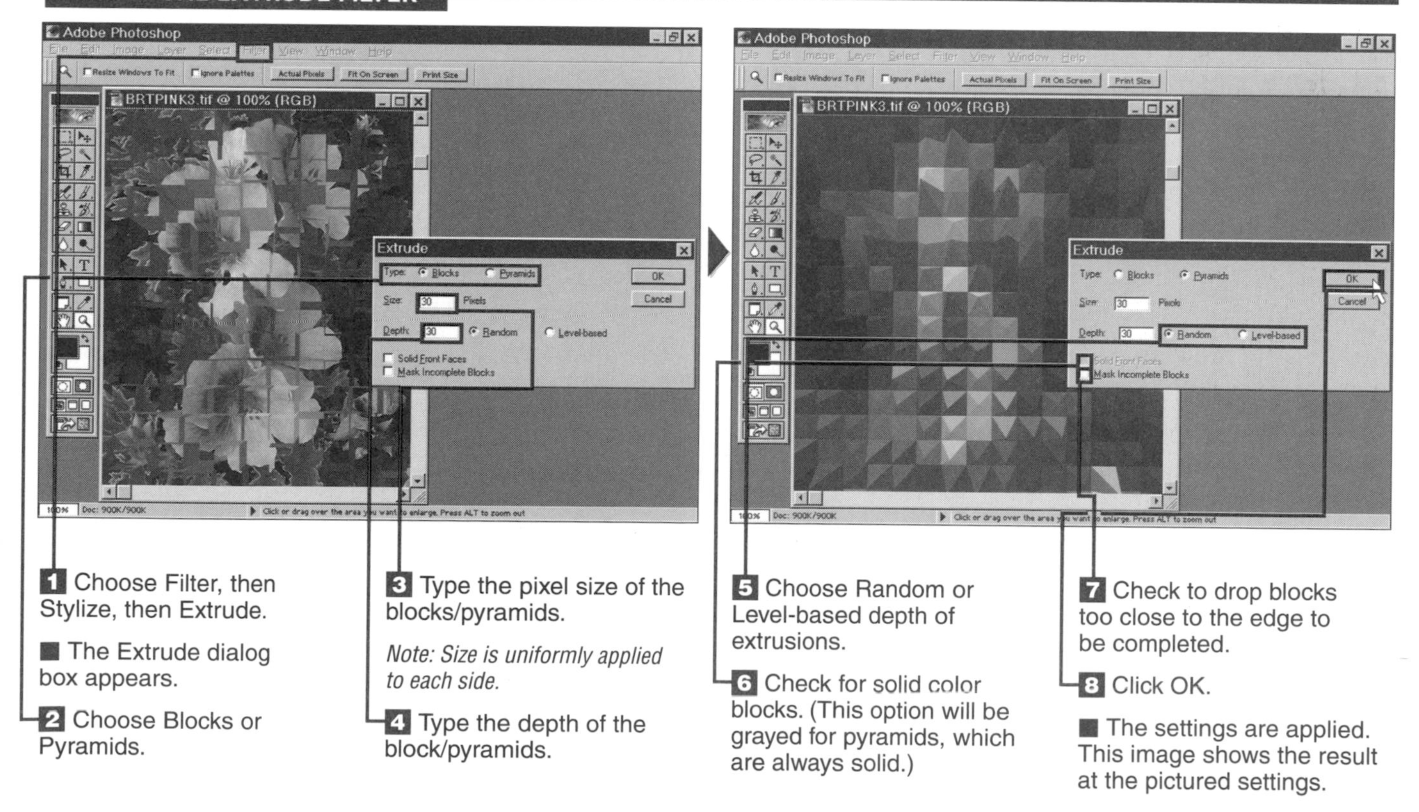

1 Choose Filter, then Stylize, then Extrude.

■ The Extrude dialog box appears.

2 Choose Blocks or Pyramids.

3 Type the pixel size of the blocks/pyramids.

Note: Size is uniformly applied to each side.

4 Type the depth of the block/pyramids.

5 Choose Random or Level-based depth of extrusions.

6 Check for solid color blocks. (This option will be grayed for pyramids, which are always solid.)

7 Check to drop blocks too close to the edge to be completed.

8 Click OK.

■ The settings are applied. This image shows the result at the pictured settings.

APPLY THE FIND EDGES FILTER

With the Find Edges filter, you can accentuate the edges of the pixels in an image. The Find Edges filter traces contrasting edges with a dark line and converts all the other shades in the image to a highlighted pastel of whatever was the image's former color. The filter causes low-contrast areas of an image to appear white, medium-contrast areas to appear gray, and high-contrast areas to appear black.

The Find Edges filter does not have settings controls and is fully automatic.

The Find Edges filter is both a fun filter and one that can yield terrific illustrations from photographs. Because this filter essentially outlines in color every edge, you are left with all the major shapes in an image, minus the small details.

Try this filter on a photo of a harbor filled with boats or on a shot of a crowded city sidewalk with lots of strong light and shadow. With the details of all objects (boats, people) removed, the result is a much greater focus on the first, overall impression that you want the image to give the viewer, rather than on tiny details.

APPLY THE FIND EDGES FILTER

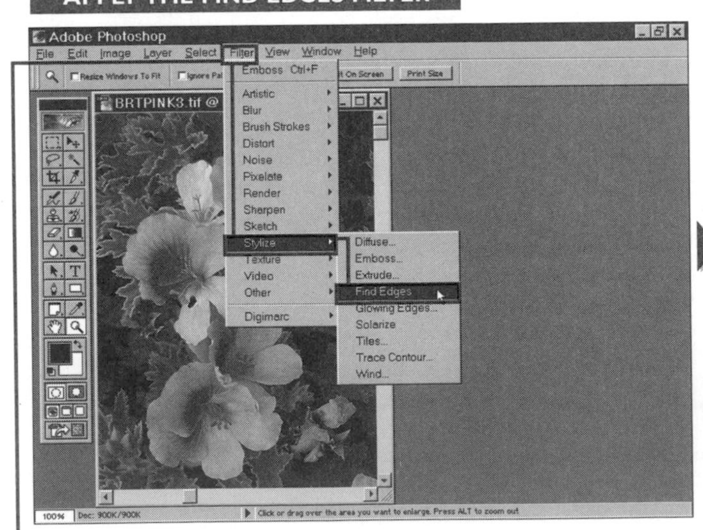

1 Choose Filter, then Stylize, then Find Edges.

■ After rendering, something similar to the effect shown here appears.

APPLY THE GLOWING EDGES FILTER

You can trace contrasting edges with a bright line and convert all the other shades in the image to a charcoal color with the Glowing Edges filter.

The Glowing Edges filter dialog box has three controls:

- Edge Width does the expected, setting the span of the edges between strongly contrasting colors.
- Edge Brightness is less obvious because the brighter the edge, the wider.
- Smoothness controls how sharp or blurred the line forming the edge will be.

You should adjust these three controls together, because one can alter the effect of the others. If you are experimenting, writing down the number settings each time you use the filter is a good idea.

If you want more control over the effects of the Find Edges filter (discussed in the previous exercise), use Glowing Edges. After using Glowing Edges, press ⌘/Ctrl+I to invert the image. Also, try duplicating the layer, running Glowing Edges on both, and then inverting the top layer. Afterward, use the Hard Light Blend mode on the top layer.

APPLY THE GLOWING EDGES FILTER

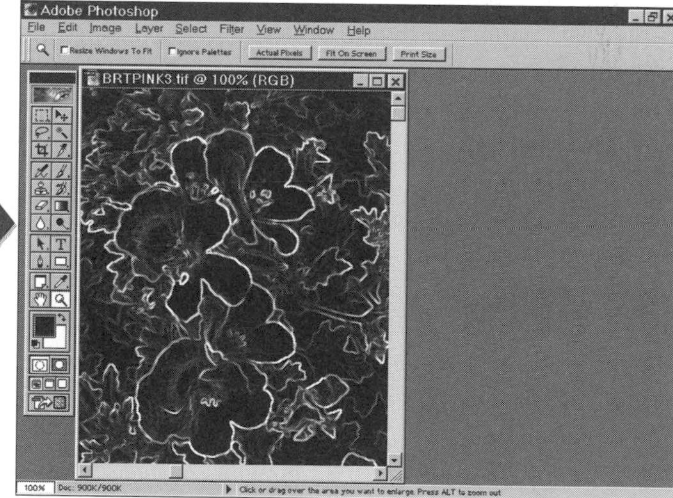

1 Choose Filter, then Stylize, then Glowing Edges.

■ The Glowing Edges dialog box appears.

2 Drag to determine the broadness of the edges.

3 Drag to determine the brightness of the edges (the brighter, the broader).

4 Drag to determine the smoothness of the edges.

5 Click OK.

■ The designated effect appears.

APPLY THE SOLARIZE FILTER

If you are familiar with traditional chemical darkroom techniques, you know that solarization results when an image is exposed to light during the developing process. This technique causes the undeveloped portion of the image to invert so that the image is half normal, half negative, or somehere in between. With Photoshop 6, you can use the Solarize filter to produce an effect similar to this process, achieving in seconds what photographers used to spend hours doing in darkrooms.

The Solarize filter is an automatic filter, meaning it does not have a dialog box for specifying settings. Although the Solarize filter is automatic, you can temper its effect by using it on a duplicate layer, putting the unchanged, original layer on top of the solarized layer, then adjusting the opacity of the original layer with the slide bar.

You can get a much more dramatic effect by choosing Image, then Adjust, then Auto Levels immediately after running the Solarize filter. Solarization can also be interesting when used to texturize the original image.

APPLY THE SOLARIZE FILTER

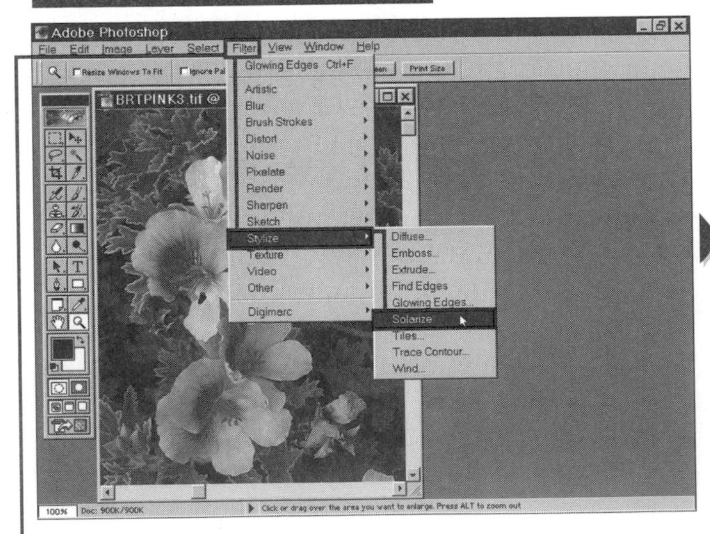

1 Choose Filter, then Stylize, then Solarize.

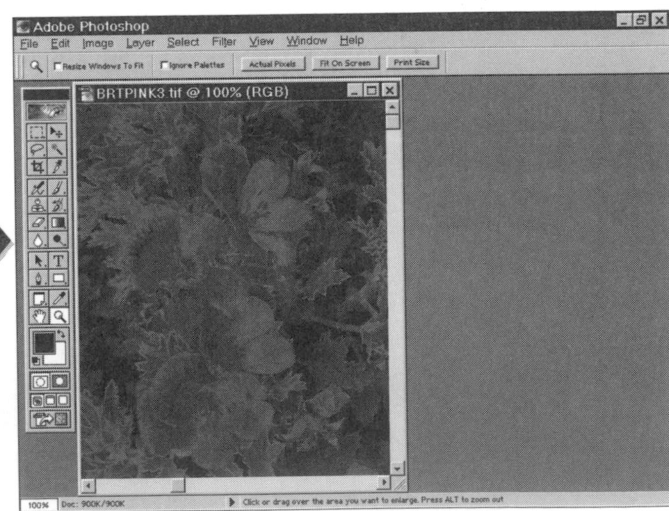

■ The result of running the Solarize filter appears.

APPLY THE TILES FILTER

You can, with the Tiles filter, produce an effect that looks similiar to a mosaic, dividing the image into somewhat irregular square tiles. The "grout" (space between the tiles) can be in the foreground or background, or can take its color from the image or the inverse of the image.

The Tiles filter dialog box, which you can access by choosing Filter, then Stylize, then Tiles, has three controls. Two entry fields let you specify the number of tiles across and the percentage of maximum offset between the tiles. The third control is a set of four radio buttons that enable you to choose how the space between tiles will be filled: Background Color, Foreground Color, Inverse Image, or Unaltered Image.

You can try making a real mosaic with solid-color tiles, by first running the Mosaic filter and then the Tiles filter. The trick is in figuring out how to make the tiles in each filter the same size. (Hint: Choose Window, then Show Info, and drag a rectangular marquee around a tile.)

APPLY THE TILES FILTER

1 Choose Filter, then Stylize, then Tiles.

■ The Tiles dialog box appears.

2 Type the desired number of tiles across the image.

3 Type a percentage of image width for maximum distance between tiles.

4 Click to choose what will fill the space between tiles.

5 Click OK.

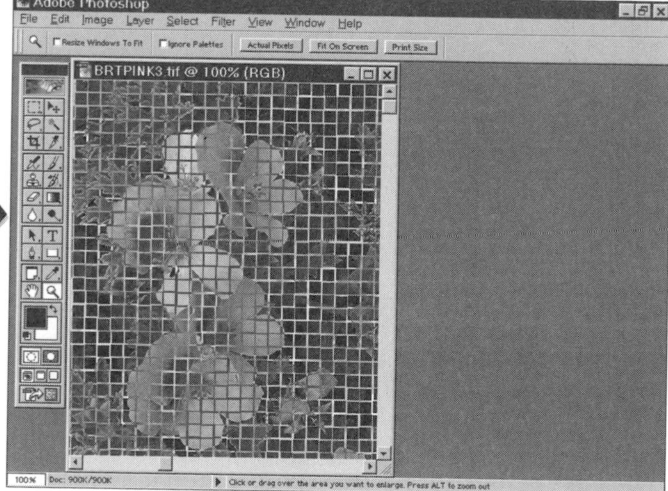

■ This result of running the Tiles filter is displayed.

APPLY THE TRACE CONTOUR FILTER

The Trace Contour filter draws a single-pixel line to trace edges and then drops out all the other colors in the image.

The Trace Contour filter dialog box, which you summon by choosing Filter, then Stylize, then Trace Contour, has a couple of controls. One is a Level slider that sets the threshold for finding an edge. Dragging this slider changes the amount of detail and influences the number of colors you see in the tracing. The pair of Edge radio buttons determine whether the edge is chosen from pixels just above or just below the threshold line.

The preview area of the dialog box can be moved around your image with the hand cursor. Just remember that if you change the adjustments to maximize what you see in the preview, those adjustments will affect the entire current selection.

You can make several duplicates of the target layer and run Trace Contour at different threshold settings on each. Next, use the Multiply Blend mode to combine all the traced edges into a more complex result.

APPLY THE TRACE CONTOUR FILTER

1 Choose Filter, then Stylize, then Trace Contour.

■ The Trace Contour dialog box opens.

2 Drag to set the edge contrast threshold level.

3 Click to choose whether the edge is determined by pixels just above or below the threshold.

4 Check to preview changes in the workspace, then click OK.

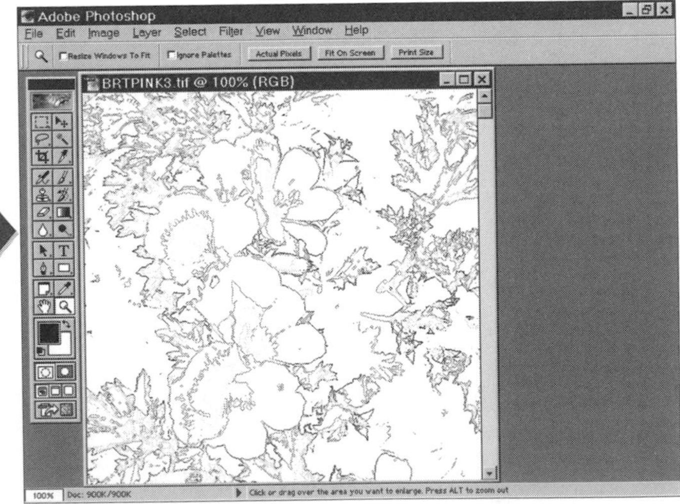

■ The result of running the Trace Contour filter appears.

APPLY THE WIND FILTER

The Wind filter is closely related to the Motion Blur filter. (Why the Wind filter is not found on the Blur Filters menu is a mystery that may haunt versions of Photoshop for years to come.) The Wind filter is more of a comic-strip motion blur, with streaked edges — at least, that is the default look. Several variations are available.

The Wind filter dialog box has two sets of radio buttons that determine the specific effect you get. The Method buttons are Wind, Blast, and Stagger. The Blast method might work for an atomic explosion type of effect, while the Stagger method almost looks like the starship *Enterprise* was beaming something up.The Direction buttons dictate whether the smears move to the left or to the right from the edge.

This filter works on all edges, especially edges that are more perpendicular to the left or right direction you set in the dialog box. The greater the contrast of an edge, the longer are the cartoonish wind streaks. Solid color or gradient backgrounds, such as skies, are not affected by the Wind filter.

APPLY THE WIND FILTER

1 Choose Filter, then Stylize, then Wind.

■ The Wind dialog box appears.

2 Choose a method (see introduction, above).

3 Choose a direction for the smear.

4 Click OK.

■ The effect of the filter settings is displayed. Notice the result of running the Wind filter at the pictured settings.

Note: Brighter edges streak farther than darker ones.

CREATE, SAVE, AND LOAD CUSTOM FILTERS

You can make and save your own filters if Photoshop does not provide one that does quite what you want. The Custom command also provides you with a way to load any of the hundreds of custom-made filters that others have posted for free on their Web sites.

Note that the Custom filter is not a particularly easy-to-use feature of Photoshop. The filter interface is fairly obscure. Try to understand the guidelines laid out here, read about some specific applications on the following pages in this chapter, and then experiment.

The Custom filter creates filters by mixing pixels within a 5-pixel radius according to the numbers you input into a 5 x 5 matrix and two additional fields, Scale and Offset. The filter multiplies the brightness of the pixels by the numbers you enter in the matrix; the numbers normally equal 1. The Scale value should always equal the sum of the matrix numbers, to maintain overall color balance. Think of Offset as a threshold control.

When creating Custom filters, check the Preview box so that you can see the result of your entries almost immediately.

CREATE, SAVE, AND LOAD CUSTOM FILTERS

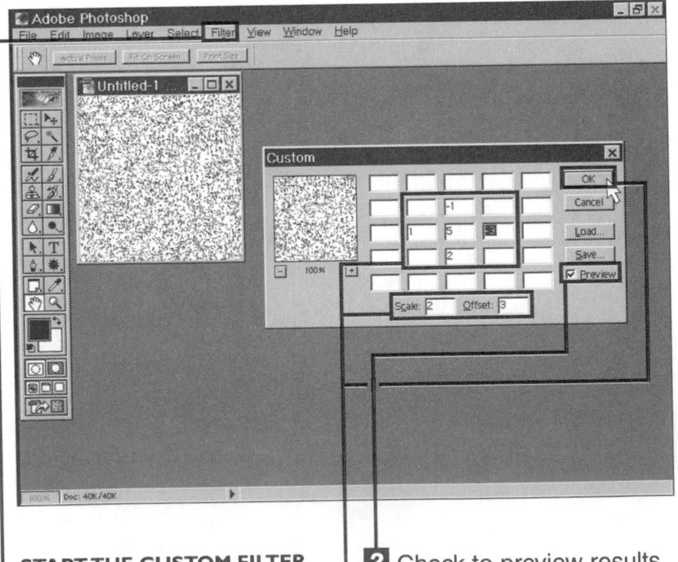

START THE CUSTOM FILTER

1 Choose Filter, then Other, then Custom.

■ The Custom dialog box appears.

Note: With the default settings, all the numbers in the matrix add up to 1, which results in no change.

2 Check to preview results in the workspace before rendering.

3 Make any desired entries in the matrix, Scale, and Offset fields.

4 Click OK.

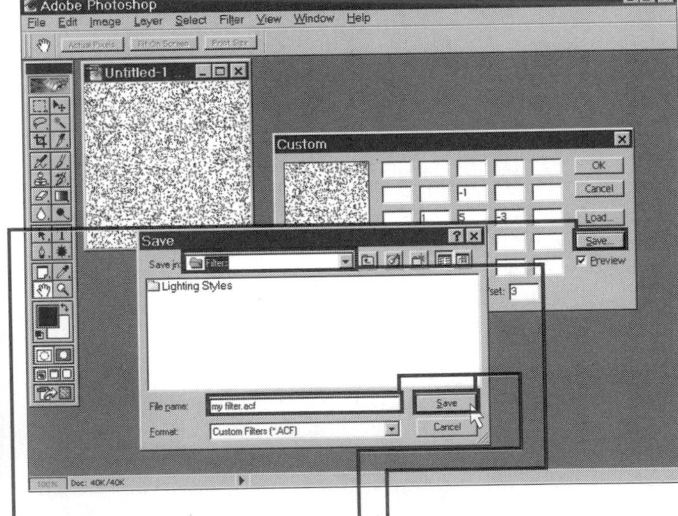

SAVE A CUSTOM FILTER IN WINDOWS

1 Click Save in the Custom dialog box.

■ The Save dialog box appears.

2 Navigate to the directory where you want to save the filter.

3 Type a name for the filter.

4 Click Save.

For what types of effects is the Custom filter best suited?

✔ Sharpening, blurring, edge detection, and embossing.

Can I apply my custom filter and then go back and save it?

✔ Save the filter first, the moment you are satisfied with the effect in the preview area, and before you render the settings by clicking OK in the Custom dialog box.

I do art, not databases. There are 27 matrix fields into which I can key numbers. How can remember the numbers I used for each custom filter?

✔ You do not have to! After you save a filter, you can always bring it back to the Custom dialog box simply by clicking the Load button.

Should I share my filters with others?

✔ Absolutely! First, save it using a descriptive name. Next, create a before and after picture, write a small blurb about how others might find it useful, put both on your Web site, and then let users click to download the file.

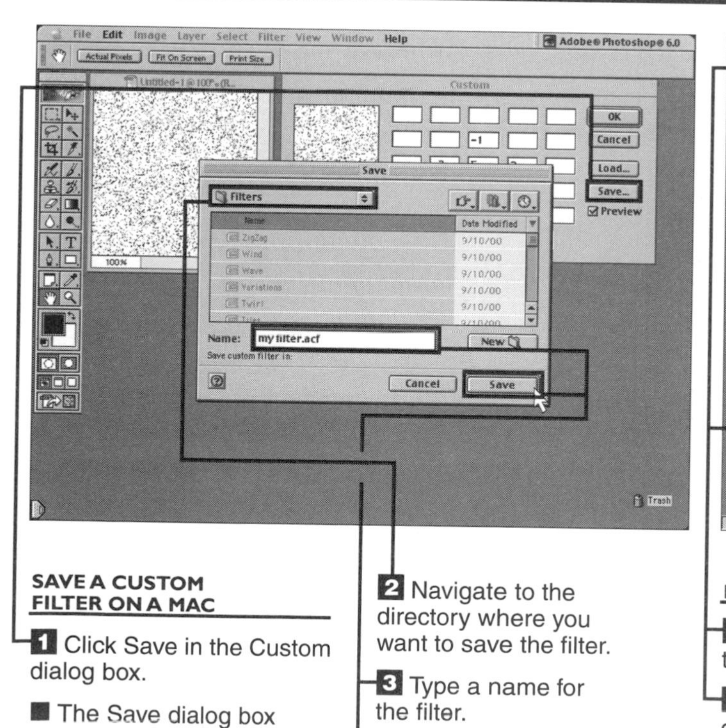

SAVE A CUSTOM FILTER ON A MAC

1 Click Save in the Custom dialog box.

■ The Save dialog box appears.

2 Navigate to the directory where you want to save the filter.

3 Type a name for the filter.

4 Click Save.

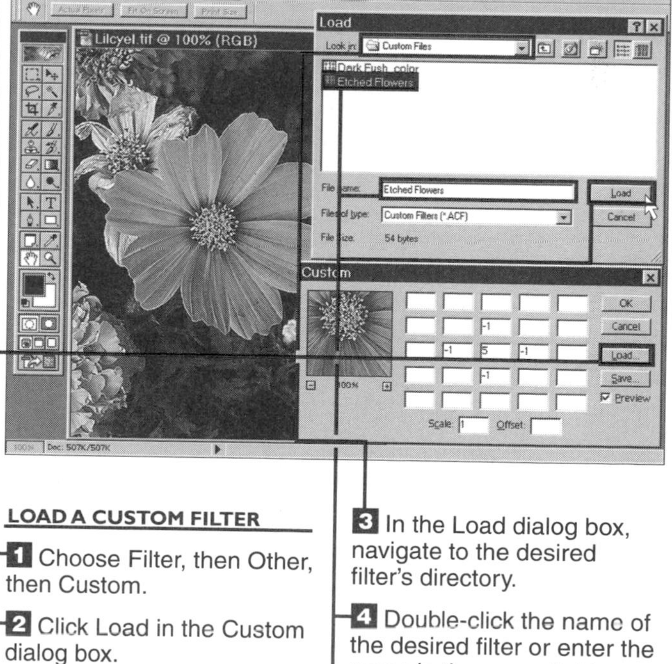

LOAD A CUSTOM FILTER

1 Choose Filter, then Other, then Custom.

2 Click Load in the Custom dialog box.

3 In the Load dialog box, navigate to the desired filter's directory.

4 Double-click the name of the desired filter or enter the name in the name field.

5 Click Load.

SHARPEN WITH THE CUSTOM FILTER

You can take, with the Custom filter, Photoshop's Unsharp Masking capabilities to different levels and create extreme effects.

You may not ever need to use more than Photoshop's usual sharpening tools, but some professionals like and need the ability to customize sharpening by the numbers, rather than with the standard tools.

Sharpening is accomplished by entering a large number in the center value field of the Custom filter dialog box and surrounding it with small numbers that add up to the center value (or come within 20 percent of it).

If you want to take sharpening to a more exaggerated state, enter the value in the outside row and increase the center value while leaving the Scale value at 1 (or very low).

The figures in this section show examples of mild and extreme sharpening. Experiment by using different numbers in the same positions for different sharpening effects.

SHARPEN WITH THE CUSTOM FILTER

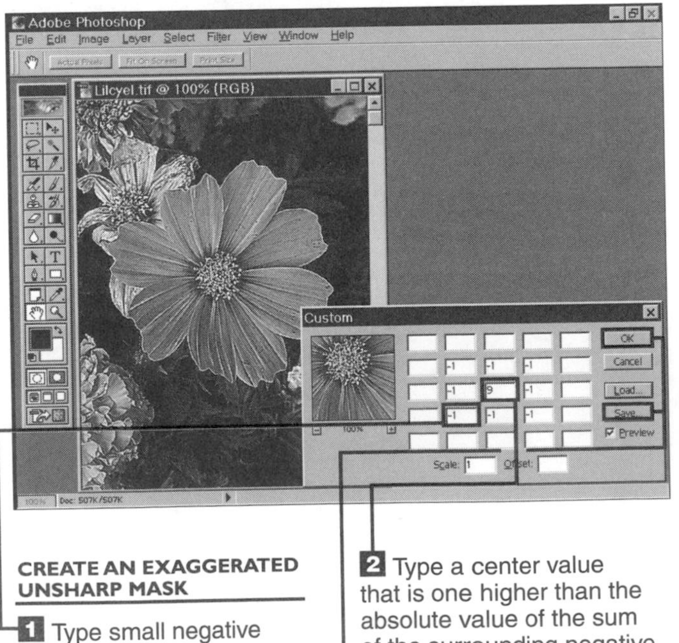

CREATE AN EXAGGERATED UNSHARP MASK

1 Type small negative numbers around the center value in the Custom dialog box.

2 Type a center value that is one higher than the absolute value of the sum of the surrounding negative numbers.

3 Save the effect if you like it.

4 Click OK to render the effect.

MAKE THE SHARPENING EFFECT MORE SUBTLE

1 Increase the center value in the Custom dialog box.

2 Type a number that equals the difference between the sum, expressed as a positive, of the matrix numbers and the center value.

3 Click OK to render the effect.

CREATE DIRECTIONAL BLURS WITH THE CUSTOM FILTER

You can end up with a directional blurring effect if you enter all your values in the Custom filter dialog box in a row rather than surrounding the center value. To create a blur, make the center value 1, set the other values higher, and make the Scale higher than the total of all the values. To sharpen, use a higher center value, negative matrix values, and a Scale value of 1.

Before creating a custom blur filter, be sure you have already tried Photoshop's various blur filters: Blur, Blur More, Gaussian Blur, Motion Blur, Radial Blur, and Smart Blur (see Chapter 13).

The two examples below show blurring in a horizontal direction and blurring in a vertical direction. Notice that you have to lay out a column of numbers to achieve a horizontal motion blur, and you must make a row of numbers to get a vertical motion blur.

CREATE DIRECTIONAL BLURS WITH THE CUSTOM FILTER

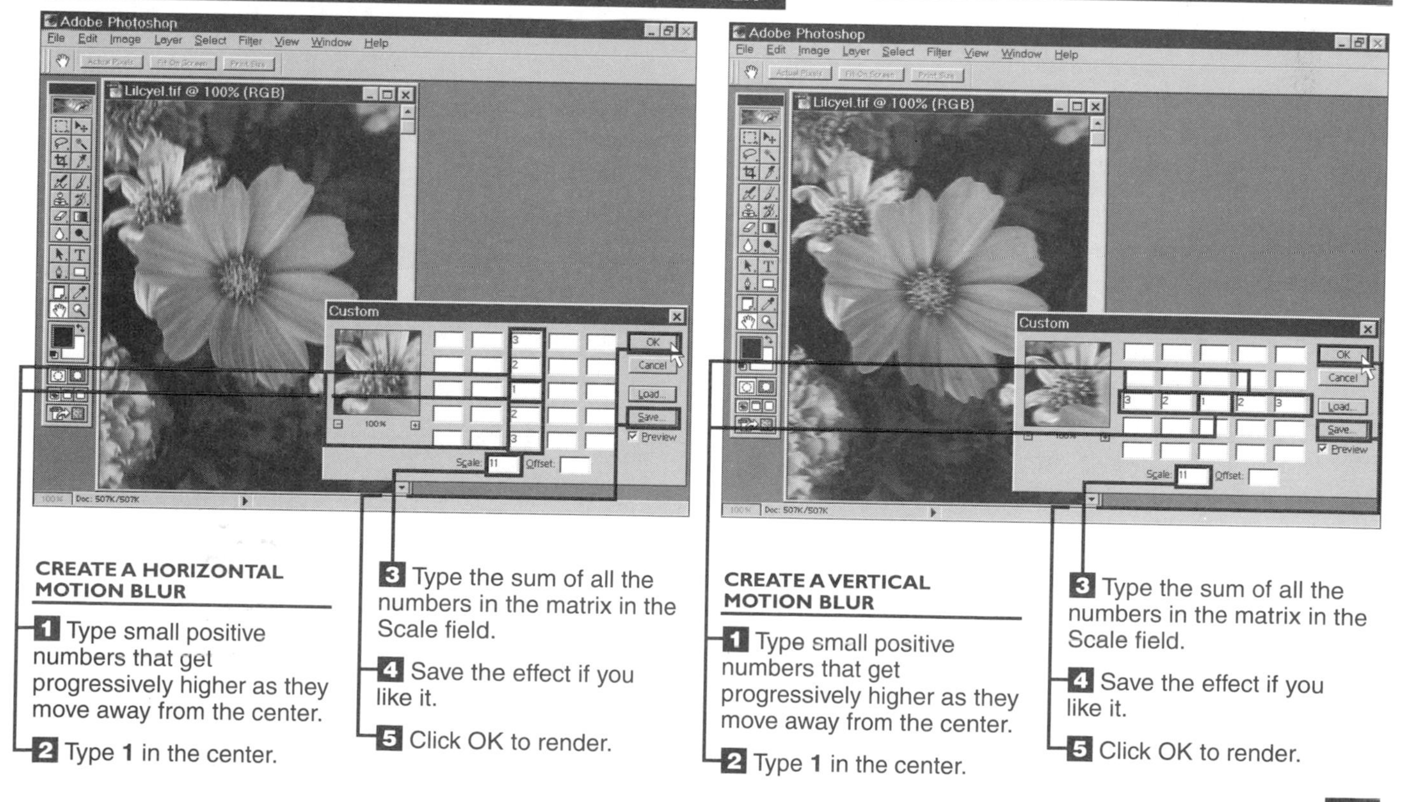

CREATE A HORIZONTAL MOTION BLUR

1 Type small positive numbers that get progressively higher as they move away from the center.

2 Type **1** in the center.

3 Type the sum of all the numbers in the matrix in the Scale field.

4 Save the effect if you like it.

5 Click OK to render.

CREATE A VERTICAL MOTION BLUR

1 Type small positive numbers that get progressively higher as they move away from the center.

2 Type **1** in the center.

3 Type the sum of all the numbers in the matrix in the Scale field.

4 Save the effect if you like it.

5 Click OK to render.

EMBOSS WITH THE CUSTOM FILTER

You can enter asymmetrical numbers into the Custom filter dialog box matrix to create embossing effects. For example, enter positive numbers on one side of the center value and negatives of the same numbers on the other side. You can go berserk with this effect by experimenting with wildly random numbers, as long as the opposite numbers are on the other side of the matrix. To put it another way: Be sure to put positive numbers on one side of the center value and negative numbers on the other.

This concept can be confusing to grasp, but playing with variations in the following exercises should clear things up. Start by keeping the Scale value set at 1 and leaving the Offset field blank.

Be sure to first experiment with the existing Emboss filter (see "Apply the Emboss Filter" earlier in this chapter).

With the Emboss filter's Angle dial, Height, and Amount adjustment sliders, you really should be able to achieve the embossing effect you are seeking without resorting to a custom filter.

EMBOSS WITH THE CUSTOM FILTER

CREATE AN EMBOSSING EFFECT

1 Type positive and negative versions of the same matrix numbers on opposite sides of the center.

2 Type **1** in the center.

3 Type **1** in the Scale field.

4 Save the effect if you like it.

5 Click OK to render.

CHANGE HIGHLIGHT AND SHADOW ANGLES

1 Type the opposing numbers in the direction of lighting.

2 Type **1** in the center.

3 Type **1** as the Scale value.

4 Save the effect if you like it.

5 Click OK to render.

APPLY THE MEDIAN FILTER

You can use the Median filter to blur your image. The only downside to the filter is that the effect sometimes spreads the highlights into the shadows. The result is something of an alternative to the Watercolor filter (see Chapter 15) without the extremely dark shadows that Watercolor produces.

If the Median filter is so similar to the Watercolor filter, why have the Median filter at all? The beauty of Photoshop is that the program often offers several ways to achieve the same end. For some, the Median filter is more straightforward to use than the Watercolor filter.

The effects of the Median filter are fairly easy to predict. The filter's dialog box only has one control, which sets the radius of spread of the average mid-tone in the current selection.

Try using this filter with the Watercolor Paper texture on the CD-ROM that accompanies this book, which will give you a good idea of what this filter can do. Run the Median filter and then choose Filter, then Texture, then Texturizer (see Chapter 14 for more information on working with textures).

APPLY THE MEDIAN FILTER

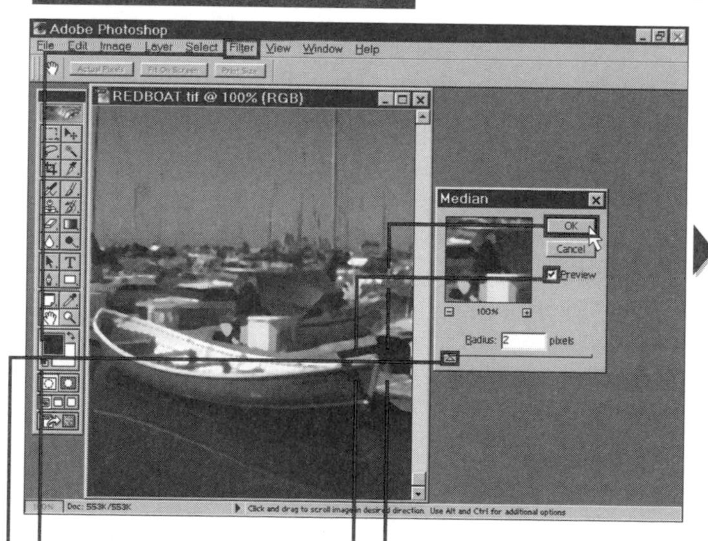

1 Choose Filter, then Noise, then Median.

■ The Median dialog box appears.

2 Drag to increase or decrease the amount of blurring.

3 Check if you want to preview the effect of the Radius setting in the workspace.

4 Click OK to render.

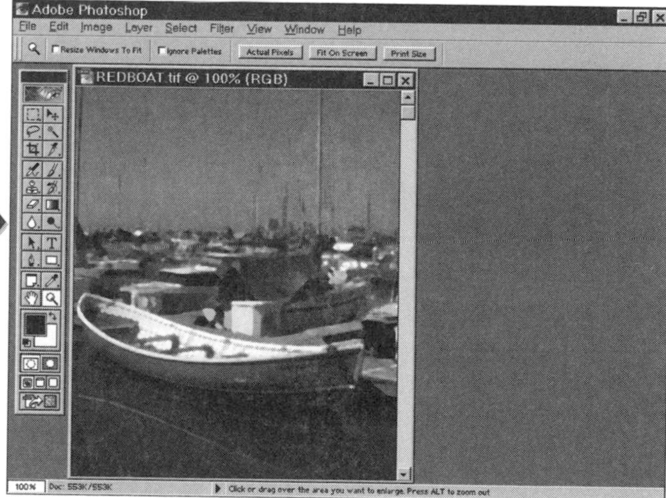

■ This example shows what happens to the image when I apply the Median filter with a radius of 2 pixels, select Filter, then Texture, then Texturizer, load the Watercolor paper texture, and then click OK.

SECTION V

18) USING LAYERS TO COMBINE EFFECTS

19) AUTOMATING PHOTOSHOP WITH ACTIONS

20) PREPARING IMAGES FOR A COMPOSITE

COMBINE FILTER EFFECTS USING LAYERS

You can duplicate layers forever in Photoshop. The variety and versatility of Photoshop's filter effects is considerably enriched by this capability. You can put a different effect on each duplicate layer. You can then combine these layers in a number of ways.

For example, you can erase or partially erase parts of various layers so that other parts show through; you can vary the Transparency setting for layers; and you can use one of the 17 layer Blend modes. Moreover, because you can hide as many layers as you want, you can try variations of the same effect, ultimately choosing to use one or more.

Combining effects by erasing parts of layers is a simple idea that you can use to produce some very complex effects. Although only four layers are used in the following exercise, you will find no end to the number of layers you can employ in this way. The advantage of erasing parts of layers, rather than creating the effect in a selection, is that the process is interactive, making visualizing the end result easier.

COMBINE FILTER EFFECTS USING LAYERS

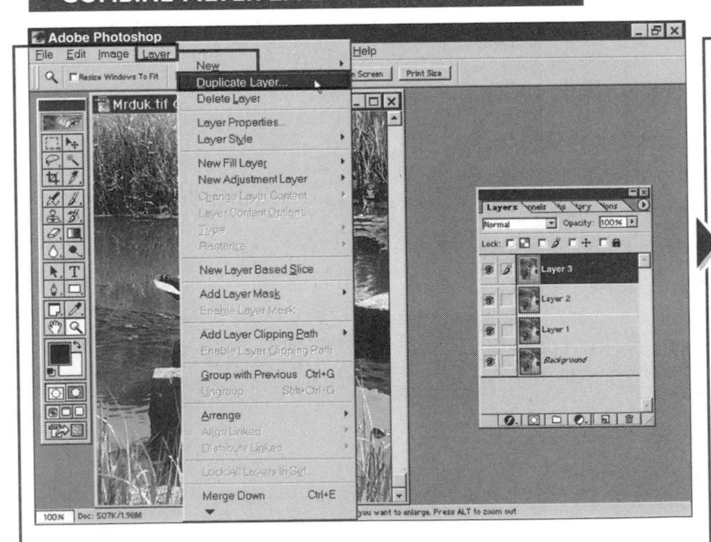

Note: Make sure the target layer is active.

1 Choose Layer, then Duplicate Layer.

■ A dialog box appears in which you can name the layer.

Note: You can also choose Duplicate Layer from the Layers palette menu, or drag the target layer onto the New Layer icon.

2 Name the layer and click OK.

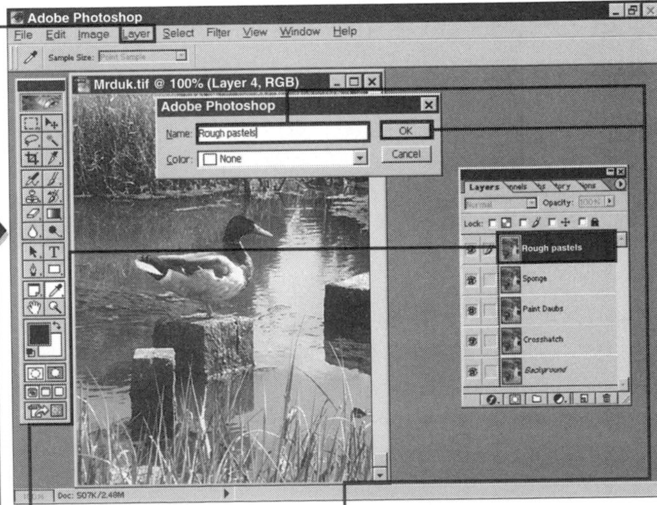

3 Click to select each layer in turn and run a different filter (or the same filter with different option settings) on each.

4 Choose Layer, then Layer Properties

■ The Layer Properties dialog box appears.

5 Type the name of the filter used on that layer.

6 Click OK.

What is another layer technique?

✔ Chapter 9 discusses blending selections and layers. On the Layers palette you can directly choose Layer Blend modes and adjust Opacity. Alternatively, choose Blending Options from the Layers palette menu. The Layer Style dialog box appears, containing the General Blending tools plus many more Advanced Blending tools.

Can I use Layer Masks to erase parts of layers?

✔ In fact, that method is an even more powerful way to do the job. Layer Masks make gradually erasing parts of the image and controlling the feathering of the edges of erasures easy. See Chapter 8 for more on masking.

I am blending one layer into another using the Paintbrush, but the results are not as I expected. What might I be doing wrong?

✔ Did you customize the Paintbrush options AND the Layer options? The Mode and Opacity settings for both yield additive effects. Try setting the Layer to Normal mode and 100% opacity, while adjusting the Paintbrush settings as you want. The results will be as you expected.

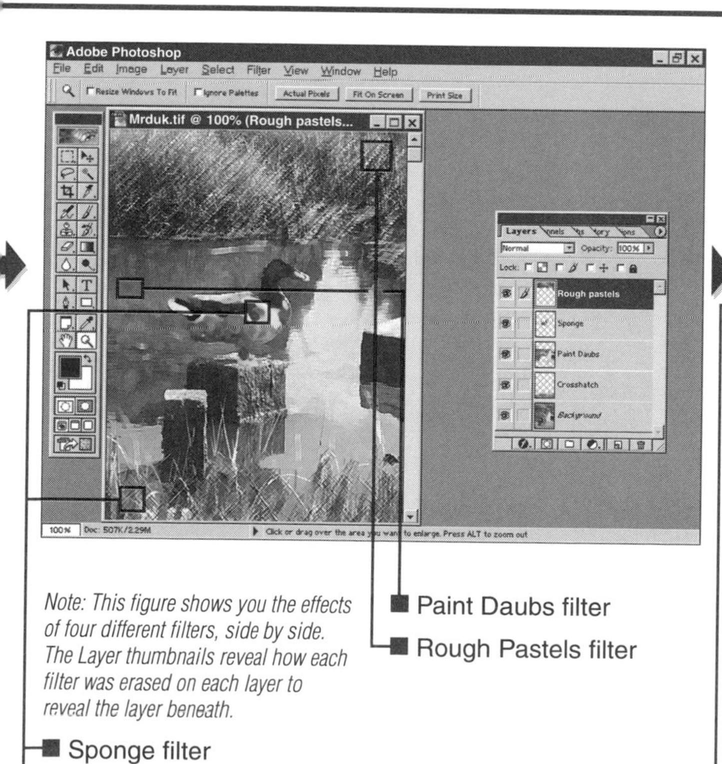

Note: This figure shows you the effects of four different filters, side by side. The Layer thumbnails reveal how each filter was erased on each layer to reveal the layer beneath.

■ Paint Daubs filter

■ Rough Pastels filter

■ Sponge filter

■ Crosshatch filter

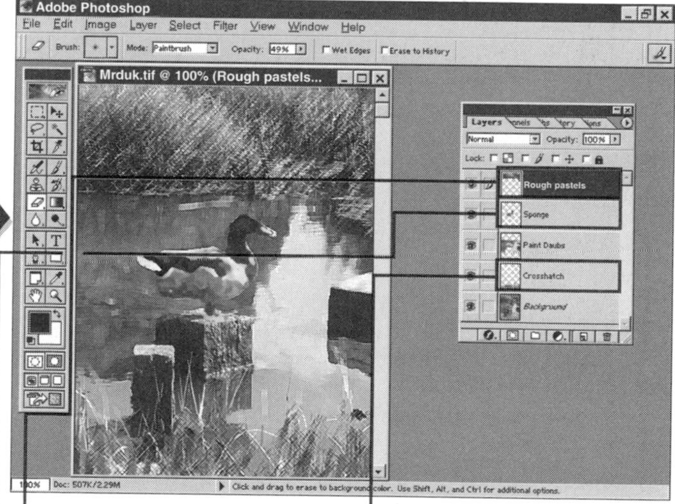

7 Activate each layer in turn.

8 Select the near objects in the image, invert, and press Delete/Backspace.

9 In the next layer, select everything below the water line, invert, and press Delete/Backspace.

10 To make the cross-hatching blend with the rough pastels on the duck, erase by using a large brush set at 50 percent.

DEFINE AND SAVE PATTERNS

A pattern, as defined by Photoshop, is all or part of any raster image that fits inside a rectangular selection marquee. You can do all sorts of things with patterns. For instance, you can make patterns by selecting part of photo of a fabric, carpet, or wallpaper pattern. You could do the same with sand or grass.

To define a pattern in Photoshop, just open the file that contains it, make a rectangular selection within that file (this includes the use of the Select All command), and then choose Edit, then Define Pattern.

If you think you may want to reuse that specific pattern, the very next thing you should do is press ⌘/Ctrl+C (to copy the contents of the selection to the Clipboard), choose File, then New, and click OK. The new file will automatically be the same size as the Clipboard. Press ⌘/Ctrl+V to paste the Clipboard contents into the new file and then save it under a new name (preferably inside a folder named Patterns). Now, any time you want to reuse the pattern, open the file, press ⌘/Ctrl+A to Select All, and then choose Edit, then Define Pattern. You need to use this method each time you change patterns.

DEFINE AND SAVE PATTERNS

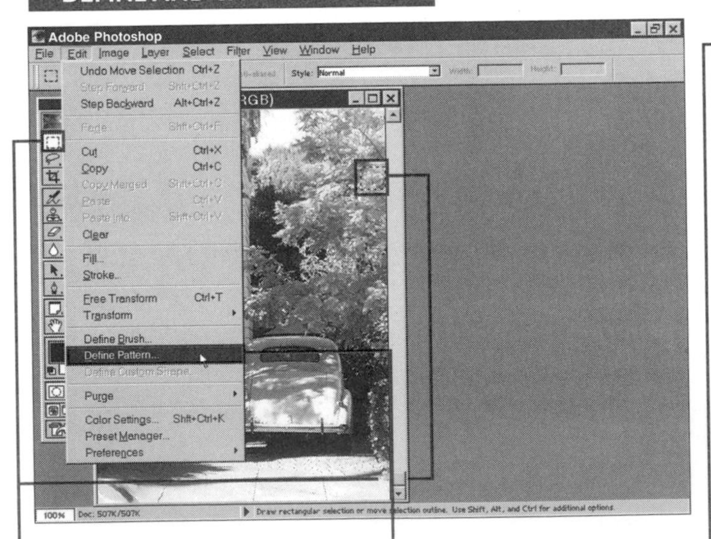

MAKE A PATTERN FROM A SECTION OF AN IMAGE

1. Click the Rectangular Marquee tool (⬚).
2. Drag to select the image area to be used as a pattern.
3. Choose Edit, then Define Pattern.

■ The Define Pattern Name dialog box appears.

4. Type a name that you can remember for this pattern and click OK.

■ Photoshop saves the pattern in the Pattern Library.

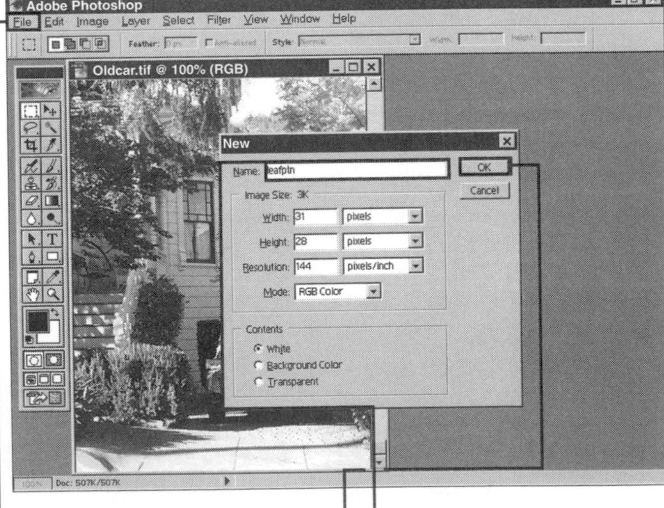

SAVE THE PATTERN FOR LATER

1. Choose File, then New.
2. Type a name for the new file.
3. Click OK.

Note: You must do these steps before exiting Photoshop or defining another pattern.

Do I have to make all my own patterns?

✔ No. Several Web sites distribute free seamless tile patterns. Some of these are given away to attract people to a particular site, and others are sold commercially (usually at very reasonable prices).

Can I edit my newly created patterns?

✔ Edit away! Your pattern files are just standard Photoshop files and may be modified.

What can I do with patterns?

✔ You can fill any layer or selection with them. You can use the Paint Bucket to fill colors with them. You can paint with them by choosing Use Pattern as an option for the Rubber Stamp tool. You can also convert a pattern file to grayscale and then use it as a texture file. (See Chapter 14 for information on creating and saving new textures.)

How do I make the edges of patterns blend together so no obvious break from tile to tile exists?

✔ See "Create Seamless Pattern and Texture Tiles" in Chapter 14.

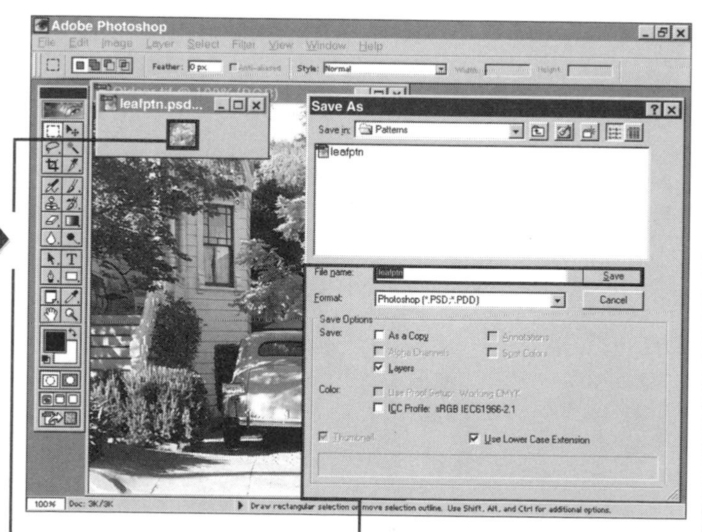

Note: An empty window opens for the new file. Make sure this window is the active window.

4 Choose Edit, then Paste.

■ The contents of the Clipboard are pasted into the new file as a new layer.

5 Choose File, then Save As.

6 In the Save As dialog box, type an appropriate filename and click Save.

Note: Creating a folder called Patterns and storing all pattern files in that folder is a good idea.

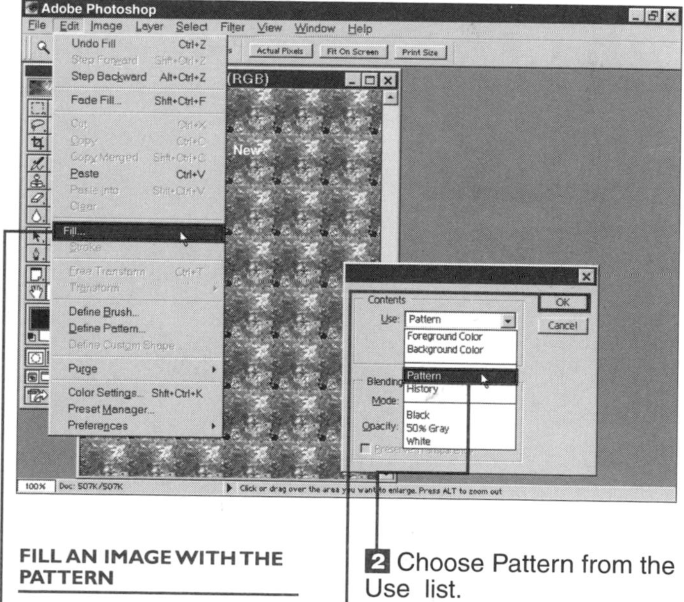

FILL AN IMAGE WITH THE PATTERN

1 Choose Edit, then Fill.

2 Choose Pattern from the Use list.

3 Click OK.

PAINT WITH FILLS

You can paint sizable areas of an image instantly simply by making use of one of the several methods Photoshop provides for automatically filling images, layers, channels, and selections. You can also fill areas of color without having to first make a selection.

Photoshop also lets you fill with solid colors, gradients, or patterns, or with the contents of any snapshot in the History palette. You can fill with the current foreground, background, and pattern with either the Paint Bucket tool or the Fill command on the Edit menu.

You can fill with a snapshot from the History palette only by choosing Edit, then Fill. You can fill with gradients only with the Gradient Fill tool.

You can also apply fills by using Blend modes. To use these, you must specify the Blend mode in either the Tools Options palette for the Paint Bucket tool or Gradient tool or in the Fill dialog box for the Fill command on the Edit menu before the fill is applied.

PAINT WITH FILLS

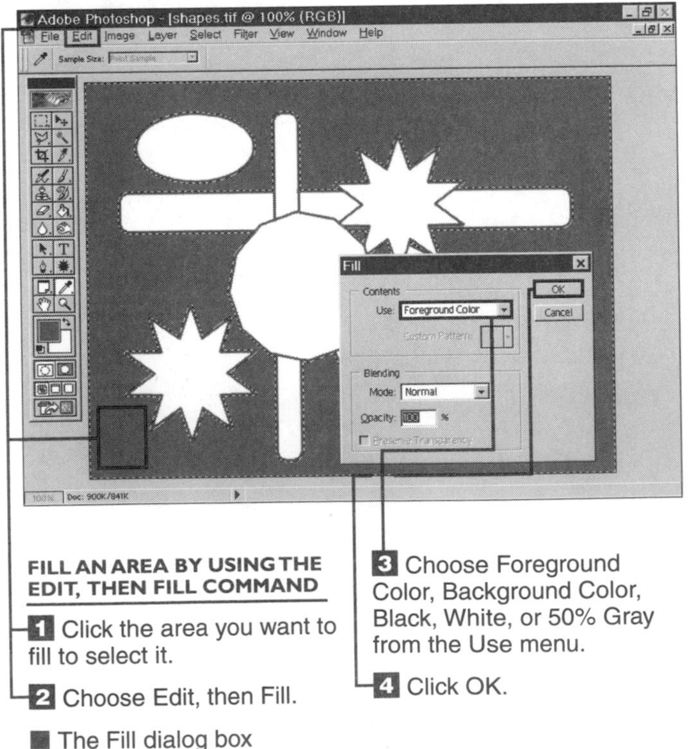

FILL AN AREA BY USING THE EDIT, THEN FILL COMMAND

1 Click the area you want to fill to select it.

2 Choose Edit, then Fill.

■ The Fill dialog box appears.

3 Choose Foreground Color, Background Color, Black, White, or 50% Gray from the Use menu.

4 Click OK.

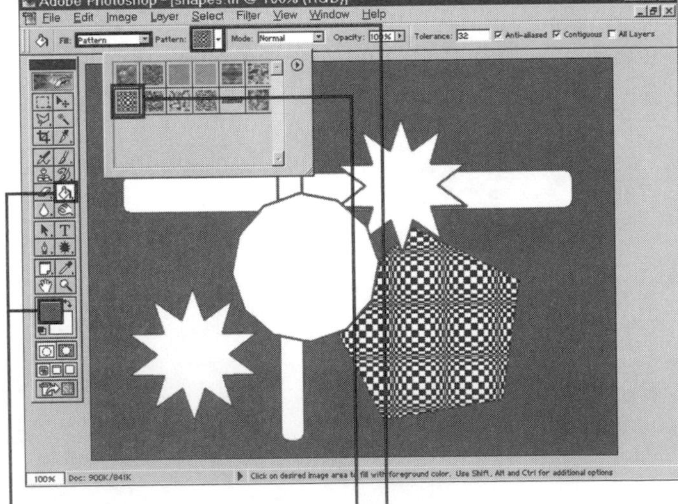

FILL AN AREA BY USING THE PAINT BUCKET TOOL

1 Click the color you want to use as the foreground color.

2 Click the Paint Bucket (Fill) tool (🪣).

3 Choose Foreground or Pattern from the Fill menu.

4 Choose a pattern from the Pattern Library.

5 Click in any area of color.

Is a Linear gradient the only type of Gradient fill?

✔ No, but Linear gradients are an excellent way to shade masks, simulate the shading in a blue sky, or simulate the change in tonalities from dark to light as a cue to the depth in an image (use the gradient with one of the Blend modes). See the other layouts on using gradients.

Can I blend a fill with the underlying image?

✔ The easiest way is to do the fill and then choose the Fade command from the Edit menu to enter a percentage of transparency in the fill. Of course, you can also use the Blend Modes menu in the Fill Options bar (see "Using Layer Blend Modes" in Chapter 9).

When I fill selections, how can I make them blend along the borders of contiguous selected areas?

✔ Make the selections slightly larger and feather the edges. Continue to do this each time you make a new selection. This way the selected areas that bump into one another cross-fade, and edges that do not run into any others blend more smoothly with their surroundings.

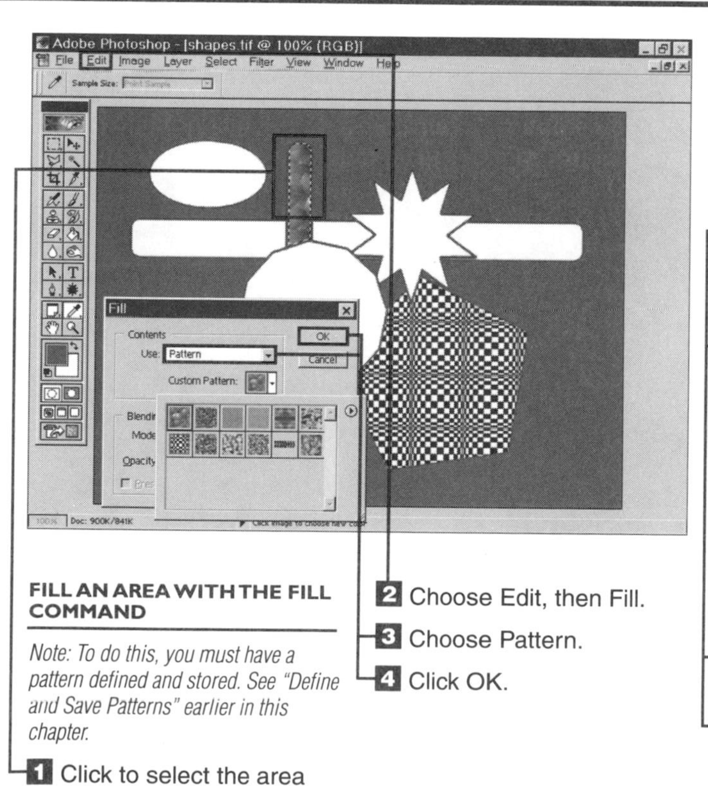

FILL AN AREA WITH THE FILL COMMAND

Note: To do this, you must have a pattern defined and stored. See "Define and Save Patterns" earlier in this chapter.

1 Click to select the area you want to fill.

2 Choose Edit, then Fill.

3 Choose Pattern.

4 Click OK.

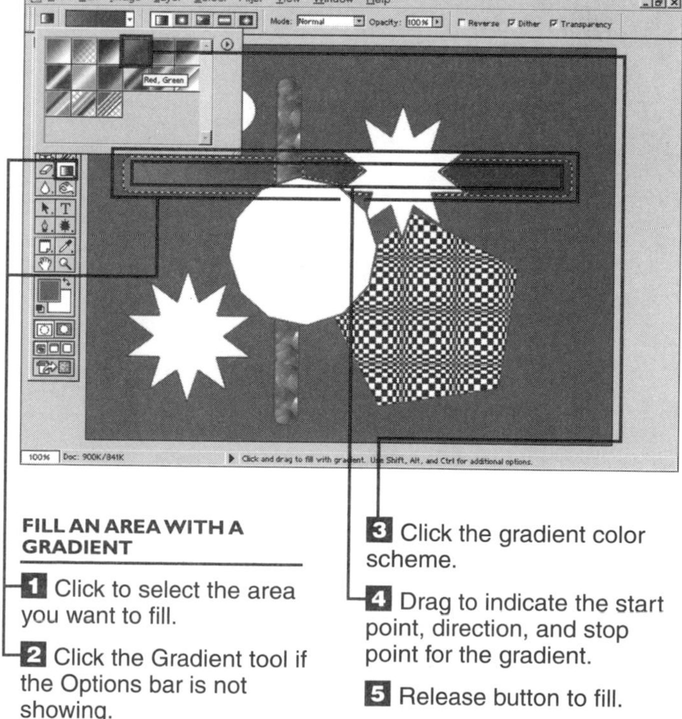

FILL AN AREA WITH A GRADIENT

1 Click to select the area you want to fill.

2 Click the Gradient tool if the Options bar is not showing.

3 Click the gradient color scheme.

4 Drag to indicate the start point, direction, and stop point for the gradient.

5 Release button to fill.

MAKE NONLINEAR GRADIENT FILLS

You can make gradient fills in a variety of shapes. After you choose the Gradient tool from the toolbox, five variations on it appear in the Gradient Tool Options bar:

- Linear Gradient shades in a straight line, perpendicular to the drag line, in even steps from the foreground color to the background color.
- Radial Gradient shades in a circular pattern.
- Angle Gradient shades in a counterclockwise direction from the start point (as though you are looking down on a shaded cone).
- Reflected Gradient mirrors the same linear gradient on either side of the start point.
- Diamond Gradient shades from the starting point outward in a square pattern, with one corner of the square attached to the drag line.

Each Gradient tool has three check boxes in its Gradient Options palette: Reverse, Dither, and Transparency. Checking Transparency enables the transparency mask that is stored with each gradient style. Checking Dither eliminates banding between shades. Checking Reverse makes the gradient go from background to foreground color.

MAKE NONLINEAR GRADIENT FILLS

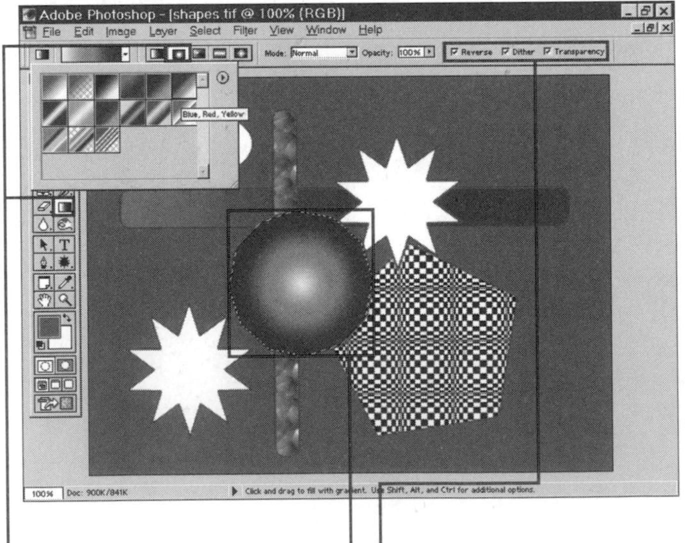

MAKE A RADIAL GRADIENT FILL

1 Click the Gradient tool (▣).

2 Choose the Radial Gradient style from the Gradient Options bar.

3 Check any option(s) you want to employ.

4 Drag to indicate the center of the circle and the distance to the end of the circle.

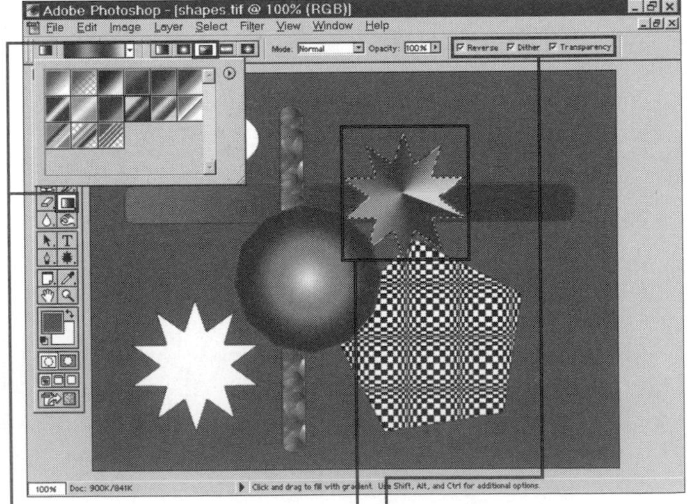

MAKE AN ANGLE GRADIENT FILL

1 Click the Gradient tool.

2 Choose the Angle Gradient style in the Gradient Options bar.

3 Check any option(s) you want to employ.

4 Drag to indicate the start of the gradient, the angle, and the distance to the end of the gradient.

How can I put a gradient into a mask?

✔ Choose Window, then Show Channels. When the Channels palette appears, click the channel name of the alpha channel mask you want to graduate. The image of the mask then fills the workspace. Click to select the area you want to fill with a gradient, and then proceed as shown in "Make a Reflected Gradient Fill" below.

Can I use gradients to affect a Blend mode between layers?

✔ Yes. Make a layer mask for the layer to which you want to apply the Blend mode and then edit the layer mask from the Channels palette.

Can I use gradients in Quick Mask mode?

✔ Yes. Black masks 100 percent and white is completely transparent (you can choose the reverse as an option), even though you see these as shades of orange in Quick Mask mode. You can also fill a selection in Quick Mask mode, as well as using any of the other Paint tools (Pen, Paintbrush, and so on). For more on Quick Mask mode, see Chapter 8.

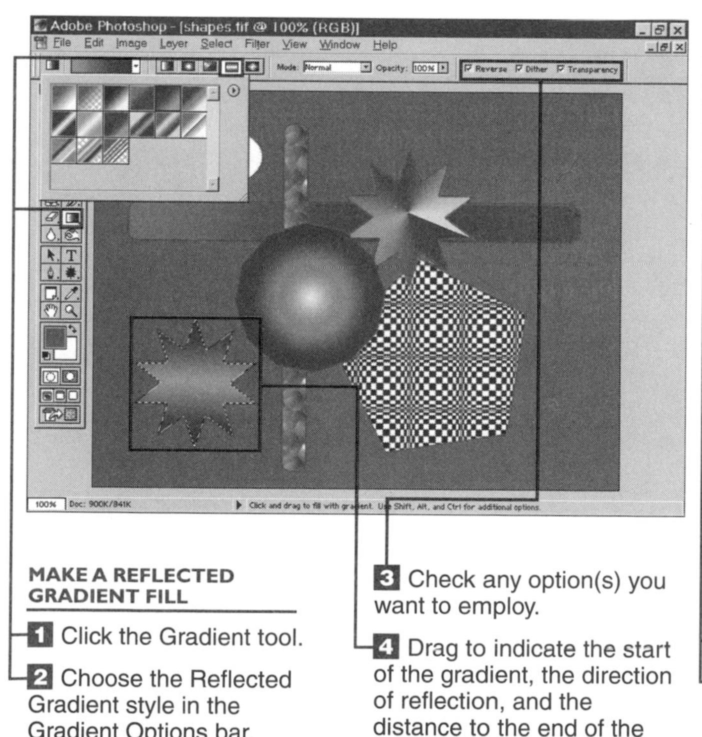

MAKE A REFLECTED GRADIENT FILL

1 Click the Gradient tool.

2 Choose the Reflected Gradient style in the Gradient Options bar.

3 Check any option(s) you want to employ.

4 Drag to indicate the start of the gradient, the direction of reflection, and the distance to the end of the gradient.

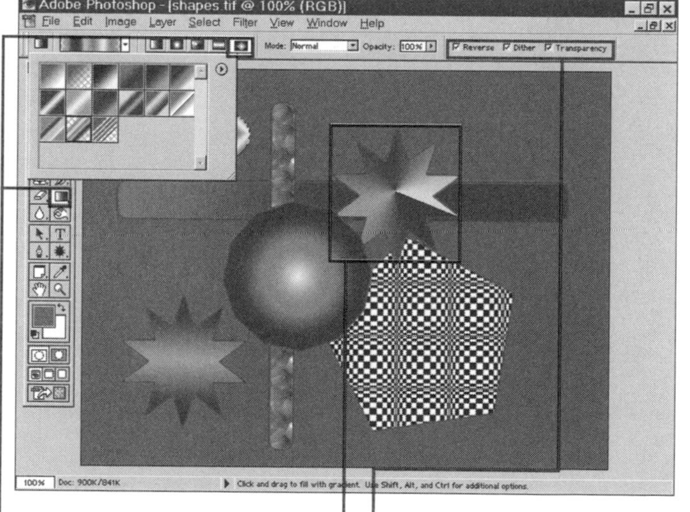

MAKE A DIAMOND GRADIENT FILL

1 Click the Gradient tool.

2 Choose the Diamond Gradient style in the Gradient Options bar.

3 Check any option(s) you want to employ.

4 Drag to indicate the start of the gradient, the direction of reflection, and the distance to the end of the gradient.

MAKE AND EDIT GRADIENT STYLES

You can create virtually any type of gradient. Photoshop 6 enables you to create gradients that blend from any color to any other color with any number of gradients in between. You can even have part or parts of the gradient fade into transparency so that the gradient fades in to the underlying image.

The following gradient styles come with the program: Foreground to Background, Foreground to Transparent, Black-White, Red-Green, Violet-Orange, Blue-Red-Yellow, Blue-Yellow-Blue, Orange-Yellow-Orange, Violet-Green-Orange, Yellow-Violet-Orange-Blue, Copper, Chrome, Spectrum, Transparent Rainbow, and Transparent Stripes. (All of these styles are shown in the color section of this book.)

You can make new styles by starting with any of the premade styles and editing them. Click the Gradient tool button to show the Gradient Options palette. Next, pick a style from the Gradient menu and click in the sample area to display the Gradient Editor. Finally, click in a blank area to create a new gradient, or click and modify an existing gradient.

You can also create new gradients by duplicating preexisting gradients, renaming them, and modifying each duplicate.

MAKE AND EDIT GRADIENT STYLES

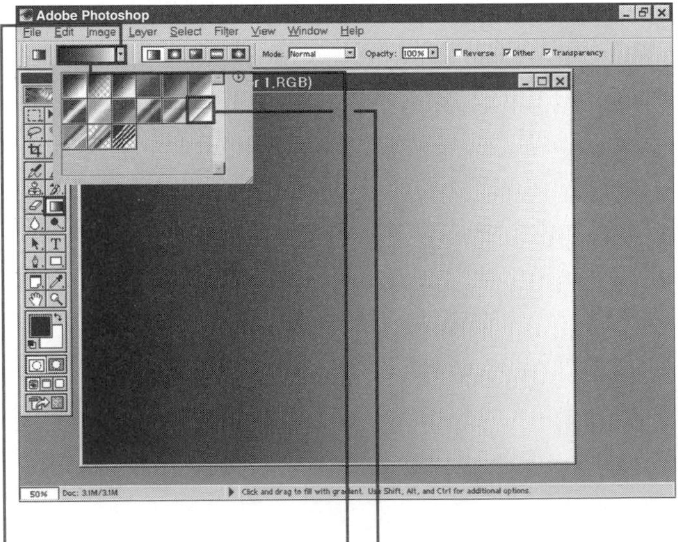

Note: Even if you want to create a new gradient, you start by editing an existing one.

1 Click the Gradient tool (▣).

■ The Options bar appears.

2 Click ▾ to view gradient styles.

3 Click the style closest to the gradient you want to make.

4 Click here.

■ The Gradient Editor appears.

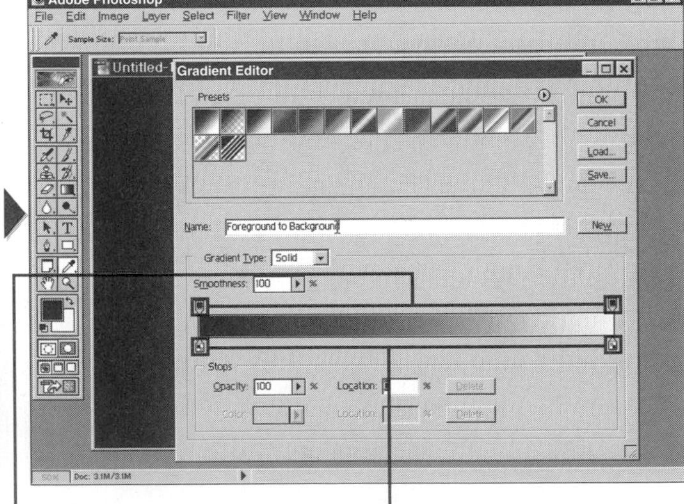

5 To change the opacity (transparency), drag these sliders.

6 To space colors, drag the slider for one or both of the colors whose spread you want to move.

What happens when I click the New button?

✔ You get a Gradient Name dialog box, in which you can name the new gradient. Next, a completely black Gradient bar with a blank New Color pointer at each end appears. Simply follow the steps outlined here to create an entirely new gradient.

How do I place and remove pointers?

✔ Click just below the Gradient bar at the place where you want a new pointer to appear. To dump a pointer, click to select it (the tip turns black) and then drag it away from the bar.

What do the New Color, F, and B pointers do?

✔ You can switch any of these pointer types to any other by first selecting the pointer on the Gradient bar and then clicking the desired Pointer Type icon. F is always the current foreground color, and B is always the current background color. A New Color pointer always retains the same color, which you pick from the standard Color Picker.

How do I change the median blending point between two colors?

✔ Drag the diamond-shaped pointer that is just above the Blending bar, or select the pointer and specify a percentage in the Location field.

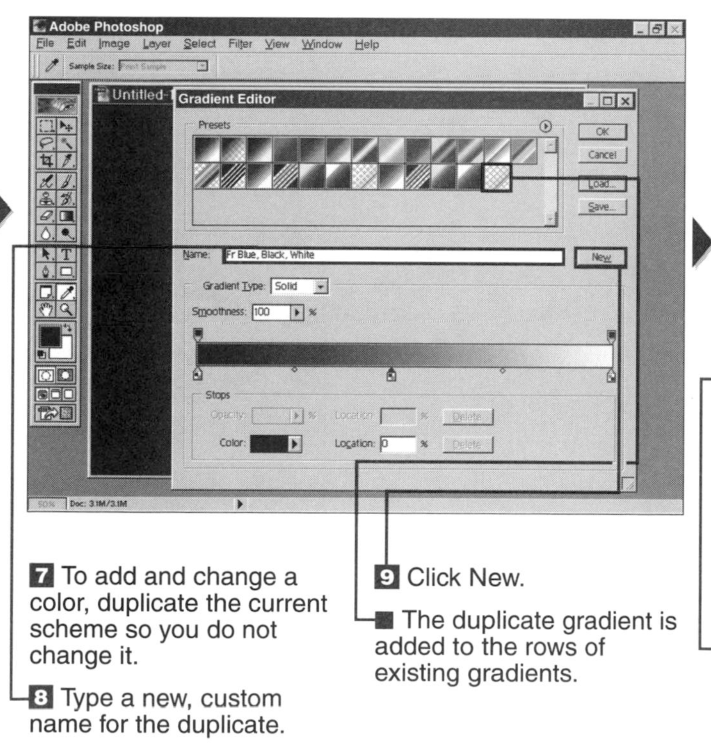

7 To add and change a color, duplicate the current scheme so you do not change it.

8 Type a new, custom name for the duplicate.

9 Click New.

■ The duplicate gradient is added to the rows of existing gradients.

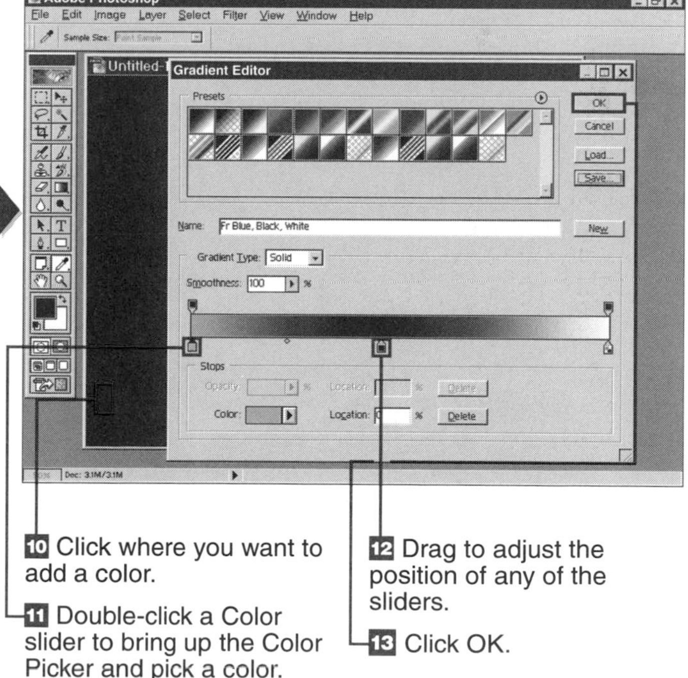

10 Click where you want to add a color.

11 Double-click a Color slider to bring up the Color Picker and pick a color.

Note: You can also double-click the Color slider after it has been placed.

12 Drag to adjust the position of any of the sliders.

13 Click OK.

CHOOSE COLORS

You can choose the colors you want to paint with in Photoshop in several ways: You can use the Eyedropper tool, select from the Color Picker, select from the Colors palette, or choose from the Swatches palette.

The Eyedropper is a tool found not only in the Toolbox but also in many Photoshop commands, such as by choosing Select, then Color Range and Image, then Adjust, then Levels/Curves.

The Eyedropper is always used to designate a color by clicking on that color in the active layer of the working image. This tool is the one to use when you need an exact match for an existing color.

The Color Picker lets you choose any of the 16.8 million colors available to a 24-bit color operation. You can also choose swatch book colors from the Color Picker or choose any color from the Colors palette.

The Swatches palette can contain any number of predefined colors. It is best used for painting and text fills when you need to quickly choose from one of several frequently used colors.

CHOOSE COLORS

CHOOSE A COLOR WITH THE EYEDROPPER

1 Click the Eyedropper tool ( ).

2 Click the pixel that is the color you want to use.

■ The color appears as the foreground color.

Note: To choose a background color, use Opt/Alt+click. If you want to exchange the foreground and background colors, press X.

CHOOSE A COLOR FROM THE SWATCHES PALETTE

1 Choose Window, then Show Swatches (or click the Swatches tab if it is visible under another palette).

2 Click the preferred swatch to choose your foreground color.

Note: See "Make Custom Swatch Palettes," later in this chapter.

What if I want subtle changes in color when I make a stroke?

✔ You have to use a pressure-sensitive digitizing tablet, such as one from Wacom. In the Options palette for the brush you are using, check the Color box. When you stroke and scrub, the color alternates subtly between the foreground and background colors.

The options menu on the Swatches palette has a long list of premade swatches to choose from. How do I learn more about them?

✔ A good place to start is Appendix A of this book. An understanding of color management for many types of output devices will explain why Photoshop comes with so many color options.

Can I choose colors that have been mixed, as one would on a traditional palette?

✔ Yes. Create a new, small file. Place your basic colors in this new file. Choose the Smudge tool and a fairly large brush, and mix the colors together. Next, use the Eyedropper to pick colors from the mixture. The chosen colors remain the same when you switch windows.

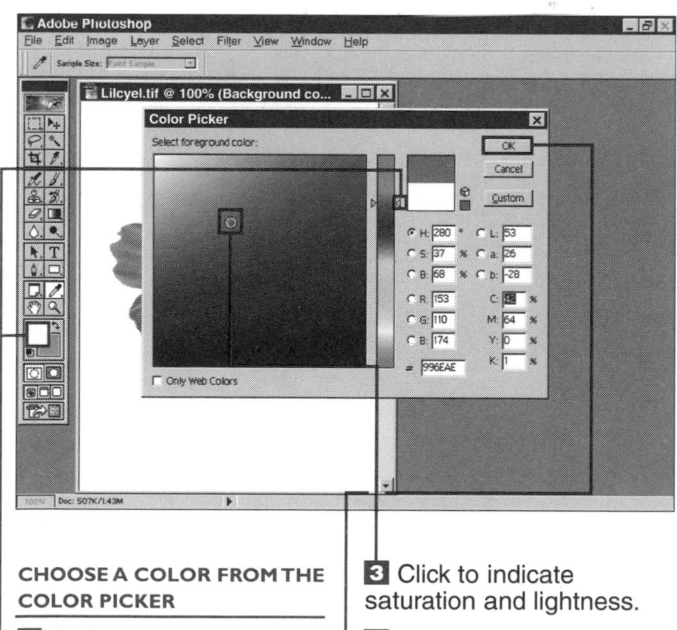

CHOOSE A COLOR FROM THE COLOR PICKER

1 Click the foreground or background color swatch.

2 Drag to pick the base color.

3 Click to indicate saturation and lightness.

4 Click OK, and the color appears in the appropriate color swatch.

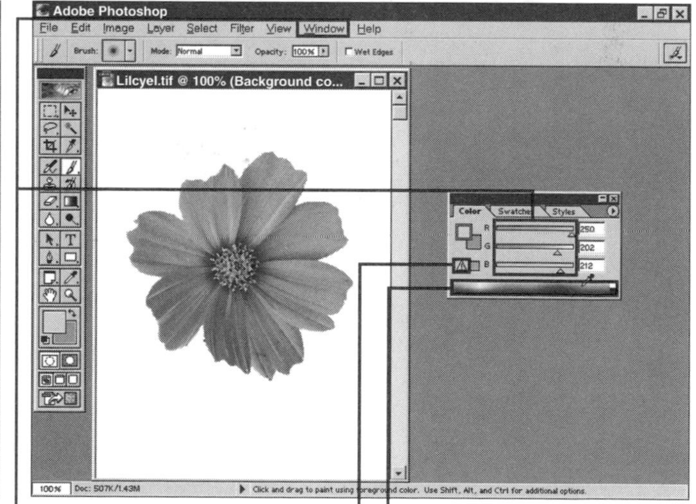

CHOOSE A COLOR IN THE COLORS PALETTE

1 Choose Window, then Show Color.

2 Drag sliders to adjust the color.

■ Alternatively, you can click in the Spectrum bar to choose a color.

■ This icon appears if you have chosen a color that is beyond printable range (out of gamut).

MAKE CUSTOM SWATCH PALETTES

You can easily create new swatch palettes. If you are creating an original image as opposed to touching up an existing one, you will no doubt want to create a custom swatch palette that enables you to quickly choose the colors you need most often. To change the color in an existing swatch, press Shift (the pointer turns into the Paint Bucket icon) and click the swatch. The color changes to that of the existing foreground color.

You can also insert a new swatch between two existing swatches. Press Shift+Opt/Alt and click a swatch. To add a new swatch without altering any existing swatches, just click the empty area below the swatches. A new swatch in the foreground color is automatically added.

Moreover, you can switch from one set of swatch colors to another, just by clicking the Swatch palette options button.

How do you choose which color will appear in the new swatch? Before you make the new swatch, use any of the methods shown in the previous section, "Choose Colors."

MAKE CUSTOM SWATCH PALETTES

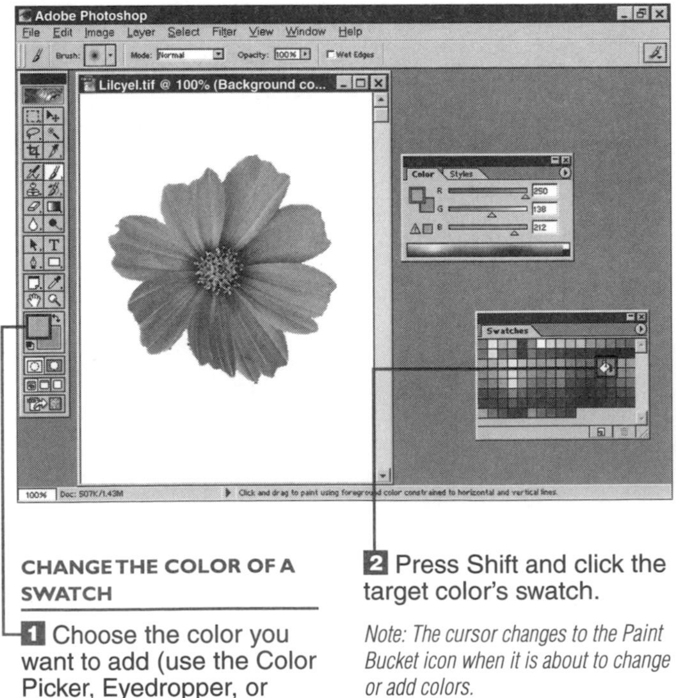

CHANGE THE COLOR OF A SWATCH

1 Choose the color you want to add (use the Color Picker, Eyedropper, or Colors palette).

2 Press Shift and click the target color's swatch.

Note: The cursor changes to the Paint Bucket icon when it is about to change or add colors.

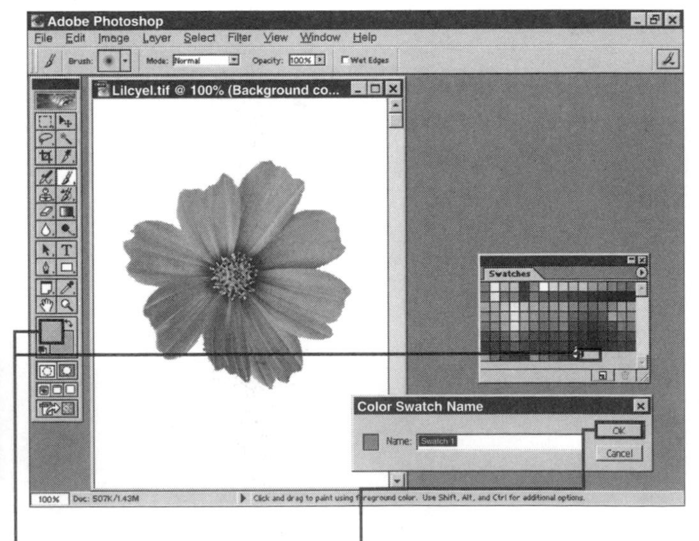

ADD A SWATCH

1 Choose the color you want to use as the foreground color.

2 Click.

■ The Color Swatch Name dialog box appears.

3 Type a name for the new swatch and click OK.

Can I quickly choose colors when I want to create a new palette?

✔ The fastest way to choose colors for a custom palette is to drag the Colors palette alongside the Swatches palette.

What should I do if I want to create a new palette without using any of the current colors?

✔ Press ⌘/Ctrl and click all the colors in the palette. Now you can add colors by simply choosing new foreground colors and clicking in the Swatches palette for each change.

How do I save the new palette?

✔ From the Swatches palette menu, choose Save Swatches. If you have made a new palette, give it a new name so you will not erase the default palette. When you want to reuse the palette, choose either Load Swatches or Replace Swatches from the palette menu. Load Swatches adds the colors to the existing palette.

What if I make a mess of the Swatches palette?

✔ From the Swatches palette menu, choose Reset Swatches.

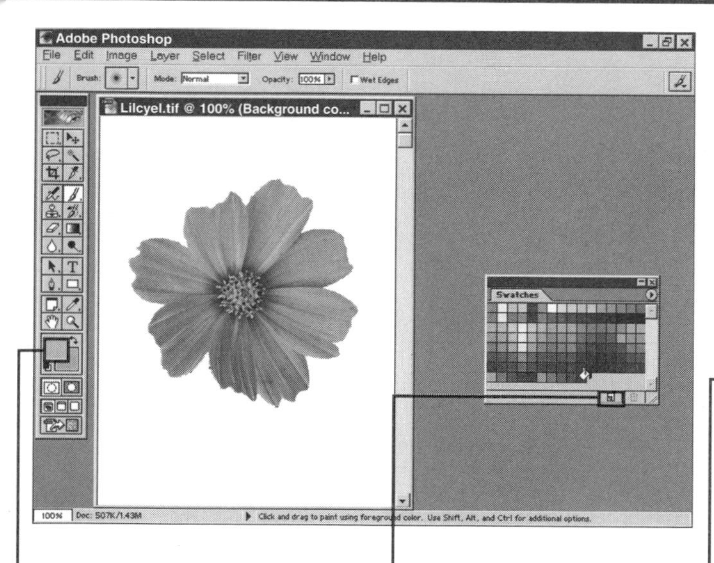

ADD A SWATCH

1 Choose the color you want to add.

2 Click the New Swatch icon (◻) at the bottom of the Swatches palette.

3 If you don't like the default name, rename the new swatch in the resulting dialog box.

■ A new swatch is added.

DELETE A SWATCH

1 Press ⌘/Ctrl and click the swatch you want to delete.

■ The cursor changes to a gray scissors icon and the swatch is deleted.

CREATE A NEW ACTION

You can execute almost any imaginable combination of commands in Photoshop 6 with a single keystroke or button click.

You do this with a capability called *Actions*. Actions save you time; help you avoid the tension that comes with having to perform repetitive tasks one command at a time; and, most importantly, help you eliminate mistakes in complicated procedures, because actions never forget the necessary sequence of commands and never exclude a needed command.

This exercise shows you how to create and record a new action on your own.

Virtually any task you perform in Photoshop more than a couple of times should be turned into an action. For example, if you have a lot of JPEG format images that you want to convert into TIFF format before archiving, create an action to do the conversion automatically.

CREATE A NEW ACTION

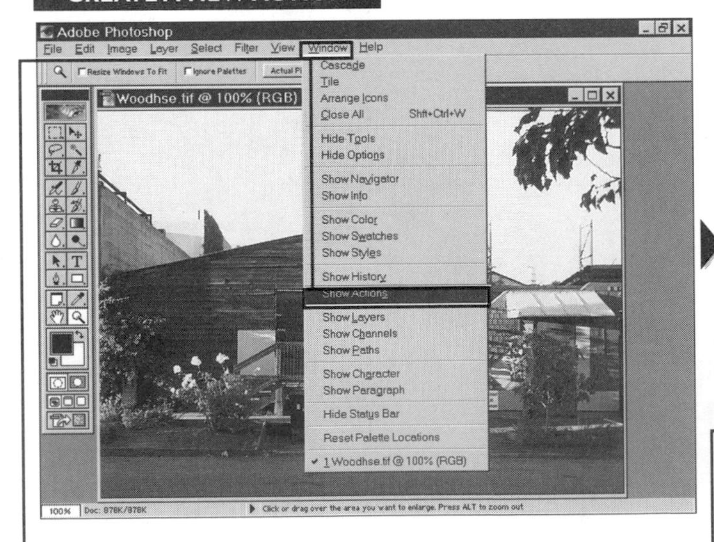

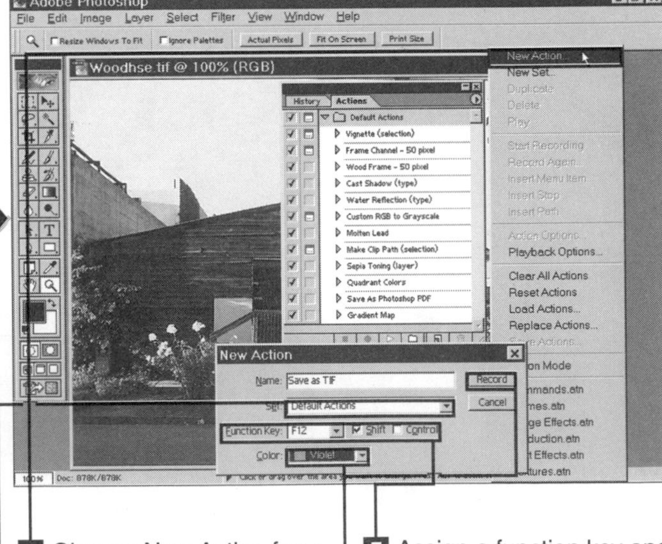

1 Open a file that is a typical target for the Action you want to open.

2 Choose Window, then Show Actions.

■ The Actions palette appears.

Note: The Actions palette must be visible before you can create, edit, and manage Actions.

3 Choose New Action from the Actions palette menu.

■ The New Action dialog box appears.

4 Choose a set to associate with the new Action.

5 Assign a function key and modifier key(s).

6 Choose a color for the button.

7 Click Record to begin recording the new Action.

What if I forget to save my Actions?

✔ Photoshop saves your Actions automatically in the default palette. To remove an Action from the default set, you can create a new set, drag the Action into that set, and then save the new set.

What commands cannot be recorded?

✔ You cannot record commands involving painting tools (Airbrush, Paintbrush, Rubber Stamp, Pencil, Eraser), focus tools (Blur, Sharpen, Smudge), and toning tools (Dodge, Burn, Sponge), or Tool options, View commands, and Preferences.

What if I want to create an Action that uses a painting, focusing, or toning tool?

✔ You cannot record the functions of these tools, but you can insert a stop in your Action. This way the Action pauses to let you manually use the tool. You can even write a customized message instructing what tool to use at what setting and for what purpose. You can also tell the Action to continue when you have finished using the tool.

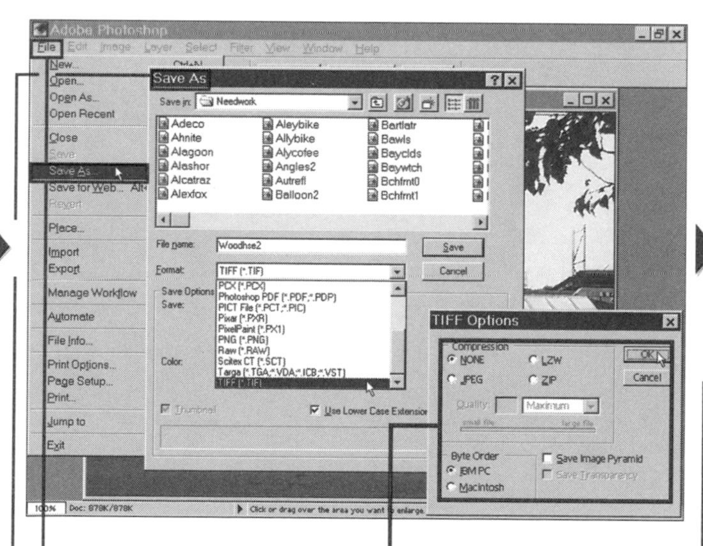

8 Choose the command you want the Action to execute first.

9 If the command has an associated dialog box, make the choices you want to repeat.

10 Click and enter the appropriate information in any subsequent dialog box, then click OK.

11 Repeat steps 8 through 10 for as many commands as you want to include in this Action.

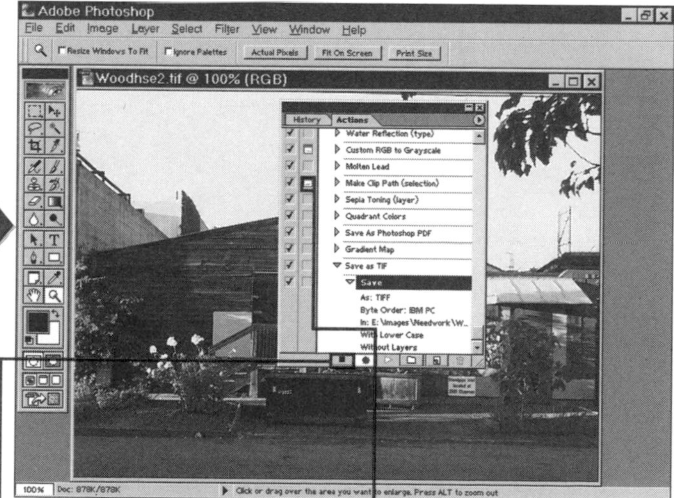

■ A command to close the file was entered after the Save As command in this example.

12 When you have finished adding commands, click Stop Recording (■).

13 Click to turn on modal control if you want to change information in a dialog box.

■ Your Actions are recorded.

SAVE AND LOAD A SET OF ACTIONS

Actions are automatically saved in a set called Actions Palette.psp (the Mac uses the same filename but does not add the .psp extension). However, at times you might want to move an Action to a different set.

You cannot save or load individual Actions, only sets of Actions.

If you want to save one Action and place it into several sets, you can create a new set and record only one Action (or move only one Action into it) and save the set.

If you move an Action out of a set but do not save the set, the Action remains in the original set for future use.

Two commands enable you to load Actions in Photoshop:

- Load Actions
- Replace Actions

Load Actions adds the chosen set to the current set. Replace Actions deletes the current set from the Actions palette and adds the newly chosen palette.

SAVE AND LOAD A SET OF ACTIONS

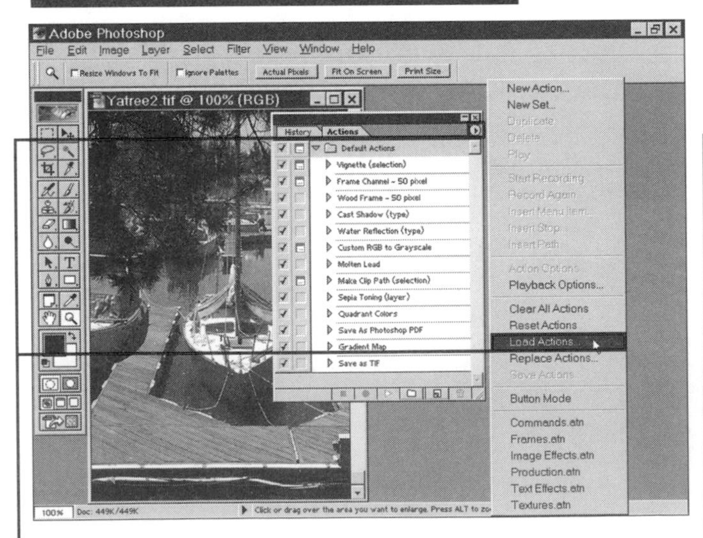

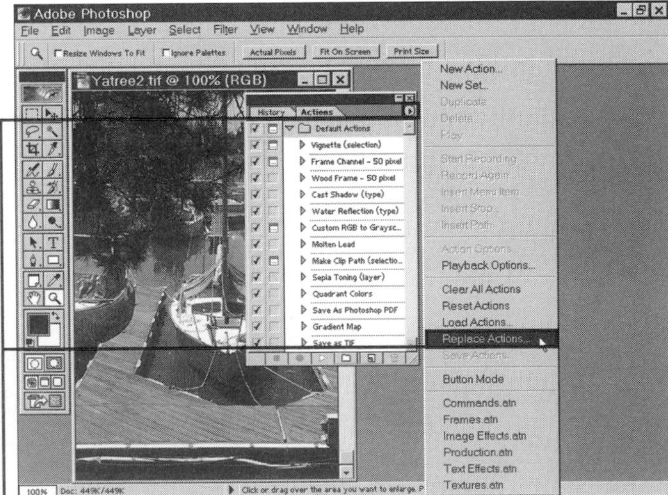

ADD ACTIONS TO THE CURRENT SET

1 Click ▶ and choose Load Actions from the Actions palette menu.

■ The Load Actions dialog box appears.

2 Navigate to the folder containing the Action sets (Windows and Mac use .atn extensions) and double-click the filename of the Action set.

■ The new Action set loads in the Actions palette.

REPLACE AN ACTION SET

1 Click ▶ and choose Replace Actions.

■ The Replace Actions dialog box appears.

2 Navigate to the folder containing the Action.

3 Double-click the filename of the Action you want to exchange.

■ The new Action set replaces any sets already loaded into the Actions palette.

Can I assign the same function key to different Actions in different sets?

✔ You can as long as both sets are not loaded into the same palette. Unfortunately, Photoshop does not alert you to problems with function keys assigned to more than one Action in a set.

How do I rename a set?

✔ You can rename a set the same way you rename any Photoshop palette item: Double-click the item's name bar in the palette. When the Set Options dialog box appears, enter a new name.

How do I copy an Action to several other sets without removing it from the original set?

✔ Drag the Action to the New Action icon at the bottom of the Actions palette. A new Action appears, with *copy* appended to the original name. Drag the copy to another set, double-click its name bar, and then rename it in the Options dialog box. Now save the set to which you moved the copy. Repeat for as many different sets as you like.

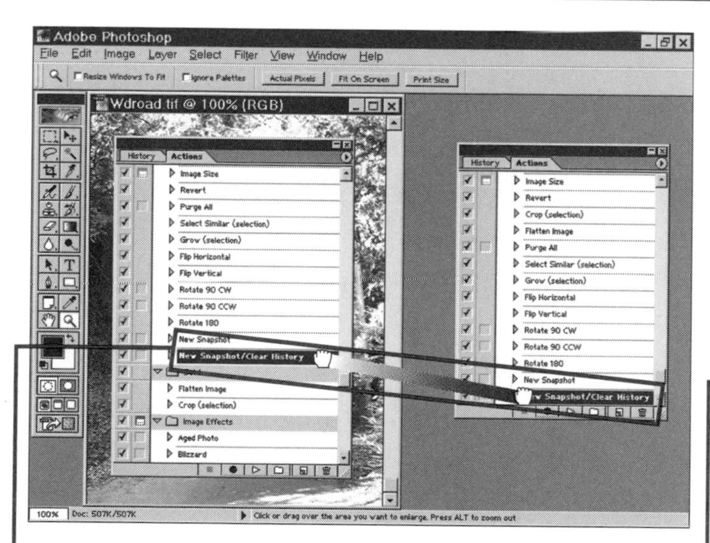

MOVE AN ACTION FROM ONE SET TO ANOTHER

1 Load both sets.

Note: See "Add Actions to the Current Set" on the facing page for more on loading sets.

2 Drag the Action from the current set to another.

■ Selecting each set and saving it makes the new location permanent.

■ You can also change an Action's position within a set by dragging it to a new location within the set.

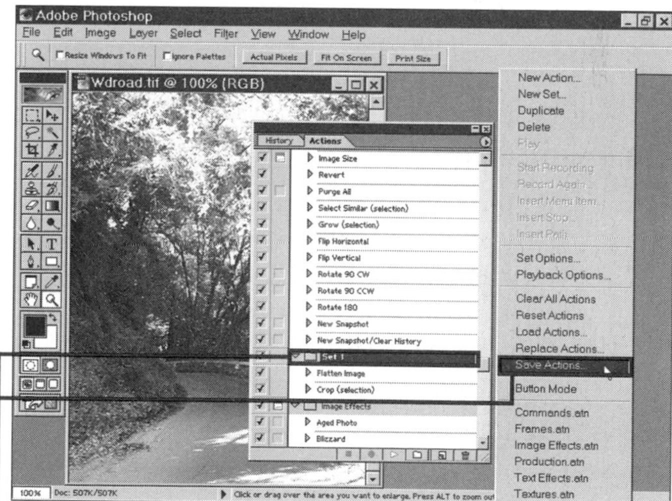

SAVE AN ACTIONS SET

1 Click to highlight the target set.

2 Click ⊙ and then choose Save Actions.

■ The standard Save dialog box appears.

3 Navigate to the desired folder and click Save.

■ Photoshop saves the action.

EDIT AN ACTION

After you record an Action, you can do several things to modify it.

- You can add new commands at any point in the Action.
- You can change the values for any commands associated with dialog boxes.
- You can change the Action Options (Action Name, Button Color, Shortcut Key and modifiers).
- Finally, you can remove commands from the Action.

If you are new to editing Actions, first make a duplicate of the Action you want to edit and work on the duplicate. If you dislike your edits, you can discard the duplicate and revert to the original Action.

The preceding exercise in this chapter demonstrates how to move a command from one Action set to another. You use the same drag-and-drop technique to move commands within the same Action, except you just drag them to a new location in that Action's queue. Commands are always executed in top-to-bottom order.

EDIT AN ACTION

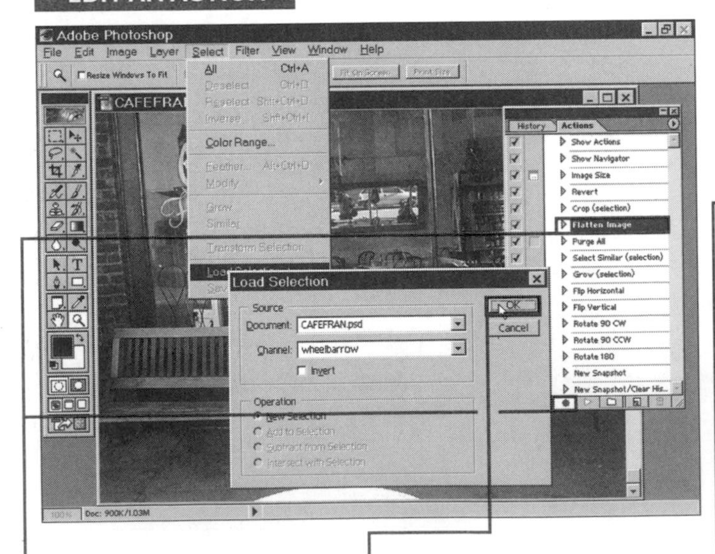

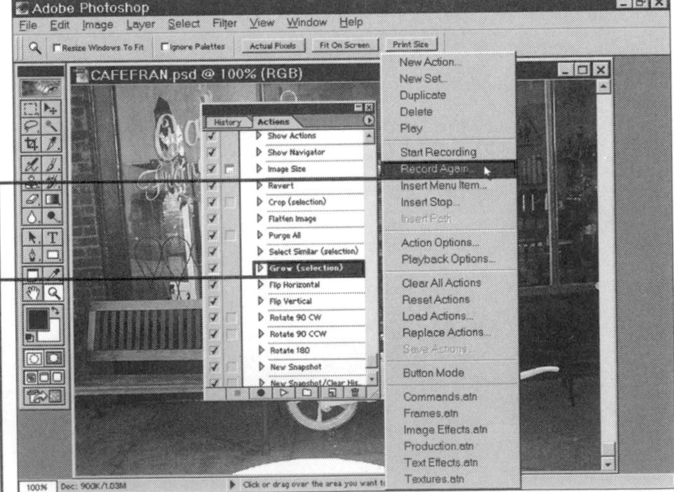

INSERT A NEW COMMAND IN AN EXISTING ACTION

1 Click the command after which you want to insert any new command(s).

2 Click the Begin Recording button (●).

3 Execute as many new commands as you would like to add.

4 Click Stop Recording (■) when you want to stop adding commands.

5 Click OK.

CHANGE AN EXISTING COMMAND

1 Click the command whose parameters you want to change.

2 Click ▶ and choose Record Again from the Actions palette menu.

Note: Any associated tool or dialog box immediately appears.

3 Change any parameter.

4 Click OK.

■ Recording stops automatically.

How can I duplicate an item on the Actions palette list?

✔ There are three ways to duplicate an item on the Actions palette list. You can drag the item to the New Action icon at the bottom of the Actions palette. You can press Opt/Alt-drag the item to a new location in the Actions palette. You can select as many commands as you like (Shift-click for noncontiguous items; Ctrl/Cmd-click for noncontiguous items) and choose Duplicate from the Actions palette menu.

I have some Actions that perform similar function yet are not identical. What do I do?

✔ Too much of a good thing can lead to chaos. Consider creating unique names for your Actions and sets so that you know their specific purpose and function.

What if I want to delete all the Actions in the palette?

✔ Choosing Clear Actions from the Actions palette menu cleans the palette. The actions are all still in the disk file unless you save the empty set under the same name. You can always retrieve the default Actions, even if you do this to them.

What do I do when I find the default set of Actions too crowded with Actions?

✔ Move all the Actions you want to keep into other sets. Next, choose Reset from the Actions palette menu. The original default Actions will reappear.

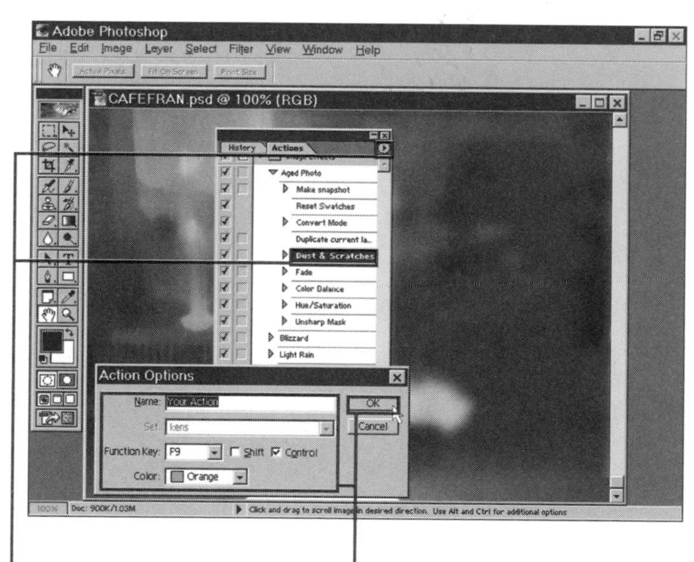

CHANGE THE ACTION OPTIONS

1 Click the Action name bar of the Action whose options you want to change.

2 Click ▶ and choose Change Options.

■ The Action's dialog box appears.

3 Change name, keyboard shortcut, and button color where needed.

4 Click OK to make the change.

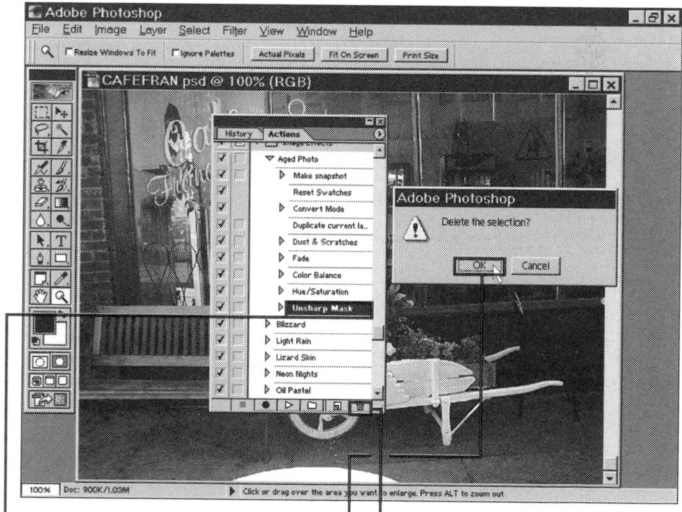

DELETE A COMMAND, ACTION, OR SET

1 Choose the name bar of the command, Action, or set you want to delete.

2 Click Delete (🗑).

3 Click OK.

■ Photoshop deletes the selection from the set.

PLAY ACTIONS

With Photoshop, you control how Actions play. You can decide whether the Actions start when you press a function key, click an Action's mode button, or double-click the Action in the editable list.

You can also

- Control how the Actions behave after they play
- Opt to play any of the commands in the Action's list
- Process a single file or, by playing the Action in Batch mode, process a whole folder of files
- Tell Photoshop to play an Action at the fastest speed possible
- Slow an action down so that you can study how it affects your work

You can even pause the Actions to use a tool that cannot be recorded. You can even opt not to play an entire Action.

You might have one command among several in an Action that you want to run by itself.

PLAY ACTIONS

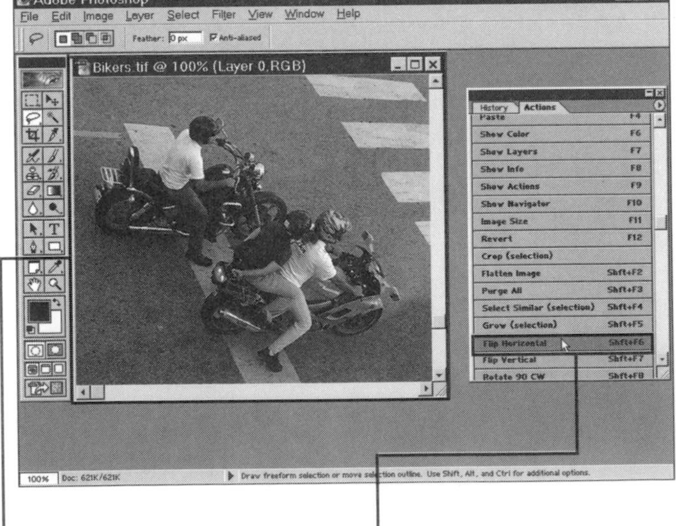

PLAY AN ACTION AT NORMAL SPEED

1 Click the window containing the file(s) you want to affect.

2 Click ⊙ and choose Button mode.

3 Click the button of the Action you want to play.

■ Or, press a function key, if available.

■ The Action plays at normal speed.

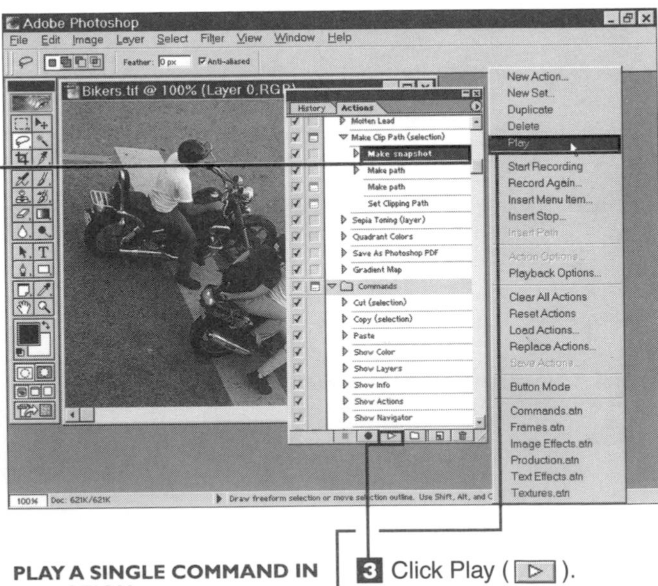

PLAY A SINGLE COMMAND IN AN ACTION

1 Make sure that you are not in Button mode.

2 Click the command you want to play.

3 Click Play (▷).

■ Optionally, choose Play from the Actions palette menu.

■ Photoshop plays the selected command.

Can I play a whole set of Actions on a single file?

✔ Yes. Just select the name of the set instead of an individual Action, and then follow the steps under the section "Play an Action at Normal Speed." This method works best in sets you have created to work in a logical "flow" on your images.

Why would I want to slow down playback of an Action?

✔ You can slow down the playback to demonstrate to someone else how you did something (such as creating a composite photo). You can use the slow playback to determine why an Action does not behave as you expected.

What if I want to undo an Action?

✔ Playing an Action does not record all the subsequently executed commands to the History palette. Give yourself a margin of safety by recording a snapshot of the state of the file before you play the Action. This way you can return to the snapshot later. To record a snapshot, choose Window, then Show History, and then choose New Snapshot from the History palette menu.

EXCLUDE PLAYBACK ACTIONS

1 Click to turn off the command (☑ changes to ☐).

Note: You can uncheck as many commands or Actions as you want to turn off. To turn them back on, click the same box again.

■ When you play an Action, Photoshop skips the selected command.

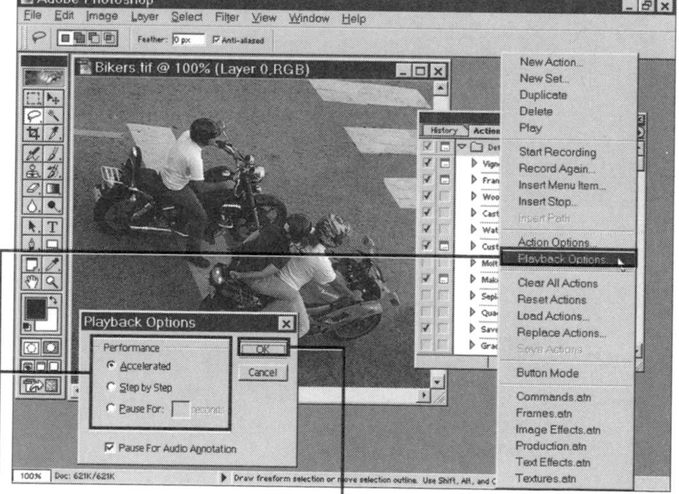

SET PLAYBACK SPEED

1 Choose Playback Options from the palette menu.

2 Select a Performance option (○ changes to ◉).

■ Accelerated plays the Actions faster, Step by Step shows individual changes to the image, and Pause stops the Actions for a selected time, which you type in the seconds box.

3 Click OK.

PLAY ACTIONS IN BATCHES

You can batch Play Actions to save time in processing images in Photoshop. For example, you can batch your conversion process when you capture dozens of frames from a video camera or digital camera.

Applications for batch processing are endless. You can apply almost any Action to a batch of figures or convert all your files to a lossless format. You can make a set of thumbnails or thumbnail contact sheets, run AutoLevels on all of them, and store them all in the folder of your choice.

Before starting a batch conversion, organize your target folders: Place all the files that you want to be converted on the same level of folders. If you want to store the results of the batch conversion to a different folder, make sure that the target folder exists before you start the Action.

Also, be sure to check that you have sufficient storage space (usually your hard disk or a volume on a hard disk) for the newly created files.

PLAY ACTIONS IN BATCHES

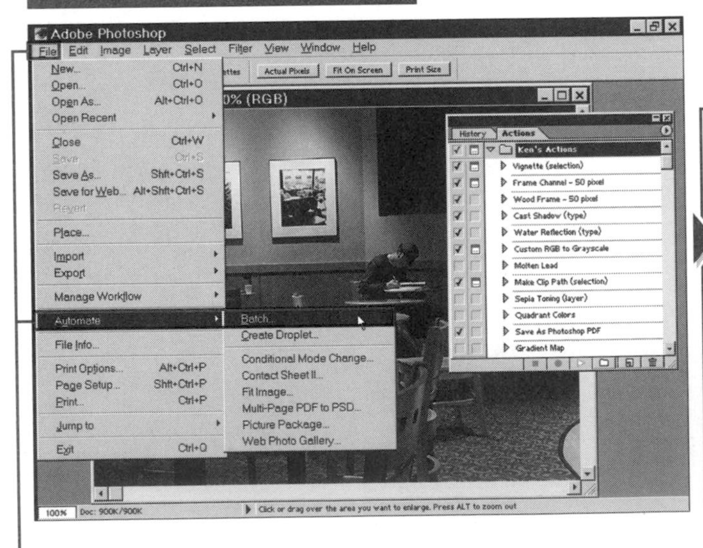

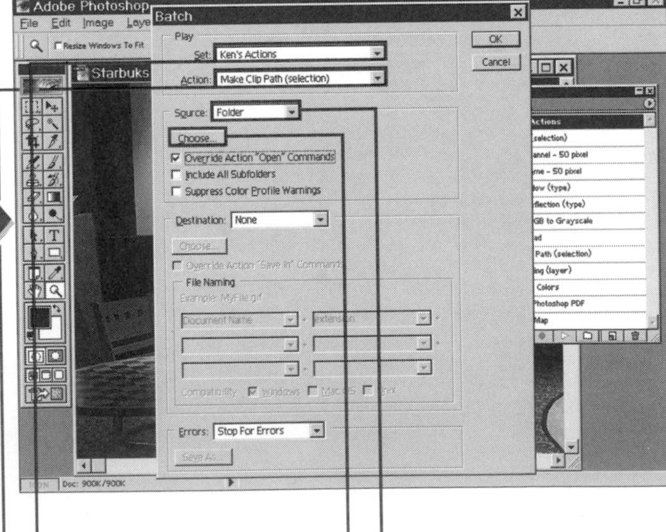

1 Choose File, then Automate, then Batch.

■ The Batch dialog box appears.

2 Choose a set from the Set menu.

3 Choose an Action from the Action menu.

4 Choose Folder (existing folder), Import (from a camera/scanner), or Opened files (currently opened files).

5 If Folder is the choice, click Choose and navigate to the folder that contains the files you want processed.

What if I want to apply just one command to a batch of files?

✔ If it is a command that is one of only a few in an Action, simply turn off all the others by unchecking their On/Off boxes. You can also record a single command as an Action.

Does any way exist for applying a complete set to a batch?

✔ You can drag all the commands in that set into a single Action. However, consider testing this new, complex Action on a few test files before applying it to many.

What if I want to process the file but do not want it to overwrite the original?

✔ Make sure you choose Folder from the Destination menu in the Batch dialog box. It is also mandatory that you either uncheck any Save or Save As commands included in the Action or check the Override Action "Save In" Commands box—unless you want the files saved in two different places.

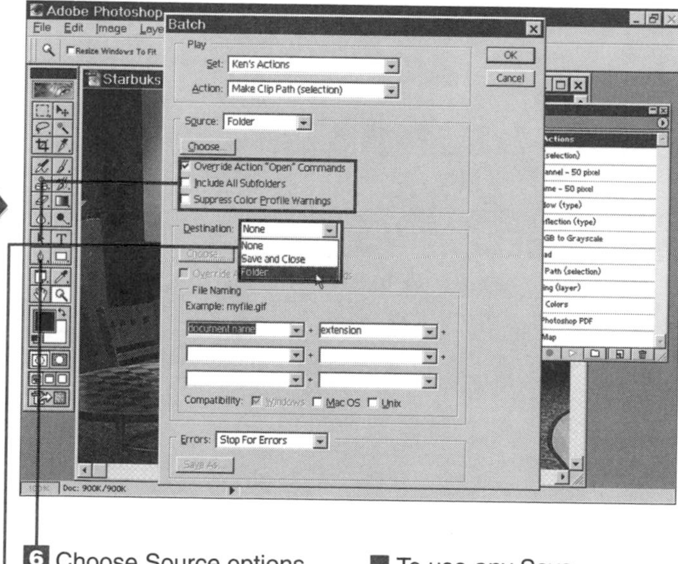

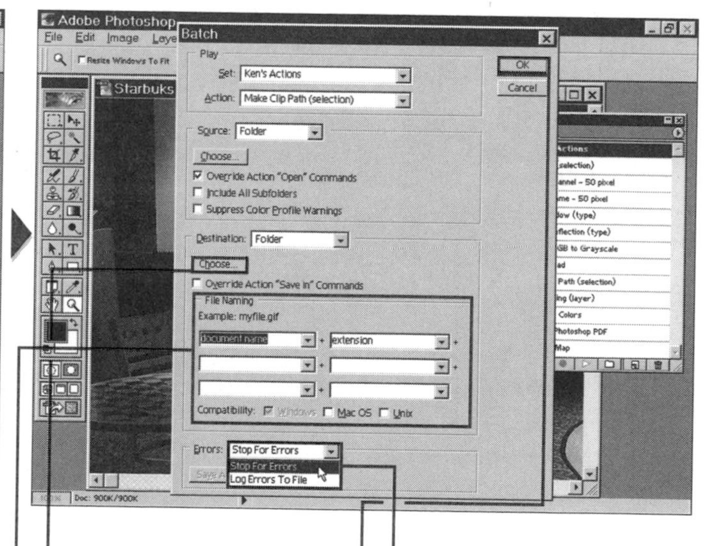

6 Choose Source options (☐ changes to ☑).

7 Choose a destination.

■ To use any Save command included in the Action or to leave files open, choose None. To save and close files after the Action is complete, select Save and Close. To save and close files into a new folder, select Folder.

■ If you chose Folder, you can click Choose and navigate to the folder you created earlier.

8 Select or type any specific rules or text required for naming the output files.

9 Choose an Errors option.

10 Click OK.

■ Photoshop saves your Batch options.

INSERT UNRECORDABLE ACTIONS

Although you cannot record some tools and commands in Actions, you can accommodate the Actions. Think of this situation as a modern, high-tech version of a master-apprentice relationship. Back in the days of the great classic painters (Raphael, for example), the apprentice did the routine work of prepping an easel and even some background painting. The master would then take over. Today, you can use Photoshop Actions to serve as your apprentice, stopping routine procedures to permit you, the master (of course!), to address your image, painting tool in hand.

The following is a partial list of tools and commands that cannot be recorded:

- Paint Tools (Paintbrush Tool, Pencil)
- History Brush Tool (Art History Brush)
- Eraser Tool (Background Eraser Tool, Magic Eraser Tool)
- Airbrush
- Clone Stamp Tool (Pattern Stamp Tool)
- Tool options
- View menu commands
- Preferences

INSERT UNRECORDABLE ACTIONS

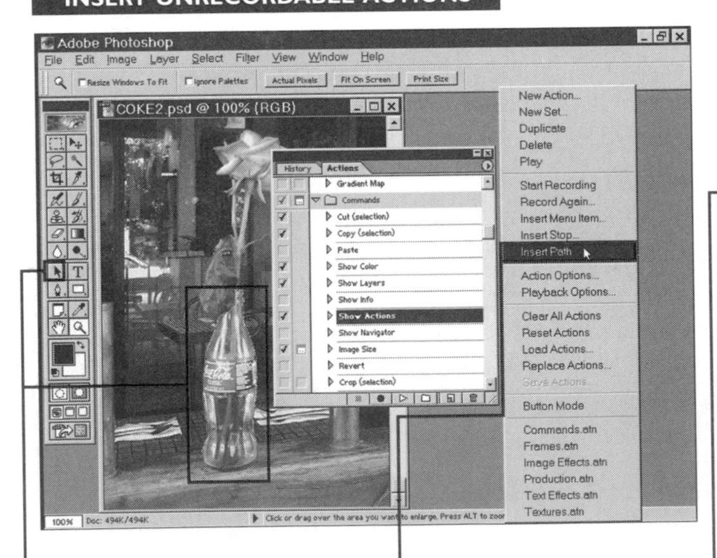

RECORD A PATH

Note: Make sure you have a path drawn on the active layer.

1 Choose the Path Component Selection tool.

2 Click the desired path to select it.

3 Choose Insert Path from the Actions palette menu.

Note: Regardless of which file an Action processes, the inserted path appears on that file's active layer.

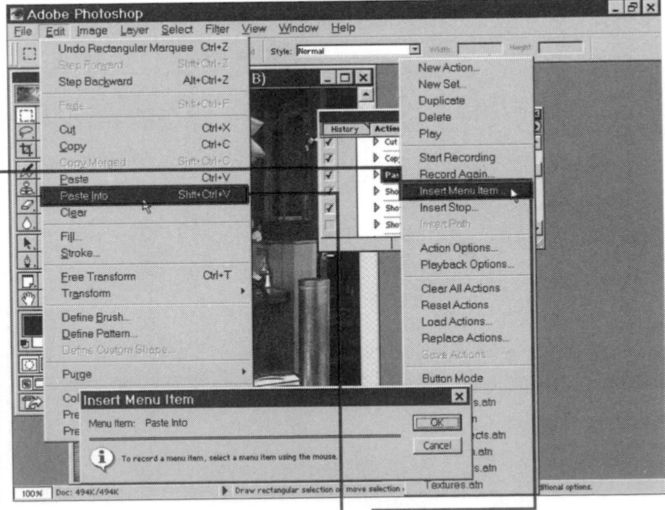

INSERT A NONRECORDABLE MENU ITEM

Note: See "Create a New Action" to finish recording the Action.

1 Click to select the recorded command to follow the inserted command (example: Edit, Paste Info).

2 Choose Insert Menu Item from the Actions palette menu.

3 Choose any menu item or tool that has an Options dialog box.

Why are some inserted commands unavailable when I try to play back the Action?

✔ The inserted command might not be available due to the process or the nature of the image at the time you play the Action. Because Photoshop does not know what the state of a given image will be when a given Action plays, Photoshop enables you to insert all commands. Photoshop always gives you the choice of continuing if you cannot access a command.

My Actions do not always work. What is going on?

✔ Bear in mind that the successful playback of an Action depends on variables that are not controlled by the Action itself. Variables such as foreground and background colors, active layers, and color modes might prevent an Action from working.

Am I limited in which commands I can insert?

✔ You can choose any command, so long as the command has an associated dialog box, and the dialog box appears without having to choose the Modal icon in the Actions palette. If there is no associated dialog box (most notably for the Undo, Cut, Copy, Paste, and Clear commands), the command simply executes.

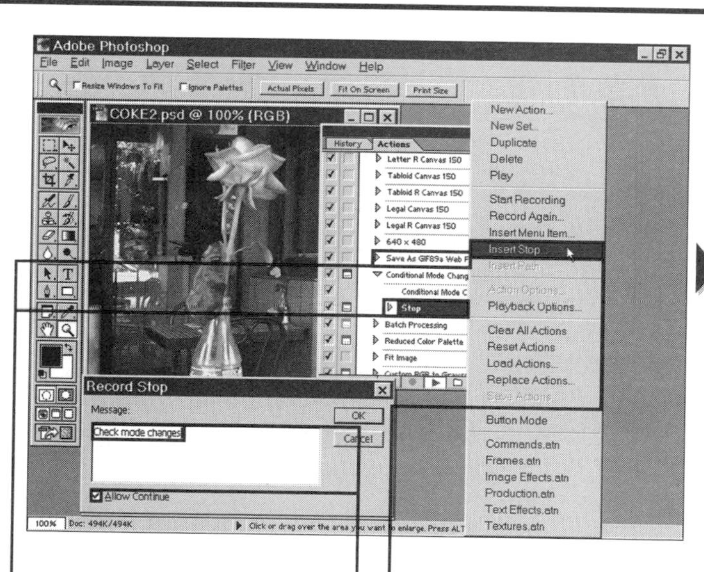

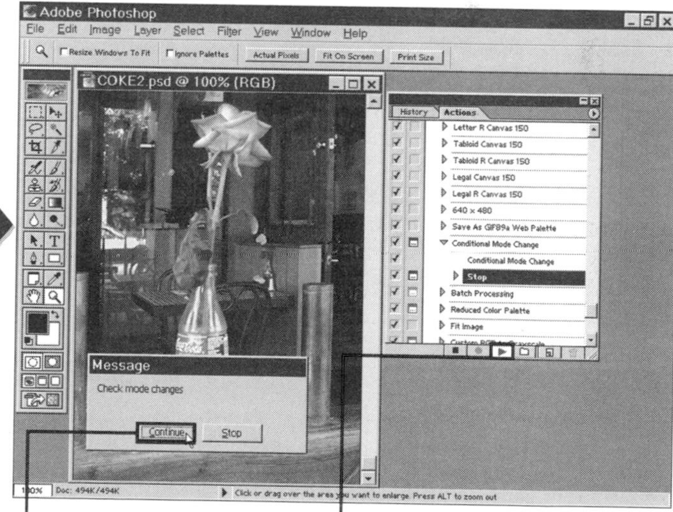

INSERT A PAUSE IN AN ACTION

1 Select the recorded command that precedes the inserted stop.

■ Or, select the Action if you want the stop to occur at the end of the Action.

2 Choose Insert Stop.

3 Type a description of what to do during the pause.

■ You can check Allow Continue if you want the Action to resume after the pause (☐ changes to ☑).

■ When you play back an Action with a stop inserted, the Action stops and a message appears.

■ When the message appears, you can click Continue to continue, or Stop to perform your selected task.

■ You can click the Play button to resume the Action.

PLACE A CONDITIONAL MODE CHANGE INTO AN ACTION

You may find yourself in a situation that requires your image(s) to be in a particular color mode in order to work with a particular command. If you need to convert a series of images to the required mode, an Automate command in Photoshop 6 (introduced in 5.5) can help you out.

The Conditional Mode Change command is so called because it can change the mode of a file only if it needs to be changed.

The Conditional Mode Change command changes the color mode of the action's target images on two conditions:

- The selected images are not already in a particular mode
- The images' current mode is different from the target mode

If the conditions are not met, the file is simply left unmodified.

PLACE A CONDITIONAL MODE CHANGE INTO AN ACTION

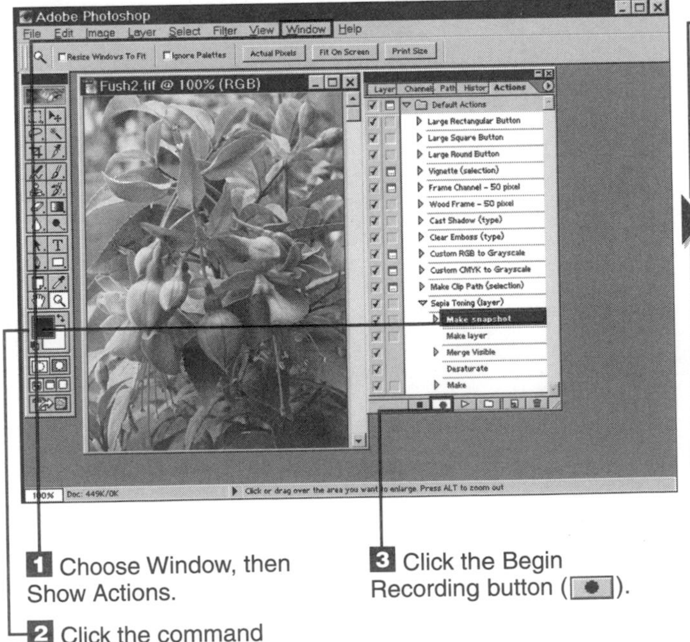

1 Choose Window, then Show Actions.

2 Click the command preceding the point where you want to add the conditional mode change.

3 Click the Begin Recording button (●).

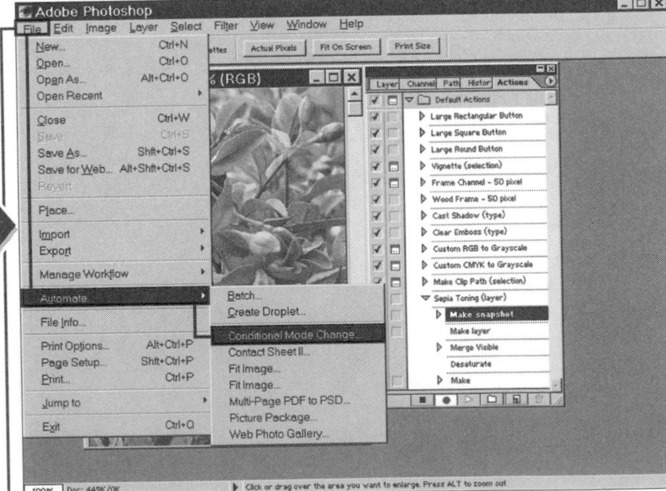

4 Choose File, then Automate then Conditional Mode Change.

What happens to the original file when I use a Conditional Mode Change?

✔ This command permanently changes the file it affects. If you do not want to change the mode of the original, be sure to organize your files so that you are working on a copy.

What happens if I click the None button?

✔ You will not make any conversions. The purpose of having the None button is to clear all previous entries so that you can start fresh.

Why can I not select more than one Target Mode?

✔ Because there is no need. You are only changing modes here so that you can perform a command that would not operate in any other mode.

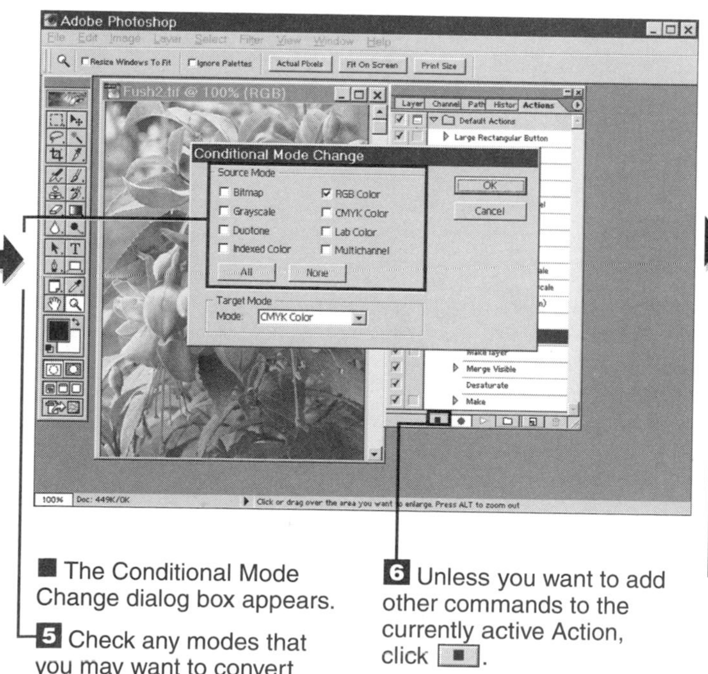

■ The Conditional Mode Change dialog box appears.

5 Check any modes that you may want to convert from.

6 Unless you want to add other commands to the currently active Action, click ■.

■ The mode change is made and is recorded in the History palette

COLLECT AND PREP IMAGES

Composite images include both *collages* (multiple images combined so that each is distinct but contributes to an overall message and composition) and *montages* (images combined to create the illusion of a scene that never happened). Collecting and prepping images for use in a collage or montage is not mandatory, but saves you time, makes it easier to move the project to another computer, and makes it easier to keep track of your work if you decide to back up your project to CD-ROM.

When collecting and prepping images for a composite project, make a special folder and then copy all the files you are going to use in the composite to the new folder. Notice the word *copy*. Then if you resize, crop, or modify the copied files, you will not have destroyed your originals.

The second most important thing is to make all the components roughly the size they will be in the composite, which means resizing and trimming them. When you resize, be sure not to make the file any smaller than you could possibly want it to be. If you do, and you have to enlarge it later, you will lose definition. (Of course, you could always copy the original back in.)

COLLECT AND PREP IMAGES

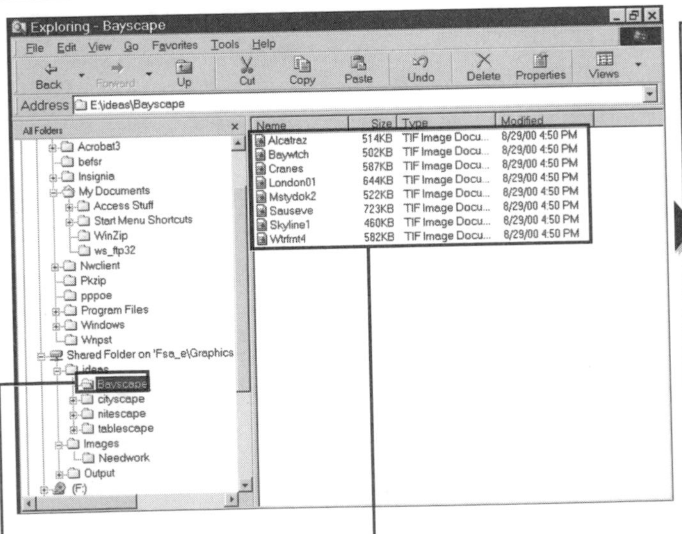

Note: Use your thumbnails or contact sheets to find the images you want in your composite.

1 Create a folder and name it after your project.

2 Copy all the needed files into this folder.

■ Windows users, remember, do not cut and paste or move them. Mac users, hold down the option key when dragging the icons to the new folder so that they will be copied.

3 Open the folder's files in Photoshop.

Note: Open the folder and then drag all the files onto the Photoshop icon.

4 Choose Window, then Tile.

Note: This command is not available in the Mac version. Just arrange windows so you can see all the needed files.

5 In turn, click to activate each image.

6 Press /Ctrl+(-) to zoom out until you can see the entire image in the window.

How do I make my montage look more realistic?

✔ A montage is more realistic when you shoot all the images under the same lighting conditions and with the light coming from the same direction. Ideally, you should collect images whose elements can be easily separated from their backgrounds because other elements are not in front of them.

Duplicating all these files uses a lot of hard disk space. How can I keep it to a minimum?

✔ Crop each of the originals to the portion used in the target image. This method keeps the size of your project folder as small as possible.

What is the best tool for making the initial quick cuts?

✔ I zoom all the way out. If I just want to lop off a portion of a layer, I use the Marquee. Otherwise, I just make a quick freehand selection with the Lasso. Press Delete/Backspace, and you are ready to perform refined edge cutouts and blending.

■ Decide which image is going to be the main image or background. You want to place all images inside this one, the target image.

7 Decide what portion of each image you want to use.

8 Click the Move tool (or press V).

9 Drag the selected portion onto the target image.

■ Each of the dragged-in selections automatically becomes a new layer in the target image.

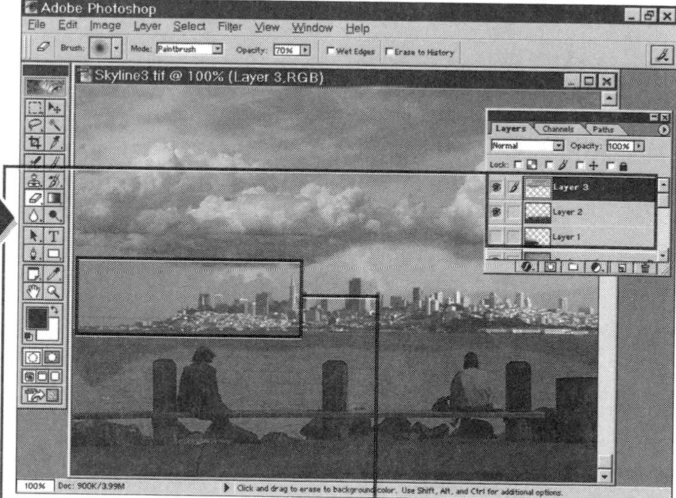

10 Choose Window, then Show Layers.

11 Drag the layers into their required stacking order.

12 Click to reveal the Opacity slider, then drag the Opacity slider to change transparency to see which portions overlap.

13 Make a rough selection of the portion of each layer that will not be needed and press Delete/Backspace to cut.

■ Now you are organized for the considerable fine-tuning needed to make your collage.

INTEGRATE IMAGES IN A MONTAGE

You can make montages that are so well integrated that most viewers will think that all the objects originated from the same photograph. Part of the reason is the capability to control exposure, transparency, and Blend mode, but the biggest difference is that images can be made to fade into one another.

The three techniques for doing such edge blending, shown in the exercise here, are quite simple:

- You can erase the edges with a highly feathered paint brush eraser.
- You can make a feathered selection.
- You can make a layer mask and then place a gradient in it.

Note that the difference between a montage and a collage is that a collage does not require you to make the images look as though they are part of the same photo. In fact, as in traditional collage, simply rough-cutting images and then scaling and placing them to make your composition is often effective.

INTEGRATE IMAGES IN A MONTAGE

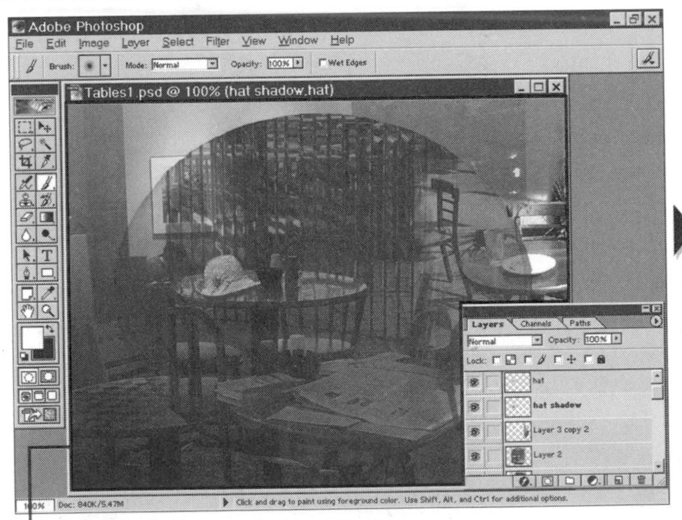

1 Assemble the images of your montage.

■ Make sure each of your images resides on its own layer.

Note: To assemble your images and check their layer position, see the section "Collect and Prep Images."

■ In this example, all the images of the montage fade into one another.

FADE AN IMAGE EVENLY

2 Make a selection that surrounds the image.

Note: To select an image, see Chapter 6.

3 Choose Select, then Feather and enter a high number (typically 10 to 60) of pixels in the Feather dialog box.

4 Invert the selection (press ⌘/Ctrl+I or choose Select, then Inverse).

5 Press Delete/Backspace.

Are there other techniques for integrating images in a montage?

✔ Scribble with the Eraser, both with and without checking the Use History box in the Eraser Options. This technique places sketches of the underlying layers within the active layer (and vice versa), and yields a different feel to the integration of your images.

Can I fade an image on both sides by using the Gradient tool?

✔ Sure. The width of your gradient is determined by how far you drag. The gradient is made from the foreground color to the background color in the direction you drag; to make a two-sided fade, just make a gradient on both edges of the mask.

Can Blend modes and filters also affect the effectiveness of a montage?

✔ There is no end to the creative ways you can use Photoshop to enhance (or mess up) your collages and montages. Using various filters and Blend modes (see Chapters 8 and 9, and Chapters 13 through 17) can certainly enrich texture and mood and do more to bring an original touch to the work.

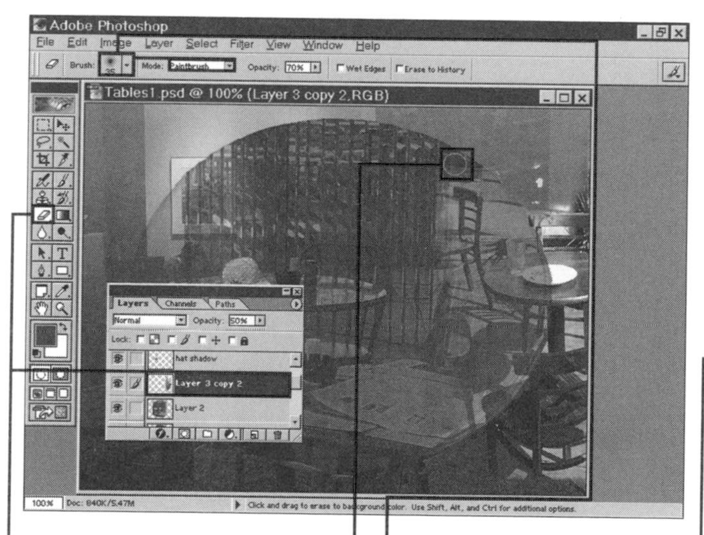

BLEND EDGES WITH THE ERASER

1 Click to activate the layer you want to erase.

2 Click the Eraser tool ( ).

3 Choose the Paintbrush mode from the Options palette and use a highly feathered brush.

4 Erase wherever you want to see an underlying image show through.

MAKE A FADING LAYER MASK

1 On the Layers palette, activate the layer you want to fade.

2 Click the Make Layer Mask icon ( ).

3 Click the Channels tab, activate the layer mask channel, and make all channels visible.

4 Click the Gradient tool ( ) and drag to make a gradient that fades from black to white.

CLEAN UP THE EDGES

If you are making a collage and you have already collected and prepped the needed images, the next step is to cut out and prepare the components that will be blended together.

The routine goes like this: First, select the obviously easy-to-delete portions you know you are not going to need. If your selection makes a clean edge, fine, but do not waste time on this task until you have gotten rid of the bulk of the stuff to be discarded. You will then have a much easier time positioning items so that they blend into one another as smoothly as possible. You should leave some portions of the original image surrounding the part you want to keep. These portions will be deleted later with the eraser.

Second, position and scale the individual layers as close to their final relative places and sizes as possible.

When everything is in position, use the Eraser and brush tools to retouch any edges as needed.

CLEAN UP THE EDGES

1 In each layer, cut out material that will not appear in the composite.

■ See Section II, "Making Image Adjustments" for more on editing images.

2 Make a loose lasso selection around the material to be kept.

■ See Chapter 6 for more on making selections.

3 Press /Ctrl+Shift+I to invert the selection.

4 Press Delete/Backspace to delete the unwanted material.

5 Choose Select, then Color Range, and click OK.

6 Press Delete/Backspace to clear the selected area.

7 Choose Layer, then Matting, then Defringe.

■ The Defringe dialog box appears.

8 Type 1 or 2 in the Width field, and then click OK.

How do I know how much width to specify in the Defringe dialog box?

✔ If in doubt, enter 1 pixel. If that setting does not do the job, repeat the command until the fringe is all gone. Do not overdo it, or parts of your image will start to disappear. Remember, you can retouch with the Eraser tool.

Why should I not make my selections before I put the image into the composite file?

✔ You will end up having to tweak it with the Eraser tool anyway. You may as well save time by doing it all in one step.

Why do you use the Eraser to fine-tune edges instead of just making a selection and inverting it?

✔ Lots of people use selection and inversion, and it is often a good technique. Unfortunately, what works in theory sometimes does not work in practice. A correctly selected edge may look too sharp in some places and too soft in others. By using the Eraser, you can control the edges visually. It is like painting the object into place.

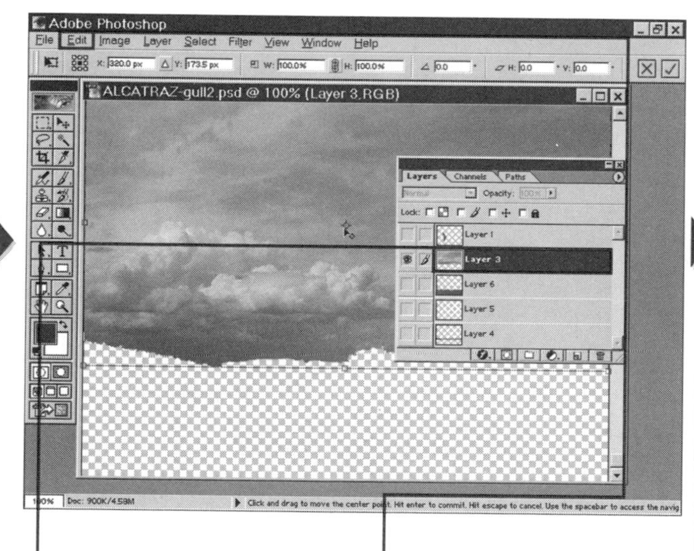

9 After you make rough trims for all the layers, use the Layers palette to stack the layers in the order in which you want them to appear.

■ See Chapter 9 for more on working with layers.

10 Choose Edit, then Free Transform, and rescale the layer.

■ Scale layers to the size they will be in the final composite.

11 Click the Eraser tool ( ).

12 Choose Paintbrush from the Mode menu (in the Options Bar).

13 Choose a fairly small brush with a slightly feathered edge.

14 Enter about 200% to zoom in and stroke the image to erase the exact edge you want.

REARRANGE ITEMS ON A LAYER

You can copy a selected portion of a layer to a new layer in one keystroke. Then, you can move an item on one of the layers in a composite so that the item is not covered by another item, or layer.

You can also move an item into a more visually prominent place or to improve the composition.

Here is how you do it: Select the item. Press ⌘/Ctrl+J to lift the contents of the selection to a new layer. Next, turn off everything but the originating layer and clone the original items. Now you can move and transform the new layer any way you like.

After you have cloned, moved, and edited the item in question, then you can return to the original layer and, using the Rubber Stamp tool, eliminate the item from that layer. This task should not be difficult, unless that item is on a very complex background.

REARRANGE ITEMS ON A LAYER

1 Click the Eye icons (👁) to turn off the layers above the target layer.

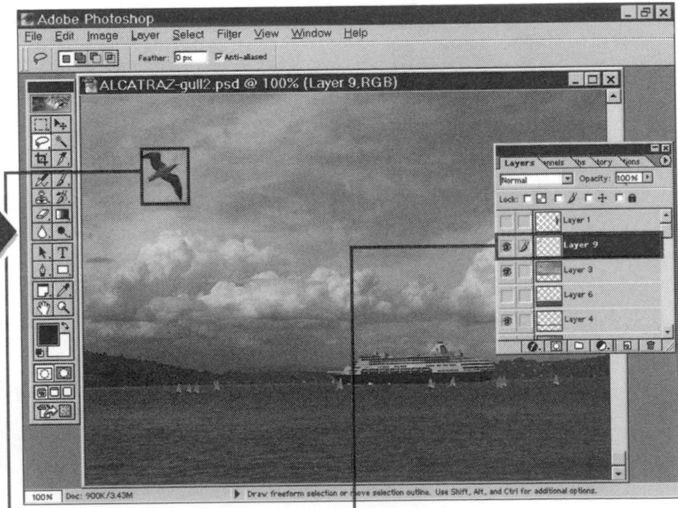

2 Make a rough selection around the subject you want to move.

Note: See Chapter 6 to learn more about selecting an item.

Note: Reflections and water tracks must be included, otherwise the subjects will not look natural in their relocated surroundings.

3 Press /Ctrl+Opt/Alt+D to feather the selection.

4 Press /Ctrl+J to lift the selection to a new layer.

What is the best way to keep the results of the cloning from being obvious?

✔ Use a feathered brush so you do not get sharp borders. Paint into the same general area from several points of origin; otherwise, you are likely to get repeating patterns, or you will push lighter areas into darker areas, which results in the appearance of an obvious border.

How much should I feather the selection?

✔ That depends on the overall size of the image and even more on the size of the object you are moving. Generally, anything less than a 5-pixel feather is going to make a visible break.

Can I keep the original item and create more than one clone of it?

✔ What is your purpose with this image? If you want to make a realistic flock of birds or create a forest of trees, cloning one or two original items just will not cut it. On the other hand, this technique may be fine for a humorous or child's illustration.

5 Click the Move tool ( ).

6 Click to activate the new layer.

7 Drag to move the item.

Note: In this case, the item blends perfectly with the clouds, but this is seldom the case. If you have to blend edges, see the previous exercise.

8 Click the Eye icons to the left of the Layer Name bars ( ) to make the original subject disappear, then turn off the layer(s) above it.

9 Click , the Rubber Stamp tool (or press S).

10 Check the Aligned check box.

11 Press Opt/Alt+click to set the origin point and paint out the original subject.

CAST SHADOWS

You can change the apparent angle of the light so that all objects in photo montages look as if they were shot in the same place and at the same time.

The first giveaway in many montages that the image is indeed a montage is inconsistent lighting. Professionals who make montages generally have well-equipped studios, so for them, this inconsistency is easy to avoid. They adjust the lighting in their studios to match the background shot and then shoot the components. If you are shooting outdoors, try to shoot all the components at the same time of day. If you cannot do that, shoot in the shade. This way you will have a fairly evenly lit subject, and you can add your own shadows. Better yet, shoot your background scene(s) on an overcast day (or at least while the sun is behind a cloud).

If you have shot on an overcast day and the lighting is fairly even (the more so, the better), you will be able to fake some shadows and highlights in Photoshop.

CAST SHADOWS

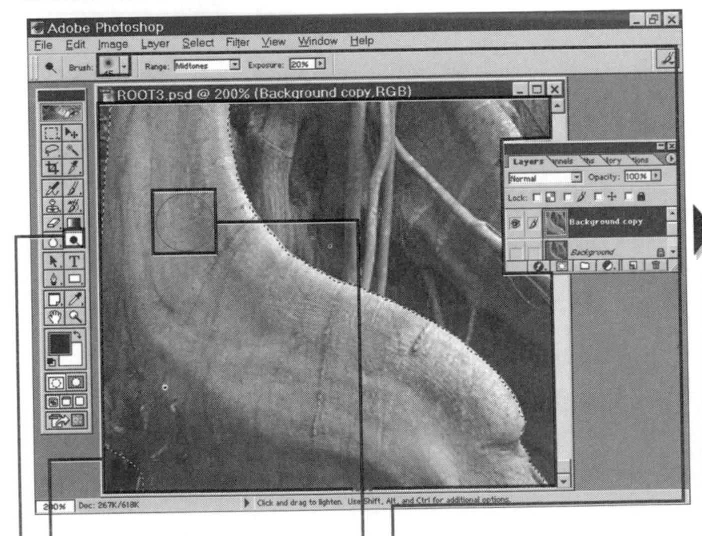

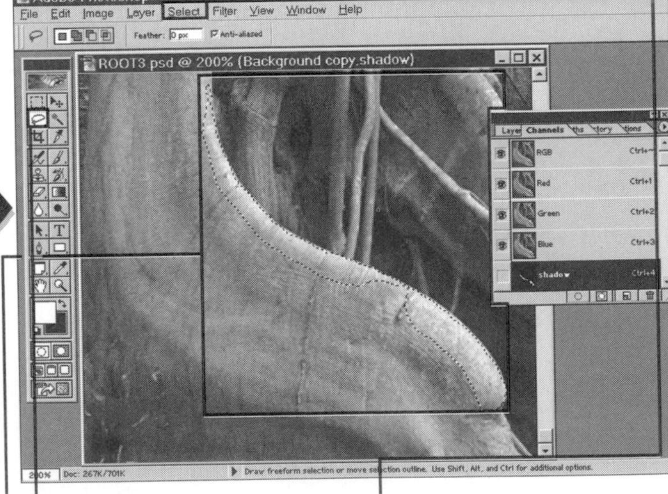

1 Select the item for which you want to change the lighting direction.

Note: See Chapter 6 to learn more about selecting an item.

2 Click the Dodge tool (🔍).

3 Choose a fairly large, highly feathered brush.

4 Scrub the shadow areas until they come close to matching the highlights.

Note: Subjects with very strong contrast between highlight and shadow are poor candidates.

5 Click the Lasso tool (🔍).

6 Select the area where you want a new shadow to be cast.

Note: See Chapter 6 to learn more about selecting an item.

7 Choose Select, then Save Selection.

■ This creates a new alpha channel, which you will need for blending the edges of the selection.

How do I control the feathering of the edge of the shadow mask?

✔ You can feather the selection, but this rarely looks natural because the edges of shadows are sharper near the object that casts them and softer at a distance. Soften the edges by painting on the mask with highly feathered brushes of different sizes. Press [and] to change brush sizes. Press D to choose the default colors. Press X to switch the foreground and background colors. Remember, black makes the mask more opaque; white makes it more transparent.

Should I save all of my selections?

✔ Always save your selections in your in-house Photoshop file. You may be able to use all or part of them again, giving new life to an image you may have used for a different client.

My initial results do not look very good. Now what?

✔ Photoshop and this book have provided you with the tools and techniques to achieve very realistic shadows. The next three things you must do are practice, practice, and practice.

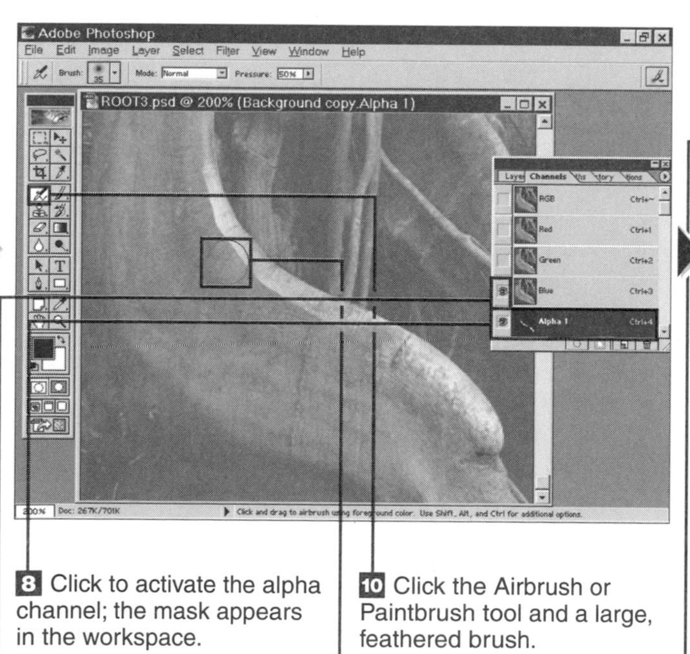

8 Click to activate the alpha channel; the mask appears in the workspace.

9 Click to make one of the color channels visible.

■ The mask changes to the chosen overlay color. Make sure none of the other channels are active.

10 Click the Airbrush or Paintbrush tool and a large, feathered brush.

11 Paint to soften the edges as needed.

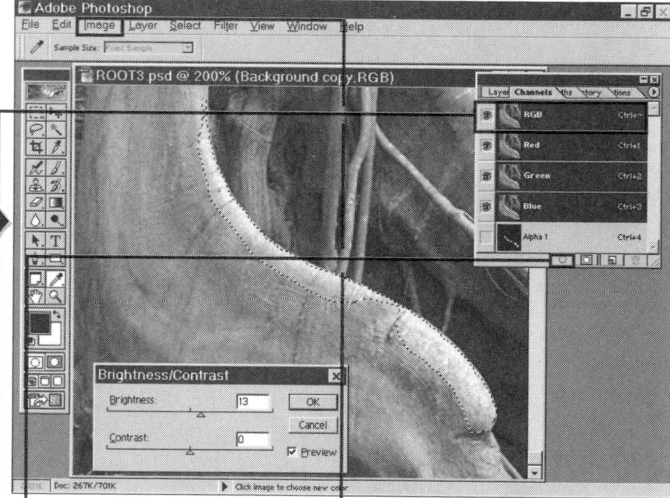

12 Drag the mask channel to the Load Channel as Selection icon.

13 Activate the RGB channel.

14 Press /Ctrl+H to hide the selection marquee so you can see how well your effect blends.

15 Choose Image, then Adjust, then Brightness/Contrast and darken as necessary.

SECTION VI

21) PREPARING AND PREVIEWING WEB PAGES

22) DESIGNING INTERACTIVE GRAPHICS

23) MAKING ANIMATIONS FROM PHOTOGRAPHS

OPTIMIZE GIF FILES

Optimization means making a graphics file as small as possible without losing too much quality. Smaller files take up less space and download more easily. You can optimize graphics files with both Photoshop 6 and an included program called ImageReady 3.0.

Both Photoshop and ImageReady offer you the same optimization capabilities and the same LiveView options. The difference is that in Photoshop, you have to choose File, then Save For Web to see the LiveView interface and the Optimization palette, whereas both are always present in ImageReady.

Although there are many optimization options, those shown in this task cover most situations. However, the LiveViews (seen in the Optimized, 2-Up, and 4-Up tabs) instantly show you the effect of any changes you make in settings. So always experiment to find the best results.

This task focuses on saving GIF (Graphics Interchange Format) images. GIF is the most widely used graphics format on the Internet because it maintains the sharp edges and solid colors needed for effective depiction of graphical text and of interactive elements such as buttons and banners.

OPTIMIZE GIF FILES

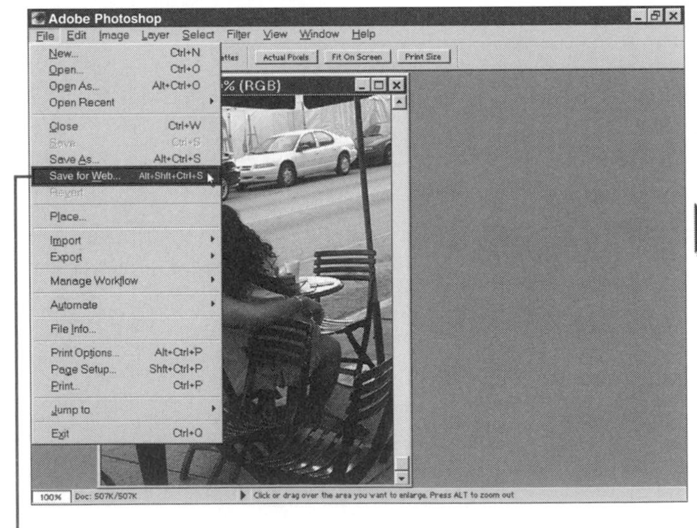

1 Choose File, then Save for Web.

■ The Save for Web dialog box appears.

2 Click the Optimized tab.

3 Click the Image Size tab.

4 Enter maximum height and width for the Web image.

5 Choose Smooth (Bicubic) from the Quality box and click Apply.

GIFs are limited to a 256-color (8-bit) graphics space. Which 256-color palette should I choose?

✔ If you are optimizing a continuous-tone image, such as a photograph, use an *adaptive* palette. Ditto if you have to maintain color fidelity with the original. If you want to make sure that your colors are seen consistently in all browsers, choose Web as the palette type.

When should I choose dithering and which type should I choose?

✔ If your graphic has hard edges and solid colors (or fewer than eight colors), choose None. Most photos look best when you choose Diffusion for dithering, but the other two choices produce smaller files.

My normal-size photos of 5–40MB take forever to resize when using the Save For Web command on the File menu. Is there a better way?

✔ This is a problem for users with slower computers and less than 96MB of RAM. Save time by resizing the image before choosing File, then Save for Web. Be sure not to save the resized original unless you save it under another name.

How can I tell how much I have improved loading time when I change settings?

✔ Choose View, then Show Optimization Info and take a look at the information displayed under the image.

6 Click the 4-Up LiveView tab.

7 Click the Color Table tab so that you can see the effect of further changes on the color table.

8 Click each window in turn and choose Dithered scheme with fewer colors for each until the result is unacceptable, then add colors.

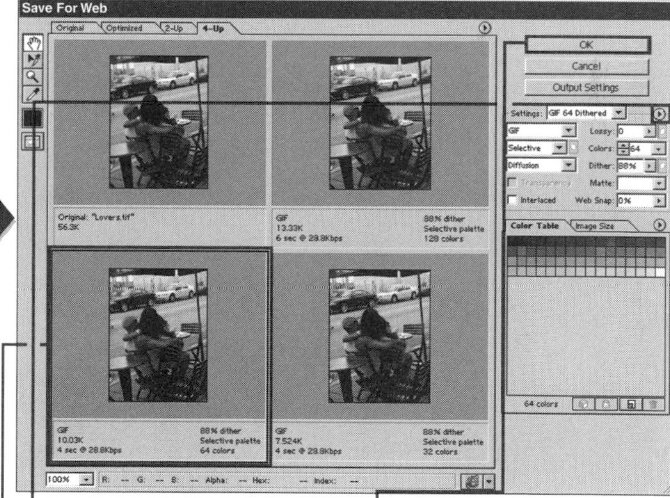

9 Click the Optimize palette menu button and choose Repopulate Views.

10 Click the fastest file.

Note: In this example, two options are equally fast. I chose the one that looks the best.

11 Click OK.

■ A standard File Save dialog box appears.

12 Name and save the optimized file to the location of your choice.

OPTIMIZE PNG-8

You can optimize 8-bit files to a new Web file format called PNG-8. Both ImageReady 3.0 and Photoshop 6 provide for PNG-8 optimization.

In fact, anything you read in this book about optimization now applies equally to either program. The only difference is whether you start in Photoshop 6 and then choose File, then Save for Web, or start in ImageReady 3.0 and use the Optimization palette and then choose File, then Save Optimized.

Optimizing to PNG-8 is essentially the same operation as optimizing in GIF (see "Optimize GIF Files" in this chapter). You may wonder why you should use it. PNG-8 is a newer format and its optimization routines result in smaller files. Only the latest browsers, however, can recognize the format. Stay away from it unless you know your audience has version 4.6+ of Internet Explorer or Netscape Navigator/Communicator.

This exercise assumes you have your image opened in Photoshop and that the image contains a transparent background. (If the image you are using does not have a transparent background, be sure you do not check the Transparency box.)

OPTIMIZE PNG-8

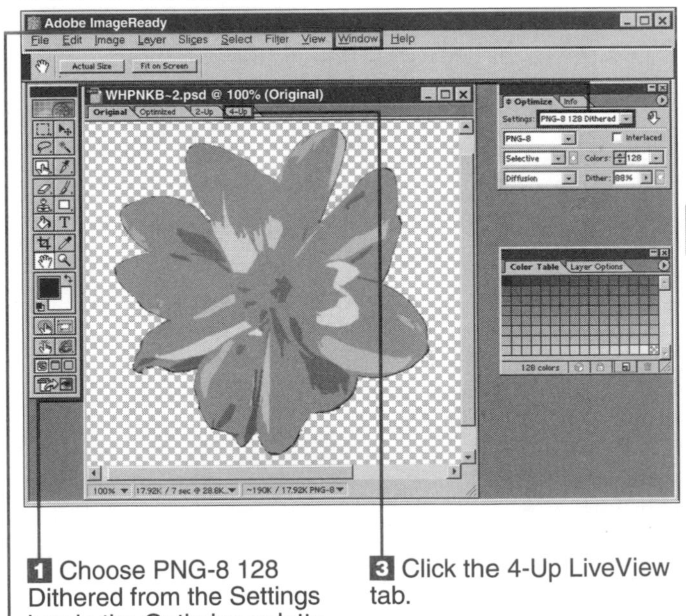

1 Choose PNG-8 128 Dithered from the Settings box in the Optimize palette.

2 Choose Window, then Show Color Table.

3 Click the 4-Up LiveView tab.

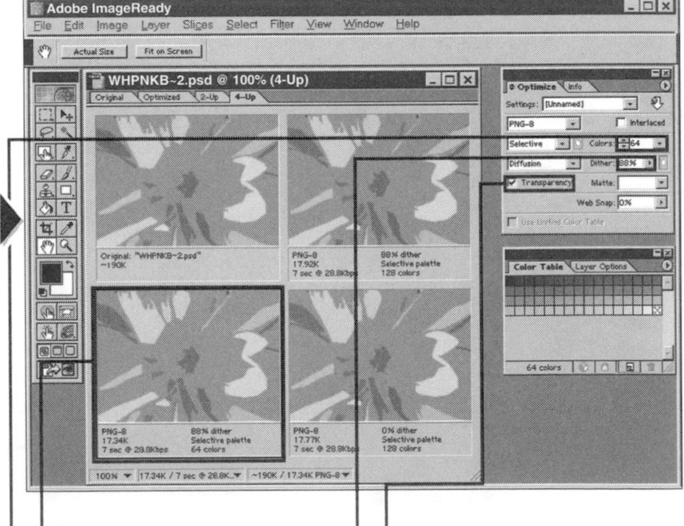

4 Click a view for experimentation.

5 Click to insert fewer colors.

Note: Always view the image in one of the Optimized views, so you can immediately see the result of adjustments. If you insert too few colors, for instance, you can back off.

6 Check Transparency (you may have to first select Show Options from the palette menu button).

7 Enter a dither percentage.

OPTIMIZE PNG-24

You can optimize 24-bit files to the new Web file format called PNG-24. Both ImageReady 3.0 and Photoshop 6 provide for PNG-24 optimization. Of course, PNG-24 optimization works the same way in Photoshop 6 as in Internet Explorer 3.0.

PNG-24 is much more suited to photographs than PNG-8. It also supports transparency, so you can have PNG-24 vignetted shapes that reveal the background wherever they do not fill a rectangle. Also, PNG-24 is the native raster-graphics file format for Macromedia Flash (Flash can *output* the graphics to GIF format) so you may find a great deal more use for this format than for PNG-8.

If you want people to see your graphics that are embedded in HTML pages on the Web, however, you can only count on the latest generations of popular browsers (4.6 and later).

This exercise assumes that you have your image opened in ImageReady 3.0 and that the image contains a transparent background. (If the image you are using does not have a transparent background, be sure that you do *not* check the Transparency box.)

OPTIMIZE PNG-24

1 Click the Optimized tab (or the 2-Up or 4-Up tabs).

2 Click PNG 24.

3 Click to check/uncheck the Transparency box.

■ Click the Transparency box if your image has transparent areas and you want the HTML background to show through.

4 Click the Interlaced box. to make a low-resolution version of the image appear in the browser while the full-resolution image finishes loading.

■ You immediately see the results of your settings in the Optimized window.

OPTIMIZE JPEG FILES

Because JPEG and PNG-24 are built to accommodate a full range of continuous tones and are less prone to posterization, you can usually optimize continuous-tone images (such as photos) more effectively in the JPEG or PNG-24 formats than in GIF or PNG-8. Also, JPEG and PNG-24 are often able to create a smaller acceptable file size when images must be larger than thumbnail-size.

The most frequently used of the formats mentioned above is JPEG. Like GIF, JPEG is almost universally understood by the installed browser base, so there is little risk that a viewer cannot see your image.

If the file you want to optimize is a painting, whether you choose JPEG or GIF will depend on the number of colors used and whether they blend into continuous tones between bordering colors. If in doubt and too short on time to experiment, JPEG is the safer bet.

Once again, it does not matter whether you use Photoshop 6 or ImageReady 3.0 to optimize your JPEGs. Just remember that in Photoshop 6 you should choose File and then Save for Web to reach the LiveView interface shown below.

OPTIMIZE JPEG FILES

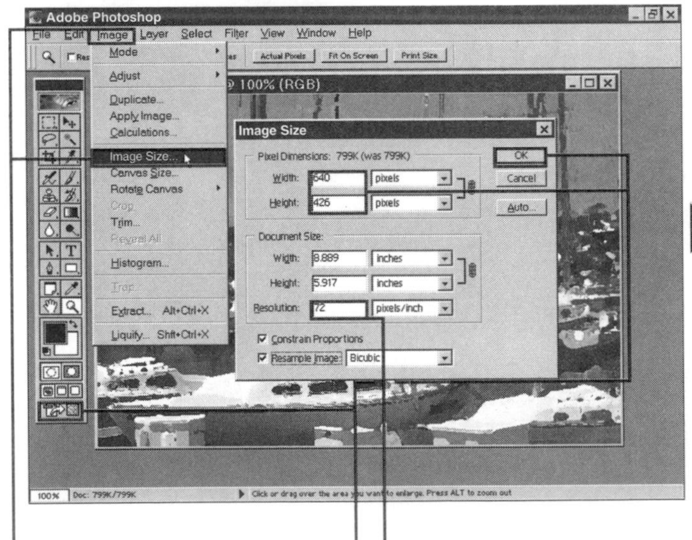

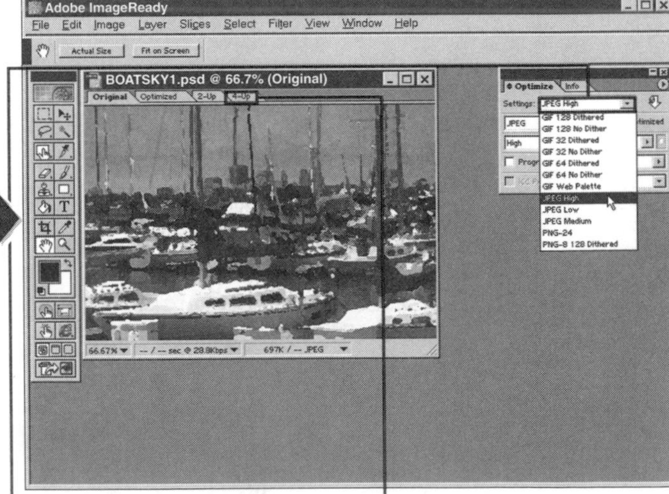

1 Choose Image, then Image Size.

■ The Image Size dialog box appears.

2 Enter a screen resolution of 72 dpi.

3 Enter new Width or Height and click OK.

4 Click the ImageReady button. (You may be prompted to save the file.)

5 Choose JPEG High from the Optimize menu's Settings box.

6 Click the 4-Up View tab.

Why is the Color Table not open?

✔ If it were, you would not see a color table because there is no need to index colors in a true-color file.

Is there a fast way to get to an even smaller, faster file?

✔ Choose Optimize to File Size from the Optimize palette menu's Settings box. Because you get to preview the result before you save it, you will know if you have picked too small a file size.

Should I always try blurring the file?

✔ No. Blurring blurs. You will probably know whether your image can tolerate that. If you can, reduce the size of the file. You have been asked to do it here so that you can see the effect.

Can I use an Action to optimize a whole folder of files at once?

✔ Yes, and it will save you LOTS of time. However, your optimization will likely not be optimal for each image. On the other hand, this is a good option for a series of images shot at the same time under similar lighting circumstances.

7 Click the Hand tool and drag in any window to center the image.

8 Choose the lowest-quality acceptable image and try an even lower Quality set.

9 Click Progressive.

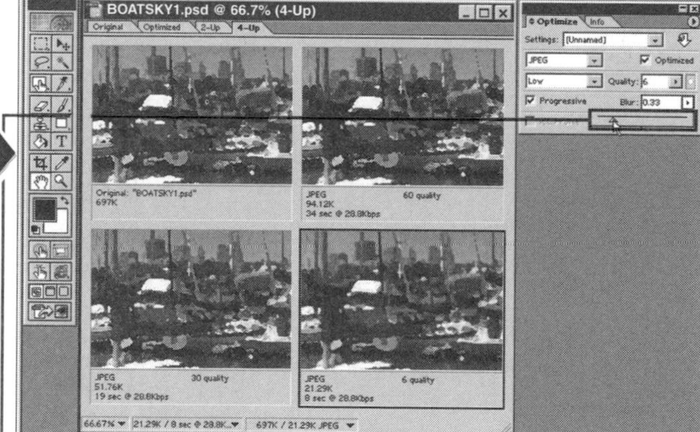

10 Drag to try the Blur slider.

■ If you can get away with a blurred image, you will get a smaller file.

11 Choose File, then Save Optimized.

SLICE AN IMAGE

Slicing an image means cutting up an image into smaller files that display edge-to-edge so that together they look like one big image. The two reasons to slice an image are speed and interactivity. You can optimize each slice separately so the total file loads faster. You can also assign mouse events to the slices.

Technically, an ImageReady-created slice is any rectangular area of an image that the program turns into a table cell in the HTML table code that is automatically created when you make an image slice. That HTML code is part of the code ImageReady writes for each image saved for the Web. Anytime you create new slices in the same image, ImageReady rewrites the code to reflect the creation of the new slice or slices.

The two types of slices are

- Those you draw (called *user slices*)
- Those Photoshop auto-creates to fill in empty spaces (called *auto slices*)

All auto slices are linked to one another and are optimized in the same way. User slices can be categorized as Image or No Image. No Image slices can contain a solid color or HTML text.

SLICE AN IMAGE

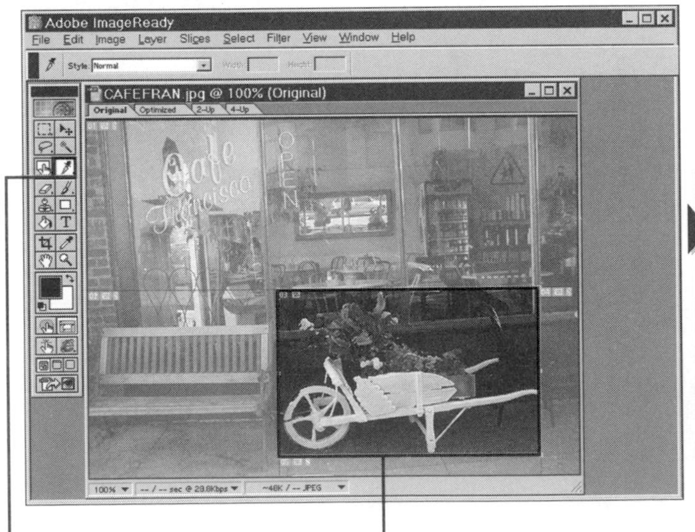

1 Open and size the file you want to slice.

2 Click the Slice tool ( ).

3 Drag to indicate slice size.

4 Repeat to indicate other major user slices.

5 ImageReady automatically divides the rest of the image into auto slices.

What goes on behind the scenes when I slice an image in ImageReady?

✔ Technically, ImageReady converts a sliced image into an HTML table, and each slice is part of that table. ImageReady automatically and invisibly writes the HTML code for each cell in the image table. Anytime you create new slices in the same image, ImageReady rewrites the code to reflect the creation of the new slice or slices.

Can you create slices from guides you drag in from the rulers?

✔ Sure. Except for how the guides are placed, it is the same process. You just choose Slices, then Create Slices from Guides.

Is there any other way to create slices?

✔ You can also create them from rectangular selections. Choose the Marquee and drag diagonally to indicate the area you want to include in the main slice. Then choose Slice, then Create Slice from Selection. You can do this technique as many times as you like.

How many different categories of slices does ImageReady allow?

✔ Two: Image (a slice that is all or part of a picture) or No Image (a slice that contains a solid color or HTML text). See "Specify Slice Options and Optimize Slices" later in this chapter for more on specifying slice types and entering slice text.

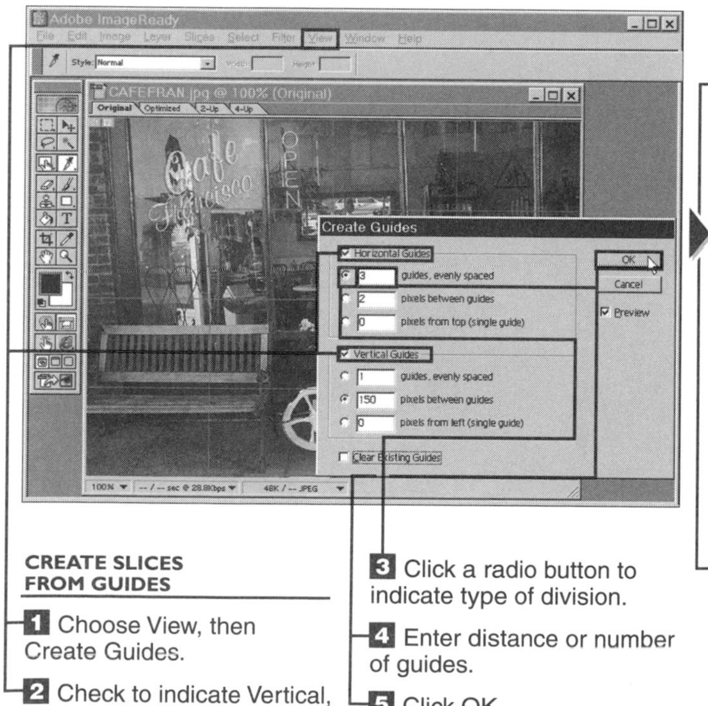

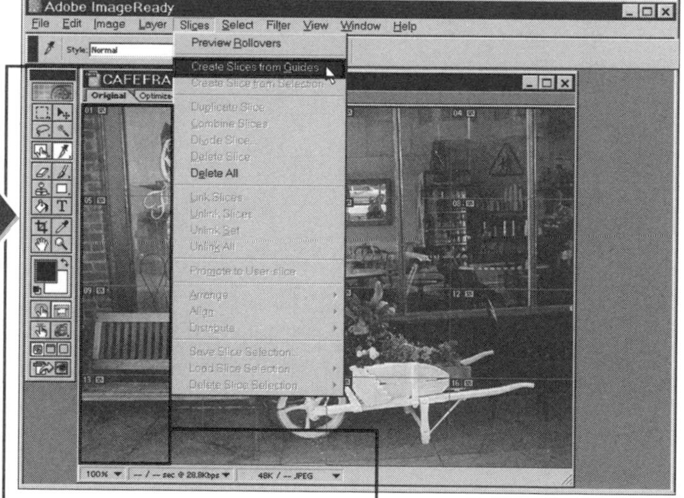

CREATE SLICES FROM GUIDES

1 Choose View, then Create Guides.

2 Check to indicate Vertical, Horizontal, or both.

3 Click a radio button to indicate type of division.

4 Enter distance or number of guides.

5 Click OK.

6 Choose Slices, then Create Slices from Guides.

■ The slices will be drawn as shown.

MODIFY SLICES

ImageReady provides a bevy of ways in which you can modify the boundaries and characteristics of slices. (It is important to note that none of the following affect the *content* of the slice.) To do any of the following, you must first choose the Slice Select tool and then click the slice number to choose the slice. In ImageReady, you can:

- Duplicate the slice to create an identical slice boundary with the same links and of the same type as the original. A duplicated slice automatically becomes a user slice and is stacked on top of the original. The original becomes an auto slice.
- Move the slice boundaries so that your framing is more precise.
- Resize the slice boundaries again to make sure that your framing is more precise. ImageReady automatically readjusts the boundaries of all the other slices.
- Divide the slice to make more than one slice.
- Combine slices so that you can redivide them differently or so you can make fewer slices whenever you have extras.
- Restack slices so that the topmost slice is always fully visible.
- Align slices by clicking the appropriate align icon in the Options bar.
- Delete slices you do not want. When you delete a slice, ImageReady and Photoshop will automatically redraw the supporting slices to compensate.

MODIFY SLICES

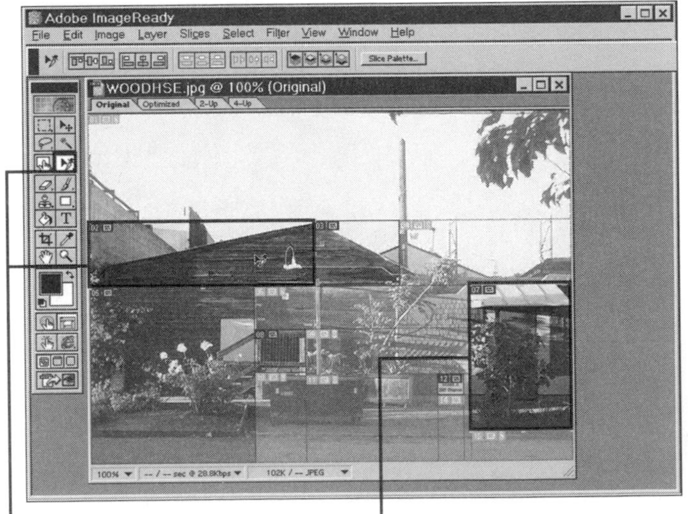

SELECT A SLICE

1 Click the Slice Selection tool ( ).

2 Click to select a single slice.

■ (Optional) Shift+click to select multiple discontiguous slices.

■ (Optional) Click and drag to select multiple contiguous slices.

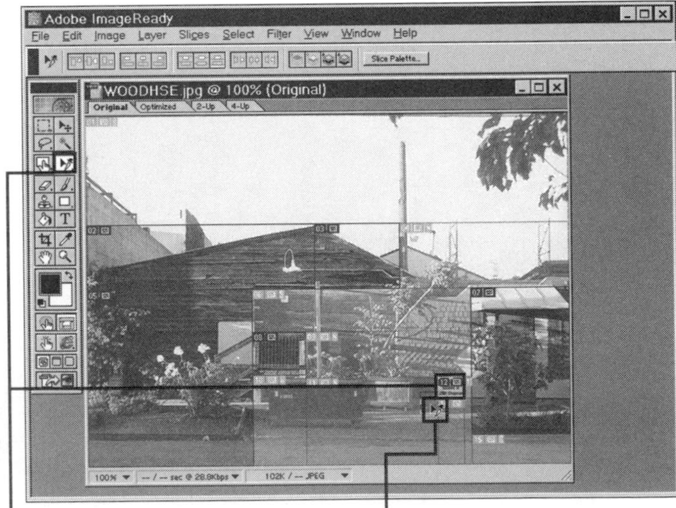

MOVE A SLICE

1 Click the Slice Selection tool.

2 Click to select the slice.

3 Drag inside the slice borders.

Note: Auto slices are redrawn automatically as you move the selected slice.

Can I duplicate a slice?

✔ Sure. Choose Slices, then Duplicate Slice. The duplicate will appear over the original, offset 10 pixels down and right. You can also duplicate by pressing Opt/Alt and dragging the Slice Selection tool from inside the slice.

What if I want to select an underlying (sub) slice?

✔ You can click on any visible part of the underlying slice to select it in its entirety.

How do I promote an auto slice to a user slice?

✔ Choose Slices, then Promote to User-slice(s). If you select multiple auto slices, you can promote them all at the same time.

What if I want to move a slice, but keep it in horizontal alignment with the original location?

✔ Press Shift while dragging. This method restricts movement to horizontal, vertical, or 45-degree diagonal from the original location.

If I move a slice, can I make it snap to the edges of other slices?

✔ Choose Slices, then Snap to Slices. If the command is checked when you open the menu, it is already turned on.

SCALE A SLICE

1 Click to select a slice.

2 Drag a handle.

3 When the slice is at the desired size, release the handle.

Note: Adjacent slices will be automatically resized to match the resized slice.

DIVIDE A SLICE

1 Select the slice.

2 Choose Slices, then Divide Slice.

■ The Divide Slice dialog box appears.

3 Check the dimensions you want to divide and select a method for making the division.

4 Enter numbers and dimensions and click OK.

CONTINUED

MODIFY SLICES CONTINUED

Any changes you make to slices causes ImageReady to automatically regenerate the HTML code for that image so that it reflects the changes to and redrawing of all auto slices.

Two of the slice modifications that are hardest to grasp a use for are changing the stacking order and aligning slices.

You may choose to avoid stacked slices whenever possible because it is harder to predict what will happen when the viewer clicks a linked and stacked slice. If you must stack slices, place the one whose link is most important and obvious on the top layer.

If you align slices, you may want to resize the slices to eliminate small, unneeded slices that are automatically made when you do the alignment.

Remember, you can only align User slices. Trying to align auto slices yields no result.

MODIFY SLICES (CONTINUED)

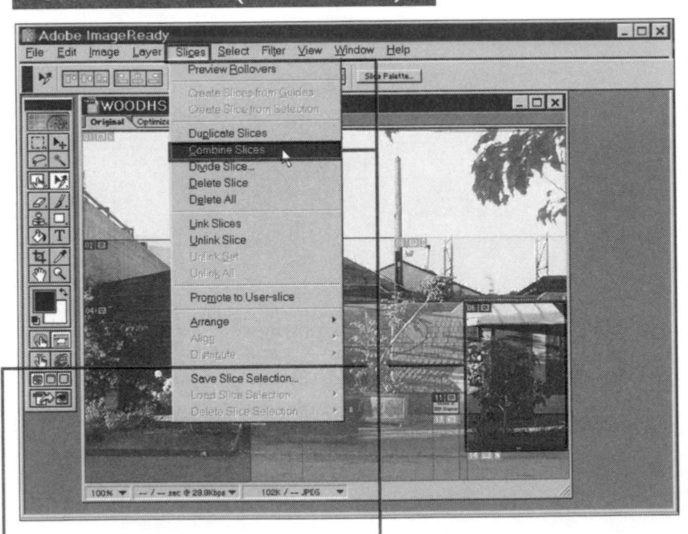

COMBINE SLICES

1 Click to select one slice and shift+click to select adjacent slices.

2 Choose Slices, then Combine Slices.

Note: Combined slices are optimized to the level of the first slice chosen.

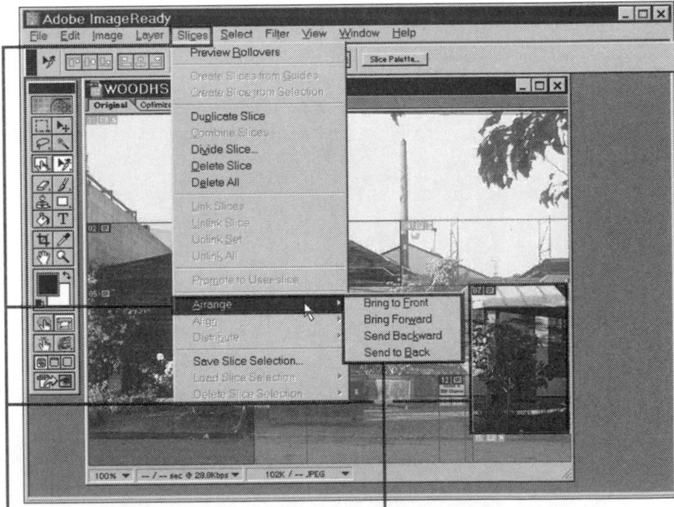

ARRANGE STACKING ORDER OF SLICES

1 Click (or shift+click) to select the slice (or slices) you want to arrange.

2 Choose Slices, then Arrange.

3 Click the appropriate command on the Arrange submenu.

■ Choose Bring to Front or Send to Back to place the slice at the top or bottom. Or choose Bring Forward or Send Backward to move the slice one level.

How do I delete a slice or slices?

✔ Choose Slices, then Delete Slice(s). If you want to delete all slices and do not want to take any chances that you have not preselected one, just choose Slices, then Delete All slices.

What happens if you change the stacking order of overlapping slices?

✔ ImageReady rewrites the HTML to reflect which slices have been subdivided.

How can I tell what the stacking order is?

✔ The last slice created is always the one on top. To put it another way, slices are piled atop one another as they are created. The slice with the smallest number is the one on the bottom.

Is there a way to select all the slices at once?

✔ Choose the Slice Selection tool and drag a rectangle that covers the entire image. You can select any number of slices in this way—just drag to enclose those you want to select.

ALIGN SLICES

1 Click to select two or more slices.

2 Choose Slices, then Align.

3 Choose an option.

Note: Aligning slices can eliminate small, unneeded slices to produce a smaller file.

DELETE ALL SLICES

1 Choose Slices, then Delete All.

SPECIFY SLICE OPTIONS AND OPTIMIZE SLICES

The ImageReady Slice palette lets you easily change a slice's type and options. When you finish editing the slice, you can then optimize the slice several different ways.

You can designate a slice as an Image (the slice is part of a picture) or No Image. (The slice contains a solid color, with or without HTML text.) Both types enable you to enter a URL, a frame name that serves as a target in the designated URL, and a background color.

Image slice option choices include an ALT tag message (to designate what appears in the browser while waiting for the file to load), Alt (assigns an alternative image to appear in place of this slice), and Precision (give *x-y* coordinates for the slice within the browser window). No Image options include the Precision option, an area to enter text that appears in the slice, and slice alignment.

You optimize images slices with options identical to those for optimizing any individual image. The difference is that each slice can be optimized differently.

GIF is generally used for graphics that have hard edges and flat (rather than shaded or graduated) colors. JPEG should be used for continuous-tone graphics—especially photos—unless they are very small. PNG-8 and PNG-24 also have their uses.

Read more about these formats in Chapter 21.

SPECIFY SLICE OPTIONS AND OPTIMIZE SLICES

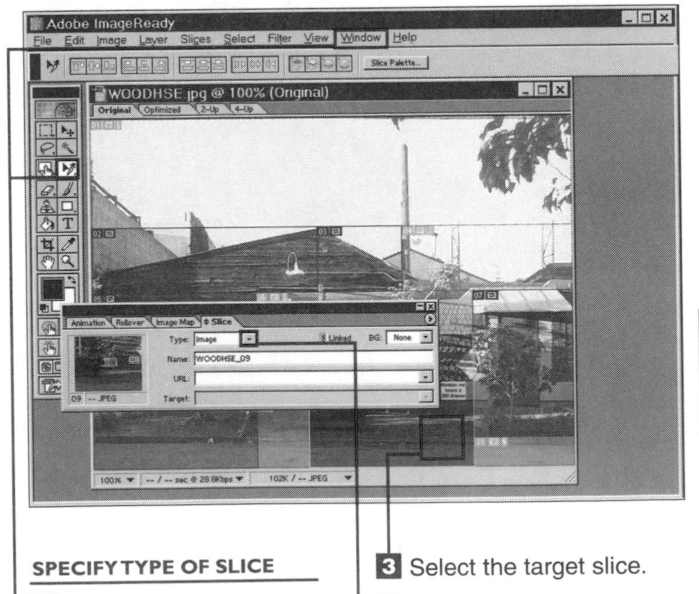

SPECIFY TYPE OF SLICE

1 Click the Slice Selection tool (icon) in the Tool box.

2 Choose Window, then Show Slice to make the Slice palette visible.

3 Select the target slice.

4 Choose the type (Image or No Image) from the palette menu.

SET OPTIONS FOR IMAGE SLICES

1 Show the Slice palette.

2 Choose Show Options from the palette menu.

■ The Slice palette expands to show additional options.

3 Choose your options.

How do I target a frame when I link a URL to a slice?

✔ Do not bother unless you know the HTML structure of the page you are targeting, because you will need to know the name of the frame you are targeting. If you do know the name of the frame, choose View, then Slices (or double-click the slice with the slice selection tool) to show the Slices palette. Then, type the name of the URL in the URL field and the name of the targeted frame in the Target field. When a Web viewer clicks the slice, it automatically links to the designated URL and frame.

What is a URL?

✔ *URL* stands for Uniform Resource Locator. In English, a URL represents a specific page on a Web site.

How do I designate the background color for a No Image slice?

✔ Click the menu button at the right of the BG field to produce a color swatches menu. Click the color you want to use. The Slice Type icon changes from mountains to an X (in the upper-left corner, next to the slice number). You can see the color change by previewing the image in a browser.

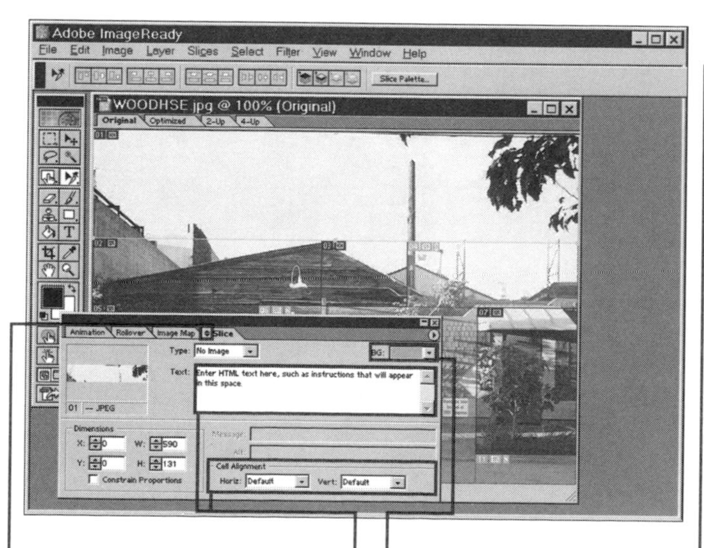

SET OPTIONS FOR NO IMAGE SLICES

1 Choose Window, then Show Slice or click the Slice tab.

■ The Slice palette appears.

2 Choose a background color.

3 (Optional) Enter HTML text to appear in the slice and appropriate HTML formatting directives.

4 Choose Cell Alignment.

OPTIMIZE SLICES

1 Click to select one or more slices.

2 Choose Window, then Show Optimize.

3 Choose an optimization scheme from the Settings box.

Note: The advantage of optimizing slices individually is that less-important areas can tolerate greater image reduction.

ASSIGN ROLLOVERS TO SLICES

Rollovers are effects that can be made to happen when you use the mouse to move over a specific slice of the image. You can create many different animation effects for rollovers and you can create them for different mouse states or events.

The seven mouse states are Normal, Over, Down, Click, Out, None, and Custom. Rollovers can cause the image in the specified slice to change in some aspect. Best of all, ImageReady writes its own JavaScript routines for creating mouse rollover events.

To create a rollover, you simply copy the image in that slice to a new layer and change the copied layer in any way you want. Finally, assign that layer to whatever mouse event you would like by simply creating an activating event in the Rollover palette.

The exercise here will also make an image appear elsewhere (called a secondary rollover) and turn a button into an animation.

ASSIGN ROLLOVERS TO SLICES

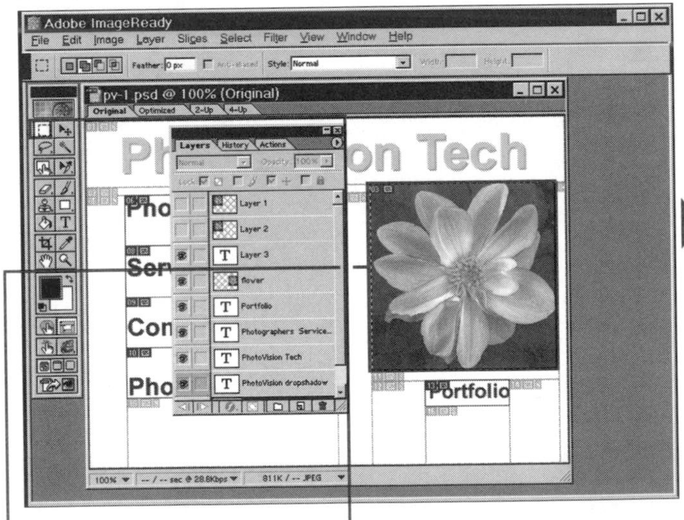

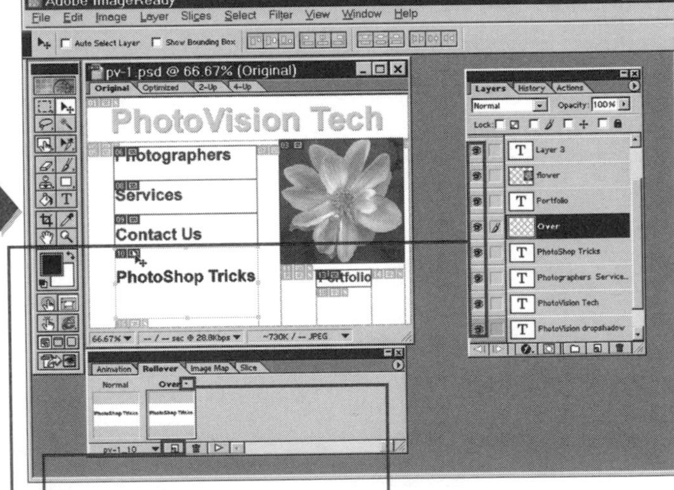

1 Design or open an image that you would like to place into a Web page.

2 Divide the image into slices.

3 Click the Marquee tool and drag to select an area of a slice.

4 Press /Ctrl+C, then /Ctrl+V to copy the area to as many new layers as you will have mouse events.

5 Click the New State button to create a new event.

6 Click the eye icons to turn off all but the layer for the rollover state you want to create.

7 Choose the type of event from the Rollover State menu.

8 Change the selected layer as you want it to appear in the new state.

Should I size and optimize images I am going to import before I import them?

✔ Yes. Planning ahead if you are going to import an image onto a layer you are assigning to an event is best. You can, however, size and optimize it in ImageReady after the fact.

Could an event bring up another menu?

✔ Sure. Just hide everything in the slices where the menu items will appear. Then put the menu on the layer that responds to the Up mouse event. Make the menu an image map and assign a different URL to each menu choice.

Can you suggest some things I might do to change a layer for an event?

✔ Some easy changes include rescaling, distorting, running a filter over the image, breaking apart the image as though it had exploded, and so on.

Do I have to create a new layer for each event?

✔ Depends on what you want to do. Yes, to add new art; no, if you change the layer by executing a layer command, such as a Blend mode or changing opacity. Whenever you create a new layer for an event, renaming the layer for the event is a good idea.

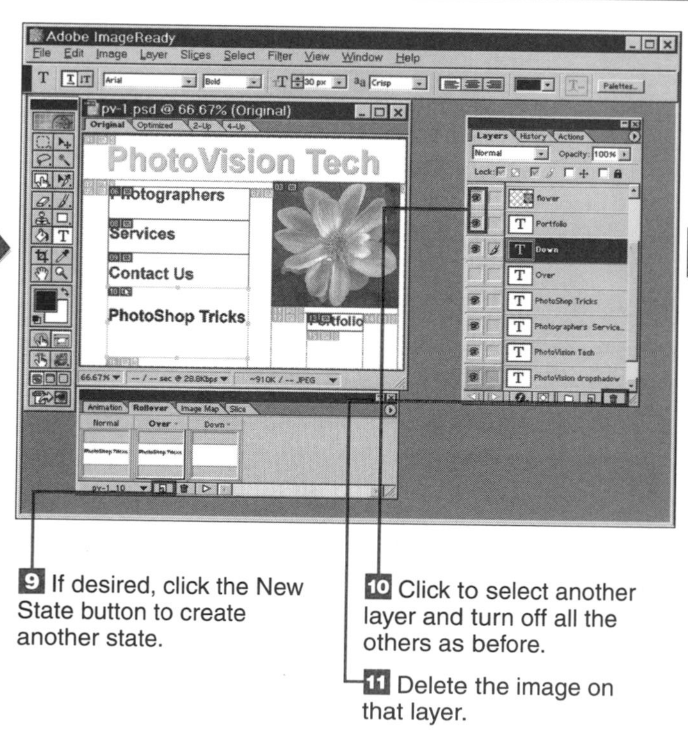

9 If desired, click the New State button to create another state.

10 Click to select another layer and turn off all the others as before.

11 Delete the image on that layer.

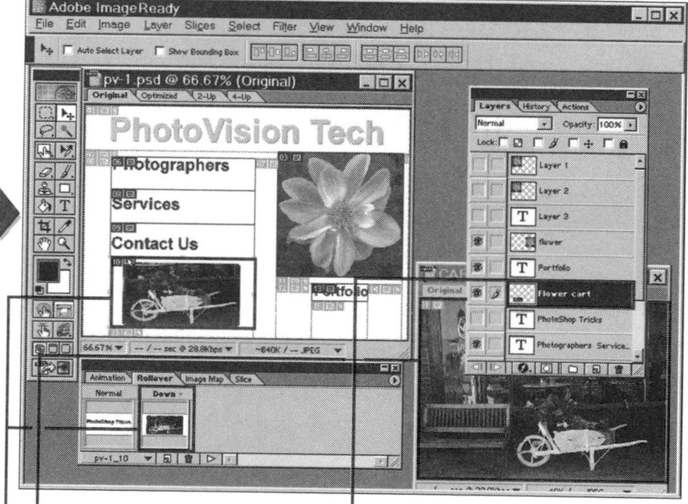

12 To have another image appear in another location, open another image.

13 Drag it onto the target image in the position where you would like it to appear.

14 Select the new state.

15 Select and name the layer created when the image was dragged in.

■ Draw, type text, or import a selection from another file.

ANIMATE A ROLLOVER STATE

You can animate a rollover state by doing little more than creating an animation in the Animations palette (or importing one), then substituting the animation for the layer in the rollover state.

You can get very elaborate with this procedure. For example, you can import an animation. Simply create your animation in another file using multiple layers. When finished, choose Select All Frames from the Animation Palette menu. Switch to the file you want to place the animation and choose Copy Frame from the Animation menu. Finally, switch back to your current file and choose Paste Frame from the Animation menu.

One note of caution: Remember that the more complex your efforts, the bigger your files are likely to grow. Larger files can adversely affect loading times for many Web visitors.

ANIMATE A ROLLOVER STATE

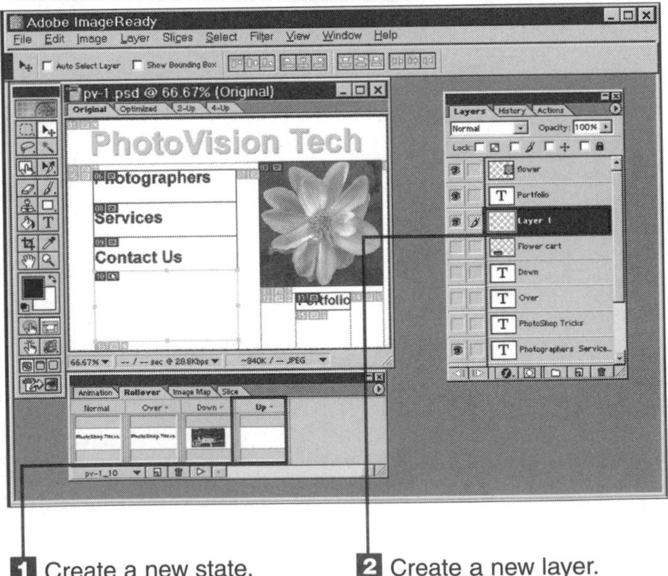

1 Create a new state.

■ See "Assign Rollovers to Slices," earlier in this chapter.

2 Create a new layer.

■ See Chapter 9.

3 Place content in the layer.

4 Make sure that the layer stays selected.

5 Turn off layers created for other states that will not be visible in this state.

Note: Be sure you do not turn off layers that contain information that will display in other slices.

How do I prevent something that was moved outside the frame in an animated layer from showing up during the preview?

✔ Create a mask (see Chapter 8) for that layer before saving the file. The layer mask should reveal only the contents of the slice.

Can I include multiple layers in the animation?

✔ Yes. Just as you do with rollover states, but in the Animation palette. Select a frame. Turn off (click the eye icon) the layer that was shown in the previous frame. Turn on a different frame. If you create multiple frames for the animation in a state, make sure only the layer that should be showing in a particular frame is chosen.

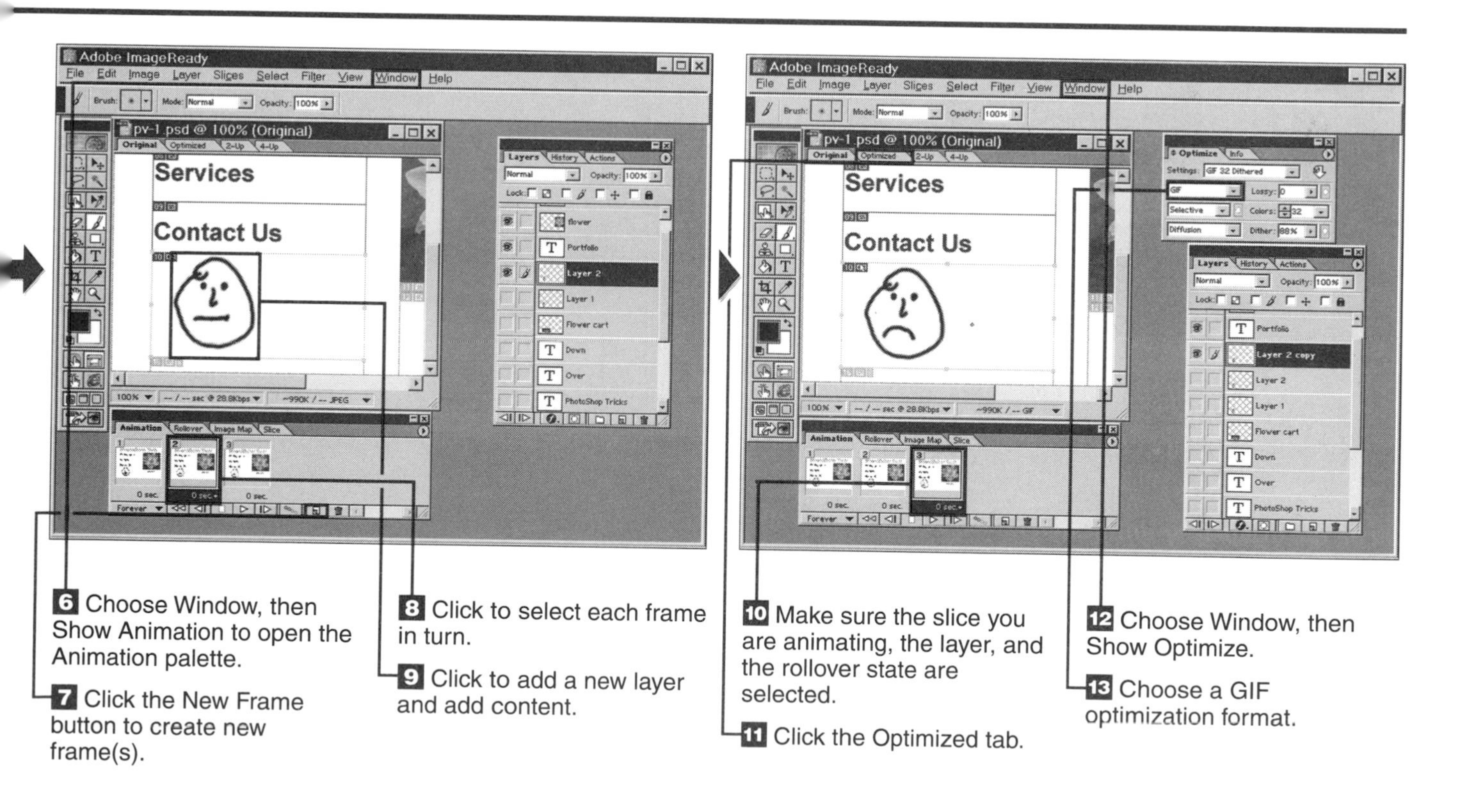

6 Choose Window, then Show Animation to open the Animation palette.

7 Click the New Frame button to create new frame(s).

8 Click to select each frame in turn.

9 Click to add a new layer and add content.

10 Make sure the slice you are animating, the layer, and the rollover state are selected.

11 Click the Optimized tab.

12 Choose Window, then Show Optimize.

13 Choose a GIF optimization format.

CREATE MOTION TWEENS

One of the easiest ways you can produce an effective animation is by creating a motion tween. *Tweening* is an animation industry term that refers to the drawing of frames in-between the start and the peak of a movement.

With ImageReady, you draw or photograph the start and stop frames and ImageReady automatically draws the tweens. ImageReady is only capable of drawing tweens for two types of changes between keyframes (the start and peak frames):

- Motion
- Opacity

Motion tweening just moves the static contents of a layer from one location to another. Do not expect it to animate motion within the object, such as expressions or body movements.

This exercise shows you how to automatically tween motion. The principle is simple: You create two frames for a layer, move the content of that layer to a different position in each frame, and then have the program draw frames that move the item between the two points.

CREATE MOTION TWEENS

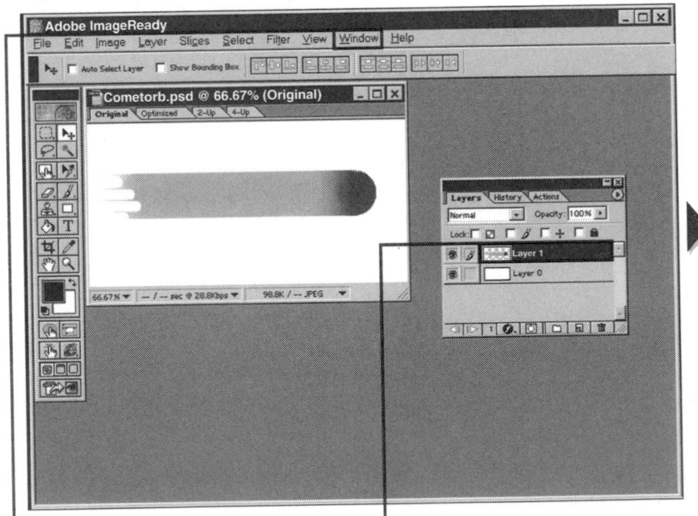

1 Open an image from which you want to make a motion tween.

2 Choose Window, then Show Layers.

■ The Layers palette appears.

3 Click Layer 1.

4 Choose Window, then Show Animation.

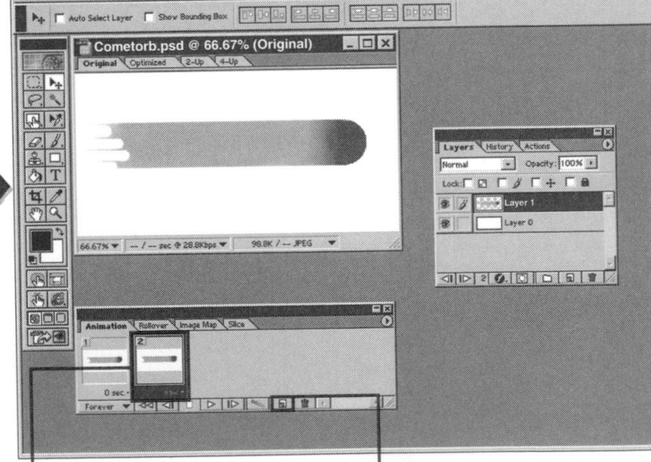

■ The Animation palette appears. The selected layer is shown as one frame in the animation.

5 Click the New Frame icon ( ) to copy the selected frame.

What if I want to do more complex tweens, such as morphs?

✔ Several third-party animation programs are available that will do more sophisticated tweening. (Macromedia's Director [bitmap] and Flash [vector] programs, are some examples; Adobe LiveMotion is another) You can create the tweens in those programs and then export their animations frame by frame to Photoshop-compatible formats (GIF is the best candidate), then place the sequence on layers in Photoshop and use ImageReady to animate them.

What if I want to animate the movement of limbs or facial expressions?

✔ The easiest method is to shoot the movement you want to animate with a video camera. Use video capture hardware and software (the Snappy device is a good low-cost option for Windows, and most Macs these days come with iMovie). Then save individual frames to GIF format, import them into Image Ready 3.0, place each on a layer, and follow the instructions for creating a GIF animation.

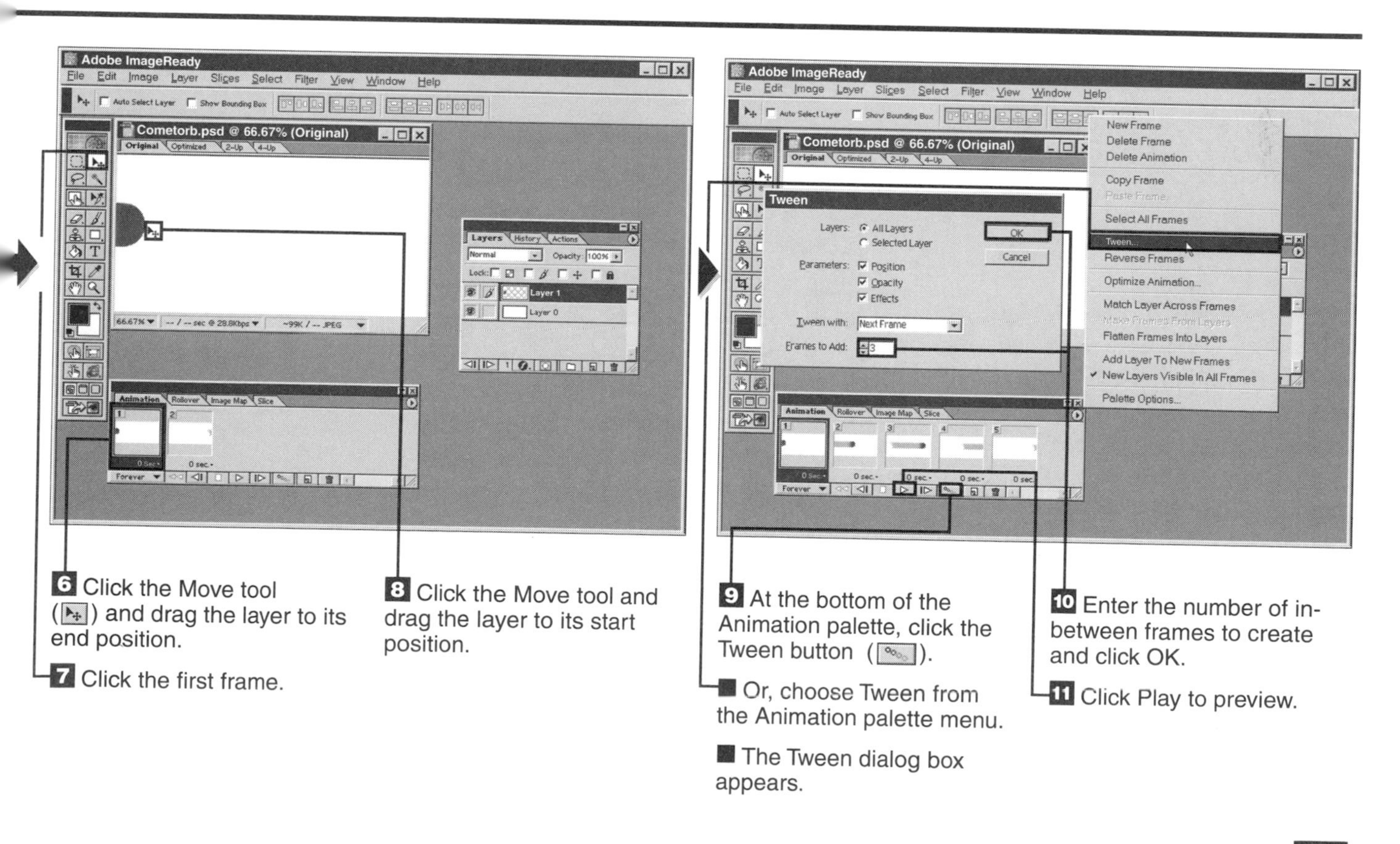

6 Click the Move tool (▸+) and drag the layer to its end position.

7 Click the first frame.

8 Click the Move tool and drag the layer to its start position.

9 At the bottom of the Animation palette, click the Tween button ( ).

■ Or, choose Tween from the Animation palette menu.

■ The Tween dialog box appears.

10 Enter the number of in-between frames to create and click OK.

11 Click Play to preview.

TWEEN A CROSS-FADE

Because ImageReady's Animation palette can tween opacity, making an image fade to black or fade to white is very easy. You just have the tween occur between an image frame and a black or white frame (or any other color frame).

You use almost exactly the same technique to cross-fade from one image to the next. This technique can give your animation a cinematic look.

Be careful, though. You can easily create animations that take several minutes to load. Doing so is a sure way to encourage impatient viewers to leave your Web site. Keeping that in mind, keep the number of frames in the transition between 3 and 5.

If you want to cross-fade between two entirely different scenes, scale two photos to the exact same size and place them in the same folder. Then choose File, then Import, then Folder as Frames.

TWEEN A CROSS-FADE

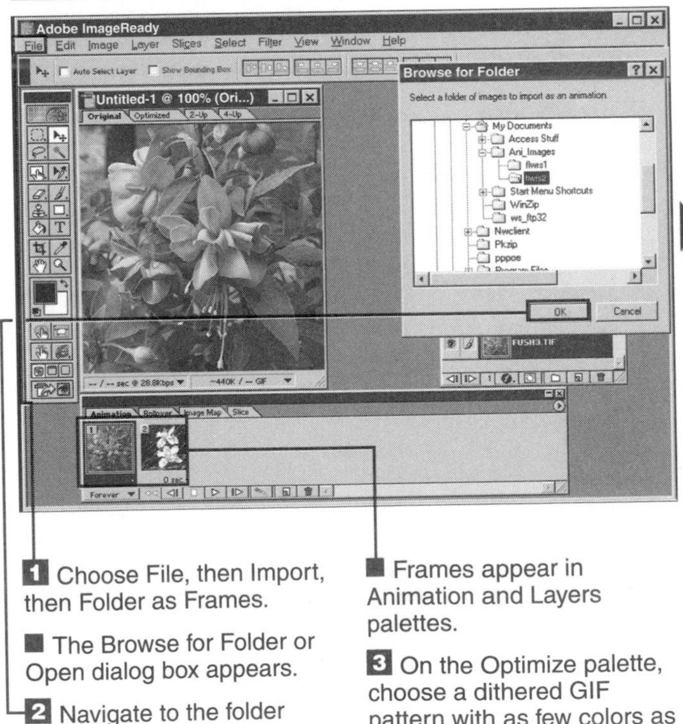

1 Choose File, then Import, then Folder as Frames.

■ The Browse for Folder or Open dialog box appears.

2 Navigate to the folder where frames are stored and click OK or Choose.

■ Frames appear in Animation and Layers palettes.

3 On the Optimize palette, choose a dithered GIF pattern with as few colors as possible.

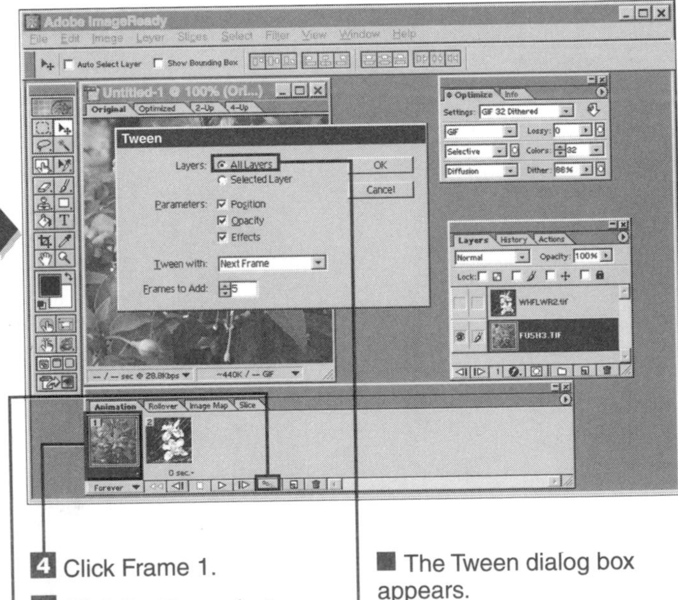

4 Click Frame 1.

5 Click the Tween button ( ).

■ The Tween dialog box appears.

6 Choose All Layers.

Do I need to optimize each frame?

✔ No. If you choose a GIF optimization when you first load the folder into the Animation palette, all the frames will be optimized to that level. You can also experiment with the other settings in the Optimize palette.

How do I make the first and last frames stay on-screen longer?

✔ Each frame has a delay menu in the lower-right corner of its icon. Choose a longer time from that menu.

How do I avoid a computer crash when importing a folder of images?

✔ Either increase the memory partition (on a Mac) or increase the total RAM availability (Windows). Problems do arise on Windows machines with only 64MB of RAM and on Macs with default 17MB allocated to ImageReady. You may also have Mac problems if your system lacks enough contiguous free RAM to launch the browser with ImageReady and other programs already running.

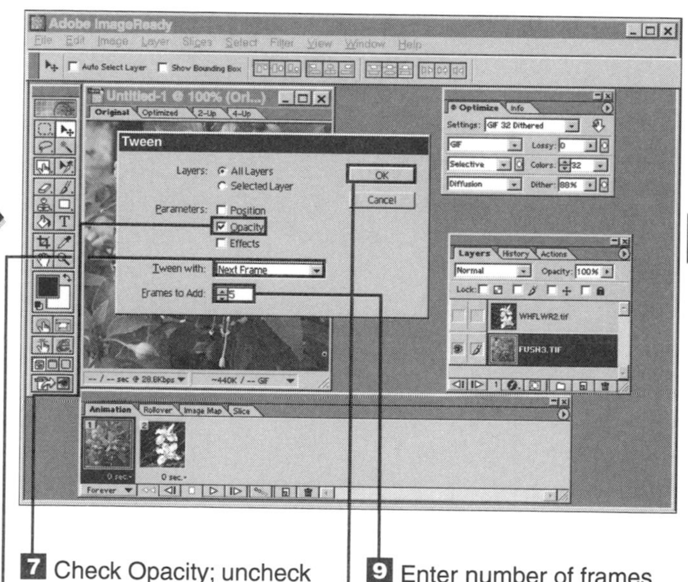

7 Check Opacity; uncheck the other Parameters options.

8 Choose Next Frame from the Tween with box.

9 Enter number of frames to insert in between.

10 Click OK.

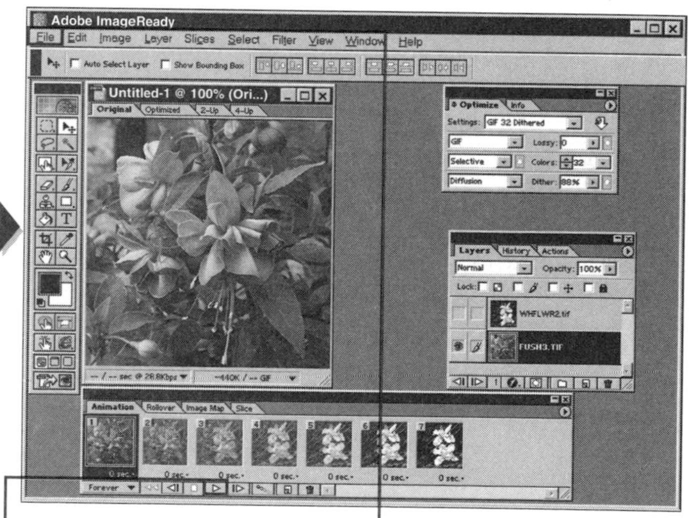

■ The Frames are inserted, and you can see the transition between frames.

11 Click the Play button to preview the animation.

12 Choose File, then Preview In, then Your Browser to preview the animation in a browser.

ANIMATE A SERIES OF PHOTOS

ImageReady cannot automate the tweening of parent-child motions, such as the movement of limbs. You can, however, take a series of still photos of a sequence.

You can also

- Capture a series of stills from videotape frames
- Shoot with a motorized still camera
- Use burst mode in a digital camera
- Or just carefully pose your subject and shoot one frame at a time

This last technique is especially suitable for time-lapse sequences that show slow actions, such as a flower growing or a caterpillar morphing into a butterfly.

After you have the photos, naming the files sequentially (for example, Laura01, Laura02, and so on) and storing them in the same folder is wise. Sizing them to their final size before storing them is also a good idea.

ANIMATE A SERIES OF PHOTOS

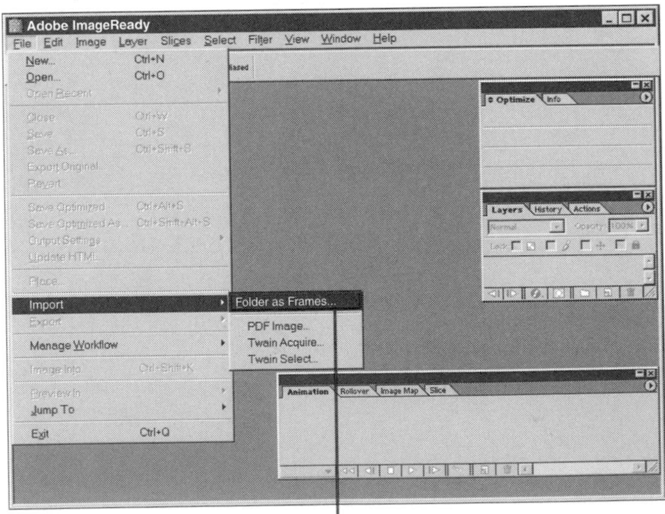

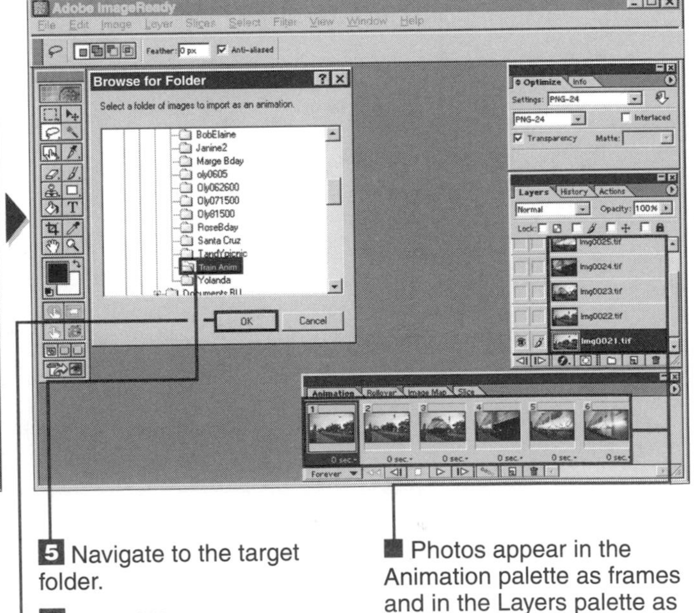

1 Choose Window, then Show Optimize.

2 Choose Window, then Show Layers.

3 Choose Window, then Show Animation.

4 Choose File, then Import, then Folder as Frames.

5 Navigate to the target folder.

6 Click OK.

■ Photos appear in the Animation palette as frames and in the Layers palette as layers.

How can I speed up the process of sizing, naming, and storing the files in the same folder?

✔ Choose Window, then Show Action and then choose New Action from the Actions palette. Name the Action in the dialog box and then do everything you need to do to resize, sharpen, and save the images. Put a pause in the Save command so that you can place the file in the new folder and enter the right name.

What file formats can you import into an animation?

✔ Any file format that Photoshop supports. However, the resulting animations are usually animated GIFs, so you probably want to remember to choose a GIF optimization in the Optimize palette before attempting to preview in a browser.

Can I import stills from a video?

✔ Yes, but doing so requires third-party hardware that is made for capturing video frames. A few computers—especially recent Mac models—have this capability built in. You also need video-editing software, such as Adobe Premiere, which lets you export individual frames.

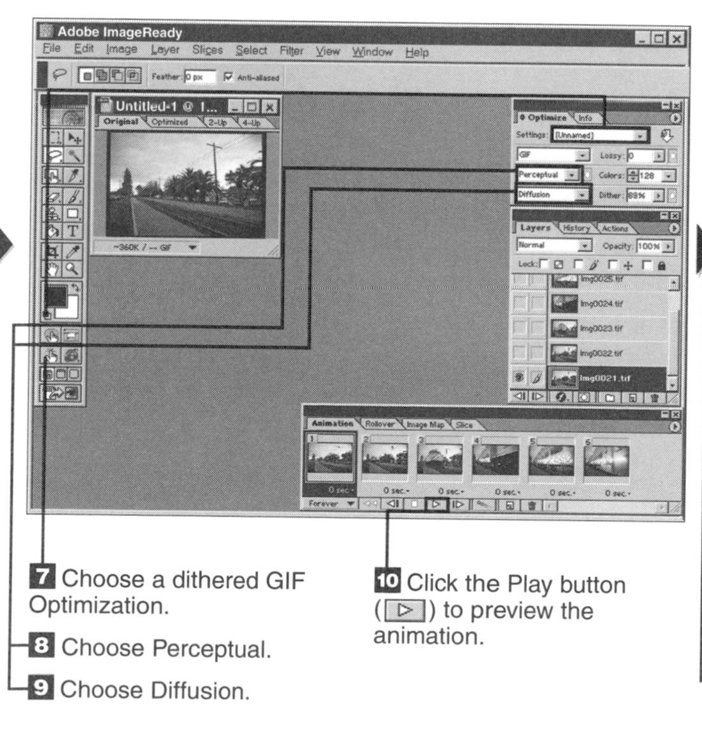

7 Choose a dithered GIF Optimization.

8 Choose Perceptual.

9 Choose Diffusion.

10 Click the Play button (▷) to preview the animation.

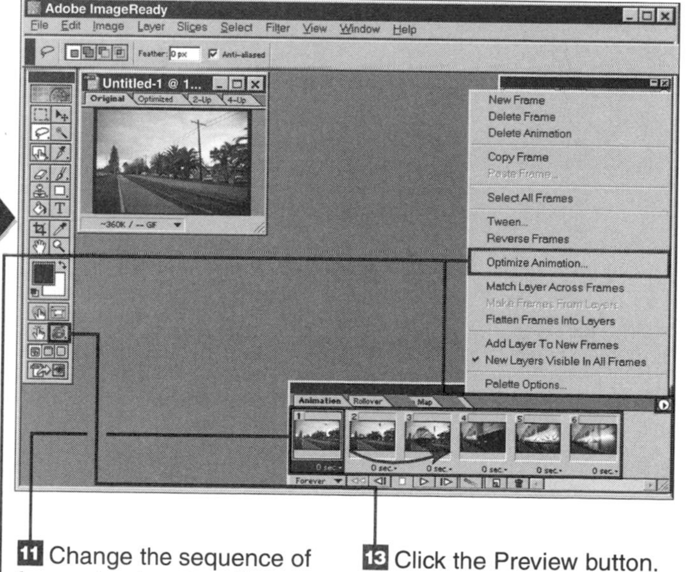

11 Change the sequence of frames by dragging, if needed.

12 Choose Optimize Animation from the Animation palette menu.

13 Click the Preview button.

14 Choose File, then Save As GIF to save the file.

CREATE A SLIDE SHOW

You can use the Animation palette in ImageReady to create something that looks more like a slide show than a movie.

Actually, a slide show is one of the most effective types of animated GIFS. A slide show is made in the same way as any other animation, but there is a much longer pause between frames. Also, within a slide show you may want frames to stack on top of one another. (In other words, several are visible at the same time.) You could also have simultaneously visible frames appearing in different places on your screen.

Slide shows are especially useful if you want to show a series of products or if you need to show larger images in the animation than would be efficient in a full-motion animation.

When you have finished the animation and like the preview, choose Optimize Animation from the Animation palette menu. Then choose File, then Save Optimized, and name and place the file.

CREATE A SLIDE SHOW

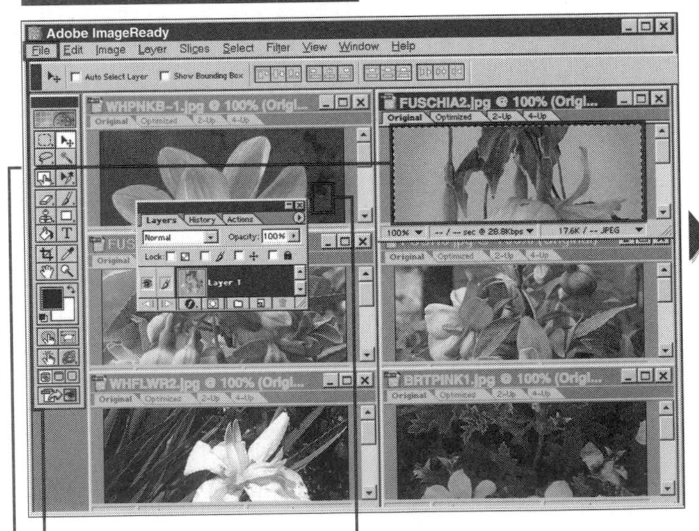

1 Open all the files you want to include in the slide show.

2 Click to select each open window except the first. Press ⌘/Ctrl+A to Select All.

3 Press ⌘/Ctrl+C to Copy.

4 Click in the window of the file you want to turn into the animation and press ⌘/Ctrl+V.

■ The copied image is pasted as a new layer in the target window.

5 Repeat until all images are pasted into the same window.

6 Choose Make Frames From Layers from the Animation palette menu.

7 Click sec to choose a delay time for each frame.

The canvas seems to be enlarged in this example. Why did you enlarge it?

✔ So that there would be room to move the images off-center from one another. The idea is to make the animation look as though the images are randomly dropped on top of one another.

Any special tips for making a slide show?

✔ Several. Put text on separate layers and then include the text in the slide show so that it becomes a presentation. Another nice effect is to tween the position of the slide so that it moves onto the screen, then set a delay in the last frame of the tween so that it stays on screen. You can also tween a cross-disolve between slides (individual frames) and then put a delay in the last frame.

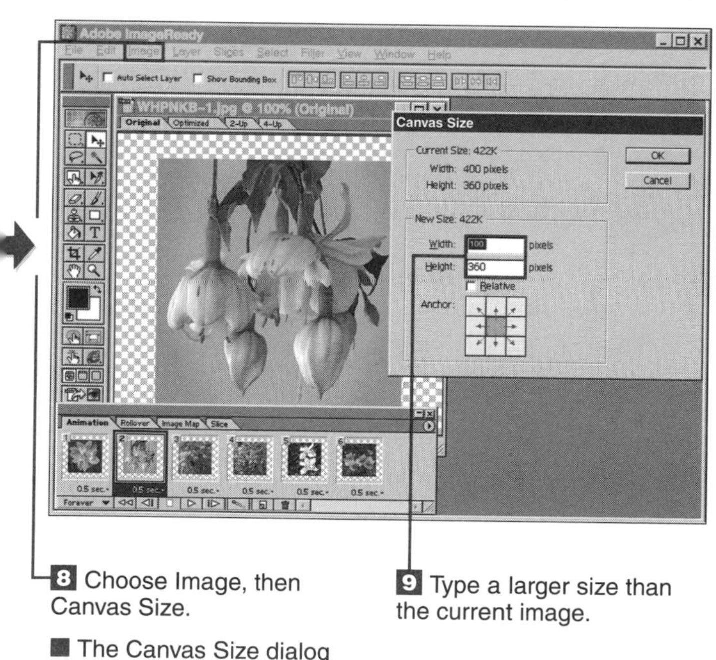

8 Choose Image, then Canvas Size.

■ The Canvas Size dialog box appears.

9 Type a larger size than the current image.

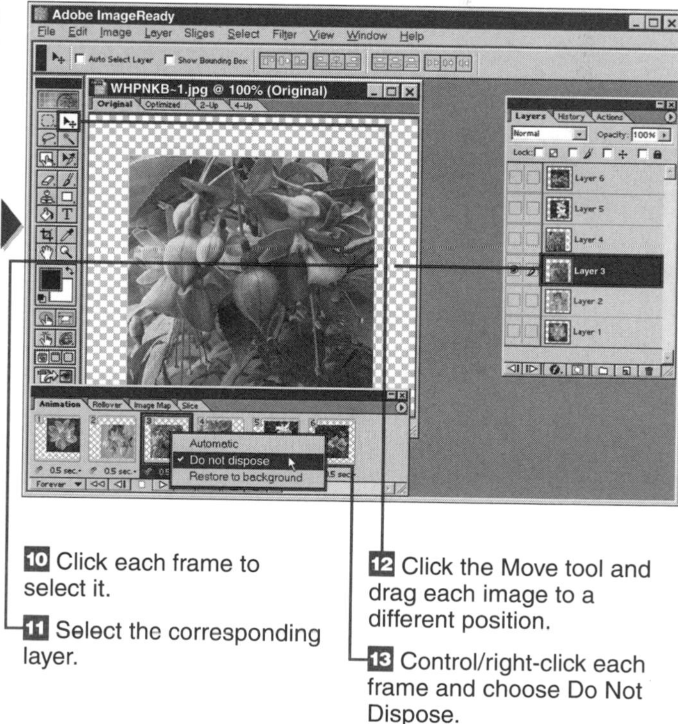

10 Click each frame to select it.

11 Select the corresponding layer.

12 Click the Move tool and drag each image to a different position.

13 Control/right-click each frame and choose Do Not Dispose.

SECTION VII

APPENDIX A

APPENDIX B

APPENDIX C

APPENDIX D

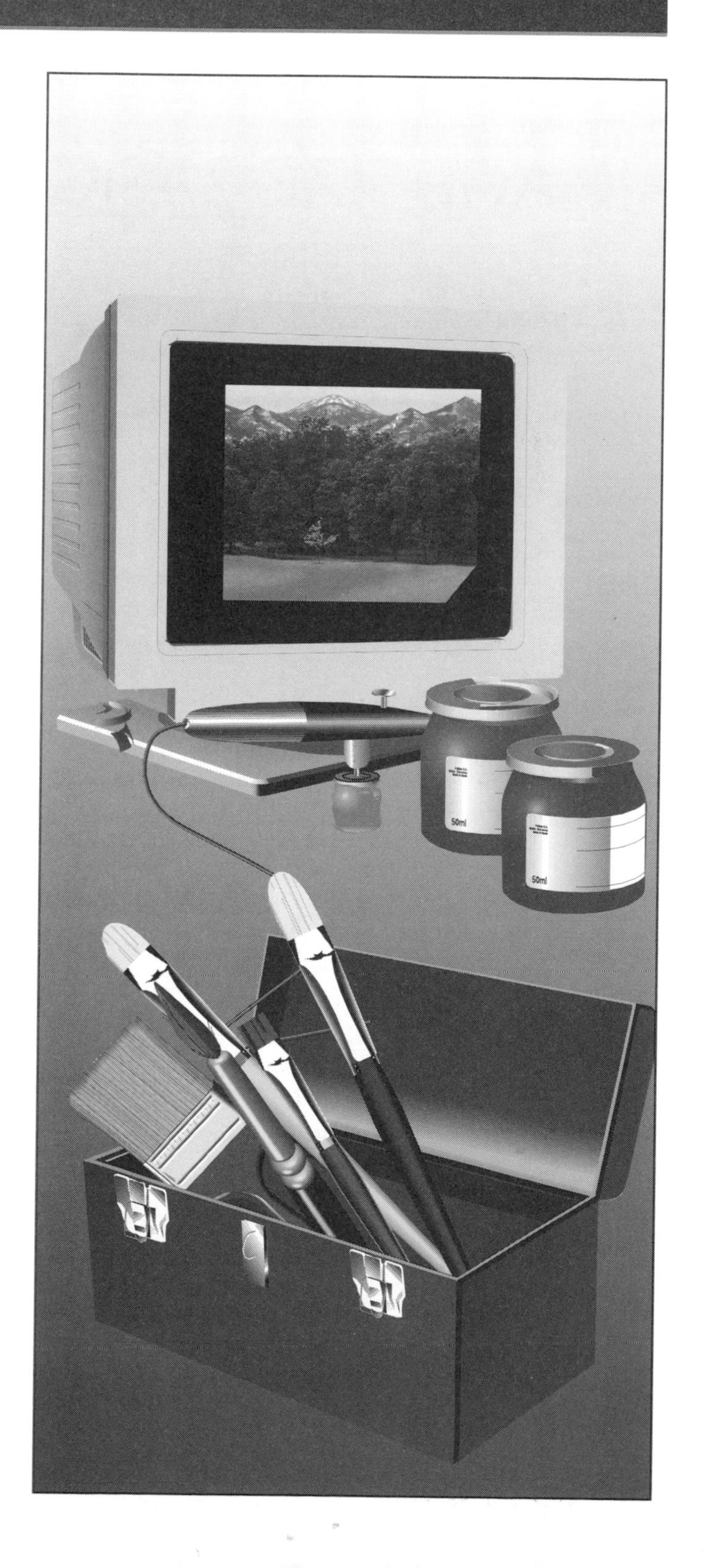

IMAGE SIZE BASICS

Before you consider changing the size of an image (see Chapter 3), you should understand that any Photoshop image consists of a fixed number of *pixels* (tiny square dots of image data) placed in a matrix made up of rows of pixels of a fixed number and columns of pixels of a fixed number. Each pixel is assigned a specific color.

Now, if you make the picture smaller, you have to remove pixels (remember, the size of the pixels themselves is fixed). Which pixels are thrown out is determined by a mathematical formula built into Photoshop, and the choices might not always be the ones you would make. Nevertheless, you usually get less loss of image quality when you reduce an image than when you enlarge it.

If you make the image larger, Photoshop must duplicate some pixels. If you make it much larger, Photoshop has to duplicate lots of pixels. How Photoshop duplicates those pixels depends on the resampling method you choose from the Resample Image menu in the Image Size dialog box, as shown in the following figure. Resampling blends the colors of added pixels so that they make a smooth transition between sharply contrasting original pixels.

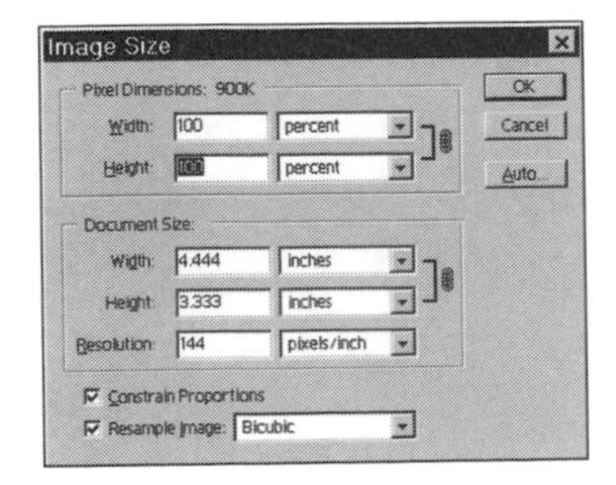

The three resampling methods are Nearest Neighbor, Bilinear, and Bicubic. Nearest Neighbor, as shown in this figure, is fastest, but most pixelated.

The next figure illustrates Bilinear resampling, which is faster than Bicubic; however, transitions between neighboring pixels are not as smooth. (These figures appear at 800 percent enlargement over the original image.)

CONTROL OVERALL IMAGE QUALITY

You control overall image quality primarily via the commands found by choosing the Image, then Adjust command. Those commands are shown in the following menu.

You can apply all these commands (except, as noted, a few that do not work with adjustment layers) to the following:

- An entire layer
- Any specific part of the image enclosed by a selection
- An adjustment layer, which affects the entire image

The advantages of making image adjustments on adjustment layers are threefold:

- All the layers below the adjustment layer are equally affected (otherwise, image adjustments work on only one layer at a time).
- You can change the adjustment at any time (or delete it), because it does not actually change any of the pixels in the underlying layers (unless, of course, you flatten the image).
- You can specify the transparency (Adobe calls it *opacity*) of the effect.

In Photoshop 6, you can change an adjustment layer from one type to another by choosing Layer, then Change Layer Content and then choosing the new layer type. This method saves steps because you no longer have to delete one Action Layer and then create an entirely new one in its place

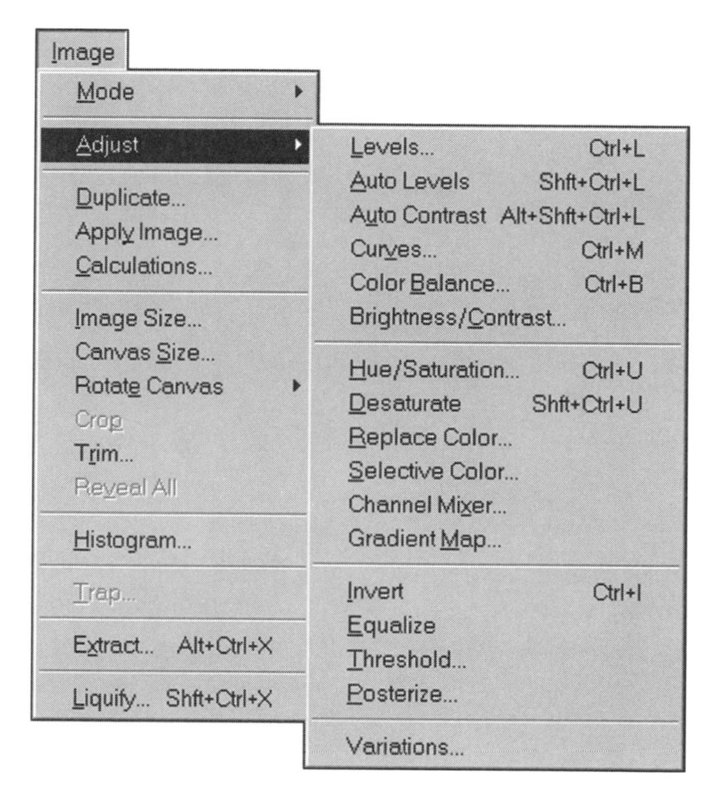

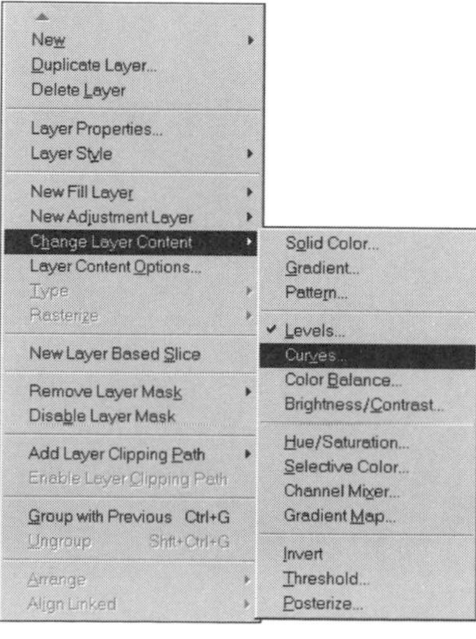

CONTROL OVERALL IMAGE QUALITY CONTINUED

Levels

You use the Levels command to compress or expand the image's range of brightness values by moving any of three input sliders in the Levels dialog box, one each for shadow, midtone, and highlight, as shown in the accompanying figure. The histogram shows the density of the pixels within a given tonal range. This color correction tool is one of the easiest and most powerful, and is usually the best place to start working in color correction after an image has been digitized.

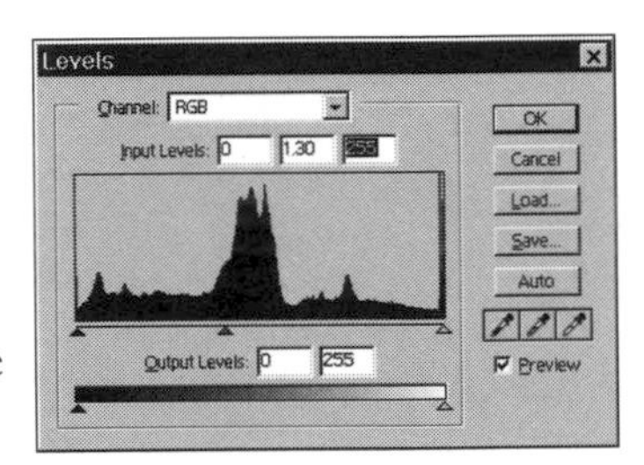

Levels Dialog Box Contents

Component	Function
Channel menu	Enables you to change the entire image or a particular color channel.
Input Levels fields	Specify the shadow, midtone, and highlight points by exact number.
Histogram	Reflects the population of pixels at a particular brightness level.
Input Levels sliders	Indicate the level of the darkest, median, and brightest pixels in the image.
Output Levels fields	Specify by exact number the darkest and lightest tones to be output.
Output Levels bar	Displays a smooth blend from black to white to help you judge where you are setting the output sliders.
Output Levels sliders	Enable you to decrease image contrast in highlights and shadows.
Load button	Loads previously stored levels setting.
Save button	Stores the current levels setting.
Auto	Executes the Auto Levels command.
Sample Eyedroppers	Each Eyedropper — Shadow, Midtone, and Highlight — enables you to select a pixel to specify the matching tone.

Curves

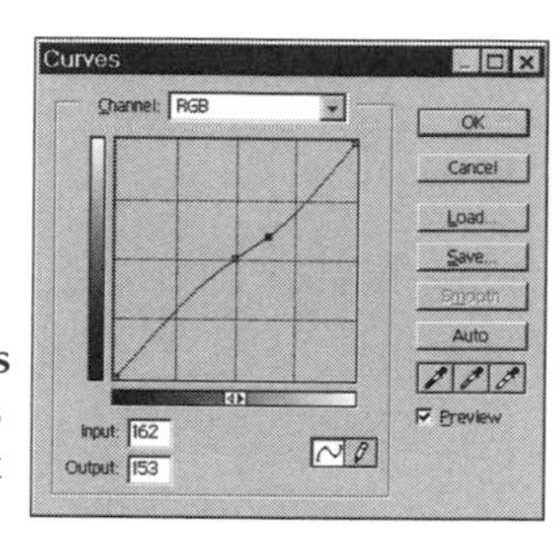

The Curves command is another powerful image adjustment command that gives you control over every aspect of an image's brightness, contrast, and color. The Curves command enables you to move the mid- and end points of the gamma spectrum for the composite channel or any of the color channels. Through this command, you can also change the brightness value of any color of any pixel in the image to any other brightness value. You do so by specifying a brightness curve along the input/output axis. Create this curve either by dragging control points or by drawing it freehand. The Curves dialog box is shown here.

Curves Dialog Box Contents

Component	*Function*
Channel menu	Enables you to change the entire image or a particular color channel.
New Brightness Values bar	Indicates the direction in which new values are displayed by the graph.
Curves graph	Reflects any redistribution of the brightness range of pixels.
Input field	Displays a numerical value for the input. You can enter a value from 1 to 255.
Output field	Displays the numerical value for the output. You can enter a value from 1 to 255.
Curve Point button	Enables you to change the shape of the curve by clicking to enter a point, and then dragging the point to change its value. Always results in a smooth curve.
Load button	Loads a previously stored levels setting.
Save button	Stores the current levels setting.
Smooth button	Converts a freehand curve to one with control points.
Auto	Executes the Auto Levels command.
Sample droppers	Each dropper — Shadow, Midtone, and Highlight — enables you to select a pixel to specify the matching tone. Shadow, Midtone, and Highlight droppers select a pixel as the matching tone.

CONTROL OVERALL IMAGE QUALITY
CONTINUED

Color Balance

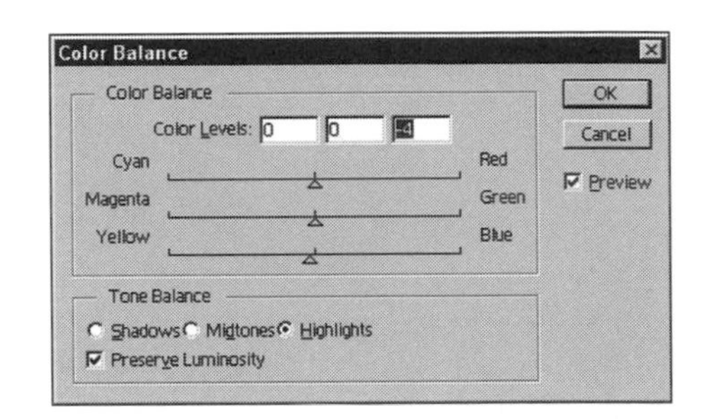

The Color Balance command makes generalized color corrections. You can control shadows, midtones, and highlights individually through the Color Balance dialog box, shown here. To change the balance of any of the primary colors, you simply drag a slider. This tool is excellent for beginners, as well as for those who want instant feedback on overall color balance changes.

Color Balance Dialog Box Contents

Component	*Function*
Color Levels fields	Indicate, from left to right, the levels of cyan/red, magenta/green, and yellow/blue. Enter a positive number to move the slider toward the primary color (for example, red), negative to move toward the complement (for example, cyan).
Color Levels sliders	Enable you to interactively set the color level for each channel.
Tone Balance radio buttons	Determine which range of tones will be affected by your settings. You can set controls at different levels for each range, one at a time.
Preserve Luminosity check box	If checked, prevents alteration of luminosity when color is changed.

Brightness/Contrast

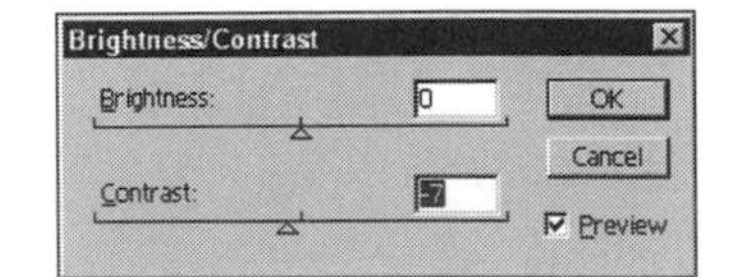

Brightness/Contrast is the simple command for controlling brightness and contrast. A pair of sliders makes the whole area lighter or darker and more or less contrasting as illustrated here.

Brightness/Contrast Dialog Box Contents

Component	*Function*
Brightness slider	Increases or decreases overall lightness.
Contrast slider	Increases or decreases overall contrast.

Hue/Saturation

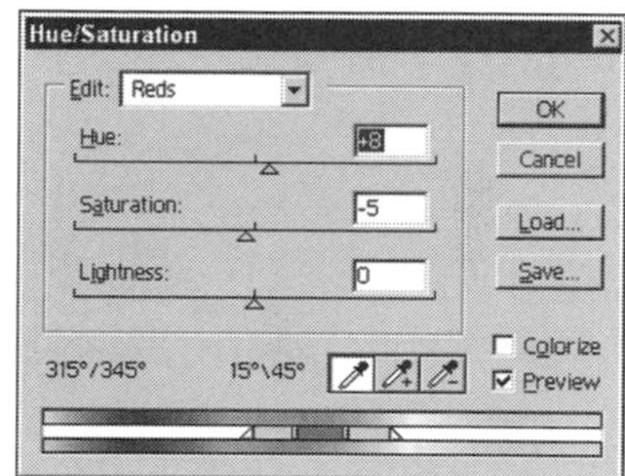

The Hue/Saturation command is especially useful for pepping up the colors in an image. This command enables color correction through independent control of Hue, Saturation, and Lightness values, as the dialog box shown here indicates. You can control all colors simultaneously or any of the primary and complementary colors individually. You can also designate which colors are to be affected by selecting them from the Edit menu, and then targeting a particular range of pixels by clicking them with the three Eyedropper tools. The Hue/Saturation command can also color the entire image if you click the Colorize check box.

Hue/Saturation Dialog Box Contents

Component	*Function*
Edit menu	Enables simultaneous or individual editing of all primary and complementary colors.
Hue slider	Infuses the image with the hue, causing a shift in color balance.
Saturation slider	Intensifies or mutes the intensity of colors.
Lightness slider	Intensifies or mutes the brightness of colors.
Input Hues bar	(The top gradient bar at the bottom of the box.) Represents the normal spectrum of colors.
Output Hues bar	(The bottom gradient bar at the bottom of the box.) Represents the shift of the spectrum according to the position of the Hue slider.
Load button	Loads a previously stored levels setting.
Save button	Stores the current levels setting.
Colorize check box	Makes a monochrome tint of the slider settings.

CONTROL OVERALL IMAGE QUALITY
CONTINUED

Replace Color

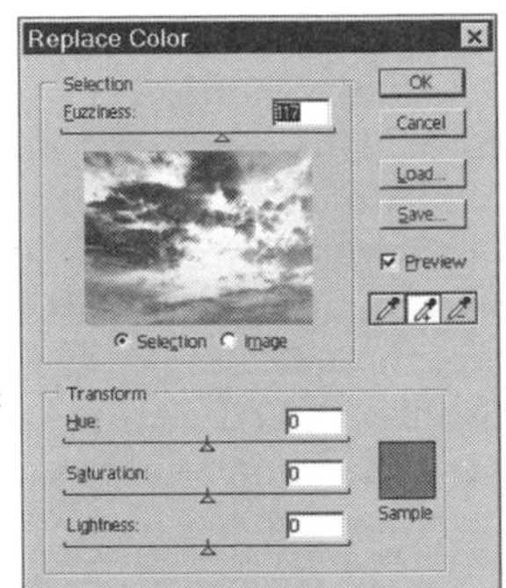

The Replace Color command enables you to replace all the pixels within a given range of color with pixels from another range of color. You use the droppers to select the color(s) you want to change; indicate a range of brightness surrounding that color with the Fuzziness setting; and then use the Hue, Saturation, and Lightness sliders to change the color in the Sample box to a shade that pleases you. If you want to change the color of one particular object in a scene, but the scene contains other objects of that color, be sure to mask the target object with a selection marquee first.

Replace Color Dialog Box Contents

Component	*Function*
Fuzziness field	Indicates spectrum range of color. Enter a number from 1 to 200.
Fuzziness slider	Enables you to specify spectrum range of color by dragging the slider.
Preview area	Shows selected colors as white (selection) or as adjusted (image).
Selection radio button	Preview area will display current selection.
Image radio button	Preview area will display full image.
Hue slider	Infuses the image with the hue, causing a shift in color balance.
Saturation slider	Intensifies or mutes the intensity of colors.
Lightness slider	Intensifies or mutes the brightness of colors.
Output Color Sample box	Previews the color that will be substituted for the selected pixels.
Load button	Loads a previously stored levels setting.
Save button	Stores the current levels setting.
Color droppers	Enable you to select a pixel that represents the color to be substituted. Plus and Minus droppers add to or subtract from the selected range of colors.

Selective Color

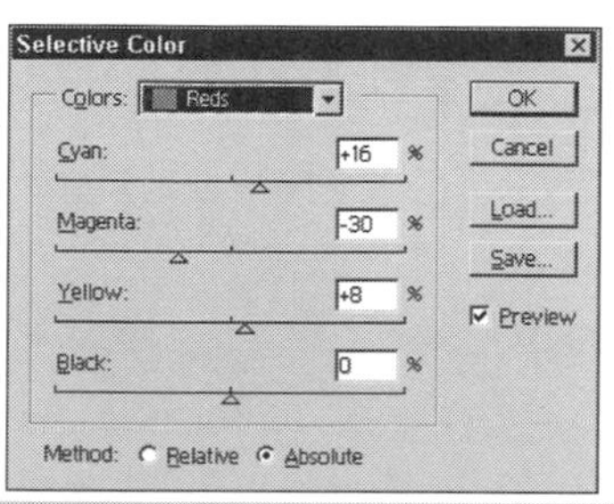

The Selective Color command lets you substitute any CMYK color for any of the primary or complementary colors as well as neutral colors, blacks, or whites. Used primarily in press applications for controlling CMYK ink levels, this command is also capable of producing unusual visual effects. The Selective Color dialog box is shown here.

Selective Color Dialog Box Contents

Component	*Function*
Colors menu	Lets you choose area of color to be adjusted.
Color sliders	Control the amount of cyan, magenta, yellow, or black ink that will be applied to the chosen color range.
Method radio buttons	Determine whether indicated changes will be relative to amount of ink color or an absolute percentage of ink color.
Load button	Loads a previously stored levels setting.
Save button	Stores the current levels setting.

Channel Mixer

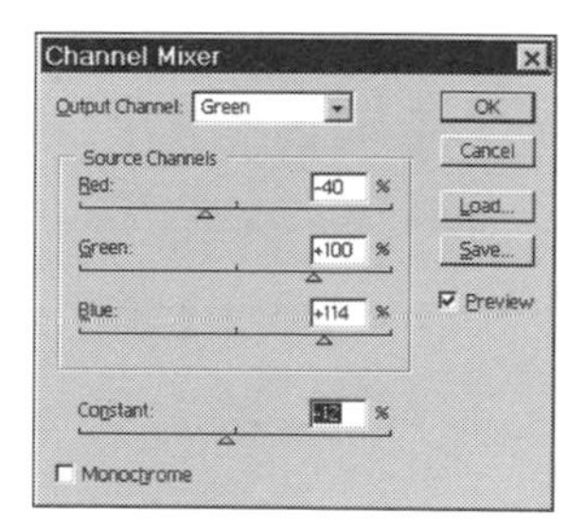

The Channel Mixer command makes mixing the color from multiple channels possible. This command is particularly handy for rescuing images from the blahs after they have been converted to CMYK from RGB or Lab color. By checking the Monochrome check box, you can also use this command to create a monochrome image from a color image while remaining in a true-color color space, thus enabling control of color values based on the information contained in one or more specific color channels. This command is disabled when in Lab Color mode.

Channel Mixer Dialog Box Contents

Component	*Function*
Output Channel menu	Lets you choose the color channel into which the colors from other channels will be mixed.
Color sliders	Control the amount of color that will be infused from existing channels.
Constant slider	Adds an opacity channel to the output channel. Drag to the left to decrease opacity, to the right to increase it.
Monochrome check box	If checked, creates a monochrome image within the current color space.
Load button	Loads a previously stored levels setting.
Save button	Stores the current levels setting.

CONTROL OVERALL IMAGE QUALITY CONTINUED

Variations

The Variations command lets you control brightness and color balance by clicking on preadjusted thumbnails. You can control values for shadows, midtones, and highlights separately in the Variations dialog box shown here. This command is very easy to use and can be a good place to start experimenting with adjustments in color, saturation, and gamma. Be aware, however, that judging the precise effect of these adjustments from the relatively small thumbnails that are your only means of previewing the image is difficult. You may want to note your settings, and then choose File, then Revert or use the History palette to restore your image to its previous state after examining the result at full size. You can then make corrections by using the Curves or Levels commands to make more precise adjustments to the final image.

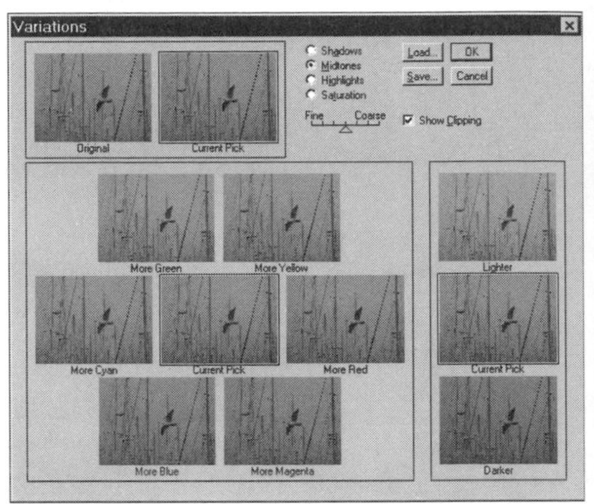

Variations Dialog Box Contents

Component	*Function*
Original thumbnail	Shows the image as unaffected by any variations.
Current Pick thumbnail	Shows the image as altered by any series of choices you have made.
More Color thumbnails	Clicking any of these thumbnails infuses an even measure of that color into the original image. You can multiply the effect by clicking more than once, and you can click on multiple color thumbnails. The effect is cumulative, and is displayed in the Current Pick thumbnail in the center of the section.
Lighter and Darker thumbnails	Make the image lighter or darker according to the position of the Fine/Coarse slider. The current effect is displayed in the Current Pick thumbnail in the center of the section.
Tonal Range radio buttons	Enable you to restrict changes to one of the listed tonal ranges.
Saturation radio button	Enables you to restrict variation thumbnails to changing only the level of color saturation.
Fine/Coarse slider	Sets the intensity of the effect that occurs when you click a thumbnail.
Load button	Loads a previously stored levels setting.
Save button	Stores the current levels setting.

Threshold

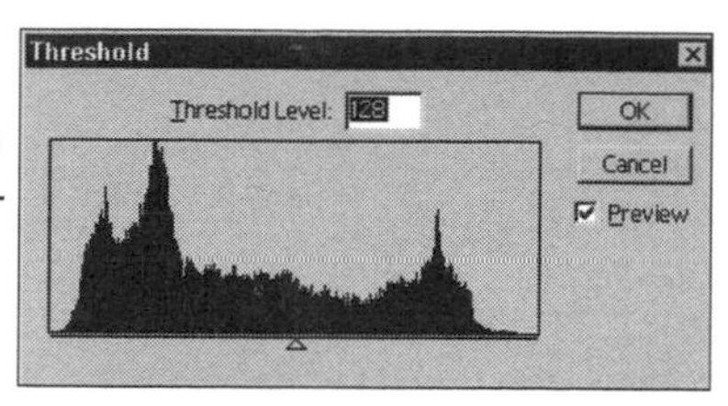

The Threshold command creates a black-and-white image by pushing all the pixels brighter than a certain level to white and all those below a certain level to black — a capability you can take advantage of to automatically make certain types of masks. Also, for an instant line drawing, try using this command in conjunction with the Find Edges filter. The dialog box for this command is shown here.

Threshold Dialog Box Contents

Component	*Function*
Threshold Level field	Indicates the value of the grayscale level. Enter a value from 0 to 255.
Histogram	Displays a graph of pixel density at a given level of brightness.
Threshold slider	Enables you to set the threshold. The value for the level automatically appears in the Threshold Level field.

Posterize

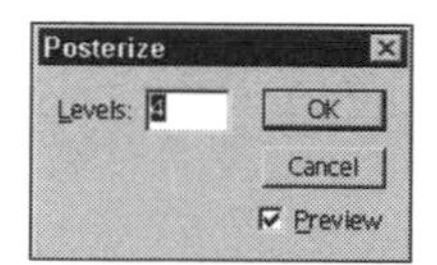

The Posterize command reduces all the colors in the image to a particular number of brightness values, as specified in the Posterize dialog box shown here. The result looks like a high-impact color poster drawn with hard edges and flat-colors.

Posterize Dialog Box Contents

Component	*Function*
Levels field	Enter any number of brightness values from 0 to 255.

Adjustment Commands Without Dialog Boxes

The following commands work automatically, with no intervention from dialog boxes. Note that none of these commands work on adjustment layers.

- **Auto Levels:** Automatically defines the lightest pixel as white and the darkest as black, and then proportionately distributes those pixels that are in between.
- **Desaturate:** Lets you turn an area into grayscale without leaving a true-color mode, so all commands available in RGB will still be available.
- **Equalize:** Interprets the brightest pixel as white, the darkest as black, and then evenly distributes the brightness values of all the pixels in between. This command is potentially useful for maximizing the detail in highlights and shadows.
- **Invert:** Reverses the light and dark tones, as well as changes colors to their complements. In other words, this command creates a color negative (but with no orange mask).

CORRECTING MISTAKES

This section deals with the tools, commands, and techniques in Photoshop that you use to correct mistakes in an image. The tools you use for retouching are, aside from the Clone tool, the same tools you would use to create an original image from scratch. The Photoshop tools used primarily for retouching include the brushes (Paintbrush, Airbrush, and Pencil); the Rubber Stamp (also called the Clone tool); and the Smudge and Blur tools.

Airbrush

The Airbrush has an associated Options palette, which is almost identical to the brush options. The Airbrush Options bar is shown here. See the "Paintbrush" section for more information about common options.

Airbrush Tool Modifiers

Icon	*Shortcut*	*Modifier: Result*
[Airbrush icon]	J	Shift: Produces straight line at any 15-degree angle from the origin of the stroke.
		⌘/Ctrl: Switches to the Move tool.
		Opt/Alt: Switches to the Eyedropper tool.

Airbrush Options

Component	*Function*
Pressure field and slider	Changes the transparency of the airbrush stroke according to the percentage entered in the field. You may enter this information numerically or by dragging a slider that pops up when you click the button.

Paintbrush

The Paintbrush's Options bar is shown here.

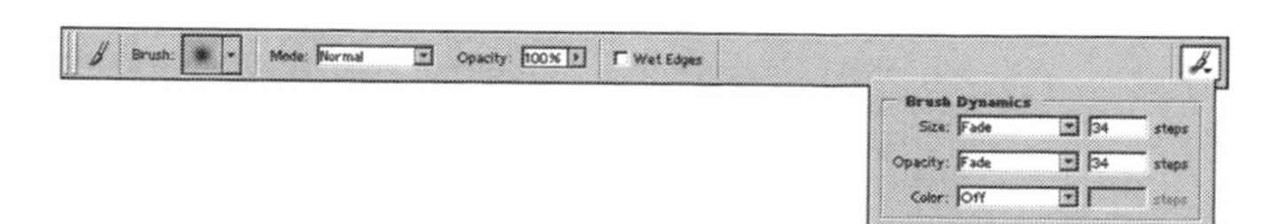

Paintbrush Tool Modifiers

Icon	Shortcut	Modifier: Result
[Paintbrush icon]	B	Shift: Produces straight line at any 15-degree angle from the origin of the stroke.
		⌘/Ctrl: Switches to the Move tool.
		Opt/Alt: Switches to the Eyedropper tool.

Paintbrush Options

Component	Function
Paintbrush icon	Resets all options to default values.
Brush Shape button	Summons the Brush Options dialog box. The button to the immediate right brings up the Brushes palette.
Mode menu	Causes the foreground color to be applied according to the method assigned to that Apply (Blend) mode.
Opacity field and slider	Changes the transparency of the brush stroke according to the percentage entered in the field. You may enter this information numerically or by dragging a slider that pops up when you click the button.
Wet Edges check box	If checked, causes the edges of the stroke to blend with surrounding pixels in a manner reminiscent of watercolors.
Brush Dynamics Size menu	Off means there will be no effect on size; Fade means that the size of the brush will be reduced over the number of steps indicated; Stylus indicates that size will be affected by stylus pressure. This last option is grayed if no stylus is present in the system.
Brush Dynamics Opacity menu	Off means there will be no effect on size; Fade means that the size of the brush will be reduced over the number of steps indicated; Stylus indicates that size will be affected by stylus pressure. This last option is grayed if no stylus is present in the system.
Brush Dynamics Color menu	Off means there will be no effect on size; Fade means that the size of the brush will be reduced over the number of steps indicated; Stylus indicates that size will be affected by stylus pressure. This last option is grayed if no stylus is present in the system.

CORRECTING MISTAKES CONTINUED

Pencil

The Pencil distinguishes itself from the other brush tools in two respects: Its strokes are always hard-edged, regardless of the brush chosen, and it can be set to automatically erase. The Pencil has an associated Options bar, shown here. The only Pencil option that differs from the Paintbrush options is the Auto Erase check box. See the "Paintbrush" section, earlier in this appendix, for more information about common options.

Pencil Tool Modifiers

Icon	*Shortcut*	*Modifier: Result*
	N	Shift: Produces straight line at any 90-degree angle from the origin of the stroke.
		⌘/Ctrl: Switches to the Move tool.
		Opt/Alt: Switches to the Eyedropper tool.

Pencil Options

Component	*Function*
Auto Erase check box	Makes painting the background color over any areas that already have been sketched with the foreground color possible.

Rubber Stamp (Clone) Tool

The Rubber Stamp (Clone) tool uses the currently chosen brush to paint a copy of the image it finds in a specific location of the image at a specified place. This specified place may be either a specific brush-sized area that is painted no matter where you lay the brush down (if the aligned box is checked in the Options dialog box), or a specific distance and angle from the brush that is always maintained, no matter where you start the stroke. The Rubber Stamp tool has an associated Options bar that is shown here. See the "Paintbrush" section, earlier in this appendix, for more information about common options.

Rubber Stamp Tool Modifiers

Icon	*Shortcut*	*Modifier: Result*
	S	Shift: Produces straight line at any 15-degree angle from the origin of the stroke.
		⌘/Ctrl: Switches to the Move tool.
		Opt/Alt: Places the pickup point for cloning.

Rubber Stamp Options

Component	*Function*
Mode menu	Causes the foreground color to be applied according to the method assigned to that Apply (Blend) mode. See the color insert section of this book for a visual description of what each Apply mode does.
Opacity field and slider	Changes the transparency of the brush stroke according to the percentage entered in the field. You may enter this information numerically or by dragging a slider that pops up when you click the button.

CORRECTING MISTAKES CONTINUED

Blur Tool

The Blur tool has an associated Options bar, shown here. See the "Paintbrush" section, earlier in this appendix, for more information about common options. Note: The letter-key shortcut for the Blur, Sharpen, and Smudge tool is R. Repeated pressing of this key cycles through the three tools.

Blur Tool Modifiers

Icon	*Shortcut*	*Modifier: Result*
[icon]	R	Shift: Produces straight line at any 15-degree angle from the origin of the stroke.
		⌘/Ctrl: Switches to the Move tool.
		Opt/Alt: Switches to the Layer Picker (double-headed arrow tool).

Blur Tool Options

Component	*Function*
Mode menu	Causes the foreground color to be applied according to the method assigned to that Apply (Blend) mode. See the Color Plates section of this book for a visual description of what each Apply mode does. Apply modes for this tool are limited to Normal, Darken, Lighten, Hue, Saturation, Color, and Luminosity.
Pressure field and slider	Changes the transparency of the brush stroke according to the percentage entered in the field. You may enter this information numerically or by dragging a slider that pops up when you click the button.
Use All Layers check box	If checked, causes the blur stroke to affect all underlying layers.

Smudge Tool

The Smudge tool has an associated Options bar, shown here. See the "Paintbrush" section, earlier in this appendix, for more information about common options. Note: The letter-key shortcut for the Blur, Sharpen, and Smudge tool is R. Repeated pressing of this key cycles through the three tools.

Smudge Tool Modifiers

Icon	*Shortcut*	*Modifier: Result*
	R	Shift: Produces straight line at any 15-degree angle from the origin of the stroke.
		⌘/Ctrl: Switches to the Move tool.
		Opt/Alt: Switches to the Eyedropper tool

Smudge Tool Options

Component	*Function*
Mode menu	Causes the foreground color to be applied according to the method assigned to that Apply (Blend) mode. See the Color Plates section of this book for a visual description of what each Apply mode does.
Pressure field and slider	Changes the transparency of the brush stroke according to the percentage entered in the field. You may enter this information numerically or by dragging a slider that pops up when you click the button.
Use All Layers check box	If checked, causes the blur stroke to affect all underlying layers.
Finger Painting check box	If checked, causes the tool to smudge using the foreground color, rather than whatever color happens to be immediately under the pointer.

MAKING SELECTIONS

If image adjustments are the heart of Photoshop and filters are its brains, then selections are the soul of Photoshop. Selections make creating irregularly shaped layers, isolating any part of the image, and blending images along their edges to make them continuous possible.

You can use selections to isolate the effect of almost any Photoshop command, and you can use them to graduate the effect of almost any Photoshop command.

Things to Remember About Selections

Although selections enable you to manipulate Photoshop's effects to their full extent, here are a few things you should remember about them:

- You can turn any selection into a mask.
- You can turn any mask into a selection.
- A selection is a mask, except it is only temporary and you cannot reuse it unless you first turn it into a mask. This happens automatically when you save the selection.
- You can blur the edges of any selection with a command known as feathering. You can set the amount of feathering for any selection tool.
- A selection has to be accurate to be effective (in other words, to be believable).
- Almost all accurate selections require that you use a mixture of tools and techniques.
- No single recipe exists for making accurate selections. Almost every situation is a unique case.
- Settings in a selection tool's Options palette remain in effect until you purposely change them or until you reset the tool.
- You can also make selections with the brushes by painting into a channel, by creating a path, or by using QuickMask. Often, these tools are the best for creating the selection you want.

The Right Tool for the Job

Each Photoshop selection tool or Select menu command gives you access to a different technique for making selections. The following table describes each tool, along with the types of images most likely to benefit from use of that tool.

Another method of making a selection, outside of using one of the selection tools, is by painting in a mask in Quick Mask mode. Because this method can be one of the most powerful methods for making selections (and for saving them as permanent mask channels), be sure to read the section "Using Quick Mask Mode" in Chapter 6.

Photoshop's Selection Tools

Icon	*Name*	*What It Does*
	Marquee	Makes a rectangular or square (when pressing Shift) selection. Good for making buttons and filling areas that will be used as backgrounds for text. Also very useful as preliminary selection to be refined by editing.
	Elliptical Marquee	Makes oval or circular (when pressing Shift) selections. Good for same purposes as Marquee tool, where desired shape is closer to an oval. Excellent for vignettes and radial blurs.
	Single Row Marquee	Makes a horizontal selection one pixel thick from edge to edge.
	Single Column Marquee	Makes a vertical selection one pixel wide from edge to edge.
	Magic Wand	Selects all pixels within a given lightness (not color) range. Good starting point for isolating items from solid-color backgrounds.
	Lasso	Makes a completely freehand selection. The most useful tool for editing rough selections.
	Polygon Lasso	Makes straight-edged, many-sided selections. Ideal for many manufactured objects and for making rough selections quickly.
	Magnetic Lasso	Shrinks to fit or expands to fit, depending on value of first pixel selected.
	Select All (on Select menu)	Selects everything in the image. It is the easiest way to copy everything onto a new layer or to drag an image from one file to another.
	Color Range (on Select menu)	Selects everything in the image that falls within the same brightness range as the target pixels. Great for selecting complex shapes, such as lace and hair, from solid or near-solid backgrounds.

Moving and Feathering Selections

The following applies to all selections, regardless of the tool used:

- To move the selection marquee, but not its contents, drag from inside the selection or exactly on its border.
- To move the selection marquee in exact increments, use arrow keys to move the marquee 1 pixel per press or Shift+arrow key to move 10 pixels per press.
- ⌘/Ctrl+dragging cuts the selection from the background and floats it (places the selection into a temporary layer that hovers or "floats" above the surface of the image).
- ⌘/Ctrl+Opt/Alt+dragging copies the contents (pixels) inside the marquee without cutting a hole in the image.
- Changing the feathering in the Options dialog box must take place before you make the selection.
- You can increase feathering after the selection is made, but you cannot decrease it below the amount shown in the Options dialog box.
- To decrease the feathering, change the amount in the dialog box. This change will not take effect until you make the next selection. If you need to decrease feathering on the current selection, you are out of luck.

PATHS

Photoshop 6 gives you virtually the same drawing tools as an illustration program in its Path tools feature, accessible through a toolbar slot menu. Each of the eight tools has an associated Options palette for setting that tool's behavior parameters. Here is a quick overview of each Path tool.

The Pen Tool

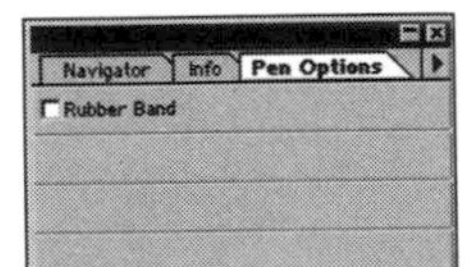

The Pen tool is the tool you will use most often for drawing smooth, efficient paths. Click to start a line segment, move the cursor and click to end the line segment, and drag to curve and shape the line. Releasing the button enables you to make the next line segment. If you make a mistake, press Delete/Backspace.

The Pen Options palette is shown here.

Pen Tool Shortcuts

Icon	*Shortcut*	*Result*
	Cursor over point	Deletes Point arrow
	Cursor over path	Adds point
	Shift	Forces a straight line at 45-degree angles from last point
	⌘/Ctrl	Switches to Direct Selection tool (arrow)
	Opt/Alt	Switches to Convert Point tool
	⌘/Ctrl, then ⌘/Ctrl+Opt/Alt	Switches to Select Path arrow

Pen Tool Options

Component	*Function*
Rubber Band	Enables you to preview the path following the entry of the last point as the cursor moves. Path does not become permanent until you click a new point.

The Magnetic Pen Tool

The Magnetic Pen tool acts almost exactly like the Magnetic Lasso: It automatically makes a path that follows the edges closest to the cursor that contrast most sharply with one another. The Magnetic Pen Options palette is shown in the following figure.

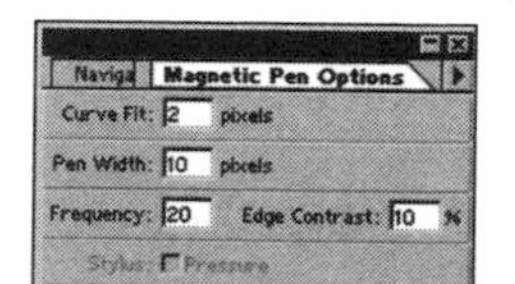

Magnetic Pen Tool Shortcuts

Icon	*Shortcut*	*Result*
	Cursor over point	Deletes Point arrow
	Cursor over path	Adds point
	⌘/Ctrl	Switches to Close Path if drawing or switches to Direct Selection tool (arrow) if editing
	Opt/Alt	Switches to Convert Point tool
	⌘/Ctrl, then Cmd/Ctrl+Opt/Alt	Switches to select Path arrow

Magnetic Pen Tool Options

Component	*Function*
Curve Fit	Enter a value between 1 and 10. Lower numbers enter more control points, making the curve fit the path more accurately. Be careful, though — too much accuracy may reflect any lack of precision on your part and cause too many points to be entered, resulting in a rougher, less accurate selection.
Pen Width	Enter a number between 1 and 40. This is the pixel width of the path that will be scanned for a contrasting edge. If several possible edges are within close range of your cursor, keep this number as low as possible. Note: Pressing [while Magnetic Pen is in use decreases pen width by 1 pixel. Pressing] increases pen width by 1 pixel.
Frequency	Enter a number between 1 and 100 to determine the speed with which new points are placed. A high number causes more points to be placed over a given path length in a given amount of time.
Edge Contrast	Enter a percentage between 1 and 100 to determine the level of contrast between adjacent pixels before they are considered an edge.
Stylus Pressure	If checked, an increase in stylus pressure shrinks the lasso width.

PATHS CONTINUED

The Freehand Pen Tool

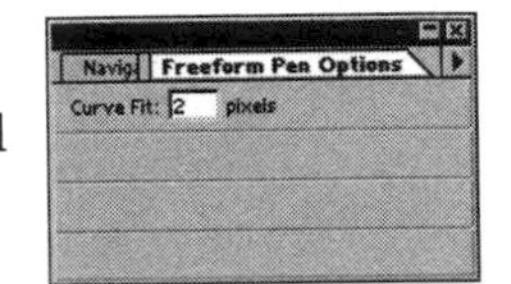

The Freehand Pen tool lets you draw a path freehand. The Freehand Pen tool is best used by those with a steady hand and a pen tablet; otherwise, you end up with too many control points. The Freeform Pen Options palette is pictured here.

Freehand Pen Tool Shortcuts

Icon	*Shortcut*	*Result*
[icon]	Cursor over point	Deletes Point arrow
	Cursor over path	Adds Point arrow
	⌘/Ctrl	Switches to Close Path if drawing or switches to Direct Selection tool (arrow) if editing
	Opt/Alt	Switches to Convert Point tool
	⌘/Ctrl, then ⌘/Ctrl+Opt/Alt	Switches to Select Path arrow

Freehand Pen Tool Options

Component	*Function*
Curve Fit	Enables you to control the frequency of control points along the freeform path. The higher the number, the more distant the points are from one another.

The Add Point Tool

The Add Point tool adds a control point whenever you click an existing path.

Add Point Tool Shortcuts

Icon	*Shortcut*	*Result*
[icon]	Cursor over point	Deletes Point arrow
	⌘/Ctrl	Switches to Direct Selection arrow
	Opt/Alt	Switches to Select Path arrow

The Delete Point Tool

The Delete Point tool removes a control point whenever you click on an existing point or an existing path.

Delete Point Tool Shortcuts

Icon	*Shortcut*	*Result*
[icon]	Cursor over point	Deletes Point arrow
	Cursor over arrow	Brings up Selection path
	⌘/Ctrl	Switches to Direct Selection tool
	Opt/Alt	Switches to Select Path arrow

The Direct Selection Tool

The Direct Selection tool, or arrow, selects a control point and shows any attached direction points (handles). If a + appears alongside, all control points are selected, and dragging moves the entire path rather than a single point or handle. You can select several points at once by dragging a marquee around them.

Direct Selection Tool Shortcuts

Icon	*Shortcut*	*Result*
[icon]	A	Selects control point(s)

The Convert Point Tool

The Convert Point tool lets you convert any type of control point to any other. Click once to remove all handles, drag from the control point to make a smooth curve, and drag handles to make an asymmetrical curve or cusp point (handles not diametrically opposed).

Convert Point Tool Shortcuts

Icon	*Shortcut*	*Result*
[icon]	Cursor over point	Brings up Direct Selection arrow
	Opt/Alt	Switches to Direct Selection tool

The Path Component Selection Tool

The Path Component Selection tool (black arrow) selects an entire component or individual path within the current workpath (which can consist of several path entities or components).

Path Component Selection Tool Shortcuts

Icon	*Shortcut*	*Result*
[icon]	A	Selects entire subpath

MASKS

Masks are one of the most powerful tools Photoshop has to offer. Masks make restricting any of Photoshop's commands, tools, or filters to the unmasked portion of the current layer possible. Selections and masks are essentially the same, with two distinctions:

- A selection does not become a mask until you save it to an alpha channel. An *alpha channel* is one that is not needed for recording a file's color information and that is not a composite channel.
- Masks are more editable than selections (although both are highly editable), because masks are actually bitmapped images that you can modify with any of Photoshop's tools and commands.

To visualize the basics of how masks work, take a look at the first figure, which shows a mask made by saving a selection. The image is that of the alpha channel resulting from saving a selection made with the Lasso tool and then editing it with the Elliptical Marquee tool. The selection made with the Lasso tool was feathered by 20 pixels, so the mask, white on the inside, fades to black on the outside. The selection made with the Elliptical Marquee tool is unfeathered and was subtracted from the first selection, so it cuts a sharp-edged hole into the center of the mask.

Prior to saving, the selection from which the mask in the first figure was made would behave just as the mask would: The black areas would totally block the effect of any Photoshop command or tool. The white areas would be affected 100 percent by those same commands. The gray areas would be partially affected, in direct proportion to their brightness. On the theory that a picture is worth more than a paragraph, look at the following figures.

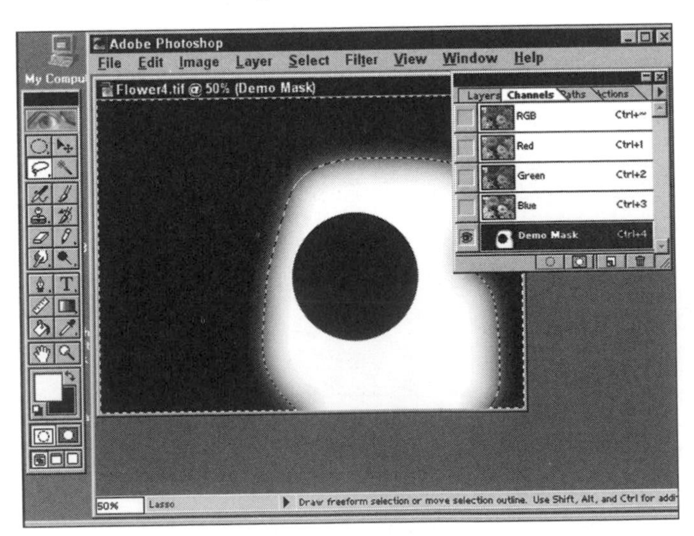

The tools and commands described in this section include the following:

- The Channels palette
- Quick Mask mode and options
- The Feather Selection dialog box
- The Save Selection dialog box
- The Load Selection dialog box

The Channels Palette

The Channels palette, shown in this figure, is the centerpiece of Photoshop's masking operations.

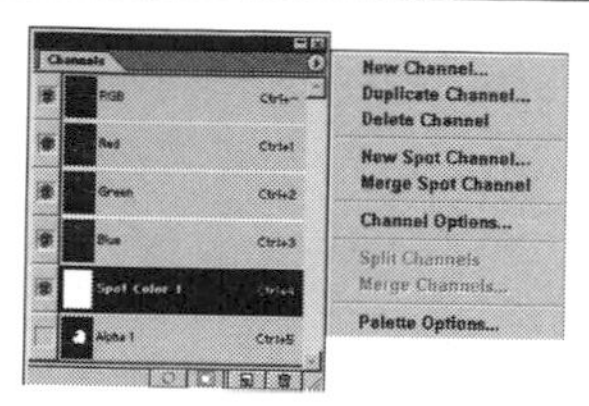

Channels Palette Contents

Component	*Function*
Visibility icon	Indicates what an option is, providing the user with a cue as to what the option does and when to use it.
Composite channel	Actually not an independent channel, but a composite of the color channels. In other words, this channel shows a preview of what the final result of any channel manipulations will be.
Channel name bar	Click to select. When selected (highlighted), the image from this channel appears in the workspace and can be edited with the full power of Photoshop 6.
Color channels	The three or four (depending on the color mode in which you are operating) independent channels that make up the primary colors in your image. You can edit each of these channels independently of one another.
Alpha (mask channel)	A grayscale bitmap that indicates areas to be masked. Black is 100 percent opaque, white is 100 percent transparent, and grays are translucent.
Make Selection icon	Drag a channel to this icon to turn its image into a selection, or select the channel and then click the icon.
Make Mask icon	Click to turn the current selection into a new alpha channel. To put it another way, clicking this icon saves the current selection.
New Channel icon	Creates a new, empty channel. You may then use any of Photoshop's tools or commands to place an image in that channel. Often used to create an empty channel into which a mask will be painted. You can also duplicate a channel by dragging its name bar to this icon.
Delete Channel icon	Drag a channel to this icon to delete it, or select the channel and then click the icon.
Channels palette menu button	Pops up the Channels palette menu.
Channels palette menu	Through this menu, you can access the commands listed in the table that follows.

Channels Palette Menu Commands

Command	*Result*
New Channel	Creates a new, empty channel. You may then use any of Photoshop's tools or commands to place an image in that channel. Often used to create an empty channel into which a mask will be painted.
Duplicate Channel	Duplicates the currently selected channel as an alpha channel.
Delete Channel	Deletes the currently selected channel.
New Spot Channel	Creates a new spot color channel. If a selection is active, the spot color appears inside the selection. If not, you can paint the spot color into the channel.

MASKS CONTINUED

Channels Palette Menu Commands (continued)

Command	*Result*
Merge Spot Channel	Merges the selected spot channel with the primary channels.
Channel Options	The dialog box that appears after you choose this command depends on the type of channel selected. If a color channel is selected, the command is unavailable. Different Options dialog boxes exist for spot channels and alpha channels. (See the text that follows for specifics.)
Split Channels	Creates a new file window for each channel.
Merge Channels	Brings up a Merge Channels dialog box. By default, reunites color channels that have been split.
Palette Options	Enables you to pick from small, medium, or large thumbnail sizes.

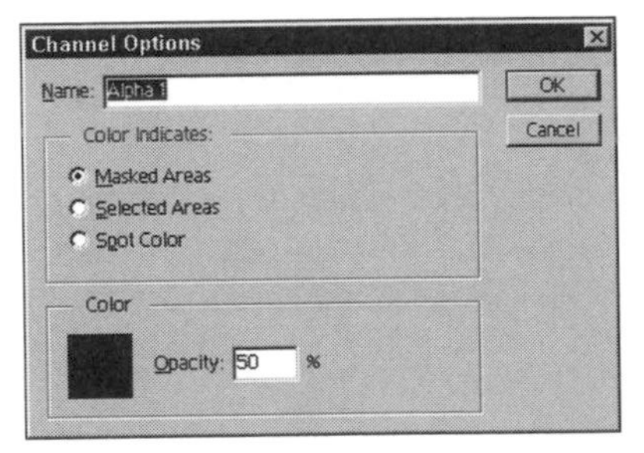

Options for Alpha Channels

An alpha channel is a channel that is not needed for recording a file's color information and that is not a composite channel. The Channel Options dialog box that appears when an alpha channel is selected enables you to specify color, opacity, and what the colors indicate in the alpha channel.

Channel Options Dialog Box Contents

Component	*Function*
Name field	Area in which you enter a name for the channel.
Color Indicates radio buttons	Mutually exclusive choices indicate whether colors in the channel represent masked or unmasked areas or spot colors. If the Spot Color option is chosen, the alpha channel changes to a spot color channel.
Color Swatch	Takes you to your operating system's Color Picker. If you are choosing spot color, you probably want to choose from an industry-standard spot color palette, such as those from Pantone, ANPA, DIC, and Focaltone.
Opacity/Solidity field	Enter a number between 1 and 100 to indicate the percentage of opacity or the solidity of the spot color.
OK button	Applies the current settings.
Cancel button	Closes the dialog box without applying any setting changes to the image.

Options for Spot Channels

You can add a new Spot channel to an image in Photoshop. When you select New Spot Color in the Channels palette menu, the Spot Channel option dialog box appears.

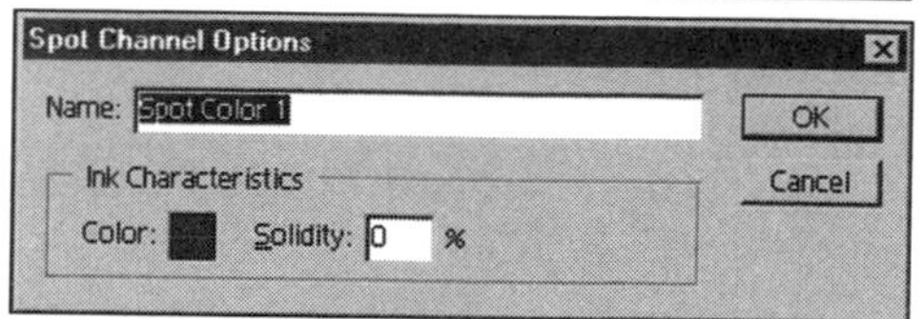

Spot Channel Options Dialog Box Contents

Component	Function
Name field	Enter any name of your choice. Use a name that will help you identify this channel's purpose.
Color Swatch	Clicking the swatch takes you to your operating system's Color Picker. If you are choosing spot color, you probably want to choose from an industry-standard spot color palette, such as those from Pantone, ANPA, DIC, and Focaltone.
Solidity field	Enter a number between 1 and 100 to indicate the percentage of solidity of the spot color.

Quick Mask Mode

Quick Mask mode is handy when creating masks for a couple of reasons:

- It lets you edit a selection using any of the Photoshop tools without forcing you to first save the channel.
- It lets you edit a mask while viewing it superimposed over the image. You can choose a contrasting color for the mask and the degree of opacity to be used.

You can also edit an alpha channel mask in Quick Mask mode. To do so, click the channel in the Channels palette, click the Make Selection icon at the bottom of the Channels palette, and then click the Quick Mask mode icon.

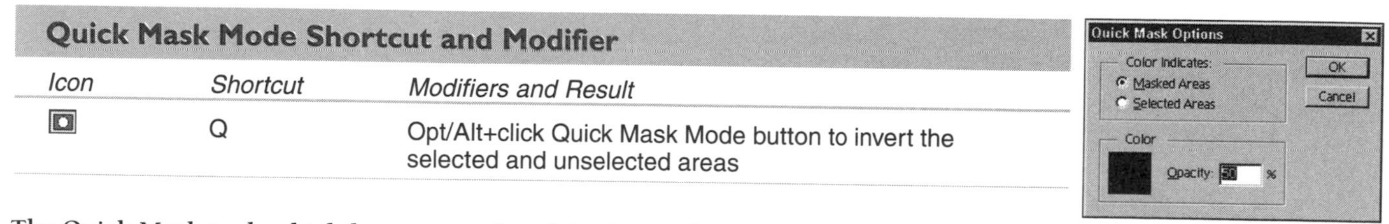

Quick Mask Mode Shortcut and Modifier

Icon	Shortcut	Modifiers and Result
	Q	Opt/Alt+click Quick Mask Mode button to invert the selected and unselected areas

The Quick Mask tool, which has an associated Options palette, is depicted here. Double-click the Quick Mask button to bring up the Quick Mask Options dialog box.

Quick Mask Dialog Box Contents

Component	Function
Color Indicates radio buttons	Click a radio button to indicate whether colored area represents the masked or unmasked areas of the image.
Color Swatch	Click here to access your operating system's Color Picker. You can choose any color as a color for the mask. Choosing a color that is not present (or, at least, not prevalent) in the image you are masking is best.
Opacity field	Enter a number between 0 and 100 to indicate the percentage of opacity of the masking color. Note: This number does not determine the opacity of the mask itself. The mask opacity is determined by the shade of gray used to paint or fill the mask.

MASKS CONTINUED

Feather Selection Dialog Box

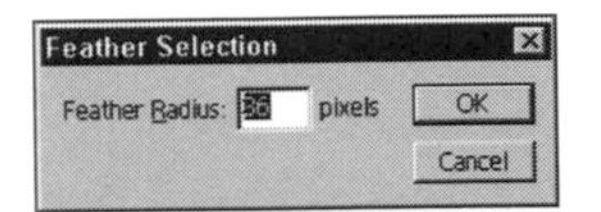

The Feather Selection dialog box, shown here, appears when you feather an existing selection. To feather an existing selection, choose Select, then Feather (Opt/Alt+⌘/Ctrl+D).

Feather Selection Option

Component	*Function*
Feather Radius field	Enter a number of pixels to indicate the width of feathering. Feathering (graduating the edges of the mask from black to white or, to put it another way, from opaque to transparent) is always centered on the selection marquee.

Two techniques are available for feathering different parts of a selection to different degrees:

- Make two selections. After making the first, which should not encompass what will be the edge of the second selection, feather it (as detailed in the preceding table). Press Shift and make a second selection that does encompass the edge you want to feather to a different degree. Now, specify a different number of pixels for feathering.
- Set a given degree of feathering in the selection tool's Options dialog box Feather field. Make a selection. Double-click the selection tool a second time to bring up its options and set a different pixel width for feathering. Now press Shift and add to the first selection. Once again, the second selection must fall outside the first selection.

Save Selection Dialog Box

When you save a selection by choosing Select, then Save Selection from the menu bar, the Save Selection dialog box shown here appears.

Save Selection Options

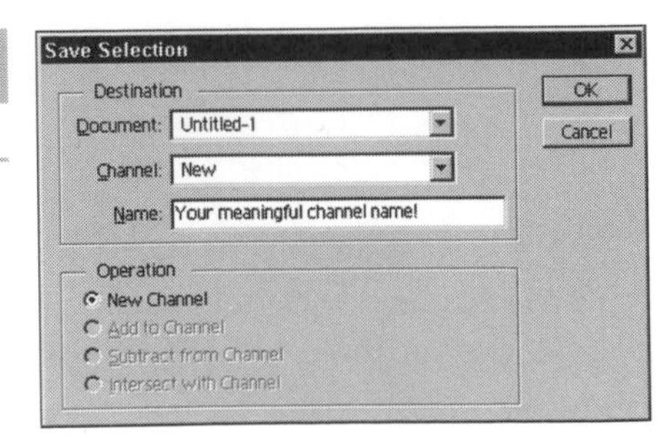

Component	*Function*
Document menu	Lets you choose the document into which you want to store the current selection. One way you can transfer channels between files is to open both files, turn the channel into a selection, save the selection, and choose the other open document as the destination using this menu. You can only choose a currently open document as a destination.

Component	Function
Channel menu	Lets you either create a new channel for this selection or merge this selection with the mask in an existing channel. The method of merging is determined by your choice of Operations radio buttons (the specific buttons are described next).
Name field	Enter any name that will help you remember the purpose of this channel.
New Channel operation	Creates a new channel for the current selection.
Add to Channel operation	Adds the current selection to the mask stored in an existing channel (be sure you have chosen the desired target channel from the Channel menu).
Subtract from Channel operation	Removes the current selection from the mask stored in an existing channel (be sure you have chosen the desired target channel from the Channel menu).
Intersect with Channel operation	Leaves only the area shared in common between the current selection and the mask stored in an existing channel (be sure you have chosen the desired target channel from the Channel menu).

Load Selection Dialog Box

When you load a selection by choosing Select, then Load Selection from the menu bar, the Load Selection dialog box appears, as shown here.

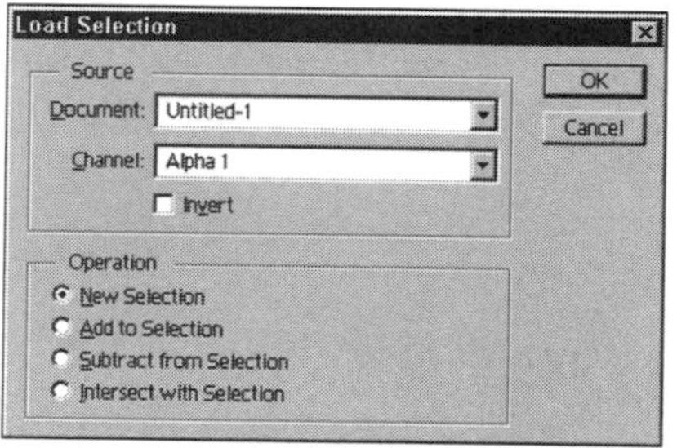

Load Selection Options

Component	Function
Document menu	Lets you choose the document from which you want to load the current selection.
Channel menu	Lets you choose to either load a new channel as the current selection or merge a current selection with the mask loaded from an existing channel. The method of merging is determined by your choice of Operations radio buttons (the specific buttons are described next).
Invert check box	Makes an inverted selection when the selection is retrieved. In other words, everything that was not selected will be selected and vice versa.
New Selection operation	Creates a new selection from the channel chosen in the Channel menu.
Add to Channel operation	Adds the mask stored in an existing channel (be sure you have chosen the desired target channel from the Channel menu) to the current selection.
Subtract from Channel operation	Removes the mask stored in an existing channel (be sure you have chosen the desired target channel from the Channel menu) to the current selection.
Intersect with Channel operation	Leaves only the area shared in common between the current selection and the mask stored in an existing channel (be sure you have chosen the desired target channel from the Channel menu).

LAYERS

Layers are another of Photoshop's strongest features. Layers make showing a client (or you) several variations or interpretations of a composition possible. They make seamlessly combining several images and testing or combining special effects from multiple processes into the same image much easier. They make dealing with part of the image independent of the rest of the image possible. Finally, they enable you to move, scale, rotate, stretch, slant, or give perspective to an image. You can mask layers. You can change their stacking order and their

transparency. You can assign each layer its own Blend mode so that it creates a special effect in combining with the layer beneath it.

Yet despite all this power, there is little you can do with layers that Photoshop will not let you do without them. Layers, however, provide ease of use, convenience, and interactivity. They also let you experiment without endangering the whole file, as almost all Photoshop commands apply only to the active layer, as shown in the first figure. Of course, if the active layer is an adjustment layer, all adjustments affect all layers; but you can always toss out the adjustment layer, and the rest of the image stays intact.

Layers Palette

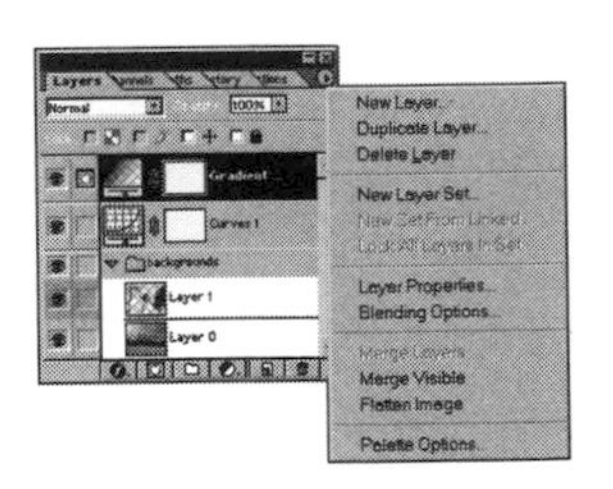

The Layers palette (shown here) provides control over layers. You can rearrange the stacking order of layers by dragging the name bar of any given layer to a new location in the Layers palette as long as that location is in between any two existing layers. To place a layer above the top layer, for example, drag it to a position between the top and second layers, and then drag the top layer below the new second layer.

If you place layers in sets, you can drag the whole set to a new location in the layers palette.

Layers Palette Contents

Component	*Function*
Blend modes menu	Setting a Blend mode for an active layer affects all underlying layers. See the color insert section of this book for a visual indication of the effect of all Blend modes.
Preserve Transparency check box	Check this box to keep tools and commands in this layer from affecting transparent areas.
Layer Visibility box	When the Eye icon is visible, the layer is visible. Click to toggle hiding and revealing of the layer.
Linked/Masked/Paint box	Can contain one of three icons: brush, which indicates the layer is active; chain link, which means the layer is linked to another one or more layers; or mask, which indicates the mask is active.
Layer thumbnail	You can change these to any of three sizes with the Layer Palette Options dialog box.

Component	Function
Make Layer Mask icon	Masks the layer with the current selection. If no selection is active, creates a new, blank mask.
Make New Layer icon	Creates a new layer when clicked. Duplicates any layer that is dragged onto it.
Delete Layer icon	Deletes the active layer or any layer or layer mask that is dragged onto it (it prompts you whether to apply or discard).
Mask Lock icon	Click to toggle capability to move mask or image independently.
Mask icon	Click to activate and edit mask.
Adjustment Layer symbol	Indicates that this layer is an adjustment layer. Default layer name indicates the type of adjustment layer.
Layer name	Double-click to rename a layer in the Layer Options palette. Also, a double-click here will turn a "background" (flat) layer into one that can have transparency.
Layer bar	Click to make a layer active. Double-click to bring up Layer Options palette.
Opacity slider	The Opacity slider appears when you drag the Opacity menu. Click and drag to change opacity percentage or type a number between 1 and 100.
Layers palette menu	Click and drag to choose menu options.

Layers Palette Menu

Many of the commands that are found in the Layers menu (discussed next) are duplicated on the Layers palette menu, as shown here, where they may be handier if the Layers palette is open. Of course, many of these commands are duplicated by the functions of the icons at the bottom of the Layers palette, which are even handier.

New Layer...
Duplicate Layer...
Delete Layer
New Layer Set...
New Set From Linked...
Lock All Layers in Set...
Layer Properties...
Blending Options...
Merge Layers
Merge Visible
Flatten Image
Palette Options...

Some commands on this menu are new to Photoshop 6: New Layer Set, New Set from Linked, Lock All Layers in Set, and Blending Options.

Layers Palette Menu Contents

Command	Shortcut	Function
New Layer	Shift+⌘/Ctrl+N	Creates a new, empty, transparent layer after bringing up the Duplicate Layer dialog box.
Duplicate Layer		Duplicates the active (selected) layer after bringing up the Duplicate Layer dialog box.
Delete Layer		Eradicates the active (selected) layer.
New Layer Set		Creates a new layer set after bringing up the New Layer Set dialog box.
New Set From Linked		Creates a new set of layers consisting of any that are linked when the command is issued. Also brings up the New Layer Set dialog box.
Lock All Layers in Set		Protects all the layers in the currently selected set from the effects of any strokes or other edits.
Merge Layers/Linked		Merges all the layers in the image. If layers are linked, command reads Merge Linked and links only those layers.
Merge Visible		Merges only those layers whose Eye icon is present.
Flatten Image		Merges all layers with the background. Using this command whenever you want to reduce the file to its smallest possible size is wise. (After applying this command, editing layers independently is no longer possible.)
Palette Options		Enables you to choose from small, medium, or large thumbnail sizes.

LAYERS CONTINUED

Layers Menu

Several commands that affect layers you can access only from the menu bar in the Layers menu. Those that are not duplicated in the Layers palette menu are listed in the following table.

Layers Menu Contents

Command	*Function*
New, then Layer	Creates a new empty layer. (Shortcut to command: Shift+⌘/Ctrl+N)
New, then Layer From Background	Creates a new layer that is the current background layer.
New, then Layer Set	Brings up the Layer Set dialog box so that you can name a new Layer Set. Clicking OK creates the set. A layer set has the same organizational functionality as a folder.
New, then Layer Set From Linked	Creates a new layer set from any layers that are currently linked.
New, then Layer via Copy	Copies the contents of the current selection to a new layer. The area outside the selection will be transparent in the new layer.
New, then Layer via Cut	Copies the contents of the current selection to a new layer and simultaneously deletes the content of that selection from the original layer.
Duplicate Layer	Duplicates the layer that is currently selected in the Layers palette.
Delete Layer	Deletes the currently active layer (the one highlighted in the Layers palette).
Layer Properties	Brings up the Layer Properties dialog box.
Layer Style	Brings up a menu of all the individual style options that are available in the Layer Style dialog box. Choosing any of these options brings up the full dialog box.
New Fill Layer	Brings up a menu of all the individual style options that are available in the Fill Layer dialog box: Solid Color, Gradient, Pattern. Choosing any of these brings up the Fill Layer Properties dialog box.
New Adjustment Layer	Brings up a menu of all the individual Image Adjust commands: Levels, Curves, Color Balance, Brightness/Contrast, Hue/Saturation, Selective Color, Channel Mixer, Gradient Map, Invert, Threshold, and Posterize. Choosing any of these commands brings up the same dialog box as if the command were chosen from the Image then Adjust menu — but the adjustment affects all underlying layers.
Change Layer Content	Brings up a menu of all the different types of content layers. Your choice replaces the content type of the currently selected layer.
Layer Content Options	Brings up the Options dialog box that is in context with the type of content layer for the currently selected layer. In other words, if it is an adjustment layer that has been assigned to Curves, the Curves Options dialog box appears.

Command	Function
Type, then Create Path	Converts the type on the currently selected layer to a workpath. This workpath Work could be used as a clipping path to mask any underlying visible content.
Type, then Horizontal/Vertical	Horizontal and Vertical are actually separate choices, with Horizontal as the default. You can switch highlighted text between horizontal and vertical orientation by choosing the state that is not preceded by a check mark.
Type, then Anti-Alias None/Crisp/Strong/Smooth	Each of these options is a separate menu choice indicating the level of edge-smoothing that will be employed along the edges of text. Can make all the difference in readability of text, especially in small sizes, on the Web — also on the maximum level of practical optimization.
Type, then Convert Paragraph	Converts the currently selected type to automatic word-wrapping and to hyphenation within the type box.
Type, then Warp Text	Brings up the Warp Text dialog box, which lets you choose from among 15 variations of text warping styles and control whether the effect is vertical or horizontal, the degree of bend, and the direction of perspective distortion.
Type, then Update All Type Layers	Updates the type on all layers.
Type, then Replace All Missing Fonts	Substitutes the closest relative for any missing font.
Rasterize, then Type	Converts all type to a bitmapped image with the balance of the layer transparent. You can then use any of the filters or painting commands on that layer.
Rasterize, then Shape	Converts all shapes to bitmapped images with the balance of the layer transparent. You can then use any of the filters or painting commands on that layer.
Rasterize, then Fill Content	Changes the contents of a fill layer to a bitmap.
Rasterize, then Layer Clipping Path	Rasterizes a layer that contains clipping paths.
Rasterize, then Layer	Use this command to Rasterize a layer that contains several element types.
Rasterize, then Linked Layers	Rasterizes all linked layers, regardless of layer type.
Rasterize, then All Layers	Rasterizes all layers, regardless of layer type.
New Layer-based Slice	Automatically creates a slice based on the boundaries of the contents of this layer. If those boundaries change (as a result of adding a style, for instance) the boundaries of the slice automatically change. Generally, you should not use layer-based slices for animations because boundaries must change to encompass the entire animation. In-place animations are okay, though.
Add Layer Mask, then Reveal All/Hide All/Reveal Selection/Hide Selection	Add appears here if no mask is assigned to the currently selected layer. The fastest way to add a layer mask is to make a selection, then choose Add Layer Mask, then Reveal/Hide Selection.
Remove Layer Mask,then Discard/Apply	Remove appears here if a mask is already assigned to the currently selected layer. Choosing Discard completely deletes the mask without imposing any effect Choosing Apply makes the hidden part of the layer transparent and removes the mask.
Enable/Disable Layer Mask toggle	Disable turns off the layer mask (Link icon disappears) so that the effect is not visible; click Enable to turn it back on.

(continued)

LAYERS CONTINUED

Layers Menu Contents *(continued)*

Command	*Function*
Add Layer Clipping Path, then Reveal All/Hide All/Current Path	Adds a clipping path to the currently selected layer. If an active workpath exists, choosing Current Path makes it the clipping path for this layer.
Enable/Disable	Toggles activation of the currently selected layer's clipping path.Layer Clipping Path
Group with Previous	Causes the clipping path on the currently selected layer to be imposed on all underlying layers. Clipping groups only affect underlying layers.
Ungroup	Reverses the effect of grouping layers.
Arrange	Lets you move the currently selected layer to the top or the bottom of the stack or to move it up or down one layer. Just dragging the layer to a new position in the Layers palette is much easier — unless making the Layers palette visible is not convenient.
Align Linked	Allows you to align partially transparent layers (buttons or thumbnails, for example) along their horizontal or vertical sides or centers. Layers must be linked in order for alignment to take effect, but the layers can be unlinked once aligned.
Distribute Linked	Makes evenly distributing linked layers between the location of the top and bottom layers in the linked set possible. You may distribute layers horizontally or vertically by sides or centers.
Merge Down	Merges the currently selected layer with the one immediately below it.
Merge Linked	This command replaces the preceding one if layers are linked in the Layers palette. Combines all linked layers into one.
Merge Visible	Merges all image layers with the Eye icon currently visible in the Layers palette. Clicking the Eye icon's box toggles it on and off.
Flatten Image	Perhaps the most frequently used command on the Layers menu. Collapses all layers of all types into one. A good habit to get into when shipping a file out for final production or when preparing an image for use on the Web.
Matting, then Defringe	Automatically replaces a selection's fringe pixels (those left from cutting the image from another background) with those of the color(s) that currently surround the selection. A dialog box lets you enter the pixel width that Photoshop should examine for defringing.
Matting, then Remove Black Matte	Automatically removes black pixels found on the borders of a selection.
Matting, then Remove White Matte	Automatically removes white pixels found on the borders of a selection.

Blending Options

You can apply Layer Blending options to any layer that is not a Fill or Adjustment layer. Choosing the Blending Options command in the Layers Palette menu accesses the Layer Style dialog box. You can then change the selected layer's Blend mode, alter its transparency and opacity. and choose from any of the advanced options shown in the following illustration. You can also access this dialog box by any of the following methods:

- Choose Layer, then Layer Style, then Blending from the menu bar.
- Choose Blending Options from the Layers palette menu.
- Double-click the layer name bar in the Layers palette.

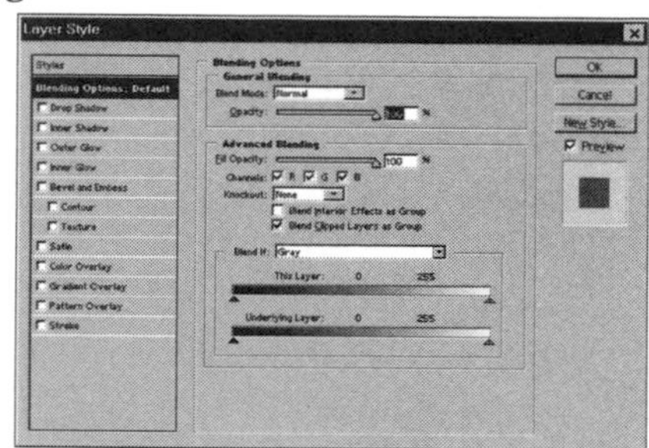

Remember, the opacity and mode settings for tools and layers interact with one another. So if you have a layer opacity of 30 percent and a brush opacity of 50 percent, the opacity of the paint will be only 15 percent (or 50 percent of 30 percent).

Blend Options Dialog Box Contents

Component	*Function*
Blend Mode menu	Alternative way to set the Blend mode for the currently selected layer. Exactly the same menu as is at the top of the Layers palette.
Opacity slider/field	Alternative way to set the opacity for the currently selected layer. Performs identically to the Opacity slider/field in the Layers palette.
Fill Opacity slider/field	Determines the opacity of a Fill layer.
Channels check boxes	Lets you choose which channels will be affected by Blend Modes. You can choose the composite channel as well as individual channels for the current image's Color Mode (for example, RGB, CMYK, Lab).
Knockout menu	Lets you select knockout options for the currently selected layer. The currently selected layer's shape knocks out (trims to its shape) the layers below it that are within its layer set. If the Pass Through option is checked or if no Layer Sets exist, then the knockout will affect all underlying layers except the background layer.
Blend Interior Effects check box	Applies Blending Modes only to those portions of the image falling inside the top layer's boundaries (silhouette).
Blend Clipped Layers check box	Causes grouped layers to use the Blend Mode of the bottom layer of the group.
Blend If menu	Lets you choose which channel to apply the Blend Modes to. Grey refers to the composite channel. The other channels will be named for the primary colors in whatever Color Mode you are in.
This Layer slider	Drag this slider to indicate the brightness range of pixels to be affected on this layer by the Blend Modes choice. Possible values are between 1–255.

(continued)

LAYERS CONTINUED

Blend Options Dialog Box Contents *(continued)*

Component	*Function*
Underlying Layer slider	Drag this slider to indicate the brightness range of pixels to be affected on visible underlying layers by the Blend Modes choice. Possible values are between 1–255.
New Style button	Saves the current settings to a new style in the Styles Library. Brings up a dialog box that allows you to choose whether to include/exclude Blending Options and Style Options.
Preview check box	Causes the effect of the current style settings (including Blending Options) to be seen instantaneously in the image itself. Can slow operations on slower computers or when file size is excessive.
Thumbnail preview	Shows how the current style, including whatever blending options are set, will look when applied to this button. Useful because this dialog box often covers too much of the screen to make using the Preview check box practical.

New Layer Dialog Box

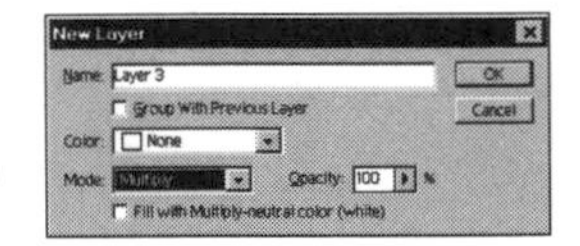

The New Layer dialog box, depicted here, is, for the most part, a subset of the Layers palette menu. This dialog box appears only if you choose New Layer from the menu bar. Those methods of creating a new layer afforded by the Layers palette do not bring up this dialog box, but you can always bring up the Layer Options dialog box after the fact by double-clicking the layer name bar in the Layers palette. The two settings unique to this palette are Group With Previous Layer and Fill With. The following table lists the uses for these settings.

New Layer Dialog Box Contents

Component	*Function*
Name field	Enter a meaningful name that will help you remember the purpose of this layer. You can rename this layer at any time by entering a new name.
Group With Previous Layer check box	If checked, the new layer is grouped with the layer immediately below it.
Color menu	Choose a color for the layer's Layer Name bar in the Layer's palette. This color does not affect actual colors in the image — it is to be used only for organizational purposes.

Component	Function
Mode menu	Lets you specify a Blend menu mode that determines how this layer interacts with layers below it. See the Color Plates section of this book for a picture of how each Blend mode works.
Opacity field/slider	Enter a number between 0 and 100 to indicate the percentage of overall transparency for this layer. Clicking the down arrow and dragging the slider produces the same result.
Fill with neutral check box	Fills the layer with a color that is unaffected by the current Blend Mode (usually black, white, or gray). The exact name of this check box changes in context with the currently chosen Blend mode.

Duplicate Layer Dialog Box

You can only reach the Duplicate Layer dialog box, shown here, if you choose the Duplicate Layer command from the menu bar. When you choose the command in this way, you can send the duplicated (copied) layer to a document other than the current document. To do so, you must make sure that the target document is also open in Photoshop. You then choose the name of the target document from the Document menu. You can also choose New from this menu, and Photoshop will automatically create a new document that contains only the layer to be duplicated.

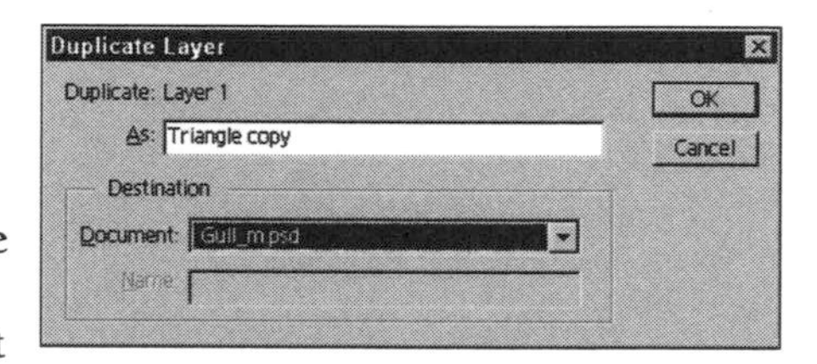

Duplicate Layer Dialog Box Contents

Component	Function
As field	The word *copy* is added automatically to the name of the layer being duplicated. If you want, you can enter a new name in this field.
Destination Document menu	Lets you choose the current document, a new document, or any open Photoshop document as the target for the duplicated layer.
Destination Name field	Lets you assign a name to the new document. This field is unavailable unless you are targeting a new document.

Adjustment Options

Each type of adjustment, which you find by choosing Layer, then New Adjustment Layer, has its own Adjustment Options dialog box. The corresponding options are Levels, Curves, Brightness/Contrast, Color Balance, Hue/Saturation, Selective Color, Channel Mixer, Gradient Map, Invert, Threshold, and Posterize.

CHANNEL OPERATIONS

Channel operations are those functions created by causing one Photoshop channel to interact with another according to a specific mathematical formula. Many of the special effects in Photoshop are due to preprogrammed channel operations. Channel operations can make use of any combination of Photoshop's channels, whether they are color channels or alpha channels.

Although all masks are channels, not all channels are masks. First, there is the composite channel, which is not really a channel but a screen image that represents the combination of all the individual color channels. Then there are the individual color channels, the number of which varies from color model to color model. For example, the RGB model has three color channels: Red, Green, and Blue; the CMYK model has four color channels: Cyan, Magenta, Yellow, and blacK. Bitmap, grayscale, duotone, and indexed-color images have only one channel.

In addition, any Photoshop file (except bitmap images) can have a total of up to 24 channels. Those that are not color channels are called *alpha channels*.

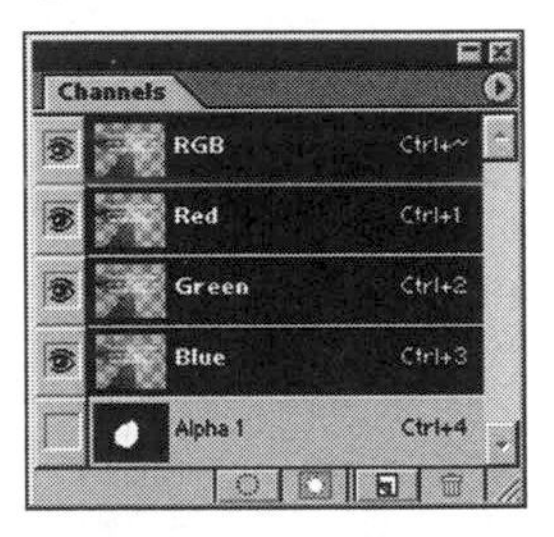

The Channels Palette

You access the Channels palette, shown here, by choosing Window, then Show Channels. Every channel in a particular image appears in the Channels palette.

Channels Palette Contents

Component	*Function*
Selection icon	Click to make selection from active channel (load channel), or drag channel to icon to make selection from channel.
Mask icon	Click to make mask channel from active channel, or drag channel to icon to make mask (alpha) channel from channel.
New Channel icon	Click to make new (blank) channel, or drag channel to icon to duplicate (copy) a channel.
Trash icon	Click to delete the currently active channel, or drag any channel to icon to delete it.
Palette menu button	Drag to open menu and choose menu item (see the following section, "Channels Palette Menu").

Channels Palette Menu

The Channels palette menu is a fly-out menu accessed by clicking the right arrow in the upper-right corner of the palette. The Channels palette menu offers a list of additional channel commands.

Channels Palette Menu Contents

Component	*Function*
New Channel	Creates a new, empty channel and brings up the New Channel dialog box.
Duplicate Channel	Makes a copy of the currently active channel and brings up the Duplicate Channel dialog box.
Delete Channel	Deletes the active channel.
New Spot Channel	Creates a new channel for a spot color. Spot colors are specific colors from ink makers' swatchbooks (Photoshop 6 supports ANPA, DIC, Focoltone, Pantone, Toyo, and Trumatch). If you specify a channel to print in one of these colors, you will get an exact match from the printers. Useful for printing solid text and logos that must meet corporate specs.
Merge Spot Channel	Converts the spot channel to the current color mode and merges it with the existing color channels. This command automatically flattens the image. The merged channels will be affected by solidity settings made in the New Spot Channel Options dialog box.
Channel Options	Enables you to rename the layer, choose the masking color, and indicate whether it covers masked, unmasked, or spot color areas of the image. You can also set the opacity of the mask color. (Double-clicking the channel also brings up this dialog box.)
Split Channels	Automatically exports each channel to a separate file. Command is inactive if only one channel exists in the file.
Merge Channels	Active only if channels have been split and the window for each of the split channels is still open. Merges all the split channels back into one channel. Enables you to reassign channels through several dialog boxes (see "Merge Channels," later in this section).
Palette Options	Enables you to choose the size of the thumbnail.

New Channel

The New Channel dialog box, depicted here, appears when you choose the New Channel command from the Channels palette menu. Use this dialog box to select the type of channel you want to create.

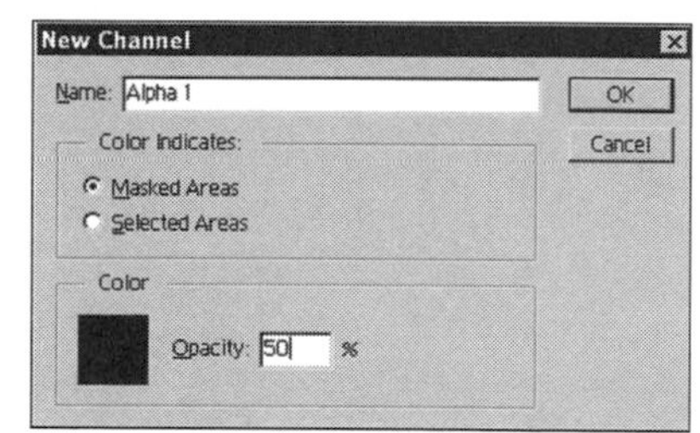

New Channel Dialog Box Contents

Component	*Function*
Name field	Enter new name for channel or accept default.
Color Indicates radio buttons	Click to choose whether the mask color indicates masked or unmasked (selected) areas of the channel.
Color swatch	Click to bring up the Color Picker dialog box. You can change color any time you like.
Opacity field	Enter desired percentage of transparency for the masking color.

CHANNEL OPERATIONS CONTINUED

Duplicate Channel

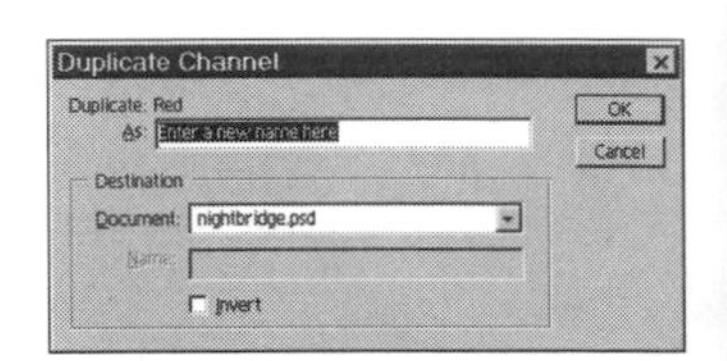

The Duplicate Channel dialog box, shown here, appears when you choose Duplicate Channel from the Channels palette menu. Use this dialog box to select the name and destination for your duplicated channel.

Duplicate Channel Dialog Box Contents

Component	*Function*
Duplicated channel	Enter a name for the copied channel.
Duplicate name field	As Enter a name that is meaningful to you for the duplicate channel or accept the automatically entered name.
Destination menu	Choose the destination file for the duplicated channel (the current document is the Document default). All documents that are open are listed on this menu, or you can choose New if you want to send the channel to a new document.
Name field	Enter the name for the new document. This field is grayed if you are duplicating to an existing document.
Invert check box	If checked, the image in this channel is inverted (made a negative).

Saving alpha channels to a new file is a great way to keep selections for a particular file in a different file. This way they are always available, but you do not have to increase your file size (and therefore your need for system memory).

New Spot Channel

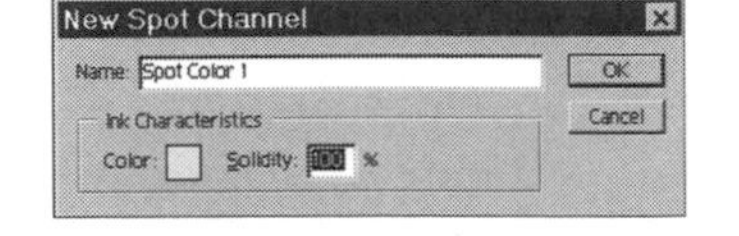

The New Spot Channel dialog box, shown here, appears when you choose New Spot Channel from the Channels palette menu. Each spot color channel prints on a separate color plate. In this dialog box, you can select the color and solidity (the opacity of the ink) of the channel.

New Spot Channel Dialog Box Contents

Component	*Function*
Name field	Accept the default name for the new color channel, or enter your own.
Color swatch	Click to bring up the Color Picker. When the Color Picker appears, be sure to click the Custom button so you can pick the spot color from one of Photoshop's swatch booklets.
Solidity field	Enter a percentage of coverage (roughly equivalent to transparency) for this spot color. The number you enter here affects the influence the spot color has if this channel is merged into the color channels. The idea here is to tell the imagesetter what percentage of a particular ink you want on that plate. How it affects the merge is less important, because the purpose of the feature is for spot color, which will not be merged. If you play with this feature, you will notice that Photoshop 6 always puts 100 percent black in the channel but displays a rendition of the spot color in its specified percentage. The percentage info is not displayed (as opacity or percentage of gray) in the channel itself.

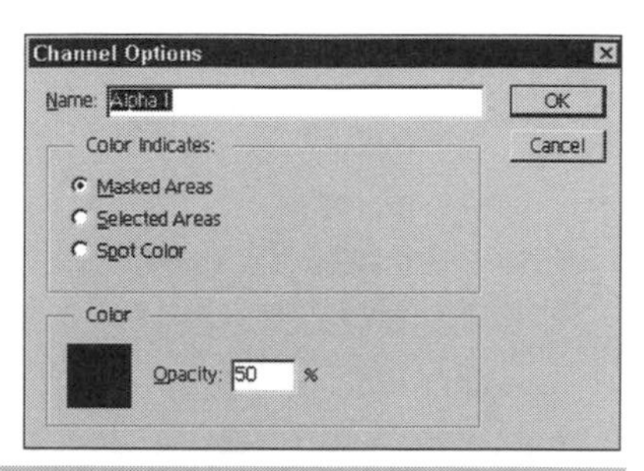

Channel Options

Access the Channel Options dialog box, shown here, by selecting the Channel Options command from the Channels palette menu. Choose this command to change the settings assigned to a spot color or mask channel.

Channel Options Dialog Box Contents

Component	*Function*
Name field	Accept the default name for the new color channel, or enter your own.
Color Indicates radio buttons	Click to indicate whether you want the color to be a spot or mask color and whether the mask color will cover selected or unselected areas of the layer.
Color swatch	Click to bring up the Color Picker so you can change the mask or spot color.
Opacity field	Enter the opacity of the masking color (the number will be translated as the solidity if this is to be a spot color).

Merge Channels

The Merge Channels dialog box, shown here, appears by choosing the Merge Channels command in the Channels palette menu. The Merge Channels command — available only if any files are open that were from previously Split Channels — enables you to merge several images into a single multichannel image.

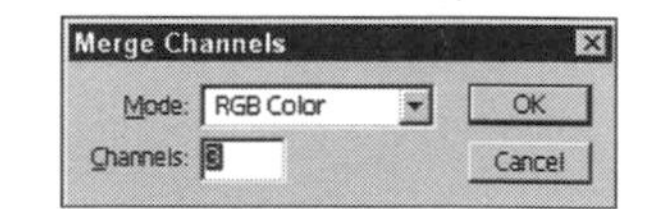

Merge Channels Dialog Box Contents

Component	*Function*
Mode menu	Drag to choose a color mode from the menu.
Channels field	Enter the number of channels (this can be no more than the number of currently open grayscale files of exactly the same pixel dimension).

Channel Palette Options

The Channel Palette Options dialog box, shown here, enables you to choose the size of the thumbnail image that appears in the Channels palette.

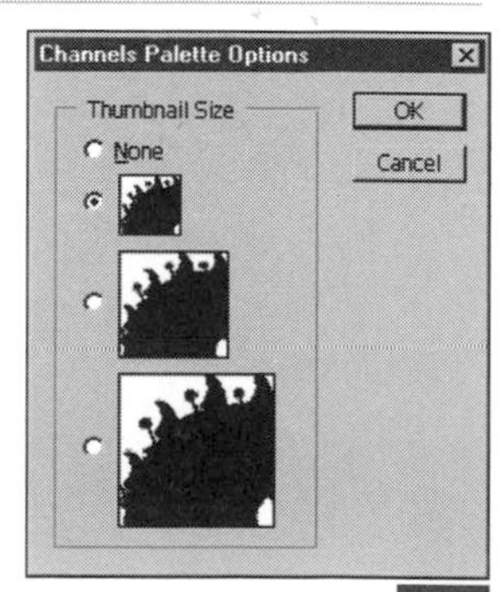

Channels Palette Options Dialog Box Contents

Component	*Function*
Thumbnail Size radio buttons	Click to choose size of channel thumbnail.

TEXT

Text control is more comprehensive than ever in Photoshop 6. When you enter text, it is placed directly on the image. What you see is what you will get from your printer. You can control *leading* (the space between lines) and *kerning* (the space between letters), change the *baseline shift* (where to place the bottoms of letters after the initial capital letter), and control *tracking* (the spacing between letters in a word or line of type). You can edit the text or change any of these specs at any time, as long as the text is maintained on its own layer. You can also change the color of text after it has been entered, but you cannot mix colors in the same entry. You can, however, mix text styles in the same entry.

In Photoshop 6, you can apply all of the above controls to any part of a line of type. New controls include paragraph type with automatic word-wrapping and hyphenation, control over minimum word size for hyphenation, minimum number of characters on either side of a hyphen, and even the maximum number of consecutive hyphens.

Full type layer features, such as post-entry editing, are available only when editing in Color modes that support layers. This excludes multichannel, bitmap, or indexed-color modes, as these modes do not support layers. You can still enter text, but it is merged directly into the underlying bitmap.

The Text Tools

A submenu of text tools no longer exists. Instead, you can access the same capabilities from the Text tool Options bar. Please see Appendix B for a complete explanation.

The Character Palette

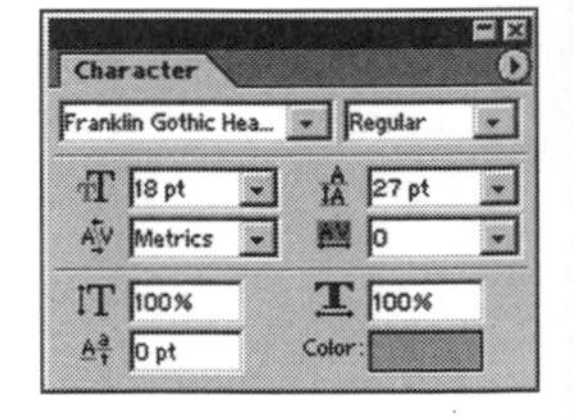

The Type Tool dialog box has been replaced in Photoshop 6, its functions distributed between the Text tool Options bar, the Character palette and the Paragraph palette. See Appendix B for more information on the Text tool options.

Access the Character Palette, shown here, by clicking the Palettes button at the right side of the Text tool Options bar.

Character Palette Contents

Component	*Function*
Font menu	All the fonts in your system are listed on this menu. Click the button to drop the menu and drag to choose a font. Upon choosing a font, any text that is highlighted in the entry area (or subsequently entered) displays in that font. You can access this same menu from the Text tool Options bar.
Style menu	Lists all the style variations for the chosen font. These vary from font to font. You can access this same menu from the Text tool Options bar.
Size field/menu	Enter any whole number or click the button to choose between points and pixels.

Component	Function
Kerning field/menu	Each unit is equal to 1/1,000 of an em space. Enter 100 units to equal 1 point in a 10-point font. This field is grayed out (unavailable) when Metrics is checked.
Vertical Scale entry field	Enter a percentage of the original size to scale highlighted characters.
Baseline entry field	Enter a number to shift the default baseline for a font by that number of points. Enter a minus number to shift the baseline down. You can shift the baseline for part of a word or phrase by highlighting only those letters that you want to shift.
Leading field/menu	Define the space between baselines. Measured in points or pixels, depending on which you picked in the Size menu. To change leading for existing type, choose Auto or choose any of the point spacing on the menu. If you prefer, highlight the type and then enter a new number for leading.
Tracking field/menu	Tracking is used to space letters evenly between the start and stop of a highlighted word or phrase. Like leading, tracking is measured in em spaces. This field is grayed (unavailable) unless you have some text selected (highlighted).
Horizontal Scale entry field	Enter a percentage of the original size to scale highlighted characters.
Color swatch	Click to bring up the Color Picker dialog box. You can choose any standard or custom color.

The Paragraph Palette

You use the Paragraph Palette to set the parameters for how paragraph text is presented.

You can also access the Paragraph Palette (shown here) by clicking the Palettes button at the right side of the Text tool Options bar.

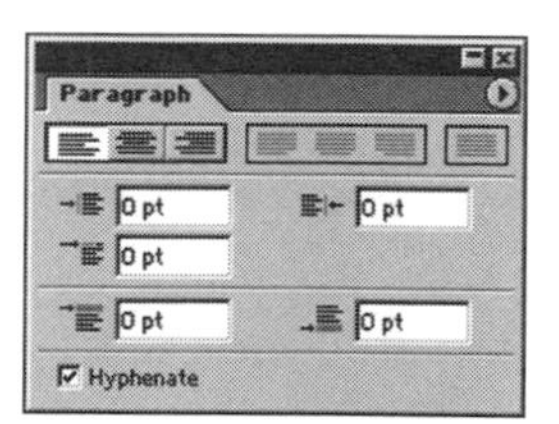

Character Palette Contents

Component	Function
Justification buttons	Choose the button that depicts the type of paragraph justification you want to use. From left to right: Left, Center, Right, Justify Last Left, Justify Last Centered, Justify Last Right, Justify All.
Indent Left Margin	Indents the left margin by the specified number of points from the left side of the paragraph marquee.
Indent First Line	Indents the first word in the first line by the specified number of points.
Space Before	Adds the specified number of points before the first paragraph.
Indent Right Margin	Indents the right margin from the limits of the paragraph marquee by the specified number of points.
Space After	Adds the specified number of points before the first paragraph.
Hyphenate check box	Toggles automatic hyphenation.

TEXTURES

One of the principal professional uses for Photoshop is creating textures, most often used as backgrounds or combined with other images to give greater depth and a more textured feel. A whole industry exists of folks who create textures in Photoshop to be used as object surfaces in 3D modeling and animation applications.

Textures can be anything from natural surfaces — such as skin, paper, and concrete — to computer-generated patterns of all sorts. You can create textures in a multitude of ways: take a texture out of a photograph, scan a surface, use a pattern-making filter, or use a texture-making tool such as Real Texture Tools from CGSD, Terrazzo from Xaos Tools, and the Texture Explorer in Kai's Power Tools.

See Chapter 14 for more on using the specific filters.

Note that some filter dialog boxes contain preview windows. These preview windows are often accompanied by + and – buttons underneath. Clicking the buttons zooms the image in the window in (+) or out (–).

Craquelure Filter

Craquelure is a stucco-like texture that is also useful for making artwork resemble old, cracked paintings. You access its dialog box, shown here, by choosing Filter, then Texture, then Craquelure.

Craquelure Filter Dialog Box Contents

Component	*Function*
Crack Spacing field/slider	Drag left to narrow or right to widen the width of the cracks. You can also enter a number directly into the field.
Crack Depth field/slider	Drag left to heighten or right to deepen the cracks. Cracks get darker in color, and highlights and shadows on the edges of the cracks become more pronounced as cracks get deeper. You can also enter a number directly into the field.
Crack Brightness field/slider	Drag left to brighten or right to darken the cracks. You can also enter a number directly into the field.

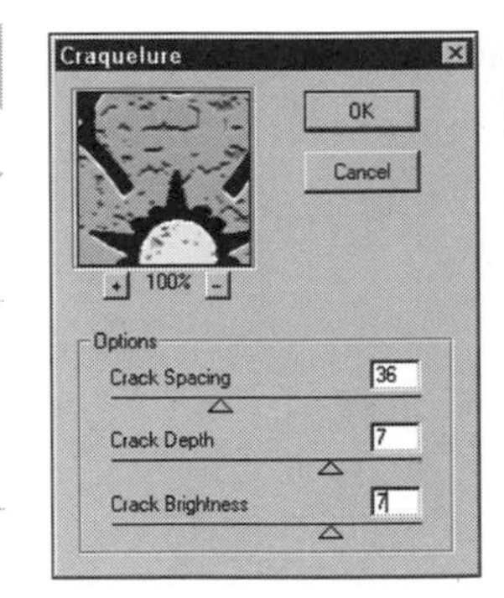

Grain Filter

The Grain filter dialog box, depicted here, actually lets you choose between film grain and several other similar effects: Soft, Sprinkles, Clumped, Contrasty, Enlarged, Stippled, Horizontal, Vertical, and Speckle. Sliders control the intensity and contrast of the effect. To access the Grain filter, choose Filter, then Texture, then Grain.

Grain Filter Dialog Box Contents

Component	*Function*
Intensity slider	Drag left to minimize or right to maximize the size of the grain clumps. You can also enter a number for the size of the clumps between 0 (smallest) and 100 (biggest) directly into the field.
Contrast slider	Drag left to narrow or right to widen the width of the clumps. You can also enter a number (between 0 and 100) directly into the field.
Grain Type menu	Choose between any of ten different grain patterns.

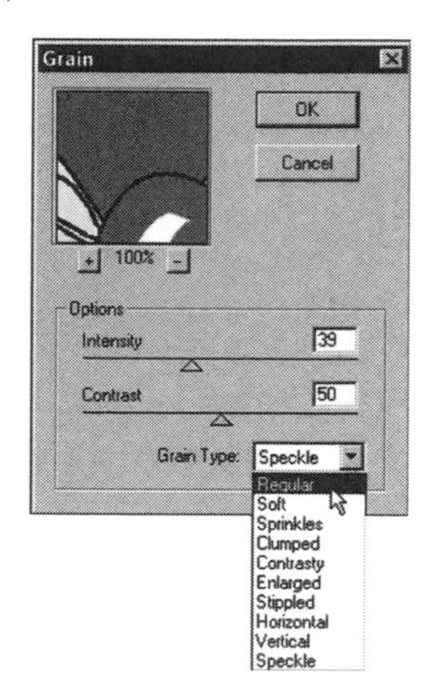

Mosaic Tiles Filter

The Mosaic Tiles texture gives images a cool effect, similar to the Craquelure filter and reminiscent of cobblestone. To access the Mosaic Tiles filter dialog box, shown here, choose Filter, then Texture, then Mosaic Tiles.

Mosaic Tiles Filter Dialog Box Contents

Component	*Function*
Tile Size field/slider	Drag left to narrow or right to widen the width of the tiles. You can also enter a number directly into the field.
Grout width field/slider	Drag left to heighten or right to deepen the space between the tiles. The grout (area between tiles) gets darker in color, and highlights and shadows on the edges of the cracks become more pronounced as the cracks gets deeper. You can also enter a number directly into the field.
Lighten Grout field/slider	Drag left to brighten or right to darken the grout. You can also enter a number directly into the field.

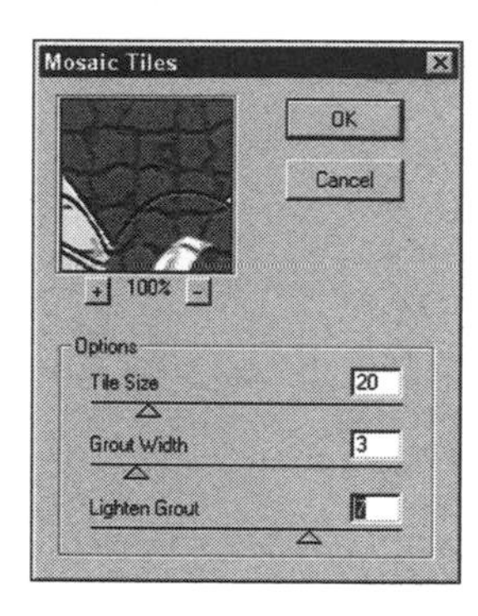

TEXTURES CONTINUED

Patchwork Filter

If you ever need to create a view through a screen or a net, the Patchwork filter might do the trick. This texture makes an image look similar to a mosaic with tiny square tiles. To access the Patchwork filter dialog box, shown here, choose Filter, then Texture, then Patchwork.

Patchwork Filter Dialog Box Contents

Component	*Function*
Square Size field/slider	Drag left to shrink or right to enlarge the size of the tiles. You can also enter a number directly into the field.
Relief field/slider	Drag left to heighten or right to deepen the space between the tiles. The grout (area between tiles) gets darker in color and highlights and shadows on the edges of the cracks become more pronounced as cracks get deeper. You can also enter a number directly into the field.

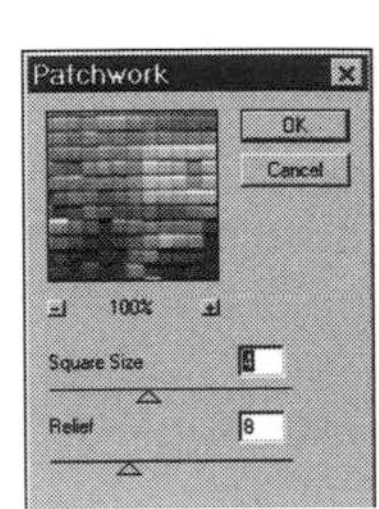

Stained Glass Filter

The Mosaic Tiles and Patchwork effects may not look much like their namesakes, but Stained Glass resembles the real thing. Each cell is a solid color, and the individual pieces of "glass" are of different sizes and shapes. To access the Stained Glass filter dialog box, shown here, choose Filter, then Texture, then Stained Glass.

Stained Glass Filter Dialog Box Contents

Component	*Function*
Cell Size field/slider	Drag left to shrink or right to enlarge the size of the panes of colored glass. You can also enter a number directly into the field.
Border Thickness field/slider	Drag left to shrink or right to enlarge the width of the space between the panes of glass. You can also enter a number directly into the field.
Light Intensity field/slider	Drag the slider or enter a number to determine which panes of colored glass should appear dark and which should appear light. (Zoom out and experiment with this one.)

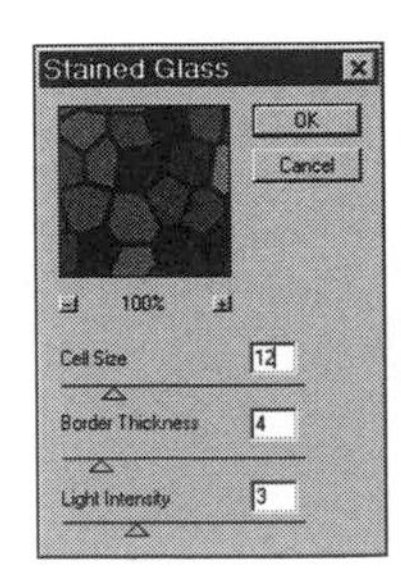

Texturizer Filter

Choose Filter, then Texture to get to the Texturizer, which comes with the premade textures Canvas, Burlap, and Sandstone. The Texturizer filter dialog box is shown here.

Texturizer Filter Dialog Box Contents

Component	Function
Texture menu	You can load any texture of your own from this menu or use one of the three built-in textures: Burlap, Canvas, or Sandstone.
Scaling field/slider	Enlarges or reduces the percentage of magnification of the texture file.
Relief field/slider	Makes the texture appear to be more or less pronounced by increasing the contrast between highlights and shadows in the texture file.
Light Direction menu	Changes the apparent direction of the light falling on the texture pattern. Choices are Bottom, Bottom Left, Top Left, Top, Top Right, Right, and Bottom Right.
Invert check box	If checked, reverses the highlight and shadow areas of the texture.

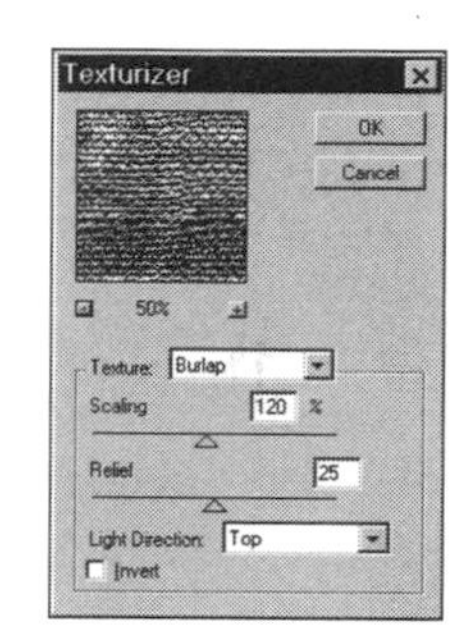

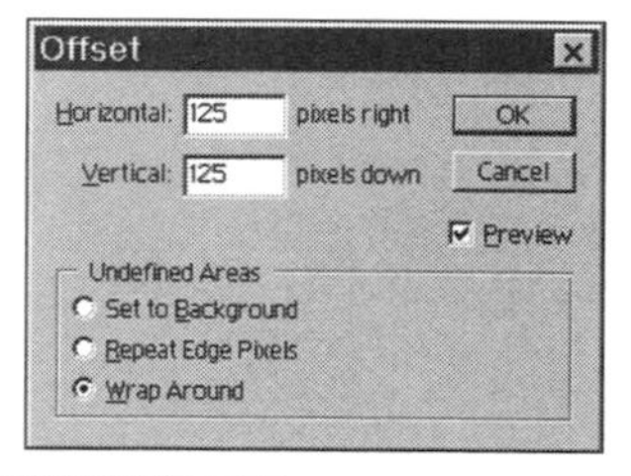

Offset Filter

You can use the Photoshop 6 Offset filter to shift your image horizontally or vertically. To access the Offset filter dialog box, depicted here, select Filter, then Other, then Offset.

Offset Filter Dialog Box Contents

Component	Function
Horizontal offset field	Enter any number to shift the selected image that number of pixels to the right.
Vertical offset field	Enter any number to shift the selected image that number of pixels down.
Set to Background radio button	If selected, fills area vacated after the shift with the background color.
Repeat Edge Pixels radio button	If selected, fills area vacated after the shift by repeating the row of pixels at the outermost edges of the selection in the direction of the offset(s). Usually creates a streaked look.
Wrap Around radio button	If selected, fills area vacated after the shift with the pixels that were moved outside the selection by the shift.
Preview check box	If checked, results occur immediately in the workspace (file window).

PAINTERLY FILTERS

Photoshop's built-in Artistic filters make converting photos and scans into something vaguely resembling a traditional painting easy. That is not to say, by any means, that Photoshop automatically knows how to paint well. The better artist you are, the more useful these tools will be. On the other hand, sometimes just being able to put some texture in part of an image, make a background or button-surface look hand-painted, or use the various filters in conjunction with selections to vary the texture in an image is enough.

Of course, any filter or other Photoshop tool could be labeled artistic. In this section, you look at those filters that fall under the Artistic, Brush Strokes, and Sketch submenus. For more on using the painterly filters, see Chapter 15.

Note that many of these dialog boxes contain field/slider settings with numeric values. Unless otherwise noted, the smallest number is the least of the effect that you can apply; the highest number is the most of the effect that you can apply. The more numbers in the range, the more variations that can be applied.

Colored Pencil Filter

The effect of the Photoshop 6 Colored Pencil filter looks similar to a cross-hatched rubbing made with sharpened pastels. The Colored Pencil dialog box is shown here.

Colored Pencil Filter Dialog Box Contents

Component	*Function*
Pencil Width field/slider	Drag to determine a pixel width for the cross-hatched strokes, or enter a number from 1 (narrowest) to 24 (widest).
Stroke Pressure field/slider	Drag to determine the area colored by the cross-hatched strokes, or enter a number from 0 (narrowest) to 15 (widest).
Paper Brightness field/slider	Drag to make the unstroked sections brighter (right) or darker (left), or enter a number from 0 (darker) to 50 (brighter).

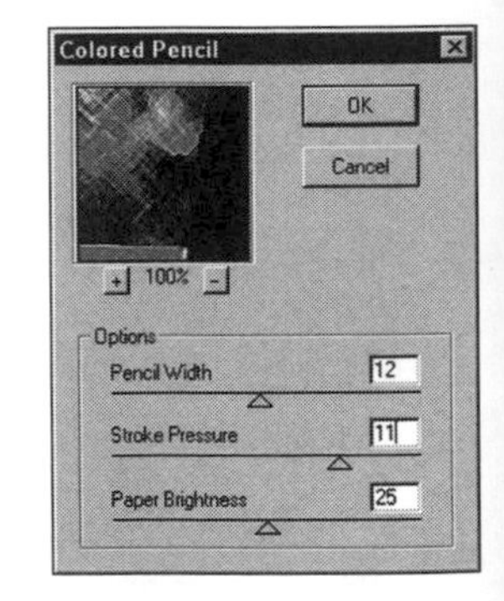

Cutout Filter

The Cutout filter reduces the number of colors in an image to the number of colors you specify in the dialog box and then smoothes the edges. The Cutout filter dialog box is shown here.

Cutout Filter Dialog Box Contents

Component	*Function*
Number of Levels field/slider	Drag to indicate the number of levels of color to appear, or enter a value from 2 to 8.
Edge Simplicity field/slider	Drag to indicate the jaggedness or smoothness of edges, or enter a value from 0 to 10.
Edge Fidelity field/slider	Drag to indicate how closely edges should follow the actual shapes in the image, or enter a value from 1 to 3.

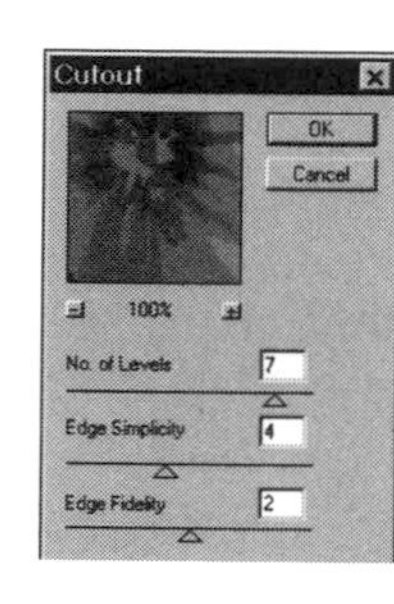

Dry Brush Filter

The Dry Brush filter produces an effect similar to that of the Cutout filter. However, with the Dry Brush filter, the edges are softer, you can have more levels (up to 10) of detail, and you can add a level of stroke texturing. The filter's dialog box is shown here.

Dry Brush Filter Dialog Box Contents

Component	*Function*
Brush Size field/slider	Drag to indicate the width of strokes, or enter a value from 1 to 10.
Brush Detail field/slider	Drag to indicate the amount of color and detail to be retained, or enter a value from 0 to 10.
Texture field/slider	Drag to indicate the amount of texturization, or enter a value from 1 to 3.

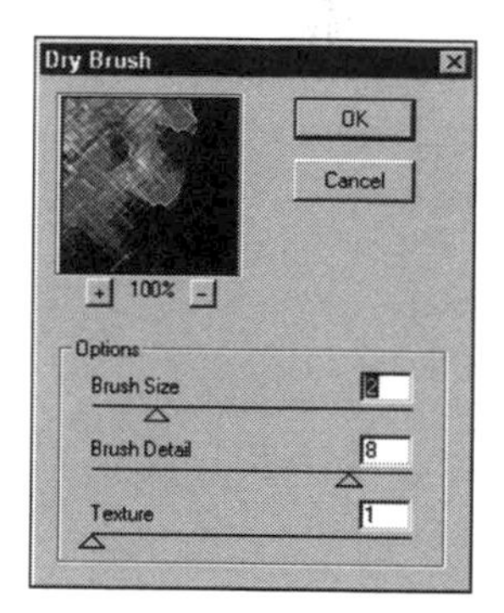

PAINTERLY FILTERS CONTINUED

Film Grain Filter

The Film Grain filter is really more of a photo effect or darkroom filter than an artistic one, but the filter is contained within the Artistic filters menu. The Film Grain filter is one of the few filters that does exactly what you expect of it; that is, it produces an effect that looks like the grain in photographic film. The following figure shows the Film Grain filter dialog box.

Film Grain Filter Dialog Box Contents

Component	*Function*
Grain field/slider	Drag to indicate the amount of grain to be infused into the image, or enter a value from 1 (least grain) to 20 (most grain).
Highlight Area field/slider	Drag to spread or narrow highlight areas of the image, or enter a value from 0 (narrowest) to 20 (widest).
Intensity field/slider	Drag to raise or lower overall image contrast, or enter a value from 0 (lowest) to 10 (highest).

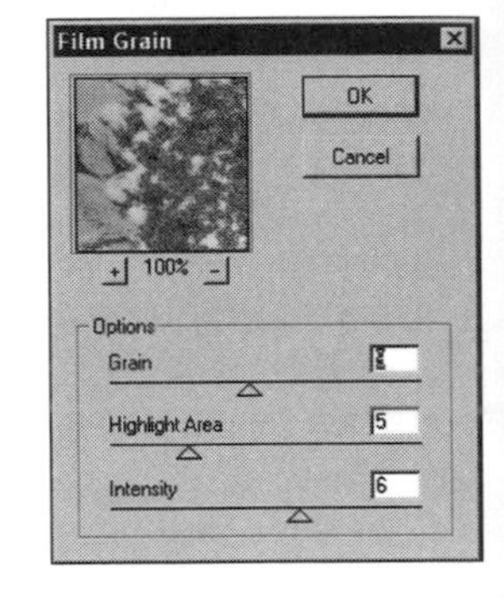

Fresco Filter

The Photoshop Fresco filter is meant to imitate the effect of painting on wet plaster. The figure here shows the associated dialog box.

Fresco Filter Dialog Box Contents

Component	*Function*
Brush Size field/slider	Drag to indicate the width of strokes, or enter a value from 0 (narrowest) to 10 (widest).
Brush Detail field/slider	Drag to indicate the amount of color and detail to be retained, or enter a value from 0 to 10.
Texture field/slider	Drag to indicate the amount of texturization, or enter a value from 1 to 3.

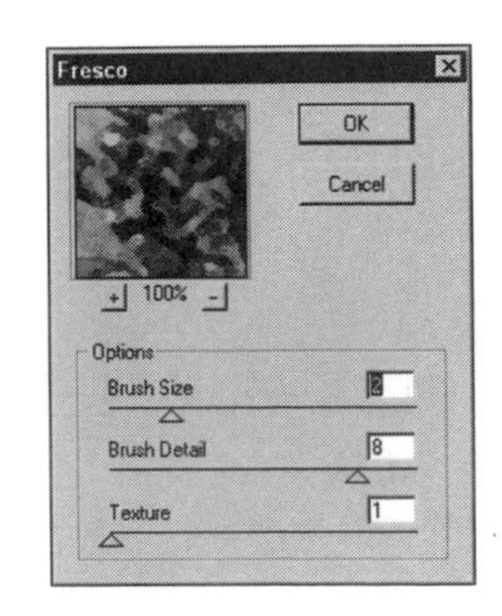

Neon Glow Filter

The Neon Glow filter gives everything in an image a bluish, fuzzy tint. This figure shows the dialog box for this filter.

Neon Glow Filter Dialog Box Contents

Component	*Function*
Glow Size field/slider	Drag right to spread the highlight area (which glows in the color chosen in the Glow swatch), or enter a value from –24 to 24.
Glow Brightness field/slider	Drag to brighten or darken the glow area, or enter a value from 0 to 50.
Glow Color swatch	Click to bring up the Color Picker.

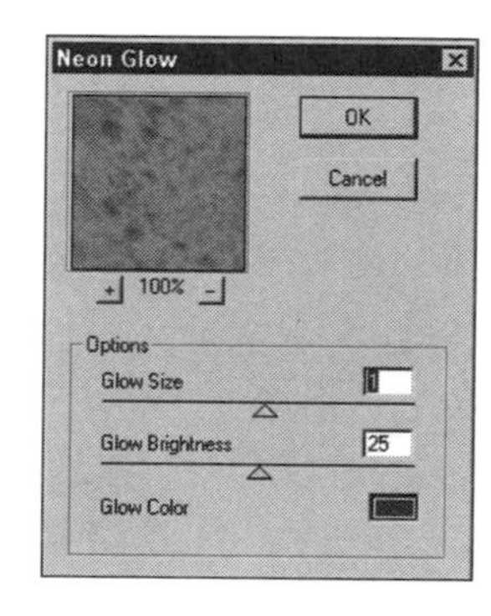

Paint Daubs Filter

The basic idea of the Paint Daubs filter is as follows: The strokes created imitate those made by a brush dipped into heavy paint and then applied by tapping the end of the brush on the canvas. The figure here shows the associated dialog box.

Paint Daubs Filter Dialog

Component	*Function*
Brush Size field/slider	Drag to increase or decrease areas of flat color, or enter a value from 1 to 50.
Sharpness field/slider	Drag to harden or soften borders between colors, or enter a value from 0 to 40.
Brush Type menu	Choose between the options Simple (default), Light Rough, Dark Rough, Wide Sharp, Wide Blurry, or Sparkle.

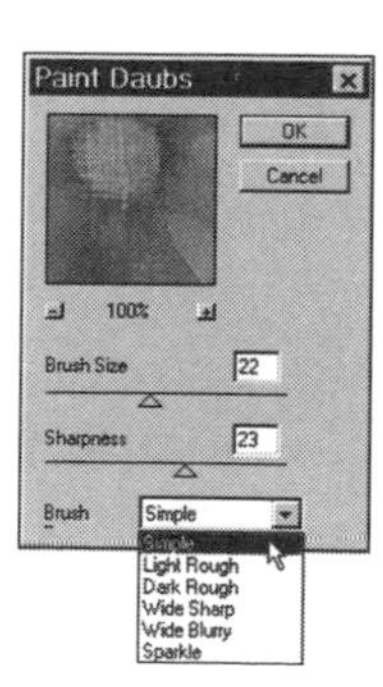

Palette Knife Filter

The Palette Knife filter is really just another way to flatten colors into broad strokes. You can vary the softness of edges and the amount of apparent detail in the strokes through the associated dialog box, depicted here.

Palette Knife Filter Dialog Box Contents

Component	*Function*
Stroke Size field/slider	Drag to increase or decrease areas of flat color, or enter a value from 1 to 50.
Stroke Detail field/slider	Drag to increase or decrease the number of flat colors, or enter a value from 1 to 3.
Softness slider/field	Drag to harden or soften the borders between colors, or enter a value from 0 to 10.

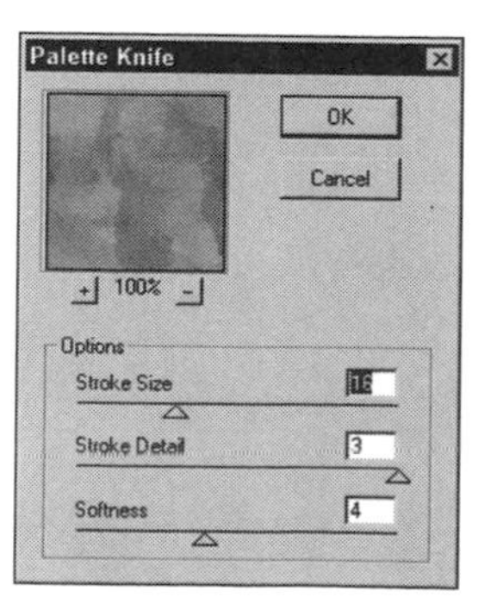

PAINTERLY FILTERS CONTINUED

Plastic Wrap Filter

The Plastic Wrap filter can create a three-dimensional look to an image, which is useful for giving depth and roundness to textured areas of a photo. The following figure shows the Plastic Wrap filter dialog box.

Plastic Wrap Filter Dialog Box Contents

Component	*Function*
Highlight Strength field/slider	Drag to increase or decrease size of highlights, or enter a value from 0 to 20.
Detail field/slider	Drag to increase or decrease areas of flat color, or enter a value from 1 to 15.
Smoothness field/slider	Drag to harden or soften the edges of areas of flat color, or enter a value from 1 to 15.

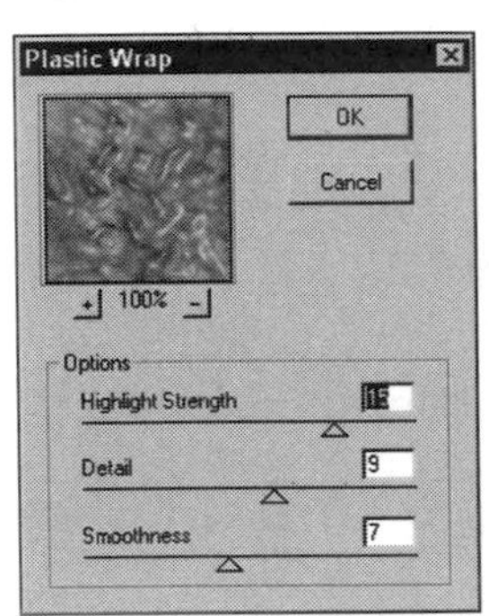

Poster Edges Filter

With the Photoshop Poster Edges filter, colors are flattened and then outlined with dark edges. The figure here shows the Poster Edges filter dialog box.

Poster Edges Filter Dialog Box Contents

Component	*Function*
Edge Thickness field/slider	Drag to indicate average width of black stroke that defines edges between highly contrasting colors, or enter a value from 0 to 10.
Edge Intensity field/slider	Drag to indicate darkness and brightness of edges, or enter a value from 0 to 10.
Posterization field/slider	Drag to specify levels of color, or enter a value from 0 to 6.

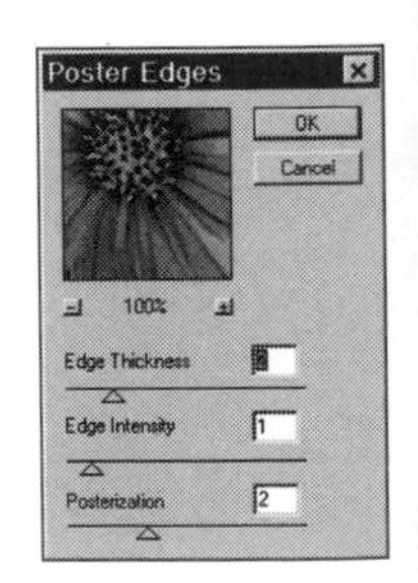

Rough Pastels Filter

The look of the Rough Pastels filter is a bit like oil pastels, but with all the strokes moving in a parallel direction. Unfortunately, the associated dialog box, depicted here, does not have an angle control, which would enable you to make the result more natural by filtering selected areas one at a time.

Rough Pastels Filter Dialog Box Contents

Component	*Function*
Stroke Length field/slider	Drag to indicate length of cross-hatched strokes, or enter a value from 0 to 40.
Stroke Detail field/slider	Drag to indicate number of colors to be interpreted, or enter a value from 1 to 20.
Texture menu	Choose from Burlap, Canvas, or Sandstone, or load a user-defined texture file.
Scaling field/slider	Drag to resize the texture image.
Relief field/slider	Drag to change emphasis of highlights and shadows in texture.
Light Direction menu	Choose from Top, Top Right, Right, Bottom Right, Bottom, Bottom Left, Left, Top Left.
Invert check box	Inverts the highlights and shadows in the texture.

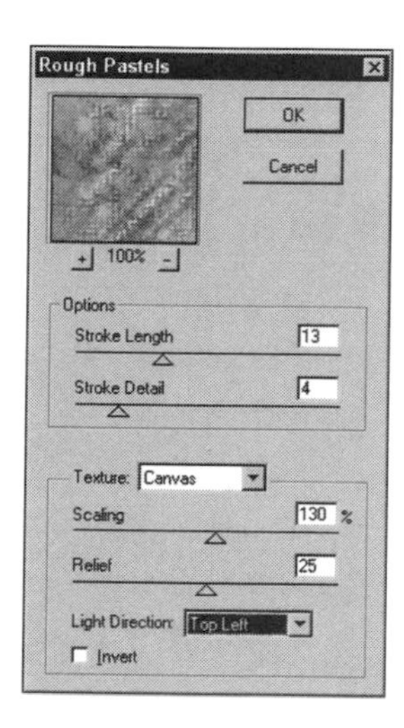

Smudge Stick Filter

The Smudge Stick filter is a little like Rough Pastels, but without the texture. The image is highly posterized (you have no direct control over the number of levels of color) and is smeared in diagonal strokes. The filter dialog box is shown here.

Smudge Stick Filter Dialog Box Contents

Component	*Function*
Stroke Length field/slider	Drag to specify distance pixels are smudged, or enter a value from 0 to 10.
Highlight Area field/slider	Drag to increase or decrease size of highlight area, or enter a value from 0 to 20.
Intensity field/slider	Drag to indicate overall contrast, or enter a value from 0 to 10.

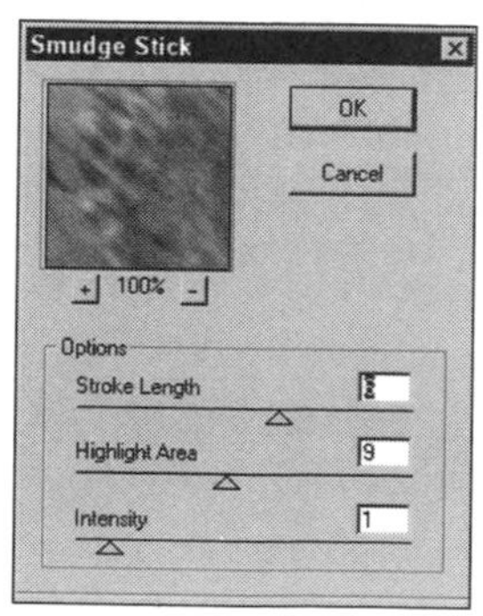

PAINTERLY FILTERS CONTINUED

Sponge Filter

With the Sponge filter, colors are flattened and posterized, and darker blotches are imposed in a seemingly random pattern to give the image a look as if it has been dabbed with a wet sponge. The associated dialog box is shown here.

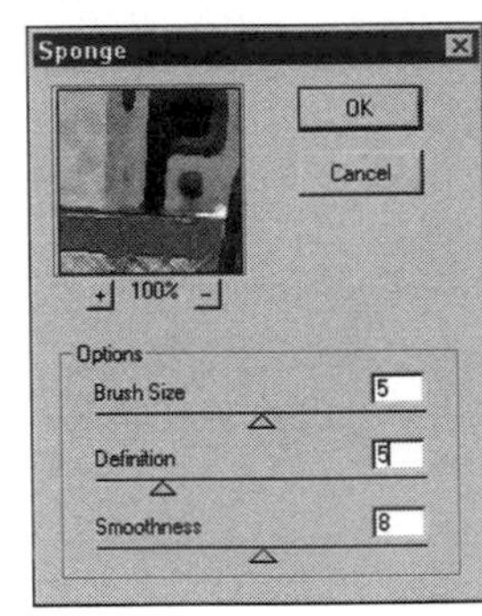

Sponge Filter Dialog Box Contents

Component	*Function*
Brush Size field/slider	Drag to increase or decrease size of the color blotches, or enter a value from 0 to 10.
Definition field/slider	Drag to specify the amount of detail that can be discerned, or enter a value from 0 to 25.
Smoothness field/slider	Drag to indicate the degree to which edges between colors blend, or enter a value from 1 to 15.

Accented Edges Filter

The Accented Edges filter reduces colors and outlines the edges with an uneven dry-brush stroke. The following figure shows the associated dialog box.

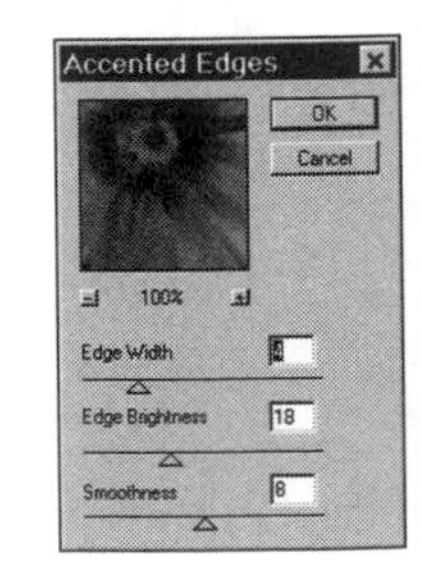

Accented Edges Filter Dialog Box Contents

Component	*Function*
Edge Width field/slider	Drag to specify the average thickness of accented edges, or enter a value from 1 (thinnest) to 14 (thickest).
Edge Brightness field/slider	Drag to change brightness of edges from black to white, or enter a value from 0 to 50. Adjustment also determines the number of accented edges.
Smoothness field/slider	Drag to specify the degree to which the edges blend with their surroundings, or enter a value from 1 to 15.

Watercolor Filter

The Watercolor filter's job is to make your Photoshop image look painted with watercolors. The figure here shows the associated dialog box.

Watercolor Filter Dialog Box Contents

Component	*Function*
Brush Detail field/slider	Drag to indicate the degree of detail you want to see in the image, or enter a value from 1 to 14. Interacts with Shadow Intensity.
Shadow Intensity field/slider	Drag to specify the size of areas that will go to black, or enter a value from 0 to 10.
Texture field/slider	Indicates level of texturization, with a value from 1 to 3.

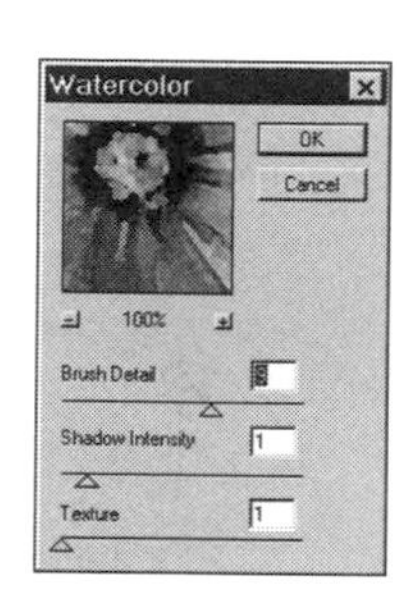

Underpainting Filter

The Underpainting filter does a credible job of making an image look as if it were washed onto a textured surface with highly thinned paints. This basic technique for starting an oil painting is a good first step in combining Artistic filters that are increasingly detailed or textured. The figure here shows the associated dialog box.

Underpainting Filter Dialog Box Contents

Component	*Function*
Brush Size field/slider	Drag to increase or decrease size of broad areas of color, or enter a value from 0 to 40.
Texture Coverage field/slider	Drag to increase or decrease the amount of the image in which texture shows through paint colors, or enter a value from 0 to 40.
Texture menu	Choose from Burlap, Canvas, or Sandstone, or load a user-defined texture file.
Scaling field/slider	Drag to resize the texture image.
Relief field/slider	Drag to change emphasis of highlights and shadows in texture.
Light Direction menu	Choose from Top, Top Right, Right, Bottom Right, Bottom, Bottom Left, Left, Top Left.
Invert check box	Inverts the highlights and shadows in the texture.

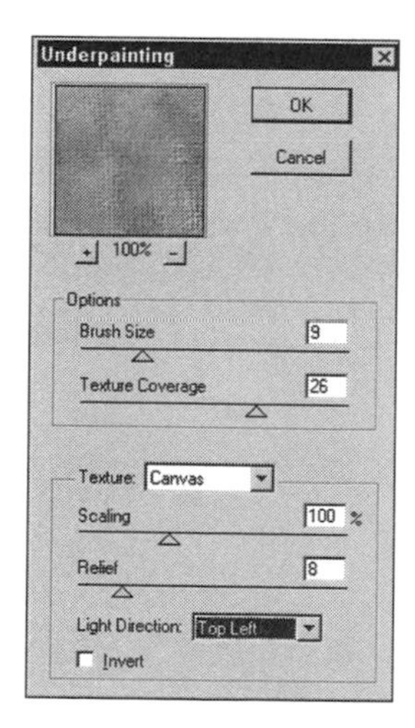

PAINTERLY FILTERS CONTINUED

Angled Strokes Filter

The Angled Strokes filter creates an effect similar to the Rough Pastels filter, but you can control the main direction of the strokes in the filter dialog box, shown here. Strokes are automatically angled in different directions in contrasting areas of the image, giving the image the appearance of having been created with a very dry, very thick oil brush.

Angled Strokes Filter Dialog Box Contents

Component	*Function*
Direction Balance field/slider	Drag to change the direction of the strokes, or enter a value from 0 to 100.
Stroke Length field/slider	Drag to lengthen or shorten relative distance over which the stroke travels, or enter a value from 3 to 50.
Sharpness field/slider	Drag to indicate anti-aliasing of edges of strokes, or enter a value from 0 to 10. Eventually strokes blend to more of a palette knife effect.

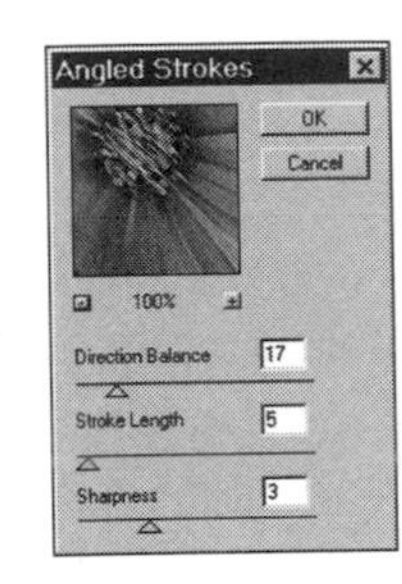

Crosshatch Filter

The Crosshatch filter creates cross-stroked color etching. The figure here shows the associated dialog box.

Crosshatch Filter Dialog Box Contents

Component	*Function*
Stroke Length field/slider	Drag to change the relative distance over which the stroke travels, or enter a value from 3 to 50.
Sharpness field/slider	Drag to indicate anti-aliasing of edges of strokes, or enter a value from 0 to 10. Eventually strokes blend to more of a palette knife effect.
Strength field/slider	Drag to specify overall contrast after strokes are applied, or enter a value from 1 to 3.

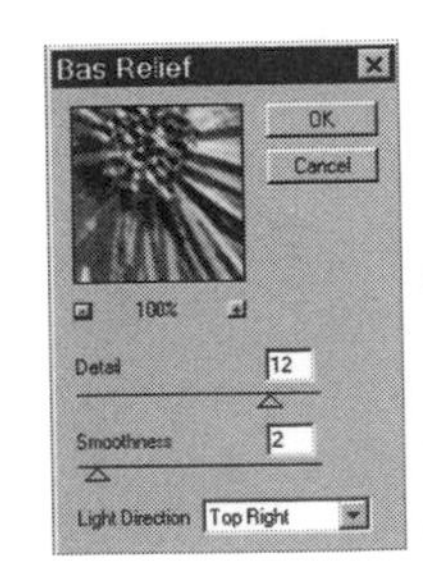

Dark Strokes Filter

The Dark Strokes filter makes angular smudged strokes and greatly heightens the difference between highlights and shadows, whereas midtones are left more or less alone. The figure here shows the associated dialog box.

Dark Strokes Filter Dialog

Component	Function
Balance field/slider	Drag to change the distribution of black and white strokes, or enter a value from 0 to 10.
Black Intensity field/slider	Drag to increase or decrease the shadow contrast (amount of black visible in the image), or enter a value from 0 to 10.
White Intensity field/slider	Drag to increase highlight contrast (amount of white visible in the image), or enter a value from 0 to 10.

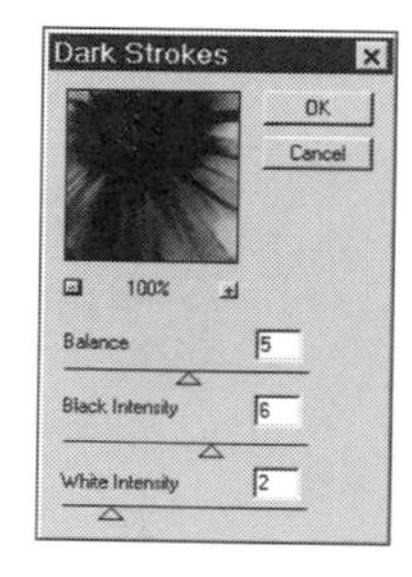

Ink Outlines Filter

The Ink Outlines filter is a great filter for making images look as if they were painted into inked sketch lines. Similar to the Dark Strokes filter, it darkens the background and increases saturation and contrast. The filter dialog box is shown here.

Ink Outlines Filter Dialog Box Contents

Component	Function
Stroke Length field/slider	Drag to influence boldness, thickness, and continuity of black outlines, or enter a value from 1 to 50.
Dark Intensity field/slider	Drag to increase or decrease shadow contrast (amount of black visible in the image), or enter a value from 0 to 50.
Light Intensity field/slider	Drag to increase or decrease highlight contrast (amount of highlights visible in the image), or enter a value from 0 to 50.

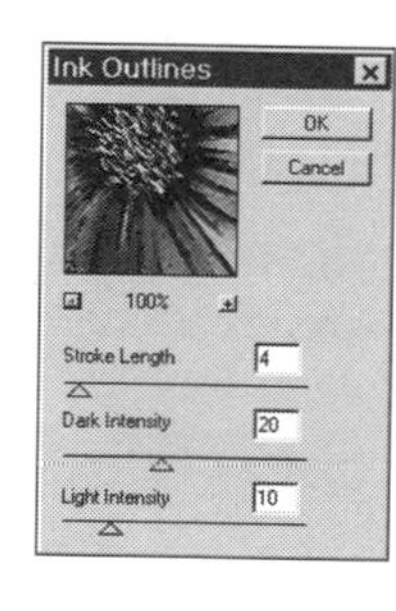

Spatter Filter

The Spatter filter creates an effect that looks like something between spraygun painting and pointillism. (How far in-between depends on where you set the filter dialog box sliders, shown here.) This filter can be excellent for giving a softening effect to an image.

Spatter Filter Dialog Box Contents

Component	Function
Spray Radius field/slider	Drag to increase diameter of paint spatters, or enter a value from 0 to 25.
Smoothness field/slider	Drag to indicate degree of blending of spats with surrounding colors, or enter a value from 1 to 15.

PAINTERLY FILTERS CONTINUED

Sumi-e Filter

The Sumi-e filter produces an effect similar to the Dark Strokes filter, but with significantly softer edges and colors. The strokes created are diagonal daubs whose size and intensity you can vary over a wide range. The filter's dialog box is shown here.

Sumi-e Filter Dialog Box Contents

Component	*Function*
Stroke Width field/slider	Drag to specify average width of stroke, or enter a value from 3 (narrowest) to 15 (widest).
Stroke Pressure field/slider	Drag to indicate number and darkness of strokes, or enter a value from 0 to 15.
Contrast field/slider	Drag to increase or decrease overall image contrast, or enter a value from 0 to 40.

Bas Relief Filter

The Bas Relief filter creates a grayscale embossed effect (grayscale if you leave colors at default; otherwise, whatever colors are there for foreground and background). The figure here shows the associated dialog box.

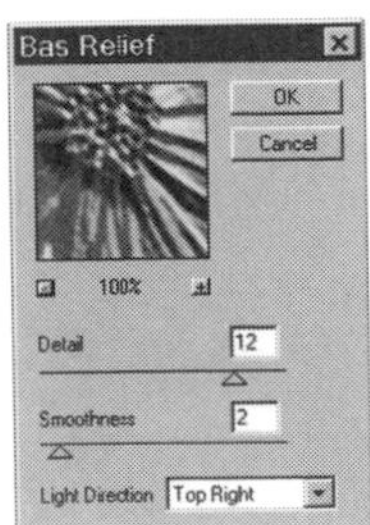

Bas Relief Filter Dialog Box Contents

Component	*Function*
Detail field/slider	Drag to increase or decrease the number of ridges that will be apparent in the relief, or enter a value from 1 to 15.
Smoothness field/slider	Drag to increase or decrease the degree of blending between edges, or enter a value from 1 to 15.
Light Direction menu	Choose from Top, Top Right, Right, Bottom Right, Bottom, Bottom Left, Left, Top Left.

Chalk & Charcoal Filter

The Chalk & Charcoal filter creates a duotone version of the Rough Pastels filter. The angular strokes are a mixture of chalk (foreground color) and charcoal (background color) smudges. The filter's dialog box is illustrated here.

Chalk & Charcoal Filter Dialog Box Contents

Component	*Function*
Charcoal Area field/slider	Drag to specify predominance of foreground color, or enter a value from 0 to 20.
Chalk Area field/slider	Drag to specify predominance of background color, or enter a value from 0 to 20.
Stroke Pressure field/slider	Drag to change overall contrast of image, or enter a value from 0 to 5.

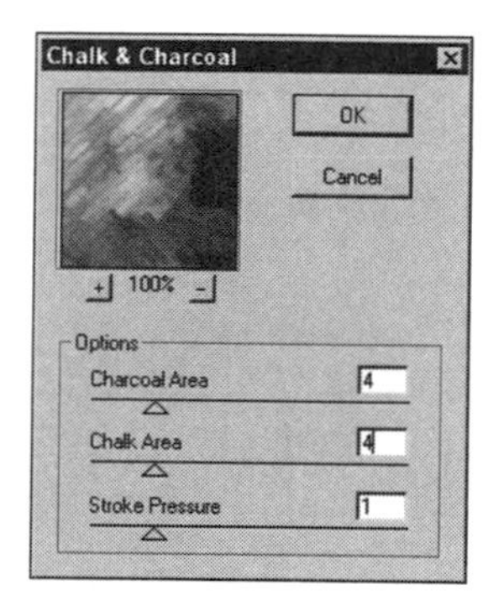

Charcoal Filter

As with the Chalk & Charcoal filter, the Charcoal filter also uses the foreground and background colors of the image (as do all the Sketch submenu filters), but the strokes are finer and crosshatched. Borders between colors are more emphasized, which gives the result a more authentic feel of charcoal on newsprint.

Charcoal Filter Dialog Box Contents

Component	*Function*
Charcoal Thickness field/slider	Drag to change the average thickness of foreground color strokes, or enter a value from 1 (thinnest) to 7 (thickest).
Detail field/slider	Drag to increase or decrease the detail of strokes in lighter-toned areas, or enter a value from 0 to 5.
Light/Dark Balance field/slider	Drag to indicate threshold, or enter a value from 0 to 100.

Chrome Filter

The Chrome filter is basically the same as a grayscale version of the Plastic Wrap filter. The Chrome filter can produce some lovely impasto effects when used with the Texturizer filter (in fact, all the Sketch filters are useful for creating texture effects with any of the filters that can use a grayscale texture).

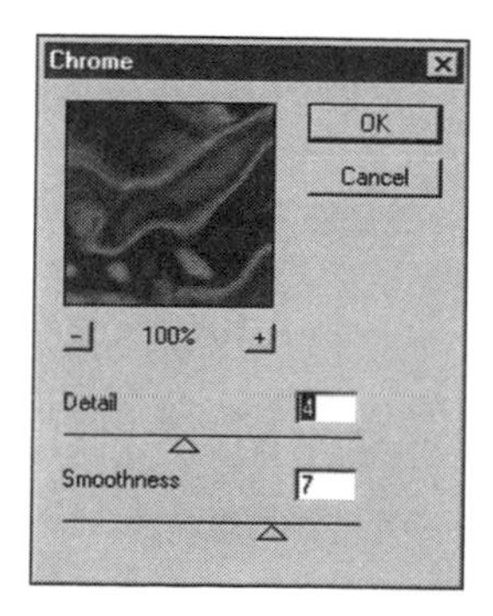

Chrome Filter Dialog Box Contents

Component	*Function*
Detail field/slider	Drag to specify amount of detail that can be discerned, or enter a value from 0 to 10.
Smoothness field/slider	Drag to dictate the degree to which edges between colors blend, or enter a value from 1 to 10.

PAINTERLY FILTERS CONTINUED

Conté Crayon Filter

The Conté Crayon filter can produce interesting results when you are reducing an image to a few duotones (made up of the foreground and background colors of the image). The following figure shows the associated dialog box.

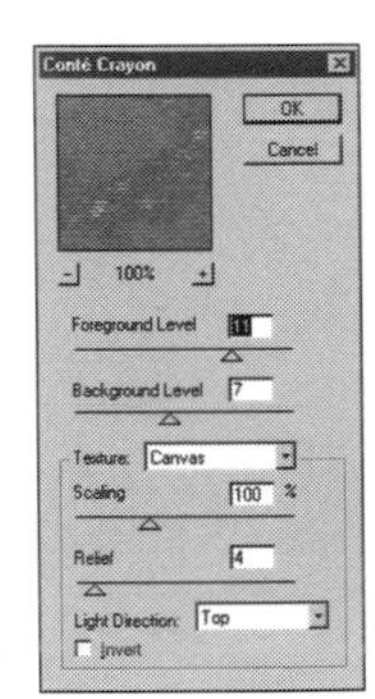

Conté Crayon Filter Dialog Box Contents

Component	*Function*
Foreground Level field/slider	Drag to increase or decrease intensity of foreground color, or enter a value from 1 to 15.
Background Level field/slider	Drag to increase or decrease the intensity of background color, or enter a value from 1 to 15.
Texture menu	Choose from Burlap, Canvas, or Sandstone, or load a user-defined texture file.
Scaling field/slider	Drag to resize the texture image.
Relief field/slider	Drag to change emphasis of highlights and shadows in texture.
Light Direction menu	Top, Top Right, Right, Bottom Right, Bottom, Bottom Left, Left, Top Left.
Invert check box	Inverts the highlights and shadows in the texture.

Graphic Pen Filter

The Graphic Pen filter produces something that looks like a pen-and-ink etching made with unidirectional strokes. The figure here shows the associated dialog box.

Graphic Pen Filter Dialog Box Contents

Component	*Function*
Stroke Length field/slider	Drag to change the relative distance over which the stroke travels, or enter a value from 3 to 50.
Light/Dark Balance field/slider	Drag to specify threshold, or enter a value from 0 to 100.
Stroke Direction menu	Choose from any 45-degree direction: Vertical, Right Diagonal, Horizontal, Left Diagonal.

Halftone Pattern Filter

The Halftone Pattern filter produces a halftone pattern atop the image. The figure here shows the associated dialog box.

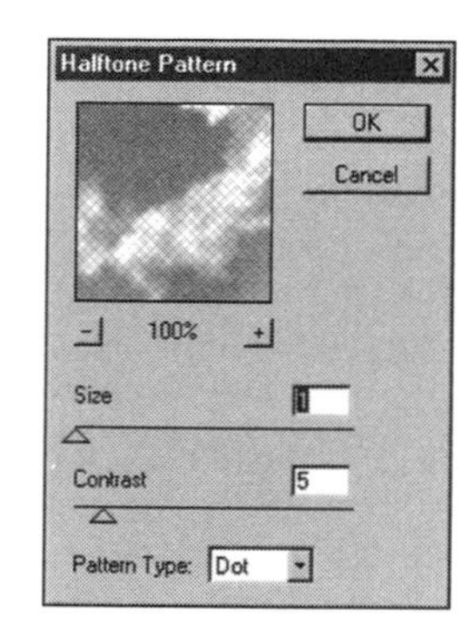

Halftone Pattern Filter Dialog Box Contents

Component	*Function*
Size field/slider	Drag to specify dot size, or enter a value from 1 to 12.
Contrast field/slider	Drag to change overall contrast, or enter a value from 0 to 50.
Pattern Type menu	Choose between Circle, Dot, Line.

Note Paper Filter

The effect of the Note Paper filter is a textured two-color (foreground/background) high-contrast rendition of the image on textured paper. You can control the graininess of the paper texture, but not the texture pattern. The dialog box is shown here.

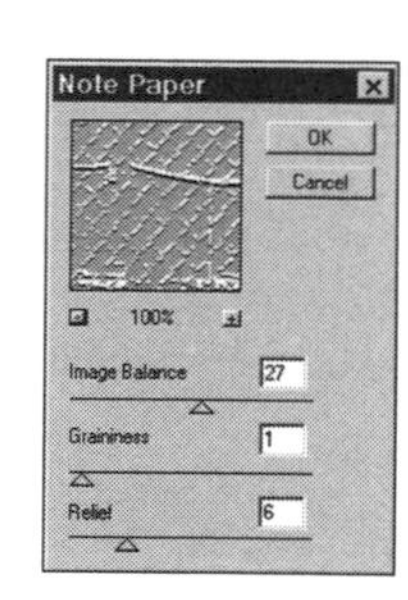

Note Paper Filter Dialog Box Contents

Component	*Function*
Image Balance field/slider	Drag to specify threshold, or enter a value from 0 to 50.
Graininess field/slider	Drag to increase or decrease amount of texture in the image, or enter a value from 0 to 20.
Relief field/slider	Drag to increase or decrease intensity of edge highlights and shadows, or enter a value from 0 to 25.

Photocopy Filter

The Photocopy filter makes the image look as if it were copied on a copy machine incapable of producing grays. The figure here shows the Photocopy filter dialog box.

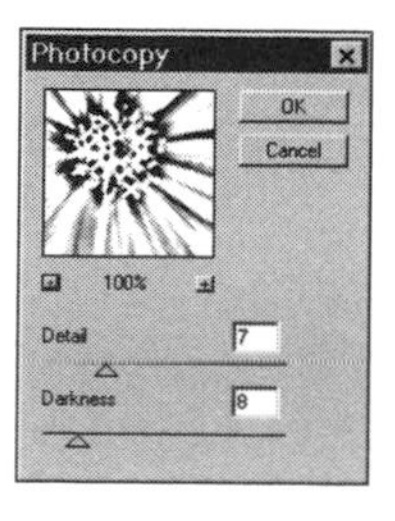

Photocopy Filter Dialog Box Contents

Component	*Function*
Detail field/slider	Drag to indicate threshold, or enter a value from 1 to 24.
Darkness field/slider	Drag to change brightness and contrast, or enter a value from 1 to 50.

PAINTERLY FILTERS CONTINUED

Plaster Filter

The Plaster filter reduces the image to a few tones below an adjustable threshold in shades of the background color and embosses the shapes over a solid foreground color. The figure here shows the associated dialog box.

Plaster Filter Dialog Box Contents

Component	Function
Image Balance field/slider	Drag to specify threshold, or enter a value from 0 to 50.
Smoothness field/slider	Drag to adjust the degree to which edges between colors blend, or enter a value from 1 to 15.
Light Direction menu	Choose from Top, Top Right, Right, Bottom Right, Bottom, Bottom Left, Left, Top Left.

Reticulation Filter

The Reticulation filter imitates what happens when photographic film is overheated during processing and film grain clumps together in worm-like forms. The effect, which you apply through the dialog box shown here, can produce interesting results when used as a texture.

Reticulation Filter Dialog Box Contents

Component	Function
Density field/slider	Drag to increase or decrease the population of grain clumps, or enter a value from 0 to 50.
Black Level field/slider	Drag to indicate threshold for black, or enter a value from 0 to 50.
White Level field/slider	Drag to indicate threshold for white, or enter a value from 0 to 50.

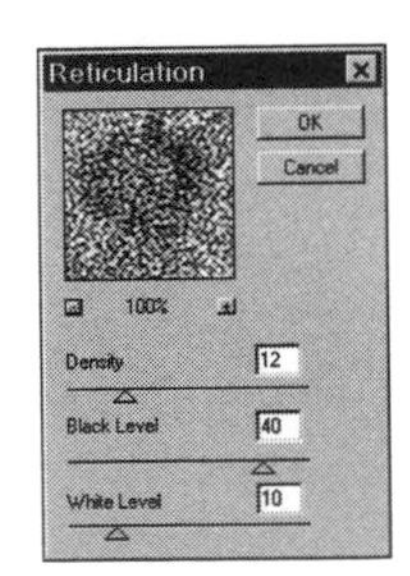

Stamp Filter

The Stamp filter carves the image out in much the same way as rubber is carved to make a rubber stamp; thus, its name. You can control the smoothness of lines and the point at which black and white divide by using the Stamp filter dialog box shown here.

Stamp Filter Dialog Box Contents

Component	*Function*
Light/Dark Balance field/slider	Drag to specify threshold, or enter a value from 0 to 50.
Smoothness field/slider	Drag to control the blending of edges, or enter a value from 1 to 50.

Torn Edges Filter

The Torn Edges filter is a Threshold filter that converts everything in the image to the exact foreground or background color. The figure here shows the Torn Edges filter dialog box.

Torn Edges Filter Dialog Box Contents

Component	*Function*
Image Balance field/slider	Drag to specify threshold, or enter a value from 0 to 50.
Smoothness field/slider	Drag to increase or decrease graininess of edges, or enter a value from 1 (smoothest) to 15 (grainiest).
Contrast field/slider	Drag to change the overall image contrast, or enter a value from 1 to 25.

Water Paper Filter

The Water Paper filter is the only Sketch filter that works in full color. It makes your image look like an ink image painted on fibrous paper and soaked in water. The figure here shows the associated dialog box.

Water Paper Filter Dialog Box Contents

Component	*Function*
Fiber Length field/slider	Drag to increase or decrease length of the threads in the texture weave, or enter a value from 3 to 50.
Brightness field/slider	Drag to change overall image brightness, or enter a value from 0 to 100.
Contrast field/slider	Drag to change overall image contrast, or enter a value from 0 to 100.

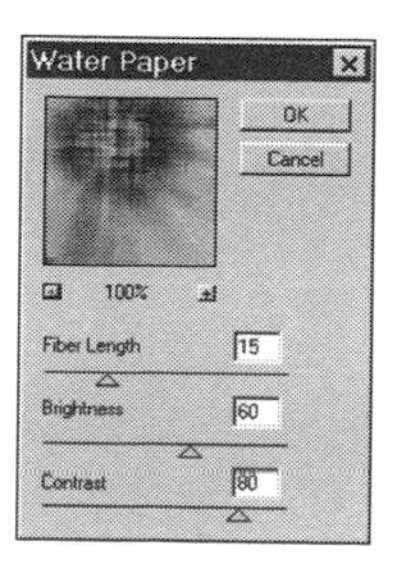

WARPING AND MORPHING

The warping and morphing filters act somewhat like funhouse mirrors by enlarging some pixels, shrinking some pixels, and moving still others. A variety of reasons exist for wanting to use these techniques, including that doing so is just plain fun. More often, though, you may have a more serious reason. For example

- You may need to composite two images so that one seems to wrap around the other.
- You may need to make a surface look as if it has been blown by the wind or rippled by raindrops.
- You may want an image to follow multiple contours, like the folds in a windblown flag.

Photoshop's twelve Distort filters perform all these functions and more. For more on how to apply these filters, see Chapter 16.

Note that some filter dialog boxes contain preview windows, which are often accompanied by + and – buttons underneath. Clicking the buttons zooms the image in the window in (+) or out (–).

Also, many of these dialog boxes contain field/slider settings with numeric values. Unless otherwise noted, the smallest number is the least of the effect that you can apply; the highest number is the most of the effect that you can apply. The more numbers in the range, the more variations that can be applied.

Diffuse Glow Filter

The Diffuse Glow filter is unique among the Distort filters in that it does not really distort at all. Instead, it "bleeds" the current background color into the lighter (highlight) areas of your image. The figure here shows the Diffuse Glow filter dialog box.

Diffuse Glow Filter Dialog Box Contents

Component	*Function*
Graininess field/slider	Increases the overall graininess of the image. Drag right to increase grain. You cannot use this control to remove any graininess that is already present in the image.
Glow Amount field/slider	Infuses the current background color into the area surrounding the highlights. This effect is very different if the background color is darker than the highlights than if it is the same or brighter.
Clear Amount field/slider	Drag to adjust the radius of the glow.

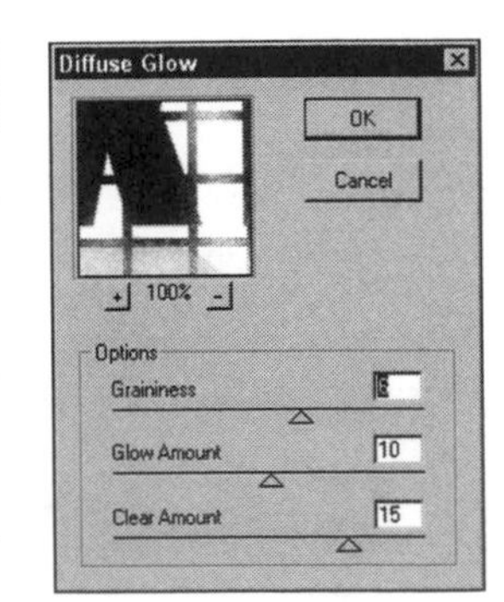

Displace Filter

The Displace filter enables you to add texture to an image by moving the colors of a certain selection in a direction and distance you specify. The Displace filter — the dialog box for which is shown here — is one of the most powerful filters in Photoshop's arsenal.

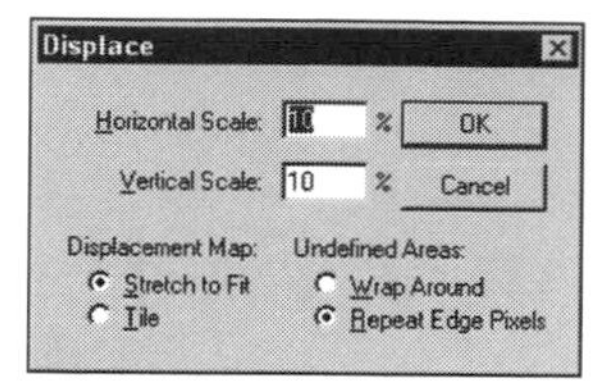

Displace Filter Dialog Box Contents

Component	Function
Horizontal Scale field	Specify a percentage of the image's size by which the displacement should occur in a horizontal direction.
Vertical Scale field	Specify a percentage of the image's size by which the displacement should occur in a vertical direction.
Stretch to Fit radio button	If chosen, the displacement map image file is resized to match the size of the current image's file.
Tile radio button	If chosen, repeats the displacement map image horizontally and vertically as needed to fill a larger image.
Wrap Around radio button	Fills any edge of the image that has been left vacant by a displacement with the part of the image that the displacement has pushed past the opposite border.
Repeat Edge Pixels radio button	Repeats the outermost row of pixels in the edge of the displaced image to the edge of the border.
OK button	When you click the OK button in this dialog box, it does not execute the displacement until you use a file loading dialog box to locate the file you want to use as a displacement map.

Glass Filter

The Glass filter makes your image look as though you are viewing it through textured glass. Some portions of the image are magnified, some reduced, and all are distorted. Its effects are similar to those of the Ocean Ripple filter, described later in this appendix. The figure here shows the Glass filter dialog box.

Glass Filter Dialog Box Contents

Component	Function
Distortion field/slider	Drag to the right to increase the bumpiness, or enter a number between 0 and 20.
Smoothness field/slider	Drag to the right to soften the edges of the texture bumps (that is, to cause them to blend with the image), or enter a number between 1 and 15.
Texture menu	Choose your own texture file or from one of the built-in textures: Canvas, Frosted, or Tiny Lens.
Scaling field/slider	Drag to enlarge or reduce the texture map tile, or enter a number between 50 and 200.
Invert check box	If checked, inverts the texture map. What was formerly a peak becomes a valley, and vice versa.

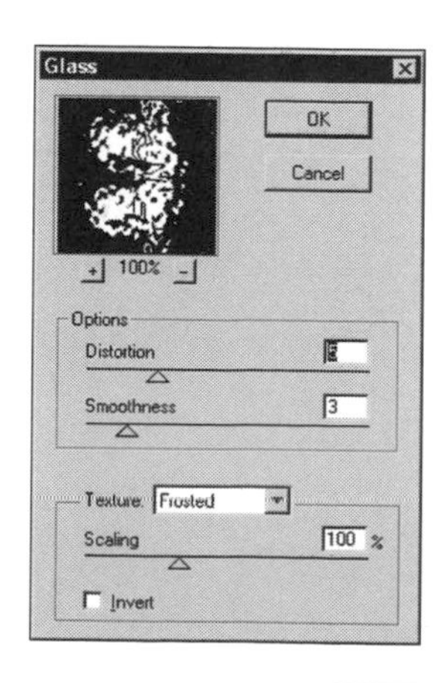

WARPING AND MORPHING CONTINUED

Ocean Ripple Filter

The Ocean Ripple filter produces a distortion that is much like the distortion created by the Glass filter, but it creates ripple shapes that are more random in size. The associated dialog box is shown here.

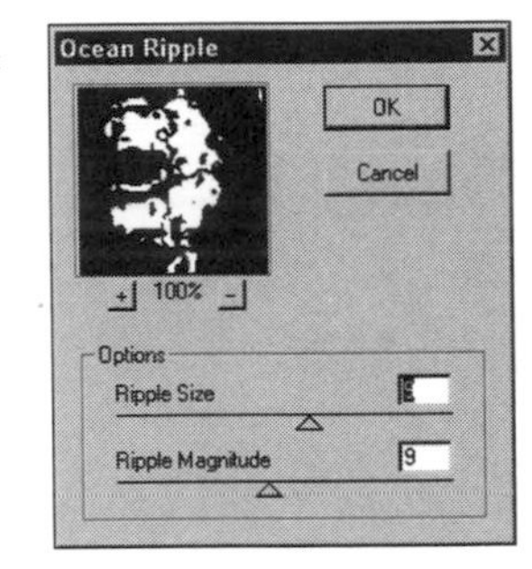

Ocean Ripple Filter Dialog Box Contents

Component	*Function*
Ripple Size field/slider	Drag to increase the instance between bumps, or enter a number between 1 and 15.
Ripple Magnitude field/slider	Drag to increase the apparent height of the bumps, or enter a number between 0 and 20.

Shear Filter

The Shear filter is a powerful and highly useful warping tool that lets you "wrinkle" the surface of anything, producing a skewed image. The figure here shows the associated dialog box.

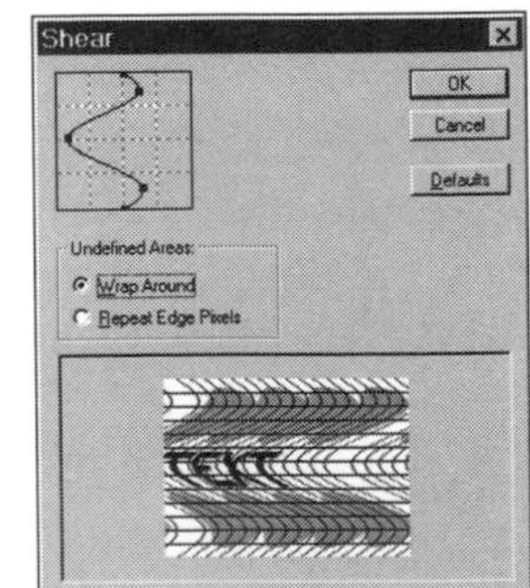

Shear Filter Dialog Box Contents

Component	*Function*
Wrap Around radio button	Choose to cause pixels pushed off one edge of the image to reappear on the opposite edge.
Repeat Edge Pixels radio button	Choose to extend pixels along a displaced edge to be repeated until they fill the space vacated by the displacement.
Distortion Curve grid	Click anywhere on curve line to enter a point. Drag a point to indicate direction and amount of displacement. You can enter any number of points, and the path can be as straight or wavy as you care to make it.
Preview window	Previews the effect of distorting along the path you have entered. Always shows thumbnail of the entire image within its boundaries.

Pinch Filter

The Pinch filter maps an image to the inside of a sphere, making an image appear as if it is printed on a piece of rubber sheeting that has been made to sag in the center. The Pinch filter is a good filter for stretching an object so that you can blend it with a concave or convex surface in a photo composite. The figure here shows the Pinch filter dialog box.

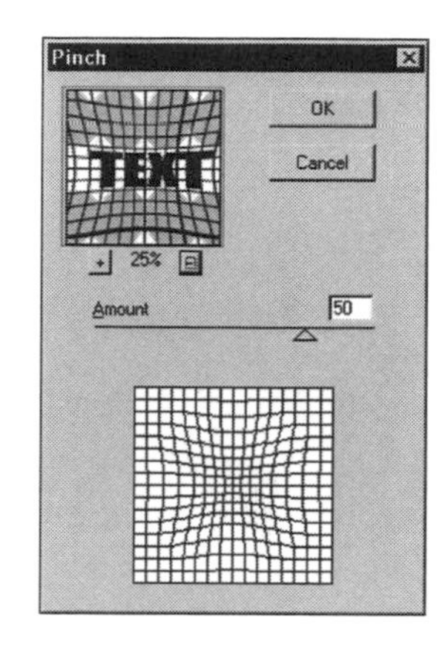

Pinch Filter Dialog Box Options

Component	*Function*
Amount field/slider	Drag to left of center to make image bulge, to right of center to push center away, or enter a number between –100 and 100.
Preview grid	Preview changes in the Amount field here.

Polar Coordinates Filter

The Polar Coordinates filter can stretch an image over a sphere, with the perspective changing so that you seem to be looking at this object from above, much like viewing Earth from space. The Polar Coordinates filter is often seen as one of the coolest distortion filters, yet one of the most difficult to understand, because you can map an image from rectangular to polar coordinates or from polar to rectangular, as shown in the dialog box here.

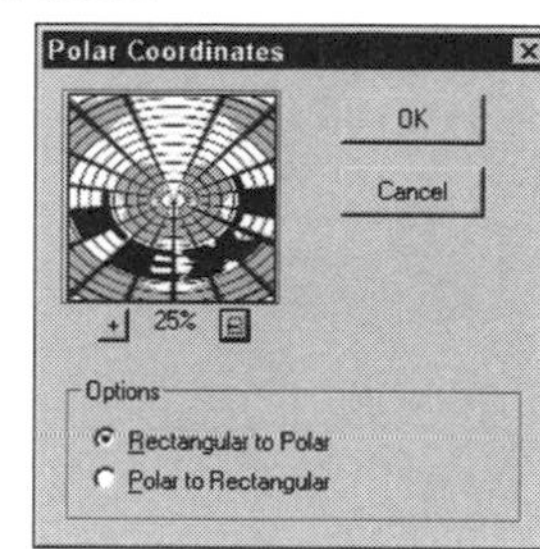

Polar Coordinates Dialog Box Contents

Component	*Function*
Rectangular to Polar radio button	Pulls all the outer edges into a single dot at the center of the image.
Polar to Rectangular radio button	Moves all the center pixels to the outer edge and pulls all the outer edge pixels to the center.

Ripple Filter

The Ripple filter is nearly identical to the Ocean Ripple filter and produces an effect similar to the Sprayed Strokes filter, but the wavy edges it creates are much lower in frequency and are more rounded. The ripples are regular in frequency (evenly spaced), and you can adjust them for a wide variety of wave heights, as shown in the following figure.

Ripple Filter Dialog Box Contents

Component	*Function*
Amount field/slider	Drag to adjust the amplitude (width) of individual ripples, or enter an amount between –999 and 999.
Size menu	Use this menu to change the height (or length, if it is easier to visualize them) of the ripples. Choose from small, medium, or large ripples.

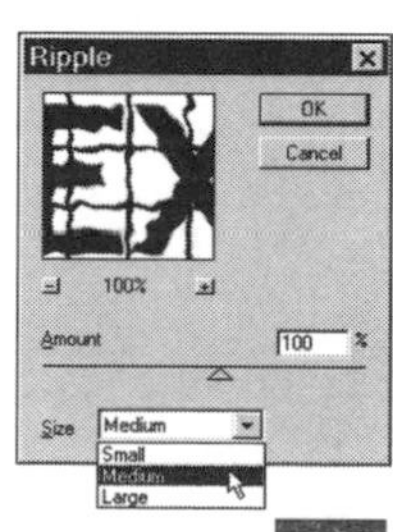

WARPING AND MORPHING CONTINUED

Spherize Filter

The Spherize filter warps the image halfway around a globe, on the outside of a sphere. This effect is similar to that of the Pinch filter, but the image protrudes outward, rather than inward. The figure here shows the associated dialog box.

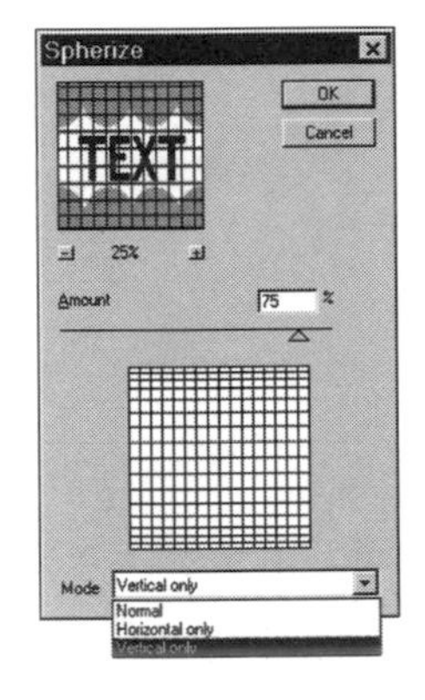

Spherize Filter Dialog Box Contents

Component	*Function*
Amount field/slider	Drag to the left for a concave distortion, to the right for a convex distortion, or enter a value between –100 and 100.
Preview grid	Previews the curvature of the distortion as the amount is changed.
Mode menu	Choose from Normal, Horizontal, and Vertical. Horizontal and Vertical make the distortion tubular, rather than spherical.

Twirl Filter

The Twirl filter rotates the center of an image, producing a spiral effect, as if the image were being sucked down a giant drain. The figure here shows the Twirl filter dialog box.

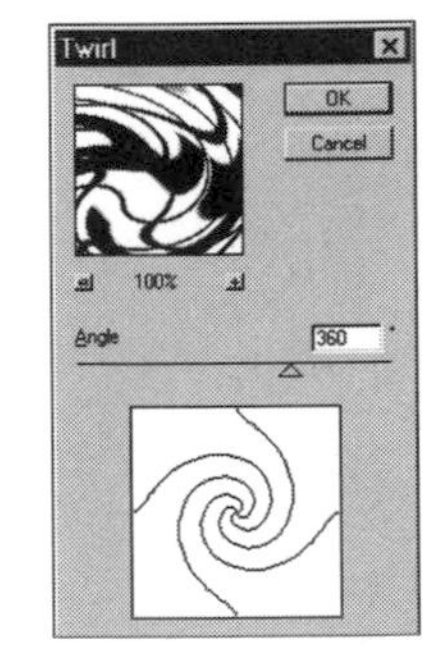

Twirl Filter Dialog Box Contents

Component	*Function*
Angle field/slider	Drag to determine the rotation and direction of the twist from the center.
Twirl preview	Shows the result of moving the Angle slider.

Wave Filter

The Wave filter contains several options that are among the most complex Photoshop has to offer. If you want to "smoosh" the elements of the image to create a watery, marbley, or zigzag texture, this filter is the one to use. Think of it as a much more powerful and less predictable version of the Ocean Ripple and Ripple filters. The associated dialog box is shown here.

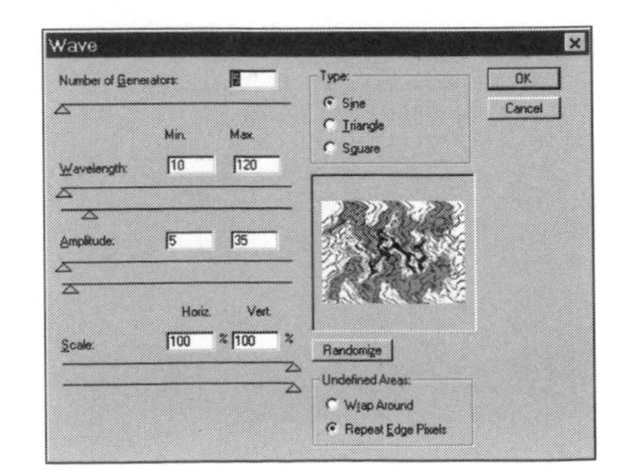

Wave Filter Dialog Box Contents	
Component	*Function*
Number of Generators field/slider	Drag to determine the number of energy centers that will create wave ripples. One generator will create a pond ripple, many will create roiling water.
Wavelength field/slider	Drag the arrows to indicate the minimum and maximum height of the individual waves. (The Mac dialog box has only one bar, but adjustments produce the same result.)
Amplitude field/slider	Drag the arrows to indicate the minimum and maximum width of the individual waves. (The Mac dialog box has only one bar, but adjustments produce the same result.)
Horizontal scale field/slider	Increases the effect by a percentage in the horizontal direction; drag the slider or enter a value between 1 and 100.
Vertical scale field/slider	Increases the effect by a percentage in the vertical direction; drag the slider or enter a value between 1 and 100.
Wrap Around radio button	Click to cause pixels pushed off one edge of the image to reappear on the opposite edge.
Repeat Edge Pixels button	Click to extend pixels along a displaced edge to be repeated until they fill the space radio vacated by the displacement.
Sine Type radio button	Generates natural-looking, watery ripples.
Triangle radio button	Generates sharply peaked ripples.
Square radio button	Generates square tiles instead of ripples.
Preview window	Always shows 100 percent thumbnail of the image.
Randomize button	Re-randomizes the already random pattern of the waves. Produces a somewhat different effect each time you click it.

ZigZag Filter

Rather than create a bunch of alternating points, as in a lightning bolt, the ZigZag filter effect resembles what happens to a quiet pond if you pitch a stone into it: It produces a ripple effect, with a zigzag of color emanating from the center of the image. The figure here shows the associated dialog box.

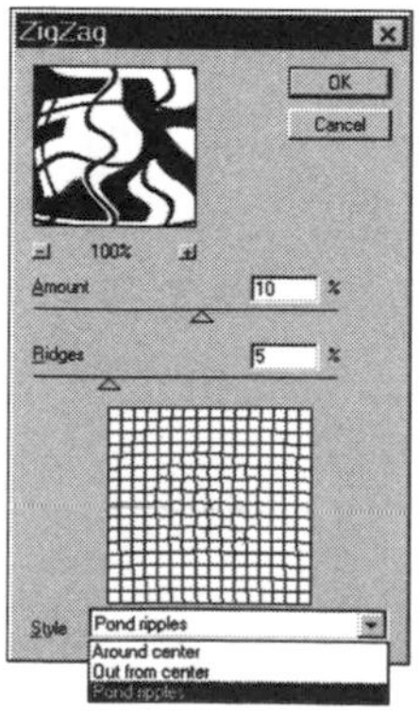

ZigZag Filter Dialog Box Contents	
Component	*Function*
Amount field/slider	Drag to indicate a positive or negative wave height, or enter a number between –100 and 100.
Ridges field/slider	Drag to indicate the number of wave peaks, or enter a value between 0 and 20.
Preview grid	Distorts the grid according to the adjustments of the sliders.
Style menu	Choose from Around Center, Out from Center, and Pond Ripples.

NOISE FILTERS

A number of Photoshop's built-in filters are dedicated to fragmenting or stylizing the image in different ways. Four of these are in the Noise filters submenu: Add Noise, Despeckle, Dust & Scratches, and Median. Another seven appear in the Pixelate filters submenu: Color Halftone, Crystallize, Facet, Fragment, Mezzotint, Mosaic, and Pointillize. The nine filters in the Stylize filter submenu enable you to add interesting stylistic effects: Diffuse, Emboss, Extrude, Find Edges, Glowing Edges, Solarize, Tiles, Trace Contour, and Wind.

Some of these filters *pixelate* an image (add "noise" to it), whereas others remove noise from an image. These filters also serve a variety of practical and artistic purposes, such as matching or creating film grain, retouching scratches, killing moiré patterns (a visible wavy distortion in an image), simulating the look of a halftone, and even imitating the look of a pointillist painting.

For more on using these filters, see Chapter 17.

Note that some filter dialog boxes contain preview windows, which are often accompanied by + and – buttons underneath. Clicking the buttons zooms the image in the window in (+) or out (–).

Also, many of these dialog boxes contain field/slider settings with numeric values. Unless otherwise noted, the smallest number is the least of the effect that you can apply; the highest number is the most of the effect that you can apply. The more numbers in the range, the more variations that can be applied.

Add Noise Filter

The Add Noise filter granulates an image regardless of the image's content. In fact, you can create textures by adding grain to a solid-color image and then use other filters to smear, grow, or move it. The figure here shows the Add Noise filter dialog box.

Add Noise Filter Dialog Box Contents

Component	Function
Amount field/slider	Drag the slider right to increase the amount of noise (graininess), left to decrease it. Or, you can specify amount by entering any whole number between 1 (less) and 999 (more) in the Amount field.
Distribution radio buttons	Click Uniform to make an even grain pattern. Click Gaussian if you want the grain pattern to spread in the highlights and clump in the shadows — as it does on film.
Monochromatic check box	If checked, all noise dots are black or white. This setting does not affect the coloration of the image itself — only of the grain pattern.
Preview check box	If checked, shows the effect of all settings on the image in the workspace.

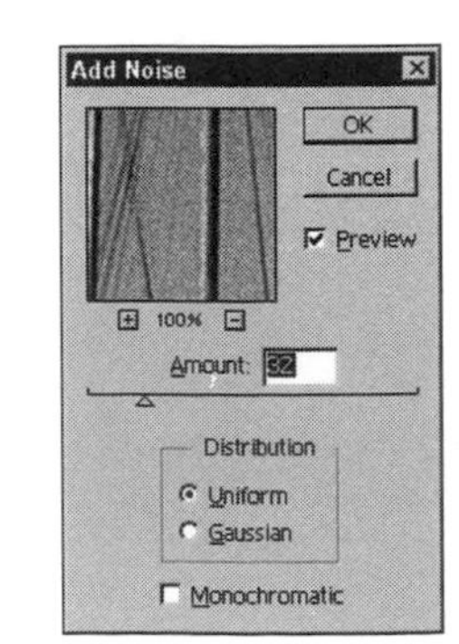

Dust & Scratches Filter

The Dust & Scratches filter looks for abrupt breaks in the overall pattern of the image and blends those breaks together. (Call it automated retouching.) You can use it on the overall image, but it the filter is likely to blur the image in unpredictable areas. The figure here shows the Dust & Scratches dialog box.

Dust & Scratches Filter Dialog Box Contents

Component	*Function*
Radius field/slider	Determines the pixel width of the faults that will be eliminated.
Threshold field/slider	Sets the level of contrast that must exist before a clump of pixels will be considered a defect.
Preview check box	If checked, shows the effect of all settings on the image in the workspace.

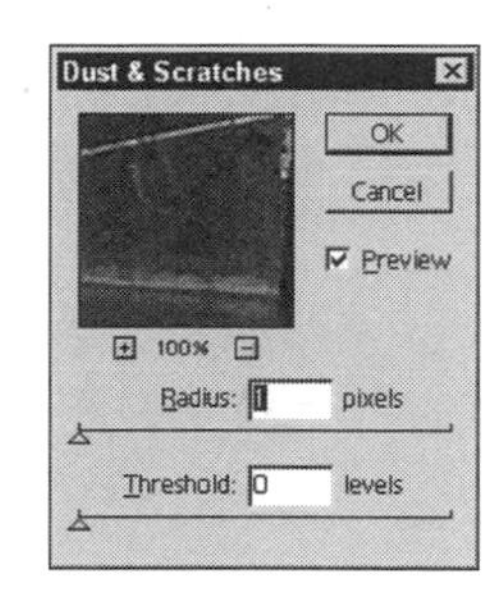

Median Filter

The Median filter blurs the image but spreads the highlights into the shadows in the process. The result can be an alternative to the Watercolor filter, without the extremely dark shadows Watercolor produces. The figure here shows the Median filter dialog box.

Median Filter Dialog Box Contents

Component	*Function*
Radius field/slider	Drag to determine the radius over which highlight pixels will be pushed into shadow pixels, or enter any number between 1 and 16.
Preview check box	If checked, shows the effect of all settings on the image in the workspace.

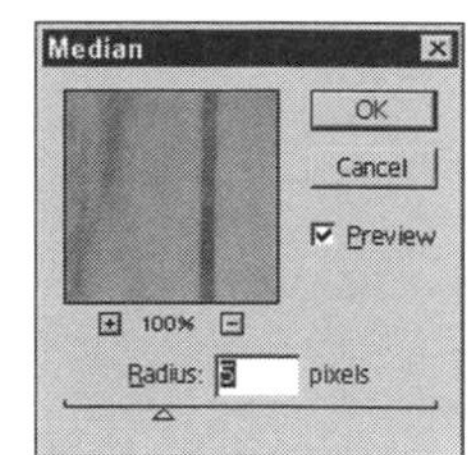

Color Halftone Filter

The Color Halftone filter is a pop-art effects filter, not actually usable for making color-separation halftones for color printing. Photoshop does have that capability, but first you need to make the separations and then make a grayscale halftone screen for each separation. The figure here shows the Color Halftone filter dialog box.

Color Halftone Filter Dialog Box Contents

Component	*Function*
Max. Radius field	Enter a whole number between 4 and 127 to determine the size of the largest halftone dots.
Screen Angles fields	Experiment with these settings for different effects.
Defaults button	Click to reset all settings to their defaults. (This feature often proves very useful, because it is easy to forget what you did when you were experimenting with the screen angle settings.)

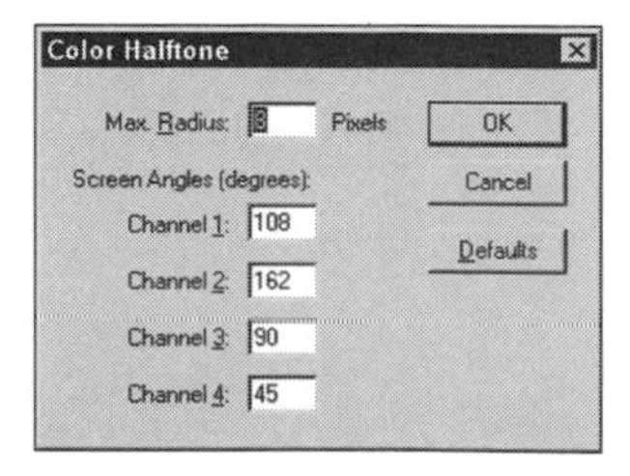

NOISE FILTERS CONTINUED

Crystallize Filter

The Crystallize filter averages a clump of pixels into irregular solid-color polygons. The effect is a reduction of colors and a variation on pointillist expressionism as an artistic style. The figure here shows the Crystallize filter dialog box.

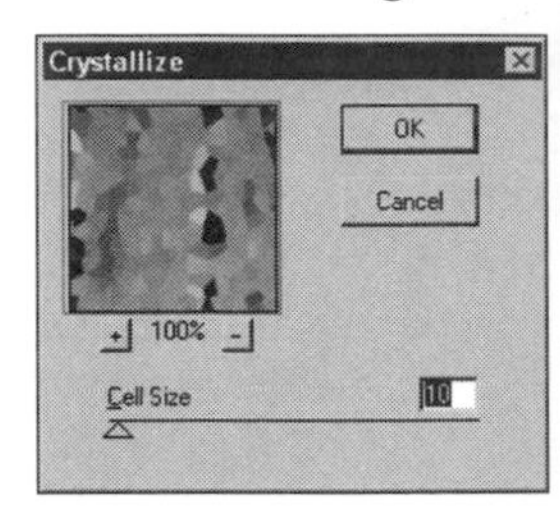

Crystallize Filter Dialog Box Contents

Component	*Function*
Cell Size field/slider	Determines the size of each crystal. You can directly enter any number between 3 (smallest) and 300 (largest) in the field.

Mezzotint Filter

The Mezzotint filter offers nine variations of a "noisy" special effect. The figure here shows the Mezzotint dialog box.

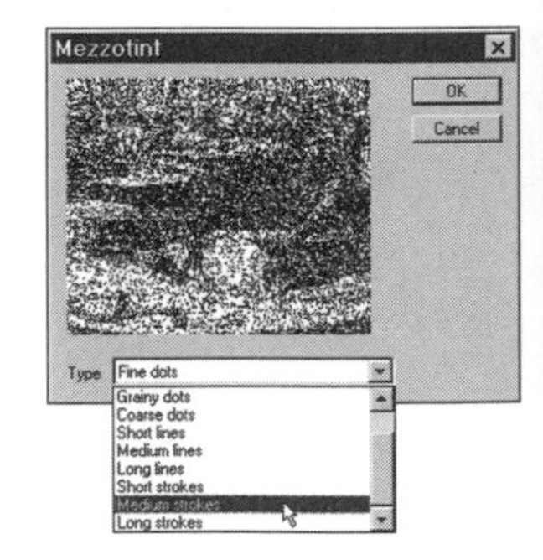

Mezzotint Filter Dialog Box Contents

Component	*Function*
Type menu	Choose from the following styles: Fine dots, Grainy dots, Coarse dots, Short Lines, Medium lines, Long lines, Short strokes, Medium strokes, or Long strokes.

Pointillize Filter

The Pointillize filter actually does a fairly credible job of turning your image into a pointillist painting. The following figure shows the Pointillize filter dialog box.

Pointillize Filter Dialog Box Contents

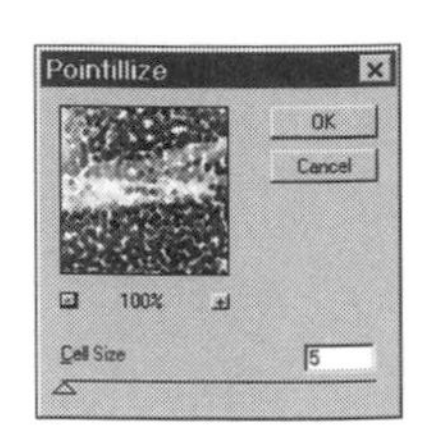

Component	*Function*
Cell Size field/slider	Determines the size of dots in the pointillist representation of the image. You can enter any number in the field between 3 (smallest) and 300 (largest).

Diffuse Filter

The Diffuse filter makes an image look as if it were sprayed with paint from an aerosol can. The filter produces a sort of diffused grainy effect. The figure here shows the Diffuse filter dialog box.

Diffuse Filter Dialog Box Contents

Component	*Function*
Normal radio button	Click to give a slightly sandy textured or spray-painted effect without shifting tones.
Darken Only radio button	Flattens and roughens shadows, with little or no effect on highlights. Tends to darken shadow areas.
Lighten Only radio button	Flattens and roughens the highlights, with little or no effect on the shadows. Tends to lighten highlight areas. Edges between strongly contrasting areas are less speckled.
Preview check box	If checked, effect is previewed in the workspace window. Greatly slows down the preview in the Preview window.

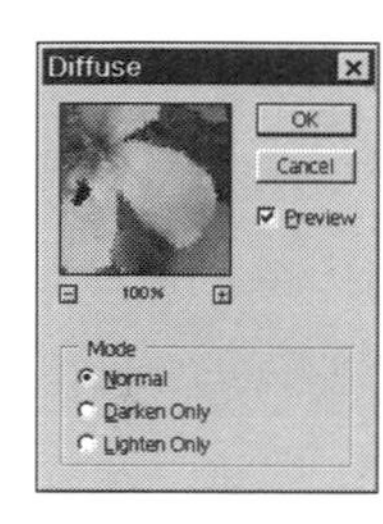

Emboss Filter

The Emboss filter creates a monochrome image that looks as if the elements in the image are stamped into paper — similar to embossed stationery. The following figure shows the Emboss filter dialog box.

Emboss Filter Dialog Box Contents

Component	*Function*
Angle field	Enter any number between 0 and 360 to indicate the angle of lighting.
Angle control	Drag dial to indicate "lighting" angle.
Height field/slider	Drag to indicate width of highlight and shadows on the edges of shapes, or enter a number between 1 (narrowest) and 10 (widest).
Amount field/slider	Also increases or decreases the apparent depth of the embossing.
Preview check box	If checked, shows the effect of all settings on the image in the workspace.

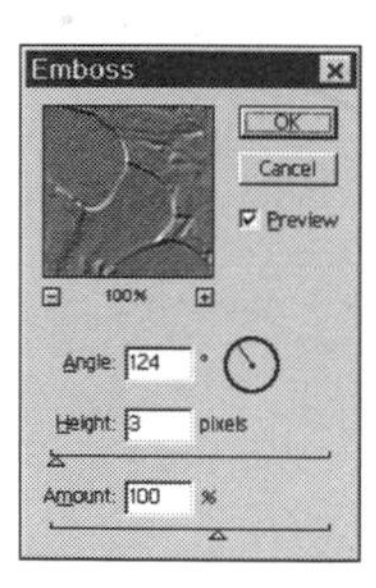

NOISE FILTERS CONTINUED

Extrude Filter

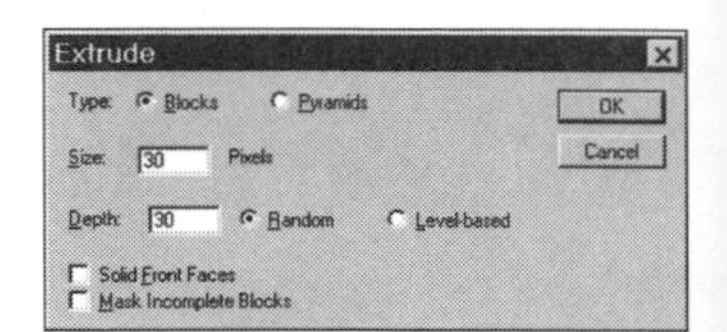

The Extrude filter makes the image look as if it has been glued to raised blocks. You can also use this filter to convert the image to solid color 3D blocks or pyramids. The following figure shows the Extrude filter dialog box.

Extrude Filter Dialog Box Contents

Component	*Function*
Blocks radio button	Click to extrude image onto flat-colored square blocks that radiate away from the center of the image.
Pyramids radio button	Click to extrude image onto pyramids that radiate away from the center of the image.
Size field	Enter a number between 2 and 255 for the number of pixels square for the extruded shape.
Depth field	Enter a number between 2 and 255 for the height in pixels of the extruded shape.
Random radio button	Click to make the apparent height of the extruded shape vary throughout image.
Level-based radio button	Click to make the apparent height of the extruded shape uniform, based on the number entered in the Depth field.
Solid Front Faces check box	Unavailable if the Pyramids button has been chosen. If checked, makes all front faces a solid color. Otherwise, front faces are the same as the original image.
Mask Incomplete Blocks check box	If checked, any blocks that do not fall completely within the selection (or the boundaries of the image) are not extruded or otherwise changed.

Glowing Edges Filter

The Glowing Edges filter traces contrasting edges with a bright line and converts all the other shades in the image to a charcoal shade. The figure here shows the Glowing Edges filter dialog box.

Glowing Edges Filter Dialog Box Contents

Component	*Function*
Edge Width	Drag to determine the width of the glowing edges, or enter a number between 1 field/slider (narrowest) and 14 (widest).
Edge Brightness	Drag to determine the brightness of the glowing edges, or enter a number between 0 (dullest) field/slider and 20 (brightest). Edge Brightness and Edge Width will often seem to have the same effect.
Smoothness	Drag to make glowing edge blend more or less sharply with surrounding image, or enter a field/slider whole number between 1 and 15.

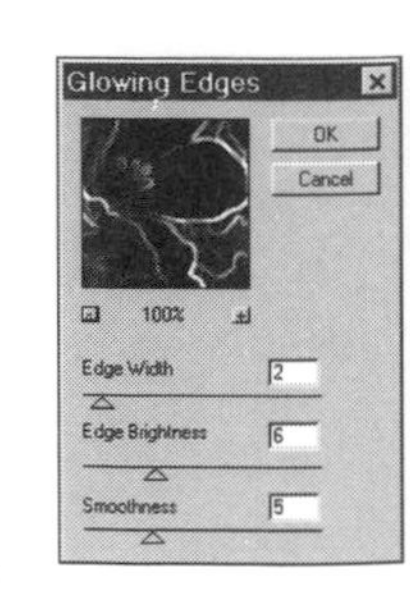

Tiles Filter

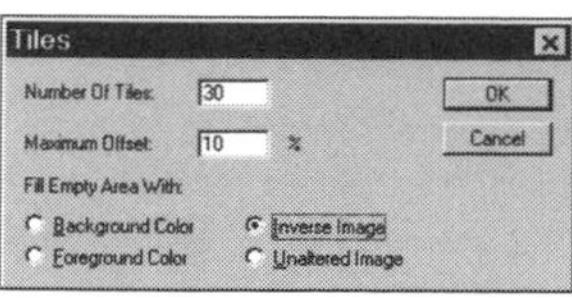

The Tiles filter produces an effect that looks similar to a mosaic, dividing up the image into somewhat irregular square tiles. The figure here shows the Tiles filter dialog box.

Tiles Filter Dialog Box Contents

Component	*Function*
Number of Tiles field	Enter a number between 1 and 99 to specify number of tiles. The size of the tiles will be dependent on the size of the image.
Maximum Offset field	Enter any number between 1 and 99 to determine the percentage of the tile size that will be assigned to the space between tiles.
Fill Empty Area With radio buttons	Click one of these buttons to determine whether the space between tiles will be filled with the current background color, the current foreground color, the negative of the image, or an offset (but otherwise unchanged) rendition of the original image.

Trace Contour Filter

The Trace Contour filter draws a single-pixel line to trace edges and then drops out all the other colors in the image. The figure here shows the Trace Contour filter dialog box.

Trace Contour Filter Dialog Box Contents

Component	*Function*
Level field/slider	Drag to set threshold for definition of edges, or enter a value between 1 and 255.
Edge radio buttons	Determines whether the edge will be traced on the upper or lower side of the threshold (edge) pixel.
Preview check box	If checked, shows the effect of all settings on the image in the workspace.

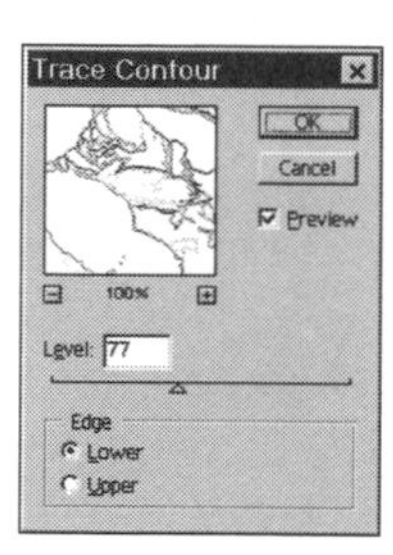

Wind Filter

The Wind filter is closely related to the Motion Blur filter. This filter produces an effect reminiscent of a comic-strip motion blur, with streaked edges. The figure here shows the Wind filter dialog box.

Wind Filter Dialog Box Contents

Component	*Function*
Wind radio button	Creates a streaking of darker pixels into the lighter areas of the image.
Blast radio button	Same as preceding radio button, but the streak is longer.
Stagger radio button	Streaks shadows into highlights in one direction and highlights into shadows in the other. Creates a sort of jarred, jagged effect.
From the Left radio button	Specifies that the streak is smudged from the left and tapers to the right.
From the Right radio button	Specifies that the streak is smudged from the right and tapers to the left.

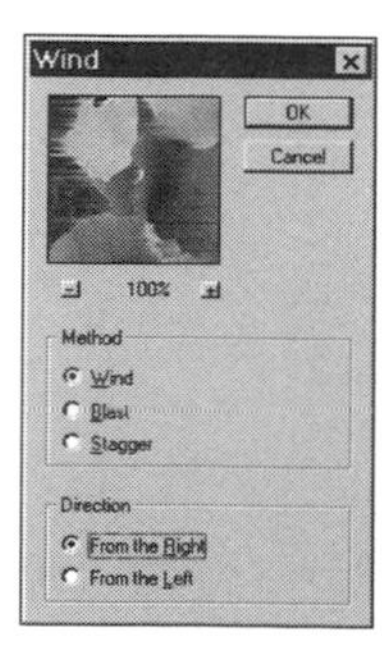

EXPRESSIVE EFFECTS

These tips and techniques are on how to create expressive, creative effects with the components of Photoshop. This section also contains a brief overview of the Color Picker dialog box and the Custom Colors dialog box, as you will use them often when experimenting with Photoshop.

The Color Picker

The Color Picker is an extremely flexible tool, as shown by the following figure. Within it, you can choose colors in several ways. You can drag the Color slider and then click in the color spectrum, or you can enter numeric values. You can also enter numbers for RGB, HSB (Hue, Saturation, and Brightness), Lab, and CMYK (Cyan, Magenta, Yellow, and blacK) color models or pick colors from the swatch books of all the most widely used color systems (ANPA, Pantone, DIC, Toyo, and Trumatch) in the Custom Colors dialog box. You can also click in the Only Web Colors check box to limit your choice of colors to those seen by Web browsers.

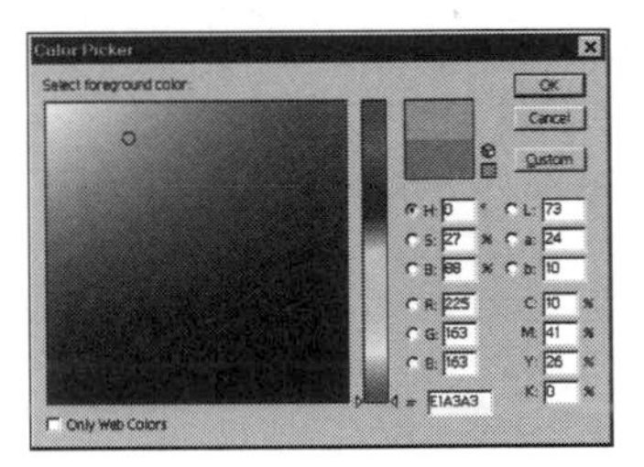

Color Picker Dialog Box Contents

Component	*Function*
Color field	This window shows you the range of colors you can choose according to the selected Color Mode buttons.
Color marker	Indicates the position of the currently chosen replacement color. You can choose a different replacement color simply by clicking a different point in the Color field.
Previous color	The color you last chose.
New color	The currently chosen color.
Color slider	Indicates the values of colors available to the currently chosen Color Mode component radio button. If you click inside the Color slider, the arrows automatically move to that position.
Color slider arrows	Drag the arrows up and down the Color slider to change the value of the colors shown in the Color field.
Color Mode component radio buttons and fields	Click a button to change the color schemes shown in the Color field and Color slider.
Custom color button	Switches to the Custom Colors dialog box.
Only Web Colors check box	Limits color choices to those viewable in Web browsers.

Custom Color

When you click the Custom button in the Color Picker, the Custom Colors dialog box appears, shown here. In this dialog box, you are able to select from a set of predefined colors. These colors are from brand-name color libraries.

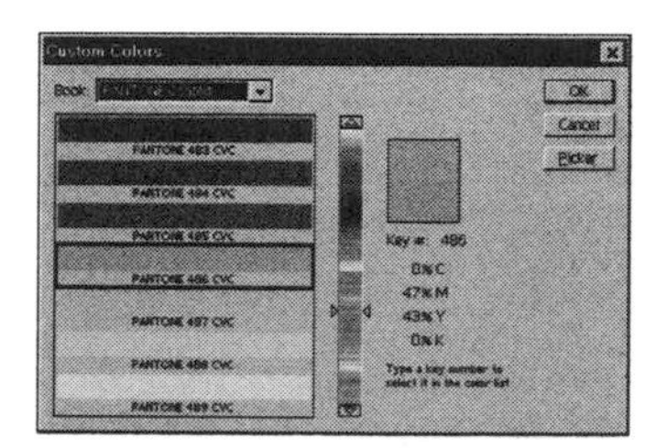

Custom Colors Dialog Box Contents

Component	*Function*
Book menu	Chooses a proprietary spot color book.
Color swatch panel	Shows exact colors available within the range indicated by the Color slider.
Color slider	Displays all the colors available in the currently chosen book. Click a color to change the colors in the Color swatch panel.
Color slider scroll buttons	Click the buttons to scroll colors upwards or downwards.
Color slider arrows	Drag to change the colors in the Color swatch panel.
Previous color	The color you last chose.
New color	The currently chosen color.
Color Key number	The code number assigned by the Color swatch book manufacturer to the currently chosen color.
CMYK color value	The percentages of cyan, magenta, yellow, and black contained in the currently chosen color.
Picker button	Switches to the Color Picker.

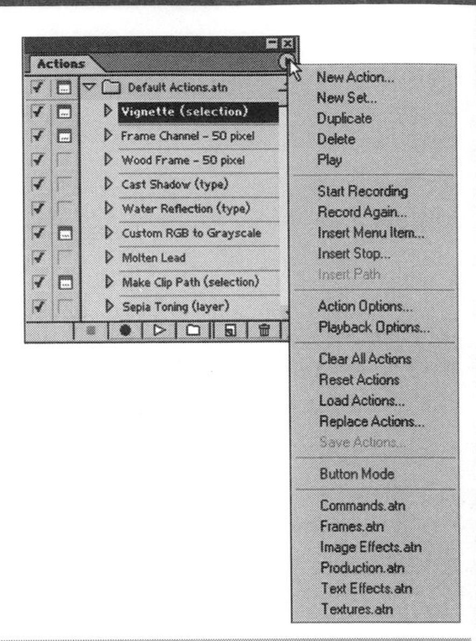

ACTIONS

Actions are lists of Photoshop edits that you can perform at a single keystroke or mouse click.

You can apply Actions to either the current file or to all the files in a given folder, making batch-processing a whole series of files possible. You could, for example, resize a whole folder of images so they fit within the confines of a Web page. The same command could reduce the colors in all those files to a given level and then convert them all to GIF file format. Please see Chapter 19. To record an Action, you must first display the Actions palette, shown here.

Actions Palette Contents

Component	*Function*
On/Off check box	Click to toggle command or Action on/off (checked is on).
Modal icon	Click to toggle modal control on/off (appearance of icon indicates on). Modal control enables the command to stop for input during its execution. Essential for operations where settings or filenames vary from one execution of an Action to another.
Set name bar	You can place Actions in sets so that you can execute a whole series of Actions by choosing the set name bar, and then clicking the Play button. You can save and retrieve sets from disk.
Action name bar	Displays the name of the Action (you enter this before recording). You can execute an Action by selecting it and clicking the Play button or by choosing the Play command from the Actions palette menu.
Recorded Command	Displays the name bar command names (entered automatically as recorded), making it easy to see what an Action does and to edit it later.
Stop button	Click to stop playing or recording.
Record button	Click to record or resume recording (you can add commands to the highlighted Action).
Play button	Plays the highlighted Action. You can also play part of an Action by highlighting a Command name bar and clicking the Play button to play the rest of the commands in the Action.
New Set button	Brings up the New Set dialog box, through which you can create a new set of Actions.
New Action button	Opens the New Action dialog box.
Trash icon	Deletes the selected command or Action. You can also delete a command or Action by dragging its name bar to the Trash icon.
Actions Palette menu button	Click to drop down the Actions Palette menu.
Actions Palette menu	Drag to select a menu item.
New Action	Brings up the Actions dialog box. Choose this command before starting a new Action.

Actions Palette Menu Contents

Command	*Function*
New Set	Brings up the New Set dialog box. Choose this command if you want to create a new set of Actions.
Duplicate	Makes a copy of the selected Action.
Delete	Eradicates the selected Action.
Play	Executes the selected Action.
Start Recording	Starts recording a new Action or inserts commands after the selected command in an Action.
Record Again	Rerecords an existing Action so you can enter a different sequence of commands.
Insert Menu Item	Inserts a command that cannot be recorded, so that you can execute it at the proper time during playback.
Insert Stop	Inserts a stop so you can perform a nonrecordable task while the Action is paused.
Insert Path	Inserts any previously selected path so that the path is recreated when the Action is played on any subsequent file.
Action Options	Opens the Action Options dialog box.
Playback Options	Opens the Playback Options dialog box.
Clear Actions	Removes all the Actions from the Actions palette.
Reset Actions	Restores the default list of Actions and dumps all others.
Load Actions	Adds a set of Actions to the current list by loading them from disk.
Replace Actions	Dumps all the Actions in the current list and loads another from disk.
Save Actions	Saves the currently selected (highlighted) Actions to disk.
Button Mode	Toggles Button mode on/off.
Saved Actions list	Lists all sets of saved Actions. Click to load a set.

Rules and Guidelines for Actions

Remember the following when working with Actions in Photoshop 6:

- Actions can include functions of the following tools: Gradient, Marquee, Crop, Polygon Lasso, Lasso, Move, Magic Wand, Paint Bucket, and Type. Palettes whose functions you can record include the Paths, Channels, Layers, and History palettes.
- Modal commands and tools all provide the user an option to interact with an Action if the Modal icon is turned on. What commands can make use of modal control? Any command that normally requires pressing Return/Enter and the function of any tool that depends on position (Gradient, Magic Wand, Lasso, Marquee, Path, and Type).
- Remember that the effect of some commands may depend on such things as the current choice of foreground/ background color, image size, current Color mode, currently active layer, and overall image size (horizontal and vertical pixel measurements).
- Although you cannot record every single Photoshop command, you can use the Insert command to add nonrecordable commands to the Action after the fact.
- Recordable commands you might normally think could not be recorded include Play on the Actions palette menu, which lets an Action start another Action; and choosing File, then Automate, then Batch, which would start a batch operation partway through the execution of a command. You can record all the Automate commands in an Action, too.
- All recorded Actions are automatically saved in the default Actions file: Actions Palette.psp (no three-letter extension is added to the Mac filename).

CONTACT SHEETS

Once you've digitized hundreds of images so that they can be worked on in Photoshop, finding exactly the right image gets to be a problem. After all, file names are seldom descriptive enough to evoke a precise image in your mind. The situation gets worse if you are trying to find the right images from among dozens of pictures of the same subject.

The easiest (and most portable) way to solve this is to print the equivalent of a photographer's contact sheet. Contact sheets get their name from the fact that the processed film is placed face down over photo paper and a sheet of glass placed atop them to press them into contact with the paper. When exposed to light and developed, small images the size of the film frame are printed in rows and columns across the paper.

Photoshop's Contact Sheet II command (choose Automate, then Contact Sheet II) creates a digital version of a contact sheet (or sheets) for all the images in a folder. In Photoshop 6, you can even choose to have all the images labeled with their file names to make it even easier to find the right image.

The Contact Sheet dialog box

Choosing File, then Automate, then Contact Sheet II brings up the Contact Sheet dialog box (see the following figure). The dialog box contains options for opening a folder full of images and assembling them on a single page.

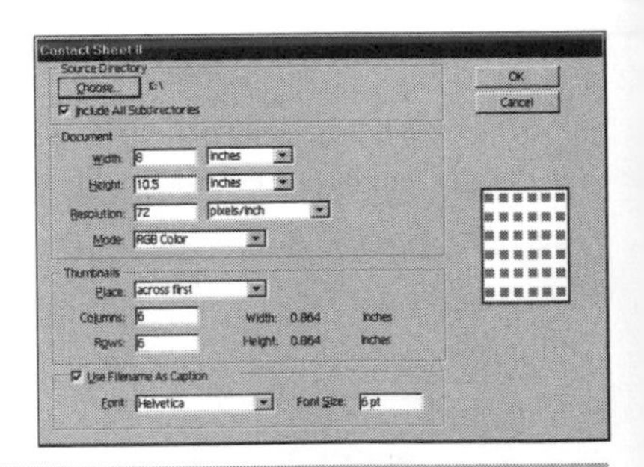

Contact Sheet Dialog Box Contents

Component	*Function*
Source Directory menu	Click to open a file browsing window. Navigate to find the folder you want to make contacts from and click.
Include All Subdirectories check box	If checked, adds images from all subdirectories of the target directory to the contact sheet.
Width and Height fields	Enter the width and height of the area into which you want all the thumbnails placed. The most typical size is 8 x 10 because that is the size used by most photographers, and because it fits on the most commonly used size of paper, which is letter size.

Component	*Function*
Width and Height units menus	Choose from inches, centimeters, or pixels.
Resolution field	This should be the resolution of the thumbnail images. Make this setting as high as your printer is capable of printing, divided by the number of primary colors in the current color (3 for RGB, 4 for CMYK, and so on).
Resolution units menu	Choose from pixels per-inch or pixels per centimeter.
Mode menu	Choose from RGB, CMYK, or Lab color modes for printing.
Place menu	Choose Across First or Down First to determine whether images will be placed in left-to-right horizontal order or in top-to-bottom vertical order.
Layout preview window	Shows you the aspect ratio of the thumbnails, the number of rows and columns that will result from the specifications you have chosen and size of the margins between thumbnails.
Columns field	Enter the number of columns across you want. Entering a number of rows and columns that will result in a square thumbnail preview is best. Otherwise, some images may be smaller than others because verticals or horizontals may need to be shrunk to fit one of the dimensions.
Rows field	Enter the number of rows across you want. If the number of rows and columns you enter results in fewer thumbnails per page than there are images in the chosen folder, Photoshop simply creates multiple contact sheets.
Thumbnails width and height	The figures shown in this area of the dialog box result from the numbers entered in the Rows and Columns fields.
Use Filename as Caption check box	If checked, filename automatically appears on a type layer below the image. This feature makes editing or adding to the labels easy.
Font menu	Lets you choose the font the filename will be typed in.
Font size field	Lets you enter a number of points (no fewer than 6) for the type size of the labels. The larger the font size, the smaller the thumbnails become because they must have room for a 39-character filename.

IMAGEREADY

The primary purpose of ImageReady, now that you can accomplish slicing and optimization so easily within Photoshop 6, is rollovers and animations. ImageReady acts as a stand-alone, feature-rich program. However, many of its functions duplicate Photoshop 6 functions.

In addition to having terrific facilities for optimizing the performance of still Web images, ImageReady features a complete GIF animation program (which has its own tricks for super-optimization) and lets you slice images and create image maps.

You can link slices to URLs or to JavaScript. ImageReady writes its own JavaScript routines for creating mouse rollover events. You can also modify the image for each event so that when the event occurs, the slice changes its appearance. You can also specify that changes occur in other slices. (For example, on mouse down, an instruction graphic could appear in another slice.) You can even have an animation appear in another slice.

The ImageReady Interface

The ImageReady 3 interface is so similar to Photoshop's that it may at first fool you into thinking that you are still working in Photoshop. With the advent of Photoshop 6, the similarities in interface have become even more prevalent. This similarity was created intentionally to help keep the learning curve between programs at a minimum.

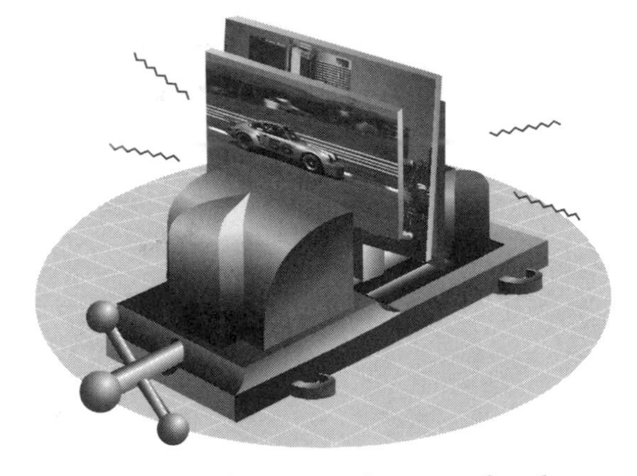

What Is Optimization and Why Is It So Important?

Optimization is the term that has come into general acceptance among Web designers for all the "tricks" that can be used to make a graphics file as small as possible without losing too much quality.

How much loss of quality is tolerable will vary considerably from image to image, author to author, client to client, and intended purpose to intended purpose. Traditionally, graphics have been optimized by performing several separate operations (image resizing, color reduction, dithering, and compression) independently. These are usually performed on several copies of each image, each using different settings. The results are compared and the smallest image that looks good enough is the one that ends up being used on the Web.

ImageReady saves you a lot of time by letting you apply up to four different sets of compression settings, each including all the categories named previously, at the same time. You can see them all side-by-side. Furthermore, you see the results of all the settings nearly instantly, which makes changing a setting or two and looking at the results again easy. As soon as you are sure that one of the four is the best you can do for that image, you select that view of the image. Only then do you need to save the file.

Which File Format?

If you are new to preparing graphics for Web publication, understanding which of the four graphics formats supported by ImageReady is most appropriate for optimizing a given image helps.

Four different file formats (actually three, one of which has two distinctive "flavors") have come into wide acceptance on the Web. In order of popularity, these include GIF (Graphics Interchange Format), JPEG (Joint Photographic Experts Group), PNG-8, and PNG-24. PNG stands for Portable Network Graphics. GIF and PNG-8 are used for 8-bit (256-colors or less) images.

- **GIF:** Use this format for graphic text (logos and such), graphic elements, technical drawings, and most hand-executed art (unless lots of soft edges and smooth gradations of color exist).
- **JPEG:** Use for almost all photos and any other artwork with lots of colors, soft edges, and smooth transitions. This format is 24-bit, so all colors are legal. Because most computers in use today have true-color display systems, you do not need to worry about Web-safe colors for this type of art work.
- **PNG-8:** Lossless compression makes this format good for highly detailed, flat-color artwork. Also, multi-level background transparency ensures smooth blending of transparent image edges with the background. (However, GIF files have much more universal browser support.)
- **PNG-24:** This format is capable of lossless compression and can store alpha channels. Use for technically critical photographs when your audience is willing to wait for the file to load in order to be able to judge the quality of your portfolio or to study a technical or scientific photo. PNG-24 is also invaluable when you need to display partial or graduated transparency. (Note: This format is supported only in the very latest generations of Web browsers.)

The PNG format is supported directly in the browser only by Internet Explorer 4.0 and later. Versions 2.0 and later of both Netscape and Microsoft browsers can use PNG plug-ins. PNG Live is a popular plug-in that works with both browsers.

LiveViews

ImageReady (and Photoshop 6 Save for Web) LiveViews are what you see as a result of choosing one of the tabs in the active document window that show an optimized version of the image. These are four tabs: Original, Optimized, 2-up, and 4-up. You can see the same views in Photoshop 6 if you choose File, then Save for Web.

You can preview the optimization ImageReady does to an image in one of these LiveViews. You can see information about the performance of the optimization settings for a given view at the bottom of that window. LiveViews are so called because any time you change an optimization setting, the selected LiveView shows the resulting changes in the image.

The layout of 2-up and 4-up LiveViews is automatically determined by ImageReady as a result of the width:height ratio of the image, the aspect ratio of the window, and whether annotations or rules are shown.

IMAGEREADY CONTINUED

The Optimize Palette

All the settings that are reflected in the currently selected LiveView are made in the Optimize palette. The contents of the Optimize palette are different for each of the four types of optimized files. (Refer to the following tables for explanations of each of the settings.) The contents of the Optimize palette menu, accessed by clicking the arrowhead in the upper-right corner of the Optimized tab, are the same for all four versions.

The Optimize Palette (8-bit Color)

Item	*What It Does*
Droplet arrow	Creates a droplet (batch processing icon) that will apply the current settings to any folder you drop on the icon.
File type menu	Lets you choose the file format (GIF, JPEG, PNG-8, or PNG-24) for optimization.
Color Reduction Algorithm menu	Choose from Perceptual, Selective, Adaptive, Web, Custom, MacOS, or Windows.
Dither Algorithm menu	Determines how to simulate colors not in the table. Choose from No Dither, Pattern (uses a halftone pattern), or Diffusion (dither effects randomly diffused).
Transparency check box	Indicates a transparent color will be assigned to the file.
Interlaced check box	Check indicates that an interlaced (low resolution) preview image should be created.
Lossy slider (GIF only)	If applied, allows loss of some image data in exchange for smaller file size.
Maximum Colors menu and field	Enter any number between 1 and 256.
Dither Percentage field/slider	Drag to indicate the amount of dithering to be applied.
Matte Color swatch and menu	Displays a swatches palette that enables you to choose a background color to use to match edge halo pixels to browser background color.
Web Snap Tolerance field/slider	Determines how close a color must come to a color in the Web-safe palette before it will be converted to that color.

The Optimize Palette (True Color)

Settings menu	Enables you to choose from any previously saved settings. (Adobe includes quite a few of the most commonly used.)
Compression Quality and menu (JPEG only)	Enables you to quickly pick between four compression levels: Low, medium, high, maximum.
Progressive/Interlaced check box	Check indicates that an interlaced (low resolution) preview image should be created.
ICC Profile checkbox(JPEG only)	Preserves any pre-existing ICC profile to be saved with the image. May increase file size.
Quality slider (JPEG only)	Drag the slider or enter a number between 1 and 100 to determine the exact amount of loss to be tolerated.

Blur field/slider (JPEG only)	Applies Gaussian blur to reduce detail and permit greater compression.
Matte Color swatch and menu	Displays a swatches palette that enables you to choose a background color to use to match edge halo pixels to browser background color.

Optimize Palette Menu	
Hide Options	Expands the palette to show additional controls.
Create Droplet	Enables you to save the current settings as a Droplet (an application file that will automatically batch process all the files in any folder you drop on it according to the current optimization settings).
Save Settings	Saves the current settings.
Delete Settings	Deletes saved settings.
Optimize to File Size	Optimizes to a specific file size in one step. Option for sticking with the current file type or enabling ImageReady to choose between GIF and JPEG.
Repopulate View	4-up view only: Regenerates optimization alternatives for all but original and selected views.
Auto Regenerate	Toggles. Automatically regenerates selected windows according to any changes in the settings.
Regenerate	Forces regeneration of the selected (or Optimized) view if Auto Regenerate is toggled off. Use when you want to edit the image without waiting for regeneration after each stroke.

Understanding Color Palettes

If you are compressing your files in true-color (JPEG or PNG-24), you need not worry about palettes. GIF and PNG-8, on the other hand, are limited to the production of 8-bit, 256 (or fewer) indexed palette colors. Because the number of colors is limited, very specific colors must be assigned to the limited number of locations available in a palette. The color of a given pixel in the image is actually assigned to a specific location in the palette matrix.

When you optimize a file in Photoshop 6 or ImageReady, you are given a choice of seven different palette types (which Adobe also calls Color Reduction Algorithms):

- Perceptual. Creates a color table based on the colors in the image, but weighted for colors that are most critically perceived by the human eye.
- Selective. Default. The choice that is usually most faithful to an original photo. Also creates a color table based on colors in the original image, but favors the preservation of Web colors and those colors that occupy large areas of the image.
- Adaptive. Bases selection of colors entirely on the frequency of their appearance in the original image. Very useful for images with one or two highly predominant colors, such as a field of grass.
- Web. Uses the Web-safe palette for the color table. All colors in the original are snapped to the closest Web-safe color. Ensures that the target browser will not dither colors. Can result in larger file sizes. Best used for logos and graphic elements with limited colors.
- Custom. You have to choose Perceptual, Selective, or Adaptive first. Creates a table from the original image that is maintained regardless of any subsequent changes you make.
- Mac OS. The color table is based on the Macintosh Operating System's uniform sampling of 256 RGB colors.
- Windows. The color table is based on the Windows operating system's uniform sampling of 256 RGB colors.

IMAGE SLICING

ImageReady 3.0 and Photoshop 6 make it possible to divide an image that is destined for the Web into several images. You can load these parts onto a Web page so that no seam is visible, yet each slice can have its own optimization characteristics and can be assigned its own Web links. This process is known as *image slicing*.

Image slicing (see Part VI) provides you with both performance advantages and interface design advantages. Performance may be enhanced for any or all of three reasons:

- You can individually optimize each slice.
- You can make slices contain no image. (You can still make the slice match the HTML page's background color and you can enter HTML text and links into non-image slices.)
- Several smaller images may load into most browsers faster than one large image.

The Interface design advantage is that you can assign JavaScript programming routines, called rollovers, to any individual slice. The purpose of rollovers is to make the interface come alive when you move your mouse over to a menu choice.

Technically, an ImageReady-created slice is any rectangular area of an image that the program turns into a cell in HTML code. That HTML code is part of the code ImageReady writes for each image saved for the Web. Anytime you create new slices in the same image, ImageReady rewrites the code to reflect the creation of the new slice or slices.

User Slices and Auto Slices

Any time you create a slice, ImageReady creates extra slices so that the whole image will fit back together. The slice you created is called a *user* slice. User slices are flexible in that they can have more properties assigned to them. The slices the program creates automatically are called *auto* slices. At any time, you can select an auto slice and promote it to a user slice. You can also create a new slice and the program will automatically reassign the slices and renumber them.

Image Slice Options Defined

The Slice palette, especially when expanded by choosing Show Options from the Slice palette menu, offers you the opportunity to choose from many settings. Their purpose and the directions for use follow.

Name and Appearance

ImageReady names slices automatically according to the preferences you set in the dialog box you get to by choosing File, then Preferences, then Slices.

You can change the naming default of DOC.NAME_## by choosing from any of the slice naming menus. You can also simply enter your own specifications in the fields, but remember that you will want SLICE NO. somewhere in the name if you want to be able to tell where the slice belongs in the image and in what order it was created.

You can also choose to show the lines without symbols and can choose the color of the lines. You can also choose whether the numbers and symbols will appear in the upper-right corner of the slice, as well as their opacity and their size.

Finally, you can choose the relative brightness of user slices and auto slices.

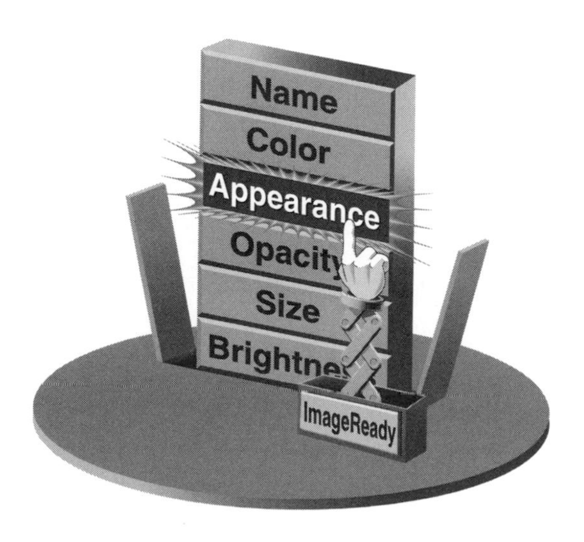

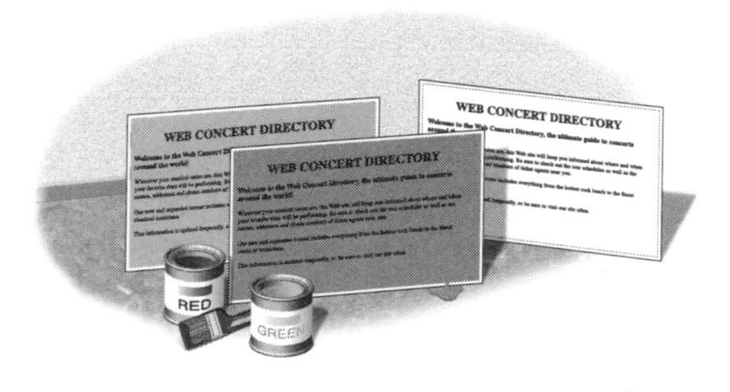

Background Color

When you choose from the Background Color menu, the color does not appear in your image. You will not see it until you preview the image in a browser.

The background color is the color you see in a browser before the other contents of a page have loaded. You can choose to use a different background color for a given slice than that of your Web page. Also, if you have a partly transparent image in your slice, it is this background color that shows through.

To choose a background color, use the menu in the Slices palette and drag to pick one of the choices shown.

- The colors in the swatches palette of the Background Color menu are all Web-safe colors.
- If you choose None, the background color of the target Web page will be used.
- If you choose Matte, you will get the Matte color specified in the Optimize palette.
- Foreground Color and Background Color refer to the colors currently chosen in the Toolbox Swatches.

IMAGE SLICING CONTINUED

URL

You can assign URLs (Uniform Resource Locators) to link the slice to another file. If you have already created URLs for other objects in the current file, they will be listed on the menu. You can choose one of those or you can type in a new link.

Target

This option is grayed unless frames exist in the image's HTML document. Frames are HTML instructions that divide a Web page into windows, each containing different content.

If you enter a frame name, it must match that of an actual frame in the HTML document. Otherwise, you can choose one of the following:

- **_blank:** Shows the linked file in a new browser window without closing the current window.
- **_self:** Places the linked file in the same frame as the original link.
- **_parent:** Puts the linked file into the frameset of the original parent. Of course, the document must contain parent/child frames.
- **_top:** Removes all the current frames and replaces the current browser window's contents.

Message

By default, when an image begins to load in a given location in an HTML page, the browser displays the name of the file that is loading. If you enter anything else in the message field, that will appear instead.

Alt

Lets you enter text that will appear in place of the slice in non-graphical browsers and in place of the image while the image is loading in graphical browsers.

Text

This field is available for non-image slices. Enter text that you would like to have appear as HTML text in the table cell occupied by the non-image slice.

If you understand how to code HTML, you can also enter code here. If you do not, but have a Web authoring program such as Adobe GoLive or Dreamweaver, you could create the content you want, then cut and paste the code into this field.

Linking Slices

If you do not want to optimize every single slice separately, there is salvation. You can link them, then apply the optimization settings to all. Linked slices also share the same color palette and dither pattern — so they will match in appearance.

Auto slices automatically link when you create them. If you manually link an auto slice to a user slice, the auto slice will be automatically promoted to a user slice.

To link slices, select them with the Slice Select tool. Shift+click to select multiple slices or drag a marquee to surround several. Next, choose Slices, then Link Slices. Unlinking slices is just a matter of selecting the slices to be unlinked and choosing Slices, then Unlink Slices. If you want to Unlink a set or sets of slices (those that were linked at the same time), you can simply choose one slice in the set and choose Slices, then Unlink Set(s). To make sure that no slices are linked, choose Slices, then Unlink All.

Changing the Appearance of Slices

ImageReady employs several visual devices to help you identify and manage slices, including colored slice lines, contrast and brightness, and name and type symbols.

To turn off all characteristics except the slice lines, choose Edit, then Preferences, then Slices and check Show Lines Only. To Change the color of lines, choose Edit, then Preferences, then Slices and choose a color from the Line Color menu. To change the contrast and brightness of user and autoslices, choose File, then Preferences, then Slices and pick a percentage from the appropriate Color Adjustments menu. To show/hide slices, click the Show Slices or Hide Slices buttons in the Toolbox.

THE PHOTOSHOP AND IMAGEREADY TOOLBOXES

Both Photoshop 6 and ImageReady 3.0 (included with Photoshop) feature a handy (and redesigned) Toolbox. This Toolbox is the repository of all the tools that are applied to specific parts of the image by moving the cursor over that part of the image.

The Photoshop Toolbox

The Photoshop Toolbox includes all the Marquee selection tools, brushes, darkroom tools (for such things as sharpening, blurring, burning, and dodging), the text tools, annotation tools, drawing tools, and zooming tools. At the bottom of the Toolbox are the color swatches, editing mode buttons, and viewing mode buttons. The toolboxes also have buttons that take you to Adobe online or let you work in ImageReady using the file on which you are currently working.

You can initiate most of the Toolbox tools by pressing a single letter key; no modifier key, such as Ctrl or ⌘, is needed. If a slot has more than one tool (often the case), pressing the letter key will rotate you through all the tools in that slot.

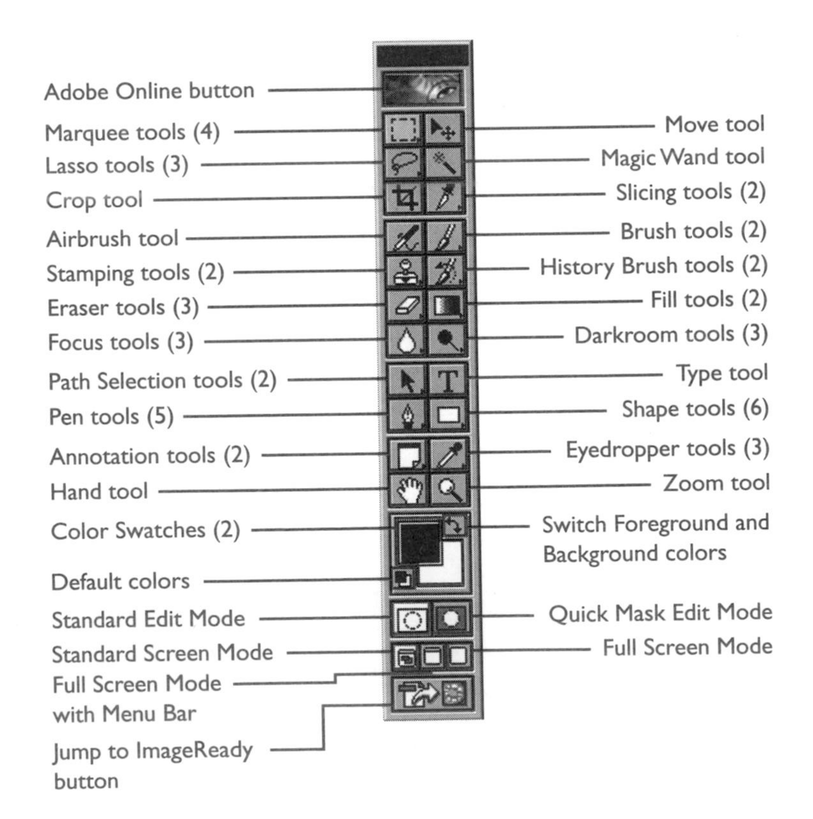

The Photoshop Toolbox Tools

Group	Tool	Keyboard Shortcut	What It Does
Adobe Online button			Takes you directly to the Adobe site, provided you are online when you click the button.
Marquee tools			Click and hold the mouse button (left, in Windows) to see a menu showing each of the following four tools:
	Rectangular Marquee tool		Click and drag diagonally to indicate the location of the upper-right and lower-left corners of a rectangular selection marquee. To restrict the marquee to a square, press Shift while dragging.
	Elliptical Marquee tool		Click and drag diagonally to indicate the location of the upper-right and lower-left corners of a elliptical (oval-shaped) selection marquee. To restrict the marquee to a circle, press Shift while dragging.
	Single Row Marquee tool		Makes a selection marquee one pixel wide across the entire horizontal width of the image.
	Single Column Marquee tool		Makes a selection marquee one pixel wide across the entire vertical height of the image.
Lasso tools		L	Click and hold the mouse button (left, in Windows) to see a menu showing the following three tools:
	Lasso tool		This is the tool for making freehand selections. Drag to outline the shape you want to select.
	Polygonal Lasso tool		Makes freehand selections composed of a series of connected straight lines. Click each point where you want a straight line to end or drag to stretch and position the straight line. Very useful for selecting straight edges.
	Magnetic Lasso tool		Automatically selects the highest point of contrast between adjacent pixels within a given number of pixels on either side of the cursor. You set this range in the Options bar.
Crop tool		C	To indicate a rectangular area to crop, drag diagonally from the upper-left corner of the rectangle to the lower-left corner. You can then adjust the exact size of the cropping marquee by dragging one of the small square "handles" found in each corner and at the mid-point of each side of the marquee. The area that will be trimmed away is automatically darkened so that it becomes much easier to see. Press Enter or click the Commit button in the Options bar to execute the crop.

Continued

The Photoshop Toolbox Tools (Continued)

Group	Tool	Keyboard Shortcut	What It Does
Airbrush tool		J	Creates a softer edge stroke that builds in intensity the longer you keep the brush pointer in the same place while the mouse button is depressed.
Stamping tools		S	Click and hold the mouse button to see a menu showing each of the following two tools:
	Clone Stamp tool		Picks up parts of the image in one area and paints a duplicate in another area. You can also uncheck the Aligned box in the Options bar to make each stroke start from a new point but at a consistent angle and distance from the brush. Unaligned cloning is a good way to move the color and texture from one area into another area — especially if you keep resetting the pickup point. To set the Clone Stamp's pickup point, press Alt+Click.
	Pattern Stamp tool		The Pattern Stamp tool paints with the currently defined pattern. To define a pattern, make a rectangular selection and choose Edit, then Define Pattern.
Eraser tools		E	Click and hold the mouse button to see a menu showing each of the following three tools:
	Eraser tool		Either replaces whatever colors are in the image with the background color or with transparency (if the Lock transparency box is checked for the current layer). You cannot erase the Background Layer to transparency unless you rename it as a layer.
	Background Eraser tool		Lets you erase pixels sampled within a radius and brightness range (set in the Options bar). This tool is especially useful for cleaning up stray edge pixels leftover from an Image Extract command or after extracting a shape using a selection marquee.
	Magic Eraser tool		Works a bit like the Magic Wand tool, but instead of just selecting pixels within the specified range of the pixel you click on, the Magic Eraser erases them.
Focus tools		R	Click and hold the mouse button to see a menu showing each of the following three tools:
	Blur tool		Intermingles the pixels within the radius of the brush, causing them to bleed into one another — much like pouring water on a watercolor painting. You can control the amount of blurring by the number of new strokes you apply to the same area.

Group	Tool	Keyboard Shortcut	What It Does
Focus tools *(continued)*			
	Sharpen tool		Has the same effect as the simple Sharpen filter, but the Sharpen tool is restricted to the area within the radius of the brush. You can control the amount of sharpening by the number of new strokes you apply to the same area.
	Smudge tool		Picks up the color found under your current brush shape and pulls it along as you drag, mixing colors in the process. Think of it as digital finger painting. Using a bigger brush means you are using a bigger finger (or your fist, maybe).
Path Selection		A	Click and hold the mouse button to see a menu showing each of the following two Path Selection tools.
	Path Component Selection tool		Selects an entire path component so that you can do such whole-path edits as moving or transforming.
	Direct Selection tool		This tool (white arrow) is used to select individual control points and their handles so that you can change the shape and size of the curves that approach and leave the control point.
Pen tools		P	Click and hold the mouse button to see a menu showing each of the following five tools:
	Pen tool		Draws the lines and curves that make up a vector path — one line at a time between control points. If you click and drag, the control point handles extend to indicate the direction and severity of the curve that will be drawn between the current control point and the next control point (which is instantly created the next time you click or click and drag). In order to close the path to complete a shape, you must place the last control point immediately atop the first control point.
	Freeform Pen tool		Acts just like the Lasso tool — except that the Freeform Pen creates a path instead of a selection. Control points are added automatically, according to the frequency you set in the Curve Fit field in the Options bar.
	Add Point tool		Adds a point at the exact spot where you click an existing path.

Continued

The Photoshop Toolbox Tools (Continued)

Group	Tool	Keyboard Shortcut	What It Does
Pen tools (continued)			
	Delete Point tool		Removes existing point when you click on it.
	Convert Point tool		Converts the existing point you click to its opposite number. In other words, if the current control point is a curve, the point is converted to a corner (the path approaches it in a straight line). Also, you can use the Convert Point tool to drag control handles asymmetrically. That is, each point can be placed where you would like without affecting its opposite number. This allows you to create curves that approach the control point at a steeper angle on one side of the control point than on the other.
Annotation tools		N	Click and hold the mouse button to see a menu showing the following two tools:
	Notes tool		Lets you add typed comments to an image. You can assign an author name to any comment, so if the file is passed around in a workgroup, you know who made which comments. As soon as you choose the Notes tool and click in the image, a small window appears and you can begin typing. When you click the close box, a small note icon appears at the point where you clicked. You can choose View, then Show, then Annotations to toggle the visibility of these icons.
	Audio Annotation tool		If you have a sound card and microphone attached to your system, this tool allows you to simply speak your annotations.
Hand tool		H	Allows you to pan and scroll an image that is larger than your current workspace window. The Hand tool is extremely useful when you have zoomed in so that you can work accurately on small details.
Color Swatches			These are the Set Foreground Color (top) and Set Background Color (behind) icons. You change these colors in either of two ways: by clicking the swatch you want to change to bring up a Color Picker dialog box or by choosing any color in the Swatches palette.

Group	Tool	Keyboard Shortcut	What It Does
Default colors			Clicking this miniature Color Swatches icon instantly changes the Foreground Color to black and the Background Color to white, the Photoshop default colors.
Standard Edit			Places Photoshop in the Standard Edit Mode in which no mask is shown when making selections.
Standard Screen			Leaves the Toolbox, Options bars, and Palettes Mode visible — except for those that you have hidden.
Full Screen Mode with Menu Bar			All the palletes, Options bars, and the Toolbox disappear, but the menu bar stays in place so that you can choose commands without having to go back to Standard Screen Mode.
Jump to ImageReady button			Opens ImageReady 3.0. If you have a file open in Photoshop, the file also opens in ImageReady.
Move tool		V	Allows you to drag the contents of any layer to any position you like. Any portion of the layer outside the boundaries of the current workspace will remain recorded in the file as long as the layers are not flattened.
Magic Wand tool		W	Allows you to select any areas of a similar color at a single click. You use the Options bar to set the desired similarity of colors to be chosen and whether all the chosen pixels must touch one another (be contiguous).
Slicing tools		K	Click and hold the mouse button to see a menu showing the following two tools:
	Slice tool		Used to sub divide an image into different files, each numbered so that a viewer's browser knows to reassemble the images as a seamless whole. All you need do to designate a slice is drag a rectangular marquee after choosing the Slice tool. Photoshop automatically subdivides the image into as many other images as needed to complete the whole.
	Slice Select tool		Highlights a specific slice (or slices) so that it can be deleted, moved, resized or converted between User and Auto slice.

Continued

The Photoshop Toolbox Tools (Continued)

Group	Tool	Keyboard Shortcut	What It Does
Brush tools		B	Click and hold the mouse button to see a menu showing the following two tools, both of which can be used to paint the foreground color onto the image's active layer:
	Paintbrush		Paints with an anti-aliased edge that, regardless of the "hardness" of the brush chosen from the Brushes library, is still not as "soft" as if the Airbrush had been used instead. The Paintbrush also gives you the option of painting with "Wet Edges," which make the edges of the stroke darker than its median.
	Pencil		Paints with absolutely hard edges (that is, no aliasing). Using this brush when doing pixel-by-pixel retouching is necessary.
History Brush tools		Y	These tools are used to allow to replace whatever is under the brush with whatever that image contained at another stage of is history (as well as content from other images). Click and hold the left mouse button to see a menu showing these two tools:
	History brush		Works like the Clone Stamp, in that it simply takes the pixels that would be under the brush in one version of the image to replace those that are under the brush in the currently chosen layer of the current version of that image.
	Art History brush		Also uses information stored (as a snapshot or state in the History palette) to replace pixels in the current version of that image. However, Photoshop simultaneously reinterprets the original pixel size, layout, and blending according to any of ten preset styles that can be chosen from a menu in the Options bar.
Fill tools		G	Click and hold the mouse button to see a menu showing these two tools:
	Gradient tool		Fills the current selection (or layer, if there is no selection) with the gradient currently chosen in the Gradients library.
	Paint Bucket tool		Fills the current selection (or layer, if there is no selection) with the current foreground color. You can also fill with a pattern.

Group	*Tool*	*Keyboard Shortcut*	*What It Does*
Darkroom tools		O	Changes the tonal values under the portion of the image under the currently chosen brush. The amount of change is cumulative as you continue to make new strokes over the same area. Click and hold the mouse button to see a menu showing the following three Darkroom tools:
	Dodge tool		Lightens the area under the brush by the percentage specified in the Options bar.
	Burn tool		Darkens the area under the brush by the percentage specified in the Options bar.
	Sponge tool		Heightens or removes color saturation (intensity) in the area under the brush by the percentage specified in the Options bar.
Type tool	T		Creates either horizontal or vertical type — either as a single line or as a paragraph. Photoshop 6, unlike previous versions, has only one Text tool, and all the variations can be controlled from the Options bar. Photoshop 6 automatically creates type on its own layer and preserves the vector outlines of the type so that it (or the overall image) can be rescaled. When an image is rescaled, the vector outlines are used to re-render the type into pixels. Thus, even though the type is rasterized into the image, edge sharpness is always as good as possible, given the resolution of the final image.
Shape tools		U	Draws preselected geometric shapes using vectors. There are six of these tools. Five are built-in, predefined shapes. The sixth allows you to use any shape you have created using the path tools or imported from another compatible illustration, CAD, or drawing program. The six Shape tools — which you can access by clicking and holding the left mouse button — are the following:
	Rectangle		Draws a rectangle or (by pressing the Shift key while dragging) square when you click and drag.
	Rounded Rectangle		Draws a rectangle with user-definable rounded corners or (by pressing the Shift key while dragging) a square when you click and drag.

Continued

The Photoshop Toolbox Tools (Continued)

Group	*Tool*	*Keyboard Shortcut*	*What It Does*
Shape tools *(continued)*			
	Ellipse		Draws an oval or (by pressing the Shift key while dragging) circle when you click and drag.
	Polygon		Draws a regular (uniform) straight-edged geometric shape. The number of sides can be any number between 3 and 100 you enter in the Options bar's Sides field.
	Line		Draws a single straight line of any length you choose.
	Custom Shape		Draws any shape that you have saved from the Paths palette as a custom shape. To save a custom shape, select the shape's name bar in the Paths palette. Next, choose Edit, then Define Custom Shape. When the Shape Name dialog box appears, enter a name for the shape and click OK.
Eyedropper tools		I	Pick up information about pixels within a given radius of the cursor and then enter that information as either the foreground color or as a measurement in the Info palette. The three eyedropper tools are
	Eyedropper tool		Simply picks up the color or colors immediately under the cursor. If you choose to sample a single pixel, that pixel's color becomes the foreground color. If you choose to sample over a multipixel radius, the colors are averaged and that average becomes the foreground color.
	Color Sampler tool		Works the same way as the Eyedropper tool, except that it allows you to place the color information from as many as four different points into the Info palette.
	Measure tool		Lets you measure the length and angle of a line between any two points using the units currently chosen in the Preferences settings.
Zoom tool		Z	Magnifies or reduces your current view of the image. By default, you magnify when you click or drag. To reduce the viewing size of the image, press Alt while you click or drag.
Switch Foreground and Background Colors		X	Switches the colors in the foreground and background.
Quick Mask Edit Mode		Q	Click to edit any selection as a mask. This allows you to edit the selection with any of the Photoshop 6 tools and commands.
Full Screen Mode		F	Hides the Menu bar as well as the Toolbox and all palettes, so that all you see is the image itself.

The ImageReady Toolbox

The following table covers only those Toolbox tools unique to ImageReady 3.0. For information about tools shared with Photoshop, see "The Photoshop Toolbox," earlier in this appendix.

The ImageReady Toolbox works much like the Photoshop Toolbox, except that the IR Toolbox contains a few different tools and leaves out a few others.

To use the missing tools, just click the Jump To button at the bottom of the Toolbox and do the operation in Photoshop. The missing tools are

- Magnetic Lasso
- Pattern Stamp
- All the Pen and Path tools
- The Custom Shape tool
- The Background Eraser
- The Annotations tools
- The Gradient Fill tool

Of course you can use any of the tools that are unique to ImageReady when you are working in Photoshop by jumping to ImageReady. The unique tools are

- Rounded Rectangle Marquee
- Vertical Text tool (found in Photoshop 5.5, but appearing in the Options bar in Photoshop 6 instead of as a separate tool)

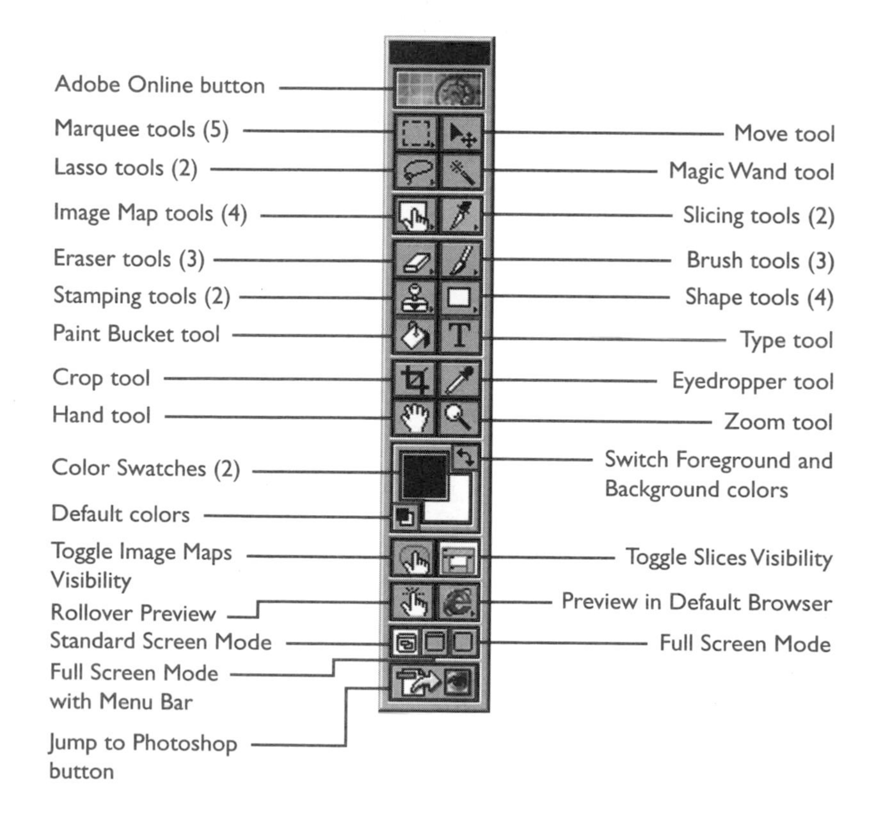

THE TOOL OPTIONS BARS

In Photoshop 6, there are no longer Options palettes for each tool. Instead, each tool has its own Options bar. By default, this bar appears at the top of the workspace at the instant when you choose a particular tool.

Marquee Tool Options

These tools make rectangular or columnar (one row of pixels) selections and Elliptical Marquees.

Rectangular Marquee Tool

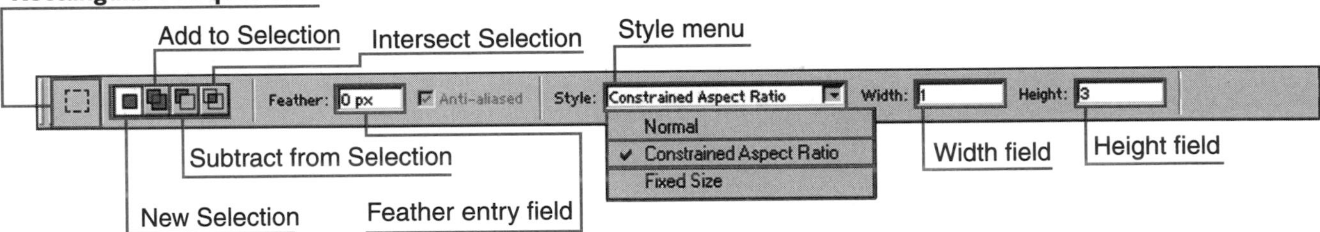

Elliptical Marquee Tool

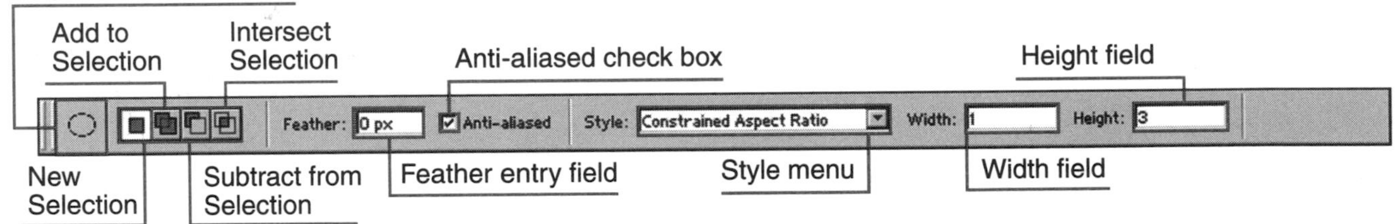

Single Row and Single Column Marquees

These make a selection exactly one pixel wide that runs the full width or height of the image. They are useful for making edge-to-edge straight line strokes.

Single Row Marquee

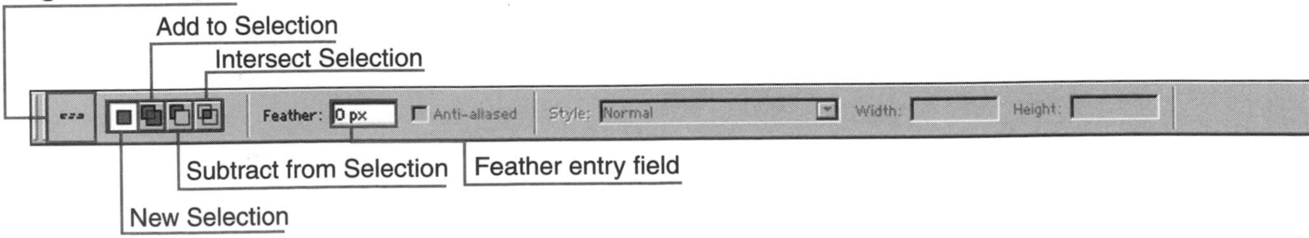

Single Column Marquee

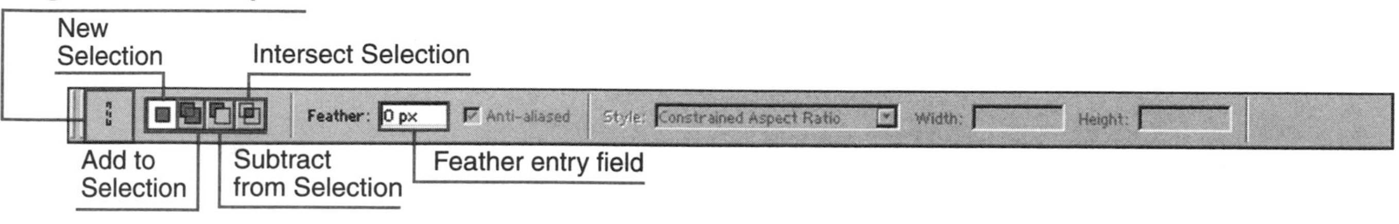

Move Tool Options

Move Tool

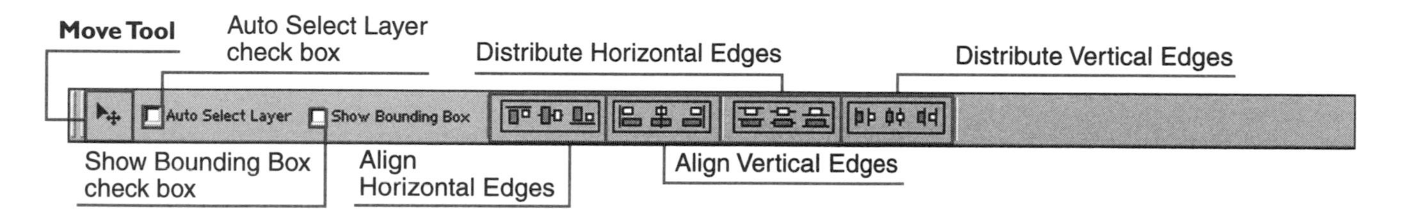

Lasso Tool Options

Lasso Tool

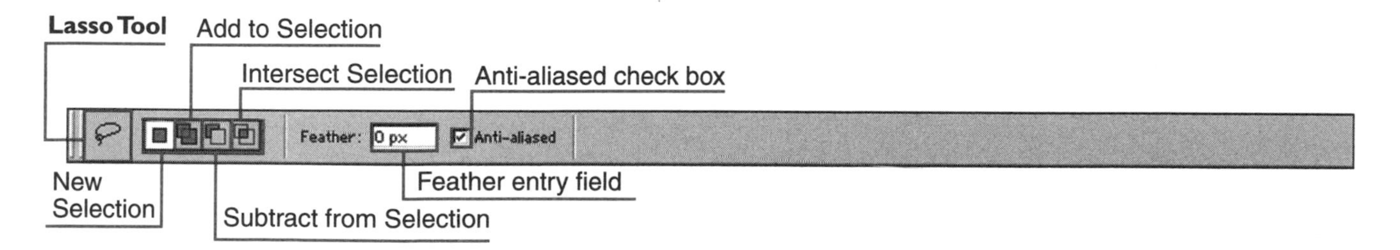

Polygon Lasso Tool

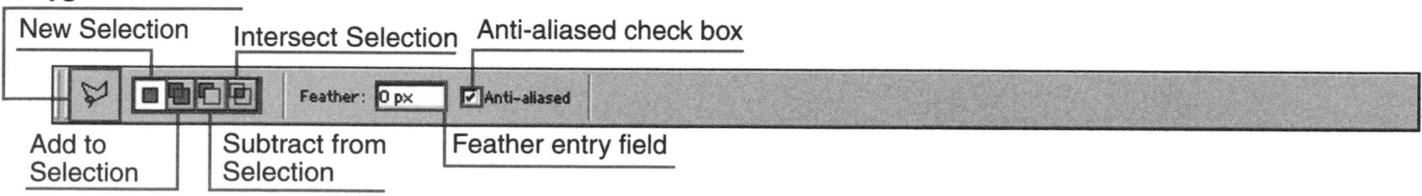

Magnetic Lasso Tool

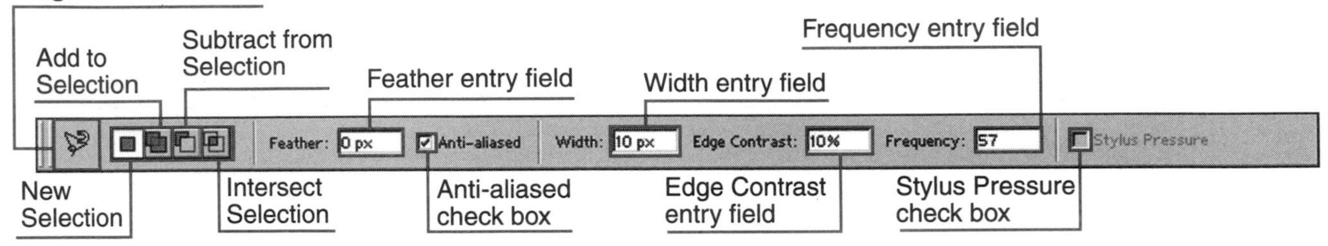

Magic Wand Tool Options

Magic Wand Tool

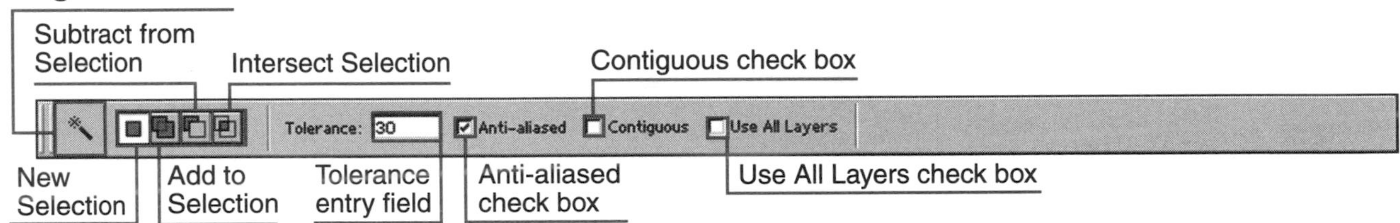

Crop Tool Options

Crop Tool

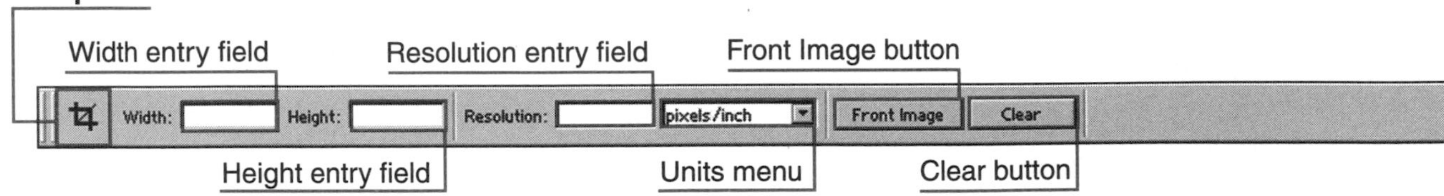

Crop Tool with Area Selected

These options appear after you drag the Crop tool to indicate the area to be cropped. Note that the location of the cancel and commit buttons is reversed on a Mac.

Crop Tool

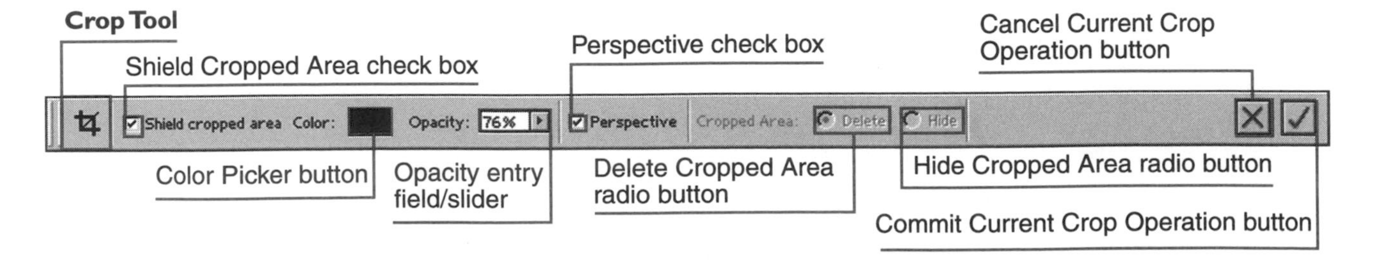

Slice Tool Options

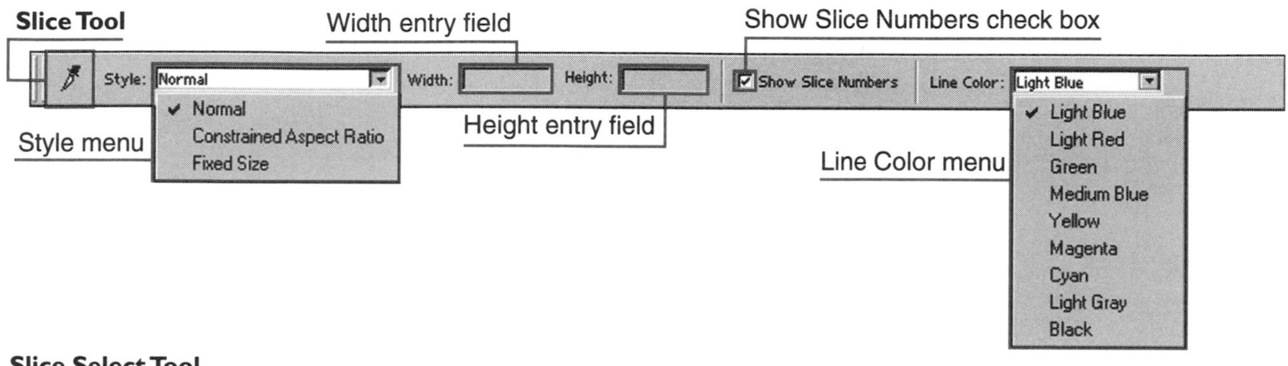

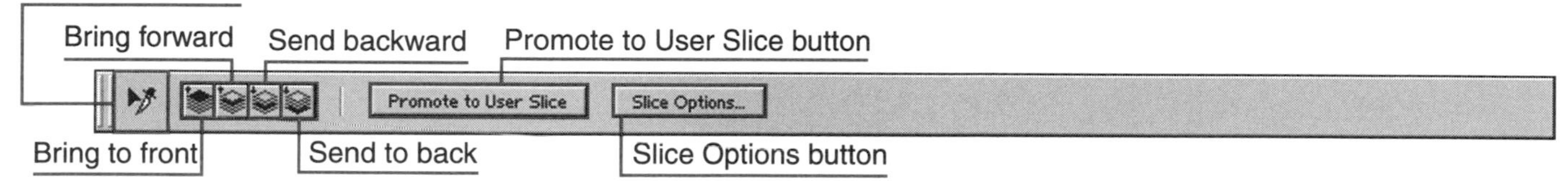

Airbrush Tool Options

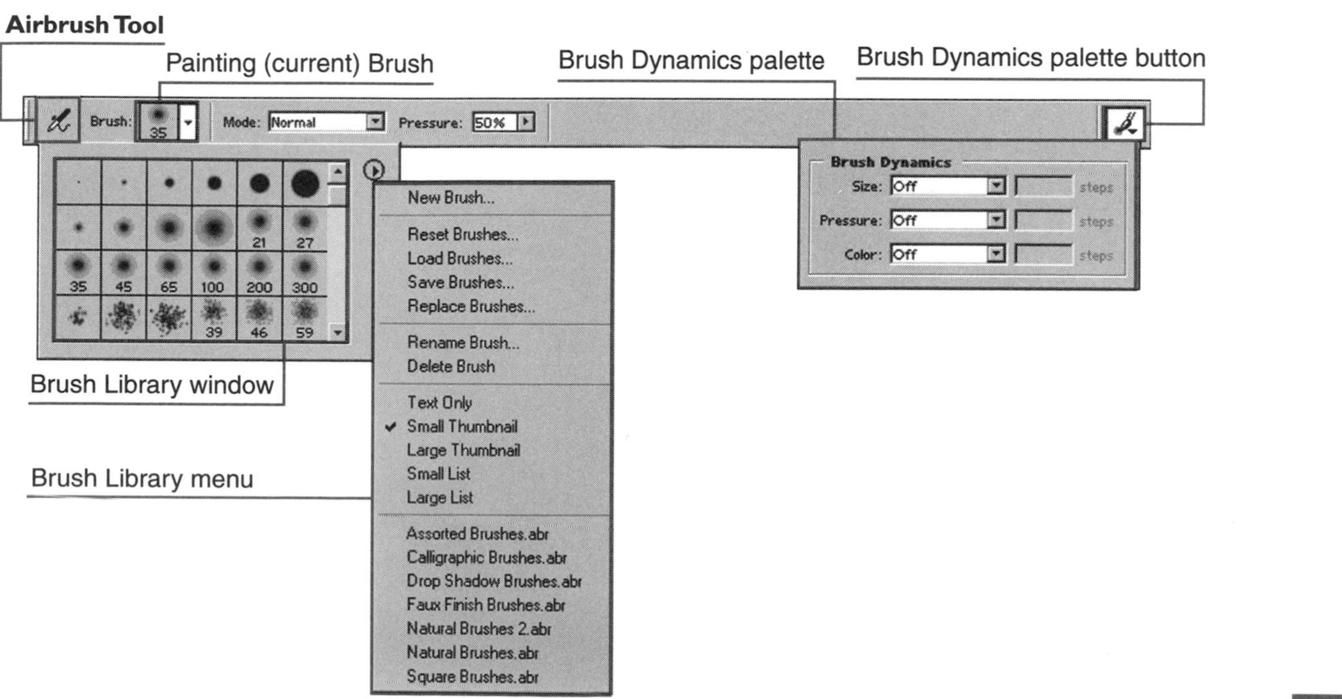

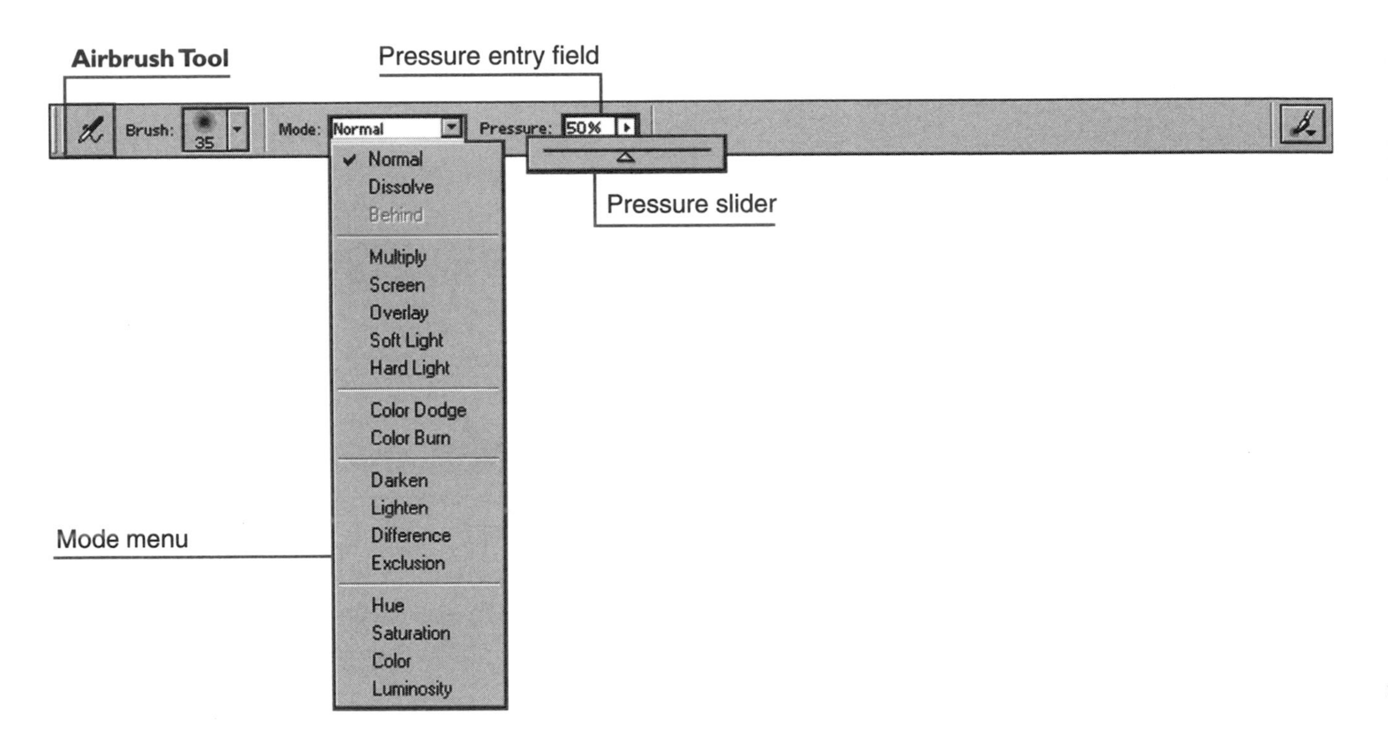

Brush Tool Options

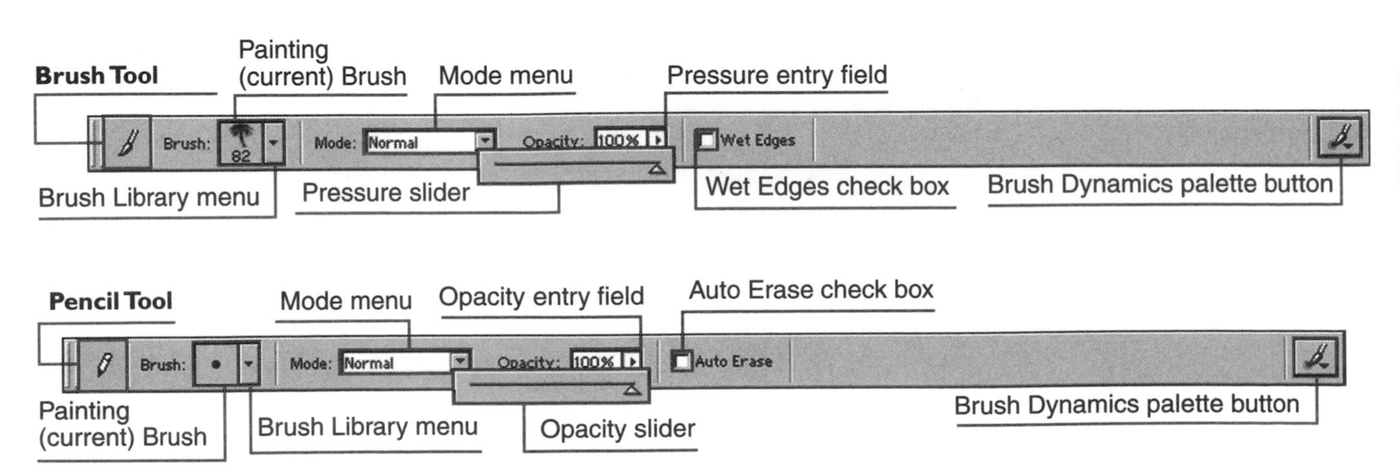

Stamping Tool Options

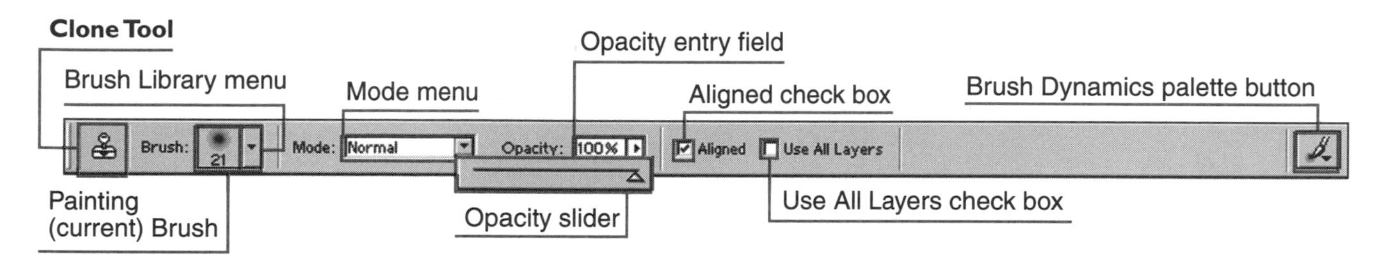

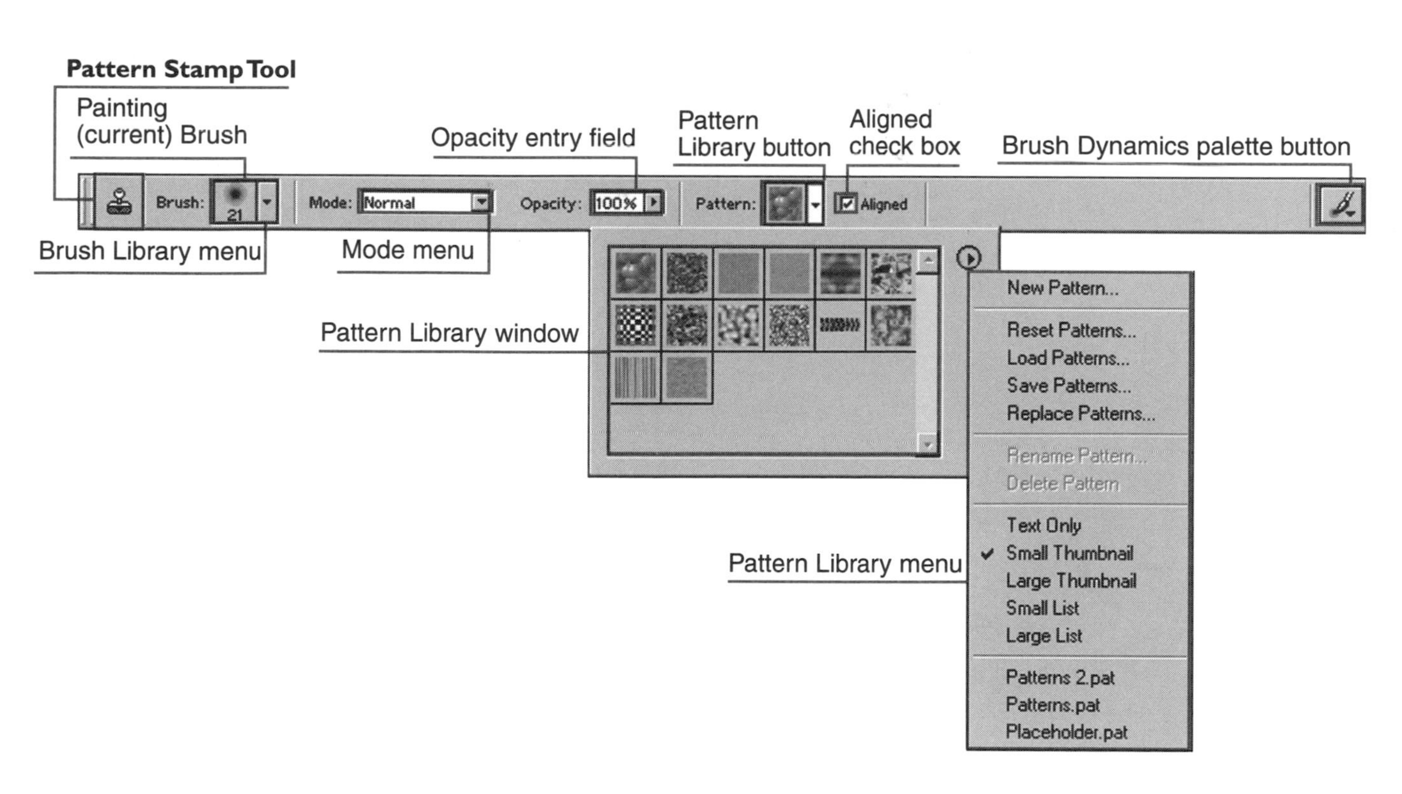

History Brush Tool Options

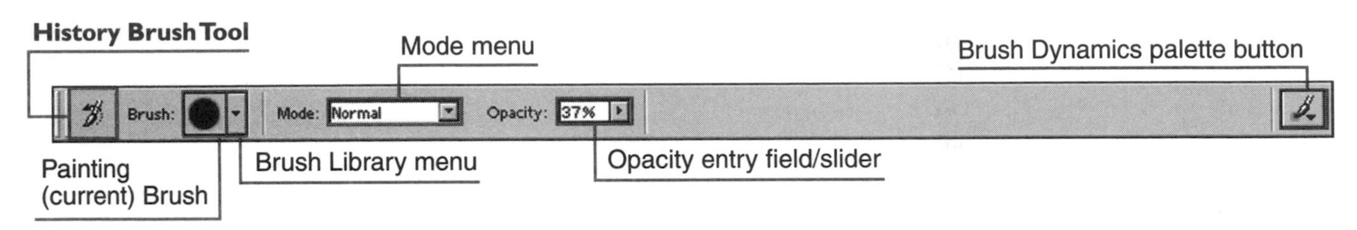

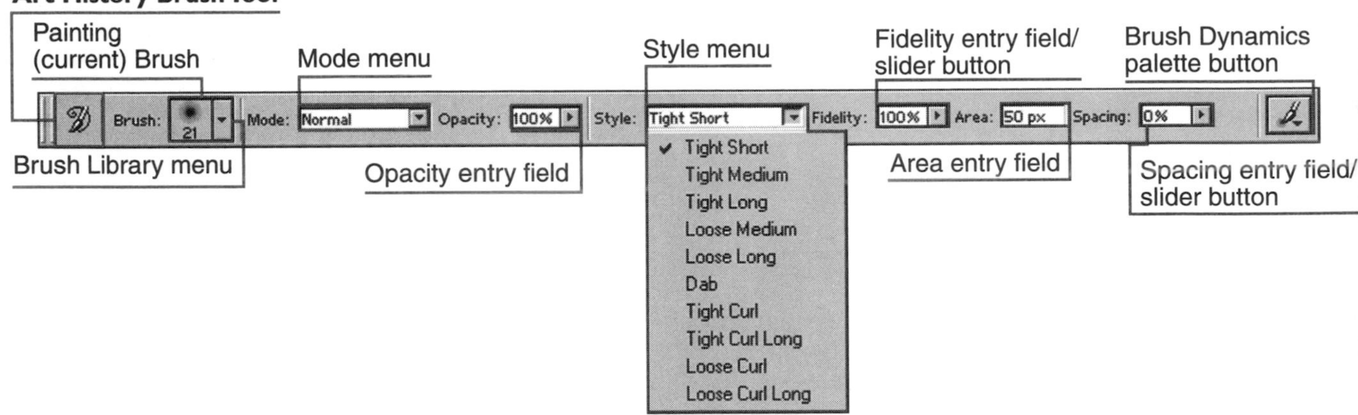

Eraser Tool Options

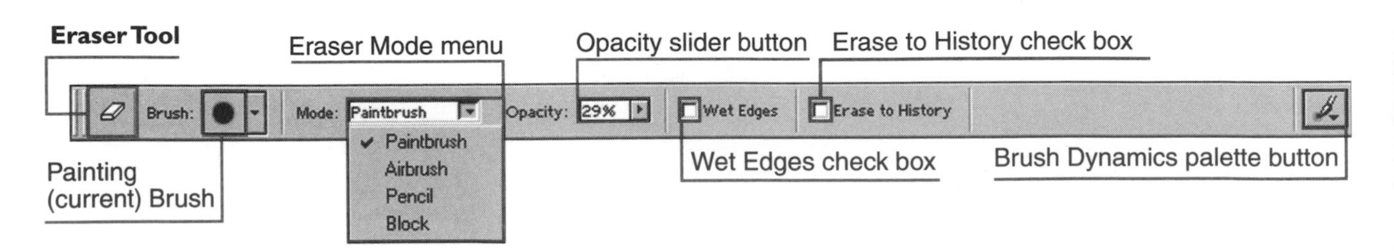

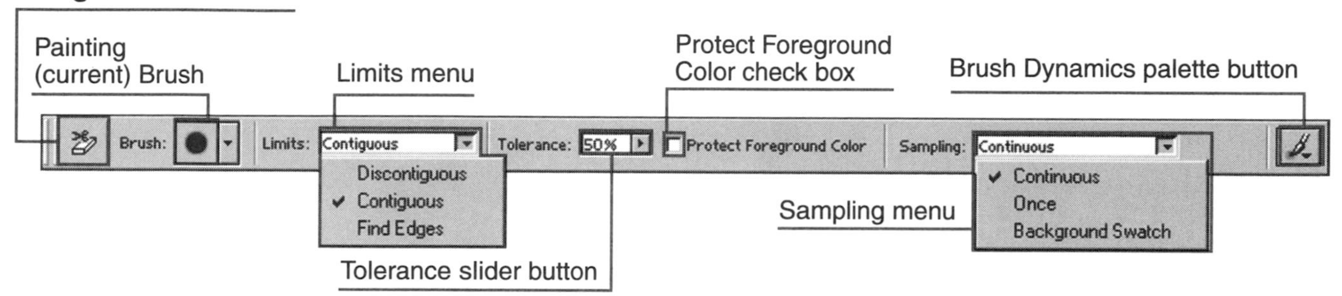

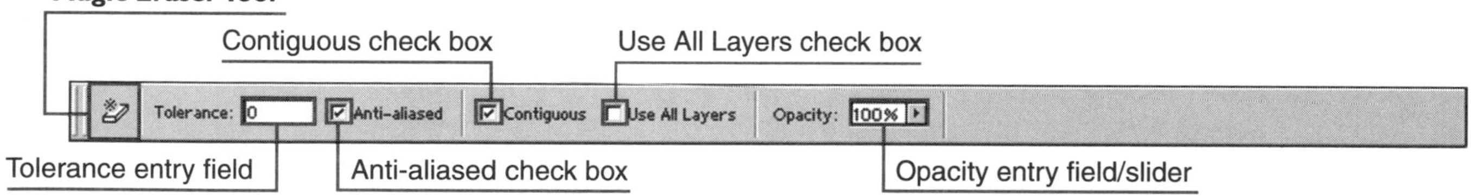

Fill Tool Options

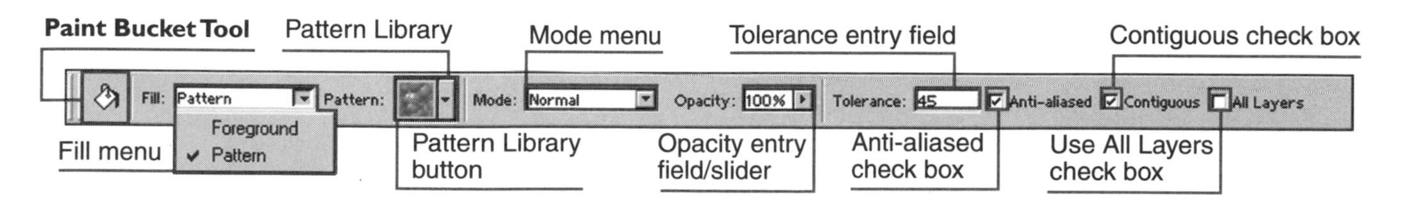

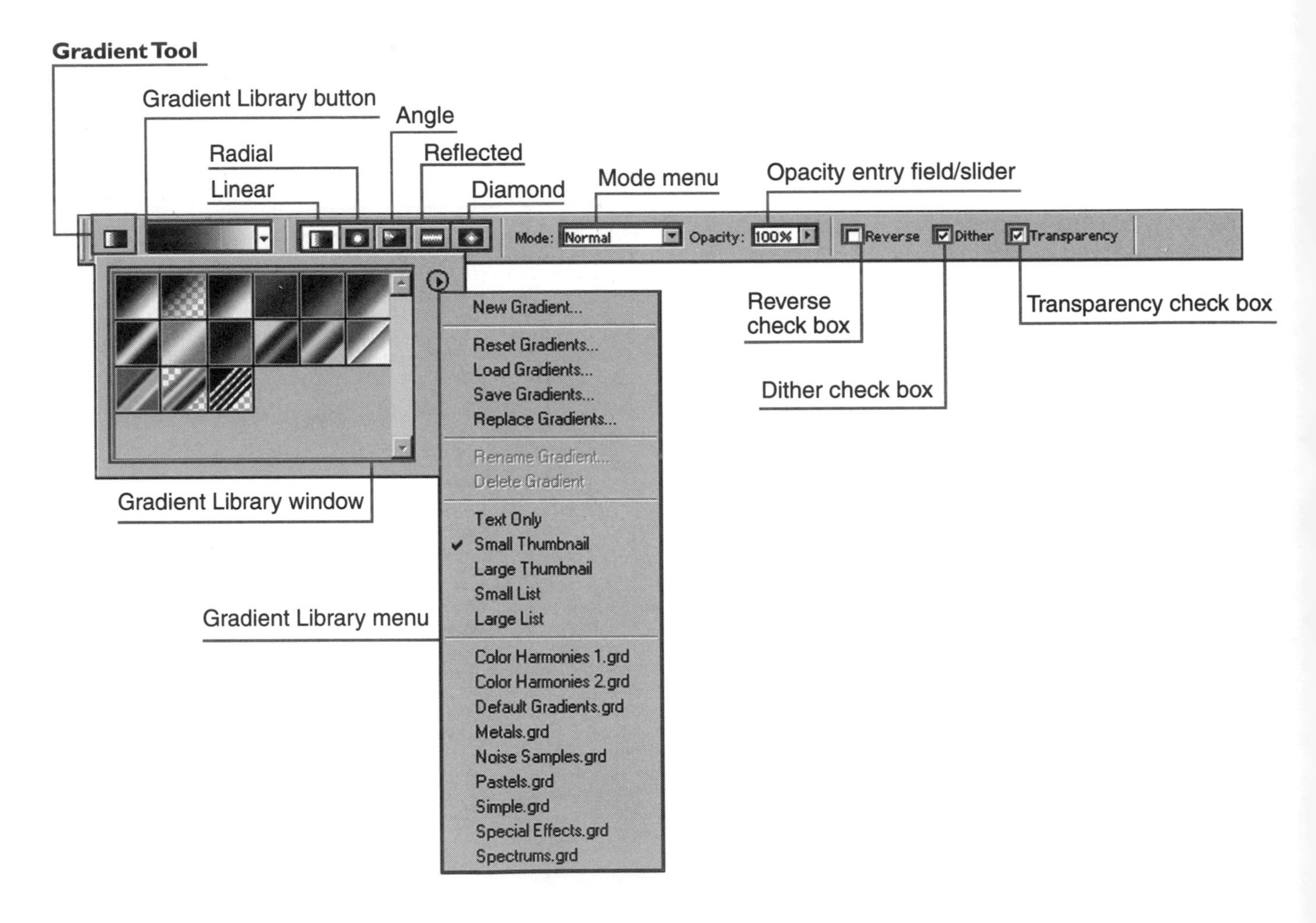

Focus Tool Options

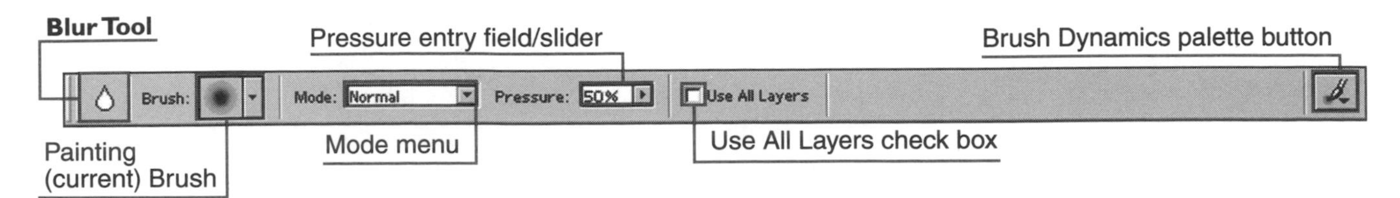

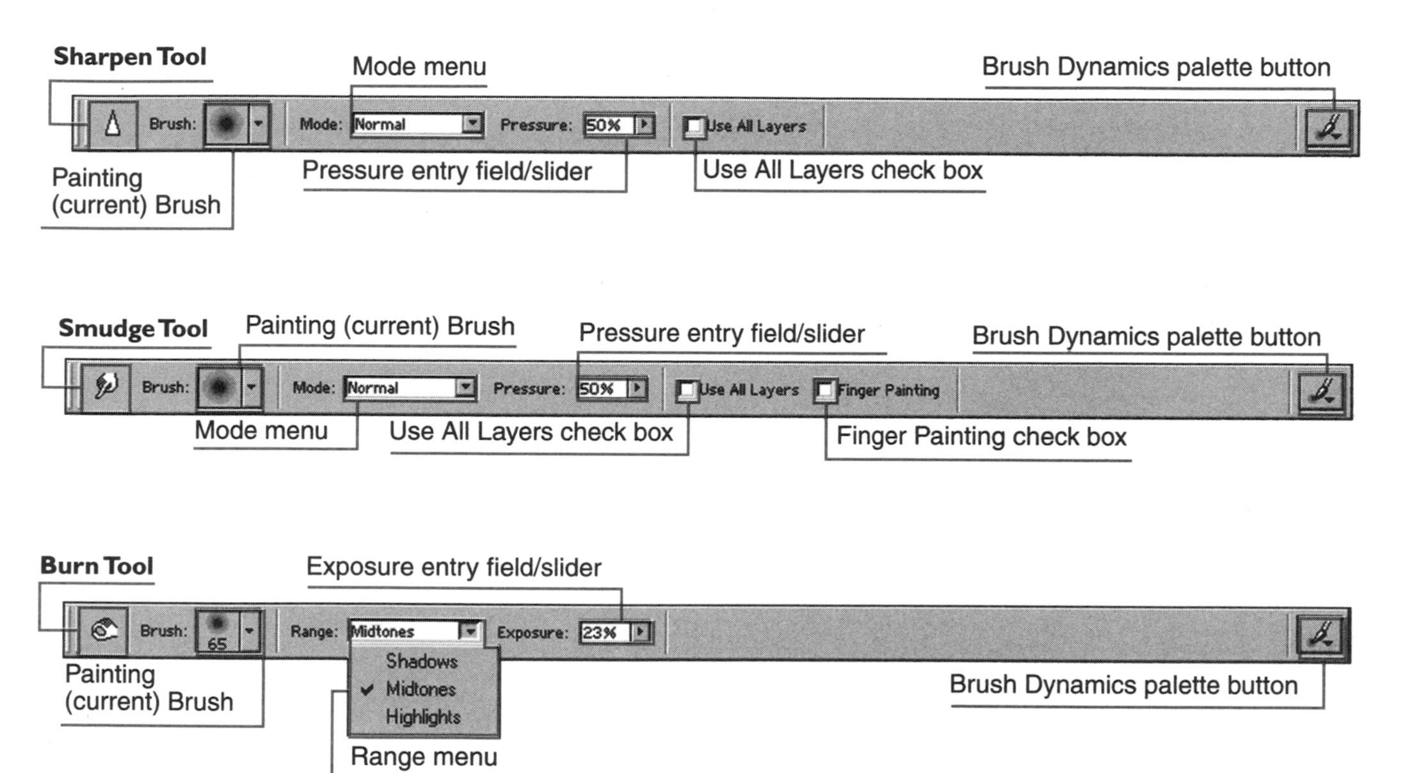

Darkroom Tool Options

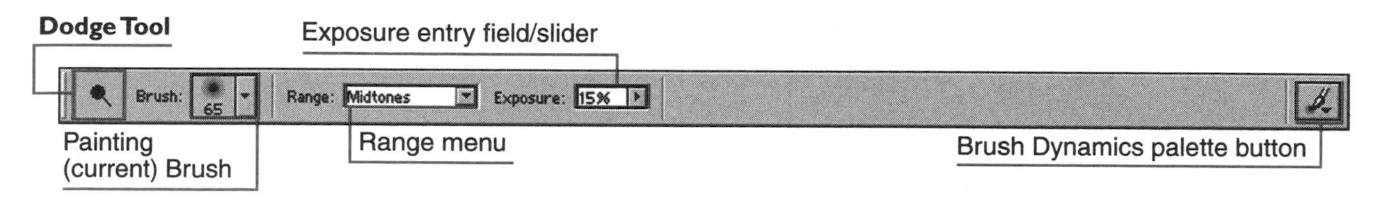

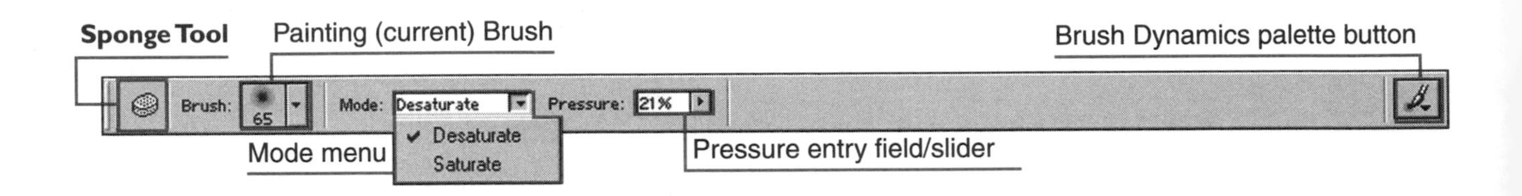

Path Selection Tool Options

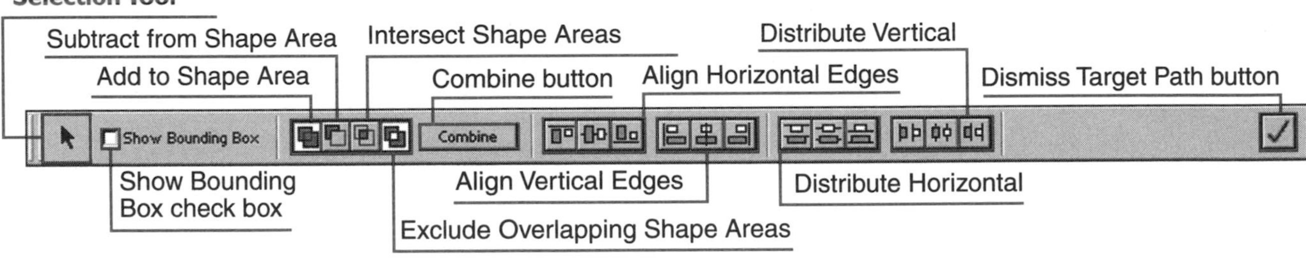

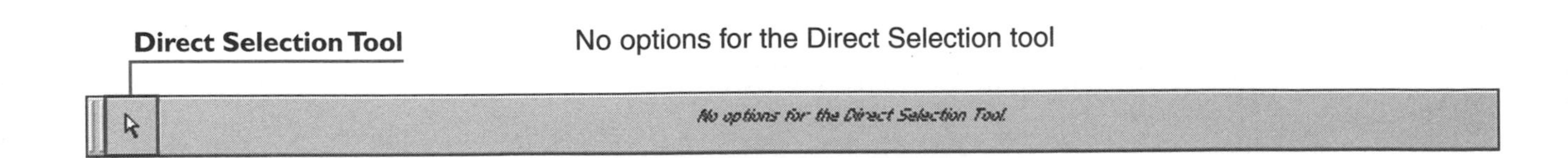

Type Tool Options

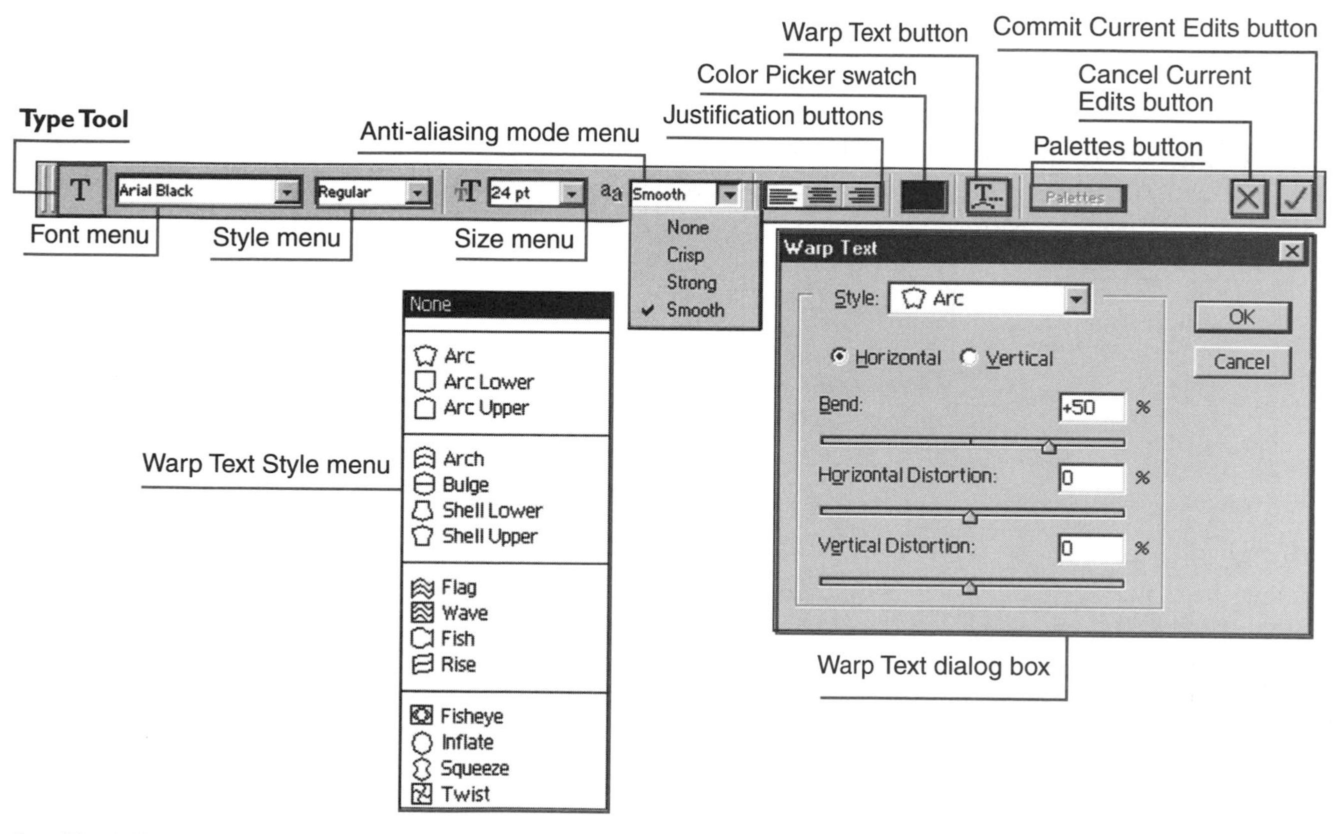

Pen Tool Options

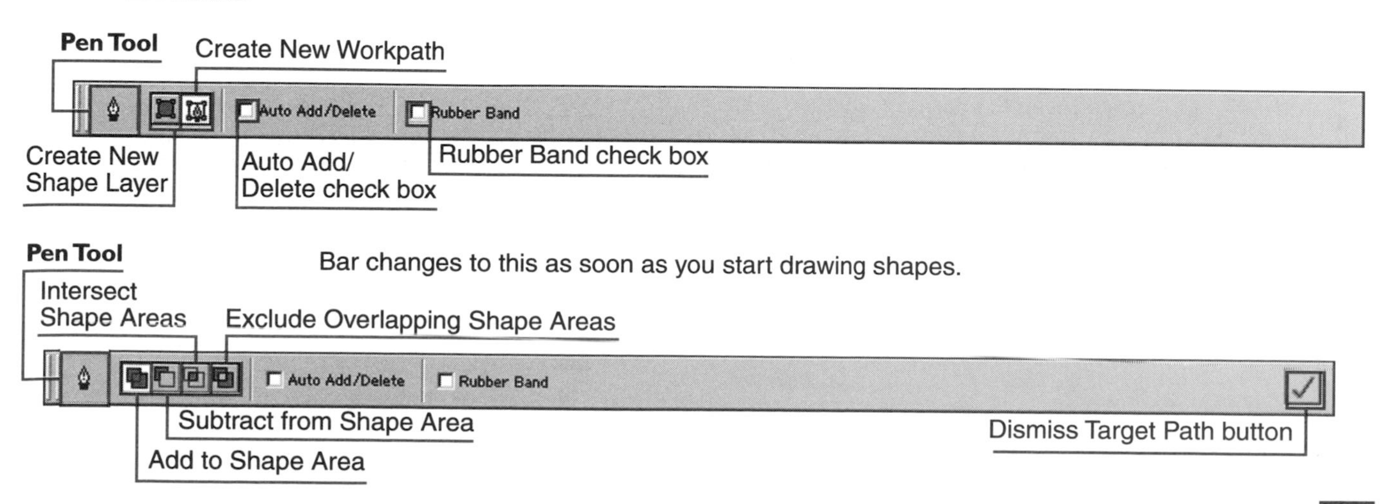

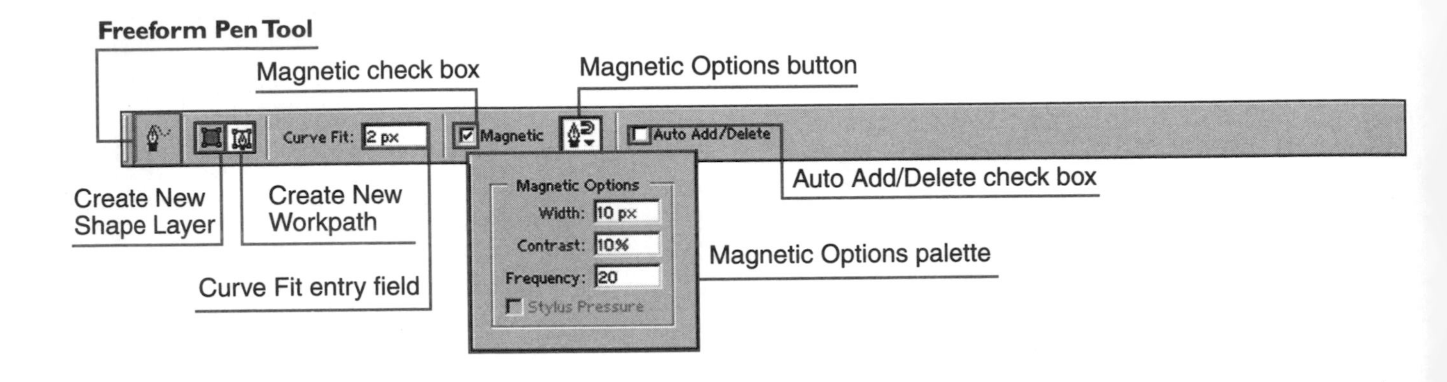

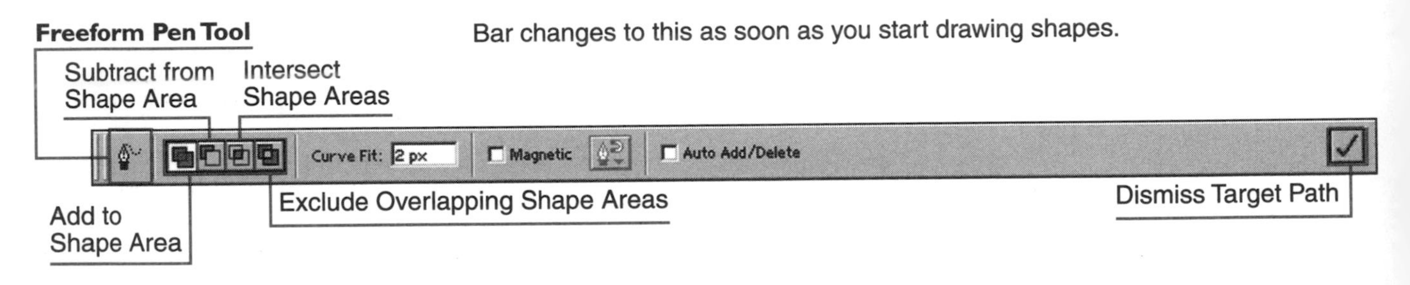

Shape Tool Options

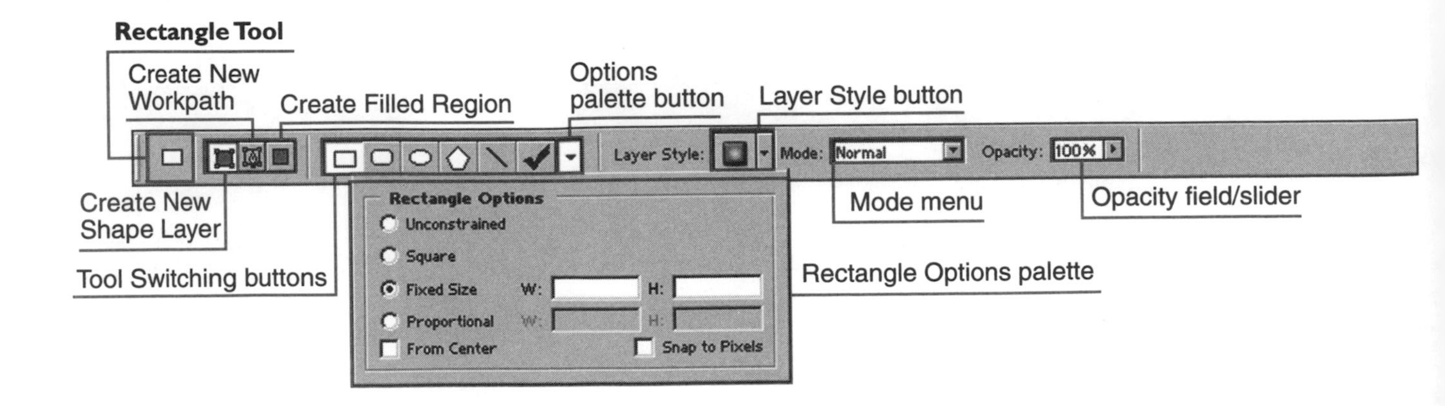

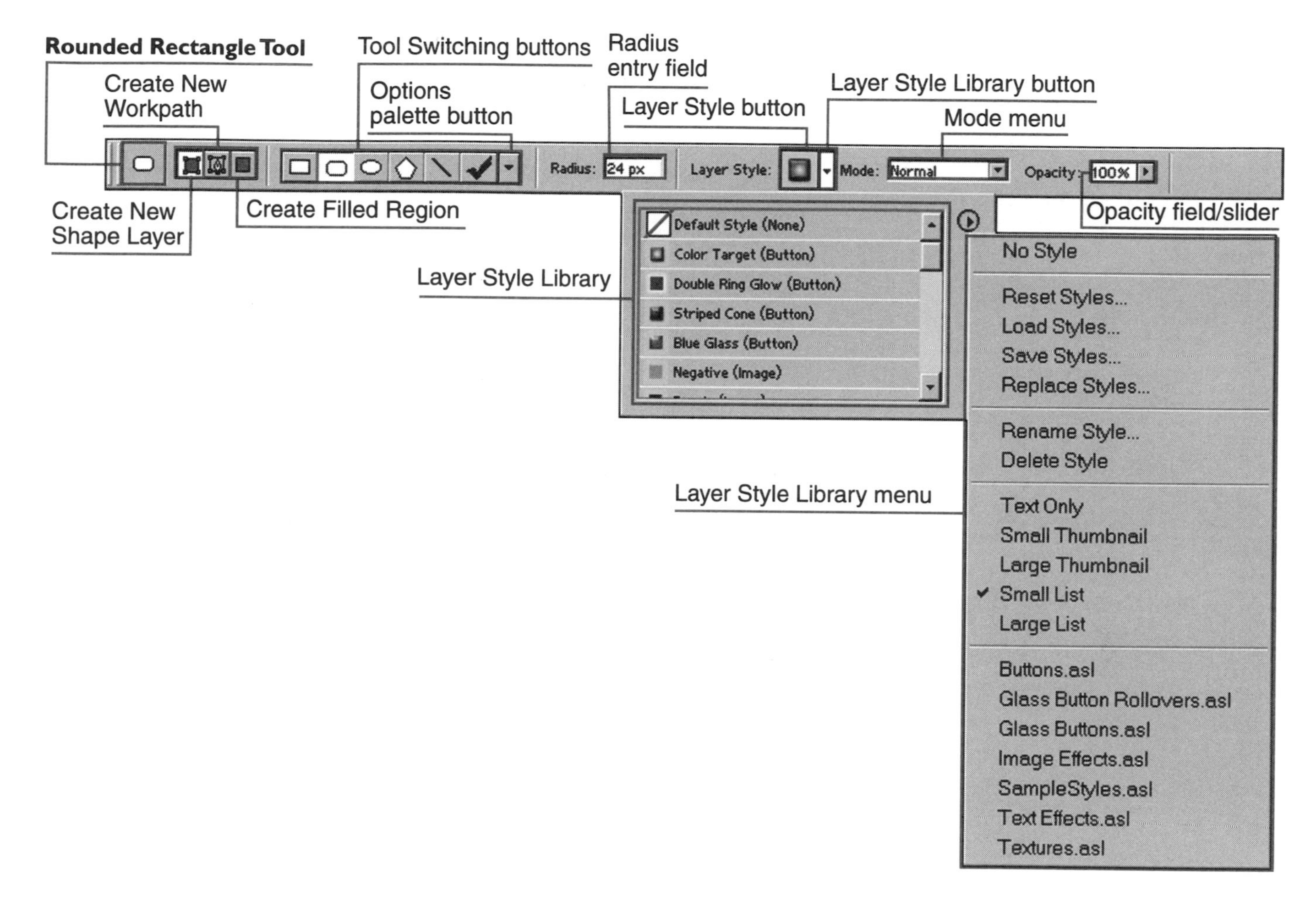
Rounded Rectangle Tool
Tool Switching buttons
Radius entry field
Create New Workpath
Options palette button
Layer Style button
Layer Style Library button
Mode menu
Radius: 24 px
Layer Style:
Mode: Normal
Opacity: 100%
Create New Shape Layer
Create Filled Region
Opacity field/slider
Default Style (None)
Color Target (Button)
Double Ring Glow (Button)
Striped Cone (Button)
Blue Glass (Button)
Negative (Image)
Layer Style Library
No Style
Reset Styles...
Load Styles...
Save Styles...
Replace Styles...
Rename Style...
Delete Style
Layer Style Library menu
Text Only
Small Thumbnail
Large Thumbnail
Small List
Large List
Buttons.asl
Glass Button Rollovers.asl
Glass Buttons.asl
Image Effects.asl
SampleStyles.asl
Text Effects.asl
Textures.asl

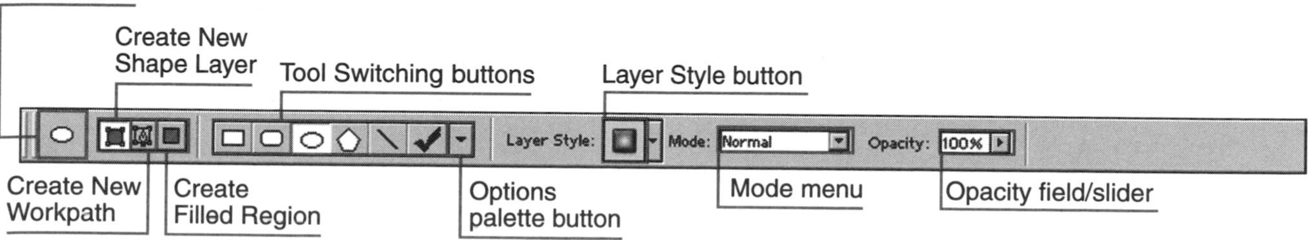
Ellipse Tool
Create New Shape Layer
Tool Switching buttons
Layer Style button
Layer Style:
Mode: Normal
Opacity: 100%
Create New Workpath
Create Filled Region
Options palette button
Mode menu
Opacity field/slider

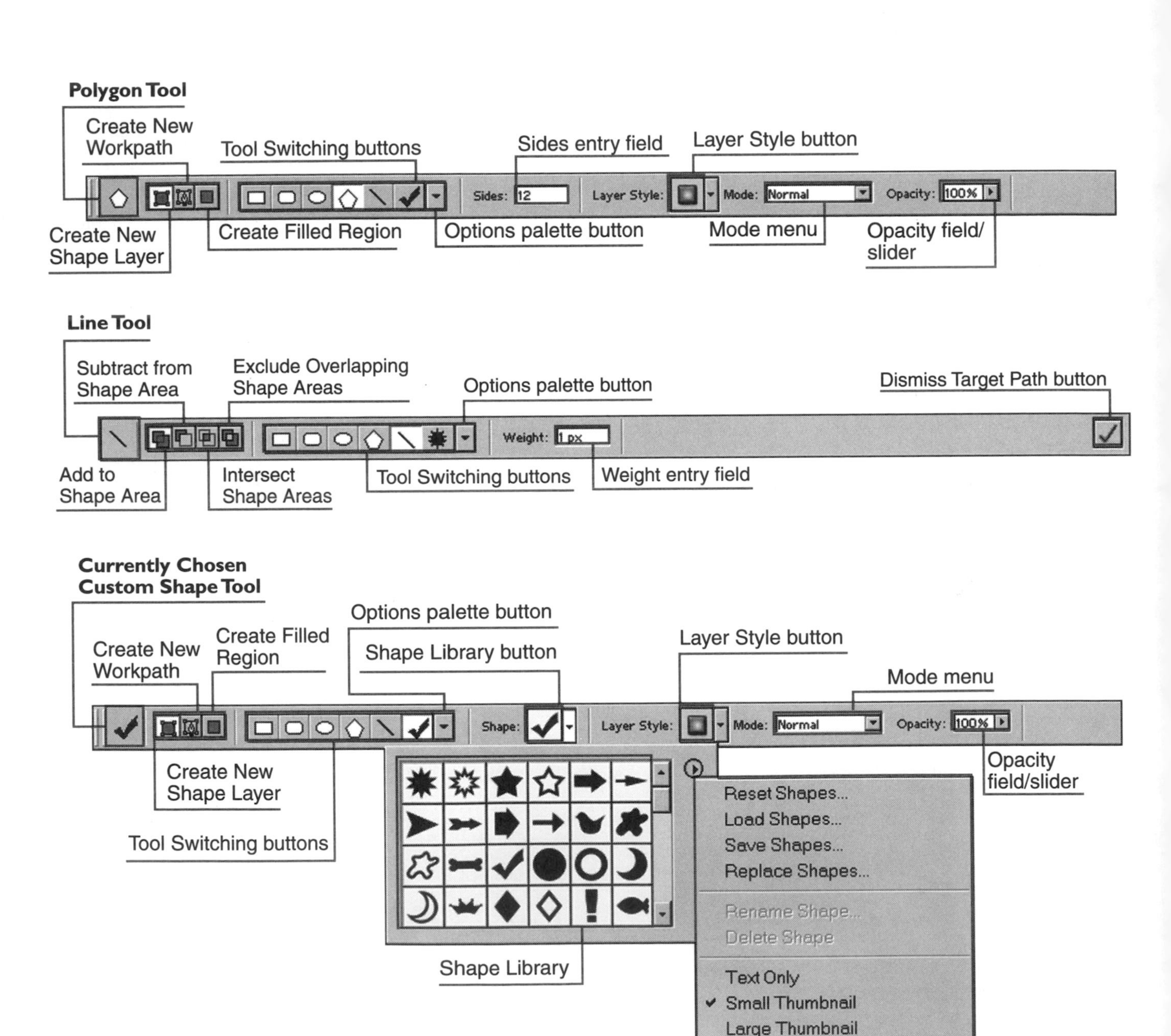
Polygon Tool
Create New Workpath
Tool Switching buttons
Sides entry field
Layer Style button
Sides: 12
Layer Style:
Mode: Normal
Opacity: 100%
Create New Shape Layer
Create Filled Region
Options palette button
Mode menu
Opacity field/ slider
Line Tool
Subtract from Shape Area
Exclude Overlapping Shape Areas
Options palette button
Dismiss Target Path button
Weight: 1 px
Add to Shape Area
Intersect Shape Areas
Tool Switching buttons
Weight entry field
Currently Chosen Custom Shape Tool
Options palette button
Create New Workpath
Create Filled Region
Shape Library button
Layer Style button
Mode menu
Shape:
Layer Style:
Mode: Normal
Opacity: 100%
Create New Shape Layer
Opacity field/slider
Tool Switching buttons
Reset Shapes...
Load Shapes...
Save Shapes...
Replace Shapes...
Rename Shape...
Delete Shape
Text Only
Small Thumbnail
Large Thumbnail
Small List
Large List
Custom Shapes.csh
Default Custom Shapes.csh
Shape Library
Shape Library menu

Annotation Tool Options

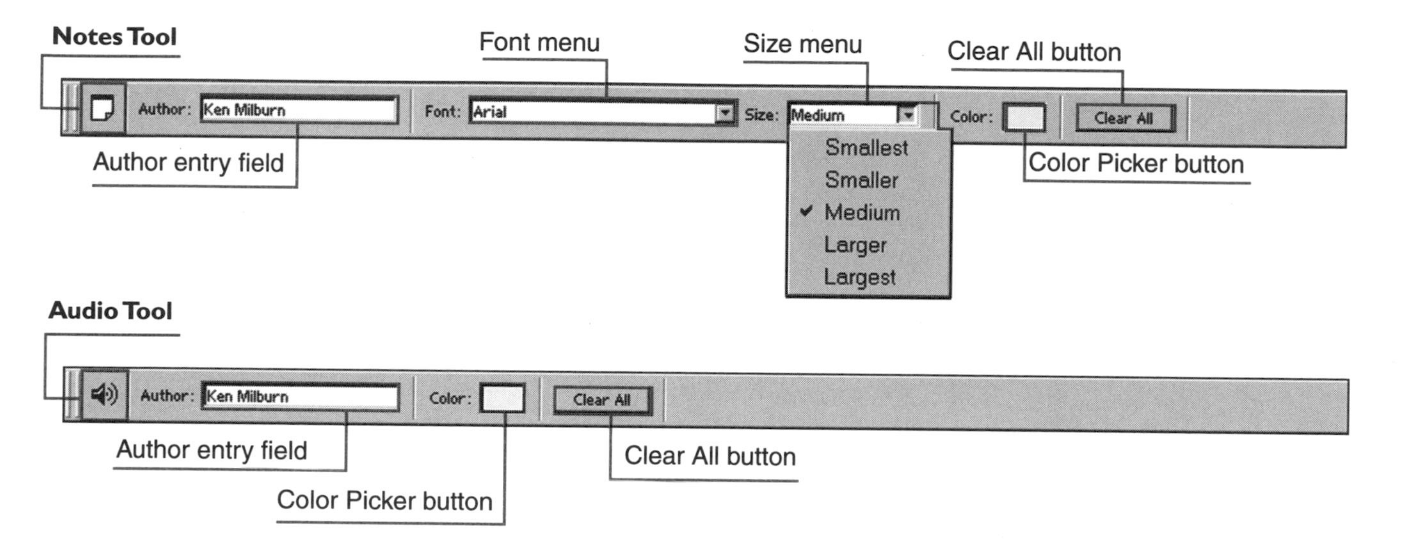

Eyedropper Tool Options

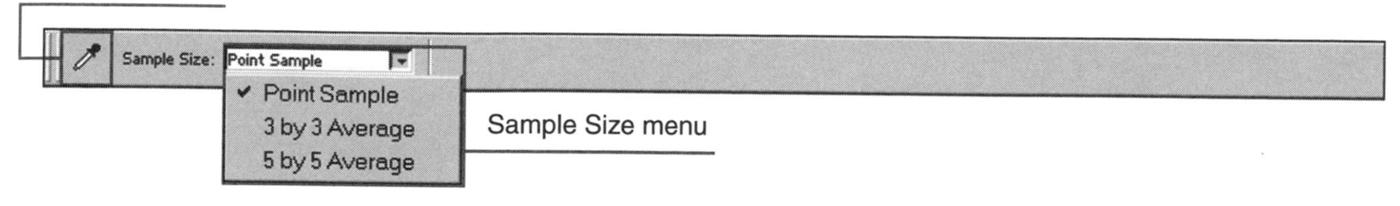

Color Sampler Tool
Sample Size menu
Sample Size: Point Sample
Clear

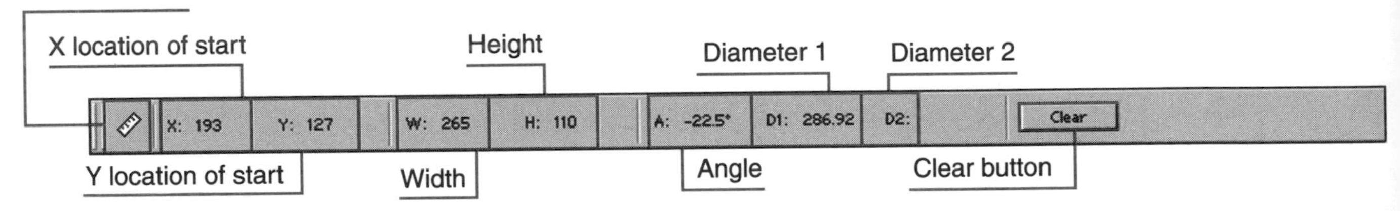

Hand Tool Options

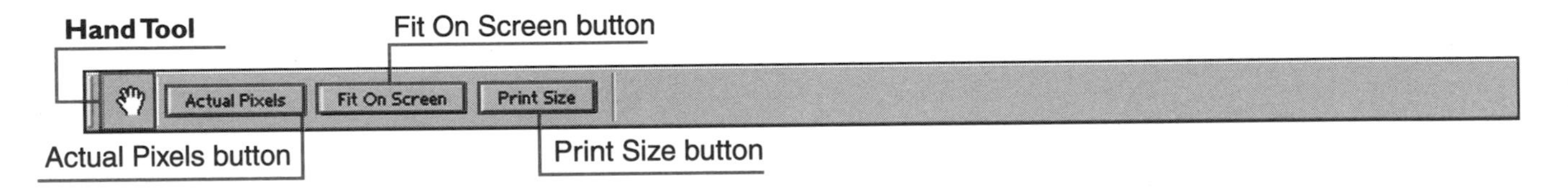

Zoom Tool Options

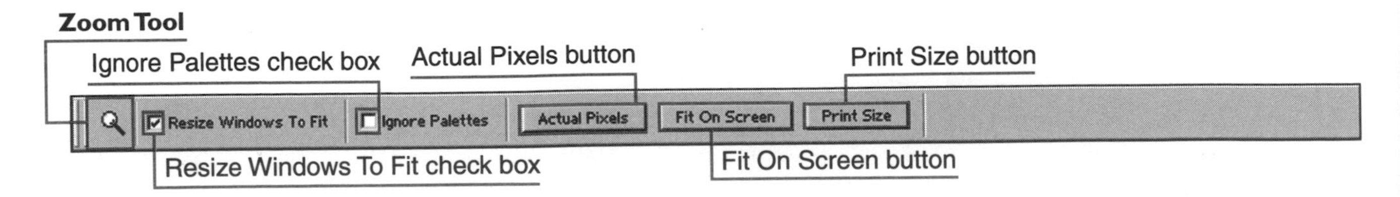

COMMAND OPTIONS BARS

The Photoshop Toolbox is not the only thing that has associated Options bars. Two of the Photoshop commands, Transform and Place, have them as well.

Transform

To access the Transform commands, click Edit, then Transform, then the name of the command you want.

Note that the position for the cancel and commit buttons are reversed on a Macintosh.

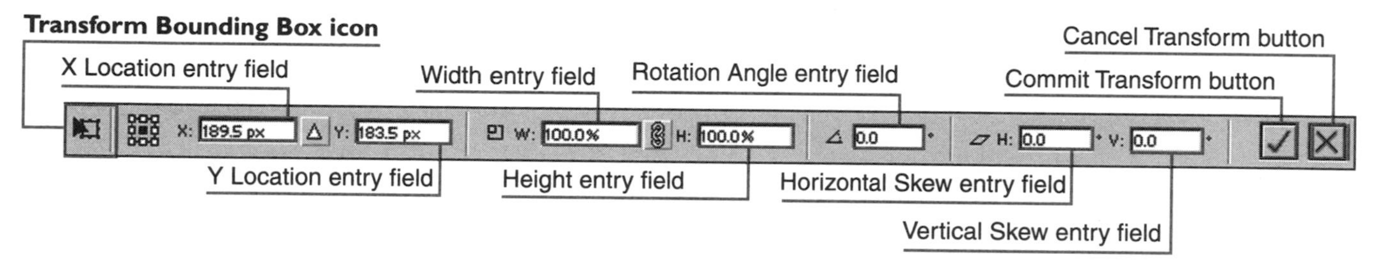

Place

To access the Place command, click File, then Place. The Place command is used to insert the contents of a specialized file format into a Photoshop or ImageReady composition on its own layer. That layer is automatically rasterized if the incoming file was from a vector format, such as EPS or PDF. In Photoshop, you can immediately transform the new layer in any way that suits you. In fact, the Photoshop Place options are identical to the Transform options shown earlier. In ImageReady, you have to issue the Transform commands independently, so there is no Options bar associated with the Place command. Note that the position for the cancel and commit buttons are reversed on a Macintosh.

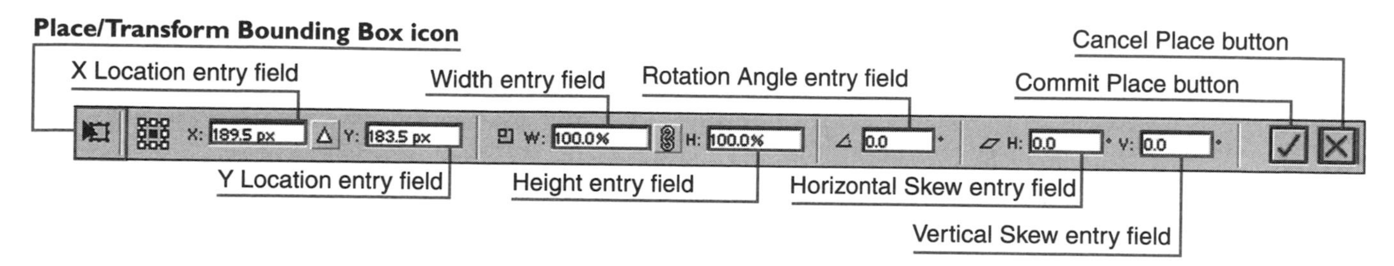

KEYBOARD MODIFIERS AND SHORTCUTS

Photoshop has always been infamous for its large array of keyboard *shortcuts* — the number of things that you can make happen just by poking a couple of keys. Keyboard shortcuts can do such things as changing a tool's performance characteristics or executing a palette command without your having to bring up the palette.

In Photoshop, you also use the keyboard to change tools while working. These keys are called *keyboard modifiers*. For example, pressing Opt/Alt while using the Magnetic Lasso changes the tool to a plain Lasso; pressing Opt/Alt while using a brush changes the brush to an Eyedropper so that you can change the foreground color just by clicking in the image.

Keyboard shortcuts are even more important in graphics programs than in office-type programs because you do not have to cover your artwork with palettes and menus as often. Therefore, keyboard shortcuts allow you to work faster, not only because you can access many of the commands faster, but because you do not have to move windows and menus out of the way in order to see a part of the picture that you want to be working on.

The following tables group the keyboard shortcuts by job category, with each table representing one category.

PAN AND ZOOM

KEYSTROKE	*EFFECT*
⌘/Ctrl+0	Fits the image in the Photoshop window.
Opt/Alt+⌘/Ctrl+0	Displays the image at its actual pixel size (100%).
⌘/Ctrl+ (+ or -)	Zooms in or out.
⌘/Ctrl+Spacebar	Zooms in.
Opt/Alt+Spacebar	Zooms out.
Spacebar+Drag	Pans and scrolls the image with the Hand tool.
Page Up/Down	Scrolls the image up or down one screen.
Shift+Page Up/Down	Scrolls up or down by 10 units.
Home	Slides the picture to the upper-left corner.
End	Slides the picture to the lower-right corner.
\	Toggles the layer mask on/off as rubylith (transparent red).
⌘/Ctrl+drag	Zooms in on that specific part of the image in the Navigator palette.

WORKING WITH SELECTIONS

KEYSTROKE	*EFFECT*
Shift+Drag (using a selection tool)	Lets you use any selection tool to add to an existing selection.
Shift+Drag (using a Marquee tool)	Constrains the rectangular and elliptical marquee to a square or circle.
Opt/Alt+Drag	Lets you use any selection tool to subtract from an existing selection.
Shift+Opt/Alt+Drag	Draws rectangular and elliptical marquees from the center while constraining them to a circle or square.
Opt/Alt+Drag	Changes the Magnetic Lasso to the Lasso.
Opt/Alt+Click	Changes the Magnetic Lasso to the Polygon Lasso.
⌘/Ctrl+Opt/Alt+Drag	Creates a copy of a selection and moves the copy.
Arrow keys	Each press moves the selection one pixel in the direction of the arrow. If you hold down the arrow key, the selection moves continuously in the direction of the arrow.
Arrow keys (using the Move tool)	Each press moves the selection contents one pixel in the direction of the arrow. If nothing is selected on that layer, each press moves the entire layer one pixel. If you hold down the arrow key, the selection contents move continuously in the direction of the arrow.
[or]	When the Magnetic Lasso is in use, increases or decreases the detection width.
Opt/Alt+Drag	With the Measure tool, becomes a protractor (measures angles).
Shift+Drag Guide	Snaps the guide to ruler ticks.
Opt/Alt+Drag Guide	Toggles the guide from horizontal to vertical.

PAINTING

KEYSTROKE	*EFFECT*
Opt/Alt+Any paint tool	Causes the brush to become an Eyedropper. You can then pick a foreground color from any pixel in the image, release the key, and continue to paint in the new color.
Opt/Alt+Click*	With Eyedropper**: Picked-up color becomes the background color.
Shift+Click*	With Eyedropper**: Picked-up color becomes color sample.
Shift+Opt/Alt+Click*	With Eyedropper** over color sample sign: Deletes existing color sample.
Opt/Alt+Click	With Color Sampler over color sample sign: Deletes existing color sample.

(continued)

PAINTING *(continued)*

KEYSTROKE	*EFFECT*
Number keys	With any brush: Sets opacity or pressure. Typing two number keys in rapid succession produces an exact number (for example, 47%); typing one number changes transparency by 10% (for example, 3=30%).
Shift+ (- or +)	Changes blending modes. Works for either brushes or layers. You can look at the Blend Mode menu bar in the current palette to see what the current Blend Mode is after pressing these keys.
Opt/Alt+Delete/ Backspace	Fills the current selection with the foreground color.
⌘/Ctrl+Delete/Backspace	Fills the current selection with the background color.
Opt/Alt+⌘/ Ctrl+Delete/Backspace*	Fills from the currently selected History snapshot.
Shift+Delete/Backspace	Brings up the Fill dialog box, so you can choose Foreground, Background, Pattern, History, Black, 50% Gray, or White.
/	Toggles the lock on transparent pixels.
Shift+Click	Any painting tool: Connects a straight line from the last stroke made.

*Not in ImageReady.

**Works only when you have chosen the Eyedropper tool from the Toolbox — not when you have converted a paint tool to an Eyedropper by pressing Opt/Alt.

EDITING TYPE

KEYSTROKE	*EFFECT*
⌘/Ctrl+Drag (when type is selected)	Moves the entire current block of text — whether all the text is selected or not.
Shift+⌘/Ctrl+L	Left aligns the current block of text (when text is oriented horizontally).
Shift+⌘/Ctrl+C	Center aligns the current block of text (when text is oriented horizontally).
Shift+⌘/Ctrl+R	Right aligns the current block of text (when text is oriented horizontally).
Shift+⌘/Ctrl+L	Top aligns the current block of text (when text is oriented vertically).
Shift+⌘/Ctrl+C	Center aligns the current block of text (when text is oriented vertically).
Shift+⌘/Ctrl+R	Bottom aligns the current block of text (when text is oriented vertically).
Arrow keys	Move one character or line per stroke in the direction of the arrow.
Shift+Right/Left Arrow	Selects one character in the direction of the arrow.

KEYSTROKE	*EFFECT*
Shift+Up/Down Arrow	Selects one line in the direction of the arrow.
Shift+⌘/Ctrl+Left/Right Arrow	Selects one word or the balance of paragraph in the direction of the arrow.
Shift+⌘/Ctrl+Up/Down Arrow	Selects the balance of paragraph in the direction of the arrow.
Double-click	Selects the word.
Triple-click	Selects the line.
Quad-click	Selects the paragraph.
⌘/Ctrl+H	Toggles showing selection. If selection is hidden, it is still active. This works whether the selection is highlighted text or selected pixels.
Shift+⌘/Ctrl+U	Toggles underline on/off.
Shift+⌘/Ctrl+/	Toggles strikethrough on/off.
Shift+⌘/Ctrl+K	Toggles all uppercase on/off.
Shift+⌘/Ctrl+H	Toggles small caps on/off.
Shift+⌘/Ctrl++	Toggles superscript on/off.
Shift+⌘/Ctrl+Opt/Alt++	Toggles subscript on/off.
Shift+⌘/Ctrl+X	Scales 100% Horizontal.
Shift+⌘/Ctrl+Opt/Alt+X	Scales 100% Vertical.
Shift+ Opt/Alt+⌘/Ctrl+A	Turns on auto leading.
Shift+⌘/Ctrl+Q	Turns off tracking.
Shift+⌘/Ctrl+J	Justifies the paragraph with the last line left aligned.
Shift+⌘/Ctrl+Q	Justifies the paragraph with the last line forced to justify on both ends.
Shift+ Opt/Alt+⌘/Ctrl+H	Toggles hyphenation.
Shift+ Opt/Alt+⌘/Ctrl+T	Toggles single-line/every-line composer.
Shift+⌘/Ctrl+<	Decreases the type size by 2 units.
Shift+⌘/Ctrl+>	Increases the type size by 2 units.
Opt/Alt+↑	Decreases the leading by 2 units.
Opt/Alt+↓	Increases the leading by 2 units.
Opt/Alt+Shift+↑	Increases the baseline shift by 2 units.
Opt/Alt+Shift+↓	Decreases the baseline shift by 2 units.
Opt/Alt+←	Increases kerning.
Opt/Alt+→	Decreases kerning.

PATH EDITING

KEYSTROKE	*EFFECT*
Direct Selection tool+Shift+Click	Selects multiple anchor points, which need not be contiguous.
Direct Selection tool+Opt/Alt+Click	Selects the whole path.
Pen tool+Opt/Alt+⌘/Ctrl+Drag	Simultaneously duplicates and moves the path.
Pen tool+⌘/Ctrl	Switches to Direct Selection tool.
Direct Selection tool+Opt/Alt+⌘/Ctrl	Switches to Convert Point tool when immediately over an anchor point.
Pen tool (or Freeform Path tool)+Opt/Alt	Switches to Convert Point tool when immediately over an anchor point.
Magnetic Pen tool+Double-click	Closes path, making "best guess."
Magnetic Pen tool+Opt/Alt+Double-click	Closes path in a straight line.

*Path Editing is not available in ImageReady.

WEB SLICING AND OPTIMIZING

KEYSTROKE	*EFFECT*
Shift+⌘/Ctrl+Y	Toggles dithering in browser for the image in the currently selected optimization pane.
Opt/Alt+⌘/Ctrl+Y	Repeat to shuffle through gamma previews in the currently selected optimization pane.
⌘/Ctrl+Y	Repeat to shuffle through the optimization views: Original, Optimized, 2-Up, 4-Up.
Slice tool+⌘/Ctrl	Toggles between the Slice and Slice Selection tools.
Slice tool+Shift+Drag	Restricts the slice to a square.
Slice tool+Opt/Alt+Drag	Starts drawing the slice from center out.
Slice tool+Opt/Alt+Shift+Drag	Draws a square slice from the center out.
Slice tool+Spacebar+drag	Moves the slice as drawn and then allows you to resume drawing when the spacebar is released.
Slice tool+⌘/Ctrl+drag	Toggles snap to slices.
Control+click/	Opens the context-sensitive Right-click on slice Slice menu.

TOOL KEYS

KEY	*TOOL CHOSEN*
M	Shuffles between Rectangular and Elliptical Marquee.
V	Move.
L	Shuffles between Lasso, Polygon Lasso, and Magnetic Lasso.
W	Magic Wand.
C	Crop.
K	Shuffles between Slice and Slice Select.
J	Airbrush.
B	Shuffles between Paintbrush and Pencil.
S	Shuffles between Clone Stamp and Pattern Stamp.
Y	Shuffles between History Brush and Art History Brush.
E	Shuffles between Eraser, Background Eraser, and Magic Eraser.
G	Shuffles between Gradient and Paint Bucket.
R	Shuffles between Blur, Sharpen, and Smudge.
O	Shuffles between Dodge, Burn, and Sponge.
A	Shuffles between Path Component Selection and Direct Selection.
T	Type tool.
P	Shuffles between Pen and Freeform Pen.
U	Shuffles between Rectangle, Rounded Rectangle, Ellipse, Polygon, Line, and Custom Shape.
N	Shuffles between Note and Audio Annotation.
I	Shuffles between Eyedropper, Color Sample, and Measure.
H	Hand.
Z	Zoom.
X	Switches current foreground/background colors.
D	Restores default foreground/background colors (black/white).
Q	Toggles editing in Standard or Quick Mask modes.
F	Shuffles screen modes: Standard, Full with Menu Bar, Full.

COMMAND KEY COMBINATIONS

KEY	*TOOL CHOSEN*
Shift+⌘/Ctrl+M	File, then Jump to (ImageReady/Photoshop).
⌘/Ctrl+N	File, then New.
⌘/Ctrl+O	File, then Open.
Alt+Ctrl+O	File, then Open Recent.
⌘/Ctrl+W	File, then Close.
⌘/Ctrl+S	File, then Save.
Shift+⌘/Ctrl+S	File, then Save As.
Opt/Alt+Shift+⌘/Ctrl+S	File, then Save for Web.
Opt/Alt+⌘/Ctrl+P	File, then Print Options.
Shift+⌘/Ctrl+P	File, then Page Setup.
⌘/Ctrl+P	File, then Print.
⌘/Ctrl+Q	File, then Exit (Windows); File, then Quit (Macintosh).
⌘/Ctrl+Z	Edit, then Undo (last step).
Shift+⌘/Ctrl+Z	Edit, then Step Forward.
Opt/Alt+⌘/Ctrl+Z	Edit, then Step Backward.
Shift+⌘/Ctrl+F	Edit, then Fade (previous command).
⌘/Ctrl+X	Edit, then Cut (to Clipboard).
⌘/Ctrl+C	Edit, then Copy (to Clipboard).
Shift+⌘/Ctrl+C	Edit, then Copy Merged.
⌘/Ctrl+V	Edit, then Paste (Clipboard contents).
⌘/Ctrl+T	Edit, then Free Transform.
Shift+⌘/Ctrl+T	Edit, then Transform, then Transform Again.
Shift+⌘/Ctrl+K	Edit, then Color Settings.
⌘/Ctrl+L	Image, then Adjust, then Levels.
Shift+⌘/Ctrl+L	Image, then Adjust, then Auto Levels.
Opt/Alt+Shift+⌘/Ctrl+L	Image, then Adjust, then Auto Contrast.
⌘/Ctrl+M	Image, then Adjust, then Curves.
⌘/Ctrl+B	Image, then Adjust, then Color Balance.
⌘/Ctrl+U	Image, then Adjust, then Hue/Saturation.
Shift+⌘/Ctrl+U	Image, then Adjust, then Desaturate.

KEY	*TOOL CHOSEN*
⌘/Ctrl+I	Image, then Invert (toggle from positive to negative).
Opt/Alt+⌘/Ctrl+X	Image, then Extract.
Shift+⌘/Ctrl+X	Image, then Liquify.
Shift+⌘/Ctrl+N	Layer, then New, then Layer.
⌘/Ctrl+J	Layer, then New, then Layer via Copy.
Shift+⌘/Ctrl+J	Layer, then New, then Layer via Cut.
⌘/Ctrl+G	Layer, then Group with Previous.
Shift+⌘/Ctrl+G	Layer, then Ungroup.
⌘/Ctrl+E	Layer, then Merge Layers.
Shift+⌘/Ctrl+E	Layer, then Merge Visible.
Shift+⌘/Ctrl+]	Layer, then Arrange, then Bring to Front.
⌘/Ctrl+]	Layer, then Arrange, then Bring Forward.
⌘/Ctrl+[	Layer, then Arrange, then Send Backward.
Shift+⌘/Ctrl+[	Layer, then Arrange, then Send to Back.
⌘/Ctrl+A	Select, then All.
⌘/Ctrl+D	Select, then Deselect.
Shift+⌘/Ctrl+D	Select, then Reselect.
Shift+⌘/Ctrl+I	Select, then Inverse.
Opt/Alt+⌘/Ctrl+D	Select, then Feather.
⌘/Ctrl+Y	View, then Proof Colors.
Shift+⌘/Ctrl+Y	View, then Gamut Warning.
⌘/Ctrl++	View, then Zoom In.
⌘/Ctrl+-	View, then Zoom Out.
⌘/Ctrl+O	View, then Fit on Screen.
Opt/Alt+⌘/Ctrl+O	View, then Actual Pixels (100%).
⌘/Ctrl+H	View, then Show Extras.
⌘/Ctrl+;	View, then Toggle Snap on.
Shift+⌘/Ctrl+H	View, then Show, then Target Path.
Opt/Alt+⌘/Ctrl+'	View, then Show, then Grid.
⌘/Ctrl+'	View, then Show, then Guides.
Shift+⌘/Ctrl+W	Window, then Close All.
⌘+? (Mac) or F1 (Win)	Help.

WHAT'S ON THE CD-ROM

The CD-ROM included in this book contains many useful files and programs. Before installing any of the programs from the disc, make sure that a newer version of the program is not already installed on your computer. For information on installing different versions of the same program, contact the program's manufacturer.

Acrobat Reader, from Adobe Systems, Inc.

For *Macintosh* and *Windows*. Trial Version. Acrobat Reader is a program and plug-in that can be used to display, Search, and print PDF files.

Installing and Using the Software

For your convenience, the software titles appearing on the CD-ROM are listed alphabetically.

Author's Sample Picture Files

For Macintosh and Windows. These images include most of the screen shots in the book. Although the excercises are designed so that you can use your own files, you may find it handy to have a library of photos with which you can practice. *Note: These photos are copyrighted by the author and are not to be used in whole or in part for any commercial or promotional use.*

BladePro 2.14, from Flaming Pear Software

For Macintosh and Windows. Demo. This software creates a wide variety of beveled edges and textures that are especially useful with clip art and type. BladePro features an incredible number of textures, all of which can be given virtually endless variations. You can also control the radius, height, texture, color, gloss, glare, reflection, glassiness, causticity, iridescence, tarnish, angle, color, and brightness of the light. Finally, you can adjust the shape of the edge bevel. You can even import a PICT file to use as a background texture. The copy on the CD-ROM is a fully functioning demo version of a shareware product.

Cinematte, from Digital Dominion

For Windows. Demo. Cinematte is handy for blue or green screen compositing. This excellent plug-in enables you to do highly automatic masking of objects shot or modeled in front of solid blue or green backgrounds. Cinematte automatically masks translucent, transparent, or hairy objects, and works with homemade blue and screens made from standard paints or fabrics. Also provides for automatic color spill removal.

Deep Paint 1.1, from Right Hemisphere Ltd.

For Windows. Demo. Deep Paint is a Photoshop plug-in that adds complete natural media painting tools within the Photoshop interface context. You get extensive natural-media brush tools, as well as the ability to paint with textured and lighted paints, so you get the feel of real paint build-up. You can also control the lighting type and angle from within the plug-in.

Digital Darkroom 1.2, from MicroFrontier

For Macintosh and Windows. Demo. Digital Darkroom is an introductory image-editing program. With it you can create your own images, improve existing images, apply 3D effects, and generate Web graphics.

Eye Candy 4000, from Alien Skin Software

For Macintosh and Windows. Demo. The Eye Candy filters are Photoshop 6-compatible and fully scriptable with Photoshop actions. These filters include the following: Antimatter, Carve, Chrome, Cutout, Drop Shadow, Fire, Fur, Glass, Glow, USE Noise, Inner Bevel, Outer Bevel, Perspective Shadow, Smoke, Squint, Star, Swirl, Water Drops, and Weave.

Four Seasons, from RAYflect S.A.

For Macintosh and Windows. Plug-in. This filter plug-in creates the effects of natural elements and atmospheres. Four Seasons comes with 150 skies and is wonderful for creating interesting skies in photos shot on gray days. Four Seasons is also useful for creating haze, fog, and rainbows.

Image Book 2.5, from Gamut Imaging

For Macintosh and Windows. Demo. This portfolio-type image manager catalogs folders with thumbnail images. You can annotate the images with keywords and file information, and then print the whole thing as a contact sheet or even a CD-ROM cover. The software automatically recognizes over 40 bitmap image formats.

LensDoc, from Andromeda Software, Inc.

For Macintosh and Windows. Demo. The ideal program for correcting lens distortion — especially prevalent in consumer-level digital cameras when shooting with the lens zoomed out. This product does a much better job of correcting distortion than one could accomplish by hand using Photoshop's Transform command. You can, for instance, remove both barrel or pincushion distortion and perspective distortion (often a problem when photographing buildings and products) in the same image.

nik Color Efex!, from TECHnik – USA

For Macintosh. This filter provides automatic color depth and detail enhancements. It is excellent for creating corrected files for photos taken in mixed or poor lighting situations and for maximizing the clarity of digital photos taken with contrast enhancement turned off.

nik Sharpener!, from TECHnik – USA

For Macintosh. Demo. Highly sophisticated image sharpening with presets for the most commonly used output types: offset printing, color laser printers, inkjet printers, and Internet images. You can do batch processing to sharpen multiple files according to a uniform set of rules. The program also features protection of anti-aliasing when sharpening in order to reduce the risk of unecessary "jaggies."

PowerTone 1.5, from Creo Products

For Macintosh and Windows. Plug-in. This plug-in generates duotones that can be printed with two inks but look like full-color images — a good trick for saving a lot of money on your next printing job.

Segmation, from Xaos Tools

For Windows. Demo. Produces outlines along the edges of your image. The outlines are vector paths and you can specify many variables — including curve smoothness and thickness. The program can also reduce the image to vector fills that can be printed at any size without showing jaggies. This plug-in is an excellent way to abstract an image before turning it into a painting using natural-media programs such as Corel Painter or Right Hemisphere Deep Paint.

Series 2 Three-D Luxe, from Andromeda Software

For Macintosh and Windows. Demo. A much more sophisticated version of Andromeda's highly respected Three-D filter. This version lets you specify transparency, texture, as well as Stressed, Riveted, Aged, Mesh, and Alien sculpted surfaces. This filter is extremely useful for artists who must composite images together that create a whole new fictitous reality for the viewer.

SilverTone, from Creo Products

For Macintosh. Plug-in. Here's a plug-in for producing metallic-color separations. You can add channels for special spot colors, such as metallic inks.

SmartGIF 1.0.2, from SiteJazz Corp.

For Macintosh. Demo. SmartGIF distinguishes itself from other plug-ins that create optimized GIFs in two significant ways. First, you can cut up an image into separate GIFs that will appear as one. This can make large images appear to load more quickly and enables you to assign a different link to each section of the image. Second, you need not flatten the image before exporting it as a GIF.

VariFocus Filter, from Andromeda Software

For Macintosh and Windows. Demo. Lets you add depth-of-field effects to photos that were made with short focal-length lenses.

Xenofex 1.1, from Alien Skin Software

For Macintosh and Windows. Demo. Xenofex contains 16 texture filters, including natural phenomena effects such as baked earth and lightning. Also has many nice texture effects, such as jigsaw puzzle pieces, turning a selection into a water stain, and many different crumpling effects.

TROUBLESHOOTING

We have tried our best to compile programs that work on most computers with the minimum system requirements outlined for this book. Your computer, however, may have components or software installed that is in conflict, and some programs may not work properly for some reason.

The two most likely problems are that you do not have enough memory (RAM) for the programs you want to use, or you have other programs running that are affecting installation or running of a program. If you get error messages like `Not enough memory` or `Setup cannot continue`, try one or more of these methods and then try using the software again:

- Turn off any anti-virus software.
- Close all running programs.
- In Windows, close the CD-ROM interface and run demos or installations directly from Windows Explorer.
- Have your local computer store add more RAM to your computer.

If you still have trouble installing the items from the CD-ROM, please call the Hungry Minds, Inc. Customer Service phone number: 800-762-2974 (outside the U.S.: 317-572-3342).

MASTER VISUALLY PHOTOSHOP 6 ON THE CD-ROM

You can view *Master VISUALLY Photoshop 6* on your screen using the CD-ROM included at the back of this book. The CD-ROM allows you to search the contents of the book for a specific word or phrase. The CD-ROM also provides a convenient way of keeping the book handy while traveling.

You must install Acrobat Reader on your computer before you can view the book on the CD-ROM. This program is provided on the disc. Acrobat Reader allows you to view Portable Document Format (PDF) files. These files can display books and magazines on your screen exactly as they appear in printed form.

To view the contents of the book using Acrobat Reader, display the contents of the disc, open the PDFs folder. Then double-click the chapter you would like to view.

USING THE E-VERSION OF THE BOOK

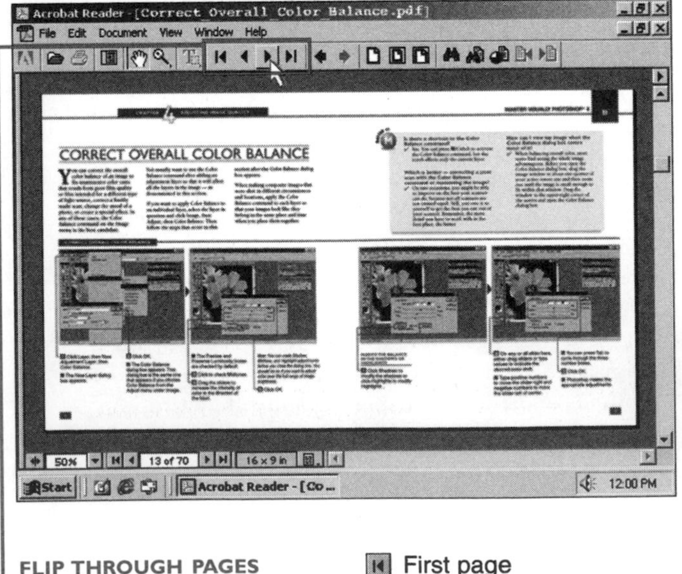

FLIP THROUGH PAGES

1 Click one of these options to flip through the pages of a section.

- First page
- Previous page
- Next page
- Last page

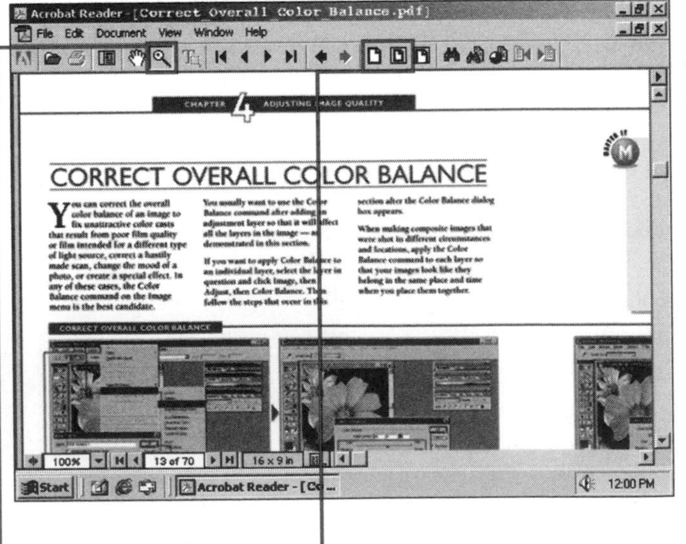

ZOOM IN

1 Click to magnify an area of the page.

2 Click the area of the page you want to magnify.

■ Click one of these options to display the page at 100% magnification ( ) or to fit the entire page inside the window ( ).

How do I install Acrobat Reader?

✔ Open the Software\Reader folder on the CD-ROM disc. Double-click the AR405eng.exe file and then follow the instructions on your screen. Or, you can use the visual interface to install Acrobat Reader. (Begin by clicking the idg.exe icon.)

How do I search all the sections of the book at once?

✔ You must first locate the index. While viewing the contents of the book, click in the Acrobat Reader window. Click Indexes and then click Add. Locate and click the index.pdx file, click Open and then click OK. You need to locate the index only once. After locating the index, you can click to search all the sections.

How can I make searching the book more convenient?

✔ Copy the Acrobat Files folder from the CD-ROM disc to your hard drive. This enables you to easily access the contents of the book at any time.

Can I use Acrobat Reader for anything else?

✔ Acrobat Reader is a popular and useful program. There are many files available on the Web that are designed to be viewed using Acrobat Reader. Look for files with the .pdf extension.

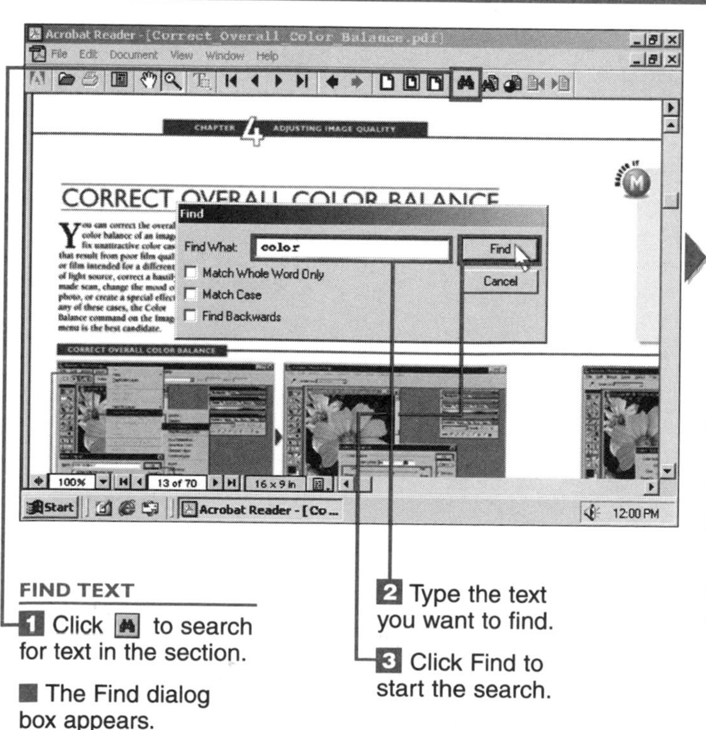

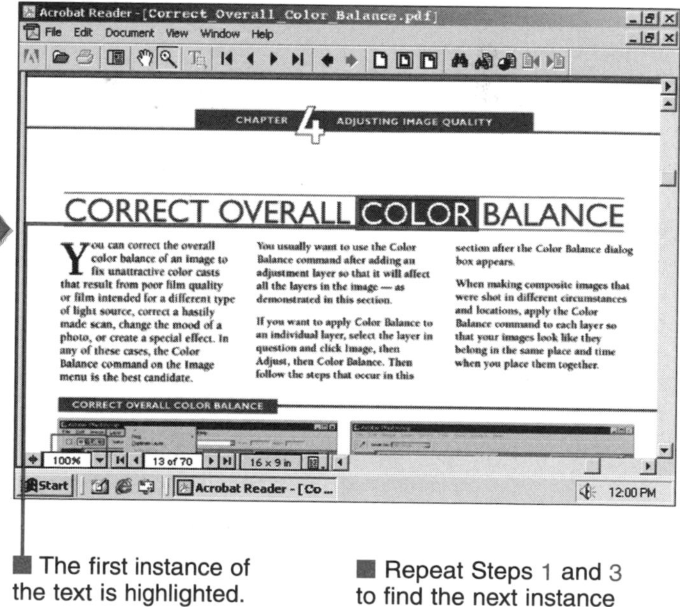

FIND TEXT

1 Click to search for text in the section.

■ The Find dialog box appears.

2 Type the text you want to find.

3 Click Find to start the search.

■ The first instance of the text is highlighted.

■ Repeat Steps 1 and 3 to find the next instance of the text.

READ THIS. You should carefully read these terms and conditions before opening the software packet(s) included with this book ("Book"). This is a license agreement ("Agreement") between you and Hungry Minds, Inc. ("HMI"). By opening the accompanying software packet(s), you acknowledge that you have read and accept the following terms and conditions. If you do not agree and do not want to be bound by such terms and conditions, promptly return the Book and the unopened software packet(s) to the place you obtained them for a full refund.

1.License Grant. HMI grants to you (either an individual or entity) a nonexclusive license to use one copy of the enclosed software program(s) (collectively, the "Software") solely for your own personal or business purposes on a single computer (whether a standard computer or a workstation component of a multi-user network). The Software is in use on a computer when it is loaded into temporary memory (RAM) or installed into permanent memory (hard disk, CD-ROM, or other storage device). HMI reserves all rights not expressly granted herein.

2.Ownership. HMI is the owner of all right, title, and interest, including copyright, in and to the compilation of the Software recorded on the disk(s) or CD-ROM ("Software Media"). Copyright to the individual programs recorded on the Software Media is owned by the author or other authorized copyright owner of each program. Ownership of the Software and all proprietary rights relating thereto remain with HMI and its licensers.

3.Restrictions On Use and Transfer.

(a)You may only (i) make one copy of the Software for backup or archival purposes, or (ii) transfer the Software to a single hard disk, provided that you keep the original for backup or archival purposes. You may not (i) rent or lease the Software, (ii) copy or reproduce the Software through a LAN or other network system or through any computer subscriber system or bulletin-board system, or (iii) modify, adapt, or create derivative works based on the Software.

(b)You may not reverse engineer, decompile, or disassemble the Software. You may transfer the Software and user documentation on a permanent basis, provided that the transferee agrees to accept the terms and conditions of this Agreement and you retain no copies. If the Software is an update or has been updated, any transfer must include the most recent update and all prior versions.

4.Restrictions on Use of Individual Programs. You must follow the individual requirements and restrictions detailed for each individual program in Appendix D of this Book. These limitations are also contained in the individual license agreements recorded on the Software Media. These limitations may include a requirement that after using the program for a specified period of time, the user must pay a registration fee or discontinue use. By opening the Software packet(s), you will be agreeing to abide by the licenses and restrictions for these individual programs that are detailed in Appendix D and on the Software Media. None of the material on this Software Media or listed in this Book may ever be redistributed, in original or modified form, for commercial purposes.

5.Limited Warranty.

(a)HMI warrants that the Software and Software Media are free from defects in materials and workmanship under normal use for a period of sixty (60) days from the date of purchase of this Book. If HMI receives notification within the warranty period of defects in materials or workmanship, HMI will replace the defective Software Media.

(b)HMI AND THE AUTHOR OF THE BOOK DISCLAIM ALL OTHER WARRANTIES, EXPRESS OR IMPLIED, INCLUDING WITHOUT LIMITATION IMPLIED WARRANTIES OF MERCHANTABILITY AND FITNESS FOR A PARTICULAR PURPOSE, WITH RESPECT TO THE SOFTWARE, THE PROGRAMS, THE SOURCE CODE CONTAINED THEREIN, AND/OR THE TECHNIQUES DESCRIBED IN THIS BOOK. HMI DOES NOT WARRANT THAT THE FUNCTIONS CONTAINED IN THE SOFTWARE WILL MEET YOUR REQUIREMENTS OR THAT THE OPERATION OF THE SOFTWARE WILL BE ERROR FREE.

(c)This limited warranty gives you specific legal rights, and you may have other rights that vary from jurisdiction to jurisdiction.

6.Remedies.

(a)HMI's entire liability and your exclusive remedy for defects in materials and workmanship shall be limited to replacement of the Software Media, which may be returned to HMI with a copy of your receipt at the following address: Software Media Fulfillment Department, Attn.: *Master Visually Photoshop 6*, Hungry Minds, Inc., 10475 Crosspoint Blvd., Indianapolis, IN 46256, or call 1-800-762-2974. Please allow four to six weeks for delivery. This Limited Warranty is void if failure of the Software Media has resulted from accident, abuse, or misapplication. Any replacement Software Media will be warranted for the remainder of the original warranty period or thirty (30) days, whichever is longer.

(b)In no event shall HMI or the author be liable for any damages whatsoever (including without limitation damages for loss of business profits, business interruption, loss of business information, or any other pecuniary loss) arising from the use of or inability to use the Book or the Software, even if HMI has been advised of the possibility of such damages.

(c)Because some jurisdictions do not allow the exclusion or limitation of liability for consequential or incidental damages, the above limitation or exclusion may not apply to you.

7.U.S. Government Restricted Rights. Use, duplication, or disclosure of the Software for or on behalf of the United States of America, its agencies and/or instrumentalities (the "U.S. Government") is subject to restrictions as stated in paragraph (c)(1)(ii) of the Rights in Technical Data and Computer Software clause of DFARS 252.227-7013, or subparagraphs (c) (1) and (2) of the Commercial Computer Software - Restricted Rights clause at FAR 52.227-19, and in similar clauses in the NASA FAR supplement, as applicable.

8.General. This Agreement constitutes the entire understanding of the parties and revokes and supersedes all prior agreements, oral or written, between them and may not be modified or amended except in a writing signed by both parties hereto that specifically refers to this Agreement. This Agreement shall take precedence over any other documents that may be in conflict herewith. If any one or more provisions contained in this Agreement are held by any court or tribunal to be invalid, illegal, or otherwise unenforceable, each and every other provision shall remain in full force and effect.

INDEX

Symbols and Numbers

A

INDEX

B

D

E

F

G

H

I

(continued)

J

K

L

P

INDEX

S

INDEX

T

U

V

W

X

Y

Z

ORDER FORM

TRADE & INDIVIDUAL ORDERS

Phone: (800) 762-2974
or (317) 572-3993
(8 a.m.–6 p.m., CST, weekdays)
FAX : (800) 550-2747 *or* (317) 572-4002

EDUCATIONAL ORDERS & DISCOUNTS

Phone: (800) 434-2086
(8:30 a.m.–5:00 p.m., CST, weekdays)
FAX : (317) 572-4005

CORPORATE ORDERS FOR VISUAL™ SERIES

Phone: (800) 469-6616
(8 a.m.–5 p.m., EST, weekdays)
FAX : (905) 890-9434

Qty	ISBN	Title	Price	Total

Shipping & Handling Charges

	Description	First book	Each add'l. book	Total
Domestic	Normal	$4.50	$1.50	$
	Two Day Air	$8.50	$2.50	$
	Overnight	$18.00	$3.00	$
International	Surface	$8.00	$8.00	$
	Airmail	$16.00	$16.00	$
	DHL Air	$17.00	$17.00	$

Subtotal ______________

CA residents add applicable sales tax ______________

IN, MA and MD residents add 5% sales tax ______________

IL residents add 6.25% sales tax ______________

RI residents add 7% sales tax ______________

TX residents add 8.25% sales tax ______________

Shipping ______________

Total ______________

Ship to:

Name ______________________________

Address ______________________________

Company ______________________________

City/State/Zip ______________________________

Daytime Phone ______________________________

Payment: ☐ Check to Hungry Minds (US Funds Only)
☐ Visa ☐ Mastercard ☐ American Express

Card # ______________ Exp. ________ Signature ______________